Law and Medical Ethics

'It would not be correct to say that every moral obligation involves a legal duty; but every legal duty is founded on a moral obligation.'

LORD CHIEF JUSTICE COLERIDGE
in *R v Instan* [1893] 1 QB at 453

Law and Medical Ethics

Fifth Edition

J K Mason CBE MD LLD FRCPath FRSE
Regius Professor (Emeritus) of Forensic Medicine
at the University of Edinburgh

R A McCall Smith LLB PhD
Professor of Medical Law
at the University of Edinburgh

with additional material by
G T Laurie LLB PhD
Lecturer in Law
at the University of Edinburgh

Butterworths
London, Edinburgh, Dublin
1999

United Kingdom	Butterworths, a Division of Reed Elsevier (UK) Ltd, Halsbury House, 35 Chancery Lane, LONDON WC2A 1EL and 4 Hill Street, EDINBURGH EH2 3JZ
Australia	Butterworths, a Division of Reed International Books Australia Pty Ltd, CHATSWOOD, New South Wales
Canada	Butterworths Canada Ltd, MARKHAM, Ontario
Hong Kong	Butterworths Asia (Hong Kong), HONG KONG
India	Butterworths India, NEW DELHI
Ireland	Butterworth (Ireland) Ltd, DUBLIN
Malaysia	Malayan Law Journal Sdn Bhd, KUALA LUMPUR
New Zealand	Butterworths of New Zealand Ltd, WELLINGTON
Singapore	Butterworths Asia, SINGAPORE
South Africa	Butterworths Publishers (Pty) Ltd, DURBAN
USA	Lexis Law Publishing, CHARLOTTESVILLE, Virginia

Typeset by Doyle & Co, Colchester
Printed and bound in Great Britain by Butler & Tanner Ltd, Frome and London

Visit Butterworths LEXIS *direct* **at: http://www.butterworths.com**

*This book is dedicated to
two Elizabeths*

Preface

Since this is probably the last edition of this book in which the first author will participate, it is difficult to resist the temptation to consider the changes that have occurred in the field of medical jurisprudence in general and to the book in particular over the last 15 years.

The most obvious is the sheer size of the subject. This edition is twice the size of the first yet, interestingly, the chapter headings have scarcely changed – something attributable, we hope, to factors other than authorial inertia. The problems with which medical law concerns itself were, of course, well recognised two decades ago. What has happened in the meantime is that their scope has widened and the legal response has correspondingly matured in its concern to reach a consensus view compatible with that of society in general – a task which has become something like the search for the end of the rainbow as medical capacity escalates and public attitudes oscillate. All of which is crystallised in the explosion of medical case law and the considerable broadening of the debate in medical ethics. We have attempted to take into account both of these developments, even if at the cost of excluding basic regulatory health care law; in our view, legal and ethical considerations are so closely intertwined in this area that it would be unhelpful to dwell on one to the exclusion of the other. Another marked feature of this debate is the extent to which it has promoted a variety of views. More than perhaps any other area of the law, medical law is a broad discipline, with strong differences of opinion being expressed on virtually every topic involved. One of us recently delivered a paper in which an attempt was made to choose, and justify the choice of, the five most significant decisions in the United Kingdom over the past 30 years. The fact that the choice of *Re B* (1981),[1] *Gillick v Norfolk and Wisbech Area Heath Authority*,[2] *Re MB (adult: medical treatment)*,[3] *A-G's Reference (No 3 of 1994)*[4] and *R v Cox*[5] would be unlikely to be that of any other interested observer goes simply to illustrate the enormous diversity of this academic field.

In much the same way, one can look back, as we did in the last Preface, to the topics which were of major concern at the time of each edition. The first was dominated by selective non-treatment of the newborn and the second by the introduction of new methods of assisted reproduction; issues of consent were paramount in 1991 and euthanasia held centre-stage in 1994. Surprisingly, the

---

1   *Re B (a minor)*(1981) [1990] 3 All ER 927, [1981] 1 WLR 1421.
2   [1986] AC 112, [1985] 3 All ER 402, HL.
3   [1997] 2 FCR 541, (1997) 38 BMLR 175, CA.
4   [1998] AC 245, [1997] 3 All ER 936, HL.
5   (1992) 12 BMLR 38.

abortion debate has been persistently topical and still represents one of the largest chapters in this edition; this may reflect something of a subliminal, but increasing, interest in fetal 'rights' which we sense as a persistent theme. Retrospection reveals another important development – the growth of public and political interest in medico-legal issues. These matters are no longer the exclusive preserve of the medical and legal professions; there has been a profound 'democratisation' of the whole debate, often fuelled, it must be admitted, by sensationalist media interest. Yet whatever misgivings one might have about the scare tactics of the press, it is surely a healthy sign that society as a whole is striving to take a view on matters which in the past might have been left largely unexamined or, possibly, resolved by the courts without any recourse to public debate.

A glance at the chapter headings shows, however, that, in this edition, we acknowledge the surge in importance of genetics as a source of medical jurisprudential concern and, to this end, our colleague Dr Graeme Laurie has contributed the completely new and significant chapter 7. We also record our grateful thanks to Dr Laurie for providing the innovative chapter 20 and for his wholehearted assistance in editing and updating throughout the book; he will be the new co-author of any future edition.

It is, perhaps, a measure of the increasing complexity of the subject that this edition has, probably, been the most difficult to write since the first and we must thank our publishers, once more, for their forbearance and helpfulness in the face of the customary set-backs and tantrums associated with publication. We can only hope that the book will maintain its evident popularity despite its ever-increasing girth.

Edinburgh   JKM
December 1998   RAMcS

Contents

Preface   vii
Table of statutes   xv
Table of foreign enactments   xix
Table of cases   xxi

INTRODUCTION
1 **Introduction**   3
A basis for medical ethics   4
The organisation of modern medicine   10
Public relations   13
Modern medical technology and the law   14
The doctor's position   18
The darker sides of medicine   19
The acquired immune deficiency syndrome (AIDS)   21

REPRODUCTIVE MEDICINE
2 **Aspects of sex law**   29
Sexual freedom   29
Incest   30
Homosexuality   33
Transsexualism   37
Respect for privacy and the right to marry   43
Labour law and discrimination   44
Application to family law   47
Deliberate transmission of sexually transmitted disease   50

3 **The management of infertility and childlessness**   56
Artificial insemination   57
The infertile or childless woman   67
The surplus embryo   73
The control of assisted reproduction   74
The surplus fetus   77
Surrogate motherhood   77

4 **The control of fertility**   89
Sterilisation   89
Other forms of contraception   107

5 Abortion 113
The evolution of the law on abortion 114
The comparative position 118
The rights of the fetus 124
Other people's rights 139
Abortion and the incompetent 144
Reduction of multiple pregnancy and selective reduction 145

6 Prenatal screening and wrongful life 147
Types of genetic disease 147
Genetic counselling 150
Controlled pregnancy 152
Counselling and negligence 158
Diminished or wrongful life actions 160

7 Genetic information and the law 167
Individual and family interests in genetic information 168
Other parties' interests in genetic information 174
The state interest in genetic information 182
Gene therapy 184
Cloning 186

MEDICAL PRACTICE
8 Medical confidentiality 191
Relaxation of the rule 193
Confidentiality and the legal process 205
Patient access to medical records 209
The patient's remedies 211

9 Medical negligence 215
The basis of medical liability 219
What constitutes negligence? 221
Protecting patients from themselves 233
Res ipsa loquitur 233
Causation 235
Injuries caused by medical products 239
Criminal negligence 240

10 Consent to treatment 244
Non-consensual treatment 245
Refusal of treatment by adults 261
Refusal of treatment in late pregnancy 265
Other vulnerable groups 269
Consent to testing for HIV infection 271
Proceeding without consent – the consequences 274
The concept of informed consent 277
The consent doctrine in the future 286

11 Health resources and dilemmas in treatment 289
Global distribution of resources 289
The allocation of national resources 290
Treatment of the individual 299

12 Treatment of the aged 310
Autonomy and paternalism in the treatment of the aged 311
The individual patient 315

DEATH
13 The diagnosis of death 327
Brain function as a measure of death 328
The legal effect of applying brain stem death criteria 333
The case for legislation 336

14 The donation of organs and transplantation 338
Technical aspects of transplantation 338
The living donor 342
Cadaver donations 350
The fetus or neonate as a transplant donor 357
Fetal brain implants 361

**15 Medical futility (or non-productive medical treatment):
1 The beginning of life** 363
The concept of medical futility 364
Selective non-treatment of the newborn 366
Selective non-treatment in infancy 372
Reversal of the trend? 377
Futility or scarcity of resources? 379
Comparative common law experience 382
Is the treatment of infants a separate issue? 385
A need for legislation? 388
The interests of others 391

16 Medical futility: 2 Later life 393
The patient in the permanent vegetative state 394
The English cases 396
The position in Scotland 401
The best interests test 403
A more honest approach? 406
PVS in the United States 409
'Do not resuscitate' orders 411

17 Euthanasia 413
Voluntary and involuntary euthanasia 414
Active and passive euthanasia 415
Suicide and attempted suicide – the current law 421

Active euthanasia 426
Passive euthanasia 427
The terminally ill patient 437
The incurable patient 438
Criminal liability for withholding treatment 442
A need for legislation? 442
The 'do not resuscitate' order 445
Feeding as a part of treatment 447

RESEARCH AND EXPERIMENTATION
18 Biomedical human research and experimentation 451
Ethical codes in human biomedical experimentation 451
What is research? 453
The design of experiments 455
Informed consent 462
The unethical researcher 466
Compensation for personal injury in research 468
Random sample testing 469

19 Research on children and fetal experimentation 471
Non-therapeutic research on children 471
Fetal experimentation 476
Embryonic research 480

20 The body as property 485
Property in living human material 485
Property in cadavers and cadaver tissues 492
Intellectual property law and the human body 494
Conclusion 496

PSYCHIATRY AND THE LAW
21 Human rights, psychiatry and the law 501
The grounds for intervention 503
Controlling treatment 509
Consent to treatment 516

22 Psychiatry and the criminal law 523
Mental illness and crime 526
The insanity plea 528
Diminished responsibility 534
Psychiatry and the sex offender 545
A delicate balance? 547

APPENDICES
Appendix A The Hippocratic Oath 551
Appendix B Declaration of Geneva 552
Appendix C International Code of Medical Ethics 553

Appendix D Declaration of Tokyo   555
Appendix E Declaration of Oslo   557
Appendix F Declaration of Helsinki   558

Index   561

Table of statutes

References in this Table to *Statutes* are to Halsbury's Statutes of England (Fourth Edition) showing the volume and page at which the annotated text of an Act may be found.

                                                    PAGE
Abortion Act 1967 (12 *Statutes* 366) 77, 81,
                                    103, 111, 113, 118, 119,
                                    123, 124, 129, 140,
                                    144, 146, 204, 361
  s 1(1)(a) 31, 115, 116, 358
    (b) 115, 116
    (c) 115
    (d) 31, 115, 143, 156, 165, 367
    (2) 117
    (3) 116
    (3A) 116, 130
  4 .... 139, 141, 391
  5(1) 117, 131, 358
Access to Health Records Act 1990
    (6 *Statutes* 974) 211
  s 4-6 210
Access to Medical Reports Act 1988
    (28 *Statutes* 261) 25
  s 2-5 210
Adoption Act 1976 (6 *Statutes* 220)
  s 51 66
  57 78
    (1), (3) 80
Adoption (Scotland) Act 1978
  s 24(2) 80
  45(5) 66
  51 80
Age of Legal Capacity (Scotland) Act 1991
  s 2(4) 259, 270, 475
  4(2) 253
AIDS (Control) Act 1987 (30 *Statutes* 977) : 198
Anatomy Act 1984 (28 *Statutes* 185) 488
Animals (Scientific Procedures) Act 1986
    (2 *Statutes* 483) 340
Births and Deaths Registration Act 1953
    (37 *Statutes* 722)
  s 29 38
Children Act 1989 (6 *Statutes* 387) 97, 208,
                                    254, 258, 260, 371
  s 1(1) 144
  2(9) 79
  8(1) 102, 249
  31 249

                                                    PAGE
Children Act 1989—*contd*
  s 100 249
    (3) 378
Children and Young Persons Act 1933
    (6 *Statutes* 18)
  s 1 369
Children and Young Persons Act 1969
    (6 *Statutes* 136)
  s 1(2)(a) 136
  28 82
Children (Scotland) Act 1995 97
  s 57 249
Chiropractors Act 1994 (28 *Statutes* 423) ... 11
Chronically Sick and Disabled Persons
    Act 1970 (40 *Statutes* 62)
  s 2 312
Community Care (Residential Accommo-
    dation) Act 1992 (40 *Statutes* 789) : 313
Company Securities (Insider Dealing) Act
    1985 (8 *Statutes* 789) 466
Congenital Disabilities (Civil Liability) Act
    1976 (45 *Statutes* 868) 66, 125, 126
  s 1 72
    (1) 161
    (2)(b) 164
    (4) 162
Consumer Protection Act 1987 (39 *Statutes*
    150)
  s 1(2) 240
  3(1) 239
    (2)(b) 239
  4(1) 239
  45(1) 240
Contempt of Court Act 1981 (11 *Statutes*
    185)
  s 10 209
Crime and Disorder Act 1998 20
Criminal Justice (Northern Ireland) Act
    1945
  s 25 .... 116, 118
Criminal Justice and Public Order Act
    1994 (12 *Statutes* 141)
  s 146(4) 35

PAGE

Criminal Justice (Scotland) Act 1980
  s 80 33
Criminal Law Act 1967 (12 *Statutes* 316)
  s 5(5) 195
Criminal Law (Consolidation) (Scotland)
    Act 1995 (12 *Statutes* 1609)
  s 1 31
Criminal Procedure (Insanity and Unfitness
    to Plead) Act 1991 (12 *Statutes* 1272) .. 534
Criminal Procedure (Scotland) Act 1995
    (12 *Statutes* 1708)
  s 18, 19 21
Damages (Scotland) Act 1976 126
Damages (Scotland) Act 1993 126
Data Protection Act 1984 (6 *Statutes* 899): 66, 209
Data Protection Act 1998 .... 174, 209
Disability Discrimination Act 1995 174
  Pt I (ss 1–3) 180
  s 1(1) 181
  Sch 1 181
      para 8(1)(a) 24
  Sch 2 181
Disabled Persons (Services, Consultation and
    Representation) Act 1986 (40 *Statutes*
    172) 318
Domestic Violence and Matrimonial Pro-
    ceedings Act 1976 (27 *Statutes* 812): 202
Employment Act 1980
  s 6 33
Employment Protection (Consolidation) Act
    1978 (16 *Statutes* 100)
  s 57(1)(b) 33
    (3) 33
Enduring Powers of Attorney Act 1985
    (1 *Statutes* 99) 319, 434
Family Law Reform Act 1969 (6 *Statutes* 128)
  s 8 .... 344, 475, 517
    (1) 258, 259, 260, 346
    (3) 258, 259
Family Law Reform Act 1987 (6 *Statutes*
    363)
  s 27 64
Family Law (Scotland) Act 1985
  s 1(1) 311
Fatal Accidents Act 1976 (31 *Statutes* 251): 125
Guardianship of Minors Act 1971
  s 1 371
Health and Social Services and Social Security
    Adjudications Act 1983 (40 *Statutes*
    135)
  s 17 314
  Sch 9
    Pt II 312
Health Service Commissioners (Amendment)
    Act 1996 218
Health Services Act 1980 (30 *Statutes* 945)
  s 6 296

PAGE

Health Services and Public Health Act 1968
    (40 *Statutes* 59)
  s 45 312
Homicide Act 1957 (12 *Statutes* 266)
  s 2(1) 535, 536

Hospital Complaints Procedure Act 1985
    (30 *Statutes* 970) 194
Housing Act 1985 (21 *Statutes* 35)
  s 59 313
Human Fertilisation and Embryology Act
    1990 (28 *Statutes* 316) 17, 61, 129,
                                        483, 485, 486
  s 1(2) 60
  2 87
    (3) 112
  3(3)(d) 187
    (4) 76
  4 87
    (1)(b) 60, 62, 63
  5 74
  13(5) 64, 72, 86
    (6) 88
  14(3) 60, 76
    (4) 76
  23(3) 48
  25(6) 64
  27 .... 64, 65, 70, 343
    (1) 69
  28 .... 70, 79, 343
    (2) 64, 65, 85
    (3) 48, 63, 64, 65
      (a) 62
    (4), (5) 65
    (6)(a) 66
      (b) 58
  29 .... 64, 343
    (1), (4) 65
  30 .... 64, 79, 80
  31(2) 66
  34, 35 66
  36 80
  37 .... 115, 131
    (3) 116, 130
    (4) 117, 130, 132, 154
    (5) 77, 145
  Sch 1
    para 4 74
  Sch 3 .... 287, 477
    para 2(2) 58
      3 60
        (1)(a) 88
      5 60
      6 .... 60, 75
        (3) 487
      7 76
      8 60

PAGE

Human Fertilisation and Embryology Act
    1990—*contd*
  Sch 4
    para 8 65
Human Fertilisation and Embryology
    (Disclosure of Information) Act 1992 ... 81
Human Organ Transplants Act 1989 (28
    Statutes 268) 485, 486, 488
  s 1(1), (2) 348
    2 65
    (2) 343
    7 342
Human Tissue Act 1961 (28 *Statutes* 52) 351,
                         353, 357, 488
  s 1(1) 350
    (2) 350, 355
    (4) 352
    (5), (9) 350
Infant Life (Preservation) Act 1929 (12
    Statutes 189) 116, 119, 358
  s 1 479
    (1) 114, 131
Infanticide Act 1938 (12 *Statutes* 205) : 369, 537
Law Reform (Miscellaneous Provisions)
    (Scotland) Act 1990
  s 71 .... 319, 434
Law Reform (Year and a Day Rule) Act 1996
    (12 *Statutes* 1776) 334
Limitation Act 1980 (24 *Statutes* 648)
  s 11 94
Matrimonial Homes (Family Protection)
    (Scotland) Act 1981 202
Medical Act 1858 10
Medical Act 1978 11
Medical Act 1983 (28 *Statutes* 101) 509
Medical (Professional Performance) Act 1995
    (28 *Statutes* 472) 12, 217
Medicines Act 1968 (28 *Statutes* 504) 11
Mental Health Act 1959 (28 *Statutes* 831) .. 253,
                         254, 396, 509
Mental Health Act 1983 (28 *Statutes* 846) .. 103,
                         266, 267, 510
  s 1(2) 514, 516, 539
    (3) 514, 516, 522
    2 .... 317, 511
    3 .... 511, 517
    (2) 504
      (b) 540
    4 317
    (3) 511
    7 317
    12(2) 268
    20(4)(a), (b) 511
    37 514
    57 .... 518, 519, 521, 522
    58 .... 517, 518, 519
    60 519

PAGE

Mental Health Act 1983—*contd*
  s 61(3) 519
    62(1)(a)–(d) 519
    63 .... 139, 270, 517, 518
    72 504
    76 196
    117 512
    131 509
    135, 136 317
    139 513
    148 517
Mental Health (Patients in the Community)
    Act 1995 (28 *Statutes* 1049) 501, 509,
                               512
Mental Health (Scotland) Act 1960
  s 2 509
Mental Health (Scotland) Act 1984 (28
    Statutes 1025) 514
  s 21 509
    24 .... 317, 511
    26 317
    97 519
    117 317
Ministry of Health Act 1919 (10 *Statutes* 277)
  s 2 96
National Assistance Act 1948 (40 *Statutes* 18)
  s 21, 26 313
    47 .... 316, 317
National Assistance (Amendment) Act 1951
    (40 *Statutes* 51)
  s 1(1) 315
National Health Service Act 1977 (30 *Statutes*
    788) 240, 298
  Pt V (ss 106–120) 194
  s 3 295
    97A 296
National Health Service and Community Care
    Act 1990 (40 *Statutes* 242) 291, 298
  s 47 312
Offences Against the Person Act 1861 (12
    Statutes 92) 51, 116, 118, 122, 129
  s 20 29
    23, 24 53
    47 29
    58 .... 112, 114, 479
    59 114
Osteopaths Act 1993 (28 *Statutes* 373) 11
Parliamentary and Health Service Commissioners
    Act 1987 (10 *Statutes* 443) 194
Patents Act 1977 (33 *Statutes* 138)
  s 1(1) 494
Police and Criminal Evidence Act 1984 (12
    Statutes 801) 20, 47, 206
  s 55 21
Prevention of Terrorism (Temporary Provisions)
    Act 1989 (12 *Statutes* 1132)
  s 18 206

PAGE

Prohibition of Female Circumcision Act 1985
(12 *Statutes* 930) 90
Public Health (Control of Disease) Act 1984
(35 *Statutes* 514)
s 17 53
Public Interest Disclosure Act 1998 13
Race Relations Act 1976 (6 *Statutes* 828) 180
Registered Homes Act 1984 (35 *Statutes*
577) 313
Registered Homes (Amendment) Act 1991
(35 *Statutes* 982) 313
Registration of Births, Deaths and Marriages
(Scotland) Act 1965
s 42 38
Road Traffic Act 1988 (38 *Statutes* 781) 470
s 172 206
Road Traffic Offenders Act 1988 (38 *Statutes*
1046)
s 15(2) 470
Sex Discrimination Act 1975 (6 *Statutes*
753) 40, 45, 46, 47, 180
s 1(1)(a) 33
Sexual Offences Act 1956 (12 *Statutes* 229)
s 6 110
10, 11 31

PAGE

Sexual Offences Act 1956—*contd*
s 28 110
30 41
Sexual Offences Act 1967 (12 *Statutes* 329) .. 33
s 7 29
Social Security Contributions and Benefits
Act 1992 (40 *Statutes* 269)
s 64, 70 312
71, 75 312
108(2) 238
Social Work (Scotland) Act 1968 (6 *Statutes*
106)
s 14 312
Still-Birth (Definition) Act 1992 357
Suicide Act 1961 (12 *Statutes* 297) 421
s 2 425
(1) 422, 444
Supreme Court Act 1981 (11 *Statutes* 966)
s 32, 34 207
Surrogacy Arrangements Act 1985 (12 *Statutes*
935) 88
s 1A 80
2(2), (3) 81
Trade Union and Labour Relations Act
1974 10

Table of foreign enactments

The Enactments in this Table are listed in order of countries and their respective territorial jurisdictions.

PAGE

AUSTRALIA
NEW SOUTH WALES
Ambulance Services Act 1976
   s 14A 248
Anti-Discrimination Act 1977 25
Artificial Conception Act 1984 64
Crimes Act 1900 41
   s 36 50
Human Tissue Act 1983
   s 4 351
   10 345
   33 336

NORTHERN TERRITORY
Rights of the Terminally Ill Amendment Act
   1996 419

QUEENSLAND
Surrogate Parenthood Act 1988 87
Voluntary Aid in Emergency Act 1973 248

SOUTH AUSTRALIA
Family Relationships Act Amendment Act
   1988
   s 6 81
Sexual Reassignment Act 1988
   s 7(8)(b) 41
Transplantation and Anatomy Act 1983
   s 24 333

VICTORIA
Children (Amendment) Act 1984 69
Human Tissue Act 1982
   s 41 .... 331, 336
Infertility (Medical Procedures) Act 1984 17
   s 6(5) 75, 481
   30 81
Medical Treatment Act 1988
   s 3 .... 433, 448
   5, 6, 9 432
Medical Treatment (Enduring Power of Attorney)
   Act 1990 432
Status of Children (Amendment) Act 1984 64

PAGE

WESTERN AUSTRALIA
Artificial Conception Act 1985 64
   s 5(1) 69
   7(1) 69
Criminal Code 122
   s 27 531
Human Tissue and Transplant Act 1982
   s 12, 13 345
   24(2) 352

BELGIUM
Penal Code
   art 458 193

CANADA
Charter of Rights and Freedoms 423
   art 7 122
Civil Code of Lower Canada 423
Criminal Code 1971 423
   s 16 531
   180 52
   251 121

ONTARIO
Human Tissue Gift Act 344
Mental Health Act 508

QUEBEC
Civil Code 423

CYPRUS
Criminal Code
   s 190 51

FRANCE
Penal Code
   art 378 193

GERMANY
Embryonenschutzgesetz (Embryo Protection
   Act) 1990

PAGE

GERMANY—*contd*
s 1(1)(vii) 81
Penal Code
para 223, 223a 51

NEW ZEALAND
Contraception, Sterilisation and Abortion
Act 1977 142
Crimes Act 1961 243
s 151(1) 424
164 424
Evidence Amendment Act 1980
s 31–33 193

REPUBLIC OF IRELAND
Non-Fatal Offences Against the Person Act
1997 50

SOUTH AFRICA
Children's Status Act 1987 64

UNITED STATES
Child Abuse Amendments 1984 382
Child Abuse Prevention and Treatment Act
1974 .... 382, 391
Emergency Medical Treatment and Active
Labor Act 1992 383

PAGE

UNITED STATES—*contd*
Genetic Confidentiality and Non-
Discrimination Act 180
Genetic Non-Discrimination in the
WorkplaceAct 180
Genetic Privacy Act 1995 .... 172, 173, 491
Genetic Protection in Insurance Coverage
Act 180
Insanity Defense Reform Act 1984 533
Patient Self Determination Act 1991 443
Rehabilitation Act 1973 383
s 504 382
Uniform Determination of Death Act 1980 .. 336
Uniform Parentage Act 1973 64
Uniform Rights of the Terminally Ill Act 1985: 443

CALIFORNIA
Natural Death Act 1976 443

ILLINOIS
Statute of 1989 51

OREGON
Death with Dignity Act 1994 .... 419, 444

PENNSYLVANIA
Abortion Control Act 1982 121

Table of cases

A

PAGE

A, Re [1992] 3 Med LR 303 .... 334, 388, 441
A (Northern Health and Social Services Board v AMNH), Re [1991] 2 Med LR 274 118
A v C [1985] FLR 445, 8 Fam Law 170; revsd [1985] FLR 445, [1984] Fam Law 241, CA: 82
A v EC Commission: T-10/93 [1994] ECR II-179, [1994] 3 CMLR 242, CFI 25
A v Tameside & Glossop Health Authority [1996] 45 LS Gaz R 30, CA 23, 199
AB v CD (1851)14 D 177 212
AB v CD (1904) 42 SLR 213, 7 F 72, 12 SLT 599 .... 209, 212
AB v Glasgow and West of Scotland Blood Transfusion Service (1989) 15 BMLR 91, 1993
     SLT 36 207
AC, Re 533 A 2d 611 (DC, 1987); affd 573 A 2d 1235 (1990) 137, 138, 265
Adoption Application, Re [1987] Fam 81, [1987] 2 All ER 826, [1987] 3 WLR 31, [1987]
     FCR 161, [1987] 2 FLR 291, [1987] Fam Law 382, 131 Sol Jo 409, [1987] LS Gaz R
     1333, [1987] NLJ Rep 267 .... 79, 80, 81, 82, 88
Airedale National Health Service Trust v Bland [1993] 1 All ER 821, 12 BMLR 64, [1992]
     NLJR 1648; affd [1993] 1 All ER 821, [1994] 1 FCR 485, 12 BMLR 64, [1992]
     NLJR 1755, CA; affd [1993] AC 789, [1993] 1 All ER 821, [1993] 2 WLR 316,
     [1994] 1 FCR 485, [1993] 1 FLR 1026, [1993] Fam Law 473, [1993] Crim LR 877,
     [1993] 4 Med LR 39, 12 BMLR 64, [1993] NLJR 199, HL... 16, 363, 389, 393, 394, 396,
                                                        397, 398, 399, 400, 404, 405,
                                                        406, 408, 409, 426, 427, 430,
                                                   431, 432, 434, 438, 440, 448, 518
Akron (City of) v Akron Center for Reproductive Health 462 US 416 1983 (1983) 120
Alcock v Chief Constable of South Yorkshire Police [1992] 1 AC 310, [1991] 4 All ER 907,
     [1991] 3 WLR 1057, 8 BMLR 37, [1992] 3 LS Gaz R 34, 136 Sol Jo LB 9, HL .. 238
Allan v Greater Glasgow Health Board 1998 SLT 580, OH 95
Allan v New Mount Sinai Hospital (1980) 109 DLR (3d) 634, 28 OR (2d) 356, 11 CCLT 299;
     revsd 125 DLR (3d) 276 274
Allcard v Skinner (1887) 36 Ch D 145, 56 LJ Ch 1052, 36 WR 251, [1886-90] All ER Rep
     90, 57 LT 61, 3 TLR 751, CA 262
Allen v Bloomsbury Health Authority [1993] 1 All ER 651, [1992] 3 Med LR 257, 13 BMLR 47,
     [1992] PIQR Q 50 .... 91, 94
Amadio v Levin 501 A 2d 1085 (Pa, 1985) 125, 478
American Academy of Paediatrics v Heckler 561 F Supp 395 (DDC, 1983) 382
American College of Obstetricians and Gynaecologists Pennsylvania Section v Thornburgh
     476 US 747, 106 S Ct 2169 (1986) 120, 132
American Hospital Association v Heckler 105 S Ct 3475 (1985) 382
Ampthill Peerage Case [1977] AC 547, [1976] 2 All ER 411, [1976] 2 WLR 777, 120 Sol
     Jo 367, HL 69
Anderson v Forth Valley Health Board (1998) 44 BMLR 108, 1998 SLT 588, 1998 SCLR
     97, OH 96, 160, 165
Andrews v DPP [1937] AC 576, [1937] 2 All ER 552, 35 LGR 429, 26 Cr App Rep 34, 101
     JP 386, 106 LJKB 370, 81 Sol Jo 497, 53 TLR 663, sub nom R v Andrews 30 Cox
     CC 576, 156 LT 464, HL 242
Appleton v Garrett [1997] 8 Med LR 75, 34 BMLR 23, [1996] PIQR P1 275
Ardnt v Smith [1996] 7 Med LR 108 275

PAGE

Ashcroft v Mersey Regional Health Authority [1983] 2 All ER 245; affd [1985] 2 All ER
    96n, CA 222, 236
Associated Provincial Picture Houses Ltd v Wednesbury Corpn [1948] 1 KB 223, [1947] 2
    All ER 680, 45 LGR 635, 112 JP 55, [1948] LJR 190, 92 Sol Jo 26, 177 LT 641,
    63 TLR 623, CA 297
A-G v Able [1984] QB 795, [1984] 1 All ER 277, [1983] 3 WLR 845, 78 Cr App Rep 197,
    [1984] Crim LR 35, 127 Sol Jo 731 422
A-G v Guardian Newspapers Ltd (No 2) [1990] 1 AC 109, [1988] 3 All ER 545, [1988] 2
    WLR 805, 132 Sol Jo 566, [1988] NLJR 47, CA; affd [1990] 1 AC 109, [1988] 3
    All ER 545, [1988] 3 WLR 776, [1988] NLJR 296, HL 191, 211
A-G v X [1992] 2 CMLR 277, 15 BMLR 104 118
A-G for Northern Ireland v Gallagher [1963] AC 349, [1961] 3 All ER 299, [1961] 3 WLR
    619, 45 Cr App Rep 316, 105 Sol Jo 646, HL 539
A-G of Queensland (ex rel Kerr) v T (1983) 46 ALR 275, HC of A 142
A-G's Reference (No 6 of 1980) [1981] QB 715, [1981] 2 All ER 1057, [1981] 3 WLR 125,
    73 Cr App Rep 63, 145 JP 429, 125 Sol Jo 426, CA 30, 245, 343, 454
A-G's Reference (No 2 of 1992) [1994] QB 91, [1993] 4 All ER 683, [1993] 3 WLR 982,
    [1993] RTR 337, 99 Cr App Rep 429, 158 JP 741, [1994] Crim LR 692, [1994] Crim
    LR 692, [1993] 27 LS Gaz R 36, [1993] NLJR 919, 137 Sol Jo LB 152, CA 545
A-G's Reference (No 3 of 1994) [1996] QB 581, [1996] 2 All ER 10, [1996] 2 WLR 412,
    [1996] 1 Cr App Rep 351, [1996] 2 FLR 1, [1996] Fam Law 464, [1996] Crim LR
    268, 140 Sol Jo LB 20, CA; affd [1998] AC 245, [1997] 3 All ER 936, [1997] 3 WLR
    421, [1998] 1 Cr App Rep 91, [1997] Crim LR 829, [1997] 36 LS Gaz R 44, [1997]
    NLJR 1185, HL 126, 127, 128, 266, 479
Auckland Area Health Board v A-G [1993] 4 Med LR 239, [1993] 1 NZLR 235 424
Australian Mutual Provident Society v Goulden (1986) 160 CLR 330, 65 ALR 637, 60 ALJR
    368, HC of A 25
Azzolino v Dingfelder 337 SE 2d 528 (NC, 1985) 158, 163

B

B (a minor), Re (1981) [1990] 3 All ER 927, [1981] 1 WLR 1421, 80 LGR 107, 3 FLR 117,
    12 Fam Law 25, 125 Sol Jo 608, CA 371, 372, 384
B (a minor), Re [1988] AC 199, [1987] 2 All ER 206, [1987] 2 WLR 1213, 86 LGR 417, [1987]
    2 FLR 314, [1987] Fam Law 419, 131 Sol Jo 625, [1987] NLJ Rep 432, HL: 98, 100, 105
B (wardship: abortion), Re [1991] FCR 889, [1991] 2 FLR 426, [1991] Fam Law 379 144
B (parentage), Re [1996] 3 FCR 697, [1996] 2 FLR 15, [1996] Fam Law 536 63
B (Nancy) v Hôtel-Dieu de Québec (1992) 15 BMLR 95, 86 DLR (4th) 385 .... 422, 432
B v B 355 NYS 2d 712 (1974) 42
B v Children's Aid Society of Metropolitan Toronto [1995] 1 SCR 315 250
B v Croydon Health Authority [1995] Fam 133, [1995] 1 All ER 683, [1995] 2 WLR 294,
    [1995] 1 FCR 662, [1995] 1 FLR 470, [1995] Fam Law 244, 22 BMLR 13, [1994]
    NLJR 1696, CA 270, 518
B v France (1992) 16 EHRR 1, [1992] 2 FLR 249 43
B v United Kingdom Application 16106/90, DR 64, p 278 34
Baby K, Re 832 F Supp 1022 (ED Va, 1993); affd 16 F 3d 590 (4th Cir, 1994); cert den 1994
    US App Lexis 5461 383
Baby M, Re 525 A 2d 1128 (NJ, 1987); on appeal 14 FLR 2007, 109 NJ 396, 537 A 2d 1227
    (NJ Sup Ct, 1988) 81, 83
Baby R, Re (1989) 53 DLR (4th) 69 135
Bagley v North Herts Health Authority [1986] NLJ Rep 1014 .... 125, 478
Banks v Goodfellow (1870) LR 5 QB 549, 39 LJQB 237, [1861–73] All ER Rep 47, 22 LT
    813 319
Barbara v Home Office (1984) 134 NLJ 888 269
Barber v Superior Court 147 Cal App 3d 1006, 195 Cal Rptr 484 (1983) 442
Barnett v Chelsea and Kensington Hospital Management Committee [1969] 1 QB 428,
    [1968] 1 All ER 1068, [1968] 2 WLR 422, 111 Sol Jo 912 228

PAGE

Battersby v Tottman and State of South Australia (1985) 37 SASR 524 282
Beardsley v Wierdsma 650 P 2d 288 (Wyo, 1982) 162
Becker v Schwartz 46 NY 2d 401, 413 NYS 2d 895, 386 NE 2d 807 (1978) 158
Bell v Devon and Cornwall Police Authority [1978] IRLR 283 33
Benarr v Kettering Health Authority [1988] NLJR 179 91
Bland v Stockport Metropolitan Borough Council [1993] CLY 1506 .... 135, 161
Black v Forsey 1988 SC (HL) 28, sub nom B v Forsey 1988 SLT 572 511
Blake v Cruz 698 P 2d 315 (Idaho, 1984).. 163
Bliss v South East Thames Regional Health Authority [1987] ICR 700, [1985] IRLR 308, CA : 212
Blyth v Bloomsbury Health Authority (1985) Times, 24 May; on appeal [1993] 4 Med LR
    151, 5 PN 167, CA 108, 283
Bolam v Friern Hospital Management Committee [1957] 2 All ER 118, [1957] 1 WLR 582,
    101 Sol Jo 357, 1 BMLR 1 .... 91, 104, 223, 224,
                                             231, 255, 280, 282,
                                           388, 398, 408, 468
Bolitho v City and Hackney Health Authority [1998] AC 232, [1997] 4 All ER 771, [1997]
    3 WLR 1151, 39 BMLR 1, [1997] 47 LS Gaz R 30, 141 Sol Jo LB 238, HL .. 226, 225, 283
Bone v Mental Health Review Tribunal [1985] 3 All ER 330 513
Borowski v A-G of Canada and Minister of Finance of Canada (1984) 4 DLR (4th) 112,
    [1984] 1 WWR 15, 8 CCC (3d) 392; on appeal sub nom Borowski v A-G of Canada
    39 DLR (4th) 731, [1987] 4 WWR 385, Sask CA 122, 125
Bouvia v Superior Court of Los Angeles County 179 Cal App 3d 1127, 225 Cal Rptr 297
    (1986) 422, 425
Bowen v American Hospital Association 106 S Ct 2101, 476 US 620 (1986) 382, 384
Boychuk v H J Symons Holdings Ltd [1977] IRLR 395, EAT 33
Brady v Hopper 751 F 2d 329 (1984) 201
Braisher v Harefield and Northwood Hospital Group Management Committee (13 July 1966,
    unreported), CA 228
Bratty v A-G for Northern Ireland [1963] AC 386, [1961] 3 All ER 523, [1961] 3 WLR 965,
    46 Cr App Rep 1, 105 Sol Jo 865, HL 530, 542
Bravery v Bravery [1954] 3 All ER 59, [1954] 1 WLR 1169, 98 Sol Jo 573, CA 90, 204, 343
Breen v Williams (1996) 138 ALR 259, 70 ALJR 772 211
Brophy v New England Sinai Hospital 497 NE 2d 626 (Mass, 1986) 436
Brotherton v Cleveland 923 F 2d 661 (1991) 490
Bruggeman v Schimke 718 P 2d 635 (Kan, 1986) 163
Burke v Rivo 406 Mass 764, 551 NE 2d 1 (1990) 93
Burton v Islington Health Authority [1993] QB 204, [1992] 3 All ER 833, [1992] 3 WLR
    637, [1992] 2 FLR 184, [1993] Fam Law 19, [1993] 4 Med LR 8, 10 BMLR 63, [1992]
    17 LS Gaz R 51, [1992] NLJR 565, [1992] PIQR P 269, 136 Sol Jo LB 104, CA.. 126, 161

C

C (a minor), Re [1985] FLR 846, [1985] Fam Law 191, [1985] NLJ Rep 106 82
C (a minor), Re [1990] Fam 26, [1989] 2 All ER 782, [1989] 3 WLR 240, [1990] FCR 209,
    [1990] 1 FLR 252, [1990] Fam Law 60, 133 Sol Jo 876, [1989] 28 LS Gaz R 43,
    [1989] NLJR 612, CA 372, 391, 438
C (adult: refusal of treatment), Re [1994] 1 All ER 819, [1994] 1 WLR 290, [1994] 2 FCR
    151, [1994] 1 FLR 31, [1994] Fam Law 131, 15 BMLR 77, [1993] NLJR 1642 .. 261, 263,
                                              270, 433, 507
C (adult patient: restriction of publicity after death), Re [1996] 1 FCR 605, [1996] 2 FLR
    251, [1996] Fam Law 610 .... 214, 400
C (a baby), Re [1996] 2 FCR 569, [1996] 2 FLR 43, [1996] Fam Law 533, 32 BMLR 44.. 375, 377
C (a minor) (detention for medical treatment), Re [1997] 3 FCR 49, [1997] 2 FLR 180, [1997]
    Fam Law 474 270
C (medical treatment), Re [1998] 1 FCR 1, [1998] 1 FLR 384, [1998] Fam Law 135, 40
    BMLR 31 .... 250, 257, 375, 377
C v C [1946] 1 All ER 562 193

PAGE

C v S [1988] QB 135, [1987] 1 All ER 1230, [1987] 2 WLR 1108, [1987] 2 FLR 505, [1987] Fam Law 269; affd [1988] QB 135, [1987] 1 All ER 1230, [1987] 2 WLR 1108, [1987] 2 FLR 505, [1987] Fam Law 269, 131 Sol Jo 624, [1987] LS Gaz R 1410, CA 130, 131, 142

C v S 1996 SLT 1387, Ct of Sess, sub nom C and C v GS 1996 SCLR 837 .... 79, 80, 83

CES v Superclinics (Aust) Pty Ltd (1995) 38 NSWLR 47 122

CH (contact: parentage), Re [1996] 1 FCR 768, [1996] 1 FLR 569, [1996] Fam Law 274. . 65

Camden London Borough Council v R (a minor) (1993) 91 LGR 623, 137 Sol Jo LB 151, sub nom R (a minor), Re [1993] 2 FCR 544, [1993] 2 FLR 757, [1993] Fam Law 577, 15 BMLR 72 249

Cameron v Greater Glasgow Health Board 1993 GWD 6-433 95

Canadian Pacific Rly Co v Kelvin Shipping Co Ltd, The Metagama (1927) 17 Asp MLC 354, 72 Sol Jo 16, 138 LT 369, 1928 SC (HL) 21, 1928 SLT 117, 1927 SN 175, 29 Ll L Rep 253 223

Canterbury v Spence 464 F 2d 772 (DC, 1972); on appeal 409 US 1064, 34 L Ed 2d 518, 93 S Ct 560 (1972) 280, 281

Carraher v HM Advocate 1946 JC 108 516

Cassidy v Ministry of Health [1951] 2 KB 343, [1951] 1 All ER 574, 95 Sol Jo 253, [1951] 1 TLR 539, CA 235

Castel v De Greef 1994 (4) SA 408 284

Cataford v Moreau (1978) 114 DLR (3d) 585 91

Cavan v Wilcox (1973) 44 DLR (3d) 42 .... 228, 235

Chappel v Hart [1998] HCA 55 284

Chatterton v Gerson [1981] QB 432, [1981] 1 All ER 257, [1980] 3 WLR 1003, 124 Sol Jo 885, 1 BMLR 80 .... 274, 277, 281, 285

Children's Aid Society of Kenora and JL, Re (1982) 134 DLR (3d) 249 135

Chin Keow v Government of Malaysia [1967] 1 WLR 813, 111 Sol Jo 333, PC 223, 228

Ciarlariello v Schacter [1993] 2 SCR 119, 151 NR 133, 100 DLR (4th) 609, 62 OAC 161. . 422

Cicero, Re 421 NYS 2d 965, 101 Misc 2d 699 (1979) 382

Clark v MacLennan [1983] 1 All ER 416 .... 222, 236

Clarke v Hurst [1994] 5 Med LR 177 411

Clunis v Camden and Islington Health Authority [1998] 3 All ER 180, [1998] 2 WLR 902, 40 BMLR 181, [1998] 02 LS Gaz R 23, 142 Sol Jo LB 38, CA 505

Cobbs v Grant 8 Cal 3d 229, 104 Cal Rptr 505, 502 P 2d 1(1972) 276

Cockrum v Baumgartner 447 NE 2d 385 (Ill, 1992) 93

Coco v A N Clark (Engineers) Ltd [1968] FSR 415, [1969] RPC 41 191

Coe v Gerstein 41 L Ed 2d 68 (1973) 142

Coffee v Cutter Biological 809 F 2d 191 (1987) 240

Coker v Richmond, Twickenham and Roehampton Area Health Authority [1996] 7 Med LR 58: 107

Colautti v Franklin 439 US 379 (1979) 132

Coles v Reading and District Hospital Management Committee (1963) 107 Sol Jo 115 ... 228

Collins v Hertfordshire County Council [1947] KB 598, [1947] 1 All ER 633, 45 LGR 263, 111 JP 272, [1947] LJR 789, 176 LT 456, 63 TLR 317 230

Collins v Wilcock [1984] 3 All ER 374, [1984] 1 WLR 1172, 79 Cr App Rep 229, 148 JP 692, [1984] Crim LR 481, 128 Sol Jo 660, [1984] LS Gaz R 2140 103

Colman v General Medical Council [1989] 1 Med LR 23; on appeal sub nom R v General Medical Council, ex p Colman 4 BMLR 33, CA 11

Colyer (Bertha), Re 99 Wash 2d 114, 660 P 2d 738 (1983) 436, 442

Comber v Greater Glasgow Health Board 1992 SLT 22n, Ct of Sess 285

Commonwealth v Introvigne (1982) 150 CLR 258, 56 ALJR 749, HC of A 220

Compassion in Dying v State of Washington 79 Fed 3d 790 (1996) 420

Connelly v HM Advocate 1991 SLT 397, 1990 SCCR 504 536

Conroy (Claire C), Re 464 A 2d 303 (NJ, 1983); on appeal 98 NJ 321, 486 A 2d 1209 (NJ, 1985) 322, 435, 436

Conservatorship of Valerie N, Re 707 P 2d 760 (Cal, 1985) 97

Cook v Cook (1986) 162 CLR 376, 68 ALR 353, HC of A 231

Cooper v R (1980) 110 DLR (3d) 46 531

PAGE

Corbett v Corbett (otherwise Ashley) [1971] P 83, [1970] 2 All ER 33, [1970] 2 WLR 1306,
    114 Sol Jo 131 .... 38, 40
Corbett v D'Alessandro 487 So 2d 368 (Fla, 1986) 436
Cossey v United Kingdom (1990) 13 EHRR 622, [1993] 2 FCR 97, [1991] 2 FLR 492,
    [1991] Fam Law 362, ECtHR 38, 43, 45
Cowe v Forum Group Inc 575 NE 2d 630 (1991) 163
Craig v Glasgow Victoria and Leverndale Hospitals Board of Management (22 March 1974,
    unreported) 247
Crawford v Board of Governors of Charing Cross Hospital (1953) Times, 8 December, CA: 227
Crichton v Hastings (1972) 29 DLR (3d) 692, Ont CA 283
Crivon v Barnet Group Hospital Management Committee [1958] CLY 2283, (1958) Times,
    19 November, CA 228
Crosby v Sultz 592 A 2d 1337 (Pa, 1991) 197
Crouchman v Burke (1997) 40 BMLR 163 .... 91, 94
Cruzan v Director, Missouri Department of Health 110 S Ct 2841 (1990) 410, 435
Curlender v Bio-Science Laboratories 165 Cal Rptr 477 (1980) 143, 163
Curran v Bosze 566 NE 2d 1319 (Ill, 1990) 344

D

D (a minor) (wardship: sterilisation), Re [1976] Fam 185, [1976] 1 All ER 326, [1976] 2
    WLR 279, 119 Sol Jo 696 .... 97, 98, 99
D (a minor), Re [1987] AC 317, [1986] 3 WLR 1080, 85 LGR 169, [1987] 1 FLR 422,
    [1987] Fam Law 202, 151 JP 313, 130 Sol Jo 984, [1987] LS Gaz R 574, [1986]
    NLJ Rep 1184, sub nom D (a minor) v Berkshire County Council [1987] 1 All ER
    20, HL 136
D (adult: medical treatment), Re [1998] 1 FCR 498, [1998] 1 FLR 411, 38 BMLR 1 .. 400, 405, 407
D (medical treatment: consent), Re [1998] 2 FCR 178, [1998] 2 FLR 22, 41 BMLR 81, [1997]
    48 LS Gaz R 30, 142 Sol Jo LB 30 .... 248, 376, 377, 445
D v National Society for the Prevention of Cruelty to Children [1978] AC 171, [1977] 1 All
    ER 589, [1977] 2 WLR 201, 121 Sol Jo 119, HL 203
Danns v Department of Health (1995) 25 BMLR 121, [1996] PIQR P 69 96
Davie v Edinburgh Magistrates 1953 SC 34, 1953 SLT 54 526
Davis v Davis 842 SW 2d 588 (1992) 76, 486
Davis v Hubbard 506 F Supp 915 (1980) 244
De Freitas v O'Brien [1995] 6 Med LR 108, 25 BMLR 51, [1995] PIQR P281, CA 226
de Martell v Merton and Sutton Health Authority [1993] QB 204, [1992] 3 All ER 833,
    [1992] 3 WLR 637, [1992] 2 FCR 845, [1992] 2 FLR 184, [1993] Fam Law 19,
    [1993] 4 Med LR 8, 10 BMLR 63, [1992] 17 LS Gaz R 51, [1992] NLJR 565,
    [1992] PIQR P269, 136 Sol Jo LB 104, CA 126, 161
Derby & Co Ltd v Weldon (Nos 3 and 4) [1990] Ch 65, [1989] 2 WLR 412, 133 Sol Jo 83,
    sub nom Derby & Co Ltd v Weldon (No 2) [1989] 1 All ER 1002, CA 208
Devi v West Midlands Regional Health Authority [1981] CA Transcript 491 247
Dewar v HM Advocate 1945 JC 5 492
Diamond v Chakrabarty 66 L Ed 2d 144, 447 US 303 (1980) 494
DiMarco v Lynch Homes-Chester County 583 A 2d 422 (Penn, 1990) 54
Dinnerstein, Re 380 NE 2d 134, 6 Mass App Ct 466 (1978) 320
Dobson v North Tyneside Health Authority [1996] 4 All ER 474, [1997] 1 WLR 596, [1997]
    1 FLR 598, [1997] Fam Law 326, [1996] 31 LS Gaz R 29, [1996] NLJR 1458, 140
    Sol Jo LB 165, sub nom Dobson v North Tyneside Health Authority and Newcastle
    Health Authority [1997] 2 FCR 651, CA 492
Docherty v Brown 1996 SLT 325 112
Doe v Bolton 410 US 179, 35 L Ed 2d 201, 93 S Ct 739; 410 US 959, 35 L Ed 2d 694, 93
    S Ct 1410 (1973) 119
Doe v Doe 314 NE 2d 128 (Mass, 1974) 142
Doe v Kelly 106 Mich App 169, 307 NW 2d 438 (Mich, 1981) 78

PAGE

Doiron v Orr (1978) 86 DLR (3d) 719 . . . .   91, 93
Donoghue v Stevenson. See M'Alister (or Donoghue) v Stevenson
Doodeward v Spence (1908) 6 CLR 406, 15 ALR 105, 95 R (NSW) 107 . . . .   492, 493
Drake v Chief Adjudication Officer: 150/85 [1987] QB 166, [1986] 3 All ER 65, [1986] 3
    WLR 1005, [1986] ECR 1995, [1986] 3 CMLR 43, 130 Sol Jo 923, [1987] LS Gaz
    R 264, ECJ   312
Dudgeon v United Kingdom (1982) 4 EHRR 149, ECtHR 33, 35
Dumer v St Michael's Hospital 69 Wis 2d 766, 233 NW 2d 372 (1975) 159, 163
Duncan v Medical Practitioners Disciplinary Committee [1986] 1 NZLR 513   198
Dunn v British Coal Corpn [1993] ICR 591, [1993] IRLR 396, [1993] 15 LS Gaz R 37,
    [1993] PIQR P275, 137 Sol Jo LB 81, CA   208
Dunning v United Liverpool Hospitals' Board of Governors [1973] 2 All ER 454, [1973]
    1 WLR 586, 117 Sol Jo 167, CA   207
Durflinger v Artiles 673 P 2d 86 (Kan, 1983); affd 727 F 2d 888 (1984)   506
Durham v United States 214 F 2d 862 (1954)   532
Duval v Seguin (1973) 40 DLR (3d) 666, 1 OR (2d) 482   161
Dwan v Farquhar [1988] 1 Qd R 234   227
Dwyer v Roderick (1983) 127 Sol Jo 805, 80 LS Gaz R 3003, CA   222

E

E (a minor), Re (1990) 9 BMLR 1   262
E (a minor), Re [1991] FCR 771, [1991] 2 FLR 585, [1992] Fam Law 15, 7 BMLR 117; on
    appeal [1993] Fam Law 15, CA   102
E v Australian Red Cross Society [1991] 2 Med LR 303, 99 ALR 601   224
Eberhardy's Guardianship, Re 102 Wis 2d 539, 307 NW 2d 881 (Wis, 1981)   105
Ebsworth v HM Advocate 1992 SLT 1161, 1992 SCCR 671   544
Elizabeth, Re (1989) 13 Fam LR 47, [1989] FLC 92-023   106
Ellis v Sherman 515 A 2d 1327 (Pa, 1986)   163
Ellis v Wallsend District Hospital [1990] 2 Med LR 103, 17 NSWLR 553 . . . .   220, 276
Emeh v Kensington and Chelsea and Westminster Area Health Authority (1983) Times,
    3 January; revsd [1985] QB 1012, [1984] 3 All ER 1044, [1985] 2 WLR 233, 128
    Sol Jo 705, CA 91, 94, 95, 151
Eve, Re [1986] 2 SCR 388, 31 DLR (4th) 1, Can SC 98, 105, 254
Eyre v Measday [1986] 1 All ER 488, [1986] NLJ Rep 91, CA 92, 93

F

F (in utero), Re [1988] Fam 122, [1988] 2 All ER 193, [1988] 2 WLR 1288, [1988] FCR 529,
    [1988] 2 FLR 307, [1988] Fam Law 337, 132 Sol Jo 820, [1988] NLJR 37, CA . .   136
F, Re [1990] 2 AC 1, [1989] 2 WLR 1025, [1989] 2 FLR 376, [1989] Fam Law 390, 133
    Sol Jo 785, [1989] NLJR 789, sub nom F v West Berkshire Health Authority (Mental
    Health Act Commission intervening) [1989] 2 All ER 545, 4 BMLR 1, HL . .   16, 60, 100,
                                                                                    103, 105, 107,
                                                                                    249, 253, 255,
                                                                                    318, 403
F, Re, F v F (2 July 1986, unreported)   384
F v R (1983) 33 SASR 189 . . . .   92, 281, 282, 284
F v Riverside Mental Health NHS Trust [1994] 2 FCR 577, 20 BMLR 1, sub nom Riverside
    Mental Health NHS Trust v Fox [1994] 1 FLR 614; revsd sub nom F v Riverside
    Mental Health NHS Trust [1994] 2 FCR 577, 20 BMLR 1, sub nom Riverside Mental
    Health NHS Trust v Fox [1994] 1 FLR 614, [1994] Fam Law 321, CA 270, 518
Falcon v Memorial Hospital 462 NW 2d 44 (Mich, 1990)   238
Fallows v Randle [1997] 8 Med LR 160, CA   92
Farrell (Kathleen), Re 108 NJ 335, 529 A 2d 404 (NJ, 1987) 422, 425, 432

PAGE

Fiori, Re 652 A 2d 1350 (Pa, 1995) 411
Finlayson v HM Advocate 1979 JC 33, 1978 SLT (Notes) 60 .... 333, 442
Fleming v Reid (1991) 82 DLR (4th) 298 508
Fletcher v Bench [1973] 4 BMJ 117, CA 234
Forrester v HM Advocate 1952 JC 28 205
Franklin v Franklin (otherwise Jones) unreported 40
Freeman v Home Office (No 2) [1984] QB 524, [1984] 1 All ER 1036, [1984] 2 WLR 802,
    128 Sol Jo 298, CA 269
Frenchay Healthcare NHS Trust v S [1994] 2 All ER 403, [1994] 1 WLR 601, [1994] 3 FCR
    121, [1994] 1 FLR 485, [1994] Fam Law 320, 17 BMLR 156, [1994] NLJR 268, CA: 399
Friedman v Glicksman 1996 (1) SA 1134 .... 143, 166
Frost v Chief Constable of South Yorkshire Police [1998] QB 254, [1997] 1 All ER 540,
    [1997] 3 WLR 1194, [1997] IRLR 173, 33 BMLR 108, [1996] NLJR 1651, CA: 238

G

G (adult patient: publicity), Re [1996] 1 FCR 413, [1995] 2 FLR 528, [1995] Fam Law 677: 214, 400
G v G 1961 SLT 324 58
GF, Re [1991] FCR 786, [1992] 1 FLR 293, [1992] Fam Law 63, [1993] 4 Med LR 77, sub
    nom F v F 7 BMLR 135 .... 16, 102
GWW and CMW, Re (1997) 21 Fam LR 612 254
Gardiner v Mounfield and Lincolnshire Area Health Authority [1990] 1 Med LR 205, 5 BMLR 1: 228
Garner v Garner (1920) 36 TLR 196 209
General Medical Council v BBC [1998] 3 All ER 426, [1998] 1 WLR 1573, 43 BMLR 143,
    [1998] 25 LS Gaz R 32, [1998] NLJR 942, 142 Sol Jo LB 182, CA 11
Gilgunn v Massachusetts General Hospital No 92 - 4820 (22 April 1995, unreported), (Mass
    Super Ct) 365
Gillick v West Norfolk and Wisbech Area Health Authority [1984] QB 581, [1984] 1 All ER
    365, [1983] 3 WLR 859, [1984] FLR 249, [1984] Fam Law 207, 147 JP 888, 127 Sol
    Jo 696, [1983] LS Gaz R 2678, 133 NLJ 888; on appeal [1986] AC 112, [1985] 1 All
    ER 533, [1985] 2 WLR 413, [1985] FLR 736, [1985] Fam Law 165, 129 Sol Jo 47,
    [1985] LS Gaz R 762, [1985] NLJ Rep 81, CA; revsd [1986] AC 112, [1985] 3 All
    ER 402, [1985] 3 WLR 830, [1986] 1 FLR 224, [1986] Crim LR 113, 129 Sol Jo 738,
    2 BMLR 11, [1985] LS Gaz R 3551, [1985] NLJ Rep 1055, HL 15, 35, 108, 109, 144,
                                                    203, 249, 252, 258, 475
Giurelli v Girgis (1980) 24 SASR 264 228
Glass v Cambridge Health Authority [1995] 6 Med LR 91 234
Gleitman v Cosgrove 296 NYS 2d 687, 227 A 2d 689, 49 NJ 22 (1967) 162
Gold v Essex County Council [1942] 2 KB 293, [1942] 2 All ER 237, 40 LGR 249, 106 JP
    242, 112 LJKB 1, 86 Sol Jo 295, 167 LT 166, 58 TLR 357, CA 221
Gold v Haringey Health Authority [1986] 1 FLR 125, [1987] Fam Law 16; revsd [1988] QB
    481, [1987] 2 All ER 888, [1987] 3 WLR 649, [1988] 1 FLR 55, [1987] Fam Law 417,
    131 Sol Jo 843, [1987] LS Gaz R 1812, [1987] NLJ Rep 541, CA 93, 94, 276, 283
Goodwill v British Pregnancy Advisory Service [1996] 2 All ER 161, [1996] 1 WLR 1397,
    [1996] 2 FCR 680, [1996] 2 FLR 55, [1996] Fam Law 471, 31 BMLR 83, [1996]
    05 LS Gaz R 31, [1996] NLJR 173, 140 Sol Jo LB 37, CA 91
Gowton v Wolverhampton Health Authority [1994] 5 Med LR 432 93
Grady, Re 405 A 2d 851 (1979); on appeal 426 A 2d 467, 85 NJ 235 (1981) 96
Grant v South-West Trains Ltd: C-249/96 [1998] ECR I-621, [1998] All ER (EC) 193,
    [1998] 1 CMLR 993, [1998] ICR 449, [1998] IRLR 206, [1998] 1 FCR 377, [1998]
    1 FLR 839, [1998] Fam Law 392, ECJ 34, 35, 46, 65
Gray v Mid Herts Hospital Management Committee (1974) 118 Sol Jo 501 230
Gregory v Pembrokeshire Health Authority [1989] 1 Med LR 81 .... 131, 143, 150, 159
Grieve v Salford Health Authority [1991] 2 Med LR 295 125
Griswold v Connecticut 381 US 479, 14 L Ed 2d 510, 85 S Ct 1678 (1965) 322
Grodin v Grodin 301 NW 2d 869 (Mich, 1981) 135

PAGE

Guardianship of Grant, Re 747 P 2d 445 (Wash, 1987)   436

H

H (a patient), Re [1992] 2 FCR 707, [1993] 1 FLR 28, [1993] Fam Law 131, [1993] 4 Med
    LR 91   283
H (adult: medical treatment), Re [1998] 3 FCR 174, 38 BMLR 11 ....   401, 407
H v Royal Alexandra Hospital for Children [1990] 1 Med LR 297 ....   227, 240
HG, Re [1993] 1 FCR 553, [1993] 1 FLR 587, [1993] Fam Law 403   101
HIV Haemophiliac Litigation, Re [1990] NLJR 1349, CA   207
HL v Matheson 101 S Ct 1164 (1981) 119, 144
Hallmark Clinic v North Carolina Department of Human Resources 519 F 2d 1315 (1975):   144
Halushka v University of Saskatchewan (1965) 53 DLR (2d) 436, 52 WWR 608   463
Hamilton v Fife Health Board [1993] 4 Med LR 201, 13 BMLR 156, 1993 SC 369, 1993
    SLT 624, 1993 SCLR 408 ....   126, 161
Hampson v Department of Education and Science [1991] 1 AC 171, [1990] 2 All ER 513,
    [1990] 3 WLR 42, [1990] ICR 511, [1990] IRLR 302, 134 Sol Jo 1123, [1990] 26
    LS Gaz R 39, [1990] NLJR 853, HL   25
Harbeson v Parke-Davis Inc 656 P 2d 483 (Wash, 1983)   163
Harnish v Childrens Hospital Medical Center 387 Mass 152, 439 NE 2d 240 (1982)   277
Harrington v Essex Area Health Authority (1984) Times, 14 November   225
Harris v McRae 100 S Ct 2671 (1980)   120
Harrison v Cornwall County Council (1990) 90 LGR 81, 11 BMLR 21, CA   313
HARVARD/ONCOmouse, Re [1990] EPOR 4, 525   495
Haughian v Paine [1987] 4 WWR 97, 37 DLR (4th) 624, Sask CA   281
Hay v University of Alberta Hospital [1991] 2 Med LR 204   209
Hayes, Re 608 P 2d 635 (Wash, 1980)   97
Hayward v Board of Management of the Royal Infirmary of Edinburgh 1954 SC 453, 1954
    SLT 226   221
Hecht v Kane 16 Cal App 4ᵗʰ 836 (1993)   486
Hendy v Milton Keynes Health Authority (No 2) [1992] 3 Med LR 119   230
HM Advocate v Brady (1996) unreported   416
HM Advocate v Cunningham 1963 JC 80, 1963 SLT 345   544
HM Advocate v Dingwall (1867) 4 SLR 249, 5 Irv 466   535
HM Advocate v Kidd 1960 JC 61, 1960 SLT 82   533
HM Advocate v McDougall 1994 Crim LB 12 – 3   126
HM Advocate v Savage 1923 JC 49   536
HM Advocate v Watson (1991 Scotsman, 11 June, p 8   415
Herskovits v Group Health Co-operative of Puget Sound 664 P 2d 474 (1983)   238
Hewer v Bryant [1970] 1 QB 357, [1969] 3 All ER 578, [1969] 3 WLR 425, 113 Sol Jo 525,
    CA 249, 252
Hickman v Group Health Plan Inc 369 NW 2d 10 (1986).......................   159
Hier (Mary), Re 464 NE 2d 959 (Mass, 1984)   436
Hills v Potter [1983] 3 All ER 716, [1984] 1 WLR 641n, 128 Sol Jo 224 ....   223, 274, 281
Hodgson v Minnesota 110 S Ct 2926 (1990)   144
Holmes v Board of Hospital Trustees of City of London (1977) 81 DLR (3d) 67, 17 OR (2d) 626:   235
Hopp v Lepp (1979) 98 DLR (3d) 464; revsd 112 DLR (3d) 67, CA   282
Hotson v East Berkshire Area Health Authority [1987] AC 750, [1987] 2 All ER 909, [1987]
    3 WLR 232, 131 Sol Jo 975, [1987] LS Gaz R 2365, [1987] NLJ Rep 638, HL ...   237
Houston, Applicant, Re (1996) 32 BMLR 93, 1996 SCLR 943, Sh Ct   270
HOWARD FLOREY/Relaxin, Re [1995] EPOR 541   495
Hsuing v Webster 1992 SLT 1071n   285
Hughes v Waltham Forest Health Authority [1991] 2 Med LR 155, CA   224
Hunter v Hanley 1955 SC 200, 1955 SLT 213 ....   224, 280, 388
Hunter v Mann [1974] QB 767, [1974] 2 All ER 414, [1974] 2 WLR 742, [1974] RTR 338,
    59 Cr App Rep 37, [1974] Crim LR 260, 118 Sol Jo 171 ....   191, 206

PAGE

Hyde v Tameside Area Health Authority (1981) 2 PN 26, [1981] CLY 1854, [1981] CA
    Transcript 130, CA 233

I

I v United Kingdom (1997) 23 EHRR CD 66, ECtHR 42, 44
Ibrahim (a minor) v Muhammad (21 May 1984, unreported) 230
Infant Doe, Re GU 8204-004 A (1982); on appeal 52 USLW 3369 (1983) 382
Inquiry into the death of of Emma Jane Hendry, Re (15 January, unreported), Sh Ct 203, 204

J

J (a minor), Re [1991] Fam 33, [1990] 3 All ER 930, [1991] 2 WLR 140, [1991] FCR 370,
    [1991] 1 FLR 366, [1990] 2 Med LR 67, 6 BMLR 25, [1990] NLJR 1533, CA:166, 251, 257,
                                371, 372, 373,
                                375, 376, 377,
                                385, 400, 405,
                                406, 446, 447
J (a minor), Re [1993] Fam 15, [1992] 4 All ER 614, [1992] 3 WLR 507, [1992] 2 FCR 753,
    [1992] 2 FLR 165, [1993] Fam Law 126, 9 BMLR 10, [1992] 30 LS Gaz R 32,
    [1992] NLJR 1123, 136 Sol Jo LB 207, CA 7, 17, 251, 257, 302, 306,
                                373, 376, 377, 379, 390, 441
James v Eastleigh Borough Council [1990] 2 AC 751, [1990] 2 All ER 607, [1990] 3 WLR
    55, 88 LGR 756, [1990] ICR 554, [1990] IRLR 288, [1990] 27 LS Gaz R 41, [1990]
    NLJR 926, HL.. 33
Jane, Re [1989] FLC 92-007, 13 Fam LR 47 .... 100, 106
Jefferson v Griffin Spalding County Hospital Authority 247 Ga 86, 274 SE 2d 457 (Ga, 1981): 137
John F Kennedy Memorial Hospital Inc v Bludworth 452 So 2d 921 (Fla, 1984) 436
Johnson v Calvert 851 P 2d 776 (1993) 84
Johnston v Wellesley Hospital (1970) 17 DLR (3d) 139 .... 109, 252
Jones (Nancy Ellen), Re 529 A 2d 434 (NJ, 1987) 436, 442
Jones v Lanarkshire Health Board 1990 SLT 19, 1989 SCLR 542; affd 1991 SLT 714, 1991
    SCLR 806 95
Jones v Manchester Corpn [1952] 2 QB 852, [1952] 2 All ER 125, 116 JP 412, [1952] 1 TLR
    1589, CA 232
Jorgensen v Meade-Johnson Laboratories 483 F 2d 237 (1973) 162
Junor v Inverness Hospital Board of Management and McNicol (1959) Times, 26 March, HL: 232

K

K (a minor) (Northern Health and Social Services Board v F and G), Re [1991] 2 Med LR 371. . 118
K and Public Trustee, Re (1985) 63 BCLR 145, 19 DLR (4th) 255, [1985] 4 WWR 724; affd
    [1985] 4 WWR 757, Can SC.. 98
KB (adult) (mental patient: medical treatment), Re (1994) 19 BMLR 144 517
Kaimovitz v Michigan Department of Mental Health 42 USLW 2063 (1973) 520
Kay v Ayrshire and Arran Health Board [1987] 2 All ER 417, sub nom Kay's Tutor v
    Ayrshire and Arran Health Board 1987 SC 145, 1987 SLT 577, HL 237
Kelly v Hazlett (1976) 75 DLR (3d) 536 276
Kelly v Kelly [1997] 2 FLR 828, 1997 SLT 896, 1997 SCLR 749, Ct of Sess 125, 142
Kenyon v Bell 1953 SC 125, 1952 SLT (Notes) 79 237
Kingsbury v Smith 442 A 2d 1003 (1982) 93
Kirkham v Chief Constable of the Greater Manchester Police [1989] 3 All ER 882; affd
    [1990] 2 QB 283, [1990] 3 All ER 246, [1990] 2 WLR 987, 134 Sol Jo 758, [1990]
    13 LS Gaz R 47, [1990] NLJR 209, CA 233, 502

PAGE

Kjeldsen v R [1981] 2 SCR 617, 131 DLR (3d) 121, 17 Alta LR (2d) 97, 39 NR 376, [1982]
  1 WWR 577, 64 CCC (2d) 161, 24 CR (3d) 289 531
Knight v Home Office [1990] 3 All ER 237, 4 BMLR 85, [1990] NLJR 210 502
Knoop, Re (1893) 10 SC 198 311
Kondis v State Transport Authority (1984) 154 CLR 672, 55 ALR 225, 58 ALJR 531, HC of A: 220
Kong Cheuk Kwan v R (1985) 82 Cr App Rep 18, [1985] Crim LR 787, 129 Sol Jo 504,
  [1985] NLJ Rep 753, PC 241
Kwok Chak Ming v R [1963] Crim LR 748, [1963] HKLR 349 479

L

L, Petitioner, Re 1996 SCLR 538 .... 102, 403
L and M (Sarah's Case), Re (1993) 17 Fam LR 357 107
LC (medical treatment: sterilisation), Re [1997] 2 FLR 258, [1997] Fam Law 604 105
La Fleur v Cornelis (1979) 28 NBR (2d) 569 219
Langley v Campbell (1975) Times, 6 November 229
Lanphier v Phipos (1838) 8 C & P 475, [1835–42] All ER Rep 421 223
Largey v Rothman 540 A 2d 504 (NJ, 1988) 280
Lask v Gloucester Area Health Authority (1985) 2 PN 96, (1985) Times, 13 December, CA: 208
Laskey, Jaggard and Brown v United Kingdom (1997) 24 EHRR 39, ECtHR 30
Lausier v Pescinski 226 NW 2d 180 (1975) 344
Law Hospital NHS Trust v Lord Advocate [1996] 2 FLR 407, [1996] Fam Law 670, 39 BMLR
  166, 1996 SLT 848, Ct of Sess; on appeal [1996] 2 FLR 407, 1996 SLT 869, OH : 254, 374,
                                                               396, 402, 404, 407
Lazevnick v General Hospital of Monro County Inc 499 F Supp 146 (MD, 1980) 162
Lee v South West Thames Regional Health Authority [1985] 2 All ER 385, [1985] 1 WLR
  845, 128 Sol Jo 333, [1985] LS Gaz R 2015, [1985] NLJ Rep 438, CA 208
Lindsay v Greater Glasgow Health Board (1990) Scotsman, 14 March 95
Lipari v Sears, Roebuck & Co 497 F Supp 185 (Neb, 1980) 505
Long v Adams 175 Ga App 538, 333 SE 2d 852 (1985) 54
Lovato v District Court 601 P 2d 1072 (Colo, 1979) 442
Loveday v Renton [1990] 1 Med LR 117 236
Lovelace Medical Center v Mendez 803 P 2d 603 (1991) 93
Lowery v R [1974] AC 85, [1973] 3 All ER 662, [1973] 3 WLR 235, 58 Cr App Rep 35,
  117 Sol Jo 583, PC 525
Ludlow v Swindon Health Authority [1989] 1 Med LR 104 234
Lybert v Warrington Health Authority [1996] 7 Med LR 71, 25 BMLR 91, [1995] 20 LS
  Gaz R 40, [1996] PIQR P45, CA 93, 286

M

M, Re [1988] 2 FLR 497, [1988] Fam Law 434 101
M v Chief Constable of West Midlands Police (1996) unreported 46
MB (an adult: medical treatment), Re [1997] 2 FCR 541, [1997] 2 FLR 426, [1997] Fam
  Law 542, [1997] 8 Med LR 217, 38 BMLR 175, [1997] NLJR 600, CA 126, 139, 266
MT v JT ABAJ 1195, 140 NJ Super 355 A 2d 204 (1976); cert den 364 A 2d 1076, App Div: 42
M'Alister (or Donoghue) v Stevenson [1932] AC 562, 101 LJPC 119, 37 Com Cas 350, 48
  TLR 494, 1932 SC (HL) 31, sub nom Donoghue (or McAlister) v Stevenson [1932]
  All ER Rep 1, 1932 SLT 317, sub nom McAlister (or Donoghue) v Stevenson 76
  Sol Jo 396, 147 LT 281 54
McAllister v General Medical Council [1993] AC 388, [1993] 1 All ER 982, [1993] 2 WLR
  308, [1993] 5 LS Gaz R 42, 137 Sol Jo LB 14, PC 11
McAllister v Lewisham and North Southwark Health Authority [1994] 5 Med LR 343 ... 285
McCandless v General Medical Council [1996] 1 WLR 167, 30 BMLR 53, [1996] 05 LS
  Gaz R 31, 140 Sol Jo LB 28, PC 11

PAGE

McClusky v HM Advocate [1989] RTR 182, 1989 SLT 175 .... 126, 479
MacDonald v Glasgow Western Hospitals Board of Management 1954 SC 453, 1954 SLT 226: 221
MacDonald v York County Hospital Corpn (1972) 28 DLR (3d) 521, [1972] 3 OR 469;
    varied (1973) 41 DLR (3d) 321, 1 OR (2d) 653, Ont CA; affd [1976] 2 SCR 825,
    sub nom Vail v MacDonald 66 DLR (3d) 530, Can SC 235, 229
McFarlane v Tayside Health Board 1997 SLT 211, OH; revsd 1998 SC 389, 1998 SLT 307,
    1998 SCLR 126 95
McGhee v National Coal Board [1972] 3 All ER 1008, [1973] 1 WLR 1, 13 KIR 471, 116
    Sol Jo 967, HL 235, 236
McKay v Bergstedt 810 P 2d 617 (1990) 432
McKay v Essex Area Health Authority [1982] QB 1166, [1982] 2 All ER 771, [1982] 2 WLR
    890, 126 Sol Jo 261, CA 143, 164, 165
McLelland v Greater Glasgow Health Board (1998) Times, 14 October, OH 160
MacLennan v MacLennan (or Shortland) 1958 SC 105, 1958 SLT 12 61
Mcleod v Napier 1993 SCCR 303 544
McNulty, Re No 1960 Probate Court (Mass, 1980) 382
Mahon v Osborne [1939] 2 KB 14, [1939] 1 All ER 535, 108 LJKB 567, 83 Sol Jo 134, 160
    LT 329, CA 235, 230, 231
Maine Medical Center v Houle No 74-145 Sup Ct (Me, 1974)..................... 382
Male v Hopmans [1967] 2 OR 457, 64 DLR (2d) 105, Ont CA 276
Malette v Shulman (1990) 72 OR (2d) 417, 67 DLR (4th) 321, [1991] 2 Med LR 162, Ont CA: 432
Marion (No 2), Re (1992) 17 Fam LR 336 106
Marriage of Moschetta, Re 30 Cal Rep 2d 893 (1994) 84
Marshall v Curry [1933] 3 DLR 260, 60 CCC 136, 6 MPR 267 247
Maynard v West Midlands Regional Health Authority [1985] 1 All ER 635, [1984] 1 WLR
    634, 128 Sol Jo 317, [1984] LS Gaz R 1926, 133 NLJ 641, HL 92, 224, 276
Medhurst v Medhurst (1984) 46 OR (2d) 263, 9 DLR (4th) 252 142
Metagama, The. See Canadian Pacific Rly Co v Kelvin Shipping Co Ltd, The Metagama
Milton v Cary Medical Center 538 A 2d 252 (Me, 1988) 125
Modinos v Cyprus (1993) 16 EHRR 485, ECtHR 35
Morgan Estates v Fairfield Family Counselling Center 673 NE 2d 1131 (Ohio, 1997) 505
Moyes v Lothian Health Board [1990] 1 Med LR 463, 1990 SLT 444 .... 278, 285
Mughal v Reuters Ltd [1993] IRLR 571, 16 BMLR 127, 137 Sol Jo LB 275 238
Mulloy v Hop Sang [1935] 1 WWR 714 274
Murphy v R (1989) 167 CLR 94, 86 ALR 35, 63 ALJR 422, HC of A 524
Murray v McMurchy [1949] 2 DLR 442, [1949] 1 WWR 989 247

N

Naylor v Preston Area Health Authority [1987] 2 All ER 353, [1987] 1 WLR 958, 131 Sol
    Jo 596, [1987] LS Gaz R 1494, [1987] NLJ Rep 474, CA 207
Netherlands v EC Council and EU Parliament: C–377/98 unreported 496
Newell and Newell v Goldenberg [1995] 6 Med LR 371 .... 92, 160, 286
Ng Chun Pui v Lee Chuen Tat [1988] RTR 298, 132 Sol Jo 1244, PC 234
Noccash v Burger 290 SE 2d 825 (Va, 1982) 143, 159
Norfolk and Norwich Healthcare (NHS) Trust v W [1997] 1 FCR 269, [1996] 2 FLR 613,
    [1997] Fam Law 17, 34 BMLR 16 .... 139, 266
Nottinghamshire County Council v Bowly [1978] IRLR 252 33

O

O (a minor) (medical treatment), Re [1993] 1 FCR 925, [1993] 2 FLR 149, [1993] Fam Law
    454, [1993] 4 Med LR 272, 19 BMLR 148, 137 Sol Jo LB 107 249
Ochs v Borelli 445 A 2d 883 (Conn, 1982) 93
Ohio v Akron Center for Reproductive Health 110 S Ct 2972 (1990) 144

O'Malley-Williams v Board of Governors of the National Hospital for Nervous Diseases   PAGE
    (1975) 1 BMJ 635 234
Open Door Counselling and Dublin Well Woman Centre v Ireland (1992) 18 BMLR 1, ECtHR: 118
Oskenholt v Lederle Laboratories 656 P 2d 293 (1982) 240
Oxfordshire County Council v M [1994] Fam 151, [1994] 2 All ER 269, [1994] 2 WLR 393,
    [1994] 1 FCR 753, [1994] 1 FLR 175, CA 208

P

P (a minor), Re (1986) 80 LGR 301, [1986] 1 FLR 272, [1982] CLY 2077 .... 144, 253
P (a minor), Re [1987] FCR 123, [1987] 2 FLR 467, [1987] Fam Law 385, 151 JP 635, CA: 136
P (minors) (wardship: surrogacy), Re [1988] FCR 140, [1987] 2 FLR 421, [1987] Fam Law
    414 .... 82, 85
P (a minor), Re [1989] 1 FLR 182, [1989] Fam Law 102 101
P v P (1994) 19 Fam LR 1 107
P v S and Cornwall County Council: C-13/94 [1996] ECR I-2143, [1996] All ER (EC) 397,
    [1996] 2 CMLR 247, [1996] ICR 795, [1996] IRLR 347, sub nom P v S (sex
    discrimination): C-13/94 [1997] 2 FCR 180, [1996] 2 FLR 347, [1996] Fam Law
    609, ECJ 34, 45
P's Curator Bonis v Criminal Injuries Compensation Board (1997) 44 BMLR 70, 1997 SLT
    1180, OH 165
Page v Smith [1996] AC 155, [1995] 2 All ER 736, [1995] 2 WLR 644, [1995] RTR 210,
    [1995] 2 Lloyd's Rep 95, 28 BMLR 133, [1995] 23 LS Gaz R 33, [1995] NLJR 723, HL: 238
Palmer v Tees Health Authority (1998) 44 BMLR 88 506
Parpalaix v CECOS (1984) unreported 486
Paton v British Pregnancy Advisory Service Trustees [1979] QB 276, [1978] 2 All ER 987,
    [1978] 3 WLR 687, 142 JP 497, 122 Sol Jo 744 .... 90, 125, 136, 141, 204
Paton v United Kingdom (1980) 3 EHRR 408 141
People (ex rel Wallace) v Labrenz 104 NE 2d 769 (Ill, 1952); on appeal 344 US 824, 97
    L Ed 642, 73 S Ct 24 (1952) 250
People v Davis 872 P 2d 591 (Cal 1994) 125
People v Lyons Sup Ct No 56072, Alameda Co (Cal, 1974) 333
People of the State of Illinois v Russell 630 NE 2d 794 (Ill, 1994) 51
Perreira v State 768 P 2d 1198 (Colo, 1989) 505
Peter (Hilda M), Re 529 A 2d 419 (NJ, 1987) 435
Peterson v State 671 P 2d 230 (Was, 1983) 201
Pickford v Imperial Chemical Industries plc [1998] 3 All ER 462, [1998] 1 WLR 1189,
    [1998] ICR 673, [1998] IRLR 435, [1998] 31 LS Gaz R 36, [1998] NLJR 978,
    142 Sol Jo LB 198, HL 238
Pizzey v Ford Motor Co [1993] 17 LS Gaz R 46, [1994] PIQR P15, CA 209
Planned Parenthood of Missouri v Danforth 428 US 52, 69 (1976) 142
Planned Parenthood of SE Pennsylvania v Casey 112 S Ct 2791 (1992) 121, 142, 144, 204
Plaza Health and Rehabilitation Center of Syracuse, Re S Ct, Onandaga Cty, NY (1984) .. 322
Pollock v Lanarkshire Health Board (1987) Times, 6 January 95
Practice Note [1993] 3 All ER 222, [1993] 2 FCR 657, [1993] 2 FLR 222, [1993] 4 Med LR
    302, [1993] 35 LS Gaz R 35, [1993] NLJR 1067, 137 Sol Jo LB 154 102
Practice Note [1994] 2 All ER 413, [1995] 1 FCR 463, [1994] 1 FLR 654, 18 BMLR 159 :   434
Practice Note (persistent vegetative state: withdrawal of treatment) [1996] 4 All ER 766,
    34 BMLR 20, sub nom Practice Note (Official Solicitor: vegetative state) [1996] 3
    FCR 606, [1996] 2 FLR 375 399
Proffitt v Bartolo 412 NW 2d 232 (Mich, 1987)............................... 159, 163
Prokanik v Cillo 478 A 2d 755 (NJ, 1984) 163
Public Health Trust v Brown 388 So 2d 1084 (1980) 93

Q

Q (parental order), Re [1996] 2 FCR 345, [1996] 1 FLR 369, [1996] Fam Law 206 ... 62, 66, 79, 80

PAGE

Quinlan, Re 355 A 2d 647 1976, 70 NJ 10 (1976) 409, 435, 442

R

R (a minor), Re [1992] Fam 11, [1991] 4 All ER 177, [1991] 3 WLR 592, [1992] 2 FCR 229,
    [1992] 1 FLR 190, [1992] Fam Law 67, [1992] 3 Med LR 342, 7 BMLR 147, [1991]
    NLJR 1297, CA 249, 251, 252, 257, 258, 259, 376, 475
R (adult: medical treatment), Re [1996] 3 FCR 473, [1996] 2 FLR 99, [1996] Fam Law 535,
    31 BMLR 127 446
R v Aarons [1964] Crim LR 484, CCA 540
R v Adams [1957] Crim LR 365 437
R v Adomako [1994] QB 302, [1993] 4 All ER 935, [1993] 3 WLR 927, 98 Cr App Rep 262,
    [1993] 4 Med LR 304, 15 BMLR 13, [1993] 25 LS Gaz R 36, 137 Sol Jo LB 145,
    CA; affd [1995] 1 AC 171, [1994] 3 All ER 79, [1994] 3 WLR 288, 158 JP 653,
    [1994] Crim LR 757, [1994] 5 Med LR 277, 19 BMLR 56, [1994] NLJR 936, HL: 242
R v Ahluwalia [1992] 4 All ER 889, 96 Cr App Rep 133, [1992] NLJR 1159, [1993] Crim
    LR 63, CA 538
R v Arthur (1981) 12 BMLR 1 .... 16, 363, 368, 369, 370, 405, 415
R v Bailey [1983] 2 All ER 503, [1983] 1 WLR 760, 77 Cr App Rep 76, 147 JP 558, [1983]
    Crim LR 533, 127 Sol Jo 425, CA 542
R v Bateman (1925) 19 Cr App Rep 8, 89 JP 162, 94 LJKB 791, 28 Cox CC 33, [1925] All
    ER Rep 45, 69 Sol Jo 622, 133 LT 730, 41 TLR 557, CCA 223, 241
R v Borg [1969] SCR 551 532
R v Bourne [1939] 1 KB 687, [1938] 3 All ER 615, 108 LJKB 471, CCA 114
R v Bournewood Community and Mental Health NHS Trust, ex p L [1998] 3 All ER 289,
    [1998] 3 WLR 107, [1998] 2 FCR 501, [1998] 2 FLR 550, [1998] Fam Law 592,
    [1998] 29 LS Gaz R 27, [1998] NLJR 1014, 142 Sol Jo LB 195, HL 318, 509
R v Braithwaite (1991) Times, 9 December, CA 524
R v Brown [1994] 1 AC 212, [1993] 2 All ER 75, [1993] 2 WLR 556, 97 Cr App Rep 44,
    157 JP 337, [1993] Crim LR 583, [1993] NLJR 399, HL 29, 243, 454
R v Brown [1996] AC 543, [1996] 1 All ER 545, [1996] 2 WLR 203, [1996] 2 Cr App Rep
    72, [1996] Crim LR 408, [1996] 10 LS Gaz R 21, [1996] NLJR 209, 140 Sol Jo LB
    66, HL 245, 485
R v Burgess [1991] 2 QB 92, [1991] 2 All ER 769, [1991] 2 WLR 1206, 93 Cr App Rep 41,
    [1991] Crim LR 548, 135 Sol Jo 477, [1991] 19 LS Gaz R 31, [1991] NLJR 527, CA: 543
R v Byrne [1960] 2 QB 396, [1960] 3 All ER 1, [1960] 3 WLR 440, 44 Cr App Rep 246,
    104 Sol Jo 645, CCA 536
R v Cambridge District Health Authority, ex p B [1995] 1 FLR 1055, [1995] Fam Law 480,
    25 BMLR 5; revsd sub nom R v Cambridge Health Authority, ex p B [1995] 2 All
    ER 129, [1995] 1 WLR 898, [1995] 2 FCR 485, [1995] NLJR 415, sub nom R v
    Cambridge District Health Authority, ex p B [1995] 1 FLR 1055, [1995] Fam Law
    480, 23 BMLR 1, CA 251, 297, 379
R v Canons Park Mental Health Review Tribunal, ex p A [1995] QB 60, [1994] 2 All ER 659,
    [1994] 3 WLR 630, 18 BMLR 94, [1994] 13 LS Gaz R 35, 138 Sol Jo LB 75, CA: 514
R v Carr (1986) Sunday Times, 30 November 415
R v Central Birmingham Health Authority, ex p Collier (6 January 1988, unreported) 297
R v Central Birmingham Health Authority, ex p Walker (1987) 3 BMLR 32, CA 296
R v Charlson [1955] 1 All ER 859, [1955] 1 WLR 317, 39 Cr App Rep 37, 119 JP 283, 99
    Sol Jo 221, CCA 541
R v Cogley [1989] VR 799 41
R v Collins, ex p S [1998] 3 All ER 673, [1998] 2 FCR 685, [1998] 2 FLR 728, [1998] Fam
    Law 526, [1998] 22 LS Gaz R 29, [1998] NLJR 693, 142 Sol Jo LB 164, CA ... 267, 432
R v Collins, ex p S [1998] 3 WLR 936, [1998] Fam Law 662, CA 267
R v Coney (1882) 8 QBD 534, 46 JP 404, 51 LJMC 66, 15 Cox CC 46, 30 WR 678, 46 LT
    307, CCR 343
R v Cooper (1979) 13 CR (3d) 97, Can SC 539
R v Cox (1992) 12 BMLR 38 .... 415, 426, 438

PAGE

R v Crown Court at Cardiff, ex p Kellam (1993) 16 BMLR 76 206
R v Crozier (1990) 12 Cr App Rep (S) 206, [1991] Crim LR 138, 8 BMLR 128, CA 197
R v Cuerrier [1996] BCJ No 2229, BCCA 52
R v Davidson [1969] VR 667 114
R v Department of Health and Social Security, ex p Darnell (1986) 293 BMJ 322 11
R v Dhingra (1991) Daily Telegraph, 25 January 112, 129
R v Dobinson [1977] QB 354, [1977] 2 All ER 341, [1977] 2 WLR 169, 64 Cr App Rep 186,
    141 JP 354, 121 Sol Jo 83, CA 242, 369
R v Donovan [1934] 2 KB 498, 32 LGR 439, 25 Cr App Rep 1, 98 JP 409, 103 LJKB 683,
    30 Cox CC 187, [1934] All ER Rep 207, 78 Sol Jo 601, 152 LT 46, 50 TLR 566, CCA: 30, 245
R v Dudley and Stephens (1884) 14 QBD 273, 49 JP 69, 54 LJMC 32, 15 Cox CC 624, 33
    WR 347, [1881-5] All ER Rep 61, 52 LT 107, 1 TLR 118, CCR 306
R v Ealing District Health Authority, ex p Fox [1993] 3 All ER 170, [1993] 1 WLR 373,
    11 BMLR 59, 136 Sol Jo LB 220 503
R v Ethical Committee of St Mary's Hospital (Manchester), ex p H (or Harriott) [1988]
    1 FLR 512, [1988] Fam Law 165, [1987] NLJ Rep 1038 .... 72, 456
R v Falconer (1990) 171 CLR 30, 65 ALJR 20, HC of A 544
R v Gardner, ex p L [1986] QB 1090, [1986] 2 All ER 306, [1986] 2 WLR 883, 130 Sol Jo
    204, [1986] LS Gaz R 786 512
R v Gaud unreported 53
R v General Medical Council, ex p Gee [1987] 1 All ER 1204, [1986] 1 WLR 226, 130 Sol
    Jo 144, [1986] LS Gaz R 125; on appeal [1987] 1 All ER 1204, [1986] 1 WLR 1247,
    130 Sol Jo 484, [1986] LS Gaz R 2001, CA; affd sub nom Gee v General Medical
    Council [1987] 2 All ER 193, [1987] 1 WLR 564, 131 Sol Jo 626, [1987] LS Gaz R
    1652, HL 11
R v Gibbins and Proctor (1918) 13 Cr App Rep 134, 82 JP 287, CCA 369
R v Gloucestershire County Council, ex p Barry [1997] AC 584, [1997] 2 All ER 1, [1997]
    2 WLR 459, 36 BMLR 69, [1997] NLJR 453, 141 Sol Jo LB 91, HL 298, 299
R v Gottschalk (1974) 22 CCC (2d) 415 544
R v Hallstrom, ex p W [1986] QB 1090, [1986] 2 WLR 883, 130 Sol Jo 204, [1986] LS Gaz R
    786, sub nom R v Hallstrom, ex p W (No 2) [1986] 2 All ER 306 512
R v Hamilton (1983) Times, 16 September 133
R v Handley (1874) 13 Cox CC 79 131
R v Harris (1988) 35 A Crim R 146 41
R v Harrow London Borough Council, ex p D [1990] Fam 133, [1990] 3 All ER 12, [1989]
    3 WLR 1239, 88 LGR 41, [1989] FCR 729, [1990] 1 FLR 79, [1990] Fam Law 18,
    133 Sol Jo 1513, [1989] NLJR 1153, CA 202
R v Hennessy [1989] 2 All ER 9, [1989] 1 WLR 287, [1989] RTR 153, 89 Cr App Rep 10,
    [1989] Crim LR 356, 133 Sol Jo 263, [1989] 9 LS Gaz R 41, CA 542
R v Herbert (1960) 25 JCL 163 486
R v Human Fertilisation and Embryology Authority, ex p Blood [1997] 2 All ER 687, [1997]
    2 WLR 806, [1997] 2 FCR 501, [1997] Fam Law 401, 35 BMLR 1, [1997] NLJR 253, CA: 58, 60
R v Hurst [1995] 1 Cr App Rep 82, CA 524
R v Instan [1893] 1 QB 450, 57 JP 282, 62 LJMC 86, 17 Cox CC 602, 5 R 248, 41 WR 368,
    [1891-4] All ER Rep 1213, 37 Sol Jo 251, 68 LT 420, 9 TLR 248, CCR 191
R v Isitt [1978] RTR 211, 67 Cr App Rep 44, [1978] Crim LR 159, CA 545
R v Jennion [1962] 1 All ER 689, [1962] 1 WLR 317, 46 Cr App Rep 212, 106 Sol Jo 224, CCA: 540
R v Johnson (1961) 1 Med Sci Law 192 416
R v Joint Committee on Higher Medical Training and Specialist Advisory Committee on
    Rheumatology, ex p Goldstein (1992) 11 BMLR 10, CA 14
R v K (1971) 3 CCC (2d) 84 544
R v Kelly [1998] 3 All ER 741, CA 492, 493
R v Kemp [1957] 1 QB 399, [1956] 3 All ER 249, [1956] 3 WLR 724, 40 Cr App Rep 121,
    120 JP 457, 100 Sol Jo 768 .... 530, 541
R v Kreider (1993) 140 AR 81 52
R v Lambeth London Borough Council, ex p Carroll (1987) 20 HLR 142 313
R v Lodwig (1990) Times, 16 March, p 3 426

PAGE

R v Lupien (1970) 9 DLR (3d) 1 525
R v McGuinness (1988) 35 A Crim R 146 41
R v MacKenney (1980) 72 Cr App Rep 78 523
R v McNaughton (1843) 1 Car & Kir 130n, 1 Town St Tr 314, 4 St Tr NS 847, sub nom
    M'Naghten's Case 10 Cl & Fin 200, [1843–60] All ER Rep 229, sub nom Insane
    Criminals 8 Scott NR 595, HL 530
R v Malcherek [1981] 2 All ER 422, [1981] 1 WLR 690, 73 Cr App Rep 173, [1981] Crim
    LR 401, 125 Sol Jo 305, CA 333, 442
R v Masih [1986] Crim LR 395, CA 524
R v Matheson [1958] 2 All ER 87, [1958] 1 WLR 474, 42 Cr App Rep 145, 102 Sol Jo 309,
    CCA 526
R v Mental Health Commission, ex p X (1988) 9 BMLR 77 .... 521, 547
R v Mental Health Review Tribunal, ex p Clatworthy [1985] 3 All ER 699 516
R v Mental Health Review Tribunal, ex p Macdonald (1998) Crown Office Digest 205 ... 514
R v Mercer (1993) 84 CCC (3d) 41.. 52
R v Mersey Mental Health Review Tribunal, ex p D (1987) Times, 13 April 504
R v Mid Glamorgan Family Health Services Authority, ex p Martin (1993) 16 BMLR 81,
    [1993] 27 LS Gaz R 35, 137 Sol Jo LB 153; affd [1995] 1 All ER 356, [1995] 1 WLR
    110, [1995] 2 FCR 578, [1995] 1 FLR 283, [1994] 5 Med LR 383, 21 BMLR 1,
    [1994] 38 LS Gaz R 42, 138 Sol Jo LB 195, CA 210, 211
R v Ministry of Defence, ex p Smith [1996] QB 517, [1996] 1 All ER 257, [1996] 2 WLR
    305, [1996] ICR 740, [1996] IRLR 100, [1995] NLJR 1689, CA 35
R v Norfolk County Council Social Services Department, ex p M [1989] QB 619, [1989]
    2 All ER 359, [1989] 3 WLR 502, 87 LGR 598, [1989] FCR 667, [1989] Fam Law
    310, [1989] NLJR 293, sub nom R v Norfolk County Council, ex p X [1989] 2 FLR
    120 202
R v North West Thames Regional Health Authority, ex p Daniels [1993] 4 Med LR 364,
    19 BMLR 67 .... 296, 299
R v Oommen [1994] 2 SCR 507, 19 Alta LR (3d) 305, 168 NR 200, [1994] 7 WWR 49,
    91 CCC (3d) 8, 155 AR 190, 30 CR (4th) 195, 73 WAC 190 529
R v Parks (1990) 73 OR (2d) 129, 56 CCC (3d) 449, 78 CR (3d) 1, 39 OAC 27, [1992] SCR
    871... 543
R v Prentice [1994] QB 302, [1993] 4 All ER 935, [1993] 3 WLR 927, 98 Cr App Rep 262,
    [1994] Crim LR 598, [1994] 4 Med LR 304, 15 BMLR 13, [1993] NLJR 850, 137
    Sol Jo LB 145, CA 242
R v Price [1969] 1 QB 541, [1968] 2 All ER 282, [1968] 2 WLR 1397, 52 Cr App Rep 295,
    132 JP 335, 112 Sol Jo 330, CA 111
R v Quick [1973] QB 910, [1973] 3 All ER 347, [1973] 3 WLR 26, 57 Cr App Rep 722,
    137 JP 763, [1973] Crim LR 434, 117 Sol Jo 371, CA 542
R v Rabey [1980] SCR 513, sub nom Rabey v R 114 DLR (3d) 193, 54 CCC (2d) 1, Can SC: 544
R v Raghip (1991) Times, 9 December, CA 524
R v Registrar General, ex p P and G [1996] 2 FCR 588, sub nom Re P and G (transsexuals)
    [1996] 2 FLR 90, [1996] Fam Law 469 .... 44, 46
R v Rivett (1950) 34 Cr App Rep 87, CCA 532
R v Roberts [1990] Crim LR 122, CA 524
R v Rothery [1976] RTR 550, 63 Cr App Rep 231, CA 486
R v Salford Health Authority, ex p Janaway [1989] AC 537, [1988] 2 WLR 442, [1988] 2
    FLR 370, [1988] Fam Law 389, 132 Sol Jo 265, [1988] 6 LS Gaz R 36, CA; affd
    sub nom Janaway v Salford Area Health Authority [1989] AC 537, [1988] 3 All ER
    1079, [1988] 3 WLR 1350, [1989] 1 FLR 155, [1989] Fam Law 191, 3 BMLR 137,
    [1989] 3 LS Gaz R 42, HL 141
R v Sanderson (1993) 98 Cr App Rep 325, [1993] Crim LR 857, CA 536
R v Sang [1980] AC 402, [1979] 2 All ER 1222, [1979] 3 WLR 263, 69 Cr App Rep 282,
    143 JP 606, 123 Sol Jo 552, HL 470
R v Secretary of State for Defence, ex p Perkins [1997] 3 CMLR 310, [1997] IRLR 297,
    141 Sol Jo LB 84 35
R v Secretary of State for Health, ex p Goldstein [1993] 2 CMLR 589 14

PAGE

R v Secretary of State for Scotland 1997 SLT 555, OH; revsd 1998 SC 49, 1998 SLT 162,
Ct of Sess 514

R v Secretary of State for Social Services, ex p Hincks (1979) 123 Sol Jo 436; affd 1 BMLR
93, CA 296

R v Seers (1984) 79 Cr App Rep 261, 149 JP 124, [1985] Crim LR 315, CA 536

R v Senior [1899] 1 QB 283, 63 JP 8, 68 LJQB 175, 19 Cox CC 219, 47 WR 367, [1895–9]
All ER Rep 511, 43 Sol Jo 114, 79 LT 562, 15 TLR 102, CCR 250, 385

R v Seymour [1983] RTR 202, 76 Cr App Rep 211, [1983] Crim LR 260, CA; affd [1983]
2 AC 493, [1983] 2 All ER 1058, [1983] 3 WLR 349, [1983] RTR 455, 77 Cr App
Rep 215, 148 JP 530, [1983] Crim LR 742, 127 Sol Jo 522, HL............... 241

R v Sheffield Health Authority, ex p Seale (1994) 25 BMLR 1 71

R v Silcott (1991) Times, 9 December, CA 524

R v Smith [1974] 1 All ER 376, [1973] 1 WLR 1510, 58 Cr App Rep 106, 138 JP 175, 117
Sol Jo 774, CA 116

R v Ssenyonga (1993) 81 CCC (3d) 257 52

R v Steel [1981] 2 All ER 422, [1981] 1 WLR 690, 73 Cr App Rep 173, 125 Sol Jo 305,
CA 333, 442

R v Stone [1977] QB 354, [1977] 2 All ER 341, [1977] 2 WLR 169, 64 Cr App Rep 186,
141 JP 354, 121 Sol Jo 83, CA 242, 369

R v Sullivan [1984] AC 156, [1983] 2 All ER 673, [1983] 3 WLR 123, 77 Cr App Rep 176,
148 JP 207, 127 Sol Jo 460, HL 543

R v Sullivan (1991) 63 CCC (3d) 97 126

R v Summer (1989) 69 Alta LR (2d) 303, 99 AR 29, 73 CR (3d) 32, CA 52

R v Tan [1983] QB 1053, [1983] 2 All ER 12, [1983] 3 WLR 361, 76 Cr App Rep 300,
147 JP 257, [1983] Crim LR 404, 127 Sol Jo 390, CA 41

R v Tandy [1989] 1 All ER 267, [1989] 1 WLR 350, 87 Cr App Rep 45, 152 JP 453, [1988]
Crim LR 308, 132 Sol Jo 90, [1988] 5 LS Gaz R 36, CA 536

R v Taylor [1979] CLY 570 416

R v Thornton [1992] 1 All ER 306, 96 Cr App Rep 112, [1992] Crim LR 54, CA 538

R v Thornton [1993] 2 SCR 445, 154 NR 243, 13 OR (3d) 744, 82 CCC (3d) 530, 21 CR
(4th) 215 52

R v Tunbridge Wells Health Authority, ex p Goodridge (1988) Times, 21 May 296

R v Turner [1975] QB 834, [1975] 1 All ER 70, [1975] 2 WLR 56, 60 Cr App Rep 80, 139
JP 136, 118 Sol Jo 848, CA 523

R v Wald (1971) 3 DCR (NSW) 25 114

R v Weightman (1990) 92 Cr App Rep 291, [1991] Crim LR 204, CA 523

R v Weise [1969] VR 953 529

R v Welsh [1974] RTR 478, CA 486

R v Wentzell (8 December 1989, unreported) 52

R v Windle [1952] 2 QB 826, [1952] 2 All ER 1, 36 Cr App Rep 85, 116 JP 365, 96 Sol Jo
379, [1952] 1 TLR 1344, CCA 531

R v Wolfson [1965] 3 CCC 304 532

R v Yogasakaran [1990] 1 NZLR 399 243

REL (otherwise R) v EL [1949] P 211, sub nom L v L [1949] 1 All ER 141, [1949] LJR 275,
93 Sol Jo 42, 65 TLR 88 58

Rabey v R. See R v Rabey

Ragsdale v Turnock 763 F 2d 1532 (1985)...................................... 120

Rahman v Kirklees Area Health Authority [1980] 3 All ER 610, [1980] 1 WLR 1244, 124
Sol Jo 726, CA 207

Raleigh Fitkin-Paul Morgan Memorial Hospital v Anderson 42 NJ 421, 201 A 2d 537 (NJ,
1964); on appeal 377 US 985, 12 L Ed 2d 1032, 84 S Ct 1894 (1964) 137

Rance v Mid-Downs Health Authority [1991] 1 QB 587, [1991] 1 All ER 801, [1991] 2 WLR
159, [1991] Fam Law 24, [1990] 2 Med LR 27, 5 BMLR 75, [1990] NLJR 325 .. 131, 143

Rawnsley v Leeds Area Health Authority (1981) Times, 17 November 159

Reed v Campagnola 630 A 2d 1145 (Md, 1993) 143

Rees v United Kingdom (1986) 9 EHRR 56, [1993] 2 FCR 49, [1987] 2 FLR 111, [1987]
Fam Law 157, ECtHR 43

PAGE

Reeves v Metropolitan Police Comr [1998] 2 All ER 381, [1998] 2 WLR 401, [1997] 46 LS
    Gaz R 29, 141 Sol Jo LB 239, CA 502
Reibl v Hughes [1980] 2 SCR 880, 114 DLR (3d) 1, 14 CCLT 1, Can SC .. 225, 274, 276, 282, 284
Reisner v Regents of the University of California 37 Cal Rep 2d 518 (1995) 54, 201
Renslow v Mennonite Hospital 67 Ill 2d 348, 10 Ill Dec 484, 367 NE 2d 1250 (1977) 162
Requena, Re 517 A 2d 893 (NJ, 1986) 436
Rice v Connolly [1966] 2 QB 414, [1966] 2 All ER 649, [1966] 3 WLR 17, 130 JP 322,
    110 Sol Jo 371, DC 195
Riverside Mental Health NHS Trust v Fox. See F v Riverside Mental Health NHS Trust
Robak v United States 658 F 2d 471 (1981) 143, 163
Rochdale Healthcare (NHS) Trust v C [1997] 1 FCR 274, [1996] 3 Hempson's Lawyer 505: 139, 266
Rodriguez v A-G of British Columbia (1993) 82 BCLR 2d 273, [1993] 3 SCR 519, 158 NR 1,
    [1993] 7 WWR 641, 85 CCC (3d) 15, 107 DLR (4th) 342, 24 CR (4th) 281, 56 WAC 1,
    34 BCAC 1, 17 CRR (2d) 193 .... 423, 424
Rodych v Krasey [1971] 4 WWR 358 223
Roe v Minister of Health [1954] 2 QB 66, [1954] 1 WLR 128, 98 Sol Jo 30; affd [1954]
    2 QB 66, [1954] 2 All ER 131, [1954] 2 WLR 915, 98 Sol Jo 319, CA 221
Roe v Wade 410 US 113, 35 L Ed 2d 147, 93 S Ct 705 (1973) 119
Rogers v Lumbermen's Mutual Cas Co 119 So 2d 649 (La, 1960) 248
Rogers v Whittaker (1992) 175 CLR 479, 109 ALR 625, 67 ALJR 47, [1993] 4 Med LR 79,
    HC of A 225
Rogers v Whittaker [1993] 4 Med LR 79, 16 BMLR 148, 175 CLR 479, 109 ALR 625, 67
    ALJR 47, HC of A 279, 280, 282, 283, 284
Rose v R [1961] AC 496, [1961] 1 All ER 859, [1961] 2 WLR 506, 45 Cr App Rep 102,
    105 Sol Jo 253, PC 536
Ross v HM Advocate 1991 SLT 564, 1991 SCCR 823 544
Rothwell v Raes (1988) 54 DLR (4th) 193; affd 76 DLR (4th) 280, CA 220
Royal College of Nursing of the United Kingdom v Department of Health and Social Security
    [1981] AC 800, [1981] 1 All ER 545, [1981] 2 WLR 279, 125 Sol Jo 149, 1 BMLR
    40, HL 140

S

S, Re [1993] Fam 123, [1992] 4 All ER 671, [1992] 3 WLR 806, [1992] 2 FCR 893, [1993]
    1 FLR 26, [1993] Fam Law 221, [1993] 4 Med LR 28, 9 BMLR 69, [1992] 43 LS
    Gaz R 31, [1992] NLJR 1450, 136 Sol Jo LB 299 .... 138, 265
S (medical treatment: adult sterilisation), Re [1998] 1 FLR 944, [1988] Fam Law 325 105
S v United Kingdom (Application 11716/85, DR 47, p 274) (1985) unreported 34
SG, Re [1991] FCR 753, [1991] 2 FLR 329, [1991] Fam Law 309, [1993] 4 Med LR 75,
    6 BMLR 95 145
SY v SY (otherwise W) [1963] P 37, [1962] 3 WLR 526, sub nom S v S (otherwise W) (No 2)
    [1962] 3 All ER 55, 106 Sol Jo 467, CA 41
Saha and Salim, Re (1992) unreported 241
St George's Healthcare NHS Trust v S [1998] 3 All ER 673, [1998] 2 FCR 685, [1998]
    2 FLR 728, [1998] Fam Law 526, [1998] 22 LS Gaz R 29, [1998] NLJR 693, 142
    Sol Jo LB 164, CA 126, 267, 432
St George's Healthcare NHS Trust v S [1998] 3 WLR 936, [1998] Fam Law 662, CA: 267, 433, 434
Salgo v Leland Stanford Junior University Board of Trustees 317 P 2d 170 (Cal, 1957) .. 277
Salih v Enfield Health Authority [1990] 1 Med LR 333; on appeal [1991] 3 All ER 400,
    [1991] 2 Med LR 235, 7 BMLR 1, CA 143, 159
Saunders v Leeds Western Health Authority [1993] 4 Med LR 355, 129 Sol Jo 225, [1985]
    LS Gaz R 1491 235
Saunders v Scottish National Camps Association Ltd [1980] IRLR 174, EAT; on appeal
    [1981] IRLR 277 33
Schloendorff v Society of New York Hospital 211 NY 125, 105 NE 92 (NY, 1914) 245
Schultz v R [1982] WAR 171 524

PAGE

Schweizer v Central Hospital (1974) 53 DLR (3d) 494 274
Scuriaga v Powell (1979) 123 Sol Jo 406; affd (24 July 1980, unreported), CA 94, 143
Secretary, Department of Health and Community Services v JWB and SMB (1992) 175 CLR
    218, 106 ALR 385, 66 ALJR 300 .... 106, 254
Secretary of State for the Home Department v Robb [1995] Fam 127, [1995] 1 All ER 677,
    [1995] 2 WLR 722, [1995] 1 FCR 557, [1995] 1 FLR 412, 22 BMLR 43, [1994]
    NLJR 1695 269
Selfe v Ilford and District Hospital Management Committee (1970) 114 Sol Jo 935, (1970)
    Times, 26 November 233
Severns, Re 425 A 2d 156 (Del, 1980) 436
Sheffield and Horsham v United Kingdom [1998] 3 FCR 141, [1998] 2 FLR 928, ECtHR :   44
Sidaway v Board of Governors of the Bethlem Royal Hospital and the Maudsley Hospital
    [1984] QB 493, [1984] 1 All ER 1018, [1984] 2 WLR 778, 128 Sol Jo 301, [1984]
    LS Gaz R 899, CA; affd [1985] AC 871, [1985] 1 All ER 643, [1985] 2 WLR 480,
    129 Sol Jo 154, 1 BMLR 132, [1985] LS Gaz R 1256, HL 223, 225, 248, 278, 281,
                                                                        283, 287, 468, 491
Siemieniec v Lutheran General Hospital 512 NE 2d 691 (Ill, 1987) 158
Simms and H, Re (1980) 106 DLR (3d) 435 142
Skinner v Oklahoma 316 US 535 (1942) 97
Smart v HM Advocate 1975 JC 30, 1975 SLT 65 .... 245, 454
Smith, Petitioner, Re 1985 SLT 461 95
Smith v Auckland Hospital Board [1964] NZLR 241; revsd [1965] NZLR 191, NZCA ... 276
Smith v Cote 513 A 2d 341 (NH, 1986) 159, 163
Smith v Gardner Merchant Ltd [1998] 3 All ER 852, [1998] IRLR 510, [1998] 32 LS Gaz R
    29, 142 Sol Jo LB 244, CA 39
Smith v Tunbridge Wells Health Authority [1994] 5 Med LR 334 225
Society for the Protection of Unborn Children Ireland Ltd v Grogan: C-159/90 [1991] ECR
    I-4685, [1991] 3 CMLR 849, 9 BMLR 100, ECJ 118
Sodeman v R [1936] 2 All ER 1138, 80 Sol Jo 532, 55 CLR 192, PC 531
South Glamorgan County Council v W and B [1993] 1 FCR 626, [1993] 1 FLR 574, [1993]
    Fam Law 398, 11 BMLR 162 260
State v Green 781 P 2d 678 (Kan, 1987) 125
State v McAfee 385 SE 2d 651 (Ga, 1989) 432
Stephens v Avery [1988] Ch 449, [1988] 2 All ER 477, [1988] 2 WLR 1280, [1988] FSR
    510, 132 Sol Jo 822, [1988] NLJR 69 191
Stewart v Long Island College Hospital 296 NYS 2d 41, 58 Misc 2d 432 (1968) 163
Stobie v Central Birmingham Health Authority (1994) 22 BMLR 135 93
Storar, Re 52 NY 2d 363, 438 NYS 2d 266, 420 NE 2d 64; on appeal 454 US 858, 70 L Ed
    2d 153 , 102 S Ct 309 (1981) 435
Strangways-Lesmere v Clayton [1936] 2 KB 11, [1936] 1 All ER 484, 105 LJKB 385, 80
    Sol Jo 306, 154 LT 463, 52 TLR 374 230
Strunk v Strunk 445 SW 2d 145 (1969) 344
Superintendent of Belchertown State School v Saikewicz 373 Mass 728, 370 NE 2d 64 (1977) : 374, 405
Superintendent of Family and Child Service and Dawson, Re (1983) 145 DLR (3d) 610 .. 368, 375,
                                                                        384, 405
Superintendent of Family and Child Service and McDonald, Re (1982) 135 DLR (3d) 330:   135
Surrogate Parenting Associates Inc v Commonwealth of Kentucky 704 SW 2d 209 (Ky, 1986):   79
Sutherland v United Kingdom (1997) 24 EHRR CD 22, ECtHR 37
Sutkin v Beck 629 SW 2d 131 (1982) 93
Swindon and Marlborough NHS Trust v S [1995] 3 Med LR 84 .... 400, 407

T

T (adult: refusal of treatment), Re [1993] Fam 95, [1992] 4 All ER 649, [1992] 3 WLR 782,
    [1992] 2 FCR 861, [1992] 2 FLR 458, [1993] Fam Law 27, 9 BMLR 46, [1992]
    NLJR 1125, CA 17, 126, 248, 261, 262, 265,
                                                278, 419, 422, 432, 433, 434

PAGE

T (a minor) (wardship: medical treatment), Re [1997] 1 All ER 906, [1997] 1 WLR 242, 96 LGR 116, [1997] 2 FCR 363, [1997] 1 FLR 502, 35 BMLR 63, [1996] 42 LS Gaz R 28, [1996] NLJR 1577, 140 Sol Jo LB 237, CA 248, 251, 371, 377, 378
T, Petitioner, Re 1997 SLT 724 34
T v T [1988] Fam 52, [1988] 1 All ER 613, [1988] 2 WLR 189, [1988] 1 FLR 400, 131 Sol Jo 1286, [1987] LS Gaz R 2456 103
TACP, Re 609 So 2d 588 (Fla, 1992) 359
TK v Australian Red Cross Society [1989] WAR 335 23
TW, Re 551 So 2d 1186 (Fla, 1989) 144
Taft v Taft 388 Mass 331, 446 NE 2d 395 (Mass, 1983) 138
Tameside and Glossop Acute Services Trust v CH [1996] 1 FCR 753, [1996] 1 FLR 762, [1996] Fam Law 353, 31 BMLR 93 . . . . 139, 266
Tarasoff v Regents of the University of California 529 P 2d 55 (Cal, 1974); on appeal 551 P 2d 334, 17 Cal (3d) 358, 425 (Cal, 1976) 201, 505
Taylor v R (1978) 22 ALR 599 526
Teece v Ayrshire and Arran Health Board 1990 SLT 512 95
Teenager, a, Re [1989] FLC 92-006 . . . . 105, 106
Terrell v Garcia 496 SW 2d 124 (1973) 93
Thake v Maurice [1986] QB 644, [1984] 2 All ER 513, [1985] 2 WLR 215, 129 Sol Jo 86, [1985] LS Gaz R 871; revsd [1986] QB 644, [1986] 1 All ER 497, [1986] 2 WLR 337, 129 Sol Jo 894, [1986] LS Gaz R 123, [1986] NLJ Rep 92, CA 92, 95, 219
Thorne v Northern Group Hospital Management Committee (1964) 108 Sol Jo 484 233
Tiller v Atlantic Coast Line Railroad Co 318 US 54 (1943) 278
Tomkins v Bexley Area Health Authority [1993] 4 Med LR 235 228
Toohey v Metropolitan Police Comr [1965] AC 595, [1965] 1 All ER 506, [1965] 2 WLR 439, 49 Cr App Rep 148, 129 JP 181, 109 Sol Jo 130, HL 523
Tremblay v Daigle (1989) 59 DLR (4th) 609; on appeal 62 DLR (4th) 634, Can SC 122, 142
Troppi v Scarf 186 NW 2d 511 (1971) 93
Truman v Thomas 611 P 2d 902 (Cal, 1980) 286
Tuffil v East Surrey Area Health Authority (1978) Times, 15 March 229
Turpin v Sortini 182 Cal Rptr 377 1982 (1982); on appeal 643 P 2d 954 (1982) 163

U

U v W (A-G intervening) [1998] Fam 29, [1997] 3 WLR 739, [1997] 2 CMLR 431, [1998] 1 FCR 526, [1997] 2 FLR 282, 38 BMLR 54, [1997] 11 LS Gaz R 36, 141 Sol Jo LB 57 . . . . 62, 65
US v Brawner 471 F 2d 969 (1972) 532
US v Holmes 26 Fed Cas 360 (1841) 306
Udale v Bloomsbury Area Health Authority [1983] 2 All ER 522, [1983] 1 WLR 1098, 127 Sol Jo 510 94
Upjohn Co (Kirton's) Application [1976] RPC 324 130
Urry v Bierer (1955) Times, 15 July, CA 231

V

VS (adult: mental disorder), Re [1995] 3 Med L Rev 292 270
Vacco v Quill 117 S Ct 2293 (1997) 419, 425, 444
Vanessa F, Re 351 NYS 2d 337 (1974) 135
Venner v North East Essex Area Health Authority (1987) Times, 21 February 91
Viccaro v Milunsky 551 NE 2d 8 (Mass, 1990) 143, 163

W

W (minors), Re [1991] FCR 419, [1991] 1 FLR 385, [1991] Fam Law 180 . . . . 79, 83

PAGE

W (a minor) (medical treatment), Re [1993] Fam 64, [1992] 4 All ER 627, [1992] 3 WLR
758, [1992] 2 FCR 785, [1993] 1 FLR 1, [1992] Fam Law 541, 9 BMLR 22, [1992]
NLJR 1124, CA 259, 260, 344, 346, 475, 517
W (a minor) (adoption: homosexual adopter), Re [1998] Fam 58, [1997] 3 All ER 620, [1997]
3 WLR 768, [1997] 3 FCR 650, [1997] 2 FLR 406, [1997] Fam Law 597, [1997]
24 LS Gaz R 32, 141 Sol Jo LB 137   34
W (EEM), Re [1971] Ch 123, [1970] 2 All ER 502, [1970] 3 WLR 87, 114 Sol Jo 549 ...   318
W v Egdell [1990] Ch 359, [1989] 1 All ER 1089, [1989] 2 WLR 689, 133 Sol Jo 570; affd
[1990] Ch 359, [1990] 1 All ER 835, [1990] 2 WLR 471, 134 Sol Jo 286, 4 BMLR
96, [1990] 12 LS Gaz R 41, CA 191, 195, 196, 208, 212, 504, 506
W v L [1974] QB 711, [1973] 3 All ER 884, [1973] 3 WLR 859, 117 Sol Jo 775, CA   515
Waldron, ex p [1986] QB 824, [1985] 3 WLR 1090, 129 Sol Jo 892, [1986] LS Gaz R 199,
sub nom R v Hallstrom, ex p W [1985] 3 All ER 775, CA   513
Walkin v South Manchester Health Authority [1995] 4 All ER 132, [1995] 1 WLR 1543,
25 BMLR 108, CA 94, 160
Wall v Livingston [1982] 1 NZLR 734, NZCA   142
Ward, a, Re [1996] 2 IR 79, 2 ILRM 401 .... 254, 400
Washington v Glucksberg 117 S Ct 2258 (1997) 419, 432, 444
Watson v M'Ewan [1905] AC 480, 74 LJPC 151, [1904–7] All ER Rep 1, 42 SLR 837, 93
LT 489, 7 F 109, 13 SLT 340, HL   209
Watt v Rama [1972] VR 353   161
Waugh v British Railways Board [1980] AC 521, [1979] 2 All ER 1169, [1979] 3 WLR 150,
[1979] IRLR 364, 123 Sol Jo 506, HL   208
Weber v Stony Brook Hospital 456 NE 2d 1186 (NY, 1983) 382, 384
Webster v Reproductive Health Services 109 S Ct 3040 (1989) 120, 130
White v British Sugar Corpn [1977] IRLR 121   40
Whiteford v Hunter [1950] WN 553, 94 Sol Jo 758, HL   229
Whitehouse v Jordan [1980] 1 All ER 650, CA; affd [1981] 1 All ER 267, [1981] 1 WLR
246, 125 Sol Jo 167, HL 17, 222, 229
Whitlock v Duke University 637 F Supp 1463 (NC, 1986); affd 829 F 2d 1340 (1987)   463
Williamson v East London City Health Authority (1997) 41 BMLR 85   286
Wilsher v Essex Area Health Authority [1987] QB 730, [1986] 3 All ER 801, [1987] 2 WLR
425, 130 Sol Jo 749, [1986] LS Gaz R 2661, [1986] NLJ Rep 1061, CA; revsd [1988]
AC 1074, [1988] 1 All ER 871, [1988] 2 WLR 557, 132 Sol Jo 418, [1988] 15 LS
Gaz R 37, [1988] NLJR 78, HL 207, 220, 223, 229, 231, 236,
Wilson v Pringle [1987] QB 237, [1986] 2 All ER 440, [1986] 1 WLR 1, 130 Sol Jo 468,
[1986] LS Gaz R 2160, [1986] NLJ Rep 416, CA   103
Wilson v Swanson (1956) 5 DLR (2d) 113   223
Wimpey Construction UK Ltd v Poole [1984] 2 Lloyd's Rep 499, 128 Sol Jo 969, 27 BLR 58:   232
Winch v Hayward [1986] QB 296, [1985] 3 All ER 97, [1985] 3 WLR 729, 129 Sol Jo 669, CA: 513
Winch v Jones [1986] QB 296, [1985] 3 All ER 97, [1985] 3 WLR 729, 129 Sol Jo 669, CA: 513
Winnipeg Child and Family Services (Northwest Area) v G (DF) [1997] 2 SCR 925,
152 DLR (4th) 193 .... 135, 250, 266
Wooley v Henderson 418 A 2d 1123 (Md, 1980)   280
Woolley v Ministry of Health [1954] 2 QB 66, [1954] 2 All ER 131, [1954] 2 WLR 915,
98 Sol Jo 319, CA   221
Worster v City and Hackney Health Authority (1987) Times, 22 June   92

X

X (a minor), Re [1975] Fam 47, [1975] 1 All ER 697, [1975] 2 WLR 335, 119 Sol Jo 12, CA: 214
X, Re (1987) Times, 4 June   145
X, Re [1991] 2 NZLR 365   98
X Petitioner, Re 1957 SLT (Sh Ct) 61   39
X v Y [1988] 2 All ER 648, [1988] RPC 379, 3 BMLR 1, [1987] NLJ Rep 1062   199
X v United Kingdom Application 7215/75, DR 19, p 66   37

PAGE

X, Y and Z v United Kingdom (1997) 24 EHRR 143, 39 BMLR 128, ECtHR   47

Y

Y (mental incapacity: bone marrow transplant) Re, [1997] Fam 110, [1997] 2 WLR 556,
    [1997] 2 FCR 172, [1996] 2 FLR 787, [1997] Fam Law 91, 35 BMLR 111   254
Yeager v Bloomington Obstetrics and Gynaecology Inc 585 NE 2d 696 (1992)   162
Yepremian v Scarborough General Hospital (1980) 110 DLR (3d) 513, 28 OR (2d) 494 . .   220
Yuen Kun-yeu v A-G of Hong Kong [1988] AC 175, [1987] 2 All ER 705, [1987] 3 WLR
    776, 131 Sol Jo 1185, [1987] LS Gaz R 2049, [1987] NLJ Rep 566, PC   456

Z

Zeitzoff v Katz [1986] 40 (2) PD 85, Supreme Court of Israel   166

Introduction

1 Introduction

Productive moral discourse should consist of more than a mere statement of conviction. It should, rather, be a matter of feeling one's way towards moral understanding and towards an appreciation of what is morally right. This book is concerned with such a moral discourse, one which has embraced not only philosophers, doctors and lawyers but also members of the lay public. This symbiosis of law and medicine has caught the public attention in a remarkable way, and this has shown little sign of diminishing in vigour.[1] Indeed, the two most closely associated, and relatively new, disciplines – bioethics and medical law – are now respectable components of the curricula of universities and colleges throughout the world.

The intensity of the debate is explained in part by the very nature of the subject matter with which it is concerned. This is a debate which touches upon people's most intimate interests. It deals with matters of human reproduction and human mortality – or sex and death – both of which have traditionally involved our religious convictions and have provoked the most intense emotions. In addressing these issues, the debate becomes involved in many fundamental questions. What is it to be a person? What is the value of human life? How, if at all, should we attempt to influence the future biology of the species?

There is no shortage of conviction on any of these issues. Most major religious traditions have firm views on such matters, and are frequently prepared to assert them as being valid for all. Those who approach these matters from the viewpoint of individual freedom are just as vigorous in their assertion of values, arguing that moral issues of this sort are clearly within the confines of the private. The antagonism between these two positions is sometimes intense and it often seems as if there is little prospect of common ground. Yet, in so far as we have to live in a community, we are obliged to identify what is permissible and what is not – and this means that the law becomes involved.[2] So we do need, for example, a law concerning artificial reproduction because, unless the law pronounces on the issue, society can be seen to be endorsing a non-interventionist approach which allows for unrestricted freedom of choice. In some cases, this may be what society actually wants, but, in others, it will not represent

---

1 A fact which is confirmed by the extensive bioethical literature now available. Constraints of space prevent reference to more than a few examples of this genre, but of the general works available, T L Beauchamp and J F Childress *Principles of Biomedical Ethics* (4th edn, 1994) has established itself as a classic. More general introductory works include M Phillips and J Dawson *Doctors' Dilemmas* (1985); R Gillon's useful *Philosophical Medical Ethics* (1986); A V Campbell's *Moral Dilemmas in Medicine* (1984); and the same author's *Medical Ethics* (1997). *The Value of Life* by John Harris (1985) has been extremely influential, as has his recent exploration of the moral implications of biotechnology, *Wonderwoman and Superman* (1992). On the same theme, see A Dyson and J Harris *Ethics and Biotechnology* (1994).
2 For the argument that in a liberal, pluralistic society there may be no consensus as to many core values, see M Charlesworth *Bioethics in a Liberal Society* (1993).

society's communal position, which also deserves protection. To take another example, termination of pregnancy can only be left legally unregulated if one is prepared to accept that the fate of the human fetus is entirely a matter for the discretion of the pregnant woman. In fact, there are very few people who would endorse that extreme view; the majority of supporters of a liberal attitude to abortion none the less accept the need for some restrictions on the time during which maternal choice can be exercised unreservedly.

Inevitably, then, the law is drawn into the debate, and this is especially so when there is a conflict of individual interests. An example of such a case would be a dispute involving the parents and hospital authorities or social workers as to the medical treatment of a child. The law cannot avoid taking a view in such cases; the alternative is an irrational and inconsistent approach to their solution. In a liberal society, however, the legislature and courts may seek to keep legal intervention in medically-related matters to a minimum. Such a society may take a positivist stance and view the function of the law as being that of the neutral adjudicator – a role in which the moral content of legal decisions is kept to a minimum. This conception of the law's role has proved largely unrealistic in the area with which we are concerned. Medical law is catalysed by moral issues. The debate on abortion, for example, is essentially an exposition of different moral views; yet, in practice, it becomes one concerning what the law should be. It is pointless to attempt to disengage the moral from the legal dispute – when we talk about legal rules, we are inevitably drawn into a discussion of moral rules.

Thus, we often find ourselves engaged in debating not what the law is, but what it should be. This requires us to engage in moral evaluation and this, in turn, raises the question of how we are to identify the right. More specifically, we are confronted with a need to identify an ethical basis for the practice of medicine and its regulation by the law. And this is no easy task, living, as we do, in a pluralist, secular age.

A basis for medical ethics

There is a plethora of theories on hand that are designed to help us decide what is morally right. These range from authoritarian, revelatory theories at one extreme to subtly nuanced visions of existential ethics at the other. In between these options – each of which, in its own way, discourages meaningful moral debate – there is a range of categories to which moral responses might be allocated. Of course there is always the possibility of eclecticism; morality, it seems, is sometimes not so much a maze as a smorgasbord.

Religious theories

Many accounts of medical ethics are strangely silent as to the importance of religious theories of medical ethics – the element of surprise stemming from the fact that medicine and religion have been intertwined from the earliest times, when priests were also recognised as physicians. As a direct result, religious theories historically constitute a major element of thinking in medical ethics and their influence continues to be felt. The common feature of such theories is a vision of man as involved in a dialogue with a divine creator as to the way in which the human body should be treated. This vision may manifest itself in an insistence on ritualistic practices, for example, in relation to burial. Such examples should not, however, be dismissed as an exercise of power based on superstitious reverence – many religious practices, especially those of orthodox Judaism, are, in fact, based on sound principles of public health. It may, on the other hand, be expressed at a higher level of abstraction, fashioning a view of the sanctity of human life which is capable of resolving a whole raft of practical issues. The Judaeo-Christian religious tradition has had the greatest impact in the Western world and is one which continues to influence much of the contemporary debate.

Religiously-based medical ethics have a clear sense of fundamental values. In the Christian tradition, these include not only a belief that human life is a divine gift which cannot be disposed of by mortals but also include a strong attachment to the importance of monogamous, enduring marriage. These values are translated into practical rules in the shape of an antipathy to abortion and euthanasia – an antipathy that amounts to prohibition in orthodox Roman Catholic thinking – and of a belief that various forms of artificial control of fertility are morally wrong. Inherent in many of these traditions is a strong sense of the *natural*, which proposes a teleology for man. In the light of this, it is often seen as wrong to interfere with the manifest destiny which has been prepared for man. This may result in the rejection of an everyday practice such as family planning just as much as it might lead to a blanket refusal to contemplate interference in the genetic endowment of mankind.

It would be wrong to assume that those who approach medical ethics from a religious viewpoint are uncritical and authoritarian in their moral thinking. Indeed, many of the more sensitive contributions to the literature of medical ethics have been made by those who come to the subject from this background. One thinks, for example, of the Protestant theologian, Paul Ramsey, whose work anticipated many of the questions which have since become the staple of contemporary debate in medical ethics.[3]

The currents of medical ethics
Contemporary medical ethics is a tapestry in which an array of philosophical theories interweave with one another. The two strands of deontological thought and utilitarianism, however, are particularly evident. Deontological theories focus on the rightness or wrongness of an act in itself. They are not concerned with the consequences which an act will have; rather, they are concerned with identifying those features of the act which mark it as morally acceptable or otherwise. The classical exposition of such a theory is that by Kant, who stressed that every person must be treated as an end in him- or herself, rather than as a means to an end. Thus, the essential message of Kantian moral teaching is that we should not use others but should respect their integrity as individuals. Modern theories of autonomy find their roots in this background and, as we shall see later, autonomy has come to be associated closely with the liberal individualism which has exerted massive influence on the philosophical climate of the latter decades of the twentieth century.

Critics of deontological theories of morality, particularly of those in the Kantian mould, often stress what is seen as a rigidity of approach. The 'strict' Kantian does

3   See eg P Ramsey *The Patient as Person* (1970).

not give sufficient weight, it is said, either to human intuitions as to what is right at the time or to the virtues. An alternative, and more flexible, approach might be one which was more sensitive to the human feelings involved in any moral dilemma and one which also paid more attention to the consequences which flow from our actions. One such approach is that adopted by utilitarianism, a philosophy which has played a major role in the medical debate and which is regarded by many as underpinning ethical medicine today.

Utilitarians are accustomed to being misrepresented by those who believe that utilitarianism is a philosophical theory which started, and ended, with the work of Jeremy Bentham. Classic utilitarianism of the Benthamite school held that the test of the morality of an action was the extent to which it promoted good consequences (pleasure) or bad (pain). The utilitarian measure of good is, therefore, the maximisation of happiness, although modern utilitarians, in particular, would stress that this does not necessarily lead to unrestricted hedonism. Modern utilitarianism acknowledges the importance of rules in identifying moral goals and, in this way, prevents the happiness of the many from overshadowing the rights of the few. Preference utilitarianism, a further modification of the classical theory, allows for the judging of the good of individuals according to their own values, a position perhaps best elucidated in modern bioethics through the work of the Peter Singer.[4]

Liberal individualism leans towards a utilitarian or consequentialist approach, in that it measures the effect of a decision on individuals. To the liberal individualist, the good which society should pursue is the fulfilment of the individual. The ideal society is, then, one in which each person makes his own decisions as far as is possible and 'creates himself'. In this way, the individual exercises and enhances his autonomy – how autonomy is used is not a major concern to the liberal individualist, so long as it is not used in a way which restricts others from exercising their own autonomy.

Autonomy is by far the most significant value which has been promoted by contemporary medical ethics. The concept which has dominated medical ethics more than any other over the final four decades of the twentieth century is that the individual should have control over his own body, should make his own decisions relating to his medical treatment and should not be hindered in his search for self-fulfilment. The acknowledgment of autonomy has served to discredit medical paternalism and has led to the promotion of the patient from the recipient of treatment to being the partner in a therapeutic project – and this change has been reflected in the legal regime by which medical treatment is regulated.

In one sense, the philosophical apotheosis of autonomy has brought liberation. It has enhanced the freedom of those whose vulnerability, physical or mental, may have exposed them to insensitive treatment or even to exploitation; it has imparted dignity to the lives of those who might, otherwise, have felt themselves to be powerless in the face of the articulate and the professional. Yet, from another view, the acceptance of autonomy as the benchmark of the good has led us to ignore other values, and this may have negative effects. Even if self-fulfilment does shine through the development and the exercise of autonomy, there is a social dimension to life which is potentially

---

4   Singer's contribution to contemporary applied ethics has been considerable. In the field of bioethics, he is associated with challenges to the traditional sanctity of human life view; on which, see his *Rethinking Life and Death* (1994).

equally enriching.[5] Autonomy must be qualified by the legitimate interests and expectations of others, as well as by economic constraints. In the medical context, the claims of autonomy must be moderated so as to accommodate the sensitivities of others, including those of the doctor – who is, after all, also an autonomous agent. It may be that respect for individual autonomy points in the direction of allowing voluntary euthanasia – but another moral agent has to administer the drug that ends life, and that person may be affected by the task. There are also the interests of others in being protected against involuntary euthanasia; it is possible that, in providing such protection, we may have to deny self-determination to those who are truly volunteers. Personal autonomy must also be measured against the needs of society as a whole. In an ideal world, a sick person should be able to demand the treatment of his or her choice. A moment's reflection, however, is enough to show us that this is an impossible goal. Society itself demands a just distribution of resources and this cannot be achieved in an ambience of unrestricted 'rights' – put another way, we can only realise our autonomy within the framework provided by society.[6]

Even so, the concept of rights has many proponents and, like autonomy, rights theory plays an important part in contemporary moral debate. Yet the language of rights may also become unduly assertive and combative and may hinder, rather than promote, moral consensus.[7] This is not to suggest that rights are unimportant. Many of the central moral positions defended in this book can be couched in terms of rights. Once again, however, rights-talk is peculiarly suited to an individualistic moral tradition and conflicts of rights tend to lead to moral impasse. Most discussion centres on the rights of the patient – but has the doctor no rights when choosing treatment in accordance with his Hippocratic principles and his training? The law, itself, is prepared to recognise this as a de facto situation. The one-time Master of the Rolls, Lord Donaldson, expressed this unequivocally when he said:

> [I cannot, at present, conceive of any circumstances] in which the court should ever require a medical practitioner to adopt a course of treatment which in the bona fide clinical judgment of that practitioner is contraindicated as not being in the best interests of the patient.[8]

In the same passage, Lord Donaldson described the fundamental duty of the doctor as being to treat the patient in accordance with his own clinical judgment – which opens the way to an alternative dialogue through the language of obligations. The way to a satisfactory doctor/patient relationship is not through the confrontational profession of rights but, rather, through a realisation of the obligations incumbent upon each side to work towards the ideal.[9]

5   For discussion, see D T Meyers *Self, Society, and Personal Choice* (1989). Also of interest is T E Hill 'The Importance of Autonomy' in his *Autonomy and Self-respect* (1991). The limits of the doctrine of autonomy are discussed in A McCall Smith 'Beyond Autonomy' (1997) 14 J Contemp Health Law and Policy 23.
6   See A V Campbell 'Dependency: the foundational value in medical ethics' in K V M Fulford and G J M Gillett (eds) *Medicine and Moral Reasoning* (1994).
7   In the view of some philosophers, rights can be reduced to principles which form the real content of morality. For a sceptical view, see R Frey *Rights, Killing and Suffering* (1983); to be contrasted with L W Sumner *The Moral Foundation of Rights* (1987) and with the outstanding contribution of K Cronin *Rights and Christian Ethics* (1992).
8   In *Re J (a minor) (wardship: medical treatment)* [1992] 2 FLR 165 at 172, (1992) 9 BMLR 10 at 17.
9   For a useful discussion in depth, see H Teff *Reasonable Care* (1994) and, in particular, his discussion of medical models in ch 3.

Intuitions, experience and morality

There are grounds, then, for doubting the practicality or effectiveness of applying a broad deontological brush to medical ethics. Each case is unique, and its individual features may change with each consultation. Recent moral philosophy supports this approach, stressing the importance of imagination as a means of navigating our way through the moral landscape.[10] This moral imagination may, to an extent, rely on metaphors rather than on rules – all of which points to a role, even if a circumscribed one, for moral intuitions. Intuition may have a limited appeal as a basis for moral philosophy but it should not be wholly discounted and this, for the reasons given above, is especially so in the field of health care.[11] Intuitions may point in the direction of a value which may not always be articulated formally but which may none the less be very important

Our own view is that medical ethics is perhaps not best served by a rigid attachment to an undiluted vision of patient autonomy, and neither was it well served by the paternalistic philosophy of the past. What is required is an openness to the complexity of moral decisions, and an awareness of the sensitive, contextual nature of the doctor-patient relationship. An understanding of the demands of this relationship is not necessarily something that philosophers can teach or lawyers prescribe. The insights of cognitive science and psychology in general increasingly recommend a model of moral reasoning which gives a large role to learned moral responses. These moral abilities – if one might call them that – are acquired through education within a particular ethos and through hands-on experience in dealing with people and their suffering. There is all the difference in the world between, say, the experienced nurse who has spent years working in a hospice setting and the lay person who approaches the issue of end-of-life decisions from an entirely theoretical perspective. A moral response which discounts the validity of the insights of the former would be unlikely to be helpful. Those involved in caring for patients are moral beings who must be encouraged to develop and express their sense of the moral demands of a particular situation. There is not necessarily one right answer to the dilemmas which they encounter, and this should perhaps be recognised more extensively than it is today. There may be two right answers, or even more, depending on the people involved and the circumstances. A moral strait-jacket is hardly helpful. Having said which, we should, perhaps go on to examine the practical environment in which health carers set about their work.

The Hippocratic influence

For the origins of our current medical practice – with its emphasis on the one-to-one relationship between doctor and patient within the confines of the home, surgery or hospital – we must look to Greece where, by 500 BC, the originally strong influence of the priest/physician had waned; a predominantly religious discipline had been taken over by the philosophers who, through the processes of logical thought,

10 See M Johnson *Moral Imagination: Implications of Cognitive Science for Ethics* (1993); L May, M Friedman and A Clark (eds) *Mind and Morals: Essays on Ethics and Cognitive Science* (1996).
11 For expression of this view, see T B Brewin 'How Much Ethics Is Needed to Make a Good Doctor?' (1993) 341 Lancet 161. Also G Gillett 'Euthanasia, Letting Die and the Pause' (1988) 14 J Med Ethics 61.

observation and deduction, transformed the concepts of medicine. Inevitably, this led to the formation of schools involving the close association of practitioners, paternalism and the elements of the 'closed shop'; a code of intraprofessional conduct evolved, heralding the dawn of what has become known as medical etiquette. In addition, the new concepts dictated that the physician went to the patient rather than the patient to the temple. A standard of practice relevant to the new ideals was required and has survived as the Hippocratic Oath.[12]

While Hippocrates remains the most famous figure in Greek philosophical medicine, he was not alone and it is probable that the Oath predates his own school. It therefore indicates a prevailing ethos rather than a professorial edict and it is still regarded as the fundamental governance of the medical profession. Much of the preamble relates to medical etiquette and is clearly outmoded – very few ageing medical professors now anticipate social security by way of the generosity of their students! This, however, is not our concern here – and it is to be distinguished clearly from medical ethics. As to the latter, the Oath lays down a number of guidelines. First, it implies the need for co-ordinated instruction and registration of doctors – the public is to be protected, so far as is possible, from the dabbler or the charlatan. Secondly, it is clearly stated that a doctor is there for the benefit of his patients – to the best of his ability he must do them good and he must do nothing which he knows will cause harm. Thirdly, euthanasia and abortion are proscribed; the reference to lithotomy probably prohibits mutilating operations (castration) but has been taken by many to imply the limitation of one's practice to that in which one has expertise. Fourthly, the nature of the doctor-patient relationship is outlined and an undertaking is given not to take advantage of that relationship. Finally, the Oath expresses the doctrine of medical confidentiality.

In fact, the Hippocratic Oath did not become an integral part of ethical teaching until well into the Christian era; it lapsed with the decline of Greek civilisation and was restored with the evolution of university medical schools. It is doubtful if any British medical school now requires a reiteration of the Oath at graduation – although most Scottish universities require assent by students to a modified version – but, avowed or not, all doctors would admit to its persuasive influence. The language of the Oath is, however, archaic and a modernised version was introduced by the World Medical Association as the Declaration of Geneva. This was last amended at Stockholm in 1994[13] and provides the basis for an International Code of Medical Ethics.[14]

We have seen that Greek medicine was essentially a private matter and, indeed, its mode of practice was scarcely attuned to the needs of public health. For the origins of this, we must turn to the Judaeo-Christian influence which, certainly in the Israeli tradition, expressed itself most powerfully in accepting that the rights of the individual must sometimes be sacrificed for the good of the community – there was strong emphasis, for example, on the isolation of infectious cases, including those of venereal disease, the regulation of sewage disposal and the like – and the principles of public health medicine were born. As we have already noted, the fact that medicine was dominated by religion turned out to be mutually advantageous. Much of this attitude passed to the Christians, who were also forced into the group life-style, and

12 See Appendix A.
13 See Appendix B.
14 See Appendix C.

were fortified by the concepts of equality, charity and devotion to the less fortunate – concepts which still underlie the ethical practice of medicine in Christian countries. It is unsurprising that, during the Dark Ages, medicine was virtually kept alive in the monasteries which provided the template for the voluntary hospitals of later years.

The organisation of modern medicine

Probably the single most important feature which distinguishes 'modern medicine' is the importance attached to experimentation and research and it was this change in emphasis which dictated most urgently that medical practice should be subject to central control.

The age of medical research can be said to have begun with the Renaissance and, since that time, the practice of medicine has become increasingly scientifically based. New dimensions are, thus, introduced and new dilemmas posed. It is obvious that scientific medicine cannot improve without extensive research while, on the other hand, that process tends to turn medical practice into a series of problem-solving exercises – a diversion which, even now, stimulates some of medicine's severest critics.

Perhaps the first practical effect of the scientific approach was to convince doctors that they have an expertise worth preserving and, as early as the sixteenth century, we find the establishment of the Royal College of Physicians of London, together with a general tightening of the rules governing the practice of surgery. The early Royal Colleges had considerable powers of examination and registration. The latter function has now gone and the major purpose of the colleges – which now represent some eight specialities with additional faculties – is to maintain a standard of excellence among specialised practitioners – a matter of current importance to which we return below.

As organisation proceeded, fortune began increasingly to depend upon fame, and fame in its turn upon academic superiority over one's colleagues – from all accounts, British medicine in the eighteenth and early nineteenth centuries was not the happiest of professions. Even so, it was not so much medical ethics, as they are understood today, that were found wanting but, rather, medical etiquette. Something had to be done to ensure the status of the profession and this need was first met by the formation of the British Medical Association (BMA) in 1832. The BMA has always been deeply concerned with the way medicine is practised but its present main function is the protection of doctors' interests – today, it is a non-affiliated registered trade union.[15] Clearly, an interested party could not represent the public need for control of a profession with such power and it was largely due to the lobby of the BMA itself that the General Medical Council (GMC) was established by the Medical Act 1858.[16]

15 Trade Union and Labour Relations Act 1974.
16 The General Medical Council at present consists of 102 members. Fifty-four of these are elected (by statute, the number of elected members must exceed the combined total of all others). A further 35 are appointed by the universities which have medical schools, by the Royal Colleges and Faculties and by the Society of Apothecaries. Thirteen further members are nominated by the Queen in Council, of whom the majority must be lay people; by convention, 11 of the 13 are lay people and the other places are filled by two of the Chief Medical Officers.

The control of medical practice[17]
It is emphasised that, while the GMC is the governing body of the medical profession,[18] its most significant public function is to regulate the standards of the profession. Until comparatively recently, it could have been said that professional negligence was of no direct concern to the Council unless it brought the profession of medicine into disrepute[19] but, as we will see below, this is now no longer true. The basic function of the GMC is to maintain the official register of medical practitioners and, thus, to protect the public from those who have not undergone recognised training; unlike the practise of dentistry, no specific offence lies in an unqualified person practising medicine in the United Kingdom – the offence is that of pretending to be a registered medical practitioner[1] or of usurping functions which are statutorily limited to registered practitioners – such as prescribing 'prescription only' medicines.[2] Other functions include supervision of standards of education, the laying down of standards of fitness to practise and the exercise of professional discipline over medical doctors. As to the last, the Council has, until recently, refused to comment on the propriety of specific intended or past actions; guidelines have been issued but detailed advice has been a matter for the doctors' protection or defence societies. Since the passing of the Medical Act 1978, however, the Council itself has undertaken to advise when so requested by registered practitioners.

The Professional Conduct Committee (PCC) is the ultimate tribunal in respect of professional standards and is subject only to appeal to the Privy Council.[3] A doctor appearing before the PCC may be found guilty or not guilty of 'serious professional misconduct'. This has been defined as conduct such as 'would reasonably be regarded as disgraceful or dishonourable by his professional brethren of good repute and standing' – a definition which is so wide as to be virtually non-exclusive. Thus, so far as this book is concerned, one of the most important functions of the GMC is to fill

17 Professional standards within the National Health Service are regulated within a complex framework of disciplinary committees: see National Health Service (Service Committees and Tribunal) Regulations 1974, SI 1974/45. Incompetence by hospital practitioners is investigated under the terms of Ministry of Health Circular HM(61)112(1961) as amended by HC(90)9(1990). The actions of a disciplinary inquiry are subject to judicial review (*R v Department of Health and Social Security, ex p Darnell* (1986) 293 BMJ 322).
18 The increasing status afforded to 'alternative medicine' is to be noted. These practitioners have their own controlling bodies: see, for example, Osteopaths Act 1993; Chiropractors Act 1994.
19 Although it was, in fact, held that seriously negligent treatment could amount to serious professional misconduct: *McCandless v General Medical Council* [1996] 1 WLR 167; (1996) 30 BMLR 53.
1 Occasionally, the Council lapses in this respect. A recent example is that of an unqualified person from overseas who managed to obtain registration with the GMC; he received £450,000 in salary from the NHS before being detected through the vigilance of a pharmacist: J Ironside 'Five Year Sentence for Fake General Practitioner' (1992) 304 BMJ 1652.
2 A further case, prosecuted and convicted under the Medicines Act 1968, has come to light: C Dyer 'Bogus British Professor Sentenced to Prison' (1993) 306 BMJ 1499.
3 The conduct of the GMC is also open to judicial review both as to its 'advice' (*Colman v General Medical Council* [1989] 1 Med LR 23, QBD; sub nom *R v General Medical Council, ex p Colman* (1989) 4 BMLR 33, CA) and as to the actions of the PCC (*R v General Medical Council, ex p Gee* [1987] 1 All ER 1204, CA; on appeal from [1986] 1 WLR 226, QBD). It is of passing interest that the conduct of the PCC is governed by English law irrespective of where the Committee is sitting; save in unusual circumstances, the standard of proof required is that applicable to civil proceedings: *McAllister v General Medical Council* [1993] 1 All ER 982, PC. While exercising a judicial power, the PCC is not part of the judicial system of the state: *General Medical Council v BBC* (1998) 43 BMLR 143.

the gap in constraining such actions as are not actionable yet which would not be expected of the ethical practitioner. For example, the law on medical confidentiality is in many ways unclear, but few doctors would wish to tangle with the GMC on the issue of professional secrecy. There is nothing criminal in adultery; yet the public cannot expect family relationships to be destroyed as a result of the doctor's privilege to enter the bedroom and, accordingly, adulterous conduct with a patient is dealt with exceptionally severely by the PCC.

The GMC has, however, been subject to considerable criticism, which has been but little allayed by the changes in structure – both imposed and self-regulatory – that have arisen in the last 15 years. Much of this criticism centred on the belief that such a form of 'peer control' provides inadequate protection for the public[4] but, perhaps more, on the specific public conviction that, whether it had the powers or not, the Council *ought* to be responsible for the technical efficiency of those it registered as being competent to practice. This has now been remedied by the passing of the Medical (Professional Performance) Act 1995.

In summary, the Act establishes two further committees of the GMC – the Assessment Referral Committee and the Committee on Professional Performance – which parallel the two committees set up to oversee practitioners' professional conduct.[5] The function of these committees is to establish whether a doctor's standard of professional performance is seriously deficient and whether, as a consequence, patients are at risk of sustaining serious harm. While the Committee on Professional Performance has the power to suspend a doctor's registration, the aim is to remedy the deficiencies and the doctor may be responsible for part or the whole of his or her retraining expenses.[6] We would have preferred to see these powers placed in the hands of the Royal Colleges, but there is no doubt that the statute has gone at least some way to satisfying the evident public demand for appropriate measures

A further criticism of the GMC is that it has very little power to institute disciplinary proceedings itself; effectively, the Council can act only on complaints received. Something of a lacuna develops when the only likely informants would be fellow doctors – for example, when treatment of doubtful validity is being dispensed.[7] Most professional men and women are inherently unwilling to denounce their colleagues and the distinction between disparaging the skill of another doctor, which the GMC would regard adversely, and informing of behaviour which raises a question of patients' well-being, which is approved,[8] may be tenuous. This reservation does not, however, apply where other health care professionals are involved and, indeed, most reports of dubious behaviour on the part of doctors stem from outraged nursing

4   A major review is to be found in M Stacey *Regulating British Medicine* (1992).
5   General Medical Council *GMC's Performance Procedures* (1997). The two functions may, however, appear to overlap. A surgeon has been suspended by the PCC for failing to obtain consent to an operation – a matter which would previously have been a matter for civil litigation: C Dyer 'Consultant Suspended for not Getting Consent for Cardiac Procedure' (1998) 316 BMJ 955.
6   For criticism of the terms, see S Brearley 'Seriously Deficient Professional Performance' (1996) 312 BMJ 1180.
7   R Smith 'Doctors, Unethical Treatment, and Turning a Blind Eye' (1989) 298 BMJ 1125. See also criticism of the management of a case of doubtful practice associated with advertising: A B Kay 'Alternative Allergy and the General Medical Council' (1993) 306 BMJ 122; R Smith 'GMC in the Dock Again' (1993) 306 BMJ 82.
8   General Medical Council *Good Medical Practice* (1995) para 18. See also Appendix C.

staff. Many such protests are based on grounds of conscience, these being related especially to life or death decisions and, although such informants often attract little local sympathy, the strong probability is that the great majority are motivated by the genuine belief that they are protecting the public against undisclosed violations of the moral, professional and criminal codes. The government has now issued draft guidelines which stress that, in so far as the interests of patients are of paramount importance, NHS staff have a right and a duty to raise issues concerning patient care; the right depends, however, on following a prescribed procedure which, for example, relegates contact with the press to a last resort.[9] A less acceptable variation on this practice – which is now known popularly as 'whistle blowing' – stems from the increasing dichotomy between the clinical and managerial arms of the health service and manifests itself as public criticism – predominantly of the latter by the former. Whether disclosure of defects in the system, which may be real or imaginary and no more than indirectly associated with patient safety, is regarded as a legitimate duty in the public interest or as a breach of a contract of employment entered into in mutual good faith is open to debate[10] – and the answer may depend very much on the particular community's attitude to freedom of information.[11] Clearly, there are difficulties in distinguishing genuine concern from malcontent but, here, we are moving some way from the doctor-patient relationship.

Public relations

The importance of the overall relationship between the medical profession and the public cannot, however, be gainsaid. The growth of the cult of patient autonomy and self-regulation has carried with it a parallel claim to a right to personal assessment of one's doctor's expertise and quality. This has added a new dimension to the GMC's attitudes to advertising by the medical profession. Time was when, for example, a doctor discussing medical matters of public interest on the radio had to do so anonymously for fear of disciplinary action on the part of the GMC. There is little doubt that such restrictions were based on a fear of competitive doctors 'touting' for patients; the advent of the National Health Service virtually eliminated any need for such behaviour and the antipathy of the GMC was steadily relaxed.

Solution of the matter was, however, catalysed by the reference of the GMC's ban to the Monopolies and Mergers Commission who held that the rule forbidding

---

9 J Warden 'New Guidance for Whistleblowers' (1992) 305 BMJ 977; 'Speaking Out in the NHS' (1992) 305 BMJ 1180; S Handysides 'Health Workers who Protest Face Disciplinary Action' (1993) 306 BMJ 1710.

10 The growth of managed care in the United States seems to have led to an interesting variation whereby doctors' contracts can prevent them discussing 'unauthorised' treatments with patients: J A Martin and L K Bjerknes 'The Legal and Ethical Implications of Gag Clauses in Physician Contracts' (1996) 22 Am J Law Med 433.

11 D Greene and J Cooper 'Whistle Blowers' (1992) 305 BMJ 1343; R Smith 'Whistle Blowing: A Curse on Ineffective Organisations' (1992) 305 BMJ 1308. The Public Interest Disclosure Act 1998, which seeks to prohibit discrimination against those who so act in good conscience, is currently before Parliament. The case of Dr Chapman, whose allegation of wrongful dismissal for questioning a colleague's research was rejected after eight years' investigation, is in point: H Spencer '"Never again" says NHS whistleblower' (1997) 314 BMJ 626.

advertising in the press by general practitioners was against the public interest.[12] At the same time, the Commission recommended considerable restraint – including a ban on disparaging other doctors and on claiming special aptitudes. The Commission, fearing exploitation, declined to extend its recommendations to advertising to the general public by specialists – although it allowed that specialists could inform their medical colleagues of the services they offered.

These recommendations, which were designed for the benefit of patients and for the improvement of specialist services, were opposed by the BMA[13] but seem logical and in accord with modern custom. They have been accepted by the GMC,[14] whose advice currently reads:

> The Council encourages doctors to provide factual information about their professional qualifications and services . . . in any form, to the public or other members of the profession . . . General practitioners publishing information about their services should not abuse the trust of patients or attempt to exploit their lack of medical knowledge . . . Advertising material should contain only factual information.[15]

Even so, the GMC remained opposed to the public recognition of medical specialists and, together with the Royal Colleges, has resisted the publication of a distinct 'specialist register'. It was, however, accepted that, in doing so, the United Kingdom was breaching the directives of the European Commission[16] and the policy has now been changed. A Specialist Register, referring to 53 medical specialties, is now held and constitutes the bench-mark for those claiming a particular expertise – although the relevant Order does not stipulate that consultants may practice only in the specialty(ies) which appear in their entry in the specialist register.[17]

Modern medical technology and the law

The late twentieth-century picture of medical practice is one of rapidly advancing technology which is effected in a strongly research orientated environment and which exists within an increasingly hedonistic and materialistic society. Society, for its part,

12 T Delmonthe 'GP's May Advertise' (1989) 298 BMJ 774. Interestingly, the Court of Appeal subsequently upheld that the recommendation did not render the GMC's advice unreasonable (*Colman* (1992) 4 BMLR 33, CA). An important issue was whether or not the English courts should apply the principles of the European Commission on Human Rights in reaching decisions, despite the fact that the latter had not been incorporated in United Kingdom law – the claim, which is still sub judice, was rejected by the European Commission on Human Rights: C Dyer 'Ban on Newspaper Advertising by Doctors Upheld' (1989) 299 BMJ 1482; A Rogers 'Court Case Rejected' (1993) 341 Lancet 366.
13 J D J Havard 'Advertising by Doctors and the Public Interest' (1989) 298 BMJ 903.
14 L Beecham 'Advertising – No Longer a Dirty Word' (1990) 300 BMJ 1420. The history of the GMC's changing attitude is outlined in D H Irvine 'The Advertising of Doctors' Services' (1991) 17 J Med Ethics 35.
15 General Medical Council *Professional Conduct and Discipline: Fitness to Practise* (1993) paras 59-61, 97-115.
16 See *R v Secretary of State for Health, ex p Goldstein* [1993] 2 CMLR 589. Followed by *R v Joint Committee on High Medical Training and Specialist Advisory Committee on Rheumatology, ex p Goldstein* (1992) 11 BMLR 10.
17 European Specialist Medical Qualifications Order 1995, SI 1995/3208.

demands more and more esoteric methodology, and personal involvement in medicine is encouraged on all sides. The law, however, moves more slowly than either medicine or the public mores. As a result, doctors frequently find themselves operating in an atmosphere of legal uncertainty which promotes confrontation – typified by such comments as:

> It is a crushing indictment of our legal system that men such as Aleck Bourne [who was found not guilty of illegal termination of pregnancy] and Leonard Arthur [who was acquitted of attempted murder] should be subjected to criminal prosecution for carrying out with great devotion and skill procedures which are accepted by the profession as in the best interests of patients.[18]

Whether or not one agrees with this view, it cannot be denied that it reveals an unsatisfactory state of affairs – a state which self-perpetuates as new attitudes and new techniques evolve.

Legal intervention in medicine

Even so, the practice of medicine is constrained by outside influences and the conduct of doctors is circumscribed by the public conscience

Thus, we see the general rules of doctoring as being developed within a moral framework which is constantly being restructured by contemporary society. Whether the law has a right to impose morality is a well-known and controversial issue in jurisprudence[19] but, for present purposes, we would argue that the public conscience, as embodied in the law, provides a useful foundation for medical ethics. This, however, is not to say that the law should dictate to the profession and, particularly, not that it should dictate by means of restrictive statute. Effectively, we are suggesting that medicine must operate within broadly stated legal rules – such as those embodied in the common law – and, as Lord Scarman has indicated,[20] the law must be flexible in the absence of parliamentary direction.

The crucial question, then, is that of determining the *extent* to which medical decisions should be the object of legal scrutiny and control. At one extreme there are those who hold that the medical profession should be left to regulate itself and that it alone should decide what is acceptable conduct. According to this view, intervention by the law is too blunt a way of tackling the delicate ethical dilemmas which doctors have to face: the individual, guided by personal experience and by prevailing public and professional standards, must confront and resolve the day-to-day ethical issues of medical practice.

The contrary view, frequently expressed just as firmly, denies that there is any reason why doctors alone should regulate their relationship with their patients. In this view, reserving to the medical profession the right to decide on issues of life and death is an improper derogation from an area of legitimate public concern and an encroachment by clinicians into what is, properly, social policy. According to the

18 J D J Havard 'Legal Regulation of Medical Practice – Decisions of Life and Death: A discussion paper' (1982) 75 J Roy Soc Med 351.
19 For discussion of this, including many medico-legal examples, see S Lee *Law and Morals* (1986).
20 In *Gillick v West Norfolk and Wisbech Area Health Authority* [1986] AC 112, [1985] 3 All ER 402, HL.

proponents of this opinion, the law, even if it is an imperfect and often inaccessible weapon, is at least one means of controlling the medical profession in the interests of the community as a whole.[1]

We will see as we go through the various problem areas discussed in this book that the relationship between the law and medicine, which, at one time, had all the trappings of confrontation, has now settled into a classical domestic state in which mutual trust is, occasionally, interspersed with outbursts of disaffection. Certainly, the law is content to allow doctors as free a hand in carrying out their duties as is possible. Thus, we have Farquharson J in his charge to the jury in *R v Arthur*:[2]

> I imagine that you will think long and hard before deciding that doctors, of the eminence we have heard, representing to you what medical ethics are . . . have evolved standards which amount to committing crime.[2]

And, again, Lord Brandon:

> The application of the principle which I have described means that the lawfulness of a doctor operating on, or giving treatment to, an adult patient disabled from giving consent will depend not on any approval or sanction of a court but on the question whether the operation or other treatment is in the best interests of the patient concerned.[3]

and, in *Re GF*[4] the President of the Family Division declined to make a declaration of lawfulness in a sterilisation case on the grounds that, to do so, might give a false impression to doctors that a court application was needed in cases where the treatment was clearly therapeutic.

The courts have also been quick to recognise their position in relation to the legislature in face of the speed of evolution of modern technology – as Lord Browne-Wilkinson put it: 'Existing law may not provide an acceptable answer to the new legal questions [raised by the ability to sustain life artificially].'[5] He went on to question whether judges should seek to develop new law to meet a wholly new situation and to suggest that it was a matter which required society, through the democratic expression of its views in Parliament, to reach its decisions on the underlying moral and practical problems and then reflect those decisions in legislation – and, in this, he was strongly supported by Lord Mustill.[6]

The co-operation of the courts with clinical freedom is clearly desirable, but it is equally unacceptable that doctors should have to work in a 'legal vacuum' in which they may be uncertain as to whether or not they face the prospect of a civil action or, again in the words of Lord Mustill, they take the risk of having to validate their conduct after the event in the context of a trial for murder. For these reasons, some may see it as preferable to have certain general rules set out clearly by way of statute

---

1 'I would expect medical ethics to be formed by the law rather than the reverse' *Airedale NHS Trust v Bland* [1993] 1 All ER 821 at 858, (1993) 12 BMLR 64 at 103 per Hoffmann LJ.
2 The Times, 6 November 1981, pp 1, 12; (1993) 12 BMLR 1 at 22.
3 *Re F* [1990] 2 AC 1 at 56, sub nom *F v West Berkshire Health Authority* (1989) 4 BMLR 1 at 8, HL.
4 [1992] 1 FLR 293, [1993] 4 Med LR 77.
5 In *Airedale NHS Trust v Bland* [1993] 1 All ER 821 at 878, (1993) 12 BMLR 64 at 124.
6 (1993) 12 BMLR 64 at 135.

and we have, in fact, concrete examples of the benign effect of legislative involvement in medical issues – it is through statute, for example, that the legal uncertainties which once surrounded the new reproductive technology have been largely dispelled.[7] The way in which this has been achieved varies according to jurisdiction. In Victoria, Australia, for instance, the relevant statute[8] spells out in detail what the clinician may or may not do. The British approach, by contrast, has been for Parliament to state its general aims and to demit their refinement to officially appointed Authorities on which the profession and the public are adequately represented.[9] This approach serves to circumvent one of the most cogent arguments against introducing legal rules into human affairs – which is, that once rules acquire a specific meaning, they allow little room for manoeuvre and can turn out to be more restrictive than was originally intended by the framer of the rule. An effect of this can be to distort people's behaviour through the fear of litigation or prosecution. One may then be concerned, not with doing what one feels to be right, but with what one feels to be the legally safest thing to do.

Doctors in the United Kingdom may be particularly fortunate in this respect as compared with their counterparts in other jurisdictions. As we intimated at the beginning of this section, the courts are inherently reluctant to interfere in clinical matters. While they will accept the absolute right of a patient to refuse treatment,[10] they will, at the same time, refuse to dictate to doctors what treatment they should give.[11] Indeed, the fear could be that, if anything, the pendulum has swung too far in favour of therapeutic immunity.[12]

But when there are no alternative methods of resolving disputes between doctors and patients, other than complaints procedures which have no financial implications for the patient, the courts are bound to be drawn into acting as mediators in complex and frequently distressing matters. Once again, however, there seems to be little enthusiasm for the task and judicial hostility to medical negligence claims in this country has occasionally been overt. In *Whitehouse v Jordan*,[13] for example, Lord Denning MR took the somewhat controversial step of considering an individual claim for damages in general terms. In making his decision, he had one eye on the picture of medical litigation in the United States – and it might be noted in passing that the picture has not changed greatly over the years:

> There, the damages are colossal . . . Experienced practitioners are known to have refused to treat patients for fear of being accused of negligence. Young men are even deterred from entering the profession because of the risks involved . . .

Similar remarks were made in the same case by Lawton LJ,[14] who expressed the view that the system of fault-based litigation was compelling judges to make

7 Human Fertilisation and Embryology Act 1990.
8 Infertility (Medical Procedures) Act 1984, amended in 1987.
9 Eg the Human Fertilisation and Embryology Authority established under the Human Fertilisation and Embryology Act 1990.
10 *Re T (adult: refusal of medical treatment)* [1992] 4 All ER 649, (1992) 9 BMLR 46.
11 *Re J (a minor) (wardship: medical treatment)* [1992] 2 FLR 165, (1992) 9 BMLR 10.
12 For a general overview, see J K Mason 'Master of the Balancers: Non-voluntary Treatment Decisions under the Mantle of Lord Donaldson' [1993] JR 115.
13 [1980] 1 All ER 650 at 658, CA.
14 At 661-662.

decisions 'which they prefer not to make'. The legal system then is faced with the classic problem of doing justice to both parties. The fears of the medical profession must be taken into account while the legitimate claims of the patient cannot be ignored, and our impression has been that the balance has been shifting incrementally in favour of the patient in recent years.

The doctor's position

There is no doubt, too, that the defining of a relationship, such as that of doctor and patient, in legalistic terms leads to a subtle but important change in the nature of the relationship. Trust and respect are more likely to flourish in one which is governed by morality rather than by legal rules and, no matter how appropriate the law may be for the regulation of many of the other ordinary transactions of life, the injection of formality and excessive caution into the relationship between doctor and patient cannot be in the patient's interest if it means that each sees the other as a potential adversary.

Where, then, does the doctor stand today in relation to society? To some extent, he is a servant of the public, a public which is, moreover, widely – though not always well – informed on medical matters. Society is conditioned to distrust paternalism and the modern medical practitioner has little wish to be paternalistic. The new talk is of 'producers and consumers' and the concept that 'he who pays the piper calls the tune' is established both within the profession and in its relationships with patients. The competent patient's inalienable rights to understand his treatment and to accept or refuse it are now well established.

Changes in the doctor-patient relationship are also much affected by the economic context in which it exists. Doctors and patients will undoubtedly view one another differently when medical treatment is provided free by the state, as compared with when it is obtained on a commercial basis. Attempts to graft a consumerist philosophy on to the former may be made but are unlikely to have any real impact on the altruistic ethic of care which, despite early opposition from the medical profession, has motivated the National Health Service over the past five decades. By contrast, the development of medical care along business lines in the United States appears to have led to dubious practices such as costly over-investigation and the unnecessary referral of patients to facilities owned by the doctors themselves.[15] Rodin's analysis of this problem concludes bleakly that money's corrupting role is difficult to avoid, even by a profession which acknowledges a high degree of responsibility for the welfare of the community. It is not surprising that, in a climate where the doctor is seen as a businessman, eager to make as much profit as possible, the patients should be ready to claw back, through litigation, what might be seen as the profession's undue gains.

A relationship of conflict – or of mutual suspicion – is in the interests of neither doctor nor patient. What is needed is one of mutual understanding in which doctors acknowledge the interests of patients and patients, for their part, reciprocate this respect while appreciating the pressures, both physical and mental under which a

---

15 M A Rodin *Medicine, Money and Morals* (1993).

health carer must work. The public has also to understand the broader issues in medicine. The profession must experiment and research if it is to improve its art and many would hold that a slight loss of autonomy on the part of patients is a small price to pay for a useful advance in therapeutic skills. The profession must also teach, or there will be no doctors to serve future generations; some loss of confidentiality can be looked upon as a return for the best treatment and the best investigative facilities. Clearly, these opposing attitudes cannot be reconciled so long as they are polarised or if the claims of one party are accepted to the exclusion of the other.[16] A middle way, based on respect and trust, must be found and this is the function of medical jurisprudence which we attempt to express in the chapters which follow.

The darker sides of medicine

Even so, society itself occasionally demands questionable practices of doctors. The extreme ethical problem of the late twentieth century relates to what are described as cruel, inhuman or degrading treatments or punishments. Political violence is all around us and the doctor cannot wholly dissociate himself from this; an international attempt to define his position is to be found in the Declaration of Tokyo,[17] which shows well the difficulties of drafting ethical codes of an academic nature – definitions of principle can only be interpreted in the mind of the individual. Who is to define a degrading procedure? Whether or not a caning is ethically preferable to deprivation of liberty is a matter of personal opinion. Is it self-evident that the well-being of an indiscriminate terrorist bomber is as valuable as is that of his potential victim? Granted that unethical biological measures are to be used in interrogation, could it not be that a doctor's presence, although disapproving, might be to the benefit of the victim? And, one might ask, by what right can the doctor command complete clinical independence when, in some circumstances, he may be ignorant of the widespread effect his decision may have on others? The motivation of the Declaration of Tokyo is impeccable in condemning the excesses of politically motivated punishment and torture, but it fails in its general purpose because it was drafted with that rather narrow end in view. Clause (8) states that the doctor 'shall in all circumstances be bound to alleviate the distress of his fellow men and no motive . . . shall prevail against this higher purpose'. Carried to its logical conclusion, this would ostracise all those who assist in bringing criminals to justice and punishment – yet, surely, forensic medicine must be seen as providing an ethical service to the community.

An exception to this rule should, however, be drawn in respect of the death penalty. We have some sympathy with the argument that life imprisonment in present-day conditions is, itself, classifiable as inhumane and degrading treatment;

16 Do documents such as *The Patients' Charter* (1993) assist in this or do they serve to amplify the potential for conflict? The problem has not gone unnoticed and a new NHS Charter is in preparation: J Wise 'Patient's Charter will Emphasise Patients' Responsibilities' (1997) 315 BMJ 971. Going a stage further, should the conditions set out in such charters be legally enforceable? See M H W Silver 'Patients' Rights in England and the United States of America' (1997) 23 J Med Ethics 213.
17 See Appendix D.

yet, on balance, it must be preferable to the barbarism – and uncertainties – of the death penalty. The doctor's position in this respect is certainly less acute in areas which practice judicial hanging than it is in the federal prisons of the United States, where the preferred method of execution by lethal injection must involve medical or paramedical intervention. However, if one can legitimately recruit a hangman, it should also be possible to engage a lethal phlebotomist and, following extensive lobbying by medical organisations, the US Department of Justice has dropped its requirement for physician participation in an execution. Although the American Medical Association accepts that doctors may attend to certify death, this absolute need has also been dropped in the United States – at which point, one may well ask, who certifies the *fact* of death? Fortunately, by the time we come to publication, such problems should be of historic interest only in the United Kingdom, for Parliament is in the process of abolishing the death penalty in the very few instances in which it could still be available.[18]

On a more prosaic level, there has always been something of an armed truce between the medical profession and the police as to confidentiality. The anxiety engendered here has been summed up: 'Although doctors in general wish to co-operate with the police, they must be sure that any information divulged *in confidence* will not be used in court unless they are aware at the time of interview that that information might be so used.'[19]

The matter of the professional relationship between doctors and the police has, to a large extent been solved in the Police and Criminal Evidence Act 1984. The major contentions centred not only on confidentiality but also on the problems associated with intimate body searches. As to the latter, the BMA considered that, in the absence of consent, they should be carried out only by medical practitioners and, then, only when there was a possibility of the secreting of a dangerous article. It could not, however, approve of compulsory searches for evidentiary reasons:

> The ethical position of a doctor invited to carry out an intimate body search for the purpose of providing evidence in support of a criminal prosecution is that it should be done only with the full, free and informed consent of the subject

wrote the Secretary of the BMA who, further, thought that written consent was insufficient to protect the doctor in the absence of confirmation that an 'informed' consent had been obtained.[20]

This controversy exemplifies the difficulties we have already noted of relying on individual conscience as a guide to ethical medical practice. The leadership of the BMA agreed with those politicians who regarded the legal permit to make searches as 'an oppressive and objectionable new statutory power [which was] a serious affront to a person's liberty'.[1] Many others, including ourselves, would consider drug peddling, with its potential catastrophic effect on many young people, as being a

---

18 Crime and Disorder Act 1998.
19 The problem is discussed further in chapter 8 below.
20 J D J Havard 'Doctors and the Police' (1983) 286 BMJ 742.
 1 W Russell 'Intimate Body Searches – for Stilettos, Explosive Devices, et al' (1983) 286 BMJ 733.

crime which merits draconian preventive methods. In the event, honours can be said to have been even. The BMA – and other interested groups – succeeded in protecting medical records from the powers of police search; the Act retained the legal right of the authorities to ask for an intimate search but stipulated that the actual operation must be performed by a medical practitioner when it is related to a Class A drug offence (s 55). The fact that s 55 has not been challenged in the European Court of Human Rights suggests that it has been operated reasonably well.[2]

The small cadre of police surgeons, or forensic medical examiners, comes into closest contact with the police[3] but it is, perhaps, the prison medical service which most magnifies and brings into focus many of the problems associated with codified ethics. Given an abnormal population, is it possible to apply to it normal methods? One would have hoped that this would be so, but there is little doubt that prison doctors are under considerable stress which results, in summary, from attempting to answer the question: are they there to serve the prisoners or the prison?[4] Smith believed that those in the service who regard their problems as exaggerated delude themselves; there is no reason to suppose that conditions have changed greatly[5] and the frequent allusions to prisoners made in this book – particularly as to consent to examination and treatment – testify to the strength of this suggestion. The number and proportion of mentally disordered prisoners has increased steadily over the years and are likely to escalate still further with the current encouragement of community care.[6] It is hard to imagine that sedative treatments are never given without the consent of the prisoner and the procedure may be justifiable on occasion. We would suggest, however, that any fault to be found in such practices lies not so much in their doing, which is a matter of clinical judgment, but, rather, in their secrecy – and that is a criticism which can also be applied to the introduction and use of many modern medical techniques. The current call is for administrative and clinical 'transparency' and there can be few circumstances in which this would not represent the preferred policy.

Every now and again, however, events overtake the medical profession and do so with such an impact as to enforce a radical alteration to its relationship with the public. The epidemic of infection by the human immunodeficiency virus (HIV) is archetypal of such an occurrence and, although it has now been with us for decades and shows signs of levelling off, it still merits special consideration.

The acquired immune deficiency syndrome (AIDS)

The human immunodeficiency virus is transmitted from person to person in three main ways – through sexual intercourse, by the exchange of contaminated blood and

---

2 Comparable powers are available in Scotland by way of the Criminal Procedure (Scotland) Act 1995, ss 18 and 19 or by obtaining a Sheriff warrant.
3 For a critical editorial comment, see The Lancet 'Three-faced Practice: Doctors and Police Custody' (1993) 341 Lancet 1245.
4 R Smith 'Prison Doctors: Ethics, Invisibility, and Quality' (1984) 288 BMJ 781.
5 J Reed and M Lyne 'The Quality of Health Care in Prison: Results of a Year's Programme of Semistructured Inspections' (1997) 315 BMJ 1420.
6 R Bluglass 'Mentally Disordered Prisoners: Reports but No Improvements' (1988) 296 BMJ 1757.

by maternal to fetal transmission. The first of these is predominant, although this depends to a large extent on the local social ambience. Male homosexual intercourse retains its pre-eminent importance, although, again, this is not universal – heterosexual spread is increasingly significant and may predominate in some areas. The result of transmission through the transfer of infected blood or blood products is to place at high risk those who *court* transfer – essentially, the intravenous drug abusers – and those who *need* it – for example, haemophiliacs. Congenital infection is said to occur in some 18-24% of infants born to infected mothers,[7] but the role of breast-feeding in transmission remains uncertain. HIV infection is, of itself, symptomless, despite the fact that the virus is transmissible. However, after a long incubation period – a mean of seven years[8] – 30-50% of these will develop clinical AIDS or pre-AIDS. The mortality of the full-blown disease is still probably 100%, although modern treatments give, at least, a hope of moderating the progress of the disease.[9]

The almost inevitable result has been that scientific attempts to control the disease have been clouded by emotion and the process has been amplified by reason of the unusual sexual connotations of the disease. In addition, however, there is a political dimension – the homosexual lobby is powerful and suspicious of discrimination on the grounds of illness; civil rights and AIDS have become inseparable issues in the United States.[10] Thus, the bid to control the disease is being made in difficult circumstances and there is less than complete agreement that all the measures taken are ideal. In essence, this dilemma stems from the need, on the one hand, to protect the public from infection and, on the other, to ensure that patients are not deterred from seeking medical help for fear of the consequences of diagnosis. The issue has crystallised into one of balancing the individual's right to privacy against the degree of coercion which the state may properly impose.

In theoretical terms, this is nothing new. All public health measures embody an involuntary element which has been accepted as inevitable since the middle of the last century – although, it has to be said that the tide of liberalism is now starting to erode this precept.[11] In practice, the politicisation of AIDS has led to a varied response to preventive measures, which run from the determinedly 'hands-off' approach in the United Kingdom to the draconian measures applied in Cuba, where the result of testing positive for HIV may be detention for an indefinite period.[12]

In general, however, most governments have chosen the way of self-control backed by education and protection from discrimination. Even so, attitudes may be changing as a result, particularly, of the epidemiological, clinical and social developments of recent years. In a short, but admirably concise, article, Danziger has put the case for the increasingly promoted values of social responsibility rather than

---

7 See eg European Collaborative Study 'Mother-to-child Transmission of HIV Infection' (1988) 2 Lancet 1039; T Rutter 'Short Course of Zidovudine Cuts Transmission of HIV' (1998) 316 BMJ 645.
8 R M Anderson and G F Medley 'Epidemiology of HIV Infection and AIDS: Incubation and Infection Periods, Survival and Vertical Transmission' (1988) 2 AIDS 57. For the American scene, see N Mueller 'The Epidemiology of the Immunodeficiency Virus Infection' (1986) 14 Law Med Hlth Care 250.
9 L Dillner 'Study Shows Two Drugs are Best for HIV Infection' (1995) 311 BMJ 827.
10 For a general review, see P Sieghart *AIDS and Human Rights* (1989).
11 See, in particular, M Brazier and J Harris 'Private Health and Public Lives' (1996) 4 Med LR 17.
12 R Bayer and C Healton 'Controling AIDS in Cuba: The Logic of Quarantine' (1989) 320 New Engl J Med 1022. Many other countries provide for quarantine of those who pose a health risk to others.

those of individual rights.[13] It is suggested that more and open testing should now be encouraged in that 'the health benefits of knowing one's serostatus now significantly outweigh the potential social and psychological harms'.[14] There is evidence of such a movement and this is particularly so in the approach to congenital HIV infection, where there is little doubt that early maternal diagnosis and treatment significantly reduces the risk of neonatal disease. As a consequence, testing of newborns may become compulsory, say, in the United States.[15] Other jurisdictions have also taken a more coercive attitude to HIV infection. The Australian response, for example, has been to endorse restriction of freedom of those HIV carriers who pose an unreasonable threat to the safety of others.[16] Powers of supervision and, indeed, of detention of persons who have knowingly exposed others to a risk of infection and have failed to change their behaviour when counselled to do so already exist in individual states where procedures have been developed to ensure that those affected have rights of review and of appeal against their exercise in an inappropriate way.[17] We doubt if such measures would ever be introduced in the United Kingdom but, even there, the impression is of some pressure to de-politicise AIDS and to look on the problem as no more than one of general public health to be tackled on established epidemiological principles.

It may well be that viral infections such as those associated with Hepatitis B and C are, in fact, of more pressing concern than is HIV and this is particularly so in what is, for present purposes, the most important aspect – that is, the relationships between the doctor and the HIV-positive patient and that between the HIV-positive doctor and his patient. It is the latter problem which predominates in the public mind and which is amplified by the frequent publication of the names of doctors suffering or dying from AIDS.[18] All the health authorities involved have emphasised the negligible risk to their patients – in which case, the simultaneous setting up of incident rooms and helplines does little more than testify to the illogical thinking that is so often applied to the disease, even to the extent of alleging negligence in providing information of possible contact by letter rather than by personal interview.[19] Calls for the routine testing of health care workers for both HIV and Hepatitis B infection have arisen – and have, to a considerable extent, been implemented in the United States.[20] The

13 R Danzinger 'An Epidemic like any Other? Rights and Responsibilities in HIV Prevention' (1996) 312 BMJ 1083.
14 Ibid. See also F S Rhame and D G Maki 'The Case for Wider Use of Testing for HIV Infection' (1989) 320 New Engl J Med 1248.
15 J Rovner 'HIV Tests for Babies to be Mandatory in USA' (1996) 347 Lancet 1325.
16 For discussion, see H Watchirs 'HIV/AIDS and the Law: The Need for Reform in Australia' (1993) 1 J Law Med 9.
17 Watchirs (1993) 1 J Law Med 9 at 20.
18 See eg the banner headlines in a quality newspaper: B Christie 'Hunt for AIDS Scare Patients' Scotsman, 27 May 1993, p 1. It seems that the doctor's name was published by the paper despite the fact that the Health Board intended to preserve anonymity – a far cry from *X v Y* [1988] 2 All ER 648, (1992) 3 BMLR 1 (see p 199 below). The merits of unofficial public admission of infection must also be considered. See A W Logie '"Coming Out" – a personal dilemma' (1996) 312 BMJ 1679. The privacy of AIDS patients has also been protected by the Australian courts: *T K v Australian Red Cross Society* [1989] WAR 335.
19 In *A v Tameside and Glossop Health Authority* [1996] 45 LS Gaz R 30, a finding by the trial judge of negligence in so doing was overturned on appeal.
20 M Morris 'American Legislation on AIDS' (1991) 303 BMJ 325.

British government has set its face against such a policy and puts its faith in those health workers who are infected or who have been exposed to infection appreciating and acting upon their responsibilities. The imposition of an ethical duty to inform the employers of any invasive contact with patients is balanced by the admonition that information as to the HIV status of health care personnel should be kept confidential – though practical experience indicates that this is scarcely possible. The revised guidelines also distinguish contacts by way of exposure-prone invasive procedures from those of normal 'social' type between physician and patient; patients in the former category should be offered HIV testing.[1]

It is fair to say that these guidelines have not gone uncriticised, particularly as to the true extent of the risks; simply to deny the presence of a risk is not to ensure that none exists.[2] We feel, however, that there is sufficient negative evidence to indicate that widespread testing of contacts with infected doctors would be unjustified – and might be interpreted as random testing through the back door.[3] Whatever the precise danger to patients may be, all authorities will agree that the risk to health care workers from infected patients is far greater; we return to this subject below.

The HIV-positive patient, the doctor and the law may, however, become interconnected in other fields. One such area is employment law which, because of its close association with discrimination, is particularly emotive. There is no anti-discrimination legislation in the United Kingdom directly related to homosexuality[4] but HIV infection is a progressive disease specifically governed by the Disability Discrimination Act 1995, Sch 1, para 8(1)(a). The overall effect of the Act in protecting infected persons is, however, doubtful, as a pre-symptomatic HIV carrier is not disabled for the purposes of the Act and has, therefore, no redress if discriminated against on this ground for the purposes of employment.[5] The infected person is protected once his ability to carry on a normal day-to-day existence is impaired to

1   UK Health Departments *AIDS-HIV Infected Health Care Workers: Practical Guidance on Notifying Patients* (1993); Department of Health *AIDS-HIV Infected Health Care Workers: Guidance on the Management of Infected Health Care Workers (interim)* (1993). Infected doctors who do not abide by the guidelines (now *HIV and AIDS: The Ethical Considerations* (1995)) may be subject to the GMC's disciplinary procedure ((1993) 341 Lancet 1407). The risks have been analysed in: Royal College of Pathologists *HIV Infection: Hazards of Transmission to Patients and Health Care Workers during Invasive Procedures* (1992). In a closely debated case, an otorhinolaryngologist who performed 'hands-off' surgery was allowed to continue to practice when HIV seropositive: see B Christie 'HIV Positive Surgeon Allowed to Operate' (1996) 313 BMJ 1279.
2   See, eg A G Bird, S M Gore, A J Leigh-Brown and D C Carter 'Escape from Collective Denial: HIV Transmission during Surgery' (1991) 303 BMJ 351; A G Bird and S M Gore 'Revised Guidelines for HIV Infected Health Care Workers' (1993) 306 BMJ 1013. Two allied papers giving full discussion of the US attitudes are: L Gostin 'The HIV-Infected Health Care Professional: Public Policy, Discrimination, and Patient Safety' (1990) 18 Law Med Hlth Care 303; M Barnes, N A Rango, G R Burke and L Chiarello 'The HIV-Infected Health Care Professional: Employment Policies and Public Health' (1990) 18 Law Med Hlth Care 311 – neither supports routine testing.
3   See p 273 below.
4   Subject to the probable ratification of the Treaty of Amsterdam, which introduces such legislation by way of the Treaty of European Union, s 6a.
5   It is, however, arguable, that he could claim indirect sex discrimination in that more men are HIV-seropositive than are women – although the gap is closing fast. See N Fagan and D Newell 'AIDS and Employment Law' (1987) 137 NLJ 752; J Kelly 'The AIDS Virus at the Workplace' (1991) 141 NLJ 88. This is not, however, agreed everywhere: B W Napier 'AIDS, Discrimination and Employment Law' (1989) 18 ILJ 84.

some, if not to a substantial, extent – but, by this time, a health authority would have little difficulty in showing that discrimination was justified.[6] The issue would be very much to the present point were a health authority to insist on pre-employment testing of health carers, but there has been no test of the proposition. Considerable public interest was aroused, however, when it was disclosed that British Airways was operating such a policy in relation to its aircrew;[7] this was never challenged in the courts. It can be assumed that at least part of the justification lies in the possibility that the change from asymptomatic to symptomatic HIV infection may first manifest itself in the central nervous system[8] – the same arguments as apply to the airline pilot could then be raised in respect of the doctor. Whether or not an employee could be discharged on being discovered to be HIV-positive is equally difficult to prejudge as, again, the 1995 Act would probably not apply; in practical terms, the relevant NHS trust or authority would probably offer the doctor alternative employment, for instance, in medical administration. It is, however, a problem that is most likely to arise in relation to breach of confidentiality and is better discussed under that head.

A collateral issue, which is very much to the heart of medical jurisprudence, is that of the relationship between HIV-seropositivity and life insurance policies. British insurers take a more interventionist stance than do their trans-Atlantic counterparts, who cannot take into account any negative or unknown result when assessing their premiums and who may be statutorily barred from asking about any previous tests at all.[9] The Association of British Insurers has attempted to soften its attitude in saying: 'having had a negative HIV test will not, of itself, prevent someone from obtaining life insurance or even affect the cost, providing there are no adverse factors present'[10] – but, clearly, the qualification implies an enduring right to investigate the appellant's life-style. The doctor is in some difficulty if questioned on the point; the BMA has advised doctors not to speculate on their patients' life-styles or risks of infection on behalf of insurance companies – such things are for the patient himself to disclose. Any reports of this type are, of course, subject to the provisions of the Access to Medical Reports Act 1988.[11]

There have been no British cases where an insurer's decision has been challenged in court. A leading Australian ruling has, however, shown the courts' reluctance to interfere with the insurers' right to manage their own affairs;[12] since anti-discrimination

---

6 Presumably, on making a balance between the degree of discrimination and the employer's need – which would be very compelling in the context: cf *Hampson v Department of Education and Science* [1991] 1 AC 171, [1990] 2 All ER 513. Refusal to employ a symptomatic sufferer has been accepted as justified by the Court of First Instance of the European Communities: *A (supported by Union Syndicalle, intervener) v EC Commission* [1994] ECR II-179.

7 J Ashworth 'Charter Condemns Jobseekers' Aids Test' The Times, 10 July 1992, p 1.

8 In support, see eg M E Appleman, D W Marshall, R L Brey et al 'Cerebrospinal Fluid Abnormalities in Patients without AIDS who are Seropositive for the Human Immunodeficiency Virus' (1988) 158 J Infect Dis 193; there are, however, as many papers to the contrary: eg A O Seines, E Miller, J MacArthur et al 'HIV-1 Infection: No Evidence of Cognitive Decline during the Asymptomatic Stages' (1990) 40 Neurology 204.

9 B Simon and P Roth 'Life Insurance and HIV Antibody Testing' (1992) 305 BMJ 902.

10 L Dillner 'Asking about HIV' (1991) 303 BMJ 327. See also N Hulme, R Smith and S E Barton 'Insurance and HIV Antibody Testing' (1992) 339 Lancet 682.

11 See p 210 below.

12 *Australian Mutual Provident Society v Goulden* (1986) 160 CLR 330. The case was brought under the Anti-Discrimination Act 1977 (NSW) which deals with physical and mental impairment in general; it was not associated with HIV infection.

policy in this respect is far stronger in Australia than it is in the United Kingdom, it is unlikely that an appellant would fare any better here. By and large, the problem of insurance provides a prime example of the need for adequate counselling before anyone subjects himself to testing.

Even if courts and legislatures have been at pains to protect the rights of HIV/ AIDS patients within their own jurisdictions, little restraint has been shown in limiting the rights of infected outsiders. Many jurisdictions are taking measures designed, at least, to prevent the importation of the HI virus – such very different cultures as the United States and Russia require HIV testing of short- and long-term visitors, as do several of the Gulf States. It was revealed in an early Canadian study that over 50 countries restricted the entry of HIV-positive persons.[13] In some cases, the main purpose of the regulations is to prevent immigration of HIV positive persons and, in several of these, deportation follows a seropositive test. Once again, the issue is by no means novel or specific to HIV infection. For years, it has been well recognised that a state may insist on minimum health standards in its immigrants – particularly in relation to infective disease; in most countries, permission to immigrate has depended upon the likelihood that the immigrant will not tax the local resources unduly. Yet the politically charged nature of the AIDS debate has resulted in that specific issue being treated in isolation. At the Pan-Commonwealth meeting on 'AIDS and Human Movement' in 1989, the policy of denying entry to HIV-positive applicants was roundly condemned, even when the purpose of entry was permanent residence.[14] It was resolved that such a policy amounted to an abuse of the would-be immigrant's human rights and, in the words of the meeting's resolution: 'could have consequences for the enjoyment of the rights of other members of [the immigrant's] family and obstruct the implementation of the fundamental human rights principle of respect for family unity.' It is difficult to accept such a position unless one chooses to regard AIDS as an infectious disease to which exceptional rules are applicable.

In practice, there is little doubt that much of the public's fear of AIDS stems from the belief that it is a highly infectious disease. This is not so – a fact which justifies, say, infected children attending school; the benefits of normal schooling greatly outweigh the risks of transmission of the disease.[15] One senses a widespread, albeit vague, mistrust of many aspects of modern medicine, but the greater part of that distrust, be it of AIDS or of genetic engineering, is founded upon ignorance. There is a need for publicity in these matters but, in its provision, the medical and legal professions must shed some of their essentially paternalistic seclusion and take the lead themselves – the alternatives are subjective television and radio presentations which often do little more than pile confusion on misunderstanding. The eventual resolution of these questions should be the product of open medico-legal debate – unhampered by political considerations.

---

13 M Duckett and O J Orkin 'AIDS-related Migration and Travel Policies and Restrictions: A Global Survey' (1989) AIDS, supp 3, s 231.
14 Commonwealth Secretariat *AIDS and Human Movement: Report of a Pan-Commonwealth Meeting* (1990).
15 For a general exposition, see A Orr 'Legal AIDS: Implications of AIDS and HIV for British and American Law' (1989) 15 J Med Ethics 61. For an American view, see W E Parmet 'AIDS and the Limits of Discrimination Law' (1987) 15 Law Med Hlth Care 61.

Reproductive medicine

2 Aspects of sex law

Sex law is one of those wide-ranging areas of the law which crosses the boundaries of, amongst others, the criminal law, family law and human rights law. It also clearly has a medical dimension, as the debate about sex is, in one sense, a debate about what can be done with the human body – and this is something in which doctors, and medical lawyers, may claim a legitimate and functional interest.

Sexual freedom

Probably the most frequently quoted reference in jurisprudence is to Mill,[1] who said:

> The only purpose for which power can rightfully be exercised over any member of a civilised community against his will is to prevent harm to others. His own good, either physical or moral, is not a sufficient warrant. He cannot rightfully be compelled to do or forebear because it would be better for him to do so, because it would make him happy or because, in the opinion of others, to do so would be wise, or even right.

This libertarian sentiment is now widely endorsed in an age in which the notion of interfering with others for their own good is deeply distrusted. Sexual behaviour has come to be regarded as a private matter in our society and, even if there is still some room for an ethics of sex, the role of the law in regulating sexual conduct is significantly constrained. In this non-paternalistic climate, the guiding principle is that of consent: the law seeks to distinguish those sexual acts which are mutually consensual from those in which one of the parties is an objector or is, at least, non-consenting. In the former situation, the law should only intervene if it is believed that autonomous consent cannot or, as a matter of public policy, should not be given. It is clear that these criteria may open the doors to jurisprudential conflict – a dilemma which was well demonstrated in the dramatic, albeit unsavoury, case of *Brown*.[2]

Here, a group of homosexual men indulged in a series of sado-masochistic sessions and were indicted – and convicted – under the Offences Against the Person Act 1861, ss 20 and 47.[3] By the time the matter reached the House of Lords, the issue had become essentially that of the role of consent in legitimating what were agreed to be injurious sexual practices – injurious, that is, short of killing or inflicting

---

1   J S Mill *On Liberty and Representative Government* Blackwell's Political Texts (1948) p 8.
2   *R v Brown (Anthony)* [1994] 1 AC 212, [1993] 2 All ER 75, HL. For a critique of this judgment, see E Edwards 'No Defence for a Sado-masochistic Libido' (1993) 143 NLJ 552.
3   A charge of indecent assault being time-barred: Sexual Offences Act 1967, s 7.

grievous bodily harm.[4]   In the event, the House of Lords held that, although a prosecutor had to prove absence of consent in order to secure a conviction for mere assault, it was not in the public interest that a person should wound or cause actual bodily harm to another for no good reason and that, in the absence of such a reason, the victim's consent afforded no defence to the charges. All the defendants had admitted causing hurt or injury calculated to interfere with the health of another party and the gratification of sado-masochistic desires did not constitute a legitimate excuse for so doing. It is to be noted that this rejection of an appeal against conviction was on the basis of a 3:2 majority, the dissenting opinions, effectively, maintaining that it was a matter for Parliament rather than the courts to legislate for what was seen as a new offence.

Brown is not an easy decision to analyse. The activities of the accused had generated no complaints, they involved adults only, the incidents took place on private property and there was no danger that they would ever be seen by the public – as a result, the decision was hotly debated in the academic literature.[5] In so far as it purports to restrict the freedom of adults to pursue sexual satisfaction in private, it is hardly consonant with the prevailing endorsement of that freedom. It is, however, easier to justify if one treats it as a decision which sets out to affirm the general principle that the physical integrity of the human body should be respected. Much will depend upon one's view of the role of the criminal courts as declarors of moral rules. If one believes that the criminal law should act as the guardian of certain moral values, then *Brown* is not more than an example of a court being prepared to do just that. If, on the other hand, one feels that it is no business of the criminal courts to make general statements about violence and the symbolic degradation of the human body – even if consensual – then *Brown* becomes an example of unacceptable moral perfectionism.

On the face of things, the decision strikes at the heart of Millian philosophy – and it is both surprising and significant that it was upheld in the European Court of Human Rights,[6] which accepted that national authorities were entitled to consider the prosecution and conviction of the applicants as being necessary in a democratic society for the protection of health.[7]

Incest

Incest – defined in the *Concise Oxford Dictionary* as 'Sexual commerce of near kindred' – is, perhaps, the most illogical of sexual offences.

---

4   The majority in the House of Lords accepted that consent does not elide the unlawfulness of inflicting such injuries: *R v Donovan* [1934] 2 KB 498; *A-G's Reference (No 6 of 1980)* [1981] QB 715, [1981] 2 All ER 1057.
5   Although mainly as to the role of consent as a 'defence' to the charges: L Bibbings and P Alldridge 'Sexual Expression, Body Alteration, and the Defence of Consent' (1993) 20 JLS 356; S Hedley 'Sado-masochism, Human Rights and the House of Lords' (1993) 52 CLJ 194.
6   *Laskey, Jaggard and Brown v United Kingdom* (1997) 24 EHRR 39.
7   As a result, the court did not find it necessary to consider whether the interference could also be justified on the ground of protection of morals.

The primary difficulty lies in its scope – 'near kindred' must be interpreted before any law is applied. Most jurisdictions which maintain the concept limit the offence to intercourse between three generations of relations in the direct line of descent or ascent and between siblings; the relationship persists in the illegitimate state and siblings of half blood are included. This is the situation in England and Wales – with a curious dispensation for grandmothers and grandsons.[8] But around this norm there are variations ranging from an absence of the offence as such in France to the relatively wide relationships which are proscribed in Scotland.[9] No one can be happy when a relationship is legal south of the River Tweed but attracts a potential sentence of life imprisonment to the north. In the face of such variations, it is reasonable to question the rationale of the offence for which there is, undoubtedly, an innate public distaste.

Few of the common reasons adduced for the so-called 'incest-taboo' provide good grounds for legislation in modern times. Socio-anthropological theories depend, in many ways, on the supposed advantages to the tribe or clan of 'breeding out'; such imaginings have no place in modern society, with its easy access to the opposite sex outside the immediate family. More often, the case against incest is based on genetic grounds; this, we suggest, is a fundamental misunderstanding. In the first place, genetics can have no place in the historic development of an incest taboo because genetic considerations would only have been apparent to those communities who regularly practised in-breeding and, therefore, suffered from no restrictive 'horror'. Secondly, genetics are related to procreation, while incest is a matter of sexual intercourse; genetic considerations are more properly directed at the marriage laws. Thirdly, there is no certainty that an isolated incestuous pregnancy will result in congenital abnormality. In the worst imaginable case – that of father/daughter incest with both carrying a deleterious recessive gene – the chances of a manifestly abnormal offspring are 1:4. Even so, this, taken with the intermediate possibility of multi-factorial disease,[10] would, in any case, be sufficient to render an incestuous pregnancy legally terminable under s 1(1)(d) of the Abortion Act 1967 – in addition to the obvious indications under s 1(1)(a); many jurisdictions specifically include pregnancy arising from rape or incest as a justification for legal termination but the wide scope of the 1967 Act makes this unnecessary in Great Britain. Far more cogently in relation to the present era, incest must be disruptive of the family; the same can, however, be said about adultery, yet we do not judge it as a criminal offence. A high proportion of wives to husbands indulging in incest will say that they are quite prepared to resume normal family relationships 'if only he will stop it'. Here, the argument is edging towards what must be the family's and society's basic revulsion to incest – that it exemplifies the exploitation of those in the care of, or under the authority of, the perpetrators. Not even apparent consent can be truly autonomous in such circumstances; effectively, incest is often an insidious form of rape.

Once that is accepted, the way to modernising the law becomes very much clearer. Age becomes a significant factor; it seems irrational to allow consenting homosexual practices between adults in private yet to criminalise consenting normal intercourse

8 Sexual Offences Act 1956, ss 10, 11.
9 Criminal Law (Consolidation) (Scotland) Act 1995, s 1.
10 See chapter 6.

between two adults who are closely related yet in a loving relationship.[11] On the other hand, increasing disparity in age increases the degree of subordination and, thus, the severity of the offence. But this is not the only feature bearing on authority. A father, in effect, has inherent authority which persists through life; a ban on father/daughter intercourse should, therefore, be absolute. Similar authority, albeit only until approximately school-leaving age, rests in the stepfather or the mother's partner; the same can be said of the foster father, while the authority of an adopting father corresponds closely to that of the genetic father. None of these is related in blood to the child, yet intercourse is, in every case, within the family and the effect on the child is the same – she is being sexually abused by someone she trusts.

Scottish legislation[12] provides an example of how some of these principles may be effected. Prohibited relationships are now defined and are restricted, as regards the offence of incest, to those which are consanguineous and adoptive – sexual intercourse between a man and his adopted daughter or former adopted daughter is now characterised as incest, as are the other permutations of the adopting state; half-blood and illegitimate relationships are now included. A separate offence of having intercourse with a step-child is created when the step-child is either under the age of 21 or has, at any time before attaining the age of 18, lived in the same household and been treated as a child of the step-parent. A further offence of having intercourse with a child under the age of 16 who is a member of the same household and over whom a position of trust or authority exists is also enacted, provided that the person concerned is over 16 years old. A number of defences, including that of ignorance as to relationship or age, are specified.

These provisions are a compromise between strict logic and public policy. Thus, the potential right of adult brothers and sisters to behave themselves in private as they please is not yet recognised, while uncles and aunts could equally well be caught in the 'trust and authority' net. More importantly, the legal obsession with defloration is perpetuated. We cannot help feeling that to force deviant sex on a young girl or homosexual acts upon a young boy is as offensive as it is to enforce 'natural' heterosexual sex; once the overall importance of trust and authority is recognised, they all become of the same nature and they should, accordingly, be treated as a group.[13] The use of the word 'incest' to cover a wide spectrum of relationships may also be considered unwise; it should, if retained, be limited to that act which is objectionable on any rationale – a sexual relationship between parent and child. Otherwise, we will continue to argue in favour of an all-embracing concept of assault with sexual intent to cover those sexual offences that are governed, directly or indirectly, by the concept of consent.

11 As suggested by the Criminal Law Revision Committee, 15th Report *Sexual Offences* (Cmnd 9213) para 8.22.
12 See n 9 above.   Prohibitions under Scots law still include uncle/aunt and great-grandparent relationships. Otherwise, the CLRC (n 11 above) was clearly concerned to avoid major deviations between the English and Scots law of incest; the Scottish offence under 'trust and authority' was not, however, accepted.
13 As, indeed, they are in many jurisdictions. See D A Batten 'Incest – A Review of the Literature' (1983) 23 Med, Sci & L 245 to indicate how the definition has been widened in the medical literature.

Homosexuality

We have hinted above at the apparent illogicality in using the criminal law to constrain the private lives of adult siblings while, at the same time, acknowledging the virtually unrestricted sexual autonomy of other adults, particularly as related to their sexual orientation. Indeed, it is probably fair to say that the increasingly liberal attitude to sex in the United Kingdom has been driven by the rapidly changing attitudes to homosexuality that have developed over the last half-century. The Sexual Offences Act 1967, permitting male homosexual practices by two consenting adults in private, was passed amid considerable public concern;[14] 27 years later, the age of consent was lowered from 21 to 18 years and the intense Parliamentary debate on the measure was concentrated not on whether this change should be made but, rather, on whether the more appropriate age was 16 years. The Sexual Offences Acts are, however, primarily concerned with actual sexual activity. In the present context, interest centres on the effects of homosexual orientation on a person's social well-being and, here, the law remains, in some respects, ambivalent.

First, as to earning one's living, it is not illegal in the United Kingdom to refuse employment on the grounds that a person has homosexual tendencies,[15] but to refuse to employ only male homosexuals would almost certainly contravene the Sex Discrimination Act 1975, s 1(1)(a).[16] Once employed, however, the fairness of dismissal on the grounds of homosexuality would be a matter of proof which would be governed by the Employment Protection (Consolidation) Act 1978, s 57(1)(b) and (3).[17] Here, much would depend upon the nature of the employment. In *Nottinghamshire County Council v Bowly*,[18] a male schoolteacher was dismissed fairly having been convicted of gross indecency although this was unrelated to his pupils; in *Boychuk v Symons Holdings Ltd*[19] an employer was found to have acted reasonably in dismissing a lesbian who refused to remove her Gay Liberation badge; but, in *Bell v Devon and Cornwall Police Authority*,[20] a homosexual canteen worker was found to have been unfairly dismissed because, inter alia, there was insufficient evidence to show that customers would have been upset by knowing he was homosexual.

A marked advance in the recognition of the homosexual's status has been seen in the field of family law. Thus it has been established both in England and in Scotland that there are no statutory or public policy reasons why a single person should be barred from adopting a child simply because he or she was living in an established

---

14 Scotland came into line with England and Wales through the otherwise unrelated Criminal Justice (Scotland) Act 1980, s 80; the impact on the public was minimal. Change in the law of Northern Ireland was, however, precipitated by an appeal to the European Court of Human Rights: *Dudgeon v United Kingdom* (1982) 4 EHRR 149, followed, as a result, by Homosexual Offences (Northern Ireland) Order 1982, SI 1982/1536 (NI 19).

15 B W Napier 'AIDS, Discrimination and Employment Law' (1989) 18 ILJ 84. In many common law jurisdictions – eg Australia, United States – homosexuals are specifically protected by the anti-discrimination laws.

16 *James v Eastleigh Borough Council* [1990] 2 All ER 607, HL.

17 As amended by the Employment Act 1980, s 6.

18 [1978] IRLR 252.

19 [1977] IRLR 395.

20 [1978] IRLR 283. See also *Saunders v Scottish National Camps Association Ltd* [1980] IRLR 174, EAT; on appeal [1981] IRLR 277.

homosexual relationship.[1] In so far as it is 'the court's duty to give first consideration to the need to safeguard and promote the welfare of the child'[2] and that, therefore, the interests of the adopters fall to be considered also, these cases go a long way to vindicating the homosexual family in the eyes of the law – the days when the 'reasonable parent' would be expected to 'protect to child from the dangers associated with a homosexual lifestyle' are numbered.[3]

A number of cases related to discrimination against homosexual men and women have come to the European jurisdiction and the results have not been as consistent as might have been anticipated. In *S v United Kingdom*,[4] the applicant, who had been living in a lesbian relationship 'as man and wife', appealed against an eviction order from her council accommodation that was issued on the death of her partner – an order which could not have been made had she been of the opposite sex. The European Commission found that the relevant housing legislation was designed to protect the family; the difference in the treatment of the applicant from that which would have been given to a person of the opposite sex could, therefore, be justified reasonably and objectively. *B v United Kingdom*[5] was an immigration case concerning the repatriation of a homosexual partner who could have remained lawfully in the United Kingdom had he been a woman. The Commission held that a state whose immigration laws provided better treatment for heterosexual couples did not practise discrimination; again, it was decided that the difference in treatment had a legitimate aim – the protection of the family – and the resultant action was proportionate to that aim.

The most recent case in point demonstrates the somewhat grey area that is apparently developing in relation to the rights of homosexuals on the one hand and of transsexuals on the other. *Grant v South-West Trains Ltd*[6] touched on the rather mundane subject of concessionary fares for railway employees. The applicant drew heavily on the judgment in *P v S and Cornwall County Council*,[7] the judgment on which, as we will see below, was, essentially, based on the claim that equality for all was a fundamental principle of European Community law. This ruling is clearly subject to open-ended interpretation and it is unsurprising that it was relied on to uphold the proposition that, if discrimination was to be avoided, homosexual couples were entitled to the same industrial benefits as were heterosexuals when the benefit in question was payable to those involved in a meaningful common law opposite sex spousal relationship. The European Court of Justice would, however, not go that far – a surprising stance in that it was contrary to the recommendation of their Advocate General. In reaching their conclusion, the court observed that, in the present state of the law within the Community, stable relationships between two persons of the same sex are not regarded as equivalent to marriages or stable relationships outside marriage between persons of opposite sex. Consequently, an employer was not required to treat the two situations as similar – it was for the

---

1   *T Petitioner* 1997 SLT 724, 1996 SCLR 897; *Re W (a minor) (adoption: homosexual adopter)* [1997]
    3 All ER 620, [1997] 3 WLR 768.
2   Per Singer J in *Re W* [1997] 3 All ER 620 at 627, [1997] 3 WLR 768 at 775.
3   See C Barton 'Will gays get their way?' (1997) The Times, 27 May.
4   European Commission for Human Rights Application 11716/85, DR 47, p 274.
5   European Commission for Human Rights Application 16106/90, DR 64, p 278.
6   Court of Justice of the European Communities Case C-249/96 [1998] IRLR 206.
7   [1996] IRLR 347.

legislature alone to adopt measures that might affect the position. Most importantly in the present context, the court firmly distinguished discrimination on the ground of gender reassignment from differences of treatment based on a person's sexual orientation.[8] Thus, it seems that, at least for the present, the European Courts will not press the United Kingdom into legislation in respect of sexual orientation alone; at the same time, there is a strong impression that they would regard it as desirable.

The key issues in any legislation lie, first, in privacy and, secondly, on the age of consent to homosexual practices. The United Kingdom Parliament's response to the former has already been outlined. In addition, the sexual privacy of those in the enclosed worlds of the armed forces and the merchant navy have also been recognised,[9] which is not only equitable but, given the increasing integration of women within the core structure of the forces, also appears logical. It is to be noted that the 1994 Act still allows for a homosexual act to be a ground for discharge from the armed forces or, where it occurs in conjunction with other acts or circumstances, to constitute an offence under the Service Discipline Acts.[10] It is, however, a long step to include under this head the power to discharge persons from the armed forces who have not committed any offence but whose sexual orientation is homosexual; this has been declared a rational ministerial decision but the policy is currently before the European Court of Justice.[11]

There is no doubt as to the position of the European Court of Human Rights, which has confirmed that it regards any legislation restricting the rights of adults to act as they please in private as an infringement of the European Convention on Human Rights, art 8 – which bars interference by a public body in the right to respect for private and family life, home and correspondence. The mere fact that prosecutions have not been taken in recent years under such legislation is considered immaterial – the threat is sufficient to affect peoples' private lives and is disproportionate to any aims that might be sought to be achieved.[12]

The question of the age at which homosexual sexual activity should be lawful has been the subject of extensive Parliamentary debate since the last edition of this book was published. Very few have denied that the right to sexual activity of one's own choice should not be withheld until the age of 21 – it is surely a matter of majority and the age of majority has been set at 18 years. Rather, the problem is whether the age at which it is lawful to engage in homosexual activity should be reduced to 16 years. The argument proceeds at two levels – first, on grounds of discrimination between sexes and, second, on the capacity of young men and women to consent to sexual activity. As to the first, it is important to remember that there is no such legal concept as an age of female consent to sexual intercourse.[13] The rule is that it is an offence

---

8 But the court did not rule out the possibility that discrimination on the basis of sexual orientation might be proscribed when the Treaty of Amsterdam (2 October 1997) came into force.

9 Criminal Justice and Public Order Act 1994, s 146.

10 Section 146(4).

11 See, currently, *R v Secretary of State for Defence, ex p Smith* [1996] QB 517, [1996] 1 All ER 257, CA; *R v Secretary of State for Defence, ex p Perkins* [1997] IRLR 297. The exclusion of sexual orientation as a measure of sex in the former case was questioned in the latter; the problem has been at least partially solved by *Grant v South-West Trains Ltd* Case C-249/96 [1998] IRLR 206, ECJ.

12 *Modinos v Cyprus* (1993) 16 EHRR 485. Confirming *Dudgeon v United Kingdom* (1982) 4 EHRR 149.

13 See Lord Brandon in *Gillick v West Norfolk and Wisbech Area Health Authority* [1986] AC 112 at 198, [1985] 3 All ER 402 at 431.

to have sexual intercourse with a girl aged less than 16 years; thus, the law is protective of children and there is no discrimination against boys in respect of heterosexual sexual activity on the ground of age. The question is, then, whether greater protection is needed in respect of homosexual relationships and, here, the arguments as to discrimination and capacity overlap. In so far as there can be no sexual intercourse within the legal definition of the act between homosexual women, there is inherent discrimination against boys; the fundamental issue can then be seen as whether the resultant paternalism on the part of the state is justified.

A legal system which allows a 16-year-old heterosexual boy to have intercourse with a woman over the age of 16 but which, at the same time, prevents a 16-year-old homosexual from engaging in sexual activity with another male is undoubtedly discriminatory. The discrimination lies in the fact that the heterosexual 16-year-old is allowed to express his sexuality in his chosen way, whereas the same courtesy is not extended to the adolescent homosexual. The only justifications for a higher age of homosexual consent then lie either in the paternalistic belief that boys between 16 and 18 should be protected from exploitation by others, or in the assumption that they should be shielded from making a choice which they are not yet mature enough to make. The validity of both of these grounds is hotly disputed. Those in favour of a lower age of consent argue that boys of 16 are mature enough to look after themselves and do not need any more protection than is given to girls. They also argue that the suggestion that boys will somehow be drawn into homosexuality if the law allows them to engage in homosexual activity before the age of 18 simply does not accord with that is known about the development of sexual identity. Proponents of a lower age of consent contend that sexual orientation is settled by the age of 16 and nothing that happens thereafter will change the individual's sexual preferences.[14] Needless to say, there are those who refute both of these points and who argue that the experiences of adolescence are crucial to the choice of an adult lifestyle. In this view, society may well feel entitled to protect its young people from making premature decisions as to their sexual future.

Rather surprisingly, an attempt to lower the age for homosexual consent to 16 failed in Parliament in 1998. It is understood, however, that the government intends to reintroduce the measure in the near future. This will accord with informed medical opinion in the United Kingdom, which has published its opposition to an age differential between lawful hetero- and homosexual activity. A leading article in the Lancet argued the case for equality very strongly.[15] Several of the arguments used seem to us to have been based on the conclusions; none the less, the article pointed out that both the Royal College of Psychiatrists and the British Medical Association believed that homosexual activity in men should be legal from the age of 16.[16] In opting for the age of 18, therefore, our legislators appear to have been motivated by the instincts of the concerned layman; parliamentary discussion was, however, both deep and lengthy.

Opinions change rapidly in the current socio-political maelstrom and European opinion is no exception. In 1975 the European Commission on Human Rights was

---

14 J Hindley 'The age of consent for male homosexuals' [1986] Crim LR 595
15 Editorial Comment 'Legislating Fairly for Consenting Homosexuals' (1994) 343 Lancet 185.
16 The problem of special relationships, particularly in respect of positions of trust, deserves closer attention than it has received – should there, in other words, be a particular homosexual offence analogous to incest and related offences? There does seem to be much merit in such a proposition.

happy to concede that it was for individual jurisdictions to fix for themselves an appropriate extension of the age of consent in relation to homosexual conduct.[17] In 1997 the same Commission found, by a majority of 14:4, that there was no objective or reasonable justification for the maintenance of a higher minimum age of consent to male homosexual than to heterosexual acts and that the application under consideration disclosed discriminatory treatment in the exercise of the applicant's right to respect for his private life under art 8 of the European Convention on Human Rights.[18] The matter will now go before the European Court of Human Rights. Meanwhile, the temptation to reproduce the dissenting opinion of Martinez J is irresistible:

> I should like to stress that the British Parliament is better placed than the members of the majority of the Commission to determine what suits best the people and the society which that Parliament democratically represents.

Transsexualism

Although the civil law in the United Kingdom currently takes little note of sex, the problems of transsexualism – or the gender dysphoria syndrome – are being raised with increasing frequency and carry serious issues in medical jurisprudence in their wake. Transsexuals are not necessarily homosexual; the great majority are heterosexual – the basic issue being that they have, so to speak, been dressed in the colours of the opposing team. The transsexual does not necessarily demonstrate any anatomical or physiological abnormality but, nevertheless, suffers from an intense wish to be, and be accepted as being, of the opposite sex. A proportion of transsexuals may pass through a phase of homosexuality, but the two states differ in that, while homosexuals are content with their own sexuality but prefer to express it in their own way, transsexuals are convinced that nature has made a mistake in their case and they are intent on rectifying it. It follows that homosexuality and transsexualism pose distinct ethical and sociological questions.

The fully developed syndrome must lead to severe distress. Nevertheless, living with a problem is a personal matter and, in the absence of identification cards, National Service and the like, society is scarcely concerned to regulate the outward trappings of transsexualism such as transvestism. But when it comes to rectification, public morality is concerned at three heads: the treatment of the condition; the recognition of treatment; and, most particularly, the final legal status of the transsexual with its multiple ramifications.

Psychiatric treatment of the fully fledged syndrome is generally ineffective; the patients need to change their sex organs and this goal can be achieved only by radical surgery. This includes castration in both males and females which, in some jurisdictions, may be unlawful in itself without judicial approval.[19] An artificial vagina can be

---

17 *X v United Kingdom*, European Commission on Human Rights Application 7215/75, DR 19, p 66.
18 *Sutherland v United Kingdom* (1997) 24 EHRR CD22.
19 S Gromb, B Chanseau and H J Lazarini 'Judicial Problems Related to Transsexualism in France' (1997) 37 Med, Sci & L 27.

fashioned in the male but, for obvious reasons, surgery is more likely to satisfy such a male-to-female convert than the female-to-male.[20] None the less, at least in the former case, the cosmetic results can be very good – the patient can finish up, as did two of the principals in reported British court cases, as a pin-up beauty or a 'Bond girl';[1] as it has been put: 'the pastiche of femininity can be very convincing'.[2]

As we will see later, some countries have wide-ranging legislation in place, but it is by no means uniform.[3] Elsewhere, the legality of consent to sex reassignment is generally based on a tacit understanding between medicine and the law. Operations are, nowadays, nearly everywhere justified under the doctrine of 'necessity' or of 'genuine medical treatment'. The ethical problem then becomes that of case selection and, in practice, a comparatively small number of applicants are, in fact, recommended for operation. Nevertheless, while some foreign national centres have a very high turnover – of anything up to 800 cases per year – well over 2,000 total cases, including some 400 females, have been operated upon within the British National Health Service and the threat of judicial review has been sufficient to cause a change of heart in health authorities which originally refused funding for the purpose.[4] There is, therefore, nothing unlawful about sex reassignment in the United Kingdom.

The diagnosis of sex

We must be clear as to the terminology if we are to speak of a person's 'sex'. Ormrod's four criteria[5] are well known but are worth recapitulating briefly. A person's sex can be identified in a number of ways or, more often, in a combination of ways:

(a) *External genitalia* – which is the way sex is diagnosed at birth and is, therefore, the basis on which a person is registered. The appearance of the external genitalia is, however, subject to developmental abnormality and to maternal or fetal hormonal dysfunction. There are also a number of genetically controlled biochemical disorders related to the synthesis of the sex hormones which may cause confusion. Such errors are often discovered only at puberty and they constitute the great majority of reasons for correction of the register.[6]

(b) *Gonads* – this is clearly a poor test in practice. In the absence of exploratory surgery, it is impossible to distinguish between the internal gonads of the female and undescended testes in the male.

(c) *Chromosomes* – As is well known, the normal female carries XX sex chromosomes and the normal male XY. The sex chromosomes are, however,

20 The surgery is well described for the non-medical by J J Hage 'Medical Requirements and Consequences of Sex Reassignment Therapy' (1995) 35 Med, Sci & L 17.
1 April Ashley in *Corbett v Corbett (otherwise Ashley)* [1971] P 83 and Caroline Cossey in *Cossey v United Kingdom* (1990) 13 EHRR, [1991] 2 FLR 492.
2 Paraphrased from Professor Dewhurst in *Corbett v Corbett (otherwise Ashley)* [1971] P 83 at 104.
3 For a resumé, see A Rogers 'Legal Implications of Transsexualism' (1993) 341 Lancet 1085.
4 C Dyer 'Transsexuals Challenge Rationing Decision' (1996) 313 BMJ 319.
5 R Ormrod 'The Medico-legal Aspects of Sex Discrimination' (1972) 40 Med-leg J 78.
6 Births and Deaths Registration Act 1953, s 29; Registration of Births, Deaths and Marriages (Scotland) Act 1965, s 42.

notorious for trisomies or deletions – that is, numerical variations on the normal number of two corresponding genes – and such abnormalities are responsible for a number of cases of difficulty in defining sex. Conceptual difficulties also arise. It is usually said that the possession of a Y chromosome indicates maleness; it might, equally, be said that the possession of XX chromosomes indicates femaleness. Where, then does one place the trisomy XXY? It will be seen later that these problems have greatly influenced the courts of the European Community.

(d) Finally, we can look at the person's *gender* – a concept which is difficult to define and one which means different things to different people. Ormrod, whose influence has been so surprisingly profound, probably hit the nail on the head when, speaking of the treatment of 'intersex' – or the presence of characteristics of both sexes – he commented that doctors would ask which gender should the patient be *encouraged* to assume.[7] In short, gender is, first, the expression of one's sex within the social construct and this is, to an extent, fashioned by the individual's psyche. Transsexualism represents the ultimate in the 'assumption' of a sexual identity and, as a result, gender has come to be identified as the sex to which the individual thinks he or she does or ought to belong.[8] The condition of transsexualism is, therefore, more descriptively named alternatively as the gender dysphoria syndrome. It is, however, a *positive* mental state – the individual *wants* to be of the opposite sex and actively seeks a coincidence between his/her physical and psychological sex; thus, we can distinguish, say, the 'tomboy' who is simply not fond of the sex she has been given.

Sexual orientation is simply the way in which an individual prefers to practice his or her sexuality. Accordingly, it does not come into the diagnosis of that person's sex[9] – a distinction which, as we have already seen (and to which we will revert), has been of major significance in interpreting European law.

Seeds of a medico-legal conflict
Faced with a conflict of evidence, the medical solution is to 'assign' a person to the sex which they are most likely to be able to support in society, the function of the chromosomal sex being then relegated to that of an indicator of the direction in which to steer an infant's upbringing. In later life, the one characteristic of sex or gender which is apparent to no one, including the principal, is the state of a person's chromosomes. Unfortunately, because of its immutability, that is the feature which appeals most to the lawyer.

The law, both in England and Wales and in Scotland[10] has resolutely turned its face against 'sex change'; only a genuine mistake at birth can justify an alteration on one's birth certificate, which is regarded as documentation of an immutable historical fact. In practice, this matters surprisingly little. United Kingdom law is relatively unconcerned with sex and the registration of 'corrected' transsexuals in their 'new'

7 Ormrod (1972) 40 Med-leg J 78.
8 The definition of gender has been discussed recently by A C Loux 'Is he our sister? Sex, Gender and Transsexuals under European Law' [1997] 3 Web J of Current Legal Issues 1 (http://webjcl.ncl.ac.uk).
9 *Smith v Gardner Merchant Ltd* [1998] 3 All ER 852.
10 *X Petitioner* 1957 SLT (Sh Ct) 61.

sex for National Insurance and employment purposes is relatively common. [11] The ultimate test, however, lies in marriage, which is the union between a man and a woman. The leading British case in this context is *Corbett v Corbett*,[12] in which it was held that:

(a) marriage is a relationship which depends on sex and not on gender;
(b) sex is determined by the consideration of the chromosomal pattern, the original gonadal status and the pre-operative genitalia; and
(c) if these are not congruent – as they were in *Corbett* – the genitalia will be preferred to the other two.

It is very widely supposed that Ormrod J held that a person's sex depended on his/her chromosomes but he did *not* say that. He *did*, however, add:

> The biological sexual constitution of an individual is fixed at birth and cannot be changed either by the natural development of organs of the opposite sex or by medical or surgical means.[13]

But, since the organs and the genitalia of a converted transsexual *have* been changed, the chromosomes are the last immutables and have, therefore, assumed an importance which Ormrod probably never intended. The other inherent difficulty with the *Corbett* decision is that it failed to define genitalia which, in a woman, can run from the fallopian tubes to the vulva. This particular aspect has to be stressed because it leads directly to consideration of the testicular feminisation syndrome (TFS) – a condition in which the *Corbett* criteria disintegrate. In the TFS we have an apparently normal woman, with an undeveloped vagina, no uterus, undescended testes and a male chromosomal pattern. Thus, in calling such a person a woman, we are pitting the possession of a vulva against all the other *Corbett* criteria which, surprisingly, take no account of personal appearances. Yet no one would dream of attempting to impose a 'true' sex on someone who is by upbringing, self-assessment and popular acclaim clearly a woman. The practical importance of the testicular feminisation syndrome in the context of this text is that the TFS patient is, effectively, a *naturally converted transsexual*. If, therefore, we accept such persons in their apparent sex without demur – as we must on both medical and social grounds – we are providing considerable logical ammunition to those who press for acceptance of the *artificially converted transsexual*. And this is a point which has been taken up by the European Court of Human Rights.

As something of a collateral issue – but of major significance to the present discussion – it was held in *Corbett* that, notwithstanding the validity of the marriage or of the sex of the 'wife', she was physically incapable of consummating a marriage

11 In *White v British Sugar Corpn* [1977] IRLR 121, for example, a woman who was treated as a 'man' for national insurance needs was regarded as a woman for the purposes of the Sex Discrimination Act 1975. The case was, however, clouded with allegations of deceit.
12 [1971] P 83, [1970] 2 All ER 33. The 'marriage' took place in Gibraltar. An unreported case, *Franklin v Franklin (otherwise Jones)*, is said to have been the first involving a 'marriage' in England; it was annulled: Scotsman, 9 November 1990, p 2.
13 [1971] P 83 at 104, [1970] 2 All ER 33 at 47.

by the use of an artificial cavity. The case was thus distinguished from *SY v SY*,[14] in which a decree of nullity had been refused on the grounds that a vestigial vagina could have been corrected by forming an artificial passage; Wilmer LJ commented:

> If a woman with an artificial vagina is incapable of true sexual intercourse she cannot be raped or commit adultery. I would regard such a result as bordering on the fantastic.[15]

The irony of the distinction between the two cases is that it would seem to have been made on the basis that SY was an imperfect woman – today, it is almost certain that she would have been diagnosed as a case of testicular feminisation and, accordingly, as a chromosomal male.

The simple expediency of the chromosomal test has led to some unfortunate consequences – in particular, the application of *Corbett* to the criminal law. This arose in *R v Tan*,[16] in which a converted male to female transsexual who was living as a woman was considered to be a man for the purposes of the Sexual Offences Act 1956, s 30; the case, however, does no more than demonstrate the dangers of extrapolating a judicial decision from its true ambience. It was left to the Australians to re-emphasise that criminal activity is to be judged by behaviour. This was demonstrated in two cases which interact almost as scientific controls.[17] In *Cogley*, circumstances very similar to those envisaged by Wilmer LJ in *SY v SY* were tested and the converted transsexual complainant was considered to possess a vagina. The trial judge found that the conformity of the current genitalia and the 'core' identity constituted the essential ingredient for establishing the 'sex' of a person. The Court of Appeal, however, in an obiter opinion, thought that judges' expressions in such cases laid down no legal principles and that the determination of disputed sex was a matter for the legislature.[18] In *Harris*, two male to female transsexuals were accused of attempting to procure an act of indecency by a male. One had undergone reassignment surgery and was held to be a female within the meaning of the Crimes Act 1900 (NSW); the other, although psychologically a female, had not had surgery and was considered male. The importance of the existing genitalia was, thereby, emphasised, Mathews J saying:

> The criminal law is concerned with the regulation of behaviour . . . I cannot see that the state of a person's chromosomes can or should be relevant . . . in the determination of his or her criminal liability . . . How can the law sensibly ignore the state of [the external] genitalia . . . simply because they were artificially created or were not the same at birth?

14 [1963] P 37, [1962] 3 All ER 55, CA.
15 [1963] P 37 at 60.
16 [1983] 2 All ER 12.
17 *R v Cogley* [1989] VR 799; *R v Harris, R v McGuinness* (1988) 35 A Crim R 146: discussed in H Finlay 'Transsexuals, Sex Change Operations and the Chromosome Test: *Corbett v Corbett* not Followed' (1989) 19 UWAL Rev 152 and in R Bailey-Harris 'Sex Change in the Criminal Law and Beyond' (1989) 13 Crim LJ 353 – which includes the appeal stage in *Cogley*. For an opinion published in a UK journal, see J L Taitz 'Confronting Transsexualism, Sexual Identity and the Criminal Law' (1992) 60 Med-leg J 60.
18 For pioneer Commonwealth legislation in the field, see the South Australian Sexual Reassignment Act 1988. Section 7(8)(b) states that a recognition certificate may be issued to an adult who has been reassigned.

Although the New South Wales Court of Appeal conceded that there was some doubt as to whether a similar test would be applied in civil litigation, the implications are that the Australian courts will apply the same reasoning to family law when asked.[19]

This rejection of *Corbett* emphasises that *Corbett* was about marriage – and only about marriage – but, even when it is so limited, its rigidity exposes the principles to severe criticism and it was, of course, marriage that brought UK transsexualism into the European amphitheatre. The case has, however, been criticised on the general grounds that it is unfeeling and fails to take into account the total sexual ambience of an individual.[20] Thus, in the American case of *MT v JT*[21] the transsexual partner to a marriage was held to be capable of acting within marriage as a female. In rejecting *Corbett*, Handler J could perceive:

> . . . no legal barrier, no cognisable social taboo, or reason founded in public policy, to prevent that person's identification, at least for the purposes of marriage, to the sex generally indicated.

This reasoning cannot, however, be applied to the female to male transsexual and 'marriages' involving them have been annulled in the United States.[1] Even in the unlikely event of the law being changed so as to validate a marriage between a converted transsexual and a person of the same chromosomal complement, such a 'marriage' between a female to male transsexual and a woman would, in the absence of additional legislation, be voidable in both England and Scotland on the grounds of incurable impotency.[2] None the less, it is essentially marriage, and the application of art 12 of the European Convention on Human Rights, that underlies the running conflict between the United Kingdom and the European courts in relation to transsexualism.[3]

Transsexualism in Europe

There are at least nine countries of those constituting the current Council of Europe in which the legal definition of sex is sufficiently wide to include the possibility of transsexual marriage in the 'converted' sex.[4] The fact that the United Kingdom is not among them leads to anomalous situations – as Norrie has pointed out, a German

---

19 For a comparison of the cases with *Tan* (n 15 above), see J Taitz 'The Law Relating to Consummation of Marriage when One of the Spouses is a Post-operative Transsexual' (1986) 15 Anglo-Am LR 141.

20 For criticism along these lines, see S Whittle 'An Association for as Noble a Purpose as Any' (1996) 146 NLJ 366.

21 *MT v JT* 355 A 2d 204 (NJ, 1976).

 1 *B v B* 355 NYS 2d 712 (1974).

 2 See K McK Norrie 'Transsexuals, the Right to Marry and Voidable Marriages in Scots Law' 1991 SLT 353. Although the government statement in *I v United Kingdom* (1997) 23 EHRR CD 66 suggests that a decree of nullity would not be granted on the basis of approbation.

 3 For previous discussion, see J K Mason 'United Kingdom v Europe: Current Attitudes to Transsexualism' (1998) 2 ELR 107.

 4 Denmark, Finland, Germany, Italy, Luxembourg, the Netherlands, Spain, Turkey and Sweden. The transsexual's converted condition is also formally recognised in Switzerland, Norway, Poland and the Czech Republic. See J L Taitz 'Confronting Transsexualism, Sexual Identity and the Criminal Law' (1992) 60 Med-leg J 60. The same is true of several anglophone countries outside Europe.

transsexual could be legally married in Britain but, with domicillary law applying, a British transsexual would be unable to marry in Germany[5] – and, in many ways, it is surprising that the United Kingdom was not challenged in Europe until 1986. Since then, however, there has been a gathering swell of applications to the European Court of Human Rights and to the Court of Justice of the European Communities. The main point of contention has been to the effect that, in refusing to alter a converted transsexual's birth certificate, that person has been precluded from marrying in the sex of his or her choice; more recently, however, controversy has spilled over into the fields of industrial and discrimination law.

Respect for privacy and the right to marry

The seminal case is that of *Rees v United Kingdom*,[6] in which the court noted the relatively relaxed attitude taken in the United Kingdom outside marriage – where one rarely has to produce a birth certificate and where there is no documentation comparable to the continental civil status certificate; accordingly, it dismissed the application under art 8 (the right to respect for one's private and family life) by a majority of 12:3. The application under art 12 (the right to marry and found a family) was dismissed unanimously since marriage was clearly a matter of union between two persons of opposite biological sex. The court also bowed to the seemingly inevitable in so far as the right to marry under art 12 is subject to this being 'according to the national laws governing the exercise of this right'.

However, five years later the court was, effectively, asked to overturn the *Rees* decision in *Cossey v United Kingdom*.[7] It did not do so, but, this time, the majority in respect of art 8 was reduced to 10:8, while the previous unanimity in respect of art 12 was reduced to a count of 14:4. Some of the difference may be due to the fact that *Cossey* involved a male to female conversion which is generally more acceptable to those who are physiologically minded.[8] We believe, however, that the fundamental reasons for the shift in opinion are to be found in the dissenting opinion of Martens J who based his opinion largely on the changing societal attitudes to activities that are essentially private. He drew attention to the fact that the court in *Rees* had left the door open to accommodate scientific and societal changes in the future and suggested that 'treatment' of the syndrome was incomplete without full recognition of the new status.

The regulation of sex reassignment operations in France is stricter than it is in the United Kingdom. It is not surprising, therefore, that the French government fared even worse the next year. *B v France*[9] concerned an appeal to the ECHR against a refusal of the Cour de Cassation, first, to declare that, following surgery, B was now of female sex and, second, to alter her documentation accordingly. The refusal was based largely on the grounds that she was still biologically male; any changes in her life-

---

5   K McK Norrie 'Reproductive Technology, Transsexualism and Homosexuality: New Problems for International Private Law' (1994) 43 ICLQ 757-775.
6   (1986) 9 EHRR 56, [1987] 2 FLR 111.
7   (1990) 13 EHRR 622, [1991] 2 FLR 492.
8   The result might have been even closer had it not been for Ms Cossey's unusual social history – including the use of her male identity for her own purposes.
9   (1992) 16 EHRR 1, [1992] 2 FLR 249.

style and anatomy that had come about had come about by her own choice and had been achieved without the safeguards that French law insisted upon.[10] In summary, B's appeal was upheld by a majority of 15:6. Article 8 had been violated, largely on the grounds that, in the French system, a person's sex is being constantly publicised by way of his or her social security number and that, as a result, B found herself in a position that was incompatible with the respect due to her private life. In a somewhat sophistic argument, the court maintained, on the one hand, that new elements in the debate – including recognition of the testicular feminisation syndrome and suggestions of a genetic background to transsexualism – were now apparent but that, on the other hand, the transsexual question was in a state of flux – legally, morally and socially. The court concluded that there was insufficient evidence to induce them to overturn the *Rees* and *Cossey* judgments, which had favoured the United Kingdom.

As a result, France was forced to mend its ways – though it seems that only a requirement to alter the civil status to accord with the person's appearance has been accepted. The United Kingdom, however, sails on unscathed and has recently restated the current inviolability of the British birth certificate in *P and G*[11] – though, even there, there are suggestions that 'new research' and the like might affect judicial attitudes in the future. A rather bizarre result is that, whereas a marriage between a resultant female and a normal man is void, an apparently homosexual marriage between a post-operative female and a normal woman would be perfectly legal in the United Kingdom.

We have long thought that the United Kingdom might well lose the next case brought against it under art 8, but the European Court of Human Rights has recently, and surprisingly, overturned its Commission and has decided in favour of the United Kingdom in relation to a violation of that article – albeit by the narrow margin of 11 to 9 votes.[12] In some ways, the applicants had a stronger case than those heard previously – one, for example, who had been married as a man and had a daughter by that marriage, was a pilot and was unable to obtain employment in her new sex. None the less, the court held that there had been no later developments in the field which would induce them to overturn *Cossey*. The United Kingdom was, however, firmly rapped over the knuckles for not having kept is legal measures in this area under review. Even so, this is still not the last word and a further case which has been upheld by the Commission is pending before the European Court of Human Rights.[13] Here, the applicant – a male to female conversion – contends that the failure to supply a replacement certificate of current gender places her at risk, inter alia, of being unable to re-register as a nurse and of being placed in a male hospital ward or male prison; she also maintains she can marry neither a woman nor a man. We wonder when the watershed will be reached.

Labour law and discrimination

The issue of the status of the birth certificate involves some fundamental domestic administrative law; the relatively cautious approach of the Court of Human Rights in

10 For discussion of French law, see Gromb et al (1997) 37 Med, Sci & L 27.
11 *R v Registrar General, ex p P and G* [1996] 2 FCR 588.
12 *Sheffield and Horsham v United Kingdom* [1998] 3 FCR 141. A plea of violation of art 12 was dismissed by a majority of 18 to 2.
13 *I v United Kingdom* (1997) 23 EHRR CD 66.

its dealings with the United Kingdom is, therefore, understandable. Labour and discrimination law is, however, more open to interpretation and the United Kingdom has, as a result, been criticised more readily in the European Court of Justice. For this, we must turn to *P v S and Cornwall County Council* [14] – a case which may have far-reaching implications.

The facts of the case are, briefly, that P was taken on as manager of an educational establishment run by Cornwall County Council. A year later he announced his intention of undergoing a sex-change operation and a dismissal notice was served while he was on sick leave following a preliminary operation. When he was asked to complete some of his tasks, he said he would do them dressed as a female but was told to do so at home. P completed gender reassignment before the actual date of her dismissal and appealed to the Industrial Tribunal, claiming discrimination on the grounds of sex.

The tribunal could find no discrimination based on the Sex Discrimination Act 1975, but then asked the European Court of Justice whether there was any further instruction to be obtained from Council Directive 76/207/EEC, which deals with equal treatment for men and women: did this, in fact, cover the dismissal of a transsexual for a reason related to a gender reassignment?

The opinion was delivered by Advocate General Tesauro, who started from the premise that:

> ... in a society as it is to-day, in which customs and morals are changing rapidly, citizens are guaranteed ever wider and deeper protection of their freedoms and social and legal studies are increasingly taking on present-day – and, for that very reason, real – values. [15]

The law, he said, must not fail to adjust to society as quickly as possible – and he pointed out that full rights of sex change, including marriage, are now available by virtue of special legislation in four countries of the European Community and a change of civil status is allowed in eight more by way of the courts or the administration. [16] The problem of distinguishing *Rees* and *Cossey* from *B v France* was solved by the fact that attitudes had changed and science had progressed in the interval. The Advocate General admitted that the EC directive referred to the traditional man/woman dichotomy; the problem was to decide whether it is *only* discrimination between men and women that is covered by the directive or whether it refers to *all* unfavourable treatment connected with sex.

Sex, he said, was to be regarded as a continuum between man and woman, so that it would not be right to refuse to protect those who are treated unfavourably precisely because of their sex and/or sexual identity or because they fall outside the traditional man/woman classification. Again, however, he had to admit that there was no discrimination as such because male and female transsexuals were treated in the same way. [17] But one thing, he thought, was certain: P would not have been dismissed had

---

14 [1996] IRLR 347, [1996] ICR 795.

15 Opinion of Advocate General Tesauro, Case C-13/94, *P v S and Cornwall County Council* transcript para 9.

16 These figures do not tally with those of Martens J in the dissenting opinion in *Cossey v United Kingdom* (1990) 13 EHRR 622, [1991] 2 FLR 492, but the language used differs in the two opinions.

17 It is to be noted, however, that three times as many men wish to become women as the reverse.

she remained a man – how, then, could it be denied that the cause of discrimination was precisely, and solely, sex?

> To maintain that the unfavourable treatment suffered by P was not on grounds of sex . . . because in such a case it is not possible to speak of discrimination between the two sexes would be a quibbling formalistic interpretation and a betrayal of the true essence of that fundamental and inalienable value which is equality.[18]

And, again, Advocate General Tesauro said:

> I note that the directive is nothing if not an expression of a general principle and a fundamental right.[19]

The Advocate then called on the court to make a courageous decision in the profound conviction that what is at stake is a universal fundamental value: the irrelevance of a person's sex with regard to the rules regulating relations in society. The court accepted his advice.

It seems to us that the court, in so doing, is depending on doubtful logic which runs on the lines: transsexualism is to do with sex, therefore sex was involved in the dismissal and, therefore, she was dismissed on the grounds of sex – which is discrimination. It is wholly desirable that the status of transsexuals should be settled in law, but it is less than satisfactory that it should depend upon semantic juggling.[20] Nor does it seem right that the terms of a Council directive should be significantly extended to representing 'an expression of a general principle' without reference to the Council. We have seen that the European Court of Justice is, currently, unwilling to follow this through.[1]

Even so, *P v S* has already been accepted in the United Kingdom in an interesting tribunal case involving a converted male to female transsexual who wanted to be a police woman.[2] Her application was rejected as a matter of policy in that she would be unable to carry out certain police duties since her legal sex was male. She appealed to the industrial tribunal under both the Sex Discrimination Act 1975 and the EC directive.

The tribunal first considered M's legal sex and, having pointed out that the European Court never considered whether P in *P v S* was *legally* female, it applied *ex p P and G*[3] and concluded that she had male status. But, as regards the law, they followed *P v S* and found that the applicant had been discriminated against on the grounds of sex within the meaning of the EC directive and that this was in breach of the directive.

This is no place to discuss the submission of the Chief Constable in detail. Suffice it to say that the police relied on art 2(2) of the directive – which acknowledges the right of member states to exclude from its application those occupations for which the sex of the worker constitutes a determining factor – and they also contended that there

18 Case C-13/94 at para 20.
19 Ibid at para 22.
20 The court might, for example, have stated firmly that discrimination on the ground of cross-dressing was discrimination within the meaning of the Sex Discrimination Act 1975. For discussion, see R Wintemute 'Recognising New Kinds of Indirect Sex Discrimination: Transsexualism, Sexual Orientation and Dress Codes' (1997) 60 MLR 335.
 1 See *Grant v South-West Trains Ltd* Case C-249/96 [1998] IRLR 206, ECJ.
 2 *M v Chief Constable of the West Midlands Police* (1996) IT Case 08964/96, unreported.
 3 [1996] 2 FCR 588.

was a genuine occupational qualification which excluded the applicant in so far as the terms of the Police and Criminal Evidence Act 1984 (PACE) dictated some gender-specific duties such as the searching of suspects.[4] After long discussion, the tribunal found that the Chief Constable had justified the discrimination and had satisfied the derogation provided by art 2(2) – including the demands of proportionality. They also looked at the gender-specific duties dictated under the various codes of practice and under the Police Manual and concluded that the investigation of crime was likely to be jeopardised if the officer was unable to search suspects lawfully. When it came to the Sex Discrimination Act 1975, the tribunal held that, when we are considering a male to female converted transsexual, we are not dealing with a female who has a particular characteristic which can be compared with a male, but with a person of legal male status who has a particular characteristic – the basic comparison required by the statute, namely that between a man and a woman, is not present. The tribunal was satisfied that the Act does not encompass a transsexual.

Application to family law

We have, however, yet to look at that aspect of transsexualism which is most intimately connected to *medical* law – that is, its application to family law and, here, the European scene has recently taken a surprising turn.

X, Y and Z v United Kingdom[5] concerned a female to male transsexual who had enjoyed a stable relationship with a woman for 15 years. During this time, the couple had had three children by way of artificial insemination by donor (AID). X now put in an application to the Registrar General not to have his birth certificate altered but, rather, to be recognised as the father of the eldest child for the purposes of registering her birth. The Registrar believed that only a biological man could be regarded as a father for the purposes of registration but conceded that there was nothing unlawful in the daughter bearing her 'father's' surname. The European Commission on Human Rights then, predictably, decided that there had been a violation of art 8 of the European Convention on Human Rights – that is, of respect for a person's private and family life, home and correspondence. The European Court of Human Rights noted that the application raised very different problems from those it had addressed in previous cases concerning transsexuals – these included the granting of parental rights to transsexuals and the manner in which the social relationship between a child conceived by AID and the person acting in the role of father should be defined in law. The majority opinion retreated behind the defences that there was, as yet, no clear consensus among member states, that the law was in a transitional condition and that to make an exception in national law of this type could lead to inconsistencies and confusion in family law – that is, they applied a margin of appreciation. On the other side of the coin, the court found that refusal to allow the application resulted in little,

4 Interestingly, it was debated whether PACE itself is discriminatory. This prompted the tribunal to consider sending the case to the European Court but they decided not to, as the *Corbett* test, on which they relied, has already been upheld both in the European and domestic courts and has, therefore, already overcome the discriminatory hurdle.
5 *X, Y and Z v United Kingdom* (1997) 24 EHRR 143, (1998) 39 BMLR 128.

if any, disadvantage to the principals and held, by 14 votes to six, that there had been no violation of art 8.

Somewhat strangely, both the Commission and the court felt that a decision in respect of art 8 rendered further discussion as to a violation of art 14 redundant. Since this was the only area in which the question of sex discrimination arose, it is only in the dissenting judgments that this important aspect of the application – and its relationship to the Human Fertilisation and Embryology Act 1990 – was reasonably well aired. The 1990 Act is discussed in detail in chapter 3. For the present, we can say that the effect of s 28(3) is to allow that, when a man and a woman are living in a stable relationship and the woman conceives as a result of mutually consensual artificial insemination, then that man will be regarded 'for all purposes' as the father of the child. X was, however, unable to rely on the 1990 Act once pure *Corbett* principles were applied – s 28(3) makes no provision for a converted transsexual. Here, there is a suggestion of what might be considered a significant misconception creeping into the ECHR for both the judgment (at para 21) and two dissenting opinions – those of Judges Foighel and Vilhjálmsson – translate 'man' in s 23(3) as 'the male partner'. It is well-nigh impossible, either legally or physiologically, to see X as a man; but it is far less difficult to see him as a 'male partner' – particularly as the 'pastiche' was particularly good in his case.[6] The dissenting opinion that, as a result, this constituted discrimination on the grounds of sex, then has some force – but the remedy, should one be sought, is to change the Act rather than to distort the use of language.

Conclusion

What, then, is the current position of transsexualism in a United Kingdom that is subject to European Community law?

There are now very few who would deny that transsexualism is a recognisable psychiatric abnormality, that it causes considerable suffering to those afflicted and that it deserves to be treated. A person who has a good cosmetic result is doing no public harm and is fully entitled to operate within his or her chosen sex. Reviewing the cases that have been reported, it is difficult to resist the conclusion that the opposition to transsexualism they demonstrate results not so much from appearance as from *change* of appearance. Current legal thinking in this area, however, suffers from the assumption that the end-state will always be satisfactory – and this is not always so. There are few reports in this respect but the results studied in Portugal are interesting: of seven persons treated, the result was considered good in three, reasonable in three and bad in one – not an over-impressive testimony to current therapy.[7] Before accepting sex conversion as beneficent and as something of an individual right, it is important to appreciate that the result may be social non-acceptance and, ultimately, a disaster for the patient. That may be a risk the individual is willing to accept and can be seen as insufficient grounds on which to base a

---

6   Many years ago, Thomson hinted at the same semantic distinction in respect of the Marriage Acts. J M Thomson 'Transsexualism: a legal perspective' (1980) 6 J Med Ethics 92.

7   J Costa-Santos and R Madeira 'Transsexualism in Portugal: the legal framework and procedure, and its consequences for transsexuals' (1996) 36 Med, Sci & L 221.

restrictive public policy when the popular thrust is to acknowledge the legal as well as the social consequences of a change of sex.

In that context, the United Kingdom can be seen as virtually the last bastion in defence of *Corbett*, but the defences are crumbling. Until quite recently, it could be assumed that the British courts would defend their position resolutely. But there is growing evidence that they are being worn down – both the Divisional Court in *ex p P and G* and the tribunal in *M* went out of their ways to support the *Cossey* court in stressing that times are changing.

Certainly, there are, at best, very doubtful grounds for extending and maintaining the *Corbett* standard outside administrative and family law. There can be very little support for the notion that the nature of sexual offences should be based on chromosomes rather than on gender and there are few, if any, tenable reasons why people should not work and behave in their chosen sex . A certificate of change of sex would offend no historian's sensitivities and legislation could cover its applicability to cases like that of *M*. But can we extend this essentially laissez-faire attitude to marriage?

It has been proposed[8] that a transsexual marriage should be valid if the transsexual is found to be capable of fulfilling the essential role of the sex he or she has assumed and that this should include the ability of the two partners to love and understand one another – and this attitude would attract fairly wide support. Kennedy,[9] in putting the case for legalising converted transsexual marriage, went on to extrapolate this to the authorisation of homosexual marriages – 'I have no doubt it will occur', he said, 'later if not sooner'. We feel that this stretches analogy too far. Marriage is defined as the union between a man and a woman but, problems of consummation excepted, the anatomic/physiologic completeness of either partner is seldom of major importance. A man with infantile or undescended testes is still capable of a legal marriage with his sexual opposite. Similarly, a woman without a uterus and who is unable to bear a child would rightly expect to be treated as a woman for the purposes of marriage to a man. It is at least arguable that the gap between such situations and that involving the converted male to female transsexual is bridgeable. A homosexual 'marriage', by contrast, is a bond based on the union of like with like. In short, as the European courts have been holding, there are real differences between sexual orientation and sex reassignment.

But, having thus opened the door to transsexual marriage, we must ask whether homosexual marriage should not be admitted. The argument in its favour is that people in such partnerships should be given the same legal protection as is accorded to those in a marriage. There is a strong case for this, just as there is a strong case for the giving of such protection to heterosexual partnerships outside marriage. Yet recognition of the case for such protection does not of itself make the case for homosexual marriage. If a sufficient number of people wish to preserve the heterosexual nature of marriage – and there is probably a fairly substantial majority in favour of this approach – then a pluralist society should recognise this entitlement. A liberal society, however, should at the same time recognise that there are those who wish to enter into publicly-acknowledged same-sex partnerships which have legal

8   See the early opinion in H A Finlay 'Sexual Identity and the Law of Nullity' (1980) 54 ALJ 115.
9   I M Kennedy 'Transsexualism and Single Sex Marriage' (1973) 2 Anglo-Am LR 112.

ramifications. This is a legitimate desire and, in that it will allow those involved to feel more accepted, it is churlish to stand in their way. A possible solution would be to create a form of 'registered partnership' or 'union' which, although not a marriage, has similar legal effects.

Deliberate transmission of sexually transmitted disease

The liability for deliberately infecting another person with sexually transmissible organisms is a currently live issue. Although the principles would be the same in respect of any such disease, the problem is amplified in the case of HIV infection as, here, the scenario includes the possibility of causing death and of unlawful killing.

Public health aspects of HIV infection have been discussed in chapter 1. Here, we are concerned only with issues surrounding the knowing possibility of transmission of disease from one individual to another; these can be viewed from the perspective either of the criminal law – the purpose of which is to deter by way of threatened punishment – or of the civil law – which is primarily concerned to compensate individuals for injury done to them.

There are a number of existing criminal offences which might be used as vehicles by which to prosecute the person who knowingly subjects another to a risk of HIV infection. These range from relatively minor nuisance-based offences, through assault to attempted murder. The criminal law should experience little difficulty in treating the act as a serious assault or, indeed, as attempted murder when the exposure is deliberate and arises outside the context of sexual intercourse. Thus, deliberately stabbing a person with a syringe filled with infected blood, with the intention of infecting the victim with HIV, would appear to satisfy the requirements of attempted murder, even though a lesser offence could be easier to charge. The same might be said of throwing infected blood or, possibly, spitting at another with the intention of transmitting the virus. There has been a legislative response to this type of assault in a number of jurisdictions. The high incidence of syringe attacks in the Irish Republic – usually as incidental to robbery – led to legislation which imposes a penalty similar to that for attempted murder.[10] In New South Wales, the Crimes Act 1900 has been amended to include a new offence of causing grievous bodily disease,[11] this response again being prompted by highly-publicised incidents in which blood-filled syringes were used as weapons.

A very much more difficult situation arises when a person who is aware of his HIV-positive status has unprotected sexual contact with a person to whom he has not disclosed that status. The questions are then posed: should this be a criminal offence, and if so, what offence might it be? Unsurprisingly, there has been considerable discussion of this issue and a variety of responses have been advocated and adopted. The major division lies between those jurisdictions that are prepared to introduce the concept of criminality into what is, essentially, a matter of public health and those that believe that the adverse consequences of doing so are such as to outweigh any potential advantages.

10 Non-Fatal Offences Against the Person Act 1997.
11 Crimes Act 1900, s 36.

The argument in favour of punishing the knowing sexual transmission of HIV depends on the fact that such behaviour amounts to the infliction of substantial harm on another; it is, therefore, indistinguishable from other forms of assault or, in the case of English law, from the range of offences currently prosecuted under the Offences Against the Person Act 1861.[12] There may, of course, be no actual intention to harm – indeed, one assumes that such an intention is absent in most cases. What there is, however, is recklessness in relation to the risk of serious harm. Provided that he knows of his own infection, an HIV-positive man who engages in unprotected sex is willingly subjecting his partner to a risk of infection and, ultimately, of death – and the same is true of the infected woman. There is probably broad agreement that such conduct is reprehensible and, indeed, this view has been sufficiently widely held in some jurisdictions to prompt a specific legislative response. Over 20 of the United States have amended existing statutes or have introduced new laws to make it a criminal offence to have sexual contact with another when one knows of the fact that one is HIV-positive and when this fact is unknown to one's partner.[13] Some such statutes are narrow in their scope and require that there be an intention to transmit the infection; others are prepared to punish the reckless exposure to risk which such action implies. Legislative action has also been taken in Australia: in South Australia, for example, it is now an offence for an HIV-infected person to fail to take all reasonable precautions to prevent transmitting the disease to another.[14]

There have, however, been a number of examples of prosecution in the absence of specific legislation of HIV-positive persons who have transmitted, or risked transmitting, the infection to an unsuspecting partner. Some of these have attracted considerable media attention, not least because of the severity of the sentences imposed; one such example is that of a sentence of 14 years' imprisonment being imposed by a Finnish court on an HIV-positive man who had sexual relations with over 100 women whom he had not informed of his infected status.[15] Prosecutions have also been reported in other European countries, including Denmark[16] and Germany. In Germany, a charge of attempted manslaughter might be competent but would probably fail on the grounds of an insufficient degree of intention or on proof of causation; a conviction for a life-endangering assault or for attempting to endanger a person's life could then be appropriate. A charge of assault would be precluded in the event of a valid consent to intercourse (Penal Code ss 223, 223a).[17]

12 For discussion of the possible offences committed, see S H Bronitt 'Spreading Disease and the Criminal Law' [1994] Crim LR 21; D Ormerod and M Gunn 'Criminal Liability for the Transmission of HIV' [1996] 1 Web J of Current Legal Issues (http://webjcl.ncl.ac.uk).
13 An example of the American legislative response is the Illinois Statute of 1989 (Ill Rev Stat 1989, ch 38; 720 ILCS 5/12-16.2 (West, 1992)). This statute has survived constitutional challenge: *People of the State of Illinois v Russell* 630 NE 2d 794 (Ill, 1994).
14 Public and Environmental Health Act 1987.
15 J Acher 'HIV man jailed for unsafe sex' Scotsman, 11 July 1997, p 12. Other prosecutions which attracted particular attention included that brought under s 190 of the Cyprus Criminal Code. This section makes it an offence to transmit (culpably) a disease dangerous to life, an offence originally introduced in order to combat the spread of typhoid and cholera: M Kelly 'Cypriot knowingly gave lover AIDS virus' Scotsman, 30 July 1997, p 5.
16 C Csillag 'Prison Sentence for Exposing Women to Risk of Infection' (1993) 341 Lancet 751 (23 women were involved with the accused: the sentence imposed was 18 months' imprisonment).
17 L G Nurenberg-Fürth, NJW 1988, 2311; A G Kempten, NJW 1988, 2313; AG Hamburg, NJW 1989, 2071; BGH, NJW 1989, 781; BGH, NJW 1990, 129. The issue is covered by A J Szwarc *AIDS und Strafrecht* (1996).

The most extensive discussion of the problem in the ambience of the common law is to be found in Canada, where there have been relatively numerous decisions on the point. There is no specific section of the Canadian Criminal Code that establishes an offence to communicate a disease through recklessness; prosecuting authorities have, therefore, turned to charging common nuisance, criminal negligence, assault, administering a noxious thing or attempted murder – with mixed results. Nuisance convictions, brought under the Canadian Criminal Code, s 180, were sustained in *R v Summer*,[18] *R v Kreider*,[19] and *R v Thornton*[20] (reckless blood donation), but an attempt to prosecute for common nuisance was unsuccessful in *R v Ssenyonga*,[1] even though the court was prepared to entertain a prosecution for criminal negligence. The latter crime was successfully prosecuted *in R v Wentzell*[2] and *R v Mercer*,[3] both of which demonstrate the sort of irresponsible, not to say heartless, behaviour which attracts criminal attention in this context. In *Mercer* the accused continued to have sexual intercourse with, and infected, a 16-year-old girl, despite having tested positive for HIV and having been advised by a doctor as to the risk of transmission. His original sentence of 27 months' imprisonment was increased to 11 years on appeal by the Crown.

The Canadian experience of using the assault provisions of the Criminal Code to prosecute in such cases demonstrates the theoretical difficulty which commentators have long identified as being a particular stumbling block to conviction in such cases – that is, consent. In essence, consent to intercourse on the part of a sexual partner would appear to cover the very act which is alleged to constitute the assault. The court in *Ssenyonga* held that there had, in fact, been consent to the application of that degree of force which was inherent to sexual intercourse and, moreover, that this consent was not vitiated by fraud. It is not surprising that the court should have reached this view; fraud in the context of rape has always been interpreted restrictively and has been taken to relate only to misrepresentations as to the nature of the act of sexual intercourse rather than to its implications. The issue arose once more in *R v Cuerrier*,[4] in which the accused began a sexual relationship with a woman after he had been notified that he had tested positive for HIV; he did not tell her of this fact, nor did he seek to minimise the risk to her. He was charged with aggravated assault after he began a relationship with another partner. On appeal by the Crown against Cuerrier's acquittal at trial, the Court of Appeal of British Columbia concluded that the fact that a partner is not informed of HIV infection does not vitiate consent. As Prowse JA observed:

> There is no recognised legal duty, enforceable through the criminal law power of the state, which requires a person to provide full disclosure of all known risks associated with sexual intercourse to his or her sexual partner as a condition precedent to the partner giving an effective consent to sexual intercourse. The criminal law of assault is, indeed, an unusual instrument for attempting to ensure safe sex.[5]

18 (1989) 73 CR (3d) 32.
19 (1993) 140 AR 81.
20 [1993] 2 SCR 445, 82 CCC (3d) 530.
 1 (1993) 81 CCC (3d) 257.
 2 (8 December 1989, unreported), NS Co Ct.
 3 (1993) 84 CCC (3d) 41.
 4 [1996] BCJ No 2229 (BCCA).
 5 Quoted in R Elliott *Criminal Law and HIV/AIDS: Final Report* (Canadian HIV/AIDS Legal Network Canadian AIDS Society, Montreal, 1996) Appendix B.

The court took note of the arguments of policy which could be raised against using the criminal law to induce people to behave with consideration towards others in respect of sexual behaviour but the response of individual judges was mixed. Prowse JA acknowledged that non-coercive measures could be more effective in reducing the spread of HIV, but Williams JA described the conduct of the accused as 'absolutely repellent and . . . deserving of some criminal sanction'. Such a sanction, he said, was currently lacking in the Criminal Code and should be considered for inclusion by Parliament.[6]

The criminal law has not been used to prosecute people for the reckless sexual transmission of HIV in the United Kingdom.[7] It is possible that recourse might be made in Scotland to the common law offence of reckless endangerment which, like many common law offences in Scots criminal law, is very broadly, and elastically, defined.[8] In England and Wales, there is a view that ss 23 and 24 of the Offences Against the Person Act 1861 could encompass this form of conduct. These define liability for 'unlawfully and maliciously' administering to another 'any poison or other destructive or noxious thing'. The Law Commission recommended that it should be an offence to transmit HIV recklessly,[9] but this view was not shared by the government which, early in 1998, announced its intention of drafting proposed reforms of the law relating to non-fatal offences against the person so as to allow for prosecution where the transmission of serious disease is intentional but not where it is reckless.[10] In taking this view, the government signalled its acceptance of a philosophy of non-coercion in this area[11] – a view which has been consistently advocated by many organisations working with those infected with HIV or with those in high-risk groups. A decision to treat the reckless transmission of a fatal condition to another as being beyond the scope of the criminal law may be justifiable on grounds of such pure public health expediency. At the same time, it undoubtedly represents a calculated, politically-motivated failure on the part of the criminal law to acknowledge, and act upon, the profound wrong which is done to those whose life expectancy may be drastically shortened by the deception involved.

---

6 See Report, n 5 above.
7 The nearest approach seems to be *R v Gaud*, where a surgeon who was suffering from Hepatitis B knowingly put hundreds of patients at risk. He was sentenced to one year's imprisonment, having been charged with the common law offence of causing a public nuisance. See C Dyer 'Surgeon jailed for infecting patients' (1994) 309 BMJ 896. The case is discussed in detail in M Brazier and J Harris 'Public Health and Private Lives' [1996] 4 Med LRev 174.
8 For discussion see GT Laurie 'Aids and Criminal Liability under Scots Law' (1991) 36 J Law Soc Scot 312. Brazier and Harris, n 7 above, suggest that such an offence is almost available under the Public Health (Control of Disease) Act 1984, s 17 but this applies only to notifiable diseases (which do not include HIV infection or AIDS) which are spread in a public place.
9 *Legislating the Criminal Code: Offences Against the Person and General Principles* (Law Com No 218) (Cm 2370, 1993).
10 Home Office *Violence: Reforming the Offences Against the Person Act 1861* (1998).
11 The question of whether the criminal law should be used at all to prevent the transmission of HIV through risky sexual behaviour is one on which there are, not surprisingly, divergent views. There appears to be a strong consensus amongst commentators that the criminal law should not be invoked: R Porter 'History Says No to the Policeman's Response to AIDS' (1986) 293 BMJ 1589; P Old and J Montgomery 'Law, Coercion and the Public Health' (1992) 304 BMJ 891. Will the introduction of the criminal law have much of an impact on the behaviour of those who might spread the infection? On this, see D E Woodhouse et al 'Restricting Personal Behaviour – Case Study on Legal Measures to Prevent the Spread of HIV' (1993) 4 Int J S AIDS 144.

The failure of the state to prosecute does not leave the injured person without any remedy: it is possible that an action in tort might be brought against one who infects another with HIV. There are several heads under which a claim for damages might lie,[12] of which negligence seems to be the most appropriate for discussion. A claim would be based either on a failure to conform to the standards of reasonable conduct or on the consent being flawed as a result of having been given on the basis of inadequate information as to the risks involved;[13] in either event, an action would depend upon a duty of care being owed by and to each partner in the course of sexual connection. Such a duty is established in the United States[14] but, surprisingly, the issue is by no means settled in the United Kingdom. The nearest 'authority' we can find is an extra-judicial opinion given by Lord Brandon to the effect that such a duty does exist[15] – and we feel confident that the courts would follow such a line. The infection of another with HIV is an undoubted harm, which is clearly foreseeable in *Donoghue v Stevenson*[16] terms. Even so, the plaintiff would face many hurdles, perhaps the most difficult of these being to establish causation – particularly in the case of AIDS, with its long incubation period and the shadowy nature of exposure to the virus. It is possible that a defence of volenti non fit injuria might be attempted in such an action, but this would be unlikely to be successful, given the clear knowledge of risk which the modern interpretation of that defence entails. Thus, the nature of the consent would be fundamental to the outcome and could find expression by way of contributory negligence – a concept which could be used to redress the balance of responsibility for transmission of any infectious disease.[17]

The question of whether there is a duty to warn of HIV infection is one which has caused some concern to doctors. There is a major issue of confidentiality here,[18] but there is also the question of whether an injured third party has a right to seek compensation from a doctor who could have warned him or her of the threat posed by a sexual partner. There has been no litigation on this issue in the United Kingdom but it has been addressed in the United States, first, in relation to hepatitis. In *DiMarco v Lynch Homes-Chester County*[19] a blood technician had accidentally infected herself with the hepatitis virus. Her doctor did not warn her to refrain from sexual contact with others for six months, with the result that she transmitted the infection to the plaintiff. The Supreme Court of Pennsylvania agreed that, in such a case, the doctor owed a duty of care which extended to anybody who was foreseeably physically intimate with the patient. It did not matter that the identity of the plaintiff was not known at the time.

This reasoning was extended to HIV infection in the Californian case of *Reisner v Regents of the University of California.*[20] Here, a girl of 12 had been infected as a result of the use of contaminated blood products. Her doctor, who was aware of the

---

12 See J Taitz 'Legal Liability for Transmitting AIDS' (1989) 57 Med-leg J 216.
13 'Informed consent' is discussed in detail at p 277 below.
14 Eg *Long v Adams* 333 SE 2d 852 (Ga, 1985). A short news item indicates that damages of $18m have been awarded in Florida to a man who was infected with HIV by his fiancée: Financial Times, 27 August 1993, p 1.
15 K Litton and R James 'Civil Liability for Communication of AIDS – A Moot Point' (1987) 137 NLJ 755.
16 *M'Alister (or Donoghue) v Stevenson* [1932] AC 562, [1932] All ER Rep 1.
17 See Old and Montgomerey, n 11 above.
18 Which is discussed at greater length at p 198 below.
19 583 A 2d 422 (Penn, 1990).
20 37 Cal Rep 2d 518 (1995).

fact that infection had taken place, did not inform the family that this had happened, with the result that she grew to maturity in ignorance of her plight. She engaged in a sexual relationship with the plaintiff, who sought damages from the doctor in respect of his infection with HIV, arguing that he had been owed a duty of care by the doctor. The California Court of Appeal, like the Supreme Court of Pennsylvania, sustained this argument, ruling that a doctor's duty of care might extend to those with whom he was not in a direct relationship and whose identity he might not know. Such liability would not be potentially too broad as claims by distant fourth or fifth persons could be limited by considerations of causation. This decision might be taken as creating a whole new range of duties to warn but, in fact, it does not. The negligence consists in the doctor's failure to warn *his patient*; had he done that, then she would have been in a position to avoid communicating the infection to others.[1] The decision does not, then, create a general duty to warn all those who might be at risk.

It is uncertain whether this jurisprudence is immediately transferable to the United Kingdom, where we are left in an unsatisfactory situation. There is little doubt that we have a moral duty not to infect others if it can be avoided[2] but moral obligations are of little moment to a person who is harmed but can find no means of redress. The uncertainty of the civil law suggests that there is a place for retaining, or initiating, some criminal sanction in cases where infection is deliberately or recklessly transmitted through sexual activity. Certainly, it is interesting to observe that the majority of comparable jurisdictions do, in fact, adopt such a policy. We have seen that the opposition to this is apparently not so rigid as it has been in the past – at least in relation to deliberate infection – and that some action may be in the offing.[3] We have consistently expressed our doubts as to the medical benefit of separating HIV infection from other forms of communicable disease and it may well be that, ultimately, the preferred approach to the specific problem will be through the amendment and application of the Public Health Acts. This would mean that, rather than using the sledgehammer of the law of assault, the courts could identify the protected interest as being that of community health. Such an approach would remove the stigma of conviction for assault while, at the same time, providing a measure of protection for the innocent victims of reckless behaviour.

1   See discussion by A Grubb 'HIV; Doctor's Liability to Future Partner' (1997) 5 Med L Rev 250.
2   J Harris and S Holm 'Is there a Moral Obligation not to Infect Others?' (1995) 311 BMJ 1215.
3   R Ford and P Webster 'Straw seeks jail for spreading AIDS' The Times, 6 March 1998, p 1.

3 The management of infertility and childlessness

The title of this chapter draws attention to a distinction which we believe to be of practical, as well as semantic, importance. Primary infertility is a problem of the production of gametes or of implantation of the embryo. This may be susceptible to hormone therapy – a matter which we barely consider here; ovum or sperm donation then becomes a secondary treatment of childlessness due to unsuccessful treatment of the primary condition. Similarly, the basic in vitro fertilisation (IVF) technique is most commonly used as a treatment of childlessness due to blockage of the fallopian tubes which is resistant to recanalisation therapy. The distinction appears to be narrow but it may be significant in relation to resource allocation. Thus, it could be held that, whereas the treatment of infertility is clearly a medical matter, childlessness can be seen as a social problem which should be funded from a different source.[1] While we cannot fully subscribe to this theory, it might serve to justify the relative scarcity of the latter facilities in the National Health Service.[2]

Some 10% of marriages are said to be infertile and the couple desire children in, at least, a high proportion of these.[3] In addition, there are couples who should not have children for genetic reasons, either because one may carry a dominant deleterious gene or because both are known to bear recessive characteristics (see chapter 6, below). Again, a couple may be able to conceive a child but the woman is unable to carry it for medical reasons. Opportunities for adoption are now meagre and, for many years, attention has focused on the elaboration of methods designed either to substitute the gametes of one or other person or to bypass the natural process in other ways.

The legal and moral issues involved have been considered at governmental level in many countries.[4] Overall, it is remarkable how similar have been the conclusions of the various committees of inquiry which have reported throughout the English-speaking world.

---

1 For discussion, see S Redmayne and R Klein 'Rationing in Practice: the Case of In Vitro Fertilisation' (1993) 306 BMJ 1521.
2 The *Sixth Annual Report of the Human Fertilisation and Embryology Authority* (1997) indicates that there are now 76 licensed centres offering IVF treatments but these are not broken down as to funding. It is said that almost 25% of health authorities refused to purchase IVF facilities in 1994: D Evans 'Infertility and the NHS' (1995) 311 BMJ 1586.
3 G Douglas *Law, Fertility and Reproduction* (1991) quotes comparable figures (at p 105). Recent studies, however, indicate that the true figure may be less than this: A Templeton, C Fraser and B Thompson 'The Epidemiology of Infertility in Aberdeen' (1990) 301 BMJ 148.
4 For a modern and wide-ranging review of international developments, see S A M McLean (ed) *Law Reform and Human Reproduction* (1992).

Artificial insemination

Artificial insemination by donor (AID)[5] may provide a solution where there is male infertility, a condition which accounts for roughly 50% of cases of involuntary failure to conceive. In this procedure, semen obtained from a donor is injected into the woman and this results in conception in a proportion of cases which is surprisingly low.[6] The husband's or male partner's semen may similarly be introduced into the uterus by artificial means (AIH or AIP)[7] – a need which might arise from impotence or from inadequate formation of spermatozoa, in which case treated semen would be used. Many couples who have recourse to AID are loath to abandon all hope of their own offspring. In such circumstances, the semen of the apparently infertile male partner is mixed with that of the donor so that the couple can still believe that the ovum may have been fertilised by the male partner's sperm. This form of artificial insemination is known as AIHD.

Artificial insemination by the husband or male partner

Leaving aside any aspects of family law which depend upon marital status, and excluding any consideration of the moral value of marriage, AIH and AIP give rise to no major legal or ethical problems. All that is entailed is that the woman conceives by a method other than that of normal sexual intercourse and the procedure will only be regarded as questionable if there is objection to any interference with nature in this area. AIH can, however, be used for reasons other than compromised fertility in the male and its morality may then be questionable. Pre-eminent among these is the use of AIH as a preliminary to sex selection of the conceptus and we discuss this as a separate matter below.

In addition, AIH has been refined in recent years by the introduction of micromanipulative techniques – in particular, those of intracytoplasmic sperm injection (ICSI) or sub-zonal insemination (SUZI). In these methods, a single spermatozoon is injected directly into the cytoplasm of an egg. The sperm can, thus, be preselected and the technique is a valuable adjunct to the management of male infertility due to poor quality of the semen. It involves the use of IVF[8] and its success depends to a great extent on the specific expertise of the operator; currently, the requirements for obtaining a licence to practise[9] are particularly strict. Moreover, the opportunities for pre-implantation genetic selection – a technique which, itself, poses a number of ethical issues – are greatly reduced; a matter of particular concern when the quality of the sperm, which is now enjoying a non-competitive existence, is, itself, suspect. As a result, most academic embryologists are adopting a cautious attitude to the new techniques.[10]

Otherwise, the major issue raised by AIH lies in the possibility of 'sperm banking' for use by a woman after her husband's or partner's death. There are obviously times when a woman whose partner is in a high-risk profession might wish to have this done, while semen may be available from 'banking' prior to testicular ablation, say, during

---

5 There is a movement to replace this acronym by DI (donor insemination) because of confusion with HIV infection. We will, however, continue with the established term, which is widely understood.
6 The live baby rate in 1995 was 9% of treatment cycles: HFEA *Sixth Annual Report* (1997) Table 5 – and this is a significant improvement on previous years.
7 For ease of writing, we will use the acronym AIH as shorthand for 'AIH or AIP'.
8 For which see p 68 below.
9 See p 74 below.
10 See S Mayor 'Technique for Treating Infertility may be Risky' (1996) 313 BMJ 248.

treatment of malignant disease.[11] The process has a specific moral relevance as to the effect on the child born into a single parent family.[12] Legally, it could lead to intolerable problems in relation to probate and succession. The dilemma has now been only partially resolved by the Human Fertilisation and Embryology Act 1990,[13] s 28(6)(b) of which states baldly that where the sperm of a man, or any embryo the creation of which was brought about with his sperm, is used after his death, he is not to be treated as the father of the child. It is to be noted that the process is not prohibited – indeed, Sch 3, para 2(2) allows for the relevant consent; however, the original government White Paper[14] made it clear that it was to be discouraged and, no doubt, both the statutory authority (see below) and the clinics themselves will take this into account in any cases that come within their ambit – and current indications are that a significant proportion of clinics disapprove the process.[15] The Act leaves open the related questions of the man who is reported missing but is, in fact, dead and of the woman who reasonably believes her dead partner to be alive – we think it is likely that legal paternity could be established in either case.

In fact, one of the major medico-legal *causes célèbres* which have arisen since the last edition of this book was associated with posthumous impregnation.[16]   Mrs Blood's case is, however, difficult to understand until the operation of the 1990 Act has been explored; moreover, its essential thrust relates to consent to the use of one's gametes rather than to the ethics of posthumous AIH. We will, therefore, defer discussion of *Blood* until later.[17]

A further legal problem could arise were nullity of the marriage to be mooted – as it could well be in likely circumstances calling for the use of AIH. Use of the procedure does not, however, constitute consummation of marriage and a decree of nullity can still be obtained if a woman conceives in this way; any children would still be regarded as legitimate on the grounds that the parents were married at the time of conception. Approbation might, however, preclude the granting of such a decree.[18]

A somewhat bizarre application of AIH relates to long-term prisoners whose wives may wish, or need, to conceive before their release. We have access only to a news item[19] in which the Home Office is quoted as saying that facilities for artificial insemination are not normally made available to prisoners but could be allowed in exceptional circumstances at the discretion of the minister. The rationale of the apparently purely retributive restraint is uncertain – particularly as conjugal prison

11 The problems of posthumous impregnation and intracytoplasmic sperm injection have been combined: S Trump 'Widow to Have her Husband's Child 3 Years after his Death' The Sunday Times, 3 August 1997, p 1.6.
12 It is reported that the French Centre for the Study and Conservation of Human Sperm opposed posthumous AID on these grounds – but the husband could have been HIV-positive at the time of 'banking': D Geddes 'Life, Death, and the Seeds of Judicial Controversy' Scotsman, 20 February 1991, p 12. The court subsequently overruled a contrary precedent and refused the widow's request (J Y Nau 'Le Sperme Defunt' *Le Monde*, 28 March 1991).
13 Hereafter referred to as the 1990 Act.
14 Human Fertilisation and Embryology: A Framework for Legislation (Cm 259).
15 E Corrigan, S E Mumford and M G R Hull 'Posthumous Storage and Use of Sperm and Embryos: Survey of Opinion of Treatment Centres' (1996) 313 BMJ 24.
16 *R v Human Fertilisation and Embryology Authority, ex p Blood* [1997] 2 All ER 687, (1997) 35 BMLR 1, CA.
17 See p 60 below.
18 *REL v EL* [1949] P 211, [1949] 1 All ER 141 (see also *G v G* 1961 SLT 324).
19 D Fernand 'Prisoner Calls for Right to Father a Child' The Sunday Times, 5 March 1989, p A9.

visits are commonplace in many jurisdictions; the fact that there are apparently no reports of any appeal suggests that the concession was granted in the case in point – one which related to the wife's age.

Primary sex selection

Some years ago, public concern was aroused by the entry into the market place of preconception sex selection of children. Most methods claiming scientific respectability depend upon altering the proportion of male- and female-bearing spermatozoa in the ejaculate and artificial insemination with the processed specimen. Opinions differ as to whether such methods are efficient and, if so, to what extent they can be relied upon; this, however, is not our main concern. What calls for analysis is the ethical position, given that a fully efficient method of sex selection at conception became available.[20] Discussion is then at two levels – the practical and the deontological. The fact that both are highly culture-dependent – with a very evident east/west divide – deserves emphasis. Thus, at the practical level, it is probably fair to say that preconception sex selection would have, at most, a negligible effect on the distribution and status of the sexes in the United Kingdom. But this is essentially a Western view and one which might well not be true of countries in the Far East[21] – indeed, the government of India has introduced legislation designed to criminalise an already widely available post-conception sex determination service.[1] On the ethical plane, very few, it is supposed, would oppose primary sex selection for the prophylaxis of X-linked disease.[2] Similarly, even those concerned to minimise fetal rights would see it as preferable to embryo selection or abortion for this purpose.

Beyond this, sex selection for non-medical or social reasons has been classed as anything from 'playing God' to offering an acceptable new dimension to family planning.[3] The latter view cannot be rejected out of hand – it is difficult to see why family design should not be refined in this way when so much family planning of other sorts is practised and encouraged. This, however, presupposes that the method is perfected. At present, it seems that, at best, only some 70% of choices will be effected. Couples who have been to considerable expense and discomfort to select the sex of their child will be bitterly disappointed when their wishes are unfulfilled; thus, we foresee a possibly disastrous outcome for 30% of children currently born using this technique. For this reason alone, we would advocate a legal limitation of 'gender clinics' to those licensed to undertake the practice; the potential consequences for individual children – and, perhaps, for society via a 'eugenic wedge'[4] – are too serious for the process to be left unsupervised.[5]

20 The Lancet 'Jack or Jill?' (1993) 341 Lancet 727.
21 T Marteau 'Sex Selection' (1993) 306 BMJ 1704.
  1 G Nandan 'India to Ban Prenatal Sex Determination' (1993) 306 BMJ 353. A ban has also been imposed in Turkey: B Arda 'Ethics and the Commercial Use of Genetics' (1995) 111 Bull Med Ethics 19.
  2 See p 149 below.
  3 This seems to be the view of the Dutch Health Council – the reproductive freedom of parents should be respected: 'Sex Selection for Non-medical Reasons' (1996) 119 Bull Med Ethics 8.
  4 A phrase borrowed from Marteau (1993) 306 BMJ 1704.
  5 The Human Fertilisation and Embryology Authority (see p 74 below) has no control so long as the process is carried out in private for the benefit of a man and woman together. Licensed clinics should not, however, select the sex of embryos for social reasons, nor should they use sperm sorting techniques in sex selection: HFEA *Code of Practice* (1995, 2nd revision) paras 7.20 and 7.21.

Artificial insemination by donor

Artificial insemination by donor introduces two additional concepts into the management of infertility. First, the procedure escapes the confines of a private matter between two persons in a close emotional relationship; rather, it involves a third party whose contribution lies at the heart of the matter. Secondly, in the case of the male, de-privatisation inevitably results in the production of a gross excess of gametes and, as a result, to their storage and the creation of options for their use. Legal control of private donor insemination is impossible and, since it has no more than collateral public importance, regulation is unnecessary. The same cannot be said of a public service and, accordingly, donor insemination is one of the two treatment services which are permitted only in pursuance of a licence – the other includes, broadly, any treatment which involves the creation of an embryo outside the human body and, hence, is almost entirely a matter of management of childlessness due to abnormality in the woman.[6] Ultimately, donor insemination – and ovum donation[7] – depends on the consent of the owners of gametes to their use; consent provides the plinth on which control is based and its form is detailed in the 1990 Act, Sch 3.

In summary, so-called 'effective consent' must be in writing and can apply to the use, storage and/or disposal of gametes. Thus, gametes cannot be used or received other than in accordance with the terms of an effective consent (Sch 3, para 5) and this extends to the use of any embryo created from those gametes (Sch 3, para 6); a consent to storage must specify the maximum period of storage[8] and, again, this applies to any embryo so formed (Sch 3, para 8); and the person giving consent must specify what is to be done with the gametes or created embryos in the event that he or she dies or becomes incapacitated (Sch 3, para 2(b)). In addition, the person giving consent must be given adequate information and must be counselled before doing so (Sch 3, para 3).

We could, now, look briefly at the case of *Blood*,[9] using it as an example of how such stringent conditions can complicate matters for both clinicians and relatives.[10] In essence, Mr Blood was the victim of meningitis. When he was in terminal coma, his wife requested, and obtained, a specimen of semen, which she hoped to use for insemination after his death.[11] There was some confusion – particularly in the expert evidence – as to whether he was or was not 'brain stem dead' at the time the specimen was taken[12] and, although it is, perhaps, not strictly to the present issue, the point has some general significance. If he were alive, removal of the specimen would, for example, have been treatment for a man and woman together and, thus, beyond the requirements of a licence (1990 Act, s 4(1)(b)) – aside from the difficulty of establishing that it was in 'his best interests' that it should be done,[13] there would have been nothing

6 1990 Act, ss 1(2) and 4(1)(b).
7 See p 69 below.
8 They cannot, in any event, be stored for longer than ten years (1990 Act, s 14(3)).
9 *R v Human Fertilisation and Embryology Authority, ex p Blood* [1997] 2 All ER 687, (1997) 35 BMLR 1, CA.
10 For a very readable account of the case, see D Morgan and R G Lee 'In the Name of the Father ? *Ex Parte Blood*: Dealing with Novelty and Anomaly' (1997) 60 MLR 840.
11 Surprisingly, requests for posthumous *recovery* of sperm are not all that uncommon. Something of the order of 4% of American and Canadian fertility clinics were found to have undertaken the procedure: (1997) 125 Bull Med Ethics 5.
12 See chapter 13 for discussion of 'brain stem death'.
13 It is an assault to touch a person who is incapable of consenting unless, among other possibilities, it is in his or her best interests to do so: *Re F (mental patient: sterilisation)* [1990] 2 AC 1, sub nom *F v West Berkshire Health Authority* [1989] 2 All ER 545. The law's ability to recognise best interests in an ever widening circle of circumstances is a continuing theme in this book.

to stop his wife's immediate AIH;[14] such an argument could not, however, be deployed once he was dead. In short, Mrs Blood's major hurdle was that her husband's semen was stored – ironically for the main purpose of establishing the legality of removing it – and this was unlawful in the absence of a storage licence and the consent of the sperm donor. The latter, to be 'effective', had to be given in writing and was subject to prior counselling – neither of which condition could be fulfilled. Accordingly – and in the face of something of a public outcry[15] – the Human Fertilisation and Embryology Authority (HFEA) held that the storage of the specimen was, and its use would be, unlawful; furthermore, the Authority declined to exercise its discretion to allow the gametes to be exported to another country where treatment could be given in the absence of the donor's written consent.

Mrs Blood applied for judicial review of this decision but her application was dismissed, Sir Stephen Brown P holding that the HFEA was, effectively, following the will of Parliament; more specifically, he judged that EC law did not assist the applicant. The Court of Appeal agreed with the High Court decision in so far as treatment in the United Kingdom was concerned. It did, however, conclude that, in failing to exercise its discretion to facilitate treatment abroad, the HFEA had not been properly advised as to the importance of EC law in relation to cross-border treatment and had been over-concerned with the creation of an undesirable precedent – something which was impossible given the ruling that the original storage was illegal in the absence of written consent. The case was, therefore, remitted to the Authority, who exercised their discretion in the light of the further evidence adduced in the Court of Appeal.[16]

In the end, then, *Blood* does nothing to alter or to ease the effect of existing domestic law and the almost palpable anxiety of the court to support Mrs Blood's quest for reproductive freedom has been the subject of considerable academic criticism.[17] Perhaps the best result of the case has been the establishment of a Review of the Consent Provisions in the Human Fertilisation and Embryology Act 1990 under the leadership of Professor McLean; the findings of the review have, unfortunately, not been published at the time of writing.

AID and the marital bond

Notwithstanding the restrictions imposed by the consent requirements, there are those who object strongly to AID on the grounds that the basis of the marriage bond is compromised by the wife's pregnancy through another man. It is supposed that the privity of marriage is invaded and that, in this respect, AID is little different from adultery.

The question of whether AID constitutes adultery in legal terms was debated in the Scottish case of *MacLennan v MacLennan*,[18] where it was determined that

---

14 Accepted by Lord Woolf in the Court of Appeal [1997] 2 All ER 687 at 696, (1997) 35 BMLR at 23.
15 Well described by P R Ferguson 'Posthumous Conception: Blood and Gametes' 1997 SLT 61.
16 Permission to seek help in a Belgian clinic did not end Mrs Blood's travails. The clinic in question insisted on a counselling process and did not give any guarantee that they would decide the procedure was ethical: J Lawrance 'Six Months On, Why Am I Kept Waiting to Conceive My Dead Husband's Baby ?' Independent, 25 September 1997, p 3.
17 For example, M Brazier 'Hard Cases Make Bad Law?' (1997) 23 J Med Ethics 341.
18 1958 SC 105.

adultery could not be held to have taken place because there was no sexual contact between the woman and the donor. This approach to the question would probably be acceptable now throughout the Commonwealth. AID without the consent of the husband may, however, be taken as constituting cruel and unreasonable conduct for divorce purposes. However, given the consent of both parties, the acceptance of AID can be seen as the fulfilment of the perfectly legitimate desire to have a child. The very fact of agreement to the process testifies to the strength of the bond between the parties – and this is confirmed by the comparatively low incidence of divorce in couples who have chosen AID. The marital bond is disturbed by the procedure only in a metaphysical sense and this disturbance is, in any event, actively sought by the couple.

This is not to recommend that AID be undertaken lightly. Several of the United States have introduced legislation to control the extensive use of donor insemination in America where its provision has, at least in the past, been of variable quality.[19] In the United Kingdom, it is now illegal to provide a treatment service involving AID without a licence to do so unless, as the 1990 Act, s 4(1)(b) puts it, the service 'is being provided for the woman and the man together'; counselling as to its psychological and legal implications is an integral part of the process.

It is of passing interest that the wording of s 4(1)(b) has caused some confusion. Does it mean 'together' in a geographic sense – ie that the woman and the man are physically present in the clinic? – or does it, perhaps, mean that both the woman and the man are receiving treatment? – in which case, it is reasonable to ask what 'treatment' the man is being given other than emotional support. The latter interpretation was clearly in the mind of Johnson J when he said:

> It seems plain to me that the subsection envisages a situation in which the man involved himself received medical treatment, although . . . I am not sure what treatment is envisaged'.[20]

The question was, however, thoroughly aired by Wilson J in *U v W*.[1] In this bizarre case, a woman conceived and bore twins as a result of micromanipulation of her ova and the sperm of an anonymous donor, the process having failed when using the semen of her partner. U applied to have her partner declared the father of the twins by virtue of the 1990 Act, s 28(3)(a).[2] In the process of deciding the meaning of the words 'treatment . . . together', Wilson J rejected the tentative interpretation in *Re Q* and opined:

> [W]hat has to be demonstrated is that, in the provision of treatment services with donor sperm, the doctor was responding to a request for that form of treatment made by the woman and the man as a couple, notwithstanding the absence in the man of any physical role in such treatment'.[3]

---

19 See eg R M Greenblatt et al 'Screening Therapeutic Insemination Donors for Sexually Transmitted Diseases: Overview and Recommendations' (1986) 46 Fertil Steril 351. The possibility of transmission of disease, including infection by HIV, is recognised everywhere: C L R Barratt and I D Cooke 'Risks of Donor Insemination' (1989) 299 BMJ 1178.
20 In *Re Q (parental order)* [1996] 1 FLR 369 at 371.
 1 *U v W (A-G intervening)* [1997] 2 FLR 282, (1997) 38 BMLR 54.
 2 See p 65 below.
 3 (1997) 38 BMLR 54 at 66. Wilson J also drew attention to the terms of the optional acknowledgment of paternity suggested in what is now Annex D of the HFEA *Code of Practice*.

In short, this judgment confirms the generally held view[4] that the purpose of the words 'treatment . . . together' in s 4(1)(b) is to exclude artificial insemination by the husband (AIH) or the partner (AIP) from the restrictive terms of the 1990 Act and, in s 28(3), to ensure legal paternity of the child born to a woman and her bona fide partner as a result of AID conducted in a licensed clinic. The parallel question of what constitutes a 'partner' for the purposes of the Act is discussed briefly below.[5]

Major ethical problems

It is probably fair to say that the major ethical problems associated with AID have been eliminated from the standard husband and wife or heterosexual partnership situations. It can, however, happen that a single woman requests AID or the request may come from a lesbian couple. Since there is no legal regulation of the matter, a doctor will have to decide on ethical grounds alone whether or not to proceed in these circumstances.

The Royal College of Obstetricians and Gynaecologists gives some answer to this in the guidelines it has laid down for its members. These recommend that AID be performed only on a married woman and, then, with the consent of her husband in writing. Some would say that this is excessively conservative; a single woman may feel precisely the same desire for a child as a married woman and should have the same access to a child as has her married counterpart. The same argument may be put forward on behalf of the homosexual woman, whether she is living by herself or with a partner. Should the experience of giving birth and raising a child be denied in either case because of the absence of a husband? Why should society exclude the possibility of conception in this way when it allows such women to conceive by normal means and permits them to keep their children as a normal right of parenthood?[6]

Artificial insemination is not, however, a natural process and it usually involves the medical profession. In participating in the process of procreation, the doctor is performing an act which is not morally colourless. Even if the principal objective of AID is to satisfy the desire for a child, thought has to be given to the child who is the end result; many would hold that the child's interests should be considered paramount – and that this holds throughout the spectrum of assisted reproduction.[7] The doctor must, therefore, question whether he should play a part in the deliberate creation of a child who could be disadvantaged as compared with his peers who have fathers. Whether or not such disadvantage – including any disadvantages of lesbian parenthood – are real or imaginary is undecided[8] and is, perhaps, indeterminable, for there are

4   And that expressed by Bracewell J in *Re B (parentage)* [1996] 2 FLR 15.
5   See p 65. A comparison of *Blood* and *U v W* provides a nice example of the juggling which can accompany attempts to harmonise domestic and European Community law. The topic is, however, beyond the scope of this book.
6   Inevitably, much of the literature in this area is partisan. A good review from the feminist viewpoint is provided by M MgGuire and N J Alexander 'Artificial Insemination of Single Women' (1985) 43 Fertil Steril 1982. Others have cast doubt on the motivation of single women seeking AID: eg S Jennings 'Virgin Birth Syndrome' (1991) 337 Lancet 559. In general, see M B King and P Pattison 'Homosexuality and Parenthood' (1991) 303 BMJ 295.
7   D Giesen 'Developing Ethical Public Policy on Reproduction and Prenatal Research: Whose Interests Deserve What Protection?' (1989) 8 Med Law 553.
8   For review, see S Golombok and J Rust 'The Warnock Report and Single Women: What About the Children?' (1986) 12 J Med Ethics 182.

probably proportionately as many good and bad homes regularised by church or state as there are occupied by single parents.

The 1990 Act, s 13(5) emphasises the importance of this particular problem by specifying consideration of 'the need of the child for a father' as one of the welfare principles to be satisfied before treatment is given under licence. In support of this, HFEA's *Code of Practice*[9] lists four major factors which clinics should take into account when people seek treatment using donated gametes – including such vagaries as the possible attitudes of other members of the family to the resulting child. The onus on the doctor is, therefore, considerable. We, ourselves, would fall back on the distinction we have already made between social and medical treatments. It is open to a fertile single woman, whether hetero- or homosexual, to have a child by natural means. Professional intervention in such circumstances is unarguably a matter of social, rather than medical, expedience; we doubt if a doctor ought to confuse his role as a therapist with that of a social worker or political economist – despite the manifestly interventionist attitude adopted by HFEA, the decision and its solution should be left to the woman herself.[10] On the other side of the coin, s 38 of the 1990 Act now relieves the doctor who conscientiously objects to such procedures of a duty to act. The discussion is, however, more germane to those forms of assisted reproduction which depend wholly upon medical expertise.[11] The Warnock Committee[12] (at para 2.11 of its report) was unable to conclude any more firmly than that it is, as a general rule, better for children to be born into a two-parent family. HFEA's *Code of Practice* has no legal force per se but renewal of a licence would undoubtedly be prejudiced were its recommendations to be flouted (1990 Act, s 25(6)). We suspect that, as a result, clinics will tend to be restrictive rather than liberal in their choice of unattached potential patients.

Legal considerations

The legal position of the child born as a result of AID has been established in the United States and in many parts of the Commonwealth for some time.[13] Legislation was delayed in the United Kingdom until the passage of the Family Law Reform Act 1987, s 27; the partial solution to the problem provided therein has now been extended in the 1990 Act, ss 27-30, which also resolve the anomalies previously extant between England and Wales and Scotland. Section 28(2) covers the case of the married woman – and it is to be noted that, although s 28(3) allows for 'partnership', there are no provisions for single women. In essence, the rule is that, given she has been

9 See p 59, n 5 above at para 3.18.
10 This is clearly the situation in the United States. There was apparently no difficulty in recruiting 26 single women without partners who were willing to undergo a definite research project involving pregnancy by AID: A J Peters, B Hecht, A C Wentz and R Jeyendram 'Comparison of the Methods of Artificial Insemination and the Incidence of Conception in Single Unmarried Women' (1993) 59 Fertil Steril 121.
11 See p 71 below.
12 Report of the Committee of Inquiry into Human Fertilisation and Embryology (Dame Mary Warnock, Chairman) (Cmnd 9314) referred to hereafter as Warnock.
13 Eg Artificial Conception Act 1985 (W Australia); Status of Children (Amendment) Act 1984 (Vict); Artificial Conception Act 1984 (NSW). See also Children's Status Act 1987 (RSA); Uniform Parentage Act (1973) (USA). For full discussion, see D J Cusine *New Reproductive Techniques: A Legal Perspective* (1988) chs 7 and 8.

inseminated with the sperm of a man other than her husband and provided that her husband has consented, he will be treated as the father of the child; s 28(4) emphasises that, in these circumstances, no other person is to be treated as the father of the child and the donor is covered against withdrawal of consent by the husband by s 28(6)(a).[14] The s 28(2) rule is voided if the husband can show that he did not, in fact, consent to the procedure. The frankly confusing terms of s 28(5) do, however, retain the common law principle of *pater est quem nuptiae demonstrant*; thus, the husband who does not consent to AID will still have to rebut that presumption by way of accepted methods of paternity testing. It is to be noted that the statutory provisions will prevail in the event of disagreement between the partners.[15] Section 29(4) preserves the somewhat archaic exclusion of hereditary titles, honours and the like from the general principles attaching to the AID child – although where the onus of proof or disproof of patrilinearity then lies or, indeed, how it can be discharged is a matter for speculation. An exception of greater practical importance is that, by virtue of Sch 4, para 8, ss 27-29 of the 1990 Act do not apply for the purposes of restricting live organ transplants between persons not genetically related (Human Organ Transplants Act 1989, s 2).

As noted above, s 28(3) extends the responsibilities and privileges of fatherhood to the woman's partner subject, first, to the insemination being carried out in a licensed clinic and, secondly, to their seeking treatment 'together' – a matter we have already touched upon. This section, which confers parenthood on a man who, otherwise, has neither genetic nor legal claim to that status, represents a remarkable advance in legislation and it is, in many ways, surprising that the Act makes no attempt to define a 'partner' – indeed, it does not mention the word.[16] *U v W* suggests that whether or not a couple 'qualify' for s 28(3) status is a matter to be determined on the facts[17] – although there is nothing to stop responsible bodies fixing their own arbitrary limits in other situations.[18] Clearly, however, considerable responsibility devolves on the clinic which has wide discretion as to the choice of 'suitable' parents.[19]

It will be seen, therefore, that, in normal circumstances, the child conceived by AID within the married state is spared the potential, even if vestigial, disadvantages of illegitimacy and the position of the child born out of wedlock is secured. The Act makes no specific mention as to the registration of the birth of the child but, again, this appears to be clarified by implication. Section 29(1) states that the treatment in law of a woman's husband as the father of a child resulting from consensual donor insemination is 'for all purposes' – and this must include the registration of births and marriages. At the same time, it is clear that the consent provision of the Act, in

---

14 This section also applies to inseminations done privately (or 'DIY' inseminations) as compared with s 28(3), which applies only to procedures carried out by a licensed practitioner. We find the interpretation applied in *U v W (A-G intervening)* [1997] 2 FLR 282, (1997) 38 BMLR 54, where treatment services were being provided to the public, difficult to accept.

15 *Re CH (contact: parentage)* [1996] 1 FLR 569.

16 This obviously concerned the Lord Chancellor during the debate on the Bill when he referred to 'the difficulty in distinguishing partners to stable relationships from more transitory ones': Official Reports, HL, 20 March 1990, col 209-10.

17 [1997] 3 WLR 739 at 749, (1997) 38 BMLR 54 at 66.

18 One railway company, for example, laid down two years as a period of partnership qualifying for family rebates: *Grant v South-West Trains Ltd* Case C-249/96 [1998] IRLR 206, ECJ.

19 HFEA *Code of Practice* para 3.17.

particular, are capable of creating a class of children who are legally fatherless and this must be a matter for criticism.[20]

This is compounded by the near absolute freedom from parental responsibility conferred on the donor by s 28(6)(a) of the 1990 Act, which specifically excludes the donor from paternity.[1]   Anonymity of the donor is now subject to the licensing authority keeping a register of identifiable individuals who have been treated, whose gametes have been stored or used and who were, or may have been, born as a result of treatment services (s 31(2)). As a corollary to this, a person over the age of 18 years, or a person over 16 years old and intending to marry, may now require the licensing authority to establish whether he or she might have been born as a result of treatment services and, if so, to provide such information as to parentage as is required by regulation.   The regulations cannot require the licensing authority to give any information as to the identity of a person whose gametes have been used and that prohibition will have retrospective force should it be revoked (s 31(5)).[2] We imagine that the type of available information will be limited to include, say, information as to the donor's ethnic type and genetic health.

Thus, on paper, anonymity seems to be adequately protected. Nevertheless, we have reservations as to the retention of names on the register. Apart from the fact that clandestine breach of confidentiality now seems to be an accepted feature of public administration, the mere fact that a list of names exists will be a source of inspiration to zealots in the cause of freedom of information. From the more specific aspect, a nominal register is held to be important to guard against the possibility of incest or of marriage within the prohibited degrees in later generations; the HFEA's *Code of Practice* dictates that, save in exceptional circumstances, no more than ten children should be fathered by one donor. The dangers, both real and imaginary, of such matings as a result of AID may be overstated; the disclosure provisions in the event of marriage are theoretically sound but may be an example of using a sledgehammer as a nutcracker. Outwith the intermarriage factor, claims are made that children have a right to know their true parentage and also that they have a strong psychological urge to do so;[3] much of the evidence for the latter is, however, anecdotal and no comparable study of children born by way of adultery has been, nor can be, made. If there *is* such pressure, the compromise of allowing access to limited information can only lead to frustration. The frequently drawn analogy with adoption – in which there is a statutory right to discover a true genetic relationship[4] – is flawed. In the latter

---

20 For case law, see *Re Q (parental order)* [1996] 1 FLR 369.
  1 It will be seen from what has already been said that the donor could, for example, be seen as the legal father if he provides a specimen for insemination of an unmarried couple by an unlicensed practitioner.
  2 Personal data relating to treatments under the 1990 Act are exempt from the subject access provisions of the Data Protection Act 1984 except so far as their disclosure is made in accordance with s 31. Disclosure can, however, be ordered by the courts in the interests of justice (s 34) and in the case of proceedings under the Congenital Disabilities (Civil Liability) Act 1976 or of comparable actions for damages in Scotland (s 35).
  3 See eg G D Mitchell 'In-vitro Fertilisation: The Major Issues – a Comment' (1983) 9 J Med Ethics 196. From Australia, L Waller 'The Law and Infertility – The Victorian Experience' in S McLean (ed) *Law Reform and Human Reproduction* (1991). A full review is K O'Donovan 'A Right to Know One's Parentage?' (1988) 2 Int J Law & Fam 27.
  4 Adoption Act 1976, s 51; Adoption (Scotland) Act 1978, s 45(5).

situation, some bonding with the true parents may have occurred; there is, at least in the 'stranger' process, no necessary genetic affiliation with either adopting parent; and, pragmatically, disclosure of status is almost certain once the child requires to see his or her birth certificate. The *need* for the AID child to have the same discovery rights as the adoptee is, therefore, by no means self-evident.

Very few of us ever question our paternity and still fewer will doubt their maternity – for the same regulations apply to ovum donation[5] as to sperm donation; it seems to us that the almost inevitable result of regulating for a few to question their parentage will be to encourage the majority to do so. It is doubtful if the statutory creation of children anxiously awaiting their eighteenth birthday in order to exorcise an implanted suspicion can be to the overall benefit of family relationships. Occasionally – and particularly in the event of the reason for AID lying in a genetic abnormality in a woman's husband or partner – disclosure of true parentage may be highly desirable; such situations are better met by good counselling within a responsible family environment.[6]

The infertile or childless woman

Although we appreciate that treatment for childlessness is available to unmarried women[7] – whether or not they are single or living in a partnership – the majority of requests for appropriate treatment are likely to come from married couples. It is in this sense that we speak of 'husband and wife' in what follows.

Childlessness due to abnormalities in the man is, as we have seen, largely a matter of the defective formation of spermatozoa. A woman may also suffer from primary infertility. In addition, however, she may be beset by anatomical problems which prevent her having children by natural means – of which, blockage of the fallopian tubes is the most important. The proportion of cases due to anatomical abnormality and to infertility resulting from faulty ovum production is about equal. We do not, here, discuss the purely medical treatment of the latter; its incidental legal and ethical significance is noted briefly below.[8] When hormonal treatment has failed, however, the anovular woman is in the same position as the azoospermic man and may be able to parent a child by way of gamete replacement; despite the fact that ova are far more scarce and are more difficult to handle than are spermatozoa, ovum donation is now a practical routine procedure. Even so, it is, perhaps fortunately, still impossible to develop a full-term fetus in a laboratory environment. Ovum donation is, therefore, pointless without, at the same time, providing a womb. Both may be contributed by the same woman or they may be available independently. These form the bases of the legal and moral problems complicating the treatment of the infertile woman.

---

5   See p 69 below.
6   For a novel approach to the dilemma, see S Wilson 'Identity, Genealogy and the Social Family: the Case of Donor Insemination' (1997) 11 Int J Law Pol Fam 270.
7   HFEA *Code of Practice*, paras 3.14 and 3.19a.
8   See p 77.

In vitro fertilisation (IVF)

Many modern reproductive techniques involve the fertilisation of the ovum in laboratory – or in vitro – conditions and the subsequent transfer of the embryo[9] from the petri dish to the uterus. Strictly speaking, therefore, IVF and embryo transfer (ET) are technical terms. Nevertheless, popular usage equates IVF with the standard treatment for childlessness due to blockage of the fallopian tubes and ET with the implantation of an embryo which has no genetic relationship either to the recipient or to her husband. This apparently semantic distinction is, we believe, of practical importance. If damage is to be done to the embryo, one would anticipate it being most likely while being manipulated in transit – and this is a matter of general technique rather than of a specific therapy.[10]

Standard IVF treatment involves collection of ova from the wife's abdomen, fertilisation of these with her husband's sperm in the laboratory and transfer of the resulting embryo to her uterus; the treatment is, therefore, essentially one designed to bypass diseased fallopian tubes. The actual collection of ova is now relatively simple through a laparoscope; the treatment cycle does, however, involve complex hormonal priming to ensure superovulation. This is important to the process as success is affected by the number of embryos implanted. The mean live birth rate depends to an extent on the size and expertise of the treatment centre but is currently in the order of 15% of treatment cycles; pregnancy rates vary from 7% when one embryo is transferred to 21% when three are implanted.[11] Thus, while IVF may well be the optional treatment for one of the commonest female causes of childlessness, the expectations of success are relatively low – an important point to be made when counselling childless couples. There is no significant difference between the pregnancy and live birth rates following IVF as related to the underlying reason for the treatment.

The rationale of the process corresponds closely to that of AIH and, as such, presents no legal problems. The genetic and natural parentage of the resulting infant are not disputed. All that has occurred is that a technique has been substituted for a natural process; if any would protest that this is in some way immoral, they would, at the same time, have to contend that the surgical treatment of any disease is similarly immoral.

There is, of course, no technical reason why the sperm must be those of the husband and, in the event of combined male infertility and an impassable female genital tract, donor semen could be used in the same way. In such circumstances, the legal problems would be comparable to those of AID, which have been discussed above.

9 The *First Report of the Voluntary Licensing Authority for Human In Vitro Fertilisation and Embryology* (1986) p 8, recommended the use of the term pre-embryo to distinguish the organism before differentiation into fetal and placental cells has occurred. There is, thus, physiological justification for this. We, however, prefer not to use the term as, despite protestations to the contrary, it smacks of an attempt to make a moral distinction between the pre-embryo and the embryo – which we suggest is spurious and unnecessary (see also the Australian *Report of a Senate Select Committee on the Human Embryo Experimentation Bill 1985* (1986)).

10 Cusine *New Reproductive Techniques* (1988) p 141, preferred the therapeutic distinction, referring to the 'transfer' in IVF as 'embryo replacement'.

11 HFEA *Sixth Annual Report* (1997) Table 4B. Strangely, the rate actually drops when more than three embryos are implanted and the Authority believes that there are no longer any circumstances in which there is clinical justification for implanting more than three; indeed, they are clearly considering reducing the number to two – as is now recommended, for example, in the Netherlands (see Report, Table 3).

Ovum donation

An alternative situation is that the ovum is donated by another woman. The need might arise as being the only way in which a woman with, say, abdominal adhesions could have children and it might be desirable in the event of a potential mother carrying an X-linked genetic disease;[12] about 1% of childlessness for female reasons is due to ovarian failure of uncertain origin and the ovaries may be destroyed during, say, treatment for cancer. The scenario is now that the donated egg is fertilised by the husband's semen and the embryo then transferred to the wife's womb. The process can, therefore, be looked upon as the female variant of AID.

The practical difference is that, whereas spermatozoa are plentiful and easily harvested, ova are scarce and their recovery involves some discomfort and inconvenience to the donor. Thus, the donor must be stimulated hormonally in order to coincide with the recipient's optimal menstrual state and, in many cases, a laparoscopy will be required. Ova may be obtained from women in the course of other surgery – in particular, during sterilisation. There is, however, some concern lest their consent may be flawed in that a measure of coercion is used in the latter case; the International Federation of Gynecology and Obstetrics has, in fact, declared that the process is unethical.[13] Nevertheless, centres in the United Kingdom may still offer, say, free treatments or sterilisation in return for donated eggs provided that very strict criteria as to counselling, management and consent are met; the policy is currently under review.[14] The difficulties, then, of ovum donation lie not only in the technique but, also, in finding the donors – a difficulty which is compounded by the fact that, unlike spermatozoa and early embryos, ova cannot, at present, be cryopreserved without an unacceptable risk of induced chromosomal abnormality – although this is now under consideration.

Once achieved, however, the natural – though not the genetic – parentage will be reasonably clear. It is difficult to see any circumstances in which motherhood would be challenged[15] and, in a patrilineal society, there are fewer objections to an admixture of ovum-derived genes in the family than to those which arise as a result of AID. The matter is now put beyond legal doubt; s 27(1) of the 1990 Act follows earlier Australian legislation[16] in holding that a woman who carries a child as a result of the placing in her of an embryo or of sperm and eggs, and no other woman, is to be treated as the mother of the child.

But what of the similar wife with an infertile husband? Although such a combination might be regarded as too rare for consideration, it could, theoretically, arise in about one in every 400 marriages seeking children. Such a state can be

---

12 See chapter 6 below.
13 *Recommendations on Ethical Issues in Obstetrics and Gynecology* (1997) 133 Bull Med Ethics 8. See also the stringent restrictions in Canada under the Human Reproductive and Genetics Technologies Act 1996.
14 HFEA *Sixth Annual Report* (1997) p 10. There are also unconfirmed but disturbing suggestions that ovum donation may be harmful of itself; see K Abuja et al 'Donor Eggs for Love or Money' The Sunday Times, 22 November 1998, p 120 (letter).
15 See *Ampthill Peerage* [1977] AC 547, HL, per Lord Simon at 577.
16 Status of Children (Amendment) Act 1984 (Vict). See also the Artificial Conception Act 1985 (W Aust) ss 5(1) and 7(1).

managed by embryo donation whereby an embryo performed from donated ovum and donated sperm is implanted in the sterile woman. The resultant complications then lie somewhere between those of in vitro fertilisation and those surrounding surrogate motherhood and are best discussed under that heading below. Even so, it is emotionally, morally and legally important to distinguish unrelated embryo transfer of this type from surrogate motherhood – the intense relationship between mother and fetus occurs in both but, in normal circumstances, does not progress to that between mother and child in the latter procedure.

Once again, the 1990 Act has cleared the legal air; by virtue of ss 27 and 28, the child born of embryo donation is, for all purposes, the child of the carrying mother and her consenting husband.

The availability of IVF

We have discussed some of the moral issues surrounding assisted reproduction under the heading of artificial insemination. Very much the same principles apply in the case of the infertile wife. There is, however, one major difference – while AID is a relatively simple process, IVF and its counterparts are both cost- and manpower-intensive. Problems of resource allocation are, thus, superimposed on those of ethical practice.

The response to the question of whether the effort applied to the alleviation of childlessness is well- or mis-directed is such a personal matter that specific discussion would be invidious; the general principles of resource allocation are outlined in chapter 11 below. Whether IVF, in its broad sense, should be available to fertile couples depends upon the motivation.[17] There may be good medical reasons, mainly in relation to the carriage of abnormal recessive genes, which fully justify intervention in any appropriate form on behalf of otherwise fertile couples; indeed, when combined with embryo biopsy – whereby the genetic status of embryos can be established before implantation – IVF may offer their currently *correct* management. Non-medical reasons would include the early removal of ova for use in later life, thus circumventing the increased risk of chromosomal abnormalities in the child, and, secondly, the wholly hedonistic use of 'womb-leasing' for social reasons. The latter is discussed below.[18] As to the former, there are no legal objections in the United Kingdom to preserving embryos in the same way as sperm and a case can be made out on grounds of social utility for women delaying their pregnancies. There are, however, practical difficulties. The problems introduced by limitations on the storage times for embryos have been alleviated to an extent since the maximum time was raised to ten years provided the storage was for treatment purposes.[19] Even so, there are important conditions as to the clinical status of the gamete providers which

17 K Dawson and P Singer 'Should Fertile People Have Access to In Vitro Fertilisation?' (1990) 300 BMJ 167. For a very controversial and critical review of the cost-effectiveness of the IVF programme, see M G Wagner and P A St Clair 'Are In Vitro Fertilisation and Embryo Transfer of Benefit to All?' (1989) 2 Lancet 1027.
18 See p 86.
19 Human Fertilisation and Embryology (Statutory storage period for embryos) Regulations 1996, SI 1996/375. In the event that the woman or her partner is or is likely to become prematurely and completely sterile, the period can be extended beyond ten years, subject to the clinical judgment of two practitioners.

restrict the concession to genuine cases of medical need and, of less practical concern, storage cannot continue beyond the 55th birthday of the woman involved; the limit remains at five years if these conditions are not met. Secondly, the risks of pregnancy itself rise dramatically with age – the maternal mortality rate over the age of 40 is some ten times that in the case of women aged 20-24.[20] Thirdly, the pregnancy rate following embryo transfer deteriorates with age[1] and , finally, the indications are that older women require the implantation of more embryos than do the young in order to achieve the same implantation rate.[2]

We discuss the concept of ageism later[3] and there is no doubt that there is, at least, emotional discrimination against the old that is based on little more than societal conditioning. Have we any moral right to discriminate against an older woman in denying her access to motherhood when we would provide the facilities without qualm to her younger sister in otherwise identical circumstances? It is difficult to support such a policy when the woman herself is providing the scarce resource – the eggs – as is the case in IVF provided for the premenopausal woman. The counter-argument depends, of course, on the effect on the consequent child and it is not difficult to dream up circumstances in which an 'ageing' mother could be seen as a disadvantage to a young child. Nevertheless, given that we would not consider depriving 40-year-old women of natural pregnancy, it seems paternalistic in the extreme to deny them assisted reproductive services on the grounds of age alone. It is for these reasons that we find it hard to support judicial acceptance of a health authority's decision not to purchase infertility services for women above the age of 35[4] – an age which, to one of us at least, appears to be that of golden youth! We might add here, in parentheses, that the same may not apply to the post-menopausal woman – whose search for motherhood has become apparent only recently. Quite apart from the fact that, here, we are dealing with ovum donation – and, hence, with a publicly scarce resource – treatment is not that of an unfortunate abnormality but is, rather, an interference with the natural order. Paternalism is, thus, excluded from the equation and we are free to concentrate entirely on the resultant child. None the less, the British Medical Association has declared its support for the procedure.[5]

As in the case of AID, the question of the child's well-being raises the question of the potential mother's status – single, lesbian or of doubtful suitability. Here, in contrast to the AID situation, medical involvement in the procedure is essential if it

20 Editorial Comment 'Too Old to have a Baby?' (1993) 341 Lancet 344.
 1 Figures are not available for the use of frozen embryos. Otherwise, this statement appears to be true only when the woman is using her own eggs. The live birth rate in the case of women aged 40-44 is then only 5.4% as opposed to 17.2% when donor eggs are used. There is a similar trend in the case of AID. See also A Templeton, J Morris and B Parslow 'Factors that Affect Outcome of In Vitro Fertilisation Treatment' (1996) 348 Lancet 1402.
 2 M G R Hull, C F Fleming, A O Hughes and A McDermott 'The Age-related Decline in Female Fecundity' (1996) 65 Fertil Steril 783.
 3 See chapter 12.
 4 *R v Sheffield Health Authority, ex p Seale* (1994) 25 BMLR 1. It is to be noted that HFEA imposes age limits for gamete donors. In respect of *treatment*, gametes must not be taken from women over 35 and men over 55 – though this may be lowered in the near future. Gametes must not be taken for treatment from persons below the age of 18. These limits may be relaxed when the gametes are to be used for self-treatment or in exceptional circumstances: *Code of Practice* (1995) paras 3.35-3.41.
 5 (1994) 308 BMJ 723. There are, however, misgivings in Italy – where the practice originated – and there is strong ministerial opposition in France: (1994) 308 BMJ 154, 155.

is to be undertaken; it follows that the doctor cannot opt out of judgments which involve purely social values. It is for this reason that the guidelines for assisted reproductive treatment centres included, from an early stage, the establishment, and use, of an ethical committee which has a wide remit as to the management of individual cases. No legally enforceable principles as to selection of candidates for the limited resource have been laid down, although the *Code of Practice*, as we have noted, contains a number of arguably intrusive conditions. In the only apposite case so far reported, refusal of treatment on the grounds that the patient had a history of prostitution and had been rejected as an adopter, was not considered so questionable as to provide grounds for judicial review of the decision.[6]

Nor is there, in our opinion, a great deal of help to be obtained from the 1990 Act, s 13(5). This, as noted above under AID, states that a woman shall not be provided with treatment services unless account has been taken of the welfare of any child born as a result of the treatment and of any other child who may be affected by the birth. Not only is this condition extremely wide – *any* child within the extended family might be said to be affected – but it is imprecise as to the quality and depth of account to be taken other than subtly indicating a covert disapproval of treatment outside the 'married' state. Moreover, it seems to us to have its own dangers. 'Taking account of' does not imply reaching a uniform conclusion; it is not too far-fetched to envisage 'shopping expeditions' on the part of unconventional would-be mothers to identify the most 'liberal' clinic as a source of treatment.

The legal position of the donor
The theoretical hazard which is common to all procedures involving in vitro embryo transfer is that the embryo will be damaged during manipulation and that an abnormal fetus will result. Animal experiments indicate that there is no higher incidence of abnormalities in live born neonates resulting from reimplantation than in those which are conceived normally and, so far as is known, no appreciable excess of human cases beyond the probability of chance has occurred. The HFEA's Annual Report of 1997 quoted 91 children born as a result of IVF or AID having developmental defects or syndromes – an occurrence of 0.8%, which certainly does not suggest any increased risk.[7] The outcome of litigation following such a misfortune would depend very largely on proof of causation. However, the ground rules are clear. Section 44 of the 1990 Act applies the Congenital Disabilities (Civil Liability) Act 1976, s 1 to infertility treatments in that, if a child resulting from embryo transfer, GIFT or AID is born disabled and the disability results from an act or omission in the course of the selection, or the keeping or use outside the body, of the embryo or the gametes used by a person answerable to the child, then the child's disabilities are to be regarded as damage resulting from the wrongful act of that person and actionable at the suit of the child. This does not apply if one or both parents knew of the risk of their child being

---

6   *R v Ethical Committee of St Mary's Hospital, ex p Harriott* [1988] 1 FLR 512, [1988] Fam Law 165. The possibility was not foreclosed – the greater part of the argument turned on whether the Committee was purely advisory or whether it had administrative responsibility. The case was also somewhat clouded by allegations of deceit.

7   The occurrence is very similar irrespective of the method used – 0.9% for IVF and 0.7% for AID. The rates are identical whether IVF is 'fresh' or involves the use of frozen embryos.

born disabled; particular importance is, therefore, likely to attach to the effectiveness of their consent in respect of the information given. Interestingly, this seems to open the door to an action for 'wrongful life'.[8]

The surplus embryo

It is inevitable that surplus embryos will be produced whether IVF or ovum donation is being attempted. The status and disposal of such embryos have significance which is independent of the problems of successful implantation.

The criminal law can be considered only to be dismissed. We will see later[9] that the fetus, even if it has legal significance, has no legal status. It is, therefore, inconceivable that the unimplanted embryo could be accorded any greater standing. We cannot see that any criminal offence is committed by their disposal so long as the method accords with standards of public decency.

That being so, the problem can be seen as being ethical in nature and one which devolves on the nature of the embryo. The US Ethics Advisory Board agreed that the 'human embryo is entitled to profound respect' but qualified this: 'but this respect does not necessarily encompass the full legal and moral rights attributable to persons.' Similarly, the Warnock Committee (at para 11.17) recommended only that the embryo of the human species should be afforded *some* protection in law. Such general prevarication indicates the measure of the moral difficulties involved but is, at the same time, unhelpful; in the end, one must come to a decision – either the embryo is a full human being within the rigid theological, perhaps mainly Roman Catholic, doctrine or it is a laboratory artefact.

We have argued previously that humanity is not established until implantation – this being largely on the grounds that it is only at implantation that the embryo achieves a capacity of meaningful development.[10] The acceptance of a 'specific moment' theory as to the acquisition of humanity is, however, by no means universal; an alternative approach suggested by Poplawski and Gillett[11] is to regard the process of becoming a human person as 'a progression through a series of linked developmental stages' and to attribute rights to the embryo because it represents a phase in the whole human form. The authors go on to base this moral value on the human capacity to react with others – a capacity which exists in modified form from implantation to death. We find this approach helpful, if only in a negative way, because, despite the authors' disclaimer, none of this perfectly valid analysis applies to the embryo in vitro. In the absence of implantation, there is no continuum and there is no human interaction; moreover, no moral value can be attributed to the embryo by virtue of its potential for personhood – for no such potential exists in the medium of the petri dish.[12]

---

8 See p 160 below.
9 See p 124 below.
10 For the argument based on 'ensoulment', see N M Ford *When Did I Begin?* (1988).
11 N Poplawski and G Gillett 'Ethics and Embryos' (1991) 17 J Med Ethics 62.
12 However, even if one concludes that the unimplanted surplus embryo has no moral value *of itself*, it could be that we should accord it *some* value on the grounds that it has considerable moral importance for others. This approach is sometimes referred to as 'transitivity of respect' – on which, see M A Warren *Moral Status* (1997) p 170.

It therefore seems acceptable – and both kinder and more practical – to liken the in vitro embryo to a culture of human tissue. If one accepts this premise, one simultaneously solves one's moral problem as to embryonic research which, when well done, must be valuable to the community as a whole. Nevertheless, this conclusion cannot be accepted without qualification – at the very least, the embryo must be accorded the respect due to any living human tissue. It could be replied that, in logic, there is no need to control laboratory interference with a research object that one believes has no moral status; but there *is* public disquiet over scientific involvement in the reproductive process and, on these grounds alone, it must be contained within a controlling framework. Most importantly, the morality of the argument rests upon the limitations of current technology. It is clear that our formula would be inadequate should technology advance to the state of being able to 'grow' fetuses to full term in vitro; were this to happen, we would be confronted with non-humanised human beings, which would be intolerable.

The control of assisted reproduction

It was against such a possible background that the 1990 legislation was enacted. The main thrust of the Act is to establish a Human Fertilisation and Embryology Authority (HFEA) (s 5) which is mandated to supervise and provide information and advice to the Secretary of State about embryos and about treatment services governed by the Act. The Authority maintains a Licence Committee; assisted reproductive treatment centres which provide a service for the public and which involve gamete donation or the creation of embryos outside the body are subject to the possession of a licence to do so.[13] Thus, in some contrast to the prototype Australian legislation – in which the limits of treatment are set out relatively precisely – the 1990 Act allows for a flexible development of the art under the control of peer and lay review.[14] Sections 3 and 4, however, define activities which *cannot* be licensed. These include: placing in a woman any live gametes or embryos other than those of human origin; placing a human embryo in any animal; replacement of an embryonic nucleus by a nucleus from any other person or embryo; and, of particular significance, keeping or using an embryo after the appearance of the primitive streak – by definition, later than 14 days from the day the gametes were mixed but excluding any time for which the embryo was stored. The spectre of in vitro fetal development is, thus, allayed although one inevitably asks – 'for how long?' The specific time limit has been attacked by purists, mainly on the grounds that a 13-day embryo is no less alive than is one of 15 days'

13 It will be noted that intra-fallopian transfer of gametes is not subject to licensing unless either the sperm or eggs are donated. Even so, the HFEA is maintaining a watchful eye on the process which carries its own hazards.
14 The Chairman may not be a registered medical practitioner or directly associated with the provision of treatment services; such persons must, however, constitute at least one third but not more than one half the total membership (Sch 1, para 4). The current Chairman is a senior academic administrator and the membership includes appointments from such varied professions as the religious ministry, the law, broadcasting and industry. Misgivings as to definitive legislation in the medical field are expressed by G Dworkin 'Law and Medical Experimentation: Of Embryos, Children and Others with Limited Legal Capacity' (1987) 13 Monash Univ LR 189.

gestation and that it is entitled to the same respect.[15] The counter-argument is that controlled embryonic research is essential if the attack on genetic disease – which may well be the most important single factor dictating morbidity in humans – is to be carried on in a scientifically acceptable way.

Given that the undeveloped in vitro embryo merits a certain, albeit unspecified, respect, its treatment presents a dilemma which exists in two distinct parts. The first is that of the use and, indeed, the production of embryos for research purposes; this highly emotive issue is discussed in chapter 19. The second relates to the practical problems surrounding the disposal of embryos that are surplus to immediate therapeutic needs. As already mentioned, overproduction of embryos is inseparable from the treatment of infertility by IVF; it is impossible to guarantee receptive wombs for those which remain unused in the individual case and, in many instances involving defective embryos, it could be wrong to attempt to do so. It follows that any new legislation that attempted to criminalise the bona fide destruction of embryos would, at the same time, effectively shut the door on this form of treatment. On the face of things, the pioneer Australian legislation did just that in stating that:

> a person shall not cause or permit [ova obtained from the body of a woman] to be fertilised outside the body of the woman except for the purposes of the implantation of embryos . . . in the womb of that woman or another woman.[16]

In effect, however, the section merely prohibits the production of embryos for the express purpose of non-therapeutic experimentation. Such a procedure would not be prohibited by the current United Kingdom legislation, under which the disposal of gametes and embryos depends heavily on the consent of those donating the gametes. It follows that whether or not an embryo can be used for treatment or research or whether it is to be destroyed at a certain time or in certain circumstances – eg on the death of the donor – depends upon the agreed consent of two persons (1990 Act, Sch 3, para 6). The 1990 Act, however, makes no provision for the condition most likely to cause difficulty – that is, when there is disagreement between the two parties concerned.

The need for some form of legislation is exemplified in two well-known *causes célèbres*. In the first of these, an Australian case,[17] embryos were stored against future use by a couple, one of whom was the genetic mother; both were killed before the embryos were implanted. There was such public outcry at the thought of their being destroyed that they were retained in storage pending the passage of legislation; our understanding is that they were not implanted later into volunteer women as had been intended and that, partly for technical reasons, they never will be. An example of

---

15 T Inglesias 'In vitro Fertilisation: The Major Issues' (1984) 10 J Med Ethics 32. The same issue contains a contrary view from a moralist: G R Dunstan 'The Moral Status of the Human Embryo: A Tradition Recalled' (1984) 10 J Med Ethics 38. See also M Lockwood (ed) *Moral Dilemmas in Modern Medicine* (1985) ch 1; and the philosophical argument in A Holland 'A Fortnight of My Life is Missing' (1990) 7 J Appl Philos 25. See also Giesen (1989) 8 Med Law 553. Inevitably, much of the basic discussion of the topic is now somewhat dated.

16 Infertility (Medical Procedures) Act 1984 (Vict), as amended, s 6(5).

17 The details of the Rios' case are hard to come by. Our authority is G F Smith 'Australia's Frozen "Orphan" Embryos: A Medical, Legal and Ethical Dilemma' (1985/86) 24 J Fam Law 27; B Steinbeck *Life Before Birth* (1992) p 212.

disagreement was provided in Tennessee in 1989. Here, a married couple who had provided stored embryos were divorced before the latter could be used. The father asked that they be destroyed while the mother wished to become pregnant by them. The judge at first instance ruled that the embryos were human beings – with all the rights attending that status – and that their fate should, therefore, be decided on the principle of their best interests; this meant that they should be implanted. This decision was reversed by the State Supreme Court, which held that the man's interest is not reproducing outweighed those of his spouse in procreating.[18] A rather similar case has been fought in Australia.[19] Our feeling is that similar problems will result from the British legislation and that it would be better for 'consent to disposal' to be vested in the person for whom the embryos were intended – that is, the proposed woman recipient. Parliament's remarkable concern for the embryo, in the face of some 180,000 abortions performed annually in Great Britain, is difficult to understand. Our preferred solution to embryo disposal would, at least, remove the anomaly which gives powers of disposal to the father of an embryo but allows the father of a fetus no rights as to the survival of his progeny (see chapter 5) – while this is explicable on the grounds that the equality of parental interest has altered in the transition, it seems unnecessary to have introduced a complication. In practice, the power of both gamete donors to decide the fate of the embryo is limited by statute – stored gametes must be destroyed at the end of ten years and embryos must be allowed to perish after five years' preservation (1990 Act, ss 14(3) and (4)) unless they are to be used for treatment in the special circumstances outlined above.[20] This, at least, sets a limit to the difficulties in estate planning and the like that are inherent within a permitted policy of indefinite preservation of embryos.[1]

Uterine lavage represents a somewhat unusual extension of the technique of IVF through embryo transfer. In this process, a fertile woman is impregnated with semen; the resultant embryo is washed out of the uterus before implantation and is transferred to the infertile patient. While such a process might be seen as constituting an abortion, for reasons discussed below (chapter 5), it is improbable that it would be considered so in the United Kingdom. The Warnock Committee looked at the matter from the point of view of the donor and concluded (para 7.5) that the risks were such that the technique of embryo donation by lavage should not be used at the present time. The method seems to us to be so comparable to the practice of animal husbandry that there are good policy reasons for its proscription. Nevertheless, the current British legislation clearly allows for the use of embryos formed in vivo (1990 Act, Sch 3, para 7).

18 *Davis v Davis* 842 SW 2d 588 (Tenn Sup Ct, 1992). The case was, however, clouded by the fact that Mrs Davis now only wanted to donate the embryos; the court recognised that the issue would have been closer had she still wanted to become pregnant.

19 R Cockburn 'Parents Contest Embryo Access' Times, 31 October 1989, p 12. This case seems to have been settled out of court. For discussion of it and *Davis*, see C Corns 'Deciding the Fate of Frozen Embryos' (1990) 64 L Inst J 273.

20 See p 70.

 1 For a very full and helpful review of the many legal problems introduced by artificial reproductive methods, see H Brown, M Dent, L M Dyer et al 'Legal Rights and Issues Surrounding Conception, Pregnancy, and Birth' (1986) 39 Vanderbilt LR 597. The relatively academic problems of succession of 'twin embryos' that are implanted at different times are settled by the elimination of 'storage time' from the age of an embryo (1990 Act, s 3(4)).

The surplus fetus

The management of both infertility and childlessness due to abnormalities in the female provokes a particular problem of multiple pregnancies. Hormone treatment of primary infertility can be over-successful and result in pregnancies involving anything up to sextuplets – and, occasionally, beyond. As to childlessness, the chances of in vitro fertilisation ending in a live birth are improved by the insertion of 2-3 embryos and more than one of these then implants in about 30% of those transfers that result in pregnancy.[2] Few people can afford to bring up several children at the same time. Moreover, the common scenario of high order pregnancies which lead to live birth is that the infants are of very low birthweight; they occupy the facilities of a neonatal intensive care unit to a disproportionate extent; the parents face the spectre of their children dying one by one over a period of weeks and those that survive may well be brain damaged as a result of prematurity.[3] It is largely in order to circumvent this prospect that the current United Kingdom Code of Practice now decrees that no more than three eggs or embryos are to be transferred in any one cycle in any circumstances. Nevertheless, even triplets[4] may be an unwelcome result of a successful treatment and evidence has been adduced that more eggs are being used in the GIFT process leading to a multiple pregnancy rate of over 40%.[5] Moreover, the superfetation of hormone therapy is hard to control. Thus, the clinician may well be faced with the option of pregnancy reduction in utero.

This process, which is carried out at or earlier than the twelfth week of pregnancy, is generally known as selective reduction of pregnancy, but it has been pointed out that, as the individual fetal characteristics are unknown at the time, there is no 'selection' other than that dictated by operative convenience. We prefer the suggested alternative of reduction of multifetal pregnancy[6] – a description which serves to distinguish the process from the truly selective termination that may be used, say, when one fetus of twins is found to be defective. The legality of the practice depends upon additions to the Abortion Act 1967 arising from the 1990 Act, s 37(5); its morality is inseparable from that of abortion and we return to the subject below.[7]

Surrogate motherhood

Surrogate motherhood requires the active co-operation of an otherwise uninvolved woman in the process of pregnancy and birth. It thus introduces a third party into what

2 HFEA *Sixth Annual Report* (1997) Table 4A.
3 In a particularly publicised case, a woman conceived octuplets through a series of adventures and misadventures. She decided to maintain her pregnancy and all eight were stillborn at 19 weeks: Leading Article 'The Death of Babies' Daily Telegraph, 4 October 1996, p 25. At much the same time, a furore erupted when a woman carrying twins elected to have one of them aborted: C Dyer 'Selective Abortions Hit the Headlines' (1996) 313 BMJ 380.
4 Some 8% of clinical pregnancies derived from the transfer of three embryos will result in a triple pregnancy.
5 *Sixth Report of the Interim Licensing Authority* (1991) p 15.
6 R L Berkowitz and L Lynch 'Selective Reduction: An Unfortunate Misnomer' (1990) 75 Obstet Gynecol 873.
7 See p 145.

has been, up till now, essentially a doctor-patient relationship. The fact that the third party may have a financial interest in a medical treatment has led to a general antipathy to the procedure in the United Kingdom. Commercialism is, however, accepted in American medical practice – for example, blood is bought and resold – and there is considerable activity in this field in the United States.

At its simplest, the infertile woman and her husband arrange with another woman that she will carry a child conceived by artificial insemination with the husband's semen and will surrender it to its genetic father after birth. The alternative, which also concludes with the return of the infant to its genetic parents, is that an embryo is created in vitro from the gametes of a husband and wife and is then implanted in the uterus of a 'surrogate'. There are several reasons for separating the two processes, which are often described as partial or complete surrogacy; we prefer to refer to the latter technique more descriptively as 'womb-leasing'. We return to this subject below but, for the present, we limit discussion to the more easily achieved objective of impregnating a fertile woman. That process, as defined, is akin to a pre-emptive adoption with the advantage that the 'adopted' baby shares at least half its genes with its 'adopting' parents. Since the practical possibility of following the normal process of adoption is decreasing steadily, there is much to be said, theoretically, in favour of surrogate motherhood as a treatment for the woman who is irrevocably childless. Yet the great majority of commentators and, possibly, the medical profession as a whole, shy away from accepting it as a means of satisfying an urge to parenthood – why?[8] The reason was summarised many years ago by Winslade:[9] 'The practice has a potential for economic exploitation, moral confusion and psychological harm to the surrogate mothers, the prospective adoptive parents and the children.' This view crystallises the debate which has surrounded surrogacy since it first came to the attention of British courts some two decades ago.

The legal issues
The possibility of exploitation is exemplified in the analogy between surrogate motherhood and adoption. The purchase of babies is expressly forbidden by the Adoption Act 1976, s 57, and all American states have laws prohibiting 'baby selling' or private placement of infants. Thus, even before the recent upsurge in interest, there was a real possibility that surrogate motherhood – and particularly that which involved some form of commercial transaction – was already illegal.[10] There is, however, much to be said for the view that surrogate motherhood and adoption are distinct, albeit closely linked, processes.[11] In the first place, the surrogate mother is not pregnant, nor has she a child to support at the time the proposition is put to her. She is under no pregnancy-related economic pressure and a main reason for prohibiting a trade in babies is, therefore, absent. Against this, it has been pointed out[12] that 40%

---

8 An opposing view is expressed by I Craft 'Surrogacy' (1992) 47 Brit J Hosp Med 728.

9 W J Winslade 'Surrogate Mothers: Private Right or Public Wrong?' (1981) 7 J Med Ethics 153.

10 In the first American test, the court agreed on the fundamental right to include a third party in a pregnancy arrangement but excluded the right to carry a child for payment: *Doe v Kelly* 307 NW 2d 438 (Mich, 1981).

11 I M Mady 'Surrogate Mothers: The Legal Issues' (1981) 7 Am J Law Med 323; I Davies 'Contracts to Bear Children' (1985) 11 J Med Ethics 61.

12 P Parker 'Motivation of Surrogate Mothers: Initial Findings' (1983) 140 Am J Psychiat 117.

of volunteer surrogate mothers in the United States are unemployed or are in receipt of welfare;[13] surrogacy may, therefore, be one response to economic need but the element of urgency that is a halmark of adoption is still lacking. The nature of any proposed payment is also different in the two cases. In one it is a matter of purchase of a commodity for sale; in the other it is a matter of expenses coupled with payment for services rendered[14] – not totally unlike a man paying for the support of the mother of his illegitimate child and supplementing this with a generous present on her bringing it to term. Subject to specific legislation, the legality of surrogacy associated with exchange of money depends upon the validity of this distinction which has, in fact, been accepted both in the United States[15] and in the United Kingdom;[16] thus, there is no intrinsic objection to adoption following receipt of a reasonable stipend by the surrogate. Some formula must be evolved if the commissioning couple is to receive the child – for the surrogate, at least in the United Kingdom, is clearly its mother irrespective of whether or not it is the product of her own ovum and, if she is married and conception was via consensual donor insemination, her husband is its father (1990 Act, s 28); moreover, neither can simply surrender their parental duties.[17] Adoption could provide the solution, but the procedure is often tedious and the issue of an adoption order cannot be guaranteed.[18] The 1990 Act, s 30 now offers an alternative by which the court may make an order providing for a child carried by a surrogate to be treated in law as the child of the commissioning couple, provided that the gametes of one or both have been involved and that they are married and have attained the age of 18. This is subject to the consent of the surrogate and, where applicable, the father of the child, including a man who is the father by virtue of the 1990 Act, s 28 – if they can be found;[19]; moreover, their agreement is ineffective if made less than six weeks after the child's birth. The application must be made within six months of the birth and the child must be living with the commissioning couple. Applications are heard in private and a guardian ad litem is appointed to watch over the child's interests. It is a stipulation that no money, other than reasonable expenses, has been given to the surrogate other than that authorised by the court.[20]

13 M Freeman, in a powerful exposure of the 'exploitation' theory, pointed out that a similar result would probably obtain were a matched sample of applications for a factory job to be considered: 'Is Surrogacy Exploitative?' in S A M McLean (ed) *Legal Issues in Human Reproduction* (1989) ch 7.
14 R Macklin 'Is There Anything Wrong With Surrogate Motherhood? An Ethical Analysis' (1988) 16 Law Med Hlth Care 57. For a strongly opposing view, see B Cohen 'Surrogate Mothers: Whose Baby Is It?' (1984) 10 Am J Law Med 243.
15 *Surrogate Parenting Associates Inc v Commonwealth of Kentucky* 704 SW 2d 209 (Ky, 1986). Kentucky legislation has since been altered.
16 *Re an adoption application (surrogacy)* [1987] Fam 81, [1987] 2 All ER 826; *C v S* 1996 SLT 1387, sub nom *C and C v GS* 1996 SCLR 837.
17 Children Act 1989, s 2(9).
18 S M Cretney and J M Masson *Principles of Family Law* (5th edn, 1990) p 712 regard these cases as 'in family' – though the concept seems to involve an uneasy mix of genetic, legal and social relationships.
19 For some of the difficulties, see *Re Q (parental order)* [1996] 1 FLR 369.
20 Parental Orders (Human Fertilisation and Embryology) Regulations 1994, SI 1994/2767; Parental Orders (Human Fertilisation and Embryology) (Scotland) Regulations 1994, SI 1994/2804. For analysis, see A Grubb 'Surrogate Arrangements and Parental Orders' (1995) 3 Med LRev 204; K McK Norrie 'The Parental Orders (Human Fertilisation and Embryology) (Scotland) Regulations 1994' (1995) Fam LB 13-3. The first 'order' was, in fact, made pre-emptively: *Re W (minors) (surrogacy)* [1991] 1 FLR 385.

The problem of money has, in fact, exercised the courts – particularly as to the relationship between surrogacy and adoption. *Re an adoption application (surrogacy)*[1] was heard before the s 30 regulations were in place. This was a remarkably amateurish affair. The principals met casually, the surrogate being motivated by a desire to help a childless couple, and she was impregnated naturally. A fee of £10,000 was agreed but half of this was returned by the surrogate on the grounds that she had obtained money from the sale of her story. All the principals, the judge said later, were supremely happy. They were also inexperienced and it was not for a further two and a half years that the 'parents' applied for an adoption. The issue was, thus, whether or not such 'payment or reward' would invalidate an adoption order.[2] In summary, Latey J held that a surrogacy arrangement would not contravene the Adoption Act so long as the payments made did not constitute an element of profit or financial reward; he thought that the payments in the instant case did no more than compensate for the inconveniences of pregnancy. More significantly, he showed his faith in the commissioning parents by stating that, if necessary, he would apply his powers to allow some profit and reward[3] retrospectively in the interests of the child. An adoption order was made. Despite some doubts being expressed at the time,[4] this relatively courageous decision has been followed without qualm.[5]

The conditions in the comparable, though more recent, Scottish case, *C v S*,[6] were something of an antithesis. The surrogate, who was unemployed, received £8,000 in expenses but then regretted her decision to give up the child. A parental order was, therefore, unavailable on the grounds of lack of consent by the legal mother and the commissioning couple sought to adopt the child a year after its birth. The sheriff, while holding that consent to adoption was being withheld unreasonably, none the less refused an adoption order because he considered the monetary transaction breached the terms of the statute;[7] a custody order was granted. On appeal to the Court of Session, however, it was held that the money had been paid in the expectation of a parental order rather than of adoption; the Act had, accordingly, not been contravened and an adoption order was substituted. The policy as to the authorisation of 'reasonable' payments in respect of surrogacy is, thus, harmonised on both sides of the Border.[8]

The question of consent to a parental order leads to consideration of the validity of any contract made between a commissioning couple and the surrogate. The position in the United Kingdom is now clear – no surrogacy arrangement is enforceable by or against any of the persons making it.[9] In so legislating, the United Kingdom Parliament has followed the majority trend of those countries that have

---

1   [1987] Fam 81, [1987] 2 All ER 826.
2   Adoption Act 1976, s 57(1).
3   Ibid, s 57(3).
4   C Dyer 'Babies in the Courts' The Times, 13 March 1987, p 15.
5   *Re Q (parental order)* [1996] 1 FLR 369. The sum of £8,280 was authorised retrospectively.
6   1996 SLT 1387, sub nom *C and C v GS* 1996 SCLR 837.
7   Adoption (Scotland) Act 1978, ss 24(2) and 51.
8   Although this decision may seem a trifle contrived, it was clearly motivated by the best interests of the child. It is probable that an adoption order could, in any case, have been granted on these grounds alone: L Edwards and A Griffiths *Family Law* (1997) p 174.
9   Surrogacy Arrangements Act 1985, s 1A, inserted by Human Fertilisation and Embryology Act 1990, s 36.

addressed the subject; whether it is the correct approach is open to argument. Undoubtedly, it is the nature of the contract which poses the greatest complications for surrogate motherhood. Non-commercial surrogacy is not illegal in the United Kingdom and is not, therefore, a practice which is fundamentally against public policy. To introduce deliberately the uncertainties of a breakable agreement seems to do little more than reflect an ambivalence in a Parliament which, while unable to follow the German model in outlawing the practice,[10] seems determined to oblate any signs of approval – surrogacy is to be seen as a form of legal liberty. A surrogate arrangement is clearly a difficult contract to draw up – it must allow for changes of heart on either side, illness in the surrogate, abnormalities in the resultant child and other imponderables, some of which, such as an abortion within the terms of the Abortion Act 1967, can be seen as basic rights. Nevertheless, it can be done; indeed, the judicial decision at first instance in the celebrated American case of *Baby M*[11] was based very largely on the law of contract. Rather than, in effect, hiding the issues, we feel it would be better to grasp the nettle and lay down what a surrogacy arrangement could *not* include – for example, a contract to pay an unreasonable sum of money, an undertaking not to accept a therapeutic abortion and the like. The rights and wrongs of an individual case should be subject to more than individual judicial interpretations – a point which was taken up by the judge in *Re an adoption application (surrogacy)*.[12]

Opinions may similarly differ as to the general morality of surrogate motherhood. Outside the United States, however, there appears to be a consensus which condemns the blatant commercialisation of child-bearing by way of intermediate, profit-making agencies. This aspect has been the subject of legislation in many jurisdictions[13] – it is to be found in the Surrogacy Arrangements Act 1985 in the United Kingdom. The main purpose of the Act is to prohibit the making of a surrogacy arrangement on a commercial basis.[14] The principals involved are expressly excused from criminal liability (s 2(2)); moreover, payments made to or for the benefit of the surrogate are not regarded as being made on a commercial basis (s 2(3)). On the face of it, this hurried and somewhat ill-prepared measure is broadly acceptable. It has, however, confused the position of professionals, such as doctors and lawyers, whose services in any arrangement are clearly desirable but who would probably expect some remuneration. Theoretically, they could give general advice but might be unable to be paid for intervention on behalf of any of the principals without contravening s 2.[15] One potential effect of the Act is, therefore, to discourage counselling in and supervision of surrogate motherhood.; it is on these grounds that the BMA, while still regarding surrogacy as 'a reproductive option of last resort', has recognised the

---

10 Embryonenschutzgesetz (Embryo Protection Act) 1990, s 1(1)(vii).
11 *Re Baby M* 525 A 2d 1128 (NJ, 1987).
12 [1987] Fam 81 at 85, [1987] 2 All ER 826 at 829, Latey J.
13 In Australia, see Infertility (Medical Procedures) Act 1984, s 30 (Victoria); Family Relationships Act Amendment Act 1988, s 6 (South Australia). For the situation in the United States, see R A Charo 'Legislative Approaches to Surrogate Motherhood' (1989) 16 Law Med Hlth Care 96.
14 Advertising by way of newspapers, periodicals and telecommunications is proscribed in s 3, the criminal liability resting on the proprietor, editor, publisher etc.
15 S Sloman 'Surrogacy Arrangements Act 1985' (1985) 135 NLJ 978. This may, however, be to take too pessimistic a view. I Kennedy and A Grubb *Medical Law: Text with Materials* (2nd edn, 1994) p 848 believe that the doctor can be paid legitimately when taking part in a privately arranged surrogacy. A further minor difficulty as to confidentiality has been eradicated in the Human Fertilisation and Embryology (Disclosure of Information) Act 1992.

widespread public acceptance of surrogacy and has softened its attitude to medical participation in the procedure.[16] We feel that, if required, the courts would certainly take a pragmatically sensible approach – especially in view of their generally sympathetic attitude to surrogacy, which can be traced through a progressive series of decisions.

The British cases
The earliest example, *A v C*,[17] arose some time before 'assisted reproduction' became widely acceptable. It was not fully reported but the gist is that an unmarried couple arranged for a prostitute's friend to be inseminated on the understanding that the resultant child was returned to them; a fee of £3,000 was involved. The mother changed her mind and the father applied for access; this was granted in the child's best interests. Nevertheless, the judge described the agreement as 'pernicious and void'[18] and, for reasons which are unrecorded, the Court of Appeal unanimously reversed the decision and decreed that A should not be allowed to see his son.

Re C (a minor)[19] was the first case to be fully covered but was, essentially, a matter of wardship. An American couple arranged a surrogacy in England through a commercial agency. As soon as the child was born, the local authority obtained a place of safety order under the Children and Young Persons Act 1969, s 28, in the belief that it would be abandoned by its mother; the father then initiated wardship proceedings. Latey J refused to discuss the rights and wrongs of surrogacy and concentrated solely on the welfare of the child – how she had been born was irrelevant. On these grounds, he considered that no one was better equipped than the commissioning couple to care for her; accordingly, he gave them care and control while, at the same time, continuing the wardship – even so, permission was given for the baby to live outside the jurisdiction. For present purposes, the most important aspect of the case is that the judge rejected suggestions that the commissioning couple were unfit parents because they had entertained a commercial surrogacy arrangement.

Surrogacy itself, and particularly the relationship between that process and adoption, was more directly considered in *Re an adoption application (surrogacy)*.[20] The facts and the outcome – including the liberal stance of the trial judge – have been discussed above.[1]

Re P (minors)[2] was heard contemporaneously with the adoption case. In this instance, the surrogate declined to hand over the twins she had conceived by a married professional man. The children were made wards of court and were allowed to stay with their natural mother; the court action was essentially a matter of custody. By the time the case came to be heard, the twins had been with their natural mother for five

---

16 BMA *Changing Conceptions of Motherhood – the Practice of Surrogacy in Britain* (1996). At least two surrogacies have been funded through the NHS: 'NHS Pays for Sister's Surrogacy' The Times, 10 April 1996, p 11.

17 (1985) 8 Fam Law 170. Commentators at the time saw the case as of interest from the AID aspect only.

18 From a report by D C Parker 'Legal Aspects of Artificial Insemination and Embryo Transfer' (1982) 12 Fam Law 103.

19 [1985] FLR 846.

20 [1987] Fam 81, [1987] 2 All ER 826.

 1 See p 80.

 2 [1987] 2 FLR 421.

months and the judge was strongly influenced by the degree of maternal bonding that had already arisen. Accordingly, he found 'nothing to outweigh the advantages to these children of preserving the link to the mother to whom they are bonded, and who has exercised a satisfactory degree of maternal care'. Once again, it is to be noted that there was no criticism of either the commissioning parents or of the surrogate for having entered into a surrogacy agreement. It cannot, however, have been a happy arrangement – the natural mother sought a maintenance order.[3]

One further case has been officially reported – *Re W*[4] – when, as noted above, the judge was prepared to pre-empt the law in order to ensure bonding of 'womb-leased' twins with their genetic parents. Following this, there was a dearth of new cases until the prototype Scottish case of *C v S*[5] which has been discussed already.[6] One wonders at the reason for the hiatus; the probability is that surrogacy is now so well established that cases are now no longer regarded as meriting report unless there are special circumstances. This situation may not, however, last; there have been recent newspaper reports of examples which have had a less than happy ending.[7]

The American scene

It would be impossible in a book of this size to take a comprehensive view of similar situations in America, where surrogacy appears to be relatively common – at least in the United States. It is clear that the great majority of arrangements proceed smoothly; only when there is conflict do cases come to public notice and it may well be that this is a major underlying reason for the general antipathy to the procedure. The rather different attitude to publicity which pertains in America may also contribute to its image as projected across the Atlantic. None the less, there are lessons to be learnt from some of the more notorious cases – in particular, perhaps, that of *Re Baby M*.[8]

In that case, the surrogate, who had agreed to a fee of $10,000, refused to relinquish her child and, in fact, absconded with it contrary to a court order. When the matter came to trial, the judge was concerned to limit the issues to those of strict law and, in this respect, he rejected any relevance of the adoption laws. He concluded, on the one hand, that a valid contract had been made and broken and, on the other, that the state's interest in the welfare of its children dictated that the child be adopted by the commissioning couple. The Supreme Court of New Jersey, however, had no hesitation in overturning this decision – and doing so forcibly.[9] The surrogacy

---

3   D Brahams 'Surrogacy, Adoption and Custody' (1987) 1 Lancet 817. For contemporary discussion of these cases see J Montgomery 'Constructing a Family – After a Surrogate Birth' (1986) 49 MLR 635; S P de Cruz 'Surrogacy, Adoption and Custody: A Case Study' (1988) 18 Fam Law 100.
4   *Re W (minors) (surrogacy)* [1991] 1 FLR 385.
5   1996 SLT 1387, sub nom *C and C v GS* 1996 SCLR 837.
6   See p 80 above.
7   In one, the surrogate was thought to be acting on behalf of two families at the same time; the case is said to be under police investigation: C Dyer 'Surrogate Mother Refuses to Give Up Baby' (1997) 314 BMJ 250. In the other, there were allegations that the surrogate had fabricated an abortion in order to keep the child: D Kennedy 'Minister Hints at Change in the Law' The Times, 16 May 1997, p 2. As a result, the UK ministers have set up a Review of Surrogacy Arrangements under the chairmanship of Professor Margaret Brazier. See now *Surrogacy: Review for Health Ministers of Current Arrangements for Payment and Regulation*, Report of the Review Team (Cm 4068, 1998).
8   525 A 2d 1128 (NJ, 1987).
9   537 A 2d 1227 (NJ Sup Ct, 1988).

contract was found to be against public policy and, as such, invalid; both the termination of the mother's parental rights and the adoption order were voided. None the less, the Supreme Court could find nothing in law against voluntary, non-commercial surrogacy, provided that the arrangement did not include any clause binding on the surrogate to surrender her baby. As a result, the court was able to dissociate the contractual aspects of surrogacy and the 'best interests' of the child and followed the lower court in awarding custody to the commissioning parents.[10]

A contrast is to be seen in the Californian case of *Johnson v Calvert*.[11] In this case, the surrogate was paid $10,000 to carry the embryo of a commissioning couple. After gestating for six months, she changed her mind as to handing over the child and the court was asked to decide on its parentage. The trial court held that a surrogate contract was both legal and enforceable and that the commissioning couple were the child's genetic, biological and natural parents; no parental rights attached to the surrogate. This disposition was upheld on appeal. In dismissing a further appeal, the Supreme Court of California held that it was the intention of the parties when making the arrangement which decided the issue when there were conflicting grounds on which it was possible to establish parentage – in this case, the surrogate had done no more than 'facilitate' the procreation of the commissioning couple's child. The court further stated that surrogate contracts did not violate any existing public policy as to adoption; any payments in the former were, effectively, made for services rendered and not as compensation for the transfer of parental rights.[12] Needless to say, this opinion has been severely criticised as fundamentally misunderstanding the biological realities of the surrogate's contribution.[13]

In our previous edition, we wondered as to the significance of the contrast between *Re Baby M* and *Johnson v Calvert* and some light may be shed by the more recent case of *In re Marriage of Moschetta*.[14] Here, the 'parents' of a year-old child, born by standard surrogacy, separated and the surrogate then claimed legal parentage. The Court of Appeal was, then, able to distinguish the case from *Johnson* because there was no conflict as to maternity – the surrogate was both the genetic and the gestational mother and was to be regarded as such. It is, however, to be noted that the court distinguished the definition of status from the allocation of custody.

10 See G P Smith 'The Case of Baby M: Love's Labor Lost' (1988) 16 Law Med Hlth Care 121. The contrast between *Baby M* and *Johnson v Calvert* 851 P 2d 776 (Cal, 1993) is very marked. We wonder if this really indicates a change of direction in the United States or whether it does no more than reflect a difference between Eastern and Western cultures in that country.

11 *Johnson v Calvert* 851 P 2d 776 (Cal, 1993) discussed by A Grubb 'Surrogate Contract: Parentage' (1994) 2 Med LRev 239. See also G Annas 'Using Genes to Define Motherhood: The California Solution' (1992) 326 New Engl J Med 417 discussing the decision in the lower court. Others may, however, feel as strongly as to the importance of the genetic affiliation: D R Bromham 'Surrogacy: The Evolution of Opinion' (1992) 47 Brit J Hosp Med 767.

12 The situation as to commercialism of surrogacy in the United States is hard to unravel. It seems that, while *Johnson v Calvert* clears the way in California, at least five states have passed statutes restricting the practice: R A Charo 'Legislative Approaches to Surrogate Motherhood' (1988) 16 Law Med Hlth Care 96.

13 R B Oxman 'California's Experiment in Surrogacy' (1993) 341 Lancet 1468.

14 30 Cal Rep 2d 893 (1994), discussed in detail by A Grubb 'Surrogate Contract: Parentage' (1995) 3 Med LRev 219.

The cases assessed

The British cases indicate that the public, as represented by its judiciary, will be sympathetic to surrogate motherhood – an attitude which probably derives more from the *fait accompli* nature of the proceedings than from any basic empathy with the practice. It can be taken that no decisions will be driven by antagonism.

Accordingly, it is very unlikely the a parental order will be withheld in the event of application by the commissioning parents and consent on the part of the surrogate and the legal father – if any. While it would always be possible for the court to override agreement by the parties, it is difficult to see how the motivation of the couple and their almost inevitable material status could be irrelevant to the child's 'best interests' – which is not to say that the latter will always take precedence.[15] In so far as it is possible to apply pre-1990 standards to the present day conditions, the indications are that the prime factor in the court's thinking in the event of disagreement would be the extent of family bonding – we suspect that much would depend on where the child was living at the time of adjudication. It would, however, be impossible to generalise – the single common feature would lie in the search for the child's best interests and it is this which would determine the direction and method of disposal of each case. There is no indication of what would result if the commissioning couple were to refuse to accept the infant; the precise details of each case would, again, be all-important, but it is difficult to see, in general, an alternative to intervention by the local authority by way of care proceedings. The position of the surrogate's husband under the terms of the 1990 Act, s 28(2) might then be problematical.

While there is no evidence on the point, we fancy that much the same approach would be taken whether the surrogate had incubated her own egg or that of the commissioning woman. This, however, might well not be the case in the United States where, judging from the Californian cases, major significance would be attributed to genetic status. As Grubb has put it:

> Infertile couples who seek surrogacy linked with IVF treatment can be reasonably certain they will come out of the arrangement . . . as the child's parents. By contrast, couples who resort to traditional surrogacy . . . will have no such reassurance.[16]

The morality of surrogate motherhood

What, then, is so special about the morality of surrogacy? Clearly, the most important difference lies in the inclusion of a third party to procreation – and in such a way as to provoke not only serious moral but also important socio-political questions; and, since the surrogate is, by definition, a woman, the latter are gender-based. Stripped to its essentials, surrogacy can be viewed from this perspective as being one way of exploiting women for the benefit of men[17] – a matter to which we have alluded above. The alternative is to see the outlawing of the practice as outright paternalism which denies a woman a chance to use her body as she pleases. It seems fair to say that the feminist movement is divided

---

15 See eg *Re P (minors)* [1987] 2 FLR 421.
16 (1995) 3 Med LRev 219 at 221.
17 G J Annas 'Fairy Tales Surrogate Mothers Tell' (1988) 16 Law Med Hlth Care 27.

in its approach;[18] the argument is one which we will not take further here save to note the difficulties that arise from generalising in personal and individual affairs.

The second major objection lies in the suggestion that surrogacy is 'baby-selling'. It is possible, however, to maintain that a baby is 'sold' only if persons with no genetic association purchase an infant that is already in being. It seems more logical to regard any monetary transaction in respect of surrogacy as payment for gestational expertise and, as the British cases indicate, the critical distinction lies between reasonable recompense and inducement to gestate.[19] The great majority of assisted reproduction is centred on private health care and, even within a public health service, there is indirect payment for obstetric expertise. Looked at in this way, either both surrogacy and embryo transfer are 'baby purchasing' or neither is – and there is no suggestion that sophisticated reproductive techniques are immoral on this score. Thirdly, it is widely believed that surrogacy must have an ill-effect on children in general or on the individual resultant child. The former, represented by a fear that children may become 'objects for barter', is valid only so long as surrogacy itself is categorised as objectionable; the premise disappears once it is regarded as a legitimate treatment for childlessness. Any effect on the individual child by way of confusion as to parentage is comparable to that which we have discussed in relation to other forms of assisted reproduction. Whether or not there is a detriment seems to us to be unproven but if there is, it should not be insurmountable – certainly no more than in other examples of the unconventional family. Even so, there is little doubt that the provisions of the 1990 Act, s 13(5) – discussed above[20] – are likely to discourage professional implication in surrogacy outside licensed clinics.

In favour of surrogacy, it must be remembered that, as noted above, it *is* a treatment for some forms of childlessness. Such cases may be rare, yet to encourage treatment by way of ovum donation for the woman who is childless because of ovarian inadequacy and, at the same time, to forbid surrogacy for the one who has no uterus, smacks of unfair discrimination.[1]

Surrogacy could, however, be used for purely selfish reasons – for example, a desire to have a child without interference with a career. Such hedonistic womb-leasing is so comparable to nineteenth-century wet-nursing that the process as a whole has become suspect. This is unfortunate because there are, in fact, far more conditions in which womb-leasing would be the preferred treatment of childlessness than there are those in which standard surrogacy would be indicated. Abnormality of the uterus or other causes of persistent miscarriage are commoner than loss of both uterus and ovaries; moreover, womb-leasing is the logical answer to an inability to carry, rather than to conceive, a baby – say, by virtue of heart disease, diabetes and the like. The other important difference is that, in womb-leasing, the commissioning

---

18 L B Andrews 'Surrogate Motherhood: The Challenge for Feminists' (1988) 16 Law Med Hlth Care 72. A further example of the debate is to be found in S Dodds and K Jones 'Surrogacy and Autonomy' (1989) 3 Bioethics 18.

19 The court in *Johnson v Calvert* considered many of these points and rejected the suggestion that surrogacy arrangements violated public policy. For a relatively recent debate, see A van Niekerk and L van Zyl 'Commercial Surrogacy and the Commodification of Children: An Ethical Perspective' (1995) 14 Med Law 163.

20 See p 81.

1 I Davies 'Contracts to Bear a Child' (1985) 11 J Med Ethics 61; Bromham (1992) 47 Brit J Hosp Med 767.

couple are the genetic parents. Thus, one would imagine that the surrogate, having no relationship to her fetus, would be less exposed to psychological trauma on surrendering it; the receiving parents are in precisely the same end position as natural coital patents; and the child suffers no 'genetic insecurity'. Certainly, womb-leasing involves the use of high-grade technology – but even this serves to remove some of the intuitive distaste provoked by standard surrogacy. Neither the Warnock Committee nor the resultant legislation distinguish between partial and full surrogacy; we feel, however, that the better argument lies in favour of clearly separating the two.[2]

There is, however, one aspect of womb-leasing that merits special attention – that is, the use of intrafamilial surrogates. Not only does this seriously disturb familial relationships but the procedure opens the door to emotional coercion. It appears to be a practice which should be made unlawful – although not everyone would agree.[3]

The future

At present, non-commercial surrogacy services do not come within the framework of the law but, in so far as the procedure normally involves artificial insemination, the Human Fertilisation and Embryology Authority may have indirect control of the practice. This, however, is only partial, since the 1990 Act does not cover insemination performed privately – under s 4, a licence is required by any person who carries out artificial insemination 'in the course of providing treatment services for any woman' and treatment services are defined (s 2) as meaning '. . . services provided *to the public or a section of the public* for the purpose of assisting women to carry children' (emphasis added). A further conceptual difficulty arises in that a licence is not required when '...the services are being provided for the woman and the man together'. Is a doctor who artificially inseminates a surrogate with the sperm of a commissioning father providing treatment services for the woman and the man together? If so, he does not require a licence – but it is generally agreed that this cannot be the correct interpretation. The better interpretation is that treatment for a woman and a man together is treatment for a couple who are consulting the doctor for a shared problem – that is, intra-familial or intra-partnership childlessness – or, perhaps simpler, who intend to bring up the child together. That being so, AID in the context of surrogacy is lawful only if done privately or, when provided as a public service, under cover of a licence. This leaves an unsatisfactory dichotomy, the solution of which is central to the control of the process. Most people would now agree with the minority of the Warnock Committee[4] that it should remain available as a treatment option.[5] Nevertheless, most would also agree that it must be controlled.[6]

2   Theoretically, womb-leasing should be the preferred surrogacy method for those of the Jewish faith as 'jewishness' is transferred through the female line. In fact, current Israeli law states that surrogacy is legal in that country only if the ovum does not come from the surrogate: R H B Fishman 'Surrogate Motherhood Becomes Legal in Israel' (1996) 347 Lancet 756.
3   A recent case reported from England involved a post-menopausal woman acting on behalf of her childless daughter. Lady Warnock is reported as saying 'It is a wonderful idea': D Kennedy 'Surrogacy Attempt Divides Experts' The Times, 3 July 1995, p 8. The baby was successfully delivered by caesarian section.
4   Cmnd 9314, p 64, n 12 above, 'Expression of Dissent A'.
5   So far as we know, in the English-speaking world, only Queensland has criminalised the procedure in all its forms: Surrogate Parenthood Act 1988 (Qd).
6   As agreed by the Brazier Committee: see p 83, n 7 above.

For our part, we suggest, first, that the procedure should be unlawful unless it is undertaken for a bona fide medical reason, other options having been considered and properly rejected.[7] As a corollary, any doubts as to the legality of active, paid intervention by health carers and lawyers should be dispelled by their specific exclusion from the terms of the Surrogacy Arrangements Act 1985; the possibility of unaided, amateurish attempts – exemplified in *Re an adoption application (surrogacy)*[8] – should be positively avoided. Secondly, the parties should be adequately counselled.[9] Thirdly, as discussed above, we see no advantage in merely declaring surrogate contracts unenforceable; it would not be difficult to specify such contractual clauses as would be against the public interest. Fourthly, we feel it to be essential that any anomalies between the granting of adoption and parental orders should be removed – cases in which one process seems to be played off against the other are scarcely satisfactory. Finally, we would recommend that the whole procedure be placed under the supervision and control of a central authority which could, with advantage, be established as a committee of the HFEA, under which body the ground rules are already largely laid down and in operation.[10]

Effectively, then, we are making a plea for medicalising surrogacy – thus emphasising our view that surrogacy is the treatment of choice for a specific group of causes of childlessness and is, therefore, comparable to any other 'treatment services' provided under cover of the 1990 Act. In present circumstances, it is unlikely that surrogacies will become widely available within the NHS. A major function of the central agency would be to control the 'tariff' in the private sector and, thus, to prevent the emergence of a 'market'. As Macklin[11] has put it – 'there is sufficient evidence of greed, corruption and duplicity of others in the public and private sectors to make us wary of allowing commercial practices to invade and dominate the delivery of health care'. Surrogacy has been likened by its opponents to prostitution. We reject this analogy; nevertheless, the two conditions share the common ground that it is the profit-making intermediary, not the principal, who is criminalised.

---

7 The HFEA *Code of Practice* (revised 1995) states (at para 3.20): 'The application of assisted conception techniques to initiate a surrogate pregnancy should only be considered where it is physically impossible or highly undesirable for medical reasons for the commissioning mother to carry the child.'

8 [1987] Fam 81, [1987] 2 All ER 826. It may well be that there are no real doubts (Kennedy and Grubb *Medical Law: Text with Materials* (2nd edn, 1994) p 848) but it could be made clearer.

9 A particularly blatant example of inadequate preparation of the principals was reported by G McBride 'US Battles over Surrogacy' (1990) 301 BMJ 1062. This point is, of course, covered under the 1990 Act, s 13(6); Sch 3, para 3(1)(a) and by the HFEA *Code of Practice*, Part 6, provided that the procedure is subject to licence.

10 The Brazier Committee (p 83, n 7 above), however, rejected this in favour of a Code of Practice devised by the Health Ministries.

11 (1988) 16 Law Med Hlth Care 57.

4   The control of fertility

Sterilisation

The aim of sterilisation is to end the patient's ability to reproduce. A number of surgical procedures may be used to achieve this. In males, the most common method is vasectomy, in which the vas deferens is cut and tied. Sterilisation in females is usually achieved by division or clipping of the fallopian tubes, which carry the ova between the ovary and the womb. An important feature of the operation from the legal and ethical standpoint is that it is generally intended to be irreversible; although it may be possible to repair the operation, prospective attempts to allow for reversibility are likely to result in procedures which fail in their primary purpose. Modern microsurgery has improved on this position – a development which may account for some of the apparently disparate court decisions that have been taken;[1] nevertheless, it is generally held that sterilisation will, or at least may well, bring a basic human function to an end.[2]

Ethical objections to sterilisation usually focus on this aspect of irreversible interference with the ability to reproduce. Those who object on these grounds would argue that such interference is unjustified, in that the individual may later undergo a change of mind and may wish to return to a position which is probably now closed. They would also stress that the decision to sterilise is one which is taken in the midst of subtle social and personal pressures; the likelihood of the decision being entirely free is, thereby, diminished – yet it is one that cannot easily be retracted. The objection of the Catholic Church is more direct. In Catholic teaching, sterilisation is a mutilation of the body which leads to the deprivation of a natural function and which must, therefore, be rejected. Sterilisation can only be accepted if it is carried out for strictly therapeutic purposes – that is, where it is necessary for the physical health of the patient; the performance of hysterectomy in the treatment of menorrhagia, for example, is admissible.[3] The secular counterpart lies in the concept of maim; although, historically, this refers to injuries which limit a man's capacity for military

1   See p 101 below.
2   Current methods also now allow for reversal of vasectomy – a success rate of up to 40% successful pregnancies is claimed. See A K Banergee and A Simpson 'Reversing Vasectomy' (1992) 304 BMJ 1130.
3   For a sensitive view from a Catholic clinician of this and other dilemmas, see J Poole *The Cross of Unknowing* (1989); 'Time for the Vatican to Bend' (1992) 339 Lancet 1340. On a world scale, the attitude of orthodox Islam is just as rigid: D A R Verkuyl 'Two World Religions and Family Planning' (1993) 342 Lancet 473.

service, the courts might well take exception, say, to castration on non-therapeutic grounds.[4] In so far as it is possible to identify a lay consensus on the matter, it is that sterilisation is an acceptable method of contraception provided that the person undergoing the operation is adequately informed of the implications. Very strong objections may be voiced, however, when there is any question as to the reality of the patient's consent and we return to the subject below.[5]

The legality of contraceptive sterilisation in the United Kingdom is now beyond doubt and only a small minority of other countries continue either to forbid the process altogether or to allow it only in narrowly defined circumstances. Not infrequently, there is a minimum age below which sterilisation on request will not be available; under United States federal requirements it is 21 years, in Denmark it is 25. Some jurisdictions require spousal consent, Japan being an example, but there is general resistance to this on the grounds that the decision is an individual matter to be decided by the individual. There is no doubt that this is the case in the United Kingdom; the Medical Defence Union has emphasised that the doctor owes a duty of care to the patient and not to his or her spouse[6] and the courts would never grant an injunction to stop sterilisation or vasectomy.[7] On the other hand, the very term 'family planning' implies a shared responsibility; the British Medical Association regards it as good medical practice to encourage potential patients to discuss such procedures with their partners[8] and we would certainly endorse such a policy. On purely practical grounds, the surgeon may wish to avoid involvement in divorce proceedings and the like. *Bravery*[9] is no longer an acceptable authority but Lord Evershed MR may still be regarded as correct in saying:

> It would not be difficult . . . to construct in imagination a case of grave cruelty on a wife founded on the progressive hurt to her health caused by an operation for sterilisation undergone by her husband in disregard of, or contrary to, the wife's wishes or natural instincts[10]

– and the alternative proposition would apply with equal force.

Liability for a failed sterilisation
This question of divided responsibility finds its counterpart in the first limb of legal liability – was there a duty of care and to whom was it owed? Clearly, if a man or woman seeks sterilisation independently, the doctor's duty of care is limited to that man or woman. By contrast, the doctor owes a duty to both partners if they come to

---

4 A similar legislative attitude is to be found in the Prohibition of Female Circumcision Act 1985. This raises the general question of self-inflicted injury, for which, see *R v Brown*, discussed at p 29 above.
5 See p 96.
6 (1987) 3 J Med Def Union (3) 24.
7 *Paton v British Pregnancy Advisory Service Trustees* [1979] QB 276 at 280, [1978] 2 All ER 987 at 990 per Sir George Baker P.
8 A Somerville (on behalf of the Working Party) *Medical Ethics To-day: Its Practice and Philosophy* (1993) p 110.
9 *Bravery v Bravery* [1954] 3 All ER 59, [1954] 1 WLR 1169, CA.
10 [1954] 3 All ER 59 at 62, [1954] 1 WLR 1169 at 1173.

him together seeking a limitation of fertility that is of benefit to both. It follows from either premise that the doctor cannot be held liable to a potential present or future sexual partner of his patient of whom he has no knowledge. While this would seem to be a relatively simple proposition, it has been the subject of extensive argument in the Court of Appeal. Here, it was confirmed that a woman who became pregnant by a man who had been told three years previously that he need take no contraceptive precautions had no cause of action against those who had given the advice.[11]

Given, however, that a duty of care has been established, liability for failed sterilisation will not be imposed unless it can be established that the failure to achieve contraception was due to medical negligence or to breach of contract rather than to the inherent possibility that conception might still occur after the operation due purely to the vagaries of nature. There are a number of important United Kingdom, Commonwealth and United States decisions which deal with the question.

The first problem to be solved in such circumstances is that of causation and this has, in turn, hinged upon the performance of the operator and, latterly, on the anterior advice given to the plaintiff. The question of competence is exemplified in the Canadian case of *Doiron v Orr*,[12] in which the operation agreed upon was one which was more remediable than was the conventional tubal ligation; the judge accepted that, having been bound by these conditions, the surgeon concerned had no liability for the subsequent pregnancy. By contrast, the court agreed that there had been technical negligence in the case of *Cataford v Moreau*,[13] in which there were no such extenuating circumstances. The courts in the United Kingdom show no evidence of bias against the plaintiff following negligently performed operations. Thus, in *Emeh*,[14] substantial damages were awarded for the birth of a child following sterilisation despite the fact that abortion was an available option; in *Benarr*,[15] the court went so far as to include damages to cover the private education of the resultant child.

The question of what constitutes a breach of any duty of care is addressed in detail in chapter 9. For the present, we need only draw attention to the fact that breach of duty is largely governed by the *Bolam*[16] principle, under which it is held that a doctor's action will not be held to be negligent if it conforms to a practice which would have been adopted by a responsible body of medical opinion. Thus, in *Venner*[17] a gynaecologist who accepted the patient's word that she could not be pregnant at the time of the operation was held to be not negligent on the grounds that others would

11 *Goodwill v British Pregnancy Advisory Service* [1996] 2 All ER 161, (1996) 31 BMLR 83.
12 (1978) 86 DLR (3d) 719.
13 (1978) 114 DLR (3d) 585. Discussed by R P Kouri in 'Comment' (1979) 57 Can Bar Rev 89.
14 *Emeh v Kensington and Chelsea and Westminster Area Health Authority* [1985] QB 1012, [1984] 3 All ER 1044, CA.
15 *Benarr v Kettering Health Authority* [1988] NLJR 179. As things now stand, this might well be regarded as unexceptional: see Brooke J in *Allen v Bloomsbury Health Authority* [1993] 1 All ER 651 at 662, (1993) 13 BMLR 47 at 59; *Crouchman v Burke* (1997) 40 BMLR 163.
16 *Bolam v Friern Hospital Management Committee* [1957] 2 All ER 118, [1957] 1 WLR 582.
17 *Venner v North East Essex Area Health Authority* (1987) Times, 21 February. We wonder if this would apply now. In the virtually identical case of *Allen v Bloomsbury Health Authority* [1993] 1 All ER 651, (1993) 13 BMLR 47, the authority admitted liability and the only matter in issue was the quantum of damages. In a still later case, damages of over £88,000 were awarded against a gynaecologist who failed to explain to a patient that she might be pregnant at the time of operation: *Crouchman v Burke* (1997) 40 BMLR 163.

have omitted a precautionary curettage in similar circumstances. As a result, it has come to be accepted that a judge cannot make a choice presented with two divergent expert opinions as to what was the correct procedure to adopt.[18] Despite the fact that *Bolam* is under severe attack, we will see that British courts have shown a disturbing tendency to extend its principles. A welcome halt has been called in *Fallows v Randle*,[19] in which the distinction between preferring an opinion – as in *Maynard* – and preferring an interpretation of the facts was neatly explained. In this case of failed female sterilisation, the rings occluding the fallopian tubes had either been placed negligently or had slipped off through no one's fault. In preferring the former sequence of events, Stuart Smith LJ had this to say:

> [The *Bolam* principle] has no application when what the judge has to decide is, on balance, which of the explanations [of failure] is to be preferred. This is a question of fact which the judge has to decide on the ordinary basis of a balance of probabilities.[20]

We suspect that the majority of actions based on the negligent *performance* of a sterilising operation are and will always be of this relatively simple type. Rather more interest centres on those actions in negligence and in contract which have been based on the grounds of inadequate provision of information as to the possibility of failure; there has been a steady evolution of such cases in the United Kingdom.

Often, the supposed deficit has proved to be no more than a matter of communication between doctor and patient. Thus, in the interesting case of *Thake v Maurice*,[1] the issue turned eventually on the definition of the word 'irreversible' – the defendant claiming that it implied no more than that the procedure could not be reversed by surgery while the plaintiff contended that it represented a contract to provide absolute sterility which was beyond recall by natural processes. After something of a *volte face* between the trial court and the Court of Appeal as to breach of contract, it was held that the surgeon had been negligent in his failure to warn of the possibility of natural reversal of vasectomy. A rather similar case turned on the interpretation of the words on the form signifying consent to operation which stated 'We understand that this means we can have no children' and which the plaintiffs contended amounted to a representation that the operation was foolproof; the trial judge, however, held that the words merely acknowledged that the intended effect of the operation was that the couple should not have more children and found for the defendants.[2] Such semantic difficulties had been foreseen in the important Australian case of *F v R*[3] when King CJ specifically drew attention to the need not only to warn of the possible complications of surgery but also of the risk of failure as to the intended end result.

---

18 *Maynard v West Midlands Regional Health Authority* [1985] 1 All ER 635, [1984] 1 WLR 634.
19 (1997) 8 Med LR 160.
20 Ibid at 165.
1 [1986] QB 644, [1984] 2 All ER 513; revsd [1986] QB 644, [1986] 1 All ER 497. It was later said of the trial stage of this case: 'I, for my part, think that . . . the less we say about that decision, the better' (per Slade LJ in *Eyre v Measday* [1986] 1 All ER 488 at 492).
2 *Worster v City and Hackney Health Authority* (1987) Times, 22 June. As a further hurdle, the plaintiffs may have to convince the court that they would have continued contraceptive methods if they had been informed of a risk: *Newell v Goldenberg* [1995] 6 Med LR 371.
3 (1983) 33 SASR 189, SC.

There have been further English cases involving much the same issues[4] – one of which concerned a woman who became pregnant while her husband was producing persistently negative seminal specimens[5] – but these are better discussed together under the heading of consent.[6]

A further major problem which the courts and commentators have identified in this area is that of the award of damages for the unexpected birth of a healthy child following breach of contract or negligent surgery. Objection to any award in such a context has been based on the view that a child is a blessing and that this constitutes a policy ground for the antipathy. The question was first fully addressed by the court in *Doiron v Orr*; the judge stated that he would have been prepared to award damages for mental anguish caused to the plaintiff, but was adamant in his refusal to accept that in such a case there could be liability for the cost of bringing up an unwanted child:

> I find this approach to a matter of this kind which deals with human life, the happiness of the child, the effect upon its thinking, upon its mind when it realised that there has been a case of this kind, that it is an unwanted mistake and that its rearing is being paid for by someone other than its parents, is just simply grotesque.[7]

Such rejection concentrates on the effect which an award might have on the child; in other cases, the focus has been more on the entitlement of the parents to damages. American courts have not taken a uniform approach to the problem but there are certainly several cases in which such redress has been refused; the view has, again, been that parents cannot be held to have been damaged by the blessing of children.[8] Elsewhere, a middle view has prevailed, the assumption being that it is illogical to suppose that a benefit – that of parenthood – can derive from failure to provide proper medical care.[9] The majority of states allow recovery for all losses excluding those attributable to bringing up a healthy child.[10] In still other instances, damages have been awarded not only in respect of the pain and suffering involved in an unwanted pregnancy but also to offset the cost of rearing the child to maturity.[11]

4 Eg *Eyre v Measday* [1986] 1 All ER 488, CA; *Gold v Haringey Health Authority* [1986] 1 FLR 125, revsd [1988] QB 481, [1987] 2 All ER 888.

5 *Stobie v Central Birmingham Health Authority* (1994) 22 BMLR 135. The case drew attention to the fact that the common law interpretation of paternity may be challenged by way of laboratory tests. The phenomenon is said to occur in about 1:80,000 cases – see J C Smith, D Cranston, T O'Brien et al 'Fatherhood without Apparent Spermatozoa after Vasectomy' (1994) 344 Lancet 30.

6 See chapter 10 below. It is possible to discern an incremental shift towards judicial reliance on the patients' understanding rather than on what the surgeon said: *Gowten v Wolverhampton Health Authority* [1994] 5 Med LR 432; *Lybert v Warrington Health Authority* (1995) 25 BMLR 91, [1996] 7 Med LR 71.

7 (1978) 86 DLR (3d) 719 at 722, per Garett J.

8 *Terrell v Garcia* 496 SW 2d 124 (Tx, 1973); *Sutkin v Beck* 629 SW 2d 131 (Tx, 1982). It has been agreed, however, that damages are recoverable for the birth of a defective child.

9 *Kingsbury v Smith* 422 A 2d 1003 (NH, 1982); *Ochs v Borelli* 445 A 2d 883 (Conn, 1982).

10 *Cockrum v Baumgartner* 447 NE 2d 385 (Ill, 1992).

11 *Troppi v Scarf* 186 NW 2d 511 (Mich, 1971), where an obligation to abort or offer for adoption was rejected. This rule may be modified by 'off-setting' comparable benefits flowing from the birth of a healthy child: *Burke v Rivo* 551 NE 2d 1 (Mass, 1990); *Lovelace Medical Center v Mendez* 805 P 2d 603 (NM, 1991). The 'balancing' approach was criticised in *Public Health Trust v Brown* 388 So 2d 1084 (Fla, 1980). J H Scheid 'Benefits vs. Burdens: The Limitation of Damages in Wrongful Birth' (1984-5) 23 J Fam Law 57. For a comparative review, see A Stewart 'Damages for the Birth of a Child' (1995) J Law Soc Scot 298.

The first comparable English case is that of *Scuriaga v Powell*.[12] The case was concerned with abortion rather than with sterilisation but none the less provides some authority. Here the plaintiff consulted a doctor, who agreed to perform a legal termination. A healthy child was born by caesarean section subsequent to a failure to terminate pregnancy. The court held that there was no public policy reason preventing a claim against the doctor in such a case and damages were awarded in respect of the diminution of the plaintiff's marriage prospects, pain and suffering, and anxiety and distress. There was no claim for damages in respect of the child's upbringing but the trial judge, Watkins J, foreshadowed future developments in saying:

> Surely no one in these days would argue [that damages were irrecoverable] if the child was born defective or diseased. The fact that the child born is healthy cannot give rise to a different conclusion save as to a measure of damages

and this view was supported in the Court of Appeal.

The validity of the 'wrongful pregnancy' action was upheld in *Udale v Bloomsbury Area Health Authority*,[13] in which damages were given for pain and suffering along with loss of earnings following a negligently performed operation; an award in respect of the cost of bringing up the child was, however, firmly rejected. In his judgment, Jupp J reiterated that the joy of having the child and the benefits it brought in terms of love should be set off against the inconvenience and financial disadvantages resulting from its birth – 'It is an assumption of our culture', he suggested, 'that the coming of a child into the world is an occasion for rejoicing'.

The Court of Appeal criticised this view in the later negligence case of *Emeh v Kensington and Chelsea and Westminster Area Health Authority*;[14] in addition, there was a strong rejection of the trial judge's view that the plaintiff's refusal of abortion was so unreasonable as to eclipse the defendant's wrongdoing.[15] Equally significantly, however, the Court of Appeal awarded damages for the cost of rearing the child and rejected the policy objections voiced in *Udale*. Thus, it appeared that any distinction between entitlement to damages for pain and suffering and that in respect of the cost of the child's upbringing had been laid to rest. None the less, the uncertainty remained and was, in fact, amplified in *Allen v Bloomsbury Health Authority*,[16] where it was firmly held, at first instance, that the two heads of damages were distinct; the Court of Appeal has now, however, clarified that a wrongful pregnancy is a personal injury which cannot be separated from its consequences.[17]

---

12 (1979) 123 Sol Jo 406.
13 [1983] 2 All ER 522, [1983] 1 WLR 1098. Similar sentiments were expressed in an unreported negligence case, *Jones v Berkshire Area Health Authority*, quoted in *Gold v Haringey Health Authority* [1986] 1 FLR 125; revsd [1988] QB 481, [1987] 2 All ER 888 – although damages were allowed.
14 (1983) Times, 3 January; revsd [1985] QB 1012, [1984] 3 All ER 1044, CA.
15 The possibility that refusal of an *early* abortion might be regarded as unreasonable still remains open. For a discussion of the relationship between abortion and wrongful pregnancy, see K McK Norries 'Damages for the Birth of a Child' 1985 SLT 69; A Grubb 'Damages for "Wrongful Conception"' (1985) 44 CLJ 30. More recently, see *Crouchman v Burke* (1997) 40 BMLR 163, where a woman who would have had an early termination refused one at 15 weeks 'for understandable reasons' (per Langley J at 176)
16 [1993] 1 All ER 651, (1993) 13 BMLR 47.
17 *Walkin v South Manchester Health Authority* [1995] 4 All ER 132, (1995) 25 BMLR 108. Which means, in passing, that actions for wrongful pregnancy are subject to the Limitation Act 1980, s 11.

Thus, the legal position in English law is now clear: unsought children are potential grounds for compensation. Scottish policy has evolved in its own way. Earlier reports are, for the most part, concerned with procedural matters and do not deal with the arguments or the outcomes in the cases.[18] Two cases have attracted the attention of the media,[19] both of which were based on lack of warning of the risk of failure rather than on operative negligence. Both were settled out of court; the offer of the substantial sum of £50,000 in *Lindsay v Greater Glasgow Health Board*[20] suggested that the Scottish courts might follow those of England in recognising the birth of a healthy child as a suitable matter for 'damages' and this appeared to be settled in *Allan v Greater Glasgow Health Board*.[1] In that case, the court explicitly accepted that there were no grounds – of principle or of policy – to prevent an award of damages for the upbringing of a child born in these circumstances. There is, of course, much force in the argument that such compensation amounts to a rejection of a fundamental value in our society – that of family love. On the other hand, it is implicit that the patient undergoing consensual, non-therapeutic sterilisation does not want any more children and that this may be for economic reasons. That being so, it is hard to refute the words of Peter Pain J: 'Every baby has a belly to be filled and a body to be clothed.'[2]

The steady approach to conformity on both sides of the Border was, however, disturbed in the Outer House of the Court of Session in *McFarlane v Tayside Health Board*.[3] Here, the Lord Ordinary effectively held that a normal pregnancy culminating in a healthy child was a natural event which could not be regarded as an injury – hence, it could not form a basis for damages. He also decided that the joys of the child's existence wholly compensated the financial cost of bringing up the child – he rejected the concept of 'off-set', or a balancing of some benefit against some disadvantage, in that it involved placing a specific value on the life of the child. This somewhat surprising decision was reversed in the Inner House, where the Lord Justice-Clerk declined to discuss the relationship of pregnancy to personal injury and, rather, addressed the problem in terms of the basic principles of Scots law.[4] Injuria or the invasion of a legal right – in this case the right not to become pregnant – was sustained at conception of the child. Damnum, or prejudice suffered in respect in respect of a legally recognised interest, was manifested in the effects of pregnancy and childbirth on the woman's bodily integrity. An obligation to make reparation arises when there is concurrence of injuria and damnum – and these conditions were satisfied in the instant case once the pregnancy was established.[5] The House rejected the proposition

18 *Smith, Petitioner* 1985 SLT 461; *Jones v Lanarkshire Health Board* 1990 SLT 19, 1989 SCLR 542; *Teece v Ayrshire and Arran Health Board* 1990 SLT 512.
19 *Pollock v Lanarkshire Health Board* (1987) Times, 6 January; *Lindsay v Greater Glasgow Health Board* (1990) Scotsman, 14 March.
20 (1990) Scotsman, 14 March, p 8.
 1 1998 SLT 580, OH. The court found, however, that there had been no negligence in this case. See also *Cameron v Greater Glasgow Health Board* 1993 GWD 6-433, (Lexis transcript available), in which damages of £40,000 were agreed; again, however, the action was unsuccessful.
 2 In *Thake v Maurice* [1984] 2 All ER 513 at 526, [1985] 2 WLR 215 at 230.
 3 1997 SLT 211, (1996) Times, 11 November.
 4 *McFarlane and McFarlane v Tayside Health Board* 1998 SLT 307 at 310, 1998 SCLR 126 at 131.
 5 Reiterated by Lord McCluskey 1998 SCLR 126 at 135. The House specifically held that the deliberate continuation of the pregnancy did not affect the chain of causation: cf Slade LJ in *Emeh v Kensington and Chelsea and Westminster Health Authority* (1983) Times, 3 January; revsd [1985] QB 1012, [1984] 3 All ER 1044, CA.

that the blessing of a child was an overriding benefit, pointing out that the couple were relying on sterilisation in order to avoid the additional expenditure which the birth of another child would entail and, having decided the issue by way of principle, went on to conclude that there was no overriding consideration of public policy which the awarding of damages would contravene.   Uniformity of approach is, thus, now assured within the jurisdictions of Great Britain and has been reinforced in a further decision in favour of the pursuers in the Outer House.[6]

As a coda to this section on failed sterilisation – or 'wrongful pregnancy' – we note what must be the ultimate in negligence actions backed by support from the legal aid fund.[7] A Mr and Mrs Danns, who became parents seven years after the husband's vasectomy, sued the Department of Health for failure to publicise information about the risk to them and to others in their situation.[8] The research on which they depend indicates a risk of recanalisation of the vas of some 0.05% – which would seem to lay a heavy burden on the protective arm of the civil service! In the event, and almost inevitably, the action failed on the grounds that, in general, how a minister's statutory duties are exercised is a matter for his or her discretion. By no stretch of the imagination could the civil servants and advisers to the department be regarded as being sufficiently proximate to the various members of the public who might have an interest in the topic of male sterilisation by vasectomy – and the learned judge gave several further trenchant reasons why the action could not succeed.

Non-consensual sterilisation

If consensual sterilisation raises ethical misgivings, then non-consensual sterilisation can be seen as a minefield of powerful objection. This form of sterilisation has been carried out in some countries as an official or unofficial part of programmes of eugenic improvement or birth control. In the United States, for example, the enthusiasm for eugenics which was the feature of the earlier part of this century led to legislative measures in a number of states providing for the sterilisation of mental defectives, those suffering from certain forms of genetically transmissible diseases and, in some cases, criminal recidivists.[9] Such laws were declared unconstitutional in some states and, in others, the number of operations carried out was small; nevertheless, compulsory sterilisation measures still remain on the statute books in a few jurisdictions. Interest now centres on the management of individual cases and here, despite some inevitable inconsistencies, a consensus is evolving in favour of non-consensual sterilisation given very specific criteria of justification. The seminal case is *Grady*,[10] where the power of the court to exercise jurisdiction as to the

---

6 *Anderson v Forth Valley Health Board* 1998 SLT 588, 1998 SCLR 97.
7 *Danns v Department of Health* (1995) 25 BMLR 121.
8 Relying on the archaic Ministry of Health Act 1919, s 2, which spelled out the duties of the minister in general terms – including ' . . . to secure the . . . effective carrying out . . . of measures conducive to the health of the people . . .'
9 D W Meyers *The Human Body and the Law* (1970) pp 28ff; P R Reilly 'Eugenic Sterilization in the United States' in A Milunsky and G Annas (eds) *Genetics and the Law – III* (1985), ch 17; J K Mason *Medico-legal aspects of Reproduction and Parenthood* (2nd edn, 1998) pp 69-71. for wide-ranging discussion, see K McK Norrie *Family Planning Practice and the Law* (1991) p 123.
10 *Re Grady* 405 A 2d 851 (Md, 1979).

sterilisation of an incompetent minor in the absence of statute was firmly upheld. The problem in all such cases is to strike a balance between the individual's right to bodily integrity and the right to choose an operation which, in the case of the mentally handicapped, may carry with it greater freedom of access to community life and relationships.[11] To make such a choice in surrogate fashion, however, is to invoke a 'substituted judgment' test. The great majority of courts have recognised the near impossibility of doing this in the face of congenital mental illness and have, accordingly, opted for a 'best interests' test, which is also central to the welfare principle on which the English wardship jurisdiction is founded.[12] A most important United States case in this respect is that of *Hayes*,[13] in which it was laid down that the courts could authorise sterilisation in the absence of consent so long as, inter alia, the subject was incapable of forming a judgment, was physically capable of procreation, was likely to engage in sexual activity and there was no reasonable alternative to sterilisation.

The root problem of non-consensual sterilisation, overshadowed as it is by the ghost of the eugenic movement, lies in the fact that it raises starkly the subject of what has been named the basic human right to reproduce – to which we return for general discussion.[14] The phrase seems to have originated in the American case of *Skinner v Oklahoma*[15] – which, in fact, concerned the punitive sterilisation of a man – and has, since, come into common usage throughout the English-speaking world. In the United Kingdom, the concept was first expressed in the very significant case *Re D (a minor).*[16] The minor in this case was an 11-year-old girl who suffered from a rare condition known as Sotos' syndrome. Her IQ was roughly 80, a rating which need not necessarily make it impossible for the person in question to cope reasonably well in everyday life and even to marry and raise a child. There was medical evidence to the effect that her condition showed some signs of improvement and that this improvement could continue.

In her judgment in this case, Heilbron J was strongly influenced by the medical evidence given to the court to the effect that sterilisation was not always appropriate in such cases and that such a decision was not within the scope of the clinical judgment of a single doctor dealing with the case. Also to be taken into account was the irreversibility of the operation and the significance of carrying it out on so young a person:

A review of the whole of the evidence leads me to the conclusion that in a case of a child of 11 years of age, where the evidence shows that her mental and physical condition and attainments have already improved, and where her future prospects are as yet unpredictable, where the evidence also shows that she is unable as yet to understand and appreciate the implications of this operation and could not give valid or informed consent, that the likelihood is that in later years she will be able to make her own choice, where, I believe,

---

11 In the US, see *Conservatorship of Valerie N* 707 P 2d 760 (Cal, 1985).
12 And see now the conditions underwriting the Children Act 1989 and the Children (Scotland) Act 1995.
13 *Re Hayes* 608 P 2d 635 (Wash, 1980).
14 See p 100.
15 316 US 535 (1942).
16 [1976] Fam 185, [1976] 1 All ER 326.

the frustration and resentment of realising (as she would one day) what happened could be devastating, an operation of this nature is, in my view contra-indicated.[17]

The judge in *Re D* has been criticised for not having addressed the general issues involved;[18] she did, however, refer to the 'basic human right of a woman to reproduce' and concluded that it would be a violation of that right if a girl were sterilised without her consent for non-therapeutic reasons. *Re D* remained the English authority for more than a decade and was quoted with approval in the Canadian case of *Re Eve*.[19] *Eve* is an important case because, among other reasons, the Supreme Court of Canada took several years to deliberate and, in so doing, canvassed a large number of opinions; moreover, by the time the trial had gone through all its stages, virtually every variant opinion had been supported in the judgments.

Eve was the mentally retarded adult daughter of a mother who asked that she be sterilised, a major plank supporting the request being that, in the event of Eve becoming pregnant, neither she nor her mother would be able to care for the baby. The Supreme Court was in no doubts as to its having a parens patriae jurisdiction through which to authorise sterilisation should the need arise. That power was, however, limited by the principle of its being exercised in the best interests of the girl. In the light of this, the judgment was concerned to distinguish between therapeutic and non-therapeutic reasons for sterilisation; La Forest J concluded:

> The grave intrusion on a person's rights and the certain physical damage that ensues from non-therapeutic sterilization without consent ... have persuaded me that it can never safely be determined that such a procedure is in the best interests of that person ... [I conclude that non-therapeutic sterilization] should never be authorised ... under the *parens patriae* jurisdiction.[20]

He appreciated that there could be difficulty in drawing a line between a therapeutic and a non-therapeutic operation, but was content to emphasise that: 'the utmost caution must be exercised commensurate with the severity of the procedure.' In essence, it was this problem which provoked the apparent conflict between the court in *Eve* and that involved in the comparable English case of *Re B*,[21] which was the first of its kind to reach the House of Lords.

Having been reported at much the same time, it is inevitable that the approaches in *Eve* and *Re B* have been contrasted. It is unfortunate that the English case concerned a girl aged 17 – she would, therefore, shortly have passed out of the English wardship jurisdiction and it was considered that there was no parens patriae authority

17 [1976] Fam 185 at 196, [1976] 1 All ER 326 at 335.
18 A Bainham 'Handicapped Girls and Judicial Parents' (1987) 103 LQR 334.
19 (1986) 31 DLR (4th) 1.
20 The extant case at the time, *Re K and Public Trustee* (1985) 19 DLR (4th) 255, in which the main therapeutic ground for sterilisation was a phobic aversion to blood which would be accentuated with the onset of the menses, was regarded as 'at best, dangerously close to the limits of the permissible' – this despite the fact that an Appeal Court judge in *Re K* thought that the case should never have come to the court (per Anderson JA at 277). See also the more recent New Zealand case *Re X* [1991] 2 NZLR 365.
21 *Re B (a minor) (wardship: sterilisation)* [1988] AC 199, [1987] 2 All ER 206, HL.

on which to fall back in the case of an adult such as was available to the Canadian courts. A speedy decision was, thus, dictated, and there is no doubt that Lord Hailsham LC, on it being suggested that the girl's progress could well be observed for a year, laid open his defences when he said: 'We shall be no wiser in twelve months than we are now.'[1] A massive literature has built up around the case and we are able to refer here only to those aspects that we regard as essential to its understanding.

B was a mentally handicapped epileptic with a mental age of five to six years. She had never conceived and was not pregnant but, absent being fully institutionalised, she was in danger of becoming so. Medical opinion – which, in contrast to that given in *Re D*,[2] was scarcely challenged – was that she would either have to be maintained on hormonal contraceptives for the rest of her reproductive life or her fallopian tubes could be occluded – and the court recognised this as being an irreversible procedure; it was common ground that any pregnancy that occurred would have to be terminated.

In authorising sterilisation, the House of Lords upheld the decisions of both the court of first instance and the Court of Appeal. The basic principle involved was the welfare of the girl; Lord Oliver, in particular, emphasised that there was no question of a eugenic motive, no consideration was paid to the convenience of those caring for the ward and no general principle of public policy was involved. Lord Hailsham LC made some specific comments aimed, in the main, at explaining any apparent variances from other relevant decisions. With particular reference to *Eve*, he said:

> [The] conclusion that the procedure of sterilisation should 'never be considered for non-therapeutic purposes' is totally unconvincing and in startling contradiction to the welfare principle . . . [The] distinction [drawn] between 'therapeutic' and 'non-therapeutic' purposes of this operation in relation to the facts of the present case . . . [is] irrelevant . . .

Lord Oliver also found, in effect, that there was no logic in distinguishing preventive medicine from therapy directed to the ward's interest and we would certainly agree with this. It is, however, possible to argue that 'non-therapeutic' in terms of La Forest J's judgment in *Eve* referred only to treatment designed for the benefit of others. If this be so, *Eve* and *Re B* are not greatly in conflict.[4]

The *Re B* decision has been widely criticised in the British academic literature.[5] We wonder, however, how much the *medical* aspects of the case have been taken into account. The speed with which the decision was taken has been questioned;[6] but this is, we suspect, no more than a reflection of the unanimity of professional opinion – there can be no doubt that pregnancy *is* contraindicated in some patients with mental

1 [1987] 2 All ER 206 at 212.
2 [1976] Fam 185, [1976] 1 All ER 328.
3 [1987] 2 All ER 206 at 213.
4 K McK Norrie 'Sterilisation of the Mentally Disabled in English and Canadian Law' (1989) 38 Int & Comp LQ 387.
5 See eg M Freeman 'For Her Own Good' (1987) 84 LS Gaz 949; S P de Cruz 'Sterilization, Wardship and Human Rights' (1988) 18 Fam Law 6; R Lee and D Morgan 'Sterilisation and Mental Handicap: Sapping the Strength of the State?' (1988) 15 J Law & Soc 229; J Montgomery 'Rhetoric and "Welfare"' (1989) 9 OJL Stud 395 – a particularly trenchant attack. It is fair to remark that the decision in *Eve* has not been applauded everywhere in Canada: see M A Shone 'Mental Health – Sterilization of Mentally Retarded Persons' (1987) 66 Can BR 635.
6 I Kennedy and S Lee 'This Rush to Judgment' The Times, 1 April 1987, p 12.

handicap and that B was one of them. Medically speaking, *Re B* and *Re D* are poles apart. Norrie, for example, is among those who felt that the former was a case that should never have occupied the courts' time; sterilisation was always legal by way of the doctrine of necessity – or, simply, it was a necessary part of the management of the child's health.[7] We suggest that the major conceptual difference between *Eve* and *Re B* is that the former attempts to generalise on principles, whereas the latter is determined to particularise on the facts – and we see no objection to the latter line of thinking.

Lord Hailsham, however, also addressed the question of rights and it is this issue that has so occupied the commentators. He said: 'The right [of a woman to reproduce] is only such when reproduction is the result of informed choice of which the ward in the present case is incapable'[8] and, again:

> To talk of the 'basic right' to reproduce of an individual who is not capable of knowing the causal connection between intercourse and childbirth . . . [or who] is unable to form any maternal instincts or to care for a child, appears to me wholly to part company with reality.[9]

The concept of the right to reproduce is one which deserves discussion in depth but which we cannot provide in the space available; suffice it to say that the existence of an absolute right is by no means certain. Simplistically, it is difficult to envisage a right that requires the co-operation of another person who is under no obligation to provide it; moreover, an absolute right to reproduce would entail access by right to all means of assisted reproduction including surrogate motherhood by way of womb-leasing – and this is clearly untenable. Grubb and Pearl[10] have argued very convincingly that the only such right currently recognised in English law is the right to choose whether or not to reproduce – this being grounded in the principle of individual autonomy. If this be so, given the inability of a subject to make a rational choice, there can be no objection to the courts assuming this right on his or her behalf.

An alternative approach is to regard the 'right' as one to retain the capacity to reproduce.[11] While this is still subject to the individual's ability to choose, it does, at first sight, make the justification for court interference with that right more difficult. In our view, the resolution of the dilemma rests upon the definition of reproduction which, surely, cannot be limited and impersonalised to the single aspect of giving

---

7 (1989) 38 Int & Comp LQ 387. But this definition of necessity would not always be agreed: see J E S Fortin 'Sterilisation the Mentally Ill and Consent to Treatment' (1986) 51 MLR 634. For assistance, see the opinion of Neill LJ in *Re F (Mental patient: sterilisation)* [1990] 2 AC 1 at 32.
8 [1987] 2 All ER 206 at 212.
9 Ibid at 213.
10 A Grubb and D Pearl 'Sterilisation and the Courts' (1987) 46 C LJ 439. See also Nicholson CJ in the Australian case *Re Jane* (1989) FLC 92-007. The reasoning in this case was very similar to that in *Re B*.
11 S A M McLean and T D Campbell 'Sterilization' in S A M McLean (ed) *Legal Issues in Medicine* (1981).

birth – it must include an element of after-care;[12] some mentally handicapped persons may not be able to supply this, although some can – it is, again, a question of degree and a matter of the individual medical status.[13] Moreover, the practical significance of this relative right disappears when, as in *Re B*, it is acknowledged that any pregnancy would have to be subject to therapeutic abortion.

A final comment on decisions such as that in *Re B* relates to criticism that they are sex discriminatory – 'Would the court', asked Freeman,[14] 'have sterilised a boy of 17?' The answer is certainly 'no', but this only proves the rule. Unfair it may be, but it is a fact of life that reproduction can have no immediately adverse medical effect on a man. The only bases for intentional, non-consensual, non-therapeutic sterilisation of a man would be punitive or eugenic, which is what all would agree should be avoided; the fact that decisions such as *Re B* are gender-based actually contributes to their justification.

Two very similar wardship cases were reported in the wake of *Re B*.[15] In both, sterilisation was approved at first instance and neither was appealed. Medical evidence was given at both hearings to the effect that the proposed operation was reversible[16] – in up to 75% of cases, according to the gynaecologists in *Re M* who, in disclaiming the emotive overtones of 'sterilisation', preferred to regard the operation as contraceptive in nature. We suspect that this greatly influenced the judges because the evidence in favour of early sterilisation was less than fully agreed in both cases; indeed, a change of mind on the part of one medical expert had to be specifically explained as not having been made for eugenic reasons. The most interesting feature of both *Re M* and *Re P* is that they can well be regarded as sterilisations which were authorised on social grounds for the benefit of the wards – a matter of protecting their life-styles; unless the House of Lords' interpretation of *Eve* is flawed, such decisions might well be excluded were that judgment to be followed.[17]

Almost parenthetically, note should be taken of more recent cases which indicate how rapidly judicial opinion has crystallised in this area. The ward in *Re HG*[18] was an epileptic who suffered from an unspecified chromosomal abnormality; there was no dispute that pregnancy would be disastrous for her and that long-term hormonal contraception was contraindicated. In making the order, the deputy judge said:

---

12 For full – and prophetic – discussion, see J A Robertson 'Procreative Liberty and the Control of Conception, Pregnancy, and Childbirth' (1983) 69 Va L Rev 405; A Thomas 'For Her Own Good – A Reply' (1987) 84 Law Soc Gaz 1196.

13 For a relatively recent appraisal, see L Appleby and C Dickens 'Mothering Skills of Women with Mental Illness' (1993) 306 BMJ 348.

14 (1987) LS Gaz R 949.

15 *Re M (a minor) (wardship: sterilization)* [1988] 2 FLR 497, [1998] Fam Law 434; *Re P (a minor) (wardship: sterilization)* [1989] 1 FLR 182, [1989] Fam Law 102.

16 It was said, in somewhat unusual phraseology: 'The situation to-day is that the operation is not irreversible although it is the current *ethical* practice to tell the patients that it is an irreversible operation' [our emphasis] (per Eastham J, *Re P* [1989] 1 FLR 182 at 189).

17 We should always remember that we are, in general, seeing medical ethical situations from the relative safety of an affluent Western society. The problems of congruent learning disability, menstruation and social support are amplified in, say, India: Z Imam 'Mass Hysterectomies in India' (1994) 343 Lancet 592.

18 *Re HG (specific issue order: sterilisation)* [1993] 1 FLR 587.

[My conclusion is that] a sufficiently overwhelming case has been established to justify interference with the fundamental right of a woman to bear a child. I am certainly satisfied that it would be cruel to expose T to an unacceptable risk of pregnancy and that that should be obviated by sterilisation in her interests.[19]

   Times have certainly moved on but, even so, it is still considered that virtually all cases require the sanction of a High Court judge. Applications may be made under the Children Act 1989, s 8(1) or under the inherent jurisdiction of the court – the latter being the preferred route.[20]   Recourse to the court is, however, unnecessary when sterilisation is an incidental result of medical or surgical treatment. This has been made quite clear in two very similar, and closely heard, cases where a hysterectomy was indicated for menstrual disorder. In the first of these, *Re E*,[1] concerning a 17-year-old, Sir Stephen Brown held that no formal consent of the court was necessary and that the parents were in a position to give a valid consent: 'A clear distinction is to be made between an operation to be performed for a genuine therapeutic reason and one to achieve sterilisation.'[2] In the second, *Re GF*,[3] the President declined to grant a declaration of lawfulness on the grounds that it was unnecessary when an operation was designed to improve the health of the patient. He did, however, lay down the conditions under which no application to the court was needed. These were that two doctors agreed: first, that the operation was necessary for therapeutic purposes; secondly, that it was in the patient's best interests; and, thirdly, that no practicable less intrusive treatment was available. The medical profession must welcome such unequivocal guidance.
   The problem of treatment of menstrual 'phobias' has also arisen in Scotland, where it provided a part basis for the only reported case so far in which sterilisation of an incapax was opposed. In *L, Petitioner*,[4] it was held in the Outer House of the Court of Session that sterilisation of an autistic woman would not be justified by the avoidance of pregnancy alone – other methods of contraception were available, although these had their inbuilt risks.[5] The fact that these would not prevent menstruation, with which she was unable to cope, tipped the balance in favour of sterilisation by way of partial hysterectomy. It is to be noted that Scots law is rather easier to apply in this field than it is in England, in so far as it is possible for the Court to appoint a tutor dative who can take health care decisions on behalf of the incapax.[6]
   Returning, however, to instances of deliberate sterilisation of those unable to consent for themselves, the practice note described above also applies to the mentally incompetent adult. This follows decisions in a line of cases which profoundly influenced English law.

19 Ibid at 592.
20 *Practice Note (Official Solicitor: Sterilisation)* [1993] 3 All ER 222, [1993] 4 Med LR 302.
 1 *Re E (a minor) (medical treatment)* [1991] 2 FLR 585, (1992) 7 BMLR 117.
 2 (1992) 7 BMLR 117 at 119.
 3 [1992] 1 FLR 293, [1993] 4 Med LR 77, sub nom *F v F* (1992) 7 BMLR 135.
 4 1996 SCLR 538. Other, unopposed, sterilisation applications have been granted: A Ward 'Tutors to Adults: Developments' 1992 SLT 325.
 5 For further discussion, see p 107 below.
 6 A D Ward 'Revival of Tutors-dative' 1987 SLT 69.

The first of these was *T v T*,[7] which involved an adult incompetent who was found to be pregnant; medical opinion was consistent that the pregnancy should be terminated under the terms of the Abortion Act 1967 and there was an additional application from the subject's mother for leave to sterilise her at the time of the termination. In the course of his determination, Wood J found that the Mental Health Act 1983 provided no solution to non-consensual treatment other than as to that which was aimed directly at the psychiatric condition; that even if the prerogative powers of the Crown as parens patriae in respect of adults still existed, there was no one who could now exercise it; that to perform an operation without consent and in the absence of a defence was tortuous irrespective of hostile intent,[8] and that it was not possible to rely on implied consent in such a case. The judge was unhappy with the defence of necessity, mainly on account of its ill-defined limits, and preferred to rely on the demands of good medical practice – not, in itself, the most unambiguous yardstick. In the circumstances, he fell back on the expedient of an anticipatory declaration that the performance of the two operations would not be unlawful.[9] This legal precedent, set in the Family Division, was approved in the House of Lords in the important case *Re F*.[10]

In *Re F*, the boundaries of the courts' discretion were, again, advanced, F being an adult with arrested mental development who was not pregnant; the conditions of *Re B* were, effectively, duplicated save that F was now beyond the protection of wardship. The course of the action was, by now, almost predictable. The trial judge, Scott Baker J, was prepared to see all treatment for physical conditions that was given to mental patients in good faith and in their best interests as lying within the exceptions to the law of battery which had been created so as to allow for the exigencies of everyday life.[11] His declaration that the operation would not be unlawful was upheld by the Court of Appeal where Lord Donaldson MR, likewise, saw nothing incongruous in doctors and others who had a caring responsibility being required to act in the interests of an adult who was unable to exercise a right of choice.[12] The Master of the Rolls was, understandably, reluctant to accept that serious medical treatment could be subsumed under the umbrella of actions acceptable in everyday life and preferred the formula of it falling 'within generally acceptable standards'. Neill LJ, approaching the problem from principle, concluded that if surgery was necessary, the performance of a serious operation, including an operation for sterilisation, on a patient who could not consent would not be a trespass to the person or otherwise unlawful.[13] The court was, however, unanimous as to the need for approval of the High Court before a sterilisation operation was undertaken.

The correctness of the decision to sterilise was not challenged in the House of Lords, which was, rather, concerned with the resolution of questions of law and

---

7 [1988] Fam 52, [1988] 1 All ER 613. Discussed in depth by Fortin (1986) 51 MLR 634; see also C Dyer 'Consent and the Mentally Handicapped' (1987) 295 BMJ 257.
8 Cf *Wilson v Pringle* [1987] QB 237, [1986] 2 All ER 440, CA. We are uncertain as to whether this would follow in Scotland.
9 RSC Ord 15, r 16.
10 *Re F (mental patient: sterilisation)* [1990] 2 AC 1, sub nom *F v West Berkshire Health Authority* [1989] 2 All ER 545.
11 *Collins v Wilcock* [1984] 3 All ER 374 at 378, [1984] 1 WLR 1172 at 1177, per Goff LJ.
12 [1990] 2 AC 1 at 18.
13 Ibid at 32.

of legal procedure. The House, inter alia, confirmed that the parens patriae jurisdiction no longer existed in England, and that, if it were to be recreated, it would be for the legislature to do so – something which the majority of commentators would approve. Their Lordships also ruled that the procedure by way of declaration was appropriate and satisfactory in cases of the kind,[14] the court having no power to consent to the operation. Undoubtedly, however, the most important aspect of the decision for our purposes was that the common law provides that a doctor can lawfully give surgical or medical treatment to adult patients who are incapable of consenting – provided that the operation or other treatment is in their best interests; it would be in their best interests if, but only if, it was carried out in order to save their lives or to ensure improvement, or prevent deterioration, in their physical or mental health[15] – a rather curious juxtaposition of the major emergency with mild palliation. The House went even further in indicating that it might be the common law *duty* of the doctor to provide treatment in the case of adults suffering from mental disability who were in the care of a guardian or who were detained in mental hospitals. Lord Brandon argued pragmatically that this must be so – otherwise the workload on the courts would be unbearable. Logically, this authority would also apply to sterilisation but six reasons were given for distinguishing that operation – including its general irreversibility which would almost certainly deprive the woman of 'what was widely, and rightly, regarded as one of the fundamental rights of a woman, the right to bear a child'.[16] The House considered, however, that the involvement of the court in cases of this kind was not strictly necessary as a matter of law; it was, nevertheless, highly desirable as a matter of good practice.

We see this as an unfortunate result. Apart from the fact that it is unclear whether the House was referring to medical or legal practice, it provides no *definite* lead for the medical profession and it certainly leaves the public wondering what proportion of cases has been subject to review in the past.[17] The House of Lords held[18] that whether the 'best interests' test had been met would be judged on *Bolam*[19] principles. The application of a test for negligence to a question of clinical practice has been criticised.[20] In any event, it seems to us that, having made a bid for judicial supervision, the court, in so stating, effectively handed back control of the decisions to the doctors.[1] It would surely have been better to strike a rule one way or the other

14 The procedural guidelines laid down in at the time ([1989] 2 FLR 47 and [1990] 2 FLR 530]) have now been amended: see p 102, n 20 above.
15 Per Lord Brandon.
16 [1990] 2 AC 1 at 55, 56.
17 C Dyer 'Decisions from the House of Lords' (1987) 294 BMJ 1219 indicated that some dozens of mentally disabled minors are being sterilised each year in England and Wales by way of a parent/physician decision. We know of no figures for adult incompetents but has been said that about 1,000 operations were performed annually in what was West Germany, where the doctors' position was less secure: J Shaw 'Sterilisation of Mentally Handicapped People: Judges Rule OK?' (1990) 53 MLR 91.
18 [1990] 2 AC 1 at 68.
19 *Bolam v Friern Hospital Management Committee* [1957] 2 All ER 118, [1957] 1 WLR 582.
20 D Ogbourne and R Ward 'Sterilization, the Mentally Incompetent and the Courts' (1989) 18 Anglo-Am L Rev 230. Attempts to undermine *Bolam*, especially as related to a duty to warn, have been increasing in a number of jurisdictions. The matter is discussed in further detail in chapter 9 below.
1 We do, however, appreciate that this depends to some extent on whether 'a matter of good practice' refers to good *medical* or good *legal* practice. Our interpretation has been the former, but that may be taking a blinkered view.

and, in fact, this was the only element of dissent in the House of Lords judgment – Lord Griffiths thought that the non-consensual sterilisation of a woman with healthy reproductive organs should be declared an operation that was unlawful absent the consent of the High Court;[2] he thus aligned himself with Lord Templeman in his obiter recommendations as to minors.[3] Even so, we have already noted the difficulty of distinguishing genuine therapeutic reasons with clarity and, while it is probably true that doctors and their health authorities will rarely bypass the courts for fear of later legal action,[4] such expectation is still a long way from assured uniformity.

Amongst its other reasons for advocating the intervention of the courts in the 'best interests' analysis, the House of Lords, per Lord Brandon, thought that there might otherwise be a greater risk of it being decided wrongly – thus endorsing the Master of the Rolls' analogy of a judicial 'third opinion'. With the best of wills, we cannot see that this follows any more than that it would be desirable for a highly experienced consultant physician to approve a judicial opinion. Far more important are the subsidiary reasons given – that it might otherwise be *thought* to have been decided wrongly and that the doctors should be protected from consequent adverse criticism or claims. We do not share Lord Brandon's fears that, but for the courts, there is a risk of sterilisation being carried out for improper reasons or with improper motives. There is always the General Medical Council – although we might not go so far as Cook J, who is reported as having said:

> It is not conceivable to this court that medical advisors would prostitute their Hippocratic Oath to perform unnecessary or ill-advised and untimely operations, particularly of a major kind.[5]

There is little doubt that many people distrust unbridled powers of doctors – particularly in the field of social medicine – yet only the doctors in clinical charge of a case can possess all the facts. The precedent set by *Re F* is that decisions of this nature will continue to be made on a case-to-case basis and it is because the details of each case differ that we would approve the process; calls for specific legislation[6] should, we believe, be resisted because it would, inevitably, lead to generalisation in an area where the individual is paramount. We do, however, question whether the adversarial system provides the ideal milieu for deciding problems in which morality, legality and personal well-being are so intertwined; is this not an area, *par excellence*, which would benefit from a medico-legal council approach to problem-solving?[7]

No discussion of the role of the courts and of parents in this very particular area of medical jurisprudence would be complete without a short review of the Australian

2 In *Re F* [1990] 2 AC 1 at 70. Current practice is now that all such cases must be approved by a High Court judge: see *Re S (medical treatment: adult sterilisation)* [1998] 1 FLR 944, [1998] Fam Law 325, following *Re LC (medical treatment: sterilisation)* [1997] 2 FLR 258.
3 In *Re B* [1988] AC 199 at 205.
4 C Dyer 'Ruling on Consent: Protection for Patients and Doctors' (1989) 298 BMJ 348.
5 In an Australian case *Re a Teenager* [1989] FLC 92-006.
6 In the US, see *Re Guardianship of Joan I Eberhardy* 307 NW 2d 881 (Wis, 1981); in Canada, *Re Eve* (1986) 31 DLR (4th) 1; in the UK, Shaw (1990) 53 BMLR 91, Fortin (1986) 51 MLR 634, Bainham (1987) 103 LQR 334.
7 J K Mason 'A Comparison of Medico-legal Systems in Scotland and Scandinavia' (1978) 23 JR 198. Ogbourne and Ward (1989) 18 Anglo-Am L Rev 230, for example, have suggested a useful set of guidelines which could be given great authority by such a council.

experience which, when the cases are taken in sequence, brings the problems into clear perspective. We have already noted the somewhat ingenuous attitude to the medical profession expressed by Cook J in *Re a Teenager*.[8] This was, admittedly, a 'menstruation' case and, therefore, arguably, solvable within the confines of the family acting in concert with the family medical practitioner; nevertheless, it is unsurprising that this generous view of the medical profession was modified in the very similar case of *Re Jane*,[9] in which Nicholson CJ said 'it is also possible that members of that profession may form sincere but misguided views about the appropriate steps to be taken' as to which one might again be tempted to ask whether the same might not apply to the legal profession! It was held that the consent of the court was required in such cases where the prime purpose of the procedure was non-therapeutic and a sterilisation was, in fact, authorised in the best interests of the girl. The court recognised, however, that the question of whether menstruation constituted a medical or social problem presented considerable difficulty.[10]

The evident judicial uncertainty was settled, at least to a large extent, by the High Court of Australia in *Secretary, Department of Health and Community Services (N T) v J W B and S M B (Marion's Case)*,[11] a case involving a 14-year-old epileptic girl with serious behavioural problems. Space does no admit of an analysis of the opinions delivered by the seven judges.[12] Suffice it to say that the majority of the court, while being reluctant to use the precise wording, acknowledged a distinction between therapeutic and non-therapeutic non-consensual sterilisation; the latter, it was held, required the consent of the court; and, significantly, the court considered that a non-therapeutic operation could be authorised on the grounds that it was in the girl's best interests. As we have indicated, the High Court was unhappy with the blurred distinction between therapeutic and non-therapeutic procedures but indicated their interpretation usefully in stating that *Marion's Case* was not a case where sterilisation was 'a by-product of surgery appropriately carried out to treat some malfunction or disease'.[13] It is noted, however, that this construct evades the issue of psychological trauma and, indeed, the case amplifies the difficulties in classifying 'menstruation' for, when it was remitted to the Family Court,[14] Nicholson CJ remarked:

> This case probably falls into the category where the court's consent is unnecessary . . . since the procedure was required for medical and therapeutic reasons.

Thus, the situation in Australia is clarified to the extent that, while the difficulties inherent in non-consensual sterilisation have not been ironed out, their nature has

---

8 [1989] FLC 92-006.
9 *Re Jane, Re Elizabeth* (1989) 13 Fam LR 47.
10 For discussion of these and other cases, see K Petersen 'Private Decisions and Public Scrutiny: Sterilisation and Minors in Australia and England' in S A M McLean (ed) *Contemporary Issues in Law, Medicine and Ethics* (1996) ch 4.
11 (1992) 175 CLR 218, (1992) 66 ALJR 300.
12 The case is thoroughly explored by N Cica 'Sterilising the Intellectually Disabled' (1993) 1 Med LRev 186.
13 (1992) 175 CLR 218 at 250.
14 *Re Marion (No 2)* (1992) 17 Fam LR 336.

been carefully explored.[15]   Doubt, however, still remains. In a later case discussed by Petersen,[16] one of severe disability following birth trauma, Warnick J said:

> To make a decision in this case in favour of sterilisation would be virtually equivalent to establishing a policy that all females with profound disabilities . . . should be sterilised.

It could, perhaps, be said that Australia has failed to solve the insoluble. It is clear from what has been said already, that we believe the solution of ethical problems in medicine is very much a matter of the evaluation of the individual case. If, however, one seeks for a general solution, it seems that, in reaching a position which lies somewhere between the rigid stance of the Supreme Court of Canada and the evidently paternalistic approach of the House of Lords, the High Court of Australia has reached a compromise which is probably as good as is obtainable. Perhaps its most important feature lies in its acceptance that non-therapeutic or social considerations – which we prefer to see as aspects of preventive medicine – can properly be prayed in aid of the incompetent minor. The concluding words of Lord Jauncey in *Re F* provide a suitable coda to the discussion:

> I should like only to reiterate the importance of not erecting such legal barriers against the provision of medical treatment for incompetents that they are deprived of treatment which competent persons could expect to receive in similar circumstances.[17]

Other forms of contraception

It may well be thought that many of the problems posed in the foregoing discussion of sterilisation – and particularly those of non-consensual sterilisation – could be obviated by the use of an alternative form of contraception. Few long-term contraceptive methods can, however, be applied without some risk – and the risk may be serious. Oral hormonally based contraception has been greatly refined over the years but there is no doubt that compounds with a high oestrogen content will predispose to intravascular thrombosis;[18] progestogens increase the liability to

---

15 There was extensive discussion of the principle in the Full Court of the Family Court in the appeal of *P v P* (1994) 19 Fam LR 1 in which guidelines were followed and developed. The Court, however, warned of the dangers of generalising in such highly personalised matters.

16 See p 106, n 10 above. *Re L and M (Sarah's Case)* (1993) 17 Fam LR 357. It is to be noted that the full Family Court in *P v P* (1994) 19 Fam LR 1 distinguished *Sarah's Case* from *Marion's Case* and their own.

17 [1990] 2 AC 1 at 83. And, at the same time, improve their freedom as to life-style: see the Australian Family Court in *P v P* (1994) 19 Fam LR 1.

18 While we have no intention of discussing such matters in detail, it has to be remembered that the causes of intravenous and intra-arterial thrombosis differ; the harmful effect of a given type of contraceptive on one form must be balanced against its possible beneficial effect on the other: K McPherson 'Third Generation Oral Contraception and Venous Thromboembolism' (1996) 312 BMJ 68. So far as we are aware, contraceptives have been blamed for death in only one reported case; *Coker v Richmond, Twickenham and Roehampton Area Health Authority* [1996] 7 Med LR 58; the action failed on the grounds that the risks had been properly explained – which probably accounts for the dearth of reports.

cardiovascular disease when combined with smoking;[19] 'depot' preparations may cause menstrual disturbances;[20] and a possible association between contraceptive therapy and an increased incidence of carcinoma of the breast or cervix is still debated.[1] The very effective interceptive methods are also suspect in that, although any association is certainly not a simple one, they may cause pelvic inflammation and permanent infertility – fear of litigation would now deter many physicians in the United States from fitting an intrauterine device.[2] These are, however, mainly aspects of clinical medicine; they are introduced here only to emphasise that non-surgical contraception also has its pitfalls and cannot be imposed without forethought – it will have been noted above that several of the non-consensual sterilisation cases were precipitated by the wish to discontinue contraceptives. The main legal and ethical issues relate to the provision of contraceptives for minors; although this was once a burning issue, it has now lost its urgency and the historic case of *Gillick*[3] is probably best discussed under 'Consent' below.[4] Nevertheless, the dilemma confronting the doctor who is consulted by a female minor requesting contraceptive advice and treatment still merits consideration.

The problem is essentially that of deciding whether the physician should do anything which might facilitate her engaging in sexual activity. If the patient is, say, 14 or 15, he may well be of the view that that is too young an age for sexual intercourse. This need not be on grounds of antipathy to sexual intercourse outside marriage; the disapproval is more likely to be based on the view that sexual activity at such an age may lead to emotional trauma and a risk of disease – including iatrogenic disease – which is best avoided. On the other hand, a refusal to prescribe contraceptives may ultimately be more damaging to the patient in that sexual activity may result in pregnancy – and giving birth to a child or abortion at such an age are likely to be severely disruptive of the patient's life.

The ethical dilemma by no means disappears once the decision is taken to provide contraception; the doctor then has to make the difficult decision whether or not to inform the patient's parents. This is really an issue of medical confidentiality which is discussed in detail in chapter 8, below. The decision in each case might, however, depend on the circumstances. A doctor who informed parents of the fact that their 13-year-old daughter had taken to prostitution could surely claim that it was in the

---

19 Indeed, smoking increases the associated risks of thrombosis almost irrespective of the type of oral contraceptive in use: B V Stadel 'Oral Contraceptives and Cardiovascular Disease' (1981) 305 New Engl J Med 612.

20 D R Bromham 'Contraceptive Implants' (1996) 312 BMJ 1555; *Blyth v Bloomsbury Health Authority* [1993] 4 Med LR 151, discussed at p 283 below. Insertion and removal also requires expertise and may be a source of litigation: J Roberts 'Women in US Sue Makers of Norplant' (1994) 309 BMJ 145.

1 J O Drife 'The Contraceptive Pill and Breast Cancer in Young Women' (1989) 298 BMJ 1269. For a succinct analysis of the whole field, see A Szarewski and J Guiilebaud 'Contraception' (1991) 302 BMJ 1224.

2 G R Thornton 'Intrauterine Devices: Malpractice and Product Liability' (1986) 14 Law Med Hlth Care 4 provides a good overview. But see N C Lee, G L Rubin, H W Ory and R T Burkman 'The Intrauterine Device and Pelvic Inflammatory Disease: New Results from the Women's Health Study' (1988) 72 Obst Gynaecol 1.

3 *Gillick v West Norfolk and Wisbech Area Health Authority* [1984] QB 581, [1984] 1 All ER 365; on appeal [1986] AC 112, [1985] 1 All ER 830, CA; revsd [1986] AC 112, [1985] 3 All ER 402, HL.

4 See chapter 10.

best interests of the child to do so; this may not be the case when a 15-year-old girl is doing no more than engaging in occasional sexual activity with one partner. Two distinct legal issues are raised in this connection. The first is the general question as to whether a doctor can properly treat a minor without consent of the parents and, more specifically, whether he may give advice and treatment as to birth control; the second raises the possibility that, in so doing, he may attract criminal liability as being a party to the offence committed by the man who has sexual intercourse with his female minor patient. Both these issues were partially resolved by the decision in *Gillick.*

This controversial case resulted from the publication of a circular by the Department of Health stating that practitioners could, in strictly limited circumstances, discuss and apply family planning measures to minors without the express consent of their parents; Mrs Gillick sought, inter alia, to have the instruction declared unlawful. In the absence of any binding authority, the trial judge relied heavily on the common law and on the Canadian case of *Johnston.*[5] While distinguishing between physical or surgical and medical treatment, he concluded that a person below the age of 16 was capable of consent to contraceptive therapy provided she was of sufficient mental maturity to understand the implications. The Court of Appeal, however, concentrated on the duties and rights of parents, which they considered inseparable. The trial judge's decision was overturned unanimously and the Authority, strongly backed by the BMA, appealed to the House of Lords. This final court of arbitration reverted to what might be loosely termed the 'mature minor' principle – and has come to be known as '*Gillick*-competence' – and decided against Mrs Gillick by a majority of 3:2.

We return to *Gillick* below;[6] for the present we can note the overall tenor of the judgment as expressed by Lord Scarman:

> If the law should impose upon the process of growing up fixed limits where nature knew only a continuous process, the price would be artificiality and a lack of realism in an area where the law must be sensitive to human development and social change.[7]

The thrust of the case is, however, to be found in Lord Fraser's speech, in which he said that the doctor would be justified in proceeding with contraceptive advice without the parents' consent or even knowledge provided that he was satisfied that:

(i) the girl would, although under 16, understand his advice;

(ii) he could not persuade her to inform her parents or to allow him to inform the parents that she was seeking contraceptive advice;

(iii) she was very likely to have sexual intercourse with or without contraceptive treatment;

(iv) unless she received contraceptive advice or treatment her physical or mental health or both were likely to suffer; and

(v) her best interests required him to give her contraceptive advice, treatment or both without parental consent.[8]

5 *Johnston v Wellesley Hospital* (1970) 17 DLR (3d) 139.
6 See chapter 9.
7 [1985] 3 All ER 402 at 421.
8 Ibid at 413.

Lord Fraser emphasised that the judgment was not to be regarded as a licence for doctors to disregard the wishes of parents whenever they found it convenient to do so and he pointed out that any doctor who behaved in such a way would be failing to discharge his professional responsibilities and would be expected to be disciplined by his own professional body accordingly.

The House also considered the second question posed and, despite a dissenting opinion, ruled that it was unlikely that a doctor giving contraceptive advice to a female minor would be committing an offence under the Sexual Offences Act 1956, s 28. It was pointed out that, were the contrary to be so, an offence would be committed irrespective of parental consent. In essence, only if the doctor actually intended to facilitate unlawful sexual intercourse could he be regarded as abetting an offence under s 6 of the 1956 Act – and this must be a condition which borders on the inconceivable. Moreover, as Woolf J explained in the trial stage of the case, an accessory before the fact must know the material circumstances of the offence, not merely, for example, that sexual intercourse might take place at an unidentified time with an unidentified man.[9]

The medical response to the House of Lords decision in *Gillick* was generally one of relief. Yet it is possible that it is something of a Pyrrhic victory; in the event of a complaint being laid, it may be very much harder for a doctor to show that he or she conformed to all five of Lord Fraser's conditions than merely to convince his peers that he was following his reasonable medical judgment. The General Medical Council has now modified its original attitude to confidentiality and the minor patient – possibly because the implications of the *Gillick* are so widely appreciated. The doctor undoubtedly has a difficult task in assessing whether or not his young patient has sufficient understanding and intelligence for him to treat her with equanimity. The GMC's guidelines now states that, if the doctor considers the patient to be incapable of giving consent because of immaturity, he or she may disclose relevant information to an appropriate person or authority if it is essential to do so in the patient's medical interests. This, however, is subject to the incapax having been told of the intention. Furthermore, the GMC follows Lord Fraser in emphasising that the judgment of whether patients are capable of giving or withholding consent to treatment or disclosure must be based on an assessment of their ability to appreciate what the treatment or advice being sought may involve, and not solely on their age.[10]

The narrowness of the decision in *Gillick* cannot be overlooked – it is noteworthy that, on a simple head count, more judges supported the plaintiff than opposed her. It is certainly true that the consequences of a medical refusal of contraception would probably be worse for the girls in question than would be the circumvention of parental control. But the case was about bigger issues than the limited question of avoiding unwanted pregnancies; in a significant sense, it represented an attempt to use the law to establish a moral, rather than a legal, point about sexual conduct – and the law is a bad instrument for this purpose. Yet, despite the evident progressive development of the public mood in the last 15 years, the warnings of those who supported Mrs Gillick should not be summarily dismissed as the protests of a latter-

---

9 A vast literature was built on *Gillick*. An interesting objective Australian view of the whole case is to be found in J Morgan 'Controlling Minors' Fertility' (1986) 12 Monash Univ LR 161.
10 Guidance from the General Medical Council *Confidentiality* (1995) para 10.

day Mrs Grundy; there is an undoubted tendency at present to undermine the concept of the innocence of childhood.[11]   There are many pressures which increasingly encourage the young to seek the status of miniature adults and a readiness for sexual activity is essential to this identity – to quote Lord Templeman: 'There are many things which a girl under 16 needs to practise, but sex is not one of them.'[12] All of this has an effect on the social and psychological well-being of children and the corresponding medical evidence – particularly of the increase in cervical cancer in those who have shown early sexual promiscuity – should not go unnoticed.   Mrs Gillick was, perhaps, less villainous than she was painted at the time.   She has now passed from the public eye as a defender of sexual mores; nevertheless, we will see as we go through the pages of this book that her place in history is assured as the woman who, albeit unwittingly, changed the face of adolescent medical treatment.

Post coital contraception

Certain types of contraception are designed to – or, in practice, do – work after the embryo has formed.   These are referred to as interceptive methods – or emergency contraception – of which the intrauterine device and the misnamed 'morning after' pill are prime examples.[13]   Such methods are, essentially, abortifacient rather than contraceptive and the question has arisen as to whether they offend against the Abortion Act 1967 (see chapter 5).   Much of the discussion turns on the interpretation of the word 'miscarriage' and whether or not this relates only to the displacement of the implanted embryo.   The Attorney General is quoted as having said that: 'the phrase "to procure a miscarriage'' cannot be construed to include the prevention of implantation.'[14]   Despite this, an argument can be developed to show that the processes are legally similar;[15] we, however, find it illogical to suggest that there can be miscarriage in the absence of true carriage.   In any event, to argue that interceptive methods of contraception are illegal is, in practice, unrewarding.   The use of an intrauterine device (IUD) must surely be morally preferable to the legal destruction of a recognisable human fetus and we would strongly support any move to put these methods of contraception beyond prosecution.[16] So far as we know, only one apposite prosecution has succeeded; the case did, however, concern the insertion of an IUD into a woman who was certainly pregnant.[17]   Rather more help can be gained from the

11   For a survey of this process, see M Winn *Children without Childhood* (1984).
12   [1985] 3 All ER 402 at 432.
13   It has been pointed out that the term 'morning after' implies a spurious sense of urgency; in fact, emergency hormonal contraception need only be instituted within 72 hours of sexual intercourse: F C Reader 'Emergency Contraception' (1991) 302 BMJ 801.
14   41 Official Report (6th series) col 239, 10 May 1983.
15   I J Keown '"Miscarriage": A Medico-legal Analysis' [1984] Crim LR 604.
16   For an interesting commentary, see D Crystal-Kirk 'Embryo Arrest: The "No-man's Land" between Contraception and Abortion' (1989) 57 Med-Leg J 111. Many would now call for making emergency contraception available from pharmacists without prescription: A Glasier 'Emergency Contraception: Time for Deregulation?' (1993) 100 BJ Obst Gynaecol 611; J O Drife 'Deregulating Emergency Contraception' (1993) 307 BMJ 695
17   *R v Price* [1969] 1 QB 541, [1968] 2 All ER 282.   The conviction was quashed on the grounds of a misdirection.

media in an otherwise unreported case[18] which involved a charge under the Offences Against the Person Act 1861, s 58 against a doctor who fitted a contraceptive coil to his secretary some 11 days after they had had intercourse. The judge, having heard gynaecological evidence that implantation would not have occurred, withdrew the case from the jury on the grounds that the woman could not have been pregnant 'in the true sense of the word'. It is unfortunate that this case was disposed of so summarily, as there are certain aspects which give rise to doubt as to its value as a precedent – not the least being an apparent rejection of a charge under the 1861 Act on the grounds that 'the modern techniques of interference [with reproduction] were not [then] available'.[19] The judge is also reported as saying: 'Only at the completion of implantation does the embryo become a fetus. At this stage, she can be regarded as pregnant.'[20] Which leads to the question of whether there would be any difference in fitting an IUD before or after the eleventh day following intercourse. None the less, it seems unlikely that any such prosecution would succeed in the future – and this is, pragmatically, a good thing.

A need still remains to distinguish interceptive from displanting methods of contraception – the euphemistically termed 'menstrual extraction' being a common example of the latter. The purpose here is to dislodge a possibly implanted embryo and, as such, it seems to us that it must involve an intended procurement of miscarriage under the terms of the Offences Against the Person Act 1861, s 58[1] and/or it constitutes a technical offence under the Abortion Regulations 1968.[2] Whatever may be the true situation in England, it is apparent that in Scotland a prosecution for the common law crime of abortion could hardly succeed, as proof of pregnancy is an essential element of that offence. None the less, the possibility of a prosecution for attempted abortion remains open.[3]

18 *R v Dhingra* (1991) Daily Telegraph, 25 January.
19 We wonder if this is a correct interpretation of the law. See D J Hurst 'The Problem of the Elderly Statute' [1983] LS 21.
20 He may have been considering the Human Fertilisation and Embryology Act 1990, s 2(3) which states that '*For the purposes of this Act*, a woman is not to be treated as carrying a child until the embryo has become implanted.' The emphasis is added but the wording could be persuasive in other branches of the law.
 1 A number of jurisdictions define the point at which legal pregnancy begins – usually as at implantation. For details, see K McK Norrie 'Post Coital Anti-pregnancy Techniques and the Law' in A A Templeton and D Cusine (eds) *Reproductive Medicine and the Law* (1990).
 2 SI 1968/390. For further brief discussion, see p 129 below.
 3 *Docherty v Brown* 1996 SLT 325.

5 Abortion

The current interest in legal abortion[1] in Great Britain is not whether it should be allowed; the practice has been with us since the passing of the Abortion Act 1967 and it is here to stay. In our view, the major significance of abortion in the context of medical ethics lies in the effect it has had on the medical ethos. The moment the Act was accepted by doctors was the moment the profession abrogated a main tenet of its Hippocratic conscience – as recently as 1994, the Declaration of Geneva, as amended in Stockholm, is advising: 'I will maintain the utmost respect for human life from its beginning.'[2] The Declaration of Oslo, however, while retaining this moral principle, modifies it to accord with modern attitudes: 'Diversity of response to this situation [the conflict of vital interests of the mother with vital interests of the child] results from the diversity of attitudes towards the life of the unborn child. This is a matter of individual conviction and conscience.'[3] This ethical watershed has spilled over to influence attitudes of doctors and towards doctors in relation to all aspects of life and death. Modern medicine now shows no embarrassment in toying with the concept of the wanted and the unwanted.

This is, however, something of a narrow view. In the wider context, attitudes to abortion depend almost entirely on where the holder stands in respect of, on the one hand, the fetal interest in life and, on the other, a woman's right to control her own body[4] and it is this which perpetuates a near intractable moral conflict. The trial of strength has been waged at relatively low key in Britain; whether this has been due to tolerance or to indifference is a matter for argument. Passion has, however, run high in the United States, where the protagonists have not been above resorting to serious crime in order to advance their cause;[5] moreover, the issue has been debated at an overtly political level. The political importance has been no less important nearer to home in the European Union, where it bid fair to forestall the reunification of Germany; there, it is possible to follow the arguments through the more staid deliberations of the legislature and the courts. We return to these examples later; meanwhile, we look briefly at the development of the law on abortion in the United Kingdom.

---

1   In our view, a great deal of emotion would be avoided if this were described as 'termination of pregnancy' leaving the term 'abortion' to signify non-medical or otherwise unlawful activity – and this was probably the intention of Parliament in the 1960s (see below). 'Abortion' is, however, now vernacular English and cannot readily be displaced.
2   There is, however, a subtle change of wording from the original 'from the time of conception'. See Appendix B.
3   See Appendix E.
4   The absolute nature of such a right is seldom questioned. The view that it is, in fact, restricted by correlative duties is put by H V McLachlan 'Bodies, Rights and Abortion' (1997) 23 J Med Ethics 176.
5   See Lancet 'This Is a Deadly Game' (1993) 342 Lancet 939. For an excellent study of the conflict in the US, see L H Tribe *Abortion: The Clash of Absolutes* (1992).

The evolution of the law on abortion

The evolution of legislation to decriminalise abortion is so well known as to merit only brief description. The fundamental law in England and Wales lies in the Offences Against the Person Act 1861, ss 58 and 59. The Act proscribes procuring the miscarriage of a woman by a third party, self-induced miscarriage, attempted procurement of miscarriage and supplying the means to do so – somewhat surprisingly, the word 'abortion' appears only in the marginal note to the sections.[6] The Act makes no distinction between criminal and therapeutic activity and, although it is currently under scrutiny, it has not been repealed. The proscription prior to 1967 was so strong that, in addition to being punished by the courts, a doctor involved in an abortion was extremely likely to have his name erased from the Medical Register. As a result, and because of the attitudes adopted to extra-marital pregnancy, a large number of abortions were performed by persons of varying skill and in varying conditions. The extent of this type of abortion has never been established satisfactorily: suffice it to say that, 40 years ago, it provided an appreciable contribution to forensic pathology.

The first statutory break in this chain is to be found in the Infant Life (Preservation) Act 1929, which introduced the offence of child destruction or causing the death of a child capable of being born alive before it has an existence independent of its mother. The offence was not committed, however, if the act was done in good faith for the purpose only of preserving the mother's life. This slight concession to the needs of therapy was still highly restrictive both as to reason and as to time – effectively, in the present context, it served only to decriminalise feticide in the event of an impacted labour. It was left to the case of *R v Bourne*[7] to temper the legal influence on medical practice in the field. Mr Bourne performed an abortion, with no attempt at secrecy, on a 15-year-old girl who was pregnant following a particularly unpleasant rape.[8] Although Mr Bourne was indicted under the Offences Against the Person Act 1861, the trial judge, Macnaghten J, took the opportunity to link the 1861 and 1929 statutes and ruled that, in a case brought under the 1861 Act, the burden rested on the Crown to satisfy the jury that the defendant did not procure the miscarriage of the girl in good faith for the purpose only of preserving her life: the word 'unlawful' in the 1861 Act 'imports the meaning expressed by the proviso in section 1(1) of the Infant Life (Preservation) Act 1929'.[9] Mr Bourne was acquitted, the summing-up essentially recognising that a woman's life depended upon her physical and mental health and that an abortion was not illegal if it was performed because these were in jeopardy.[10] The law and the medical profession then lived in

---

6 The distinction, if any, between 'miscarriage' and 'abortion' is of academic interest in relation to pre-implantation methods of contraception (see pp 111, above and 129, below). Some writers believe the terms to be interchangeable: see, eg, I J Keown '"Miscarriage": a Medico-legal Analysis' [1984] Crim LR 604.

7 [1939] 1 KB 687, [1938] 3 All ER 615.

8 There is a fascinating review of the trial and its ambience in B Brookes and P Roth '*Rex v Bourne* and the medicalization of abortion' in M Clark and C Crawford (eds) *Legal Medicine in History* (1994) ch 13.

9 [1939] 1 KB 687 at 691, [1938] 3 All ER 615 at 617.

10 [1939] 1 KB 687 at 694, [1938] 3 All ER 615 at 619. The Australian courts have also used the word 'unlawful' as indicating that there must be a 'lawful' reason for termination of pregnancy. See *R v Davidson* [1969] VR 667; *R v Wald* (1971) 3 DCR (NSW) 25.

harmony for many years; the *Bourne* decision was undoubtedly stretched to the limits of interpretation by many doctors but the law turned a sympathetic eye.

But it is never a good thing for any section of the public, no matter how well intentioned, to flirt with illegality; moreover, there was still no authority for termination of the pregnancy in the event of probable malformation or other handicap of the potential neonate – a proposition which many would regard as being of the first importance. The situation was resolved when the Abortion Act, which started out, more aptly, as the Medical Termination of Pregnancy Bill,[11] was put into law in 1967; despite repeated attack, it remained unchanged until 1990.

It is interesting to compare the historic attitudes in England with those prevailing in Scotland where abortion, either self- or otherwise induced, has always been a common law offence without being defined by statute. The whole subject, including a review of the 1967 Act, occupies less than three pages in *Gordon*.[12] The difference in concern lies in the Scottish emphasis on the evilness of intent in crimes at common law; by and large, doctors are assumed to be acting in good faith and there is little doubt that Mr Bourne would have been unable to provoke a test case in Scotland. It is, in fact, arguable that there was no need to extend the Act to Scotland; its inclusion was only justified in that it removed any doubt as to the limits of therapeutic abortion in that country where, in effect, a legal policy similar to that recognised in *Bourne* had been openly followed for decades.

The Abortion Act 1967

The Abortion Act 1967[13] has been significantly amended by the Human Fertilisation and Embryology Act 1990, s 37.[14] In summary, it now states that a person shall not be guilty of an offence under the law of abortion when termination is performed by a registered medical practitioner and two registered medical practitioners have formed the opinion in good faith that the continuance of the pregnancy would involve risk, greater than if the pregnancy were terminated, of injury to the physical or mental health of the pregnant woman or any existing children of her family (s 1(1)(a)); these therapeutic and social grounds are subject to the pregnancy not having exceeded its twenty-fourth week. The remaining justifications are now free of gestational restriction. These are that there is a risk of grave permanent injury to the physical or mental health of the pregnant woman (s 1(1)(b)); that the continuance of the pregnancy would involve risk to the life of the pregnant woman greater than if the pregnancy were terminated (s 1(1)(c)) – accounting for 128 cases in 1996; and, finally, that there is a substantial risk that, if the child were born, it would suffer from such physical or mental abnormalities as to be severely handicapped (s 1(1)(d)) – 1.1% of the total in 1996. Subsections (b) and (c) are not restricted by requiring the opinion of two registered medical practitioners; single persons may operate on their own initiative

---

11 The title was changed on the last day of the debate – almost, it seems, in a desperate effort to conclude the proceedings (Official Reports HC, vol 751, col 1780).
12 G H Gordon *The Criminal Law of Scotland* (2nd edn, 1978) ch 28.
13 Hereafter 'the 1967 Act'.
14 Hereafter 'the 1990 Act'.

in such circumstances.[15] Termination under the Act may be carried out in National Health Service hospitals or in places approved for the purpose by the Minister or the Secretary of State (s 1(3)). It is this clause which legalises abortions performed privately and for a fee. The demand for termination is, however, so great that, since 1981, a compromise position has been achieved whereby the private sector acts as an agency for the NHS. Twenty per cent of terminations were dealt with in this way in 1996 when a further 28% were performed independently of the NHS. The advent of medical methods for the termination of pregnancy has dictated a change in the location rules, which are now relaxed for this purpose.[16]

The great majority of legal abortions are performed under s 1(1)(a) of the 1967 Act for minor therapeutic or social reasons (97% of cases in England and Wales in 1996). It is arguable that the risks of an abortion to the health of a woman are always less than those of a full-term pregnancy – particularly if the termination is carried out in the first trimester.[17] Equally, it is obvious that the mental health of a woman who is carrying an unwanted pregnancy must suffer more damage if she is forced to carry her fetus than it would is she were relieved of her burden. It can also be argued that simple economics dictate that a *risk* to the well-being of any existing members of the family is occasioned by the advent of another mouth to feed. The indications are, therefore, that it is impossible for a doctor to perform an abortion in Great Britain[18] that can be shown to have been unlawful provided that all the administrative conditions are met. As a corollary, the doctor who applies the letter of the law must always be acting in good faith – indeed, possibly the only way in which a termination can be carried out in *bad* faith is when it is done without the woman's consent.[19] We have been able to find only one conviction under the Act[20] and this appears to have arisen mainly because of the way the operation was performed.

In any event, the medical profession as a whole tends to look on the Act as a success[1] – witness the opposition to change which continued to the last days of the Parliamentary debate on the 1990 Act. Occasionally, however, issues arise which strain the constancy even of the medical establishment – abortion on the basis of fetal sex selection provides such an example. The problem being put to him, Dr John Dawson, spokesman on medical ethics for the British Medical Association at the time, is reported as saying:

---

15 It is to be noted that s 1(1)(b) contains no comparative element – there simply has to be a risk.
16 Section 1(3A), inserted by the 1990 Act, s 37(3). There were 9,715 terminations involving the use of antiprogesterones in 1996.
17 The risks of pregnancy and childbirth are not constant. Overall, they are about equal but the risk of pregnancy increases with age. Conversely, the risks of abortion in young nulliparae are greater than of pregnancy unless the procedure is completed in the first eight weeks of pregnancy (P R Myerscough (1975) 1 J Med Ethics 310). Abortion methods have become much safer in the last 25 years but the complication rates still alter with gestation.
18 The Abortion Act 1967 does not extend to Northern Ireland, where the Infant Life (Preservation) Act 1929 is repeated in the Criminal Justice Act (Northern Ireland) 1945, s 25; conditions as to the latter are unaffected by the Human Fertilisation and Embryology Act 1990, s 37. The Channel Islands have recently adopted legislation which is similar to that of Great Britain.
19 And, even then, the charge would be under the Offences Against the Person Act 1861 rather than under the 1967 Act. See C Dyer 'Gynaecologist Acquitted in Hysterectomy Case' (1996) 312 BMJ 11.
20 *R v Smith (John)* [1974] 1 All ER 376, [1973] 1 WLR 1510, CA.
1 D Munday, C Francome and W Savage 'Twenty-one Years of Legal Abortion' (1989) 298 BMJ 1231.

To terminate a pregnancy solely on the grounds of the sex of the foetus is an abuse of medical skills. It is unethical and I believe the GMC should take a serious view . . . [of] a doctor who undertakes that sort of work.[2]

Which may well be so – the issue is of a different dimension from pre-conception selection which we have discussed above;[3] nevertheless, it is difficult to see it as illegal. The 1967 Act, at s 1(2), specifically states that, in making a determination as to the risk of injury to the woman's or her existing children's health, 'account may be taken of the pregnant woman's actual or reasonably foreseeable environment'. Given the right ethnic ambience – most particularly within Asian and Muslim cultures – there can be no doubt that the birth of a female child could affect a woman's mental health and, possibly, her physical well-being, and there is nothing in the Act which limits such risks to those directly associated with the condition of pregnancy.[4] Even an Anglo-Saxon may be mentally disturbed by the thought of a third male (or female) child and, while gender abortion may not constitute a major problem in our society, it serves to illustrate how wide is the facility for termination within the wording of the 1967 Act.

The availability of lawful termination has been further extended by s 37(4) of the 1990 Act, which amends s 5(1) of the 1967 Act so as to read:

No offence under the Infant Life (Preservation) Act 1929 shall be committed by a registered medical practitioner who terminates a pregnancy in accordance with the provisions of this Act.

The criminal associations with 'viability' of the fetus[5] and the living abortus (which we discuss briefly below[6]) are, therefore, now almost, although not quite, entirely dispelled.

There are still some who would regard abortion in Great Britain as being unreasonably restricted as compared with other jurisdictions;[7] even so, the scope of the Abortion Act 1967 probably exceeds that envisaged by its originators. The number of terminations carried out in England and Wales reached a peak in 1990, when almost 187,000 abortions were performed. The first fall since 1976

---

2   'Babies of Wrong Sex Aborted, Claims Report' Scotsman, 4 January 1988, p 2. See also J Sherman 'Child's Sex "Sways Mothers"' The Times 2 February 1987, p 3. It is noteworthy that it may well become a criminal offence in Germany for the doctor to reveal the sex of the fetus prior to abortion: D van Zyl Smit 'Reconciling the Irreconcilable? Recent Developments in the German Law on Abortion' (1994) 2 Med LR 302.
3   See p 59.
4   Similar views were expressed by D Morgan 'Foetal Sex Identification, Abortion and the Law' (1988) 18 Fam Law 355.
5   See p 130 below.
6   See p 133.
7   See eg D Paintin 'Abortion in the First Trimester' (1992) 305 BMJ 967. A recent poll has indicated that some 42% of the British public would support availability of abortion without any reason other than the woman's choice: J Wise 'British Public Supports Legal Abortion for All' (1997) 314 BMJ 627. There are suggestions that a private members' Bill may be introduced to Parliament with at least partial government backing: R Sylvester 'Labour MP Aims to Relax Abortion Law' Daily Telegraph, 20 January 1998, p 4.

occurred in 1991 and the trend continued until 1995; there was, however, a sharp rise in 1996, when the total number of legal terminations involving resident women was 167,916, giving a rate of 15.51/1000 resident women in the age group 15-44 years. The comparable figures for Scotland, where both the number and the rate of abortions have continued to rise, were 11,978 terminations involving 10.9/1000 women in 1996.

The number of terminations provided for foreign women in England and Wales in 1996 represented 5.3% of the total. This shows a marked decline from the peak in 1973 when 33.8% of legal abortions were for patients from overseas. Clearly, there have been policy changes in other countries and it is worth considering some of these briefly.

The comparative position

Northern Ireland

We have, thus far, spoken only in terms of Great Britain as far as domestic law is concerned. The position in Northern Ireland is particularly sensitive, due to its close association with the Republic of Ireland – where abortion remains illegal under art 40.3.3 of the Constitution and is not universally supported even in the event of risk to the life of the mother.[8] As a result, the Abortion Act 1967 does not run to the Province, where the law is still governed by the 1861 Act; this has, however, been modified by some important court decisions. In *Re K (a minor)*,[9] it was held that the law lay in the 1861 Act as modified by the charge to the jury in *R v Bourne*;[10] termination of a 13-week pregnancy in a severely handicapped ward of court was authorised. Again, in *Re A*,[11] the court used the reasoning in *Bourne* to apply the Criminal Justice Act (NI) 1945, s 25 to the 1861 Act; a termination was held to be in

8   A Murdoch 'Irish Doctors Row over Limited Abortion Rights' (1993) 306 BMJ 675. The law in the Republic of Ireland is in a state of flux, with a number of important decisions having been taken recently. The right of the state to prohibit the dissemination of abortion information was upheld in the Court of Justice of the European Communities: *SPUC v Grogan* [1991] 3 CMLR 849, (1992) 9 BMLR 100, but this was countered in the European Court of Human Rights: *Open Door Counselling Ltd and Dublin Well Woman Centre Ltd v Ireland* (1992) 18 BMLR 1. In addition, the Supreme Court of Ireland extended the grounds for a legal abortion to include when it was probable that there was 'a real and substantial risk to the life of the mother' in *A-G v X* [1992] 2 CMLR 277, (1992) 15 BMLR 104 – while, at the same time, affirming that Irish women had no *general* right to travel abroad to obtain an abortion. A referendum held in November 1992 confirmed the Irish people's preference for access to information and travel; a proposal to liberalise the basic law was defeated – but mainly for procedural reasons: A Murdoch 'Irish Vote Against Abortion on Their Soil' (1992) 305 BMJ 1383. For a fuller discussion of the Irish (and German, see below) scene, see the slightly outdated R Boland 'Abortion Law in Europe in 1991-1992' (1993) 21 J Law Med & Ethics 72. A detailed description of the basic Irish law is in A Sherlock 'The Right to Life of the Unborn and the Irish Constitution' (1989) 24 (NS) Irish Jurist 13.

9   *Re K (a minor) (Northern Health and Social Services Board v F and G)* (1991) 2 Med LRev 371.

10 [1939] 1 KB 687, [1938] 3 All ER 615.

11 *Re A (Northern Health and Social Services Board v AMNH)* (1991) 2 Med LRev 274.

the handicapped woman's best interests. It will be seen, below, that a very similar situation – albeit one that could be regarded as confusing – exists in New South Wales, where a particularly liberal approach to abortion has evolved. Thus, it may well be that the potential exists for homologation of abortion practice throughout the component parts of the United Kingdom. However, such a potential has not yet been realised; 1,573 women from Northern Ireland, along with 4,894 from the Irish Republic, obtained terminations in England and Wales during 1996.

The United States

Practice in the United States has been profoundly modified as a result of persistent legal intervention which has been notable for its absence in Great Britain.

Abortion laws in the mid-twentieth century differed in the various States of the United States. Some, as in New York, were wholly liberal; some, in Texas, corresponded roughly to the English Infant Life (Preservation) Act; but the majority followed variations on the United Kingdom Abortion Act. Then, in 1973, the Supreme Court altered the whole picture in the historic twin decisions of *Roe v Wade*[12] and *Doe v Bolton*.[13] The effect of these well-known cases can be summarised: it is an invasion of a woman's constitutional right to privacy to limit her access to abortion by statute – and this applies also to schoolchildren, although their parents may still be informed of the circumstances;[14] the expression 'to preserve the life' of a woman is unconstitutionally vague, although 'to preserve the life or health' is acceptable – which raises an intriguing conflict. It was suggested at the time of the decision[15] that health is inclusive of convenience and that this effectively allows for abortion on demand – and although the Supreme Court specifically stated that there was no such absolute constitutional right, there is no doubt that the result of *Roe* is that abortion during the first trimester is an inalienable prerogative of the American woman and is grounded in the right to individual privacy. To confirm the essential nature of privacy, the court also ruled that an appeal on the grounds that wholly liberal laws were invalid because they deprived unborn children of the right to life was not available to an individual. Nevertheless, the court did give some regard to the rights of the developing fetus. In the first trimester, the question of abortion was to be decided solely between the woman and her physician; during the second trimester, the State could intervene by reason of its interest in the health of the mother, no such interest being vested in the fetus – interference of this type could include stating where and by whom an abortion could be done. After 'viability', which the court assessed as somewhere between the twenty-fourth and twenty-eighth week of pregnancy, it was agreed that the State had a compelling interest in the health of the fetus and could, therefore, constitutionally intervene on its behalf excepting when the conditions threatened the life or health of the mother.

The decision in *Roe v Wade*, which has resulted in nearly one-third of pregnancies in the United States being terminated legally, has been a subject of controversy ever

12 93 S Ct 705 (1973).
13 93 S Ct 739 (1973).
14 *HL v Matheson* 101 S Ct 1164 (1981).
15 J H Ely 'The Wages of Crying Wolf: A Comment on *Roe v Wade*' (1973) 82 Yale LJ 920.

since its pronouncement.[16] In the first place, it satisfies virtually no one; the anti-abortionists have been, inevitably, outraged, while the feminist lobby sees the result as being still too restrictive of women's rights. Secondly, the trimester rule is unreliable in that it rests upon fluctuating medical expertise and medical technology.[17] This was well put by O'Connor J:

> The lines drawn [in *Roe*] have now become 'blurred' . . . The state can no longer rely on a 'bright line' that separates permissible from impermissible regulation. . . . Rather, the State must continuously and conscientiously study contemporary medical and scientific literature in order to determine whether the effect of a particular regulation is to "depart from accepted medical practice".[18]

There are, however, practical reasons why, very unusually in the field of medical jurisprudence, American attitudes have little influence on British thinking in this area. Fundamentally, and despite the emotions it engenders, abortion in the United States is not so much a philosophical issue as it is one of constitutional law.[19] Moreover, the subject has become highly politicised and the Supreme Court, which interprets the Constitution, is subject to political adjustment. Thus, the Supreme Court firmly repelled a major attack on *Roe* which was mounted in the mid-1980s.[20] However, a change in personnel encouraged a further sally towards the end of the decade[1] which was rather more successful in that, although the court was unwilling to overturn the principles laid down in *Roe*, it upheld a Missouri statute which certainly limited the availability of abortion; the implication is that other States will be able to introduce similar restrictions. Apart from some considerations as to fetal viability, the central issue in *Webster* turned on the State's right to restrict the reasons for which pregnancies could be terminated at public expense. Indeed, it has been held for some time[2] that federal funding in the form of 'Medicaid' is available for abortions only in limited circumstances – such as preserving the life of the mother or terminating pregnancies resulting from rape or incest – and that, accordingly, the individual State health systems need not contribute towards expenses incurred on other grounds.[3]

---

16 It is poignant to find that 'Ms Roe' has been converted to the 'pro-life' cause and that, in fact, she never obtained her own termination: N McCorvey 'My Legal Fight Helped Start a Generation of Child Slaughter and That Makes Me Weep' Daily Telegraph, 20 January 1998, p 4.
17 N K Rhoden 'Trimesters and Technology: Revamping *Roe v Wade*' (1986) 95 Yale LJ 639.
18 In *Akron v Akron Center for Reproductive Health* 462 US 416 (1983) at 455-456.
19 R Dworkin 'The Great Abortion Case' New York Review, 29 June 1989, p 49. See also I Loveland 'Abortion and the U.S. Supreme Court' (1992) 142 NLJ 974.
20 *American College of Obstetricians and Gynaecologists v Thornburgh* 476 US 747 (1986).
 1 *Webster v Reproductive Health Services* 109 S Ct 3040 (1989). For extensive and critical discussion, see W Dellinger and G B Sperling 'Abortion and the Supreme Court: The Retreat from *Roe v Wade*' (1989) 138 U Penn LR 83 and related papers. In J Bopp and R E Coleson 'What Does *Webster* Mean' (1989) 138 U Penn LR 157, the authors maintain, inter alia, that 'the trimester scheme may be considered *de facto* and *sub silentio* overruled'.
 2 *Harris v McRae* 100 S Ct 2671 (1980).
 3 The Supreme Court was due to hear another case involving financial pressures – in this instance, a matter of refurbishment of abortion clinics – but the matter was resolved out of court: *Ragsdale v Turnock* 763 F 2d 1532 (1985).

The struggle, however, continued. In 1992 the Supreme Court was, again, asked to pronounce on the legality of a State statute – in this case, the Abortion Control Act of Pennsylvania, which created a number of obstacles in the way of abortion 'on demand'. The issue, here, as in many of the United States cases, was not so much related to a maternal/fetal conflict as to one involving, on the one hand, the woman's right to bodily privacy and, on the other, the State's interest in the protection of life and a preference for childbirth over abortion.[4] Simplistically, the Supreme Court introduced an 'undue burden' test – which meant that the State was empowered to impose financial, medical or emotional barriers to abortion provided that these did not become a substantial obstacle, or undue burden, to choosing abortion; the basic premise of the woman's liberty of conscience and bodily integrity was, in this way, upheld. Even so, some fetal rights were maintained, in that States could restrict abortion of the 'viable' fetus save in relation to a medical emergency threatening the mother. Needless to say, this decision was by the barest of majorities and powerful dissenting opinions were handed down – including a rejection of the whole concept of a fundamental women's liberty to choose abortion. The opinion has been said to please no lobby[5] and there is every indication that the abortion debate will continue in the United States in an atmosphere of increasing acrimony and increasing subservience to political exigency.[6]

The British Commonwealth

Turning to the Commonwealth, the most interesting, and hard fought, abortion battles have been waged in Canada where, until the last decade, the law was not outstandingly liberal. Control of legal terminations was vested in hospital abortion committees under the Criminal Code 1971, s 251; in the long-running case of *R v Morgentaler*,[7] however, the Supreme Court held that this section violated the security and liberty of the pregnant woman. The Chief Justice expressed his reasons for this conclusion as follows:

> Forcing a woman, by threat of criminal sanction, to carry a fetus to term unless she meets certain criteria unrelated to her own priorities and aspirations, is a profound interference with a woman's body and thus a violation of security of the person.[8]

---

4 *Planned Parenthood of Southeastern Pennsylvania v Casey* 112 S Ct 2791 (1992). See A Charo 'Undue Burden of Abortion' (1992) 340 Lancet 44.
5 See Loveland (1992) 142 NLJ 974.
6 Most recently, the problem of the control of the method of abortion – in the form of 'partial birth abortion' – has been before Congress: J Rovner 'US Senate Puts Off Vote to Ban Abortion Method' (1995) 346 Lancet 1353. When a Bill to ban the method was eventually passed, the President vetoed the measure. Training in abortion has also come under attack: Editorial Comment (1996) 347 Lancet 1055.
7 [1988] 1 SCR 30.
8 Ibid at 56, per Dickson CJ. For discussion of this decision, see M L McConnell 'Abortion and Human Rights: An Important Canadian Decision' (1989) 38 ICLQ 905.

In parallel litigation, the Canadian Charter of Rights and Freedom, Article 7 of which guarantees the 'right to life, liberty and security of the person', was held to be inapplicable to the fetus.[9] Those opposed to abortion gained a surprise victory in *Tremblay v Daigle*[10] – in which a father gained an interlocutory injunction to prevent the abortion of his child; the decision rested on the Provincial Charter of Rights and the case was held under the civil law jurisdiction of Quebec. The situation was, however, short-lived, the full Supreme Court of Canada reversing the decision unanimously.[11] It is to be noted that neither the Supreme Court of the United States nor that of Canada will allow of a 'trade-off' or balancing act between fetal and maternal rights to life or health – it is the latter which is to be safeguarded.

The innate tendency towards liberal abortion law is also demonstrated in Australia where, other than in South Australia and the Northern Territories, which have enabling statutes, the basic law corresponds to that in the Offences Against the Person Act 1861. Judicial interpretation of the word 'unlawful' in relation to medical practice has resulted in a very wide availability of terminations – prosecution of doctors has been notable for its absence, at least in New South Wales: there is a strong possibility that abortion is not intrinsically an unlawful act in the common law States of Australia.[12] The continued presence of an offence of abortion in the Criminal Code of Western Australia has, however, given rise to uncertainty. In that state, two doctors were charged in 1998 with procuring abortion – a move which provoked a parliamentary attempt to decriminalise the procedure.[13]

The German experience

The recent history of German legislation is instructive and is of practical importance in the light of current attempts to unify abortion law throughout the European Community.[14] Here, abortion legislation was isolated as the only exception to the general reunification formula that Western institutional and legislative experience should be extended to the East.[15] Simplistically, the existing situation was that, whereas abortion during the first 12 weeks of pregnancy was controlled solely by the free choice of the pregnant woman in the East, abortion was illegal in the West save in specific circumstances dependent, in large part, on 'stage of the fetus' provisions – a situation analogous to that in Britain with 'general hardship' substituted for the

---

9 *Borowski v A-G of Canada* (1987) 39 DLR (4th) 731 (Sask, CA).

10 (1989) 59 DLR (4th) 609.

11 (1990) 62 DLR (4th) 634.

12 *CES v Superclinics* (1995) 38 NSWLR 47 per Kirby AC-J. For commentary, see K Petersen 'Medical Negligence and Wrongful Birth Actions: Australian Developments' (1997) 23 J Med Ethics 319.

13 D Reardon 'Doctors Call for Abortion Reform' The Age, 14 February, 1998. At the time of writing, the Criminal Code Amendment (Abortion) Bill 1998 (WA) appears to be stalled in Parliament. For previous Australian judicial decisions, see p 114, n 10 above. A very useful comparison is to be found in K Petersen 'Abortion Laws: Comparative and Feminist Perspectives in Australia, England and the United States' (1996) 2 Med Law Internat 77. For a complete overview, see the same author's *Abortion Regimes* (1993).

14 Where some countries have exceptionally liberal laws – eg Denmark, where woman have a right to first trimester abortions.

15 Treaty on German Unity (31 August 1990), art 31 *Family and Women*, para 4, Bundesgesetzblatt (BGbl) II, 1990, p 885.

social clause in the 1967 Act. Approximately 33% of pregnancies were terminated in East Germany but, very interestingly, abortions were at least as frequent in the West. Controversy, therefore, rested on a purely ideological base. The conflict was fuelled by a resurgence of activity by both conservative and liberal elements in West Germany but was, at the same time, dampened by an increasingly wide perception of abortion as a potentially dangerous piece of social engineering rather than a woman's right.[16]

The compromise was that the issue would be settled on a free vote in the Bundestag two years after reunification. The federal parliament duly passed a law under which a pregnant woman could choose to have an abortion in the first three months of pregnancy provided she had undergone social counselling at least three days before the termination was carried out.[17] After long deliberation, the Constitutional Court declared that the new legislation was contrary to the Basic Law in certain respects – in particular, the new law failed to meet the minimum standards for the protection of unborn human life as set out in the Constitution; these could only be satisfied if the state placed a fundamental legal duty on the woman to carry her fetus to term.[18] As an interim measure, procedures were laid down which, if followed, would render consensual abortion within the first three months of pregnancy still illegal but not subject to criminal sanction.[19] The court's decision was founded on the premise that abortion offends against that part of the German Constitution which 'guarantees the right to life and freedom from bodily harm' – a right which extends, even if in modified form, to the fetus. These provisional measures continued in force until 1996, when a new law came into effect.[20] Abortion now remains illegal, but no criminal sanctions will be applied if it is performed within specified limits. Abortion is freely available on request in the first 12 weeks of pregnancy provided the woman has been counselled by her own doctor and by staff from an independent counselling centre. In providing this counselling, the doctor must give priority to the protection of the fetus. After 12 weeks, abortion is available when the life or the health of the woman is threatened or if the fetus suffers from a serious defect.

Compromise, albeit an imperfect solution, depolarises attitudes and fosters less violent confrontation.[1] The German experience, however, reinforces the view that, in the context of abortion, it dictates some acknowledgment of fetal rights and, here, one senses a wind of change blowing against a well-established screen in several jurisdictions.

---

16 E Kolinsky 'Women in the New Germany' in G Smith et al (eds) *Developments in German Politics* (1992) ch 14.

17 A Tuffs 'Germany: Abortion, the Woman's Choice' (1992) 340 Lancet 43.

18 H Karcher 'Abortion Law Diluted Again in Germany' (1993) 306 BMJ 1566; A Tuffs 'Germany: Illegality of Abortion' (1993) 341 Lancet 1467.

19 A form of prevarication which seems to be part of the Continental jurisdictions: cf the Dutch attitude to euthanasia (see p 417 below). Other 'compromises' were introduced – eg an illegal abortion could not be funded from statutory medical insurance but the woman could, subsequently, enjoy the social welfare and unemployment benefits. A useful summary is in M Prutzel-Thomas 'The Abortion Issue and the Federal Constitutional Court' (1993) 2 German Politics 467. See also the very full commentary by D van Zyl Smit (1994) 2 Med LR 302.

20 Schwangeren-und Familienhilfänderungsgesetz (1995).

1 But cannot eliminate it – see the dogged opposition from the Bavarian Government: S Goldbeck-Wood 'Bavaria Threatens to Reduce Abortion Access' (1996) 312 BMJ 1118.

The rights of the fetus

Roe v Wade highlights the fundamental ethical issue in abortion: at what point, and in what circumstances, does a fetus become a person, and at what point, if any, does that person have rights to an existence? This, however, is only a part of the assessment of what might loosely be called 'fetal rights' and which should, logically, be considered as a whole. We intend to follow that concept in this chapter. What follows is, therefore, related to abortion only in part; nevertheless, this chapter is a convenient place in which to consider the wider spectrum of fetal/maternal relationships.

What constitutes personhood is a matter of moral decision and is not one of scientific fact. The conservative view, as exemplified, particularly by the Roman Catholic Church, lies at one extreme; this holds that personhood and the right to protection exist from the moment of conception. We suggest that there are few other than academic theologians who would support this decision; there are, in fact, relatively good reasons, based, inter alia, on the totipotential capacity of the early embryonic cells, for regarding the pre-implantation morula as being, also, pre-embryonic. At the other end of the scale, there are those who would equate personhood with intellect and with the power to make decisions.[2] We reject such an extreme, if for no reason other than that it would deprive even young infants of the rights of a person. Many attempts have been made to define the point at which the fetus is morally entitled to, at least, consideration within these brackets – the Jewish rabbinical law, for example, sets the time as when pregnancy is recognisable externally;[3] the early Christian moralists were attracted to the evidence of life exhibited by quickening;[4] and, currently, there is an increasing tendency to accord the fetus 'rights' at viability, the complications of which as to definition are discussed later in this chapter. Even today, the law itself is inconsistent: 'Tort, criminal and constitutional law all have their own working definition of "person" and the protection to which the fetus is entitled.'[5] At this point, we would only remark on the well appreciated fact that the limits of viability in terms of gestation periods will be steadily lowered to their physiological baseline as neonatal medicine improves and becomes more widely available. As O'Connor J put it in *Akron*:[6] 'The [*Roe v Wade*] framework is on a collision course with itself'; it is this inevitable trend that has sustained the many attempts to amend the British Abortion Act – and there are few indications that the conflict between the recognition of fetal rights and the promotion of increasingly permissive abortion laws is likely to abate.

As to the general law, it is everywhere accepted that, although fetal rights may be established while in utero – or even before conception – they cannot be realised unless

---

2   M Tooley 'A Defense of Abortion and Infanticide' in J Feinberg (ed) *The Problem of Abortion* (1973) and H Kuhse and P Singer *Should the Baby Live?* (1985), in particular, ch 6.

3   A Steinberg 'Induced Abortion in Jewish Law' (1980) 1 Int J Law Med 187.

4   See G R Dunstan 'The Moral Status of the Human Embryo: A Tradition Recalled' (1984) 10 J Med Ethics 38 for a comprehensive review.

5   A Peterfy 'Fetal Viability as a Threshold to Personhood' (1995) 16 J Leg Med 607 provides a most interesting overview.

6   462 US 416 (1983).

the fetus is born alive;[7] moreover, the legal concept of a separate existence is still further limited in England and Wales in the Congenital Disabilities (Civil Liberty) Act 1976, under which the neonate must survive for 48 hours before being able to recover damages in negligence. 'There can be no doubt, in my view', said Sir George Baker,[8] 'that in England and Wales the foetus has no right of action, no right at all, until birth' and the same is equally true in Scotland – Scots law recognises no right of the fetus to continue to exist in its mother's womb.[9] From Canada, we have: 'There is no existing basis in law which justifies a conclusion that foetuses are legal persons',[10] from which it follows that a stillbirth cannot benefit. No suit for wrongful fetal death is recognisable in the United Kingdom[11] and we are left with an apparent paradox – as Pace[12] has put it: 'Liability is incurred for negligent injury to the foetus but not – or, at least, not necessarily – for its deliberate destruction.' There is, however, evidence that some jurisdictions are moving towards the recognition of such suits. Thus, in the United States, we read in very similar vein:

> To deny a stillborn recovery for fatal injuries during gestation while allowing such recovery for a child born alive would make it more profitable for the defendant to kill the plaintiff than to scratch him.[13]

The tone in this case, and in others that have both preceded it and followed it, indicates not so much a shift in jurisprudential reasoning as a logical wish for punitive sanctions against the person who negligently destroys the child in utero – another form of expression of an intrinsic public concern for the status of the fetus.[14]

There are strong indications that the United Kingdom courts are also anxious to invest the fetus with as positive an identity as is possible within current legal constraints. In general terms, we have the Master of the Rolls stressing the right of an adult to refuse life-saving treatment but, at the same time, acknowledging that there

---

7 An exception probably lies in the criminal law of California, where an offence of feticide appears to be established: *People v Davis* 872 P 2d 591 (Cal 1994). The courts in other states seem to be resisting such a move: eg *State v Green* 781 P 2d 678 (Kan 1987).

8 *Paton v British Pregnancy Advisory Service Trustees* [1979] QB 276 at 279, [1978] 2 All ER 987 at 989.

9 *Kelly v Kelly* 1997 SLT 896, 1997 SCLR 749, per Cullen LJ-C. But see the suggested protection of the fetus in relation to advance refusal of treatment in the draft Incapable Adults (Scotland) Bill, c 40(b)(d).

10 *Borowski v A-G of Canada and Minister of Finance of Canada* (1984) 4 DLR (4th) 112 at 131, per Matheson J.

11 Damages have been given for a stillbirth resulting from negligent treatment: *Bagley v North Herts Health Authority* [1986] NLJ Rep 1014. These were, however, to the mother; damages in respect of bereavement under the Fatal Accidents Act 1976 were expressly disallowed on the grounds that the negligence had caused the child to die in utero. The court was, however, at pains to ensure adequate compensation notwithstanding. See also *Grieve v Salford Health Authority* [1991] 2 Med LR 295, where only the quantum of damages for negligence leading to stillbirth was considered.

12 P J Pace 'Civil Liability for Pre-natal Injury' (1977) 40 MLR 141.

13 *Amadio v Levin* 501 A 2d 1085 (Pa, 1985).

14 It seems that, while 'wrongful fetal death' statutes are uniform throughout the US, judicial interpretation varies – an action for wrongful death was dismissed in *Milton v Cary Medical Center* 538 A 2d 252 (Me, 1988) and, in general, most States operate a 'viability' limitation with recovery available only to the viable fetus. For further discussion, see B Dickens 'Wrongful Birth and Life, Wrongful Death before Birth, and Wrongful Law' in S A M McLean (ed) *Legal Issues in Human Reproduction* (1989) and Peterfy (1995) 16 J Leg Med 607.

might well be an exception to the rule were a viable fetus to be involved[15] – this was, however, an obiter statement that has been put to the test and rejected.[16] In England, it has been held that the fetus has common law rights irrespective of the Congenital Disabilities (Civil Liability) Act 1976[17] and, in Australia, this has been extended to an acceptance of a fetal right to sue its mother for negligent injury in utero.[18] The trial judge in that case said:

> I would hold that an injury to an infant suffered during . . . its journey through life between conception and parturition is not injury to a person devoid of personality other than that of the mother-to-be. Nicole's personality was identifiable and recognisable.

A similar trend has been evidenced in Scotland, where a fetus has been recognised as a person when criminally injured under the Road Traffic Act 1972,[19] while a similar extension of the statutory 'person' beyond a being 'with legal personality' has been approved under the Damages (Scotland) Act 1976:[20]

> It is perfectly common in ordinary speech to refer to a child in the womb as 'he', 'she', 'him' or 'her' . . . it was this child who sustained injuries to his person and who died in consequence of personal injuries sustained by him.[1]

But, despite the evident tone of judicial concern, all these later examples depend upon the fetus being born alive and it can be said with confidence that there is no civil action available to the fetus in the United Kingdom for its negligent death.[2] Nevertheless, the cases demonstrate a clear intention to acknowledge – or even create – a persona in the fetus when it is possible to do so,[3] a tendency which has caused some difficulty in the field of criminal law.

Strictly speaking, it could be said that *A-G's Reference (No 3 of 1994)*[4] has no relevance to abortion. Nevertheless, it is of major significance as to judicial attitudes to fetal status and this seems the most appropriate place to discuss the case. In essence, the case concerned the stabbing of a pregnant woman who gave birth to a severely premature baby two weeks later; it transpired that, contrary to what had

---

15 *Re T (adult: refusal of medical treatment)* [1992] 4 All ER 649 at 653, (1992) 9 BMLR 46 at 50. For a similar Scottish approach, see Incapable Adults (Scotland) Bill 1995, c 40(6)(d).
16 See p 139 below for further discussion. See *Re MB (caesarian section)* [1997] 2 FCR 541, (1997) 38 BMLR 175 and, more recently, *St George's Healthcare NHS Trust v S* [1998] 3 All ER 673. The problem of the enforced caesarian operation is dealt with at some length in chapter 10.
17 *Burton v Islington Health Authority; de Martell v Merton and Sutton Health Authority* [1992] 3 All ER 833, (1993) 10 BMLR 63.
18 Reported by D Brahams 'Australian Mother Sued by Child Injured in Utero' (1991) 338 Lancet 687. This being a road traffic accident, there seems no reason why such an action should not be available in England under the 1976 Act (see p 134 below).
19 *McCluskey v HM Advocate* 1989 SLT 175, [1989] RTR 182. The importance of subsequent live birth was, however, confirmed in the Sheriff Court in *HM Advocate v McDougall* 1994 Crim LB 12-3.
20 *Hamilton v Fife Health Board* 1993 SLT 624. The 1976 Act must now be read in conjunction with the Damages (Scotland) Act 1993.
1 Ibid at 629.
2 A Whitfield 'Common Law Duties to Unborn Children' (1993) 1 Med LRev 28.
3 But the Canadian courts are still resolute: see the criminal case *R v Sullivan* (1991) 63 CCC (3d) 97.
4 [1996] QB 581, [1996] 2 All ER 10, CA.

been supposed, the fetus had been injured in the assault and the infant died 120 days after birth. The attacker was charged with murder and the trial judge directed an acquittal on the grounds that no conviction for murder or manslaughter was possible under the existing law. The Attorney General then sought a ruling from the Court of Appeal, asking whether the crimes of murder or manslaughter could be committed where unlawful injury was deliberately inflicted to a child in utero or to a mother carrying a child in utero, where the child was born alive and died having existed independently of the mother, the injuries in utero having caused or made a substantial contribution to the death; the court was also asked whether the fact that the child's death was caused solely as a consequence of injury to the *mother* could remove any liability for murder or manslaughter in those circumstances.

We are concerned here not with the niceties of the criminal law but, rather, with those aspects of the judgment which relate to the status of the fetus in utero. In this respect, Lord Taylor LCJ developed a two-stage argument. First, it was held that, in the eyes of the law, the unborn fetus is deemed to be part of the mother – an intention to cause serious harm to the fetus is, therefore, an intention to cause severe injury to a part of the mother; and, this being the case, malice directed at the mother can be transferred to the fetus once it is born.[5]

This decision was greeted by many lay commentators as another step towards the recognition of a fetal right to life. In fact, it is nothing of the kind, in so far as it deprives the fetus of any individual personality it previously enjoyed. The concept of an intention directed towards a child capable of becoming a person in being was summarily rejected – as Lord Taylor put it:

> An intention to cause serious bodily injury to the foetus is an intention to cause serious bodily injury to a part of the mother just as an intention to injure her arm or her leg would be so viewed[6]

thus glossing over the difference that an arm is incapable of developing into an individual human being. And, in fact, the House of Lords would have nothing to do with that view when the case was referred to them,[7] Lord Mustill believing it to be wholly unfounded in fact.[8] Pointing to the truism that mother and fetus were unique human beings once the latter was born, his Lordship emphasised that the maternal-fetal relationship was one of bond, not of identity. In effect, the fetus was neither a 'person' nor an adjunct of its mother – it was a unique organism. Unfortunately, the House never defined the nature of that unique organism save in the negative sense that it is not a person in being while in utero – there is no offence of feticide and there never has been. At the same time:

> For the foetus, life lies in the future, not the past. It is not sensible to say that [the foetus] cannot ever be harmed or that nothing can be done to it which can ever be dangerous ...

5 For an analysis of this decision, see M Seneviratne 'Pre-natal Injury and Transferred Malice: The Invented Other' (1996) 59 MLR 884.
6 [1996] 2 All ER 10 at 18.
7 *A-G's Reference (No 3 of 1994)* [1998] 1 Cr App Rep 91, HL.
8 Ibid at 98.

It may also carry with it the effects of things done to it before birth which, after birth, may prove to be harmful.[9]

Thus, the fetus remains a person-in-waiting – or a thing which will, in due course, become something; *A-G's Reference (No 3 of 1994)*, in the end, does nothing to improve its status.

Even so, the movement towards such improvement is fuelled by two developments which cannot be ignored – the availability of fetal therapy and an increasing recognition of risks to the health of the fetus which may be taken by pregnant women. Neither affects the abortion issue directly but each may have a profound effect on instinctive reactions to the debate;[10] we discuss the relevant cases later.[11] For the present, we note only that both offend against the extreme feminist view which can be paraphrased as holding that the fetus is no more than a complex cellular appendage to its mother. There cannot be many who would sustain this interpretation – and it was certainly rejected by the House of Lords, where Lord Mustill[12] noted that the reason for the uniqueness of the fetus lies in the fact that its genes differ from those of its mother. Life is a constructive continuum from conception to birth and from infancy to adulthood and the so-called fetal-maternal conflict can be expressed in moral terms in two quotations:

> The increasing tendency to view the fetus as an independent patient or person occurs at the cost of reducing the woman to the status of little more than a maternal environment.[13]

and

> The developing human life has a great intrinsic value. It cannot be viewed purely as a part of the woman's body.[14]

Some middle view has to be reached if we are not to drift into accepting the principle that the unwanted should be destroyed simply because they are unwanted. Many years ago, Ely[15] remarked, in relation to the right to privacy, that there is not a wide difference between being inconvenienced by a fetus and being inconvenienced by an unwanted infant. There is much to commend the concept of the maternal-fetal

9 Ibid at 116, per Lord Hope.
10 See the searching article by D Callahan 'How Technology is Reframing the Abortion Debate' (1986) Hastings Center Report, February, p 33.
11 See p 134 below.
12 *A-G's Reference (No 3 of 1944)* [1998] 1 Cr App Rep 91 at 99. In the same case, Lord Hope showed that the theory becomes untenable once one admits of in vitro fertilisation (at 112).
13 J Benschol 'Reasserting Women's Rights, in 'Late Abortion and Technological Advances in Fetal Viability' (1985) 17 Fam Plan Perspect 162, quoted by Callahan (1986) Hastings Centre Report, February p 33.
14 Swedish Government Official Report 'The Pregnant Woman and the Fetus – Two Individuals' SOU 1989.51. The aborted pre-viable fetus which is recognisable as such must now be given a respectful cremation in Sweden. See K Kallenberg, L Forslin and O Westerborn 'The Disposal of the Aborted Fetus – New Guidelines: Ethical Considerations in the Debate in Sweden' (1993) 19 J Med Ethics 32.
15 (1973) 82 Yale LJ 920.

unity[16] – or symbiosis – which forces attention on the individual pregnant woman rather than simply on a woman or on a fetus, a dichotomy which serves only to polarise opinion.

The fetal status does, however, have additional important practical legal connotations at the beginning of and towards the end of pregnancy. The 1967 Act deals with the termination of pregnancy but certain procedures, in particular menstrual extraction and post-coital insertion of intrauterine devices, are performed partly because a pregnancy might exist before any definite diagnosis can be made. In the absence of any relevant amendment of the Act, it is doubtful if menstrual extraction, which deals with a problematical implantation, can be legal under the terms of the statute, which is concerned with the assessment of an established pregnancy. Nevertheless, interceptive and displanting contraception are forms of 'after the fact' action to prevent the birth of an unwanted baby which are less likely to offend the public conscience than is frank fetal destruction; it seems illogical that they could be uniquely liable to censure under the Offences Against the Person Act 1861, s 58. The acquittal in *R v Dhingra* on just such a charge has been discussed above.[17]   In withdrawing the case from the jury, the judge said:

> It is highly unlikely any ovum became implanted and only at the completion of implantation does the embryo become a fetus. At this stage she can be regarded as pregnant.[18]

Whether or not this is a binding statement of the law, it is a policy which we feel should be accepted. We have argued the importance of implantation on general ethical grounds already;[19] we also agree strongly that the ruling in *Dhingra* needs to be followed in order to harmonise the Offences Against the Person Act 1861, the Abortion Act 1967 and the Human Fertilisation and Embryology Act 1990.[20]

Consideration of early termination techniques must now include 'medical' abortion. There has been surprisingly little overt opposition to the method in Britain[1] – although, by contrast, the introduction of mifepristone in France resulted in pressure sufficient to force the manufacturers to withdraw the product until the government, as major shareholders, insisted on the resumption of research and clinical evaluation. Emotional accusations such as 'the launching of chemical warfare against unborn children' were met by emollient attempts to recategorise the process as 'contragestation' rather than abortion.[2]   It is a measure of the intensity of the abortion debate in the United States that the antiprogestin RU 486 is not available there because of

16 Originally expressed in R F R Gardner 'A New Ethical Approach to Abortion and its Implications for the Euthanasia Dispute' (1975) 1 J Med Ethics 127.

17 See p 112.

18 *R v Dhingra*: T Shaw 'GP Cleared of Procuring His Secretary's Miscarriage' Daily Telegraph, 25 January 1991, p 5. In the absence of a full report of this case, it is difficult to see why, even so, there was no offence in so far as an offence is created by s 58 'whether [the woman] be or be not with child'.

19 See p 73.

20 A Grubb 'The New Law of Abortion: Clarification or Ambiguity?' [1991] Crim LR 659.

1 Nearly 4,000 terminations using antiprogesterones were carried out in England and Wales in 1993.

2 E-E Baulieu 'RU 486 as an Antiprogesterone Steroid: From Receptor to Contragestion and Beyond' (1989) 262 J Amer Med Ass 1808.

the manufacturers' reluctance to become involved.[3] The treatment is distinguished from post-coital contraception[4] in that it is clearly abortifacient; it can, therefore, be administered only within the terms of the 1967 Act – interestingly, a company attempting to patent a similarly acting product was forced to include a disclaimer to this effect over a decade ago.[5] We view the introduction of 'contragestation' therapy with some concern as, in the same way as the 'morning after pill', it will inevitably come to be regarded as a safe form of contraceptive back-up. The result must be to blur the distinction, which we regard as essential, between contraception and abortion; while the two processes may be comparable in that they both *prevent* new life, it is only abortion that can be seen as *taking* life.

At the other end of fetal life, any criminal liability of doctors for aborting a viable fetus has now been removed.[6] None the less, practical and moral implications still surround the living abortus and a brief consideration of 'viability' is still apposite – if only to assist understanding of the comparative law. Viability is something of a legal fiction, originating in the United States, designed to define some point at which the state accepts a compelling interest to protect the lives of its unborn citizens; conceptually, therefore, viability is a term of constitutional law and it probably has no place in English law.[7] The attainment of American viability purports to coincide with the gestational age at which the fetus can be presumed to be capable of an existence separate from its mother and, as has been seen, the US Supreme Court has set this as lying between the twenty-fourth and twenty-eighth weeks of pregnancy.[8] United Kingdom legislation has, however, concentrated on the concept of being born, or being capable of being born, alive. Live birth is undefined and has generally been interpreted as the converse of stillbirth – effectively, a certificate of stillbirth cannot be issued if, having fully proceeded from its mother, the neonate breathed or showed any other sign of life. This carries no time limitation and, furthermore, leaves open what are 'other signs of life'. Williams[9] believed that they included a beating heart – in which case, every normally developed fetus delivered after 18 weeks' gestation could be said to be born alive. While we believe that this never could have held, it is obvious that such a standard requires very little of the neonate – in theory, it need only have managed one breath to have been 'born alive'. By contrast, viability is a term of medical art implying an ability to live – at least for a reasonable time. Thus, viability is a product not only of fetal maturity but also of the motivation and resources of any medical attendants at the birth. As the Supreme Court of the United States pointed out in *Webster*, viability cannot be defined legally and is a matter for medical determination.

---

3   R Boland 'RU 486 in France and England: Corporate Ethics and Compulsory Licensing' (1992) 20 Law Med Hlth Care 226. A whole issue of this journal was devoted to the subject. R Macklin 'Antiprogestin Drugs: Ethical Issues' at 215 is of particular interest.
4   Discussed at p 111 above.
5   *Upjohn Co (Kirton's) Application* [1976] RPC 324. The way is now cleared for medicinal abortion by the Abortion Act 1967, s 1(3A) (inserted by Human Fertilisation and Embryology Act 1990, s 37(3)) which extends the types of premises in which a legal abortion can be performed.
6   1990 Act, s 37(4).
7   K McK Norrie 'Abortion in Great Britain: One Act, Two Laws' [1985] Crim LR 475.
8   *Webster v Reproductive Health Services* 109 S Ct 3040 (1989).
9   G Williams *Textbook of Criminal Law* (2nd edn, 1983), p 290. In this, he is supported by the World Health Organisation: see *C v S* [1988] QB 135 at 142, [1987] 1 All ER 1230 at 1236.

Considerable confusion existed at one time in England and Wales as a result of the apparently interchangeable use of the words 'born alive' in the Infant Life (Preservation) Act 1929, s 1(1) and 'viable' in the original Abortion Act 1967, s 5(1); there are a number of cases in which the matter has been addressed.

The most widely publicised of these was *C v S*,[10] in which it was held that a fetus born following 18-21 weeks' gestation was not capable of being born alive because it was incapable of breathing by the use of its own lungs – with or without the use of a ventilator; live birth and viability were, thus, approximated, although the use of the ventilator maintained a medical resource element in the definition. The court avoided addressing the question of viability directly, a manoeuvre which was followed in the case of *Gregory*.[11] The Court of Appeal, there, was, however, not prepared to reject out of hand the notion that a fetus of 24 weeks' gestation was 'viable'.

A firmer approach was taken at first instance in *Rance*,[12] which was, like *Gregory*, a 'wrongful birth' case. Here is was held that a child was born alive if, after its birth, it existed as a live child, that is to say was breathing and living through the use of its own lungs alone. Brooke J found that the child in question would certainly have been born alive at 27 weeks' gestation. The judge also believed that the word 'viable' was used in the Abortion Act 1967, s 5(1) as convenient shorthand for 'capable of being born alive' – an interpretation which appears to us to be too facile but is, nevertheless, one which indicates that the academic argument at the time can now be regarded as a storm in a teacup. From the point of view of the criminal law, the meaning of being born alive remains as it was decided more than a century ago[13] and the word 'viability' has disappeared from the statute book following amendment of the 1967 Act, s 5(1) by way of the Human Fertilisation and Embryology Act 1990, s 37(4). A further major good to come from these cases is that 'live birth' is now clearly defined by the capacity to breathe and the confusing phrase 'any other sign of life' is, correspondingly, irrelevant.

The case of Mrs Rance demonstrates vividly the unsatisfactory state of the law prior to 1990. Her child was known to be physically abnormal but, by the time the diagnosis was established, the gynaecologists were unable to terminate the pregnancy for fear of transgressing the criminal law. But while that concern has now been removed, it has been replaced by moral considerations which are, if anything, exaggerated by the 1990 amendments to the 1967 Act.

Those who support the interests of the fetus have always been concerned to prevent the abortion, or feticide, of those capable of a free existence by lowering the fetal age above which termination is impermissible so as to keep pace with medical capabilities. They can be said to have succeeded to an extent by having this set at 24 weeks for relatively slight medical and social reasons.[14] The offset is that it may be difficult, particularly in the face of human error, to make a prognosis of serious neonatal handicap within that timescale. Accordingly, the 1990 Act removes the

---

10 [1988] QB 135, [1987] 1 All ER 1230. For discussion, see S P de Cruz 'Abortion, *C v S* and the Law' (1987) 17 Fam Law 319.
11 *Gregory v Pembrokeshire Health Authority* [1989] 1 Med LR 81.
12 *Rance v Mid-Downs Health Authority and Storr* [1991] 1 QB 587, [1991] 1 All ER 801.
13 *R v Handley* (1874) 13 Cox CC 79.
14 In passing, s 37 of the 1990 Act now brings the law, as well as the practice, of abortion in Scotland into line with that of England.

pre-existing 28 weeks' legal limit and imposes no other time restrictions on abortions performed by reason of fetal abnormality. Similar derestriction applies in the event of risk or grave injury to the pregnant woman – and such conditions are likely to arise particularly in late gestation. The *need* for late abortion thus remains and the Act is silent as to what is to be done with a live abortus. It has to be remembered that a living abortus is a creature in being; to kill such a being or to allow it to die without good reason may be murder or manslaughter – and s 37(4) of the 1990 Act absolves the gynaecologist of child destruction only.

One practical solution is to ensure that no mature abortus is given the opportunity to live. Not only may this involve the use of feticidal methods which are, at the same time, relatively dangerous to the pregnant woman but such methods may also be repugnant to all associated with the procedure – it is difficult to visualise a process which offends the Hippocratic and intuitive conscience more than the dismemberment of a relatively well-formed fetus.[15] This is precisely the situation the 'pro-life' parliamentary lobby sought to avoid and a clause designed to ensure that reasonable steps were taken to assist a mature abortus to live was introduced at a late stage in the debate on the 1990 Bill.[16] The motion was defeated, largely as a result of advice that doctors carrying out terminations after the twenty-fourth week of pregnancy 'would make every conceivable effort . . . to make sure the baby was capable of living . . . a normal and independent existence'.[17] Lord Ennals quoted a letter from 20 gynaecologists:

> If the fetus is mature enough to have a reasonable chance of survival with intensive care, all possible steps are taken to optimise the recovery of both mother and fetus. Delivery then is usually by Caesarean section.[18]

Since the avowed purpose of the clause was to control the maverick, it is surprising that the medical profession was so antipathetic to a measure approved by its senior practitioners. Moreover, the stated practice raises some interesting issues. What distinction, if any, is made between the normal and handicapped fetus? Could the doctor be required to use a process which might result in a damaged neonate and possible litigation?[19] Can a woman in such a condition give a valid consent to a serious operation? Is it right to subject a woman to an invasive procedure on behalf of the fetus and would she, in fact, consent? – a matter to which we return in chapter 6. Above all, parliament gave no indication of how the doctor was to dispose of his new patient.

The gynaecologist is certainly in a difficult position. On the one hand, he has effectively contracted to relieve a woman of her fetus. On the other, he is confronted by an infant who, on any interpretation, is entitled to a birth certificate and, if necessary, a certificate as to the cause of death.[20] Considerations as to the proper use

15 R J Lilford and N Johnson 'Surgical Abortion at Twenty Weeks: Is Mortality Determined Solely by the Outcome?' (1989) 15 J Med Ethics 82.
16 Such a condition has been declared unconstitutional in the United States: *Colautti v Franklin* 439 US 379 (1979); *American College of Obstetricians and Gynecologists Pennsylvania Section v Thornburgh* 106 S Ct 2169 (1986).
17 Official Reports (Lords) vol 522, col 1043, 18 October 1990, per Lord Walton at 1050.
18 Ibid at 1052.
19 For discussion, see R P S Jansen 'Unfinished Feticide' (1990) 6 J Med Ethics 61.
20 See Lord Wells-Pestell HL Official Reports (5th series) col 776 (12 December 1974).

of limited resources must also colour any decision-making. The principles of selective non-treatment of a defective neonate (see chapter 15) might well apply but, otherwise, we can see no theoretical objection to the view that failure to attempt to sustain a living infant could result in a charge of culpable homicide.

Legal precedents are slender in Great Britain and, what few there are, are inconsistent. In one case, an area health authority inquiry concluded that allowing an aborted fetus to die was an action which was fully within the law. In another, where an infant lived for 36 hours after having been aborted at 23 weeks, the coroner found that death was due to prematurity and that there was no culpability on the part of the medical staff. So far as we know, only one coroner, faced with such circumstances, has brought in a conclusion of death due to want of attention at birth to a premature infant;[1] no further action seems to have been taken. One prosecution is known to have been mounted by the DPP against a doctor who was alleged to have left a living abortus to die in the sluice-room; the magistrates took the unprecedented step of deciding there was no case to answer.[2] There was a further instance of a supposedly 21-week-old fetus, breathing and with a heart beat, being left to die without assistance for three hours; neither the birth nor the death were registered and the body was incinerated. In the absence of a cadaver, the coroner applied to the Home Office for authority to hold an inquest but this was refused for reasons which were not given publicly.[3] Similar uncertainty has been noted in America, where Dr Waddill, who ordered 'oxygen only' for a 26-week delivered fetus, was brought to trial for murder; two juries failed to agree, whereupon all criminal charges were dismissed.[4]

We find it illogical to distinguish in legal terms between abandonment of the newborn infant and abandonment of the living abortus. Morally, it is hard to divert further from the Hippocratic ethos than to leave to die a normal infant which is crying for the incubator simply on the grounds that it is unwanted.[5] The coroners' courts are, however, apparently happy to maintain a pragmatic approach to the problem. It was reported in 1996 that a normal infant, wrongly suspected of having severe physical abnormality and aborted at 27 weeks, survived for 45 minutes without active resuscitation. The coroner recorded a verdict of death due to legal termination[6] – which, on the face of things, is a surprisingly innovative finding and a further example of the reluctance of the law to interfere in medical practice if it can avoid doing so.

We admit to some disappointment that the 'pro-abortus' motion in the House of Lords was lost and we deprecate any movement towards equating late abortion with deliberate feticide.[7] There is, in fact, no certainty that all women seeking a

1   Inquest on Infant Campbell, Stoke-on-Trent, 19 October 1983.
2   *R v Hamilton* The Times, 16 September 1983, p 1.
3   Reported by M Fletcher The Times, 25 February 1988, p 2. The case was raised in Parliament on a motion for the adjournment: Official Reports (HC), 8 June 1989, vol 154, col 460.
4   B Towers 'The Trials of Dr Waddill' (1979) 5 J Med Ethics 205.
5   Ms Anne Widdicombe, a Parliamentary 'pro-life' activist, put the issue as lying between 'I perceive this to be a human being because I want it' or 'I perceive this not to be a human being because I do not want it': Official Reports (HC) 24 April 1990, vol 171, col 192.
6   (1996) 119 Bull Med Ethics, 4.
7   In fact, it has been government policy since 1975 that abortions beyond the twentieth week of pregnancy should be carried out only in hospitals having appropriate facilities including resuscitation equipment: Barbara Castle, Official Reports (HC), 21 October 1975, vol 898, col 245.

termination of pregnancy also seek the destruction of their fetus – indeed, it could be argued that such right as the woman may have to control her pregnancy does not extend so as to include a right to control the destiny of a 'viable' fetus. McLean, while insisting on the former right throughout pregnancy, has enlarged this concept and has suggested that much of the current rancour could be dispelled if women were given encouragement and the *opportunity* to undergo late, and salvageable, abortions.[8] We still hold to the view that, in general, 'viable' fetuses should be given a chance to live – there is no reason why such as can and do survive should not be regarded as parentless infants and offered for adoption on that basis. It is unlikely that there would be any shortage of adopting parents – particularly if the process was simplified to accord with the unusual circumstances.

Maternal responsibility to the fetus

Thus far, we have considered the fetal/maternal relationship mainly within the context of abortion; the general topic of maternal responsibility for the well-being of the fetus remains to be discussed. The Law Commission considered this question and decided that an action against its mother in respect of damage resulting from her negligence during pregnancy should not be available to a child. It was felt that a claim of this type would compromise the parent-child relationship and might also be used as a weapon in matrimonial disputes. Accordingly, the English legislation excludes claims by a child against its mother except as to injuries sustained during traffic accidents; here, special policy grounds and the availability of insurance were held to justify the admissibility of such claims.[9] The matter remains open in Scotland because there is no legislation on the subject and there is no reason in law to exclude a claim by a child against its mother in respect of prenatal injuries. It is possible, however, that the courts may be unsympathetic to such claims on policy grounds.

Discussion along these lines relates, largely, to injury to the fetus due to negligence as it is commonly understood. We have to look a degree deeper to determine the extent to which the mother's duty of care towards her unborn child might be held to limit her freedom of personal behaviour during pregnancy. Interest in this aspect of the fetal-maternal relationship has escalated in the past few decades.[10] Major attention has been directed to the use of alcohol and other drugs, including tobacco, on fetal morbidity and mortality – and it is almost certain that the last word on the subject has not been said. A few years ago, it was easy to hold that social smoking and drinking of alcohol could hardly be viewed in law as negligence. Yet there is virtually irrefutable evidence of their harmful effect on the fetus and, at least

---

8 S A M McLean 'Women, Rights and Reproduction' in S A M McLean (ed) *Legal Issues in Human Reproduction* (1989) see the same author 'Abortion Law: Is Consensual Reform Possible?' (1990) 17 J Law & Soc 106. But would it not be both medically and economically more logical to encourage the woman to carry her fetus to term?

9 An apposite case, possibly the prototype, has been reported by C Dyer 'Boy Wins Damages after Injury in Utero' (1992) 304 BMJ 1400.

10 See eg E W Keiserlingck 'A Right of the Unborn Child to Pre-natal Care – the Civil Law Perspective' (1982) 13 Rev de Droit 49; P L Hallisey 'The Fetal Patient and the Unwilling Mother: A Standard for Judicial Intervention' (1983) 14 Pac LJ 1065; J L Lenow 'The Fetus as a Patient: Emerging Rights as a Person' (1983) 9 Amer J Law Med 1.

in the former context, negligent injury to other parties has been successfully litigated or settled out of court.[11]

Scrutiny of the interplay of fetal rights and maternal lifestyle has been nowhere more intense than in the United States, where well over 6,000 children are born each year suffering from the fetal alcohol syndrome and where the occurrence of drug withdrawal symptoms in neonates increased by 450% from 1984 to 1986.[12]   There, the state has not only a right but also a duty to protect its children under the parens patriae jurisdiction and there is strong support for the view that this extends to an interest in the well-being of the 'viable' fetus.[13]   Cases of fetal neglect that have come before the courts have been assessed both under the common law and through the federal and state legislation prohibiting child abuse and neglect;[14] as might be expected, the outcomes have not been entirely consistent. The most extreme example that we have noted concerned Ms Stewart, who was found to have ingested amphetamines and cannabis before her infant was born brain damaged. The mother was charged in the criminal court with omitting to furnish necessary medical attendance or other remedial care; the case was dismissed on the grounds that there was no statutory basis for the charge.[15]   Such instances are often reported only anecdotally[16] but a number of civil actions have been officially reported; these suggest that the fetus enjoys an enhanced standing in such courts and, having been born, may be able to sue on its own behalf.[17]

The courts in Canada have also appreciated the concept of intra-uterine child abuse and have immediately placed in care and protection neonates who have been subjected seriously to drugs or alcohol during pregnancy.[18]   However, the courts will not go so far as to restrict the freedom of a woman to live her life as she would please while she is pregnant. In *Winnipeg Child and Family Services (Northwest Area) v G (DF)*[19] the Supreme Court ruled on a case involving an order which had been granted at first instance requiring that a five-month pregnant woman who was addicted to glue sniffing be detained in a health centre until the birth of her child. One of the grounds for the order was the parens patriae jurisdiction in respect of the fetus. It was argued

11 D Brahams 'Tobacco Litigation (USA, UK and Australia)' (1992) 340 Lancet 230; 'Passive Smoking' (1993) 341 Lancet 552.   *Bland v Stockport Metropolitan Borough Council* (1900, unreported), discussed by C Dyer 'UK Woman Wins First Settlement for Passive Smoking' (1993) 306 BMJ 351. See also S Chapman and S Woodward 'Australian Court Decision on Passive Smoking Upheld on Appeal' (1993) 306 Brit Med J 120 for the Australian courts' view of passive smoking.
12 For relevant data, see E J Larson 'The Effects of Maternal Substance Abuse on the Placenta and Fetus' in G B Reed (ed) *Diseases of the Fetus and Newborn* (2nd edn, 1994); W A Vega, B Kolody, J Hwang, and A Noble 'Prevalence and Magnitude of Perinatal Substance Exposures in California' (1993) 329 New Engl J Med 850.
13 For an early exhaustive review of the US scene, see J E B Myers 'Abuse and Neglect of the Unborn: Can the State Intervene?' (1984) 23 Duquesne LR 1.   An interesting feminist perspective is to be found in R I Solomon 'Future Fear: Prenatal Duties Imposed by Private Parties' (1991) 17 Amer J Law M 411.
14 As an example see M T Storall '*In re Valerie D* and State Intervention on Prenatal Drug Abuse' (1993) 25 Connecticut LR 1265.
15 For this and similar cases, see Solomon (1991) 17 Amer J Law M 411.
16 See eg N MacReady 'Fetal Homicide Charge for Drinking While Pregnant' (1996) 313 BMJ 645.
17 *Grodin v Grodin* 301 NW 2d 869 (Mich, 1981).   See also *Re Vanessa F* 351 NYS 2d 337 1974.
18 *Re Children's Aid Society of Kenora and JL* (1982) 134 DLR (3d) 249; *Re Superintendent of Family and Child Service and McDonald* (1982) 135 DLR (3d) 330.
19 [1997] 2 SCR 925.   See, also, an earlier case, *Re Baby R* (1989) 53 DLR (4th) 69 – powers to interfere with the rights of women must be given by specific legislation.

that this inherent jurisdiction of the courts to protect the vulnerable – normally incapax adults and minors – should be extended to protect the fetus in utero. The Supreme Court refused, however, to sanction such a major change to the law. Noting that this would involve conflicts of fundamental rights and interests and difficult policy issues, the court recognised that the unique relationship which a woman has with her fetus is such that 'the court cannot make decisions for the unborn child without inevitably making decisions for the mother herself'. Such a power, if it were thought desirable, had to be introduced by the legislature.

A ruling to the same effect has already been given in England in *Re F (in utero)*,[20] a case in which the local authority sought to make the fetus a ward of court so that it could be protected from its mother, who was leading a nomadic existence and who, shortly before the child was due, again went missing. The application was refused both at first instance and in the Court of Appeal on the grounds that, until the child was actually born, there would be an inherent incompatibility between any projected exercise of the wardship jurisdiction and the rights and welfare of the mother. Relying heavily on *Paton*,[1] the Court of Appeal first concluded that the fetus had no individual personality and that, therefore, there could be no jurisdiction in wardship; and, secondly, it was made clear that, in practice, it would be impossible to follow the principle of the paramountcy of the child's welfare in wardship if that conflicted with the liberty and legal interests of the mother.

The preferred course of action in such cases is to make the child a ward of court on its birth. The authority for this is the decision of the House of Lords in *D (a minor) v Berkshire County Council*,[2] in which the court upheld a decision to make a care order in respect of a child born prematurely and suffering from drug dependency. The House held that the words: '[The child's] proper development is being avoidably prevented or neglected' in the Children and Young Persons Act 1969, s 1(2)(a) referred to a continuing, rather than an instant, situation. Thus, while the court would not go so far as to make a fetus a ward of court, conditions both before birth and in the hypothetical future could be taken into account when assessing a neonate's need for care and control, the important point being that there is a genuine continuum. The decision caused considerable concern; first, on the grounds that its application to family law might be extended to the criminal field and, secondly, because it denied the drug addicted mother the right to prove her capacity for motherhood. For ourselves, we see *D (a minor)* as yet another case that was decided on its own facts; there is no reason to suppose that a similar decision would be taken in every instance – only that the remedy is there should it be needed in serious cases.[3]

D (a minor) is an example of fetal 'rights' maturing at birth. The reasons for seeking fetal protection in *Re F* were, we feel, far less pressing than were those in, say, *Re D*; the nature of any maternal improbity differed and it is possible to explain the two decisions in that simple light.[4] None the less, *Re F* is the more significant in that it

20 [1988] Fam 122, [1988] 2 All ER 193.
 1 *Paton v British Pregnancy Advisory Service Trustees* [1979] QB 276, [1978] 2 All ER 987.
 2 [1987] AC 317, [1987] 1 All ER 20, HL.
 3 The court will certainly use its power. In *Re P (a minor) (child abuse: evidence)* [1987] 2 FLR 467, CA a place of safety order was granted on the day of a child's birth into a family which had a history of sexual abuse.
 4 It is noteworthy that the Court of Appeal was unable to see any logical difference between the early and the 'viable' fetus as regards a need for protection ([1988] 2 All ER 193 at 199, per Balcombe LJ).

lays down a principle which is likely to be followed in the absence of parliamentary intervention. Any rights vested in the fetus are strictly circumscribed. Whether or not one agrees with such a loading of the odds, there is little doubt that it has to be accepted on pragmatic grounds. There is simply no way in which the criminal law could be invoked so as to control a pregnant woman's smoking, eating or sexual habits, nor is it desirable – amongst other ill-effects, doctors would be turned into police informers. We can also foresee great difficulty in proof of causation: teratogenic effects are maximal in the first trimester of pregnancy and the further in time that the cause is removed from the visible effect, the more difficult it becomes to associate the two.

Maternal/fetal conflict

The topic of parental neglect in the form of refusal of treatment in the fetal interest is becoming more controversial as the opportunities become ever more feasible. This has had comparatively little impact in Britain. We suspect that the great majority of women who have carried a fetus long enough for it to be available for treatment are anxious that it should survive to childhood – most fetal treatments, or other interventions in the pregnancy on behalf of the fetus, are carried out in a consensual medical environment. The greater publicity attracted in the United States may reflect no more than a stiffer polarisation of attitudes; this leads to more conflicts of conscience which can be resolved only in the public courtroom.[5]

A subset of this problem lies in refusal, not of treatment for the fetus itself, but of maternal treatment which, if not undertaken, will lead to fetal damage or death. In such circumstances, a conflict paradigm arises which is frequently seen as involving a choice either to respect the wishes of the woman or to disregard those wishes and treat the woman in a way which does not jeopardise fetal interests.[6] In dealing with such thorny issues most courts have been hesitant about the appropriateness of sanctioning either course of action. The classic situation is to be found in refusal of caesarian section in the fetal interest. There are a number of relatively old precedents from the United States in which a mother has been ordered to undergo such treatment[7] and, occasionally, such directions end disastrously.

The exemplar case is *Re A C*,[8] where a caesarian section was ordered against the wishes of a moribund woman suffering from malignant disease in an attempt to salvage a 26-week-old fetus – the mother survived only long enough to see her baby

---

5 There is some disagreement as to how often this occurs. L J Nelson and N Milliken 'Compelled Medical Treatment of Pregnant Women: Life, Liberty and Law in Conflict (1988) 259 J Amer Med Ass 1060 is at some odds with V E B Colder, J Gallagher and M T Parsons 'Court-ordered Obstetrical Interventions' (1987) 316 New Engl J Med 1192. See also N Rhoden 'The Judge in the Delivery Room: The Emergence of Court-ordered Cesarians' (1986) 74 Calif LR 1951. For a contrary view, see E-H W Kluge 'When Caesarian Operations Imposed by a Court are Justified' (1988) 14 J Med Ethics 206.

6 One need not, however, always approach the problem as one which necessarily involves a conflict: see J Mair 'Maternal/Foetal Conflict: Defined or Diffused?' in S A M McLean (ed) *Contemporary Issues in Law, Medicine and Ethics* (1996) ch 5.

7 Eg *Raleigh Fitkin-Paul Morgan Memorial Hospital v Anderson* 201 A 2d 537 (NJ, 1964); *Jefferson v Griffin Spalding County Hospital Authority* 274 SE 2d 457 (Ga, 1981).

8 *Re A C* 533 A 2d 611 (DC, 1987). For discussion, see D Brahams 'A Baby's Life or a Mother's Liberty: A United States Case' (1988) 56 Med-leg J 156; M A Field 'Controlling the Woman to Protect the Fetus' (1989) 17 Law Med Hlth Care 114.

die in a matter of hours. Brahams noted that the case should sound a warning bell to all interventionists in Britain; the majority of commentators adopted a similarly cautious approach to the subject on the grounds, among others, that it is nearly impossible to balance the benefits to the fetus against the reasonableness of withheld consent,[9] that unwanted intervention must injure the maternal doctor-patient relationship and that the standards of enforcement would be inequitable. This view was vindicated by the District of Columbia Appeal Court, where the court vacated the judgment in *Re A C* and, by a 7:1 majority, held that the right to informed consent encompassed a right to informed refusal of treatment; a fetus cannot have rights in this respect superior to those of a person who has already been born. Even so, the door was not quite shut:

> We do not quite foreclose the possibility that a conflicting State interest may be so compelling that the patient's interest must yield but we anticipate that such cases will be extremely rare and truly exceptional.[10]

The circumstances in *Re A C* were special – involving a dying woman carrying a barely viable fetus – and, although it will be clear that we support some notion of fetal rights, we would align ourselves with the view of the Court of Appeal on the particular facts of the case.

Subsequently, there has been something of a spate of cases in England where the issues have been less clear cut and the courts have been prepared to accept Terry J's exceptions – although with rather less reservations. The first of these was *Re S*,[11] in which a woman who had been in labour for several days with the fetus impacted in a transverse lie steadfastly refused to undergo caesarian section. The clinicians appealed to the court and a declaration was granted to the effect that, the operation being in the vital interests of the patient and the unborn child, it could be performed lawfully despite the woman's refusal to give consent. Once again, this decision was greeted with a volley of academic criticism.[12] It was, perhaps, unfortunate that Sir Stephen Brown P was not apprised of the Appeal Court decision in *Re A C* and, certainly, no analysis of the issues was contained in the decision handed down. Even so, the judge was faced with the need for an immediate answer and, apparently paradoxically, we support his decision – *Re A C* and *Re S* provide the perfect example of circumstances altering the case. While Sir Stephen Brown P emphasised that the life of the unborn child was at risk, there was also no question but that the mother would die in great pain in the absence of surgical intervention; by contrast, there was no way in which maternal death could be avoided in *Re A C*. We believe that the declaration represented the correct humane – albeit possibly not the correct jurisprudential – solution in the circumstances.

---

9 There is, none the less, a tide in favour of some sort of balancing act. Thus, in *Taft v Taft* 446 NE 2d 395 (Mass, 1983) the court refused surgical intervention but might have been prepared to accept medical treatment of the fetus. See F A Chervenak and L B McCullough 'Perinatal Ethics: A Practical Analysis of Obligations to Mother and Fetus' (1985) 66 Obst Gynecol 442. The views of F H Miller 'Maternal-Fetal Ethical Dilemmas: A Guideline for Physicians' (1991) 10 Seminars Anaesth 157 are particularly attractive.

10 *In re A C* 573 A 2d 1235 (DC, 1990), prt Terry J. See D Brahams 'Enforced Caesarian Section: A US Appeal' (1990) 58 Med-leg J 164.

11 *Re S (adult: refusal of medical treatment)* [1992] 4 All ER 671, (1992) 9 BMLR 69.

12 See eg M Thomson 'After *Re S* ' (1994) 2 Med L Rev 127.

The courts have, however, gone further in their concern for the state's interest in the preservation of life. In *Norfolk and Norwich Healthcare (NHS) Trust v W*[13] and *Tameside and Glossop Acute Services Trust v CH (a patient)*[14] the High Court upheld forced caesarian section, even justifying its action in *Tameside* by deeming the section to be 'treatment' for the woman's schizophrenia under the Mental Health Act 1983, s 63. We discuss these cases further in the more appropriate context of consent,[15] together with the Court of Appeal judgment in *Re MB (caesarian section)*.[16] It is sufficient to note for present purposes that the court held in *Re MB* that the courts have no jurisdiction to require a competent woman who refuses medical treatment to undergo that treatment *even if* the refusal might have adverse or fatal consequences for the fetus she bears. A woman carrying a fetus is entitled to the same degree of respect for her wishes as anyone else. That having been said, the continued ambivalence of the courts towards such cases is more than adequately evidenced in the actual outcome of *Re MB*. Having accepted the paramountcy of the woman's autonomy, the court promptly deemed her to be incapax because of a fear of needles which had led her to refuse the section. None the less, it was accepted that it was in the woman's own best interests to undergo the procedure and, faced with such a *fait accompli*, she 'consented'. We predict that we will continue to witness a divergence of theory and practice in this controversial area for some time to come.[17]

But, whatever compromise is reached by the lawyers, the doctor's dilemma persists whenever, and in whatever context, he seeks to protect the fetus from its mother. Once he agrees to intervene on behalf of the fetus – or, more contextually, to treat it individually – he has both a moral and a legal duty to treat it with all due care; the problem, therefore, lies in the original acceptance of the unborn as a patient. We suggest that prudence should dictate a very cautious approach to fetal therapy which could, in the great majority of instances, be properly withheld until birth.

Other people's rights

The rights of those who participate as third parties receive comparatively little attention in the abortion debate as compared with that devoted to the woman and her fetus.

Conscientious objection

This unconcern may well spring from the fact that the Abortion Act 1967 (at s 4) excuses the conscientious objector from participating in treatment by abortion unless that treatment is directed towards the saving of life or of preventing grave permanent

13 [1996] 2 FLR 613. See also *Rochdale Healthcare (NHS) Trust v C* [1997] 1 FLR 274. Both cases were decided, effectively, on the basis of 'what a reasonable person would decide'.
14 [1996] 1 FLR 762, (1996) 31 BMLR 93.
15 See p 265 below.
16 [1997] 2 FLR 426, (1997) 38 BMLR 175, CA.
17 For a similar view argued from a feminist perspective, see J Bridgeman and S Millns *Feminist Perspectives on Law: Law's Engagement with the Female Body* (1998) s 6.2.

injury to the health of the mother. But, while this would seem to be perfectly clear, the doctor's situation is not uncomplicated. The curious provision which stipulates that the English doctor must prove his conscience while his Scottish counterpart's sworn word will, quite properly, be accepted at face value is illogical but is of minor significance. The most important and unfortunate result of the 1967 Act is that some discrimination takes place against doctors, and especially those seeking to become gynaecologists, who are unable to accept its wide terms.[18] It is to be noted that, while a doctor may, in general, refuse to take part in the abortion procedure, he remains under an obligation to advise. Such advice is subject to the normal rules of medical negligence and the conscientious objector's only recourse is, therefore, to refer his patient to another practitioner, a practice which is only marginally compatible with a strong conscience and which must damage the essential bond of trust between doctor and patient. The facts that the woman may well be unaware of her practitioner's attitude and that a second referral inevitably delays the termination provide one of the most powerful arguments put forward by those who would demedicalise early abortion. It is often forgotten that a doctor's objection to abortion may be Hippocratic rather than, say, religious in origin and a logical case can be made, and a major ground for confrontation thereby removed, for delegating abortions which have no immediate therapeutic dimension to trained abortionists. The doctor's conscience does not absolve him from treating a woman when the continuation of the pregnancy is life-threatening and there is, of course, no right to conscience in treating the *results* of a legal abortion; these considerations apply equally to the nursing staff.

The nursing staff and others involved

The role of the nurse in therapy of all sorts is becoming more significant; this is exemplified in the sphere of abortion by the widespread use of prostaglandin infusions for induction of premature labour. Nurses have so great a part to play in this process that some doubt was raised as to whether they were, in fact, thus guilty of performing illegal abortions in the sense that they were not 'registered medical practitioners' as required by the Act; the Royal College of Nursing accordingly sought a declaration to the effect that the advice in a departmental circular[19] stating that, irrespective of the precise action taken, an abortion was legal provided that it was initiated by and was the responsibility of a registered medical practitioner, was wrong in law. The complexities were such that the Royal College lost its case in the High Court, won it in the Court of Appeal and, finally, lost it in the House of Lords.[20] Effectively, therefore, abortion, no matter how it is performed, is a team effort and is no different in this respect from any other form of treatment. It is, nevertheless, interesting that, in total, five out of nine judges involved took the view of the nurses.

It is easy to believe that the sensibilities of the nursing staff are inadequately recognised within the abortion debate. The damage that conscientious objection causes to their career prospects is even greater than that sustained by doctors – a doctor does not *have* to practise gynaecology but, as Lord Denning emphasised,

18 J Warden 'Abortion and Conscience' (1990) 301 BMJ 1013.
19 CMO (80) (2).
20 *Royal College of Nursing of the United Kingdom v Department of Health and Social Security* [1981] AC 800, [1981] 1 All ER 545, HL.

nurses are expected to be mobile throughout the hospital system.[1] Moreover, current methods of termination beyond the twelfth week of pregnancy involve the nursing staff in an uncompromising way – whether it be in the delivery of what is comparable to a premature birth or in counting the fragmented parts of a formed fetus;[2] there can be no doubts as to their *rights* to special consideration even if these are not always respected.

Valid conscientious objection within the terms of the Abortion Act 1967, s 4 is, however, limited by a proximity test – that is, that it covers only those involved in the therapeutic team effort. The case of Mrs Janaway, who regarded herself as having been unfairly dismissed following her refusal to type a letter referring a patient for termination of pregnancy, was considered so important that it was taken to the House of Lords.[3] In the event, Mrs Janaway failed at every step, essentially on the grounds that participation in treatment, as applied to s 4, referred to actually taking part in treatment administered in a hospital or other approved place; the suggestion in the Court of Appeal that the conscience clause applied to activities which would have been criminal absent the 1967 Act was rejected in the House of Lords – and, at any rate, a typist could not be held to be an accessory in the criminal sense. Mrs Janaway was clearly well distanced from the actual treatment but one can only guess whether others more closely involved – eg hospital porters – would be similarly excluded; the dividing line might be fine. The advent of medical termination raises the unusual position of the conscientiously objecting pharmacist who is asked to fill the necessary prescriptions; in our view, the proximity test would be satisfied, although much depends on how the relationship between the pharmacal and medical professions is viewed.[4]

The father

The anomalous position of the father in the right to life debate also falls to be considered. It is clear from current worldwide decisions that, in so far as abortion is concerned, he has, for practical purposes, *no* rights. It seems incongruous that this should be so, irrespective of the reason for the abortion, and that it should apply even in cases which do not relate to the health of the mother; a father could not, for example, save the existence of a *potentially* haemophiliac son.

The English position was established in *Paton*,[5] where it was clearly laid down that a husband cannot by injunction prevent his wife from undergoing a lawful abortion. The decision was upheld by the European Court of Human Rights; the European Court, however, was clearly worried by the possible complication of fetal 'viability' – the matter was not decided and it remains an area of potential doubt.[6] It

---

1 [1981] AC 800 at 804-805, [1981] 1 All ER 545 at 555.
2 See Lilford and Johnson (1989) 15 J Med Ethics 82. J Glover *Causing Death and Saving Lives* (reprinted 1986) p 142 points to the effects on the health carers as providing a major moral distinction between, say, contraception and abortion.
3 *R v Salford Health Authority, ex p Janaway* [1989] AC 537, CA; affd sub nom *Janaway v Salford Area Health Authority* [1989] AC 537, [1988] 3 All ER 1079, HL.
4 For analysis, see B D Weinstein 'Do Pharmacists Have a Right to Refuse to Fill Prescriptions for Abortifacient Drugs?' (1992) 20 Law Med Hlth Care 220. This is from the American view, where the matter is not addressed by statute – but the principles remain the same.
5 *Paton v British Pregnancy Advisory Service Trustees* [1979] QB 276, [1978] 2 All ER 987.
6 *Paton v United Kingdom* (1980) 3 EHRR 408.

was clarified no further in *C v S*,[7] in which the unmarried father's locus standi was firmly rejected – and was not appealed – but in which the main thrust of the hearing was to establish that the fetus in question was *not* viable. It was, at one time, mooted that the fetus in Scotland might be able to petition through its tutor – ie its father – for interdict of any threatened harm;[8] any such remote possibility has now been excluded. In *Kelly v Kelly*,[9] the Inner House of the Court of Session agreed that the remedy of interdict would be available to prevent damage being caused to a person which, if it occurred, would sound in damages to that person. However, a review of the extensive Commonwealth decisions supported the view that the fetus had no rights for the protection of which the remedy of interdict might be invoked. It followed, therefore, that the father, as the guardian of the fetus, had no standing by which to prevent his wife's abortion. Although this result was wholly predictable, permission to appeal to the House of Lords was granted; no further action was, however, taken.

Attitudes elsewhere in the English-speaking world are diverse. The firm English stance would seem to be accepted in New Zealand but the reasoning there is based more on statute than on common law.[10] It is unlikely that an injunction to prevent a maternally-desired abortion would ever be granted in Australia but the position there is, again, complicated – this time by considerations of legality.[11] There is, perhaps, more flexibility in the United States, where it has been said that the state courts believe the father to have a real interest in the fate of his fetus but that the woman's interest in her health and her freedom from unwanted pregnancy must prevail.[12] Relevant cases denying paternal rights to veto abortions are now very old[13] and the door seems, now, to have been closed in *Casey*.[14] It is, however, in Canada that the fetus has been the least unsuccessful in obtaining paternal representation. Thus, in *Medhurst*[15] a husband was given standing to seek an injunction against abortion and in *Tremblay*[16] it was considered that a potential father had as much right to speak on behalf of the fetus as anyone; neither of these cases succeeded and they probably represent no more than the general willingness of the Canadian courts to grant a locus standi to interested parties.[17] Caldwell has drawn attention to the increasingly caring role of the husband in the upbringing of his children. But it is doubtful if this will affect his future control over a pregnancy, for nothing can alter the fact that it is the woman who carries the fetus for nine months and whose health is mainly at risk during that time – and it is almost certainly this factor which explains the difference in legal attitudes to the father's interest in his fetus and in his in vitro embryo.[18] In our view, while acknowledging that the woman's right to control her body may well take precedence,

7 [1988] QB 135, [1987] 1 All ER 1230.
8 D M Yorke 'The Legal Personality of the Unborn Child' 1979 SLT 158.
9 1997 SLT 896, 1997 SCLR 749.
10 *Wall v Livingston* [1982] 1 NZLR 734, NZCA. The code of decision-making is laid down in the Contraception, Sterilisation, and Abortion Act 1977.
11 *A-G of Queensland (ex rel Kerr) v T* (1983) 46 ALR 275 indicates the difficulties.
12 J L Caldwell 'Abortion: The Father's Lack of Standing' [1988] NZLR 165.
13 *Coe v Gerstein* 41 L Ed 2d 68 (1973); *Doe v Doe* 314 NE 2d 128 (Mass, 1974); *Planned Parenthood of Missouri v Danforth* 428 US 52 (1976).
14 112 S Ct 2791 (1992).
15 *Medhurst v Medhurst* (1984) 9 DLR (4th) 252.
16 (1989) 59 DLR (4th) 609.
17 See nn 15 and 16 above. See also *Re Simms and H* (1980) 106 DLR (3d) 435.
18 See p 76.

the interests of the father still deserve more consideration than is currently afforded them. The potential harm or wrong done to the father by the destruction of his unborn child ought not to be ignored.

The nature of the doctor's duty

The nature of the doctor's duties, in relation not only to the mother but also to the fetus itself, is not completely solved – and this is particularly so in the case of the fetus that is known to be defective. It is clear that the doctor then owes a duty of care to the mother under the terms of the Abortion Act 1967, s 1(1)(d); it could, however, be held that he has a similar duty to the fetus in protecting it from a life of pain and suffering or from one which is diminished for other reasons. Actions for the dereliction, if any, of the latter duty are known colloquially as suits for 'wrongful life', which are discussed in greater detail in chapter 6. For the present, it need only be said that the British position is summed up in the words of Stephenson LJ, who asked how there could be imposed upon a doctor a duty towards the child to take away life by means of abortion:

> to impose such a duty towards the child would be to make a further inroad – in addition to that created by the Abortion Act 1967 – into the sanctity of human life which would be contrary to public policy.[19]

This view is not easy to accept as, apart from the saving of the mother's life, the 'eugenic' clause of the Abortion Act is probably that part which offends the Hippocratic conscience least.

At the same time, Stephenson LJ agreed that there could be a duty to the mother to give her an opportunity to have the life of the fetus terminated. Such an action – for wrongful birth – is of a quality different from the wrongful pregnancy cases which have been discussed under 'Sterilisation' (chapter 4). The cause has been widely upheld in the United States[20] and the near inevitability of success in the event of a negligent failure to give advice or warning probably accounts for the lack of reported cases in the United Kingdom.[1] Such as reach the legal reports are generally those which fail on the grounds of causation or of public policy.[2] It is in the nature of things that most wrongful birth actions arise from laboratory errors; the resultant children are, thus, more usually damaged mentally than physically and often grow up in a loving environment.[3]

19 *McKay v Essex Area Health Authority* [1982] 2 WLR 890 at 902, CA.
20 *Curlender v Bio-Science Laboratories* 165 Cal Rptr 477 (1980); *Robak v United States* 658 F 2d 471 (1981); *Noccash v Burger* 290 SE 2d 825 (Va, 1982); *Reed v Campagnola* 630 A 2d 1145 (Md, 1993). For a good overview, see J R Boitkin and M J Mehlman 'Wrongful Birth: Medical, Legal and Philosophical Issues' (1994) 22 J Law Med & Ethics 21.
 1 In *Salih v Enfield Health Authority* [1990] 1 Med LR 333, for example, only the quantum of damages was in issue.
 2 *Scuriaga v Powell* (1979) 123 Sol Jo 406; *Rance* [1991] 1 QB 587; *Gregory* [1989] 1 Med LR 81.
 3 It may be that wrongful birth actions are being substituted for wrongful life actions in that the families deserve compensation and success in the former is far more likely: eg *Viccaro v Milunsky* 551 NE 2d 8 (Mass, 1990). See also the South African case *Friedman v Glicksman* 1996 (1) SA 1134 – a spina bifida case in which a wrongful life action failed but a wrongful birth action was accepted.

Abortion and the incompetent

We have no reason to believe that termination of pregnancy in minors is to be regarded as different from any other aspect of medical treatment; the principles involved are, therefore, best considered within the whole spectrum of consent which is addressed in chapter 10. In theory, any concerns for the fetus must be added to the equation but, in practice, the courts will always put the interests of the young mother above those of her fetus in the event of conflict – indeed, they *must* do so.[4]

Specific problems as to confidentiality are, however, likely to arise in the unique context of under-age pregnancy and these merit consideration. These have caused particular concern in the United States, where a distinction has been drawn between a duty to inform the parents of an impending procedure[5] and a need to obtain their authority;[6] there have been a number of conflicting decisions[7] but the matter has now probably been put beyond dispute in *Casey*,[8] where the need for parental consent was confirmed.

In Britain, the concept of the 'understanding child' has gone unchallenged since it was first mooted by Butler-Sloss J in 1982.[9] There can, however, be no doubt that to perform an operation without parental permission on a child too young to understand the issues – and, hence, to give a valid consent – would constitute an assault and, logically, this applies to an abortion. In practice, short of strongly held religious views, it must be very rare for the parents of an unmarried girl below the age of 16 not to consent to termination of pregnancy[10] but the question remains – *must* the parents be informed prior to legal termination of a minor's pregnancy? The Abortion Act itself makes no distinction between age groups and, by implication, gives no grounds for supposing that the special conditions of abortion give rise to special rights to privacy. Yet it is hard to believe that all the 3,645 terminations carried out on girls aged 15 or under in 1996 (representing 2.2% of the total) were carried out with parental knowledge. Again, we can turn to practical considerations among which it is reasonable to assume that the majority of children who are old enough to *become* pregnant are also old enough to understand the consequences; the conditions which can be extrapolated from *Gillick*[11] would apply. Thus, although the knowledge and agreement of the parents are clearly desirable, it is likely that a doctor who has made

---

4   Children Act 1989, s 1(1). See the specific criticism of an expert witness in *Re B (wardship: abortion)* [1991] 2 FLR 426 at 431 per Hollis J.
5   *HL v Matheson* 101 S Ct 1164 (1981).
6   *Hallmark Clinic v North Carolina Department of Human Resources* 519 F 2d 1315 (1975).
7   In *Re T W* 551 So 2d 1186 (Fla, 1989), the court was unable to discern a compelling state interest in overriding a minor's right to privacy only when abortion was concerned. In *Hodgson v Minnesota* 110 S Ct 2926 (1990) and *Ohio v Akron Center for Reproductive Health* 110 S Ct 2972 (1990), the Supreme Court held that only one parent need be notified. In both cases, however, it was noted that a judicial process to bypass parental consent was sufficient protection for the minor. For discussion of the early cases, see H L Hirsch 'The Law Protecting Children in the United States' in J K Mason (ed) *Paediatric Forensic Medicine and Pathology* (1989).
8   112 S Ct 2791 (1992). The importance of the judicial bypass was re-emphasised.
9   *Re P (A minor)* [1986] 1 FLR 272, (1982) 80 LGR 301.
10 For a case in which a mother opposed a termination for her 12-year-old daughter, see *Re B* [1991] 2 FLR 426.
11 *Gillick v West Norfolk and Wisbech Area Health Authority* [1986] AC 112, [1985] 3 All ER 402, HL. See p 252 below for a full discussion.

reasonable efforts to induce his patient to confide in her parents and is still faced with an adamant refusal of consent to disclosure and who goes on to terminate a minor's pregnancy would be secure from action in the courts or before the General Medical Council. The trend in medical, legal and societal attitudes over the last two decades gives added support to this view.

Almost certainly, many abortions have been carried out on the mentally handicapped under the twin cover of good medical practice and legal necessity; authority for termination of pregnancy has probably also been obtained in camera on more than one occasion.[12] The legal uncertainties arising from the abolition of the English courts' parens patriae powers to care for adult incompetents have now been largely dispelled in respect of termination of pregnancy. Abortion is to be distinguished from, say, sterilisation in that the former is governed by statute which gives sufficient protection to doctors provided they comply with its terms; a formal declaration of lawfulness by the High Court, is not, therefore, needed.[13] Ethical problems, however, linger on. Thus, although the very wide terms of the 1967 Act would be met in virtually any of the circumstances under consideration, one might, on occasion, question whether the termination was being undertaken for the benefit of society rather than for the genuine good of the pregnant woman – for any supposed 'right to procreate' is violated as much by non-consensual abortion as it is by non-consensual sterilisation.[14] We can only suggest that this is an area where clinical judgment is all important; given that the Abortion Act and Regulations are followed, we would agree that the routine involvement of the High Court serves no useful purpose in the uncontested case.

Reduction of multiple pregnancy and selective reduction

The need for a reduction in the number of fetuses carried at one time has been discussed in chapter 3. Original doubts as to the legality of the process were based mainly on terminological grounds – first on whether the phrase 'termination of pregnancy' in the 1967 Act relates to the pregnancy as a whole and, if this strict interpretation is inappropriate, whether individualised feticide in situ can be regarded as an abortion.[15] Whatever the solution of this interesting academic argument may be, the situation has now been resolved in practice – both selective reduction and reduction of multiple pregnancy in utero are legal when the requirements of the Abortion Act 1967, as amended, are fulfilled in relation to the individual fetus.[16]

12 F Gibb 'Judge Orders Abortion on Woman, Aged 25' The Times, 28 May 1987, p 1 records the surprise of a judge when his decision was publicised.
13 *Re SG (adult mental patient: abortion)* [1991] 2 FLR 329, sub nom *Re SG (a patient)* (1992) 6 BMLR 95; Superseding *Re X* (1987) Times, 4 June.
14 M J Gunn 'Sex and the Mentally Handicapped: A Lawyer's View' (1986) 5 Med Law 255. The author believed that non-consensual abortion contravenes art 12 of the European Convention on Human Rights (the right to marry and to found a family) – but it seems difficult to apply this if the woman concerned is unmarried.
15 For somewhat opposing views, see J Keown 'Selective reduction of Multiple Pregnancy' (1987) 137 NLJ 1165; D P T Price 'Selective Reduction and Feticide: The Parameters of Abortion' [1988] Crim LR 199.
16 Human Fertilisation and Embryology Act 1990, s 37(5) adding to the 1967 Act, s 2.5(2).

Thus, there is now no legal difficulty in justifying pregnancy reduction on the grounds that continuance of a multiple pregnancy would have an adverse effect on a woman's foreseeable environment and, hence, would involve a risk of injury to the mental health of the pregnant woman; the conflict of economic and moral values was exposed vividly in a much-publicised case in England in which a woman insisted on reduction of a twin pregnancy involving two normal fetuses.[17] It might be equally appropriate to plead risk to the physical or mental health of the existing family – particularly if the intended remaining fetus or fetuses were regarded as 'existing children of the family'; the death of all octuplets following refusal of fetal reduction in another recent *cause célèbre* provides an extreme example.[18] Selective destruction of an abnormal fetus is, of course, justified under the serious handicap clause of the 1967 Act. Whether there is tort liability in the event of damage to a surviving fetus is arguable; the probability is that the doctor would not be liable in the absence of negligence in the operation.[19]

It scarcely needs emphasising that all the foregoing relates to legal justification – the morality of the procedure remains in doubt.[20] For our part, we find it hard to adopt a 'blanket' approach to this question. There is, clearly, a marked moral difference between reducing a twin pregnancy and reducing one involving sextuplets. To say that both are wrong in that they offend against the principle of respect for human life is to ignore the similarly valid argument that ensuring the death of all six fetuses by inaction is, equally, disrespectful of the value of human life. The subject opens up the age-old question of whether it is permissible to use unacceptable means to achieve a desirable end – at which point, one can only retire behind the defence that each case must be judged on its particular merits.

17 R L Berkowitz 'From Twin to Singleton' (1996) 313 BMJ 373.
18 Leading Article 'The Death of Babies' Daily Telegraph, 4 October 1996.
19 M Brazier 'A Legal Commentary' (1990) 16 J Med Ethics 68 in discussion of Jansen (1990) 6 J Med Ethics 61.
20 Conservative Roman Catholic opinion remains implacably opposed to the process, which is regarded as 'embryonicide' rather than abortion. See the Official Statement of the Centre of Bioethics, Catholic University of the Sacred Heart, Rome 'Against So-called Embryo Reduction' (1997) 127 Bull Med Ethics 8.

6 Prenatal screening and wrongful life

The importance of genetically dependent diseases has risen as the control of those due to infection has increased. Currently, the proportion of childhood deaths attributable wholly or partly to genetic factors runs at about 50%. And it is becoming increasingly clear, as work continues on the Human Genome Project to map the genetic code of the human species, that a genetic component may well operate in many illnesses and conditions which were previously thought to be controlled by non-genetic factors. For these reasons, and because of the social, ethical and legal implications which advances in genetics have for all of us, the treatment of the topic has been significantly expanded in this edition. The nature of genetic disease, the role of the genetic counsellor and the question of liability for negligent failure to diagnose, disclose or treat genetic abnormalities are discussed in this chapter. In chapter 7 we examine the legal responses to the social and ethical dilemmas posed for individuals and families by the increased availability of genetic information.

Types of genetic disease

Genetic diseases are of three main types. Some are chromosomal – the structure or the number of chromosomes is altered and typical disease states arise, many of these being associated with mental illness. The classic example is Down's syndrome – technically known as trisomy-21. Some chromosomal abnormalities increase markedly with maternal age. Approximately 2% of women aged 40, left to uncontrolled pregnancy, will produce a chromosomally defective child, half of these suffering from Down's syndrome; by the age of 45, the risk of trisomy-21 rises to about 4%. There is some evidence that advanced paternal age may also be a risk factor.

The second group includes those conditions described as unifactorial in origin. Genes are positioned on chromosomes which exist in the cells in pairs, one member of each pair being derived from each parent. Unifactorial disease results from the presence of a specific abnormal gene and, since either of a pair of genes can be donated at random by either parent to their offspring, it is a simple calculation to determine the statistical probability of an infant being so endowed (see Figure 6.1). The genes may be 'autosomal dominants' – in which case they will express themselves, in this case as a disease, when the pair of genes contains only one which is abnormal. Normal natural selection should lead to the eradication of dangerous dominant genes. They may arise by mutation, or spontaneous change – a process which is greatly augmented by, for example, ionising radiation – or the gene may possess some special attribute. Huntington's disease, for example, persists because the symptoms associated with the responsible gene often do not appear until after marriage and procreation. Alternatively, the gene may be an 'autosomal recessive',

147

Figure 6.1   UNIFACTORIAL DISEASE

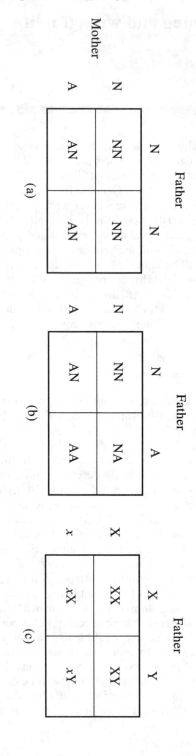

(a) The mother has an abnormal gene (A). If this is dominant, half the children will have the disease; if it is recessive, half the children will be carriers.

(b) Both the mother and the father have one deleterious recessive gene (A); half the children will be carriers and one in four will suffer from the disease.

(c) The mother is a carrier of an abnormal X-linked gene (x). Half the male children will have the disease and half the female children will continue to carry the disease.

in which case its expression is repressed by its normal dominant partner. Those persons possessing a single abnormal recessive gene will be 'carriers' of the disease with which it is associated. Frank disease will result only if an individual inherits the same two recessive genes – which means that both parents must have been carriers or one was a carrier and the other diseased; this, incidentally, provides the genetic basis for discouraging inbreeding.

Unifactorial disease may also be 'sex-linked' – or, better, 'X-linked'. Simplistically, this implies that the abnormal gene is present on part of the X chromosome which has no counterpart on the Y chromosome, the possession of which determines maleness. An abnormal recessive X-linked gene will be suppressed in the female by the dominant normal gene on the other X chromosome; it will, however, be free to express itself when coupled in the male XY configuration. Haemophilia is a classic example of such a disease.

Another group of disorders, referred to as multifactorial traits, are believed to be the result of both environmental factors and the effects of one or several genes. The environmental factors may also be of diverse types and interactions and it is, therefore, generally impossible to predict mathematically the occurrence of this commonest type of genetic disorder. Coronary heart disease, for example, is to some extent genetically determined but the occurrence of symptoms will depend upon a number of uncertain features such as the potential patient's job, diet, recreation and smoking habits. Such conditions, however, lie in the unpredictable future; we are, here, concerned with defects which can be demonstrated in utero and, in that respect, neural tube defects – spina bifida and anencephaly – are the most important multifactorial diseases.

Some form of behavioural or surgical treatment is available for those suffering from multifactorial disease and the same is true for a few unifactorial conditions. But there is no curative treatment for most of the more serious genetic disorders,[1] the control of which then depends on prevention. As the House of Commons Science and Technology Committee pointed out:

> While genetics is likely eventually to transform medicine, it may take some while before treatments based on genetic knowledge become available . . . [i]n the short term, the most widespread use of medical genetics will be, as now, in diagnosis and screening.[2]

This 'public health' objective is a central function of the genetic counsellor; its relative importance, however, poses one of the major ethical problems of modern medicine – and one which is likely to increase.[3]

---

1   N A Holtzman et al 'Predictive Genetic Testing: From Basic Research to Clinical Practice' (1997) 278 Science 602.
2   House of Commons Science and Technology Committee *Human Genetics: The Science and its Consequences* Third Report, 6 July 1995, pp 36-37, paras 71, 72. As the report makes clear, *diagnosis* is aimed at individuals; genetic *screening* is routine screening of populations, or identifiable subsets of populations (for example, men or women only, or ethnic groups at increased risk for particular diseases).
3   While 95% of the more common genetic disease can now be tested for, the number of available cures remains very low.

Genetic counselling

Assessed as an arm of public health, the task of genetic counselling seems easy; in practice, it abounds with practical, ethical and, inevitably, legal problems and the Nuffield Council on Bioethics chose to make genetic screening the subject of its first report for just such reasons.[4] Modern genetic counselling involves more than merely quoting risks. The ideal is to avoid a directive approach but, rather, to concentrate on the psychological circumstances so that couples can be led to make decisions which are right for them rather than right for the scientists. Almost inevitably, however, the counsellor's opinion will be sought and how this is reached depends particularly on whether the counselling is retrospective or prospective – are parents seeking advice because they already have an abnormal child or is the consultation based on information derived from other sources? Patient-clients who know that genetic disease might affect their family come, in the main, with a degree of preparedness and an appreciation of their future options. The role of the counsellor assumes an entirely different mantle, however, if he is privy to information of which his clients know nothing – perhaps as a result of a confidential discussion with another health care professional; the question then arises as to whether and how such information should be imparted. These complex issues are discussed in detail in chapter 7.

In directing clients towards a particular reproductive decision, the counsellor can virtually never make a firm statement as to having or not having a further child. He can take extraneous circumstances – eg religious or financial status – into consideration but, in the end, he is down to speaking about probabilities. In the case of unifactorial disease, he can give accurate figures – eg the chances of an overtly affected child are one in four pregnancies if both the mother and father carry recessive deleterious genes. The position as to chromosomal disease is rather more complicated. In the usual circumstance, the condition is due to trisomy, in which three similar chromosomes are present in the cells rather than a pair; this is a chance occurrence which cannot be predicted mathematically. Males with trisomy-21 or Down's syndrome are sterile but there is the theoretical risk that half the children of a female sufferer will also have the chromosomal defect; in practice, not only is such a pregnancy unlikely but, also, more than half of any affected fetuses would miscarry naturally. However, rather under 5% of Down's syndrome patients are not trisomic but, instead, demonstrate a chromosomal abnormality known as translocation – parts of chromosome-21 are exchanged for those of another.[5] This may also occur sporadically but, once it has done so, a carrier state can develop and affect one in three children – passage to later generations is, thus, possible and its occurrence will be independent of maternal age. The counsellor must, therefore, consider each sub-type of chromosomal disorder separately.[6]

In the event of a multifactorial condition, the probabilities can only be derived in an empirical fashion. Even then, the prospects are subject to interpretation.

4   Nuffield Council on Bioethics *Genetic Screening: Ethical Issues* (1993).
5   Some readers may require a more detailed explanation than we have space for. A very easily understood description is to be found in R F Mueller and I D Young *Emery's Elements of Medical Genetics* (9th edn, 1995) ch 3.
6   The risk is 1:3 rather than the anticipated unifactorial 1:4 because a quarter of the conceptuses will be monosomic and will die in utero. The significance of translocation disease was noted in *Gregory v Pembrokeshire Health Authority* [1989] 1 Med LR 81.

Thus, presented with a child with spina bifida, one can say there is a 10% chance that the couple will have a further child with developmental abnormality; it will sound quite different when expressed as a 90% chance of a normal infant. Moreover, nine to one are acceptable odds to many; others might regard anything less than 99 to 1 as an unacceptable risk. In the end, the choice rests with the couple and this choice is a product of their ability to understand and the skill of the counsellor.

Which is, perhaps, an easy enough thing to say but is, at the same time, a statement fraught with underlying ethical difficulty. One has to ask, first, whether the goal of free patient choice is possible, given the fact that, once genetic counselling has been offered and accepted, a likely chain of events has already been set up in the minds of all those involved.[7] Clarke also asks whether the objective is, itself, morally defensible − or have we, for fear of being labelled eugenists, 'fled so far from medical paternalism that we deny ethical responsibility for our professional activities'? Moreover, the whole concept of genetic counselling can be questioned, in so far as it increasingly involves the systematic selection of fetuses and, hence approaches children as consumer objects subject to quality control.[8] The increasing 'need' for genetic counselling can be seen as being based on the increasing number of disorders which can be diagnosed and, as Lippman has said, before long, the definition of fetal imperfection will come to mean any condition which can be diagnosed in utero. The social and economic pressures on a woman to terminate a pregnancy once an abnormality is discovered in her fetus are such that her autonomous choice is severely prejudiced. These pressures would escalate were the somewhat bizarre suggestion adopted that the cost-efficiency of a genetic counselling service could be gauged by the number of abortions performed.[9] It is astonishing to read, for example, that the House of Commons Science and Technology Committee found that, in Edinburgh, a prenatal test for late onset Huntington's disease will not be offered to a woman who is herself afflicted unless she agrees to terminate if the test proves positive.[10] The rationale is that the child is otherwise burdened by the knowledge of its early death. Yet, such a policy betrays an underlying attitude towards those affected by such a condition and ignores the fact that they can enjoy many happy asymptomatic years of life. One thing is, however, certain: no woman can be forced to destroy her fetus. There is no legislative basis for such a suggestion which has strong overtones of positive eugenics.[11]

But the counsellor has several advisory options: he can dismiss the risks, he can advise sterilisation of either partner, he can put the options of artificial insemination by donor or of ovum donation, or he can arrange for a suitably

---

7 See, particularly, A Clarke 'Is Non-directive Genetic Counselling Possible?' (1991) 338 Lancet 998. On genetic counselling in general, see the major reference: A Clarke *Genetic Counselling: Practice and Principles* (1994).

8 See A Lippman 'Prenatal Genetic Testing and Screening: Constructing Needs and Reinforcing Inequities' (1991) 17 Am J Law Med 15.

9 For discussion, and rejection, see A Clarke 'Genetics, Ethics, and Audit' (1990) 335 Lancet 1145.

10 House of Commons Science and Technology Committee, Third Report, para 90.

11 D J Galton and C J Galton 'Francis Galton: and Eugenics Today' (1998) 24 J Med Ethics 99. See also *Emeh v Kensington and Chelsea and Westminster Area Health Authority* [1985] QB 1012 at 1024, [1984] 3 All ER 1044 at 1053, per Slade LJ, CA.

controlled pregnancy coupled with the alternatives of live birth or abortion as conditions indicate.

Controlled pregnancy

The counsellor may have advised a pregnancy or he may be presented for the first time with a couple in which the wife is already pregnant. In either event, should he feel that a risk exists, he now has at his disposal a considerable technical armamentarium to help in closing the gap between probability and certainty. His methods may be non-invasive or invasive.

Non-invasive techniques

X-rays of the fetus are contra-indicated save in an emergency. The modern alternative is visualisation by means of ultrasound. This is accepted as being innocuous as far as the fetus and mother are concerned and is widely used in obstetric management – so much so that testing may well be considered to be governed by implied consent alone;[12] moreover, its use in locating the placenta is an essential prerequisite to amniocentesis, chorionic villus sampling and fetoscopy.[13] Ever-increasing technical and interpretative skills have transformed ultrsonography from a fairly crude diagnostic tool to one which is capable of demonstrating not only major external abnormalities, such as spina bifida or anencephaly, but also congenital disease of the internal organs, and minor defects such as cleft lip – not to mention the sex of the baby. The processes of obstetric management and genetic counselling are, therefore, irrevocably entwined and it is important that the woman is aware of the implications, which are similar to those we discuss below under amniocentesis. The clinician who discovers a fetal abnormality as a by-product of management can scarcely conceal his knowledge while the woman, for her part, may be ill-prepared to receive it; the case for what is commonly known as informed consent[14] to ultrasonography is strong. It is an interesting psychological side-effect of the process that many parents regard the sonogram as their first 'baby-picture' – something which tends to endow the fetus with a recognisable personality; this, in itself, has some influence on the management decision.[15]

Maternal invasion

Fetuses with neural tube defects – spina bifida or anencephaly – secrete an excess of the protein α-fetoprotein into the amniotic fluid and some of this is transferred to the

---

12 See Lippman, (1991) 17 Am J Law Med 15. It is difficult to know how seriously we should take suggestions such as ultrasound predisposing to, eg, left-handedness: K A Salvesen, L J Vatten, S H Eik-Nes et al 'Routine ultrasonography in utero and subsequent handedness and neurological development' (1993) 307 BMJ 159 – perhaps they should serve as gentle reminders.

13 See p 156 below.

14 See further chapter 10.

15 D Callahan 'How Technology is Reframing the Abortion Debate' (1986) Hastings Center Rep, February, p 33.

maternal circulation. Testing the maternal serum thus offers a simple and risk-free method of diagnosing abnormality in the fetus and is very acceptable to mothers. While 80-90% of neural tube defective fetuses can be diagnosed in this way, the test is probably best regarded as a major indication of the need for amniocentesis. Conversely, it has been recognised for some time that a low maternal concentration of α-fetoprotein is associated with Down's syndrome in the fetus. Other maternal serum constituents – eg unconjugated oestriol and human chorionic gonadotrophin – are also influenced; a very effective rate of diagnosis of Down's syndrome can be achieved by combining such analyses with consideration of the mother's age[16] and the number of appropriate markers is increasing.[17] Most practitioners, however, probably would still wish to offer amniocentesis or chorionic villus sampling to women aged over 35 years and at, generally, higher risk. None the less, the introduction of a relatively cheap and effective test raises the possibility of extending routine testing to all pregnant women rather than to the older group alone. Here, however, we enter the realm of resource allocation – a subject dealt with in detail in chapter 11. For the present, we only draw attention to the conflict which arises between those who would hold to the assumption that 'because a test is possible, testing should be implemented as a service'[18] and those who emphasise the importance of cost-effectiveness before a new policy is established – in itself, often a source of contention.[19] The potential dangers of the former policy are shown by the mounting of an action for negligence in not disclosing the merits of the improved test at a time when it was scarcely beyond the development stage.[20] What does seem to be evident is that the provision of a test without adequate back-up counselling as to the significance of the result is likely to introduce as much harm as good.[1] We also call into question the ethical propriety of making available a plethora of tests for conditions for which no treatment or cure is available, such as Down's syndrome. In these circumstances, the availability of such tests can *only* be justified to facilitate an abortion decision – otherwise, offering them can be seen as little more than a waste of resources. By contrast with what is, arguably, a dubious justification, it is possible to mount a *strong* ethical argument justifying tests which will identify illnesses likely to expose a child to suffering.

Serum tests are best performed at about 16 weeks' gestation; reliance on maternal serum for diagnosis thus leads to late terminations when a termination is indicated, whereas the current emphasis is on identifying chromosomal abnormalities in early pregnancy.[2]

16 N J Wald, A Kennard, J W Densem et al 'Antenatal Maternal Serum Screening for Down's Syndrome: Results of a Demonstration Project' (1992) 305 BMJ 391.

17 Eg Inhibin A: J Wise 'Quadruple Test Is Available for Down's Syndrome' (1996) 313 BMJ 380.

18 Editorial Comment 'Screening for Fetal Malformations' (1992) 340 Lancet 1006.

19 Eg M Connor 'Biochemical Screening for Down's Syndrome' (1993) 306 BMJ 1705. The original article sparked a massive correspondence, most of which was doubtful of the justification for extended screening; see Correspondence columns (1992) 305 BMJ 768 et seq.

20 A Ballantyne 'Mother Sues over Lack of Down's Test' The Sunday Times (1992), 23 August, p C5. The outcome of the case is not known; it may, in fact, have lapsed for want of legal aid.

1 S Vyas 'Screening for Down's Syndrome' (1994) 309 BMJ 753.

2 See p 154 below.

Uterine invasion

The commonest invasive techniques for prenatal diagnosis which involve the fetus or its environment are amniocentesis and chorionic villus sampling. The former is technically easier and carries a lesser risk to the pregnancy; despite the theoretical advantages of the latter, amniocentesis is still probably the most popular method of direct investigation in the United Kingdom.

A significant proportion of British mothers undergo amniocentesis. The process consists of needling the sac surrounding the fetus and withdrawing fluid which contains excretions and metabolites of the fetus together with representative cells; the latter can be grown in culture for chromosomal studies and to detect certain metabolic diseases; the fluid can also be used for biochemical testing.

Biochemical tests can be made rapidly and can directly diagnose some rare diseases of defective metabolism of the gargoylism type. The onset of 'rhesus disease' can also be detected. But by far the most important test in the present context is that for α-fetoprotein, by means of which an efficient laboratory can now diagnose all neural tube lesions. Cell culture can indicate the presence of chromosomal disorder in some 10-20 days. In expert hands, the presence of what are termed 'inborn errors of metabolism' can be detected after some six weeks' culture.

On the face of things, therefore, amniocentesis provides very powerful means of preventing genetic disease but, at the same time, it presents both technical and ethical problems. First, the number of centres practising amniocentesis is limited. A 'defensive' policy of amniocentesis for all would offer little or no benefit in terms of the proportion of positive results and would impose considerable strain on manpower resources; some form of selection has to be imposed. In practice, amniocentesis is now used selectively on approximately 8% of the population[3] and is used almost exclusively for the diagnosis of chromosomal abnormalities, especially Down's syndrome. In the past, amniocentesis was commonly used where routine screening of maternal serum α-fetoprotein had shown a raised level which might indicate a structural abnormality of the fetus, notably a neural tube defect; such abnormalities are now, however, readily diagnosed by the use of ultrasound. As has been discussed above, it has now been shown that the maternal α-fetoprotein level may be abnormally low in Down's syndrome, and this and other biochemical parameters are used in conjunction with the mother's age to calculate a risk score on which a decision to recommend amniocentesis may be more robustly based.[4] Having decided to test, however, it is to be noted that, even in the best hands, an adequate amount of fluid can only be obtained after about the fourteenth week of pregnancy – although the use of sophisticated ultrasonography may reduce this to 12 weeks; no fluid is obtained in some 5-10% of cases and the test must then be repeated; add to this the time required for effective cell culture and it will be seen that one is close to producing a viable infant – and a consequently more hazardous operation – in the event that termination of pregnancy is indicated.[5]

3   Based on data from the Simpson Memorial Maternity Pavilion, Edinburgh 1998 – A A Calder, personal communication.
4   For full details, see H S Cuckle and N J Wald 'Screening for Down's Syndrome' in R Lilford (ed) *Prenatal Diagnosis and Prognosis* (1990).
5   The Human Fertilisation and Embryology Act 1990, s 37(4) has eliminated the legal concern here; the aesthetic distaste for, and the comparative danger of, late abortions remains.

These concerns can, however, be reduced by the use of chorionic villus sampling – or removal and study of the early placental cells; used in conjunction with recombinant DNA techniques, it could revolutionise the diagnosis and management of genetic disease.[6] Chorionic villus sampling suffers in being of no value in the identification of neural tube defects; the incidence of doubtful chromosomal analyses is some four times greater than that following amniocentesis; it is more expensive; and, currently, the risk of miscarriage following the procedure is certainly greater – occurring in some 2-3% of examinations. Against this, chorionic villus sampling provides a good source of fetal DNA. Perhaps the most important practical consideration lies in the fear that early villus sampling may result in facial or limb abnormalities in an otherwise normal fetus.[7] For all these reasons, the early enthusiasm with which the procedure was greeted has waned somewhat. It should probably be reserved for those women who are at greatest risk – and, therefore, most likely to seek an early termination – or for cases where there is a single gene defect likely to require diagnosis.[8]

Amniocentesis itself is said to carry a fetal mortality rate of up to 0.5%; slight though this may be, it is still not inconsiderable and, again, indicates the need for case selection – particularly if fertility is already low. It, too, cannot be used in a 'blanket' fashion – only specific diseases can be sought and discovered; moreover, irrespective of negligence, some false positive or false negative tests are inevitable and will increase with the complexity of the tests undertaken. Because of this, research and, indeed, paediatric opinion are now directed towards primary prevention – for example, towards identifying the underlying environmental causes in multifactorial disease.

Limitations of technique give rise to ethical, as well as practical, problems. Although modern techniques of gene marking have reduced the toll,[9] a proportion of normal male children at risk of X-linked disease are still legally aborted. Again, a raised α-fetoprotein level does not give a clear indication of the degree of neural tube defect.[10] The routine abortion of fetuses with any detectable spinal abnormality will, therefore, result in the destruction of some salvageable – and lovable – children; on the other hand, 10-20% of 'missed' cases will have a severe defect and will require much corrective surgery. Similarly, the presence of the typical chromosomal abnormality does not indicate the likely severity of Down's syndrome. There are other problems of interpretation. For example, given a chromosomal abnormality, what does it mean? Certain arrangements are well known to be associated with severe disease but in others – notably the 'XYY syndrome' – the evidence is by no means clear.[11] XYY boys are said to be prone to vicious behaviour but 'prone' is a very relative concept.[12] Should a doctor, on the one hand, recommend abortion of such

6 For a good account of the latter, see R F Mueller and I D Young (eds) *Emery's Elements of Medical Genetics* (1995).
7 H V Firth, P A Boyd, P Chamberlain et al 'Severe Limb Abnormalities after Chorionic Villus Sampling at 56-66 Days' Gestation' (1991) 337 Lancet 762.
8 R J Lilford 'The Rise and Fall of Chorionic Villus Sampling' (1991) 303 BMJ 936.
9 Eg markers are already available for cystic fibrosis, Duchenne muscular dystrophy and Huntington's disease.
10 This situation may be improved by combining α-fetoprotein analyses with high quality ultrasonography: M J Seller 'Is Antenatal Selection for Spina Bifida Possible?' (1990) 301 BMJ 251.
11 See L Taylor 'Genetically Influenced Antisocial Behaviour and the Criminal Justice System' (1982) 33 NILQ 215.
12 On the supposed link between genetics and criminality see, generally, Ciba Foundation *Genetics of Criminal and Antisocial Behaviour* (1996).

a fetus as a 'precaution' or, on the other, say nothing and risk leaving the parents with an inexplicably 'difficult' child; alternatively, should he inform the parents, allow the pregnancy to run normally and possibly expose the family unnecessarily to an atmosphere of distrust? What is one to do when one of the other common aberrations of the sex chromosomes – for example Klinefelter's (XXY) or Turner's (XO) syndrome – is discovered? Such abnormalities are often, but not always, associated with a degree of infertility or mental dysfunction. The variations are so many that it is impossible to generalise. The essential point is that patients who request or consent to antenatal diagnoses of this type must fully understand the extent of their consent and must be aware of the potential consequent decisions to be made.[13] Some might wish to be informed of every item of information which has come to light, while others might require to know only of conditions which have a fully understood and significant prognosis; much subsequent searching of conscience can be avoided by preparatory discussion of the issues.

At the same time, as we have already intimated, the doctor's own motivation, prejudices and failings cannot be discounted. Much will depend upon whether, and to what extent, he sees himself as a community rather than a personal physician – and how much that is personal to the woman or to her progeny. We have already concluded that it is well-nigh impossible to perform an illegal therapeutic abortion in Great Britain but the clinician is still confronted with the moral problems inherent in the interpretation of 'severe handicap' in the Abortion Act 1967, s 1(1)(d) – it is, for example, even possible to construct an argument which casts doubt on the ethical justification for abortion in such a serious condition as Huntington's disease.[14] What seemed, at first sight, to be an uncomplicated and thoroughly desirable procedure presents, in the end, as a Pandora's box of moral uncertainties.

Some of the difficulties can be overcome by more modern techniques. Fetoscopy, for example, allows for direct inspection of the fetus and, thence, an assessment of the degree of abnormality; at the same time, fetoscopy carries with it a fetal mortality of about 1%. Fetal blood sampling, originally developed for the diagnosis, inter alia, of haemophilia has had a relatively short life as the need for such relatively dangerous investigations recedes with the availability of recombinant DNA techniques.[15] Mention must also be made of the potential for embryo biopsy as an answer to the very high risk pregnancy. This technique combines in vitro fertilisation with removal and genetic analysis of single cells from eight-cell embryos, followed by selection of those found to be normal for implantation. This immediately raises the question of the status of the surplus embryo which we discuss in detail below.[16] Here, it need only be noted that many, though not all, would see embryocide as preferable to – or, perhaps, less reprobate than – feticide. The procedure also carries the many difficulties associated with in vitro fertilisation of itself (see chapter 3) and we tend to doubt whether its benefits outweigh the imposed emotional and financial costs.[17] That having been

---

13 An interesting survey was reported by H Statham and J Green 'Serum Screening for Down's Syndrome: Some Women's Experiences' (1993) 307 BMJ 174.
14 S G Post 'Huntington's Disease: Prenatal Screening for Late Onset Disease' (1992) 18 J Med Ethics 75.
15 N M Fisk and S Bower 'Fetal Blood Sampling in Retreat' (1993) 307 BMJ 143.
16 See chapter 19.
17 A very good discussion is to be found in M Michael and S Buckle 'Screening for Genetic Disorders: Therapeutic Abortion and IVF' (1990) 16 J Med Ethics 43.

said, however, it is impossible to ignore the speed with which this branch of science moves forward. The range of pre-implantation diagnoses is growing such that the technique is referable to an ever widening body of patient-clients. It is now possible to screen for a large number of conditions, including cystic fibrosis, Tay Sachs disease, Duchenne muscular dystrophy and even dominant disorders such as Marfan's syndrome. Anecdotal evidence suggests that, while families affected, for example, by hereditary cancers show little interest in prenatal diagnosis, couples at risk of passing on a dominant condition generally prefer prenatal diagnosis to the option of aborting an otherwise normal pregnancy.[18]

But increasing sophistication to some extent only serves to underline the fundamental moral issue of prenatal screening which is – how far is one to go in defining abnormality? Is the 'perfect baby' to be encouraged?[19] The concept of parents obtaining a termination on the grounds of, for example, the sex of the child may seem frivolous – or unprincipled – to many; but, as we discuss above,[20] it may be medically defensible and, accordingly, legal. One can foresee more generally applicable dilemmas of conscience. Cases of Down's syndrome or of spina bifida which have not been discovered through prenatal screening are already candidates for neonaticide or local authority care. Is such disposal to run parallel with an increasing prenatal diagnostic capability when, as a result, more parents reject what will be regarded as imperfect children on increasingly demanding criteria? It is for such reasons that we argue later[1] in favour of legislation which ensures that, whatever may be the legal situation of the fetus, the best interests of the neonate are paramount.

On the other side of the coin, it is clear that genetic counsellors should not overemphasise the interests of the state in reducing the incidence of genetic disease and, as clinicians, should not join with the scientists in welcoming the genetic issue as 'unstoppable'.[2] Rather, the aim should be to concentrate on the particular circumstances and interests of the parents in wanting a child. The Nuffield Council on Bioethics,[3] the House of Commons Science and Technology Committee[4] and the British Medical Association[5] have all stressed the importance of accepting the ethical principle that screening or testing is justifiable only if based on free and informed consent. Similarly, in the United States, the National Institutes of Health Task Force on Genetic Testing has stated that '[it] is unacceptable to coerce or intimidate individuals or families regarding their decision about predictive genetic testing'.[6] An elderly couple, for example, might see a pregnancy as their last possibility and might prefer to take their chance in the ignorant way of natural parenthood – and they should

18 J D A Delhanty and J C Harper 'Genetic Diagnosis Before Implantation' (1997) 315 BMJ 828.
19 R F Chadwick 'The Perfect Baby: An Introduction' in R F Chadwick (ed) *Ethics, Reproduction and Genetic Control* (1987) p 93. See also E Yoxen *Unnatural Selection* (1986).
20 See p 116.
1 See chapter 15 below.
2 Editorial Comment 'Ethics and the Human Genome' (1991) 351 Nature, Lond 591, quoted by Clarke (1990) 335 Lancet 1145.
3 *Genetic Screening: Ethical Issues* paras. 4.6.-4.16.
4 Third Report (1995) paras 81-105, esp paras 88, 97.
5 BMA *The BMA's Views on Genetic Testing* (21 November 1995).
6 N A Holtzman and M S Watson (eds) *Promoting Safe and Effective Genetic Testing in the United States* (1997).

be allowed to do so; a woman who has managed to conceive by assisted means may rightly refuse to take the risks involved in chorionic villus sampling or amniocentesis. A refusal to accept information must be respected just as much as must the desire to receive information. To an extent, the wishes of patient-clients dictate the parameters of the duties of genetic counsellors and, indeed, of all health care professionals. In practice, the precise boundaries of such duties are established and maintained by the law through the actions for wrongful life and for wrongful birth, which are, essentially, actions for negligence brought over genetic counselling. We turn to consider these now and stress that what is said must be viewed in the light of this complex and, sometimes, conflicting moral background.

Counselling and negligence

The parents of an afflicted child may choose to raise an action in negligence against a genetic counsellor or doctor who has failed either to advise them of the risk of genetic illness in their children or to carry out, and interpret correctly, appropriate diagnostic procedures which would have disclosed abnormality in the fetus. The counsellor or doctor owes them a duty of care in which he or she has been found wanting; the parents may contend that, as a result, they have been deprived of the opportunity to terminate the pregnancy and they are now burdened with a sick or handicapped child. Such an action, brought by and on behalf of the parents, is generally known as one for 'wrongful birth'.[7] Damages may be sought in respect of the distress occasioned by the parents in respect of the existence of the defect in their child and for the extra costs which are entailed in bringing up the child.

The courts in the United States were at first divided in their attitudes to such actions but have steadily become more amenable to recognising damages for the birth of a handicapped child as a legitimate claim. In *Becker v Schwartz*[8] the New York Court of Appeals allowed a parental claim for damages in respect of the cost of the institutional care of a child suffering from Down's syndrome. The negligence in question was the failure of the doctor to recommend amniocentesis to a 37-year-old mother who, by virtue of her age, had a relatively high risk of bearing a handicapped child. They have, however, found difficulty as to the conflict of interests. On the one hand, there is the question of public policy which should, in theory, favour birth over abortion.[9] On the other, the woman's prerogative to control her own body, and the consequent acceptability of abortion, have been increasingly recognised. The general

---

7　Other related actions include an action for 'wrongful pregnancy', which we define as a claim that an unwanted implantation or pregnancy occurred because of another's negligence. Some authors distinguish an action for 'wrongful conception' which is raised on the rather narrower ground that a failed sterilisation operation has resulted in a conception: see B Dickens 'Wrongful Birth and Life, Wrongful Death before Birth and Wrongful Law' in S A M McLean (ed) *Legal Issues in Human Reproduction* (1989) ch 4. Such a distinction may be useful in limited circumstances but we prefer to use the umbrella term 'wrongful pregnancy' to encompass both. We discuss the action for 'wrongful life' at p 160ff below.

8　386 NE 2d 807 (NY, 1978).

9　See eg *Azzolino v Dingfelder* 337 SE 2d 528 (NC, 1985); *Siemieniec v Lutheran General Hospital* 512 NE 2d 691 (Ill, 1987).

rule which seems to have emerged is that, while wrongful life actions[10] will fail, the corresponding claim for wrongful birth will succeed.[11] Even so, the causation problem remains. It is, for example, still up to the plaintiff to convince the court that, given the information, she would have undergone a termination.[12] The causation issue also arises in damages; in *Noccash*,[13] for example, widely based damages were awarded for the birth of an infant with Tay-Sachs disease but costs concerned with the child's funeral were disallowed on the grounds that the fatality was the result of hereditary factors rather than of the defendant's negligence. Other difficulties relate to the fact that pregnancy has been actually sought in these cases. Should the damages awarded then reflect the full costs of rearing a defective child or should they be limited to the difference in financial burden posed by a normal and a handicapped infant? Should they extend to compensation for emotional distress? – these questions seem to be very finely balanced in the American courts.[14] While, as has been noted, the United States courts have been willing to accept a wrongful birth action in principle in most cases, some state legislatures have enacted laws stating clearly their preference for denying such causes of action.[15] Moreover, the constitutionality of a prohibition on such actions has been upheld, as we see in the judgment of the Supreme Court of Minnesota in *Hickman v Group Health Plan Inc.*[16]

Comparable cases have been rare in the United Kingdom but, in recent years, the courts have shown an increased willingness to address the problems. There is no doubt that damages will be awarded in respect of negligent counselling; in other words, a wrongful birth action is available in the United Kingdom and we suspect that most cases are settled out of court.[17] The case of *Salih*[18] is interesting as it was specifically concerned with quantum; it was held that the parents were entitled to claim for the basic cost of bringing up the child, not just the difference between normality and abnormality – the parents wanted a child but the cost of maintaining a handicapped child was something they did not want. In *Gregory v Pembrokeshire Health Authority*[19] the trial judge found that the doctors' neglect to inform of the failure of an amniocentesis was a breach of the duty of care; the action failed, however, on grounds of causation, the plaintiff being unable to convince the court, or

---

10 See p 160 below.
11 *Smith v Cote* 513 A 2d 341 (NH, 1986); *Proffitt v Bartolo* 412 NW 2d 232 (Mich, 1987) – where the inconsistency of dissociating the two types of action was vented. For a more recent discussion of these actions, see P M A Beaumont 'Wrongful Life and Wrongful Birth' in S A M McLean *Contemporary Issues in Law, Medicine and Ethics* (1996) ch 6.
12 *Dumer v St Michael's Hospital* 233 NW 2d 372 (Wis, 1975) – cf the English case of *Gregory v Pembrokeshire Health Authority* [1989] 1 Med LR 81.
13 *Noccash v Burger* 290 SE 2d 825 (Va, 1982).
14 See G G Sarno 'Recoverability of Compensatory Damages for Mental Anguish or Emotional Distress for Tortiously Causing Another's Birth' (1989) 74 ALR 4th 798.
15 As an example, consider this provision from the Utah Code Ann para 78-11-24: '[a] cause of action shall not arise, and damages shall not be awarded, on behalf of any person, based on a claim that but for the act or omission of another, a person would not have been permitted to have been born alive but would have been aborted.'
16 369 NW 2d 10 (1986).
17 *Rawnsley v Leeds Area Health Authority* (1981) Times, 17 November is an example of an unreported case. For general discussion of the liability of genetic counsellors, see M L Lupton 'The Impact of Genetics on Society: The Law's Response' (1991) 10 Med Law 55.
18 *Salih v Enfield Health Authority* [1990] 1 Med LR 333; on appeal (1991) 7 BMLR 1, CA.
19 [1989] 1 Med LR 81.

the Court of Appeal, that she would have had a second investigation had she been offered one. In *Anderson v Forth Valley Health Board*,[20] a couple sought damages in respect of the alleged negligence of a health board which led to their two sons being born suffering from muscular dystrophy. The pursuers averred that, had they been referred for genetic counselling and testing, a genetic disorder carried by the wife would have been discovered and the couple would have chosen to terminate both pregnancies. As it was, no tests were ever offered or carried out, despite the fact that the hospital had been informed of a history of X-linked Duchenne muscular dystrophy among the male members of the wife's family. The children's condition only came to light when one of the boys injured himself in a fall. After a very comprehensive review of the case law, Lord Nimmo Smith held that he could see 'no good reason' not to treat the pursuers as having suffered personal injuries 'in the conventional sense' and awarded damages accordingly under the heads of both solatium and patrimonial loss.[1]

The seminal decision of the Scottish courts in *McLelland v Greater Glasgow Health Board*[2] should be noted as to the matter of damages. In this case, a father was, for the first time, awarded damages for the shock and distress he suffered as the result of the birth of a son suffering from Down's syndrome – as in *Anderson*, the hospital had been made aware of a family history suggestive of genetic disease but had failed to offer an amniocentesis. This ruling is unprecedented because it is normally only the mother of the child who will receive damages for pain and suffering. The closest analagous authority we can find in England is *Newell v Goldenberg*,[3] in which a couple were awarded £500 for the anxiety and distress suffered when they discovered that Mrs Newell had become pregnant following the failure of her husband's vasectomy. Normally, the plaintiff must prove an element of psychiatric disturbance or illness in order to recover damages for 'nervous shock'. In *McLelland*, however, Lord MacFadyen was persuaded that this criterion goes only to the question of the existence of a duty of care; no duty of care arises if the only harm suffered is anxiety and distress, and there is no evidence that that harm is of a psychiatric nature. However, in the circumstances of the particular case, the defenders admitted to a duty of care to the father. Thus, an award of damages for the father's upset fell to be considered as would be any other head of damage when the pursuer has suffered material prejudice as a result of the defender's negligence.

Diminished or wrongful life actions

The basis of a parental claim may be clear enough, but what is the juristic nature of a claim brought on behalf of the child itself? The status of the fetus in utero is legally established – the fetus has a general right not to be injured by the wrongful act of a third party. This right was recognised at common law in Canada and in Australia in

20 (1998) 44 BMLR 108, 1998 SLT 588.
 1 Wrongful pregnancy is also regarded as a personal injury in England: *Walkin v South Manchester Heath Authority* [1995] 4 All ER 132.
 2 (1998) Times, 14 October.
 3 [1995] 6 Med LR 371.

two important decisions, *Duval v Seguin*[4] and *Watt v Rama.*[5] Similar recognition is afforded to the fetus by the common law in Scotland[6] and has been held retrospectively to have existed in England prior to the Congenital Disabilities (Civil Liability) Act 1976.[7]

The most important aspect of these rights in the present context relates to the responsibilities of the mother to her fetus. The Law Commission considered this question and decided that an action against its mother in respect of damage resulting from her negligence during pregnancy should not be available to a child. It was felt that a claim of this type would compromise the parent-child relationship and might also be used as a weapon in matrimonial disputes. Accordingly, the English legislation excludes claims by a child against its mother except as to injuries sustained during traffic accidents; here, special policy grounds and the availability of insurance were held to justify the admissibility of such claims.[8] The matter remains open in Scotland because there is no legislation on the subject and there is no reason in law to exclude a claim by a child against its mother in respect of prenatal injuries. It is possible, however, that the courts may be unsympathetic to such claims on policy grounds.

It is also difficult to determine the extent to which the mother's duty of care towards her unborn child might be held to limit her freedom of action during pregnancy. Interest in this aspect of the fetal-maternal relationship has escalated in recent years.[9] The fetus has emerged as a patient in its own right and major attention has been directed to the use of alcohol and other drugs, including tobacco, on fetal morbidity and mortality. It is almost certain that the last word on the subject has not been said. A few years ago, it was easy to hold that social smoking and drinking of alcohol could hardly be viewed in law as negligence. Yet there is virtually irrefutable evidence of their harmful effect on the fetus and, at least in the former context, negligent injury to other parties has been successfully litigated or settled out of court.[10] It seems only a matter of time before the neonate – who could not even protest at the passive smoking to which he was subjected in utero – can sue for the damage done although, admittedly, success would be difficult if not impossible in England by virtue of the Congenital Disabilities (Civil Liability) Act 1976, s 1(1).

Apart from the straightforward case of an injury to the fetus in utero, a child born with an abnormality may argue that some other sort of wrong has been done to it. First,

4 (1973) 40 DLR (3d) 666.

5 [1972] VR 353.

6 *Hamilton v Fife Health Board* (1993) 13 BMLR 156, 1993 SC 369, 1993 SLT 624.

7 See *Burton v Islington Health Authority, de Martell v Merton and Sutton Health Authority* [1992] 3 All ER 833, (1992) 9 BMLR 69.

8 An apposite case, possibly the prototype, has been reported by C Dyer 'Boy Wins Damages after Injury in Utero' (1992) 304 BMJ 1400. At least one Australian case has been successful: D Brahams 'Australian Mother Sued by Child Injured in Utero' (1991) 338 Lancet 687.

9 See eg E W Keiserlingck 'A Right of the Unborn Child to Pre-natal Care – the Civil Law Perspective' (1982) 13 Rev de Droit 49; P L Hallisey 'The Fetal Patient and the Unwilling Mother: A Standard for Judicial Intervention' (1983) 14 Pac LJ 1065; J L Lenow 'The Fetus as a Patient: Emerging Rights as a Person' (1983) 9 Am J Law Med 1.

10 D Brahams 'Tobacco Litigation (USA, UK and Australia)' (1992) 340 Lancet 230; 'Passive Smoking' (1993) 341 Lancet 552; *Bland v Stockport Metropolitan Borough Council* (unreported) – discussed by C Dyer 'UK Woman Wins First Settlement for Passive Smoking' (1993) 306 BMJ 351. See also S Chapman and S Woodward 'Australian Court Decision on Passive Smoking Upheld on Appeal' (1993) 306 BMJ 120 for the Australian courts' view of passive smoking.

he or she may claim that there was negligence prior to its conception, and that this negligence has resulted in its being born with certain abnormalities. An example of such a claim is provided by the American case of *Yeager v Bloomington Obstetrics and Gynecology, Inc.*[11] This concerned a child born suffering from brain damage due to haemolytic disease of the newborn which occurred because the hospital negligently failed to treat rhesus immunisation of the mother during a previous pregnancy; the court held it to be reasonably foreseeable that subsequent children would be injured as a result. Such a claim would also be competent in English law provided that, at the time of conception, the parents were not aware of the risk that their child would be born disabled. This exemption does not apply if, in an action by the child against its father, it is established that the father knew of the risk while the mother did not.[12]

The child may also bring a claim in respect of its *wrongful life*. The basis of this claim is that, through the negligence of the defendant, the child's parents were not afforded the opportunity to abort the fetus; as a result, the child seeks damages for the impaired existence he or she is now being forced unwillingly to lead. The negligence in question may occur either before the child's conception – as, for example, in a case of negligent genetic counselling – or after conception – as when a doctor fails to detect an abnormality in the fetus. A high proportion of such cases result from laboratory errors which are, in general, clearly recognisable as negligent.

The history of the wrongful life action can be traced through the United States courts. Attempts to extend the cause of action to merely being born have, not unnaturally, received short shrift.[13] Suits brought by defective children, however, pose difficulties with which the American legal system has been struggling for many years. In *Gleitman v Cosgrove*,[14] the plaintiff was born deaf, mute and nearly blind as a result of his mother's exposure to German measles during pregnancy. The Supreme Court of New Jersey dismissed the plaintiff's claim for damages, against the doctors who were alleged to have told the mother that there was no risk of German measles harming her child. The basis for dismissal was that its acceptance would amount to a statement that it was better not to be born at all than to be born handicapped; it was logically impossible, the court felt, to weigh the value of a handicapped life against non-existence. As it was expressed:

> It is basic to the human condition to seek life and to hold on to it however heavily burdened. If Jeffrey [the plaintiff] could have been asked as to whether his life should be snuffed out before his full term of gestation could run its course, our felt intuition of human nature tells us he would almost surely choose life with defects against no life at all 'For the living there is hope, but for the dead there is none . . .

A year later, the claim of a child similarly damaged by its mother's illness was rejected on the grounds that to allow a claim based on failure to abort the plaintiff would be the antithesis of the principles of the law of tort, which is directed towards

11 585 NE 2d 696 (Ind, 1992). For earlier examples, see *Lazevnick v General Hospital of Monro County Inc* 499 F Supp 146 (Md, 1980); *Jorgensen v Meade-Johnson Laboratories* 483 F 2d 237 (1973); *Renslow v Mennonite Hospital* 367 NE 2d 1250 (Ill, 1977).
12 Congenital Disabilities (Civil Liability) Act 1976, s 1(4).
13 *Beardsley v Wierdsma* 650 P 2d 288 (Wyo, 1982).
14 296 NYS 2d 687 (1967).

the protection of the plaintiff against wrongs. The greatest wrong, it was pointed out by the court, is to cause another person's death.[15] In other cases, the courts have chosen to reject the claims of handicapped children on the grounds that it is impossible to assess the child's damages.[16]

There is no indication that the courts, in refusing the children's claims, have intended to limit compensation for this type of negligence. Actions by the parents for emotional shock, expenses incurred in rearing a defective child and the like have been successful and the trend has been – as explained in *Robak*[17] – to focus on the family as the true object of the claim. This was emphasised in *Prokanik v Cillo*,[18] which was a rare instance of a wrongful life action being accepted; a main reason for so doing was that the parents were time-barred and could not sue on their own behalf. In line with other common law jurisdictions, the American courts will, where it is possible, allow the neonate a suit for prenatal injury while denying one for wrongful life.[19]

To our knowledge, there exists only one straightforward instance of a wrongful life action being allowed in full.[20] This case was effectively overturned by the Supreme Court of California in *Turpin*,[1] when it adopted the principle of allowing the suit to proceed and accepting a claim to special damages – ie those incurred as a result of the congenital defects – but not to general damages; the basis for the latter restriction lay in the still insoluble problem of comparing an impaired existence with not being born at all. The movement towards acceptance of the suit has, however, been arrested and there is now a definite trend in favour of rejecting such claims in toto.[2] When the plaintiff in *Bruggeman v Schimke*[3] averred that actions for wrongful life were being increasingly recognised, the court replied that this was simply not true and that any theory sustaining a legal right to be dead rather than to be alive with deficiencies was one completely contrary to the laws of the state. In practical terms, children are unlikely to be disadvantaged when an action for wrongful life fails. Since the courts allow the parents to recover the medical expenses in rearing a defective child, the child's separate claim will apply only to expenses incurred after reaching majority; in most cases, the defect will be so serious that the damaged child will never achieve that age. Even so, both the United States courts and the state legislatures appear increasingly concerned to express their preference for birth over abortion – and this to the extent that not only wrongful life but also wrongful birth actions may be rejected.[4]

15 *Stewart v Long Island College Hospital* 296 NYS 2d 41 (1968).
16 Eg *Dumer v St Michael's Hospital* 233 NW 2d 372 (Wis, 1975); *Blake v Cruz* 698 P 2d 315 (Idaho, 1984); *Smith v Cote* 513 A 2d 341 (NH, 1986); *Cowe v Forum Group Inc* 575 NE 2d 630 (Ind, 1991).
17 *Robak v United States* 658 F 2d 471 (1981).
18 478 A 2d 755 (NJ, 1984). A similar option has been left open more recently: *Viccaro v Milunsky* 551 NE 2d 8 (Mass, 1990).
19 Eg, *Cowe v Forum Group Inc* 575 NE 2d 630 (Ind, 1991).
20 *Curlender v Bio-Science Laboratories* 165 Cal Rptr 477 (1980).
 1 *Turpin v Sortini* 182 Cal Rptr 377 (1982). Also followed in *Harbeson v Parke-Davis Inc* 656 P 2d 483 (Wash, 1983).
 2 Eg *Ellis v Sherman* 515 A 2d 1327 (Pa, 1986); *Proffitt v Bartolo* 412 NW 2d 232 (Mich, 1987); *Cowe v Forum Group Inc* 575 NE 2d 630 (Ind, 1991).
 3 718 P 2d 635 (Kan, 1986).
 4 For evidence of this from state legislatures see p 159, n 15, above. Also, *Azzolino v Dingfelder* 337 SE 2d 528 (NC, 1985). For major reviews, see E H Morreim 'The Concept of Harm Reconceived: A Different Look at Wrongful Life' (1988) 7 Law & Philos 3; B R Furrow 'Actions for Wrongful Life' in J K Mason (ed) *Paediatric Forensic Medicine and Pathology* (1989) ch 26.

A similar judicial antipathy to abortion is to be seen in the only apposite English case – *McKay v Essex Area Health Authority.*[5] Prior to this Court of Appeal decision, the Law Commission had considered the merits of the wrongful life action in its Report on Injuries to Unborn Children[6] and had come to the conclusion that it should not be allowed. The gravamen of this recommendation lies in the belief that to allow such actions would place 'an almost intolerable burden on medical advisors', who might be under 'subconscious pressures' to advise abortions in doubtful cases. As a result of these recommendations, the Congenital Disabilities (Civil Liability) Act 1976, s 1(2)(b) appears to exclude the right of a child to sue in such circumstances.[7] The infant plaintiff in *McKay* was, however, born before 22 July 1976 and, therefore, did not come within the ambit of the Act; the issue of wrongful life was, therefore, open to the court.

In this case, the mother of the handicapped child had been in contact with the virus producing German measles and had consulted her doctor. A blood sample was taken but this was mislaid. A second sample of blood was taken and the mother was duly informed that neither she nor the infant had been infected with rubella; however, the infant girl was found to be severely handicapped when she was born. The plaintiffs alleged that there was negligence on the part of the defendants in that they either failed to carry out the necessary tests on the blood samples or failed to interpret them correctly. A number of claims were made as a result of this alleged negligence, including a claim by the child for damages in respect of entry into a life of distress and suffering.

The court discussed the major issues of legal policy to which this case gave rise in an extensive judgment. While recognising that there was no reason why a mother in such circumstances may not be able to claim in respect of the negligent failure to advise her of her right to choose abortion, the court was not prepared to recognise any claim by a child to damages for wrongful life. The grounds on which this decision was reached are similar to those which have appeared in the American cases.

The initial analysis is in terms of the duty of the doctor. The doctor clearly owes to the fetus a duty not to do anything to injure it, but what duty is owed to a fetus which has been damaged by some agency for which the doctor can bear no responsibility – in this case by the rubella virus? The only duty which the court could see would be an alleged duty to abort the fetus and the question then to be considered was whether this could ever be legal.[8] As to 'wrongful life', it was held that an *obligation* to abort:

[W]ould mean regarding the life of a handicapped child as not only less valuable than the life of a normal child, but so much less valuable that it was not worth preserving, and it would even mean that a doctor would be obliged to pay damages to a child infected with rubella before birth who was in fact born with some mercifully trivial abnormality. These are the consequences of the necessary basic assumption that a child has a right to be born

---

5   [1982] QB 1166, [1982] 2 All ER 771, CA.
6   Law Com no 60.
7   A good argument can, in fact, be made out that wrongful life actions are not excluded: J E S Fortin 'Is the "Wrongful Life" Action Really Dead?' [1987] J Soc Welfare Law 306. See also the commentary on *Cowe*: A Grubb [1993] 1 Med L Rev 262.
8   This attitude, particularly as related to rubella immunisation, is challenged by Morreim (1988) 7 Law & Philos 3.

whole or not at all, not to be born unless it can be born perfect or 'normal', whatever that may mean.[9]

Having declined to find a duty basis of the claim, the court also cavilled at the difficulties of assessing damages in such a case. Here, the impossibility of comparison argument was seen as a strong one: how could a court compare the value of a flawed life with non-existence or, indeed, with any 'after life' which an aborted child was experiencing? – the court declined to undertake any judgment on the conflicting views of theologians and philosophers on the latter aspect. Even faced with this conceptual difficulty, Stephenson LJ was of the opinion that it was better to be born maimed than not to be born at all except, possibly, in the most extreme cases of mental and physical disability – which provokes the questions: 'what is extremity?' and 'by what right do the courts take the view that existence is always to be preferred to non-existence?' The decision is, surely, one which should be left to the handicapped child by way of substituted judgment. It is very probable that a Scottish court would following the ruling in *McKay*.[10]

The doubtful aspect of the wrongful life action lies in the fact that it requires that the court should say to the plaintiff: 'Yes, it would be better had you not been born.' This judgment, however sympathetic to the motives behind it, would seriously compromise the value of human life which the courts are more usually called upon to endorse. The disabled should be helped and, if possible, compensated for the suffering which their lives may entail, but the moral basis for such compensation should be the desire to make life more comfortable and bearable – not the notion that they should not be in existence at all.

In line with this argument, we believe that the conceptual difficulties would largely disappear if, first, the Abortion Act 1967, s 1(1)(d) – the 'eugenic clause' – were accepted as having been drafted in the fetal, rather than the maternal, interest.[11] The 'right' of the handicapped fetus to abortion is then comparable to the defective neonate's right to refuse treatment (see chapter 15); failure to respond to the interests of either, albeit necessarily expressed by proxy, then falls into the ambit of consent-based negligence (see chapter 10) – in effect, the fetus is saying: 'but for the negligent advice given to me through my parents, I would not have chosen a disadvantaged condition; I now have to be disadvantaged and, therefore, I am entitled to compensation.' Secondly, we favour abandoning the principle of 'wrongful life' in favour of 'diminished life'; we can then look not at a comparison, whether it be between the neonate's current existence and non-existence or with normality, but, rather at the actual suffering that has been caused. There would have been no suffering in the event of an abortion, there was no abortion as a result of negligence, and it follows that the negligence has produced suffering which should be compensated according to its degree. This carries the practical advantage that the courts can understand and accommodate this form of damage, which allows for a distinction to be made between

9 [1982] 2 All ER 777 at 781, per Stephenson LJ.
10 *Anderson v Forth Valley Health Board* 1998 SLT 588 at 604, per Lord Nimmo Smith, referring to Lord Osborne in *P's Curator Bonis v Criminal Injuries Compensation Board* 1997 SLT 1180, (1997) 44 BMLR 70.
11 For discussion, see J K Mason *Medico-Legal Aspects of Reproduction and Parenthood* (2nd edn, 1998) pp 157-158.

serious and slight defect. Lord Donaldson MR, in a comment on *McKay*, has explained that the child also claimed that, if her mother had received appropriate treatment, her disabilities would have been less. She therefore sought damages based on the different between her quality of life as it was and the quality of life which she would have enjoyed if her mother had been treated – and this claim was allowed to proceed.[12] This is very close to an action for diminished life and is an aspect of *McKay* which merits closer study – though there seem to be no reports of the action.

Powerful legal and philosophical arguments can be, and are, adduced in favour of rejecting the wrongful life action – not the least of which is that, in the majority of instances, the particular neonate had no opportunity to lead a normal life. Yet intuition urges that justice is, thereby, thwarted;[13] it is interesting that at least one jurisdiction has accepted the infant plaintiff's cause when confronted with the problem de novo.[14]

12 *Re J (a minor) (wardship: medical treatment)* [1990] 3 All ER 930 at 935, (1992) 6 BMLR 25 at 31, CA.

13 See, inter alia, T K Foutz '"Wrongful Life": The Right Not To Be Born' (1980) 54 Tulane LR 480; M Slade 'The Death of Wrongful Life: A Case for Resuscitation?' (1982) 132 NLJ 874; G E Jones and C Perry 'Can Claims for "Wrongful Life" Be Justified?' (1983) 9 J Med Ethics 162; B Dickens, p 158, n 7 above.

14 *Zeitzoff v Katz* [1986] 40(2) PD 85 (Supreme Court of Israel). See J Levi 'Wrongful Life Decision in Israel' (1987) 6 Med Law 373; A Shapira '"Wrongful Life" Lawsuits for Faulty Genetic Counselling: Should the Impaired Newborn Be Entitled to Sue?' (1998) 24 J Med Ethics 369. It was, however, rejected at first hand in the Roman-Dutch jurisdiction of South Africa: *Friedman v Glickson* 1996 (1) SA 1134, where the coincident claim for wrongful birth was upheld.

7 Genetic information and the law

The rather tired adage that 'information is power' has been rejuvenated with the advent of the so-called 'new genetics'. Developments in genetic medicine over the last few years now mean that access to genetic information through genetic testing is relatively cheap and easy but, as a result, this has given rise to serious concerns about access to, and the use of, test results. While the sensitivity of medical data is an issue of general concern which we address in the context of confidentiality in chapter 8, matters are particularly complicated in the context of genetics because of certain features unique to genetic information.[1] First, a test result has implications not only for the individual who has been tested (the 'proband') but also for blood relatives of that person who share a common gene pool.[2] Second, this information has implications also for *future* relatives, in the sense that genetic disease passes vertically through generations. Thus, genetic information impacts directly on reproductive decisions. Third, genetic test results can disclose a likelihood of *future* ill-health in persons who are currently well. Fourth, because in most cases testing is carried out by analysing a person's DNA, which remains unchanged throughout their life, genetic testing can be done at any stage from the cradle to the grave – and, indeed, beyond.[3] Thus, a fetus can be tested in utero for a condition such as Huntington's Disease which might not manifest itself until middle age. Finally, underlying all of these factors is the perceived benefit which genetic testing can offer in the guise of predictability. As a result of this, there is a range of persons or bodies who might have an interest in genetic test results. Relatives might wish to know if they too will be affected by disease or, indeed, if their progeny will be so affected. Insurers have always taken family history as an index of risk in the assessment of insurance cover but, now, genetic testing offers a seemingly more accurate and more scientific means of predicting liability. Similarly, employers might harbour deep concerns about the future employability of persons likely to be struck down by genetic disease, and the state itself has an undeniable interest in promoting public health by reducing the incidence of genetic disease. In light of this range of interests, the potential for conflict over access and control of genetic information is axiomatic and it is important to

1 For a good account of the range of problems which can flow from this see T H Murray et al (eds) *The Human Genome Project and the Future of Health Care* (1996).
2 On this, see L Andrews 'Gen-Etiquette: Genetic Information, Family Relationships and Adoption' in M A Rothstein *Genetic Secrets: Protecting Privacy and Confidentiality in the Genetic Era* (1997) ch 14; R Deech 'Family Law and Genetics' (1998) 61 MLR 697; L Skene 'Patients' Rights or Family Responsibilities' (1998) 6 Med L Rev 1; and, generally, T Marteau and M Richards *The Troubled Helix: Social and Psychological Implications of the New Human Genetics* (1996).
3 For an explanation of the range of ways in which genetic tests differ from other medical tests, see Advisory Committee on Genetic Testing *Consultation Report on Genetic Testing for Late Onset Disorders* (1997) p 10.

recognise that the impact of a genetic test result on an individual's life might well be felt long before they experience the onset of disease. In its struggle to respond adequately to the dilemmas posed by advances in genetics, the law turns to ethics for guidance. It is, therefore, apposite to consider the nature and strength of the ethical arguments which both support and refute the claims of those in each of the above categories and to assess the responses of the law to date in light of this.

Individual and family interests in genetic information

The availability of genetic information is appealing because of its perceived utility: what does it allow one to do? Even so, we consider it preferable to begin our inquiry by asking the opposite question: what does genetic information *not* allow one to do? Probably the most important single factor which has a bearing on this debate is that few cures for genetic conditions exist at present. Moreover, successful treatments for many conditions remain elusive. Thus, except in rare cases, genetic information does not necessarily allow us to avoid genetic disease. This is important because it bears on the motivation of those who would seek to have access to genetic testing or test results. Let us begin by considering the claims of the proband and his or her relatives.

In the absence of treatment or cure, *preparedness* is often cited as the justificatory reason for offering or seeking genetic testing. Adults and children can ready themselves, both psychologically and in other ways, for the onset of disease and couples contemplating a family or who have a child on the way can make a more informed reproductive choice in light of all the available facts.[4] Such justification is, however, a double-edged sword for a number of reasons. First, it is by no means clear that pre-emptive knowledge of future ill health is necessarily 'a good thing'.[5] While evidence exists that this can be so,[6] there is also a growing body of evidence which suggests that adverse psychological sequelae can flow from such knowledge. Andrews has noted, for example, that the suicide rate among young Caucasians who know that they carry the Huntington's disease gene is four times as high as that of the United States national average for a comparable group.[7] The Danish Council of Bioethics warns too of the possibility of *morbidification*:

> The risk of participants in screening programmes possibly suffering from some form or other of morbidification or the notion of 'falling victim' to some inescapable 'fate' uncovered by the genetic examination in itself furnishes a basis for ensuring the

4   V English and A Sommerville 'Genetic Privacy: Orthodoxy or Oxymoron?' J Med Ethics (1999, forthcoming).
5   But knowledge in this context will be relative both as to occurrence and severity of disease.
6   M R Hayden 'Predictive Testing for Huntingon's Disease: Are We Ready for Widespread Community Implementation?' 40 Am J Med Gen 515; J Brandt et al 'Presymptomatic Diagnosis of Delayed-Onset with Linked DNA Markers: The Experience with Huntington's Disease' (1989) 216 J Amer Med Ass 3108.
7   L Andrews 'Legal Aspects of Genetic Information' (1990) 64 Yale J Biol Med 29. For other evidence of adverse results, see D Craufurd et al 'Uptake of Presymptomatic Predictive Testing for Huntington's Disease' (1989) 2 Lancet 603; K M Kash et al 'Psychological Distress and Surveillance Behaviors of Woman with a Family History of Breast Cancer' (1992) 84 J Nat Cancer Cent 24.

provision of adequate information, counselling and follow-up in connection with such programmes.[8]

While it is important to draw a distinction between genetic *testing*, which involves an individual patient being tested in his own medical interests, and genetic *screening*, which involves the testing of populations for public health or research reasons, the Danish Council's observation remains valid in both contexts. It is for reasons such as these the Advisory Committee on Genetic Testing (ACGT)[9] has issued a code of practice to regulate the availability of 'over-the-counter' genetic testing.[10] The committee has recommended strongly that only tests which reveal carrier status for inherent recessive disorders should be made available outside the NHS genetic services.[11] This is because the discovery of carrier status has no direct health implications for the proband. By contrast, testing for adult onset dominant conditions and X-linked disorders should only be provided in a clinical setting.[12] The importance of full and proper counselling in this context cannot be over-emphasised.

Knowledge of one's own genetic constitution and of possible future ill-health can have profound effects on one's sense of 'self'. And, while an individual who seeks out genetic testing might have prepared himself for possible bad news, what of that person's relatives who might suspect nothing as to the presence of genetic disease in their family? Eighty-five per cent of high risk couples are reported as having no knowledge of their condition. In such circumstances, information must come to these persons in ways which may raise issues of confidentiality. Even so, while the prevention of genetic disease may well be seen as admirable community medicine, there are difficulties when the principles are applied to the individual.[13] Should one impose knowledge on someone who has not sought it and who may, perhaps irrationally, be disturbed as a consequence? At what stage should this knowledge be used? It is arguable that premarital advice is preferable to prenatal warning, but to implement such a policy has implications which are scarcely acceptable. On the other hand, has a doctor a moral duty to impose counselling? Here the roles of the genetic counsellor and the health care professional assume paramount importance. The general practitioner who is in possession of familial genetic information is in a particularly difficult position; he has a general duty of care to all of his patients, but a specific duty of confidentiality to the proband. What should he do? It might be asked if there is a legal duty in so far as an action might be brought were parents to discover after the birth of an abnormal child that relevant information had been available but

---

8 Danish Council of Ethics *Ethics and Mapping the Human Genome* (1993) p 60.
9 The Advisory Committee on Genetic Testing was established in the UK in July 1996 with a remit to give full consideration to the ethical and social aspects of genetic testing and to advise the government accordingly.
10 The first such test made available in the UK was for cystic fibrosis: see ACGT *First Annual Report: July 1996 – December 1997* (1998).
11 ACGT *Code of Practice for Genetic Testing Offered Commercially Direct to the Public* (1997).
12 See p 174.
13 For general discussion of the implications of imparting genetic knowledge, see I Pullen 'Patients, Families and Genetic Information' in E Sutherland and A McCall Smith (eds) *Family Rights* (1990) ch 3. But not everyone would see a contradiction between concern for the genetic health of the population and concern for the problems of the individual family: see eg R F Chadwick 'What Counts for Success in Genetic Counselling?' (1993) 19 J Med Ethics 43.

not disclosed. Yet, as we discuss in chapter 8, the practitioner might find himself facing an action for breach of confidence if disclosure was made. In legal terms, no precedent exists to guide the way in such cases. We must, therefore, rely on ethical argument.

A right to know and a right not to know

The origin of this polemic lies in the fact that various parties have valid claims to the same information because, in essence, it relates to each of them. One could, in the first instance, categorise the strength of any claim to information by straightforward reference to the degree of consanguinity: the chances of a second cousin being affected by the same genetic condition are statistically smaller than those of a first cousin and the strength of any claim by the former is correspondingly weaker. This is, however, an unsophisticated approach and unhelpful in the case of the nuclear family, where claims to the information are at their strongest. Matters are complicated by the additional problem of deciding what is the best thing to do – to disclose or not to disclose? While few would argue that the risk of genetic disease should be withheld from family members when an effective treatment or cure is available, the motivation for disclosure in the absence of treatment is, once again, called into question. If it is to facilitate preparedness, then the health care professional must consider the possibility that a relative might not, in fact, wish to know that he might develop a genetic disease. Yet, even if the practitioner is confident that a relative would wish to know, he must justify any disclosing action in ethical terms if he is faced with the proband's refusal to authorise release of the information. Current ethical principles are tested to their limits in such circumstances. Why, for example, should the autonomy of the relative who wants to know trump the autonomy of the proband who wishes to keep the information private? As Ngwena and Chadwick rightly state:

> ... what has to be taken into account is the fact that respecting the autonomy of one person may have implications for the autonomy of others. As the Royal College of Physicians argue, 'Blood relatives have an interest in knowing the truth which has nothing to do with influencing their behaviour towards affected individuals in their families, but as a necessary means to finding out the truth about themselves' ... How is the choice between the autonomy of different people made? ... What is clear is that the decision cannot be taken *on autonomy grounds.*[14]

The ethical principle of respect for patient confidentiality assists the practitioner to a certain degree in that it constitutes one of his primary duties to the proband. Yet release of the information can be justified equally by reference to the principle of non-maleficence if he genuinely feels that harm will come to relatives (or even their progeny) through non-disclosure – neither in ethics nor law is the principle of confidentiality seen as absolute (see chapter 8).

If the avoidance of harm is, indeed, the paramount consideration, then the prospect of harming a relative who might be disturbed by unsolicited information must be considered. For this reason and others, we argue elsewhere that the interest

---

14 C Ngwena and R Chadwick 'Genetic Diagnostic Information and the Duty of Confidentiality: Ethics and Law' (1993) 1 Med Law Internat 73 at 77.

or right not to know deserves recognition.[15] Moreover, the basis of this interest lies not in autonomy or confidentiality but, rather, in privacy. Privacy consists of two aspects: informational privacy and spatial privacy. Informational privacy is concerned with the control of personal information and with preventing access to that information by others. An invasion of informational privacy occurs when any unauthorised disclosure of information takes place. Confidentiality is a subset of this privacy interest and is breached when confidential information which is the subject of the relationship is released to parties outside the relationship without authorisation. Informational privacy is wider than this in that it requires no relationship to exist.

Spatial privacy protects the individual's sense of 'self'. It recognises the interest which each of us have in maintaining a sense of separateness from others. Our spatial privacy is invaded when others 'invade our space' and this includes invasion of our psychological privacy which occurs, inter alia, when unsolicited information about one's self is received. An interest in *not* knowing about oneself has been recognised by the Convention for the Protection of Human Rights and Dignity of the Human Being with regard to the Application of Biology and Medicine,[16] art 10(2) of which states:

> Everyone is entitled to know any information collected about his or her health. *However, the wishes of individuals not to be so informed shall be observed.* (Emphasis added.)

Similarly, the UNESCO Universal Declaration on the Human Genome and Human Rights[17] states in art 5c that:

> The right of every individual to decide whether *or not* to be informed of the results of genetic examination and the resulting consequences should be respected. (Emphasis added.)

The efficacy of grounding such a 'right' *solely* in terms of choice is doubtful.[18] The principle of respect for autonomy requires that we see the individual as a 'moral chooser'.[19] In order to choose meaningfully we require full information about the range of options available and the consequences of any particular choice. However, this paradigm breaks down in the context of an interest in *not* knowing genetic information. Here, the choice is about knowledge itself. As Wertz and Fletcher have put it:

> [t]here is no way . . . to exercise the choice of not knowing, because in the very process of asking 'Do you want to know whether you are at risk . . . ?' the geneticist has already made the essence of the information known.[20]

15 G T Laurie 'The Most Personal Information of All: An Appraisal of Genetic Privacy in the Shadow of the Human Genome Project' (1996) 10 Int J Law Pol Fam 74.
16 Council of Europe *Convention for the Protection of Human Rights and Dignity of the Human Being with regard to the Application of Biology and Medicine: Convention on Human Rights and Medicine* Oviedo, April 1997.
17 Adopted unanimously on 11 November 1997 in Paris at the Organisation's 29th General Conference.
18 Cf J Husted 'Autonomy and A Right Not to Know' in R Chadwick, M Levitt and D Shickle, *The Right to Know and the Right Not to Know* (1997) ch 6.
19 This expression is borrowed from Stanley Benn, who explores the ideas of the 'moral chooser' and 'private life', inter alia, in *A Theory of Freedom* (1988).
20 D C Wertz and J C Fletcher 'Privacy and Disclosure in Medical Genetics Examined in an Ethic of Care' (1991) 5 Bioethics 212 at 221.

The principle of respect for patient confidentiality is similarly unhelpful in protecting the interest in not knowing. It is simply not meaningful to talk of a breach of confidence when information about the party to whom the duty is owed is disclosed *to that party*.

How then is the interest in not knowing to be protected? It is argued in more detail elsewhere that the concept of spatial privacy – which requires that a degree of respect be paid prima facie to an individual's state of separateness or, in this case, state of 'ignorance'– provides a viable mechanism.[1] Spatial privacy could be invaded legitimately, but only if good cause could be shown. The following criteria could be considered for use by any health care professional when deciding how to resolve competing claims to genetic information in the familial context:

- the availability of a cure or treatment;
- the severity of the condition and the likelihood of onset;
- the nature of the genetic disease;
- the nature of any further testing which might be required;
- the question of whether disclosure can further a legitimate public interest;
- the question of how the individual might be thought to react if offered unsolicited information (for example, whether any advance directive has been made).

A practitioner who is faced with a refusal by a proband to communicate test results to relatives when a cure or effective treatment is available would be justified in disrespecting the proband's wishes in order to protect other family members from harm. He might, however, be rightly less inclined to disclose information about a condition for which nothing can be done and which has relatively mild symptoms. This nuanced approach can be supplemented by taking a hierarchical attitude when testing families – the need to test members of the younger generation can be greatly clarified if the older generations are approached and tested first.[2]

Of course, the problem of controlling communication between family members always remains, and a particularly problematic scenario arises when members of the younger generations are tested for a genetic condition and found to be positive. This must mean that one or more parents or grandparents are also affected in some way, yet these persons may have no idea of their condition or may have chosen not to know. It can be very difficult to stem the tidal flow of information within the familial milieu.

It is in the case of children that an appreciation of these subtleties can be found among legislatures and governments. In the United States the Genetic Privacy Act was drafted in 1995 as part of the ELSI[3] division of the Human Genome Project. This is a piece of federal legislation designed for possible adoption by individual states. The draft explains the Act's remit:

---

1 G T Laurie 'Legal and Ethical Aspects of Genetic Privacy' Cambridge University Press, forthcoming.
2 See B S Wilfond et al 'Cancer Genetic Susceptibility Testing: Ethical and Policy Implementations for Future Research and Clinical Practice' (1997) 25 J Law Med & Ethics 243.
3 Part of the Human Genome Project is to establish programmes examining the 'Ethical, Legal and Social Issues' which arise from mapping of the human genome (ELSI).

[T]he overarching premise of the Act is that no stranger should have or control identifiable DNA samples or genetic information about an individual unless that individual specifically authorizes the collection of DNA samples for the purpose of genetic analysis, authorizes the creation of that private information, and has access to and control over the dissemination of that information.

The Act gives an individual from whom a sample is taken (the 'sample source') a number of rights, including the right to determine who may collect and analyse DNA, the right to determine the purposes for which a sample can be analysed and the right to order destruction of samples. Those who collect samples have a number of corresponding duties. The Act also protects genetic information from a number of potential abuses by third parties, such as the state or employers and insurers, and we return to this below.[4] For present purposes we focus on the provisions of the Act which deal with testing minors for genetic conditions.

The Genetic Privacy Act provides that an individually identifiable DNA sample source shall not be taken from a minor under 16 to detect any genetic condition which, in reasonable medical judgment, does not produce signs or symptoms of disease before the age of 16 unless an effective intervention is available to delay onset or ameliorate the severity of the disease; the said intervention must be made before the age of 16 and written authorisation has to be given by the minor's representative. The rationale behind this has been explained by the authors of the Act:

> There are two reasons for this prohibition on the exercise of parental discretion. First, if someone learns that the child is a carrier of a gene that disposes the child to some condition later in life, this finding may subject the child to discrimination and stigmatization by both the parents and others who may learn of this fact. Second, a child's genetic status is the *child's* private genetic information and should not be determined or disclosed unless there is some compelling reason to do so. (Emphasis added.)[5]

The Act is clearly designed to protect the spatial privacy interests of children, and recognises that these should not be invaded without due cause. Arguably, however, it is deficient in not recognising such interests for *all* persons about whom genetic information is known but who have not sought it themselves. By March 1998, 16 states had introduced laws regulating the privacy of genetic information and some 150 bills had been proposed in state legislatures.[6] Such frantic legislative activity reveals the depth of concern which surrounds genetic information.

In the United Kingdom, the House of Commons Science and Technology Committee, in its third report, alerted the public to the range of issues and problems which flow from the availability of genetic information.[7] The committee recommended the establishment of a Human Genetics Commission with the power, inter alia, to monitor the provision of genetic services in the United Kingdom, advise on testing

---

4 See p 174ff.
5 The Act was drafted by George Annas, Leonard Glantz and Patricia Roche of the Boston University School of Public Health. A text of the Act and the comments of the authors can be found at http://www.ornl.gov/TechResources/Human_Genome/resource/privacy/privacy1.html.
6 *The Gene Letter* vol 2, issue 2, March 1998.
7 House of Commons Science and Technology Committee *Human Genetics: The Science and its Consequences* Third Report, 6 July 1995.

and screening procedures, and prescribe the circumstances in which particular screening or diagnostic procedures are provided or proscribed. No such Commission has been established to date. However, a number of relevant bodies do exist: we have already mentioned the Advisory Committee on Genetic Testing (ACGT); the Gene Therapy Advisory Committee (GTAC) was established in 1993 as a result of the recommendations of the Clothier Committee,[8] and we discuss its work below.[9] The Human Genetics Advisory Commission was set up in December 1996 to advise on non-healthcare aspects of genetics, such as the regulation of access to genetic information by insurers and employers, privacy matters and questions surrounding intellectual property rights over genetic material.[10]

These bodies have produced a number of guidelines which show great sensitivity in respect of genetic information. In particular, the ACGT has strongly recommended that no pre-symptomatic testing for late onset disorders for which there are no clinical treatments should be carried out on minors under 16.[11] In parallel, the ACGT has recommended that no over-the-counter testing for late onset disorders be allowed. For testing which *is* permissible, suitable pre- and post-testing consultation should be made available at no extra cost by the suppliers of tests.[12]   A regulatory framework governing the quality of tests is yet to be introduced. A draft European Directive on In Vitro Medical Devices[13] extends to genetic tests and, if passed, will ensure that all medical devices falling within the provisions of the directive are in conformity with 'CE' quality standards. No specific legislation to regulate the control and use of genetic information has been introduced in the United Kingdom to date. However, as is discussed below,[14] the Disability Discrimination Act 1995 goes some way to guarding against discrimination based on genetic traits, and the Data Protection Act 1998 ensures that all records containing personal information, both manual and electronic, are subject to stringent security provisions.

Other parties' interests in genetic information

A number of parties outside the family context profess an interest in access to genetic information. These include insurers, current and prospective employers and the state itself. In this section, the nature of the interests at stake is considered and their respective weights in light of the interests of the proband and his relatives are assessed. The important issue of protection against genetic discrimination is also addressed.

8 Clothier Committee *Report of the Committee on the Ethics of Gene Therapy* Cm 1788, 1992.
9 See p 184ff.
10 The Human Genetics Advisory Commission is part of the Office of Science and Technology within the Department of Trade and Industry. It reports to industry and health ministers. The Commission produced its first annual report in March 1998. For an account of the Commission's work in the future straight from the horse's mouth, see the Chairman's views in C Campbell 'A Commission for the 21st Century' (1998) 61 MLR 598.
11 ACGT *Code of Practice* (p 169, n 11 above) Pt 7. Note, too, the Committee's *Report on Genetic Testing for Late Onset Disorders* (1998).
12 ACGT *First Annual Report* (p 169, n 10, above) pp 4 and 6.
13 *Draft Directive on In Vitro Diagnostic Medical Devices* COM(95) 130.
14 See pp 180-182.

Insurance

The forms of insurance most relevant to genetic testing are life and health insurance. Private health insurance is currently less important in the United Kingdom than in other jurisdictions because of the existence of the National Health Service. Life insurance, however, is a prerequisite for certain types of loan, including, in most cases, mortgages for the purchase of property. Moreover, most individuals take out life insurance to protect their families in the event of their own premature death. Insurance thus touches the lives of most of us and its denial can have far-reaching consequences for both individuals and families.[15]

Genetic information is clearly important to the insurance industry in order to assess the risk of providing cover at all and to determine the level of premiums if an offer of insurance is made. The nature of the interest at stake is entirely financial, and it is one that the industry may legitimately seek to protect. An insurance contract is an example of a contract uberrima fides: of the utmost good faith. In practice, this means that any information having a bearing on the assessment of risk should be disclosed to the insurer; otherwise, the contract can be avoided at any future time. Two possible avenues are open to the insurer in the context of genetic information. First, a request can be made that all test results be disclosed. Second, the insurer can require that the prospective insured undergo genetic testing. In respect of the first of these, it might be argued that this is no different to any other form of medical history. A genetic test result should be disclosed in the same way as one would disclose the removal of a melanoma or a family history of high blood pressure. This having been said, a concern has been expressed in many quarters that individuals might be deterred from seeking testing if it were to be the case that all test results should be disclosed. As the Science and Technology Committee commented:

> We accept that the insurance industry has collectively tried to deal with genetics in a responsible way; nonetheless we are concerned there is a real danger that people could decide to decline testing, even when such testing would be advantageous to them, because of the possible insurance implications.[16]

As to insurers actively requiring prospective customers to be tested, there is a fear that the increased availability of tests will lead to the 'development and proliferation of predictive genetic testing'.[17] This is to be deprecated because of the serious implications which it has for the (spatial) privacy interests of individuals required to be tested. An unacceptable degree of coercion is brought to bear in such circumstances which might vitiate any 'consent' to undergo testing.

Many commentators and organisations have advocated a moratorium on the use of genetic testing in the context of insurance. In 1993 Nys et al surveyed ten jurisdictions noting that the use of genetic test results had been excluded only in two (Belgium and the Netherlands).[18] Testing for insurance purposes *only* was thought

---

15 For an account of the respective approaches in the US and the UK see, O O'Neill 'Insurance and Genetics: The Current State of Play' (1998) 61 MLR 716.

16 Third Report (p 173, n 7 above) para 242.

17 R Chadwick and C Ngwena 'The Human Genome Project, Predictive Testing and Insurance Contracts: Ethical and Legal Responses' (1995) 1 Res Publica 115.

18 H Nys et al *Predictive Genetic Information and Life Insurance: Legal Aspects – Towards European Community Policy?* (1993).

to be unacceptable in every jurisdiction which had specifically legislated on the matter. The authors recommended action within the European Community either to ban outright or to place tight restrictions on the use of genetic testing by insurance companies. No such action has so far been taken. The Council of Europe has, however, issued a recommendation on the protection of medical data which are processed automatically;[19] genetic data are specifically included. The Council recommends that member states take steps to ensure that their laws and practices reflect certain key principles embodied in the recommendation. These provide, among other things, that medical data should, in principle, be collected only by health care professionals or their assistants and, in the context of genetic information, this should only be for preventive treatment, diagnosis or treatment of the data subject or for scientific research, judicial procedure or criminal investigation. The collection and processing of genetic data outside these categories should be permitted only for health reasons; it could be allowed in order to predict ill-health, but only in the case of an overriding interest and subject to appropriate safeguards defined by law. The drafters of the recommendation make it clear in the explanatory memorandum that:

> a candidate for employment, an insurance contract or other services or activities should not be forced to undergo a genetic analysis, by making employment or the insurance dependent on such an analysis, unless such dependence is explicitly provided for by the law and the analysis is necessary for the protection of the data subject or a third party.[20]

The Nuffield Council on Bioethics has recommended that those individuals with a known family history who decide to take a test and test positive should not be treated by the insurance company any differently from other family members – that is, they should still be assessed at the same level of risk as those family members who have not been tested[1] – it was reasoned that, since the industry tends to interpret family history cautiously,[2] 'there is unlikely to be a major difference in insurability between an individual with a family history of a genetic disorder and an individual who has had a positive genetic test result'. By corollary, the Council envisages that those who test negative should benefit from this result and be treated as persons with no family history. In this way the Council hopes that individuals will not be deterred from having genetic tests and also that insurers will not be adversely affected, since they can continue their present practice based on family history.   However, the recommendations of the Council are somewhat different in respect of population screening programmes. In such cases the majority of those taking part would not be aware of any family history of disease. The Council considers that:

---

19 Council of Europe *The Protection of Medical Data* Recommendation No (97) 5 and explanatory memorandum, 13 February 1997.
20 Ibid, para 103.
 1 Nuffield Council on Bioethics *Genetic Screening: Ethical Issues* (1993) para 7.28.
 2 Eg the Council notes that (para 7.23): 'Tables used by the insurance industry show that insurers treat 5% risk of developing Huntington's disease in the same way as a 50% risk: such individuals may be declined insurance or offered insurance at an increased premium, depending on their age at the time of application. Insurance prospects for individuals with a family history of Huntington's disease only improve when the risk is below 5%.'

[i]f insurers were to demand access to the results of population screening for polygenic or multifactorial disease (for example, for genetic predisposition to breast cancer), and premiums were increased for those who tested positive, many people would clearly be discouraged from participating in such programmes. This could have adverse consequences both for the health of individuals and for the public health,[3]

and it concludes that it is not acceptable for insurers to have access to genetic test results which arise from a population screening programme. Furthermore, because of the principle of free and informed consent (discussed in chapter 10), genetic testing should not be made a prerequisite for obtaining insurance. Thus, it can be seen that the Council is emphatic that genetic testing solely for the purposes of assessing insurance risk is unacceptable – and this is true both for those who have a family history and for those who do not.

In the absence of clear government guidelines or legislative intervention the Association of British Insurers (ABI), whose representatives account for 95% of insurance business in the United Kingdom, affirmed in 1997 that insurers will not require a genetic test as a prerequisite for insurance cover.[4] The ABI also announced that a two-year moratorium would be imposed by the industry on the use of adverse genetic test results in respect of mortgage related life insurance contracts (a ceiling limit of £100,000 would, however, be imposed). Individual companies would have the discretion to ask for test results in respect of other forms of life insurance.

The Human Genetic Advisory Commission has also reported on genetic testing and insurance.[5] While the Commission welcomes the ABI's initiative, it noted that the degree of accuracy in the assessment of risk offered by genetic tests is far from ideal and that a detailed family history can provide sufficient data for actuarial purposes. A moratorium on the use of test results was recommended for the time being. The Commission also noted a strong sense of unease among the public in respect of the way in which genetic information is interpreted by the insurance industry and a degree of concern about the risk of discrimination that was sufficient to deter people from seeking testing. The Commission endorsed the practice of the industry in not requiring testing for life insurance and recommended that any breaches of this should be dealt with promptly.

Finally, some have suggested that no access to genetic information should be granted. For example, Harper has argued that insurers should not be allowed to require disclosure of genetic test results within the ordinary run of life insurance policies.[6] Whether it is right that the increased costs of such a scheme should be passed on to the 'normal' population is probably a matter for Parliament to decide; we take the view that it would be an acceptable price to pay for a gesture of support

3 Ibid, para 7.31.
4 ABI *Policy Statement on Life Insurance and Genetics* (1997).
5 Human Genetics Advisory Commission *The Implications of Genetic Testing for Insurance* (1997).
6 P S Harper 'Insurance and Genetic Testing' (1993) 341 Lancet 224. The author points to the doubt as to whether genetic counselling can be seen as part of a 'medical assessment'. The majority approach seems to be much the same in the US: B R Furrow 'Cystic Fibrosis and DNA Tests' (Book review) (1993) 19 Am J Law Med 177. For experience elsewhere, see S Gevers 'Use of Genetic Data, Employment and Insurance: An International Perspective' (1993) 7 Bioethics 126.

178   *Genetic information and the law*

for those who, through no fault of their own, are likely to find themselves increasingly disadvantaged.[7]

Employment

An employer might have two contrasting reasons for seeking access to genetic information about his employees or future employees. First, there is a financial interest in not employing persons who are likely to become debilitated through disease and so affect profits through days lost. Second, he might have a genuine concern that the working environment could effect an employee's health adversely, perhaps by exacerbating an existing condition or by provoking symptoms in an otherwise asymptomatic individual.[8] This concern might relate to the person's health *in se*, and/or to the fear that compensation could be sought by an individual so affected. The propriety of permitting an employer or prospective employer access to genetic information must be addressed in each case. As with the insurance industry, access could be granted either to existing test results or a genetic test could be made a condition of the employment contract. Moreover, a request for genetic information could be made either pre- or post-employment.

Pre-employment requests for genetic information are the most effective means of reducing costs for the employer. Little expenditure is incurred in obtaining the information; the prospective employee is asked either to reveal existing knowledge or to take a relatively inexpensive test. No future expenditure need be incurred because the employer has no obligation to do so in the absence of an actual employment contract.

An employer who seeks genetic information from a current employee is in a very different position. Time and money may have been spent training someone who now cannot do the job, and termination of the employment contract is subject to strict requirements. All of which means that it is very much in the employer's financial interests to seek genetic information from *potential* rather than from *actual* employees. And one might argue that *future* employees can (and should) be excluded from employment if information reveals either the actual presence of, or a predisposition to, genetic disease such as is likely to pose a risk to themselves and/or others if employed.

This advantage of pre-employment screening has been considered further by the Nuffield Council on Bioethics, which has stated:

> Employees would, in principle, be empowered to avoid occupations which would increase the risk of ill health and which in the long run might be life threatening. In this way they could protect the economic security of themselves and their families.[9]

A major difficulty with such an otherwise admirable approach lies in the fact that the predictive accuracy of genetic predictive information is far from assured, and the very factors which concern employers – such as the likely date of onset and degree of

7   For a similar view, see H D C Roscam-Abbing 'Predictive Genetic Knowledge, Insurances and the Legal Position of the Individual' in O Guillod and P Widmer (eds) *Human Genetic Analysis and the Protection of Personality and Privacy* (1994).
8   Eg an environment which is dense with heavy particles is very bad for individuals suffering from or prone to α1-antitrypsin deficiency.
9   See p 176, n 1, para 6.6.

affliction – are unlikely to be known. Also, the sensitivity of such information and the apparent public misunderstanding which surrounds genetic information provoke the very legitimate fear that the information could be used to exclude individuals from employment, or to terminate employment, even when they are not affected by disease and are unlikely to be so for some time. The question thus arises as to whether access to genetic information is an acceptable way by which to ensure the interests of employers and of employees or job applicants.

The Nuffield Council has recognised the privacy implications of employer requests for genetic information,[10] as has the House of Commons Science and Technology Committee.[11] The latter, relying heavily on the views of the Nuffield Council, recommended that legislation to protect the privacy of genetic information be introduced and be drafted so as to prohibit employers testing for genetic conditions other than those which might put the public at direct and substantial risk. Furthermore, any genetic testing for employment purposes should be strictly limited to specific conditions relevant to the particular employment and samples provided for testing should not be examined for evidence of other conditions.

The clear message here is that employers' access to genetic information must be justified on the grounds that the knowledge can have a direct bearing on the job of work to be done.[12] In other words, it is unacceptable for an employer to seek access to another individual's genetic information simply to further his financial interests. This is especially true when that access is sought in order to identify some *future* risk because such a possibility does not affect the individual's current ability to perform his or her job of work.

What, however, of the argument that genetic information should be revealed in order to protect the interests of employees and job applicants themselves? The Science and Technology Committee concluded that:

> Genetic Screening for employment purposes should be contemplated only where:
> (i)   there is strong evidence of a clear connection between the working environment and the development of the condition for which the screening is conducted;
> (ii)   the condition in question is one which seriously endangers the health of the employee; and
> (iii)   the condition is one for which the dangers cannot be eliminated or significantly reduced by reasonable measures taken by the employer to modify or respond to the environmental risks.[13]

Importantly, the Committee stresses that 'employees should have the right to decide whether or not to participate in such screening'. It is unclear, however, whether the recommendations are intended to extend both to current employees and job applicants. No convincing argument could be put that this should not be the case, but the Committee only mentions 'employees'.[14]

10 See p 176, n 1, paras 6.20–6.23.
11 See p 173, n 7, paras 231–233.
12 Science and Technology Committee Report quoting Memorandum (vol II) p 52.
13 See p 173, n 7 at 233.
14 For a criticism of the Nuffield Council's recommendations, and by implications those of the Science and Technology Committee, see M A Rothstein 'Genetic Discrimination in Employment: Ethics, Policy and Comparative Law' in O Guillod and P Widmer (eds) *Human Genetic Analysis and the Protection of Personality and Privacy* (1994).

Discrimination

Perhaps the single most important concern related to genetic information lies in the potential for discrimination it generates.[15] This is relevant to both the employment and insurance scenarios, yet no specific legal regulation currently exists in the United Kingdom to control genetic testing or screening or the uses to which the results can be put.[16] The matter of discrimination must, therefore, be dealt with under the current anti-discrimination laws. In contrast, federal legislation has been proposed in the United States and some states have already introduced anti-discrimination legislation directly tailored to the problems arising from genetic information.[17] As of 1998, 14 states have introduced laws on employers' access to or use of genetic information; 11 of these prohibit outright the discharging or refusing to hire of an individual based on their genetic constitution.[18]

Anti-discrimination law in the United Kingdom is governed by three pieces of legislation: the Sex Discrimination Act 1975, the Race Relations Act 1976 and the Disability Discrimination Act 1995. The protection afforded against discrimination by the 1975 and 1976 Acts is restricted to their precise remits – that is, sexual or racial discrimination. Since many genetic conditions are sex-linked or affect particular ethnic and racial groups, differential treatment of afflicted individuals could amount to discrimination within the terms of these Acts, probably as examples of indirect discrimination. It is not clear, however, how successful such arguments would be, there being no cases on point. More opportunities for redress lie with the Disability Discrimination Act 1995, which is the first piece of United Kingdom legislation to deal directly with discrimination against disabled people. The Act outlaws discrimination in a wide range of fields – such as employment, the provision of goods, facilities and services, the sale and let of property, education and public transport.

The Act defines 'disability' and 'disabled persons' in Pt I as follows:

1(1) Subject to the provisions of Schedule 1, a person has a disability for the purposes of this Act if he has a physical or mental impairment which has a substantial and long-term adverse effect on his ability to carry out normal day-to-day activities.
1(2) In this Act 'disabled person' means a person who has a disability.

In the context of employment, the provisions of the Act ensure that it is unlawful for an employer to treat an individual less favourably than he would treat others for a reason which relates to the individual's disability and when he cannot show that the

---

15 R Hubbard and E Wald *Exploding The Gene Myth: How Genetic Information is Produced and Manipulated by Scientists, Physicians, Employers, Insurance Companies, Educators and Law Enforcers* (1997).
16 A failed Discrimination (Genetic Information) Bill was sponsored by Anne Campbell MP in the parliamentary session 1994/95. For discussion of regulation generally, see J Black 'Regulation as Facilitation: Negotiating the Genetic Revolution' (1998) 61 MLR 621.
17 Eg in 1997 the US Congress faced a number of Bills, including the Genetic Confidentiality and Non-Discrimination Act, the Genetic Non-Discrimination in the Workplace Act and the Genetic Protection in Insurance Coverage Act. For comment generally on discrimination issues in this context, see J Gaulding 'Race, Sex and Genetic Discrimination in Insurance: What's Fair?' (1995) 80 Cornell L Rev 1646 and B R Gin 'Genetic Discrimination: Huntington's Disease and the Americans with Disabilities Act' (1997) 97 Columbia L Rev 1406.
18 *The Gene Letter* (1998) vol 2, issue 2.

treatment in question is justified. Discrimination can occur, inter alia, in respect of: (a) the arrangements which an employer makes for the purpose of determining to whom he should offer employment; (b) in the terms in which he offers employment; (c) his refusal to offer, or deliberate not offering of, employment; (d) his refusal to afford an employee opportunities for promotion, a transfer, training or receiving any other benefit, or his treating the employee differently in such opportunities; (e) his dismissal of an employee, or subjecting the employee to any other detriment.

These provisions could clearly go a long way to preventing discrimination against individuals based on information about their genetic constitution[19] – note, particularly, how pre-employment discrimination is also outlawed. However, the question arises of whether the provisions of the Act extend to persons whose genome contains defective genes which do, or can have, a bearing on their ability to do their job. The crucial term here is '*can have*'. Clearly, persons who are already affected by a genetic condition come within the definition of 'disabled person'. But what of a person who merely has a predisposition to ill-health? A literal interpretation of s 1(1) excludes such a person for it speaks of one who '*has* a physical or mental impairment'. The section must, however, be read in conjunction with Schs 1 and 2, which allow for regulations to be made which will clarify the definitions in s 1. In particular, Sch 1, para 8 concerns 'progressive conditions'. The examples given of such conditions are cancer, multiple sclerosis, muscular dystrophy or infection with the human immunodeficiency virus. The paragraph provides that someone who suffers from such a progressive condition will be treated as 'disabled' provided that their condition results in an impairment which, at least, has (or had) an effect on their ability to carry out normal day-to-day activities, even if that effect is not a substantial adverse effect. Even so, the individual must still be in some way symptomatic, thus excluding those who have 'merely' a predisposition to disease at the relevant time. This means, by inference, that discrimination against persons in this last category is not unlawful under the Act. This disparity and the question of genetic testing were raised in the parliamentary debates but the minister in charge stated:

> . . . except in a few well-publicised cases, genetic tests are not as yet a useful indicator of future actual disability. Their inclusion would open up the [Act] to large numbers of people who are clearly not, and may never become disabled . . . we cannot wander into a situation whereby, for some reason or another, potentially the entire population could claim protection under the [Act].[20]

It is certainly true that genetic tests are by no means accurate at present, but that does not mean that such tests cannot be misused by employers and others, nor that they will not be used to exclude people from jobs and other services for irrelevant and irrational reasons. Legislation designed to outlaw discrimination on the grounds of disability should cover *all* forms of discrimination, whether the disability is actual or perceived, current or future. It is arguable that the provisions of the Act as they currently stand are inadequate and are potentially prejudicial to persons likely to develop genetic conditions later in life; the Secretary of State might, with advantage,

19 One limiting factor is the exemption for small business. The provisions of the Act do not apply to an employer who has fewer than 20 employees.
20 Official Reports, HC, vol 257, col 887, 28 March 1995.

use the powers given under the Act to expand the definition of disability to include such persons. The anomalies in the current provisions were summed up by Baroness Jay in the House of Lords:

> The paradox which is possible in the present situation is that where genetic counselling, genetic testing and identifying genetic markers is potentially one of the most exciting and liberating developments in medical science at the end of the 20th century, if it becomes the case that people feel that identifying those markers in their own personal situation will lead to discrimination, they will be less likely to take advantage of those extraordinary scientific advances which may help their own condition and in which medical science may be able to help future generations of children.[1]

The state interest in genetic information

The above sections have identified many varied interests in genetic information which are held by both individuals and institutions. Two particular state concerns arise from these interests: an inclination to reduce the financial burden wherever possible and a desire to minimise or eliminate harm to its citizens. The state has a role in protecting and advancing 'the public good' – that is, the collective interests of society as a whole. To what extent, then, can the state legitimately request results of genetic tests or require genetic testing?

One of the most obvious state interests in the health care setting is that of securing public health and, perhaps unsurprisingly, it has been argued that mandatory testing for genetic disorders might halt the spread of genetic disease.[2] Even if little or nothing can be done for those already afflicted, disclosure might prevent the transmission of defective genes to future persons. Set against this, however, is the potential infringement of privacy interests which such practices can represent although, in this connection, it can be argued further that the state has a positive interest in facilitating individual choice. It can adopt a more pastoral role towards individuals by providing them with information which may help them make important life decisions such as whether or not to have a child if both partners are carriers of cystic fibrosis. Not only does this make individuals more independent as moral choosers but it might also have the desired social end of preventing the further spread of genetic disease. For example, Ball et al have noted that this view is held by the Royal College of Physicians:

> [the] Royal College of Physicians report suggests that as long as individuals have the right to decide for themselves whether to bear children it could be argued that such individuals

---

1   Official Reports, HL, vol 564, col 1713, 13 June 1995.

2   See S M Suter 'Whose Genes Are These Anyway?: Familial Conflicts Over Access to Genetic Information' (1993) 91 Michigan L Rev 1854 at 1897, citing H P Green and A M Capron 'Issues of Law and Public Policy in Genetic Screening', in D Bergsma (ed) *Ethical, Social and Legal Dimensions of Screening for Human Genetic Disease* (1974). See also M Shaw 'Conditional Prospective Rights of the Fetus' (1984) 5 J Leg Med 63, in which it is argued that prospective parents should face mandatory screening for certain conditions.

should have access to the fullest possible information, including genetic, pertinent to that decision and therefore this should not be withheld.[3]

This implies that the state should seek to further its interest in facilitating choice by providing comprehensive screening programmes, a plethora of genetic tests accompanied by suitable counselling services and other support mechanisms, such as easy access to abortion. Cost implications aside, this would certainly further both individual and state interests by making free choice a market commodity. The risk of a conflict of interests would be almost entirely eliminated if such programmes were provided free of coercive measures.[4]

The situation becomes more complicated, however, if the state seeks to further the interests of its individual citizens rather than those of the public as a whole. There is real potential for conflict when prospective parents wish to know of a relative's genetic constitution in order to make a fully informed reproductive choice. This raises the question of whether the interest in the information for reproductive purposes is enough to warrant an invasion of the relatives' privacy interests.[5]

The moral basis for introducing population genetic screening programmes has been questioned when no appropriate medical intervention is possible in light of a positive result.[6] No such programmes exist in the United Kingdom for adults and the only routine screening of children relates to neonates in respect of phenylketonuria, haemoglobin disorders and hypothyroidism.[7] The availability of a plethora of tests for prenatal genetic diagnosis has been noted in chapter 6. While this can facilitate parental choices as to the continuance of a pregnancy, it still raises concern that such testing is open to abuse if parents are in any way pressurised to test for a range of conditions and to abort any affected fetuses. The prospect that parents who choose not to abort a child might come to be seen as irresponsible is deplorable. We agree with the ACGT in this regard – the aims of any programme should be clearly articulated, including any public health-related agenda on the part of the state, all programmes should be subjected to strict scrutiny by the National Screening Committee and each programme should be accompanied by impartial pre- and post-testing counselling. While it can be accepted that the state may have legitimate reasons for encouraging individuals to act responsibly in their use of any available genetic information, such encouragement should be offered only in the most moderate of terms. The autonomy and privacy interests of each of us require prima facie respect and this should be borne in mind whenever the introduction of a population screening programme is being considered. It is very difficult to justify any screening programme

---

3   See D Ball et al. 'Predictive Testing of Adults and Children' in A Clarke (ed.) *Genetic Counselling: Practice and Principles* (1994) at 77 referring to the Royal College of Physicians of London *Ethical Issues in Clinical Genetics: A Report of the Working Group of the Royal College of Physicians' Committees on Ethical Issues in Medicine and Clinical Genetics* (1991).

4   However, as the Nuffield Council has pointed out (p 176, n 1 above at 8.11): '[i]t has been argued that the availability of prenatal screening and diagnosis, together with the termination of seriously affected pregnancies, both reflect and reinforce the negative attitudes of our society towards those with disabilities. Indeed medical genetics may add a new dimension if genetic disorder came to be seen as a matter of choice rather than fate.'

5   We refer the reader to p 172 above for discussion of the factors to be considered in resolving such conflicts.

6   See, inter alia, Advisory Committee on Genetic Testing (p 167, n 3 above) Annex A and the Science and Technology Committee Third Report (p 173, n 7 above) para 83.

7   Nuffield Council on Bioethics (p 176, n 1 above) at 27.

of children or adults which is unaccompanied by an effective cure or treatment. The strength of the state interest in promoting public heath per se is insufficient to justify compromising the interests of individuals in receiving or not receiving genetic information about themselves.

Gene therapy

Advances in screening constitute only one aspect of the progress which has been made in human genetics over recent decades. Perhaps more significantly from the scientific point of view, possibilities have opened up for manipulation of the genes of existing and future individuals. This is best known as gene therapy, or, in some contexts, as genetic engineering; inevitably, it has given rise to considerable bioethical debate.[8]

Gene therapy may be of two types – somatic or germ-line.[9] Somatic gene therapy is directed towards the remedying of a defect within the patient and involves the insertion of genetic material which will perform some function which the patient's own genetic material cannot achieve. Germ-line gene therapy can be visualised in two ways: the insertion of genetic material into the pre-embryo, which is pre-emptive treatment of the future being and his or her progeny, or as the insertion of a gene into the germ cells of an individual. The latter therapy has no direct bearing on the individual but is intended to ensure that any subsequent children are born with or without certain characteristics. Although the scientific techniques involved are in their infancy, both forms of manipulation have already spawned considerable – and emotional – debate; indeed, genetic engineering is one of the few modern medical technologies in which study of the moral aspects has preceded the practical realities.

The ethical implications of somatic gene therapy were considered by the Committee on the Ethics of Gene Therapy – the Clothier Committee – which reported in 1992.[10] The Committee thought that this form of treatment was uncontroversial, if novel, and felt that it gave rise to no new ethical challenges. The Group of Advisors of Ethical Implications of Biotechnology of the European Commission similarly reported in 1994 and encouraged somatic gene therapy at a number of levels, including basic research, clinical trials and biotechnology.[11] This having been said, the group considered that, because of certain unknown risks associated with the process, research into somatic gene therapy should be restricted to serious diseases for which there is no other effective available treatment. Similar views have been expressed in the United States and in international documents concerned with the bioethics of manipulation of the human genome.[12] We can accept these assessments; the goals of

---

8 See eg P Wheale and P McNally *Genetic Engineering: Catastrophe or Utopia?* (1988).

9 For an up-to-date account of progress so far in gene therapy, see J Kinderlerer and D Longley 'Human Genetics: The New Panacea?' (1998) 61 MLR 603 at 614ff.

10 *Report of the Committee on the Ethics of Gene Therapy* (1992).

11 Opinion of the Group of Advisers on Ethical Implications of Biotechnology of the European Commission *The Ethical Implications of Gene Therapy* (1994).

12 For the US position, see *Report and Recommendations of the Panel to Assess the National Institutes of Health Investment in Research on Gene Therapy* (1995). The Council of Europe *Convention for the Protection of Human Rights and Dignity of the Human Being with regard to the Application of Biology and Medicine: Convention on Human Rights and Biomedicine* states, in art 13: 'An intervention seeking to modify the human genome may only be undertaken for preventative, diagnostic or therapeutic purposes and only if its aim is not to introduce any modification in the genome of any descendants.'

somatic gene therapy are identical to the goals of other forms of treatment and, provided that it does not involve undue risk to the patient or to others, it is as ethically acceptable as is drug therapy or surgical intervention.   There may be a need for caution if somatic gene therapy is developed so as to combat behavioural disorders; even then, however, the ethical considerations will be similar to those which already arise from the use of psychotropic drugs or psychosurgery and which are discussed in greater detail in chapter 22.[13]   It is important, however, to bear in mind that, thus far, effective gene therapy remains a vision of the future in almost all cases.[14]

The controversial nature of germ-line gene therapy – whether directed to the pre-embryo or to an individual's germ cells – rests on its capacity to change future people. Some such changes will, in themselves, be unobjectionable; it is difficult, for example, to find grounds for objection to preventive medicine which will ensure that the bearers of a serious genetically transmissible disease will not pass the condition on to their children. Such medical practice is no different from other, long-accepted, efforts to eradicate disease within the human population which, arguably, interfere with the natural order to a comparable degree.

The difficulty that some have with any form of germ-line therapy is that of the 'slippery slope' which is encountered at a number of points in medical jurisprudence.[15] If we allow germ-line therapy in relation to, say, a seriously debilitating disease, then how are we to prevent its use to eliminate characteristics which we would not, currently, label as a defect but which may be considered undesirable? Rifkin has put the question as follows:

> Once we decide to begin the process of human genetic engineering, there is really no logical place to stop. If diabetes, sickle cell anaemia, and cancer are to be cured by altering the genetic make-up of an individual, why not proceed to other 'disorders': myopia, colour-blindness, left-handedness? Indeed, what is to preclude a society from deciding that a certain skin colour is a disorder?[16]

This is a bleak view of scientific ambitions, but the concern for possible abuse that it expresses has been potent enough to cause a number of governmental or other official bodies to proscribe germ-line gene therapy. The Council of Europe was, initially, sufficiently suspicious to recommend a complete ban on such practice – on the grounds of its insult to human dignity – but later modified this to allow germ cell

---

13 Over 100 somatic gene therapy studies had been reviewed and approved in the US by late 1995. See L Walters 'Reproductive Technologies and Genetics' in R M Veatch (ed) *Medical Ethics* (2nd edn, 1997) p 229.

14 The GTAC noted in its First Annual Report (November 1993–December 1994) that '[t]he application of gene therapy in any routine sense for health care is a long way off. A prolonged period of research lies ahead and it would be wrong to expect immediate returns or instant cures in view of the time and effort that must be expended'. Similarly, the NHS Central Research and Development Committee on the New Genetics produced its first report in May 1995 (Department of Health *Report of the Genetics Research Advisory Group* (1995) in which it said (at p 17) that '[c]orrective gene therapy . . . is still a long way off'. It also laid down the following requirements before it would consider acceptable the widespread implementation of gene therapy: (a) has safety been established?; (b) is treatment possible?; (c) is effectiveness proven?

15 N Holtug 'Human Gene Therapy: Down the Slippery Slope' (1993) 7 Bioethics 402.

16 J Rifkin *Algeny* (1983) p 232, quoted in Holtug (1993) 7 Bioethics 402 at 405.

manipulation for therapeutic purposes.[17]   UNESCO has not ruled out germ-line therapies ab initio in its Universal Declaration on the Human Genome and Human Rights but, rather, prohibits 'practices which are contrary to human dignity'.[18] An arguable case can be made that germ-line research falls into this category. The total outlawing of germ-line therapy has been recommended in Germany – and this attitude was endorsed in a statement from the medical research councils of 11 European states in 1988.[19]

However, germ-line gene therapy is not without its supporters – as Harris has asked: is there anything really wrong in wanting to have a fine child?[20]   The real difficulty lies in distinguishing between eugenically-motivated, or enhancement, germ-line manipulation on the one hand and truly therapeutic intervention on the other. It should be necessary to forbid *all* work in this area only if it is felt that the demarcation line can never be held. Unfortunately, science's bad record in keeping to a narrow, acceptable track lends some force to the arguments of those who would prevent such meddling altogether. It certainly seems to us to be one of those subjects which should only be acceptable following wide and informed public discussion.

Cloning

The birth of Dolly the lamb in 1997 sparked one of the most controversial furores to affect the discipline of medical law and ethics since its beginnings some 30 years ago. Dolly was the first example of an adult vertebrate cloned – that is, genetically copied – from another adult. She was created using a 'fusion' technique whereby the nucleus from an adult cell (in this case mammarian cells) was fused with an unfertilised egg from which the nucleus had been removed. This egg was then transplanted into another adult sheep for normal gestation to take place. The benefits of such a technique include the improvement of production of transgenic livestock which can be used to produce therapeutic agents involving human proteins.

These developments also raise the spectre of human cloning, and it is in this regard that much of the controversy has arisen. The prospect that individuals could clone themselves and have children who share precisely the same genetic make-up is, for some, to go too far. Certainly, if such procedures ever became possible there would be considerable social, legal and ethical ramifications.[1] There is serious concern that the use of such a technique would alter our perception of what it means to be human. Moreover, many fear that the potential for exploitation is too great and envisage the

---

17 Council of Europe *Recommendation 934 on Genetic Engineering* (1982); *Recommendation 1100 on the Use of Human Embryos and Foetuses in Scientific Research* (1989).
18 See p 171, n 17 above, art 11.
19 M A M de Wachter 'Ethical Aspects of Human Germ-line Gene Therapy' (1993) 7 Bioethics 166. The tone of the Declaration of Inuyama and Report of a Working Group on Human Gene Therapy is cautious but not prescriptive: reproduced and discussed in J C Fletcher and W F Anderson 'Germ-line Gene Therapy: A New Stage of Debate' (1992) 20 Law Med Hlth Care 26.
20 J Harris 'Is Gene Therapy a Form of Eugenics?' (1993) 7 Bioethics 178.
 1 And one's fears are not groundless when one reads of the intention that the cells of infertile men are to be cloned so that they may have children: see S Farrar 'Maverick Fertility Expert Plans First Human Clone' The Sunday Times, 25 October, 1998.

production of human clones to be used as sources of spare parts. Others still have posited that the birth of a clone would distort beyond recognition traditional familial hierarchies and relationships. While many of these fears must be unfounded, we cannot deny that the strength of the reaction to these developments dictates a very cautious approach to the future.[2]

Governmental responses to the birth of Dolly were swift and unanimously condemnatory. The United Kingdom government quickly confirmed its position that any work which was designed to produce cloned human beings was unethical and illegal[3] – a matter which we address further below. In the United States, the National Bioethics Advisory Commission (NBAC) reported in June 1997 and concluded that the risks of research into human cloning involving clinical trials were too great and that legislation should be passed to prohibit research into cloning 'complete people'. As a result, the Cloning and Prohibition Bill 1997 was sent to Congress, but the Bill was not introduced in the first session. Since then, at least six other cloning prohibition Bills have been introduced, one of which has already failed.[4] At the state level, 19 states had proposed 22 Bills by the end of 1997, and California passed a law in that year imposing a five-year moratorium on cloning of an entire human being.[5]

Other reactions to this development have been equally antipathetic. A protocol to the Council of Europe Convention on Human Rights and Biomedicine prohibits the cloning of human beings[6] and the UNESCO Declaration on the Human Genome and Human Rights specifically disallows cloning as being contrary to human dignity.[7] Moreover, incentives to carry out research in this field in Europe have been removed with the passing of the Directive on the Legal Protection of Biotechnological Inventions,[8] art 6 of which expressly prohibits the granting of a patent for 'processes for cloning human beings'.[9]

At the domestic level, we confess to some doubts as to whether cloning is, indeed, illegal in the United Kingdom. The Human Fertilisation and Embryology Act 1990 regulates the creation, use and storage of embryos outside the human body and brings all activities involving such practices under the control of the Human Fertilisation and Embryology Authority (see further chapter 3). In so far as s 3(3)(d) of the 1990 Act criminalises only the replacement of the nucleus of a cell of an embryo with a nucleus taken from a cell of any person or embryo, the technique which was used to produce 'Dolly', and which requires only that the nucleus of an unfertilised egg be replaced, might not fall foul of the clause that was designed to prohibit cloning. None the less, the Authority has the exclusive power to license clinics for reproductive research and

2   For a measured proposal, see A L Bonnicksen 'Procreation By Cloning: Crafting Anticipatory Guidelines' (1997) 25 J Law Med & Ethics 273.
3   Official Reports, HC 26 June 1997, col 615ff.
4   I Stith-Coleman et al 'Cloning: Where Do We Go From Here?' Congressional Research Service Report for Congress, September 1998.
5   SB 1344, 1997-98 Leg, Reg Sess (Cal 1997) (enacted) (Human Cloning).
6   Additional Protocol to the Convention for the Protection of Human Rights and Dignity of the Human Being with regard to the Application of Biology and Medicine, on the Prohibition of Cloning Human Beings (Paris, January 1998).
7   Article 11.
8   *Directive of the European Parliament and of the Council on the Legal Protection of Biotechnological Inventions* No 98/44/EC of 6 July 1998, published at OJ L213, 30 July 1998, p 13.
9   It should also be noted that, inter alia, this article excludes processes for modifying the germ-line genetic identity of human beings from patentability. We discuss this directive further in chapter 20.

for the provision of reproductive treatment services. Thus, in real terms, cloning research can be restricted by the withholding of licences and the Authority would almost certainly do so in current circumstances. The point, however, is that 'Dolly' provides us with a classic example of the truism that the law in the medico-legal sphere is destined to remain behind medicine, bringing up the rear and limping a little.

In the absence of specific legislation, the United Kingdom Human Genetics Advisory Commission has produced a consultation paper which seeks views on the public's attitude towards cloning generally, as well as on the perceived benefits and risks of the technique.[10]   This move is to be welcomed wholeheartedly. When responding to developments which have consequences as far-reaching as do so many of those subsumed in the discipline of medical law, it is essential that a broad cross-section of views are obtained and, where possible, taken on board. It remains to be seen how the law will respond to the advent of cloning – but the means by which the final end is reached can be as important as the reaching of the end itself.

10 Human Genetics Advisory Commission *Cloning Issues in Reproduction, Science and Medicine* (1998).

Medical practice

8 Medical confidentiality

A general common law duty is imposed on a doctor to respect the confidences of his patients.[1] The nature of this obligation – which applies to all confidential information and not only to medical material – was discussed by the Court of Appeal in *A-G v Guardian Newspapers Ltd (No 2)*,[2] in which it was affirmed that there was a public interest in a legally enforceable protection of confidences received under notice of confidentiality. There are three elements required to establish a breach of the obligation. First, the information divulged must have the necessary quality of confidence about it; secondly, that information must have been imparted in circumstances importing an obligation of confidence; and, thirdly, there must be an unauthorised use of that information to the detriment of the party communicating it.[3] All these criteria would apply in a medical context where the duty of discretion has been endorsed judicially. Thus, in *Hunter v Mann*[4] the court accepted that:

> ... the doctor is under a duty not to [voluntarily] disclose, without the consent of the patient, information which he, the doctor, has gained in his professional capacity.

More recently, in the very significant case of *W v Egdell*,[5] which we discuss in greater detail below, the court accepted the existence of an obligation of confidentiality between a psychiatrist and his subject, an obligation which counsel submitted was based not only on equitable grounds but also on implied contract.

Whatever may be the legal basis for the duty, its moral content is considerable. Indeed, in the context of medical law in particular, it is difficult to dissociate the two disciplines – thus, we have Lord Coleridge CJ: 'A legal common law duty is nothing else than the enforcing by law of that which is a moral obligation without legal enforcement.'[6] We can, therefore, look not only at what the patient feels is his legal entitlement but also at the ethical requirements of the medical profession itself. Here there are a number of sources from which the doctor can seek guidance. The Hippocratic Oath[7] makes several demands which can scarcely be regarded as binding

---

1 The doctor-patient and priest-penitent relationships were cited as classic examples in *Stephens v Avery* [1988] Ch 449 at 455, [1988] 2 All ER 477 at 482, per Browne Wilkinson V-C.
2 [1990] AC 109, [1988] 3 All ER 545.
3 Per Megarry J in *Coco v A N Clark (Engineers) Ltd* [1969] RPC 41 at 47, repeated with approval in *Stephens v Avery* [1988] Ch 449, [1988] 2 All ER 477.
4 [1974] QB 767 at 772, [1974] 2 All ER 414 at 417 per Boreham J. For a general discussion of the duty of confidentiality in the medical context, see G Parker and M Spencer 'Confidentiality: Medical Reports' in M J Powers and N Harris (eds) *Medical Negligence* (1990) p 69.
5 [1990] Ch 359, [1990] 1 All ER 835.
6 In *R v Instan* [1893] 1 QB 450 at 453.
7 See Appendix A.

on the modern doctor; none the less, its stipulations as to professional confidentiality are still firmly endorsed. The translation cited in the *sponsio academica* at graduation ceremonials in the University of Edinburgh runs: 'Whatever things seen or heard in the course of medical practice ought not to be spoken of, I will not, save for weighty reasons, divulge.' The Declaration of Geneva (amended at Sydney)[8] imposes much the same obligation on the doctor, requiring him to 'respect the secrets which are confided in me, even after the patient has died'.

The great majority of commentators on medical ethics endorse a continued adherence to a strict principle[9] although some doubt the efficacy of an absolute rule and prefer a form of contractual obligation which, it is thought, would promote the individual patient's autonomy.[10] Most critics, however, see the concept as being something of a pretence in that bureaucracy, fired by modern administrative technology, is increasingly invasive of the principle; certainly, patients' records must circulate fairly widely – and among professionals who are less deeply indoctrinated as to confidentiality than are their medical colleagues. As a result, it has been suggested that institutions should take over custodianship of confidences and thus impose an overall standard of duty on all who work in, for example, the hospital.[11]

Even so, the special position of the doctor is unlikely to change in the foreseeable future and he is currently bound by the authority of, and is subject to the discipline of, the General Medical Council (GMC). Subject to certain exceptions, which we discuss further below[12] the GMC imposes a strict duty on registered medical practitioners to refrain from disclosing voluntarily to any third party information about a patient which he has learnt directly or indirectly in his professional capacity.[13] A breach of this duty will be a serious matter, exposing the doctor to a wide range of potential professional penalties. It is to be noted, however, that sanctions of this nature are purely intra-professional and is has long been questioned whether they give adequate protection to the aggrieved patient; thus, the Law Commission has suggested that the common law position should be strengthened by establishing a statutory offence of breach of confidence which would include those arising between doctor and patient.[14] It may well be that additional regulation

8 See Appendix B.
9 Eg J M Jacob 'Confidentiality: The Dangers of Anything Weaker than the Medical Ethic' (1982) 8 J Med Ethics 18; M H Kottow 'Medical Confidentiality: An Intransigent and Absolute Obligation' (1986) 12 J Med Ethics 117.
10 S J Warwick 'A Vote for No Confidence' (1989) 15 J Med Ethics 183.
11 D L Kenny 'Confidentiality: The Confusion Continues' (1982) 8 J Med Ethics 9; M Siegler 'Confidentiality in Medicine: A Decrepit Concept' (1982) 307 New Engl J Med 1518. See also D F H Pheby 'Changing Practice on Confidentiality: A Cause for Concern' (1982) 8 J Med Ethics 12; A W Macara 'Confidentiality: A Decrepit Concept?' (1984) 77 J Roy Soc Med 577.
12 See p 193,
13 GMC *Duties of a Doctor: Confidentiality* (1995). The advice of the BMA has no disciplinary authority but provides invaluable background to the GMC's instructions: see BMA *Philosophy and Practice of Medical Ethics* (1988) ch 3 and BMA *Rights and Responsibilities of Doctors* (1988) ch 2.
14 *Breach of Confidence* (Cmnd 8388) para 6.1. There has as yet been no government action on this report, which was issued in 1981.

will be forced upon the United Kingdom. Medical confidentiality in France and Belgium is absolute and is protected in the criminal code.[15] Future developments in the United Kingdom, in so far as they are influenced – or even driven – by European initiatives, may well reflect this attitude. Certainly, there is a strong interest in the subject in Europe which is reflected in the Council of Europe's 1997 recommendation on the protection of medical data.[16] This recommendation, which emanates from the Committee of Ministers of Member States, includes not only general principles which should guide national laws on the confidentiality of medical information, but also embraces specific recommendations relating to such matters as storage of data, its transmission across borders, and the use of data in medical research.

Relaxation of the rule

Nevertheless, all the classic codes of practice imply some qualification of an absolute duty of professional secrecy. Thus, the Hippocratic Oath has it: 'All that may come to my knowledge ... which ought not to be spread abroad, I will keep secret', which clearly indicates that there are some things which *may* be published. The Declaration of Geneva modifies this prohibition to: 'I will respect the secrets which are confided in me' and the word 'respect' is open to interpretation. The GMC, while always emphasising its strong views as to the rule dictating professional secrecy, still lists eight specific possible exceptions to the rule which provide a sound basis for discussion.

Consent to publish

The first, and most easily recognisable, exception is when the patient or his legal adviser consents to a relaxation of secrecy. The situation is simple when viewed from the positive angle. A positive consent to release of information elides any obligation to secrecy owed by the person receiving that consent;[17] equally, an explicit request that information should not be disclosed is binding on the doctor save in the most exceptional circumstances – a matter which is of major concern in relation to communicable disease.[18]

However, the position is not so clear when looked at from the negative aspect and it may, indeed, be frankly unsatisfactory. How many patients know whether the person standing with the consultant beside the hospital bedside is another doctor, a social worker or just an interested spectator? Would they have consented to their presence if they had been informed? The consultant may be responsible if, as a result,

---

15 France: Penal Code, art 378; Belgium: Penal Code, art 458. Attention is also drawn to the Evidence Amendment Act 1980 in New Zealand where, subject to minor reservations, privilege is accorded to medical confidence (ss 32, 33); the rights of the dead are specifically covered as is, incidentally, the religious confessional (s 31).

16 Council of Europe, Recommendation R (97) 5.

17 *C v C* [1946] 1 All ER 562.

18 See p 198 below.

there is a breach of confidence – but this is small consolation to the patient who feels his rights have been infringed. What patient at a teaching hospital out-patient department is likely to refuse when the consultant asks: 'You don't mind these young doctors being present, do you?' – the pressures are virtually irresistible and truly autonomous consent is impossible, yet the confidential doctor-patient relationship which began with his general practitioner has, effectively, been broken.

It is obvious that such technical breaches must be, and generally are, accepted in practice – a modern hospital cannot function except as a team effort and new doctors have to be trained, the return for a technical loss of patient autonomy being access to the best diagnostic and therapeutic aids available. The GMC recognises this in permitting the sharing of information with other practitioners who assume responsibility for clinical management of the patient and, to the extent that the doctor deems it necessary for the performance of their particular duties, with other health care professionals who are collaborating with the doctor in his patients' management. [19] The exception notes that it is the doctor's responsibility to ensure that such individuals appreciate that the information is being imparted in strict professional confidence. The doctor's duty is thereby restricted in a reasonable way; it is difficult to see how he can be expected to carry the onus for any subsequent actions by his associates. Any such infringement might be the basis of a complaint to the Health Service Commissioner. [20]

The patient's interests

The next exception – that it is ethical to break confidentiality without a patient's consent when it is in his own interests to do so and when it is undesirable on medical grounds to seek such consent [1] – is acceptable save to those who are fanatically opposed to so-called professional paternalism. The recipient of the information may be a close relative or, as in a case where the doctor suspects that the patient is a victim of neglect or physical or sexual abuse, an unrelated third party – but it remains the doctor's duty to make every reasonable effort to persuade the patient to allow the information to be given. When these situations occur, decisions rest, by definition, on clinical judgment – a properly considered clinical decision cannot be *unethical* whether it proves right or wrong and, in the event of action being taken on the basis of breach of confidence, the fact that it was a justifiable breach would offer a complete defence both in the civil courts and in the Professional Conduct Committee of the GMC; the GMC does, however, stress the need for caution when the patient has insufficient understanding, by reason of immaturity, of what the treatment or advice being sought involves; we return to this aspect later in the chapter. [2]

19 *Confidentiality* (p 192, n 13 above) para 3.
20 National Health Service Act 1977, Pt V, as amended by Parliamentary and Health Service Commissioners Act 1987. An investigation by the Health Service Commissioner will not be precluded by the Hospital Complaints Procedure Act 1985, which enforces a duty to deal with complaints and to publicise the arrangements made for so doing.
1 *Confidentiality* (p 192, n 13 above) para 10.
2 See p 203 below.

The doctor in society

In so far as it rests on subjective definitions, the doctor's overriding duty to society represents what is arguably the most controversial permissible exception to the rule of confidentiality. Society is not homogeneous, but consists of groups amenable to almost infinite classification – regional, political, economic, by age and so on. It follows that what one person regards as a duty to society may be anathema to another. Individual doctors are bound to weigh the scales differently in any particular instance while, in general, all relative weighting must change from case to case – there is, for example, a great deal of difference in respect of confidentiality between a bee sting and venereal disease. While it is clear that no rules can be laid down, some aspects of this societal conflict are of sufficient importance to merit individual consideration.

The most dramatic dilemma is posed by the possibility of violent crime. What is the doctor to do if he knows his patient has just committed rape – particularly if there is evidence that this is but one of a series of attacks on women? Perhaps even more disconcertingly, what if it becomes apparent that his patient is about to commit such an offence? Statute law is helpful here only in a negative sense – misprision of felony, other than as related to treason, is no longer an offence.[3] There is case law to the effect that the doctor need not even assist the police by answering their questions concerning his patients, although he must not give false or misleading information.[4] The obligation on the prosecution to disclose to the defence all unused material which might have some bearing on the offences charged has caused some difficulty for police surgeons. Generally speaking, an accused gives consent to disclosure of specific information only. Other information may, however, come to light during the course of the examination; once this is in the police notes, the police may feel it their duty to include it in their 'disclosure', despite the fact that there is no consent to their so doing. The police surgeon may, therefore, feel it his ethical imperative to conceal his knowledge – but the decision must, at times, be difficult to make.[5]

In the early part of the twentieth century, both medical and legal opinion was divided on the issue of disclosure of serious crime; discussion was, however, based largely on the subject of illegal abortion, which has emotional overtones of its own. Nevertheless, it was in that context that Avory J made his well-known observation:

> There are cases where the desire to preserve [the confidential relation which exists between the medical man and his patient] must be subordinated to the duty which is cast on every good citizen to assist in the investigation of serious crime.[6]

and this probably represents the foundation of the doctrine of the public interest as applied to medicine. This crystallised in the case of *W v Egdell*.[7]

Here, a prisoner in a secure hospital sought a review of his case with a view to transfer to a regional secure unit. His legal representatives secured a report from an

---

3 Criminal Law Act 1967, s 5(5).
4 *Rice v Connolly* [1966] 2 QB 414, [1966] 2 All ER 649. See also P Schutte 'Medical Confidentiality and a Police Murder Inquiry' (1989) 5 J Med Def Union (Spring) 21.
5 For discussion, see P Schutte (1993) 9 J Med Def Union 62.
6 Birmingham Assizes, 1 December 1914, reported in (1914) 78 JP 604. The judge referred to a possible moral duty in the event that the patient was not dying; his views as to strict moral duty were mainly concerned with the loss of evidence in failing to take a dying declaration from a moribund patient.
7 [1990] Ch 359, [1990] 1 All ER 835.

independent consultant psychiatrist which was, in the event, unfavourable to W; as a result, the application for transfer was aborted. W was, however, due for routine review of his detention and the psychiatrist, becoming aware that his report would not be included in the patient's notes, feared that decisions would be taken on inadequate information with consequent danger to the public. He therefore sent a copy of his report to the medical director of the hospital and a further copy reached the Home Office; W brought an action in contract and in equity alleging breach of a duty of confidence. The trial judge, Scott J, considered that, in the circumstances:

> The question in the present case is not whether Dr Egdell was under a duty of confidence; he plainly was. The question is as to the breadth of that duty.[8]

Attention was drawn to the advice of the GMC as to the circumstances in which exception to the rule of confidentiality is permitted. The GMC's guidelines which applied at the time were contained in the so-called 'Blue Book'. Para 79 stated:

> Rarely, cases may arise in which disclosure in the public interest may be justified, for example, a situation in which the failure to disclose appropriate information would expose the patient, or someone else, to a risk of death or serious harm.

Scott J based his conclusions on broad considerations – that a doctor in similar circumstances has a duty not only to the patient but also to the public and that the latter would require him to disclose the results of his examination to the proper authorities if, in his opinion, the public interest so required; this would be independent of the patient's instructions on the point.

The Court of Appeal unanimously confirmed the trial judge's decision to dismiss the action but did so with rather more reservation – particularly as expressed in the judgment of Bingham LJ. The concept of a private interest competing with a public interest was rejected in favour of there being a *public* interest in maintaining professional duties of confidence; the 'balancing' of interests thus fell to be carried out in circumstances of unusual difficulty. Doubts, which we share, were cast on the applicability of para 79 of the *Blue Book* (then para 78(b)) to a doctor acting in the role of an independent consultant; disclosure would have to be justified under para 86 (then para 78(g)) and, here, it was for the court, not the doctor, to decide whether such a disclosure was or was not a breach of contract. Moreover, there was no doubt that the Mental Health Act 1983, s 76 showed a clear parliamentary intention that a restricted patient should be free to seek advice and evidence for specific purposes which was confidential in respect of the authorities. Only the most compelling circumstances could justify a doctor acting contrary to the patient's perceived interests in the absence of consent. Nevertheless, in the instant case, the fear of a real risk to public safety entitled a doctor to take reasonable steps to communicate the grounds of his concern to the appropriate authorities.

Looked at superficially, it is easy to view *Egdell* as a serious intrusion into the relationship of confidential trust between doctor and patient; it is equally possible to perceive the principle as emerging relatively unscathed. W's case was clearly

8   [1990] Ch 359 at 389, [1989] 1 All ER 1089 at 1102.

regarded as extreme and, although we cannot exclude some concern, there is no evidence in the judgment that the courts would condone a breach of confidence on less urgent grounds. The 'danger area' seems to be better deliminated by way of independent activity on the part of doctors – as anticipated by Bingham LJ in *Egdell*. In *R v Crozier*,[9] a psychiatrist called by the accused, concerned that his opinion should be available to the court, apparently handed his report to counsel for the Crown; the now sentenced accused appealed on the grounds that the breach of confidentiality between doctor and patient had denied him the opportunity of deciding whether medical evidence would be tendered. The Court of Appeal again thought that there was a stronger public interest in the disclosure of the psychiatrist's views than in the confidence he owed to the appellant; the psychiatrist was found to have acted responsibly and reasonably in a very difficult situation. But what if a doctor acts *un*reasonably in such circumstances? The damage to the patient is done and he will get little satisfaction from the fact that the doctor is censured; it is surely a thoroughly paternalistic practice that should be carefully restrained.

On a more mundane note, the importance of disease in drivers has increased and presents a major dilemma to the conscientious doctor. The urgency of decisions is maximised by the facts that driving licences are now issued for the lifetime up to the age of 70 and that responsibility for reporting health deficiencies is placed firmly on the licence holder. Heart disease is always thought of as being paramount in this context but, in practice, very few car accidents that result in serious personal injury are caused by cardiac conditions. Moreover, the majority of cardiac patients are mature and conscious of their responsibilities. Epilepsy is a far more apposite example. Nearly half the instances of unconsciousness at the wheel of a car are epileptic in origin and the condition is found to have been undisclosed in over three quarters of these – the public need seems clear, but what is the doctor to do? The standard answer is that he should either persuade the patient to report the disability or obtain the patient's consent to disclosure, but this does not help when, as is likely, both courses are rejected. It has been suggested[10] that a doctor who knew that an unsafe patient of his was continuing to drive and who then failed to take any action on the point might be liable in damages for negligence to anyone harmed by his patient on the road. This seems unlikely to happen in a United Kingdom context and has been rejected even in the United States.[11] We conclude that doctors are not only protected against any action for breach of confidence by qualified privilege but also that they have a positive moral duty to inform the medical authorities at the vehicle licensing centre of patients who are a danger on the road by virtue of their medical condition; in the unlikely event of it being needed, *Egdell* would almost certainly be applied. This conclusion is supported by the advice proffered by the GMC in Appendix 1 to its guidelines on confidentiality, which form part of *Duties of a Doctor*. This states that a doctor should make every effort to ensure that a patient who is considered to be unfit to drive understands his or her duty to inform the DVLA. The guidelines continue:

9 (1990) 8 BMLR 128.
10 Anonymous 'Doctors, Drivers and Confidentiality' (1974) 1 BMJ 399.
11 In *Crosby v Sultz* 592 A 2d 1337 (Pa, 1991) a suit against a doctor who allowed a diabetic patient to drive was rejected on the grounds that injuries inflicted on a person who could not be notified of the driver's condition were not foreseeable.

If patients continue to drive when they are not fit to do so, you should make every reasonable effort to persuade them to stop. This may include telling their next of kin. If you do not manage to persuade patients to stop driving, or you are given or find evidence that a patient is continuing to drive contrary to advice, you should disclose relevant medical information immediately, in confidence, to the medical adviser at the DVLA.[12]

An interesting example of the problems posed has been reported from New Zealand. There, a bus driver underwent a triple coronary bypass operation and was subsequently certified as fit to drive by his surgeon. His general practitioner, however, asked that his licence to drive be withdrawn and, furthermore, warned his passengers of their supposed danger. The practitioner's activities resulted in a report to the Medical Practitioners' Disciplinary Committee and a finding of: 'guilty of professional misconduct in that he breached professional confidence in informing lay people of his patient's personal medical history.' Dr Duncan sought judicial review of this decision. The High Court accepted the propriety of breaching medical confidentiality in cases of clear public interest, but refused the application on grounds which can be summed up: 'I think a doctor who has decided to communicate should discriminate and ensure the recipient is a responsible authority.'[13] Seldom can there have been a case which demonstrates the 'need to know' principle so forcibly.

Confidentiality and HIV infection

The spread of the human immunodeficiency virus has given rise to a host of problems related to confidentiality. Sexually transmitted diseases are not new to the medico-legal arena, but what sets AIDS apart is the current absence of a proven treatment of a condition which, in its full-blown state, appears to be, if not always fatal, at best highly resistant to therapy. Its relatively specific sexual connotation, together with its serious association with drug addiction, leads to considerable stigmatisation. Those who are found to be HIV-positive may be disadvantaged in a number of practical ways which have been discussed in chapter 1 and to which we refer again below;[14] all serve to fuel the concern which many such persons harbour as to the confidentiality of their status.

Such concerns attract great sympathy, yet there are also social interests to be considered. The crucial dilemma here is whether relaxation of the confidentiality rule would lead to failure to seek advice and treatment and hence to the spread of the disease, or whether the imposition of absolute secrecy improperly denies others the opportunity to avoid the risk of exposure to infection. Should a sexual partner be told of the risk if the patient himself declines to pass on the information? What is the situation if a person known to be infected is employed in circumstances in which he might expose others to the virus? The problem of confidentiality cannot, however, be settled by the balancing of conflicting private interests alone – the public health dimension has to be taken into account. AIDS is not, at present, a notifiable disease[15] – a dispensation which certainly helps to maintain confidentiality. The rationale

---

12 *Confidentiality* Appendix 1, paras 4–5.
13 *Duncan v Medical Practitioners' Disciplinary Committee* [1986] 1 NZLR 513 at 521, per Jeffries J.
14 See p 271.
15 Under the AIDS (Control) Act 1987, health authorities must provide reports to the responsible minister. The minister can also order hospitalisation and, if necessary, detention of sufferers Public Health (Infectious Diseases) Regulations 1985, SI 1985/434.

given for this is that notifiability would inhibit persons from undergoing testing;[16] while some would doubt the validity of this, any public health 'risk' is justified on the grounds that, in the conditions of everyday social contact, HIV is transmitted only with great difficulty – if at all. As a result, it is government policy, supported by the majority of informed opinion, that any departure from the strictest anonymity in respect of HIV-related information must be subject to intense scrutiny.[17]

The English courts have declared their hand in weighting the balance between a strongly supported public policy in favour of freedom of the press against the need for loyalty and confidentiality with particular reference to AIDS patients' hospital records. In *X v Y*,[18] the names of two doctors being treated in hospital for AIDS were improperly disclosed; the health authority sought, and obtained, an injunction to prevent their publication by a newspaper. While holding that the health authority had not made out a case for forced disclosure of the source of the information, Rose J stated that such luck a second time was highly unlikely and that prison would be the probable consequence if the informer repeated his or her betrayal of confidence:

> The public in general and patients in particular are entitled to expect hospital records to be confidential and it is not for any individual to take it upon himself or herself to breach that confidence whether induced by a journalist or otherwise.[19]

The authority's action was not, as has been suggested, a 'cover-up' operation – the basic reasons underlying absolute confidentiality in AIDS-related cases should be applied irrespective of the patient's calling. The decision can be justified medically on the grounds that the risks of a well-counselled physician passing the disease to a patient are, at worst, slightly more than negligible.[20] This is, however, an area in which the media are insatiable. We have already noted[1] a rash of cases in which the names of infected doctors have been widely publicised in the press; a number of letters from the health boards concerned have testified to the fact that, given that the boards must notify all patient contacts of such practitioners, it is virtually impossible to preserve anonymity.[2] The current policy of the General Medical Council to the effect that:

> Only in the most exceptional circumstances, where the release of a doctor's name is essential for the protection of patients, may a doctor's HIV status be disclosed without his or her consent[3]

is, in practice, unworkable.

16 M W Adler 'HIV, Confidentiality and a "delicate balance"' (1991) 17 J Med Ethics 196.
17 For a general overview of the ethical position, see R Gillon 'AIDS and Medical Confidentiality' (1987) 294 BMJ 1675. A useful review is M Brazier and M Lobjoit 'AIDS, Ethics, and the Respiratory Physician' (1990) 45 Thorax 283.
18 [1988] 2 All ER 648, (1992) 3 BMLR 1.
19 [1988] 2 All ER 648 at 665, (1992) 3 BMLR 1 at 21, per Rose J.
20 It is widely accepted that only one case has been confirmed – and the patient was later found to be an intravenous drug abuser: B Mishu, W Schaffer, J M Horan et al 'A Surgeon with AIDS: Lack of Evidence of Transmission to Patrons' (1990) 264 J Amer Med Ass 467.
 1 See p 23 above.
 2 Although this information need not be given 'face to face': *A v Tameside and Glossop Health Authority* [1996] 45 LS Gaz R 30.
 3 GMC *HIV Infection and AIDS: The Ethical Considerations* (revised, 1993).

Anyone infected with HIV constitutes an undoubted danger to his or her sexual partner, although the risk of transmission depends upon the nature of the sexual activity, the frequency and diversity of exposure and the extent to which precautions are taken. Counselling of HIV cases includes such information routinely, and patients are advised as to the need to disclose their status to those whom they might have put at risk of infection. It is unsurprising that there will be some patients who are not prepared to do so nor, indeed, to inform their general practitioners; the doctor is then faced with the problem of whether or not he, himself, should inform those with 'a need to know'.

The GMC has advised doctors that patients should be persuaded of the need for their general practitioners to be informed of the diagnosis but states that the patient's wishes should be respected if consent to disclosure is refused.[4] An exception may be made, however, if the doctor believes that a failure to pass on the information may expose other health caring staff to serious risk – even so, the doctor must be prepared to justify such action. Passing information to a patient's spouse or other sexual partner in the absence of consent is allowable so long as every effort has been made to persuade the patient to do so and there is a serious and identifiable risk to a specific individual. The GMC emphasises that their paper does not represent a code; the original document has now been clarified in many ways but there are still ambiguities. What is one to make of phraseology such as 'the doctor may consider it a duty to seek to ensure that a sexual partner is informed'? In an interesting discussion of the original guidelines, the Institute of Medical Ethics has shown that two doctors could react to the issue of confidentiality in diametrically opposed ways, yet each could still be acting within the 'guidelines'.[5] The GMC concludes that the responsibility for any action taken is entirely that of the individual doctor – which tells us nothing as to how to construct that responsibility.

The Institute's solution is to rely on a relationship of mutual empowerment based on a balance between, on the one hand, the patient's proper power of decision making and, on the other, the doctor's exercise of clinical skills and, most importantly, of effective communication of information. The ideal is that the person at risk should be able to make an informed choice whether or not to accept the risk and that this choice will be offered by the patient. In the exceptional case where the patient frustrates this policy, the doctor should, in the Institute's view, base his decision as to whether or not to breach confidentiality on the strength of his judgment that, by maintaining confidentiality, he can encourage the infected patient to acknowledge his or her responsibility to respect the interests of others. In this respect, great importance is laid on whether or not the person at risk is also a patient of the doctor – the implication being that, in the first case, disclosure would be justified fairly easily but that confidentiality would be the better choice in the latter.

This may be a pragmatic solution, but it appears to us to be morally ambivalent. If it is medical beneficence to inform one's *patient* of a risk, it is scarcely justifiable to bask in the safety-net of confidentiality when one's duty of care is no more than

4   General Medical Council *HIV and AIDS: The Ethical Considerations* (1995) para 16. The BMA is silent on the question in *Philosophy and Practice of Medical Ethics* (1988).
5   K M Boyd 'HIV Infection and AIDS: The Ethics of Medical Confidentiality' (1992) 18 J Med Ethics 173.

indirect. A discussion based on moral principles, however, takes little account of the legal issues involved and it is arguable that a patient would have a right of action against a doctor who warned his or her spouse or other sexual partner of their potential risk. Despite the prima facie breach of confidence, a court would almost certainly balance the two private interests involved and hold that disclosure was justified by the intention to protect others from a possibly fatal risk. It is difficult to imagine a court awarding damages to such a plaintiff and there has been no decision directly in point taken in the United Kingdom. Conversely, it seems that there is a general common law duty and a statutory duty on the doctor in some parts of the United States and Canada to inform those at risk[6] – and the *Tarasoff* decision[7] which we discuss in chapter 21, could be taken as a pointer. A curious twist to this issue emerged in the remarkable Californian case of *Reisner*.[8] A young girl had been exposed to HIV infection through the transfusion of tainted blood. Neither she nor her parents were informed of this. Some years later she became intimate with a boyfriend, whom she infected with the virus. He raised a successful action for damages against the doctors for their failure to inform her, thereby subjecting him, as a foreseeable victim, to the risk of infection. This decision did not invoke the suggestion that the doctor had a duty to warn. It is not clear how a British court might react to a similar situation. The inference of a duty to care in respect of endangered third parties might be difficult to reconcile with existing notions in the United Kingdom. No duty to warn exists in the absence of a special relationship between the parties and it is difficult to see why the AIDS situation should constitute an exception to the general common law rule, in both England and Scotland, that there is no duty to rescue.[9] It is, however, possible that a doctor might even be held to have a *duty* – as opposed to mere justification – to warn a third party *who was also his patient*, as in this case there is a relationship which is sufficiently proximate to give rise to a duty of affirmative action.

It is impossible to leave the subject of confidentiality in HIV infection without mention of the specific problem of prisons – the environment could have been designed for the spread of the condition and the consequences of disclosure of a positive status could be disastrous for the individual. A policy of confidentiality exists but, clearly, it is difficult, if not impossible, to maintain so long as positivity is associated with segregation, provision of personalised eating utensils and the like; there has also been some limited purposeful breaching of confidentiality in respect of a 'need to know' on the part of the staff.[10] Such potentials for disclosure discourage voluntary testing and counselling and serve as barriers to effective public health

---

6 L Gostin and A Ziegler 'Review of AIDS-related Legislative and Regulatory Policy in the United States' (1987) 15 Law Med Hlth Care 5; D I Casswell 'Disclosure by a Physician of AIDS-related Patient Information: An Ethical and Legal Dilemma' (1989) 68 Can BR 225.

7 *Tarasoff v Regents of the University of California* 529 P 2d 55 (Cal, 1974); on appeal 551 P 2d 334 (Cal, 1976). Decisions following upon this include the contrasting cases of *Brady v Hopper* 751 F 2d 329 (1984) and *Peterson v State* 671 P 2d 230 (Was, 1983).

8 *Reisner v Regents of the University of California* (1995) 37 Cal Rptr 2d 518.

9 For further discussion, see A McCall Smith 'The Duty to Rescue and the Common Law' in M Menlowe and A McCall Smith (eds) *The Duty to Rescue* (1993) p 55.

10 T Groves 'Prison Policies on HIV under Review' (1991) 303 BMJ 1354. See also M Beaupré 'Confidentiality, HIV/Aids and Prison Health Care Services' (1994) 2 Med L Rev 149. The vexed question of the police's 'need to know' was discussed in J K Mason 'Recording HIV Status on Police Computers' (1992) 304 BMJ 995.

measures; they have been phased out since 1991. It has been shown that a guarantee of confidentiality results in a marked increase in identified positive subjects.[11] Such evidence tends to support the general national policy on confidentiality and HIV; at the same time, it cannot be denied that more prisoners are infected than are identified – the issue is, indeed, delicately balanced.

Confidentiality within the family

A narrower area of societal privilege lies within the family, where the doctor may be the first to recognise the signs of violence. The police are, in general, disinclined to interfere in cases of marital violence because of the unsympathetic reception they are likely to get from both sides in so doing. But this may not always be the case, and the doctor cannot be content to watch his patient suffer not only physical injury but also intense mental trauma. In the end, however, it is clear that an adult woman of sound mind is entitled to her autonomy; she has the opportunity of reporting to the police or, often more usefully, she has access to one of the many voluntary shelters which are now being established. She now has considerable protection under the law.[12] All the doctor can effectively do is to advise, and in this he may be able to help by arranging for treatment of the offender – 'wife battering' is markedly associated with alcoholism and neurotic symptoms in the husband.

The position is different in the case of child abuse. Here the victim is defenceless and the victim is the patient. Parental autonomy must be forfeited on the grounds of impropriety while the doctor is covered, legally, by the doctrine of necessity – in this case to assume consent to disclosure by one who cannot give consent – and, professionally, by the advice of the GMC that disclosure in such circumstances is justified.[13]

It has been suggested that, as a matter of law, such action probably does constitute a technical breach of the duty of confidence[14] but this proposition seems barely tenable. Rather, the doctor faces a clinical dilemma which, although less publicised, is of greater importance. The introduction of registers for infants at risk from violence and the obvious merit in nipping violence in the bud act as servo-mechanisms to one another. The possibility is increasing that truly accidental injuries are being misdiagnosed, with a consequent reluctance on the part of parents to seek help for fear of being 'branded';[15] children may, therefore, actually suffer despite the doctor's concern for their safety. A case misdiagnosed as child abuse will cause considerable distress for those accused;[16] but, equally, a missed case which ends in murder can

11 S A M Gore and A G Bird 'No Escape: HIV Transmission in Jail' (1993) 307 BMJ 147.
12 Domestic Violence and Matrimonial Proceedings Act 1976; Matrimonial Homes (Family Protection) (Scotland) Act 1981.
13 *Confidentiality* (p 192, n 13 above) para 11.
14 A Samuels 'The Duty of the Doctor to Respect the Confidence of the Patient' (1980) 20 Med Sci & L 58.
15 D M Wheeler and C J Hobbs 'Mistakes in Diagnosing Non-accidental Injury: 10 Years; Experience' (1988) 296 BMJ 1233. It seems that, at present, no action for negligence can be brought in England in such cases: C Dyer 'No Redress for Wrong Diagnosis of Sexual Abuse' (1993) 306 BMJ 881. The case noted was struck out; it is likely to go to appeal.
16 See two 'at-risk register' cases: *R v Norfolk County Council Social Services Department, ex p M* [1989] QB 619, [1989] 2 All ER 359; *R v Harrow London Borough Council, ex p D* [1990] Fam 133, [1990] 3 All ER 12, CA.

bring great recrimination on the doctor. The concern of the profession as to possible actions for defamation was certainly eased by the decision that a recognised caring authority may refuse to disclose the name of an informant.[17] In the end, however, such a right to or privilege of non-disclosure depends not so much on principles of confidentiality as on what lies in the public interest.

Confidentiality between parent and child becomes further involved at teen age. Consent to treatment is discussed in detail in chapter 10; in the present context, we are concerned only with confidentiality and, particularly, with the doctor's relationship with the family. It is possible to conceive of other medical conditions which a minor might wish to conceal from his or her parents but, in practice, such conditions are likely to be limited to their sexual affairs.[18] As has already been indicated, young persons of both sexes do have intercourse and the doctor may be confronted by requests as to contraception or abortion by young girls or for treatment of venereal disease by minors of either sex. It is therefore unsurprising that the leading case to address the question of minors' rights to confidentiality – *Gillick*[19] – should concern contraception and has, in fact, been discussed under that head.[20] The twin issues of consent to treatment and right to privacy in young people are inextricably interwoven and, again, further discussion will be found elsewhere.[1] Here, we will attempt to limit discussion to those issues in the case which are specific to confidentiality.

From this point of view, the background to the *Gillick* decision is relatively simple, yet it represents the core of the case. As we have already suggested, contraception must be seen as sociologically preferable to abortion; even so, only a few young girls are likely to consent to their parents being told they are 'on the pill' and refusal to supply is unlikely to deter those who want sexual intercourse. On this basis, the doctor who secretly supplies contraceptives on request to a girl under the age of 16 is performing a duty to society. On the other hand, most would agree that parents have a right to know what is happening to their children and should, ideally, give consent to medical treatment irrespective of the minor's capacity to understand the complexities. It is, therefore, apparent that any entitlement to consent carries with it a simultaneous entitlement to confidentiality and vice versa. The House of Lords' solution of the problem is to be found in Lord Fraser's five criteria which have been recapitulated above.[2] and which can be summarised as granting a right of confidentiality to the mature minor when the exercise of that right was in her best interests. It must, however, be emphasised that, throughout the case, an obligation was firmly imposed on the doctor to attempt to persuade the girl to inform her parents or to allow him to do so – that, in itself, constituting an important qualification of the normal rules of professional secrecy. Thus, despite the case seeming to represent a victory for the autonomy of youth, the situation remains uneasy for both the doctor and the patient.

---

17 *D v National Society for the Prevention of Cruelty to Children* [1978] AC 171, [1977] 1 All ER 589, HL. Protection of the informant is guaranteed by law in places having compulsory reporting (eg Child Welfare Act 1977 (NSW)).

18 But see the case of Emma Hendry discussed below. *Inquiry into the Death of Emma Jane Hendry* (15 January 1998, unreported), Glasgow Sheriff Court.

19 *Gillick v West Norfolk and Wisbech Area Health Authority* [1984] QB 581, [1984] 1 All ER 365; on appeal [1986] AC 112, [1985] 1 All ER 533, CA; revsd [1986] AC 112, [1985] 3 All ER 402, HL.

20 See p 109 above.

 1 See 'Consent', p 252 below.

 2 See p 109.

On the one hand, the latter cannot know the former's intentions until *after* the consultation; on the other, the doctor must be prepared to justify his decision – but to whom and in what circumstances is left unstated. The decision to respect a minor's right to confidentiality may be a delicate one, and this is particularly so when drugs are prescribed. In one Scottish Fatal Accident Inquiry concerning a 14-year-old girl's death from an overdose of tricyclic antidepressants, a doctor's decision not to inform her parents of her treatment was considered to be perfectly correct. The patient's maturity was held to be such that her desire for confidentiality in relation to her parents had to be respected.[3]

The longest established family relationship is that of the spouse – what are his or her rights in both the positive and negative aspects of confidentiality? If the treatment is for a medical condition, a married person has the same rights to confidentiality in respect of the spouse as in respect of anyone else and, since the Abortion Act 1967 refers only to medical indications, this must apply to abortion. This can be implied also on legal grounds in that, since the husband has no right of veto either in Great Britain or in the United States[4] he similarly has no right to information, and it is not hard to think of instances where disclosure of an abortion to the spouse could be construed as being malicious.

The conditions are not quite so clear, however, when treatment of an individual is not primarily based on medical considerations but, at the same time, affects the whole family – effectively, this is a matter of sterilisation. Lord Denning was in no doubt in an early, minority, opinion that the surgeon should 'approach the spouse in order to satisfy himself as to consent'.[5] This must certainly be the case when genetic considerations are involved. Either or both parties may be contributing to a multifactorial trait; genetic counselling is impossible unless both husband and wife are involved. There is, however, less certainty when sterilisation is purely a matter of convenient family planning. On the face of it, there ought to be a consensual decision, but the twenty-first-century couple are not certainly going to be together until parted by death, religious differences may prohibit agreement and there must be times when one spouse feels compelled to act for his or her individual reasons. The doctor may rightly refuse to sterilise in the absence of consent to spousal consultation but he would, we believe, be acting correctly both in law and in ethics were he to do so; adults have a right to privacy and it could probably be left to the Divorce Court, as in *Bravery*, to decide whether such unilateral action rendered marriage intolerable.[6] The matter has been discussed in greater detail in chapter 4. The very particular conditions attaching to genetic counselling are, similarly, addressed in detail in chapter 6.

3   *Inquiry into the Death of Emma Jane Hendry* (15 January 1998, unreported), Glasgow Sheriff Court.
4   *Paton v British Pregnancy Advisory Service Trustees* [1979] QB 276, [1978] 2 All ER 987; confirmed in the US in *Planned Parenthood of Southeastern Pennsylvania v Casey* 112 S Ct 2791 (1992).
5   *Bravery v Bravery* [1954] 3 All ER 59 at 67, [1954] 1 WLR 1169 at 1177, CA.
6   The BMA states that the custom of obtaining consent from the patient's spouse to operation on the reproductive organs is one of courtesy not of legal necessity: *Philosophy and Practice of Medical Ethics* (1988) p 33.

Other special groups

Finally, there are many special groups which can be conceived of as raising particular problems in relation to medical confidentiality – those which spring to mind most readily are accused persons, prisoners and members of the armed forces. Accused persons are legally innocent and therefore have the same rights as any member of the public. The police surgeon must state that the result of his examination will be reported to third parties and cannot proceed if, as a result, consent to examination is refused. In the interests of justice, however, he may make, and transmit the results of, observations which need not be confined to purely visual impressions.[7] The doctor-patient relationship is complicated in respect of prisoners and confidentiality is best considered as part of the whole spectrum of prison medicine (see chapter 1). Much loose talk is often voiced as to the status of medical officers in the armed forces. In reality, their relationship to individual patients is precisely the same as in civilian practice, with the proviso that the doctor's duty to society is accentuated when this is formulated as a duty to a fighting unit; eventually, the lives of many are dependent upon the health of individuals. There is thus a wider justification for disclosure than exists in civilian life and the serviceman has tacitly accepted this in enlisting; nevertheless, the principle of justification remains valid. Similar considerations apply, for instance, to doctors in medical charge of sports teams; the discussion has come full circle in that, basically, one's ethical standards depend upon one's definition of society.

Doctors employed by companies or other institutions to act as medical advisers on staff health occupy a special position which has been singled out by the General Medical Council. It must now be stated explicitly before carrying out a pre-employment medical examination, or for fitness to work, that the results of that examination may be communicated to the employer and the written consent of the examinee must be obtained in the light of that information. Likewise, in the case of examinations carried out for insurance purposes, the doctor must obtain the positive agreement of the patient to waive the normal obligations of confidentiality within a 'need to know' formula. In the absence of such agreement, it is unlikely that the doctor engaged in industrial or insurance medicine could justify, on either ethical or legal grounds, a breach of a patient's confidence on the grounds that he, the doctor, owed a duty as an employee to his employer.

For the purposes of medical research

Information may be disclosed if necessary for the purposes of a medical research project which has been approved by a recognised ethical committee. The matter is included in the general discussion of medical research in chapter 18.

Confidentiality and the legal process

Disclosure of confidential medical information as part of the legal process can be looked at in two main categories: statutory and non-statutory. Statutory disclosure

7   *Forrester v HM Advocate* 1952 JC 28.

presents no problem to the doctor, but is nevertheless showing signs of encroachment on traditional values. Thus, the original requirements for reporting by the doctor of infectious disease[8] or industrial poisoning[9] are clearly directed to the good of society. More recently, however, compulsory notification has become required more for statistical purposes[10] or for the protection of individuals by the state.[11] The two latter examples also show an increasing acceptance of some state control of the medical profession itself. Despite occasional protests at 'interference', there can be very little serious objection to such regulations.

It is to be noted that no immunity is granted to the doctor when a statutory duty is imposed on 'any person' to provide information. Such a situation arises, for example, under the Prevention of Terrorism (Temporary Provisions) Act 1989, s 18, which places every person under an obligation to disclose to the police information connected with acts of terrorism. Opinion is divided, however, as to the working of the Road Traffic Act 1988 when, by virtue of s 172, the doctor must provide on request any evidence which he has which may lead to the identification of a driver involved in an accident. The patient can scarcely expect the doctor to breach confidentiality; yet the doctor's liability under the law has been confirmed.[12]

There may, of course, be other times when the police would have an interest in access to medical records. Police engaged in the investigation of a serious arrestable offence may obtain a warrant to search for material which is likely to be relevant evidence. Under the Police and Criminal Evidence Act 1984,[13] magistrates cannot, however, issue a warrant to search for 'excluded material' which includes personal records relating to a person's physical or mental health and which are held in confidence; medical records are, therefore, excluded material. However, a constable may still apply to a circuit judge for an order to obtain such records. Not only must the court be satisfied of the need for access, but there must have been some statutory authority passed before the 1984 Act which would have authorised such a search. The Act illustrates some of the difficulties in applying an ethical principle by way of statute. Hospital notes are clearly excluded material and can, therefore, be withheld from the police irrespective of the purpose of their search. Thus, the police cannot obtain them even though their sole purpose is, for example, to establish the whereabouts of a potential murderer at a given time[14] – as Morland J said in *Kellam*:[15]

> Presumably Parliament considered that the confidentiality of records of identifiable individuals relating to their health should have paramountcy over the prevention and investigation of serious crime.

But one wonders if this was really in the contemplation of the legislature or of those who lobbied them so assiduously. Even so, we can see no reason within the statute

---

8 Public Health (Infectious Diseases) Regulations 1988, SI 1988/1546.
9 Reporting of Injuries, Diseases and Dangerous Occurrences Regulations 1985, SI 1985/2023.
10 Abortion Regulations 1991, SI 1991/499; Abortion (Scotland) Regulations 1991, SI 1991/460.
11 Misuse of Drugs (Notification and Supply to Addicts) Regulations 1973, SI 1973/799.
12 *Hunter v Mann* [1974] QB 767, [1974] 2 All ER 414.
13 Section 9(1).
14 *R v Cardiff Crown Court, ex p Kellam* (1993) 16 BMLR 76. The court set aside the order to produce the documents 'with considerable reluctance'.
15 (1993) 16 BMLR 76 at 80.

why a doctor who sees it as a public duty to co-operate with the police should not do so if asked – provided, of course, that he is prepared to justify this later in a court of law or before his peers.

Other than by regulations, courts of law can compel the disclosure of medical material either through the production of documents or during evidence and cross-examination.

Disclosure of documents

A patient contemplating negligence proceedings against a doctor or a health authority will usually need access to his medical records so that his claim can be evaluated by his legal and medical advisers. Those in possession of such records have been enjoined by the courts to act in a spirit of candour and not to resist disclosure – a course of action which might have the effect of delaying the resolution of a dispute and preventing a just outcome.[16] Failure to put one's 'cards on the table' can be met with an order for the discovery of documents under ss 32 and 34 of the Supreme Court Act 1981. Disclosure may be made to a medical expert or to the applicant's legal advisers. A plaintiff cannot engage in a general 'fishing expedition' to see whether he has a cause of action – an application must disclose the 'nature of the claim he intends to make and show not only the intention of making it but also that there is a reasonable basis for making it'.[17]

A person in possession of documents may be entitled to refuse disclosure on the grounds that it is not in the public interest to make the documents available. This will rarely arise in medical negligence cases, but the court may have to consider whether disclosure should be denied when there is a public health dimension to a case. This was the position in *Re HIV Haemophiliac Litigation*,[18] where the public interest in question was the confidentiality of policy documents relating to blood products policy. Similarly, in *AB v Glasgow and West of Scotland Blood Transfusion Service*,[19] the Court of Session would not order disclosure of the identity of a blood donor in an action resulting from the donation of contaminated blood – the pursuer's right to claim damages was not of such magnitude that it should take precedence over a material risk to the sufficiency of the national supply of blood for transfusion.

Court directions may also be made for the disclosure before trial of expert medical reports which it is proposed to bring in evidence. The exception to this policy once lay in cases involving a suggestion of medical negligence – the rationale being that parties should not have to disclose experts' reports which were directed to establishing liability rather than to the prognosis and quantum of damages.[20] Largely as a result of the unsatisfactory trial in *Wilsher*,[1] alterations were made to the Rules of the Supreme Court so as to bring medical negligence cases into line with others involving personal injury – prior disclosure was to become the norm rather than the exception. In general, *all* the cards must now be put down, not just those obviously concerned

---

16 *Naylor v Preston Area Health Authority* [1987] 2 All ER 353, [1987] 1 WLR 958, CA.
17 *Dunning v Board of Governors of the United Liverpool Hospitals* [1973] 2 All ER 454 at 460.
18 [1990] NLJR 1349.
19 1993 SLT 36, (1989) 15 BMLR 91.
20 *Rahman v Kirklees Area Health Authority* [1980] 3 All ER 610, [1980] 1 WLR 1244, CA.
1 *Wilshire v Essex Area Health Authority* [1987] QB 730, [1986] 3 All ER 80, CA.

with the action; the current view is that the court can deal with problems of confidentiality relating to irrelevant conditions – such as a past history of sexually transmitted disease – by limiting disclosure to the other side's medical advisers who must respect medical confidentiality except where litigation is affected.[2] Brahams[3] has suggested that the duty of pre-trial publication may be wider than is generally thought. As things stand, however, the expert is not expected to consider or anticipate every possible form of cross-examination – the need is only to disclose that evidence which he, himself, intends to give at trial.[4]

Disclosure of documents and information is, however, subject to what is commonly known as 'legal professional privilege' – a doctrine designed to allow the client unfettered access to his advisers. The concept is not without difficulties, of which the doctor should be aware. First, legal professional privilege is tightly defined and is likely to be overridden, whenever this is possible, in the interests of legal fairness.[5] Thus, disclosure of reports which are designed primarily for accident investigation and prevention and only secondarily for the purpose of seeking legal advice is likely to be ordered. It is clear that this gives rise to a conflict of interests. On the one hand, it could be held that the public good of preventive medicine must take second place to the threat of private litigation;[6] on the other, the imposition of professional privilege has, on occasion, been granted only reluctantly in that secrecy is inequitable to the person who suffers medical mishap.[7] Secondly, while professional privilege is there in order to allow the client to be uninhibited when approaching his legal advisers, there is no corresponding privilege to encourage a patient to be equally open in relation to his medical advisers. This was demonstrated forcefully in *W v Egdell*,[8] where it was concluded that a clear and important distinction was to be made between, on the one hand, instructions given to an expert and, on the other, the expert's opinion given in response to those instructions; the former was covered by legal professional privilege, while the latter was not. We have some difficulty in understanding how a question can be subject to absolute confidentiality while the answer is not; nevertheless, the ruling given at first instance was fully supported in the Court of Appeal. Thirdly, a request for information from a solicitor is not the same as an order of the court even though the conditions – eg that litigation is in progress – may seem similar; medical

---

2 *Dunn v British Coal Corpn* [1993] ICR 591, CA.
3 D Brahams 'Medical Confidentiality and Expert Evidence' (1991) 337 Lancet 1276.
4 *Derby Co Ltd v Weldon (No 2)* [1989] 1 All ER 1002, quoted by Brahams (1991) 337 Lancet 1276. Whether this will be so if the recommendations of the Royal Commission on Criminal Justice *Report* (1993) are put into operation remains to be seen. For discussion, see J P Shepherd 'Presenting Expert Evidence in Criminal Proceedings' (1993) 307 BMJ 817.
5 Professional privilege is, in a sense, a product of the adversarial system of presenting evidence and is less likely to be upheld when proceedings are more akin to inquisitorial. The classic example of the latter is the case brought under the Children Act 1989 or in wardship proceedings: *Oxfordshire County Council v M* [1994] Fam 151.
6 *Waugh v British Railways Board* [1980] AC 521, [1979] 2 All ER 1169. For discussion, see G Robertson 'Discovery of Hospital Accident Reports' (1983) 133 NLJ 1020 and, with rather different emphasis, 'Hospital Inquiries: Evidence and Privilege' (1982) 284 BMJ 519. The order to disclose may extend to specific accident report forms which might well be thought to be privileged (*Lask v Gloucester Health Authority* (1985) Times, 13 December).
7 *Lee v South West Thames Regional Health Authority* [1985] 2 All ER 385, [1985] 1 WLR 845, discussed also in 'Disclosure of Documents by Doctors' (1985) 290 BMJ 1973.
8 [1990] Ch 359, [1989] 1 All ER 1089.

practitioners have been found guilty of serious professional misconduct for making such a mistake in good faith but in ignorance.[9] Finally, it is worth noting that, while the legal representative may, of course, withhold any documents to which professional privilege applies, the adversary may have advantage of these if they are disclosed in error and it is not obvious that privilege has not been waived.[10]

The doctor in the witness box has absolute privilege and is protected against any action for breach of confidence. The Earl of Halsbury LC provides the highest possible authority: the immunity of the witness in court 'is settled in law and cannot be doubted'.[11] This privilege extends to pre-trial conferences and Scottish precognitions, the exception being that a privileged communication must not be made maliciously.[12] Judges may go to great lengths to protect the witness but, when so ordered, the doctor is bound to answer any question which is put to him;[13] refusal to answer in the absence of the court's discretion to excuse a conscientious witness must expose the doctor to a charge of contempt – and the court will take precedence even when there is a statutory obligation of secrecy.[14] In some European countries, however, the obligation to maintain confidentiality extends to the courtroom.

Patient access to medical records

The right to see one's own medical records has now been largely accepted, even if there was earlier opposition to the principle on the part of some medical practitioners. In the past, a patient has had no access to such records, although access could be obtained by a plaintiff in a legal action. Concern over the storage of information on computers gave rise to a movement for allowing public access to personal records, and it was this general development which led to the first dent in this specific form of medical secrecy. The Council of Europe's Data Protection Convention required the recognition of a right of access to personal data stored in computer banks; this gave rise to the Data Protection Act 1984, which has now been replaced by the Data Protection Act 1998. The 1998 Act was a response to the EU Data Protection Directive of 1995 and, significantly, covers not only computerised data but also data which is manually stored in filing systems. The subject has a right to information as to the purposes for which data about him is being processed and the persons who will have access to it. In other respects, the new scheme of protection is broadly similar to that which was introduced in 1984: the protection of those about whom computerised information is stored lies in preventing the holding of inaccurate information or of

---

9 See 'Medical Confidence and the Law' (1981) 283 BMJ 1062.
10 *Pizzey v Ford Motor Co Ltd* [1994] PIQR P15, CA.
11 In *Watson v M'Ewan* [1905] AC 480 at 486, HL.
12 *AB v CD* (1904) 7 F 72, per Lord Moncrief. This is the Court of Session stage of *Watson v M'Ewan*. This is the same in other Commonwealth countries. See *Hay v University of Alberta Hospital* [1991] 2 Med LR 204 (QB, Alberta), in which it was held that the plaintiff had no right to withhold consent to pre-trial discussions by the defendants with his medical attendants.
13 The exception to this requirement being disclosure of a source of information for which special rules apply (Contempt of Court Act 1981, s 10). For a robust criticism of the present status of doctors, see J D J Havard 'A Question of Privilege' (1985) 25 Med Sci & L 242 and 'The Responsibility of the Doctor' (1989) 299 BMJ 503.
14 *Garner v Garner* (1920) 36 TLR 196.

concealing the fact that information is stored at all. Subject to a fee, a patient has the right to be told by the 'registered data user' – who could be any health caring body holding records – whether any such information is held and to be supplied with a copy of that information; the patient may then ensure its accuracy. There is provision, which is generalised throughout this area of legislation, for doctors to prevent access to information that is 'likely to cause serious harm' – a condition which is left undefined.

An important development in allowing patient access to personal medical information came with the Access to Medical Reports Act 1988. This is not descended linearly from the 1984 Act, as the relevant reports are limited to those prepared by a doctor who has clinical charge of the patient for direct supply to the patient's employer, prospective employer or to an insurance company (s 2). Reports by doctors who have had only a casual, non-caring professional association with the patient are excluded. Such reports as are included have always been subject to the patient's consent but the applicant must now positively seek such consent and must inform him of his rights to access (s 3). The patient can see the report before it is sent and, unless he has done so, issue of the report must be delayed for three weeks (s 4). He has the right to ask the doctor to alter anything that he feels is inaccurate and he may add a dissenting statement should the doctor refuse to do so (s 5). Once again, access may be withheld if disclosure would cause serious harm to the patient's physical or mental health – or to that of any other person – but, in those circumstances, the patient may withdraw his consent.

Patient access to manual records was achieved through the Access to Health Records Act 1990. This extends the patient's rights to access so as to include health records relating to him that have been prepared manually and which are held by a variety of health professionals, including doctors, dentists and psychologists. The patient may now see his records and may ask the holder to correct the information contained if he forms the view that it is inaccurate (s 6). A holder who agrees that the information is, indeed, inaccurate may make an appropriate amendment; otherwise, he may make a note in the relevant part of the record setting out the respect in which the patient regards it as inaccurate. There is the standard exemption of records which are likely to cause serious physical or mental harm (s 5). The right of access under this Act does not apply to notes made before 1 November 1991 – when the Act came into operation – unless such access is needed for the understanding of a later record. A suggestion that a common law right existed before that date has been rejected by the court[15] but access to pre-1991 records has become available since the Code of Practice on Openness in the NHS came into force in 1995. This is a non-statutory code which attempts to introduce broad principles of openness in all aspects of the operation of the NHS. Doctors and other health carers are required to release a patient's own personal records on the request of that patient, even if they was stored before 1995. The Code is enforceable by the Health Service Commissioner. The legislative right of access to records under the 1990 Act extends to children provided that the child is capable of understanding the nature of his or her application for access (s 4); alternatively, the right may be exercised by a parent or guardian on behalf of the child.

---

15 *R v Mid Glamorgan Family Health Services, ex p Martin* (1993) 16 BMLR 1; affd [1995] 1 WLR 110.

While patients' access to medical records is a subject dear to the heart of civil libertarians, it has less support in the medical profession – an antipathy which is not entirely derived from professional protectionism. The majority of those giving whole-hearted support work in the field of general practice; by the very nature of primary care, reports compiled and received in that area are largely factual and, most importantly, do not include a deal of varied, and possibly contradictory, opinion. By contrast, hospital notes are fuller, they are contributed to by members of the health care team, who will be of differing experience, and the several consultative opinions will be written from differing angles with varying emphasis. It is now possible that the notes will be limited and their content 'tailored' to the possibility of disclosure; interchange of opinion may be increasingly by way of word of mouth. The disadvantage to the patient is, then, evident – in the event of a change of location, his accompanying medical documents will be of less value to his new health carers than ought to be the case.[16] There is, however, no hard evidence that the Act has affected medical practice adversely and such musings may be unduly pessimistic; certainly, an impressive body of research can be quoted which stresses the practical advantages. The Access to Health Records Act 1990 undoubtedly attracts general popular support and there is a movement towards giving patients physical possession of their records.[17] Whether this would be technically possible is uncertain because the general impression is that physical ownership of the notes is vested in ownership of the paper on which they are written; the ownership of the contained intellectual property – ie the copyright – is held by the person who has created the notes or his employer, and not by the subject of those notes. The patient is therefore unlikely ever to have a successful property claim over his or her notes.[18]

The patient's remedies

The law has been slow to develop a remedy for breach of confidentiality in spite of its clear recognition of such breaches as a proper basis for legal action. This latter has been considerably clarified and its requirements set out in the House of Lords decision in *A-G v Guardian Newspapers (No 2)*.[19] It is likely that a patient would be able to claim damages for improper disclosure of information about his health even if he suffered no financial loss as a result; this is almost implicit from *X v Y*,[20] in which it was said that 'No one has suggested that damages would be an adequate remedy in this case' – the clear implication being that they were there for the taking in the absence of a better solution. They might, of course, be only nominal; on the other

---

16 For a relatively early debate, see A P Bird and M T I Walji 'Our Patients Have Access to Their Medical Records' (1986) 292 BMJ 595; A P Ross 'The Case Against Showing Patients Their Records' (1986) 292 BMJ 578.

17 See M L M Gilhooly and S M McGhee 'Medical Records: Practicalities and Principles of Patient Possession' (1991) 17 J Med Ethics 138.

18 In *R v Mid Glamorgan Family Health Services* [1995] 1 All ER 356, [1995] 1 WLR 110, the court accepted that medical records were owned by the health authority, and a similar view was taken by the High Court of Australia in *Breen v Williams* (1996) 138 ALR 259.

19 [1990] 1 AC 109, [1998] 3 All ER 545.

20 [1988] 2 All ER 648, (1992) 3 BMLR 1.

hand, they might be considerable were it possible to show loss of society, severe injury to feelings, job loss, interference with prospects of promotion of the like. However, a distinction has to be made between actions in contract and in tort. Thus, in the trial stage of *W v Egdell*,[1] Scott J discarded the possibility of damages for shock and distress – other than nominal – largely on the particular facts of the case but also because it was based on breach of an implied contractual term;[2] the decision has no relevance to an action in tort.

The matter came before the courts in Scotland in two similarly named decisions, the *AB v CD* cases. In the earlier *AB v CD*,[3] the Court of Session considered an action for damages brought against a doctor who had disclosed to a church minister that the pursuer's wife had given birth to a full-term child six months after marriage. The court held that there was a duty on the part of the doctor not to reveal confidential information about his patient unless he was required to do so in court or if disclosure were 'conducive to the ends of science' – but, in that case, identification of the patient would be improper. In the second *AB v CD*,[4] the pursuer was seeking a separation from her husband. Having been examined by the defender at the suggestion of her lawyers, she was later examined by the same doctor who was then acting on behalf of her husband. The doctor disclosed to the husband certain information he had obtained in the course of his first examination and the wife argued that this constituted a breach of confidence. Once again, the court accepted that there was a duty on the part of a doctor not to disclose confidential information about his patient but stressed that not every disclosure would be actionable. As Lord Trayner pointed out,[5] some statements may be indiscreet but not actionable; there might be, for example, an actionable breach if the disclosure revealed that the patient was suffering from a disease which was a consequence of misconduct on his part.[6] In fact, disclosure of the background to the illness may be of greater importance than the disclosure of illness itself.

This really amounts to no more than saying that the patient is entitled to protection against defamatory statements, a protection which is hardly adequate. In both English and Scots law, the patient is not being defamed if what the doctor says is true.[7] Moreover, in England, the law of slander (spoken defamation) requires that the plaintiff should be able to prove special damage – which is, essentially, pecuniary damage – except in those limited cases of slander which are actionable per se. The protection provided by the law of defamation in cases where the doctor verbally reveals confidential information to another is thus unlikely to be significant.

Qualified privilege should, in the absence of malice or reckless unconcern as to the truth of the statement, be a defence against any action for breach of confidence, as it already is in the law of defamation – qualified privilege in this context being but

---

1   [1990] Ch 359, [1990] 1 All ER 835.
2   Quoting *Bliss v South East Thames Regional Health Authority* [1987] ICR 700.
3   (1851) 14 D 177.
4   1904 7 F 72.
5   1904 7 F 72 at 85.
6   Scots law provides a potential remedy in the form of the *actio iniurarium*. For comments on the possible application of this delict in cases of breach of confidence, see Scottish Law Commission, Memorandum No 40 *Confidential Information* (1977) p 28.
7   The doctor's most likely exposure to defamation is, of course, on an intra-professional basis. For a brief overview, see Legal Correspondent 'Doctors and Defamation' (1985) 290 BMJ 1342.

another expression of the 'need to know' principle. This is the ultimate determinant of ethical disclosure. The profession is not, or should not be, so concerned with the niceties of intra-professional relationships or of communication in good faith with paramedical or other responsible groups; what really matters is irresponsible gossip – and, here, the ultimate deterrent is the Professional Conduct Committee of the General Medical Council. Punitive action against a doctor is unlikely to be of material benefit to a wronged patient, but it is still a very effective preventive weapon.

Confidentiality and death

Final reflection might, appositely, be concerned with death. The Declaration of Sydney says: 'I will respect the secrets which are confided in me, even after the patient has died.' In practice, this is incapable of fulfilment as a death certificate, signed by a doctor, is a public document – albeit, available only on payment of a fee for a copy. Once again, the spectre of AIDS raises its head in so far as confidentiality may, here, be as important to the bereaved family as to the deceased during life. It is certain that death certification in the United Kingdom – and probably elsewhere – is inaccurate, but this can only be compounded if doctors take it upon themselves to 'sanitise' the diagnosis so as to spare the relatives distress and, maybe, harm. A government publication[8] suggests that certificates relating to recent deaths should be available only to those who may legitimately want them – but such measures are unlikely to achieve strict confidentiality.[9] The dilemma of conscience for doctors is acute in many types of death which carry a social stigma but, pending an alteration in the law, we find it hard to accept that doctors should be encouraged to falsify facts which are attested to be 'true to the best of my knowledge and belief'. Our major concerns here, however, are, first, with conditions discovered after death and, secondly, with the circumstances leading to death. The legal position is that, as the confidence is prima facie a personal matter, the legal duty ends with the death of the patient;[10] the GMC is, however, unequivocal: 'The death of the patient does not absolve the doctor from this obligation [of professional secrecy].' There can be no doubt that a post-mortem report merits the same degree of confidentiality as does the report of the clinical examination; insurance companies and the like have an obvious interest in its content but their right to disclosure is the same as the right to discovery of hospital records – in the absence of a court order, consent to disclosure from the next of kin of the deceased is essential.

But has the public any rights to details of the medical history of the dead?[11] While the principle remains irrespective of personalities, this is essentially a problem of public figures – and it is remarkable how rapidly professional ethics can be dissipated, say, in describing to the media the wounds of President Kennedy or the psychiatric history of the principals in any *cause celèbre*. It is easy to say 'History will out, let it be sooner than later' but it is less easy to decide at what point revelations become history. The GMC has suggested that whether or not disclosure after death will be

8 *Registration: A Modern Service* (Cm 531).
9 M B King 'AIDS on the Death Certificate: The Final Stigma' (1989) 298 BMJ 734.
10 However, any action for breach of confidence before the death of the patient could be transmitted to the executor.
11 See S E Woolman 'Defaming the Dead' 1981 SLT 29.

improper depends, inter alia, on the nature of the information given, the extent of previous publication and the time elapsed since death – as to the last, the Council rightly will not specify a number of years, merely remarking that a doctor who discloses such information without the consent of a surviving relative may be required to justify his action. Moreover, a bark in this context carries a bite – no less a person than a former Editor of the British Medical Journal has been taken to task for reporting information concerning the health of a well-known, albeit controversial, general after his death.[12]

Respect for the privacy of the dead seems reasonable – particularly when children or, especially, spouses are alive.[13] Indeed, the courts may apply the principles of medical confidentiality by insisting that an order imposing anonymity in judicial proceedings should remain in force after the subject's death in cases of major sensitivity – such as those involving declarations as to the withdrawal of treatment from the incompetent.[14] Not only does this appear logical but post-mortem publicity may, in turn, raise questions as to the ethics of previous non-disclosure. It has, for example, been seriously argued that Lord Moran invited criticism not so much for his disclosures after the death of Winston Churchill[15] as for his failure to draw attention to the physical state of his patient during life. Which brings us back almost to where we started – to the dilemma of the doctor's relationship to his patient vis-à-vis society.

12 S Lock and J Loudon 'A Question of Confidence' (1984) 288 BMJ 123, 125.
13 The courts are, however, concerned for a balancing of interests between those of the bereaved and of freedom to publish. See *Re X (a minor) (wardship: restriction on publication)* [1975] Fam 47, [1975] 1 All ER 697.
14 *Re C (adult patient: publicity)* [1996] 2 FLR 251 – though this may not hold if the public interest dictates otherwise. For the balance of private and public interest and the imposition of anonymity in general, see *Re G (adult patient: publicity)* [1995] 2 FLR 528.
15 Lord Moran *Winston Churchill: The Struggle for Survival, 1944-1965* (1966).

9 Medical negligence

Medical negligence is more than a matter between two parties – it is also a political issue. In both medical and governmental circles there is concern over the growing incidence of personal injury actions against doctors and over the cost to the health system of compensating the victims. It is pointed out that medical negligence actions are destructive of trust in a doctor-patient relationship and distort the practice of medicine in an over-cautious direction. From the doctor's point of view, the prospect of being sued in the event of making a mistake is stressful and demoralising. Many of those working outside medicine may face such a prospect in the course of exercising their profession but, in the case of the doctor, the fundamentally hazardous nature of the work, combined with the demanding and fraught conditions under which it has to be performed, makes the possibility of error and subsequent legal action very strong indeed. It has, for example, been revealed that some 37% of consultants and senior registrars in the NHS had been sued at least once in 1996. Legal action is, thus, a very real risk for the medical practitioner and it would be surprising if litigation at this level did not seriously compromise medical morale. Funding bodies might expect to find the picture equally bleak. Again in 1996-97, the cost of clinical negligence claims to the Department of Health was in the region of £300m.[1] This would be sufficient to fund a large health service trust for the whole of one year.

What lies behind this increase in litigation? First and foremost, modern medicine is intrusive and the chances of injury are therefore increased. Secondly, the current social climate encourages expectations of cure. When these are not met, the culture of consumerism – fuelled by patients' charters and by a press eager to disclose wrongdoing – advocates the allocation of blame and the seeking of compensation. Finally, intolerance of error, and of the fact that any complex human endeavour will inevitably involve the making of mistakes, means that the public increasingly insists on accountability and, if possible, the pinning of an adverse outcome on some identifiable human agency. There are no longer any accidents – somebody, somewhere must be made to answer for what has happened. This has created a climate which is excessively stressful for social workers, teachers and, to a marked extent, health care staff.

The current system comes under attack from other quarters. Patients, it is argued, have great difficulty seeking compensation for negligently inflicted medical injury and may face awesome hurdles in the process of suing a doctor. Only a relatively small proportion of the victims of medical negligence bring an action for damages and, currently, 83% of these fail.[2] Those who do succeed may have to wait a considerable time before damages are paid; in many cases three or more years may elapse before

---

1 Government statement, *Hansard*, 24 March 1998, cols 165-166.
2 See n 1 above.

the matter is finally settled. The current system thus seems to the patient to be flawed: he or she has suffered an injury and yet it may be difficult to recover what is seen as his or her due. Moreover, having failed to get any explanation as to what went wrong and having been offered no apology, the patient may have felt that there was no alternative to bringing an action. Both sides – if one can talk of sides in this matter – see the current system of compensation for medical injury being slow, traumatic and socially expensive, one from which it is often only the lawyers who profit. There must be a better way of dealing with this issue – a way which provides reasonably efficient compensation without destroying the doctor-patient relationship and without diverting health-targeted funds from hospitals and patient care into legal fees and damages.

A widely canvassed alternative to negligence actions, which commands much support, is to introduce a system of no-fault compensation, which will provide for the making of awards to injured patients irrespective of the requirement of proving fault on the part of medical personnel.[3] Such a scheme has operated in New Zealand since 1974 as part of an overall no-fault compensation scheme and, even if it has had its opponents, it has now survived into its third decade.[4] In the medical context, however, the New Zealand claimant must still establish that the injury resulted from 'medical or surgical misadventure', a requirement which has caused difficulties in distinguishing between those conditions which result from the physiological progress of a medical condition and those which are genuinely the result of misadventure occurring in the course of treatment. A considerable body of case law is devoted to determining just when a complication following upon a medical procedure is so rare as to amount to a misadventure.[5] It will be seen that such schemes do not do away entirely with all the difficult issues of foreseeability and causation which dog the operation of conventional tort law. It is, perhaps, significant that organisations such as the British Medical Association, whose primary concern as a trade union is for the interests of the profession, have consistently supported the introduction of a no-fault based system into the United Kingdom.[6] Under the scheme proposed by the BMA, compensation would be available for medically-induced injury but would exclude those injuries which were not avoidable through the exercise of reasonable care. The concept of negligence is therefore effectively preserved, although it would undoubtedly

3   For a survey of the alternatives to fault-based compensation, see the discussion of New Zealand, Swedish and German schemes, in D Giesen *International Medical Malpractice Law* (1988) p 529. The New Zealand scheme is discussed by J Fleming *The Law of Torts* (7th edn, 1987) p 375; see also, S A M McLean 'Liability Without Fault – the New Zealand Experience' [1985] J Soc Welfare Law 125. For the Swedish system, see C Oldertz 'The Swedish Patient Insurance System – 8 Years of Experience' (1984) 52 Med-Leg J 43.
4   Criticisms include those of unacceptably low levels of compensation, high cost to the taxpayer and the removal of deterrents to safety practices in the workplace. On the last of these, see A Lewis 'No Fault Liability – Thirty Years of Experience in New Zealand' (1996) 15 Med & Law 425.
5   The issue is fully discussed by K Oliphant 'Defining "Medical Misadventure": Lessons from New Zealand' [1996] 4 Med L Rev 1. Oliphant suggests that in a possible British scheme, medical misadventure should be equated with 'treatment error', a concept which should include errors which have occurred in spite of the exercise of reasonable skill on the practitioner's part.
6   BMA *Report of the BMA No Fault Compensation Working Party* (1987); discussed by C Dyer 'No Fault Compensation' (1988) 297 BMJ 143, (1989) 298 BMJ 143. The BMA Annual Representative Meeting again backed a call for the introduction of no-fault compensation in 1996.

be easier to establish; moreover, there would be no inference of 'fault' of quite the same nature as is inferred in a tort-based system. A no-fault system of compensation is also the preferred option in the Report of the Royal College of Physicians on the subject.[7]

For a variety of reasons, predominantly those of cost, the government has not supported the movement and a Private Member's Bill aimed in that direction was defeated in Parliament.[8] The government's attitude has not, however, been one of total inaction and the Department of Health has encouraged discussion of ways by which to make compensation more readily available and less costly. The role of arbitration in helping to reduce the time and expense involved in meeting a claim for medical injury has attracted official attention.[9] A suggested scheme involves a panel of three arbitrators – composed of one doctor nominated by each litigant and a lawyer chairman – which would work entirely on paper and which would, therefore, avoid the cost of court proceedings and witness's time. Some objections to this are foreseen; in particular, it might be difficult to avoid the need for the examination of experts in certain cases of special complexity.

The argument in favour of retaining the present system for compensating the victims of medical accident or negligence can be couched in positive as well as negative terms. One is based on the deterrent value of the law of tort, the view being taken that to remove the threat of litigation will affect adversely the care with which doctors treat their patients. There is certainly some evidence that doctors are more cautious when they are aware of the Damoclean possibility of legal action; surveys undertaken in the United States indicate that successful litigation provokes greater care – at least in the realm of diagnosis.[10] Yet there are other ways of deterring carelessness and it may be that a more extensive power of the General Medical Council to deal with doctors who fail to live up to an expected standard of competence could prove a more effective incentive to maintain high standards of practice.[11] The GMC's power to protect the public against sub-standard practice is grounded in the Medical (Professional Performance) Act 1995.[12] A major invocation of these powers was evident in the proceedings against the Bristol thoracic surgeons who were found to have had what can only be described as an unacceptable mortality rate in paediatric operations. One of the surgeons involved was removed from the Register and the other was banned from paediatric heart operations for a period of three years.[13] The political ramifications of this case could be extensive and the question of the self-regulation of the medical profession may well be subject to further review.[14] The

7 *Compensation for Adverse Consequences of Medical Intervention* (1990).
8 National Health Service (Compensation) Bill 1991. The case against no-fault compensation is summarised by B Capstick, P Edwards and D Mason 'Compensation for Medical Accidents' (1991) 302 BMJ 230.
9 Department of Health *Arbitration for Medical Negligence in the National Health Service* (Discussion Paper, 1991).
10 P M Danzon *Medical Malpractice* (1985) esp ch 1.
11 For discussion of the deterrent argument in the context of reforms in medical discipline, see M Stacey 'Medical Accountability: A Background Paper' in A Grubb (ed) *Challenges in Medical Care* (1992) p 109.
12 Explained in GMC *GMC's Performance Procedures* (1997).
13 C Dyer 'Bristol Doctors found Guilty of Serious Professional Misconduct' (1998) 316 BMJ 1924. This case also raises issues of whistle-blowing: see p 13 above.
14 See R Smith 'All Changed, Changed Utterly' (1998) 316 BMJ 1917.

existence of a clear, effective and patient-friendly system of investigating grievances may do more than satisfy those potential litigants whose principal goal is to find out what went wrong and to get an apology; it may also form a valuable element in a system of professional audit.

The power of deterrence is also qualified by the financial realities of the system in the United Kingdom. In this country, outwith private practice, the doctor has no direct contract with the patient and medical damages are usually underwritten by the state;[15] if one adds to these the surrealistic conditions surrounding legal aid – under which it may be economically preferable to settle an action out of court rather than to win a contested action – it becomes possible to raise an argument that the doctor in the United Kingdom is exposed to too little by way of stricture.

The question of compensation for medical injury in the United Kingdom has had a number of official airings. It was discussed as a special issue by the Royal Commission on Compensation for Personal Injury (The Pearson Commission),[16] which concluded that there were insufficient grounds for introducing no-fault compensation schemes. More recently, Lord Woolf addressed the matter in his wide-ranging investigation into the operation of the system of civil justice. Lord Woolf singled out medical negligence as an area for special consideration on the grounds that it was in respect of these claims that civil justice was 'failing most conspicuously'.[17] This failure was demonstrated by a variety of factors, including an unacceptable delay in the resolution of cases and a success rate which was lower than that in other personal injury litigation. The report suggested that the system could be improved by a better complaints procedure and by extending the jurisdiction of the Health Service Ombudsman to include complaints against the clinical expertise of NHS staff, both of which suggestions have been acted upon.[18] Lord Woolf was also concerned to establish what he described as a 'climate of change' that is marked by greater openness. One possible way of achieving this would be by making it incumbent upon doctors to inform patients if there has been an act or omission on their part which may have caused injury. It was questioned whether this duty already existed at common law, but Lord Woolf did not favour the imposition of this obligation on the grounds that the sensitive nature of the relationship between doctor and patient precluded it. He did, however, suggest that the GMC might explore ways of clarifying the responsibilities of the doctor in terms of candour,[19] and he also favoured the wider use of mediation schemes. It would seem, though, that, in spite of tinkering at the margins of the problem, the victims of medical negligence will have to continue to seek compensation through a fault-based tort system. Their ability to do so, however, currently depends to a very great extent on the availability of legal aid. There are indications that this may eventually be withdrawn in favour of a contingency fee system – a development attributable to the reluctance of the government to continue

15 Department of Health *Claims of Medical Negligence against NHS Hospital and Community Doctors and Dentists* (1989) HC(89) 34. See J D J Harvard 'Doctors and Medical Negligence' (1990) 300 BMJ 343. See also p 219 below.
16 Cmnd 7054-1.
17 *Access to Justice: Final Report to the Lord Chancellor on the Civil Justice System in England and Wales* (1996) 15.2.
18 For the increased powers of the Health Service Ombudsman, see Health Service Commissioners (Amendment) Act 1996.
19 See L Beecham 'GMC approves new Ethical Guidelines' (1998) 316 BMJ 1556.

to fund what it sees as a cost ineffective system of compensation.[20] In the following sections, we analyse the operation of this system and the rules it has developed for the adjudication of such claims.

The basis of medical liability

Most claims in respect of medical injury are brought in tort, that is, on the basis of a non-contractual civil wrong. The reason for this is that, within the NHS, patients are not in a contractual relationship with the doctor treating them. In the private sector, by contrast, there will be a contractual relationship and it is, therefore, possible to bring an action for damages in contract. In practice, there is very little difference between the two remedies,[1] although the law of contract may provide a remedy for an express or implied warranty given by a doctor.[2] In a Canadian case, *La Fleur v Cornelis*,[3] the court held that a plastic surgeon was bound to an express contractual warranty that he had made to the patient. This warranty arose when he was unwise enough to say: 'There will be no problem. You will be very happy.' This sort of case will be comparatively unusual and, for all practical purposes, any discussion of medical negligence can confine itself to liability under the law of torts, in which the first question to be asked is: whom do we sue?

A medical injury may have been caused to the plaintiff by any one or more of the health care personnel who have treated him. Locating negligence may be simple in some cases but, in others, the patient may have to choose the responsible party from a fairly large group, which may include a general practitioner, a hospital consultant, other hospital doctors and the nursing staff. Locating the specific act of alleged negligence which caused the injury may also involve a degree of disentanglement.

The plaintiff may proceed directly against the doctor in question if an allegation is made of negligence on the part of a general practitioner. The general practitioner in the United Kingdom is solely responsible for the treatment of his patients and there can be no question of responsibility being imposed on a health authority unless the authority has intervened in the practitioner's treatment of his patient – all partners in a practice may, however, be liable for the actions of one of their number. Normally, of course, the general practitioner will be a member of a medical defence society, to whom he will refer any claim against him; the society then advises him and undertakes the defence or settlement of the claim. General practitioners are not covered by the NHS indemnity which applies to hospital doctors[4] unless a claim arises in respect of work undertaken under a health authority contract. A general practitioner will be

---

20 Lord Chancellor's Department Consultation Paper *Access to Justice with Conditional Fees* (1998) 3.15. The current (1998) annual cost of legal aid in England and Wales for medical negligence cases is £27m.
1 For a useful discussion of the distinction between contractual and tortious remedies in this context, see M A Jones *Medical Negligence* (1991) p 15.
2 An issue which arose in *Thake v Maurice* [1986] QB 644, [1984] 2 All ER 513; revsd [1986] QB 644, [1986] 1 All ER 479.
3 (1979) 28 NBR (2d) 569 (NBSC); discussed by Jones, n 1 above, p 18.
4 See p 221 below.

vicariously liable for the negligence of staff employed by him – nurses, receptionists etc – but not for the acts of a locum tenens or a deputising doctor.[5]

The position is different if the alleged negligence occurs after the general practitioner has referred the patient for further treatment within the NHS. If the negligent act is committed by a health service employee, the patient then has the choice of proceeding either against the individual he feels has been negligent, or against the health authority, or against both in a joint action. In practice, many actions are brought against the health authority on the grounds of convenience. The liability of the authority may be based on either of two grounds: (1) the duty of a hospital to care for patients; or (2) the vicarious liability of a health authority for the negligence of its employees.

There is some doubt as to whether a hospital owes a non-delegable duty to use skill and care in treating its patients.[6] This has been addressed in some Commonwealth jurisdictions which have a somewhat different form of health care delivery to that existing in the United Kingdom. Thus, in the Australian case of *Ellis v Wallsend District Hospital*,[7] the majority held that there was a non-delegable duty in those cases where patients were permitted to go directly to the hospital for treatment and advice; no such duty would exist where the hospital merely provided services which a doctor could use to treat his own patients.[8] By contrast, the Ontario Court of Appeal has found that the hospital's duty extends no further than employing competent staff.[9] The minority view was, however, that hospitals, to a growing extent, hold out to the public that they provide medical treatment and emergency services – and that the public increasingly relies upon them to do so; Blair JA, in expressing this view, drew upon the evolution of the law in England which he thought supported the view that the hospital could be personally liable for negligent treatment in certain circumstances.[10] The English case of *Wilsher*[11] could have provided an ideal ground to decide the matter but the issue was not raised by the plaintiffs; nevertheless, the possibility clearly remains open – it was said that:

I can see no reason why, in principle, the health authority should not be [directly] liable if its organisation is at fault.[12]

The point seems to be of some importance, particularly in respect of the nursing staff, who may well be covered themselves by a common insurance policy taken out by the Royal College of Nursing on behalf of its members but who have less than

---

5 There was no vicarious liability for the negligence of a locum tenens in the Canadian case of *Rothwell v Raes* (1988) 54 DLR (4th) 193.

6 For discussion, see A M Dugdale and K M Stanton *Professional Negligence* (2nd edn, 1989) para 22.21; M Jones *Medical Negligence* (1991) p 283.

7 (1989) 17 NSWLR 553, CA.

8 The matter was also pronounced upon, obiter, by the High Court of Australia in *Commonwealth v Introvigne* (1982) 56 ALJR 749 and *Kondis v State Transport Authority* (1984) 154 CLR 672, 55 ALR 225.

9 *Yepremian v Scarborough General Hospital* (1980) 110 DLR (3d) 513.

10 Ibid at 579.

11 *Wilsher v Essex Area Health Authority* [1987] QB 730, [1986] 3 All ER 801, CA; revsd [1988] AC 1074, [1988] 1 All ER 871, HL.

12 [1987] QB 730 at 778, [1986] 3 All ER 801 at 833, per Browne-Wilkinson VC.

doctors by way of personal representation and the like; it could scarcely be denied that a hospital undertakes to provide nursing care for the patients.[13]

The discussion is, however, relatively sterile in the case of hospital doctors, the vast majority of whom are direct employees of the NHS. The health authority is, therefore, liable for their negligence under the principle of vicarious liability. This provides that an employer is liable for his employee's negligent acts, provided that the employee is acting within the scope of his employment. It should be borne in mind that the employer may still be held vicariously liable even if the employee acts in direct contradiction of his employer's instructions or prohibitions.[14] The vicarious liability of hospitals throughout their hierarchy has been clearly established for over 30 years[15] and requires no further discussion.

In the past, an agreement between the Ministry of Health and the Secretary of State for Scotland and the medical defence societies allowed for the costs of any actions to be shared between the two parties.[16] All doctors employed in the National Health Service were, accordingly, contractually bound to be members of a defence organisation; the membership fees, however, increased so dramatically that they had to be subsidised by the authorities. Crown immunity has been extended to doctors, dentists and community physicians since January 1990[17] and, as a result, the entire costs of negligence litigation are now borne by the NHS. Health authorities may, as a consequence, feel obliged to settle cases on the grounds that this is the cheapest, if not the fairest, option; moreover, there is a strong suspicion that compensation for the injured may be bought at the expense of limitations in treatment facilities for the remainder – but this is, perhaps, to take too pessimistic a view. It is to be noted that the scheme applies *only* to services provided within the NHS; doctors should, therefore, retain cover for any private or 'good Samaritan' work – and, indeed, for medico-legal activity.

What constitutes negligence?

In determining whether there has been negligence in medical treatment, the courts pursue the same line of inquiry as they pursue in any other similar claim: did the conduct of the defendant amount to a breach of the duty of care which he owed to the injured plaintiff? Expressed somewhat differently, this amounts to asking whether the standard of the treatment given by the defendant fell below the standard expected of him by the law and whether there was, therefore, any fault in the legal sense. Fault remains the theoretical underpinning of the law in this area until such time as strict liability may be imposed.

13 *Gold v Essex County Council* [1942] 2 KB 293 at 299, CA, per Lord Greene.
14 R F V Heuston and R A Buckley *Salmond and Heuston on the Law of Torts* (20th edn, 1992) p 460.
15 *Roe v Minister of Health; Woolley v Ministry of Health* [1954] 2 QB 66; *Hayward v Board of Management of the Royal Infirmary of Edinburgh* and *Macdonald v Glasgow Western Hospitals Board of Management* 1954 SC 453. For discussion, see Jones, *Medical Negligence* pp 272 et seq.
16 Ministry of Health circular HM(54)32.
17 See p 219, n 4 above.

A major difficulty for any plaintiff will be the burden which falls upon him to prove that the defendant's negligence caused his injury. This is often a difficult burden to discharge and, indeed, suggestions have been made that the patient attempting to succeed in an action against a doctor should face a heavier burden in establishing his case than that required in any other personal injury litigation. There is an indication that this occurs in practice in so far as payment is made in some 30-40% of medical cases as compared with 86% in the general run;[18] the figures may, however, conceal more than a simple cause and effect phenomenon. The legal foundation for this view, which was put forward by Lawton LJ,[19] may be tenuous and it was, in fact, strongly opposed in *Ashcroft*;[20] nevertheless, it is certainly true that there has been a degree of policy-based judicial reluctance to award damages against doctors. In *Dwyer v Roderick*,[1] May LJ suggested that it would be:

> To shut one's eyes to the obvious if one denied that the burden of achieving something more than the mere balance of probabilities was greater when one was investigating the complicated and sophisticated actions of a qualified and experienced [inter alia] doctor than when one was enquiring into the inattention of the driver in a simple running down action.[2]

At the same time, the courts have not been insensitive to the plaintiff's difficulties in a medical negligence case. The correctives applied have been the occasional invocation of the principle of res ipsa loquitur or, as in *Clark v MacLennan*,[3] an attempt to shift the burden of proof to the defendant. The observations of Kilner Brown J in *Ashcroft* on this point are revealing:

> When an injury is caused which never should have been caused, common sense and natural justice indicate that some degree of compensation ought to be paid by someone. As the law stands, in order to obtain compensation an injured person is compelled to allege negligence against . . . a person of the highest skill and reputation.[4]

We return to this problem below.[5]

The reasonably skilful doctor

There have been many judicial pronouncements by the courts on the standard of care which is expected of the doctor. As early as 1838 we see Tindall CJ ruling that:

> Every person who enters into a learned profession undertakes to bring to the exercise of it a reasonable degree of care and skill. He does not undertake, if he is an attorney, that at all

---

18 M A Jones 'Medical Negligence – the Burden of Proof' (1984) 134 NLJ 7, quoting the Pearson Report (p 218, n 16 above).
19 In *Whitehouse v Jordan* [1980] 1 All ER 650 at 659.
20 *Ashcroft v Mersey Regional Health Authority* [1983] 2 All ER 245 at 247, per Kilner Brown J.
 1 (1983) 127 Sol Jo 805, CA.
 2 See p 235 below.
 3 [1983] 1 All ER 416.
 4 [1983] 2 All ER 245 at 246.
 5 See p 223.

events you shall gain your case, nor does a surgeon undertake that he will perform a cure; nor does he undertake to use the highest possible degree of skill.[6]

An echo of this is to be found in *R v Bateman,*[7] where the court explained that:

If a person holds himself out as possessing special skill and knowledge, by and on behalf of a patient, he owes a duty to the patient to use due caution in undertaking the treatment ... The jury should not exact the highest, or very high standard, nor should they be content with a very low standard.

The doctor is thus not expected to be a miracle-worker guaranteeing a cure or a man of the very highest skill in his calling. What standard then is he expected to meet? McNair J provides us with the classic answer to this question in *Bolam v Friern Hospital Management Committee:*[8]

The test is the standard of the ordinary skilled man exercising and professing to have that special skill. A man need not possess the highest expert skill at the risk of being found negligent. It is a well-established law that it is sufficient if he exercises the ordinary skill of an ordinary man exercising that particular art.

Nevertheless, he *is* professing a particular skill and, in the immortal words of McNair J, the test of that skill 'is not the test of the man on the top of the Clapham omnibus because [that man] has not got this special skill'.[10]

The doctor having that degree of competence expected of the ordinary skilful doctor sets the standard. He is the practitioner who follows the standard practice of his profession – or, at least, follows practices that would not be disapproved of by responsible opinion within the profession; he has a reasonably sound grasp of medical techniques and is as informed of new medical developments as the average competent doctor would expect to be. The circumstances in which a doctor treats his patient will also be taken into account. A doctor working in an emergency, with inadequate facilities and under great pressure, will not be expected by the courts to achieve the same results as a doctor who is working in ideal conditions.[11] This was alluded to by Mustill J in *Wilsher*, where he said that, if a person was forced by an emergency to

6 *Lanphier v Phipos* (1838) 8 C & P 475 at 478.
7 (1925) 94 LJKB 791 at 794, CCA.
8 [1957] 2 All ER 118 at 121, [1957] 1 WLR 582 at 586.
9 A test approved in the Privy Council: *Chin Keow v Government of Malaysia* [1967] 1 WLR 813. The *Bolam* test is applied throughout medical practice – including the providing of information and warnings: *Sidaway v Board of Governors of the Bethlem Royal Hospital and Maudsley Hospital* [1985] AC 871, [1985] 1 All ER 643, HL. See also *Hills v Potter* [1983] 3 All ER 716, [1984] 1 WLR 641.
10 This is in accordance with the general principle in the law of torts that errors of judgment are more excusable in an emergency: *The Metagama* (1927) 138 LT 369 at 370. In the medical context: *Rodych v Krasey* [1971] 4 WWR 358. See also *Wilson v Swanson* (1956) 5 DLR (2d) 113 (emergency removal of suspected cancerous tissue before a firm pathological report was available).
11 [1986] 3 All ER 801 at 812

do too many things at once, then the fact that he does one of them incorrectly 'should not lightly be taken as negligence'.[12]

Usual practice

The 'custom test' – the test whereby a defendant's conduct is tested against the normal usage of his profession or calling – is one that is applied in all areas of negligence law.[13] The courts have given expression to this test in the medical context in a number of decisions. In the important Scottish case of *Hunter v Hanley*, for example, there was a clear endorsement of the custom test in Lord Clyde's dictum:

> To establish liability by a doctor where deviation from normal practice is alleged, three facts require to be established. First of all it must be proved that there is a usual and normal practice; secondly it must be proved that the defender has not adopted that practice; and thirdly (and this is of crucial importance) it must be established that the course the doctor adopted is one which no professional man of ordinary skill would have taken if he had been acting with ordinary care.[14]

This attractively simple exposition of the law, however, conceals a hurdle at the outset. It may, in many cases, be possible to prove that there is a 'usual and normal practice' – this is particularly so if there are guidelines covering a procedure, a ploy which is increasingly used in UK legislation[15] and which might be seen as helpful to the plaintiff.[16] On the other hand, there will obviously be disagreement as to what is the appropriate course to follow in a number of medical areas. In some circumstances, the existence of two schools of thought may result in more than one option being open to a practitioner. If this is so, then what are the liability implications of choosing a course of action which a responsible body of opinion within the profession may well reject? Precisely this question arose in *Bolam*,[17] where the plaintiff had suffered fractures as a result of the administration of electro-convulsive therapy without an anaesthetic. At the time, there were two schools of thought on the subject of anaesthesia in such treatment, one holding the view that relaxant drugs should be used, the other being that this only increased the risk. In this case, the judge ruled that a doctor would not be negligent if he acted 'in accordance with the practice accepted by a responsible body of medical men

12 J Fleming *The Law of Torts* (7th edn, 1987) p 109; A Linden 'Custom in Negligence Law' [1968] Can Bar Jnl 151; R B M Howie 'The Standard of Care in Medical Negligence' [1983] JR 193; K Norrie 'Common Practice and the Standard of Care in Medical Negligence' [1985] JR 145.
13 1955 SC 200 at 206. The rigid simplicity of Lord Clyde's definition is defended in an anonymous article, 'Medical Negligence: *Hunter v Hanley* 35 Years On' 1990 SLT 325. *Hunter* was specifically approved by Lord Scarman in *Maynard v West Midlands Regional Health Authority* [1985] 1 All ER 635, [1984] 1 WLR 634. For recent discussion of custom in a medical context, see *E v Australian Red Cross Society* (1990-91) 99 ALR 601 at 647 et seq.
14 B Hurwitz 'Clinical Guidelines and the Law' (1995) 311 BMJ 1517.
15 These have not proved to be as productive of litigation as might be expected: A I Hyman, J A Brandenburg, S R Lipsitz et al 'Practice Guidelines and Malpractice Litigation: a Two-Way Street' (1995) 122 Ann In Med 450.
16 [1957] 2 All ER 118, [1957] 1 WLR 582.
17 [1985] 1 All ER 635, [1984] 1 WLR 634. *Maynard* was followed in *Hughes v Waltham Forest Health Authority* [1991] 2 Med LR 155, in which the court emphasised that the fact that a surgeon's decision was criticised by other surgeons did not amount *in itself* to an indication of negligence.

skilled in that particular art'. Negligence would not be inferred merely because there was a body of opinion which took a contrary view. Subsequent cases confirm this approach. In *Maynard v West Midlands Regional Health Authority* the trial judge had preferred an alternative medical approach to that which had been chosen by the defendant, notwithstanding the fact that this latter course found support in responsible medical opinion; both the Court of Appeal and the House of Lords confirmed that this was an unsatisfactory way of attributing negligence.[18] As a corollary to this, the plaintiff will have failed to discharge the burden of proof if the court is unable to select between two possible explanations.[19]

Bolam has been the object of sustained criticism from those who object to the implication that the medical profession itself determines what is an acceptable level of care. Critics have argued that doctors themselves should not determine whether conduct is negligent; this should be a matter for the courts. In fact, courts had on occasion made precisely this point themselves[20] and a number of judges in the English High Court had not been afraid to attack the traditional view. In *Smith v Tunbridge Wells Health Authority*,[1] for example, the judge applied *Bolam* in an action based on duty to warn of risk but, despite the existence of a competent body of opposing opinion, held that the decision not to do so was neither reasonable nor responsible. Nevertheless, there had been no high level judicial attack on the *Bolam* custom test in the Commonwealth until the High Court of Australia broke down the doors in the controversial 'consent' case of *Rogers v Whittaker*:[2]

In Australia, it has been accepted that the standard of care to be observed by a person with some special skill or competence is that of the ordinary skilled person exercising and professing that special skill. But that standard is not determined solely or even primarily by reference to the practice followed or supported by a responsible body of opinion in the relevant profession or trade.[3]

The High Court of Australia has a reputation for creativity; would the English courts, with their rather more conservative reputation, follow suit? An answer – even if a hesitant one – came in the decision in *Bolitho v Hackney Health Authority*,[4] a case regarded by some commentators as representing a significant nail in *Bolam's* coffin. *Bolitho* arose out of a failure on the part of a hospital doctor to examine and intubate a child experiencing respiratory distress. Expert evidence was led by the plaintiff to the effect that a reasonably competent doctor would have intubated in such circumstances. The defendant, however, had her own expert witnesses prepared to say that non-intubation was a clinically justifiable response. Causation was also at issue: the defendant argued that, had she attended the child, she would not have intubated her and her failure to attend would not, therefore, have made any difference

18 *Harrington v Essex Area Health Authority* (1984) Times, 14 November.
19 For a similar Canadian view of the relationship, see *Reibl v Hughes* (1980) 114 DLR (3d) 1. In *Sidaway v Governors of the Bethlem Royal Hospital and the Maudsley Hospital* [1985] AC 871 at 900, [1985] 1 All ER 643 at 663, HL Lord Bridge was of the opinion that disclosure of a particular risk might be so obviously necessary that no reasonable doctor would fail to do so.
20 [1994] 5 Med LR 334.
1 (1992) 109 ALR 625, [1993] 4 Med LR 79.
2 (1992) 109 ALR 625 at 631, [1993] 4 Med LR 79 at 82.
3 [1997] 4 All ER 771, (1977) 39 BMLR 1, HL.
4 [1997] 4 All ER 771 at 778, (1997) 39 BMLR 1 at 9.

to the outcome. It is not the causation issue, however, which lends significance to this decision. What makes *Bolitho* important is the court's departure from the certainties of *Bolam*. Under *Bolam*, a doctor will not be negligent if what he has done would be accepted by a responsible body of medical opinion. According to Lord Browne-Wilkinson in *Bolitho*, however, the court must be satisfied that the body of opinion in question rests on a logical basis:

> In particular, in cases involving, as they so often do, the weighing of risks against benefits, the judge before accepting a body of opinion as being responsible, reasonable or respectable, will need to be satisfied that, in forming their views, the experts have directed their minds to the question of comparative risks and benefits and have reached a defensible conclusion on the matter.[5]

This appears to be a clear rejection of the *Bolam* rule, but it must be read in the light of the strong caveat which Lord Browne-Wilkinson attached:

> In the vast majority of cases the fact that distinguished experts in the field are of a particular opinion will demonstrate the reasonableness of that opinion ... But if, in a rare case, it can be demonstrated that the professional opinion is not capable of withstanding logical analysis, the judge is entitled to hold that the body of opinion is not reasonable or responsible ... I emphasise that, in my view, it will very seldom be right for a judge to reach the conclusion that views genuinely held by a competent medical expert are unreasonable.

Bolitho undoubtedly removes the trump card which *Bolam* presented to the doctor but it is arguably undesirable to undermine the latter test beyond a certain point. *Bolam* provides some protection for the innovative or minority opinion. If this protection is removed, then the opinion which the cautious practitioner will wish to follow will be that which involves least risk. This may have an inhibiting effect on medical progress: after all, many advances in medicine have been made by those who have pursued an unconventional line of therapy. Such doctors may quite easily be regarded as negligent by a judge given to favouring conventional medical opinion.

There is, however, the decision in *De Freitas v O'Brien*,[6] which, rather than bolstering a conservative approach in assessing the acceptability of a body of opinion, gives comfort to the so-called 'super-specialist' who may undertake procedures which others might regard as being inappropriate or even too risky. In this case, a spinal surgeon – said to be one out of only 11 such specialists in the country – claimed that surgery he performed was in line with what his fellow spinal surgeons would have considered clinically justified. The plaintiffs claimed that, in fact, 'normal' orthopaedic surgeons would not have operated in the circumstances. The Court of Appeal confirmed that the *Bolam* test did not require that the responsible body of opinion be large, thus endorsing the acceptability of acting within limits defined by a sub-speciality. One criticism of the decision in *De Freitas* is that it licenses the taking of risks. Yet, the court clearly retains it ability to declare an opinion to be unreasonable, a power which is underlined in *Bolitho*.

5   [1997] 4 All ER 771 at 778, (1977) 39 BMLR 1 at 10.
6   (1995) 25 BMLR 51, [1995] 6 Med LR 108, CA.

The doctor has a duty to keep himself informed of major developments in practice but this duty obviously cannot extend to the requirement that he should know all there is to be known in a particular area of medicine. In the case of *Crawford v Board of Governors of Charing Cross Hospital*[7] the plaintiff had developed brachial palsy as a result of his arm being kept in a certain position during an operation. Six months prior to the operation an article had appeared in the *Lancet,* pointing out just this danger but the anaesthetist against whom negligence was being alleged had not read the article in question. The Court of Appeal eventually found in favour of the anaesthetist, Lord Denning stating that:

> it would, I think, be putting too high a burden on a medical man to say that he has to read every article appearing in the current medical press; and it would be quite wrong to suggest that a medical man is negligent because he does not at once put into operation the suggestions which some contributor or other might make in a medical journal. The time may come in a particular case when a new recommendation may be so well proved and so well known, and so well accepted that it should be adopted, but that was not so in this case.[8]

Failure to read a single article, it was said, may be excusable, while disregard of a series of warnings in the medical press could well be evidence of negligence. In view of the rapid progress currently being made in many areas of medicine, and in view of the amount of information confronting the average doctor, it is unreasonable to expect a doctor to be aware of every development in his field. At the same time, he must be reasonably up to date and must know of major developments. Hindsight is, of course, a harsh judge; yet, in a number of HIV-related cases, the courts have indicated that doctors could not have been expected to have known of a risk at a time when its significance was only just being established.[9] The practice of medicine has, however, become increasingly based on principles of scientific elucidation and report and the pressure on doctors to keep abreast of current developments is now considerable. It is no longer possible for a doctor to coast along on the basis of long experience; such an attitude has been firmly discredited not only in medicine but in many other professions and callings.

Innovative techniques

Resort to an innovative therapeutic technique may be appropriate in certain cases but should be made with caution. Whether or not the use of such a technique could amount to negligence would depend on the extent to which its use was considered justified in the case in question.[10] In assessing this, a court would consider evidence of previous trials of the treatment and would also, no doubt, take into consideration any dangers

7 (1953) Times, 8 December, CA.
8 Ibid.
9 *Dwan v Farquhar* [1988] Qd R 234. In this case the risk of HIV transmission through blood transfusions was discussed in an article published in March 1983; there was no negligence in respect of a transfusion given in May of the same year. See also *H v Royal Alexandra Hospital for Sick Children* [1990] 1 Med LR 297; Jones, *Medical Negligence* p 75.
10 See also chapter 18 below.

which it entailed. It is possible that a court would decline to endorse the use of an untried procedure if the patient was thereby exposed to considerable risk of damage. Other factors which might be taken into account would be the previous response of the patient to more conventional treatment, the seriousness of the patient's condition and the attitude of the patient himself towards the novelty and risk. The standard of care to be applied in such circumstances would be expected of a doctor who is reasonably competent in the provision of *such treatment*. A doctor should not, therefore, undertake procedures which are beyond his capacity.[11]

Misdiagnosis

A doctor is expected by the law to use the same degree of care in making a diagnosis that is required of him in all his dealings with his patients. A mistake in diagnosis will not be considered negligent if this standard of care is observed but will be treated as one of the non-culpable and inevitable hazards of practice.[12] Liability may, however, be imposed when a mistake in diagnosis is made because the doctor failed to take a proper medical history,[13] failed to conduct tests which a competent practitioner would have considered appropriate, or simply failed to diagnose a condition which would have been spotted by a competent practitioner. As a minimum, the doctor must examine his patient and pay adequate attention to the patient's medical notes and to what the patient tries to tell him.[14] Telephone diagnosis is hazardous, especially if the facts as related by the patient are such as to raise in the doctor's mind a suspicion that can only be allayed by proper clinical examination.[15]

One of the problems in determining whether there has been a mistake in diagnosis turns on deciding what investigative techniques need to be used in a particular case. Ordinary laboratory tests must be used if symptoms suggest their use[16] but elaborate and expensive investigative procedures would not be expected other than in complicated or puzzling cases. Failure to X-ray, for example, might well be negligence – but even that might not be so, particularly in the light of both public and professional awareness of the major contribution made by diagnostic radiography to the background radiation in developed countries. We can turn again to Lord Denning:[17]

11 In *Tomkins v Bexley Area Health Authority* [1993] 4 Med LR 235, the patient's lingual nerve was damaged in the course of an operation for the removal of wisdom teeth. Wilcox J observed: 'When fine movements and fine judgments are the order of the day, with surgery being conducted in the confined space of the mouth, a high degree of care is needed.'
12 In *Crivon v Barnet Group Hospital Management Committee* (1959) Times, 19 November, the judge said of misdiagnosis: 'Unfortunate as it was that there was a wrong diagnosis, it was one of those misadventures, one of those chances, that life holds for people.' Courts – and patients – might be less inclined to take such a view today.
13 *Chin Keow v Government of Malaysia* [1967] 1 WLR 813 (failure to inquire as to the possibility of penicillin allergy); *Coles v Reading and District Hospital Management Committee* (1963) 107 Sol Jo 115
14 *Giurelli v Girgis* (1980) 24 SASR 264, discussed in Jones, *Medical Negligence* p 117.
15 *Barnett v Chelsea and Kensington Hospital Management Committee* [1969] 1 QB 428, [1968] 1 All ER 1068; *Cavan v Wilcox* (1973) 44 DLR (3d) 42.
16 *Gardiner v Mounfield and Lincolnshire Area Health Authority* (1989) 5 BMLR 1, [1990] 1 Med LR 205.
17 In *Braisher v Harefield and Northwood Hospital Group Management Committee* (13 July 1966, unreported), CA. See H Jellie [1966] 2 Lancet 235.

In some of the earlier cases, the doctor has been criticised for not having taken X-rays with the result that they have sometimes been taken unnecessarily. This case shows that the Courts do not always find that there has been negligence because a patient has not had an X-ray; it depends upon the circumstances of each case.

Only some 1% of radiographs taken of the ankle in casualty departments demonstrate a fracture and, of these, a high proportion would have healed in the absence of identification. The approach to and the solution of such problems is by no means easy.[18]

Langley v Campbell[19] and *Tuffil v East Surrey Area Health Authority*[20] provide instances of successful actions against doctors on the basis of failure to diagnose correctly the nature of the patient's complaint. In *Langley*, the patient had returned from East Africa shortly before the development of symptoms. The general practitioner failed to diagnose malaria and negligence was found, the judge accepting the evidence of a relative who said that the family had suggested such a diagnosis to the doctor. In *Tuffil*, the patient had spent many years in a tropical climate; the doctor failed to diagnose amoebic dysentery, which proved fatal. This failure to diagnose was held to be negligence on the doctor's part.

An example of an unsuccessful claim of this sort is provided by *Whiteford v Hunter*.[1] The defendant in this case had diagnosed carcinoma of the bladder, a diagnosis which was subsequently found to be incorrect. An important question was whether the defendant should have used a cystoscope: he did not have one in his possession and it would have been difficult to obtain one. The court found that there was no negligence in the misdiagnosis, holding that the defendant had used methods which were in common use at the time.

In cases where a doctor is doubtful about a diagnosis, good practice may require that the patient be referred to a specialist for further consideration. It may be difficult for a doctor to know when to seek specialist advice – a fact explicitly acknowledged in the case of *Wilsher v Essex Area Health Authority*[2] – but in case of doubt, it is certainly safer for a doctor to refer the patient.[3]

Negligence in treatment

The most important distinction here is that to be made between a medical mistake which the law regards as excusable and a mistake which would amount to negligence. In the former case, the court accepts that ordinary human fallibility precludes liability while, in the latter, the conduct of the defendant is considered to have gone beyond the bounds of what is expected of the reasonably skilful or competent doctor.

The issue came before the courts in the case of *Whitehouse v Jordan*.[4] In this case negligence was alleged on the part of an obstetrician who, it was claimed, had pulled

18 B Jennett 'Some Medico-legal Aspects of the Management of Acute Head Injury' [1976] 1 BMJ 1383.
19 (1975) Times, 6 November.
20 (1978) Times, 15 March.
1 (1950) 94 Sol Jo 758, HL. Note 'at the time'; such an error would be indefensible today.
2 [1987] QB 730 at 777, [1986] 3 All ER 801 at 833.
3 This would be especially so where the doctor was unable to explain some aspect of the patient's condition: *Macdonald v York County Hospital Corpn* (1973) 41 DLR (3d) 321; affd (1976) 66 DLR (3d) 530 (S Ct Can).
4 [1981] 1 All ER 267, [1981] 1 WLR 246, HL.

too hard in a trial of forceps delivery and had thereby caused the plaintiff's head to become wedged, with consequent asphyxia and brain damage. The trial judge held that, although the decision to perform a trial of forceps was a reasonable one, the defendant had in fact pulled too hard and was therefore negligent. This initial finding of negligence was reversed in the Court of Appeal and, in a strongly worded judgment, Lord Denning emphasised that an error of judgment was not negligence.[5] Implicit in Lord Denning's remarks was a strong policy-based unwillingness to find negligence against doctors, an unwillingness which is to be seen in a number of the earlier judgments of the same judge.[6] When the matter came on appeal before the House of Lords, the views expressed by Lord Denning on the error of judgment question were rejected. An error of judgment could be negligence if it is an error which would not have been made by a reasonably competent professional man acting with ordinary care. As Lord Fraser pointed out:

> The true position is that an error of judgment may, or may not, be negligent; it depends on the nature of the error. If it is one that would not have been made by a reasonably competent professional man professing to have the standard and type of skill that the defendant holds himself out as having, and acting with ordinary care, then it is negligence. If, on the other hand, it is an error that such a man, acting with ordinary care, might have made, then it is not negligence.[7]

In the event, the House of Lords held that there had not, in any case, been sufficient evidence to justify the trial judge's finding of negligence.[8]

Gross medical mistakes will almost always result in a finding of negligence. Operating mistakes such as the removal of the wrong limb or the performance of an operation on the wrong patient are usually treated as indefensible and settled out of court; hence the paucity of decisions on such points.[9] Use of the wrong drug or, often with more serious consequences, the wrong gas during the course of an anaesthetic will frequently lead to the imposition of liability, and in some of these situations the res ipsa loquitur principle[10] may be applied.[11]

Many cases deal with items of operating equipment being left inside patients after surgery. In these, generally known as the 'swab cases', the allocation of liability is made according to the principle laid down in the locus classicus of the law on this point, the decision in *Mahon v Osborne*.[12] In this case, as in subsequent decisions, the courts have shown themselves unlikely to dictate to doctors in a hard and fast way the

5 [1980] 1 All ER 650 at 658, CA.
6 For further instances, see G Robertson *'Whitehouse v Jordan* – Medical Negligence Retired' (1981) 44 Med LR 457.
7 [1981] 1 All ER 267 at 281, (1980) 1 BMLR 14 at 30.
8 A misjudgment will also be negligent if it is in respect of something 'lying within the area where only a sound judgment measures up to the standard of reasonable competence expected': *Hendy v Milton Keynes Health Authority (No 2)* [1992] 3 Med LR 119 at 127, per Jowitt J.
9 An example is *Ibrahim (a minor) v Muhammad* (21 May 1984, unreported), QBD, in which a penis was partially amputated during circumcision; only the quantum of damages was in dispute.
10 See p 233 below.
11 *Strangeways-Lesmere v Clayton* [1936] 2 KB 11, [1936] 1 All ER 484; *Collins v Hertfordshire County Council* [1947] KB 598, [1947] 1 All ER 633; *Gray v Mid Herts Hospital Management Committee* (1974) 118 Sol Jo 501.
12 [1939] 2 KB 14, [1939] 1 All ER 535, CA.

exact procedure that should be used towards the end of an operation in order to ensure that no foreign bodies are left in the patient. At the same time, however, it is clear that the law requires that there should be some sort of set procedures adopted in order to minimise the possibility of this occurring. Overall responsibility to see that swabs and other items are not left in the patient rests on the surgeon; he is not entitled to delegate the matter altogether to a nurse. This point was emphasised in *Mahon* by Lord Goddard, who said:

> As it is the task of the surgeon to put swabs in, so it is his task to take them out and if the evidence is that he has not used a reasonable standard of care he cannot absolve himself, if a mistake has been made, by saying, 'I relied on the nurse'.[13]

In the later case of *Urry v Bierer*[14] the Court of Appeal confirmed that the patient was entitled to expect the surgeon to do all that was reasonably necessary to ensure that all packs were removed and that this duty required more than mere reliance on the nurse's count.

The problem of the novice

The degree of expertise possessed by a medical practitioner obviously depends to a considerable extent on his experience and the argument has been put forward that the standard of competence of a newly qualified doctor will be less than that expected of an experienced practitioner. Although this may be the day-to-day expectation, it is not that of the law. The strict application of the *Bolam* principle[15] would lead the courts to expect the doctor to show that degree of skill which would be shown by the reasonably competent professional. This is an objective standard and it is therefore irrelevant whether the doctor has qualified the day before or ten years before the alleged incident of negligence – it should make no difference to the way in which his conduct is assessed.

The problem was considered in the case of *Wilsher v Essex Area Health Authority*.[16] The plaintiff had been born prematurely and had been admitted to a specialised neonatal intensive care unit. Extra oxygen was administered by junior hospital doctors, who made an error in monitoring the arterial oxygen tension. It was claimed that this could have caused the virtually blinding condition of retrolental fibroplasia which occurred. It was argued by the defendants that the standard of care expected of the junior doctor was not the same as that of his experienced counterpart. Extensive use, it was said, had to be made of recently qualified medical and nursing staff and it was unavoidable that such staff should 'learn on the job'; it would be impossible for public medicine to operate properly without such arrangements and to do otherwise would, ultimately, not

---

13 [1939] 2 KB 14 at 47, [1939] 1 All ER 535 at 559. Scott LJ, however, qualified this by pointing out that it might be necessary to dispense with normal precautions in an emergency.
14 (1955) Times, 15 July, CA. For discussion of further swab (and forceps) cases see Jones, *Medical Negligence* p 140.
15 [1957] 2 All ER 118, [1957] 1 WLR 582. See p 224.
16 [1987] QB 730, [1986] 3 All ER 801. For discussion of this case, see I Kennedy and A Grubb *Medical Law* (2nd edn, 1994), p 412. A lower standard of care for novices was proposed in the Australian case of *Cook v Cook* (1986) 162 CLR 376, in which it was held that an inexperienced driver might not be judged on the same standard as others. In this case, however, there were special features in the relationship between the parties.

be in the best interests of patients. The judgments in the Court of Appeal are not free of ambiguity. The majority of the judges maintained that the public were entitled to expect a reasonable standard of competence in their medical attendants. The decision of Mustill LJ, however, makes it clear that he, at least, was prepared to define the standard of care according to the requirements of the post. An inexperienced doctor occupying a post in a unit which offered specialised services would, accordingly, need that degree of expertise expected of a reasonably competent person occupying that post; the defendant's actual hospital rank – house officer, registrar etc – would not be relevant in the determination.

Glidewell LJ also stressed the importance of applying an objective standard which would not take account of an individual doctor's inexperience. The apparent harshness of this conclusion was, nevertheless, mitigated by his suggestion that the standard of care is very likely to be met if the novice seeks advice or consults with his more experienced colleagues when appropriate. Even so, this apparently simple solution does not answer the question which many juniors may ask – how am I to be so experienced as to know when I should be uncertain? And, if, I cannot tell this, am I to ask my seniors before I make any important decision? This question effectively forces us back to accepting a standard of care test which is based on the doctor of similar experience irrespective of the post in which he operates. Conversely, however, an experienced doctor occupying a junior post would be judged according to his actual knowledge rather than by the lower standard of the reasonably competent occupant of that post – the rationale being that, by reason of his superior expertise, he would be more able to foresee the damage likely to arise from any negligent acts or omissions.[17] It is important to bear in mind that *Wilsher* was very much concerned with specialist units and there is no certainty that the judgments are applicable, say, to the general practitioner in so far as delegation of responsibility, hierarchical organisation and the like are particular features of hospital practice.

Hospital authorities cannot, of course, rely too much upon junior employees; the principles of vicarious liability will, by themselves, prevent this. As Lord Denning said in *Jones v Manchester Corpn*:

> It would be in the highest degree unjust that the hospital board, by getting inexperienced doctors to perform their duties for them, without adequate supervision, should be able to throw all the responsibility on to those doctors as if they were fully experienced practitioners.[18]

Delegation of responsibility to another may, however, amount to negligence in certain circumstances. A consultant could be negligent were he to delegate responsibility to a junior in the knowledge that the junior was incapable of performing his duties properly.

A junior to whom responsibility has been delegated must carry out his duties as instructed by his superior in order to avoid liability. If he chooses to depart from specific instructions, he will be placing himself in a risky position in the event of anything going wrong.[19] At the same time, there may be circumstances in which he

17 See *Wimpey Construction UK Ltd v Poole* [1984] 2 Lloyd's Rep 499.
18 [1952] 2 QB 852 at 871, [1952] 2 All ER 125 at 133, CA.
19 *Junor v Inverness Hospital Board of Management and McNicol* (1959) Times, 26 March, HL.

is entitled to depart from instructions; obedience to manifestly wrong instructions might, itself, be construed as negligence in some cases.

Protecting patients from themselves

In certain circumstances, it is part of the duty of care of doctors and nurses to predict that patients may damage themselves as a result of their medical condition. The extent of the duty to safeguard against such damage is problematical and the decisions have not all gone the same way. In *Selfe v Ilford and District Hospital Management Committee*,[20] the plaintiff had been admitted to hospital after a drug overdose. Although he had known suicidal tendencies, he was not kept under constant observation and climbed on to the hospital roof while the two nurses on duty were out of the ward; he fell and was injured. Damages of £19,000 were awarded against the hospital.

By contrast, the plaintiff in *Thorne v Northern Group Hospital Management Committee*[1] failed to win an award of damages for the death of his wife who had left a hospital in suicidal mood. In this case, the patient had slipped out of the hospital when the nurses' backs were turned, returned home and gassed herself. The court took the view that, although the degree of supervision which a hospital should exercise in relation to patients with known suicidal tendencies is higher than that to be exercised over other patients, they could not be kept under constant supervision by hospital staff.

In *Hyde v Tameside Area Health Authority*[2] the Court of Appeal overturned a High Court award of substantial damages to a plaintiff who, believing he had cancer, made a suicide attempt in hospital. Not only did the court take the view that there had been no breach of duty on the part of the defendants, but Lord Denning stressed in his judgment that there were strong policy grounds why damages should not be awarded in respect of attempted suicide. Nowadays, that would probably be a minority view.

In *Kirkham v Chief Constable of Greater Manchester*[3] an appeal to the ex turpi causa principle – which may exclude liability where the plaintiff's act is in some way immoral – was rejected. It was held that the award of damages in respect of a suicidal death caused no affront to the public conscience – at least when the mind of the suicide was in some way unbalanced.

Res ipsa loquitur

Because it may be difficult in many personal injury actions to establish negligence on the part of the defendant, plaintiffs occasionally have recourse to the doctrine of res ipsa loquitur. This doctrine does not shift the onus of proof to the defendant, as is sometimes suggested; what it does achieve is to give rise to an inference of negligence on the

---

20 (1970) 114 Sol Jo 935.
 1 (1964) 108 Sol Jo 484. A similar decision was taken in the Scottish case *Rolland v Lothian Health Board* (1981) unreported, OH, per Lord Ross.
 2 [1981] CLY 1854, CA; (1986) 2 PN 26, CA.
 3 [1989] 3 All ER 882; affd [1990] 2 QB 283.

defendant's part.[4] If the defendant cannot then rebut this inference of negligence, the plaintiff will have established his case. It follows from this that it is considerably easier for the plaintiff to succeed in his claim when res ipsa loquitur applies.

The doctrine is most useful in cases where damage has occurred in an incident involving machinery or in the context of damage suffered while the plaintiff was involved in some sort of complex process. It applies only where the plaintiff is unable to identify the precise nature of the negligence which caused his injury and where no explanation of the way in which the injury came to be inflicted has been offered by the defendant. The injury itself must be of such a kind as 'does not normally happen' in the circumstances unless there is negligence. Thus, in a case of neurological damage following difficult aortography,[5] the plea of res ipsa loquitur was rejected on the grounds that the injury sustained was of a kind recognised as an inherent risk of the procedure.

The doctrine's application in medical cases may still be particularly apt because of the difficulty that the ordinary plaintiff sometimes experiences in unravelling the cause of an injury sustained during technical procedures of which he has little understanding; indeed, he may well have been unconscious at the relevant time. It may also be seen as a potential corrective to the tendency of the medical profession to 'close ranks' when one of their number is accused of negligence. However, it is possibly of less importance in a climate of increasing openness – or, in today's usage, transparency. It must also be borne in mind that the courts are in general reluctant to apply the res ipsa loquitur principle and that this is certainly evident in medical negligence cases. As Megaw LJ said:

> [if one were to accept the view that negligence was inevitably proved if something went wrong and it was unexplained], few dentists, doctors and surgeons, however competent, conscientious and careful they might be, would avoid the totally unjustified and unfair stigma of professional negligence probably several times in the course of their careers.[6]

An unsuccessful attempt to raise the doctrine of res ipsa loquitur was made in *Ludlow v Swindon Health Authority*,[7] in which it was stressed that the plaintiff had to establish facts which, if unexplained, would give rise to an inference of negligence. In this case the plaintiff claimed to have regained consciousness during a caesarian section operation and to have experienced intense pain. She failed, however, to establish that the pain arose at a stage during which halothane should have been administered; there was, accordingly, no inference of negligence in the administration of the anaesthetic. Nevertheless, there are cases where the injuries sustained by the patient are of such a nature that there is an inescapable inference of negligence. In *Glass v Cambridge Area Health Authority*[8] the patient suffered brain damage as a

---

4 There has been some debate as to the precise effect of res ipsa loquitur, but the current weight of opinion favours the view outlined here: see *Ng Chun Pui v Lee Chuen Tat* [1988] RTR 298, PC. For discussion, see J Fleming *The Law of Torts* (8th edn, 1992) p 322; D Giesen *International Medical Malpractice Law* (1988) p 515.
5 *O'Malley-Williams v Board of Governors of the National Hospital for Nervous Diseases* (1975) unreported, cited in [1975] 1 BMJ 635.
6 *Fletcher v Bench* (1973) unreported, CA cited in [1973] 4 BMJ 117.
7 [1989] 1 Med LR 104.
8 [1995] 6 Med LR 91.

result of suffering a heart attack under a general anaesthetic. The court held that this was not an event which normally would be expected to happen in the circumstances and that the onus therefore transferred to the defendant to provide an explanation of the event which was consistent with the absence of negligence. The Canadian case of *MacDonald v York County Hospital Corpn*[9] provides a further example. In this case, the plaintiff was admitted to hospital for treatment of a fractured ankle and left with an amputated leg. All the requirements of res ipsa loquitur were present: a leg is not usually lost in such circumstances unless there is negligence; the plaintiff was not able to explain what had happened, nor was the defendant; and the plaintiff had identified the doctor whose negligence must have been responsible for the injury.

MacDonald followed the pattern of the early English case of *Cassidy v Ministry of Health*,[10] in which the plaintiff went into hospital for an operation to remedy Dupuytren's contracture of two fingers and came out with four stiff fingers. Denning LJ (as he then was) expressed the view that the plaintiff was quite entitled to say:

> I went into hospital to be cured of two stiff fingers. I have come out with four stiff fingers and my hand is useless. That should not have happened if due care had been used. Explain it if you can.[11]

Although res ipsa loquitur will not be applied automatically, there are several 'swab cases' – as discussed above – in which it has been successfully invoked. In *Mahon v Osborne*,[12] for example, the court held that the patient could know nothing about swab procedures in the operating theatre and it was therefore for the surgeon to show that he exercised due care to ensure that the swabs were not left there.

Causation

As if the problems of fault were not enough, it will do the plaintiff no good to establish negligence on the part of a defendant doctor unless he is able to prove that the damage he has suffered was caused by that negligence. This may be particularly difficult in the context of medicine, where there may be a variety of possible independent explanations for the occurrence of a condition. Thus, if a person brings an action for 'nervous shock', it may well be arguable that the symptoms complained of are those of a psychiatric state which existed before the claimed precipitating event. Some assistance in this respect was provided to the plaintiff through the Scottish case of *McGhee v National Coal Board*,[13] in which it was held that liability will be imposed

9 [1972] 28 DLR (3d) 521.
10 [1951] 2 KB 343, [1951] 1 All ER 574, CA.
11 [1951] 2 KB 343 at 365, [1951] 1 All ER 574 at 588. Other medical cases in which res ipsa loquitur has applied include: *Saunders v Leeds Western Health Authority* (1984) 129 Sol Jo 225; *Cavan v Wilcox* (1973) 44 DLR (3d) 42 and *Holmes v Board of Hospital Trustees of the City of London* (1977) 81 DLR (3d) 67.
12 [1939] 2 KB 14, [1939] 1 All ER 535, CA.
13 [1972] 3 All ER 1008, [1973] 1 WLR 1.

if it can be established that the negligence of the defender materially increased the risk of the plaintiff being damaged in the way in question.[14]

This principle was endorsed in *Clark v MacLennan*,[15] in which it was held that, where there was a precaution which could have been taken to avoid the precise injury which occurred, the onus was then upon the defendant to establish that his failure to take this precaution did not cause the plaintiff's injury. This 'recognised risk avoidance' concept brings us very close to that of res ipsa loquitur which, as we have seen, the courts are reluctant to apply. This antipathy was demonstrated in the very comparable case of *Ashcroft v Mersey Regional Health Authority*,[16] which was heard at much the same time as *Clark*. Here, the plaintiff underwent a relatively straightforward and commonplace operation to remove granulation tissue – the result of chronic infection – from the ear; she sustained a severe paralysis of the facial nerve. Opinion was divided as to whether the surgeon had negligently pulled too hard on the nerve or whether the injury was an unfortunate accident. In the result, Kilner Brown J was, with obvious reluctance, unable to shift the burden of proof and found that, on a balance of probabilities, there was no negligence. The correctness of this view was later confirmed in *Wilsher*,[17] where the House of Lords went so far as to reverse the opinion of the Court of Appeal and to order a retrial on the grounds that the coincidence of a breach of duty and injury could not, of itself, give rise to a presumption that the injury was so caused: 'Whether we like it or not, the law . . . requires proof of fault causing damage as the basis of liability in tort.'[18]

The difficulty for the plaintiff in *Wilsher* lay in the fact there were five possible causes for the condition with which he was afflicted. One of these was medical negligence but it could not be established that this *possible* cause actually made a material contribution to the injury. It might have done so, but this fact still required to be proved by the plaintiff. The House of Lords discarded the notion that *McGhee v National Coal Board*[19] constituted an authority for transferring the onus of proof to the defendant. *McGhee* was to be distinguished from *Wilsher* in that there were several agents which could have caused the injury in the latter but only one in the former.[20] This provided an exceptional inference as to cause and, as a result, *McGhee* positively affirmed that the onus of proving causation lies on the pursuer or plaintiff.

A similar point as to proof of causation was made in the lengthy and complicated litigation over pertussis vaccination. In *Loveday*[1] the court held that establishing a mere chance that the vaccine might cause brain damage in children did not discharge the obligation on the plaintiff. It is to be noted, parenthetically, that the

---

14 [1972] 3 All ER 1008 at 1011, per Lord Reid, [1973] 1 WLR 1 at 4, per Lord Reid.
15 [1983] 1 All ER 416.
16 [1983] 2 All ER 245.
17 *Wilsher v Essex Area Health Authority* [1988] AC 1074, [1988] 1 All ER 871, HL. For a useful summary of the complicated post-*Wilsher* landscape, see Jones, *Medical Negligence* p 169.
18 [1988] AC 1074 at 1092, [1988] 1 All ER 871 at 883, per Lord Bridge.
19 [1972] 3 All ER 1008, [1973] 1 WLR 1.
20 See the dissenting opinion of Browne-Wilkinson V-C in *Wilsher v Essex Area Health Authority* [1987] QB 730 at 779, [1986] 3 All ER 801 at 834. For discussion of the issue, see J Fleming 'Probabilistic Causation in the Tort Law' (1989) 68 Can BR 661.
 1 *Loveday v Renton* [1990] 1 Med LR 117.

decision in *Loveday* was not the last word on pertussis vaccine; in *Best v Wellcome Foundation Ltd*,[2] the Supreme Court in Ireland awarded £2.75m to a young man who had suffered brain damage after its administration. The ground for the award was, however, that the particular batch of vaccine used was sub-standard and should not have been released on the market – future litigants will still have to prove that, on the balance of probabilities, their injuries were caused by the vaccine per se.

In a rather similar causation problem, both the Court of Session and the House of Lords have declared that a judge was not entitled to propound his own theory of a causative link between an overdose of penicillin and deafness; the weight of the evidence in *Kay* was that the causative factor was the meningitis for which the penicillin had been prescribed.[3]

An interesting variation on the causation theme was reintroduced in *Hotson*.[4] Here, the plaintiff was, admittedly, negligently treated following traumatic avulsion of the head of the femur and developed avascular necrosis. However, there was a 75% chance that this lesion would develop even in the event of correct diagnosis and treatment. The trial judge concluded that the matter was simply one of quantification of damages and the Court of Appeal upheld the view that the mistreatment had denied the plaintiff a 25% chance of a good recovery; damages were awarded and reduced accordingly. The House of Lords, however, declined to measure statistical chances[5] and concluded that it was the original injury which caused the avascular necrosis. Lord MacKay expressed the true situation:

> . . . the probable effect of delay in treatment was determined by the state of facts existing when the plaintiff was first presented at the hospital . . . If insufficient blood vessels were left intact by the fall, he had no prospect of avoiding complete avascular necrosis whereas if sufficient blood vessels were left intact . . . he would not have suffered the avascular necrosis.[6]

or, as put in *The Times* transcript,[7] what was meant by a chance was that if 100 people had suffered the same injury, 75 would have developed avascular necrosis and 25 would not. Thus, on the balance of probabilities, the plaintiff fell into the larger group – there being no evidence that he was one of the fortunate 25% who could benefit from treatment – and, consequently, his injury could not be attributed to the negligence of the defendants. It would be different if 51% of people sustaining the sort of injury which the plaintiff suffered could be treated with, say, a 20% chance of success. Then,

2   Irish Supreme Court, 3 June 1992: reported by D Brahamas 'Court Award for Pertussis Brain Damage' (1993) 341 Lancet 1338; C Dyer 'Man Awarded damages after Pertussis Vaccination' (1993) 306 BMJ 1365.
3   *Kay's Tutor v Ayrshire and Arran Health Board* [1987] 2 All ER 417, 1987 SLT 577, HL.
4   *Hotson v East Berkshire Area Health Authority* [1987] AC 750, [1987] 2 All ER 909, HL. A similar claim was dismissed in the early Scottish case of *Kenyon v Bell* 1953 SC 125. For discussion, see D T Price 'Causation – The Lords' "Lost Chance"' (1989) 33 ICLQ 735.
5   Statistical chances and personal chances are quite different matters: T Hill 'A Lost Chance for Compensation in the Tort of Negligence by the House of Lords' (1991) 54 MLR 511. The author regrets the fact that the House of Lords appears to leave open the possibility of future successful actions based on a *personal* loss of chance.
6   [1987] AC 750 at 785, [1987] 2 All ER 909 at 915.
7   (1987) Times, 6 July.

on the balance of probabilities, the plaintiff would have fallen into that group of 51%, and, if a hospital negligently failed to offer him the treatment, he would have personally lost that 20% chance of a successful outcome. Whether that 20% loss is something which should attract compensation in the form of 20% damages is left open by the decision in *Hotson*.

Damages for a loss of chance have been awarded in the United States. In *Falcon v Memorial Hospital*,[8] the Supreme Court of Michigan awarded damages for the wrongful death of a woman who would have had a 37.5% chance of survival had she been treated effectively. The court held that the physician's inaction had elided any chance of survival and that the appropriate measure of damages was equal to the chance of survival multiplied by the total damages available for wrongful death.

The increased attention paid in recent years to what might loosely be termed 'psychosomatic' diseases has led to some interesting developments in the field of causation. Repetitive strain injury (RSI) – now more specifically referred to as Prescribed Disease A4[9] – is one such condition. Medical opinion differs as to whether it is organic or psychiatric in origin or whether it results from a combination of causes. Thus, it is not surprising that litigation has led to some confusing results – ranging from large out of court settlements[10] to judicial comments such as: '[I agree] that RSI is, in reality, meaningless . . . Its use by doctors can only serve to confuse.'[11] In what is probably the most important judicial airing of the subject,[12] the House of Lords overturned the Court of Appeal in holding that the fact that the trial judge was unwilling to accept that the plaintiff's condition was simply that of conversion hysteria was not, of itself, sufficient ground to sustain her claim in negligence; it was essential to the success of her case that she proved that her condition had been caused by repetitive movements while typing. If it was impossible to decide what was the cause of the condition from the medical evidence alone, the court was entitled to consider all the other evidence in concluding that the plaintiff had failed to prove her case.

Other conditions that raise similar problems include post-traumatic stress disorder,[13] myalgic encephalomyelitis[14] and the purely psychiatric condition of so-called 'nervous shock'.[15] We believe that a full discussion of the law in this area, a proportion of which is based on policy considerations, is beyond the scope of a book of this size – and it is probable that, if and when the next edition appears, a major topic for discussion under this heading will be 'Gulf War Syndrome'.

---

8 (1990) 462 NW 2d 44 (Mich). See also the earlier case of *Herskovits v Group Health Co-operative of Puget Sound* 664 P 2d 474 (Wash 1983), in which the court allowed a claim for damages in respect of a cancer patient's loss of a 14% chance of survival for more than five years.
9 Social Security (Industrial Injuries) (Prescribed Diseases) Regulations 1985, SI 1985/967, Sch 1, Pt 1. There is nothing to stop an employee suing his employers in negligence despite the fact that the condition sustained is recognised as a work hazard (for which see Social Security Contributions and Benefits Act 1992, s 108(2)).
10 'Revenue to Pay £79,000 to RSI Victim' (1994) *Scotsman* 19 January, p 5.
11 *Mughal v Reuters Ltd* (1993) 16 BMLR 127 at 140, per Prosser J.
12 *Pickford v Imperial Chemical Industries plc* [1998] 3 All ER 462, [1998] 1 WLR 1189.
13 *Frost v Chief Constable of South Yorkshire Police* [1997] 1 All ER 540, (1996) 33 BMLR 108, CA.
14 *Page v Smith* [1995] 2 All ER 736, (1995) 28 BMLR 133, HL.
15 *Alcock v Chief Constable of South Yorkshire Police* [1992] 1 AC 310, (1991) 8 BMLR 37.

Injuries caused by medical products

The extensive use of drugs and other medical products in modern medical practice, coupled with the wide variety of available substances and devices, inevitably leads to a high incidence of injuries for which they are held responsible. The number of persons affected will be small in some instances due to the speedy detection of the dangers and the rapid withdrawal of the products concerned. In others, the scale of the claims may be astronomic, an example being the series of actions brought against manufacturers of intrauterine devices.[16] For these reasons, the question of compensation becomes an intensely political issue, as it has done in relation to HIV-contaminated blood and certain tranquillisers.

Compensation for injury caused by products is now largely regulated in the United Kingdom by the Consumer Protection Act 1987. This derives from the European directive on product liability,[17] the aim of which was to create strict liability for most injuries which were caused by defective products; this policy had long been advocated by commentators on compensation for personal injury. Under the terms of the Act, strict liability is borne primarily by the manufacturer of a defective product, although the suppliers will also be held liable if they cannot identify the manufacturer. Products include the components and raw materials from which a product is made and, in certain circumstances, a doctor may be a supplier of a drug. Despite strong protests from the industry, pharmaceutical products are not exempted from the system of strict liability. A drug will now be regarded as defective if it fails to measure up to that degree of safety which 'persons generally are entitled to expect' (s 3(1)).

In some circumstances, the manufacturer will be able to call on a development risk – or, in American terms, a 'state of the art' – defence. Section 4(1)(e) of the Act provides that the manufacturer will not be liable if he can show:

> that the state of scientific and technical knowledge at the relevant time was not such that a producer of products of the same description as the product in question might be expected to have discovered the defect if it had existed in his products while they were under his control.

The aim of this defence is to relieve manufacturers of liability if the existence of a defect was undiscoverable at the time.[18] Expert evidence will be important in deciding whether a manufacturer has attained this goal. The Act does not require the highest possible standards; it is suggested, for example, that a manufacturer would not reasonably be expected to know of and to act on an obscure report in a foreign language.

Is a manufacturer entitled to market a drug which will be beneficial to many but which he knows may cause harm to a minority? The traditional approach to this issue is by way of balancing the prospective benefit and risk. In general, sensitive users will have no claim to compensation if it is in the public interest that the drug should be available; much would then depend upon the presentation of the product and the nature of any warnings given. In this respect, s 3(2)(b) of the 1987 Act stipulates that,

---

16 G R Thornton 'Intrauterine Devices: Malpractice and Product Liability' (1986) 14 Law Med Hlth Care 4.
17 Council Directive 85/374/EEC.
18 C Newdick 'The Development Risk Defence of the Consumer Protection Act 1987' (1988) 47 CLJ 455. See also C J Stolker 'Objections to the Development Risk Defence' (1990) 9 Med Law 783.

in assessing what constitutes defect, consideration must be given to what might reasonably be expected to be done with, or in relation to, the product. Thus, for example, it might reasonably be expected that children could gain access to drugs intended for adult use only. It is, however, unlikely that, say, suicide could be reasonably anticipated by the manufacturer.

The litigation relating to transmission of HIV infection through contaminated blood products has been taken in breach of a statutory duty under the National Health Service Act 1977 and in negligence;[19] nevertheless, the question remains as to whether strict liability now applies to human blood and its derivatives. While, for example, concentrated Factor VIII would clearly be a pharmacological product, it is less easy to see unmodified blood as such. A reading of the 1987 Act, ss 1(2) and 45(1), however, indicates firmly that blood would be a substance included within its scope – blood being a naturally occurring substance which has not been manufactured but which has been won or abstracted.[20] In terms of the Act, the Blood Transfusion Service would normally be the producer of the 'product' but the hospital, or even the individual doctor, responsible for its transfusion would be the supplier. The application of strict liability to blood transfusion has, inevitably, been considered at greatest length in the United States, where the principle has been applied in some courts but where, in general, transfusion has been looked upon rather as the provision of a service than of a product,[1] thereby attracting potential actions in negligence – which would, of course, still be available outside the Act in the United Kingdom.[2] Clark[3] says that the majority of the United States have legislated to the effect that the supply of human blood is a service rather than a sale; the introduction of an element of 'sale' perhaps makes the distinction more urgent there than it is in the United Kingdom.

The major concern for the doctor or the pharmacist as to strict liability laws lies in the need to ensure that the manufacturer can be adequately identified in order to avoid claims being made against himself. This might entail elaborate bureaucratic procedures and the fear has been expressed it could lead to further development of the practice of defensive medicine. An interesting American twist is shown in *Oskenholt v Lederle Laboratories*,[4] where a doctor, having been successfully sued for prescribing a faulty drug, himself brought an action against the manufacturers for damage to his professional reputation – a fair example of the worm turning!

Criminal negligence

Medical negligence is predominantly a civil matter, but a spate of prosecutions in the early 1990s served to remind doctors that the loss of a patient may sometimes lead to criminal prosecution. Such prosecutions used to be rare; their increase points to

19 D Brahams 'Confidential Documents in HIV/Haemophilia Litigation' (1990) 336 Lancet 805.
20 Such commentators as we have been able to find agree with this analysis in general. See, in particular, A M Clark *Product Liability* (1989) ch 3. C Dyer 'Strict Liability Arrives: Significance for Doctors' (1988) 296 BMJ 635 is less certain, as is Jones, *Medical Negligence* p 292, n 4.
1 Eg *Coffee v Cutter Biological* 809 F 2d 191 (1987).
2 The supply of HIV-infected blood was the subject of common law-based litigation in the Australian case of *H v Royal Alexandra Hospital for Children* [1990] 1 Med LR 297.
3 *Product Liability* p 62.
4 656 P 2d 293 (Ore 1982).

heightened interest in the external regulation of medicine and to a diminution in the professional immunity which doctors may previously have enjoyed. In some respects, this process is healthy; in others, it is a matter for regret. The principle that doctors, and indeed all professionals, should be accountable for their failures is entirely acceptable; what is more dubious is that the criminal law, and particularly manslaughter prosecutions, should be the instrument chosen to perform that task. We believe that the concept of criminal liability for negligence involving a breach of duty is, at best, tenuous and that the minimum threshold for the invocation of criminal sanctions should be recklessness. We explore the implications of this below.

Criminal liability for negligence is effectively limited to prosecutions for manslaughter. The level of negligence which the doctor must have manifested is considerably above that at which civil liability may be incurred. Traditionally it has been defined as 'gross' or 'extreme' negligence and sometimes, somewhat tautologically, as 'criminal negligence'; the essential concern is that it surpasses the civil test, as was stressed in *R v Bateman*:

> In order to establish criminal liability, the facts must be such that . . . the negligence of the accused went beyond a mere matter of compensation between subjects and showed such disregard for the life and safety of others as to amount to a crime against the State and conduct deserving punishment.[5]

This, of course, does not answer the question of when conduct goes beyond the compensation level but it is probably impossible to be much more specific. It is clear that what is required is conduct which gives rise to a sense of outrage – or to the conclusion that the accused deserves *punishment* for what he did. Such a conclusion, though, is likely to be articulated in terms of a lack of regard for the patient's welfare or safety – and therein lies the problem. If criminal negligence is defined in terms of a deliberate exposure of the patient to some form of risk, then we are in the realms of recklessness rather than negligence.[6] It is one thing to punish a person for subjective recklessness; it is quite another to punish for objective negligence. In the former case the accused has effectively said: 'I knew of the risk of harm but did not care'; in the latter, he may have been quite unaware of any risk at all – the damage caused may have been the result of incompetence or ignorance, neither of which qualities necessarily deserve punishment.

The conduct involved in the relevant cases has ranged from, at one extreme, an apparent indifference with all the features of recklessness to mere incompetence at the other. In *Saha and Salim*,[7] two doctors administered an astonishing cocktail of drugs to a remand prisoner who died as a result. They were both convicted and sentenced to a term of imprisonment. By contrast, the conviction of two young and relatively inexperienced doctors for the manslaughter of a patient to whom they had incorrectly administered cytotoxic drugs was greeted with concern in medical circles and was,

5 [1925] All ER Rep 45 at 48, 19 Cr App Rep 8 at 11, per Lord Hewart LCJ.
6 A difficulty which the courts have acknowledged in those decisions where gross negligence manslaughter appears to have been replaced by reckless manslaughter: *R v Seymour* (1983) 76 Cr App Rep 211; *Kong Cheuk Kwan v R* (1985) 82 Cr App Rep 18.
7 (1992, unreported); see D Brahams 'Death of Remand Prisoner' (1992) 340 Lancet 1462.

in due course, quashed by the Court of Appeal.[8] Somewhere in between lies the case of *R v Adomako*,[9] in which an anaesthetist failed to notice the fact that his patient was in distress when this would have been glaringly obvious to any competent practitioner. There was conflicting evidence on the question of whether the accused was out of the theatre at the time; if he had been, and if there had been a failure on his part to make adequate arrangements for the monitoring of the patient, then that would surely have amounted to a degree of recklessness which was strongly deserving of punishment. If, however, he was merely incompetent, it might be more difficult to argue for his conviction of manslaughter – although, undoubtedly, professional sanctions would still be needed. These cases were heard together on appeal,[10] when it was held that the proper test in manslaughter cases based on breach of duty was that of gross negligence rather than recklessness.[11] In contrast to that of the two young doctors, Dr Adomako's appeal failed. He did, however, carry his appeal to the House of Lords where his conviction was upheld.[12] It was further clarified that, in cases of manslaughter by criminal negligence involving a breach of duty, it was a sufficient direction to the jury to adopt the gross negligence test set out by the Court of Appeal; it was not necessary to define recklessness, although it was open to the judge to use the word 'reckless' in its ordinary meaning as part of his exposition of the law.

Thus, as the criminal law now stands, a grossly incompetent doctor is liable to conviction despite the fact that there is no element of subjective wrongdoing on his part. This might well be considered inappropriate.[13] The alternative view is that the law should protect the public and that prosecution represents one way of controlling those who cannot meet minimal professional standards. Surely, however, the law should, at the same time, recognise the difference between the reckless and the inadequate practitioner. There is, indeed, some evidence that the House of Lords was prepared to concede the inherent dangers of the gross negligence test. Thus, we have Lord MacKay commending the words of the trial judge in *R v Adomako*:

> You should only convict a doctor of causing death by negligence if you think he did something which *no reasonably skilled* doctor should have done. (Emphasis added)[14]

which is a very severe definition.

But are the criminal courts the appropriate guardians of conditions in the operating theatre? The General Medical Council has been widely criticised in the past for its ineffective control of clinical standards. It now appears prepared to use its newly erupted teeth.[15] It could well be that the better route to the protection of the public from

8 *R v Prentice, R v Adomako* [1993] 4 All ER 935 (1993) 15 BMLR 13, sub nom *R v Holloway, R v Adomako, R v Prentice and Sulman* [1993] 4 Med LR 304. See C Dyer 'Manslaughter Verdict Quashed on Junior Doctors' (1993) 306 BMJ 1432.
9 [1991] 5 Med LR 277.
10 (1993) 15 BMLR 13, [1993] 4 Med LR 304.
11 (1993) 15 BMLR 13 at 21, [1993] 4 Med LR 304 at 310, per Lord Taylor, following *Andrews v DPP* [1937] AC 576, [1937] 2 All ER 552, HL and *R v Stone and Dobinson* [1977] QB 354, [1977] 2 All ER 341.
12 *R v Adomako* [1995] 1 AC 171, (1994) 19 BMLR 56, HL.
13 For expansion of this argument, see A McCall Smith 'Criminal Negligence and the Incompetent Doctor' (1993)1 Med L Rev 336.
14 (1994) 19 BMLR 56 at 64-65.
15 See p 217 above.

clinical error lies along the development of the investigative and restrictive powers of the GMC and the Royal Colleges, leaving only the subjective wrongdoer where the belongs – in the criminal courts.

If concern is felt in the United Kingdom over the prosecution of, often junior, doctors for causing of the deaths of patients, it was considerably multiplied in New Zealand where, under the Crimes Act 1961, criminal liability was imposed on a doctor who merely failed to show 'reasonable knowledge, skill and care' in the treatment of his patients. This extraordinarily low threshold of liability was applied in *R v Yogasakaran*[16] and confirmed on appeal to the Privy Council.[17] In this case, an anaesthetist had not checked the label on an ampoule of a drug which he injected into a patient. The ampoule was of the appropriate shape and size and was in the right place on the trolley but, for some reason unconnected with the anaesthetist, contained the wrong drug. Presumably, the same result would have been achieved if the anaesthetist had, in fact, read the label but had read it wrongly. Such a common mistake can hardly be seen as justification for convicting a person of a crime which carries with it a very deal of moral opprobrium – it would surely be better investigated by the Medical Practitioners' Disciplinary Committee. Concerted medical opposition to the use of the criminal law in this fashion led, in fact, to a government-sponsored amendment to the Crimes Act, which required that there should be a substantial departure from the normally-expected levels of care before liability for manslaughter could be imposed.[18] This effectively raised the standard in New Zealand to the gross negligence standard applied elsewhere. Most of the New Zealand doctors or nurses who were found guilty under the old legislation would not be convicted under the new standard.

---

16 [1990] 1 NZLR 399.
17 See D B Collins 'New Zealand's Medical Manslaughter' (1992) Med Law 221.
18 On the background, see A Merry and A McCall Smith 'Medical accountability and the criminal law' (1996) Hlth Care Anal, and, by the same authors, 'Medical Manslaughter' (1997) Med J Austral 342.

10 Consent to treatment

The paternalist might argue that there are many examples in medical practice of situations in which treatment is justified in the teeth of the patient's objection. Arguing from such a position – that the patient may be unable to appreciate that a particular treatment is in his best interest – the decision of the doctor to impose it is seen as serving the patient's interest in spite of what may turn out to be short-term objections. This, a paternalist would hold, cannot be wrong. Good health and physical comfort are preferable to ill health and physical discomfort: a patient will thus be happier treated than untreated.

Such arguments can, however, be sustained only in very limited conditions, such as when the patient is in an irrational state because of impaired or disturbed consciousness. Restraining a delirious patient is justifiable paternalism, as is the action of clearing the air passages of one who is about to choke to death. The intervention is justified by the conviction that this is what the patient would want, were he fully rational, or that such treatment is needed to restore him to a position in which he can make up his own mind.

The case for imposed treatment can also be couched in social terms. Illness is costly to the community and the individual is not entitled to refuse treatment which may minimise that cost. The community may have to support the family of a person who dies as a result of refusing treatment. Non-voluntary intervention is thereby justified. This argument is, however, also weak. Society may, indeed, be saved certain costs if a life is preserved, but it can be argued that the damage resulting from coercion convincingly outweighs that which it seeks to avert. Thus, for example, in *Davis v Hubbard*[1] the US District Court of Ohio rejected out of turn an argument that it had the power to authorise treatment of incompetent patients with psychotropic drugs on the grounds that the state had a legitimate interest in maintaining its institutions in the cheapest and most efficient manner. A coercive society can be most cost-effective – but this does not mean it is most desirable.

A possible, although uncommon, exception to this rejection of the social cost argument exists when a person is found to be suffering from a highly infectious and dangerous illness; few would then argue that he should be allowed to refuse treatment if such treatment is the sole way to reduce the risk of spreading the disease. Here, the only caveat to the application of coercive treatment is that it should be as non-coercive as is compatible with containment of the threat.[2]

---

1 506 F Supp 915 (1980).
2 See M Brazier and J Harris 'Public Health and Private Lives' (1996) 4 Med L Rev 171.

Non-consensual treatment

The legal justification

The common law has long recognised the principle that every person has the right to have his bodily integrity protected against invasion by others. Only in certain narrowly defined circumstances may this integrity be compromised without the individual's consent – as where, for example, a parent or guardian applies justifiable corporal punishment or where physical intrusion is involved in the carrying out of lawful arrest.

The seriousness with which the law views any invasion of physical integrity is based on the strong moral conviction that everyone has the right of self-determination with regard to his body. Unless there is consent to an act of touching by another, such an act will – subject to the principle *de minimis non curat lex* – constitute a battery for which damages may be awarded. Consent can make physical invasion lawful, but the reality of such consent may be closely scrutinised by the law and is, anyway, subject to certain policy limitations. Consent will not normally render legitimate a serious physical injury; thus, it was held by Swift J in *R v Donovan*:

> As a general rule to which there are well established exceptions, it is an unlawful act to beat another person with such a degree of violence that the infliction of bodily harm is a probable consequence and, when such an act is proved, consent is immaterial.[3]

This being so, it is nevertheless important to note that the degree of harm suffered goes simply to the question of damages and does not operate in constituting the tort or delict. It is the affront to bodily integrity which makes the conduct actionable. No actual physical harm need, therefore, arise. In the same way, the motive of the aggressor is irrelevant. Thus, it matters not that the touching is designed to 'help' the person and, as a consequence, every touching of the patient by way of medical treatment is potentially a battery on that patient. The classic expression is that of Cardozo J:

> Every human being of adult years and sound mind has a right to determine what shall be done with his own body; and a surgeon who performs an operation without the patient's consent commits an assault.[4]

It is the patient's consent – either implied or expressed – which makes the touching legally innocuous and there is no doubt that surgical interference is covered by this principle.[5] The theory, then, is quite simple – the reality is somewhat different. Much recent litigation in common law countries has focused on the consent issue and, as a result, the so-called doctrine of informed consent has assumed a significant role in the medical negligence debate. As will be seen later in the chapter, it is a doctrine which lies surprisingly uneasily in the medico-legal ambience of the United Kingdom.

---

3 [1934] 2 KB 498 at 507: endorsed in *R v Brown* [1996] 1 All ER 545.
4 *Schloendorff v Society of New York Hospital* 105 NE 92 (NY, 1914).
5 *A-G's Reference (No 6 of 1980)* [1981] QB 715, [1981] 2 All ER 1057. The Scots equivalent, albeit indirect, lies in *Smart v HM Advocate* 1975 SLT 65.

Is consent always necessary?

As a general rule, medical treatment, even of a minor nature, should not proceed unless the doctor has first obtained the patient's consent. This consent may be expressed or it may be implied, as it is when the patient presents himself to the doctor for examination and acquiesces in the suggested routine. This principle applies in the overwhelming majority of cases but there are limited circumstances in which a doctor may be entitled to proceed without this consent. Essentially, these can be subsumed under the heading of 'non-voluntary therapy', which has to be distinguished from involuntary treatment. The latter implies treatment against the patient's expressed wishes; the occasions on which this would be ethical are, indeed, very few, although a case can be made out when the interests of a third party or of society itself are involved.[6] Non-voluntary treatment is that which is given when the patient is not in a position to have or to express any views as to his or her management. This clearly covers circumstances in which treatment in the absence of consent is more easily justified. They include, first, when the patient is incapable of giving consent by reason of unconsciousness; second, when the patient is a minor; and, finally, when the patient's state of mind is such as to render an apparent consent invalid.

The unconscious patient

It is possible to see non-voluntary treatment as proceeding with consent, although that consent has not been expressed. Thus, when an unconscious patient is admitted to hospital, the casualty officer may argue that his consent could be implied or presumed on the grounds that if he were conscious he would probably consent to his life being saved in this way. This may be true but, while the majority of patients could be expected to endorse the decision to treat in such circumstances, it is a rather fictitious way of approaching the problem.[7]

An alternative approach is to apply the necessity principle. It is widely recognised in both criminal and civil law that there are certain circumstances in which acting out of necessity legitimates an otherwise wrongful act. The basis of this doctrine is that acting unlawfully is justified if the resulting good effect materially outweighs the consequences of adhering strictly to the law. In the present context, the doctor is justified, and should not have criminal or civil liability imposed upon him, if the value which he seeks to protect is of greater weight than the wrongful act he performs – that is, treating without consent.

Necessity will be a viable defence to any proceedings for non-consensual treatment where an unconscious patient is involved and there is no known objection to treatment. The treatment undertaken, however, must not be more extensive than is required by the exigencies of the situation – we do well to remember what Lord Devlin said, albeit in a rather different context: 'The Good Samaritan is a character

---

6 Eg in the case of the quarantine and treatment of an individual suffering from a contagious disease.
7 P D G Skegg *Law, Ethics and Medicine* (1984) is a most valuable reference; the particular point is discussed at p 99. A rather mundane example involved a dental anaesthetist who inserted an analgesic suppository while the patient was anaesthetised in order to minimise the pain from multiple extractions. He had not discussed this particular treatment before the operation. The GMC found him guilty of serious professional misconduct: see J Mitchell 'A Fundamental Problem of Consent' (1995) 310 BMJ 43.

unesteemed in English law.'[8] A doctor cannot, therefore, 'take advantage' of unconsciousness to perform procedures which are not essential for the patient's survival. This was established in two well-known Canadian cases where the courts explored the distinction between procedures justified by necessity and those which are merely 'convenient', a distinction which would, in all probability, be followed by the British courts.

In the first of these, *Marshall v Curry*,[9] the plaintiff sought damages for battery against the surgeon who had, in the course of an operation for a hernia, removed a testicle. The surgeon's case was that the removal was essential to a successful operation and that, had he not done so, the health and life of the patient would have been imperilled because the testis was, itself, diseased. Taking the view that the doctor had acted 'for the protection of the plaintiff's health and possibly his life', the court held that the removal of the testicle was necessary and that it would have been unreasonable to put the procedure off until a later date. By contrast, in *Murray v McMurchy*,[10] the plaintiff succeeded in an action for battery against a doctor who had sterilised her without her consent. In this case, the doctor had discovered during a caesarian section that the condition of the plaintiff's uterus would have made it hazardous for her to go through another pregnancy and he tied the fallopian tubes although there was no pressing need for the procedure to be undertaken. The court took the view that it would not have been unreasonable to postpone the sterilisation until after consent had been obtained, in spite of the convenience of doing it on the spot.[11]

The principle that emerges from these two cases is that a doctor is justified by necessity in proceeding without the patient's consent if a condition is discovered in an unconscious patient for which treatment is necessary in the sense that it would be, in the circumstances, unreasonable to postpone the operation to a later date. Postponement of treatment is, however, to be preferred if it is possible to wait until the patient is in a position to give consent. The distinction is, nevertheless, often delicately balanced – particularly in the light of the sometimes vague terms of written consent forms. In an unreported Scottish case[12] the patient signed to the effect: 'I hereby give permission for myself to have a general anaesthetic and any operation the surgeon considers necessary.' The operation proposed was the comparatively simple removal of a supposed branchial cyst but, on exploration, the 'cyst' was found to be a carotid body tumour. Removal of such a mass is a far more difficult procedure and the patient, in fact, sustained paralysis of half his body. The Inner House concluded that permission was not limited by seriousness and that the patient had consented to any operation to the end of removing the swelling: 'Consent must be read as covering any operation considered by the surgeon at the time to be in the patient's interest' (per Lord Robertson). None the less, the three judges concerned could all foresee different

8 Lord Devlin *Samples of Law Making* (1962) p 90.
9 [1933] 3 DLR 260.
10 [1949] 2 DLR 442. *Devi v West Midlands Regional Health Authority* [1981] CA Transcript 491 provides an almost exact British parallel.
11 Such cases seem still not infrequent and, although the formation of such pressure groups is increasingly common, it is significant that a charity – the Hysterectomy Legal Fighting Fund – has been established in the UK. See D Brahams 'Unwanted Hysterectomies' (1993) 342 Lancet 361.
12 *Craig v Glasgow Victoria and Leverndale Hospitals Board of Management*, (22 March 1974, unreported) 1st Division. See J A Cameron *Medical Negligence: An Introduction* (1983).

conclusions if the operation lay outside the procedure contemplated by the patient. It is less certain that such a decision would be reached elsewhere, particularly in the United States, where it has been considered for many years that: 'the so-called authority [of such consent forms] is so ambiguous as to be almost completely worthless.'[13] As a result, a uniform model consent form has been used throughout the NHS since 1990.[14]

It is possible that a member of the family, a partner or a close friend may be at hand when a patient is unconscious. In such a case, it may be wise for the doctor to obtain the agreement of that person largely in order to discover any anticipatory choice on the part of the patient or other details which might affect a clinical decision. It is, however, now clear that, in the case of an adult patient, no other person, not even next of kin, has an automatic *legal* right to consent to or refuse consent to treatment.[15] Indeed, the doctor who delays unreasonably while seeking the support of family or significant others is misconceiving the law. None the less, the doctor's position is often not easy and, provided that it involved no adverse effects, the fact that the spouse's, parents', partner's or friends' agreement had been obtained could be of value in that it would diminish the likelihood of the patient feeling aggrieved at the invasion of his or her bodily integrity.[16] In those common law countries which retain the parens patriae jurisdiction, the courts have the power to consent or refuse on behalf of an incapax, whether they be in that state temporarily or otherwise. This is a wide-ranging discretion which is limited only by one principle: all decisions must be taken in the best interests of the patient. We discuss this jurisdiction in more detail below.

Proxy consent and the consent of minors

Proxy *consents* are truly valid only when the patient has given express authority to another person to give or withhold consent on his behalf or when the law invests a person with such power. The commonest example of the latter would be that of parent and child. When proxy consent of this sort is available, the person vested with the power must use it reasonably; the unreasonable withholding of consent may justify a third party's ignoring such withholding. Specific court authority either to consent on behalf of a minor, or to declare a particular course of conduct or non-conduct in respect of an adult incapax lawful, can be sought when there is dispute between carer and health care professional.[17]

---

13 *Rogers v Lumbermens Mutual Cas Co* 119 So 2d 649 (La 1960).
14 NHS Management Executive *A Guide to Consent for Examination or Treatment* (1990). It is possible to make out an argument, based on *Sidaway v Board of Governors of the Bethlem Royal Hospital* [1984] QB 493, [1984] 1 All ER 1018, CA (see p 281 below), that it is wrong in law to require such detailed consent; see C Heneghan 'Consent to Medical Treatment' (1991) 337 Lancet 421. We suggest that it would be unwise to put it to the test.
15 *Re T (adult: refusal of medical treatment)* [1992] 4 All ER 649 at 653; (1992) 9 BMLR 46 at 50, CA, per Lord Donaldson MR.
16 All the United States have enacted 'good Samaritan' legislation aimed at protecting the doctor giving emergency roadside treatment; it can be argued that this interference with access to the courts is both unnecessary and unconstitutional: B Sullivan 'Some Thoughts on the Constitutionality of Good Samaritan Statutes' (1982) 8 Am J Law Med 27. See also Australian legislation: Voluntary Aid in Emergency Act 1973 (Queensland), Ambulance Services Act 1976, s 14A (NSW).
17 See eg *Re T (a minor) (wardship: medical treatment)* (1997) 35 BMLR 63, CA and *Re D (medical treatment)* [1998] 2 FCR 178.

A common occasion on which parents refuse to give consent to the medical treatment of their children is when they disapprove of it for religious reasons. The capacity of the 'mature minor' to consent to treatment on his or her own behalf is discussed in some detail below;[18] here, we are concerned only with the child who is evidently too young to take important decisions about his or her own medical treatment. A doctor taking steps to administer life-saving treatment such as a blood transfusion to the child against the wishes of its parents could rely upon the common law as above – and the current judicial climate is such that we believe a decision taken in good faith in the best interests of a child would, save in very unusual circumstances, be upheld by the courts[19] – and this is the choice hospital authorities will, in general, adopt. It is also technically possible for the medical advisers to initiate care proceedings[20] or to apply for a specific issue order.[1] An alternative approach would be invite the High Court to exercise its inherent jurisdiction and to negate the parental decision because the that power had been exercised unreasonably. There is, at present, some confusion as to the priority to be given to these possible tactics. In *Re O*,[2] it was held that the inherent jurisdiction of the High Court – by way of the 1989 Act, s 100 – was the most appropriate legal framework within which to consider a contested issue relating to emergency treatment for a child. Only a few months later, however, another judge of the Family Division opted for the invocation of a specific issue order.[3] The difference is, however, largely a matter of the interpretation of a statute and its more subtle limitations; it was admitted in *R* that the inherent jurisdiction of the court was always available should its statutory jurisdiction be found wanting.[4] It is to be noted that neither court was in any doubt that blood transfusion should be authorised when medical considerations dictated the need.

Although there would be little public sympathy for parents who refuse on religious grounds to consent to blood transfusion for a perilously ill child, it would be a mistake to reject their position out of hand. The refusal of blood in such circumstances may seem to many to be irrational and pointless, but there is no doubt that it is a strongly held minority position. Ignoring it involves overriding religious convictions and this is a major step in a free society. Such action also entails a significant interference with the principle that parents should have freedom to choose the religious and social upbringing of their children. These factors certainly suggest caution but are outweighed by the counter-arguments that there has been a redefinition of the role of the parents in respect of control of their children and that it is no longer possible to regard them as having an almost absolute power: 'Parental rights to control a child', said Lord Fraser, 'exist not for the benefit of the parent but for the child'.[5] The community interest in the welfare of children is demonstrated in a number of

18 See p 252ff.
19 By extrapolation from *Re F* [1990] 2 AC 1, sub nom *F v West Berkshire Health Authority* [1989] 2 All ER 545, HL (the *Bolam* principle, see p 280ff below, would, presumably, dictate the outcome).
20 Children Act 1989, s 31; Children (Scotland) Act 1995, s 57.
 1 Children Act 1989, s 8(1).
 2 *Re O (a minor) (medical treatment)* [1993] 2 FLR 149.
 3 *Camden London Borough Council v R (a minor).(blood transfusion)* (1993) 91 LGR 623.
 4 *Re R (a minor) (wardship: medical treatment)* [1991] 4 All ER 177.
 5 In *Gillick v West Norfolk and Wisbech Area Health Authority* [1986] AC 112, [1985] 3 All ER 402 (see p 252ff below). Following Lord Denning MR in *Hewer v Bryant* [1970] 1 QB 357 at 369: 'Parental rights start with the right of control and end with little more than advice.'

ways, some more draconian than others. Society is prepared to remove a child from its parents if it is in moral or physical danger; the child whose life is endangered by parental refusal of consent to medical treatment may be removed from its home on precisely the same grounds as may be the battered child. Any difference in the two cases lies in motives. The parent withholding consent may be doing so for what he sees as good reasons and in the interests of the child; the parent who neglects his child is unlikely to feel the same. In spite of this difference, however, there must be few who will see the parents' good faith as justifying the imperilling of the child's life; death of a child in such circumstances might result in prosecution of the parents for manslaughter[6] – as was said in a well-known American case: 'Parents may be free to become martyrs themselves. But it does not follow that they are free in identical circumstances to make martyrs of their children.'[7]

The Supreme Court of Canada has ruled that to allow parents to refuse blood transfusions for their child for religious reasons 'undermines the ability of the state to exercise its legitimate parens patriae jurisdiction'.[8] Indeed, the court continued: '[a]s society becomes increasingly aware of the fact that the family is often a very dangerous place for children, the parens patriae jurisdiction assumes greater importance.'[9]

Most recently, the Family Division of the English High Court in *Re C (a minor) (medical treatment)*[10] refused to respect the wishes of parents to continue treatment of their 16-month-old child, who was suffering from spinal muscular atrophy. Medical assessment of the infant's condition was to the effect that continued ventilation was futile, it only being a matter of time before she suffered a fatal collapse. The parents agreed that ventilation should be discontinued but were unwilling, on religious grounds, to stand idly by and watch a life wither away when further intervention could delay death. They insisted that the child be ventilated in the event of further collapse. We discuss this case below in the general context of withdrawal of treatment from handicapped neonates.[11] Its significance here lies in the attitude of the court in determining the point at which parental powers of consent fall away to be replaced by the court's power to exercise its inherent jurisdiction, and the extent to which parental power is subjugated to the clinical judgment of health care professionals. Importantly, whether we are concerned with the powers of the parents or the court, or with the duty of the medical profession towards the patient, the determining factor which limits interventions in each case is that of the subject's best interests. What exactly was in the best interests of this child? As orthodox Jews, the parents of C firmly believed that life should always be preserved where possible and could not accept the conclusion that it was in her best interests not to be reventilated if she was subsequently unable to breathe independently. The contrary attitude of the medical profession was unequivocal. Overwhelming clinical evidence testified to the 'futile' nature of continued intervention; the carers, in their turn, were unable to contemplate such a course of action in the best interests of the child. The court, in

---

6 *R v Senior* [1899] 1 QB 283. For a survey of important US decisions see 52 ALR 3d 1118.
7 *People (ex rel Wallace) v Labrenz* 104 NE 2d 769 (Ill, 1952).
8 *B (R) v Children's Aid Society of Metropolitan Toronto* [1995] 1 SCR 315 at 433.
9 But the Supreme Court will not extend the jurisdiction to the child in utero: *Winnipeg Child and Family Services (Northwest Area) v G (DF)* [1997] 2 SCR 925.
10 [1998] 1 FLR 384, (1997) 40 BMLR 31.
11 See p 375.

refusing to interfere with the medical assessment of the case, assiduously followed existing precedents which have eschewed all interference with the clinical judgment of health care professionals by the courts in cases such as this.[12] There was, however, no direct mention in this case of the place for the parents' religious views. The decision was presented as involving an objective assessment of best interests and, indeed, of what counts as futility, yet as we discuss below,[13] these notions are, in reality, highly subjective. Whichever way one looks at a case such as *Re C*, one cannot avoid the conclusion that it involves a value judgment. That the values of the parents in consenting on behalf of their child are completely ignored is at best paternalistic and, at worst, culturally imperialistic.[14] We have yet to encounter a case in the United Kingdom which displays a significant degree of sensitivity to the cultural and religious mores of parents.[15]

A first step on this path may, however, have been taken. In *Re T (a minor) (wardship: medical treatment)*[16] the Court of Appeal issued the unprecedented ruling that parents of a child suffering from biliary atresia, a life-threatening liver defect, could legally refuse a liver transplant on behalf of the infant, even although there was firmly held medical opinion that a transplant would give the child a number of years of life beyond his current prognosis. We discuss this case in depth below.[17] Suffice it to say here that the significance of the court's ruling from the perspective of the law of consent lies in its willingness *not* to equiparate the concept of best *medical* interests with the far broader notion of *overall* best interests.

In many respects, the decision in *Re T* was easier for the Court of Appeal to achieve than was that in *Re C* for the High Court.[18] While both involved a rejection of received medical wisdom, the parents in the latter case sought to force health care professionals to treat against their will, while in the former, the parents simply requested to be left alone. *Re C* was therefore, to all intents and purposes, founded on a 'right to health care' argument. For ethical and pragmatic reasons, no such right has ever been held to exist.[19] Thus, whilst parents do not have a right to demand continuous care on behalf of their child, there is scope for argument that their right to refuse on behalf of their child has been strengthened judicially. The focus in *Re T* on the effect of forced treatment on the relationship between the child and the parents may prove to be of some utility in the future for parents who would seek to refuse medical care for their child because of their personal beliefs. It could, for example, be legitimately argued that, on religious and cultural grounds, they too would come to see their child

12 *Re J (wardship: medical treatment)* [1991] Fam 33, [1990] 3 All ER 930; *Re J (a minor) (medical treatment)* [1993] Fam 15, [1992] 4 All ER 614; *Re R (a minor) (wardship: consent to treatment)* [1992] Fam 11, [1992] 1 FLR 190. We discuss these cases in detail at pp 372ff.
13 See chapters 15-16.
14 For an account of the importance of cultural and religious tenets in withdrawal cases, see M F Morrison and S G DeMichele 'How Culture and Religion Affect Attitudes toward Medical Futility' in M B Zucker and H D Zucker *Medical Futility* (1997).
15 For a useful overview, see P Morgan and C Lawton (eds) *Ethical Issues in Six Religious Traditions*, (1996).
16 [1997] 1 All ER 906, (1996) 35 BMLR 63.
17 See p 377.
18 For discussion and comparison of these two cases, see J Loughrey 'Medical Treatment – The Status of Parental Opinion' [1998] Fam Law 146.
19 Compare *R v Cambridge Health Authority, ex p B (a minor)* (1995) 25 BMLR 5 (first instance) with the Court of Appeal ruling at (1995) 23 BMLR 1, discussed below at p 379.

differently if treatment were imposed without their consent. They may regard their child as 'tainted' or 'soiled' by medical treatment which is administered against their religious beliefs, leading them to reject the child or treat him or her adversely. In such cases, the argument could be put that it is in the child's *overall* best interests not to receive the said treatment.[20]

Mature minors

The questions of positive consent to and refusal of medical and surgical procedures by relatively mature minors in the absence of parental authority – or, indeed, knowledge – is one of the more controversial issues in this field. The status of the minor between the ages of 16 and 18 is now almost settled and we return to it briefly below; discussion is, here, confined to the child below the age of 16. The common law does not exclude such a child giving consent but the validity of that consent still falls to be considered in the light of the pivotal case of *Gillick v West Norfolk and Wisbech Area Health Authority*.[1] Although, as is well known, that case was specifically concerned with the provision of contraceptives (and is also discussed under that heading and under confidentiality[2]), many of the points made in the majority opinions can be taken as relating to the consent of minors to medical treatment as a whole – indeed, the term '*Gillick* competent' is now part of medico-legal lore.[3]

The dominant opinion[4] was that the parental right to determine whether or not their minor child below the age of 16 years will have medical treatment 'terminates if and when the child achieves a significant understanding and intelligence to enable him or her to understand fully what is proposed' but, until the child attains such a capacity to consent, the parental right to make the decision continues save only in exceptional circumstances.[5] Despite the general tenor of his judgment, Lord Scarman affirmed that: 'Parental rights clearly exist and do not wholly disappear until the age of majority.' It can be taken as being now accepted that a doctor treating a child should always attempt to obtain parental authority but that, provided the patient is capable of understanding what is proposed and of expressing his or her wishes, the doctor may, in exceptional circumstances, provide treatment on the basis of the minor's consent alone. The decision to do so must be taken on clinical grounds and, clearly, must depend heavily on the severity and permanence of the proposed therapy.[6] It follows, too, that a sufficiently mature minor is also entitled to a cloak of confidentiality, part of which might cover a request from the minor that his/her parents not be told about the proposed therapy. The concurrence of Scots law on this question has

20 A D Lederman 'Understanding Faith: When Religious Parents Decline Conventional Medical Treatment for their Children' (1995) 45 Case Western Res L Rev 891.
1 [1986] AC 112, [1985] 3 All ER 402, HL.
2 See pp 109 and 203 above.
3 *Re R (a minor) (wardship: medical treatment)* [1992] 3 Med LR 342 at 347, (1992) 7 BMLR 147 at 156, CA, per Lord Donaldson.
4 [1985] 3 All ER 402 at 423, per Lord Scarman.
5 A similar approach by Lord Denning MR in *Hewer v Bryant* [1970] 1 QB 357, [1969] 3 All ER 578 was strongly approved and the common law position in Canada, as expressed in *Johnston v Wellesley Hospital* (1970) 17 DLR (3d) 139, was also quoted.
6 For a critical review of the *Gillick* decision with particular reference to the doctor's situation, see G Williams 'The *Gillick* Saga' (1985) 135 NLJ 1156, 1179.

scarcely been disputed and is enshrined in the Age of Legal Capacity (Scotland) Act 1991, s 4(2).

The court in *Gillick* took the view that it would be a question of fact to be decided in each case whether a child seeking advice had sufficient understanding to give a consent valid in law. An illustration of this is provided by a case in which the court agreed that a schoolgirl aged 15 should be allowed to have an abortion against the wishes of her parents. Butler-Sloss J said: 'I am satisfied she wants this abortion; she understands the implications of it.'[7]

Thus, the problem of consent to treatment by minors is, to all intents, settled and is well understood. We have not, however, yet touched on refusal of treatment. This is an issue which has aroused considerable controversy. We return to it in a discussion of recent cases below.[8]

The mentally incompetent

A proportion of non-consensual treatment which can be provided for involuntary mental patients is proscribed by statute and is discussed further below.[9] All such therapy is, however, specifically limited to treatment of the mental condition. Treatments of unrelated physical conditions are excluded and a therapeutic lacuna remains – how can treatment be provided legitimately to persons who are unable to consent to it?

We have already seen some of the difficulties entailed in the series of sterilisation operations which have come to the notice of the courts.[10] Nevertheless, it is these very cases which have served to clarify the medical position. In *Re F*[11] it was clearly stated that a doctor can provide treatment for a mentally handicapped person in the absence of consent so long as that treatment is in the patient's best interests – and a line of decisions has supported that view and, indeed, extended its scope. It is, however, doubtful if this professionally orientated approach acts to the advantage of the mentally handicapped; this is despite the fact that the confusion arises, at least in part, from progressive changes on mental health legislation which have been designed, with the best of intentions, to restore autonomy to the mentally impaired[12] – not the least significant of these being the removal of the parens patriae jurisdiction from the courts of England and Wales by the Mental Health Act 1959.

Parens patriae jurisdiction

The parens patriae jurisdiction – literally 'parent of the country' – is an ancient jurisdiction dating from as early as the thirteenth century. A product of the feudal system, it was originally held by the English monarch and permitted him to take care of those vassals on his lands unable to take care of themselves. Through time, the jurisdiction came to be vested in the High Court, the prerogative being passed from

7 *Re P (a minor)* [1986] 1 FLR 272, 80 LGR 301.
8 See p 257ff.
9 See p 516.
10 See chapter 4.
11 *Re F (mental patient: sterilisation)* [1990] 2 AC 1, sub nom *F v West Berkshire Health Authority* [1989] 2 All ER 545.
12 See eg C Dyer 'Who Decides for Those Who Can't?' (1991) 302 BMJ 1352.

the monarch to the Lord Chancellor by means of the Sign Manual – a regnal order authorising the Officer to exercise the jurisdiction on behalf of the Sovereign. Parallel developments occurred in a number of common law countries including Australia, Canada, Ireland and the United States, each taking its authority from English law.[13] The essential importance of the jurisdiction in the medical law context is that it permits a court to consent to or refuse medical treatment on behalf of an 'incapax', being either a minor or an incapable adult. Alternatively, the court can exercise its jurisdiction through others by appointing a guardian with powers of consent and refusal.

By something of a twist of fate, however, the jurisdiction was lost to the English and Welsh courts by the coincidence of two events in 1960. These were the passing of the Mental Health Act 1959 and the revocation by warrant under the Sign Manual of the last warrant authorising the Lord Chancellor to exercise the jurisdiction. The 1959 Act swept away previous legislative provisions dealing with incapable adults and reduced the power to treat adults suffering from mental illness to a single statutory footing. The effect of the revocation of the Sign Manual was to remove the jurisdiction from the common law completely. The net result was that no one, not even a court, can now consent to or refuse medical treatment on behalf of an incapable adult which does not fall within the provisions of the mental health legislation. The position of the minor remained unaffected, however, being governed by the courts' wardship jurisdiction. This disparity remains today – subject to the restrictions imposed by the Children Act 1989.

The same result has not occurred in other jurisdictions[14] where parens patriae has, in practice, provided a very wide-ranging prerogative. Thus, for example, in *Re Eve*[15] the Supreme Court of Canada confirmed the persistence of its parens patriae role, and that of the Canadian Supreme Courts, but refused to exercise the jurisdiction to authorise a non-therapeutic sterilisation of an incapax adult woman. The opposite conclusion was, however, reached on very similar facts by the Australian High Court in *Secretary, Department of Health and Community Services v JWB*.[16] The Australian Family Court also has the jurisdiction and has authorised the harvesting of bone marrow from a 12-year-old boy to help in the treatment of his aunt.[17] The court granted the order on being satisfied that the nature of the relationship between the donor and the donee meant that the intervention was in the minor's best interests. The jurisdiction has also been used in Ireland[18] and in Scotland[19] to authorise the removal of artificial nutrition and hydration from severely and permanently incapacitated adults. This particular use of parens patriae is discussed further in chapter 16.

13 For comment see G T Laurie 'Parens Patriae in the Medico-legal Context: The Vagaries of Judicial Activism' (1993) 3 ELR (forthcoming) and J Seymour '*Parens Patriae* and Wardship Powers: Their Nature and Origins' (1994) 14 OJLS 159.
14 Principally because the Sign Manual is a procedure unique to England.
15 [1986] 2 SCR 388.
16 (1992) 106 ALR 385.
17 *Re GWW and CMW* (1997) 21 Fam LR 612. A similar decision was reached in *Re Y (adult patient) (transplant: bone marrow)* [1997] Fam 110, (1996) 35 BMLR 111, in which it was held to be in the best interests of a 25-year-old incapax woman to donate bone marrow to her sister. We, however, have some concerns with such a use of the best interests test in England and Wales, as we discuss below at p 255.
18 *Re a Ward* [1996] 2 IR 79.
19 *Law Hospital NHS Trust v Lord Advocate* 1996 SLT 848; on appeal 1996 SLT 869.

The loss of the parens patriae jurisdiction to England and Wales was confirmed by the House of Lords in *Re F*,[20] who then proceeded to develop a necessity test – based, again, on the patient's best interests – to legitimise the medical treatment of incapable adults. We believe that this form of best interests test should be distinguished from that which lies at the heart of the parens patriae jurisdiction in other countries. This is so for two reasons. First, the use of the test in England and Wales serves merely to support the lone authority of the court to declare a particular course of conduct as being lawful or unlawful and does not represent a consent on behalf of the incapax. This leads to the second point of distinction – summed up in the question: 'Who decides what constitutes best interests, and how?' The answer in England and Wales is the medical profession. Moreover, in *Re F* the House of Lords ruled that the profession could so decide by reference to the standard of care required by the law of negligence:[1] what would a responsible body of medical opinion consider to be in the best interests of the patient? We find this doubtfully acceptable, in that it places the focus not on the patient's interests as such, but on the views of the medical profession as to those interests. Such views could be arrived at by any number of means and need not represent a consensus of views – indeed, the view of a *single* body of medical opinion is enough to satisfy the standard of care[2] and, hence, to establish what are the patient's best interests. Furthermore, the court is effectively excluded from that determination. This is to be contrasted with the test as it is applied by courts exercising the parens patriae jurisdiction. Here the only question to be determined, by the court, is that of the *overall* best interests of the patient – of which the medical opinion as to the treatment proposed and the patient's reaction to it will be only one facet. This is a far more principled approach to the question of the treatment of the incapax and one which is more easily justified on ethical grounds.

The Law Commissions' proposals

Even so, we cannot fully endorse either the parens patriae approach to consent or the concept of the best interests test as we have outlined in respect of England and Wales. It is difficult to escape the fact that a test couched in the terms of either is inherently paternalistic. It is also exceptionally vague in its content and is subject to many potential interpretations. These apprehensions are shared by the English and Scottish Law Commissions, both of which have reported on the law in this area and recommended reform.[3] These reports have provoked a wide range of responses.[4]

The Law Commission's paper addresses three main principles: (1) capacity, (2) best interests and (3) the general authority to act reasonably. We comment on capacity

---

20 [1990] 2 AC 1, [1989] 2 All ER 545.
1 Laid down in *Bolam v Friern Hospital Management Committee* [1957] 2 All ER 118, [1957] 1 WLR 582.
2 See chapter 9 for discussion of the *Bolam* principle.
3 Law Commission, *Mental Incapacity,* No 231, 1995; Scottish Law Commission, *Report on Incapable Adults,* No 151, 1995.
4 For comment on the Law Commission's work, see P Alldridge 'Consent to Medical and Surgical Treatment – The Law Commission's Recommendations' (1996) 4 Med L Rev 129 and P Wilson 'The Law Commission's Report on Mental Incapacity: Medically Vulnerable Adults or Politically Vulnerable Law?' (1996) 4 Med L Rev 227. The Lord Chancellor's Department has expressed its views for England and Wales in *Who Decides? Making Decisions on Behalf of Mentally Incapacitated Adults,* December 1997.

below in relation to case law.[5] In respect of best interests, it is recommended – and accepted by the government – that the concept be retained as the test for ensuring lawful and ethical treatment of incapax persons. The content of that test has, however, been considered at length. The Commission takes the view that, in determining what constitutes 'best interests', regard should be paid to the past and present wishes and feelings of the person concerned, to the need to permit and encourage the person to participate as fully as possible in decision-making and to consideration of the views of other appropriate people. While accepting these recommendations in principle, the government has sought further views on a range of practical considerations, such as the resolution of disputes between those consulted, the potential liability of medical staff who fail to consult fully and the role of religious and cultural factors in establishing a person's best interests. Significantly, there is no question of challenging the role of health care professionals as the principal decision-makers but, at the same time, the government has accepted the recommendation that certain types of medical intervention which are particularly invasive or which are of doubtful benefit to the health of the incapax – such as sterilisation, transplant donations and research – should require specific court approval. Finally, the proposal to establish a judicial forum with jurisdiction to deal specifically with the care and management of the incapax has also been accepted.

Like its English counterpart, the Scottish Office accepts to a large extent the recommendations of the Scottish Law Commission[6] and has issued its own consultation paper.[7] The reports of the two Commissions demonstrate an interesting attempt at symbiosis. As the Lord Chancellor's Paper comments:

> The medical aspects of the two Law Commissions' reports are sufficiently similar that careful consideration will be required of taking a common GB-wide approach in this area. Given the different existing framework of statutory and common law in Scotland, other provisions can be expected to vary, even though the underlying principles are shared.[8]

Thus we see, for example, recommendations in England that a court or an attorney can consent on behalf of an incapax; something currently possible in Scotland but not in England and Wales. Conversely, there are proposals in Scotland to establish the new office of Public Guardian, akin to the Official Solicitor, to represent and defend the interests of incapable adults. However, not all the recommendations are in tandem. Two in particular merit comment. First, the Scottish Law Commission has expressed far more concern as to the best interests test and has rejected an express reference to best interests in setting out the general principles governing its recommendations.[9] Instead, the Scottish Commission preferred to list a number of factors to be considered before treating an incapable adult. Although these reflect to a large extent the factors proposed in England,[10] the rejection of best interests is,

---

5 See p 261ff.
6 *Report on Incapable Adults*, p 255, n 3 above.
7 The Scottish Office, *Managing the Finances and Welfare of Incapable Adults*, February 1997.
8 Para 1.13.
9 Para 2.50.
10 They include eg: seeking previously expressed wishes of the incapax; consultation with relatives and other carers; and the need to show a benefit for the incapax except in the most exceptional of circumstances.

nevertheless, significant. As a 'vague concept',[11] best interests permits of wide-ranging discretion even when, as the English proposals would have it, the test is tempered by 'factors' to be taken into account.

Second, the Scottish Law Commission has recommended that an advance refusal of treatment by a female patient should be ineffective if the refusal would endanger the life of a fetus, aged 24 weeks or more, which she is carrying.[12] In stark contrast, the English Commission merely proposes a presumption against an advanced refusal of treatment from a pregnant woman if that refusal does not specifically cover the possibility of her being pregnant when incapacity supervenes.[13] A clearly worded directive would be respected. As shown below,[14] the Scottish proposal is out of line with common law developments in this area and would set Scots law apart from the rest of the United Kingdom if it were ever implemented.

The fate of all of these recommendations remains to be seen. For the present, the legal provisions governing the incapax remain those laid down at common law. Let us then consider the current position.

The cases

We noted in the previous (fourth) edition of this book that the interval between the third and fourth editions had provided a remarkable series of cases which had served to draw together, and indicate judicial attitudes to, non-voluntary treatment involving minors, mature minors and doubtfully incompetent adults. This trend has proceeded unabated. Several of these cases have far-reaching implications; here, we consider only those aspects which are directly related to refusal of and consent to treatment.

The first, albeit not chronologically, which is of importance in the present context is *Re J*.[15] This case concerned a 16-month-old brain damaged child whose condition was such that his medical attendants considered it inappropriate to provide invasive intensive care in the event that he suffered a life threatening event. The boy's mother sought, and obtained, an order that such treatment should be given if it served to prolong his life. This order was immediately stayed and this was, later, upheld on appeal. The significance of *Re J* is that, in restating[16] in the clearest terms that the medical profession could not be required to undertake treatment against its clinical judgment, it lays a base-line that, while *consent* to treatment is essential, there is no concurrent right to *demand* treatment – in short, there are 'checks and balances of consent and willingness and ability to treat'. We saw above how this ruling has been applied without question in *Re C (a minor) (medical treatment)*.[17]

---

11 The Scottish Office accepted the SLC's rejection of best interests, p 256, n 7 above at para 2.41.
12 Report *Incapable Adults*, n 3 above, paras 5.57-5.58. The Scottish Office has not endorsed this view but has simply sought further comment, p 256, n 7 above at para 6.31.
13 Law Commission *Metal Incapacity*, p 255, n 3 above, paras 5.24-5.26.
14 See p 265ff.
15 *Re J (a minor) (wardship: medical treatment)* [1992] 2 FLR 165, (1992) 9 BMLR 10.
16 The proposition had been previously stated in *Re J (a minor) (wardship: medical treatment)* [1991] Fam 33 at 41, (1992) 6 BMLR 25 at 30 and in *Re R (a minor) (wardship: medical treatment)* [1992] Fam 11 at 22, (1992) 7 BMLR 147 at 154, both per Lord Donaldson MR. The trial judge in the present case interpreted these remarks as not binding.
17 [1998] 1 FLR 384, (1997) 40 BMLR 31.

Re R[18] is something of a landmark case as it constituted the first time that the concept of the mature – or *Gillick*-competent – minor had been tested in the United Kingdom courts; it also raised, but scarcely resolved, the relationship between consent to and refusal of treatment. Briefly, the case concerned a 15-year-old girl whose increasingly disturbed behaviour required sedative treatment. However, during her lucid phases – in which she appeared rational and capable of making decisions – she refused her medication and the local authority instituted wardship proceedings, the intention being to seek authority to provide anti-psychotic treatment whether or not she consented; R appealed against an order to that effect which had been obtained.

The Court of Appeal first disposed of the distinction, if any, between parental powers and those of the court in wardship and concluded that the latter were wider; the court could override both consent and refusal of treatment by the ward if that was considered to be in his or her best interests. The court then further distinguished *Gillick,* which was concerned with the developing maturity of normal children; the test elaborated in that case could not be applied to a child whose mental state fluctuated widely from day to day. But the aspect of the case having by far the most general significance lay in its definition of parental powers. Essentially, Lord Donaldson MR considered that the parental right which *Gillick* extinguished was to *determine* the treatment of a mature minor – and this was considered to be wider in its implications than a right to consent, in so far as it included the right of veto. In explanation, Lord Donaldson introduced the concept of consent providing the key to the therapeutic door and of there being, in the case of the mature minor, two keyholders – the minor and its parents; consent by either *enabled* treatment to be given lawfully but did not, in any way, *determine* that the child should be treated. Lord Donaldson was later to regret his keyholder analogy in so far as keys can lock as well as unlock doors. It seems to us to be acceptable so long as it is modified to imply that refusal on the part of the child effectively means that the child has thrown away its key to a locked door; it is then only prudent that there should be a second key available as a fire precaution.

Re R raised a storm of academic protest. This was not, primarily, as to the assessment of mental incompetence, which the court considered should be based on the general condition of the patient rather than that at a given moment in time; nor was there great exception to the definition of the court's authority in wardship – which will, in any event, be less commonly invoked since the coming into force of the Children Act 1989. Rather, the criticism was directed at the retention of the parental right to give consent in the face of the child's refusal – an interpretation of the law which Kennedy described as 'driving a coach and horses through *Gillick*'.[19] But is this, in fact, so? Lord Donaldson's distinction between a parental ability to determine a minor's treatment – which Lord Scarman considered to be overtaken by the child's developing maturity[20] – and to consent to treatment is a legitimate one and, as we have seen, a corresponding obligation to apply that treatment was firmly rejected. Moreover,

18 [1992] Fam 11, (1992) 7 BMLR 147.
19 I Kennedy 'Consent to Treatment: The Capable Person' in C Dyer (ed) *Doctors, Patients and the Law* (1992) ch 3. See also A Bainham 'The Judge and the Competent Minor' (1992) 108 LQR 196, which is concerned more with the Family Law Reform Act 1969, s 8(1) rather than with s 8(3).
20 In *Gillick* [1986] AC 112 at 188, [1985] 3 All ER 402 at 423.

the Master of the Rolls was, arguably, doing no more than interpreting the statute law of England. The Family Law Reform Act 1969, s 8(1) gives the minor aged 16-18 powers of consent to medical and surgical treatment equivalent to those of an adult. Section 8(3), however, goes on to say:

> Nothing in this section shall be construed as making ineffective any consent which would have been effective if this section had not been enacted.

It has been widely assumed that this section does no more than confirm the common law right of competent minors to decide these questions for themselves. We have always doubted this, largely because, if this is the correct interpretation, there was never any need for s 8(1) – a view which was endorsed by the absence of any such statute in Scotland prior to the Age of Legal Capacity (Scotland) Act 1991.[1] The better view, in our opinion, is that a parental right to consent on behalf of a child existed before 1969 and that s 8(3) preserves that right in the case of all those below the age of 18; this seems to have been Lord Donaldson's interpretation,[2] on which he based his opinion. The academic response to *Re R* demonstrates, above all, the difficulties which arise when attempting to apply general philosophical principles to particular medical cases. The opinion may have further muddied the murky waters of *Gillick* but what was the alternative? This could only have been to accede to the minor's right to refuse treatment when competent and to treat her when incompetent under the mantle of necessity. This is not only bad medicine; it also smacks of a 'cat and mouse' approach which cannot be ethically sustainable. It might have been better to confine the ratio to such narrow issues and to regard the remainder of Lord Donaldson's speech as obiter; but the Master of the Rolls, albeit with some reservations, consolidated his position in the next case – *Re W*.[3]

Re W takes us one step further down the road of consent in that it concerned a 16-year-old girl who, therefore, came within the provisions of s 8(1) of the Family Reform Act 1969 which states:

> The consent of a minor who has attained the age of sixteen years to any . . . medical . . . treatment which, in the absence of consent, would constitute a trespass to the person, shall be as effective as it would be if he were of full age; and where a minor has by virtue of this section given effective consent to any treatment it shall not be necessary to obtain any consent for it from his parent or guardian . . .

W was suffering from anorexia nervosa and was refusing all treatment despite a rapid deterioration in her health. The Court of Appeal supported an order that she be treated in a specialist unit but, in essence, did so on the clinical grounds that the

1 The Age of Legal Capacity (Scotland) Act 1991, s 2(4) gives statutory power, which is rather wider even than that envisaged in *Gillick*, to the mature minor under the age of 16 to consent to medical or dental treatment. The section is, however, *enabling* in that it provides an exception to the general rule that a person under 16 has no capacity to enter into any legal transaction. For the application of the English case law to Scotland, see L Edwards 'The Right to Consent and the Right to Refuse: More Problems with Minors and Medical Consent' [1993] JR 52.
2 (1992) 7 BMLR 147 at 156.
3 *Re W (a minor) (medical treatment)* [1992] 4 All ER 627, (1992) 9 BMLR 22.

disease is capable of destroying the ability to make an informed choice – the wishes of the minor thus constituted something which, of themselves, required treatment. In the course of the judgments, however, several general issues were either clarified or reinforced. First, it was reiterated that the court had extensive powers in wardship and that these existed irrespective of the provisions of the Family Law Reform Act 1969, s 8(1); moreover, Lord Donaldson held that the exercise of the court's power to make a specific issue order did not conflict with those sections of the Children Act 1989 which give a mature minor the right to refuse psychiatric or medical treatment in defined circumstances.[4] All the opinions emphasised that this attitude did not conflict with *Gillick* which was concerned with *parental* powers only. Secondly, the court disposed in clear terms of the relationship of consent to refusal of treatment with particular reference to the 1969 Act. Lord Donaldson said:

> No minor of whatever age has power by refusing consent to treatment to override a consent to treatment by someone who has parental responsibility for the minor and a fortiori a consent by the court.[5]

Balcombe LJ said:

> I am quite unable to see how, on any normal reading of the words of the section, it can be construed to confer [an absolute right to refuse medical treatment] . . . That the section did not operate to prevent parental consent remaining effective, as well in the case of a child over 16 as in the case of a child under that age, is apparent from the words of sub-s (3).[6]

This is, of course, a legal decision and it is true, as Balcombe LJ himself said, that, in logic, there can be no difference between an ability to consent to treatment and an ability to refuse treatment. But is there not a clear practical distinction to be made? It is reasonable to suppose, paternalistic though it may sound, that a qualified doctor knows more about the treatment of disease than does a child? Thus, while consent involves acceptance of an experienced view, refusal rejects that experience – and does so from a position of limited understanding. Furthermore, a refusal of medical treatment may close down the options – and this may be regretted later in that the chance to consent has now passed. The implications of refusal may, therefore, be more serious and, on these grounds refusal of treatment may require greater understanding than does acceptance. A level of comprehension sufficient to justify refusal of treatment certainly includes one to accept treatment but the reverse does not hold; the two conditions cannot be regarded as being on a par.[7] We accept, of course, that the same could also be true for most adults. But we have no difficulty with the courts deeming the distinction to be necessary in the case of vulnerable persons – be

---

4   This has been clearly restated in *South Glamorgan County Council v B and W* [1993] 1 FLR 574, (1993) 11 BMLR 162.
5   [1992] 4 All ER 627 at 639, (1992) 9 BMLR 22 at 36.
6   [1992] 4 All ER 627 at 641, (1992) 9 BMLR 22 at 37, 38. Kennedy p 258, n 19 above at 60-61 regarded Lord Donaldson's refusal in *Re R* to accept refusal and consent as twin aspects of the single right to self-determination as bordering on the perverse; this was because he had no stated support. The presence of such support in *Re W* serves to fill the lacuna.
7   For a contrary clinico-legal view, see J A Devereux, D P H Jones and D I Dickenson 'Can Children Withhold Consent to Treatment?' (1993) 306 BMJ 1459.

they minors or incapax adults. Indeed, as we show below,[8] just such an approach has been adopted in the case of the latter by the courts after the decision of *Re C (adult: refusal of medical treatment)*.[9]

What is clear from both *Re R* and *Re W* is that, rather like Lord Denning before him, Lord Donaldson was concerned to protect the medical profession from the fire of litigation – his reference to consent providing a flak-jacket for the doctor demonstrates this vividly. It is, therefore, possible to criticise the two decisions as concentrating on this aspect and taking insufficient notice of the developing autonomy of adolescence. None the less, all the speeches in both cases are at pains to emphasise the importance of respecting the minor's wishes – and of giving them increasing value with increasing maturity. What they do is to emphasise that they are not absolute; but their tenor is such as to retain the concept of the mature minor very firmly and to insist that this is breached only in exceptional circumstances. It is very unlikely that future cases will be regressive in this sense.

Refusal of treatment by adults

The Court of Appeal was not yet done, for it still had to consider the adult who refuses treatment – this it did in *Re T*.[10] *Re T* appears to have been the first adult Jehovah's Witness case to have come before a British court. The case itself was fairly unexceptional. A pregnant woman was involved in a car accident and, after speaking with her mother, signed a form of refusal of blood transfusion. Following a caesarian section and the delivery of a stillborn baby, her condition deteriorated and a court order was obtained legalising blood transfusion on the grounds that it was manifestly in her best interests; the declaration was upheld by the Court of Appeal. The fundamental decision was to the effect that an adult patient who suffers from no mental incapacity has an absolute right to consent to medical treatment, to refuse it or to choose an alternative treatment[11] – 'it exists notwithstanding that the reasons for making the choice are rational, irrational, unknown or even non-existent'.[12] How, then, did the court reach its decision to support the provision of apparently involuntary treatment?

First, of course, it had to transform involuntary treatment into non-voluntary. This it did by finding that T's mental state had deteriorated to such an extent that she could not make a valid choice as between death and transfusion – and if there was doubt as to how the patient was exercising her right of self-determination, that doubt should be resolved in favour of the preservation of life.[13] But an additional factor of great importance to the doctors was added when it was stated that the effects of outside

---

8 See pp 263-264 and p 270.
9 [1994] 1 All ER 819.
10 *Re T (adult) (refusal of medical treatment)* [1992] 4 All ER 649, (1992) 9 BMLR 46, CA.
11 The only possible qualification mentioned by Lord Donaldson – where the choice might lead to the death of a viable fetus – is discussed below at p 265.
12 [1992] 4 All ER 649 at 653, (1992) 9 BMLR 46 at 50, per Lord Donaldson.
13 For an example of the difficulty given a patient of marginal mental capacity, see A N Wear and D Brahams 'To Treat or Not To Treat: The Legal, Ethical and Therapeutic Implications of Patient Refusal' (1991) 17 J Med Ethics 131. See, too, MA Jones and K Keywood 'Assessing the Patient's Competence to Consent to Medical Treatment' (1996) 2 Med Law Internat 107.

influence on a patient's refusal have to be taken into consideration; in short, the question of whether the patient means what he or she says has to be posed – and whether the decision was reached independently after counselling and persuasion or whether the patient's will was overborne is a matter to be decided by the doctors. At first glance, this looks suspiciously like opening the door to involuntary treatment – that is, until one comes to Staughton LJ, who said:

> I cannot find authority that the decision of a doctor as to the existence or refusal of consent is sufficient protection, if the law subsequently decides otherwise. So the medical profession . . . must bear the responsibility unless it is possible to obtain a decision from the courts.[14]

Since this will be possible only rarely in an emergency, *Re T* seems to place a well-nigh intolerable burden on the doctors, not all of whom in the middle of the night will be of consultant status. What, for example, is the young houseman to make of Lord Donaldson:

> . . . what the doctors *cannot* do is to conclude that, if the patient still had the necessary capacity in the changed situation [he being now unable to communicate], he would have reversed his decision . . . What they *can* do is to consider whether at the time the decision was made it was intended by the patient to apply in the changed situation.[15]

One of us, at least, is grateful that he is no longer likely to be faced with an uncompleted suicide attempt in a busy casualty department! Even the law is undecided on the definition of undue influence and, again, neither Lord Donaldson[16] nor Butler-Sloss LJ[17] make it any easier by including parents and religious advisers among those who might, as a result of their relationship, lend themselves more readily than others to overbearing the patient's will. The law, in fact, seems to have comparatively little difficulty in discounting religious belief. T was considered to be, at best, an uncommitted Jehovah's Witness and we have Ward J in *Re E*[18] saying of a 15-year-old '*Gillick* competent' boy who was refusing blood transfusion: 'I respect this boy's profession of faith, but I cannot discount at least the possibility that he may in later years suffer some diminution in his convictions.'

Yet, as we have already intimated, one feels that parents ought to be able to take seriously their duty to look after not only the physical but also the spiritual well-being of their children free from the potential accusation of exercising undue influence. *Re T* is, in our opinion, the least satisfactory of this series of cases and it is to be noted that,

---

14 [1992] 4 All ER 649 at 670, (1992) 9 BMLR 46 at 68.
15 [1992] 4 All ER 649 at 662, (1992) 9 BMLR 46 at 60.
16 [1992] 4 All ER 649 at 664, (1992) 9 BMLR 46 at 62.
17 [1992] 4 All ER 649 at 667-668, (1992) 9 BMLR 46 at 65-66.
18 *Re E (a minor)* (1990) 9 BMLR 1 at 8 Ward J did say he wished to avoid notions of undue influence. Perhaps feelings are not as strong as they once were: 'of all influences religious influence is the most dangerous and powerful' – *Allcard v Skinner* (1887) 36 Ch D 145, [1886-90] All ER Rep 90 at 99-100, per Lindley LJ, referred to by Butler-Sloss LJ in *Re T* [1992] 4 All ER 649 at 667, (1992) 9 BMLR 46 at 65.

in contrast to *Re R* and *Re W*, leave to appeal to the House of Lords was granted – however, it has not, as yet, been taken up.

The authority of *Re T* was applied shortly afterwards in very interesting circumstances of the case of *Re C*.[19] Despite being a decision at first instance only, the case is, nevertheless, extremely important in that it was the first in which the right to refuse treatment has been respected by the United Kingdom courts. The case concerned a 68-year-old patient suffering from paranoid schizophrenia who had developed gangrene in a foot while serving a term of imprisonment in Broadmoor. On removal of the patient to a general hospital, a consultant prognosed that he had only a 15% chance of survival if the gangrenous limb was not amputated below the knee.[20] The patient, however, refused the operation, saying that he preferred to die with two feet than to live with one. An application for an injunction restraining the hospital from carrying out the operation without his express written consent was lodged with the court on C's behalf. The hospital questioned C's capacity to exercise his autonomy in this way.

Thorpe J held that C was entitled to refuse the treatment even if this meant his death. Quoting with approval the dicta of Lord Donaldson in *Re T*, he stated that, prima facie, every adult has the right and capacity to accept or refuse medical treatment. He acknowledged that this might be rebutted by evidence of incapacity but this onus must be discharged by those seeking to override the patient's choice. When capacity is challenged, as in this case, its sufficiency is to be determined by the answer to the question: has the capacity of the patient been so reduced (by his chronic mental illness) that he did not sufficiently understand the nature, purpose and effects of the proffered medical treatment? This depends on whether the patient has been able to comprehend and retain information, has believed it and has weighed it in the balance with other considerations when making his or her choice.[1] As Thorpe J said:

> Applying that test to my findings on the evidence, I am completely satisfied that the presumption that C has the right to self-determination has not been displaced. Although his general capacity is impaired by schizophrenia, it has not been established that he does not sufficiently understand the nature, purpose and effects of the treatment he refuses. Indeed, I am satisfied that he has understood and retained the relevant treatment information, that in his own way he believes it, and that in the same fashion he has arrived at a clear choice.[2]

Several points of interest arise from this judgment. First, it reaffirms the commitment of the law to the principle of respect for patient autonomy. There is a prima facie presumption of its existence and value which can only be overridden in established circumstances.[3] Furthermore, the particular facts of the case show that incapacity in one or several areas of one's life does not preclude autonomous behaviour in others,

---

19 *Re C (adult: refusal of medical treatment)* [1994] 1 All ER 819, (1993) 15 BMLR 77.
20 This was, however, averted by intervention short of amputation: [1994] 1 All ER 819 at 821, (1993) 15 BMLR 77 at 78-79.
1 Similar to the approach proposed by the Law Commission in *Mentally Handicapped Adults and Decision-making* Consultation Paper No 129.
2 [1994] 1 All ER 819 at 824, (1993) 15 BMLR 77 at 82.
3 For a critique of the decision which doubts that it pays proper respect to patient autonomy, see M Stauch 'Rationality and the Refusal of Medical Treatment: A Critique of the Recent Approach of the English Courts' (1995) 21 J Med Ethics 162.

nor does it remove the presumption of competence to refuse. Indeed, the injunction obtained by the plaintiff extended not only to the particular operation contemplated by the hospital but to *all* future attempts to interfere with his bodily integrity without his express written consent.[4] If, however, incapacity can ever be established, then, as we have seen, the patient must be dealt with in a manner which furthers his or her own best interests.[5]

The judgment, however, suffers from its vagueness. A patient's competence can be successfully challenged if it can be shown that he does not comprehend or absorb information to the extent that he understands it or if he is thought not to believe the information or if he cannot balance this information against other considerations when making his choice. In this way, hurdles are placed in the path of those seeking to exercise their autonomy but, at the same time, it remains uncertain how high they must jump in order to clear these hurdles. For example, the requirement that the patient must actually comprehend the information is not easy to assess – it can depend as much on the amount of information which is given to the patient and the manner in which it is provided as on the capacity of the patient to understand. Yet, the test is not '*can* the patient understand?' but, rather, '*does* the patient understand?' This imposes an obligation on medical staff to ensure that actual understanding is reached and this, in itself, is paradoxical given that treatment staff might not want the patient to understand if they disagree with the nature of his or her decision – as in the present case.

Neither is it exactly clear *what* the patient must understand. The decision talks of the 'nature, purpose and effects' of the treatment. This is potentially very broad and can encompass elements ranging from the general aim of the procedure to the risks and the consequences of refusal and beyond. Arguably, as Grubb has pointed out, the category of 'autonomous persons' is reduced to only the most 'comprehending' individuals if excessive amounts of information are required to be disclosed and understood.[6]

Finally, *Re C* confirms the role of the best interests test in the medico-legal field. If self-determination is successfully challenged, then the only option left is to treat the patient in his or her best interests. However, as we have argued above, this concept is also vague and leaves considerable control and power in the hands of the health care professionals. Neither the precise nor the general nature of best interests is defined by the United Kingdom courts. Cases such as *Re T* and *Re C* demonstrate that the principle of respect for patient autonomy – and, therefore, patient choice – is, prima facie, prescribed but the tests which have been laid down give us no more than a general idea of where the limits of the principle lie. Moreover, these cases have to be read in conjunction with others in which the autonomy of the patient has been overridden and their right to choose for themselves has been denied.

---

4   The importance of this should not be underestimated. In effect, it is tantamount to judicial recognition of the validity of advance refusals of treatment.
5   Both Law Commissions have offered a new definition of capacity. The English definition proposed a presumption against lack of capacity, and preferred a 'functional' approach to the question which focuses on the understanding and ability of the patient at the time of the relevant decision (paras 3.1.-3.23.). The Scottish Law Commission's proposals roughly follow this model, adding that there should be no presumption that a person who behaves immorally or irrationally, or who has a substance addiction, demonstrates incapacity (paras 2.3.-2.17.).
6   See A Grubb 'Commentary' (1994) 2 Med L Rev 92 at 95.

Refusal of treatment in late pregnancy

The decision of the Court of Appeal in *Re T* was also not without its caveats. Lord Donaldson said:

> An adult patient who ... suffers from no mental incapacity has an absolute right to choose whether to consent to medical treatment, to refuse it or to choose one rather than another of the treatments being offered. *The only possible qualification is a case in which the choice may lead to the death of a viable foetus.*[7]

This 'possible qualification' was tested in the soon-to-follow decision of *Re S*,[8] in which a health authority applied for a declaration to authorise the surgeons and staff of a hospital to carry out an emergency caesarian section on a 30-year-old woman who was in spontaneous labour with her third child. The woman refused to submit to a section on religious grounds. The surgeon in charge was adamant that both patient and baby would die without such intervention. After six days of Mrs S's labour, the health authority sought a judgment from the High Court. The decision of Sir Stephen Brown is approximately one page in length, one half of which is concerned with relating the facts, and there is little or no legal argument or analysis in the judgment whereby the declaration was agreed. As the President said:

> I [make the declaration] in the knowledge that the fundamental question appears to have been left open by Lord Donaldson MR in *Re T* . . ., and in the knowledge that there is no English authority which is directly in point.

But it was precisely this lack of precedental authority which provoked major criticism in *Re S* in so far as the case, with all its jurisprudential limitations, bid fair to *provide* that authority. But the problems thus generated are both manifold and manifest. First, the decision was based wholly on the medical evidence. There was no discussion of how the competency of a woman to make such a choice is to be assessed. How is the choice by a woman in Mrs S's position to be validated? Secondly, when Lord Donaldson spoke of a 'viable' fetus, he was speaking in relative rather than absolute terms – for viability results from a combination of gestational age and obstetric expertise.[9] At what stage, therefore, is it regarded as legally acceptable to enforce the operation? Thirdly, we have to ask what importance is the court to place on the danger to the life of the woman herself. Strictly speaking, this should have no influence for, as was said in *Re T*, the right to decide whether or not to accept treatment persists even if refusal will lead to premature death. Yet it is asking a great deal of the health care team to stand by and watch their patient die a painful death and it is probable that such considerations were in the mind of the President when he was

---

7 [1992] 4 All ER 649 at 652-653, (1992) 9 BMLR 46 at 50, emphasis added.
8 [1992] 4 All ER 671, (1992) 9 BMLR 69. This case was decided only two and a half months after *Re T*.
9 See eg the American case *Re AC* 573 A 2d 1235 (DC, 1990) where the enforced caesarian section of a 26-week-old fetus ended, almost predictably, with the death of the neonate within hours. The case, which is discussed further in chapter 6, seems to have been unfortunately wrongly interpreted in *Re S*.

confronted with an emergency situation.[10] Finally, the decision depends on very doubtful logic in that it is well established law that the fetus in utero has no rights of its own and has no distinct human personality;[11] moreover, there is no offence of feticide in the United Kingdom. If, then, we look upon an enforced caesarian as a means of resolving a conflict between a woman who is refusing treatment and a fetus who seeks it, there is, in sporting terms, effectively 'no contest' – there can be no valid reason behind isolating this particular situation as the one occasion on which the fetus achieves legal dominance over its mother. While we have considerable sympathy with the President in the particular circumstances of *Re S*, it is hard to see his decision as other than logically untenable.

None the less, it appeared for a time as though *Re S* had, indeed, set a precedent and, despite fierce criticism of *Re S*,[12] the English courts proceeded in *Norfolk and Norwich Healthcare (NHS) Trust v W*[13] and *Tameside and Glossop Acute Services Trust v CH (a patient)*[14] to impose caesarian sections on woman against their will. Indeed, in the latter case it was held that the performance of a caesarian section on a schizophrenic woman could be 'treatment' of her mental disorder within the terms of the Mental Health Act 1983.

The relationship between a pregnant woman and her fetus was, however, fully reconsidered by the Court of Appeal in *Re MB*.[15] The court was adamant in its ruling that a woman carrying a fetus is entitled to the same degree of respect for her wishes as is anyone else and reiterated the general principle that a person of full age and sound mind cannot be treated against his or her will without the door being opened to civil and criminal legal consequences. It also endorsed strongly the view that a refusal of medical treatment can be for any reason, rational or irrational, or for no reason at all. In particular, it was stressed that circumstances in which non-voluntary treatment is permissible arise only when the patient cannot give consent and when treatment is in the *patient's* best interests. The court has no jurisdiction to declare medical intervention lawful when a *competent* pregnant woman decides to refuse treatment, *even though* this might result in the death or serious handicap of the fetus she is bearing. The question of the woman's own best interests *does not arise* in such circumstances. On the facts of the particular case, however, the pregnant woman was declared incompetent because of a fear of needles which had led her to refuse the operation – but, at the end of the day, she consented and a healthy child was delivered.

This decision clearly places the autonomy of the woman above any interests of the fetus, including an interest in being born alive. Yet, it is important to bear in mind that all of this is subject to the woman being competent when she makes her refusal. If she is not, she must be treated in her best interests. In the particular circumstances of

---

10 For some judicial sympathy, see Major J dissenting in *Winnipeg* [1997] 2 SCR 925: 'Where the harm is so great and the temporary remedy so slight, the law is compelled to act . . . Someone must speak for those who cannot speak for themselves.'
11 Most recently expressed in *A-G Reference (No 3 of 1994)* [1998] 1 Cr App Rep 91, HL.
12 See eg A Grubb 'Commentary on *Re S*' (1993) 1 Med L Rev 92.
13 [1996] 2 FLR 613, (1996) 34 BMLR 16. The same judge made a similar decision in the less well reported *Rochdale Healthcare (NHS) Trust v C* [1996] 3 Hempson's Lawyer 505.
14 [1996] 1 FLR 762, (1996) 31 BMLR 93. For analysis see A Grubb 'Commentary' (1996) 4 Med L Rev 193. An interesting selection of views is to be found under the general heading 'Caesarian Section: A Treatment for Mental Disorder?' (1997) 314 BMJ 1183.
15 *Re MB (caesarean section)* [1997] 8 Med L R 217, (1997) 38 BMLR 175, CA.

Re MB, the assessment that the operation was in her best interests is open to little question; both the woman and her husband wanted the child to be born – subject to her needle phobia. However, it still remains open to speculation how the patient's best interests should be assessed if there is no clear indication of how the mother feels about the birth. In the final analysis, *Re MB* does little to remove from the medical profession the discretion and power to decide on a patient's capacity to act autonomously – and ultimately, in cases of incapacity, to decide on the patient's best interests.

This discretion has not been removed by the latest case in this line of authority,[16] although the Court of Appeal's ruling in *St George's Healthcare National Health Service Trust v S (No 2); R v Collins, ex p S (No 2)*[17] does provide helpful guidance for health care professionals who must decide on the capacity of a patient to consent to or refuse treatment. The case concerned S, a 36-year-old pregnant woman with pre-eclampsia who was advised that she would require to be admitted. Fully cognisant of the risks, and wishing her baby to be born naturally, S refused. As a consequence, she was seen by a social worker and two doctors and admitted to a mental hospital for assessment. On her transfer to another hospital a declaration was sought and granted to dispense with S's consent and the baby was delivered by caesarian section. S discharged herself and appealed against the declaration.

The Court of Appeal upheld its ruling in *Re MB* to the extent that a mentally competent pregnant woman has the absolute right to refuse medical intervention. The actions of the hospital were a trespass and the former declaration was set aside accordingly. Moreover, the court castigated the use of the mental health legislation to treat an otherwise healthy woman:

> The Act cannot be deployed to achieve the detention of an individual against her will merely because her thinking process is unusual, even apparently bizarre and irrational, and contrary to the views of the overwhelming majority of the community at large.

Thus, the position of the pregnant woman of sound mind has been brought into line with the 'adult of sound mind' referred to in *Re T*. More significantly, the Court of Appeal sought to prevent a repeat of this case and, indeed, others involving the treatment of patients of doubtful capacity, and issued guidelines for future reference. These are of considerable importance and we repeat them here for the sake of completeness:

(i)   The guidelines have no application where the patient is competent to accept or refuse treatment. In principle, a patient may remain competent notwithstanding detention under the Mental Health Act 1983.

(ii)   An application to the High Court for a declaration will be pointless if the patient is competent and refuses consent to the treatment. In this situation the advice given to the patient should be recorded. For their own protection, hospital authorities should seek unequivocal assurances from the patient (to be recorded in writing) that the refusal represents an informed decision: that is that she understands the nature of and reasons for the proposed treatment and the risks and likely prognosis involved in the decision to refuse or accept it. If the patient is unwilling to sign a written indication of this refusal, this too should be noted in writing. Such a written

16 *St George's Healthcare National Health Service Trust v S, R v Collins, ex p S* [1998] 3 All ER 673.
17 [1998] 3 WLR 936.

indication is merely a record for evidential purposes. It should not be confused with or regarded as a disclaimer.

(iii) If the patient is incapable of giving or refusing consent, either in the long term or temporarily (eg due to unconsciousness), the patient must be cared for according to the authority's judgment of the patient's best interests. Where the patient has given an advance directive, before becoming incapable, treatment and care should normally be subject to the advance directive. However, if there is reason to doubt the reliability of the advance directive (eg it may sensibly be thought not to apply to the circumstances which have arisen), then an application for a declaration may be made.

(iv) The authority should identify as soon as possible whether there is concern about a patient's competence to consent to or refuse treatment.

(v) If the capacity of the patient is seriously in doubt, it should be assessed as a matter of priority. In many such cases, the patient's general practitioner or other responsible doctor may be sufficiently qualified to make the necessary assessment but, in serious or complex cases involving difficult issues about the future health and well-being or even the life of the patient, the issue of capacity should be examined by an independent psychiatrist, ideally one approved under s 12(2) of the Mental Health Act 1983. If, following this assessment there remains a serious doubt about the patient's competence, and the seriousness or complexity of the issues in the particular case may require the involvement of the court, the psychiatrist should further consider whether the patient is incapable by reason of mental disorder of managing her property or affairs. If so the patient may be unable to instruct a solicitor and will require a guardian ad litem in any court proceedings. The authority should seek legal advice as quickly as possible. If a declaration is to be sought, the patient's solicitors should be informed immediately and, if practicable, they should have a proper opportunity to take instructions and apply for legal aid where necessary. Potential witnesses for the authority should be made aware of the criteria laid down in *Re MB* and this case, together with any guidance issued by the Department of Health and the British Medical Association.

(vi) If the patient is unable to instruct solicitors, or is believed to be incapable of doing so, the authority or its legal advisers must notify the Official Solicitor and invite him to act as guardian ad litem. If the Official Solicitor agrees he will no doubt wish, if possible, to arrange for the patient to be interviewed to ascertain her wishes and to explore the reasons for any refusal of treatment.

(vii) The hearing before the judge should be inter partes. A declaration granted ex parte is of no assistance to the authority as the order made in her absence will not be binding on the patient unless she is represented either by a guardian ad litem, if incapable of giving instructions, or, if capable, by counsel or solicitor. Although the Official Solicitor will not act for a patient if she is capable of instructing a solicitor, the court may in any event call on the Official Solicitor, who has considerable expertise in these matters, to assist as an amicus curiae.

(viii) It is axiomatic that the judge must be provided with accurate and all the relevant information. This should include the reasons for the proposed treatment, the risks involved in the proposed treatment, and in not proceeding with it, whether any alternative treatment exists, and the reason, if ascertainable, why the patient is refusing the proposed treatment. The judge will need sufficient information to reach an informed conclusion about the patient's capacity and, where it arises, the issue of best interest.

(ix) The precise terms of any order should be recorded and approved by the judge before its terms are transmitted to the authority. The patient should be accurately informed of the precise terms.

(x)   Applicants for emergency orders from the High Court made without first issuing
       and serving the relevant applications and evidence in support have a duty to comply
       with the procedural requirements (and pay the court fees) as soon as possible after
       the urgency hearing.

Detailed though these guidelines are, it is noteworthy that they concern, primarily, procedural matters – the court was clearly disinclined to interfere in clinical matters. Indeed, it emphasised that the guidelines were, at the end of the day, guidelines only and advised that rigid compliance with them was inappropriate if to do so would put the patient's health or life at risk. The ball thus remains firmly in the health carers' court – subject, of course, to its being played according to the rules. A significant feature of the case, however, lies in its challenge to the use of mental health legislation as a means of legitimising involuntary treatment. There has been a recent increase in such cases, not only in relation to pregnant women, but also in the context of anorexics – who are discussed below.[18]

Other vulnerable groups

It is everywhere agreed that, to be valid, consent should be free, rational and unfettered; thus, prisoners constitute a further group which deserves special consideration.

The status of prisoners has been referred to briefly in chapter 1. It will be seen from this that it could be held that the incarcerated can never give a valid consent to treatment in that an element of coercion is implicit in the prison doctor-patient relationship. This proposition was considered in *Freeman*,[19] the decision in which greatly restricts this line of argument. The case turned in large measure on its own facts but the suggestion that the position of the prison psychiatrist vis-à-vis his patient voided a general consent was rejected; it was further stated that 'it was not open for it to be argued for the plaintiff that "informed consent" was a consideration which could be entertained by the courts'. While we believe that this latter opinion derived from a semantic misinterpretation of the concept which is discussed in detail below, the judgment clearly indicates that, in the absence of overt coercion, the restricted circumstances in which a prisoner's consent to treatment is given will be unlikely to affect the validity of that consent in law. An action for trespass is open to those in detention when consent to treatment has not been given[20] but mere negligence in obtaining that consent[1] will not brand the trespass as being coercive or oppressive. As an example of a valid refusal on the part of a prisoner, we have the judgment in *Secretary of State for the Home Department v Robb*,[2] a case which raised the question of whether the decision of a prisoner to go on hunger strike should be respected by the prison authorities. Somewhat unorthodoxly, the court applied a

18 See p 270.
19 *Freeman v Home Office (No 2)* [1984] QB 524, [1984] 1 All ER 1036.
20 *Barbara v Home Office* (1984) 134 NLJ 888.
 1 See pp 274-275 below.
 2 [1995] 1 All ER 677.

medical law approach to the case, even although the prisoner was not a patient, and upheld the individual's 'right to self-determination' to refuse food.

In contrast, a series of cases has sanctioned – principally under the terms of the Mental Health Act 1983 – the force-feeding of persons such as anorexics and depressives who refuse food. The rationale in each case has been that the feeding is *treatment* for the individual's *mental disorder*, this being the sole criterion under the legislation which permits health care professionals to forego consent.[3] Thus, for example, the trial judge in *Riverside Mental Health Trust v Fox*[4] held that an adult who was being treated for anorexia nervosa could be force-fed as a part of treatment for her mental condition. The Court of Appeal later overturned this decision but did so on procedural grounds and did not question the validity of the application of the 1983 Act to such a case. As if to endorse this line of reasoning, the Court of Appeal in *B v Croydon Health Authority*[5] authorised force-feeding under the 1983 Act of a woman with a borderline personality disorder, and feeding of a depressive and suicidal quinquagenarian was similarly ordered in *Re VS (adult: mental disorder)*.[6] Most recently, an anorexic 16-year-old was detained using the High Court's inherent protective jurisdiction in order that she receive 'medical treatment' including, inter alia, force-feeding.[7] This unusual procedure was justified as being in the child's best interests on the grounds that, because it was in her best interests to receive 'treatment' for her condition, it was also a part of those interests that she be detained – using reasonable force if necessary – so that the treatment could be carried out. It is to be noted that this order was not based on the detention provisions of the 1983 Act but, rather, on the common law powers of the High Court – which suggests that this jurisdiction is potentially very wide-ranging. Another interesting point is the use by Walls J of the three-stage test for competency laid down in *Re C (adult: refusal of medical treatment)*.[8] That case concerned the competency of an adult. As we have seen, the capacity of a minor to agree to or refuse medical treatment has relied up until now on the concept of *Gillick* competence, the evaluation of which lies within the discretion of the health care professional. This equiparation of the test for competency in adults and minors is, in our view, correct, and adds judicial weight to our earlier argument that refusal of treatment by minors requires a higher standard of competency than does a decision to consent.[9]

---

3 In particular, Mental Health Act 1983, s 63.
4 [1994] 1 FLR 614, (1993) 20 BMLR 1.
5 [1995] 1 All ER 683, CA.
6 [1995] 3 Med L Rev 292.
7 *Re C (detention: medical treatment)* [1997] 2 FLR 180.
8 [1994] 1 All ER 819, (1993) 15 BMLR 77.
9 In the context of minors the Scottish courts would not appear to agree with us. In *Houston, Applicant* (1996) 32 BMLR 93 Sheriff McGown interpreted s 2(4) of the Age of Legal Capacity (Scotland) Act 1991 in respect of a 15-year-old boy suffering from mental illness to mean that capacity to consent encompassed a capacity to refuse and, furthermore, it brings to an end the power of a parent to consent on behalf of the minor.

Consent to testing for HIV infection

The question of whether tests for HIV infection can be undertaken without the consent of the patient has always been controversial.[10] There may be times when a doctor would wish to carry out such tests as part of a responsible diagnostic routine but, at the same time, be reluctant to alarm or embarrass his patient by disclosing his intention. Equally, the HIV status of a patient might be an issue after a needle-stick injury or blood contamination of medical personnel; the need to know could be urgent, yet the patient might refuse to consent to testing. The legal problem is the same in each instance: does HIV testing exceed the bounds of any consent which the patient has already given to therapeutic or diagnostic investigation?

The General Medical Council has firmly rejected HIV testing in the absence of specific consent save in the 'most exceptional circumstances'.[11] The GMC believes that specific consent is required because of the serious social and financial consequences that may follow a positive diagnosis; every patient should have the opportunity to evaluate these consequences as they affect him personally. Non-consensual testing is permissible, in the GMC's view, only where it has not been possible to obtain consent and the health of others than the patient is endangered – although the memorandum defines neither 'possible' nor 'other persons'; the GMC also agrees that the best interests of a child may dictate testing even in the face of parental objection. Such advice carries great ethical weight but does not help as to the legality of such testing. Here, conflicting advice has been offered to doctors in the United Kingdom. Legal opinion sought by the Council of the British Medical Association was to the effect that, not only was non-consensual testing impermissible but also, to do so, might well constitute an assault;[12] by contrast, the Central Committee for Hospital Medical Services has been advised that the doctor may exercise his clinical judgment unless the patient asks specifically about HIV testing;[13] finally, the Medical Defence Union obtained an opinion which eliminated the possibility of assault once permission for venepuncture had been given but, nevertheless, thought that, save in exceptional circumstances – as, for instance when the expectation of a positive result was very low – specific consent for HIV should always be obtained.[14]

In seeking a way through these divergent opinions, we take the view that a patient who consults a doctor gives tacit consent to the carrying out of those diagnostic tests that the doctor considers necessary – the patient's consent to each and every test to be performed on a blood sample need not be obtained and it is unreal to speak of 'informed consent' in this context. This is not a unique view – as Dyer has reported:

10 See K M Boyd 'HIV Infection: The Ethics of Anonymised Testing and of Testing Pregnant Women' (1990) 16 J Med Ethics 173. The position in the US, where AIDS is a notifiable disease, and elsewhere, may well be different and is not considered here; see D H J Hermann 'Liability Related to Diagnosis and Treatment of AIDS' (1987) 15 Law Med Hlth Care 36. For general discussion of blood testing, see A Grubb and D S Pearl *Blood Testing, AIDS and DNA Profiling: Law and Policy* (1990).

11 GMC *HIV and AIDS: The Ethical Considerations* (1995).

12 M Sharrard and I Gatt 'Human Immunodeficiency Virus (HIV) Antibody Testing' (1987) 295 BMJ 911.

13 HMSC *Advice re HIV Testing* (1988) discussed by C Dyer 'Another Judgment on Testing for HIV Without Consent' (1988) 296 BMJ 1791.

14 Medical Defence Union *AIDS: Medico-Legal Advice* (1988). These three opinions are discussed in detail by J Keown 'The Ashes of AIDS and the Phoenix of Informed Consent' (1989) 52 MLR 790.

'some lawyers have suggested that patients with a "perplexing presentation" might be taken to have given an implied consent to any tests designed to find out what was wrong with them.'[15] The essential question is whether the HIV test is of such a nature as to remove it from the scope of those tests to which the patient may be said to consent implicitly – reportedly, it would not be excluded, say, in Germany.[16] It is true that HIV tests carry major emotional, financial and social significance; moreover, the disease to be diagnosed is currently incurable – which distinguishes the test from one for, eg, syphilis. The same could, however, be said for a hypothetical test which demonstrated the presence of incurable malignant disease. It would not be necessary for the doctor to obtain specific consent to undertake such a test, yet it could have consequences similar to a test for HIV infection. The similarity is, however, not absolute – the major distinction being that, irrespective of the result, the mere fact that an HIV test has been undertaken carries serious insurance implications and has to be disclosed as a condition of most policies.[17] We would raise, too, the potential psychological sequelae of an unexpected positive result. We cannot escape the fact that our society has constructed a stigma around this disease which makes the confirmation of a positive result all the more difficult to accept. Moreover, if such a result comes 'from the blue' when no specific consent was given, the question of the patient's right *not* to know arises.[18] These factors certainly constitute grounds for putting the HIV test into a separate category but it is doubtful if it is a sufficiently powerful argument to exclude absolutely all testing for which no specific consent was given. None the less, the patient could argue that, had he been informed of the doctor's intention, he would not have consented to giving the sample; in such circumstances, an action for negligence might be available under the general terms of the consent doctrine.[19] The critical condition, here, is that he was informed – insurance and comparable complicating factors do not arise if the patient is ignorant of the facts. Thus, there may be many, perhaps a majority of, cases in which non-disclosure would be good medical practice and, as Keown has stressed, the legality of non-disclosure is then measured in *Bolam* terms – would the action be supported by a responsible body of medical opinion?[20] Judging by the fact that a motion in favour of non-consensual clinical testing was passed by a vote of 183-140 at the 1987 annual representative meeting of the British Medical Association,[1] this support might be available despite the fact that the council of the BMA would not support the resolution. The arguments in favour of this practice, of course, meet stiff opposition in the face of a positive result and we accept that this does raise considerable difficulty. Is it, however, sufficient to overcome the evident advantages of being able to investigate the patient without, at the same time, distressing him or her unnecessarily? One way out of the impasse might be a policy of obtaining retrospective consent and, if this is not forthcoming, of maintaining secrecy. This, of course, is, at least, ethically dubious; much would

15 C Dyer 'Testing for HIV: The Medicolegal View' (1987) 295 BMJ 871. D Brahams 'Human Immunodeficiency Virus and the Law' [1987] 2 Lancet 227 shares our view so long as consent to test for HIV infection has not been specifically withheld.
16 H L Karcher 'Doctors and HIV: An International Perspective. 1 – Germany' (1991) 302 BMJ 195.
17 See chapter 1.
18 Discussed in the context of genetic information in chapter 7.
19 See p 274ff below.
20 For discussion of the principle, see p 280ff and, generally, chapter 9.
 1 BMA 'HIV Antibody Testing: Summary of Guidance' (1987) 295 BMJ 940.

depend on whether one sees a moral distinction between deception and lying.[2] But there is not a chasm of difference between silence when one strongly suspects a diagnosis and silence when one knows the answer; such a practice, although philosophically suspect, might be seen as benign pragmatism.

All the above discussion relates to consent within the clinical setting and the patient's advantage; there can, in our opinion, be no vacillation if the advantage of testing is to another party – express consent would have to be obtained in such circumstances and action in its absence would have to be defended on the grounds of necessity or public interest. Would the public interest justify coercive routine testing of some or all health carers? There is clearly a tendency in this direction in the United States,[3] which has been resisted in the United Kingdom, by both the government and the medical profession. In practice, it would be an ineffective way of solving a problem which, as we have seen, is, to all intents, insignificant. It is more than doubtful if it would be morally defensible to spend millions of pounds of health service money[4] on exorcising such an ephemeral spectre.

The issue of contamination of the health carer has been raised by the Royal Colleges of Surgeons of England and of Edinburgh.[5] The principle of the need to obtain consent to testing before operation, even in an emergency, from a high-risk patient was emphasised but the Colleges agreed to support any surgeon who undertook non-consensual testing in the interests of seriously contaminated theatre staff – serious contamination and high-risk being, again, left to the individual surgeon's interpretation. It was said that testing before the patient had recovered from the anaesthetic could count as an assault; we confess to some difficulty in accepting this – it is hard to see where would be the element of assault provided no special invasion were made for the express purpose of obtaining the blood sample. In the current climate, however, it might be hard to justify a failure to wait the few minutes needed for the patient's recovery in order to carry out a relatively lengthy test; the situation, however, seems to be one of more theoretical than practical importance.

Anonymised HIV testing, which may be of great epidemiological importance, is less controversial but still raises ethical issues.[6] Such tests involve either taking blood or saliva from random groups of patients who have not necessarily engaged in high-risk practices or using blood samples that have been obtained for other purposes. The morality of random testing for a specific condition depends, to a large extent and as discussed above, on what would be done in the event of a positive result. The dilemma can be overcome by total anonymisation but this only substitutes one potential immorality by another – the knowledge obtained cannot now be used for the benefit of the individual; obtaining useful epidemiological evidence at the expense of the deliberate exclusion of any means of helping both those who are found to be infected and their contacts is a process fraught with ethical problems. In general, however, the positive advantages of investigation seem to outweigh such objections provided that

2   See the useful debate J Jackson 'Telling the Truth' (1991) 17 J Med Ethics 5, 'On the Morality of Deception – Does Method Matter?' (1993) 19 J Med Ethics 183; cf D Bakhurst 'On Lying and Deceiving' (1992) 18 J Med Ethics 63.
3   M Morris 'American Legislation on AIDS' (1991) 303 BMJ 325.
4   K Tolley and J Kennelly 'Cost of Compulsory HIV Testing' (1993) 306 BMJ 1202.
5   A Walker 'Surgeons and HIV' (1991) 302 BMJ 136.
6   See Boyd p 271, n 10 above.

those tested are informed that their blood may be subjected to anonymised testing of any sort and that they will not be informed of the results.

Proceeding without consent – the consequences

Non-consensual medical treatment entitles the patient to sue for damages for the battery which is committed. It is also possible to base a claim on the tort of negligence, the theory being that the doctor has been negligent in failing to obtain the consent of the patient. There are important differences between the two forms of action which have given rise to much legal debate. The issue is, however, now settled and the law is reasonably clear.

An action for battery arises when the plaintiff has been touched in some way by the defendant and when there has been no consent, express or implied, to such touching. All that the plaintiff need establish in such an action is that the defendant wrongfully touched him. It is unnecessary to establish loss as a result of the touching and, therefore, there is no problem as to the causation of damage to be overcome. By contrast, in an action based on the tort of negligence, the plaintiff must establish that the defendant wrongfully touched him and that the negligence of the defendant in touching him without consent has led to the injury for which damages are sought. There is thus a problem of factual causation to be tackled and, for this reason, the action for battery is an easier option from the plaintiff's point of view. The measure of damages recoverable will also be different. All direct damages are recoverable in battery; only those damages which are foreseeable may be recovered in an action for negligence. Thus, an unforeseen medical complication arising from the procedure in question may be something for which damages are recoverable in battery but not in negligence. Clarification of the circumstances in which each action is available was provided by the Supreme Court of Canada in *Reibl v Hughes*[7] and in the first apposite English case of *Chatterton v Gerson*.[8]

An action for battery is appropriate where there has been no consent at all to the physical contact in question. Thus, an action for battery is the suitable remedy if a patient has refused to submit to a procedure but the doctor has, nevertheless, gone ahead in the face of that refusal. A number of Canadian cases illustrate the typical circumstances. Actions were sustained in *Mulloy v Hop Sang*,[9] where the plaintiff's hand was amputated without his consent; in *Allan v New Mount Sinai Hospital*,[10] where the plaintiff had an anaesthetic injected into his left arm in spite of his objection to this procedure; and, as a final illustration, in *Schweizer v Central Hospital*,[11] in which the surgeon performing an operation on the back of a plaintiff whose consent was related to an operation on his toe was held liable for battery. It will be seen that, in all of these cases, what the doctor actually did was quite unconnected with the procedure to which the patient had consented. There was no consent to an operation

7 (1980) 114 DLR (3d) 1 at 10, per Laskin CJ.
8 [1981] QB 432, [1981] 1 All ER 257. See also *Hills v Potter* [1983] 3 All ER 716, [1984] 1 WLR 641.
9 [1935] 1 WWR 714.
10 (1980) 109 DLR (3d) 634.
11 (1974) 53 DLR (3d) 494.

of the 'general nature' of that which was actually performed – thus, they lay within the courts' policy of restricting battery actions to acts of unambiguous hostility.

A claim based on negligence is apt when the plaintiff has given his consent to an act of the general nature of that which is performed by the defendant but there is a flaw in this consent and, as a result, there is no consent to certain concomitant features of the act of which he was unaware. The negligence lies in a failure to apprise the patient of such features as a result of which he has sustained damage; the damage is not due to negligent performance but results from a mishap which, in this instance, was a recognised potential hazard of the procedure. The distinction between the two forms of action was sharply outlined in *Reibl v Hughes* by Laskin CJC, who remarked in his judgment:

> I do not understand how it can be said that the consent was vitiated by the failure of disclosure of risks as to make the surgery or other treatment an unprivileged, unconsented to and intentional invasion of the patient's bodily integrity. I can appreciate the temptation to say that the genuineness of consent to medical treatment depends on proper disclosure of the risks which it entails, but . . . unless there has been misrepresentation or fraud to secure consent to the treatment, a failure to disclose the attendant risks, however serious, should go to negligence rather than battery.[12]

Similarly, it was emphasised in *Chatterton v Gerson* that an action for trespass to the person is inappropriate once the patient is informed in 'broad terms' of the nature of the procedure and consent is given; an action for negligence is the proper remedy if there is a failure to disclose risks.

This, however, is not to say that an action in assault or battery is entirely irrelevant to medical law. In *Appleton v Garrett*[13] the High Court awarded both exemplary and aggravated damages against a dentist who had actively deceived patients as to their need for treatment over a number of years. Any consent offered by the patients was vitiated by the fraudulent misrepresentation of the practitioner. The court held that information had been deliberately withheld and the defendant had acted throughout in bad faith, making an action in battery, rather than in negligence, appropriate.

The negligence action – causation problems
In essence, the aggrieved patient is claiming: 'You did not inform me of the risk which has eventuated; but for your failure, I would not have consented to the procedure; you have failed in your duty of care and, as a result, I have sustained injury.' The problem in negligence actions based on a lack of consent is, therefore, that of causation – the court must be satisfied that the defendant's failure to obtain the valid consent of the patient was, in fact, the cause of the patient's injury. To satisfy this requirement, the patient must prove that he would not have given his consent had he had the information of which he was allegedly deprived.

There are several ways by which the strength of the plaintiff's case can be assessed. The first involves a purely subjective judgment – that is, what would that particular patient have considered to be adequate information? This is clearly open

---

12 For an interesting example of a British case following *Reibl,* see *Ardnt v Smith* (1995) 7 Med LR 108.
13 [1996] PIQR P1. See also [1996] 4 Med L Rev 311.

to the abuse of hindsight. It will be only too easy for a plaintiff, once he has suffered damage, to allege that he would not have given his consent when, in reality, he may well have been quite prepared to do so, even with full knowledge of the risks entailed – as a Californian court had it: 'Subjectively he may believe [he would have declined treatment] with the 20/20 vision of hindsight but we doubt that justice will be served by placing the physician in jeopardy of the patient's bitterness and disillusionment.'[14] The subjective standard is weighted overwhelmingly in favour of the plaintiff and only a few jurisdictions have accepted it.[15]

An alternative objective approach is to postulate a standard based on a reasonable patient. Would the reasonable patient have given his consent when confronted with full information of the risks and difficulties of the procedure in question? If the answer is 'yes', then it may be inferred that the plaintiff himself would have consented. This, like all objective tests, has the disadvantage of being potentially unfair to the plaintiff. There may be specific circumstances which are unique to the individual and it may well be that he or she genuinely would not have consented. To apply the objective standard might, then, be equally unsatisfactory: 'if it is Utopian to think one must concentrate on the particular patient, the law should surely be aiming at Utopia.'[16] The reasonable patient test has practical value in that judges are, themselves, patients and can, therefore, assess the evidence at first hand rather than by proxy; at the same time, this introduces the element of personal prejudice and, in *Maynard*,[17] the trial judge was considered to have been in error in preferring one body of medical opinion to another.

A third, compromise, possibility exists. The court may opt for an objective approach but qualify it by investing the hypothetical reasonable patient with the relevant special peculiarities of the individual plaintiff. In this way the edge is taken off the objective test, while the pitfalls of the purely subjective approach are avoided. This solution is increasingly favoured in the criminal law relating to the plea of provocation.

The courts in Canada vacillated between the alternatives of the objective and subjective approaches.[18] Finally, in *Reibl v Hughes*,[19] the Supreme Court came down in favour of the compromise solution. The effect of this is that one's starting point is to determine the extent to which the balance of risks was, medically speaking, in favour of the treatment in question. This allows a decision to be made as to whether a reasonable patient would have consented and, that done, the court can proceed to

14 *Cobbs v Grant* 104 Cal Rptr 505 (1972).
15 The subjective standard was certainly used by the New Zealand Court of Appeal in *Smith v Auckland Hospital Board* [1964] NZLR 241, SC; revsd [1965] NZLR 191, NZCA, but there was no argument on the point in this very early case; a clear Antipodean preference for the subjective standard is to be found in the New South Wales Court of Appeal decision: *Ellis v Wallsend District Hospital* [1990] 2 Med LR 103. For full exposition, see D Giesen *International Medical Malpractice Law* (1988) pp 252 et seq.
16 K McK Norrie 'Informed Consent and the Duty of Care' 1985 SLT 289. Or achieving 'the ethical optimum of patient autonomy' as put by M Brazier 'Patient Autonomy and Consent to Treatment: The Role of the Law?' (1987) 7 LS 169.
17 *Maynard v West Midlands Regional Health Authority* [1985] 1 All ER 635, [1984] 1 WLR 634, HL. A rather similar judicial foray into medical decision-making was rejected on appeal in *Gold v Haringey Health Authority* [1988] QB 481, [1987] 2 All ER 888, CA.
18 See eg *Male v Hopmans* (1967) 64 DLR (2d) 105; *Kelly v Haslett* (1976) 75 DLR (3d) 536.
19 (1980) 114 DLR (3d) 1.

look at the particular patient's condition. Here the judgment in *Reibl v Hughes* emphasised the importance of taking into account the patient's questions to the doctor, as these will demonstrate his concerns and will better enable the court to assess what a reasonable patient in the plaintiff's position would have done.

The concept of informed consent

The discussion thus moves inexorably to the issue of 'informed consent' – one which will always remain a classic example of the importation of a medical philosophy from across the Atlantic. Its progress has, in fact, been remarkably slow. Thus, while the first mention of 'informed consent' in the English courts seems to have been as late as 1981,[20] the seed was sown in America in 1957 in the case of *Salgo*.[1] Here, the court concluded that the doctor had a duty to disclose to the patient 'any facts which are necessary to form the basis of an intelligent consent by the patient to the proposed treatment'.[2] It is unfortunate that the phrase 'intelligent consent' was replaced in a later passage related to therapeutic privilege:[3]

> In discussing the element of risk, a certain amount of discretion must be employed consistent with full disclosure of facts necessary to an *informed* consent (our emphasis).[4]

Informed consent was later made a requirement for all state-funded research work following a series of allegations that potentially dangerous experiments were being conducted without the consent of the experimental subjects.[5] Silverman maintains that there are, thus, two distinct forms of 'informed consent' and, certainly, this must be so as to the assessment of the quality of the information provided. Such a review *must* be prospective in the case of research whereas it can only be retrospective, for example by way of litigation, in respect of day to day patient management.

In either event, informed consent introduces a new element to medical treatment. It is no longer a simple matter of consent to a technical assault; consent must now be based on a knowledge of the nature, consequences and alternatives associated with the proposed therapy. Bray J's definition has gone relatively unchallenged[6] across the United States but it is still no more than a broad expression of principle. It goes no way to explaining either what counts as informed consent or how we tell that the circumstances surrounding a given event satisfy the requirements.[7] In so far as it defines a doctor's duties rather than the patient's reaction, the phrase is a misnomer[8]

20 *Chatterton v Gerson* [1981] QB 432, [1981] 1 All ER 257.
1 *Salgo v Leland Stanford Junior University Board of Trustees* 317 P 2d 170 (Cal, 1957).
2 Per Bray J.
3 See p 279 below.
4 We are indebted to W A Silverman 'The Myth of Informed Consent: In Daily Practice and in Clinical Trials' (1989) 15 J Med Ethics 6 for many of the historical facts.
5 Surgeon General's Memorandum *Clinical Investigations Using Human Subjects* (1966).
6 Eg *Harnish v Children's Hospital Medical Center* 387 Mass 152 (1982) where the phrase 'intelligent decision' was used.
7 G R Gillett 'Informed Consent and Moral Integrity' (1989) 15 J Med Ethics 117.
8 T K Feng 'Failure of Medical Advice: Trespass or Negligence' (1987) 7 LS 149.

which, we believe, has been applied in medical writing and, indeed, in official publications with inadequate exploration of its meaning. Moreover, the phrase is tautologous – to be ethically and legally acceptable, 'consent' must always be 'informed' and the first element of the phrase is, then, redundant. It is interesting to note, for example, that although the English text of the Council of Europe *Convention on Human Rights and Biomedicine* speaks of 'informed consent' in Article 5, the French text refers merely to 'consentment' *tout simple*.[9]

The topic recalls the remarks of Frankfurter J, albeit in a completely different context:

> A phrase begins life as a literary expression; its felicity leads to its lazy repetition; and repetition soon establishes it as a legal formula indiscriminately used to express different and sometimes contradictory ideas.[10]

Thus, we suggest that, when Dunn LJ said in the fundamental United Kingdom case of *Sidaway*: 'The concept of informed consent forms no part of English law',[11] he may well have been referring to consent based on a subjective patient test – for no one would deny that 'information' must be nowadays be passed from doctor to patient in the United Kingdom. Yet, similar disclaimers have been repeated more recently both in England[12] and in Scotland[13] – and have been echoed in Australia[14] – and the legal definition has become no clearer. The phrase 'informed consent' is, however, now part of the lore of medical ethics; we must, therefore, accept it and consider the basic nature of the information that has to be given in order to validate consent to medical treatment.

What needs to be disclosed?

Looked at from the ethical point of view, the matter is one of self-determination. A person should not be exposed to a risk of damage unless he has agreed to that risk and he cannot properly agree to – or, equally importantly, make a choice between – risks in the absence of factual information. The twin problems to be resolved are, therefore, by what general standard should the information be judged and, within that, to what extent must or should particular details be divulged?

---

9 Council of Europe, *Convention for the Protection of Human Rights and Dignity of the Human Being with regard to the Application of Biology and Medicine*, Oviedo, 4 April 1997, art 5.

10 *Tiller v Atlantic Coast Line Railroad Co* 318 US 54 at 68 (1943).

11 *Sidaway v Board of Governors of the Bethlem Royal Hospital* [1984] QB 493 at 517, [1984] 1 All ER 1018 at 1030, CA.

12 'English law does not accept the transatlantic concept of informed consent' per Lord Donaldson in *Re T (adult) (refusal of medical treatment)* [1992] 4 All ER 649 at 663, (1992) 9 BMLR 46 at 61, CA. The use of the words 'transatlantic concept' is, itself, misleading, as probably the majority of the United States still hold to the professional standard.

13 '[T]he law . . . has come down firmly against the view that the doctor's duty to the patient involves at all costs obtaining the informed consent of the patient to specific medical treatments': *Moyes v Lothian Health Board* [1990] 1 Med LR 463, 1990 SLT 444 per Lord Caplan at SLT 449.

14 '. . . nothing is to be gained by reiterating . . . the oft-used and somewhat amorphous phrase "informed consent"': *Rogers v Whittaker* (1992) 109 ALR 625 at 633, 16 BMLR 148 at 156 (High Court of Australia), per Mason CJ et al.

The general standards available are conveniently described as the 'patient standard' and the 'professional standard'. The former has already been described above in the wide context of consent to battery. Precisely the same principles apply to counselling. Thus, the extreme of this school of thought would hold that, given a rational patient, the doctor must reveal all the relevant facts as to what he intends to do. It is not for him to determine what the patient should or should not hear. Obviously, there must be some medical assessment of what is or is not significant but, apart from the exclusion of irrelevant material, the patient should be as fully informed as possible so that he or she can make up his or her mind in the light of all the relevant circumstances. This approach most fully satisfies the requirements of self-determination but can be criticised on the grounds that it leaves little scope for the exercise of clinical judgment by the doctor. It is for this reason that even those most dedicated to patient autonomy will allow the doctor the 'therapeutic privilege' to withhold information which would merely serve to distress or confuse the patient.

This concession applies only to specific items selected by the doctor for specific reasons. It does not run as far as acceptance of the alternative ethical approach to disclosure of information – that is, one based on the professional standard. Here, counselling and informing are regarded as an integral part of clinical management; the extent and detail of the information supplied is a matter for decision by the doctor who is, therein, subject to the same duty of care as when prescribing or operating. It follows that, whichever standard is adopted, litigation based on inadequate information must be taken in negligence. Any difference lies in the test to be applied. Given a patient standard, the quality of information will be judged from the viewpoint of the prudent – or the particular – patient; under the professional standard, it will be that of the prudent doctor.

The choice between a 'patient standard' and a 'professional standard' is a difficult one. There must be respect for the patient's legitimate interest in knowing to what he is subjecting himself but, at the same time, there will clearly be cases where a paternal approach is appropriate. In addition, the practicalities of the situation must be borne in mind. Although it might be ethically desirable for patients to be as fully informed as possible, the time spent in explaining the intricacies of procedures could be considerable, particularly if a doctor is expected to deal with remote risks. Doctors – and, particularly, doctors operating in a NHS – simply do not have the time to spend on unduly lengthy explanations of all the ramifications of treatment and many would regard the practice as unnecessarily disturbing for the patient.[15] It has also been pointed out that adherence to a professional standard provides a coherent body of principles;[16] courts that are subject to this standard are, therefore, at least less likely to be inconsistent in their judgment of disputes.

A final point about the nature of the doctrine of informed consent relates to 'patient understanding'. The focus of the concept is on information giving, supposedly to further the autonomy of the patient. But the consequent implication is that the health care professional has fulfilled his duty once he has proffered the information. Such a narrow interpretation, however, ignores consideration of the patient's ability

15 This, and other aspects, have been researched in Sheffield: D D Kerrigan, R S Thevasagayam, T O Woods et al 'Who's Afraid of Informed Consent?' (1993) 306 BMJ 298 and was found to be unmerited. The study, however, concerned the relatively innocuous repair of inguinal hernia – the authors concede that the results could be different in more serious circumstances.
16 C Newdick 'The Doctor's Duties of Care Under *Sidaway*' (1985) 36 NILQ 243.

to assimilate and analyse the information. If it is not also part of the doctor's duty to ensure at least a degree of understanding on the part of the patient, he can discharge his duty by offering information in a way that results in no enhancement of the patient's autonomy – the ethical basis of the doctrine is, accordingly, undermined.

The cases

Whatever standpoint one takes on this matter, a decision of some court can be found to endorse one's preferred approach. Within the Commonwealth, there are decisions ranging from the endorsement of the deliberate medical lie to the acceptance of the extreme patient- orientated approach which emphasises complete disclosure of risk. The United States, with its 51 independent jurisdictions, provides a useful overall view. Although a majority of the States still apply a professional standard, there is a recognisable national drift towards that of the prudent patient; it is worth recapitulating the reasons given for this in a typical case in which the onus was transferred.[17] These included:

(a) that conditions other than those that are purely medical will influence the patient's decision;
(b) that following the whim of the physician is inconsistent with the patient's right to self-determination; and
(c) that the professional standard smacks of anachronistic paternalism.

In addition, the court in *Largey* specifically ruled out the criticism that the prudent patient test obliges the doctor to list every possible complication of the proposed procedure. While this appears superficially disarming, it does, in fact, serve to emphasise that the professional is bound to be unsure of his precise position; as Margaret Brazier put it: 'the doctor is left to "second-guess" the courts.'[18]

The way ahead in the United Kingdom is, now, clear. The starting point must be found in the complementary cases of *Hunter v Hanley*[19] in Scotland and *Bolam v Friern Hospital Management Committee*[20] in England, both of which define the essence of medical negligence. Most of the discussion of informed consent has been couched in *Bolam* terms and we will, for the moment, confine ourselves to that case – always with the caveat that we are following the loose thinking which surrounds that concept; for, as the High Court of Australia has pointed out,[1] consent is relevant to actions framed in trespass or battery, not in negligence which is simply a matter of standards of care. For present purposes, the essential part of the *Bolam* dictum runs: 'a doctor is not negligent if he acts in accordance with a practice accepted at the time as proper by a responsible body of medical opinion.'[2] Since it is agreed that actions based on lack of consent to medical treatment should be taken in negligence, it follows that any argument as to what needs to be disclosed in British medical practice hinges

17 *Largey v Rothman* 540 A 2d 504 (NJ, 1988). The prudent patient standard was set in *Canterbury v Spence* 464 F 2d 772 (DC, 1972). For retention of the professional standard, see *Wooley v Henderson* 418 A 2d 1123 (Md, 1980).
18 M Brazier 'Patient Authority and Causent & Treatment: The Role of the Law?' (1987) 7 LS 169.
19 1955 SC 200, 1955 SLT 213.
20 [1957] 2 All ER 118, [1957] 1 WLR 582.
 1 In *Rogers v Whittaker* (1992) 109 ALR 625 at 633, [1993] 4 Med LR 79 at 83.
 2 Per McNair J [1957] 2 All ER 118 at 122.

upon whether or not the Bolam principle applies equally to both diagnosis and treatment and to the giving of information.

That it did so was upheld both in *Chatterton v Gerson*[3] and in *Hills v Potter*.[4] The acid test, however, came in the seminal case of *Sidaway*[5] where the proposition was accepted in the court of first instance but was received rather less enthusiastically in the Court of Appeal; there, Sir John Donaldson MR did not regard it as self-evident that the standards applied to diagnosis and treatment should be the same as those applied to disclosure. Concern was expressed that the definition of the duty of care was a matter for the law which 'could not stand by if the profession, by an excess of paternalism, denied their patients a real choice'.[6] The Master of the Rolls' reasons for isolating the advisory duty in this way have been questioned[7] and his colleagues were unable to follow him all the way. Browne-Wilkinson LJ, however, also believed that there was a prima facie duty on the doctor to inform the patient – the assumption of the role of adviser carried with it the duty to disclose material and unusual risks.

The House of Lords, while maintaining a professional standard of disclosure, was, similarly, prepared to modify the existing law in certain respects. Thus, Lord Bridge held:

> A judge might, in certain circumstances, come to the conclusion that the disclosure of a particular risk was so obviously necessary to an informed choice on the part of the patient that no reasonably prudent medical man would fail to make it . . .[8]

while Lord Templeman considered that:

> . . . the court must decide whether the information afforded to the patient was sufficient to alert the patient to the possibility of serious harm of the kind in fact suffered.[9]

Lord Scarman, however, delivered what was, effectively, a dissenting judgment in which he indicated that: 'it was a strange conclusion if our courts should be led to conclude that our law . . . should permit doctors to determine in what circumstances . . . a duty arose to warn.' He found great merit in the American case of *Canterbury v Spence*,[10] in which it was held that, while medical evidence on this matter was not excluded, it was the court which determined the extent of, and any breach of, the doctor's duty to inform. Information includes warning. King CJ, for example, specifically instructed that the doctor's duty extends not only to disclose any real risks in the treatment but also to warn of any real risk that the treatment may prove ineffective.[11]

3 [1981] QB 432, [1981] 1 All ER 257.

4 [1983] 3 All ER 716, [1984] 1 All ER 641.

5 *Sidaway v Board of Governors of the Bethlem Royal Hospital* [1984] QB 493 at 517, [1984] 1 All ER 1018 at 1030, CA; affd [1985] AC 871, [1985] 1 All ER 643, HL.

6 [1984] QB 493 at 513, [1984] 1 All ER 1018 at 1028, CA.

7 See eg K McK Norrie 'Standards of Disclosure' 1984 SLT 237; I Kennedy 'The Patient on the Clapham Omnibus' (1984) 47 MLR 454.

8 [1985] AC 871 at 900, [1985] 1 All ER 643 at 663, HL.

9 [1985] AC 871 at 903, [1985] 1 All ER 643 at 665.

10 464 F 2d 772 (DC 1972).

11 *F v R* (1983) 33 SASR 189, SC. Alternative treatments should also be canvassed – particularly if there is a choice between medical and surgical procedures: *Haughian v Paine* (1987) 37 DLR (4th) 624, cited in (1987) 137 NLJ 557.

Two specific aspects of the information issue are confirmed as a result of *Sidaway*. The first is that material risks of a procedure must be disclosed, subject only to therapeutic privilege which a doctor might be required to justify. Following *Canterbury*, a risk can be defined as material if a reasonable person in the patient's position, if warned of the risk, would be likely to attach significance to it. Similarly, it is material if the medical practitioner is, or should reasonably be, aware that the particular patient, if warned of the risk, would be likely to attach significance to it.[12] Quite what that means in relation to chance is impossible to assess and, indeed, generalisations may be inappropriate as the test relates to the circumstances of the particular case. Moreover, significance in this field is a function not only of incidence but also of severity; thus, in *Hopp v Lepp*,[13] it was stated that a risk, even if it is a mere possibility, should be regarded as material if its occurrence causes serious consequences. As to incidence, it was agreed in *Sidaway* that a risk of 10% of a stroke resulting – as was established in *Reibl v Hughes*[14] – was one which a doctor could hardly fail to appreciate as necessitating a warning; but non-disclosure was considered proper in Mrs Sidaway's case when the risk of damage to the spinal cord was of the order of 1% or less. We have to admit to some concern that odds shorter than 100:1 might be regarded as immaterial in the eyes of the law.[15] A great deal will, however, hang on the *patient's* requirements as expressed by way of questioning and we return to this below.

Secondly, *Sidaway* confirmed the 'therapeutic' or professional' privilege to withhold information that might be psychologically damaging to the patient. This, again, follows the direction in *Bolam*, in which the judge said in his charge to the jury:

> You may well think that when a doctor is dealing with a mentally sick man and has a strong belief that his only hope of cure is submission to electroconvulsive therapy, the doctor cannot be criticised if he does not stress the dangers, which he believed to be minimal, which are involved in the treatment . . .[16]

This principle has since been widely adopted.

It is also clear from *Sidaway* that, by way of exception to this rule, there must be particularly good reasons, which the doctor would have to justify, for failing to answer such questions as the patient puts and that there may, indeed, be a strict obligation to do so. Thus, Lord Bridge held, albeit obiter, that:

> When questioned specifically by a patient of apparently sound mind about risks involved in a particular treatment proposed, a doctor's duty must, in my opinion, be to answer both truthfully and as fully as the questioner requires.[17]

---

12 Mason CJ et al in *Rogers v Whittaker* (1992) 109 ALR 625 at 634, [1993] 4 Med LR 79 at 83 (High Court of Australia).
13 (1979) 98 DLR (3d) 464. But in the Australian case *Battersby v Tottman and State of South Australia* (1985) 37 SASR 524, the risk of blindness was considered a subject for obligatory disclosure only in a minority opinion – this may, however, have been because there was a strong possibility of suicide.
14 (1980) 114 DLR (3d) 1.
15 King JC accepted 200:1 as not being material in *F v R* (1983) 33 SASR 189, SC.
16 [1957] 2 All ER 118 at 124, [1957] 1 WLR 582 at 590, per McNair J.
17 [1985] AC 871 at 898, [1985] 1 All ER 643 at 661, HL.

'The fact that the patient asked questions revealing concern about the risk would make the doctor aware that this patient did, in fact, attach significance to the risk'[18] – and, hence, affect its materiality; it was certainly this fact which served to turn a 1:14,000 chance of blindness into a risk which it was found negligent not to disclose in the Australian case of *Rogers v Whittaker.*

This inference was, however, disturbed in England in *Blyth v Bloomsbury Health Authority.*[19] Here, the trial judge's decision in favour of the plaintiff was reversed on appeal. He was found to be in error in holding that there was an obligation, when asked, to pass on *all* the information available to the hospital; the question of what a patient should be told in response to a general inquiry could not be detached from the *Bolam* test any more than when no such enquiry was made (per Kerr LJ). Neill LJ went further:

> I am not convinced [from *Sidaway*] that the *Bolam* test is irrelevant even in relation to the question of what answers are properly to be given to specific enquiries or that Lords Diplock and Bridge intended to hold otherwise.[20]

However, the argument in *Blyth* centred largely on some rather obscure therapeutic notes written in the hospital and there has been no judicial enthusiasm to follow its line.

The House of Lords' approach in *Sidaway* has been subject to academic criticism[1] largely because of the uncertainties it left behind. A strong impression remains that the House was not entirely at ease with *Bolam* – only Lord Diplock was prepared to carry it to its conclusion. Yet ranks are closed whenever the principle is directly questioned. Thus, in *Gold,*[2] Schiemann J at first instance attempted to distinguish counselling from treatment and was firmly overruled by the Court of Appeal.[3] The House of Lords has grudgingly confirmed that, in theory at least, the courts retain the power to establish standards of care,[4] but, as we point out in chapter 9, their Lordships find it acceptable to challenge medical opinion only when the latter has no rational basis. This attitude is taking on an atmosphere of stubbornness and is becoming almost unique in face of the now universal acceptance of a patient's right to decide on his or her own treatment. The writing was already on the wall in Canada where, in *Reibl,* it was held:

---

18 Mason CJ et al in *Whittaker* (1992) 109 ACLR 625 at 631, [1993] at 4 Med LR 79 at 82.
19 (1985) Times, 24 May; on appeal [1993] 4 Med LR 151, CA. *Blyth* reminds us that the principles derived from surgical cases can apply equally to medication – implied consent to taking a drug cannot be assumed: *Crichton v Hastings* (1972) 29 DLR (3d) 692.
20 [1993] 4 Med LR 151 at 157, Neil LJ concurring at 160.
 1 For full discussion see I Kennedy and A Grubb *Medical Law: Text and Materials* (2nd edn, 1994) pp 184 et seq.
 2 *Gold v Haringey Health Authority* [1988] QB 481, [1987] 2 All ER 888, CA.
 3 The integral nature of medical attendance has been emphasised in other contexts, eg in the management of the mentally incompetent: *Re H (mental patient) (diagnosis)* [1993] 1 FLR 28, [1993] 4 Med LR 91.
 4 *Bolitho v City and Hackney Health Authority* [1997] 4 All ER 771, (1997) 39 BMLR 1.

> [The] scope of the duty of disclosure ... is not a question that is to be concluded on the basis of the expert medical evidence alone ... What is under consideration here is the patient's right to know what risks are involved in undergoing or forgoing certain surgery or other treatment.[5]

and, in 1983, it was said of warning of therapeutic failure in the Supreme Court of South Australia:

> The ultimate question ... is ... whether the defendant's conduct ... conforms to the standard of reasonable care demanded by the law. That is a question for the court and the duty of deciding it cannot be delegated to any profession or group in the community.[6]

The strongest attack on *Bolam* to date has, however, come from the High Court of Australia where its application to counselling has been firmly rejected in *Rogers v Whittaker*. In that case, we have the majority opinion saying:

> There is a fundamental difference between, on the one hand, diagnosis and treatment and, on the other hand, the provision of advice or information to the patient ... Because the choice to be made calls for a decision by the patient on information known to the medical practitioner but not to the patient, it would be illogical to hold that the amount of information to be provided by the medical practitioner can be determined from the perspective of the practitioner alone or, for that matter, of the medical profession.[7]

and even more trenchantly, Gaudron J:

> [E]ven in the area of diagnosis and treatment, there is, in my view, no legal basis for limiting liability in terms of the rule known as "the *Bolam* test" ... [It] may be a convenient statement of the approach dictated by the state of the evidence in some cases. As such, it may have some utility as a rule-of-thumb in some jury cases, but it can serve no other useful function.[8]

The ripples of *Rogers* have reached distant shores, primarily those of South Africa, where negligence is subsumed under a general heading of 'wrongfulness' for which the defence of *volenti non fit injuria* – ie voluntary assumption of risk – is available. In *Castell v De Greef*[9] the Cape Provincial Division of the Supreme Court endorsed not only the Australian High Court's patient-orientated disclosure test, but also that court's definition of material risk. It was held that, for a defence of *volenti non fit inuria* to be successful, the consenting party must have knowledge, awareness,

---

5 (1980) 114 DLR (3d) 1 at 13.
6 *F v R* (1983) 33 SASR 189 at 194, per King CJ.
7 (1992) 109 ALR 625 at 632, [1993] 4 Med LR 79 at 83. For a full discussion of the case, see D Chalmers and R Schwartz 'Rogers v Whittaker and Informed Consent in Australia: A Fair Dinkum Duty of Disclosure' (1993) 1 Med L Rev 139; R C Pincus 'Has Informed Consent Finally Arrived in Australia?' (1993) 159 Med J Austral 25; and B McSherry 'Failing to Advise and Warn of Inherent Risks in Medical Treatment: When Does Negligence Occur?' (1993) 1 J Law Med 5.
8 (1992) 109 ALR 625 at 635-636, [1993] 4 Med LR 79 at 84. Most recently, this decision has been strongly re-affirmed by the High Court in *Chappel v Hart* [1998] HCA 55.
9 1994 (4) SA 408.

appreciation and understanding of the nature and extent of the harm or risk involved, this being on the grounds that the patient has otherwise not voluntarily assumed the risks in question, ie is not *volens*. The juxtaposition of *volenti* and consent suggests that, pace *Chatteron v Gerson*[10] an action in trespass may still be available, at least in South Africa; the fact that *Castell* was taken in negligence was dictated by the nature of the pleadings. Thus, we see how a common concept of informed consent can be recognised in legal systems with varying traditions.

In the United Kingdom, however, habits die hard and the position in Scotland which was awaited with some interest, has been resolved in a way that leaves little room for doubt.[11] Lord Caplan had this to say:

> In my view . . . the appropriate tests to apply in medical negligence cases are to be found in *Hunter v Hanley* and *Bolam* . . . As I see it, the law in both Scotland and England has come down firmly against the view that the doctor's duty to the patient involves at all costs obtaining the informed consent of the patient to specific medical treatments . . . I can read nothing in the majority view in *Sidaway* which suggests that the extent and quality of warning to be given by a doctor to his patient should not in the last resort be governed by medical criteria.[12]

But, despite this, there is no doubt that a movement away from *Bolam* has developed in the years since the previous edition of this book and there is now some evidence that the British courts will not always adhere rigidly to the *Bolam* standard in disputes over information disclosure. In *Smith v Tunbridge Wells Health Authority*,[13] for example, the failure of a consultant surgeon to inform a 28-year-old man of impotence and bladder dysfunction following an operation to treat rectal prolapse was held to be negligent, despite medical support for the decision. Indeed, it was considered that disclosure of the risk was the *only* reasonable course of action.

Negligence was established in *McAllister v Lewisham and North Southwark Health Authority*,[14] when a senior consultant neurosurgeon failed to disclose the risks surrounding an operation to alleviate a weakness in the patient's leg which was linked to a neurological malformation. Among other lapses, a risk of hemiplegia was not disclosed. The trial judge held that:

> I have come to the conclusion that those who say that the warnings given . . . were inadequate are right and there has not been shown to me on the evidence any reputable body of responsible opinion to the contrary.

---

10 [1981] QB 432, [1981] 1 All ER 257.
11 *Moyes v Lothian Health Board* 1990 SLT 444, [1990] 1 Med LR 463. Two further Scottish cases are known to have failed but are very poorly reported: *Comber v Greater Glasgow Health Board* 1992 SLT 22n, *Hsuing v Webster* 1992 SLT 1071n. They are reported as news items in (1991) Scotsman, 24 April, p 4.
12 1990 SLT 444 at 449, [1990] 1 Med LR 463 at 468.
13 [1994] 5 Med LR 334.
14 [1994] 5 Med LR 343.

Newell and Newell v Goldenberg[15] was in essence a wrongful pregnancy case, involving a vasectomy which reversed and led to a fourth conception for the plaintiffs. The undisclosed risk of this happening was 1 : 2,300 and the plaintiffs argued that, had they been informed, Mrs Newell would also have been sterilised. Mantell J found for the plaintiffs in holding that a patient about to undergo elective or voluntary surgery is entitled to be told about its effectiveness. He opined that, although some doctors might not have disclosed the risk at the relevant time, they would not, in so doing, have been acting reasonably or responsibly: '[t]he Bolam principle provides a defence for those who lag behind the times . . . It cannot serve those who know better.'

In our final case from the Queen's Bench, Butterfield J held in *Williamson v East London and City Health Authority*[16] that non-disclosure of the full nature of the surgery to remove a breast prosthesis – which was, effectively, a mastectomy – constituted negligence. This was so even though the court accepted that the removal proved to be necessary. In the court's opinion, the plaintiff had wrongly been deprived of the opportunity to contemplate and agree to the possibility that mastectomy might be the outcome of her operation.

Most significantly of all, in *Lybert v Warrington Health Authority*,[17] the Court of Appeal upheld a plaintiff's action for negligent failure to disclose the risk that a hysterectomy might not provide protection against conception. Without referring explicitly to *Bolam*, the court none the less decreed that part of the duty of care owed was to ensure that a proper and effective system existed for giving sufficient warning of failure. Ideally, that warning should be oral *and* in writing and could be given either on admission of the patient, before she agreed to the operation or before her discharge. Here the court is effectively laying down the acceptable standard of care for such cases and, in this respect, the decision represents a first, tentative incursion into near-virgin territory.

Movement away from *Bolam* of this sort is unprecedented and, as the High Court of Australia so readily accepted in *Rogers v Whittaker*, is due to recognition of the fact that the advice-giving aspect of medical practice is not entirely a matter of medical knowledge and expertise. This must be correct for, unlike diagnosis and treatment, the question of whether a patient wishes to consent to a particular procedure is bound firmly to the notion of patient autonomy – the choice of the patient is crucial and a choice can only be real and valid if it is based on adequate information. This brings us full circle and back once again to the nature of the doctrine of informed consent and its future.

The consent doctrine in the future

Few would deny that the progress of the consent doctrine in the United States has shown signs of overreaction leading, in some instances, to the undue encouragement of malpractice litigation.[18] There is also little doubt that such fears have had their

15 [1995] 6 Med LR 371.
16 (1997) 41 BMLR 85.
17 [1996] 7 Med LR 71.
18 In *Truman v Thomas* 611 P 2d 902 (Cal, 1980) a doctor was, effectively, held liable for failing to convince a reluctant patient of the importance of a screening test for cancer.

influence on the British courts – Dunn LJ, for example, considered that the acceptance of 'informed consent' would be damaging to the relationship of trust and confidence between doctor and patient and might have an adverse effect on the practice of medicine.[19] Two judges in the House of Lords in *Sidaway* admitted their reliance on an article by Robertson[20] in which an American opinion was quoted:

> The requirement of informed consent to medical treatment has, for at least the past two decades, been used as a cloth from which courts slowly have begun to fashion a no-fault system for compensating persons who have suffered bad results from medical treatment.[1]

Robertson, himself, concluded that 'it is judicial policy, rather than the importance of the patient's rights, which will dictate the future development of the doctrine in the United Kingdom'. We would hope that this cynical analysis is untrue – although it is certain that, so long as *Bolam* holds sway, it is unlikely that the consent-based action will be used as widely in the British courts as it has been in those of the United States. In what is probably the most comprehensive study of the consent issue in the United Kingdom available, McLean predicted that a 'prudent patient' test will never be developed here.[2]

Even so, the wind of change is blowing and the question is not so much 'is the doctrine of informed consent coming to the United Kingdom?' as 'what can we do to improve on the American model?'

In our view, a start might well be made by dropping the phrase 'informed consent' in favour of 'rational consent' – or, perhaps better, using the word 'understanding', for a competent adult has every right to make a decision which may appear irrational to others. Both are terms which pay due deference to patient autonomy and, at the same time, provide the doctor with a yardstick as to what is expected of him.[3] We need to ensure that any emerging spirit of confrontation between the medical profession and the public is halted and abandoned in favour of the concept of what Teff described as a therapeutic alliance.[4] Diana Brahams[5] expressed the issue best when she said:

> it is up to us to persuade doctors to alter their practice so as to divulge more information routinely and bring their standards up to what a prudent patient would like to know – without intervention of law.

There are, indeed, signs that this is happening. The prudent patient and the prudent doctor standards are approximating de facto even if not de jure. A glance

19 [1984] 1 All ER 1018 at 1030.
20 G Robertson 'Informed Consent to Medical Treatment' (1981) 97 LQR 102.
 1 A Meisel 'The Expansion of Liability for Medical Accidents: From Negligence to Strict Liability by Way of Informed Consent' (1977) 56 Neb L Rev 51.
 2 S A M McLean *A Patient's Right to Know* (1989) p 85.
 3 The use of other ill-defined terms such as 'effective consent' (Human Fertilisation and Embryology Act 1990, Sch 3) do little more than compound the difficulties.
 4 H Teff 'Consent in Medical Procedures: Paternalism, Self-determination or Therapeutic Alliance?' (1985) 101 LQR 432.
 5 D Brahams '"Informed Consent" – the Thin End of the Wedge' (1985) 135 NLJ 201.

at the literature clearly shows that, even if the courts are suspicious of the doctrine of informed consent, the medical profession now accepts it as a *fait accompli*. Increasingly, the gap between what *is* revealed and what *should be* revealed to the patient is closing.

11 Health resources and dilemmas in treatment

No resources are infinite. Even if a basic material is widely available, the costs of harvesting, treating or assembling it put some restraint on its use; moreover, the manpower required for distribution and exploitation of the finished product is always going to be limited. Applying this to medicine, it is clear that it is well-nigh impossible to provide every form of therapy for everyone – some sort of selective distribution is inevitable.

The logistics of medicine get no easier despite – or, more probably, because of – the massive technological advances of the last half century. Costs of all types are rising while the world faces persistent economic difficulties. The average span of life is increasing – at least in the developed countries – and, as a result, people need treatment for longer; this treatment is not the 'easy-cure' type appropriate to infectious diseases but is rather a matter of sophisticated care for the results of degenerative change. In addition, the public are better informed on medical matters and are better able to assimilate the information they are given; the choice of treatment is increasingly influenced by the patient's demands, with proportionate erosion of the doctor's discretion – in effect, while the latter may wish to treat on a productivity basis, the former views therapy in terms of feasibility.

Somehow, a compromise must be achieved between demand and supply and, although there is little law established on the subject, the distribution of scarce resources poses some of the more complex ethical problems of modern medicine and permeates every aspect of its structure. They are not confined to the higher administrative echelons nor to the more esoteric departments of major hospitals. They may, indeed, arise and be answered subconsciously – every time a doctor travels to visit a patient he is distributing his resources in favour of one priority and this is possibly at the expense of others with which he could have dealt during his non-productive driving time.[1]

Such an example relates to the treatment of individuals. But the ethics of health service distribution can also be considered on a global scale; the problems arising on a national level occupy an intermediate position. We propose examining these as three separate issues.

Global distribution of resources

It is beyond question that the world's medical resources are distributed unevenly both in material and in human terms. The money to buy the expensive paraphernalia

---

1 This aspect is amplified in R Klein 'Dimensions of Rationing: Who Should Do What?' (1993) 307 BMJ 309.

associated with modern hospital medicine is simply not available in the developing countries; at the same time, there are inadequate facilities for the local training of doctors who must, therefore, travel to obtain experience. The result is a vicious circle in which doctors accustomed to the sophisticated methods of the developed nations return to their own countries only to depart again dissatisfied with what they have found. The response of the richer states is often to attempt to fill the vacuum by supplying the highly complex diagnostic and therapeutic apparatus which characterises modern medicine. But does such well-intentioned aid represent either good medical morals or good medical politics? – morals and politics may, indeed, be synonymous because decisions on priorities of allocation can be translated as 'politics', 'management' or 'clinical judgment', depending on whether one is speaking in terms of international, national or individual needs.

Criticism of this type is not new, nor is it confined to those with a special interest in medical jurisprudence; it has long been realised that it is absurd to spend much effort in eradicating disease in the underdeveloped areas only to allow the population to die of starvation because the necessary farming technology was not supplied at the same time. But the nature of medical aid to the developing countries cannot avoid being politically influenced and is certainly a matter beyond the control of the average doctor or lawyer.[2]

The allocation of national resources

We come closer to personal reality when discussing resource allocation on a national scale and, here, a mass of relevant literature has built up in recent years – much of which admits the near impossibility of a wholly just solution.

The primary problem, which is essentially political, is to establish what share of the national resources is to be allocated to health – and it is the open-endedness of claims to health care that leads to particular difficulties. As David Owen said many years ago:

> All the evidence there is, both national and international, suggests that if [the] need [for health care] is not infinite, it is certainly so large relative to the resources which society is able to provide now and in the foreseeable future that we can never hope to meet it completely.[3]

Ideally, resource allocation should provide equal access to health care for those in equal need. Attempts have been made in recent years to achieve this by systematically correlating the revenue given to the health authorities with their needs. These needs were originally based by the Resource Allocation Working Party on the standardised mortality rates which were taken as representing the underlying morbidity.

2 For a philosophical approach, see R Attfield 'The Global Distribution of Health Care Resources' (1990) 16 J Med Ethics 153. Attitudes are, in fact, changing and far more effort is being put into resources at the level of primary and paramedical care.
3 D Owen *In Sickness and in Health: The Politics of Medicine* (1976), quoted by D Black 'Paying for Health' (1991) 17 J Med Ethics 117.

This, in itself, is open to criticism, as it reflects the needs at hospital level rather than those of the provision of primary care which is particularly affected by external factors such as the degree of social deprivation. Nevertheless, RAWP, as the process came to be known, appeared to provide an objective, albeit rough, formula which could be readily understood; inevitably, it was subject to criticism and the major discrepancies were ironed out slowly.[4] A new formula was introduced in 1991 which weights the age adjusted population of each region by the square root of its standardised mortality rate for those under 75 years old;[5] this was based on empirical findings. One effect is, as pointed out by Sheldon, to open the doors to differential interpretation at sub-regional level and to political lobbying by health authorities who can gain from some of the many variables which can, legitimately, be fed into the resultant equation – moreover, by their nature, empirical data are unlikely to be fully contemporary. Some explicit measure of macroallocation of national resources is clearly needed – it has been suggested that one result of its use is that vote maximising policies become more obvious and are, thus, more difficult to carry out.[6] Even so, it may well be that it is better left at a relatively unsophisticated level and that further research is directed to how the allocations, once made, are actually used.

When allocation is considered at sub-regional level, equity becomes a less significant factor and gives way to the dictates of demand. This inevitably involves a choice and this choice must be, to some extent, arbitrary. The ethical control of resources then depends, first, upon the broad base of representation on the allocation committee and, secondly, on the willingness of the constituent members not to press their own interests too hard – a process which has been described, and, to an extent, approbated, as shroud waving;[7] the lay influence of community health councils is important at this point.

In any event, a change in circumstances has been dictated by the passage of the National Health Service and Community Care Act 1990. This establishes the district health authorities as purchasers of health services on behalf of the local population. In this role they must act as good housekeepers and not only provide what the people want but also do this in the most cost-effective manner. The choices can never be easy – is it possible to decide the relative importance between, say, strict economy, the avoidance of suffering or the prolongation of life? And how is one to identify the best route to the intended goal? If, for example, morbidity as a whole is taken as the yardstick, the alleviation of bronchitis and asthma has been found to take precedence; if, on the other hand, one considers total hospital in-patient days, mental health may be the single most important consideration. But to say that mental health and respiratory disease constitute the most serious burdens on the health service is not necessarily to say that they merit the greatest allocation of resources. There is a strong

---

4   N Mays 'Measuring Morbidity for Resource Allocation' (1987) 295 BMJ 703; G Bevan and J Charlton 'Making Access to Health Care More Equal: The Role of General Medical Services' (1987) 295 BMJ 764; J Smith 'RAWP Revisited' (1987) 295 BMJ 1015.
5   Department of Health *Funding and Contracts for Health Services, Working Paper 2* (1989). For discussion, see T A Sheldon, G D Smith and G Bevan 'Weighting in the Dark: Resource Allocation in the New NHS' (1993) 306 BMJ 835 – particularly for the mathematical analysis which is beyond the ambit of this book.
6   See eg A Maynard and A Ludbrook 'Applying Resource Allocation Formulae to Constituent Parts of the UK' (1980) 1 Lancet 85.
7   J Rawles 'Castigating QALYs' (1989) 15 J Med Ethics 143.

economic incentive to apply some sort of 'productivity test' in distributing the resources of society; the question is – is it ethical to do so? Analysis of the problem raises some stark and disturbing answers. Thus, it has been said that to reject opportunities to allow natural dying is costly in financial terms – in a health care service with finite resources, it is neither harsh nor unethical to accept the consequences of a financial limit.[8] And the same article expresses the grim reality of political power in the suggestion that to spend a lot on the elderly might not be supported by public opinion if it became known that younger lives were being lost because of inadequate finance.

This immediately draws attention to the major difficulty encountered in any such evaluation based on public opinion – which is that the welfare of the unproductive is likely to be regarded as secondary to that of the productive unless the views of voluntary organisations with specific interests are given particular consideration; the mentally handicapped and the elderly are, in fact, in double jeopardy – not only may they be seen as less deserving of resources, but they are less likely to be invited to subscribe to the opinion-making process. Geriatric patients, it is said, would not and should not expect priority over younger patients. Which is true enough – but they *would* expect equal consideration. Harris's argument,[9] which sees the saving of life as the main medical objective, is at its strongest when we are considering the use of life years as a parameter for the assessment of the disposal of scarce resources. The choice between a 20-year-old and an 80-year-old may be straightforward to the outsider. But, at the moment of decision, each patient values his or her life equally – and the problem, then, is how to measure that equality; a productivity test, for example, demands that treatment should be both beneficial *and* effective whereas an evaluation on the basis of social good may conclude that benefit alone is sufficient to justify the resultant costs to the community.[10]

It is inevitable that, so long as there is a restriction on resources – and there must be a limit even in Utopia – some principle of maximum societal benefit must be applied; the individual's right to equality must, to some extent, be sacrificed to the general need. The precise determination of a maximum benefit policy is difficult to make, but the decision is societal rather than medical and involves a 'cost-benefit' analysis and all that that entails as to the quality of life.[11] Essentially, there are three potential measures of a free health service – comprehensiveness, quality and availability – and the situation is that the goal of fully comprehensive, high quality medical care that is freely available to all on the basis of medical need is unattainable in the face of steadily increasing costs;[12] the temptation is to lower one standard in favour of the other two. The difficulties are formidable because what we are

8 G S Robertson 'Dealing with the Brain-damaged Old – Dignity Before Sanctity' (1982) 8 J Med Ethics 173.
9 J Harris 'Unprincipled QALYs' (1991) 17 J Med Ethics 185.
10 M A Somerville ' "Shall the Grandparents Die?": Allocation of Medical Resources with an Ageing Population' (1986) 14 Law Med Hlth Care 158.
11 A particularly poignant example is to be found in the salvage of extremely premature infants. The cost of intensive care has been put at £20,000 for each baby weighing less than 1.5kg and some 50% of these may sustain brain damage sufficient to require life-long support. Would the money be better spent on research into the prevention of prematurity? Office of Health Economics *Born Too Soon* (1992). See L Hunt 'Cost "Dilemma" Posed by Premature Babies' (1993) Independent, 20 January, p 6.
12 A Weale 'Rationing Health Care' (1998) 316 BMJ 410.

discussing at this level is essentially 'horizontal resource allocation', or priority setting between different types of service, which depends not so much on professional medical assessment and advice as on public opinion and on evidence as to cost and effectiveness[13] – and the former, at least, is a fickle measuring instrument. Not only can polls be grossly distorted by the way in which questions are put but also opinion is very subject to political and other extraneous influences; you do not sell newspapers by agreeing that treatment for varicose veins has a low priority – sales are improved by emphasising the injustice in regarding varicose ulceration as less debilitating than the peptic variety. Attempts made thus far to sacrifice comprehensiveness in favour of 'core care' by way of translating societal attitudes into standardised decision-making[14] seem to achieve less than satisfactory results. The essential dilemma stems from the fact that the categories of choice on which a consensus may be sought are indefinable save at the margins of health care.[15] However, the new emphasis on explicitness in rationing strategies is an increasingly important development and may lead to surprising results; resource allocators, it has been said, should not take it for granted that their own values are shared by the general public.[16]

Given the absence of any obvious set of principles on which to act and given that the function of district health authorities is, on the one hand, constrained by the regional or higher authority[17] and, on the other, is to provide what the public want, it is unsurprising that the distribution of the scarcer resources is uneven and that the principles invoked in decision-making are uncertain – the factors given most weight has been found to range from the availability of other funding (eg the private sphere) for the service to the more obviously laudable potential for health gain in terms of length and quality of life.[18] In his survey of six districts, Ham found that there was a general reluctance to exclude some services entirely from their contracts. But it is from a review of a service which was *not* provided by some authorities – in this case, in-vitro fertilisation – that some of the clearest evidence of the factors likely to be considered influential is to be found. These included:

(a) the presence of a prominent lobbyist for the service and the ready availability of the service;
(b) whether or not a competent public health department could be used to interpret the effectiveness of and need for the service;
(c) whether it represented a true health need;
(d) having decided that there was a need, whether the particular service offered the best way of meeting that need;

13 M Cochrane, C Ham, C Heginbotham and R Smith 'Rationing: At the Cutting Edge' (1991) 303 BMJ 1039.
14 P A Lewis and M Charny 'Which of Two Individuals Do You Treat When Only Their Ages Are Different and You Can't Treat Both?' (1989) 15 J Med Ethics 28.
15 See reply to Lewis and Charny, n 14 above: D Lamb 'Priorities in Health Care' (1989) 15 J Med Ethics 33; also B A Stoll 'Choosing Between Cancer Patients' (1990) 16 J Med Ethics 71.
16 E Nord 'The Relevance of Health State after Treatment in Prioritising between Different Patients' (1993) 19 J Med Ethics 37. The plea for transparency in decision making is still being voiced and is given urgency by the introduction of yet more potent drugs; see eg R Smith 'Viagra and Rationing' (1998) 317 BMJ 760.
17 See Klein p 289, n 1 above.
18 See the analysis provided by C Ham 'Prority Setting in the NHS: Reports from Six Districts' (1993) 307 BMJ 435.

(e) notwithstanding the effectiveness of the service, whether it should be purchased at the expense of another unrelated service;
(f) whether valid reasons could be given for selective treatment when supply fell short of demand; and
(g) whether it was right to introduce a service which could not be given to everyone.[19]

Despite the obvious difficulties, we see it as self-evident that some form of cost evaluation in health care is essential at the resource purchasing level, if only to ensure impartiality – pressure groups are bad advocates in that they take no account of the deprivation elsewhere which is the concomitant to success in their own particular sphere. District health authorities are still inexperienced in developing priority setting and, as Ham put it, the important practical feature is to concentrate on study as to the appropriateness of the use of services and as to the setting in which they are to be used. We agree with those who believe that the ethical problem does not lie in the application of economics to health resource allocation. It should, rather, be accepted that without such control there is likely to be an unethical maldistribution of resources; as Williams put it, anyone who says no account should be paid to costs is, in reality, saying no account should be paid to the sacrifices thereby imposed on others – and there are no *ethical* grounds for ignoring the effect of an action on other people.[20] Surely, everyone would agree with this – but it still leaves open the question of in which group's favour is a marginal change in resource allocation to be tilted.

We must also not lose sight of the fact that there are more reasons than cost for limiting the availability of drugs and other treatments. A health authority may, for example believe that a given therapy is useless and, accordingly, refuse to sanction its purchase. Such situations arise most commonly in those conditions for which there is, currently, no effective treatment. Sufferers from multiple sclerosis, for example, will clutch at any straw and will be unimpressed by the need for statistical evaluation of a drug before they can be given the chance to use it. Since the status of a new drug is largely a matter of individual advisory medical opinion, the result is an inequality of distribution which, in the absence of a national policy, can satisfy no-one.[1] Alternatively, the condition itself may be questioned as to its nature – is its alleviation a truly medical matter or is it one of 'life-style enhancement' only? Here, we could place, for example, assisted reproduction and gender reassignment, both of which are discussed in some detail elsewhere in this book, in the 'grey' area of the black and white scale where we are likely to get different answers from different authorities. At the more extreme, we could consider the topical question of the supply of Viagra through the NHS. We appreciate that there are occasions when impotence – as opposed to sexual inadequacy – can be seen as a proper medical concern. But this is a far cry from supplying a drug with no intention other than to improve sexual

19 S Redmayne and R Klein 'Rationing in Practice: The Case of In Vitro Fertilisation' (1993) 306 BMJ 1521. The issue of in vitro fertilisation is also taken up by the Lancet 'Rationing Infertility Services' (1993) 342 Lancet 251.
20 A Williams 'Cost-effectiveness Analysis: Is It Ethical?' (1992) 18 J Med Ethics 7. See also G Mooney 'QALYs: Are They Enough? A Health Economist's Perspective' (1989) 15 J Med Ethics 148.
1 Consider eg the availability of the interferons for the treatment of MS: J Ross 'MS Patients May Fight Drug Refusal' (1997) Scotsman, 30 July, p 10.

performance. The government can surely expect support for saying that the use of sildenafil for such a purpose is a pleasure which may be bought – but not at the expense, both financial and healthwise, of the rest of the community.[2]

Finally, it must, of course, be conceded that societies differ and, while some form of resource rationing is, as we have said, inevitable, no single system will be universally acceptable. Britain has been described as an original sin society[3] in which tribulation in the form of ill-health is expected – a statement which, incidentally, is becoming less and less true as the years pass. The United States, on the other hand, are seen as a society striving for perfectibility of man and dominated by consumerism; the demand for and the use of medical resources are bound to differ widely. That being so, it is, perhaps, anomalous that the one experiment in health care rationing that has come into force as a result of statute should have its origins in the United States.[4] The State of Oregon has, as a result of research including extensive public debate, arrived at an adaptable prioritised list of treatments which will and will not be available under Medicaid and business-related private insurance arrangements. Inevitably, the plan has had its difficulties – one of which lies in the constantly changing list of priorities and the consequent inflation of the basic healthcare package that is available.[5] Its success or failure also depends to a large extent on extraneous factors such as the strength of the state economy as a whole, which leads to fluctuation in the number of those covered. We doubt, however, if the Oregon experiment has any direct relevance to the United Kingdom. Quite apart from the very disparate populations involved, the Oregon plan is directed at those who cannot, for financial and other reasons, obtain private medical insurance, whereas the NHS is open to all in the United Kingdom as a right. There may well be valuable lessons to be learnt but, at the moment, further discussion seems unnecessary.

The legal situation

Financial restraints clearly place the Secretary of State in some difficulty in discharging his statutory duty to provide, to such extent as he thinks necessary to meet all reasonable requirements including, inter alia, hospital accommodation.[6]

In some ways it is surprising that there have not been more actions brought by patients who feel that he has failed in these duties but, on reflection, it is probable that the dearth of cases results from the extreme improbability of a successful outcome.

---

2   Britain is not the only country to take such a decision – one which has the support of the medical profession. See the review under 'Viagra Falls: The Debate over Rationing Continues' (1998) 317 BMJ 836.
3   R Klein 'Rationing Health Care' (1984) 289 BMJ 143. For an updated comparative review, see R G Lee and F H Miller 'The Doctor's Changing Role in Allocating U.S. and British Medical Services' (1990) 18 Law Med Hlth Care 69.
4   M J Garland 'Justice, Politics and Community: Expanding Access and Rationing Health Services in Oregon' (1992) 20 Law Med Hlth Care 67; S Rosenbaum 'Mothers and Children Last: The Oregon Medicaid Experiment' (1992) 18 Am J Law Med 97; J Dixon and H G Welch 'Priority Setting: Lessons from Oregon' (1991) 337 Lancet 891. New Zealand and the Netherlands are also investigating possible policies.
5   C Ham 'Retracing the Oregon Trail: The Experience of Rationing and the Oregon Health Plan' (1998) 316 BMJ 1965.
6   National Health Service Act 1977, s 3.

Such recorded cases as there are tend to be reported sporadically; the classic action is that of *Hincks*.[7] In that case, patients in an orthopaedic hospital complained that they had waited an unreasonable time for treatment because of a shortage of facilities arising, in part, from a decision not to build a new block to the hospital on the grounds of cost; accordingly, they sought a declaration that the Secretary of State and the health authorities were in breach of their duty. In dismissing the application, Wien J said it was not the court's function to direct Parliament what funds to make available to the health service and how to allocate them. The duty to provide services 'to such extent as he considers necessary' gave the minister a discretion as to the disposition of financial resources. The court could only interfere if the Secretary of State acted so as to frustrate the policy of the Act or as no reasonable minister could have acted; and no such breach had been shown in the particular case. Moreover, even if a breach was proved, the Act did not admit of relief by way of damages.

The case went to appeal[8] where, as might be expected, the judgment turned on the interpretation of 'reasonable requirements'. Lord Denning MR considered this to mean that a failure of duty existed only if the minister's action was thoroughly unreasonable. It was further thought that we should be faced with the economics of a bottomless pit if no limits in respect of long-term planning were to be read into public statutory duties; the further the advances of medical technology, the greater would be the financial burden placed upon the Secretary of State.

Since 1980, however, health authorities have been required to balance their individual budgets.[9] Inevitably, major decisions as to the provision of health care have been moved down one hierarchical step, thus bringing the decision-makers into closer contact with those affected. Society, in the form of the Community Health Council, has a statutory place in the process[10] and, as a corollary, is entitled to judicial review of decisions thought to have been taken improperly. Nevertheless, attempts to extend this privilege to individuals seeking improved access to treatment have foundered consistently on the rock of the reasonableness inherent in the adverse decisions taken.

The paradigmatic case is that of *Walker*,[11] which concerned a baby whose surgery had been postponed five times because of a shortage of skilled nursing staff. The trial judge, Macpherson J, commented that the application for judicial review took on the guise of a general criticism of the health service rather than that of an actual attack on the decision of the health authority. He deprecated any suggestion that patients should be encouraged to think that the court had a role in cases which sought to compel the

---

7 *R v Secretary of State for Social Services, ex p Hincks* (1979) 123 Sol Jo 436. A rather comparable case of 'hospital economics' is described in very human terms by Bishop B Habgood 'The Ethics of Resource Allocation: A Case Study' (1983) 9 J Med Ethics 21.

8 *R v Secretary of State for Social Services, ex p Hincks* (1980) 1 BMLR 93, CA. The case was discussed in J D Finch *Health Services Law* (1981) pp 38-39 and in 'Rationing of Resources' (1985) 290 BMJ 374 and by D Brahams 'Enforcing A Duty to Care for Patients in the NHS' [1984] 2 Lancet 1224. See also C Newdick 'Rights to NHS Resources after the 1990 Act' (1993) 1 Med L Rev 53. F H Miller 'Denial of Health Care and Informed Consent in English and American Law' (1992) 18 Am J Law Med 37.

9 National Health Service Act 1977, s 97A, inserted by Health Services Act 1980, s 6.

10 Eg *R v Tunbridge Wells Health Authority, ex p Goodridge* (1988) Times, 21 May; see also *R v North West Thames Regional Health Authority, ex p Daniels* (1993) 19 BMLR 67, [1993] 4 Med LR 364 (Community Health Council Regulations, SI 1985/304, reg 19(1)).

11 *R v Central Birmingham Health Authority, ex p Walker* (1992) 3 BMLR 32, CA.

authority to carry out an operation that was not urgent; the Court of Appeal confirmed his refusal of the application for review. Within two months, the same health authority was involved in a comparable case, the only major difference being that the child was possibly in greater immediate danger.[12] Reiterating that, to be so unreasonable as to come within the jurisdiction of the court, the Authority would have had to make a decision that no reasonable body could have reached,[13] Stephen Brown LJ said:

> In the absence of any evidence which could begin to show that there was [such a failure] to allocate resources in this instance . . . there can be no arguable case . . . It does seem to me unfortunate that this procedure has been adopted. It is wholly misconceived in my view. The courts of this country cannot arrange the lists in the hospital . . . and should not be asked to intervene.

While expressing great sympathy with the parents, Stephen Brown LJ suggested that it might have been hoped that the publicity would bring pressure to bear on the hospital and there is no doubt that this effect could and does, materialise – particularly in a life-saving situation. Dyer reported a case of a woman suffering from end-stage renal failure who was refused dialysis facilities; on her being granted legal aid to take the authority to court, an extra £250,000 was made available to the local renal units.[14] Whatever one thinks of the morality of the process, it seems to have been a very successful exercise in 'shroud waving' – and it is to be noted that the money was not 'new' but was plucked from the waiting list fund. The circumstances were such, however, as to raise a real possibility of *Wednesbury* unreasonableness. An even more spectacular 'success' concerned Laura Davies, who received, and rejected, a liver and small intestine transplant; she was then given a second transplant involving seven organs at a cost estimated as £1m, which is said to have been defrayed by a Middle Eastern potentate.[15] The intervention of philanthropists is, in fact, becoming a feature of such cases, although it is sometimes difficult to see what good such isolated gestures do for the general well-being of society. Perhaps the most publicised relevant incident in recent years has been that of 'Child B', in which funding for an essentially ineffective treatment was refused.[16] This case is discussed in detail below;[17] for the present, it is appropriate only to quote the chief executive, who was, as the mouthpiece of the health authority, taken to be responsible for the decision:

> [The] case took on a symbolic importance, helping people to grasp the reality that expectation and demand had now outstripped their publicly funded systems' ability to pay without regard to the opportunity cost.[18]

12 *R v Central Birmingham Health Authority, ex p Collier* (6 January 1988, unreported, available on Lexis). The case is discussed by D Brahams 'Seeking Increased NHS Resources Through the Courts' (1988) 1 Lancet 133. See also Newdick p 296, n 8 above; Miller p 296, n 8 above for this case and *Walker*.
13 *Associated Provincial Picture Houses Ltd v Wednesbury Corpn* [1948] 1 KB 223 at 229, [1947] 2 All ER 680 at 683, per Lord Greene MR, CA.
14 C Dyer 'Going to Law to Get Treatment' (1987) 295 BMJ 1554.
15 For a critical lay view of such disposal of both financial and organic resources, see K Muir 'Can Saving the Life of Little Laura Really Be Worth £1 million?' (1993) The Times, 22 September, p 15.
16 *R v Cambridge Area Health Authority, ex p B* (1995) 25 BMLR 5; revsd (1995) 23 BMLR 1, CA.
17 See p 339.
18 S Thornton 'The Child B Case – Reflections of a Chief Executive' (1997) 314 BMJ 1838.

It is, perhaps, worth noting that the NHS has not been singled out for judicial cheeseparing. In a case brought under the Chronically Sick and Disabled Patients Act 1970, it was held that the costs of the arrangements and the authority's resources were proper considerations in assessing whether a person had a need and whether it was necessary to make arrangements to meet it.[19] The case concerned the *removal* of social services from a disabled man; some of the difficulties involved are crystallised in the dissenting opinion of Lord Lloyd:

> How can resources help to measure [the man's] need? . . . It cannot, however, have been Parliament's intention that local authority B should be able to say "because we do not have enough resources, we are going to reduce your needs". His needs remained exactly the same. They cannot be affected by the local authority's inability to meet those needs.[20]

Even so, as in the medical cases, the court was not minded to interfere with the tactics of resource allocation.

A further problem concerns the effect of the National Health Service and Community Care Act 1990 on the legal rights of patients and doctors in access to health service resources. For present purposes, the significant feature of the Act is to introduce what appear to be commercial concepts into the provision of care under the NHS. Care now reaches the patient through purchasers – that is, the general practitioners who are encouraged to function as fund holders – and suppliers or hospitals which may become self-governing trusts. There can be no doubt that the new regulations revamp the traditional setting of the health service – though whether this is by way of restricting the medical profession's clinical integrity in favour of managerial expertise or by imposing increased financial responsibility on doctors is open to question.[1] The new administration intends to revise the current organisation in the next parliamentary session.

Alterations in the structure of the service also alter the confrontational ground and the opportunity for, if not the likelihood of, litigation in terms of health care delivery is now considerable. In a most comprehensive review, Newdick[2] has pointed to the difficulties in maintaining the precepts of the National Health Service Act 1977 which are introduced by transferring much of the decision-making to managers of both practices and hospitals. Newdick points out that no policy reason exists to abolish the rights that patients currently enjoy and he pleads that the *Bolam* principle[3] be shielded from administrative interference. An interesting observation is that much responsibility is now laid directly on the family health service authorities, who are exposed to claims in negligence and to judicial review. New avenues to litigation against hospitals are also opened up – for example, has a hospital a duty of care to patients on its waiting list and can it, accordingly, be sued for faulty prioritisation arrangements? And as a coda, Miller, in an equally useful contribution, suggests that patients themselves now have an opportunity to 'shop around' and that failure to explain the lack of a resource may result in actions for negligence based on flawed consent.[4]

19 *R v Gloucestershire County Council, ex p Barry* (1997) 36 BMLR 69, HL.
20 (1997) 36 BMLR 69 at 96.
 1 R Klein 'The Politics of Change' (1991) 302 BMJ 1102.
 2 Newdick p 296, n 8 above.
 3 See p 223 above.
 4 Miller p 296, n 8 above. See also pp 277 et seq above.

No actions related to the specific provisions of the 1990 Act have been reported[5] and the forecasts of potential confrontation have something of a 'Doomsday' atmosphere about them – many of the scenarios painted are, at least, very unlikely to materialise[6] and there seems no reason why professional health economists should not be subject to their own *Bolam*. But, whether or not the direct influence of economists turns out to benefit a national system of health care delivery, there is little doubt that a main effect of the 1990 legislation is to convert the covert rationing which has always occurred into a process which is open to public scrutiny and debate – and this must be a good thing. The extent of public involvement in the Oregon experiment may never be matched in the United Kingdom but increasing attention is likely to be paid to the voice of the consumer.[7]

A recent poll indicated that more than half the British public favoured unlimited funding of the NHS.[8] While this is clearly impossible, it can be argued that, once it is established that there is a reasonable requirement for a particular service, no further qualification exists upon the Secretary of State's duty to provide it and that inadequate resources do not absolve him from this duty.[9] This may well be so but, in so far as one cannot make a pot of tea without tap water unless one takes the water from the coffee urn, it adds little to the solution of the problem. Clearly, however, a further major ethical dilemma centres on the imposed medical limitations on treatment of the individual and it is to that aspect that we now turn.

Treatment of the individual

In discussion of the medical treatment of the individual, we are faced not with the hypothetical patient who may become ill but with one who is actually at risk. Objectivity is no longer the main arbiter and is replaced by need – itself described as an imprecise and elastic concept – and, in the event of enforced discrimination, the assessment of relative needs dictates a value judgment.

How, then, is that judgment to be made? In practice, many decisions are made instinctively and without the need for profound analysis – thus, the single-handed doctor will unhesitatingly choose the patient in greater pain for treatment, despite the fact that this will simultaneously delay the treatment of those in lesser pain. There may well be moral arguments against such a policy – it does, for example, act to the detriment of the stoic – but the circumstances are acute and, the urgency being comparable, the doctor has selected a single criterion on which to base his judgment.

---

5 The report of the *Daniels* case, (1993) 19 BMLR 67, [1993] 4 Med LR 364 includes no mention of any action in negligence in respect of the closure of the unit which had agreed to treat the child for the rare metabolic condition of infantile Batten's disease.

6 For a thoroughly pessimistic appraisal, based on English and American experience, see R D Persaud 'What Future for Ethical Medical Practice in the New National Health Service?' (1991) 17 J Med Ethics 10.

7 M Dean 'The Oregon Trail Reaches Britain' (1991) 338 Lancet 1133.

8 T Groves 'Public Disagrees with Professionals over NHS Funding' (1993) 306 BMJ 673.

9 G P Morris 'Enforcing a Duty to Care: The Kidney Patient and the NHS' (1983) 80 Law Soc Gaz 3156. But an extrapolation of *ex p Barry* (1997) 36 BMLR 69 suggests that this would be unlikely to be sustained.

Moral agonising is, in practice, reserved for the treatment of chronic, life-threatening diseases, not only because they offer the opportunity for analysis but because they attract the use of expensive resources and will consume these for a long time – at which point the dilemma extends not only to the allocation of resources but also to their withdrawal. In practice, the treatment of chronic renal diseases and of brain injury provide good examples on which to base discussion.

It is easy to say that enough dialysis machines should be made available to treat all cases of chronic renal failure but, in existing circumstances, this may merely mean that some other financially dependent resource must be curtailed. Costs can be cut by, for example, changing a policy of hospital dialysis to one of home treatment, but the fact of financial restraint is not thereby removed – only its degree is altered. But, at the same time, the modern patient undoubtedly regards access to high technology medicine as his individual right and such a view is readily tenable when there is an urgent need. If the doctor is, perforce, to qualify those rights, his reason for so doing must be beyond reproach and therein lies the problem – which we admit to finding virtually insoluble.

It is possible to discuss the allocation of resources in terms of triage. Triage is a curiously derived expression meaning, in the present context, the separation of casualties into priority treatment groups. It is essentially a military concept, the current British policy being to allocate four categories of casualty, ranging from those whose slight injuries can be managed by self-care to those who cannot be expected to survive even with extensive treatment and who are, therefore, treated on a humanitarian basis only; the policy is closely associated with that of casualty evacuation. Triage in this sense is not only good emergency surgical practice but is also ethically acceptable because it is directed to a single discernible end – that is, to win the war or the battle, and we accept that this, in itself, is a morally acceptable objective with which the medical branch of the armed services can quite properly associate itself. It may, however, have unusual applications. The story is told that, with the advent during the Second World War of the new and scarce drug penicillin, instructions were given in an allied army that top priority was to be given for its use in the treatment of venereal disease rather than of battle wounds on the grounds that this represented a maximum return by way of military efficiency. The story may well be apocryphal but it serves to illustrate two features. First, given the fact that there is an easily definable and ethically desirable objective, the logical means taken towards that end may still be suspect. Secondly, it reinforces the view, which we share, that the concept of triage, which is an emergency procedure, cannot be simply transferred to civilian practice.[10] It may be possible to do so in special circumstances – it is, for example, a recognised practice following a major disaster, when the single most pressing objective is to mitigate the effects of that disaster. But the term triage, and its underlying principles, cannot be used as a convenient substitute, or subterfuge, for resource allocation and should be abandoned for that purpose. What, then, does one put in its place?

---

10 Not everyone would agree with this view: eg J Cubbon 'The Principle of QALY Maximisation as the Basis for Allocating Health Care Resources' (1991) 17 J Med Ethics 181. See also K M Boyd and B T Potter 'Priorities in the Allocation of Scarce Resources' (1986) 12 J Med Ethics 197.

Alternative models

There have been many attempts to solve the problem[11] but none is satisfactory – all generalisations fail when applied to the particular but we will briefly outline some proposals which have been made. It is, perhaps, easiest to progress from those parameters which we consider to be least appropriate at the individual patient level.

We do not believe that cost-benefit should be a major influence here. It needs no profound philosophical analysis to make one appreciate instinctively that it is right to deploy a helicopter to rescue a man on a drifting pleasure raft, despite the fact that his danger is of his own making, despite the expense and despite the fact that the helicopter is designed to carry ten persons. The immediacy of the situation has placed a very high value on life which it would be quite immoral to ignore. The value cannot, however, be infinite – otherwise, faced with the choice of saving one man on a raft or ten men in a sinking dinghy, the grounds for the 'value choice' would be equal whereas, in practice, few would doubt the correctness of choosing the larger number – always provided the operational circumstances were similar. Such choices must, however, be very rare in practice. In the chronic situation, as exemplified by dialysis, we are effectively confronted with a one-to-one choice between two individuals; at this point it is possible to introduce a cost-benefit argument which takes the form of assessing the relative gain to society of saving one or the other. In practice, this would invoke the use of some formula such as 'earning capacity x (65 - age)'. We believe that neither age nor income group should be primary criteria regulating choice per se – it might be that the aged respond less well to treatment than do others but that would be a different consideration. Such an assessment would, in addition, offend 'moral' practices which have almost attained the force of common law and of which 'women and children first' is an obvious example; women would, in general, come out worst if such objective cost-benefit criteria were to be applied. But this is not to say that some concern for quality or expectation of life should not be thrown into the prognostic balance.

The corollary to this line of thought is that scarce resources should be distributed on the basis of the 'deserts' or basic merits of the recipients. One aspect of this is discussed further in chapter 14, where we note a United States experiment which attempts to distribute a very scarce resource – human kidneys – to those hospitals which have, themselves, provided organs; while such a system has much to commend it, any benefit accrues to the hospital rather than to the individual patient who still has to be 'chosen' by some other method. Others would look at this criterion from the opposite point of view and would exclude those who could positively endanger the treatment programme – a group who are exemplified by those carrying the virus of hepatitis or of the acquired immune deficiency syndrome. Such reasoning is a purely technical matter and is, in a sense, a criticism of the dialysis unit itself as being unable to contain the potential hazard. A rather more moralistic variant on this theme would hold it to be acceptable for a society which was providing the facility to exclude persons who increased the cost of care through their own choice;[12] while this is

11 An exhaustive analysis of the alternatives is given by H J J Leenen 'The Selection of Patients in the Event of a Scarcity of Medical Facilities: An Unavoidable Dilemma' (1979) 1 Int J Med Law 161. For a more recent appraisal, see M J Langford 'Who Should Get the Kidney Machine?' (1992) 18 J Med Ethics 12.

12 H T Engelhardt 'Allocating Scarce Medical Resources and the Availability of Organ Transplantation' (1984) 311 New Engl J Med 66.

certainly arguable, it is a concept that is probably more applicable to communities in which the health of only a proportion is being supported by the taxes paid by the remainder – the beneficiaries of a national health service are more likely to see themselves as all in the same leaky boat.

More often, the assessment of 'deserts' is taken to apply to the intrinsic worth of the subject to society – and, again, we may look at this from the negative or positive aspect. First, there could be patients, who, by reason of some other disability, could be regarded as being unlikely to benefit from treatment in a societal sense; this group, however, is essentially included among those falling to be assessed under the 'medical benefit' test and is best discussed within that context. The alternative, positive, approach in the event of shortage of facilities for treatment is to select those who offer the greatest contribution to society now and in the future. In our view, allocation tests which attempt to distinguish between, for example, the philanthropic mafia millionaire and the contestant for an international prize in applied mathematics serve no useful purpose in that they are hopelessly subjective. Choices so based are clearly beyond the capacity or function of the individual doctor – and a 'committee decision', which is sometimes advocated, is no more than a sum of individual subjective assessments; we reject the concept.

The one 'deserts-related' issue which is most commonly raised is that of age. It is very widely held that the older a patient is, the less can he or she command equal opportunity in a competition for therapy. The reasons for this acquiescence differ. Some will rely on the argument 'he's had his innings' – but even this depends, to an extent, on one's position in the batting order; others, more rationally, will point to the fact that results of treatment are generally better in the young than in the old – but simply because the results of coronary surgery are commonly more satisfactory in the middle-aged patient does not mean that surgery is not worthwhile in the 75-year-old. There is, moreover, a tendency to forget that not every therapy is effective for a full life-span; if we anticipate a likely five-year survival, it matters not whether the patient is aged 20 or 60. We suspect that the reason underlying the common assumption is that those responsible for decision-making are, by definition, below retiring age; it has been said, rightly, that there is often a wide discrepancy between the optimum solution of a problem from the perspective of society as a whole and that of the individual within that society.[13] Lewis and Charny [14] have tried, by means of an opinion poll, to establish the points at which the public would be prepared to accept age-based choices and, thus, to map out decision-making boundaries which will reflect the values of society as a whole. This is a praiseworthy effort which is obviously open to criticism;[15] for ourselves, while appreciating the value of uniformity and accepting the need for the development of guidelines established by way of wide societal involvement, we find it difficult to support a cold actuarial basis for making what is still a human clinical decision.

Clearly, the most widely acceptable criterion of selection would be that determined by medical benefit.[16] But, once again, this is easier to believe than to put into practice.

13 Lewis and Charny, p 293, n 14 above.
14 Ibid.
15 See Lamb, p 293, n 15 above; P Whitaker 'Resource Allocation: A Plea for a Touch of Realism' (1990) 16 J Med Ethics 129.
16 The choice made, inter alia, by Professor Gillon's remarkably prescient daughter: see R Gillon 'Justice and Allocation of Medical Resources' (1985) 291 BMJ 266. It was also the implicit choice of the court in *Re J (a minor) (wardship: medical treatment)* [1992] 2 FLR 165, (1992) 9 BMLR 10.

Unless one is dealing with a recoverable condition – and dialysis, which is providing the main theme for discussion, is only palliative – medical benefit is a relative matter and, moreover, prognosis is unpredictable. It is also difficult to avoid the conclusion that the individual's social status may influence the outcome of any therapy – despite the ultimate medical basis for any decision, access to scarce resources is, then, governed by economic considerations.

But, even if the clinician claims absolute responsibility for allocation of his expertise, he must consider the quality of the life he is extending and it is here that he may obtain guidance from – or suffer the interference of – the health economist. Perhaps the greatest influence in this field over the last decade has been the introduction of the concept of quality adjusted life years – or QALYs.[17]

Quality adjusted life years

The principle of the QALY is simple enough. A year of healthy life expectancy is scored as 1 and a year of unhealthy life as less than 1, depending upon the degree of reduction in quality; while death is taken as zero, a life considered to be worse than death can be accorded a minus score. The 'value' of treatment in terms of 'life appreciation' can then be assessed numerically. Thus far, in fact, QALY's seem to be doing little more than expressing the intuitive findings of the competent clinician in a mathematical formula. And, therein lies the rub – for the 'quality scoring' will still be founded on a 'best interests' assessment made by a third party and the paternalistic element in that assessment has been scarcely modified. It is, for example, hard for a middle-class doctor not to see a middle-class life as being of higher quality than one sustained on social security; a young physician may see a short life on the golf course as preferable to a long one tied to the television set – but this may well not be the patient's evaluation. It is thus apparent that, at this level, a QALY can only be truly evaluated with the patient's co-operation; it can then be used to decide between two possible treatments for the same condition. Here, in what has been described as 'vertical priority setting', one is on more level ground insofar as one is comparing like with like.[18] Used in this way, QALYs may actually augment the patient's autonomy by explicitly involving him or her in the process of rational consent to therapy.[19] Even so, a note of caution may be sounded as it is not difficult to confuse the objectives. The easy phrase 'not clinically indicated' may mean either that the treatment is not considered to be of overall benefit to the patient or it may imply an inappropriate allocation of resources.[20] The distinction is conceptually important; in the latter case, the professional has a legitimate prior interest in decision making while, in the former, the choice is one for the individual patient.

There are other more specific objections to QALYs as they are currently developed. Clearly, they operate to the disadvantage of the aged; they measure only

17 A Williams 'The Economic Role of "Health Indicators" ' In G Teeling-Smith (ed) *Measuring the Social Benefits of Medicine* (1983).
18 Cochrane et al p 293, n 13 above.
19 See p 287.
20 See T Hope, D Sprigings and R Crisp '"Not Clinically Indicated": Patients' Interests or Resource Allocation?' (1993) 306 BMJ 379.

the end-point of treatment without considering the *proportional* loss or gain in the quality of life; and there are parameters other than simple health which need to be fed into the equation. Possibly the most important moral criticism is that the QALY sets no value on life per se.[1] Harris considers that we should be saving as many lives, not life years, as possible – a proposition which simplifies the argument by removing it from the ambit of life-saving treatment which should, then, be apportioned only on a 'first come, first served' basis; we also suggest that the customary use of the term 'life-saving', when what is really meant is 'death-postponing', can lead to false reasoning. What this view certainly does, however, is to emphasise that QALYs can never be used to compare the value of 'life-saving' therapies with those which are merely life-enhancing. Indeed, it may well be asked whether we have any right to pronounce on the quality of other people's lives and, hence, whether abstract formulae should ever be used to compare the management of individual persons or different disease states. We should be very careful lest we find that we have unwittingly written into the equation a constant such as that the mentally handicapped, for example, are, by definition, possessed of less QALYs than are those with no inherent deficit.

In view of these many criticisms, it is not surprising that alternatives to the QALY are being actively sought. One such system is the saved young life equivalent, in which saving the life of a young person and restoring him or her to full health is regarded as the unit of measurement – on the grounds that most people would regard that as the maximum benefit that a single individual can obtain.[2] The comparative values of treatments is than assessed in terms of how many expected outcomes of each treatment would be equivalent to one SAVE. Such a system may or may not be easier to understand than are QALYs and its evaluation would certainly require a vast amount of empirical field-work. Our specific criticism would be that, even by its title, it actively promotes 'ageism', which is little more than an unfortunate, though inevitable, incidental to the QALY concept; and, in general – and in common with all such formulae – it reduces persons to numbers and tends to dehumanise medical practice.

This criticism hardens when the health economists tie cost to their preferred process of analysis – something which they must do in order to guide those responsible for macroallocation of resources. It may well be salutary for physicians and surgeons to be forced into knowing the cost-effectiveness of any given procedure. What health economists should not do, in our view, is to attempt to dictate the resolution of clinical problems in financial terms – to allow this is, as Rawles has put it, to condone: 'the development by health economists of fairer methods of denying patients treatment.'[3]

To some, the answer to the resource allocation dilemma is simply to increase the resources;[4] others regard this as a dangerous assumption – Klein, for example, suggests that it is only a slight exaggeration to say that the demand for health care is

1 See, in particular, J Harris 'QALYfying the Value of Life' (1987) 13 J Med Ethics 117; Rawles, p 291, n 7 above.
2 E Nord 'An Alternative to QALYs: The Saved Young Life Equivalent (SAVE)' (1992) 305 BMJ 875.
3 J Rawles and K Rawles 'The QALY Argument: A Physician's and A Philosopher's View' (1990) 16 J Med Ethics 93.
4 Rawles, n 1 above.

what the medical profession chooses to make it.[5] We believe that the transfer of funds from, say, nuclear weapon production to health care, while being admirable in itself, does no more than move the problem one incremental stage further. The majority would agree that some form of structured distribution of facilities at microallocation level is essential even though equity and efficiency may, at times, lie together uneasily. Harris, for example, makes a powerful case against the QALY[6] but this is, in our view, insufficient to convince one that the best method of resource allocation is on the basis of 'first come, first served'. McKie and his colleagues, in a continuing debate with Harris, see QALY's, on the other hand, as a sensitive and egalitarian method of distributing scarce resources among competing individuals.[7] We doubt if they should be used in this way. To say that 'the QALY approach is egalitarian because no one's QALYs count for more than anyone else's' takes no note of the fact that, when the chips are down, the QALYs available to each player are unequally stacked. McKie et al are at their fairest when they say that they would restrict the QALY method of assessment if it was shown in a particular case to have a 'divisive and corrosive effect on the sense of community'. But to do so is to reintroduce subjective preferences into what was intended to be an objective exercise and is, to that extent, self-defeating. In the end, QALYs as they stand are no more than aids to decision-making and they are but one of a number of models that are currently being looked at.[8] All are there to be developed and improved upon; possibly their most useful current feature is that they trigger debate as to how priorities in health care should be set rationally.

We should exclude from this discussion, and treat as a special case, the patient who is using a scarce resource but who is obtaining no benefit. The most clear example of this is one who is brain damaged and is being maintained in intensive care – a situation discussed in detail in chapter 16 below. We believe that, once treatment is clearly of no avail, it is not only permissible but positively correct to discontinue heroic measures. Of the many reasons for taking this view, the one which is presently apposite is that a resource, even if couched in terms of man-hours only, is thereby released for someone who is likely to benefit.

Random selection

In our search for an equitable and efficient method of providing limited treatment, we have left for discussion only the option of random selection of patients – or of lottery, or 'first come, first served', which come to much the same thing in slightly different circumstances.

Such a policy has the advantage of apparent objectivity and, as we have seen, it could be regarded as the morally desirable choice in the context of potentially fatal disease. It is, however, a bad medical option because it takes no account of the gravity of the patient's condition and no account of 'medical benefit' – it concentrates on justice and ignores 'welfare'; moreover, the sheer length of waiting lists may prevent the most acceptable cases from the physician's point of view from ever obtaining

5 Klein, p 289, n 1 above.
6 Most recently in J Harris 'Would Aristotle Have Played Russian Roulette' (1996) 22 J Med Ethics 209.
7 J McKie, H Kuhse, J Richardson and P Singer 'Double Jeopardy, the Equal Value of Lives and the Veil of Ignorance' (1996) 22 J Med Ethics 204.
8 For a useful summing up, see R Robinson 'The Policy Context' (1993) 307 BMJ 994.

treatment. As an option, it is also socially suspect in that it treats human beings as 'things' and pays no attention to human values and aspirations. And, finally, its acceptance may be a cloak for no more than abrogation of responsibility. Nevertheless, it may be the way of allocating scarce resources that the public prefer.[9]

It is surprising that there is no recent precedental case law on which to judge the attitudes of society in respect of allocation of resources at the micro, or individual, level. The most likely reason for this is that decisions are taken in good faith and are based on principles which would be acceptable to a responsible body of medical opinion – there is, therefore, no action available in negligence; moreover, there is a remarkable tendency for well-publicised and apposite instances to be solved pragmatically.[10] For any assistance, we suspect we must go back to the classic case of *US v Holmes*.[11] In this instance, a ship's officer ordered a number of passengers to be ejected from a sinking lifeboat; Holmes, who helped effect the instructions, was convicted of manslaughter. A main argument for the prosecution was that the passengers, at least, should have been chosen by lot. It seems fair to assume that this decision would lend support to a policy of randomisation in the event of competition for scarce medical resources; the inferred element of an 'appeal to God' certainly adds a moral weight to the argument. A rather similar English incident is reported in relation to a ferry-boat disaster. Here, a passenger assumed a position of authority and may well have occasioned the sacrifice of one man in order to save the lives of several other passengers; the case never came to court and the coroner thought that such killing would not necessarily be criminal. The commentator, however, considered that such authority as exists is to the effect that the killing of one to save the lives of others cannot be justified or even excused.[12] But such precedents are, at best, only loosely applicable to the present discussion.

As to the withdrawal of resources from a patient already using them, both United Kingdom and United States law is discussed in chapters 15 and 16. It is to be noted, however, that nowhere is there any authority for such action on the grounds of competing medical benefit – that is, that a further latecomer to the scene would be likely to do better. Indeed, there are strong indications that the contrary holds. In *Re J*,[13] Balcombe LJ said:

> I would stress the absolute undesirability of the court making an order which may have the effect of compelling a doctor or health authority to make available scarce resources (both human and material) to a particular child, without knowing whether or not there are other patients to whom the resources might more advantageously be devoted ... [It might] require the health authority to put J on a ventilator in an intensive care unit, and thereby possibly to deny the benefit of those limited resources to a child who was much more likely than J to benefit from them.

9 The calls for more public participation and debate are increasing: R Smith 'Rationing Health Care: Moving the Debate Forward' (1996) 312 BMJ 1553.
10 See the report by D Brahams 'When is Discontinuation of Dialysis Justified?' (1985) 1 Lancet 176.
11 26 Fed Cas 360 (1841), No 15383.
12 Our authority is J C Smith and B Hogan *Criminal Law: Cases and Materials* (4th edn, 1990), p 231. The well-known case of *R v Dudley and Stephens* (1884) 14 QBD 273, [1881-5] All ER Rep 61, CCR was essentially a matter of killing and cannibalism for self-preservation and is too far removed to be appropriate to the present discussion.
13 *Re J (a minor) (wardship: medical treatment)* [1992] 2 FLR 165 at 176, (1992) 9 BMLR 10 at 20.

The implication is clear – withdrawal of treatment will only be condoned when the patient can receive no further benefit.

A solution of the insoluble?

We have thus reached a position where no single parameter seems entirely satisfactory. Gordon[14] in a discussion of the doctrine of necessity, speaks of it as offending 'against the feeling that no human being has a right to decide which of his fellows should survive in any situation'; but, while most would agree with this proposition, doctors cannot opt out of such decisions. Some idea of the complexity of the dilemma was given in an interesting study of dialysis decisions.[15] In this, 40 specimen patients' records were sent to 25 renal units with the request that ten patients be rejected on the grounds of inadequate treatment resources. Only 13 patients would have been accepted in all the units, but, at the same time, none was rejected by all; in the event, it was discovered that six of the ten most commonly rejected cases had already been successfully treated by the authors! Something of a lottery must have been operating despite the most earnest endeavours of physicians to improve upon the system – and it has to be noted that far more sophisticated approaches to organ allocation are now being operated.[16]

We have not discussed a final possible criterion of selection – that is, the ability to pay for a resource. The omission probably derives from a natural repugnance to such an idea, particularly among those accustomed to a national health service. But, on reflection, we wonder if a modified concept of this type does not have its attractions as a way of alleviating scarcity while still retaining moral respectability – indeed, Dworkin has suggested that one criterion for the allocation of resources might be based on what the public *would* pay for given the need.[17] There is no shortage of dialysis machines from the manufacturing point of view; it is the shortage of money to pay for them within the confines of a 'free' medical service which lies at the root of the problem. In these circumstances, it might not be unreasonable to allow patients to contribute to the purchase of 'engineering hardware' according to their means, on the principle that a machine which is bought releases another for the use of others who cannot do so. Such a system operates in the United States as regards dialysis where, admittedly, it was introduced for precisely the opposite reasons – that patients with chronic renal disease would be destroyed financially unless public assistance was given; but whatever the reason, it is probable that the overall provision of dialysis resources is better when distributed as a joint private and public enterprise.

Such a policy would be, we admit, difficult to apply with absolute equity. In particular, it could be argued that it would draw off in an unequal manner the personnel required to operate the machines and who have been trained at public expense.[18] To which one could answer that one does not expect a university graduate

14 G H Gordon *The Criminal Law of Scotland* (2nd edn, 1978) p 422.
15 V Parsons and P Lock 'Triage and the Patient with Renal Failure' (1980) 6 J Med Ethics 173. In fairness, however, it should be remarked that this is a very dated reference.
16 R W S Chang 'How Should Cadaver Kidneys Be Allocated?' (1996) 348 Lancet 453 and associated papers.
17 For discussion, see R Smith 'Being Creative about Rationing' (1996) 312 BMJ 391.
18 An effective case can be made out for an 'all or nothing' policy for health service employees: D W Light 'The Real Ethics of Rationing' (1997) 315 BMJ 112.

in law to accept only legal aid cases; one could also point out that a greater number of cases – of dialysis cases, at least – would be treated at home and that, by and large, the efficiency of domiciliary treatment and the financial status of the patient are closely related. In short, in certain circumstances, there may be a logical case for including private medicine within the public sector with possible benefit to the latter.

We appreciate that, at the end of this fairly lengthy discussion, we have come to little in the way of firm conclusions. We have approached the issues from the position of doctor and lawyer and it is, in some ways, comforting to find that philosophers may be in much the same dilemma.[19] Gillon probably sums up the debate correctly when he implies that, provided decisions are made taking into account fundamental moral values and principles of equity, impartiality and fairness, and provided the bases for decision-making are flexible in relation to the times, then the underlying system is just and is likely to yield just results. Alternatively, we can simply be stoical and acknowledge that: 'to live with circumstances that are unfortunate but not unfair is the destiny of men and women who have neither the financial nor the moral resources of gods and goddesses.'[20]

The responsibility of the individual
No discussion of this type would be complete without a passing reference to the responsibility of the individual to avoid the need for medical resources. The argument that prevention is better than cure has been widely popularised. No one would deny the importance of the theory at all levels but, equally, it is difficult to decide when friendly persuasion ceases and restriction of liberty begins. It follows that a good case can be made out for a right to choose to be unhealthy – and this not only on Kantian but also on utilitarian grounds, for every sudden death in late middle age that is prevented is potentially a long-term occupation of a bed in a psychogeriatric ward; it could well be that the quest for dementia that is inherent in many of the currently popular limitations on habit will turn out to be remarkably cost-inefficient.

What does *not* follow is that there is a concomitant right to health resources when the consequences of that choice materialise. It seems that the public have little sympathy for the cavalier approach – in Williams's experience, the least unacceptable reason for discrimination in prioritisation was that the prospective patients had not cared for their own health.[1] In making such value judgments, however, the public are not constrained by principles of professional ethics and the issue is certainly not so easily solved by health care providers. Various views were put forward in an interesting debate in the British Medical Journal on whether or not coronary bypass surgery should be offered to smokers.[2] The attitude of the surgeons was conditioned by the poor results obtained in smokers and the fact that they spent longer in hospital. Non-treatment could, therefore, be justified on the grounds that treatment of non-smokers deprived others of more efficient and effective surgery. An alternative

19 Gillon, p 302, n 16 above.
20 Engelhardt, p 301, n 12 above.
 1 Williams, p 294, n 20 above.
 2 'Should Smokers Be Offered Coronary Bypass Surgery?' (1993) 306 BMJ 1047: M J Underwood and J S Bailey 'Coronary Bypass Surgery Should Not Be Offered to Smokers' at 1047; M Shiu 'Refusing to Treat Smokers Is Unethical and a Dangerous Precedent' at 1048; R Higgs 'Human Frailty Should Not be Penalised' at 1049; J Garfield 'Let the Health Authority Take the Responsibility' at 1050.

medical view was that non-treatment of symptomatic patients is often less effective in terms of overall cost to society than is operation, that there are many other 'self-inflicted' conditions which one would not hesitate to treat and that, at least in some cases, smoking is an addictive disease which merits sympathy. A warning was also sounded that, in regarding those who have brought medical ills upon themselves as, somehow, less deserving, the doctor is coming perilously close to prescribing punishment. We would accept the view expressed that the patient should be offered the chance when a positive therapeutic advantage – albeit a less than ideal advantage – may be attainable. The solution to the problem thus comes down to the 'best interests' of the individual; we believe, moreover, that this is the route that would be taken by the courts were such a case to be litigated – but no doubt *Bolam* would be left holding the stakes.

12 Treatment of the aged

Old age used to present no particular medico-ethical problems – senescence carried with it an increasing susceptibility to infection and the majority of the aged died at home within the family circle, having strayed not too far from their biblical allocation of three score and ten years.

Today, the physical health of the elderly is improving along with that of other age groups; longevity itself and the expectation of longevity are both increasing. Figures from America are probably valid for most well-developed countries. There, 4% of the population were aged over 65 years at the turn of the century; this proportion had grown to 12.7% by 1990 and is expected to reach 21.8% in 2050 – at which time 5% of the total population will be aged 85 or over. The elderly population is also growing older – while one third of those aged more than 65 were aged more than 75 in 1960, the proportion is likely to be 50% in 2001.[1] The proportion of persons over pensionable age in Great Britain rose from 6% in 1900 to 18% in 1991 – interestingly, the proportion of children under the age of 16 fell from 35% to 20% in the same period.[2] The proportion of women also enlarges with increasing age; British men reaching the age of 50 in the year 2000 are projected to have a 50% chance of reaching 75, while the figure for women is likely to be 74%.[3] Improved physical status, however, is not necessarily paralleled by improved mental capacity; indeed, a longer life provides more time during which the inevitable wastage of a limited supply of brain cells can occur. The stage is then set for a swelling proportion of the population which is suffering from various degrees of dementia; this may, itself, be of primary degenerative type or be secondary to disease of the cerebral vasculature. Long-stay is likely when such patients are admitted to hospital and the dilemma in respect of resource allocation scarcely needs emphasis[4] – up to 20% of all medical and surgical beds in the United Kingdom may be occupied by people over the age of 75 years, although the current redeployment of resources for the chronically sick (for which, see below[5]) may alter the picture. Population projections are now sufficiently

---

1 E S Cohen 'Realism, Law and Aging' (1990) 18 Law Med Hlth Care 183. Different views can, however, be taken of statistics. M Jefferys (ed) *Growing Old in the 20th Century* (1989), introduction, points out that there were 11 persons aged over 85 per 1,000 UK population in 1981; there will only be 17 in 2001 – which should not put too great a burden on an advanced society.

2 P Johnson and J Falkingham 'The Demography of Ageing' in *Ageing and Economic Welfare* (1991) ch 2. The same authors point out that the most important factor determining the proportion of elderly people in the population is not the improvement in the ability to survive to old age but, rather, the changes in size of the generations available to survive – ie the fertility rate.

3 M Dean 'Towards a Healthy Third Age' (1992) 339 Lancet 1403. The 'third age' referred to here is an artificial category of persons aged 50-75.

4 See K Andrews 'Demographic Changes and Resources for the Elderly' (1985) 290 BMJ 1023 for an analysis.

5 See p 313.

sophisticated to indicate the problems likely to be met in deciding on the means by which to cope with conditions in the future – those means cannot be determined on the basis of administrative convenience alone but must involve both ethical and legal considerations.

Autonomy and paternalism in the treatment of the aged

The conflict between autonomy – or the exercise of choice – and paternalism – or the efforts of others to protect those who they consider to be in need of protection – lies at the heart of the dilemma and is far more complex in the context of geriatric medicine than it is, say, in the relatively simple field of consent to surgical treatment by a competent adult. The elderly person is constrained in his choice of action by many factors, some of which are endogenous – such as the effects of early dementia – but others of which are extraneous – for example poverty. The impetus to paternalistic protection of the aged, no matter how it is ultimately applied, is likely to come from that person's family and, although the factor may be minimised in individual cases, it remains an undeniable general fact that it is easier to live without the burden of caring for one's ageing parents; children become paternalists in seeking institutional care for their parents and there is no way in which subjectivity can be wholly eliminated from such action. It is arguable that children have no obligation to support their parents[6] and, regrettable as it may seem, such an obligation has never existed in English law; moreover, the common law duty which existed previously in Scotland has been removed by statute.[7] The public is probably insufficiently aware of the extent of intrafamilial abuse of the elderly; the degree of ignorance – or, in this case possibly, of indifference – is comparable to that which applied to child abuse 40 years ago. There can be little doubt that abuse is extensive and that it occurs in various forms including verbal, physical and by way of neglect or deprivation; figures of between 5% and 65% of elderly persons being at risk are quoted, the incidence depending on the criteria used by the reporting agencies.[8] In one prospective study in England, 45% of carers admitted to some form of 'elder abuse'.[9] It follows that any attempt to enforce a filial duty of care for the aged would be likely to exacerbate domestic violence or neglect and, thus, provoke further deterioration in the geriatrics' conditions. Much of the care of the elderly must, therefore, devolve on the medical and social services and both of these must be supported by the law.[10]

6 N Daniels 'Family Responsibility Initiatives and Justice Between Age Groups' (1985) 13 Law Med Hlth Care 153. This US article specifically applauds the general direction of geriatric health care in the UK. Also by the same author *Am I My Parents' Keeper?* (1988).
7 Family Law (Scotland) Act 1985, s 1(1). But this is not universal. A duty to care for one's indigent parents exists, say, in South Africa: P Q R Boberg *The Law of Persons and the Family* (1991) quoting *In re Knoop* (1893) 10 SC 198.
8 B Pitt 'Abusing Old People' (1992) 305 BMJ 968.
9 A C Homer and C Gilleard 'Abuse of Elderly People by their Carers' (1990) 301 BMJ 1359. It is fair, however, to say that such figures are not always obtained: J Ogg and G Bennett 'Elder Abuse in Britain' (1992) 305 BMJ 998.
10 See A Griffiths, R H Grimes and G Roberts *The Law and Elderly People* (1990).

Institutional treatment

Medical treatment of the aged in the United Kingdom has, as in all advanced societies, moved a long way since the chronically sick, including those who were simply homeless, were almost arbitrarily assigned to hospital wards which have been described as little more than 'human warehouses'.[11] Attention is now concentrated on maintaining the old person's environment as far as is possible. Such a policy must include as a starting point a system of pre-admission home visits by specialists in geriatric medicine; the fact that an inability to appreciate one's disablement is a concomitant of dementia has also dictated positive case-finding.[12] Both these activities may raise problems of etiquette, if not of ethics, between specialists and general practitioners; moreover, there is a strong possibility that case finding imposes an excessively heavy load on general practitioners – which may account for the relatively slight impact the Edinburgh example has had on a national scale.[13] Antipathy to institutionalising the psycho-geriatric patient simultaneously calls for improvements in home help. Given a good relationship, much of this can be provided by the family particularly if they are given assistance. The local authority has a duty to assess the needs of anyone who appears to be in need of community care[14] and, once the authority is satisfied of that person's needs, it has a duty to make suitable arrangements.[15] These are available by way of rather complex legislation. In essence, a disability living allowance, divided into care and mobility components, is payable to a person who, inter alia, is so physically or mentally disabled as to require the constant attention of another person by day (or prolonged or repeated attention at night) to assist with his or her bodily functions or for his or her protection from danger. Disability living allowance is payable only if the disability arose before the age of 65; it is replaced by attendance allowance if it arose later – and there is no age limit applied to this benefit.[16] Elective and temporary admission to hospital, thus allowing the carers time for relaxation, can be a most useful adjunct. By and large, however, home assistance must be a function of the social services and the local authority is under an obligation to provide such aid in a 'preventive' mode. This includes help with the design of the house and the provision of meals, facilities for recreation and home helps. Boarding accommodation, which is something less than residential care, can also be provided.[17] It may be that such treatment is cost ineffective and is difficult to apply. The economic return depends to an extent on the degree of dependency – the expense of domicillary care increases with increased dependency and, at some point,

11 T Howell 'The Birth of British Geriatrics' (1983) 13 Geriat Med 791.
12 M Arcand and J Williamson 'An Evaluation of Home Visiting of Patients by Physicians in Geriatric Medicine' (1982) 283 BMJ 718.
13 S Barley 'An Uncompromising Report on Health Visiting for the Elderly' (1987) 294 BMJ 595.
14 National Health Service and Community Care Act 1990, s 47. The quality of such assessment and the consequent disposal of the subjects is open to criticism: E Dickinson 'Long Term Care of Older People' (1996) 312 BMJ 862.
15 Chronically Sick and Disabled Persons Act 1970, s 2.
16 Social Security Contributions and Benefits Act 1992, ss 71, 75 and 64. These benefits are to be distinguished from invalid care allowance which is paid to the carer (s 70). The rights of married daughters to invalid care allowance have been upheld by the European Court of Justice: *Drake v Chief Adjudication Officer* [1986] 3 All ER 65, [1986] ECR 1995.
17 Health and Social Services and Social Security Adjudications Act 1983, Sch 9, Pt II; Social Work (Scotland) Act 1968, s 14. A general duty to care for the welfare of the elderly also rests on the local social service authority (Health Services and Public Health Act 1968, s 45).

it will become inequitable for a disabled person to expect cost-ineffective support at the expense of others who are, thereby, deprived of care;[18] clearly, however, the wishes – or autonomy – of the subject must be fed into the balance. The current proliferation of privately run nursing homes, which derives from government policy that most institutional care should be provided on a private commercial basis, makes it very difficult to generalise as to the comparative prognosis of those cared for at home and those institutionalised. Inevitably, much depends upon the degree and efficiency of supervision of residential and nursing homes and we return to the subject below.

Nevertheless, some old people, who are fit other than in the mind, must be institutionalised to an extent which will depend upon the severity of dementia. The simplest form of such care is by way of sheltered housing – which may be provided by the local authority, housing associations or as a private venture – but the degree of available supervision is generally so low as to eliminate it as a resort for persons who are anything greatly less than fully independent; sheltered housing might, however, be the ideal refuge for the elderly person who is subject to domestic abuse and, thereby, eligible for priority accommodation.[19] Beyond this, it may be possible to arrange for residential care in accommodation which the local authority has a duty to provide by virtue of the National Assistance Act 1948, s 21. Practice, however, falls short of the theoretical ideal. The local authority has no obligation to provide specialist or hospital-type medical facilities in such institutions, which are already accepting patients whose requirements exceed those for which this method of disposal was designed; so-called 'Part III accommodation' tends to revert to the conditions which are less than ideal.

The result has been a growth of private homes, which has been encouraged by government policy that the local authorities should utilise the private sector.[1] Homes are divided into those which provide only accommodation and those which, in addition, provide either board and personal care to those in need of it[2] (residential care homes) or nursing care (nursing homes). It is only the last two which require to be registered under the Registered Homes Act 1984.[3] The extension of private nursing homes, with governmental assistance as to charge, has provided some sort of solution to the problem of the scarcity of residential accommodation – a problem which was fast becoming beyond the ability of the NHS to contain. At the same time, the pressure to empty hospital beds into residential and nursing homes is increasing and, since there are very few nursing homes run by the NHS, financial strains on the elderly are similarly increasing – effectively, a person who has a capital of £16,000 or more, which includes the value of his or her own home, has to pay his or her charges in full; the local authority will pay the difference between their basic and the actual costs until

---

18 J G Evans 'Institutional Care and Elderly People' (1993) 306 BMJ 806.
19 Housing Act 1985, s 59. Vulnerability can only be defined following wide-ranging inquiry: *R v Lambeth Borough Council, ex p Carroll* (1987) 20 HLR 142.
 1 Community Care (Residential Accommodation) Act 1992, amending National Assistance Act 1948, s 26.
 2 The fact that a person is not receiving assistance with bodily functions does not mean that he or she cannot be in need of personal care: *Harrison v Cornwall County Council* (1990) 11 BMLR 21.
 3 In response to public disquiet, small homes (with fewer than four residents) providing such services must now be registered: Registered Homes (Amendment) Act 1991.

the person's savings have been reduced to £3,000; the authority will then pay the full fee.[4]

Something of a conflict may, therefore, develop between the local health authorities, who are anxious to clear their bed-space, and the elderly, backed by their families, many of whom would, quite reasonably, wonder why they have been singled out as a group to whom the facilities of a comprehensive health service are denied when most needed – one commentator estimates that some 40,000 houses are sold each year in order to finance long-term nursing care.[5] Health authorities may, and do, claim that their duty of care is limited by the resources available and, as a result, policies on the limitation of long-term care are variable; at the same time, the social services cannot find places for an indefinite number of persons discharged from hospital. In general, many would maintain that the time limits projected for in-patient nursing care are too short.

Paradoxically, however, the academic specialist in geriatric medicine may well regard an institutionalising policy as being likely to counter that of care within the community; moreover, the process is one which, as discussed above, may or may not be wasteful of scarce financial resources.[6] The modus operandi of the geriatric unit is based on rehabilitation and the return of patients to their natural environment. In 1987 only 7% of those assessed for ideal disposal in Edinburgh were, in fact, admitted to residential care[7] and less than 20% of patients admitted to the geriatric medical wards remained in long-term care. The ideal situation is, however, hard to come by. A recent report on the national scene indicated that some one-third of nursing home residents were unsuitable for this form of care and that this was mainly associated with inadequate assessment. Perhaps even more disturbingly, the poor quality of institutional care was found to be a major contributor to the high costs involved.[8] But, while the overall management of psychogeriatric patients may seem to be less than satisfactory, the conditions are not confined to the United Kingdom. Kapp,[9] writing of the United States, appealed for direction of, and rationality in, long-term care policy. He wrote:

4   Health and Social Services and Social Security Adjudications Act 1983, s 17. J Kellett 'Long Term Care in the NHS: A Vanishing Prospect' (1993) 306 BMJ 846.; J Warden 'The Lottery of Long Term Care' (1994) 308 BMJ 742.

5   M Dean 'UK's Long-term Nightmare on Nursing-care Costs' (1996) 347 Lancet 681. Predictably, the NHS denies that it is neglecting the long-term health care of the elderly: Community Care Unit, NHS Executive *NHS Responsibilities for Meeting Longterm Health Care Needs* (1994). However, some form of insurance scheme seems inevitable for the twenty-first century: M Mulube 'Plan for Insurance to Fund Elderly Care' (1996) 313 BMJ 709. See also T Richards 'Ageing Costs' (1998) 317 BMJ 896.

6   D Challis, R Darton, I Johnson et al 'An Evaluation of an Alternative to Long-stay Hospital Care for Frail Elderly Patients. II. Costs and Effectiveness' (1991) 20 Age and Ageing 245.

7   J Rafferty, R G Smith and J Williamson 'Medical Assessment of Elderly Persons Prior to a Move to Residential Care: A Review of Seven Years' Experience in Edinburgh' (1987) 16 Age and Ageing 10.

8   E Dickinson 'Long Term Care of Older People' (1996) 312 BMJ 862. In the UK, the whole issue of the financial burden of care in old age is being reviewed at the time of writing by a Royal Commission established by the government under the chairmanship of Sir Stewart Sutherland which is due to report in early 1999.

9   M B Kapp 'Financing Long-term Care for the Elderly; Am I *Your* Parents' Keeper?' (1985) 13 Law Med Hlth Care 188. Experience in Australia seems to be similar but rather more satisfactory: T Smith 'Old Age in the Sun' (1984) 288 BMJ 1515.

Our principles and the choices – that must deal simultaneously with the forces of autonomy, quality and cost – that carry out these principles, must be developed and made public.

The resolution of, on the one hand, demands for unlimited long-term care and, on the other, our willingness to arrange payment for the associated benefits are matters of universal concern.

The individual patient

So far, we have considered the problems of the aged in general terms only; they become even more acute when applied to the individual patient. Thus, in the conditions of Part III housing, injuries due to falls and other mishaps in an unsupervised situation are likely to arise; deaths which occur later, and which are no more than temporarily associated, are likely to be the subject of inquiry by either the Coroner or the Procurator Fiscal.[10] Many such incidents may be beyond the control of inadequate staff, notwithstanding their dedication; yet the fear of culpability can rebound to the overall detriment of the patient – 'defensive' action by the nurses may result in unnecessary restraint of their charges.[11] Of greater immediate importance are the ethical problems surrounding those old persons who want to retain their independence and who resist removal to an institution. The danger, then, is double-sided – either the 'cussedness' of old age may be designated as mental illness and the aged person be compulsorily restricted or, as has occurred in some of the United States, the senile dement may be determinedly excluded from the social benefits which are available to those who can lay claim to a recognisable mental illness.

In the United Kingdom, the legal resolution of the problem of compulsory disposal of the inadequate aged person rests, primarily, on the National Assistance Act 1948, s 47. This allows the compulsory removal from their homes of persons who are not mentally ill but who are suffering from grave chronic disease or, being aged, infirm or physically incapacitated, are living in insanitary conditions and are unable to devote to themselves, and are not receiving from other persons, proper care and attention. Removal may be effected in the person's own interest or in order to prevent injury to the health of, or serious nuisance to, other persons. The district community physician, or community medicine specialist, can apply for a magistrate's order giving seven days' notice of removal. The order allows for detention in a 'suitable hospital or other place' for up to three months; emergency removal for a period of three weeks can be achieved on the recommendation of the community physician if this is backed by another practitioner – who is normally the person's general practitioner – and the removal is in the interests of the person concerned.[12] The fact that this accelerated procedure is used in the majority of cases is a cause of anxiety as to the operation of the legislation.

---

10 For an up to date review of accidents in the home, see S M Cordner and J Ozanne-Smith 'Accidental Death and Injury in the Home' in J K Mason and B Purdue (eds) *The Pathology of Trauma* (3rd edn, 1999).

11 A very full discussion is to be found in S H Johnson 'The Fear of Liability and the Use of Restraints in Nursing Homes' (1990) 18 Law Med Hlth Care 263.

12 National Assistance (Amendment) Act 1951, s 1(1).

It is estimated that the powers under s 47 are invoked annually less than some two hundred times in England[13] and 15 times in Scotland. The reasons for this marked selectivity are both practical and ethical. As to the former, the order does not provide for compulsory treatment and the subject is likely to be removed to a geriatric hospital rather than to a geriatric unit; worse, admission may be to a general hospital where treatment and investigation are not likely to be strongly motivated and will be looked on as contradictions in terms unless the admission is on the grounds of grave chronic disease. The moral issues were elegantly argued by Gray[14] who, first, questioned the justifiability of removing an elderly person from his or her home for the benefit of 'other persons' – as he pointed out, powers of compulsory home cleaning and the like are already available under the Public Health Acts 1936-1961. Secondly, the arguments balancing paternalism against personal liberty, which have been discussed above, are raised in a particularly acute form. Thirdly, the use of statutory powers may be little more than a cloak for inadequate social services or family care – which, taken together, are to be preferred to institutionalisation. And finally, and perhaps of greatest importance, there is a strong implication that the powers are based on disapproval of deviant rather than of dangerous behaviour.[15]

The contrary view was put by Greaves[16] who concluded that reference to the standard philosophical alternatives do not do justice to the moral issues at stake; he saw the answer to the problem lying somewhere between the application of rational principles and personal prejudices. Greaves gave no firm answer as to how this level is to be achieved, but accepted that, in certain circumstances, a decision must be taken by proxy on behalf of the old person – and that this is best done by a doctor whose personal ethical sensitivity is unlikely to be suppressed by the blanket application of a principle. Gray[17] in fact, pointed out that s 47 was seen as essentially a mechanism for protecting the elderly against the whims of officialdom and the Medical Officer of Health was thought to be the best person to do this. While criticising the draconian powers available under s 47, he did not believe that it should be repealed – but this is largely because other coercive or frankly immoral practices would evolve in order to persuade old people to resign their homes; there is an ingrained way of public thought that, given the same abnormality, old people 'must' be protected while others merely 'ought' to be so persuaded. There is, in fact, no easy solution. In a more recent attack on the current legislation, it is admitted that there are underlying problems involving individuals in need of care which cannot, at present, be answered in any other way than by the use of s 47 and it is asked whether it is right to deny what may be the best, albeit imperfect, option to one person in the hopes of improving the law

13 P Nair and J F Mayberry 'The Compulsory Removal of Elderly People in England and Wales under Section 47 of the National Assistance Act and its 1951 Amendment: A Survey of its Implementation in England and Wales in 1988 and 1989' (1995) 24 Age and Ageing 180.
14 J A M Gray 'Section 47' (1981) 7 J Med Ethics 146.
15 For further criticism, see J D Fear, P Hatton and E B Renvoize 'Section 47 of National Assistance Act: A Time for Change?' (1988) 296 BMJ 860.
16 D A Greaves 'Can Compulsory Removal Ever Be Justified for Adults Who Are Mentally Competent?' (1991) 17 J Med Ethics 189.
17 J A M Gray 'Section 47 – Assault On or Protection Of the Freedom of the Individual ?' (1991) 17 J Med Ethics 195.

for others. None the less, the author concluded that all suggested justifications for the use of s 47 fail.[18]

The alternative procedures available must also be considered critically. Foremost among these are the statutory provisions within the Mental Health Act 1983 and the Scottish equivalent of 1984. There are, first, the extensive powers available under s 135 (s 117 in Scotland) whereby a justice, acting on information from an approved social worker, can authorise the police to enter and remove to a place of safety a mentally disordered person who is at risk and living alone (this can only be done in Scotland after a mental health officer or a medical commissioner has been refused entry). The subject can then be detained for only 72 hours and, unsurprisingly, the section is used very rarely.[19] Very much more important are the powers relating to compulsory admission to hospital for assessment (s 2 (s 24(S)) or for emergency assessment (s 4 (s 26(S)). These are discussed in greater detail in chapter 21; for the present it is necessary only to note that there would be little or no difficulty in invoking them in cases where s 47 was appropriate – indeed, the Mental Health Act can be seen as the preferred route in an emergency.[20] We take the view, however, that committal under the 1983 and 1984 Acts inevitably classifies the elderly and confused as being mentally abnormal – and, to many, such classification represents a stigma; despite the simultaneous provision of a recognised system of appeal, the use of what is, effectively, a ruse as a matter of administrative convenience seems to us to be more morally reprehensible than is the use of the more straightforward s 47.

The possibility of an application for guardianship remains[1] – the purpose being to empower the guardian, who may be the local authority, to dictate the place of residence of the disordered person. Once again, the practice is seldom adopted due, largely, to the fact that the essential function of a guardian is to maintain the incompetent in the community; to order removal to residential care is something of a contradiction in terms. Moreover, the guardian has no power to order treatment and the guardianship can be challenged by the subject's next-of-kin.

Thus, no current way of achieving compulsory residential care of the elderly is wholly satisfactory. The unfortunate result is that, in the majority of cases, legal process is avoided and the elderly person is 'talked into' abrogating his, or more commonly her, independent status.

The removal of an elderly person to a home or hospital does not, of course, solve all treatment dilemmas. He or she may, like any other, refuse to accept treatment. Compulsion from the legal point of view is out of the question so long as the subject is competent, although, in practice, relatives and others may resort to pressure of various sorts to ensure compliance. The position of the doctor, though, is clear: treatment against the will of the patient could constitute an assault in criminal law or an actionable civil wrong. Thought should also be given to the moral inappropriateness of compelling treatment in such cases; no matter what they feel about apparently

18 S J Hobson 'The Ethics of Compulsory Removal under Section 47 of the 1948 National Assistance Act' (1998) 24 J Med Ethics 38. Repeal of s 47 was envisaged in the Law Commission's draft Mental Incapacity Bill 1995. See p 319, n 9 below.
19 Section 136, which refers to persons in public places, is being used increasingly as residential patients are returned to community care as a matter of public policy.
20 E Murphy 'What to do with a Sick Elderly Woman Who Refuses to go to Hospital' (1984) 289 BMJ 1435.
1 Mental Health Act 1983, s 7.

irrational refusal, few doctors would now attempt to force treatment upon a patient who is mentally competent and who does not want it.

The position of one who is dementing will, however, be different. Almost by definition, such a patient is unlikely to understand fully the nature of his condition and the treatment available. It might be argued that an analogy with the unconscious patient is applicable and, in that case, a doctor may justify the non-consensual treatment of his patient on the grounds of necessity. A dementing patient, however, is not unconscious. His comprehension may be affected by dementia but, equally, he may still be capable of holding and articulating views.[2] It might be better, then, to consider such treatment as an acceptable instance of paternalistic intervention of the sort under which children who are incapable of full understanding are treated. A 'best interests' argument could be advanced should specifically legal justification be called for.

The incompetent patient who is admitted to hospital under the Mental Health Acts may be treated compulsorily for the mental disorder which forms the basis of his admission. Treatment for other conditions is not permitted by the legislation unless it can be seen as being part of that which is appropriate for the mental disorder. This apparently restrictive attitude is compensated by the common law – the lawfulness of a doctor operating on, or giving other treatment to, an adult person disabled from giving consent would depend not on any approval or sanction of a court, but on the question whether the operation or other treatment was justified on the basis of necessity and was in the best interests of the patient concerned.[3]

Legal protection

Any demented person, and certainly anyone for whom compulsory admission to an institution is justified, is unlikely to be able to manage his or her affairs. The law has, therefore, made special provision to ensure that the interests of incompetent elderly people are protected. In English law, the task of administering the affairs of such people may be performed by the Court of Protection. This court, which is an office of the Supreme Court of Judicature, has powers under the Mental Health Act to act on behalf of those who are incapable as a result of mental disorder, a category which would include those suffering from dementia. Application for the appointment of a receiver may be made by a relative or by some other person with a legitimate interest in the matter, including a creditor. During the period in which the receiver acts for the incapable person, the court exercises overall control and supervision of his or her activities.[4] In Scotland, where there is no comparable body solely concerned with

---

2   For an exhaustive study, see M J Gunn 'Treatment and Mental Handicap' (1987) 16 Anglo-Am L Rev 242.

3   *Re F (mental patient: sterilisation)* [1990] 2 AC 1, sub nom *F v West Berkshire Health Authority* [1989] 2 All ER 545 at 551 per Lord Brandon at AC 55, HL. It will be seen throughout this book that this case has been cited as the basis for treatment of the incompetent in a number of ways. This includes admission to hospital for psychiatric treatment: *R v Bournewood Community and Mental Health NHS Trust, ex p L* [1998] 3 All ER 289, [1998] 3 WLR 107. The subject is treated at length in chapter 21.

4   For powers of the Court of Protection, see *Re W (EEM)* [1971] Ch 123 at 143, per Ungoed-Thomas J. Statute, when enforced, will make a new provision for the appointment of an authorised representative with the power to negotiate on behalf of a disabled person with the local authority as to the general provision of welfare services (Disabled Persons (Services, Consultation and Representation) Act 1986).

these matters, the normal method of dealing with the affairs of an incompetent person is to petition the Court of Session for the appointment of a curator bonis, who carries out the same duties as a receiver in England. Neither the receiver nor the curator bonis has powers over the person of the incompetent, which means that neither would be able to authorise medical treatment on the incompetent person's behalf or to take any action with respect to the living conditions of their charge. In Scots law, the Court of Session has recently affirmed the persistence of its common law facility to appoint a tutor dative, who has such a power over the person, in respect of an adult incompetent; in one such instance, a couple successfully applied for tutorship of their mentally handicapped adult son.[5] There seems no reason why the principle should not be applied more extensively to the incompetent elderly – one advantage being that the powers of the tutor dative can be as limited or as broad as the Court of Session decides.

Outwith the context of these rather formal legal institutions, the law also takes some account of the particular situation of the elderly person. Contractual capacity may be denied to one who cannot understand the implications of a contract and contracts which are entered into by persons whose mind is affected by dementia may, of course, be set aside. Similarly, testamentary capacity is restricted to those who can comprehend the nature and extent of their estate and the claims which people may have upon them. In assessing such capacity, however, the law is not so much concerned to place a psychiatric label on a testator as to determine the impact which an apparent specific delusion may have on the contents of the will.[6]

The rules of testamentary capacity were developed with the interests of others in mind. The same focus of attention can be detected in the other areas of the law in which special regard has been paid to the needs of the elderly. Continuance of the property control arrangements which the elderly person him- or herself has made may now extend beyond the onset of incompetence.[7]

The law protecting the elderly, dementing person is, thus, well-intentioned but seriously fragmented; as a result, it is unsatisfactory from the view of both the patient and society. It is against this background that the Law Commissions of both England and Scotland have been studying the total legal environment of the incapacitated[8] and have proposed draft Bills by which to consolidate the existing legislation.[9] The contained proposals as to the provision of treatment are very similar. Both recognise a general mandate for treatment to be given that is, either, reasonable in the circumstances or clearly for the benefit of the incapax – this being subject to restriction in the case of certain procedures which would require specific authority. The English Commission, however, foresees the establishment of a reorganised Court of Protection which has the power to appoint 'managers' to make decisions, including health care decisions, on behalf of incapable individuals; in Scotland, the comparable duties would be undertaken by the Public Guardian acting in association with the Mental Welfare Commission and appointed 'continuing attorneys' and 'welfare attorneys' – the latter being concerned

---

5 A D Ward 'Revival of Tutors-dative' 1987 SLT 69. For further, general discussion, see A D Ward *The Power to Act* (1990).
6 *Banks v Goodfellow* (1870) LR 5 QB 549.
7 Enduring Powers of Attorney Act 1985. Similar arrangements are now available in Scotland: Law Reform (Miscellaneous Provisions) (Scotland) Act 1990, s 71.
8 Law Commission *Mental Incapacity*, Law Com no 231 (1995); Scottish Law Commission *Report on Incapable Adults* no 151 (1995).
9 Mental Incapacity Bill 1995; Incapable Adults (Scotland) Bill 1995.

with health care issues only. In both jurisdictions, the individual would retain the right to appoint a manager or welfare attorney whose authority would survive the granter's loss of capacity and both Commissions set great store by expressions of intent provided by advance statements or directives. The two proposed Bills would undoubtedly help to ease the health management of the aged incapax – but it is to be noted that both still allow the medical profession considerable discretion.

Ethical considerations

There remain for consideration the practical and ethical aspects of the treatment of geriatric patients. These are often discussed in the context of euthanasia which we deal with later in chapter 17. But, while it is true that many old persons may be suffering from terminal physical disease, an equal or greater number may be the victims of no more than intellectual deterioration; the greater part of geriatric medicine relates, in fact, to the management of incurable, rather than of terminal, disease. If the patient's best interests represent the therapeutic yardstick – as they should – the inner world of the geriatric must be assessed subjectively and not related to the observer's own youthful or middle-aged experience. The demented but otherwise physically capable old person is not in pain and, for all we know, is passing a reasonably contented life. The parallel in controversial treatment issues is to be found in the uncomplicated Down's syndrome infant who, as we have already argued, is as entitled to medical treatment as is his mentally normal counterpart. Glib phrases such as 'pneumonia is the old man's friend' come easily to the lips in this discussion and can be dangerously emollient unless they are qualified; death may certainly be a blessed relief to the patient in severe pain but problems raised in the treatment, say, of intercurrent infection in the contented dement are of the same order as are those faced by the mentally competent – one wonders if the more honest aphorism is not that 'pneumonia in an old man is his associates' best friend'.

We would, therefore, disagree to an extent with those who, effectively, call for a policy which is generally biased towards non-treatment of the elderly demented patient on grounds of the 'quality of cognitive life'.[10] At one time, this was frequently expressed by including in the hospital notes the instruction 'do not resuscitate', the morality and practicality of which is discussed below.[11] Similar instructions to withhold resuscitative measures in the event of cardiorespiratory arrest are known as 'No-code orders' in the United States where their validity has been upheld.[12] The judicial reliance on good medical practice that is evident on both sides of the Atlantic emphasises the importance of considering each patient as an individual problem. Following our analogy with the newborn, there is a case to be made out for selective non-treatment of the aged – but selection must be based on the individual patient's circumstances rather than on unfeeling demographic rationalisation.[13]

10 G S Robertson 'Ethical Dilemmas of Brain Failure in the Elderly' (1983) 287 BMJ 1775.
11 See p 445.
12 *Re Dinnerstein* 380 NE 2d 134 (Mass, 1978). See, for a general American review, T A Brennan 'Do-not-resuscitate Orders for the Incompetent Patient in the Absence of Family Consent' (1986) 14 Law Med Hlth Care 13, and, for attempts in the US to codify the process, see T E Miller ' Do-Not-Resuscitate Orders: Public Policy and Patient Autonomy' (1989) 17 Law Med Hlth Care 245.
13 For a useful brief discussion, see Lancet 'Do Doctors Short-change Old People?' (1993) 342 Lancet 1.

The issues crystallise in the place of the elderly in the allocation of resources which, as we have seen, is inevitable in an expanding medical technological ambience – and the arguments are finely balanced. The views of Callahan are particularly interesting in this context.[14] In brief, Callahan sees the need for objective planning if the otherwise certain breakdown in resources is to be avoided. The aged, it is said, have some claim to public funds but these are not unlimited – the goal is a balanced, affordable system of care for the elderly which admits of a good balance between length and quality of life. Effectively, we should see ageing as an inevitable part of life and accept that society discharges its principal duty to the elderly by avoiding premature death. Callahan admits that any serious form of setting limits to treatment will be unpleasant but, since the possibilities of spending money in an attempt to turn old age into permanent middle age are infinite, we should impose an age limit upon ourselves. These views, needless to say, have attracted opposition particularly from those who see the welfare of the individual as transcending a policy of general societal benefit[15] – the argument that we should *always* prefer a younger patient before an older one on the grounds that society's net life gain is, thereby, more evenly distributed is attractive but too dispassionate for comfort. While we would agree that difficult decisions may have to be taken, we prefer the egalitarian philosophy which will avoid positive discrimination against the elderly – expressed as the age-indifference principle which asserts that each person is entitled to the same concern, respect and protection of society as is accorded to any other person in the community.[16] Therapeutic decisions are intensely individual matters which cannot be covered by way of restrictive formulae; age may be one factor in the decision to treat but it cannot be the only factor. To quote Harris again:

> All of us who wish to go on living have something that each of us values equally although for each it is different in character . . . This thing is of course 'the rest of our lives'. So long as we do not know the date of our deaths then for each of us the 'rest of our lives' is of indefinite duration. Whether we are 17 or 70 . . . so long as we each wish to live out the rest of our lives . . . we each suffer the same injustice if our wishes are deliberately frustrated and we are cut off prematurely.[17]

Such problems may confront the surgeon with particular force; the application of the productive/non-productive test[18] must always affect his decision whether or not to operate on the elderly. A negative response to advanced malignant disease may be a simple matter but the improvement in operative techniques is such that the results of elective general surgery in the aged, even of an advanced technological nature such as coronary artery replacement, may be both satisfactory and rewarding – the fact that results may be generally better in the young does not mean that the same procedure in the old is necessarily not worthwhile. It has, in addition, been suggested that

---

14 D Callahan *Setting Limits* (1987). This sort of view is, undoubtedly, taking hold but are well criticised by H R Moody 'Should We Ration Health Care on Grounds of Age?' in *Ethics in an Ageing Society* (1992) ch 9.

15 See eg R W Hunt 'A Critique of Using Age to Ration Health Care' (1993) 19 J Med Ethics 19.

16 J Harris 'The Principle of Age Indifference' in Age Concern Millennium Paper *Values and Attitudes in an Ageing Society* (1998).

17 J Harris *The Value of Life* (1985) p 89.

18 See p 431.

relatively risky surgery, offering either good health or a quick death, may be particularly attractive to the old who should not be denied the choice.[19] In any event, it is relatively unlikely that considerations of productivity can be applied to an acute surgical emergency occurring in an elderly patient with no other mortal disease. The only acceptable test is then one of feasibility – there can seldom be an ethical alternative to treatment if it can be given but, inevitably, high morbidity and mortality rates must be accepted.[20]

The dilemma of what to do in the event that a geriatric patient refuses treatment appears to be less urgent in the United Kingdom than it is in the United States – a difference which possibly reflects that which separates the financial consequences of prolonged medical care in the two countries. There can be no doubt as to the rights of the competent adult to refuse treatment under both jurisdictions and these rights would certainly include opposition to forced feeding. The difficulty, as we know, is that the borderline between competence and incompetence is often indistinct in old age.[1] Court judgments or decisions on the part of guardians may be sought in dramatic situations such as the removal of life-support but are unlikely to be invoked for apparently trivial matters like oral feeding; it is probable that many old people, no matter what their situation, are fed with a varying degree of force but the action is taken on the assumption that refusal to eat is non-volitional. The process is degrading both to the staff and to the patient and, moreover, carries considerable hazard. It is, however, difficult to see the alternative to compassionate and moderate coercion in such cases. Positive refusal of treatment by the competent old person is a different matter and one which has attracted considerable attention in the courts of the United States. There, the right to be let alone has been described as 'the most comprehensive of rights and the right most valued by civilised men'[2] and the courts have, in general, upheld such rights – perhaps the most apposite case being that concerning an 85-year-old, yet alert, man who frankly chose suicide by self-starvation in preference to medical care.[3] The problem of the management of the partially competent geriatric who depends upon artificial feeding can be more difficult; this is well exemplified in the various stages of *Conroy*,[4] which we discuss in greater detail below.[5] Here, it need only be noted that, although the appellate courts disagreed on the definition of medical treatment, both had misgivings as to the possible impact that the decision to

---

19 T Hope, D Sprigings and R Crisp '"Not Clinically Indicated": Patients' Interests or Resource Allocation?' (1993) 306 BMJ 379.

20 J E Robb, I Murray and C MacKay 'Is Elective Surgery in the Elderly Worthwhile?' (1987) 32 Scot Med J 79; A V Pollock and M Evans 'Major Abdominal Operations on Patients Aged 80 and Over: An Audit' (1987) 295 BMJ 1522.

1 In an interesting unpublished paper: C Heginbotham 'Mental Disorder and Decision Making: Respecting Autonomy in Substitute Judgments' (1992) Paper presented to the UK Forum on Health Care Ethics and the Law, London, the author draws attention to the distinction between capacity, which hinges on cognitive and volitional attributes of the individual, and competence. Capacity, being a necessary, though insufficient, condition for competence is, thus, the more important.

2 *Griswold v Connecticut* 381 US 479 (1965).

3 *Re Plaza Health and Rehabilitation Center of Syracuse* S Ct, Onandaga Cty, NY, 4 Feb 1984.

4 *Re Claire C Conroy* 464 A 2d 303 (NJ, 1983), CA, 486 A 2d 1209 (NJ, 1985), SC. For an overview of US cases, see H L Hirsh and M K Cuneo 'Who shall Live, Who shall Die. Who Decides?' (1986) 5 Med Law 111. See also N Rhoden 'How Should We View the Incompetent?' (1989) 17 Law Med Hlth Care 264.

5 See p 436.

abandon nasogastric feeding might have on the general treatment of the elderly incompetent. Indeed, in attempting to resolve the ethical issues in this area, it has been rightly said that: 'Society should be wary of moving from a recognition of an individual's right to die to a climate of enforcing a duty to die.'[6] Our sympathy would be with Murphy,[7] when she says that loss of dignity derives from the way that we care for our sufferers from dementia, not from the illness itself; the condition is a challenge to society's attitudes to the aged and is to be met by the provision of appropriate facilities. Unfortunately, this is a counsel of perfection which, in the prevailing economic climate, is unlikely to be followed until the proportion of the elderly in the population has grown to represent a significant voting force – and, even then, it may be a matter of crying for the moon.

6   M Siegler and A J Wiesbard 'Against the Emerging Stream' (1985) 145 Arch Int Med 129.
7   E Murphy 'Ethical Dilemmas of Brain Failure in the Elderly' (1984) 288 BMJ 61.

Death

13 The diagnosis of death

Death is defined in *Chambers Twentieth Century Dictionary* as 'the state of being dead; extinction or cessation of life'. *Steadman's Medical Dictionary* adds to this 'in multicellular organisms, death is a gradual process at the cellular level with tissues varying in their ability to withstand deprivation of oxygen'. There is, therefore, a conceptual conflict between layman and doctor, the latter being forced to accept an academic formula such as death being 'a permanent state of tissue anoxia'. Tissue anoxia arises naturally in two ways – either respiration ceases, in which case there is a failure to harvest oxygen, or the heart fails, when oxygen is no longer distributed to the tissues. In either case, the diagnostic problem lies in the definition of permanence.

In practice, it is astonishing how often the moment of 'death' is perfectly clear. One can tell immediately when a loved one or a carefully observed patient 'dies' in cardiorespiratory terms. The patient has 'breathed his or her last' and the heart stops beating; this is 'somatic' death. But the individual cells of the body are not dead; they will continue to function until their residual oxygen is exhausted. How long this takes depends upon their oxygen consumption which, in turn, is correlated with their specialised activity. Theoretically, therefore, there should be evidence of cellular death before the state of permanence is accepted but, in practice, the doctor can rely on his senses and on his stethoscope because death is to be expected and is accepted on the vast majority of occasions when it visits. Even so, one is left with the disquieting realisation that brain cells will withstand anoxia for a time, albeit for only a few minutes. If we are to accept the concept of 'brain death', as argued below, we should treat the patient in irreversible cardiorespiratory failure as dying rather than dead – for the true agonal period in natural death is that which lies between cardiac and cerebral failure.

But what if death is unheralded and unexpected? It is common knowledge that the apparent permanence of cessation of the respiration or blood flow can, in many instances, be challenged by physical or mechanical intervention. Thus, sudden heart failure due to the common 'coronary attack' may, in suitable cases, be reversed by electrical stimulation (cardioversion) or by cardiac massage coupled, perhaps, with artificial respiration or ventilation. But, while the patient has been 'saved from the dead', the process of cellular death has been initiated by the temporary failure of oxygen distribution. The majority of organs will recover from such an insult but the cells of the brain are outstandingly the most sensitive in the body to oxygen deprivation and, moreover, they are irreplaceable. Thus, a situation may arise whereby the body as a whole is brought back to life but where it is now controlled by a brain which is damaged to an uncertain degree. The decision to restore an interrupted cardiac function is not, therefore, a simple choice between the good (life) and the bad (death). It poses serious and urgent ethical problems which provide a base from which to discuss the more measured, and in some ways more complicated, issues arising from ventilator deaths.

When death strikes unexpectedly on its second front – by way of acute respiratory failure – it may be countered by the use of artificial ventilation. This may be accomplished by a mechanical respirator which simulates the movements of the chest wall or, more commonly in the context of the present discussion, by a ventilator which forces air in and out of the lungs.

Brain function as a measure of death

The mechanisms underlying acute heart failure and respiratory failure need to be distinguished. Given an adequate oxygen supply, the heart will continue to beat independently of higher control – it did, for instance, commonly beat for some 20 minutes following the broken neck of judicial hanging; the cause of acute cardiac failure, therefore, lies within the heart itself. Respiration, on the other hand, is controlled by the respiratory centre – a nervous 'battery' situated in the brain stem. Moreover, now that acute anterior poliomyelitis ('infantile paralysis') has been virtually eradicated, there are very few extra-cerebral causes of acute respiratory failure that cannot be corrected by the ventilator. Acute respiratory failure of the type which is important in the present context is almost invariably the result of central damage – that is, damage to the brain stem. Oxygenation of the tissues, or cellular life, is, thus, based on a servo-type mechanism: the heart depends for its own tissue oxygen on the lungs which, in turn, are useless without the heart; together they supply oxygen to the brain which, therefore, cannot function in the absence of competent heart and lungs; yet the lungs are, themselves, dependent upon a functioning brain stem. The only segment of this triad which cannot be substituted is the brain. There are, therefore, strong logical arguments for defining death in terms of brain death rather than in the generally accepted terms of cardiorespiratory failure; indeed, Pallis holds that all death is, and always has been, brain stem death and that circulatory arrest just happens to be the commonest way to bring such death about[1] – a point to which we have alluded in the introduction to this chapter. Be that as it may, it is clear that we *must* turn to the brain when the natural functional condition of the lungs – or, occasionally, of the heart – is obscured by the intervention of a machine.

The brain itself is not uniformly sensitive to hypoxia.[2] Simplistically, it can be divided into three main areas: the cortex, which is responsible for our human intellectual existence and is the least able to withstand oxygen deficiency; the thalamus, which roughly regulates our animal existence; and the brain stem, which controls our purely vegetative functions including breathing. The brain stem is least affected by hypoxia; if it is so damaged, it can be assumed, as near certainly as is possible, that the rest of the brain is damaged to a similar or greater extent.[3] Generalised hypoxia will affect all tissues of the body but to a varying extent – the

1   C Pallis 'Return to Elsinore' (1990) 16 J Med Ethics 10.
2   The relative term 'hypoxia' is used advisedly to emphasise that oxygen lack need not be absolute – 'anoxia' – in order to cause brain damage.
3   Lesions which affect the lower brain and leave the cortex intact are the result of local vascular damage – not of generalised hypoxia.

brain being pre-eminently at risk. Conditions producing such hypoxia may be natural – eg heart failure or severe internal haemorrhage – or unnatural, of which drug overdose or a reduced oxygen intake, due, for instance, to a poorly given anaesthetic, are probably the most important in the present context. Violence may be such as to reduce the chest movement or, more likely, will cause 'surgical shock', in which a lowered blood pressure results in inadequate oxygen perfusion of the tissues. Other causative lesions – which can be natural or associated with injury – may be localised within the skull and injure the brain in secondary fashion by occupying the confined space and, effectively, squeezing the vessels carrying the blood. Whatever the cause, hypoxic *anatomic damage* to the brain is irreversible; but further damage is prevented once an efficient oxygen supply is restored. In such a situation, therefore, one can speak of *degrees* of brain damage and resultant coma but not of *stages* of coma because, once the oxygen supply is restored, the condition is no longer progressive.

The clinical appearances in a person who is brain damaged but treated will vary with the degree of hypoxic insult sustained. Four degrees of coma were recognised by the early French writers:[4] *coma vigile,* which represents no more than a blurring of consciousness and intellect; *coma type* and *coma carus,* which are characterised by increasing loss of relative functions followed by vegetative functions; and, finally, *coma depassé* – something beyond coma in which all functions are lost and the patient can only be maintained by artificial means.

Thus, while all appropriate cases may properly be given intensive care for the purposes of diagnosis and assessment, it would be well-nigh impossible to justify long-term treatment for a patient who was likely to end up with no cortical and minimal thalamic function remaining. The identification of such a case presents a formidable technical dilemma because some *functional* or *physiological* damage may be recoverable while some 'dormant' brain cells may have survived to become activated later. This potential for apparent recovery underlies the distinction between a persistent and a permanent stage of cerebral dysfunction; it also accounts, at least in part, for the fact that recovery of brain function is more likely when it has been lost as a result of direct head injury than when a comparable loss is due to pure hypoxic damage.[5]

The wholly decorticated patient falls into the category originally defined by Jennett[6] as the persistent vegetative state – in layman's terms, the 'human vegetable'. Such a person will have periods of wakefulness but is, nevertheless, permanently unconscious; the state has been described as eyes-open unconsciousness.[7] The definition and management of such persons is discussed in detail in chapter 16. For the present, it will be clear that a human who has lost cortical function has, simultaneously, lost his human personality but, in so far as he is capable of existing without mechanical support, he is equally certainly not dead – indeed, he is in some ways more 'alive' than was the fully conscious sufferer from poliomyelitis who existed only by virtue of the respirator. There have been serious suggestions that the decorticated patient should be regarded as dead – may not *homo sapiens* be weakened in its own fight for survival if it devotes strength and resources to maintaining *homo*

4 P Mollard and M Goulon 'Le Coma Depassé' (1959) 101 Rev Neurol 3.
5 R S Howard and D H Miller 'The Persistent Vegetative State' (1995) 310 BMJ 341.
6 B Jennett and F Plum 'Persistent Vegetative State after Brain Damage' (1972) 1 Lancet 734.
7 R E Cranford and D R Smith 'Consciousness: The Most Critical Moral (Constitutional) Standard for Human Personhood' (1987) 13 Am J Law Med 233.

when he is no longer *sapiens*?[8] These were very advanced views at the time they were expressed, but the equation of permanent loss of personality with no longer being alive is a philosophy that is gaining relatively wide acceptance.[9] Such an attitude may be tenable in a general discussion on euthanasia but, when related to the definition of death, it can only confuse the issue and enhance the already strong public apprehension of premature disposal of the body; a particularly influential article, for example, concluded that, while neocortical death may be compatible with our current concepts of death, it should not be introduced as public policy simply because the general public would not understand the issues and it would be needlessly divisive for society.[10] Put another way, could a non-cognitive, decorticated person with continuing cardiopulmonary function be buried?[11] We feel strongly that similar considerations should dictate one's attitudes to the anencephalic infant who, in some circumstances, may represent a naturally occurring persistent vegetative state. Death must remain an absolute; there is no place in medical jurisprudence for conditional phrases such as 'at death's door' or 'as good as dead'. The definition of death has not – or should not have – changed; and, if we are to alter our diagnostic methods, the diagnosis of death must be as sure as it was when we were using the heart and lungs as its sole parameters.[12]

It follows that, if we are to adjudge death by death of the brain, we must be certain that there is *permanent* physical destructive damage to the *whole* brain – and, as we will see later, this must include the brain stem. This principle has been unintentionally confused semantically by the Harvard group, who introduced the term 'irreversible coma'.[13] One's first reaction would be to equate such a condition with the persistent vegetative state – or decorticated patient – or an even lesser degree of cerebral incompetence.[14] It is, however, clear that the committee was describing what other Americans and, later, the British Royal Colleges dubbed 'brain death'.[15] Even this term is capable of misinterpretation – in particular, it can be taken as including 'partial brain death'. The alternative is to speak only in terms of 'brain stem death', a term which derives from the logical assumption that somatic life is impossible in the absence of a functioning brain stem. Conceptual difficulties still remain which are

---

8 Lord Scarman 'Legal Liability in Medicine' (1981) 74 J Roy Soc Med 11.

9 For a comparatively early exposition, see D R Smith 'Legal Recognition of Neocortical Death' (1986) 71 Cornell L Rev 850.

10 R J Devettere 'Neocortical Death and Human Death' (1990) 18 Law Med Hlth Care 96. This paper also summarises the views of others in the field.

11 D J Powner, B M Ackerman and A Grenvik 'Medical Diagnosis of Death in Adults: Historical Contributions to Current Controversies' (1996) 348 Lancet 1219.

12 J M Stanley 'More Fiddling with the Definition of Death ?' (1987) 13 J Med Ethics 21. It is disturbing to read in the modern literature '[This] reflects the medical community's use of the terms "brain dead" or "clinically dead" for persons who are unconscious, comatose, and terminally ill without any reasonable prognosis of recovery': G J Banks 'Legal and Ethical Safeguards: Protection of Society's Most Vulnerable Participants in a Commercialized Organ Transplantation System' (1995) 21 Am J Law Med 45.

13 H K Beecher (chairman) 'A Definition of Irreversible Coma', Report of the ad hoc Committee of the Harvard Medical School to examine the definition of brain death (1968) 205 J Amer Med Ass 337.

14 The most recent authoritative report in the UK emphasises the distinction to be made between coma and the permanent vegetative state: Working Group of the Royal College of Physicians 'The Permanent Vegetative State' (1996) 30 J R Coll Physicians Lond 119. Coma classically presents as eyes-closed unconsciousness.

15 Conference of Medical Royal Colleges and their Faculties in the UK 'Diagnosis of Brain Death' [1976] 2 BMJ 1187.

concerned, for the most part, with such differences as there may be between 'brain stem death' and 'whole brain death'.[16] We are very doubtful whether the distinction needs to be emphasised. Natural diseases in the form of destructive primary lesions of the brain stem which do not simultaneously affect the rest of the brain are rare and are either partial in type or, more commonly, rapidly fatal; the 'locked in' syndrome is probably the least uncommon and, certainly, the most terrifying example but its existence is well appreciated by neurologists.[17] The only unnatural ways in which death or destruction of the brain stem can reasonably be expected in the presence of a normal cerebrum are following accident, judicial hanging or beheading – none of which are germane to the present discussion. For the rest, it is well-nigh impossible to conceive of a generalised, fundamentally hypoxic condition destroying the brain stem while sparing the highly specialised tissue of the cerebral cortex;   and, even were this possible, continued attempts to maintain such a body artificially would be hopelessly non-productive and positively unethical. We believe that the common terms used to define the irreversible cessation of all brain function – 'brain stem death' and 'whole brain death' – can be regarded as synonymous in both practice and theory.[18] But, since the tests devised for diagnosis are, essentially, tests of brain stem function, we prefer the former term which is, in addition, in general use in the United Kingdom.

We do, however, accept that many misconceptions are founded on misunderstanding of the British standards for the diagnosis of brain stem death. These include three equally important phases. First, there is the exclusion of coma being due to reversible causes including drug overdose, hypothermia and metabolic disorders while, at the same time, making a positive diagnosis of the disorder which has caused the brain damage and ensuring that this, in turn, is irremediable. Secondly, there is the carrying out of a number of tests specifically designed to demonstrate destruction of the several components of the brain stem – which include the respiratory centre and, hence, the ability to breathe naturally. Thirdly, there is a carefully controlled system whereby a patient's inability to breath spontaneously is proved.   These tests should be repeated although the recommendations are, of necessity, somewhat open on this point and depend, mainly, on the nature of the precipitating condition.

These criteria have been criticised on the grounds that the patient is 'being asked to prove he is alive' rather than that the physician is proving death. Positive tests, such as an electroencephalogram (EEG) or an angiogram – by which cessation of the blood flow in the brain can be visualised – are therefore sought and one or other is, indeed, mandatory in some countries of the European Community.[19] It is almost incredible

16 C Pallis *ABC of Brain Stem Death* (1983).
17 J M S Pearce 'The Locked In Syndrome' (1987) 294 BMJ 198. For general discussion, see C M C Allen 'Conscious but Paralysed: Releasing the Locked-in' (1993) 17 Lancet 130.
18 This is often the case in practice. Victorian legislation, for example, speaks in terms of irreversible cessation of all function of the brain (Human Tissue Act 1982, s 41) while, at the same time assessing this by way of tests for death of the brain stem – and this is acceptable: J L Dixon (chairperson) Parliament of Victoria Social Development Committee *Report upon the Inquiry into Options for Dying with Dignity* (1987).
19 Pallis, n 16 above, quoted France, Greece and Italy as so requiring. The UK, Eire, Belgium, Germany and the Netherlands are said to accept medical criteria alone as being diagnostic of brain stem death. Among countries in which there is specific legal recognition of the brain as an indicator of death are at least 33 of the United States, Canada and the States of Australia although this relates only to transplantation procedures in Queensland and Western Australia.

that an EEG, which measures the surface electrical activity of the cerebral cortex, should be positive in the presence of properly performed confirmatory tests for brain stem death but there is no reason why such a test should not be added if it would serve to allay any fears among the next of kin as to the certainty of death.

There is little doubt that any residual public misgiving would be lessened if the purposes of defining brain stem death were more fully understood. Certainly, it is a valuable tool in the provision of high quality organs for transplantation (see chapter 14) but this is only part of the story. The major purpose of the procedure is to establish a consensus by which patients who can no longer benefit can be removed from ventilator support. This is essential if the patient is to die with dignity, if the relatives are to be spared wholly unnecessary suffering and if resources, both mechanical and human, are to be properly apportioned. Accepting brain stem death is not a way of 'hurrying death along'; rather, the ventilator allows the pace of investigation, assessment and prognosis to be slackened; when it comes to the point, the diagnosis of brain stem death is, in the great majority of cases, only confirming what is clear from clinical observation – that the patient is dead.

In view of the very widespread international agreement that exists, it came as something of a surprise to find the Danish Council of Ethics rejecting the principle of brain death in 1989.[20] It may well be that the Council has no political power, but its observations are useful to look at as an example of the confused thinking which sometimes attaches to the issue. Reduced to a summary, the Council's view is that death should be defined in terms of what a particular community regards as death – few people, it states, would refer to a warm, pink body as a corpse; the loss of brain function should be regarded as the irreversible onset and that of cardiac function as the termination of the process of death. Clearly, such a formula can apply only when the patient is maintained on a ventilator and, even within that limited parameter, it positively excludes cardiac transplantation as an ethically acceptable procedure. More dangerously, it tends to perpetuate a suspicion that different concepts of death are being used by the profession and the public and that special criteria apply in association with transplantation.[1] Understanding, or its lack, lies at the root of the problem. Evans, who has been a major opponent of the brain stem death concept, has suggested that our moral convictions stand independent of rational account or explanation[2] – and has been criticised for, thereby, rendering philosophical inquiry superfluous.[3] Yet, in simply calling for better 'education' of the public, it is easy to overlook or to minimise the importance of religious and cultural traditions. Transplant operations involving brain dead donors are performed only exceptionally in Japan and a major reason for this must lie in the unique attitude to death that is widely held in that country. The Japanese medical profession itself may share some responsibility for the failure to recognise brain stem death; even so, one feels that caution should prevail before centuries of cultural tradition are swept aside in the name of modern medical technology.[4]

20 B A Rix 'Danish Ethics Council Rejects Brain Death as the Criterion of Death' (1990) 16 J Med Ethics 5.
 1 For further commentary on the Danish recommendations, see R Gillon 'Death' (1990) 16 J Med Ethics 3 and D Lamb 'Wanting It Both Ways' (1990) 16 J Med Ethics 8.
 2 M Evans 'A Plea for the Heart' (1990) 3 Bioethics 227; 'Death in Denmark' (1990) 16 J Med Ethics 191.
 3 D Lamb 'Death in Denmark: A Reply' (1991) 17 J Med Ethics 100.
 4 For discussion, see J Nudeshima 'Obstacles to Brain Death and Organ Transplantation in Japan' (1991) 338 Lancet 1063; M Takao 'Brain-death and Transplantation in Japan' (1992) 340 Lancet 1164; K Hoshino 'Legal Status of Brain Death in Japan: Why Many Japanese Do Not Accept "Brain Death" as a Definition of Death' (1993) 7 Bioethics 234.

Perhaps we *are* 'fiddling with definitions' and should, rather, concentrate on what it is or is not ethical to do with a dying or a dead body. Gillett[5] has summarised the situation in that we do not and cannot require to prolong a life that will never again be engaged with the world; that we require that life to be terminated decently; and that we require that human remains should be treated with respect – and there is much to commend this rationalisation. Within such a framework, the problems of removal from the ventilator become technical rather than ethical. It has been advised that the diagnosis of brain stem death should be made by two doctors, one of whom should be the consultant in charge of the case and the other suitably experienced and clinically independent of the first;[6] but, while the vast majority of practitioners would abide by authoritative guidelines, there is no United Kingdom law on the point.

The legal effect of applying brain stem death criteria

The application of brain stem death criteria has obvious implications as to causation in cases of unlawful killing. But any difficulties disperse once it is conceded that brain stem death means somatic death.[7] It then becomes clear that the effect of intensive treatment has been simply to delay the inevitable result of the initial insult to the brain and there is no break in the chain of causation. This was accepted, first, in America in *People v Lyons*[8] where it was found that the victim of a shooting incident was legally dead before being used as a transplant donor. The British position has been summed up in two leading cases to which we return in chapter 17. Thus, in Scotland, it was held:

> Once the initial reckless act causing injury has been committed, the natural consequence which the perpetrator must accept is that the victim's future depended on a number of circumstances, including whether any particular treatment was available and, if it was available, whether it was medically reasonable and justifiable to attempt it and to continue it.[9]

The later English decision was fully confirmatory:

> Where a medical practitioner, using generally acceptable methods, came to the conclusion that the patient was for all practical purposes dead and that such vital functions as remained were being maintained solely by mechanical means, and accordingly discontinued treatment, that did not break the chain of causation between the initial injury and the death.[10]

---

5 G Gillett 'Fiddling and Clarity' (1987) 13 J Med Ethics 23. For a rather similar US view, see D Wickler and A J Weisbard 'Appropriate Confusion over "Brain Death"' (1989) 261 J Amer Med Ass 2246.
6 Lord Smith (chairman of Working Party) *The Removal of Cadaveric Organs for Transplantation: A Code of Practice* (1979). There is such legislation, for example, in the Australian States and in South Africa (eg Transplantation and Anatomy Act 1983 (South Australia), s 24). A very useful protocol for the diagnosis of brain stem death is to be found in M D O'Brien 'Criteria for Diagnosing Brain Stem Death' (1990) 301 BMJ 108.
7 Conference of Royal Medical Colleges and their Faculties in the United Kingdom 'Diagnosis of Death' (1979) 1 BMJ 332.
8 *People v Lyons* Sup Ct No 56072, Alameda Co (Cal, 1974).
9 *Finlayson v HM Advocate* 1978 SLT (notes) 60 at 61, per Lord Emslie LJ-G.
10 *R v Malcherek; R v Steel* [1981] 2 All ER 422 at 428-429, CA, per Lord Lane LCJ.

It is therefore clear that the law has no intention of regarding doctors who remove a brain stem dead patient from the ventilator as being, thereby, responsible for his death.

Although it is doubtful if it was needed, there is now case law which confirms the medical view that persons whose brain stems are dead are, themselves, dead. In the unusual case of *Re A*[11] – in which the parents of a child sought to have him retained on a ventilator for medico-legal reasons – the judge made a declaration that A, who had been certified as brain stem dead, was dead for all legal as well as all medical purposes and that a doctor who disconnected the apparatus was not acting unlawfully; the fact of death was emphasised when the judge held that he had no inherent jurisdiction over a dead child who could not be made a ward of court for the same reason.

The major legal problem still outstanding relates to the precise time that death occurs in such circumstances; there are several issues which depend upon that determination, and it is surprising that none appears to have been brought to the courts.

Lawyers are inclined to dismiss the problem of when death occurs on the assumption that the time of death can be equated to the time the diagnosis is made or to the time the ventilator support is removed. But a moment's reflection makes it clear that the diagnosis of brain stem death, and the consequent ending of treatment, must be retrospective – death has already occurred and the precise time at which it occurred is unknown and unknowable. Moreover, the choice of the time at which the necessary tests are undertaken is as likely to be based on convenience as on anything else. It is difficult to see how the doctor can conscientiously certify the 'date and time of death' – which is not the same as the 'date and time of death certification' – but it is easy to think of occasions on which he might be called upon to do so urgently.

One very real difficulty lay in the 'year and a day' rule, under which death could not be attributed to murder, manslaughter, infanticide or suicide if it occurred more than a year and a day after the precipitating cause. This rule has now been repealed by the Law Reform (Year and a Day Rule) Act 1996 – a statute which was introduced for the specific reason that the time when 'death on the ventilator' occurs is largely in the hands of the intensive care team. Time-related factors in the payment, or withholding, of life or personal accident insurance policies remain as being possibly important; one example could concern the application of a suicide clause which would be lifted on a given day. Problems as to the payment of estate duty might also arise.

But the most intractable issue would seem to be that related to succession and the possibility of disputed survival. What is to be said as to the deaths of a husband and wife who are injured in the same accident, who are both ventilated and who are both declared brain stem dead? One thing is certain – survivorship cannot be judged on the basis of the technical diagnosis because the order in which death is determined could well be purely arbitrary. To remove ventilator support from both simultaneously and measure the time for the individual heart to stop beating would be confusing and would raise considerable difficulties in those jurisdictions which allow for *alternative* means of diagnosing death (see below); it is essential to hold on to the premise that the patients have been certified as being *already* dead. It would be wholly illogical to vary one's criteria to accommodate a specific situation – alternative methods in diagnosis are acceptable but double standards of death are not.[12] The rules of succession are bound by statute and, accordingly, this is one aspect of brain stem

11 *Re A* [1992] 3 Med LR 303.
12 See P D G Skegg *Law, Ethics, and Medicine* (1984) ch 9; Lamb, p 332, n 3 above.

death which could be subject to legislative action. It seems to us that a positive solution to 'ventilated commorientes' is currently impossible; but a negative direction on the lines that evidence as to the time of removal of ventilator support cannot, by itself, be regarded as sufficient to rebut the statutory presumptions might, at least, be equitable and, at the same time, relieve the doctor of one moral problem.

The ethical position of the doctor

Thus, while we have said that the act of terminating treatment once brain stem death is diagnosed is a technical problem which raises no ethical issues, the time at which this is done unfortunately may do so. It is facile merely to remark that the doctor's decisions should be uninfluenced by extraneous factors because, in practice, he can scarcely avoid being aware of them – and influence is inseparable from awareness. The moral problems posed, say, by insistent pressure from relatives concerned for an insurance policy could be insoluble. A further question arises in respect of how long can a corpse be kept in a state of cellular preservation while still maintaining an acceptable ethical standard. For how long, for example, would it be proper to await a suitable heart transplant recipient?

In recent years, however, doctors and the public have been confronted by the picture of women being retained on support for several weeks for the main purpose of bringing a fetus to viability. There can be little doubt that the fetus of a pregnant woman who is being ventilated in her own interests should, subject to the woman's medical condition, be given the chance to survive. Rather less certainty attaches to the woman who would be removed from intensive care on the grounds of medical futility (see chapter 16) were it not that she was pregnant and that there was a chance that the fetus could be sustained to viability; in the absence of special factors, our feeling is that to do so would be an unacceptable invasion of a dying woman's privacy.[13] The ultimate proposition is to continue to ventilate a brain stem dead woman purely for the benefit of the fetus and there have been a number of instances in which this is said to have been done; the morality of so doing would depend very much on the gestational age of the fetus. This seems to have been the issue in an instance from Germany which concerned an unmarried, brain stem dead 18-year-old who was only 15 weeks' pregnant; the hospital ethics committee (see chapter 21) recommended continuation of the pregnancy – a decision which was, in our view surprisingly, widely supported by all other than women's groups. The fetus was still born after six weeks of intensive effort. The President of the Federal Chamber of Physicians is reported as commenting: 'Due to scientific advances, medicine will, again and again, have to infringe ethical borders';[14] the alternative view, which we share, sees such actions as incremental nudges which may, ultimately, push this branch of medicine into areas of doubtful morality unless they are held firmly in check.

This is not the place to expand on the ethics of comatose or post-mortem gestation, as we are concerned, here, with the diagnosis of death. The procedure has, however, considerable interest within that context. Jennett has said that, even with intensive

13 In one English case, a woman's partner threatened to sue the hospital for so doing: D Kennedy 'Father may Sue over Coma Baby' (1996) The Times, 4 July, p 5. For full discussion, see J A Robertson 'Posthumous Reproduction' (1994) 69 Indiana LJ 1027.
14 H L Karcher 'German Doctors Struggle to Keep 15 Week Fetus Viable' (1992) 305 BMJ 1047; A Tuffs 'Keeping a Brain-dead Pregnant Woman "Alive"' (1992) 340 Lancet 1029.

care, cardiac function can be maintained for a few days at most once the brain stem is dead.[15] Many of these cases are said to have been ventilated for more than 50 days – which strongly suggests the possibility of a misdiagnosis. This being so, attempts to incubate a fetus to viability in a dead woman may not only be unethical but may also contribute to the confusion and distrust which, even today, colour the concept of brain stem death.

The case for legislation

It is because of this latent unease that the case for a modern statutory definition of death has been widely canvassed and is applied in many jurisdictions.

The main difficulty in framing legislation is to allow for all modes of death – from the elementarily obvious to the complex ventilator case; it would be absurd to demand that criteria designed for the latter be applied to the former. As a result, most statutes, either existing or proposed, have applied some form of dual criteria of proof of death.[16] A typical expression is to be found in the United States Uniform Determination of Death Act 1980, which reads:

> An individual who has sustained either (1) irreversible cessation of circulatory and respiratory functions, or (2) irreversible cessation of all functions of the entire brain, including the brain stem, is dead. A determination of death must be made in accordance with accepted medical standards.

And, as an example of Commonwealth legislation, we quote the Human Tissue Act 1982 (Victoria), s 41:

> A person has died when there has occurred:
> (a) Irreversible cessation of the circulation of the blood in the body of the person, or
> (b) Irreversible cessation of all functions of the brain of the person.

There are similar provisions in the Human Tissue Act 1983 (NSW), s 33.

But, in essence, all these measures do is to spell out good medical practice within a legal framework – and many would feel this to be unnecessary. They lay down no specific methods; these being relegated to codes of practice – and this, we believe, is rightly so. We would certainly agree with the great majority of commentators that any statutory definition of death must be limited to an enabling concept. Medical facilities and expertise alter and do so faster than can the law; it is, therefore, essential that the evaluation of diagnostic techniques remains in the hands of the medical profession.

---

15 B Jennett 'Brain Death 1981' (1981) 28 Scott Med J 191.
16 D W Meyers *Medico-Legal Implications of Death and Dying* (1981) divides state statutes in the USA into three categories: those which provide for brain death as an express alternative to heart-lung orientated death, those which admit the use of brain-based criteria when a cardiorespiratory diagnosis is obviated by artificial maintenance; and those which recognise brain death simply as a means of determining or defining death. All States have now adopted brain death either by statute or by court recognition.

In fact, the ethical, philosophical and social problems inherent in the definition of death seem to have been largely solved in recent years;[17] definitive legislation might do little more than reanimate concerns which have long been put to rest and might, as a result, be self-defeating. The stethoscope and the CT scanner have it in common that both depend upon the expertise of their user – no Act of Parliament can alter that basic fact.

17 Pallis, p 331, n 16 above.

14 The donation of organs and transplantation

The juxtaposition of chapters on the diagnosis of death and on transplantation of organs should not be taken to indicate that they are *necessarily* associated. It is again emphasised that the concept of brain stem death is as important to neurosurgeons, who can now allow their hopeless patients to die in peace, and to the relatives, who can now accept the fact of death with good conscience, as it is to the transplant surgeon. Nevertheless, and despite the relatively recent introduction of new techniques to which we refer later, optimum transplantation – and, with it, maximum saving of lives – depends upon the acceptance of brain stem death; furthermore, the two conditions are closely linked in the public mind. This is, therefore, a not inappropriate point at which to discuss the ethics and legality of a procedure which, although now firmly established as accepted medical treatment, nevertheless still provokes some public disquiet.

Technical aspects of transplantation

There are three major biological hurdles to be overcome in successful transplantation therapy: neutralising the 'tissue immunity' reaction; ensuring that the donated organs are healthy; and preserving the viability of those organs in the period between their becoming available and their reception.

A tissue immunity reaction results from the recognition by the body of antigenically foreign material which it will then reject with a degree of determination which depends, to a large extent, on *how* different is the donated tissue from that of the recipient. From this point of view, we can distinguish three main forms of the procedure:

(a) Autotransplantation, or the resisting of portions of the same body. This is effectively limited to skin or bone grafting and poses only the difficulties of highly complex surgery. It is of no concern in the present context.
(b) Homotransplantation or allografting, which involves the transfer of viable tissue from one human being to another.
(c) Heterotransplantation or xenotransplantation – that is, the successful transplantation of organs from one species to another.

Xenotransplantation
Clearly, xenotransplantation is that form of organ grafting which will stimulate the maximum immune reaction. The reaction will be quantifiably different between so-called concordant species – for example, within the primates – and when the species

338

are widely unrelated, or discordant, as in pig to man transplants; the reaction is then of a quite different order to that seen with the customary allograft and is known as hyperacute rejection of the donated organ. As a result, xenografting – xenografting and xenotransplantation are interchangeable terms – is a highly complex and experimental procedure; it will be convenient to discuss it and to dismiss it before proceeding to the major topic of homotransplantation.

In the third edition of this book, we referred to xenografting as being, currently, a practical impossibility and we dismissed a well-publicised attempt in 1984 to transplant a baboon's heart into a human neonate[1] as being so doomed to failure as to have no practical significance in a discussion of organ replacement therapy. We cannot, however, be so cavalier today. As we have suggested above, the major *clinical* barrier to xenografting lies in the intense immune reaction that is established when organs from different species share the same blood supply. The increasing sophistication of immunosuppressant drugs and of immunosuppressant techniques – in particular that of genetic replacement whereby transgenic animals, modified so as to contain human genetic material, are produced[2] – are, however, changing the scene to the extent that a man has survived for 70 days following the transplantation of a baboon's liver.[3] These rapid advances have precipitated precautionary governmental action which has, thus far, culminated in the establishment of a Xenotransplantation Interim Regulatory Authority (UKXIRA); the Authority will oversee the development of xenotransplantation and its co-ordination pending the introduction of primary legislation. The government's approach to this new therapy is, therefore, very similar to that it adopted in respect of assisted reproduction (see chapter 3). One of the first actions of the UKXIRA has been to declare a moratorium on clinical trials of xenografting pending further research. Thus, while we must now take a rather more detailed look at the process than we did in previous editions of this book, it can still be pitched at a relatively superficial level. This, however, should not cloud the fact that xenotransplantation stimulates a host of ethical problems in addition to those which are severely practical.

As to the latter, in addition to the establishment of an immune response in the individual case, the community-based possibility of transmitting animal micro-organisms – in particular, viruses – to humans, and of their becoming adapted to the new environment, is very real and constitutes one of the main reasons why xenotransplantation is suspect.[4] A corollary to this, which crosses the ethical/practical boundary, is that animals destined to be donors would have to be reared in 'pathogen-free' environments which are hard, if not impossible, to define and maintain but which would also involve much animal suffering – and the morality of xenotransplantation depends on there being a positive balance in favour of human advantage over animal disadvantage.[5] Given that

---

1   L L Hubbard 'The Baby Fae Case' (1987) 6 Med Law 385.
2   A James 'Transplants with Transgenic Pig Organs ?' (1993) 342 Lancet 45.
3   T E Starzl, J Fung, A Tzakis et al 'Baboon-to-human Liver Transplantation' (1993) 341 Lancet 65. Even so, we remain unconvinced that such a result should be classified as a success. For more recent analysis from the US, see J K Fredrickson 'He's All Heart . . . and a Little Pig Too: A Look at the FDA Draft Xenotransplant Guidelines' (1997) 52 Food Drug LJ 429; J M Kress 'Xenotransplantation: Ethics and Economics' (1998) 53 Food Drug LJ 353.
4   See Nuffield Council on Bioethics *Animal-to-Animal Transplants* (1996) ch 6. Also M Fox and J McHale 'Regulating Xenotransplantation' (1997) 147 NLJ 139.
5   That such a balance exists was accepted by both the government appointed Advisory Group on the Ethics of Transplantation *Animal Tissue into Humans* (1996) and the Nuffield Council, n 4 above. Individuals are less convinced: see R Downie 'Xenotransplantation' (1997) 23 J Med Ethics 205.

it is acceptable to use animals in this way, one has to ask – what sort of animals? Clearly, tissue rejection would be minimised if non-human primates were used. It is, however, widely accepted that primates have special characteristics and constitute such a natural resource as to exclude them as organ donors.[6] Current interest, therefore, centres on the pig – an animal which has no antigenic but remarkable physiological affinities with man.[7] Modern molecular biological techniques have already produced transgenic pigs, in which at least one of the mechanisms leading to graft rejection appears to have been eliminated; there is little doubt that clinical trials using such organs are on the horizon, albeit not just around the corner.

All of which may be good scientific medicine but, like so many such 'advances', it raises both intuitive and philosophical doubts. Undoubtedly, there is a 'gut' distaste for being maintained by a porcine heart. More importantly, one must wonder at the morality of maintaining and, worse, breeding animals for the express purpose of substituting human body parts. The simple response that this is no different from eating pork in order to avoid starvation seems unsatisfactory – Downie,[8] for example, sees a moral difference between 'natural' feeding and 'unnatural' organ substitution. We feel, however, that the subject – which should include an analysis of the philosophy of speciesism – is too wide for a book of this type. In fact, while very much appreciating the potential human advantages of xenotransplantation, we are equally concerned as to the possible ill effects on our human society. It is not wholly unreal to foresee human organs being replaced by those of animals as they fail in sequence; we are then left with the unedifying picture of replacement therapy being continued until the irreplaceable and paradigmatic human organ, the brain, wears out. Moreover, since no health service could contain the costs of such a programme, longevity would become the prerogative of the rich; the structure of human society could be altered dramatically. In practical terms, no xenografts have, as yet, been performed in the United Kingdom; it is to be noted, however, that current government policy on the subject is very cautious but is by no means exclusive.[9]

Even so, the great majority of commentators would prefer to see improvements in the homotransplantation programme and the remainder of this chapter is devoted to organ replacement as it is generally understood.

Homotransplantation

Here, despite the fact that we are dealing with tissues from the same species, an immunity problem persists because, for practical purposes, no two persons other than monovular twins are genetically identical; the body can still recognise, and will reject,

---

6 While stating this firmly, the Advisory Group, p 339, n 5 above, considered primates could, in strictly circumscribed conditions, be used for research into xenotransplantation. They would, of course, be protected by the Animals (Scientific Procedures) Act 1986.

7 See eg D White and J Wallwork 'Xenografting: Probability, Possibility, or Pipe Dream?' (1993) 342 Lancet 879.

8 See p 339, n 5 above. Others are less convinced: eg J Hughes 'Xenografting: Ethical Issues' (1998) 24 J Med Ethics 18. For a comprehensive analysis, see M Fox and J McHale 'Xenotransplantation: The Ethical and Legal Ramifications' (1998) 6 Med L Rev 42.

9 Official Reports HC, 15 February 1993, vol 219, col *80*. See also *Government Response to "Animal Tissue into Humans"* (1997).

tissues of the same species which are 'non-self'.[10] This intra-species immune reaction can be increasingly well suppressed with the use of the cyclosporine group of drugs and monoclonal antibodies. The general principle remains, however, that such suppression will be effective – and will have less adverse side effects – in proportion to the genetic similarity of donor and recipient. Thus, sibling donation will be especially satisfactory and intrafamilial exchanges in general are likely to show less antigenic discrepancies than are those between random strangers. Other variables, however, intrude and complicate the picture. Immunosuppression is non-specific; therefore, while the graft rejection process is being controlled, other desirable immune reactions – such as the body's defence against microbiological invasion – are also affected. Moreover, the greater the *quantity* of foreign material transplanted, the greater will be the need for immunosuppression and, as a corollary, micro-organisms that are normally resisted with ease will be increasingly able to establish themselves in the vulnerable body – the most specifically significant of these are viruses which are responsible for certain forms of malignant disease of the lymphoid system. Enhanced success of transplantation therapy is not, therefore, simply a matter of discovering more powerful immunosuppressants.

It is axiomatic that an organ intended as a replacement for a diseased tissue must be normal itself. The practical result is that donors should be relatively young and they must either be living or have died from accident or from localised natural disease which has no effect on the donated tissue. This implies a pragmatic limitation on the age of the donor but this is higher than might be expected – 70 in the case of kidneys, 50 for livers and 40 for donors of hearts[11] – and may be extended as the general health of the aged steadily improves.

Viability is that essential element which combines most clearly the technical and ethical problems of transplantation surgery. As has been discussed in chapter 13, the cells of the body will deteriorate when deprived of oxygen; the process of deterioration can be slowed markedly by chilling the organ, the viability, or competence, of which then depends on the 'warm anoxic time' – that is, the interval between cessation of the circulation and chilling of the specimen. In terms of practical transplantation, it becomes increasingly pointless to transplant a kidney after more than one hour's warm anoxia. Even so, the acceptable cold anoxic time is also finite and varies with the tissue involved – not only as regards its metabolic activity but also as to the urgency with which it must assume full function after transplantation; the heart and lungs can be used up to four hours after harvesting, the liver up to 8-12 hours and the kidneys can be maintained in vitro for more than 24 hours.[12] Imposed delays must, therefore, jeopardise the validity of the operation.[13]

10 The alternative – where the transplanted material attacks the host – is a difficulty of bone marrow transplantation. See A M Denman 'Graft versus Host Disease: New Versions of Old Problems?' (1985) 290 BMJ 658.
11 W B Ross 'Increasing Organ Donation – A Review' (1989) 34 Scott Med J 451. The Exeter Protocol (see Feest et al, p 355, n 20 below) includes no overriding age limitation.
12 J Wallwork 'Organs for Transplantation' (1989) 299 BMJ 1291.
13 Cold perfusion of the whole body or of individual organs in situ is now used to reduce these difficulties. The non-heart beating donor may be returning and improving the supply of organs. J P Cachera, D Y Loisance, O Tavolaro et al ' Hypothermic Perfusion of the Whole Cadaver: A Response to the Question of the Multiple-organ Donor' (1986) 18 Transplant Proc 1407; G Kootstra, R Wijnen, J P van Hooff and C J van der Linden 'Twenty Percent More Kidneys through a Non-heart Beating Program' (1991) 23 Transplant Proc 910.

It will be evident that organs can be provided for transplantation by the living or by the dead. Living donation offers many technical advantages – tissue compatibility can be measured at leisure, the operation can be elective and the warm anoxic time can approach zero. In theory, potential cadaver donors are widely available but, in practice, their recovery is capricious and both donor and recipient operations must take on the character of emergency surgery. The recognition of brain stem death, however, offers the possibility of a variation on cadaver donation – the 'beating heart donor' – which bridges the gap between the living and the conventionally dead and carries with it many of the advantages of both types of donor. The legal and ethical limitations of all three methods must be considered.

The living donor

The donation of tissues which can be replaced rapidly – such as blood and bone marrow – presents, in practice, few technical or ethical problems other than that of commercialism to which we refer below.[14] We are concerned here only with non-regenerative tissues.

The legal regulation of living donations in the United Kingdom lies in both common and statute law. As to the former, the starting-point must be the principle that no person is to be deemed capable of consenting to his being killed or seriously injured. The living donation of a heart is, thereby, precluded. This, of course, is the extreme case and, beyond it, legality would depend upon the presumed risk-benefit ratio involved in the procedure – and assessment of this is difficult because the technological boundaries of medicine are always expanding. A few years ago, one would have said the same about the liver as about the heart; today, the use of segments of adult liver in paediatric transplantation therapy is so far beyond the experimental stage that a leading American surgeon can say: 'We estimate that maybe 50 per cent of our paediatric liver transplants will be done that way'[15] – in fact, since the liver regenerates both anatomically and functionally,[16] it may be that segmental liver donation is more akin to bone marrow donation rather than organ transplantation.[17] None the less, ethical problems, especially as to the relative risks and benefits to donor and recipient, abound and must now be applied to live donation of lung tissue where perhaps the main precautionary principle should be that live donation of this severity should be used only to supplement cadaver donation.[18] The common law legality and morality of live organ donations which will not necessarily cause grave harm to the

14 Though bone marrow donation is certainly a procedure which cannot be undertaken light-heartedly.
15 G McBride 'Living Liver Donor' (1989) 299 BMJ 1417. See also P A Singer, M Siegler, P F Whitington et al 'Ethics of Liver Transplantation with Living Donors' (1989) 321 New Engl J Med 620; C E Droelach, P F Whitington, J C Emond et al 'Liver Transplantation in Children from Living Related Donors' (1991) 214 Ann Surg 428.
16 S Kawasaki, M Makuuchi, S Ishizone et al ' Liver Regeneration in Recipients and Donors after Transplantation' (1992) 339 Lancet 580.
17 The Human Organ Transplants Act 1989, s 7 defines an organ as any part of the human body consisting of a structured arrangement of tissues which, *if wholly removed*, cannot be replicated by the body (our emphasis). This would include a liver but not necessarily a segment of liver.
18 L R Shaw, J D Miller, A S Slutsky et al 'Ethics of Lung Transplantation with Live Donors' (1991) 338 Lancet 678.

donor is now settled; consent to a surgical operation which is, in itself, non-therapeutic will be valid so long as the consequent infliction of injury can be shown not to be against the public interest.[19]

The statutory regulation of live donation is to be found in the Human Organ Transplants Act 1989,[20] which creates an offence if a live organ transplant between persons who are not genetically related is undertaken without the agreement of the Unrelated Live Transplant Regulatory Authority (s 2).[1] Section 2(2) defines a genetic relationship. This can be so wide – it includes, for example, uncles and aunts by half blood – as to raise the suspicion that family loyalties are preferred to genetic niceties[2] – even so, it is surprising that interspousal donation of kidneys, and donation by 'in-laws', are still subject to restriction. Genetically related transplantation is not subject to statutory control. Authority for an unrelated donation is, however, subject to very strict rules as to the absence of commercial involvement and as to the consent of the donor and counselling of both parties – additionally, the Authority must be informed of any difficulties in communication between the counsellor and the donor and/or recipient.[3] An interesting variation on the normal conditions for consent (for which see chapter 10) is that the donor *must* understand the processes involved – there is no scope here for 'professional privilege' in providing information; live organ donations involving unrelated incompetents are, therefore, very nearly legally impossible – the position as regards minors is discussed below. These rules, other than those associated with non-payment, are waived in the event that the donation is part of the treatment of the donor[4] – a circumstance which arises most commonly in what is known as the 'domino transplant'. Thus, in the treatment of cystic fibrosis, for example, it is clinically more satisfactory to use a heart/lung preparation obtained from a cadaver rather than a lung alone; this leaves the live recipient's heart available for donation in what will almost certainly be a non-related context. A major proportion of approved unrelated donations are, in fact, of this type.[5]

Rather surprisingly, the proportion of live/cadaver renal transplants is falling in the United Kingdom and, in 1992 was 5.4%, which compares with 24.1% in the United States.[6] Despite the fact that there is no statutory protection for the *related*

---

19 *R v Coney* (1882) 8 QBD 534. The obiter remarks of Denning LJ in *Bravery v Bravery* [1954] 1 WLR 1169 at 1180 have been endorsed: *A-G's Reference (No 6 of 1980)* [1981] QB 715, [1981] 2 All ER 1057.

20 An Order in Council made under the Northern Ireland Act 1984 extends the conditions to Northern Ireland.

1 See also particularly Human Organ Transplants (Establishment of Relationship) Regulations 1989, SI 1989/2107 and Human Organ Transplants (Unrelated Persons) Regulations 1989, SI 1989/2480.

2 Human Fertilisation and Embryology Act 1990, ss 27-29 (see pp 64, 70) do not apply for the purposes of the section. It is, however, fair to say that, consequent upon the major improvements in immunosuppression, not everyone is uncritical of the current restrictions: eg M Evans 'Organ Donation Should not be Restricted to Relatives' (1989) 15 J Med Ethics 17.

3 Human Organ Transplants (Unrelated Persons) Regulations 1989, SI 1989/2480 reg 3(2)(e).

4 SI 1989/2480, n 3 above, reg 3(1)(c)

5 B New, M Solomon, R Dingwall and J McHale *A Question of Give and Take: Supply of Organs for Transplantation* (1994), p 35.

6 New et al, n 5 above. The proportion was over 12% in 1989: G D Chisholm 'Time to End Softly Softly Approach on Harvesting Organs for Transplantation' (1988) 296 BMJ 1419. The very high proportion of live transplants in the Scandinavian countries is remarkable. It should be noted that live donation is the preferred method in some societies. In Japan, for example, where, as discussed at p 352, the concept of brain stem death is unacceptable, some 70% of donations are of live type. Virtually all transplants in India are 'live' but this is probably an administrative rather than cultural consequence (see p 349 below).

donor, there can be no doubt as to the legality of the removal of a kidney from a live adult for the purpose of saving the life of a seriously ill patient – subject, of course, to free and rational consent to the operation (see chapter 10). Living donation by children, however, raises a number of thorny issues.

The minor as a donor

The donation of organs is required surprisingly often from children and, clearly, the advantages of live donation will apply here as well as they will in the adult situation. The legality of such operations on children below the age of 16 has not been decided by British courts and the issue must thus be considered in the light of the general legal principles applied to the medical treatment of minors. As discussed in chapter 10, consent to an operation on a minor below the age of 16 years should normally be obtained from the parents, subject only to the possible common law rights of the child.[7] Valid parental consent, however, refers to treatment for the advantage of the child; troublesome questions arise in relation to procedures which are not calculated to be to his or her benefit – does parental consent in such circumstances constitute an abuse of parental power?

It has been argued that the principle that a minor cannot legally be subjected to any procedure which is not to his advantage is not an absolute one. It is also possible that a court might consider that the donation of an organ is not only in the public interest but is also in the interest of the minor donor, who will, almost certainly, be a sibling of the recipient. Each such case would stand on its own merits but, in such circumstances in general, it might be supposed that it is in the interests of the minor that a member of his family should be saved rather than that his relative should die. This line of argument was successfully pursued in the important American decision in *Strunk v Strunk*.[8] In this case, the donor, who, although adult, had a mental age of six, was chosen to donate a kidney to his brother, who was critically ill. The court came to the conclusion it would be in the donor's best interests for his brother's life to be saved after hearing evidence of the close relationship which existed between the two boys. Consequently, the operation was allowed although the donor was not in a position to give consent.

Many jurisdictions are reluctant to allow the taking of organs from minors. In Canada, for instance, the Ontario Human Tissue Gift Act provides an example of statutory prohibition of donation by minors.[9] A policy of limitation was advised by the Australian Law Reform Commission in their report on transplantation. The Commission took the view that the donation by minors of non-regenerative tissue

---

7   P D G Skegg 'English Law relating to Experimentation on Children' (1977) 2 Lancet 754 took the view that the Family Law Reform Act 1969, s 8 has no application to non-therapeutic procedures and that the rules of non-statutory law do not vary with different categories of persons. See now, Lord Donaldson in *Re W (a minor) (medical treatment)* [1992] 4 All ER 627, (1992) 9 BMLR 22, discussed p 346 below.

8   445 SW 2d 145 (Ky, 1969). The donor's best interests were considered in the English case *Re Y (adult patient) (transplant: bone marrow)* [1997] Fam 110, (1996) 35 BMLR 111 (remarked on at p 254, n 17) – authority was given for a bone marrow transplant involving an incapax donor whose mother would, thus, be able to devote more time to her. A different result was reached in a US case where the court refused permission for a bone marrow transplant involving three-year-old twins; the court ruled that this was not in the best interests of the donor: *Curran v Bosze* 566 NE 2d 1319 (Ill, 1990).

9   B M Dickens *Medico-legal Aspects of Family Law* (1979) p 96.

should not be forbidden without exception but that the circumstances in which it should be allowed should be circumscribed. The enabling conditions were suggested as being: when the donor and recipient are members of the same immediate family; when there is independent medical evidence that the prospective recipient will die unless the transplant is carried out; where the parents of the donor (or those in loco parentis) agree to the donation; where the donor has sufficient mental capacity and agrees to the donation; and, finally, when an ad hoc committee consisting of a judge and two other persons comes to the conclusion that the donation is desirable and in the interests of the donor. In the event, none of the individual states accepted this proposal and, indeed, applied some of those qualifications to the donation of *regenerative* tissue; it is not lawful in Australia to remove non-regenerative material from the body of a living child for the purpose of transplantation.[10] A blanket ban on the use of minors as organ donors has been advocated by the World Health Organisation.[11]

While the complete exclusion of minor donors would seem to many to be too extreme, there are powerful reasons why some limits should be placed on the use of children as donors of non-regenerative tissue and very great caution should be exercised in the case of young children in whom there is unlikely to be any significant understanding of what the donation entails. Even if a minor shows a reasonable degree of understanding of the donation and of the risks involved, a sharp distinction is to be made between instances when the recipient is a member of the immediate family and when he is not. It might be regarded as ethically acceptable for a minor to be used as a donor in the former case; generosity towards a brother or sister is to be encouraged and may even be regarded as a social duty.[12] The situation is less clear with relatives other than siblings. Should one apply the same rule to a situation where the prospective recipient is a cousin in the first degree? It is possible that the minor donor may be as fond of such a cousin as he is of a brother or sister and the illness of the cousin may be as distressing to him as would be the illness of a sibling. Nevertheless, a policy of limiting approved donation by minors to the immediate family has the attraction of certainty and, in practice, the clinical limitations must be taken into account – donation to an adoptive brother, for example, would be ethically suspect simply because, other than by chance, genetic incompatibility might compromise the success of the operation.

The law in France[13] illustrates an acceptable compromise statutory position. There, a living minor may only donate to his brother or sister; consent must be given by the donor's legal representative; and the procedure must be authorised by a committee composed of at least three experts two of whom must be doctors, one of whom must have practised for 20 years. If the minor can be consulted, refusal on his part must be respected in all cases. The caution shown by countries subject to both

10 See eg Human Tissue and Transplant Act 1982, ss 12, 13 (Western Australia). The Human Tissue Act 1983, s 10 (NSW) forbids it by omission.

11 World Health Organisation *Guiding Principles on Human Organ Transplantation* (1994) principle 4, discussed by M N Morelli 'Organ Trafficking: Legislative Proposals to Protect Minors' (1995) 10 Am U J Int Law Pol 917.

12 L F Ross 'Moral Grounding for the Participation of Children as Organ Donors' (1993) 21 J Law Med & Ethics 251 introduces the interesting concept of the family as an autonomous unit which can aspire to a collective purpose. Intrafamilial donation by a child advances the family's interests, which is a means of promoting the child's own interests.

13 Law of 22 December 1976.

common and civil law jurisdictions is noteworthy and, while statute is either ambivalent or silent on the matter in the United Kingdom, some clarification of the current legal position here has come recently from the Court of Appeal.

The case of *Re W*[14] dealt with consent to treatment by a 16-year-old and was concerned, in the main, with the application of the Family Law Reform Act 1969, s 8(1).[15] The problem of organ transplantation was not in issue but was touched upon by the Master of the Rolls; his views must, we feel, be regarded as obiter but are, nevertheless, persuasive. Lord Donaldson first disposed of the statute on the grounds that the section related to treatment and diagnosis; it could not, therefore, extend to the donation of organs as this did not satisfy either condition in respect of the donor. He went on:

> Organ donations are quite different and, as a matter of law, doctors would have to secure the consent of someone with the right to consent on behalf of a donor under the age of 18 or, if they relied on the consent of the minor himself or herself, be satisfied that the minor was '*Gillick* competent' in the context of so serious a procedure which would not benefit the minor.[16]

As to the latter, he added, somewhat equivocally: 'This would be a highly improbable conclusion.' The whole passage is, in fact, a trifle confusing as, logically, '*Gillick*-competence' applies only to the under 16 -year-old, whereas s 8(1) of the Act relates to the 16–18-year-old. However, Lord Donaldson continued:

> It is inconceivable that [the doctor] should proceed in reliance solely upon the consent of an under-age patient, however '*Gillick*-competent', in the absence of supporting parental consent and equally inconceivable that he should proceed in the absence of the patient's consent. In any event he will need to seek the opinions of other doctors and may be well advised to apply to the court for guidance . . .[17]

which seems clear enough until we look at the summary provided by the Master of the Rolls:

> A minor of any age who is *Gillick*-competent in the context of a particular treatment has a right to consent to that treatment which again cannot be overridden by those with parental responsibility, but can be overridden by the court. Unlike the statutory right this common law right extends to the donation of blood or organs.[18]

We can only suggest that, however this is interpreted, it would be a brave surgeon who ignored Lord Donaldson's advice-in-chief. The minor's right to refuse is, however, clearly preserved.

It appears, in fact, that transplant surgeons in general have pre-empted the Master of the Rolls. Our inquiries indicate that no currently practising British transplant

14 *Re W (a minor) (medical treatment)* [1992] 4 All ER 627, (1992) 9 BMLR 22.
15 Already discussed in greater detail at p 259 above.
16 [1992] 4 All ER 627 at 635, (1992) 9 BMLR 22 at 31.
17 [1992] 4 All ER 627 at 635, (1992) 9 BMLR 22 at 31.
18 [1992] 4 All ER 627 at 639, (1992) 9 BMLR 22 at 35.

surgeon would accept a live child as an organ donor; only one such instance, involving an identical twin aged 17 years, has arisen in the United Kingdom in the last 15 years. Only five living minor donors have been used in the Eurotransplant catchment area and none has been recorded in France, despite the enabling legislation; similarly, none is recorded by Scadiatransplant.[19] Discussion of the matter thus lies at the academic rather than the practical level.

Nothing, however, is static in modern medicine. There have been reports that couples are now having children for the express purpose of providing genetically compatible sibling donors of, at present, regenerative tissue only.[20] Whatever one feels about such a practice, the pragmatic answer is that it cannot be prevented. Medico-legally, any such child, when born, would be protected by the rules governing donation by living minors. But, speaking ethically, it cannot be denied that the process does little credit to the doctrine of free consent – there is a strong impression that human life is being used as a means to an end.

Patients in the permanent vegetative state
In ordinary circumstances, we would not feel it necessary to distinguish consideration of any single form of cerebral incompetence from our attitudes to the unconscious patient in general. However, such is the current pressure to accept cognitive death as equivalent to somatic death[1] that we feel a word on the permanent vegetative state is needed. It is, perhaps, necessary only to recapitulate our view that, tragic as their state may be, persons in the persistent vegetative state are existing by means of their own cardiovascular system and are not dead – and none of the standard defences of lawful killing could be applied to them. There is, of course, no reason why permanently vegetative patients should not be used as organ donors within the existing framework of the law when they die – although the manner of their dying may cast doubt on the quality of the organs thus made available;[2] but there can be no question of killing them – or limiting their existence – for the express purpose.[3] Predictably, this view is shared by the British Medical Association.[4] Times, however, change and a recent paper authorised by an International Forum for Transplant Ethics infers that to exempt PVS patients from the normal legal prohibitions against 'killing' would be humanitarian in that it would obviate the futile use of resources and would release organs that were suitable for transplantation.[5] We have to admit to strong doubts as to such a policy. To confuse the concept of brain stem death and to associate the permanent vegetative state with transplantation could only fan any embers of public distrust for 'premature

19 J K Mason 'Legal Aspects of Organ Transplantation' in C Dyer (ed) *Doctors, Patients and the Law* (1992).
20 G McBride 'Keeping Bone Marrow Donation in the Family' (1990) 300 BMJ 1224. The case is discussed by J Rachels 'When Philosophers Shoot from the Hip' (1991) 5 Bioethics 67.
.1 See p 329 above.
2 See p 406 below for further discussion.
3 Discussed by J Downie 'The Biology of the Persistent Vegetative State: Legal. Ethical, and Philosophical Implications for Transplantation' (1990) 22 Transplant Proc 995.
4 BMA 'Guidelines Relating to the Persistent Vegetative State' reproduced in (1993) 3 Bull Med Ethics, 8, para 9.
5 R Hoffenberg, M Lock, N Tilney et al 'Should Organs from Patients in Permanent Vegetative State Be Used for Transplantation?' (1997) 350 Lancet 1320.

grave robbing' which still remain. Burke and Hare attracted much sympathy in their role of exhumers; it was when they became pre-emptive that they fell from grace!

The donor as vendor

The most urgent issue in the context of living donation is now that of the commercialisation of transplant surgery. This is, essentially, a matter of consent and, on this score, it is to be distinguished from payment for cadaver organs – the latter being better considered as an aspect of the availability of organs.

Inevitably, a British view on donation for recompense must be coloured by one's experience of a national health service. Within that framework, it is difficult to see the sale of organs as other than a way for the rich to obtain priority essential care, the inequity being compounded by the corollary that the poor, who would form the pool of such donors, would be positively disadvantaged in the role of supplier. But it is only fair to remark that those working in a health care system that is governed by a market economy could see the situation as one in which an anxious buyer meets a willing seller. It is not easy to occupy an objective middle ground.

The problem may have existed in England before 1989 but it was then that it presented acutely. It transpired that impoverished Turkish donors were being recruited and paid to donate their kidneys to genetically and ethnically unrelated recipients; there were wide-ranging repercussions at both legislative and professional levels and these, of themselves, provoke further ethical debate.

The response of the legislature was to rush through the Human Organ Transplants Act 1989, which prohibits the exchange of money, other than legitimate expenses, for the purpose of organ donation by the living (s 1(1)); it is also an offence to advertise for the purpose (s 1(2)). Clearly, the legislative intention is to distinguish altruism from commercialism and to approve the former while condemning the latter. The distinction is dictated by the consent doctrine in that it is assumed that a free, uncoerced consent is impossible in the face of financial inducement. To which one might add the widely held moral objection to *any* commercialisation of the human body.[6]

The great majority would accept these restrictions on the individual's power over his or her own body – and yet: cannot this be seen as unacceptable paternalism? Is it impossible that a commercial donor could make his decision in a reasoned manner and on his own altruistic grounds?[7] And who, in quest of unfettered consent, is to distinguish between external financial pressure and moral pressure exerted within the family? It is at least arguable that, in closing the door on the use of an inessential part of one's body for gain, Parliament is striking at the individual publican's autonomy in favour of the corporate pharisee's inner virtue.[8]

---

6 We are unconvinced by the philosophical argument that the wrong lies in the invasion of bodily integrity – a wrong which is offset by the good of altruism but which finds no such exculpation in the commercial situation: S Wilkinson and E Garrard 'Bodily Integrity and the Sale of Human Organs' (1996) 22 J Med Ethics 334. The money that accrues can be put to good use (see p 356 below).
7 It is reported that one of the donors intended to devote the proceeds to the medical treatment of his daughter. See a sympathetic contribution by J Harvey 'Paying Organ Donors' (1990) 16 J Med Ethics 117.
8 For expression of such doubts, see Evans, p 343, n 2 above.

The professional reaction to the 'Turkish affair' was no less positive. The name of one of the doctors concerned was erased from the Medical Register while the professional freedom of two others was severely curtailed.[9] The GMC has now issued definitive guidelines, which include:

> In no circumstances may doctors participate in or encourage in any way the trade in human organs from live donors. They must not advertise for donors nor make financial or medical arrangements for people who wish to sell or buy organs . . . Doctors must also satisfy themselves that consent to a donation has been given without undue influence of any kind, including the offer of financial or material benefit.[10]

It has been said that to allow payment would be to open up a traffic in organs. Yet it is difficult to see why this could not be obviated by legalising paid donations only by way of the Unrelated Live Transplant Regulatory Authority. There is some empirical evidence that public opposition to payment is not as strong as might be supposed – between 40% and 50% may find the practice permissible[11] and it has been noted that: 'As long as there are adequate safeguards, any ethical or legal fastidiousness demanding that donation be only gratuitous could condemn the sick.'[12] In any event, a traffic in organs cannot now be confined within one jurisdiction. It is reported[13] that a network for the commercial provision of organs is already in existence; clearly any restrictions on the practice must be international if they are to be effective and the European Parliament has now asked the Council of Ministers to ban the sale of organs throughout the European Community.[14] A British minister has said that: 'the concept of kidneys for sale is entirely unacceptable in a civilised society'[15] and many would undoubtedly agree – but, at the same time, it is difficult to identify the precise moral basis for so doing. As the International Forum has said:

> [F]eelings of outrage and disgust that led to an outright ban on kidney sales . . . typically have a force that seems to their possessors to need no further justification. Nevertheless, if we are to deny treatment to the suffering and dying we need better reasons than our own feelings of disgust.[16]

Moreover, the fact that this antipathy is a specifically Western view merits repetition. It is at least arguable that, in a country such as India, where there is no cadaver transplant programme and where long-term dialysis is impracticable, paid organ donation may be not only ethical but also desirable. As has been said, the ethical

9 C Dyer 'GMC's Decision on "Kidneys for Sale"' (1990) 300 BMJ 961.
10 GMC 'Guidance for Doctors on Transplantation of Organs from Live Donors' (1992) News Review, December, Supplement.
11 A Guttmann and R D Guttmann 'Attitudes of Health Care Professionals and the Public towards the Sale of Kidneys for Transplantation' (1993) 19 J Med Ethics 148.
12 I Davies 'Live Donation of Human Body Parts: A Case for Negotiability?' (1991) 59 Med-Leg J 100.
13 A Dorozynki 'European Kidney Market' (1989) 299 BMJ 1182; H D C R Abbing 'Transplantation of Organs: A European Perspective' (1993) 21 J Law Med Ethics 54.
14 A Dorozynski 'Europe Condemns Sale of Organs' (1993) 307 BMJ 756.
15 See J Warden 'Kidneys Not for Sale' (1989) 298 BMJ 1670.
16 J Radcliffe-Richards, A S Daar, R D Guttmann et al 'The Case for Allowing Kidney Sales' (1998) 351 Lancet 1950.

distinction between allowing one poor and needy citizen to run the risk of brain damage in the boxing ring and denying another the right to sell a kidney may prove hard to define.[17]

Cadaver donations

The deceased has very limited rights as to the disposal of his body in common law and the wishes of the executors would normally be supported rather than those of the dead person in the event of conflict. Statute law is, however, replacing common law and the use of cadaver organs and tissues is now regulated in Great Britain by the Human Tissue Act 1961. This provides, in s 1(1), that removal of an organ is authorised if there has been a specific request to this effect by the deceased; the removal may be for therapeutic, educational or research purposes. In the absence of such a request, s 1(2) provides for the authorisation of organ removal if the person 'lawfully in possession of the body' has, after making such 'reasonable enquiry as may be practicable', no reason to believe that the deceased had expressed any objection to organ removal or that the surviving spouse or 'any surviving relative' of the deceased objects to the body being so dealt with.

The somewhat loose wording of the Act has caused occasional difficulty in its implementation. This was particularly so as to the definition of the person in lawful possession. For some time it was considered that the term implied one with a right to possession, that is, the executors. The alternative view is that it refers to the person who has physical possession of the body who is, in practical terms, the hospital administrative officer. This latter interpretation is supported by the wording of other sections of the Act and is now widely accepted by the administration, the legal profession and the BMA but the point has not been tested in the courts. The more recent legislation which has been passed throughout Australia puts the question beyond doubt by vesting the powers in a designated officer within the hospital. Clarity on the point is important in that, were the executors to be in lawful possession, they could overrule any specific request made by the deceased. Even allowing for the fact that the relatives have no locus standi to object to the removal of organs under s 1(1), which is clearly paramount, the doctor is in a difficult position in the event of their objections being voiced. On the one hand, he has legal justification to proceed and he may, rightly, be thinking of the potential recipients. On the other, it would be extremely hard to justify in ethical terms a decision to add further suffering to the bereaved. It is fortunate that such conflicts are very rare in practice but we return to the point when considering the shortfall in organs available for treatment. It should be noted, in passing, that the coroner or procurator fiscal may veto any authorisation if the death comes within their jurisdictions (s 1(5) and (9)).

The concept of 'such reasonable enquiry as may be practicable' is also vague, reasonableness being a matter of highly subjective judgment. The partial solution is to consider what is *un*reasonable – and it would clearly be unreasonable to prolong one's enquiries until the intended donor organ was non-viable. Such a pragmatic approach is, however, less tenable in the context of the beating heart donor, which is

17 J Bignall 'Kidneys: Buy or Die' (1993) 342 Lancet 45.

discussed below. Finally, the wording 'any surviving relative' is confusingly open-ended and must again be interpreted in a practical sense – the phrase must be taken to mean 'any relative who can reasonably be contacted within the limited time available', which effectively limits one to the immediate next of kin. This difficulty has also been noted in Australia, where 'next of kin' are specified in order of 'seniority'; responsibility for consent is then vested in the most senior next of kin who can be contacted.[18]

The Human Tissue Act 1961 is unpopular on theoretical and practical grounds within both the legal and medical professions and it is, therefore, interesting to note that at least one academic commentator has questioned whether there is any offence committed in its non-observance;[19] the same authority suggests that an apparently unauthorised action to save the life of a recipient might be justified on the basis of necessity. From the civil aspect, there seems no reason in principle why an action in tort for nervous shock should not be available to relatives who believe that the conditions of reasonable inquiry have not been met; the majority opinion is that, while such actions have succeeded in the United States, they would be unlikely to do so in the United Kingdom.[20]

Beating heart donors

It is apparent that the major technical criticisms levelled at the Human Tissue Act 1961 relate to the prolongation of the warm anoxic time entailed in strict adherence to its terms. But such objections are valid only when death is measured by the irrevocable failure of the cardiovascular system. In practice, the overwhelming proportion of cadaver-donated material will come from patients who have been maintained on ventilator support and in whom it will be appropriate to reach a diagnosis of death by means of brain stem criteria. There is no logical reason why ventilation should not be continued after death and the heart beat be maintained during an operation for organ donation. The ideal situation of the living donor is thus achieved in a cadaver.

The technical advantages of a beating heart donation are not in dispute and the process is essential to the success of some transplantations.[1] Why, then, is there such antipathy to the procedure? Much must stem from an inherent revulsion at performing what is a lethal operation amid the conditions pertaining to a living patient, but this is irrational once the concept of brain stem death has been accepted – any emotional

18 Eg Human Tissue Act 1983, s 4 (NSW).
19 P D G Skegg 'Liability for the Unauthorized Removal of Cadaveric Transplant Material' (1974) 14 Med Sci & L 53.
20 I M Kennedy 'Further Thoughts on Liability for Non-observance of the Provisions of the Human Tissue Act 1961' (1976) 16 Med Sci & L 49. While we appreciate the pitfalls on the way, we feel that the necessary conditions of proximity would be satisfied if a close relative was confronted with what he or she regarded as a mutilated corpse.
 1 But the use of non-heart beating donors may be dictated by the shortage of organs, see p 341, n 13 above and the discussion which follows. The question may then arise as to whether the use of a 'second-best' organ is better than no transplant. The current attitude of transplant surgeons would be essential to the resolution of any dispute. See the *Bolam* principle discussed in chapter 9. In fact, any differences in outcome between non-heart beating and beating heart donations appear to be of a subtle nature only: R M H Wijnen, M H Booster, B M Stubenitsky et al 'Outcome of Transplantation of Non-heart-beating Donor Kidneys' (1995) 345 Lancet 1067.

bias should be directed towards the recipients. Perhaps the major problem lies in the fact that there are still those who, in all good conscience, cannot accept the technical criteria advocated for the diagnosis of brain stem death – and these include some eminent doctors;[2] some surgeons, while accepting a ventilated donor, will not operate until the patient is disconnected from the machine and shows a flat electrocardiogram. While fully accepting that every doctor is entitled to his own clinical judgment, we do suggest that the subject would be, so to speak, defused were it to be made compulsory for a death certificate to be issued, and the notification handed to the next of kin, before any donation could be effected. This would serve, first, to ease matters for the professionals involved – it is not entirely satisfactory for the surgeon undertaking a beating heart donation to have to 'satisfy himself by personal examination of the body that life is extinct' (Human Tissue Act 1961, s 1(4)) from a mere perusal of the hospital notes; secondly, we feel the process would set the minds of the relatives at rest. An alternative is to dissociate the problems of the definition of death from those of transplantation and to legislate purely for the latter contingency. Thus, the Human Tissue and Transplant Act 1982, s 24(2) of Western Australia makes no mention of death but ordains that two medical practitioners with specific qualifications must certify that irreversible cessation of all functions of the brain has occurred before organs can be removed from the body of a person whose respiration and circulation are being maintained artificially.

In any event, relatives must be confused and distraught unless given sympathetic counselling and, in practice, this should always be possible in modern circumstances when, as a result of ventilator support, relatives will have been aware of the impending death for some time and will, no doubt, have been attending at the hospital – transplant co-ordinators are now widely established and can assist in the task to great advantage. Every assistance should be given. Thus, while we accept the view that an electroencephalogram is not necessary to establish the fact of death, we also believe that the relatives should have the right to such evidence should they ask for it. It is only by such adaptations of the principle of informed consent that beating heart donation will become fully accepted and that, as a consequence, the best therapy will be available to those in dire need.

As indicated above, however, in some countries, notably Japan,[3] there is an inherent antipathy to the concept of brain death which is shared to a major extent by the medical profession. A Japanese doctor has, in fact, been charged with murder for performing a cardiac transplant and, although the case was dropped, it did nothing to encourage the evolution of a programme.[4] It is in such circumstances that non-heart beating donation, aided by developments in hypothermic preservation, may well be regarded as the procedure of choice.

2 N Hodgkinson 'When Does a Beating Heart Die?' (1986) The Sunday Times, 7 December, p 1.
3 J Nudeshima 'Obstacles to Brain Death and Organ Transplantation in Japan' (1991) 338 Lancet 1063. By contrast, it is to be noted that Muslim law now allows donation and receipt of organs using a brain stem death approach: V Choo 'UK Shariah Council Approves Organ Transplants' (1995) 346 Lancet 303.
4 M Yamauchi 'Transplantation in Japan' (1990) 301 BMJ 507.

The availability of suitable organs

It has been calculated that there are enough suitable cadaver kidneys available in America to satisfy the demand but that the requirements are still not met because only one in eight potentially useful organs are obtained in practice.[5] An unsatisfactory situation also persists in the United Kingdom. Over 4,460 patients were awaiting kidney transplants in 1997;[6] by the same year, the number of cadaver transplants performed had fallen from a high of 1,645 in 1995 to a decade-low figure of 1,535. It has been reported that nearly half the potential donors fail to become actual donors[7] and it is this deficit which needs to be corrected. The problem has been addressed by a Government Working Party[8] and new initiatives are promised but, despite the urgency of the situation, no satisfactory solution has emerged as yet. In the meantime, the International Forum have stated: '[I]t is morally unjustified to perpetuate a system that falls short of increasing the availability of organs to people who might benefit from transplantation.'[9]

There are essentially two avenues to explore: to reform the law or to change professional and public attitudes. As to the former, it is clear that a main source of cadaver organs under the Human Tissue Act 1961 results from a system of 'contracting in' to the transplant service, something which dictates a conscious effort that many healthy persons – and particularly young persons – find difficult to make. It is widely suggested that the Act could profitably be altered to hold a 'contracting out' position – that is, one in which consent to donation is presumed unless it is specifically withheld. Such a system operates in several European countries, although with varying rigidity. Thus, a right of veto is still vested in the next of kin in Italy and Spain, while the sensitivities of the relatives are deeply respected in Belgium – very few transplant centres would apply the law in that country in the face of their opposition. The views of the next of kin are held at a minimum in Austria where, interestingly, the cadaver kidney donor rate is the highest among the leading 'transplant countries'.[10] Thus, a good case for 'presumed consent' can be made out – and contracting out on the Belgian model is clearly the preferred choice of the International Forum;[11] nevertheless, it carries with it a hint of coercion and it is hard to foresee a British government making such a major policy change, particularly in the light of the statement – admittedly by a different administration:

> We must accept that nobody has a right to anybody else's organs. If something untoward happens, our organs may be of value to someone else but that should be the result of an altruistic decision about how we want our bodies to be used when we die. It should not be

5 For an overview of US attitudes, see H S Schwartz 'Bioethical and Legal Considerations in Increasing the Supply of Transplantable Organs: From UAGA to "Baby Fae"' (1985) 10 Amer J Law Med 397.
6 (1998) 137 Bull Med Ethics 7. The cost of hospital dialysis averages £25,000 per year and of home dialysis £15,000; following an initial operative cost of between £10,000 and £15,000, the follow-up treatment of the transplant recipient costs around £3,000 per year.
7 Wallwork, p 341, n 12 above.
8 R Hoffenberg (chairman) *Report of the Working Party on the Supply of Donor Organs for Transplantation* (1987).
9 I Kennedy, R A Sells, A S Daar et al 'The Case for "Presumed Consent" in Organ Donation' (1998) 351 Lancet 1650.
10 New et al, p 343, n 5 above, fig 11.
11 See p 347, n 5 above.

as a result of a right of the recipient. . . . It is the responsibility of the living whose organs may be of use to someone else; it is not anyone else's job to claim the organs.[12]

Whether objections from the next of kin would remain at the same level given a change of policy is uncertain. Kennedy et al[13] point out that there is a difference for the relatives between making a decision and simply confirming the fact that the deceased had not registered an objection, but many doctors would still find the resulting pressure on relatives to be distasteful. At the same time, this fear may be being exaggerated to the detriment of the programme. It is quite clear that signing the donor card is a written expression in life of a request that one's body should be used for therapeutic purposes,[14] yet the great majority of transplant surgeons will be reluctant to press the matter if the relatives express an objection. While this may be very good and sympathetic medicine, it is, paradoxically, doubtful medical ethics – effectively, the last autonomous wish of the individual is being thwarted simply because he or she is in no position to object. Whether or not a firmer attitude would result in significantly more donations is uncertain, but it is scarcely fair to blame the law for any shortcomings if the law is being disregarded; it has been said, in a slightly different context, that the kidney donor card is not dead but may require intensive care to restore it to more robust health.[15]

Such professional antipathy to or apathy in seeking the co-operation of relatives may be an important factor; this has led to a movement in favour of 'required request' for organ donation – a format which imposes a legal obligation on doctors to seek permission from the relatives for the removal of tissues from suitable dead persons. This is now the subject of federal law in the United States;[16] a Transplant Notification Bill having the same objectives was introduced in the House of Commons in 1988 but made no progress. There is, in fact, considerable debate in the United Kingdom as to the efficacy of this type of legislation.[17] Moreover, 'required request' undoubtedly compromises the clinical autonomy of the medical staff concerned. It has to be appreciated that, in addition to the difficulties associated with grieving relatives, maintaining a brain dead beating heart donor is effort-intensive, particularly as regards multi-organ donation, and facilities may simply not be available in the acute care unit.[18] Even so, it is significant that failure to ask about donation still constitutes the second most important reason for the loss of useable organs.[19]

12 Official Reports, HC, 28 March 1991, vol 188, col 1142 per Stephen Dorrell.
13 See p 353, n 9 above. Much the same point is made by S Eaton 'The Subtle Politics of Organ Donation: A Proposal' (1998) 24 J Med Ethics 166.
14 This was the, admittedly extra-judicial, view of Lord Edmund Davies more than a quarter of a century ago: 'A Legal Look at Transplants' (1969) 62 Proc Roy Soc Med 633.
15 R M R Taylor 'Opting In or Out of Organ Donation' (1992) 305 BMJ 1380.
16 US Public Law 99-509 9318.
17 G D Chisholm p 343, n 6 above regards it as 'positive'; R M R Taylor and J H Salaman 'The Obligation to Ask for Organs' (1988) 1 Lancet 985 see it as the only answer to a dialysis 'crisis'; A Bodenham, J C Berridge and G R Park 'Brain Stem Death and Organ Donation' (1989) 299 BMJ 1009 are doubtful.
18 But some writers would see these merely as difficulties to be overcome. For particularly trenchant support of required request, see Taylor and Salaman, n 17 above.
19 S M Gore, D J Cable and A J Holland 'Organ Donation from Intensive Care Units in England and Wales: Two Year Confidential Audit of Deaths in Intensive Care' (1992) 304 BMJ 349.

A recent addition to the melting pot of professional attitudes and ethical values has been the introduction of 'elective ventilation' as a means of widening the supply of organs. Essentially, the concept involves extending the source of donors from accident and emergency departments so as to include the medical wards. Deeply comatose patients dying from strokes or other cerebral medical conditions are transferred to the intensive care unit and are there supported until brain stem death supervenes and organ retrieval can be arranged. The procedure was pioneered in Exeter,[20] where the original research involved between three and 41 hours' intensive care for eight donors who would, otherwise, have been missed. A rigid protocol was drawn up but, while appreciating that great care had been put into the drafting of the protocol – and accepting the caution expressed by the authors – we believe that the procedure does raise a number of legal and ethical difficulties.[1] As to the former, we wonder if the authority vested in the hospital and the surviving relatives by the Human Tissue Act 1961, s 1(2) can be assumed before a person is dead. That is, perhaps, a minor point and it could be argued that no *authority* is being claimed by consenting to removal to the intensive care unit. Ethically, however – and despite the precondition of deep coma – we wonder if it is right to alter radically the mode of death, and to prolong the dying process, purely for the benefit of others.[2] Whether intensive care beds should be utilised in this way is, in our view, a purely practical matter to be resolved by the doctors in charge. In the event, it has been widely agreed that the procedure is unlawful given the current regulations[3] and it has, for the time being, been discontinued. Despite the obvious advantages to the organ harvest, we believe this to be correct – one cannot exorcise a feeling that death is being pre-empted and it is certain that this form of organ husbandry must be very carefully controlled if a backlash of public reaction is to be avoided.[4]

This is of immense overall importance as it is probable that British policy in the quest for more donated organs will depend upon public education for the foreseeable future. One still has to wonder at the basic reasons underlying the refusal of some 30%

20 T G Feest, H N Riad, C H Collins et al 'Protocol for Increasing Organ Donation after Cerebrovascular Deaths in a District General Hospital' (1990) 335 Lancet 1133. The protocol was also used elsewhere: M A M Salih, I Harvey, S Frankel et al 'Potential Availability of Cadaver Organs for Transplantation' (1991) 302 BMJ 1053. These authors suggested that, realistically, including potential medical donors aged 50-69 would have provided a harvest of 36 kidneys per million population per year, which is coming somewhere near the need for 48 kidneys per million population per year.

1 For similar misgivings, see J V McHale 'Elective Ventilation – Pragmatic Solution or Ethical Minefield?' (1995) 11 Prof Neg 23; S A M McLean 'Transplantation and the "Nearly Dead": The Case of Elective Ventilation' in S A M McLean (ed) *Contemporary Issues in Law, Medicine and Ethics* (1996).

2 This is denied on the grounds that it is a corpse that is being ventilated: A Nicholls and H Riad 'Organ Donation' (1993) 306 BMJ 517. But the patients are not dead when the ventilation is instituted. The Exeter group have put up a strong defence of their procedure, only to be contradicted: see H Riad and A Nicholls 'Elective Ventilation of Potential Organ Donors' (1995) 310 BMJ 714 and associated debate.

3 S Ramsay 'UK Organ-retrieval Scheme Deemed Illegal' (1994) 344 Lancet 1081. For support for changing the law to accommodate elective ventilation, see A B Shaw 'Non-therapeutic (Elective) Ventilation of Potential Organ Donors: The Ethical Basis for Changing the Law' (1996) 22 J Med Ethics 72.

4 G Routh 'Elective Ventilation for Organ Donation – The Case Against' (1992) 8 Care Crit Ill 60. For the opposite view, see C H Collins 'Elective Ventilation for Organ Donation – The Case in Favour' (1992) 8 Care Crit Ill 57. The BMA took a very cautious stance: Annual Report 1992.

of relatives to consent to donation[5] – the same public will flock to donate their blood at the sight of a poster advertising an appropriate time and place. Ignorance may be one factor, antipathy on the part of the entertainment media another and, undoubtedly, the suggestion of ambivalence, as regards both techniques and ethics, among the medical profession plays its part. Attitudes may, however, be changing as the results of the more exotic transplant operations improve.[6] We now believe that the concept of the multiple organ donor should be maximised. It is not easy to enthuse about a treatment whereby one family's joy at the availability of a donor must be balanced against another's tragedy; the public's imagination might well be fired were it generally appreciated that one regrettable death could be compensated by the salvage of four or more lives. This process will undoubtedly be reinforced as increasingly experienced transplant co-ordinators are established as major points of contact with the public.

Payment for tissues

Any discussion on the availability of organs must take into account the possibility of their provision on a commercial basis. We have discussed the ethics of donation for reward by the living and have concluded that this is essentially a matter of valid consent by the donor. But the selling of cadaver organs is, at root, directed to the enticement of the next of kin. Put this way, the proposition can be seen as appealing to the baser human instincts and as something with which the medical profession should have no truck – typically put:

> A shift into any form of commercialism or its currently more fashionable cousin 'rewarded gifting' holds the potential of threatening the entire spiritual structure upon which organ transplantation is based at present.[7]

The possibility is, however, by no means excluded and seems to be gaining momentum in the United States. Manoeuvres to avoid ethical restrictions such as wholesale to kidney banks rather than to individuals have been mooted; standardised cash awards in various forms – such as payment of donors' funeral expenses – have been suggested; and an 'insurance policy' in the form of preferred status is, perhaps surprisingly, the top-ranked option in the United States, where over half those responding to a survey approved the introduction of incentives to improve the supply of organs.[8] Commenting on this, Peters, who supports payment of a fixed death benefit to donors through an organ procurement organisation, suggests that those in the transplant field have wrongly adhered to certain moral values of their own – values which are not necessarily accepted by those at the giving and receiving end of the

---

5   Gore et al, p 354, n 19 above.
6   Eg N Brousse and O Goulet 'Small Bowel Transplantation' (1996) 312 BMJ 261.
7   F T Rapaport 'Progress in Organ Procurement: The Non Heart-beating Cadaver Donor and Other Issues in Transplantation' (1991) 23 Transplant Proc 2699.
8   D S Kittur, M M Hogan, V K Thukral et al 'Incentives for Organ Donation?' (1991) 338 Lancet 1441. The 'carrot' of preferred treatment for registered donors is discussed and approved by R Jarvis 'Join the Club: A Modest Proposal to Increase Availability of Donor Organs' (1995) 21 J Med Ethics 199, but is rejected in the same issue by R Gillon 'On Giving Preference to Prior Volunteers when Allocating Organs for Transplantation' (1995) 21 J Med Ethics 195.

process;[9] Sells also points out that antagonism to incentive represents an essentially Western view of ethics as we think they ought to be practised:

> Western societies have prescribed for the rest of the globe without giving much thought, evidently, to the differing ethical and medical circumstances in which our less-affluent colleagues have to operate.[10]

This is not to say that we approve of a traffic in human organs – in fact, we find payment for the organs of the dead far less easy to justify than payment to the living donor. Given, however, that the process was strictly controlled – say, through a restructured Unrelated Live Transplant Regulatory Authority – and supposing that it *succeeded* in providing life-saving treatment for those dying on the waiting list, reward for donation of cadaver organs appears in a less scandalous light than it did at first sight. The following observation from America is, perhaps, indicative of the trend in that country:

> It is only a matter of time before this country will be forced to decide on *the type of commercial system* which should be adopted in order to meet the demand of transplantable human organs. (emphasis added)[11]

The fetus or neonate as a transplant donor

Transplantation therapy in the neonatal period is now a standard part of paediatric surgery. Suitable organs, such as the liver, may become available from other newborn infants suffering from fatal conditions; such opportunities are rare but no new issues are then involved because the infant is subject to the conditions of the Human Tissue Act 1961 in just the same way as is the adult or the minor. This, however, is not always so in the case of the fetus who may be involved as an organ donor at maturity or as a cell donor at an early stage of development.

In the former circumstance, the fetal organs must be both mature and viable if they are to be used to good purpose. One potential source of mature organs is the stillbirth which, by definition, must be of more than 24 weeks' gestation.[12] Equally by definition, however, the stillbirth must neither have breathed nor shown any other sign of life once separated from its mother. It follows that its organs must have been

---

9 T G Peters 'Life or Death: The Issue of Payment for Cadaveric Organ Donation' (1991) 265 J Amer Med Ass 1302. For criticism of his arguments, see E D Pellegrino 'Families' Self-interest and the Cadaver's Organs: What Price Consent?' (1991) 265 J Amer Med Ass 1305. Opposition also comes from R W Evans 'Incentives for Organ Donation' (1992) 339 Lancet 185; 'Organ Procurement Expenditures and the Role of Financial Incentives' (1993) 269 J Amer Med Ass 3113. For support from an unlikely source of payment for cadaveric organs, see G P Smith 'Market and Non-market Mechanisms for Procuring Human and Cadaveric Organs: When the Price is Right' (1993) 1 Med Law Internat 17.

10 R A Sells 'Commerce in Human Organs: A Global Review' (1990) 19 Dialysis Transplant 10.

11 G J Banks 'Legal and Ethical Safeguards: Protection of Society's Most Vulnerable Participants in a Commercialized Organ Transplantation System' (1995) 21 Am J Law Med 45.

12 Still-Birth (Definition) Act 1992.

anoxic for an uncertain, but probably significant time; the chances of their being viable in the sense of being transplantable are, therefore, very slight and, save in the exceptional circumstances hypothesised below, the stillbirth can be ignored as a possible source of *organs*. The exception lies in the stillbirth who was known to be alive shortly before a catastrophe during birth; in our view, the practicalities of dealing with a distraught mother, coupled with the absence of a ready recipient, preclude even these stillbirths as donors. It follows that the 'fetal' donor must be alive when born and we are, in fact, considering the neonate as a donor. None the less, it is convenient to retain the term 'fetal donor' in order to distinguish him or her from the neonate that has been under treatment for a significant time.

The 'live fetal' donor might then derive from a therapeutic abortion – a possibility which is rendered more real by the 1990 amendments to the Abortion Act 1967 which, inter alia, permit an abortion on the grounds of fetal abnormality without limit of gestational age (s 1(1)(a)) and absolve the doctor from liability under the Infant Life (Preservation) Act 1929 when terminating a pregnancy within the provisions of the 1967 Act (s 5(1)). The use of a living abortus as a transplant donor would be constrained by the terms of the Polkinghorne Report and is best regarded as an aspect of fetal research.[13] Ultimately, therefore, discussion of the fetal organ donor is limited to that of the anencephalic fetus; new ethical ground is, thereby, broken.

The status of the anencephalic neonate is considered further in chapter 15. Here, it need only be said that treatment of the infant who exists only by virtue of a residual brain stem is, perhaps, the quintessential example of medical futility. On the other hand, the anencephalic is, by existing standards, legally a 'creature in being' to whom the existing rules of homicide apply. Thus, the neonate must be allowed a natural death which, save in exceptional circumstances, will occur within about one week.[14] Two major difficulties arise from this – first, as to the diagnosis of death in such circumstances and, secondly, as to the unpalatable corollary that the dead neonate or abortus must be reanimated if it is to provide undamaged organs. As to the former, the Royal Colleges and their Faculties in the United Kingdom have concluded that: 'organs for transplantation can be removed from anencephalic infants when two doctors who are not members of the transplant team agree that spontaneous respiration has ceased.'[15] On the face of things, this seems to be doing no more than restating a diagnostic test for death which has been, and still is, the norm – moreover, the test is equally applicable to fetuses who have been fatally brain damaged during delivery and who might, exceptionally, be considered as donors. More importantly, perhaps, it pre-empts suggestions that anencephaly per se should carry a presumption of death[16] – for the surviving anencephalic neonate is in the same position as is the adult in the persistent vegetative state.[17] It is, therefore, both unnecessary and impracticable to attempt to introduce a brain death standard. There is, however, a practical difficulty in that fetal tissues – and particularly the heart – are extremely sensitive to 'warm anoxia' – the best results from the small number of cases reported are said to have come from those infants who were placed on life support and the organs used as soon

---

13 For which see p 477 below.
14 P A Baird and A D Sadovinich 'Survival in Infants with Anencephaly' (1984) 23 Clin Pediat 268.
15 Report of the Working Party of the Conference of Medical Royal Colleges and their Faculties in the United Kingdom on Organ Transplantation in Neonates (1988).
16 D Brahams 'Transplantation, the Fetus and the Law' (1988) 138 NLJ 91.
17 See chapter 16.

as possible without regard to the existence of brain stem activity.[18] The time required to satisfy the Royal Colleges' criterion of cessation of respiration may, therefore, dictate an unacceptable deterioration in the quality of the donor organs which, in general, must be recovered from a 'beating heart' donor. But this practice depends, as we have seen, on the acceptance of 'brain stem death' and the transplant surgeon is left with a well-nigh insoluble dilemma – so much so that at least one authoritative commentator has questioned whether it is possible to establish death legally in an anencephalic and, at the same time, preserve the best interests of the recipient of its organs.[19] Attempts to redefine death in the anencephalic as a state of 'brain absence' or to regard such a neonate as 'not being a reasonable creature in being' seem to us to be examples of semantic juggling which should be resisted; the same applies to the more extreme suggestion that the definition of death should be extended so as to include anencephalics as a distinct group[20] – as McCullagh has observed:

> Classification as 'dead' will not cause an anencephalic who is breathing to cease doing so . . . One would require also to accept the burial of a spontaneously breathing patient.[1]

The more honest approach is to accept that, at the least, the legality and morality of anencephalic donations are matters for concern and that it is probable that their eventual solution will be founded on strongly utilitarian rather than strict deontological principles.

The implicit result of using the Royal Colleges' criteria is that anencephalic donation must involve some form of 'reanimation ventilation'. This inevitably introduces moral qualms – not the least being that the period of 'deanimation' will be unacceptably short – and, at the end of the day, one has to ask whether the manifest invasion of normal ethical standards is justified by results. It has been estimated that not more than 20 suitable donors will be available each year in the United Kingdom;[2] the surprisingly low yield of organs which would accrue in the United States has been emphasised[3] as has their poor quality and associated distressingly bad therapeutic success rate.[4]

All these factors were considered in what appears to be the only extant judicial consideration of the status of the anencephalic – at least in the English speaking jurisdictions.[5] The circumstances of T's birth were widely publicised. She was born anencephalic and, during her life of nine days, her parents sought to have her declared dead so that her organs could be used to save other lives. The circuit court judge held that she was not brain dead but, nevertheless, gave permission for a single kidney to be removed on the grounds that this was not harming her. This ruling was upheld in

---

18 The Medical Task Force on Anencephaly 'The Infant with Anencephaly' (1990) 322 New Engl J Med 669.
19 S McLean 'Facing the Dilemma of a Life and Death Issue' (1991) Scotsman, 26 August, p 9. For a similar US view, see J L Peabody, J R Emery and S Ashwal 'Experience with Anencephalic Infants as Prospective Organ Donors' (1989) 321 New Engl J Med 344.
20 For review, see W F May 'Brain Death: Anencephalics and Aborted Fetuses' (1990) 22 Transplant Proc 885.
1 P McCullagh *Brain Dead, Brain Absent, Brain Donors* (1993) p 168.
2 See J R Salaman 'Anencephalic Organ Donors' (1989) 298 BMJ 622.
3 See May, n 20 above, reporting the findings, in particular, of Shewmon.
4 D A Shewmon, A M Capron, W J Peacock and B L Schulman 'The Use of Anencephalic Infants as Organ Sources' (1989) 261 J Amer Med Ass 1773.
5 *In re T A C P* 609 So 2d 588 (Fla, 1992).

the District Court of Appeal but, despite the fact that the baby was now dead, the Supreme Court of Florida then agreed to accept the case as one which 'raised a question of great public importance requiring immediate resolution'. Much of the court's deliberation concerned the common and statute law of Florida but questions of principle were also addressed. Having established that T was legally alive at the relevant time, the parents' request that an additional common law standard of death applicable to anencephalics was considered in the light of current technology. It was held:

> Our review of the medical, ethical, and legal literature on anencephaly discloses absolutely no consensus that public necessity or fundamental rights will be better served by granting this request. [6]

and, later:

> We acknowledge the possibility that some infants' lives might be saved by using organs from anencephalics who do not meet the traditional definition of 'death' we affirm to-day. But weighed against this is the utter lack of consensus, and the questions about the overall utility of such organ donations. The scales clearly tip in favor of not extending the common law in this instance. [7]

Thus, the essential ethical problem is to decide whether the utilitarian advantages stemming from anencephalic organ donation are sufficient to offset the inherent deontological doubts raised by the procedure.[8] A 'cost-benefit' analysis inclines us to the view that, in current circumstances, the price is too high. The balance is, however, finely adjusted;[9] there might well be a case for further consideration should transplantation techniques improve to the extent that it can be shown clearly that, once obtained, organs from anencephalics offer a genuine prospect of life to those who are otherwise condemned to death.

The question would then remain whether a woman can properly choose to carry an affected baby close to term purely to provide transplantable organs. Such a programme appears, at first sight, to be unethical on the grounds that a human being is being used as a means. Yet, to prevent it could be seen as unreasonable paternalism. A veto not only *might* deprive potential recipients of life but it would also strike a direct blow at a woman's right to control her body. We would not support a total ban on what may be a truly altruistic endeavour – but it is an aspect of transplantation therapy which must merit very careful scrutiny.

6   Ibid at 594.
7   Ibid at 595.
8   M Harrison 'Organ Procurement for Children: The Anencephalic Fetus as Donor' (1986) 2 Lancet 1383. For criticism of the utilitarian view, see A Davies 'The Status of Anencephalic Babies: Should Their Bodies Be Used as Donor Banks?' (1988) 14 J Med Ethics 150.
9   For an international assessment, see L S Rothenberg 'The Anencephalic Neonate and Brain Death: An International Review of Medical, Ethical and Legal Issues' (1990) 22 Transplant Proc 1037.

Fetal brain implants

Normal adult nerve cells cannot replicate, whereas fetal cells are actively growing and multiplying; theoretically, therefore, an implanted fetal nerve cell will grow and provide a source of important cellular metabolites that are often deficient in the aged. When the previous edition of this book was published, the use of fetal neural tissue for the treatment of Parkinsonism[10] in the elderly – and its extension to the treatment of other degenerative diseases of the ageing brain – was a burning issue. Much of the urgency has now been dispelled as a moratorium has been agreed as to further clinical trials. None the less, the procedure raises a number of legal and ethical problems which merit an airing – and we see four of these as being of major importance.

In contrast to fetal organs, fetal brain cells must be immature and are ideally harvested at 10-14 weeks' gestation. Thus, the first problem is that, excluding the rare opportunities derived from natural spontaneous miscarriage – and all commentators accept that there is a clear moral distinction to be made – the process is inextricably linked to abortion. The legal consequence is that fetal brain therapy is largely governed by the Abortion Act 1967; morally speaking, those who are opposed to abortion can accept fetal brain implantation only on the basis that it is desirable to extract some good from an intrinsically bad action if it is possible to do so[11] – and by no means all moralists would agree to such a proposition.[12] Certainly, virtually everyone would agree that a termination of pregnancy and any subsequent transplantation must be dissociated; the prospect of a woman becoming pregnant in order to provide therapeutic material for an aged relative is scarcely acceptable – as Nolan has put it, it involves seeing fetuses as valuable primarily for their medicinal properties rather than for their stunning developmental potential. Secondly, it is obvious that the individual brain cells must be viable in themselves; can it then be said that the fetus is dead when subjected to surgery? Here, we must rely to an extent on semantic and pragmatic arguments. A 10-14 week-old fetus is not viable – it has no organised heart beat, its lungs cannot conceivably function as oxygenators and, once delivered, it is so clearly not born alive that its existence will go unrecorded save in respect of the abortion regulations; it follows that it is born dead. Moreover, in practice, the technique of abortion will have been so traumatic to the fetus as to preclude any form of life as it is generally accepted. But, be that as it may, it is still very difficult to answer the question: 'Is it brain dead?' in the affirmative.

Thirdly, we cannot overlook the revulsion with which most people view any form of tampering with the brain and particularly the idea of 'brain transplants' – as well

---

10 Note that there is a clinical distinction to be made between idiopathic Parkinson's disease and the signs of Parkinsonism which occur in several other conditions: Editorial Comment 'Parkinson's Disease: One Illness or Many Syndromes? (1992) 339 Lancet 1263.

11 J A Robertson 'The Ethical Acceptability of Fetal Tissue Transplants' (1990) 22 Transplant Proc 1025 argues, persuasively, that the physician using the material has no complicity in obtaining it. The discussion is continued by K Nolan 'The Use of Embryo or Fetus in Transplantation: What There Is to Lose' (1990) 22 Transplant Proc 1029, who concludes that the use of fetal tissues obtained after elective abortion is justified only as a last resort.

12 See R Gillon 'Ethics of Fetal Brain Cell Transplants' (1988) 296 BMJ 1212 for a brief report of expressed attitudes. For extended analysis, see D G Jones 'Fetal Neural Transplantation: Placing the Ethical Debate Within the Context of Society's Use of Human Material' (1991) 5 Bioethics 23.

they might when it is seriously argued that a severed and perfused head might exist more happily than one attached to an aching body.[13] There is; of course, no suggestion that such developments are remotely upon us; nevertheless, the BMA's recommendation that nervous tissue should only be used for transplantation in the form of isolated neurones or tissue fragments[14] should be fully endorsed.[15] Finally, there is some moral repugnance to the use of tissues from the very young to sustain the aged. This is unfair in the present context for the aged are just as entitled to available treatment as is any other population group. But we must ensure that it is true treatment designed to ameliorate specific disease processes. Dr Faustus, in his quest for eternal youth, is scarcely admirable but there are few who have passed middle age who could honestly deny at least a touch of sympathy for his objectives; it is important that we do not seek to force the role of Mephistopheles upon the neurosurgeon.[16, 17]

13 C Fleming 'If We Can Keep a Severed Head Alive . . .' (1988) 297 BMJ 1048.
14 Medical Ethics 'Transplantation of Fetal Material' (1988) 296 BMJ 1410.
15 The question of the persona and brain tissue transplants is discussed in G Northoff 'Do Brain Tissue Transplants Alter Personal Identity? Inadequacies of some "Standard" Arguments' (1966) 22 J Med Ethics 174. See the associated editorial comment R Gillon 'Brain Transplantation, Personal Identity and Medical Ethics' (1996) 22 J Med Ethics 131.
16 For an excellent review of the agonies of a Research Review Committee, see A S MacDonald 'Foetal Neuroendocrine Tissue Transplantation for Parkinson's Disease: An Institutional Review Board Faces the Ethical Dilemma' (1990) 22 Transplant Proc 1030.
17 During the processing of this chapter, our attention has been drawn to the Dutch Organ Donation (Wet op de Orgaandonatie) Act 1998. Under the statute, everyone over the age of 18 is invited to register with a central registry. The individual can register one of four options as to post-mortem donation – a consent to donate any or specified organs, a refusal to donate, delegation of consent to the next of kin or delegation to a nominated person. The choice may be altered at any time. Access to the Central Register is available 24 hours a day. Living donation of organs and bone marrow is also covered by the Act. This appears to be a remarkable legislative advance. It is also fully acceptable on ethical grounds in so far as a coercive element is avoided by providing an equal opportunity to consent or refuse. Up until now, some 30% of the adult population has accepted the opportunity.

15 Medical futility (or non-productive medical treatment): 1 The beginning of life

One of the certainties of life is that we must all die, yet it is surprising how often this is forgotten in the popular view of modern medical practice. We are repeatedly told, for example, that we can 'save our lives' by, say, adopting a given dietary regime or by avoiding some otherwise pleasurable pastime. But, of course, we cannot – the best we can do is to alter the time of our natural death. Sometimes, as when the proximate potential cause of death is *un*natural – say, accidental or homicidal – we can 'save a life' by way of emergency treatment. Again, however, we are, in reality, doing no more than restoring the life span to its natural conclusion.

Conditions such as these provide examples of the intuitive medical urge to prolong life until we can do no more. There is, however, another side to the coin in that, occasionally, the value of that supposed imperative comes into question. The question may be posed by the patient him- or herself – in which case we are in the field of euthanasia, which we discuss in chapter 17. Alternatively, the health carers may raise the question which, then, evolves into a decision as to whether it is in the patient's interests not so much as to whether he or she should live or die but, rather, should his or her death be prolonged by medical treatment. In other words, are there times when treatment should be considered futile and should be abandoned?

When the first edition of this book was written, selective non-treatment of the newborn and, most particularly, withholding the means of survival from mentally handicapped infants were burning issues; it is fair to say that the legal and ethical standards in this area are, now, relatively stabilised. In the interim, however, a comparable flurry of interest has developed around the management of the incompetent adult, with greatest importance attaching, in this instance, to the patient in the persistent or permanent vegetative state. Categories have become blurred in the process. Much as we predicted originally, selective non-treatment of the newborn has progressed to the selective non-treatment of the defective child, while the infant whose brain has been destroyed by meningitis can be used as a model for the adolescent who is similarly affected. It is somewhat ironic that the long and careful deliberations of the House of Lords in *Bland*[1] can trace their origins to the thoroughly unsatisfactory case of *Arthur*.[2]

All these situations, which form a continuum from neonatal deformity, through the persistent vegetative state, to the catastrophically afflicted adult, have it in common that treatment may be contraindicated on the grounds either that it is achieving no medical effect or that continued treatment can be seen as being against the patient's best interests. These can be subsumed together under the general heading

---

1 *Airedale NHS Trust v Bland* [1993] 1 All ER 821, (1993) 12 BMLR 64, Fam D, CA, HL.
2 *R v Arthur* The Times, 6 November 1981, pp 1, 12, (1981) 12 BMLR 1.

of futility. Simple as this analysis appears to be, attempts to reach a universally satisfactory definition of 'futility' do little more that open a Pandora's box of conflicting moral values – for it cannot be denied that it raises the curtain on what is no more and no less than the first Act in the wider drama of euthanasia. Thus, while we find the concept useful, albeit in a restricted way, we cannot introduce it without some consideration of its limitations.

The concept of medical futility

Before starting the discussion, however, it is well to clear up what may become a source of trans-Atlantic misconception. The term in the United States is seen generally as a shorthand way to describe the situation in which a patient demands and a physician objects to the provision of a particular medical treatment on the ground that the treatment will provide no medical benefit to the patient.[3] This definition, in introducing an element of conflict, is restrictive and, we believe, self-defeating. Conflict there may be, but an essential aspect of the regime is that it should be carried out, so far as is possible, in an atmosphere of mutual understanding and agreement – and it is with this aim in mind that we address the subject.

The basis for the concept of futility is certainly not new. More than a quarter of a century ago, it was said:

> The whole resources of an advanced medical service are currently deployed in the pursuit of the preservation of life. It is becoming obvious that the costs of this policy are becoming insupportable . . . We must face an inescapable duty to let some patients die.[4]

The philosophy behind this approach was widely accepted during the 1980s but has since been challenged on several grounds. First, it confuses futility or non-productivity of treatment with rationing of resources; secondly, it suggests that doctors can and should select their patients by way of their own value judgments as to their relative worth; thirdly, the statement, as it stands, conflicts head-on with the rapidly evolving respect for the principle of patient autonomy; and, finally, it speaks in the language of duty while, at the same time, failing to identify the beneficiary of that duty. All of which lead us directly to the question – what do we mean by futility?

Even then, this question can be formulated in a number of ways. Who is to make the definition – the patient, his surrogate or the doctor? And, if it is the last, what is his objective standard – for one man's futility is another's courageous effort.[5] Equally, reliance on, say, the surrogate is bound to end in conflict for, as we will see

---

3   J F Daar 'Medical Futility and Implications for Physician Autonomy' (1995) 21 Am J Law Med 221.
4   E Slater 'Severely Malformed Children: Wanted – A New Approach' (1973) I BMJ 285.
5   See, eg, the case of *Baby Nguyen* referred to in W Prip and A Moretti 'Medical Futility: A Legal Perspective' in M B Zucker and H D Zucker *Medical Futility* (1997) ch 13. One hospital was prepared to treat aggressively an infant with kidney failure, bowel obstruction and brain damage who had been rejected for treatment by another. A very similar case is discussed by J J Paris, R K Crone and F Reardon 'Physicians' Refusal of Requested Treatment: The Case of Baby L' (1990) 322 New Engl J Med 1012.

later – and despite some moral doubts on the part of respected American bioethicists[6] – no doctor in the United Kingdom can be compelled to provide a particular treatment against his better judgment.[7]

Can we refine this choice more closely by considering the quality of the decision to be made? We could, for example, define futile treatment as care that does not accomplish its intended purpose – in which case, a respirator that kept a person breathing could never be classed as providing futile treatment irrespective of the status of the patient. Despite later legal intervention,[8] this is clearly not how the medical profession intended the term to be used; Jecker and Pearlman[9] reviewed the literature and identified four major alternative definitions of futility:

(a) treatment which was either useless or ineffective;
(b) that which fails to offer a minimum quality of life or a modicum of medical benefit;
(c) treatment that cannot possibly achieve the patient's goals; or
(d) treatment which does not offer a reasonable chance of survival.

This mix demonstrates very well the fundamental distinction which must be made between, on the one hand, the *effect* of a treatment – which is no more than an alteration in some bodily function – and, on the other, the *benefit* of a treatment – which is something that can be appreciated by the patient.[10] Put another way, the need is to distinguish between physiological and normative futility[11] – in which case, it is arguable that the former is to be decided on purely medical grounds while the latter involves a quality or value judgment which is the prerogative of the patient or his surrogates.[12] Against which, it has been said that medical judgments are never value-free and that to abandon such judgments at the behest of the patient is to subvert the core of medical professionalism.[13] The doctor's dilemma can, perhaps, best be appreciated in terms of objective. When the primary aim of the health carer is to preserve life, futility only has a role to play when life can no longer be preserved. This is a relatively straight forward issue – either life can be saved or it cannot. However, matters become altogether more complicated when the doctor assumes the role of

6 Eg R M Veatch and C M Spicer 'Futile Care: Physicians Should Not Be Allowed to Refuse to Treat' in T L Beauchamp and R M Veatch *Ethical Issues in Death and Dying* (1996) p 392. It is to be noted that the vast majority of analysis of 'futility' currently derives from America.
7 The situation in the US is complicated by the varying conditions in 'advance directive' or 'living will' legislation. Thus, in 11 States, there is provision for indicating what treatment persons wish to receive in the event of permanent unconsciousness. See Prip and Moretti, p 364, n 5 above. On the other hand, a line of decisions justifying withdrawal of futile treatment in the face of objection is developing – culminating in *Gilgunn v Massachusetts General Hospital* No 92-4820 (Mass Super Ct, Suffolk Co, 22 April 1995), see T Rutter 'US Doctors Win Life Support Lawsuit' (1995) 310 BMJ 1223.
8 See p 383 below.
9 NS Jecker and R A Pearlman 'Medical Futility: Who Decides ?' (1992) 152 Arch Intern Med 1140.
10 L J Schneiderman and N S Jecker 'Futility in Practice' (1993) 153 Arch Intern Med 437.
11 Veatch and Spicer, n 6 above.
12 The major part of an issue (1992) 20 Med Law Hlth Care was given over to the problem. See, in particular, R Cranford and L Gostin 'Futility: A Concept in Search of a Definition' at 307.
13 J F Drane and J L Coulehan 'The Concept of Futility: Patients Do Not Have a Right to Demand Medically Useless Treatment' (1993) 74 Hlth Prog 28; H Brody 'Medical Futility: A Useful Concept?' in Zucker and Zucker, p 364, n 5 above, ch 1.

quality of life provider – futility then assumes an image which is far less clear cut and this is particularly so when decisions are made as to life or death. In such cases, medical intervention *may* keep the patient alive but, none the less, futility is advanced as a justification for allowing him or her to die. Futility then becomes not futility in the face of death – which is an easily appreciated absolute – but, rather, futility in the face of an unacceptable quality of life, which is a far more subjective construct.

Thus, the whole topic of medical futility – when seen as a concept rather than as a series of problem-solving exercises – is fraught with difficulties and contradictions. It has been said that futility is not only a word which is foreign to the families of defective neonates but it is also one which is unacceptable because of its hopelessness; its use militates against achieving the proper societal response.[14] Gillon believes that 'when judgments are to be used as a basis for withholding or withdrawing potentially life prolonging treatment, they had better be made rather precisely and preferably expressed in terms that are less ambiguous, complicated and distressing'.[15] While it is clear that we accept the *medical* principles behind selective non-treatment of the newborn,[16] of 'do-not-resuscitate' orders and of withdrawal of treatment from persons in the permanent vegetative state, we have great sympathy with those who object to *futility* on semantic and philosophical grounds. We much prefer to speak of non-productive treatment, which places the problem firmly in the medical field and, as a result, carries the added advantage of clarity of intention.[17] Meantime, it is suggested that non-productivity and futility can be reconciled if the latter concept is confined to Schneiderman and Jecker's summary definition:

> A treatment which cannot provide a minimum likelihood or quality of benefit should be regarded as futile and is not owed to the patient as a matter of moral duty.[18]

Schneiderman and Jecker also remind us that there are *positive* dangers of abuse if the term 'futile treatment' is adopted uncritically within the medical vocabulary. These include the resurgence of inappropriate paternalism, the erosion of patient autonomy, the unjustified avoidance of the duty to treat – or, we might add, the creation of an ephemeral duty *not* to treat – and the introduction of disguised and arbitrary rationing of resources. Many of these pitfalls are revealed in the cases which follow.

Selective non-treatment of the newborn

It is apparent that we regard the problem of non-productive treatment as one that is common to all ages; nevertheless, selective non-treatment of the newborn retains

14 B Anderson and B Hall 'Parents' Perceptions of Decision Making for Children' (1995) 23 J Law Med & Ethics 15; C Weijer and C Elliott 'Pulling the Plug on Futilty' (1995) 310 BMJ 683.
15 R Gillon '"Futility" – Too Ambiguous and Pejorative A Term?' (1997) 23 J Med Ethics 339.
16 We have retained this expression because it is well established. Paediatricians will, however, point out that it covers a period of care which demands particular clinical and nursing skills. Everyone should read I Laing 'Withdrawing from Invasive Neonatal Intensive Care' in J K Mason (ed) *Paediatric Forensic Medicine and Pathology* (1989).
17 We discuss this concept in greater detail at p 431 below.
18 See p 365, n 10 above.

some unique features. First, it is intimately bound up with the subject of abortion – in so far as a large proportion of conditions which call for 'futile' neonatal treatments were present and were diagnosable in utero and, as such, constituted grounds for legal termination of pregnancy by way of the Abortion Act 1967, s 1(1)(d). What, then, of those affected fetuses which come to full term undiagnosed? Where does public opinion and the law stand between the opposite extremes, on the one hand, of an absolute right to life and, on the other, of a positive policy of elimination of the imperfect? There has to be a middle road but, in the case of the neonate, we must find it without the aid of statute.

Secondly, treatment decisions taken immediately after birth concern human beings who are at the most vulnerable period of their lives – human beings, moreover, who cannot express their feelings for the present or the future and whose surrogates have no experience on which to base their health care decisions. This may explain the relative dearth of court decisions concerning treatment of the neonate. Parents faced with decision-making at this point are likely to agree with their medical advisers simply because they have no evidence on which to *disagree*. It is only when the bonds of adversity have been cemented between the parents and the defective infant that the former can be said to have developed opinions of their own. As a result, the majority of cases in which the court is called upon to adjudicate concern defective infants rather than neonates.

In either case, however, the 'futility' debate is, as discussed above, likely to be conducted at the 'quality of life' level. We have, however, not yet considered whether this is, of itself, a morally tenable level. Have we the right to place relative values on lives or is all life sacrosanct? This question represents the foundation stone of the futility argument and, while it is applied throughout the spectrum of selective treatment, it is convenient to discuss it in the context of the early stages of human development.

Sanctity or quality of life?

The doctor's dilemma is self-evident – is he or she practising truly 'good' medicine in keeping alive a neonate who will be unable to take a place in society or who will be subject to pain and suffering throughout life? In short, is one to displace a concept of the sanctity of life based on a Hippocratic and theological foundation by a standard related to the quality of life which is, essentially, justified by a utilitarian ethos?[19] The situation gives rise to a catalogue of questions – of which the first might well be to ask if there is, in fact, any solid basis for what has become known as the 'sanctity of life doctrine'. This seems to us to be, at least, doubtful. The Hippocratic Oath proscribes euthanasia but neither it, nor the more contemporary Declaration of Geneva impose an obligation to provide treatment at all times; rather, the emphasis is on doing no harm – an approach which clearly allows for pragmatic interpretation. A persuasive case can also be made out for there being no theological imperative to regard human life as sacrosanct.[20]

19 A very full review of the whole question is to be found in L Gostin 'A Moment in Human Development: Legal Protection, Ethical Standards and Social Policy in the Selective Non-treatment of Handicapped Neonates' (1985) 11 Am J Law Med 31.
20 K Boyd 'Euthanasia: Back to the Future' in J Keown (ed) *Euthanasia Examined* (1995) ch 7.

Even so, the concept of the sanctity of life is widely endorsed; the debate continues raising, in its turn, a number of derived questions, many of which are unanswerable in the abstract. Who is to determine the minimum quality of life? Whose life are we considering – the infant's? or are we also taking into account that of the parents or, indeed, the well-being of society? Do we, in fact, *want* a society in which the right to life depends upon achieving a norm which is largely measured in material terms? Should the abnormal infant who resolutely refuses to die be helped on its way? – and, if so, is this help to be a matter of omission or should positive steps be taken to end life? In the discussion of euthanasia which follows in chapter 17, stress is laid on the relationship between the quality of life and the proportionate or disproportionate treatment which is needed to maintain that quality. But the quality of the therapeutic environment at the beginning of life is very hard to assess. Not only can the patient express no opinion but, were it possible, he or she has no yardstick by which to judge; as put by the Canadian McKenzie J:

> . . . he would not compare his life with that of a person enjoying normal advantages. He would know nothing of a normal person's life having never experienced it.[1]

As an inevitable result, parents must be invited to make 'life or death' decisions on behalf of their abnormal offspring – and they will be guided by the doctor whose advice is likely to be on the lines that consideration for the preservation of life is secondary to that of preventing suffering. Medical leadership has supported this parental responsibility – 'in the absence of a clear code to which society adheres, there is no justification for the courts usurping the parents' rights'[2] – and it has been backed by influential academic legal thought - 'the criminal law should stay its hand. The decision of the parents should prevail'.[3] These are, however, generalisations and the cases which follow demonstrate that generalisations provide no easy answers to individual problems.

In particular, the early cases fail to address the solution of conflict between the medical carers and the parents. As we have seen, this underlies the concept of medical futility which, as a result, can be seen as developing in the United Kingdom only since the 1980s. Thus, we have the evidence of Dr Dunn at the trial of Dr Arthur: 'no paediatrician takes life but we do accept that allowing babies to die is in the baby's interest at times'[4] – and the wealth of distinguished supporting evidence showed that this paediatric practice was clearly acceptable at the time. It does, however, involve a number of assumptions:

(a) that there is an essential difference between activity and passivity when the same end – death – is realised by either and, arising from this, that passivity does not

---

1 *Re Superintendent of Family and Child Service and Dawson* (1983) 145 DLR (3d) 610 at 621.
2 Editorial Comment 'The Right to Live and the Right to Die' (1981) 283 BMJ 569.
3 G Williams 'Life of a Child' (1981) Correspondence, The Times, 13 August.
4 *R v Arthur* (1981) 12 BMLR 1 at 18. Dr Dunn would now limit withholding life-saving treatment only in three groups of neonate: those with severe malformations, those with severe hypoxic/traumatic brain damage; and those of extreme prematurity with major problems such as brain haemorrhage: P M Dunn 'Appropriate Care of the Newborn: Ethical Dilemmas' (1993) 19 J Med Ethics 82.

conflict with the doctor's duty to 'maintain life from the time of conception';[5] moreover, passivity is clinically preferable from the patient's viewpoint;

(b) that there is a point at which death is preferable to life; and

(c) that some, as yet unidentified person, can decide that point in surrogate fashion and that it is right and proper for others to act on that judgment.

Yet this seems to come perilously close to breaking the law. To kill a living human being deliberately is murder and, except as to the specific crime of infanticide,[6] the age of the victim has no relevance. Killing a child by omission could be prosecuted under the Children and Young Persons Act 1933, s 1;[7] it is more likely to be charged as manslaughter although it could be murder[8] – the paramount considerations being whether or not there is a duty of care and, if there is, what is the extent of that duty.[9] It is difficult to see how the consultant in charge of the paediatric ward does not have a duty of care to his patients. Yet, anything up to 30% of deaths in a neonatal intensive care unit follow the deliberate withdrawal of life support[10] and we have Farquharson J charging the jury in the leading apposite criminal case:

> I imagine that you will think long and hard before concluding that doctors, of the eminence we have heard . . . have evolved standards that amount to committing a crime.[11]

Moreover, we have not yet fed the rights of the neonate into the equation. In our view, the newly born baby has the same rights to self-ownership of the body as has every human being. This proposition is, however, increasingly under attack as the definition of personhood in terms of intellect is developed. We have already observed that, if it is valid to treat the fetus as a non-person, it is also valid to use the same parameters by which to deny personhood to the neonate; there are, indeed, those who are prepared to equate the status of 'infanticide' with that of 'feticide'[12] – or even of contraception. It is against this conflicting legal and ethical background that we can trace the absorption of the concept of medical futility into the medical jurisprudence of the United Kingdom as, first, related to the neonate and infant.

Futility or a duty not to treat?

Although *R v Arthur*[13] was, chronologically speaking, not the first instance of selective non-treatment of the newborn to come before the English courts, it was

---

5 Declaration of Geneva (see Appendix B).

6 Infanticide Act 1938.

7 There is some doubt as to whether the section applies only to parental obligations. If this be so, it would not constitute a potential sanction against the health care team. See I M Kennedy and A C Grubb *Medical Law: Text with Materials* (2nd edn, 1994), p 1249.

8 *R v Gibbins and Proctor* (1918) 13 Cr App Rep 134, CCA.

9 *R v Stone; R v Dobinson* [1977] QB 354, [1977] 2 All ER 341, CA.

10 A Whitelaw 'Death as an Option in Neonatal Intensive Care' [1986] 2 Lancet 328; C H M Walker '. . . Officiously to Keep Alive' (1988) 63 Arch Dis Child 560.

11 *R v Arthur* (1981) 12 BMLR 1 at 22.

12 See in particular H Kuhse and P Singer *Should the Baby Live?* (1985) ch 6. Other observations along the same lines include J G Bissenden 'Ethical Aspects of Neonatal Care' (1986) 61 Arch Dis Child 693; C Wells 'Whose Baby Is It?' (1988) 5 J Law & Soc 323.

13 (1981) 12 BMLR 1.

undoubtedly that which brought the whole subject before the public conscience. In so far as it was taken through the criminal courts, it is an unsatisfactory prototype; nevertheless, it has been said that there are surprisingly few substantive issues in medical ethics that Dr Arthur's case does not raise[14] and it remains an important landmark.

Put briefly, the salient features of the case are that a baby was born with apparently uncomplicated Down's syndrome and was rejected by his parents; Dr Arthur, a paediatrician of high repute and impeccable professional integrity, wrote in the notes 'Parents do not wish it to survive. Nursing care only'; the baby died 69 hours later. Dr Arthur was charged with murder but, during the course of the trial, medical evidence was adduced to the effect that the child had not been physically healthy; accordingly, the charge was reduced to one of attempted murder and Dr Arthur was acquitted.

The central question raised by the trial is why, in the light of the acknowledged developments in neonatal intensive care, was Dr Arthur singled out for prosecution?[15]

In our view, the most logical answer lies in the application of a 'treatability' test. Dr Arthur's patient was in no physical pain and, so far as was known prior to autopsy, he required no treatment. Death in such circumstances depends on the withholding of nourishment and to take away such a life is to make a social rather than a medical decision – the fact that it was taken by a doctor rather than a member of the public should be irrelevant. The prosecution of Dr Arthur led to a storm of resentment on the part of the leaders of the medical profession but this was almost entirely due to a failure to appreciate that there is a world of difference between withholding treatment from a dying patient and refusing sustenance to one who shows firm evidence of a will to live.[16] Any confusion as to the doctor's role is dispersed once it is appreciated that there is a fundamental distinction to be drawn between physical defect – for which invasive treatment remains an option – and mental defect for which no curative treatment is available. The failure of the medical establishment in this respect is exemplified in the statement of the President of the Royal College of Physicians:

> Where there is an uncomplicated Down's case and the parents do not want the child to live . . . I think there are circumstances where it would be ethical to put it upon a course of management that would end in its death . . . I say that with a child suffering from Down's and with a parental wish that it should not survive, it is ethical to terminate life.[17]

By any standards, this is a remarkable interpretation of both medical and parental responsibilities and powers. In the light of later judicial decisions, which are discussed below, it is unlikely that Dr Arthur's regime would be acceptable today and the case has lost any credibility as a precedent. In our view, the management pattern disclosed in *R v Arthur* is best seen as an example of the dangers of

---

14 R Gillon 'An Introduction to Philosophical Medical Ethics: The Arthur Case' (1985) 290 BMJ 1117.
15 Only a few weeks previously, the Director of Public Prosecutions had decided that no action would be taken against a doctor who had allegedly refused to sustain a baby, Stephen Quinn, who was suffering from spina bifida: (1981) The Times, 6 October, p 1.
16 Eg Editorial Comment 'Paediatricians and the Law' (1981) 283 BMJ 1280.
17 (1981) 12 BMLR 1 at 21-22. See also the leading article at the time, 'After the Trial at Leicester' (1981) 2 Lancet 1085.

extrapolating the concept of 'futility' to one of an obligation not to treat in the face of parental pressure.

Case law other than Arthur

With, perhaps, one major exception,[18] the law in this area has shown a remarkably steady development in the last 15 years. None the less, the template was undoubtedly established in the prototype case of *Re B (a minor)*,[19] the judgment in which has been said still to represent the law in this particular field.[20] Thus, despite its antiquity, *Re B* still merits close consideration.

In essence, B was an infant suffering from Down's syndrome complicated by intestinal obstruction of a type which would be fatal per se but which was readily amenable to surgical treatment. The parents took the view that the kindest thing in the interests of the child would be for her not to have the operation and for her to die – in passing, a decision which was later described by Dunn LJ as 'an entirely responsible one'. The infant was made a ward of court and, in the face of both judicial indecision and medical disagreement, the question 'to treat or not to treat?' came before the Court of Appeal.

The summary answer to the basic question was provided by Dunn LJ in saying: 'She should be put in the position of any other mongol child and given the opportunity to live an existence.'[1] For the major analysis, however, we must look to Templeman LJ who, adhering to the general principles relating to the affairs of minors,[2] concluded that the judge of first instance, in refusing to authorise the operation, had been too much concerned with the wishes of the parents; the duty of the court was to decide the matter in the interests of the child. In coming to the conclusion that these interests were best served by treatment, he said:

> . . . it devolves on this court . . . to decide whether the life of this child is demonstrably going to be so awful that in effect the child must be condemned to die or whether the life of this child is still so imponderable that it would be wrong for her to be condemned to die. . . . Faced with [the] choice, I have no doubt that it is the duty of this court to decide that the child must live.[3]

and it was this that led Lord Donaldson to look upon *Re B* as close to a binding authority for the proposition that there is a balancing exercise to be performed in assessing the course to be adopted in the best interests of such children.

Templeman LJ did, however, clearly leave the door open for an alternative decision in saying:

18 *Re T (a minor) (wardship: medical treatment)* [1997] 1 All ER 906, discussed in greater detail at p 377, below.
19 (1981) [1990] 3 All ER 927, [1981] 1 WLR 1421, CA.
20 *Re J (a minor) (wardship: medical treatment)* [1990] 3 All ER 930, (1990) 6 BMLR 25, CA paraphrasing Lord Donaldson MR [1990] 3 All ER 930 at 938, (1990) 6 BMLR 25 at 34.
 1 [1990] 1 All ER 927 at 929, [1981] 1 WLR 1421 at 1425.
 2 Guardianship of Minors Act 1971, s 1. See, now, Children Act 1989, s 1.
 3 [1990] 1 All ER 927 at 929, [1981] 1 WLR 1421 at 1424. The case is well discussed by D D Raphael 'Handicapped Infants: Medical Ethics and the Law' (1988) 14 J Med Ethics 5.

There may be cases ... of severe proved damage where the future is so certain and where the life of the child is so bound to be full of pain and suffering that the court might be driven to a different conclusion.[4]

Thus, the court clearly accepted that there is an essential prognostic difference between mental and physical handicap and, as to the latter, laid the foundations for a quality of life therapeutic standard rather than one based on a rigid adherence to the principle of the sanctity of human life.

Even so, the medical profession was now left in a cleft stick. Allowing for the fact that they relate to different jurisdictions, *Re B* and *Arthur* are virtually impossible to reconcile. Legally speaking, it is difficult to see why the parents' wishes as to the death of their offspring should be overruled when major surgery is involved, yet be regarded as ultimately decisive when it is not and, in a clarification which seems only to add to the confusion, the Attorney General said shortly after Dr Arthur's trial:

I am satisfied that the law relating to murder and to attempted murder is the same now as it was before the trial; that it is the same irrespective of the age of the victim; and that it is the same irrespective of the wishes of the parents or of any other person having a duty of care to the victim. I am also satisfied that a person who has a duty of care may be guilty of murder or attempted murder by omitting to fulfil that duty, as much as by committing any positive act.[5]

This unsatisfactory situation persisted for almost a decade but has now been greatly clarified in the series of cases overseen by Lord Donaldson MR.[7] The decisions in these cases relate to treatment of infants rather than of the newborn. They can, therefore, be taken as early examples of the application of medical futility across the whole span of life.

Selective non-treatment in infancy

Re C[7] concerned a moribund child and the essence of the decision was that the hospital were given authority to treat her so as to allow her life to come to an end peacefully and with dignity; such treatment as would relieve her from pain, suffering and distress would be given but it was specifically said to be unnecessary to use antibiotics or to set up intravenous infusions or nasogastric feeding regimes. It was emphasised that the decision was based on the paramountcy of her welfare, well-being and interests. *Re C* thus represents the antithesis of *Re B* in respect of physical disability and, in retrospect, neither case was difficult to decide.

Baby J[8] was, however, not dying and the case illustrates more clearly the real dilemma presented by these cases. The situation was that the brain-damaged child suffered from repetitive fits and periods of cessation of breathing for which he

---

4   [1990] 3 All ER 927 at 929, [1981] 1 WLR 1421 at 1424.
5   19 HC Official Reports (6th series) written answers, col 349 8 March 1982..
6   For review of these cases, see J K Mason 'Master of the Balancers: Non-voluntary Therapy under the Mantle of Lord Donaldson' [1993] JR 115.
7   *Re C (a minor) (wardship: medical treatment)* [1990] Fam 26, [1989] 2 All ER 782.
8   *Re J (a minor) (wardship: medical treatment)* [1990] 3 All ER 930, (1992) 6 BMLR 25.

required ventilation. There was no doubt that he could be rescued in the probable event that he sustained further episodes of respiratory failure but it was equally certain that he would die if the necessary treatment was withheld. Non-treatment in these circumstances cannot be dressed in such euphemisms as 'allowing a peaceful and dignified death' and the question before the court was what was to be done if he sustained a further collapse. The Court of Appeal had little difficulty in agreeing with the judge of first instance that:

> it would not be in J's best interest to reventilate him [by machine] in the event of his stopping breathing unless to do so seems appropriate to the doctors caring for him given the prevailing clinical situation. [9]

In the course of his judgment, the Master of the Rolls made several observations which we see as being of particular importance. In the first place, he stressed that, while there was a strong presumption in favour of a course of action that will prolong life, nevertheless, the person who makes the decision must look at it from the assumed view of the patient. Following on from this, consideration must be given to the prognosis in terms of pain and suffering – including the distress caused by any treatment of itself; in J's case, the quality of life, even without the added effect of further hypoxic episodes, was extremely low. Thirdly, the court held that decision making was a co-operative effort between the doctors and the parents – or, in the case of wardship, between the doctors and the court with the views of the parents being taken into consideration;[10] any choice must be made solely on behalf of the child in what was believed to be his best interests. Finally – and this we see as especially significant – it was emphasised that any decision taken was one which would affect death by way of a side-effect; the debate was not about terminating life but solely about whether to withhold treatment designed to prevent death from natural causes:

> The court never sanctions steps to terminate life. That would be unlawful. There is no question of approving, even in a case of the most horrendous disability, a course aimed at terminating life or accelerating death. The court is concerned only with the circumstances in which steps should not be taken to prolong life.[11]

Re C and *Re J* must, however, be looked at in conjunction with a third case which was unfortunately also named *Re J*[12] – and called here *Re J(2)*. Here, a mother attempted to enforce the intensive care of her child who had sustained severe brain

9 [1990] 3 All ER 930 at 933, (1992) 6 BMLR 25 at 29.
10 The nurses were singled out for praise in the Court of Appeal in *Re C,* where there were clear indications that their views should also be considered.
11 [1990] 3 All ER 930 at 943, (1990) 6 BMLR 25 at 40, per Taylor LJ. In *Re C*, the Court of Appeal would not even tolerate the expression 'treat to die'.
12 *Re J (a minor) (medical treatment)* [1993] Fam 15, [1992] 4 All ER 614. Two very similar decisions have been reached in Scotland. The determination in the fatal accident inquiry concerning the death of Rebecca Cassidy supported a decision not to treat an extremely low birth-weight premature infant: see S English 'Doctor was Right not to Resuscitate "Unviable" Baby' (1997) The Times, 27 June, p 11. The decision not to provide a liver transplant for a teenage girl was accepted as good medical practice in the inquiry into the death of Michelle Paul: see G Bowditch 'Surgeon Right to Refuse Teenager a Liver Transplant' (1997) The Times, 23 July, p 7.

damage as a result of a fall. The Court of Appeal, however, refused to entertain the suggestion that it should direct clinicians to provide treatment against their best clinical judgment:

> I agree with Lord Donaldson that I can conceive of no situation where it would be proper ... to order a doctor, whether directly or indirectly, to treat a child in the manner contrary to his or her clinical judgment. I would go further. I find it difficult to conceive of a situation where it would be a proper exercise of the jurisdiction to make an order positively requiring a doctor to adopt a particular course of treatment in relation to a child.[13]

Thus, this series of cases indicates a strong judicial belief in the doctor's clinical autonomy. It also shows a very determined stance in favour of a quality of life standard which is founded on the principle of the patient's 'best interests'.

The use of this standard is best considered under the management of the permanent vegetative state.[14] For present purposes, we consider only the relationship between 'best interests' and 'no interests' in which we are, in fact, reverting to the problem of distinguishing mental from physical disability. It may well be permissible to see death as a blessed relief from severe pain or unacceptable bodily invasion and, therefore, an outcome of a treatment that is in the patient's 'best interests'. By contrast, the patient who has sustained brain damage of such degree as to permanently deprive him or her of sensation and cognition has no immediate interests as between death or survival.[15]

We believe that some other test is called for in the latter circumstance and that it is there, in particular, that we can legitimately call on the concept of medical futility to guide our therapeutic programming. However, as we have seen, this can conflict with the respect due to *patient* autonomy and, to avoid this, it may be preferable to rely on the principle of substituted judgment – or, in other words, to follow the regime that one assumes the patient him- or herself would have opted for if given the chance.[16] The objections to such a test are discussed in greater detail above/below.[17] For the present, we will only observe that its acceptance relieves one of an element of hypocrisy that is inherent in the 'best interests' test. We are constantly assured that judicial treatment/non-treatment decisions are founded on the best interests of the patient alone and that the interests of the relatives, carers and, indeed, the state are irrelevant – yet, in all honesty, it is hard, if not impossible, to separate these extraneous interests. Substituted judgment allows us to take the latter into consideration with a relatively clear conscience. A competent patient may opt for non-treatment rather than treatment and the effects of the decision on his or her family can legitimately form part of its foundation; there is no reason why this should not be incorporated in the substituted judgment.

---

13 [1993] Fam 15 at 29, [1992] 4 All ER 614 at 625, per Balcombe LJ.
14 See p 394 below.
15 Although Dworkin, for one, speaks in terms of critical interests which persist despite the loss of appreciative capacity: R Dworkin *Life's Dominion* (1993), discussed extensively by A Grubb 'Commentary on *Law Hospital NHS Trust v The Lord Advocate*' (1996) 4 Med L Rev 301. We see this, however, as having academic rather than practical consequences.
16 'Donning the mental mantle of the incompetent patient': see *Superintendent of Belchertown State School v Saikewicz* 370 NE 2d 64 (Mass, 1977).
17 See pp 404-405.

In fact, the English courts, in their anxiety to maintain the welfare principle, have tended to confuse the two tests. Thus, we have Lord Donaldson[18] quoting the Canadian McKenzie J: [19]

> It is not appropriate for an external decision maker to apply his standards of what constitutes a liveable life . . . The decision can only be made in the context of the disabled person viewing the worthwhileness or otherwise of his life in its own context as a disabled person.[20]

Although it was taken as expressing the best interests of J, this is as clear a description of the principle of substituted judgment as one is likely to find. It also re-emphasises the mental/physical divide – a divide which has become even more apparent in some relevant cases which have been reported since the era of Lord Donaldson.

Important cases post-Donaldson

Re C (a baby)[1] concerned a premature infant who developed meningitis resulting in her being blind and deaf and suffering from repeated convulsions. She could survive only by virtue of artificial ventilation but, given that support, it was thought that she could live for months or even up to two years. Meantime, her pain and distress were expected to increase. She was described as not being in coma but as having 'a very low awareness of anything, if at all'; Sir Stephen Brown P summed up her condition as 'almost a living death'. Medical opinion was that she had no independent existence and that it was in her interests that ventilation should be discontinued – in which case she would die within hours. The President had no doubt that he should grant leave to the medical staff to adopt this recommended regime.

The President was invited to make observations as to when it would be appropriate for doctors placed in this position to seek the leave of the court; he thought, however, that it would not be appropriate to make any general observation abut that matter – medical and legal opinion concurred in believing that each case should be considered on its particular facts.

The parents in *Re C (a baby)* agreed with the recommendations of their medical advisers. In the second important case, *Re C (a minor)*,[2] however, the parents were orthodox Jews, who firmly believed that life should always be preserved. Their child, aged 16 months, suffered from spinal muscular atrophy – a progressive condition for which it was agreed there was no curative treatment. Nevertheless, she was conscious, able to recognise her parents and was able to smile. The recommended plan was to undertake a form of therapeutic test by removing her from supportive ventilation; if, as was probable, she suffered a further respiratory relapse, she would not be reventilated but would be allowed to die. The parents accepted the first part of the plan but were unable to consent to the second. The stage was, thus, set for the classic American 'futility' scenario.

18 In *Re J* [1990] 3 All ER 930, (1990) 6 BMLR 25.
19 In *Superintendent of Family and Child Services and Dawson* (1983) 145 DLR (3d) 610.
20 [1990] 3 All ER 930 at 936, (1990) 6 BMLR 25 at 32.
 1 *Re C (a baby)* [1996] 2 FLR 43, (1996) 32 BMLR 44.
 2 *Re C (a minor)* (1997) 40 BMLR 31.

In the event, the President relied heavily on Lord Donaldson's leading cases[3] in defining the legal limits of the doctor's duties. In particular:

> [To follow the wishes of the parents] would be tantamount to requiring the doctors to undertake a course of treatment which they are unwilling to do. The court could not consider making an order which would require them so to do.[4]

The situation was defined as one in which the hospital trust sought the court's consent in the absence of consent by the parents. The medical evidence was not in dispute and was backed by the general recommendations issued by the Royal College of Paediatrics and Child Health[5] – under the terms of which, spinal muscular atrophy would be regarded as a 'no-chance situation' in which medical treatment may be deemed inappropriate. Leave was granted to the hospital to withdraw treatment and to exclude resuscitation in the event of respiratory arrest – such a regime being justified as being in C's best interests.

It is appropriate here to note one further 'futility related' case, despite the fact that it concerns an adult patient. The subject of *Re D*[6] was a 49-year-old man suffering from chronic renal failure whose long-standing mental disability and drug abuse problems made it impossible for him to co-operate with dialysis treatment except by being anaesthetised for each session. Sir Stephen Brown held that, where the weight of medical opinion supported the view that treatment would not be practicable, it would be lawful, as being in the patient's best interests, for doctors to refrain from imposing such treatment notwithstanding that the patient was unable to consent to or refuse treatment due to mental disability.

Thus, while all the cases cited could be subsumed under the rubric of medical futility, we see them as illustrating a relatively steady – and significant – extension of the conditions which render non-treatment lawful. Two common threads are to be seen. On the one hand, the courts will not, and are unlikely ever to, order doctors to provide treatment against their better judgment – especially for those who are severely brain damaged. As a corollary, it is clear that, no matter what may be the practical clinical situation, parents and other guardians have no *legal* right to demand treatment which the doctors regard as being inappropriate. This, however, depends upon the weight of the medical opinion expressed. It is to be noted that the medical evidence has never been seriously challenged by the amicus curiae in the reported cases and one wonders what would be the outcome were it to be otherwise. The general tenor of the decisions since *Re B* through the two *Re Js* suggests that the courts would opt for the salvaging of life – as Lord Donaldson put it: 'There is without doubt a very strong presumption in favour of a course of action which will prolong life' albeit adding the rider 'but . . . it is not irrebuttable'.[7]

3   *Re J (a minor)* [1990] 3 All ER 930, (1992) 6 BMLR 25; *Re J (a minor)* [1993] Fam 15, [1992] 4 All ER 614; *Re R (a minor) (wardship: medical treatment)* [1992] Fam 11, (1991) 7 BMLR 147.
4   (1997) 40 BMLR 31 at 37.
5   Royal College of Paediatrics and Child Health *Withholding or Withdrawing Life Saving Treatment in Children: A Framework for Practice* (1997).
6   *Re D* (1997) 41 BMLR 81.
7   *Re J (a minor) (wardship: medical treatment)* [1990] 3 All ER 930 at 938, (1990) 6 BMLR 25 at 34.

At the same time, the more recent *Re C* cases raise the possibility of a subtle change of emphasis leading to supremacy of the 'quality of life' as a unit of assessment. It is true that all life and death decisions have been based on a 'best interests' test, but the facts of each successive case seem to point to an incremental erosion of the pure concept – is it not, in fact, possible to discern the glimmers of a legal recognition of the 'personhood' construct? The *C* and *J* cases can also be distinguished in that, while the latter are concerned with the non-provision of treatment that interferes with the natural process, the former relate to the withdrawal of treatment that is already in place; it is difficult in the extreme to deny that the *C* cases sanction a regime designed to bring about a death which would not otherwise have occurred – barely distinguishable from that which Taylor LJ excluded in *Re J*[8] and which was foreseen by Balcombe LJ in *Re J (2)*.[9] Can this be a tentative step towards legalised euthanasia?

Finally, the more recent cases illustrate vividly the difficulties surrounding the whole concept of futility. Continued treatment was futile from the perspective of the doctors in *Re C (a baby)*,[10] *Re C (a minor)*[11] and *Re D*[12] and this constitutes the justification of its withdrawal; it is, surely, carrying sophistry too far to plead 'best interests' – especially in the case of *Re D*, in which non-treatment decisions were, in effect, enforced. But, if a procedure is to be regarded as futile, it must be devoid of utility and, certainly, treatment would have been beneficial to D had it been possible to provide it. Moreover, the 'futile' treatment of C in *Re C (a minor)* was not only useful but was essential to her parents. In short, there is a practical as well as a theoretical distinction to be made between futile treatment and *medically* futile treatment. The doctor is entitled to assess the latter and to argue in favour of its non-provision or withdrawal. But , in the end, to do so is no more than a powerful contribution to the overall assessment of the former – which goes some way to supporting Sir Stephen Brown P in his resistance to generalising in this field.[13]

Reversal of the trend?

We have noted above the inclination of the courts to follow the medical opinion whenever it is possible to do so; the case of *Re T (a minor) (wardship: medical treatment)*,[14] in which the trend was reversed, is, therefore, of considerable interest.

---

8 [1990] 3 All ER 930 at 943, (1990) 6 BMLR 25 at 40.
9 [1993] Fam 15 at 30, (1992) 9 BMLR 10 at 20, CA.
10 (1996) 32 BMLR 44.
11 (1997) 40 BMLR 31.
12 (1997) 41 BMLR 81.
13 *Re C (a baby)* (1996) 32 BMLR 44. See also Waite LJ: ' All these cases depend on their own facts and render generalisations ... wholly out of place' in *Re T (a minor) (wardship: medical treatment)* [1997] 1 All ER 906 at , (1996) 35 BMLR 63 at 75. At the time of writing, the BMA is seeking general guidelines comparable to those issued by the Royal College of Paediatrics and Child Health (p 376, n 5 above). *Withdrawing and Withholding Treatment: A Consultation Paper from the BMA's Medical Ethics Committee* (1998).
14 [1997] 1 All ER 906, (1996) 35 BMLR 63. For discussion, see M Fox and J McHale 'In Whose Best Interests?' (1997) 60 MLR 700; A Bainham 'Do Babies Have Rights?' (1997) 56 CLR 48; A Grubb 'Commentary' (1997) 4 Med LRev 315.

Here, the child curiously designated as C, was born with biliary atresia – a condition likely to be fatal within $2^1/_2$ years in the absence of transplantation therapy. Remedial surgery at the age of $3^1/_2$ weeks produced no improvement but medical opinion was unanimous in its belief that the chances of a successful transplant were good and that the operation was in C's best interests. This included the opinion of a consultant engaged on behalf of the mother who opposed a further operation on the grounds of the pain and suffering C had sustained following the first procedure and who even took her child abroad where there were no facilities for a liver transplant. The child's local authority then raised the matter as a special issue under the terms of the Children Act 1989, s 100(3). As a result, the trial judge found that the mother's conduct was not that of a reasonable parent and directed that C be admitted to a hospital that was prepared to undertake a transplant operation.

The Court of Appeal, however, unanimously reversed this decision, largely on the grounds that the judge had failed to give adequate weight in the necessary balancing exercise to the objections of the parents – which were supported by qualities of devotion, commitment, love and reason. These included an assessment of the pain and suffering likely to be imposed by a second major operation and of the chances and consequences of failure. In addition, the court agreed with one expert opinion that passing back responsibility for parental care to the mother and expecting her to provide the essential commitment to the child after the operation in the face of her opposition was, in itself, fraught with danger for the child. How would the mother cope with having to remain in England? asked Butler-Sloss LJ. The mother and the child were one for the purposes of the case and the decision of the court to assent to the operation jointly affected the mother and son and also the father. Waite LJ went so far as to hold that the child's subsequent development could be injuriously affected if his day-to-day care depended upon the commitment of a mother who had suffered the turmoil of her child being compelled against her will to undergo a major operation 'against which her own medical and maternal judgment wholeheartedly rebelled'.[15] The appeal was upheld and the orders of the trial judge to the effect that surgery should be performed notwithstanding the refusal of the mother to consent were set aside.

Re T raises a number of questions – both general and particular. It is, first, reasonable to question whether it is right to place discussion of the case within a section devoted to medical futility. Our view is that it represents one side of the wide concept – albeit the rather unusual reverse in which the parents, on behalf of their child, are claiming treatment to be futile in so far as it is, on balance and in their view, offering minimal benefit. It will be seen below that we reject this prognostic assessment and it may be that the importance of the case lies in providing a measure of how far the concept of futility can be stretched without incursion into areas such as euthanasia – it is possible, but it is certainly not easy, to accommodate phrases such as: '. . . the prospect of forcing the devoted mother of this young baby to the consequences of this major invasive surgery . . . '[16] within the envelope of the child's unaffected best interests. Equally to the point, one has to ask if the decision in *Re T* does, in fact, represent a watershed in the medico-legal symbiosis that has developed in this area. C's parents were described as health professionals; their status is unstated but the Court of Appeal was clearly impressed by their understanding of the situation

15 [1997] 1 All ER 906 at 917, (1996) 35 BMLR 63 at 75.
16 *Re T* [1997] 1 All ER 906 at 916, (1996) 35 BMLR 63 at 74, per Butler-Sloss LJ.

– so much so that, at times, the mother's views appear to take on the significance of another expert medical opinion. Moreover, previous court decisions represent not so much a judicial submission to the medical will as, rather, a reluctance to impose a duty to treat on unwilling doctors. *Re T* was an antithetical proposition, the end result of which was to place an embargo on treatment which at least some experts were willing to provide. It may not, therefore, be a decision taken against the stream.

Whether it was a 'good' decision in medical jurisprudential terms is, again, questionable. Despite the protestations of all three judges, and despite the court's repeated assurance as to the responsibility and devotion of the parents, an unavoidable impression remains that their interests weighed heavily in the balance at the expense of the paramountcy of those of the child. Certainly, there is great good sense in the opinion of the trial judge. There are few fields of modern medicine in which progress is as fast as it is in transplantation therapy. It is at least possible that additional technology would become available during the several years of good quality life available within the current state of the art; not only might these then be extended beyond current expectation but, in the interim, the mother's attitude might well change. It is hard to dismiss such gains as medically futile objectives.

Futility or scarcity of resources?

We have suggested already that the concept of futility carries with it the real danger that it can be used as a means to the disguised and arbitrary rationing of resources. This may well be so but, before accepting this as wholly pejorative, it is well to note the underlying practicalities.

In the first place, the one necessarily follows the other. Thus, if one patient is removed from futile treatment, that resource automatically becomes available to another for whom it will be useful – but the motive behind the exchange remains subject to interpretation. Secondly, given that resources are not infinite, therapeutic merit is a good candidate for the most acceptable basis for their distribution; as we discuss in chapter 11, the 'first come, first served' regime fails as a principle because it dictates the provision of treatment in medically futile circumstances. Thirdly, the law clearly accepts that resource allocation forms a proper part of medical decision making. Thus, we have Balcombe LJ:

> [M]aking an order which may have the effect of compelling a doctor or health authority to make available scarce resources . . . to a particular child . . . might require the health authority to put J on a ventilator in an intensive care unit, and thereby possibly to deny the benefit of those limited resources to a child who was much more likely than J to benefit from them.[17]

None the less, the seeds of conflict are there to be sown and are well illustrated in *R v Cambridge Health Authority, ex p B*,[18] which concerned a 10-year-old child who had been suffering from lymphoma since the age of five. By the time of the action,

---

17 *Re J (a minor) (wardship: medical treatment)* [1993] Fam 15 at 30, (1992) 9 BMLR 10 at 20.
18 (1995) 25 BMLR 5; revsd (1995) 23 BMLR 1, CA.

she had received two courses of chemotherapy and had undergone whole body irradiation and received a bone marrow transplant before she suffered a further relapse. At this point, her doctors determined that no further treatment could usefully be given and estimated her life expectancy as between six and eight weeks. Her father had, meantime, obtained a second opinion from the United States which, effectively, suggested that further treatment carried an 18% chance of a full cure. Doctors who were prepared to continue treatment in the United Kingdom regarded this as unduly optimistic and set the chance of success at anything between 10% and 2.25% – which was, of course, to be set against the risk to the patient's life and the distress associated with the proposed treatment; due to a shortage of beds, this would have to be carried out in the private sector and the cost was estimated to be in the region of £75,000. Taking into account the judgment of their own clinicians, the nature of the treatment and its chances of success, the health authority declined to provide the funding, giving as its reasons, first, that the treatment would not be in B's best interests and, second, that the expenditure of so much money with so little prospect of success was an ineffective use of their limited resources bearing in mind the present and future needs of other patients. The father sought judicial review of this decision.

In the High Court hearing, Laws J began his determination with the words: 'Of all human rights, most people would accord the most precious place to the right to life itself.' In our view, this is a contentious premise. We suggest that there is no rights-based entitlement to any particular treatment; the 'right to life' in this context means no more than the right not to have one's life taken away and this right is in no sense infringed if it is agreed that the available treatment is either futile or against the patient's best interests. In confronting such criticism, Laws J opined that, in contrast to the position in criminal law, public law allowed no difference of principle between act and omission and, accordingly, the decision of the health authority assaulted the child's right to life. He then considered the justification for such an assault and concluded that, while the doctors could rightly assess the chances of success of the proposed treatment and its objective disadvantages in terms of risk and suffering, the assessment of the patient's best interests was not, in the end, a medical question at all. Rather, it was a matter to be decided by the child's father acting as a surrogate responsible for her overall care. Thus, in the end, the issue turned on the provision of funds – and the learned judge considered that, when the question was whether the life of a 10-year-old might be saved, by however slim a chance, the authority should do more than 'toll the bell of tight resources'. In conclusion, while admitting that there might still be cogent reasons for withholding funding which had not been explored, Laws J ordered that the authority's decision be reconsidered in the light of his judgment.

Almost predictably in the light of previous decisions in which the allocation of resources formed a part,[19] the Court of Appeal reversed this order emphasising, in general, that its function was to rule upon the lawfulness of decisions – not to express opinions as to the merits of medical judgment. In particular, the court rejected the suggestion that the wishes of the parents had been inadequately considered; in fact, the authority was under great pressure from the parents and had taken its decision in response to that pressure. Secondly, Sir Thomas Bingham MR considered that, by any showing, the treatment was at the frontier of medical science. Thirdly, he held:

19 See chapter 11, p 296 above.

I have no doubt that in a perfect world any treatment which a patient ... sought would be provided if doctors were willing to give it, no matter how much it cost ... It would, however, be shutting one's eyes to the real world if the court were to proceed on the basis that we do live in such a world.[20]

And, further, the court cannot make a judgment as to how a limited budget is to be best allocated. In the end, it was open to the health authority to reach the decision they had already reached. We should, as a coda, note that B's treatment was ultimately funded from both private and public sources; she died 14 months after the hearing. All the doctors involved agreed that B's life under treatment was likely to be oppressive; can one say that the gain of a year of such life negates the imprint of medical futility? – we have our doubts.

The case of Child B provided the perfect setting for 'shroud-waving' in the popular press; an in-depth analysis of the media coverage shows the extent of the pressures exerted.[1] It was, of course, unfortunate that clinical and economic considerations became entwined and, inevitably, the press saw the issue almost exclusively in financial terms; the situation was, however, bound to arise as the funding for what are known as 'extra-contractual referrals' – or the purchase of medical services outside the particular health authority – is subject to special regulation. But was *ex p B* an attempt to impose resource rationing under the cloak of medical futility? We think not. An authority must abide by the decisions of its expert advisers who were unanimous that the suggested treatment was contraindicated. In the circumstances, the authority might well have been regarded as behaving unreasonably if it *had* persisted with treatment. At the most, its attitude could be seen as part of the now familiar balancing exercise; we will never know what would have been the decision had the proposed regime not been quite so extravagant of public money – or, on the other side of the coin, had not involved quite such risk and discomfort to the patient.

Re T and *ex p B* may seem to be at odds, in that the Court of Appeal recognised the interests of the parents as having a high priority in the former and rejected them in the latter. The cynic might say that this is simply a matter of health care economics – that parental interests will be supported when they pose no threat to the pocket of the NHS. The alternative and, in our view, better approach is to see the two decisions as consistent. We do not disguise our suspicions as to the correctness of that in *Re T*. The fact remains that the court conducted a balancing act in both cases and, rightly or wrongly, concluded that the risks and suffering involved in treatment outweighed the chances of success. Certainly, the decisive evidence came from opposing corners but, at the end of the day, the lesson is that the courts will not impose what they, having heard the medical evidence, regard as medically futile – or, better, non-productive – treatment of children who are central to a conflict of opinion.

20 (1995) 23 BMLR 1 at 8-9.

1 V A Entwistle, I S Watt, R Bradbury and L J Pehl ' Media Coverage of the Child B Case' (1996) 312 BMJ 1587.

Comparative common law experience

The American experience in this field of neonatal and paediatric medicine demonstrates a somewhat turbulent history. Three cases in the late 1970s indicate that there was, at that time, a strong legal bias in favour of the infant's right to a sanctity of life approach. Opinions were handed down such as: 'If there is any life-saving treatment available, it must be given regardless of the quality of life that will result'[2] or 'Children are not property whose disposition is left to parental decision without hindrance'[3] and, in general, extensive surgery was ordered so long as it was feasible. However, a change appeared in the next decade. In *Weber v Stony Brook Hospital*,[4] the Court of Appeal in New York would not overturn a judgment to the effect that, in refusing permission for surgery, the parents had 'elected a treatment which was within accepted medical standards'; 'to allow [a guardian]' it was said 'to bypass the statutory requirements would catapult him into the very heart of a family circle to challenge the parents' responsibility to care for their children'. The decision in *Re Infant Doe*[5] was that the value of parental autonomy outweighed the infant's right to live when 'a minimally adequate quality of life was non-existent' – this despite the fact that the anatomic abnormality present in association with Down's syndrome was amenable to relatively routine surgery; moreover, the case arose in Indiana, which was, at the time, the only state in which the life of the newborn was protected by statute. It has been described as a case: 'in which a baby whose life could almost certainly have been saved was starved to death under color of law'.[6]

The position then became even more turbulent. *Infant Doe* provoked presidential reaction on the grounds that selective non-treatment contravened federal laws protecting the handicapped; hospitals receiving federal aid were reminded that they were prohibited from withholding life-saving medical or surgical treatment from handicapped infants. Particular attention was paid to the provision of nourishment, fluids and routine nursing care – items which were not considered options for medical judgment: 'no health care provider should take it upon itself to cause death by starvation or dehydration.' Nevertheless, the United States District Court for the District of Columbia rapidly invalidated these rules by declaring, inter alia, that the Rehabilitation Act 1973, s 504, which protects the rights of the handicapped, 'could never be applied blindly and without any consideration of the burdens and intrusions which might result'.[7] The Federal regulations were, therefore, revised but were again struck down.[8]

Subsequently, the call for legislation has been strong in the United States and has ultimately been met by the Child Abuse Amendments of 1984 which amend the Federal Child Abuse Prevention and Treatment Act 1974.[9] The essential thrust is that,

2   *Re McNulty* No 1960 Probate Court (Mass, 1980) following *Maine Medical Center v Houle* No 74-145, Sup Ct (Me, 1974).
3   *Re Cicero* 421 NYS 2d 965 (1979).
4   456 NE 2d 1186 (NY, 1983).
5   (1982) GU 8204-004 A (Monroe County Cir, 12 April), cert denied 52 USLW 3369 (US, 1983). See G P Smith 'Defective Newborns and Government Intermeddling' (1985) 25 Med Sci & L 44.
6   N Lund 'Infanticide, Physicians and the Law' (1985) 11 Am J Law Med 1.
7   *American Academy of Paediatrics v Heckler* 561 F Supp 395 (DDC, 1983),
8   *American Hospital Association v Heckler* 105 S Ct 3475. The death knell was sounded in *Bowen v American Hospital Association* 106 S Ct 2101 (1986).
9   The onus of monitoring and enforcing the Act remains with the individual states.

having defined medical neglect, the amendments lay down the circumstances in which withholding medically indicated treatment would not be so described. These include the presence of irreversible coma, when treatment would merely prolong dying and when treatment would be futile or inhumane – but correction of a simple complication of Down's syndrome is not included as an exception.

There have been two notable developments in more recent years. First, the United States appears to be the only country in which xenotransplantation has been actually attempted as a treatment of last resort. Given the current state of the art, we would regard the procedure as an outstanding example of medical futility; the subject in general and the case of Baby Fae in particular are, however, discussed in chapter 14.[10] Second, and very much to the point in the present discussion, we have had the case of *Baby K*.[11]

Baby K was born an anencephalic and, accordingly had no cognitive abilities or awareness; she was, however placed on a ventilator because of respiratory distress. Given a prognosis of death within a few days, the hospital doctors recommended supportive care only; in so far as there is no cure for anencephaly and, hence, there was no remedy for the child's mental state, treatment was considered futile and both medically and ethically inappropriate. However, her mother, who had already refused a recommended termination of pregnancy, had a firm belief in God's unique responsibility for human life, insisted on mechanical ventilation when required – and this was, in fact, provided on at least three occasions. The hospital then sought a declaration that it was not required to provide respiratory support and this application was refused by the district court. It is, for present purposes, unfortunate that the Appeals Court was constitutionally unable 'to address the moral or ethical propriety of providing emergency stabilizing medical treatment to anencephalic infants' and the issue became one of the interpretation of statute – EMTALA[12] – which, effectively, requires hospitals to provide 'stabilising' treatment in an emergency situation to any person who comes to hospital and requests treatment.

In the event, the case was decided in favour of the mother on the narrow ground that the statute applied – but this was because the treatment requested was for respiratory distress rather than for anencephaly. But, in so concluding, a number of other problems were addressed. First, it was held that the parents have a constitutional right to make medical decisions on behalf of their children[13] and that no such right is accorded to physicians in their choice of treatments. At first glance, this seems

---

10 See p 339 above.
11 *In the matter of Baby K* 832 F Supp 1022 (ED Va, 1993), affd 16 F 3d 590 (4th Cir, 1994); cert denied 1994 US App Lexis 5461. The greater part of the information on this case is taken from E J Flannery 'One Advocate's Viewpoint: Conflicts and Tensions in the *Baby K* Case' (1995) 23 Law Med & Ethics 7 and E W Clayton 'Commentary: What is Really at Stake in *Baby K*?' (1995) 23 Law Med & Ethics 13. For further commentary, see 'Anti-dumping Law: Application to Anencephalic Infants' (1993) 19 Am J Law Med 548.
12 Emergency Medical Treatment and Active Labor Act 1992. Other statutes were cited including the Rehabilitation Act 1973, which prohibits health providers from discriminating on the basis of handicap or disability in the provision of medical care.
13 This cannot, however, be absolute, as argued by Clayton, n 11 above. It is to be noted that exceptions such as those associated with the management of children of Jehovah's Witnesses (see p 249 above) can be explained in that these may cause harm to the child who is, then, covered by the child abuse laws.

entirely contrary to the British position as expressed in *ex p B*;[14] it has to be remembered, however, that the court in *Baby K* was concerned only with statute and not the 'best interests' of K. Second, the courts in *Baby K* rejected the hospital's submission on the grounds that its proposals for non-treatment were based on the child's disability rather than on its respiratory condition. Although the reasoning was different, this is, to an extent, a reflection of the seminal English case of *Re B*; there is, however, a world of difference between Down's syndrome and anencephaly – there is little doubt that, were a *Baby K* case to come to the English courts, it would be treated as one of Templeman LJ's exceptions destined to a demonstrably awful life.[15] Finally, *Baby K*, again, leads us to the definition of futility. It is arguable that intensive care was 'useful' to K in that it restored her respirations. Equally, however, it was 'futile' in that that was not a worthwhile achievement from the patient's point of view. We are then faced with the recurring problem – ought we, and can we, isolate the patient's interests from those of other involved parties, including those of the state? And if we cannot, ought treatment decisions to be left solely in the hands of the physician? In the end, the *Baby K* decision was policy-based – the courts were unwilling to undermine a general statute in order to solve a particular dilemma; the outcome might have been very different had the courts been able to consider the patient's 'best interests'. We suggest that *Baby K* will not be the last American word on the subject.

The Canadian courts have also addressed the problem. In the most influential case,[16] it was held that parental refusal to allow replacement of a shunt for the alleviation of hydrocephalus might result in increasing disability and pain for the child and the operation was ordered. In discussion of this case, Dickens[17] suggested that the court was concentrating on the brain, and particularly its capacity to experience pain, as the central focus of human personality.

An apposite case to come before the Australian court is *Re F*.[18] In his judgment, Vincent J put it:

> No parent, no doctor, no court, has any power to determine that the life of any child, however disabled that child may be, will be deliberately taken from it . . . [the law] does not permit decisions to be made concerning the quality of life, nor does it enable any assessment to be made as to the value of any human being.

The judge was addressing himself to the specific problem of feeding, but, nevertheless, it would seem to state clearly the law as it stands in Australia.

---

14 For discussion, see F H Miller 'Infant Resuscitation: A US/UK Divide (1994) 343 Lancet 1584. *Baby K* is a very interesting case in the present context but is probably not a particularly influential US case in relation to parental rights – for which see *Weber v Stony Brook Hospital* 456 NE 2d 1186 (NY, 1983); *Bowen v American Hospital Association* 476 US 620, 106 S Ct 2101 (1986).
15 *Re B (a minor)* (1981) [1990] 1 All ER 927 at 929, [1981] 1 WLR 1421 at 1424.
16 *Re Superintendent of Family and Child Service and Dawson* (1983) 145 DLR (3d) 610 at 621. The case was quoted with particular approval in *Re J*.
17 B M Dickens 'Withholding Paediatric Medical Care' (1984) Can BR 196.
18 *Re F, F v F* (2 July 1986, unreported), Supreme Court of Victoria.

Is the treatment of infants a separate issue?

Thus far, we have concentrated on the neonate and the infant. The discussion has been long and we must ask if there is good reason for this emphasis. There are at least two good reasons for isolating the issues in early life from those in adulthood or those which are essentially perimortal. In the first place, decisions in the first situation rest almost entirely on prognosis, which is another way of expressing an informed guess as to the future. This may, in any event, be difficult and, while we know that we are dealing with only short-term survival at the end of life, this is not the case at birth – we may be confident of what will be the state of affairs next week but we cannot say the same about the next decade. Moreover, the neonate is not passing from a settled norm into a progressively less satisfactory condition; he is developing in a sub-optimal milieu which is his norm – can one say with any certainty that the mongol, who has never known anything different, is dissatisfied with his existence within himself? Thus, we would take issue with the reasoning of Professor Williams, who wrote: 'If a wicked fairy told me she was about to transform me into a Down's baby and would I prefer to die I should certainly answer yes',[19] because this is not the question being asked of the infant. The better view is that of Lord Donaldson – that the starting point in analysing the defective's condition is not what might have been but what is.[20]

The second major distinction between life and death decisions at the extremes of life is that, while the adult sufferer is likely to be able to express an opinion or, save in a few cases, to have previously intimated his wishes, there is no way in which the neonate can consent to treatment, suffering or death. Consent must be parental and one then asks where, in fact, do lie the parents' rights that it is feared will be usurped by the courts? Have they any more right to reject a child than to abandon it? If it can be criminal to disbar an older child from treatment,[1] why is it less culpable to fail, or to connive at failure, to provide the minimum of neonatal treatment – infant feeding? How do these rights differ when exercised in the light of medical advice rather than by way of simple intuition in the privacy of the home? Is it likely that a blind eye would be turned on parents who, on their own initiative, decided to abandon their defective child? And can the parents who are, in addition to their emotional involvement, economically and socially concerned, make a truly objective decision on behalf of the child?[2]

These questions have, in the main, an ethical or social dimension. *Re C* and the *Re J* cases have, we suggest, clarified the criminal aspects of neonaticide and there is little doubt that non-treatment decisions are now taken on a daily basis.[3] Campbell,[4] writing on severely brain damaged children, believed that anything, including

---

19 G Williams 'Down's Syndrome and the Duty to Preserve Life' (1981) 131 NLJ 1020.
20 In *Re J (a minor) (wardship: medical treatment)* [1990] 3 All ER 930 at 936, (1990) 6 BMLR 25 at 32, paraphrasing McKenzie J.
1 *R v Senior* [1899] 1 QB 283, CCR. The accrual of rights with age is discussed by C Wells 'Whose Baby Is It?' (1988) 5 J Law & Soc 323.
2 A useful modern overview is to be found in S Moor 'Euthanasia in Relation to Newborn Babies – A Comparative Study of the Legal and Ethical Issues' (1996) 15 Med Law 295 and 537.
3 For an up-to-date review, see A G M Campbell and H E McHaffie 'Prolonging Life and Allowing Death: Infants' (1995) 21 J Med Ethics 339.
4 A G M Campbell 'Children in a Persistent Vegetative State' (1984) 289 BMJ 1022.

feeding, that prolongs such non-human or artificial life is 'wrong for the child, wrong for the family and wrong for society'. This, however, clearly depends on a value evaluation of the quality of life and, consequently, on a largely undefined discretion.[5] While it may well be an expression of the current state of the law, we suggest that decision-makers in the field should be wary of extending the bounds of *Re J* with impunity – life clearly carried great weight in Lord Donaldson's balance pan and does so in those of his successors.

What we *have* seen, is that the English courts are resolute in distinguishing between non-treatment and euthanasia and, in this respect, the fundamental distinction to be made is between, on the one hand, infants with pure mental defects and, at the other extreme, those with severe physical incapacity resulting, for example, from neural tube defects. Treatment of the latter is a matter of careful medical management which must incorporate an element of selection.[6] Many such handicapped children will inevitably die and many should be allowed to do so; the principle of 'allowing nature to take its course' on the basis of a shared decision between doctor and parents is acceptable in both a moral and a legal sense provided that the decision is taken in the best interests of the child.[7] By contrast, if the mentally handicapped child is not to live, it must be encouraged and guided towards death. There is no non-treatment for the anatomically normal Down's baby because it needs no treatment and failure to feed in the latter instance can only be categorised as neonaticide – ie *killing* of the neonate, which brings us back to the question of whether there is, in fact, any true difference between non-treatment and euthanasia. Kuhse[8] has argued most persuasively that there is no moral or legal distinction to be drawn between activity and passivity in this area of medical practice. Gillon[9] put it:

> While there may be some social benefit in distinguishing between actively 'allowing to die' and painlessly killing such infants, there is, I believe, no other moral difference and doctors who accept such 'allowing to die' of severely handicapped newborn infants should not deceive themselves into believing that there is such a difference.

Elsewhere, the same author emphasised that, while there is no *necessary* moral difference between killing and letting die, it does not follow that there is a moral equivalence.[10] Were this so, we would have to approve the spectre of the paediatrician

---

5 See, in particular, C Wells '"Otherwise Kill Me": Marginal Children at the Edges of Existence' in R Lee and D Morgan (eds) *Birthrights* (1989) ch 11.

6 For a philosophical assessment, see J Harris 'Ethical Problems in the Management of Some Severely Handicapped Children' (1981) 7 J Med Ethics 117. Results from the coalface are reported in A Whitelaw 'Death as an Option in Neonatal Intensive Care' [1986] Lancet 328 and, more recently, I M Balfour-Lynn and R C Tasker 'Futility and Death in Paediatric Medical Intensive Care' (1996) 22 J Med Ethics 279.

7 D D Raphael 'Handicapped Infants: Medical Ethics and the Law' (1988) 14 J Med Ethics 5 pointed out the conceptual difficulty in attributing any *interest* in death – 'the most you can say is that someone would prefer to die'.

8 H Kuhse 'A Modern Myth. That Letting Die is not the Intentional Causation of Death: Some Reflections on the Trial and Acquittal of Dr Leonard Arthur' (1984) 1 J Appl Philos 21. The same point is made by Harris, n 6 above.

9 R Gillon 'Conclusion. The *Arthur* Case Revisited' (1986) 292 BMJ 543.

10 R Gillon 'Euthanasia. Withholding Life-Prolonging Treatment and Moral Differences between Killing and Letting Die' (1988) 14 J Med Ethics 115.

armed with a lethal syringe – and the concept is quite unacceptable. As we discuss in chapter 16, in relation to the permanent vegetative state, it is hard to assail the logic which says that a quick death is preferable to one which depends upon the vagaries of nature; nevertheless, we believe that natural death is the only acceptable concomitant of a decision not to treat a severely physically defective infant – and we also believe that food and water should be provided for any child which is capable of taking nourishment by mouth. In so saying, we admit to being guided, to a very considerable extent, by moral intuition alone – as a well-respected medical philosopher has put it: 'We are, here, noting a deep human inhibition which it might be unwise to tamper with in the name of logic.'[11] Clinicians are similarly beset by the illogic of intuition:

> There is a powerful psychological distinction [between 'killing' and 'allowing to die'] which is important to the staff of intensive care units. To them, there is a big difference between not using a respirator to keep an infant of 600 g alive and giving a lethal injection, although the end result is the same.[12]

And, whatever logic may tell us, *Re J* spells out clearly what is the law. The situation is one in which the most acceptable course is not, unhappily, the kindest.

Advances in modern medicine have, at the same time, brought their own problems to the neonatal period. It is increasingly possible to maintain and rear premature infants of low birth weight and evidence is accumulating that a number of such children are disadvantaged to an extent which is inversely proportionate to their birthweight – thus, some 12-19% of extremely low birthweight babies (less than 1 kg) who have survived will be severely handicapped.[13] The discussion of selective non-treatment is, accordingly, being extended to include attitudes to intensive care of the premature infant. It is trite medicine to say that premature births should be prevented by improved ante-natal care. The fact remains that they will continue and their numbers will be augmented not so much due to poor maternal care as by the improved medical management of high-risk pregnancies. In these circumstances, we can see little alternative but to agree with those who believe that, since an accurate prognosis is generally impossible, such infants should always be offered treatment until such time as it is clearly ineffective – the test for treatment is, on these terms, one of feasibility – not of futility. The difficulty of such a rule is that, while resuscitation may be successful, the end result may be a severely handicapped survivor; quite apart from the individual clinical result, there may also be a serious problem of resource distribution:

> The ability to preserve the lives of these infants must be weighed against the resultant increase in the numbers of impaired children, the distress and suffering caused by lengthy

11 R S Downie 'Modern Paediatric Practice: An Ethical Overview' (1989) in Mason, p 366, n 16 above, ch 31.
12 A G M Campbell 'Ethical Issues in Child Health and Disease' in J O Forfar (ed) *Child Health in a Changing Society* (1988).
13 V Yu 'The Extremely Low Birthweight Infant: Ethical Issues in Treatment' (1987) 23 Austral Paediatric J 97; L W Doyle, L J Murton and W H Kitchen 'Increasing the Survival of Extremely-immature (24-28 weeks' gestation) Infants – At what Cost ?' (1989) 150 Med J Austral 558.

treatment and hospitalisation, their eventual expected quality of life, and the socio-economic consequences for society as a whole.[14]

We have discovered only two relevant cases – strangely, both from Scottish fatal accident inquiries and, accordingly, poorly reported. In the first, the decision not to resuscitate an extremely premature infant was regarded as a reasonable medical option – legal intervention resulted only from a failure in communication between physicians and parents.[15] A similar finding was recorded in the second which involved the death of a 23-week-old neonate. The sheriff ruled that 'the doctor's decision not to resuscitate was made in the best interests of the child and was a reasonable clinical decision in the circumstances . . . The doctor's clinical judgment had to take precedence over the wishes of the parents'. Since this is one of the clearest judicial statements on the relative rights of the parents to come from Scotland, it is something of a pity that the case went no further.[16] Any similar actions in negligence brought in the civil courts would almost certainly fail on the application of the *Bolam* and *Hunter v Hanley* principles of approved medical practice.[17]

A need for legislation?

Despite the doubts expressed above, it is not difficult to argue that the medical practitioner still needs more official guidance and legal protection when undertaking selective non-treatment decisions. The current vogue in the United Kingdom when the common or statute law is unclear as to detail is for the creation of 'guidelines' by an authoritative body. These generally do not have the force of law but their non-observance will reflect adversely on the person who fails to follow them. As we have already noted, such a document relating to paediatric practice is now available.[18] In summary, this outlines five situations where the withholding or withdrawal of curative medical treatment might be considered:

(a) *The brain dead child.* Once the diagnosis of brain death has been made, it is agreed within the profession that treatment in such circumstances is futile and withdrawal is appropriate.[19]
(b) *The permanent vegetative state.* We discuss this state below.[20]

---

14 J Griffin, quoted by L Hunt 'Cost "Dilemma" Posed by Premature Babies' (1993) Independent, 20 January, p 6 in discussion of Office of Health Economics *Born Too Soon* (1993).
15 D Brahams 'No Obligation to Resuscitate a Non-viable Infant' [1988] 1 Lancet 1176.
16 S English 'Doctor Was Right not to Resuscitate "Unviable" Baby' (1997) The Times, 27 June, p 11.
17 *Bolam v Friern Hospital Management Committee* [1957] 2 All ER 118, (1957) 1 BMLR 1; *Hunter v Hanley* 1955 SC 200, 1955 SLT 213, for which see chapter 9.
18 See p 376, n 5 above.
19 It will be seen from chapter 13 that we regard this as something of a contradiction in terms; the child is dead and you cannot *treat* a corpse. There is specific case law to the effect that the health carers cannot be compelled to do so: *Re A* [1992] 3 Med LR 303.
20 See p 394.

(c) *The 'no chance' situation.* The child has such severe disease that life sustaining treatment simply delays death without alleviation of suffering. Medical treatment may, thus, be deemed inappropriate.
(d) *The 'no purpose' situation.* Although the patient may be able to survive with treatment, the degree of physical or mental impairment will be so great that it is unreasonable to expect them to bear it. The child in this situation will never be capable of taking part in decisions regarding treatment or its withdrawal.
(e) *The 'unbearable' situation.* The child and/or family feel that, in the face of progressive and irreversible illness, *further* treatment is more than can be borne. These wishes are irrespective of the medical opinion on its potential benefit.

In situations that do not fit these five categories, or where there is dissent or uncertainty about the degree of future impairment, the child's life should be safeguarded in the best possible way.

Contemporaneously, the Dutch Paediatric Association have issued guidelines which include prognostic implications based on function:

– what communicative abilities will the child have later?
– will he or she be able to lead an independent life?
– will the child be continuously dependent on medical care?
– will he or she suffer, mentally or physically?
– how long is the life expectancy?

As a result, four options are regarded as being available: to continue intensive care and extend if necessary; to maintain the status quo (which can only be a temporary measure); to stop the most intensive treatment; or to stop all life-prolonging measures.[1] The code stresses the importance of the parents' wishes and of the involvement of the whole health care team. Such a code of practice would be generally acceptable and the principles are no doubt being followed widely even if not 'codified'. The majority of decisions are, often, not difficult to make but there is always the core of problem cases where a severely disabled infant is able to survive without intensive therapy. The Dutch solution, here, might well be active euthanasia.[2] This, however, would currently be unacceptable in the United Kingdom and judicial opinion voiced in *Bland*[3] is firmly of the view that the legality of euthanasia – including by way of withdrawal of sustenance – should be a matter of legislation.[4]

Equally, however, there is ample authority supporting the premise that there are some infants who *ought* not to be assisted to live by invasive methods. The incapacitated child has as much right to die in peace as has his grandfather and there

1 Working Group of the Dutch Paediatric Association (C Versluys, chairman) *To Do or Not to Do? Boundaries for Medical Action in Neonatology* (1992). See C Versluys 'Ethics of Neonatal Care' (1993) 341 Lancet 794.
2 See chapter 17 for discussion of the Dutch approach to ending life.
3 *Airedale NHS Trust v Bland* [1993] 1 All ER 821, (1993) 12 BMLR 64.
4 A Select Committee of the House of Lords has reiterated its opposition to euthanasia in the absence of legislation: *Report of the Select Committee on Medical Ethics* HL Paper 21, 1994.

are times when it is clear that that right should be exercised. Moreover, it is now clear that a responsible clinician who believes that to be the right course cannot be compelled to provide treatment with which he disagrees.[5] Nevertheless, while there is probably now sufficient case law to justify non-treatment decisions, many would hold that clarifying legislation is still desirable if only to do no more than relieve the clinician of an *accusation* of homicide in such circumstances. Moreover, legislation can anticipate and forestall the 'domino effect'. It does not need much imagination, for example, to envisage parental rejection of the newborn as being justified by a club foot or even unattractive features.

The case of *Baby K* has already demonstrated the difficulties that surround *positive* legislation in fields such as this and, in our view, statute law ought not to create new offences – it should do no more than lay down the conditions under which a doctor who withholds or withdraws treatment commits no offence. Furthermore, since legislation is always difficult to adapt to changing circumstances, it should be relatively non-specific and should allow for the free exercise of clinical decision-making in individual cases. If there were to be legislation – and we discuss the need further under the heading of the permanent vegetative state[6] – we suggest the inclusion of a clause to the effect:

> In the event of positive treatment being necessary for a neonate's survival, it will not be an offence to withhold such treatment if two doctors, one of whom is a consultant paediatrician, acting in good faith and with the consent of both parents if available, decide against treatment in the light of a reasonably clear medical prognosis which indicates that the infant's further life would be intolerable by virtue of pain or suffering or because of severe cerebral incompetence.

We believe that, on the one hand, this emphasises the interests of the infant while, on the other, it clarifies and protects the legal position of paediatricians who are forced into making particularly stressful clinical decisions. Open legislation is best backed by guidelines for decision-making and we have attempted to evolve a consensus view.[7] Essentially, this proposes that positive treatment which is needed for the infant's survival may be withheld when: (a) there is corroborated opinion that the decision is medically proper; (b) there is adequate written explanation of the decision; (c) the parents have been enabled to give, or refuse, an information-based consent; and (d) the decision is made with the interests of the child providing the guiding principle. We also suggest that any treatment of the newborn which has been instituted may be abandoned if death is highly probable regardless of treatment, or if there is no reasonable possibility that the infant will be able to participate in normal

---

5   *Re J (a minor) (medical treatment)* [1993] Fam 15, (1992) 9 BMLR 10. Interestingly, one of the reasons given was that to do so might require the health authority to use intensive care resources and, thereby, to deny them to someone who might derive greater benefit ([1993] Fam 15 at 29, (1992) 9 BMLR 10 at 20, per Balcombe LJ). The implication is that the courts see a difference between not starting a life-saving treatment and withdrawing it (see chapter 17).
6   See p 407 below.
7   J K Mason and D W Meyers 'Parental Choice and Selective Non-treatment of Defective Newborns: A View from Mid-Atlantic' (1986) 12 J Med Ethics 67.

human relationships, or if the treatment cannot alleviate a level of chronic pain which makes continued life-preserving therapy inhumane.[8]

None of these codes really address the critical dilemma of the infant who satisfies all the requirements but still survives without treatment. We find it difficult, if not impossible, to disagree with those who hold that normal feeding, not involving medical intervention, should be continued whenever the infant is capable of taking nourishment by mouth – yet we have to acknowledge that there are times when this does not seem to be in the neonate's best interests in terms of suffering. The status of normal feeding is, however, again best discussed under the heading of PVS, where the problem has been fully addressed in the courts.[9]

The interests of others

No practical solutions to the ending of life can be applied without giving thought to those who must participate in any process and, in particular to those who have a conscientious objection to the procedures. Were there to be any legislation which legalises the withholding or withdrawal of treatment in specified circumstances, it must, in our view, include a discretionary clause similar to that in the Abortion Act 1967, s 4. We draw particular attention to the role of the nursing staff and to the importance of safeguarding their position both now and in the event of legislation. It is the nurses, not the doctors, who will bear the brunt of selective non-treatment; not only must they be spared responsibility for carrying out instructions but, also, their sensitivities must be fully respected. We strongly commend the increasingly accepted principle of a team approach to neonatal intensive care.[10]

We believe that current court decisions have done much to define parental powers in this area. No one would deny that the parents' views should be ascertained, nor that they should carry great weight – but they cannot be determinative. It has to be reiterated that non-treatment decisions are taken routinely with complete co-operation between the health care team and the parents – it is only when there is disagreement that cases attract the publicity of the courts. None the less, common attitudes to the disposal of abnormal infants are based on the assumption of marital harmony, in that they relate so firmly to the wishes of 'the parents' – what if there is disagreement? We suggest that terminating the life of the neonate differs distinctly from abortion in that, while the father has no decision-making right in the latter, he should have a voice equal to the mother's as to the management of an abnormal baby once it is born.

Fortunately, the situation must arise only rarely. Nevertheless, while the birth of a defective child may uncover qualities of goodness in the parents that are beyond

---

8 Although reached independently, these conclusions are very similar to those found in the amendments to the US Child Abuse Prevention and Treatment Act 1974 (see p 382 above) and to those set out by the Canadian Paediatric Society; they are also compatible with the teaching of the Roman Catholic Church: *Care of the Handicapped Newborn: Parental Responsibility and Medical Responsibility* (1986).

9 See p 447 below.

10 The point was well taken in the judgment in *Re C (a minor) (wardship: medical treatment)* [1990] Fam 26, [1989] 2 All ER 782.

expectation, there can be no doubt that an opposite reaction can be provoked.[11] Raphael[12] concluded that the current medical perspective in this field differs markedly from that of the common law; it is essential that the medical and legal professions – as well as society at large – should make sure of the lines they intend to draw in the face of potential conflict, whether this be inter-professional of inter-parental.

11 See B Shepperdson 'Abortion and Euthanasia of Down's Syndrome Children – The Parents' View' (1983) 9 J Med Ethics 152. And, for an interesting debate: 'Informed Dissent': M Simms 'The Views of Some Mothers of Severely Mentally Handicapped Young Adults'; A Davis 'The View of a Disabled Woman' (1986) 12 J Med Ethics 72, 75.
12 (1988) 14 J Med Ethics 5, p 371, n 3 above.

16 Medical futility: 2 Later life

We have suggested in the previous chapter that the concept of medical futility can be applied as a continuum across the whole range from the neonate to the terminally ill. The full picture is, however, not quite so simple, as the underlying reasons for, and the management of, non-treatment will vary according to age. Thus, non-treatment in infancy has been, at least in part, a matter of the management of physical disability. But this has been morally permissible only because treatment of itself would result in an intolerable life which it would be inhumane to enforce on the child who would, at the same time, die naturally if it were untreated. Such conditions are uncommon in adult life and, when they do occur – as, for example, in accidental quadriplegia – their management is more allied to euthanasia[1] than to selective non-treatment.

Disability due to brain damage is, however, common to both infancy and adulthood and we have seen that, while the courts will not tolerate the deliberate shortening of life, they are fully prepared to accede to non-treatment of associated lethal disease in the severely brain-damaged child – and to base this on an undeniably 'quality of life 'standard as measured by a 'best interests' test. It is of some interest to speculate on why it is that this has been accepted relatively easily in the case of children while the legal attitude to the management of the brain damaged adult has taken so long to mature and has done so amid so much controversy. Is it that we give greater weight to life that has 'been lived' than to life which has no past? Do we see a sustainable distinction between starting on a disabled life and continuing life in a disabled state? Are we less concerned with any residual cognitive ability in the infant than we are with comparable but expressible brain activity in the adult? And are we frightened of an ever-widening definition of what is perceived as intolerable in the adult? Possibly the most important delineator lies in the purely pragmatic reason that fatal intercurrent disease is simply less common in the brain damaged adult in whom, accordingly, non-treatment moves ever closer to euthanasia and, as a result, becomes less acceptable.

Yet we are constantly assured that we are *not* practising euthanasia in allowing such persons to die. Thus, we have Hoffmann LJ saying:

> This is not a case about euthanasia because it does not involve any external agency of death. It is about whether, and how, the patient should be allowed to die.[2]

It is for this reason that we have detached the management of the brain damaged adult – and, particularly, the adult in the permanent vegetative state – from our

---

1 See Chapter 17.
2 In *Airedale NHS Trust v Bland* [1993] 1 All ER 821 at 856, (1993) 12 BMLR 64 at 101, CA.

discussion of euthanasia. Legally – if less certainly logically – it sits easier under the heading of 'futile treatment'; as Lord Goff put it in the House of Lords in *Bland,* 'it is the futility of the treatment [of Anthony Bland] which justifies its termination'.[3]

The patient in the permanent vegetative state

We have already discussed the effect of hypoxia on the various segments of the brain. In clinical terms, this means that depriving the brain of oxygen can result in anything from mild intellectual deterioration to death – the outcome being determined almost exclusively by how rapidly normal oxygenation can be established. How much consciousness or cognitive ability is retained then depends on the degree of cortical damage and this can be of very considerable moral and medico-legal significance. In any event, the brain stem – which controls our vegetative functions – will survive an hypoxic insult better than will the cortex, and the truly critical situation arises when the cortex is wholly destroyed but the brain stem continues to function. This is the condition which was originally described as the 'persistent vegetative state' by Jennett and Plum.[4] The patient then has no consciousness and the critical nature of the condition is summed up in the phrase: 'Consciousness is the most critical moral, legal, and constitutional standard, not for human life itself, but for human personhood'[5] – the unconscious or comatose patient is incapable of fulfilling his human function in a way which transcends the loss of any other capacity; it follows that the whole status of the person in a position of persistent unconsciousness is in doubt.

It is notoriously difficult to identify a satisfactory definition of the persistent vegetative state. The distinguishing features include an irregular but cyclic state of circadian sleeping and waking unaccompanied by any behaviourally detectable expression of self-awareness, specific recognition of external stimuli, or consistent evidence of attention or inattention or learned responses.[6] It is important to note that patients in this state, while generally being in a spastic condition, are not immobile and, to a varying extent, retain both cranial-nerve and spinal reflexes, including those related to visual and auditory stimuli. Again, this reflects the degree of brain damage; we can, therefore, speak in terms of degrees of vegetativeness, although it requires skilled neurological expertise to distinguish retained – or recovered – cortical function from sub-cortical reflex activity. It is also to be noted that the persistent vegetative state is to be distinguished from coma.

Even so, the concept has its own semantic difficulties, the most urgent of which lies in the word 'persistent'. A persistent state is one which persists until it is relieved – from which it follows that the diagnosis of the persistent vegetative state envisages a potential for recovery; this was the understanding of those who coined the term. It is, in our opinion, essential that discussion – and any legislation based upon it – should

---

3   [1993] 1 All ER 821 at 870, (1993) 12 BMLR 64 at 116.
4   B Jennett and F Plum 'Persistent Vegetative State after Brain Damage' (1972) 1 Lancet 734.
5   R E Cranford and D R Smith 'Consciousness: The Most Critical Moral (Constitutional) Standard for Human Personhood' (1987) 13 Am J Law Med 233.
6   Multi-society Task Force on PVS 'Medical Aspects of the Persistent Vegetative State' (1994) 330 New Engl J Med 1499 (Pt 1), 1572 (Pt 2).

be devoted to the management of the permanent vegetative state (PVS).[7] Even then, the difficulties are not all eliminated. Permanence is a presumption rather than a certainty; whether or not that presumption is acceptable depends on empirical evidence which must, also, bow to practicality. Thus, the Multi-society Task Force in America defined the persistent vegetative state as a vegetative state present one month after acute traumatic or non-traumatic brain injury; it concluded that a permanent state can be assumed if the patient has been vegetative for one year.[8] But to say that a state is permanent if it has been present for a year[9] involves a balancing act between reasonableness and certainty. The compromise, no matter how high is the degree of clinical certainty, is unlikely to satisfy everyone and the possibility of exceptions to the rule cannot be denied; nevertheless, the advantages of establishing a cut-off point outweigh the disadvantages of prolonging the decision indefinitely. Of equal importance is the fact that, as we have already noted, the word 'vegetative' fails to define the degree of brain damage involved. Therapeutic decisions in PVS thus depend not only on its permanence but also on the definition of vegetative which must, to an extent, involve a value judgment.

Having reached a diagnosis, however, we are left with what may well be regarded as the ultimate tragedy in human life – a human being who is alive in the cardiovascular sense in that he or she can breathe and maintain a heart beat, and who is, equally, not brain stem dead, but who, at the same time, has no contact with the outside world and will never have such contact again. We have discussed the concept of neocortical death above.[10] At this point we need only reiterate that it has no place in the law of the United Kingdom. The law as to killing is unaffected by the mental state of the victim – dements and aments are still protected in so far as the term 'reasonable being' implies no more than 'human being' – and persons in the permanent vegetative state still represent 'persons in being'. They present an extra jurisprudential difficulty in that, being unconscious, they are free from pain – or, at least, pain cannot be expressed in a manner which makes it treatable; the doctrine of 'double effect' cannot, therefore, be applied within their management – and, in this respect, it is to be noted that, absent an intercurrent infection or similar complication, well-managed PVS patients have a life expectancy that is to be measured in years. Lord Scarman,[11] while appreciating –

> that there are great social problems not only in the life support of the human vegetable but also in the survival of barely sentient people who cannot look after themselves,

also added:

> there are implications in the right to terminate another's existence of which it is well to be fearful in the absence of a more prolonged analysis of the problem than that which it has received.

---

7 See, especially, 'The Permanent Vegetative State – Review by a Working Group Convened by the Royal College of Physicians and Endorsed by the Conference of Medical Royal Colleges and their Faculties of the United Kingdom' (1996) 30 J R Coll Physicians Lond 119.
8 See p 394, n 6 above.
9 Agreed by the BMA: *BMA Guidelines on Treatment Decisions for Patients in Persistent Vegetative State* (1996) and by the Working Party of the Royal College of Physicians, n 7 above.
10 See p 330.
11 Lord Scarman 'Legal Liability and Medicine' (1981) 74 Proc Roy Soc Med 11.

These extra-judicial remarks were made some time ago and, since then, the topic has been subject to intense moral scrutiny and, recently, to extensive legal analysis. We have spent some time on the definitional difficulties of the condition because, without an understanding of them, it is impossible to appreciate the distinctions which have been made in the various cases that have come before the courts in recent years and the reasons underlying them. All those that we discuss have it in common that the courts were being invited to pronounce on the lawfulness of withdrawing physiological support from severely brain-damaged patients.

The English cases[12]

The first, and most important case in which the matter was addressed in the United Kingdom was *Airedale NHS Trust v Bland*.[13]   Anthony Bland was crushed in a football stadium in April 1989 and sustained severe anoxic brain damage; as a result, he relapsed into the persistent vegetative state. There was no improvement in his condition by September 1992 and, at that time, the hospital sought a declaration[14] to the effect that they might lawfully discontinue all life-sustaining treatment and medical support measures, including ventilation, nutrition and hydration by artificial means; that any subsequent treatment given should be for the sole purpose of enabling him to end his life in dignity and free from pain and suffering; that, if death should then occur, its cause should be attributed to the natural and other causes of his present state; and that none of those concerned should, as a result, be subject to any civil or criminal liability. This declaration – save for the final clause, which was considered inappropriate[15] – was granted in the Family Division essentially on the grounds that it was in AB's best interests to do so; the court considered there was overwhelming evidence that the provision of artificial feeding by means of a nasogastric tube was 'medical treatment' and that its discontinuance was in accord with good medical practice. An appeal was unanimously dismissed in the Court of Appeal. From three exceptionally well-considered opinions, we extract only that of Hoffmann LJ:

> This is not an area in which any difference can be allowed to exist between what is legal and what is morally right. The decision of the court should be able to carry conviction with the ordinary person as being based not merely on legal precedent but also upon acceptable ethical values.[16]

12 We have discussed these and other apposite cases in some detail in J K Mason and G T Laurie 'The Management of the Persistent Vegetative State in the British Isles' [1996] JR 263.

13 [1993] 1 All ER 821, (1993) 12 BMLR 64, Fam D, CA, HL.

14 The English courts have been in something of a dilemma in such cases since their authority under the parens patriae jurisdiction was removed by way of the Mental Health Act 1959 and revocation of the last warrant under the sign manual. The court cannot now give effective consent to medical treatment on behalf of a mentally incompetent adult unless that treatment is directed to the cause of the incompetence. The court can, however, make an anticipatory declaration as to the lawfulness or otherwise of a proposed action: see discussion of *Re F* at pp 253-254 above.

15 This problem was considered in greater detail in the comparable Scottish case *Law Hospital NHS Trust v Lord Advocate* 1996 SLT 848, (1996) 39 BMLR 166, for which see p 401ff below.

16 [1993] 1 All ER 821 at 850, (1993) 12 BMLR 64 at 95.

and, later:

> In my view the choice the law makes must reassure people that the courts do have full respect for life, but that they do not pursue the principle to the point at which it has become almost empty of any real content and when it involves the sacrifice of other important values such as human dignity and freedom of choice. I think that such reassurance can be provided by a decision, properly explained, to allow Anthony Bland to die.[17]

The inherent difficulty of the declarator procedure is that it is concerned only with the *lawfulness* of an action[18] and, when the *Bland* case came to the House of Lords, Lord Browne-Wilkinson and Lord Mustill were at particular pains to emphasise that the ethical issues should be considered and legislated for by Parliament:

> [I]s this a matter which lies outside the legitimate development of the law by judges and requires society, through the democratic expression of its views in Parliament, to reach its decisions on the underlying moral and practical problems and then reflect those decisions in legislation? I have no doubt that it is for Parliament, not the courts, to decide the broader issues which this case raises.[19]

It was, therefore, not surprising that, although the House could not entirely avoid addressing the ethical and moral problems involved, it did so to a lesser extent than did the Court of Appeal. In this respect, the fundamental conflict lies in the inevitable distortion of the principle of the sanctity of life which would result from a decision to terminate the care on which life depended.[20] The majority of the House was able to dispose of this on the grounds that the principle was certainly not absolute. Moreover, since the right to refuse treatment – including life-sustaining treatment – is now firmly part of common law and medical ethics, the principle of the sanctity of life must yield to that of the right to self-determination and, of the many lines of argument considered, it is this which seems to us to bind all five Law Lords most closely together. As Lord Goff put it,[1] the right to self-determination should not be eclipsed by the fact of incompetence – it must always be present. This also forms the basis of Lord Mustill's reasoning, which is summarised below and which, essentially, justifies the withdrawal or withholding of treatment. We are less happy with the alternative view taken, in particular, by Lord Lowry and Lord Browne-Wilkinson. In essence, this also started from the premise that non-voluntary treatment was lawful only so long as it was justified by necessity; but, once necessity could no longer be claimed – by reason of the futility of treatment – further invasion of the patient's body constituted either the crime of battery or the tort of trespass. On this view, any potential medical offence lies not in *withholding* treatment but in *continuing* it to no purpose. This argument seems to us to be dangerously open-ended in relation to conditions less clear-cut than the persistent vegetative state – a situation which Lord

17 [1993] 1 All ER 821 at 855, (1993) 12 BMLR 64 at 100.
18 See J Bridgeman '"Declared Innocent?"' (1995) 3 Med L Rev 117.
19 [1993] 1 All ER 821 at 878, (1993) 12 BMLR 64 at 124, per Browne-Wilkinson.
20 For major discussion, see J Keown 'Restoring Moral and Intellectual Shape to the Law after *Bland*' (1997) 113 LQR 481.
 1 [1993] 1 All ER 821 at 866, (1993) 12 BMLR 64 at 112.

Mustill was clearly anxious to avoid. It is better that a doctor, trained to preserve life, should be required to defend himself against failure to do so rather than for following his natural inclinations.

The greater part of the opinions was, accordingly, concerned for the doctors' position vis-à-vis the criminal law. First, it was essential to elide the possibility of murder by classifying removal of support as an omission rather than as a positive act.[2] There was wide agreement that, while there was no moral or logical difference, a distinction was certainly to be made in law. The House came to a unanimous conclusion that discontinuance of nasogastric feeding was an omission; their Lordships achieved this in various ways but, in general, it was considered impossible to distinguish between withdrawal of and not starting tube feeding – and the latter was clearly an omission. Next, the problem of the duty of care had to be addressed. Lord Mustill's argument can be summarised:

(a) Treatment of the incompetent is governed by necessity and necessity is, in turn, defined in terms of the patient's best interests.
(b) Once there is no hope of recovery, any interest in being kept alive disappears and, with it, the justification for invasive therapy also disappears.
(c) In the absence of necessity, there can be no duty to act and, in the absence of a duty, there can be no criminality in an omission.

This, however, leads to what was, perhaps, the major hurdle – can feeding be regarded as medical treatment and, therefore, a fit subject for medical decision-making, or is it always such a fundamental duty that it can never be wilfully withheld? The Lords in Bland had rather more trouble with this than have had their counterparts in the United States and we return to the subject in a little more detail below.[3] Eventually, however, a consensus was reached that nasogastric feeding at least formed part of the general medical management. While it is certainly more difficult to see nasogastric feeding as medical treatment than it is to accept gastrostomy feeding as such, we do not share some of the academic distrust of the concept that has been expressed.[4]

At the end of the day, the House of Lords was able to justify their unanimous decision on the basis of the patient's best interests. All the opinions stressed that it was not a matter of it being in the best interests of the patient to die but, rather, that it was not in his best interests to treat him so as to prolong his life in circumstances where 'no affirmative benefit' could be derived from the treatment.[5] We confess to some difficulty in accepting a 'best interests' test in these circumstances and we return to the matter below.[6] For the present, we point out that its application dictates the concurrent acceptance of 'good medical practice' as the yardstick of assessment. This led the House of Lords to conclude that the *Bolam* test [7] – that the doctor's decision

---

2   For further discussion of which, see chapter 17, p 430 below.
3   See p 408.
4   See, eg, J M Finnis 'Bland: Crossing the Rubicon?' (1993) 109 LQR 329.
5   [1993] 1 All ER 821 at 883, (1993) 12 BMLR 64 at 130, per Lord Browne-Wilkinson. See also [1993] 1 All ER 821 at 865, (1993) 12 BMLR 64 at 115.
6   See p 403ff.
7   *Bolam v Friern Hospital Management Committee* [1957] 1 WLR 582, (1957) 1 BMLR 1.

should be judged against one which would be taken by a responsible and competent body of relevant professional opinion – applied in the management of PVS. This means, in effect, that the medical profession will decide what amounts to the patient's best interests by reference to its own standards[8] and, in deciding that artificial feeding was, at least, an integral part of medical treatment, the House of Lords opened the door to the health carers to withdraw alimentation. Nevertheless, the requirement to seek court approval in every case was maintained[9] – subject to the hope that the restriction might be rescinded in the future – and there was, in fact, a strong undercurrent to the effect that the decision was specific to *Bland* rather than a general statement on the removal of alimentation from brain damaged persons.

English cases post-Bland
Consideration of the later cases suggests that a note of caution may not have been misplaced. Almost exactly a year later, we had the case of *Frenchay Healthcare NHS Trust v S*.[10] This concerned a young man who had been in apparent PVS for $2^1/_2$ years as a result of a drug overdose. When it was discovered that his gastrostomy tube had become detached, a declaration was sought that the hospital could lawfully refrain from renewing or continuing the alimentary and other life-sustaining measures and could restrict any medical treatment to that which would allow him to die peacefully and with the greatest dignity. The declaration was granted and the decision was upheld on appeal.

Frenchay v S differs from *Bland* in a fundamental respect – that, although the prospect had been mooted, the actual decision to discontinue treatment was not a considered one but was one forced by events. As a corollary, the judicial inquiry was certainly hurried and this was the factor which most concerned Waite LJ in the Court of Appeal. The decision has also been subject to academic criticism on these grounds.[11] More importantly, Sir Thomas Bingham MR considered it plain that the evidence in *Frenchay* was neither as emphatic nor as unanimous as that in *Bland*'s case.[12] We must also consider the potential results of failing to make or countermanding the declaration sought – either the doctors would have been forced into an operation which was, in the opinion of the consultant in charge, of no benefit to the patient and which possibly verged on criminal intervention or they would have had to do nothing and take their chance with the law.

Sir Thomas accepted such medical opinion as was provided but was, himself, conscious of a qualitative difference between the two cases. The question thus arises as to whether *Frenchay* represents a 'slippery slope' on which we could descend from PVS to little more than physical or mental disability when assuming that the patient's 'best interests' lie in non-treatment; alternatively, is it a judicial effort to homogenise non-treatment decisions – during which process, PVS becomes merely the end-point

8   See [1993] 1 All ER 821 at 883, (1993) 12 BMLR 64 at 130, per Lord Browne-Wilkinson: '... on an application to the court for a declaration that the discontinuance of medical care will be lawful, the courts only concern will be to be satisfied that the doctor's decision to discontinue is in accordance with a respectable body of medical opinion and that it is reasonable ...' (emphasis added).
9   *Practice Note* [1996] 4 All ER 766, (1996) 34 BMLR 20.
10   [1994] 2 All ER 403, (1994) 17 BMLR 156, CA.
11   See eg A Grubb 'Commentary' (1994) 2 Med L Rev 206.
12   [1994] 2 All ER 403 at 411, (1994) 17 BMLR 156 at 163.

for decision-making rather than a condition to be considered on its own? We discuss below[13] the difficulties in harmonising the 'specific-case' stance adopted in *Bland* with the relatively open-ended direction as to withholding 'futile' treatment that was provided in *Re J*.[14] Meantime, perhaps the main inference to be drawn is that each case is special and must be judged on its own facts.[15]

Later English cases have been reported only spasmodically. We comment briefly on some of these mainly to indicate the quality of the evidence.

Re C[16] concerned a 27-year-old man who had been in PVS for four years following an anaesthetic disaster. Clinically, the case was of great severity and the judge appears to have accepted without demur the evidence provided by the relatives as to the likely wishes of the patient.

Re G[17] related to a young man whose brain damage, sustained in a motorcycle accident, was intensified by a later anoxic episode. The case was of particular interest in that there was some dispute amongst the relatives as to the course to be adopted. Sir Stephen Brown P concluded that the dissenting views of the patient's mother should not be allowed to operate as a veto when his best interests – as defined by the surgeon in charge – favoured removal of nutrition. It seems likely, therefore, that the comments of Lord Goff in *Bland*[18] to the effect that the attitudes of relatives, while due great respect, should not be determinative will be followed in the event of conflict.

Swindon and Marlborough NHS Trust v S[19] was unique among reported cases in being concerned with a patient who was being nursed at home. Rather as in *Frenchay*, however, the issue was forced by blockage of the gastrostomy tube; further treatment would, therefore, have involved hospitalisation. Ward J held that, given the certain diagnosis of PVS, to discontinue life-sustaining measures would be in accordance with good medical practice as recognised and approved within the medical profession. Once again, as in *Re G*, the court firmly adopted *Bolam* as the benchmark – there is a strong suggestion that good medical practice is being seen as a test of lawfulness.

There was no doubt as to the diagnosis in any of these three cases. *Re D*,[20] however, concerned a 28-year-old woman who sustained very severe brain damage for uncertain reasons following serious damage due to a head injury some six years before. Again, an emergency arose when her gastrostomy tube became displaced. All medical opinion was to the effect that D was totally unaware of anything or anyone but she did not fully satisfy the conditions laid down by the Royal College of Physicians for the diagnosis of the permanent vegetative state.[1] The President of the

13 See p 406ff.
14 *Re J (a minor) (wardship: medical treatment)* [1990] 3 All ER 930, (1990) 6 BMLR 25.
15 A point which was emphasised in *Bland* and also in the even more doubtful Irish case of *In the matter of a Ward* (1995) 2 ILRM 401. Precisely the same result was achieved in this case although the reasoning was complicated by considerations of Irish constitutional law. For discussion, see Mason and Laurie, p 396, n 12 above; J Keown 'Life and Death in Dublin' [1996] CLJ 6.
16 R Ford 'Patient in coma may die in dignity' (1995) The Times, 18 November, p 1. The importance of continued post-mortem anonymity was considered in *Re C (adult patient: restriction of publicity after death)* [1996] 2 FLR 251.
17 [1995] 3 Med L Rev 80. In passing, it was held that the public interest in these cases determined that they should be heard in open court: *Re G (persistent vegetative state)* [1995] 2 FLR 528.
18 [1993] 1 All ER 821 at 872, (1993) 12 BMLR 64 at 118.
19 [1995] 3 Med LR 84.
20 (1997) 38 BMLR 1.

Family Division regarded her as suffering 'a living death' and was unable to accept that, because she did not fulfil one of the diagnostic criteria, she was not in a permanent vegetative state. He, therefore, did not believe he was extending the range of cases in which a declaration as to the removal of feeding and hydration might properly be considered. It was appropriate and in her best interests to make such a declaration.

The final English case to be mentioned, *Re H*,[2] involved a 43-year-old woman who had existed for three years in a severely brain damaged state following a vehicular accident. She, too, was agreed to be wholly and unalterably unaware of herself or her environment but, equally, it was agreed that she did not fit squarely within one of the College of Physicians' diagnostic criteria. Sir Stephen Brown P thought that, in this instance 'it may be that a precise label is not of significant importance'. Indeed, the whole area is prey to semantic juggling – one expert, while agreeing that the case did not fit the criteria for the permanent vegetative state, nevertheless thought that H was in a vegetative state which was permanent. The court reiterated that, while it was aware of the consequences that would follow the suspension of treatment, it did not in any sense sanction anything which is *aimed* at terminating life:

> The sanctity of life is of vital importance. It is not, however, paramount and . . . I am satisfied that it is in the best interests of this patient that the life sustaining treatment . . . should be brought to a conclusion.[3]

Thus, while all these cases show distinctive variations, they also have common features which may serve as pointers to the future. The first is that, the precedents having been set, the baseline lies in the confirmed diagnosis of PVS. Once that is made, the conclusion follows automatically that the patient's best interests dictate the termination of assisted feeding and, indeed, there may well be an obligation on the doctor to discontinue treatment.[4] Second, and following from this, the Official Solicitor will no longer oppose any applications for withdrawal of support once the diagnosis is confirmed. Complete medicalisation of treatment decisions in the condition may, then, be only a short step away.

The position in Scotland

The outcome of a similar case in Scotland was awaited with some interest accentuated in part by some very real jurisdictional variations between the two countries. The difficulty of deciding what were, essentially, criminal matters in a civil court were common to both jurisdictions. The House of Lords, while being unanimously wary on the point,[5] was quite prepared to accept a fait accompli: 'This appeal', said Lord Mustill, 'has reached this House, and your Lordships must decide it'. There was,

1 See p 395, n 7 above.
2 *Re H (adult: incompetent)* (1997) 38 BMLR 11.
3 (1997) 38 BMLR 11 at 16.
4 Following the argument put forward by Professor Grubb in Commentary [1995] 3 Med L Rev 83, 85.
5 See [1993] 1 All ER 821 at 864-865, 876, 880, 886-887, (1993) 12 BMLR 64 at 110, 122, 127, 133-134, per Lord Goff, Lord Lowry; Lord Browne-Wilkinson and Lord Mustill respectively.

however, no certainty that such pragmatism would be available to the Scottish courts. On the other hand, the English court in Bland was undoubtedly hampered by the absence of any residual powers of parens patriae and, again, the issue was in some doubt in Scotland. This, then, was the uncertain position when Scotland's first PVS case to come to the Court of Session by way of *Law Hospital NHS Trust v Lord Advocate*,[6] in which authority was sought by relatives of a middle-aged woman in PVS (Mrs Johnstone), and by the hospital treating her, to discontinue feeding.

In the event, the Inner House confirmed that it was not competent to issue a declarator to the effect that a proposed course of action was or was not criminal – it could, however, authorise a declaration in the knowledge that it would not bar proceedings in the High Court but in the hope that it would, in practice, ensure that no prosecution was undertaken there.[7] The court did, however, find that, in contrast to the position in England, the parens patriae jurisdiction survived in Scotland and that any authority thus given would have the same effect in law as if consent had been given by the patient. In this respect, it is to be noted that the Scottish courts have a further string to their bow, which is not available to their counterparts in England, in that they may appoint a tutor dative to oversee the interests of an incompetent adult[8] – and this includes the power to consent to medical treatment on behalf of the incapax.[9] In fact, there is no need to appoint a tutor dative to look after the long-term interests of the patient in PVS as the book is effectively closed once the decision to discontinue feeding and hydration has been taken – the Inner House held that the court, in so deciding, could act on its own initiative and would do so in the future.

The tutor dative procedure is, however, designed to overcome any difficulties as to *consent to treatment* on the part of the incompetent. The court in PVS cases is effectively refusing treatment and no authority exists as to the capacity of a tutor dative to authorise action which leads, inevitably, to the death of the patient. The Inner House considered the numerous rulings that had been reached in several common law jurisdictions as to the correct test for exercising the power of consent or refusal of treatment on behalf of incompetents and concluded that the common denominator is that the decision should be taken in the patient's best interests. It followed that if, as in Mrs Johnstone's case, treatment could be of no benefit, then there were no longer any best interests to be served by continuing it.[10] Accordingly, the Lord Ordinary was authorised to provide a declarator to the effect that removal of life-sustaining treatment from Mrs Johnstone would not be unlawful in respect of its civil law consequences.[11]

The Lord President also remarked that nothing in his opinion was intended to suggest that an application must be made in every case where it is intended to withdraw treatment:

6 *Law Hospital NHS Trust v Lord Advocate* 1996 SLT 848, (1996) 39 BMLR 166. The case was reported by Lord Cameron from the Outer House to the Inner House without any preliminary judgment.
7 1996 SLT 848 at 855, (1996) 39 BMLR 166 at 176, per Lord President Hope.
8 See A Ward 'Tutors to Adults: Developments' 1992 SLT 325.
9 For commentary on the parens patriae jurisdiction in Scotland and elsewhere, see G T Laurie 'Parens Patriae in the Medico-legal Context: The Vagaries of Judicial Activism' (1999) 3 ELR (forthcoming).
10 1996 SLT 848 at 859, (1996) 39 BMLR 166 at 182-184, per Lord Hope.
11 It is clear that such a complex manoeuvre will be unnecessary in the future when the Inner House will use its parens patriae powers but it was convenient to use it in the instant case. See *Law Hospital NHS Trust v Lord Advocate (No 2)* 1996 SLT 869, (1996) 39 BMLR 166 at 197.

The decision as to whether an application is necessary must rest in each case with those who will be responsible for carrying that intention into effect, having regard in particular . . . to any statements of policy which may, in the light of this case, be issued by the Lord Advocate.[12]

And it is here that we run into some difficulties following a statement by the Lord Advocate[13] to the effect that the policy of the Crown Office will be that no criminal prosecution will follow a decision to withdraw feeding but that this is subject to authority to do so having first been obtained by way of the civil law. This appears to pre-empt the direction by the Inner House. However, the Lord Advocate did not say he *would* prosecute in any case that was not so authorised and he went on to say, admittedly in an unofficial ambience:

In Scotland, a decision to withdraw treatment in any case cannot be *guaranteed* immunity from [prosecution] unless the withdrawal has first been authorised by the Court of Session.[14] (emphasis added)

Thus, both the Lord President and the Lord Advocate of the time agreed that decisions could be made on medical grounds and independently of the courts – but neither gave any guidance as to when it would be either necessary or unnecessary to seek judicial approval. The latter concluded in his paper: '. . . it is for doctors and relatives involved in such tragic situations to decide which course of action they wish to adopt.'

We would hope, and expect, that good common sense would prevail but, meanwhile, we suggest that not many doctors will be prepared to trust to chance that they have 'got it right'. It is reasonable to expect the criminal law to set out the boundaries of impermissible conduct in advance. Vagueness in criminal law offends the widely recognised principle of legality, which requires that crimes should be clearly defined. The situation has now arisen where the doctor may be required to second guess the criminal law – a position that is hardly defensible.

The best interests test

The best interests test has been widely accepted as the measure of good practice in surrogate medico-legal decision-making not only as to PVS but also as to allied problems confronting those caring for incompetent adults.[15] We have, however, to express our doubts as to its validity in respect of the removal of feeding and hydration from PVS patients. This is so for three main reasons.

---

12 1996 SLT 848 at 860, (1996) 39 BMLR 166 at 184.
13 J Robertson 'Policy on right to die welcomed' (1996) Scotsman, 12 April, p 1.
14 Lord Mackay of Drumadoon 'Decision on the Persistent Vegetative State: Law Hospital' (1996), paper presented at the Symposium on Medical Ethics and Legal Medicine, Royal College of Physicians and Surgeons of Glasgow, 26 April 1996.
15 Eg in sterilisation of the mentally incompetent: *Re F (mental patient: sterilisation)* [1990] 2 AC 1; *L, petitioner* 1996 SCLR 538.

First, it lends itself to semantic juggling. Certainly, Lord Goff in *Bland* was of the opinion that the correct framing of the question in these cases was of crucial importance. He said:

> The question is not whether the doctor should take a course which will kill his patient, or even take a course which has the effect of accelerating death. The question is whether the doctor should or should not continue to provide his patient with medical treatment or care which, if continued, will prolong his patient's life . . . [T]he question is not whether it is in the best interests of the patient that he should die. The question is whether it is in the best interests of the patient that his life should be prolonged by the continuance of this form of medical treatment or care.[16]

Then, we have Lord Hope in *Law Hospital*[17] using the negative approach – 'there are no longer any best interests to be served by continuing treatment' – which can be compared with Lord Browne-Wilkinson's medical orientation in *Bland*:[18] 'unless the doctor has reached the affirmative conclusion that it is in the patient's best interest to continue the invasive care, such care must cease.' Our sympathies lie with Lord Clyde:[19]

> [W]hile in the context of some medical situations expressions [such as for the welfare of or in the best interests of] may be of value, I find less assistance in such language when the choice is between life of a sort and death.

Secondly, it is difficult to accept Lord Goff's argument in *Bland* as to the nature of the question to be asked: 'we are not saying that it is your best interests to die, just that it is in your best interests not to receive essential physiological support.' How can these two can be separated?[20] How can one avoid the conclusion that to argue that it is in one's best interests to be starved is to say anything other than that it is in one's best interests to die? To ask the truly honest question fatally undermines the best interests test. How, then, can one depend upon such a test?

Thirdly, we believe that the concept of consent is of major importance to the jurisprudence of the vegetative state and it is difficult to fit 'consent' into the inherently paternalistic concept of 'best interests'. It is possible to hold that the best interests of the patient are best served by respecting his autonomy but the argument has something of a hollow ring. We believe that an alternative basis on which to decide what an incompetent person would have consented to or refused must be found and, here, we suggest that the use of the 'substituted judgment' test might be a preferred alternative in the circumstances under consideration.

---

16 [1993] 1 All ER 821 at 869, (1993) 12 BMLR 64 at 115.
17 1996 SLT 848 at 859, (1996) 39 BMLR 166 at 183.
18 [1993] 1 All ER 821 at 883, (1993) 12 BMLR 64 at 129.
19 In *Law Hospital* 1996 SLT 848 at 863, (1996) 39 BMLR 166 at 196. The case against reliance on 'best interests' in the context of PVS is argued by A J Fenwick 'Applying Best Interests to Persistent Vegetative State – A Principled Distortion?' (1998) 24 J Med Ethics 86. An alternative view is given in the same issue: R Gillon 'Persistent Vegetative State, Withdrawal of Artificial Nutrition and Hydration, and the Patient's "Best Interests"' (1998) 24 J Med Ethics 75.
20 Lord Lowry in Bland had similar reservations: [1993] 1 All ER 821 at 887, (1993) 12 BMLR 64 at 123.

The English courts, at least, have consistently rejected this approach in favour of a best interests test but, like it or not, an element of substituted judgment pervades many of the relevant cases.[21] Our reasons for seeking what is, in effect, compliance with the patient's supposed wishes are several. In so far as substituted judgment acknowledges the autonomy of the patient, it is ethically preferable to a best interests test which is, at base, paternalistic. The absolute right of a competent adult to consent to or refuse treatment is now established in all common law jurisdictions; it is wrong to deprive a person of his or her rights to autonomy on the grounds that he or she is incompetent to express that freedom of choice.[1] Moreover, it eliminates many of the more obvious objections to the latter formulation – 'how can it be in the best interests of anyone to die?'; 'how can a person with no interests have any best interests?', and the like.

The main ground for objection lies in its inapplicability to those who have never been competent to take such decisions.[2] But to limit its application to a subjective evaluation of the patient's previously expressed wishes – an interpretation that is very much a part of the doctrine as used in the United States – is, we believe, to take too narrow a view of the test. Judgments on which treatment decisions are made do not have to be substituted for written or clearly expressed preferences on the part of the patient; nor must they be rejected simply because no such declarations of intent are available. In the absence of indications of any sort, there seems no reason why an objective assessment cannot be made – what would a reasonable person of similar type and character have decided in the prevailing circumstances? It could be said that this is no more than semantic pedantry as, given no previous indications, it is almost impossible to conceive of a situation where the 'substituted judgment' and the 'best interest' tests would not coincide.[3] There is also the view that the best interests test – sensitively applied – may take the claims of autonomy into account. It is surely not in a person's best interests to have his explicit or implicit preferences ignored.[4] Even so, on balance, substituted judgment fits the concept of consent more closely and this is particularly so when considering how consent by proxy can be applied.

The PVS cases do, in fact, suggest that judicial antipathy to this approach is less rigid than it once was. The words of Lord Clyde in *Law Hospital* merit repetition:

21 See eg the reasoning of the Master of the Rolls in *Re J (a minor) (wardship: medical treatment)* [1990] 3 All ER 930 at 936, (1990) 6 BMLR 25 at 32, quoting McKenzie J in *Superintendent of Family and Child Services and Dawson* (1983) 145 DLR (3d) 610. Substituted judgment was quite clearly used in *Re D* (1997) 38 BMLR 1 on the evidence of her mother.
 1 See Lord Goff in *Bland* [1993] 1 All ER 821 at 866, (1993) 12 BMLR 64 at 112, quoting the Supreme Judicial Court of Massachusetts in *Superintendent of Belchertown State School v Saikewicz* 373 Mass 728 (1977).
 2 But the test has academic support otherwise. See I Kennedy, and A Grubb 'Commentary on Airedale NHS Trust v Bland' (1993) 1 Med L Rev 359 at 362; D Tomkin and P Hanafin 'Medical treatment at life's end: the need for legislation' (1995) 1 Med-Leg J Ireland 3.
 3 An exception could lie in the management of the mentally disabled neonate. See discussion of *R v Arthur* (1981) 12 BMLR 1 in chapter 15.
 4 It is to be noted that the Law Commission include the ascertainable past and present wishes and feelings of the person among the criteria of 'best interests': Law Commission Mental Incapacity (1995) Law Com no 231, para 3.28.

It seems to me that, in a case such as the present, the question for the court is whether . . . it is or is not just and proper to grant the authorisation in the circumstances as viewed from the position of the patient.[5]

A more honest approach?

A further alternative is to approach the truth and to admit that the deliberate removal of sustenance from a vegetative patient is indistinguishable from euthanasia. In order to circumvent this, the courts in England, Scotland and the Republic of Ireland have been at pains to emphasise that the cause of death in PVS cases is the original injury. But, while it is true to say that this was the ultimate cause of death, the proximate cause, given that the patient has survived for a minimum of a year, must be the results of starvation – otherwise, there would be no death and, hence, no cause of death. There would be no difficulty in certifying death as being due to (a) inanition due to lawful removal of support due to (b) severe brain damage due to (c) cerebral hypoxia. A further practical advantage would be that the mortality statistics should be maintained correctly – and it would be possible to discover how often such decisions are made.

The fears of the judiciary are summed up by Lord Goff in *Bland,* who declined to allow active steps to bring about death in PVS patients because this would be to authorise euthanasia and: 'once euthanasia is recognised as lawful in these circumstances, it is difficult to see any logical basis for excluding it in others.'[6] We question this view, first, on the grounds that, once the concept of substituted judgment is accepted, removal of sustenance from PVS patients equates, at most, to passive, voluntary euthanasia which is already practised widely under one name or another. PVS cases occupy a unique niche in the spectrum of euthanasia. All higher brain function has been permanently lost, there is no awareness and no sensation. There is no alternative of palliative care because there are no senses to palliate – as Lord Goff put it: 'there is no weighing operation to be performed.' Only the vestiges of the person remain as the breathing body and, once the patient's close relatives have come to terms with the situation, it is futile to maintain that respiration.

All this, however, depends upon the certainty of definition and diagnosis. Anthony Bland's and Mrs Johnstone's conditions were unequivocal but one cannot avoid the impression that the precedents laid down in their cases are being extended to include less well defined conditions than was intended at the time. The House of Lords distinguished *Bland* from other 'quality of life' cases such as *Re J.*[7] The two cases have very different ratios. In the former, a wholly insensate patient was deemed to have no interest in continued treatment which could, therefore, be discontinued as being futile. In the latter, it was accepted that some benefit could be derived from treatment of a patient who was not insensate but it was held that non-treatment was to be preferred when any supposed benefit

5   1996 SLT 848 at 863, (1996) 39 BMLR 166 at 196.
6   [1993] 1 All ER 821 at 867, (1993) 12 BMLR 64 AT 113.
7   [1990] 3 All ER 930, (1990) 6 BMLR 25, discussed in chapter 15.

was weighed against other considerations such as pain and suffering. *S*,[8] *Re D*[9] and *Re H*,[10] in particular, demonstrate a shift in thinking from that adopted in *Bland* towards that involved in *Re J* and one wonders if this is not something of a move towards acceptance of active euthanasia; the cases provide the most impressive example to date of the willingness of the British courts to take 'quality of life' decisions and, in our view, represent a significant step in this area of law. At the end of the day, all the cases discussed, from *Bland* to *Re H*, represent variations on what is meant by 'best interests'; the fundamental question is, then, whether the jump from 'no interests' to 'a balance of interests' is acceptable in the management of the vegetative state or whether it represents a quantum leap onto the slippery slope of ending 'valueless lives'.

It has to be remembered that all the post-*Bland* cases have been scrupulously examined and all were supported not only by respected medical opinion but also by the Official Solicitor. All the patients were, by any standards, existing in appalling conditions and we have the gravest doubts as to whether the failure of a single arbitrary clinical test should be allowed to distinguish them in any significant way – and it is at least arguable that the near-vegetative state is a more horrifying condition than is PVS itself.[11] In short, we submit that the approach adopted by the courts in *Re J* could properly be applied to the withdrawal of feeding (or other vital treatment) from severely damaged adult patients. *Re J* and its allied cases went a long way to medicalising the whole approach to termination of treatment decisions and, provided medical authority is tempered by the sensitive handling of close relatives, there seems to be no fundamental reason why it should not be applied irrespective of age – the courts would then be involved only in those cases in which there is serious dispute between or within the health caring and family groups. Public acceptance of this policy would be greatly eased by an open acceptance by the medical profession of the futility of treatment of vegetative patients.[12] This may be an outcome of the major inquiry now being conducted by the BMA.[13]

Inevitably, however, one is reminded of the calls in the House of Lords and the Court of Session for Parliamentary intervention – and, while this has its attractions, the proposal is not of unquestionable merit. To legislate for PVS alone would be to concentrate on its particular clinical status and to segregate it from the general euthanasia debate – which is as it should be.[14] Other advantages of legislation could be that the limits of PVS were statutorily determined[15] and that a clear framework could be devised within which doctors withdrawing treatment could be seen to be acting lawfully without the need for routine approval by a court. A line could thus be drawn between unequivocal and

8 *Swindon and Marlborough NHS Trust v S* [1995] 3 Med LR 84.
9 (1997) 38 BMLR 1.
10 (1997) 38 BMLR 11.
11 R Cranford 'Misdiagnosing the Persistent Vegetative State' (1996) 313 BMJ 5.
12 See K R Mitchell, I H Kerridge and T J Lovat 'Medical Futility, Treatment Withdrawal and the Persistent Vegetative State' (1993) 19 J Med Ethics 71.
13 BMA's Medical Ethics Committee *Withdrawing and Withholding Treatment; A Consultation Paper* (1998).
14 J K Mason and D Mulligan 'Euthanasia by Stages' (1996) 347 Lancet 810.
15 Perhaps based on the guidelines of the Royal College of Physicians, p 395, n 7 above.

doubtful cases and a barrier placed at the edge of any developing slippery slope. On the other hand, legislation of this type could be seen as disadvantageous in that it would be restrictive – while withdrawal of support from the *Bland*-type patient would be permissible, non-treatment options might be barred in many cases of brain damage in which only minimal cognitive function remained such as in *S, D* and *H*. To many, this would represent the primary function of the legislation; to others, it might seem an unacceptable price to pay for the loss of individual judgment – as we have already suggested, generalisations are difficult to apply in a medical context. It might, therefore, be thought preferable to introduce purely enabling legislation along much the same lines as we have suggested in chapter 15.

To do so, however, would be to move towards the diametric alternative of complete medicalisation of the subject – something which was, admittedly, in the contemplation of Lord Goff in *Bland* and Lord Hope in *Law Hospital*.[16] This solution also makes sense in that it is the doctor who has to make the diagnosis and the doctor who is familiar with the associated difficulties[17] – as Lord Browne-Wilkinson said in *Bland*: 'In the past, doctors exercised their own discretion, in accordance with medical ethics, in cases such as these',[18] and he added that this was to the great advantage of society. Moreover, the courts are, ultimately, dependent on the medical evidence. Again, however, PVS decisions carry more than purely medical implications[19] and there is a powerful impression that the public is uneasy when confronted with unbridled autonomy of the medical profession:

> Although essentially the decision [to treat or not to treat] is one for the clinical judgment of responsible medical practitioners . . . it is desirable as a safeguard and for the reassurance of the public that the court should be involved in the way I have indicated.[20]

It is impossible to deny that doctors vary in their intellectual abilities and moral application. The familiar ghost of *Bolam*[1] is, perhaps, not the ideal preceptor in such sensitive territory – it could well be a mistake to tamper with our current pragmatic resolution of the problems involved:

16 It is to be noted that the Americans find no difficulty in seeing artificial feeding as a medical matter: see eg B Brody 'Special Ethical Issues in the Management of PVS Patients' (1992) 20 Law Med Hlth Care 104. A Meisel 'A Retrospective on *Cruzan*' (1992) 20 Law Med Hlth Care provides a comprehensive list of apposite court decisions and statements from learned societies.

17 For discussion, see a series of papers: K Andrews 'Recovery of Patients after Four Months or More in the Persistent Vegetative State' (1993) 306 BMJ 1597, 'Patients in the Persistent Vegetative State: Problems in their Long Term Management' (1993) 306 BMJ 1600; R Gillon 'Patients in the Persistent Vegetative State: A Response to Dr Andrews' (1993) 306 BMJ 1602.

18 [1993] 1 All ER 821 at 880, (1993) 12 BMLR 64 at 126.

19 See M Angell 'After Quinlan: The Dilemma of the Persistent Vegetative State' (1994) 330 New Engl J Med 1524.

20 *Airedale NHS Trust v Bland* [1993] 1 All ER 821 at 833, (1993) 12 BMLR 64 AT 77, Per Sir Stephen Brown P. This applied to all PVS cases but later judges were prepared to limit court hearings to those cases in which there was conflict: eg Lord Goff [1993] 1 All ER 821 at 874, (1993) 12 BMLR 64 at 120.

1 *Bolam v Friern Hospital Management Committee* [1957] 2 All ER 118, (1957) 1 BMLR 1.

Provided the legal process continues to provide solutions that accord with sound medical ethics and commonsense, there should be no tension between those who provide or withhold life-prolonging treatment and those who ultimately judge their decisions.[2]

PVS in the United States

There are more than 50 jurisdictions in the United States where PVS decisions are, to an extent, governed by constitutional and statute law. This, together with the sheer volume of work involved,[3] makes it difficult to follow the more important cases and to identify a definite trend in the development of the relevant common law in that country.

In fact, this is not of major concern to the British reader, as this appears to be one area in which the United Kingdom courts are forging a particularly independent path. Due respect is paid to United States decisions[4] but, such is their diversity, that a selective approach is inevitable. The fundamental distinction between the two main jurisdictions seems, to us, to lie in the test by which to justify termination of treatment which, we have seen, is firmly held to be that of the best interests of the patient in the United Kingdom. By contrast, three standards for surrogate decision-making under this heading are available in the United States[5] – the subjective, substituted judgment and best interests standards, the inference being that these are adopted in descending order of acceptability. Thus, the substituted judgment test – in which the surrogate makes his or her best approximation of what management schedule the patient would have wanted – is adopted only if the subjective test, which is based on what wishes the patient actually expressed, is not available; contrary to the position in the United Kingdom, the best interests test is, then, to be regarded as something of a last resort. Clearly, the tests run into one another and the standards of proof can be manipulated – what, for example, constitutes an 'expression of intention'? The scope for interpretation is, therefore, very wide and, for that reason, we are limiting our discussion to only a few cases which are of comparative interest.

Consideration of the American scene must include a brief reference to the old, but fundamental, case of *Re Quinlan*;[6] this involved a 21-year-old girl who was in what was described at the time as a chronic persistent vegetative state and who existed on ventilator support. Given a hopeless prognosis, her parents sought to remove her from intensive care against the advice of the health care team. The Supreme Court of New Jersey found, however, that Ms Quinlan's right to privacy would allow her to refuse further ventilator therapy were she competent and that this right persisted when she was incompetent. It concluded that evidence from her friends was insufficiently probative to establish what her actual wishes would be but, interestingly, rescinded

2   D Collins 'Prescribing Limits to Life-prolonging Treatment' [1994] NZLJ 246.
3   It was estimated that, from 1975 to 1989, between 2,900 and 7,000 life-sustaining medical treatment cases were heard by the American judiciary and some 50 to 75 went to appeal. These derive from an estimated 13.6m apposite deaths: T L Hafemeister et al 'The Judicial Role in Life-sustaining Medical Treatment Decisions' (1991) 7 Issues in L & Med 53, quoted by Meisel p 408, n 16 above.
4   See eg Sir Thomas Bingham MR in *Bland* [1993] 1 All ER 821 at 836-837, (1993) 12 BMLR 64 at 80-81.
5   Meisel, p 408, n 16 above.
6   *Re Quinlan* 355 A 2d 647 (NJ, 1976).

this assessment a decade later.[7] Her father was appointed her guardian with authority to act on her behalf and to withdraw treatment, subject to the agreement of the attending physicians and of the hospital ethics committee. The function of the ethics committee was seen as, first, effectively covering the physician against any subsequent challenge by a family member and, secondly, as protection against any 'less than worthy motivations of family or physician' – indeed, the court was happy to turn over assessment of future cases to such tribunals.[8]

Quinlan was not appealed to the US Supreme Court and it was not until 1990 that Ms Cruzan's case was heard there.[9]   *Cruzan* was, therefore, awaited with great interest but, in the end, the decision was disappointing in its depth and scope – it has been said that perhaps the chief problem with the majority decision was its almost complete lack of attention to medical reality.[10] Ms Cruzan's situation was very similar to that of Ms Quinlan, save that the former, while requiring tube-feeding in order to survive, had no need of ventilator support; after three years in PVS, her parents requested that feeding and hydration be discontinued – this being justified on the basis of their interpretation of her wishes when competent and in accordance with previous precedent.[11] The Supreme Court of Missouri overturned the trial judge's permissive order and the case went to the Supreme Court of the United States. The question before the Supreme Court, however, was simply whether the Constitution debars a State from requiring 'clear and convincing evidence' of a person's expressed decision while competent to have hydration and nutrition withdrawn in such a way as to cause death – that is, to insist on the highest subjective test for decision-making. The court decided, by the narrow majority of 5:4, that it had but it has been pointed out consistently that it did not dictate the use of such a standard which has, subsequently, been rejected by all States other than Missouri and New York. *Cruzan* thus made no effective change to the law as it had previously evolved and, in fact, the case withered away as the State did not contest a second hearing based on new evidence and Ms Cruzan was allowed to die.

Some observations in the Supreme Court are, however, significant even though they might be regarded as obiter. First, the majority opinion held that the principle that a competent person has a constitutionally protected liberty interest in refusing unwanted medical treatment can be accepted by inference.[12] Secondly, Justice O'Connor, who sided with the majority, agreed with the minority that artificial feeding cannot be distinguished from other forms of medical treatment; as a consequence, refusal of the artificial delivery of food and water is protected by the Constitution. In view of these, most commentators are agreed that, paradoxically, the power of the family and health care team to make agreed decisions as to withdrawal of treatment from the incompetent is, at least, unaltered and, possibly, strengthened by *Cruzan*.

---

7 In *In the matter of Claire Conroy* 486 A 2d 1209 (NJ, 1985).
8 For a modern appraisal of shared decision making, see B Spielman 'Collective Decisions about Medical Futility' (1994) 22 J Law Med & Ethics 152.
9 *Cruzan v Director, Missouri Department of Health* 110 S Ct 2841 (1990).
10 G J Annas 'Nancy Cruzan and the Right to Die' (1990) 323 New Engl J Med 670.
11 See Meisel, p 408, n 16 above.
12 110 S Ct 2841 at 2851. The question as to whether the 'right' is based on liberty or privacy interests is a very US-orientated argument.

Following from this, we have selected one further case which seems to us to be significant. In *re Fiori*[13] concerned a man who had been in PVS for some 15 years and was tube-fed but not ventilated. In allowing his mother's request to withdraw gastrostomy feeding, the Superior Court of Pennsylvania specifically rejected the need for a prior express statement by the patient as the test. Indeed, in holding that the surrogate decision-maker can consider 'the patient's personal value system for guidance' in the absence of an expressed view as to the use of life support, the court positively approved the use of an objective standard much as we have suggested above.[14] Of greater general importance, it held that there is no need for a court to intervene in the decision-making process unless there is disagreement between the interested parties and, while limiting itself strictly to the permanent vegetative state of a patient who had never clearly expressed a preference for termination, the court concluded that the surrogate consent of a close family member, backed by the written approval of two physicians, protects the patient's interests sufficiently.

Fiori thus seems a major step towards accepting the family's ultimate responsibility for taking treatment withdrawal decisions in the United States. There are, however, two provisos to consider. First, the decision was strictly limited to the patient satisfying the PVS criteria. Secondly, despite the importance attached to the family, it is at least arguable that the concept of family decision-making is illusory, given the overwhelming power of the medical advisers – and the procedure envisaged by the Superior Court of Pennsylvania will only operate successfully when there is complete agreement. One suggested alternative method of decision-making is to *assume* that no one would wish to be maintained in the PVS and that, once the diagnosis was made, we could act on that assumption.[15] It would then be up to families seeking to continue treatment to justify their stance.[16] This has a ring of certainty about it but, at the same time, it re-introduces the image of unrestrained medicalisation which we have raised doubts about above. Perhaps the better way of looking at the dilemma of PVS is to remind ourselves that perhaps several hundred commonsense decisions are taken for every one that is argued in the courts.[17]

'Do not resuscitate' orders

The last aspect of medical futility that falls to be discussed is the so-called 'do not resuscitate' (DNR) order. There can be no doubt that it is often undesirable, effectively, to prolong the process of dying – irrespective of the competence of the

---

13 652 A 2d 1350 (Pa, 1995).
14 See pp 406-409.
15 C H Baron 'Why Withdrawal of Life-support for PVS Patients Is not a Family Decision' (1991) 19 Law Med Hlth Care 73.
16 A similar attitude to the burden of proof is shown by Angell, p 408, n 19 above.
17 Other jurisdictions have followed the general trend. In South Africa, for example, 'the feeding of the patient in PVS did not serve the purpose of supporting human life as it is commonly known' and it would not be acting wrongfully to discontinue artificial feedings: *Clarke v Hurst* [1994] 5 Med LR 177.

patient at the time.[18] Nevertheless, in extending the concept of non-treatment to the incapacitated rather than the incompetent, it is possible that our attitudes are being moulded overly in favour of death, rather than treatment, as a management option. Moreover, we have to ask ourselves whether the DNR option is a valid example of an exercise of the principle of futility – there is a physical and moral divide between the PVS patient and the patient who is reaching the end of life in a natural fashion, albeit often in a state of diminished competence. Where one places the DNR order is a matter of ethical importance. After much consideration, we doubt if it is correctly sited under 'futility' and will discuss the matter under the heading of euthanasia.[19]

18 A particularly effective series of commentaries is to be found related to E L Schucking 'Death at a New York Hospital' (1985) 13 Law Med Hlth Care 261. See also the papers associated with R F Weir 'Betty's Case: An Introduction' (1989) 17 Law Med Hlth Care 211.
19 See chapter 17.

17 Euthanasia

Thus far, we have looked at the ending of life in the general context of withdrawal of treatment that was regarded as inappropriate. The legal insistence that this did not constitute euthanasia has been a feature of all the cases discussed – and, indeed, it is this which underwrites their legality. In this chapter, we consider the occasions when the premature termination of life is the intended aim – and this is, at least, one definition of euthanasia. Euthanasia can, however, also be seen as providing a 'good' death or 'easing the passing' and we will, where necessary, include this in our discussion. We have already considered the infant or young child as a separate issue and have explained our reasons for isolating such cases; here it is proposed to discuss the subject only in relation to the adult patient.

Conditions at each end of life differ significantly from both the legal and ethical viewpoints. Unlike the infant, the adult patient may well be able to express his wishes as to the quality of his own life. In default of this, those responsible for the patient's management have a background of previous abilities and aspirations from which to measure the likely shortfall; clinical decisions can be based on history rather than on clairvoyance. On the other hand, the aged present a bewildering array of mental and physical variations which virtually preclude generalisations as to management – and attitudes to the elderly are inevitably coloured by the fact that their potential for meaningful relationships is waning rather than developing.

The prohibition of the taking of human life is based on fundamental and deeply held ethical and religious convictions. We have broached the question of the sanctity of human life in chapter 15. In the Judaeo-Christian tradition, the concept is founded on the notion that life is a gift over which we have stewardship but no final control. This conviction is expressed in many ways, the common feature of which is that there is a value in life which must be taken as a moral absolute. The right of each person to life is something which is intrinsic to his status as a human being and which is a necessary concomitant of human existence.[1] Those with a religious outlook believe that human life itself is of divine origin and is, therefore, outwith human disposal. Those who deny the existence of a creator can, however, maintain a similarly strict view.[2] It is not difficult to construct a utilitarian argument in favour of such a position which is founded on the proposition that the consequences of allowing the taking of life are, ultimately, destructive of greater societal happiness.

Nevertheless, few of those who recognise its value will deny that life may be taken in at least some circumstances. The principle of self-defence – either in the private context or in the course of a just war – may admit the killing of others. Similarly, those

---

1 Linacre Centre, *Report of a Working Party Euthanasia and Clinical Practice* (1982) p 37.
2 For a discussion of non-religious grounds for opposition to euthanasia, see P Foot *Virtues and Vices* (1978) p 33 et seq. A short appraisal for the lawyer is to be found in J Wilkinson 'The Ethics of Euthanasia' (1990) 35 J Law Soc Scot 243.

who would normally condemn murder might, none the less, see legal execution as an appropriate part of the process of criminal justice. In medicine, too, stout opponents of euthanasia may accept the legitimacy of abortion – a process which, by any standards, involves the taking of *some* form of life. We admit the right of a person to commit suicide and do this on the grounds that, in general, the right to self-determination is the most fundamental of all human rights. The door is thereby opened for considering euthanasia in some forms as a morally acceptable practice.

Voluntary and involuntary euthanasia

The subject of euthanasia is, in our opinion, clouded by uncertainties of definition. *Stedman's Medical Dictionary* has two citations – a quiet, painless death and the intentional putting to death by artificial means of persons with incurable or painful disease. The former is etymologically correct but the latter more closely mirrors the public view. Thus, *Collins' English Dictionary* confines itself to 'the act of killing someone painlessly, especially to relieve suffering from an incurable illness'. To hide behind semantics is obfuscatory. Any useful discussion of euthanasia must accept the, admittedly unpalatable, fact that it involves some form of killing; it is only by so doing that the moral and legal implications can be reviewed in a clear light.

The major thrust of those concerned to legalise the termination of life on medical grounds has always been concentrated on what is generally known as voluntary euthanasia. This form of words implies that the patient specifically requests that his life be ended. It is everywhere agreed that to attain any semblance of validity, this request must come from one who is either subject to intolerable pain or disability or who is suffering from an illness which is agreed as being terminal. It may be made prior to the development of the illness in question or during its course. In either case, it must not result from pressure of any sort from relatives or from those looking after the patient. We follow earlier authorities[3] in distinguishing non-voluntary euthanasia as a sub-variety of voluntary euthanasia. This involves the death, ostensibly for his or her own good, of someone who cannot express any views on the matter and who must, therefore, use some sort of proxy – be it the family or the actual medical attendant – to request that his or her life be ended. As Glover has pointed out, it is this form of euthanasia which most intimately concerns the medical profession. In practice, non-voluntary euthanasia presents only as an arguable alternative to non-treatment which we have discussed in detail in the preceding chapters.

Involuntary euthanasia is a quite different concept and is one from which most groups pressing for reform of the law have been careful to distance themselves. An act of involuntary euthanasia involves ending the patient's life in the absence of either a personal or proxy invitation to do so. The motive – the relief of suffering – may be the same as that involved in voluntary euthanasia but its only justification lies in a paternalistic decision as to what is best for the victim of disease. In extreme cases, indeed, there may be no claim to individual advantage – or the patient's consent may be expressly withheld – and the grounds may be no more than those of social

3   Notably, J Glover *Causing Death and Saving Lives* (1977, reprinted 1986) p 191.

convenience. It is examples of this last type which provide the major armamentarium of those who oppose the legalisation of euthanasia – the contained threat to the old or to the mentally or physically infirm scarcely needs emphasis.

Criminal cases are rarely reported unless they demonstrate some specific point of law. Even so, we would hope that the dearth of truly apposite trials of doctors under this heading also reflects the generally law-abiding ethos of the profession.[4] Even including the remarkable Dr Adams,[5] whose case we discuss below,[6] the vast majority of the few who have come to trial on charges of murder, manslaughter or culpable homicide have been accused of using therapeutic drugs in overdose[7] and all the relevant verdicts have indicated the reluctance of British juries to convict a medical practitioner of serious crime when the charge arises from what they see as his considered medical judgment. In *R v Carr*[8] a doctor was accused of attempted murder by injecting a massive dose of phenobarbitone into a patient whose lung cancer had been declared inoperable some seven months previously. He was acquitted of the charge but, in the course of the summing-up, Mars-Jones J had this to say:

> However gravely ill a man may be . . . he is entitled in our law to every hour . . . that God has granted him. That hour or hours may be the most precious and most important hours of a man's life. There may be business to transact, gifts to be given, forgivenesses to be made, 101 bits of unfinished business which have to be concluded.

which is as good a comment on misplaced paternalism as is likely to be found. The pattern of acquittal was, however, changed dramatically by the case of *R v Cox*[9] in which a consultant rheumatologist was convicted of attempted murder. The case is discussed in greater detail below.[10]

Active and passive euthanasia

A patient's life may be terminated, or death accelerated, either actively or passively. This distinction – or whether there is, indeed, any true distinction – is one of the most hotly argued issues in the euthanasia debate and one which can be addressed on either the legal or the moral plane.

---

4 But we note below the surprising number of doctors who claim to have taken part in some form of euthanasia. We privately wonder how many Walter Mittys were involved in the relevant surveys.
5 H Palmer 'Dr Adams' Trial for Murder' [1957] Crim LR 365.
6 See p 437.
7 We would except Dr Arthur: see *R v Arthur* (1981) 12 BMLR 1, discussed in chapter 15.
8 *R v Carr* (1986), The Sunday Times, 30 November p 1. In Scotland, a doctor who injected an elderly patient with ten times the normal dose of diamorphine was acquitted of culpable homicide – the defence was, however, one of accidental error: *HM Advocate v Watson* (1991) Scotsman, 11 June, p 8, 14 June, p 3. More recently, a Newcastle doctor who admits to giving large doses of painkillers to terminally ill patients has been charged with murder but the case has not yet been heard: C Dyer 'Newcastle GP Charged with Murder' (1998) 316 BMJ 1849.
9 *R v Cox* (1992) 12 BMLR 38.
10 See p 426.

Despite the rarity of cases involving the medical profession, there is no ambiguity in the attitude of the law in the United Kingdom towards a positive act of euthanasia. It is summed up in the words of Devlin J:

> If the acts done are intended to kill and do, in fact, kill, it does not matter if a life is cut short by weeks or months, it is just as much murder as if it were cut short by years.[11]

and we have Glanville Williams writing: 'The law does not leave the issue in the hands of doctors; it treats euthanasia as murder'.[12] While motive is irrelevant, intention is all-important. If a doctor intends to kill, he is as liable to prosecution as is the layman. There have been recommendations for the introduction of a specific offence of 'mercy-killing'[13] and, although these have not been translated into legislation – and although there is, apparently, no intention so to do[14] – there is an innate reluctance on the part of the courts to convict the genuine 'mercy-killer' of an offence which carries a mandatory sentence of life imprisonment. This is particularly so when relatives have cared for the sick with great devotion and have ultimately decided to release them from misery. In such circumstances, the prosecutor may well exercise his discretion and accept a plea of manslaughter;[15] alternatively, the court may accept a plea of diminished responsibility on the grounds of mental abnormality[16] – psychiatrists are just as ready to diagnose or to infer a reactive depression in the accused.[17]

Until quite recently, one would have supposed that the public were content with such a practical solution and had little or no wish to see it extended. The euthanasia debate has, however, now been reopened in full force; some of the impetus has undoubtedly come from the Netherlands, where it appears that active euthanasia is widely practised. In point of fact, active euthanasia is still illegal in the Netherlands and the political argument as to its correct status continues.[18] In 1991, it was said that nearly 2% of deaths in the Netherlands resulted from euthanasia; these involved approximately 2,300 cases of euthanasia and 400 of assisted suicide each year.[19] The journey towards legislation in Holland has been stormy and, in our opinion, provides a cautionary tale for those intent on a rush down the 'libertarian' slopes. Thus, we have the Royal Dutch Medical Association advocating 'life termination' in 1991 without, apparently, considering whether their proposals

11 Palmer, p 415, n 5 above.
12 G Williams *Textbook of Criminal Law* (2nd edn, 1983) p 580.
13 See R Leng 'Mercy Killing and the CLRC' (1982) 132 NLJ 76.
14 J Warden 'No New Law Planned on Mercy Killing' (1993) 306 BMJ 1150.
15 Eg *R v Johnson* (1961) 1 Med Sci & L 192. A typical Scottish case, *HM Advocate v Brady* (1996 unreported), involved a man who smothered his brother who was suffering from Huntington's disease; he was found guilty of culpable homicide and was admonished: B Christie 'Man Walks Free in Scottish Euthanasia Case' (1996) 313 BMJ 961.
16 See p 534 et seq.
17 S Dell *Murder into Manslaughter* (1984) p 35 et seq. In *R v Taylor* [1979] CLY 570, a man who battered his autistic child to death was placed on probation for 12 months. Perhaps the most remarkable example comes from the USA, where no charges were pressed against a man who held the staff at gun-point while disconnecting his son from the ventilator: see eg J D Lantos, S H Miles and C K Cassel 'The Linares Affair' (1989) 17 Law Med Hlth Care 308.
18 M A M de Wachter 'Euthanasia in the Netherlands' (1990) 300 BMJ 1093.
19 H Hellema 'Euthanasia – 2% of Dutch Deaths' (1991) 303 BMJ 877.

conform with Dutch law.[20] From a study undertaken at much the same time, it appeared that medical decisions concerning the end of life were taken in 38% of all deaths – the sole conclusion being that such decisions should get more attention in research, teaching and public debate.[1] Two years later, the Dutch Commission for the Acceptability of Life Terminating Action called for public debate on whether the life of a patient suffering from severe dementia without serious physical symptoms might be terminated with or without having executed an advance directive on the point[2] and, in the same year, the concept of life-terminating acts without the specific request of the patient (LAWER) was clearly being accepted as a normal part of medical practice.[3] While such data may suggest a 'slippery slope', the true underlying problem seems to have been that of uncertainty[4] and it was not until 1993 that legislation passed the Second Chamber. The legal position now is that euthanasia, with or without the explicit request of the patient,[5] remains a criminal act and doctors engaging in life-terminating acts will be punishable by penal law unless they conform to relatively strict guidelines[6] – these include: that all other treatment options must have been exhausted or refused by the patient; that the patient has made specific requests and that his or her decision is well-informed, free and enduring; that the patient's mental or physical suffering is very severe and without prospect of relief; and that the doctor has taken others into consultation. Even if a prosecution is brought, the courts will accept a defence of *force majeure* – or necessity – when the guidelines have been followed. Thus, despite a quarter of a century's political manoeuvring, the precise legal situation is still unclear. It has been commented that, following the final acceptance of the 1993 Act by the Senate, doctors are now 'legally obliged to give evidence of a criminal act they have committed' in the face of 'an active prosecution policy' on the part of the justice ministry.[7] As a result, the extent to which euthanasia is used remains uncertain, largely because many doctors do not follow the requirement to refer their cases to the police – research indicates, however, that 3,200, or 2.4% of all deaths, resulted from explicitly requested euthanasia in

20 H Hellema '"Life Termination" in The Netherlands' (1991) 302 BMJ 984.

1 P J van der Maas, J J M van Delden, L Pijnenborg and C W N Looman 'Euthanasia and Other Medical Decisions Concerning the End of Life' (1991) 338 Lancet 669.

2 H Hellema 'Dutch Doctors Support Life Termination in Dementia' (1993) 306 BMJ 1364.

3 L Pijnenborg, P J van der Maas, J J M van Delden and C W N Looman 'Life-terminating Acts without Explicit Request of Patient' (1993) 341 Lancet 1196. In subsequent correspondence B Pollard suggested that the only legal category for LAWER in the Netherlands, as elsewhere, was murder.

4 See H Rigter, E Borst-Eilers and H J J Leenen 'Euthanasia Across the North Sea' (1988) 297 BMJ 1593; H Rigter 'Euthanasia in the Netherlands: Distinguishing Fact from Fiction' (1989) Hastings Center Report, Spec Supp Jan/Feb, p 31. The same issue contains a trenchant criticism of the Dutch ethos: R Fenigsen 'A Case Against Dutch Euthanasia' at p 22. Major problems lie in definitions and the interpretation of statistics: J J M Van Delden, L Pijnenborg and P J Van der Maas 'Dances with Data' (1993) 7 Bioethics 323.

5 The Dutch had, previously, made a firm distinction between euthanasia, which involves positive action following a well-considered request from the patient for the doctor to end his or her life on account of unbearable and hopeless suffering, and termination of life without request because of, say, mental incompetence. The removal of the distinction has been criticised: H Hellema 'Dutch Confused over Euthanasia' (1993) 306 BMJ 415.

6 M Spanjer 'Netherlands: Euthanasia Legislation' (1993) 341 Lancet 426.

7 T Sheldon 'Euthanasia Law Does Not End Debate in the Netherlands' (1993) 307 BMJ 1511.

1995.[8] It is to be noted that the states of Washington and California have rejected legalised euthanasia[9] – and, at least in the case of the former, this was for fear that the safeguards were inadequate. Such concerns do not appear ill-founded when one reads that a Dutch psychiatrist has been found to be medically justified in assisting the suicide of a physically healthy woman who was depressed[10] – precisely the situation foreseen by those who oppose legalising the termination of life. The Dutch experience could, in fact, be taken as an object lesson rather than as a paradigm.[11]

We have seen that a major difficulty in assessing the Dutch experience lies in definition and this, in turn, probably derives from their use of the term 'medical decisions concerning the end of life (MDEL).[12] MDEL includes a wide spectrum of activity ranging from manifest euthanasia, through the concept of 'double effect'[13] to the most controversial, and hard to unravel, group involving termination of life without an explicit request. Griffiths extrapolated the available data to suggest that, on these grounds, an MDEL is the immediate cause of death in more than half all the deaths in Holland due to chronic disease. Only some 5% of MDELs are, however, euthanasia and, while much of the terminology is confused, there is no doubt that euthanasia in the Netherlands includes both the active killing of the patient and assisting the patient to precipitate his or her own death – a procedure which would be known as physician assisted suicide (PAS) in most anglophone jurisdictions. Is there, in fact, a distinction to be made?

Physician-assisted suicide

Once again, we are confronted with problems of definition. Take, for example the doctor who responds to a request to disconnect the ventilator in a case of progressive neurological disease – is this to be classed as refusal of treatment by the patient or as assisted suicide? Or, what of the doctor who performs the venepuncture and then holds the syringe while the patient presses the plunger? – is this assisted suicide or is

8 This has now 'improved' so that some 41% of cases are now reported to the authorities: T Sheldon 'Euthanasia Reporting is Increasing but is Still Low' (1996) 313 BMJ 1423. As would be expected, the proportion of euthanasia cases depends very much on the diagnosis – apart from AIDS, euthanasia is most commonly used in cases of intractable neurological disease: G Van der Wal and B D Onwuteaka-Philipsen 'Cases of Euthanasia and Assisted Suicide Reported to the Public Prosecutor in North Holland over 10 Years' (1996) 312 BMJ 612.
9 M Morris 'Washington State Rejects Euthanasia' (1991) 303 BMJ 1223; R Rhein 'California Says No to Euthanasia' (1992) 305 BMJ 1175.
10 'Mercy-killing Doctor Freed' (1993) Scotsman, 22 April, p 8.
11 For a major advocate of the Dutch system, see P Admiraal 'Voluntary Euthanasia' in S A M McLean (ed) *Death, Dying and the Law* (1996) ch 7. A forceful opposition view is to be found in J Keown 'Some Reflections on Euthanasia in the Netherlands', 'Further Reflections on Euthanasia in the Netherlands in the Light of the Remmelink Report and the Van der Maas Survey' in L Gormally (ed) *Euthanasia, Clinical Practice and the Law* (1994) chs 4 and 5. For a good factual review, see J Griffiths 'The Regulation of Euthanasia and Related Medical Procedures that Shorten Life in the Netherlands' (1994) 1 Med Law Internat 137. An interesting critique of the Dutch experience, which reveals how the availability of euthanasia can obscure other options, is H Henden *Seduced by Death: Doctors, Patients and the Dutch Cure* (1997).
12 Griffiths, n 11 above, supports the suggestion that this would be better expressed as 'medical procedures that shorten life'.
13 See p 437 below.

it active euthanasia?[14]   Clearly, there is no bright dividing line between refusal of treatment, suicide, assisted suicide and euthanasia yet, in practice and, perhaps, intuitively, most people would perceive a distinction. Sometimes this may be subtle – as between the first two, for example, we have Lord Donaldson saying:

> This appeal is not in truth about 'the right to die'. There is no suggestion that Miss T wants to die . . . This appeal is about the 'right to choose how to live'. This is quite different, even if the choice, when made, may make an early death more likely.[15]

which, taken in the context of refusal of a life-saving blood transfusion, attracts something of an aura of legal expediency. Again, we have the Court in the American case of *Vacco v Quill*:[16]

> [The] distinction between assisting suicide and withdrawing life-sustaining treatment in hopeless cases is logical, widely recognized and endorsed by the medical profession and by legal tradition.

and we only wish it were always so. On other occasions, however, the difference may be obvious. In respect of assisted suicide and euthanasia, for example, it is not difficult to see a practical difference between the classic ploy of 'leaving the pills' and undertaking a lethal injection – and it is this sort of comparison that most people have in mind when addressing the subject.[17]

There is also legislative precedent for distinguishing physician-assisted suicide as a separate entity. Having seen initiatives designed to decriminalise active voluntary euthanasia fail in both California and the state of Washington by narrow majorities,[18] Oregon introduced its Death with Dignity Act of 1994, which concerned assisted suicide only. This was passed by an even more slender majority but, after a series of stays on constitutional grounds, the measure was re-enacted by a voting majority of 60-40%.[19]   Thus, the isolation of assisted suicide appears to be a significant requirement if legislation on euthanasia is to succeed. The chances of legislation legalising active euthanasia being accepted, say, in the United Kingdom are very slim;[20] but opposition might be very much less were it possible to legislate for PAS

---

14 These examples are taken from D W Meyers and J K Mason 'Physician Assisted Suicide: A Second View from Mid-Atlantic' (1999) Anglo-Am L Rev (in press), in which the comparative Anglo-American scene is discussed in detail.
15 *Re T (adult: refusal of medical treatment)* [1992] 4 All ER 649 at 652, (1992) 9 BMLR 46 at 49.
16 117 S Ct 2293 (1997).
17 For commentary, see L R Churchill and N M P King 'Physician Assisted Suicide, Euthanasia, or Withdrawal of Treatment' (1997) 315 BMJ 137.
18 Only one jurisdiction has passed such legislation: Rights of the Terminally Ill Amendment Act 1996 (NT, Australia). Four persons died under its provisions before the Australian Senate declared the measure to be unconstitutional.
19 The United States Supreme Court has decreed that statutes which *prohibit* assisted suicide are not unconstitutional; the arguments are, however, essentially based on US constitutional law and have very little relevance outside the US: *Vacco v Quill* 117 S Ct 2293 (1997), *Washington v Glucksberg* S Ct 2258 (1997). Assisted suicide is unlawful in at least 43 of the United States.
20 House of Lords *Report of the Select Committee on Medical Ethics* (HL Paper 21-1, 1994) – which, admittedly, would have no truck with physician assisted suicide either.

alone – an electorate that, rightly, could not accept the doctor as an executioner might be less hostile to a doctor who could be regarded as a friend in need.[1]

We are on less sure ground, however, when we take a theoretical rather than practical approach. We are then thrown back once again to the commission/omission debate, which we have referred to in chapter 15 and address more closely below,[2] and have to ask what is the *moral* distinction between, say, writing a prescription for a lethal dose and injecting a lethal dose of barbiturates when the objective – the patient's premature death – is the same in each case? Again, it seems that we can only revert to our intuition that action is morally more potent than inaction and to the classic words of Capron:[3]

> I never want to have to wonder whether the physician coming into my hospital room is wearing the white coat (or the green scrubs) of a healer, concerned only to relieve my pain and restore me to health, or the black hood of the executioner. Trust between patient and physician is simply too important and too fragile to be subjected to this unnecessary strain.

Even then, one is left with the uncomfortable possibility that the doctor who will practice PAS but not active euthanasia can be justifiably accused of moral cowardice. On balance, however, we feel that this would be too harsh a judgment; there is much to be said in favour of the proposition that the final *action* in a life terminating procedure should be in the hands of the person who wants his or her *own* life to end prematurely.

Whatever the reason, there is some evidence that both doctors and the public will accept the distinction. In a major survey undertaken in Scotland, McLean and Britton[4] found that, given a change in the law, 43% of doctors across the United Kingdom would opt for PAS – defined as the person's action leading to their own death – and 19% for active euthanasia in which the actions of other persons leads to death; the high proportion of undecided respondents (38%) should be noted. As opposed to this, 42% of Scottish people would prefer voluntary euthanasia while 28% would choose PAS. It is very difficult to avoid the conclusion that, in this very sensitive situation, most people would wish to pass the ultimate responsibility to others.

It is hard to define the public attitude to either euthanasia or PAS – indeed, the public itself can appear confused. Thus, in McLean and Britton's survey, 67% thought that human beings should have the right to choose when to die (with 20% opposed) but only 55% (with 30% opposed) agreed that PAS should be made legal in Great Britain.[5] Perhaps the most powerful evidence as to current opinion in Great

1   See p 446 below for further discussion.
2   See p 428.
3   A M Capron 'Legal and Ethical Problems in Decisions for Death' (1986) 14 Law Med Hlth Care 141. See also the view of a hospice practitioner R C Twycross 'Assisted Death: A Reply' (1990) 336 Lancet 796.
4   S A M McLean and A Britton *Sometimes a Small Victory* (1996).
5   It was stated in *Compassion in Dying v State of Washington* 79 Fed 3d 790 (1996) that US opinion polls show majorities of between 64% and 73% in favour of physician assisted suicide. In a study involving oncologists and oncology patients, the latter were consistently more in favour of PAS than were their physicians: E J Emanuel, D L Fairclough, E R Daniels and B R Clarridge 'Euthanasia and Physician-Assisted Suicide: Attitudes and Experiences of Oncology Patients, Oncologists, and the Public' (1996) 347 Lancet 1805,

Britain is to be found in the survey carried out by Social and Community Planning Research in 1996,[6] where 82% of the survey population thought that doctors should be allowed to end a person's life when requested. The opinion was, however, selective. Thus, while 86% supported the procedure in comatose, incurably ill patients who were on ventilator support, the proportion dropped to 42% when the patient had and incurable, painful but not fatal illness – the situation faced by Dr Cox.[7] It does seem that there is a groundswell in favour of a change in the law,[8] although it would be useful, were it possible, to survey the opinions of those who are close to death – even so, generalisations can never provide a satisfactory template in such intensely individualised conditions.[9]

There are also uncertainties as to the attitude of the medical professions. McLean's survey disclosed only 30% of doctors opposed to a change in the law to allow physician-assisted suicide; by contrast, this rose to 57% in a study carried out at much the same time by the BMA.[10] Similarly, 55% of the BMA sample would not take part in PAS if asked while only 37% of McLean's study group would never do so. Whatever one is to make of these figures, it is interesting to note that the majority of Western anglophone medical 'establishments' – as represented by their national Associations – want nothing to do with PAS or euthanasia.[11] Nor, one might perhaps reflect, are moral questions to be determined on the basis of straw polls. The fact that a majority believes that something is right does not *make it* morally right.

Suicide and attempted suicide – the current law

Suicide and attempted suicide are no longer criminal offences.[12] Whether or not this implies a legal right to end one's life is debatable but it is, at least, now firm law that the refusal of life-sustaining treatment is not a matter of attempted suicide.[13] The major interest, here, lies in the residual offence of counselling, procuring, aiding and abetting suicide which remains an offence in England and Wales by virtue of the

6 See J Wise 'Public Supports Euthanasia for Most Desperate Cases' (1996) 313 BMJ 1423.
7 See p 426 below.
8 R Smith 'Euthanasia: Time for a Royal Commission' (1992) 305 BMJ 728.
9 Although, in fact, a group of American oncology patients (ie with malignant disease) did not differ in any significant way from the general public: see Emanuel et al, p 420, n 5 above.
10 J Coulson 'Doctors Oppose Legal Mercy Killing for Dying' (1995) BMA News Review (March) p 15. The BMA sample was, however, small and, one suspects, relatively selected. However, in a poll taken by the BMA only six months later, the gap between the two series narrowed – eg 46% of doctors opted for a change in the law to allow active medical intervention to terminate life if asked as opposed to 44% who were against. The proportion who would not intervene if so requested fell to 48%: J Coulson 'Till Death Us Do Part?' (1996) BMA News Review (September) p 23.
11 Eg C-G McDaniel 'US Doctors Reaffirm Opposition to Euthanasia' (1996) 313 BMJ 11. A Working Party of the British Medical Association concluded, in 1988, that the deliberate taking of a human life should remain a crime and that the doctor who feels compelled by conscience to end a patient's life must take his chance with the scrutiny of the law.
12 Suicide Act 1961.
13 For a discussion of the relationship between suicide and the refusal of treatment, see J Fletcher 'The Courts and Euthanasia' (1987/88) 15 Law Med Hlth Care 223. D Lanham 'The Right to Choose to Die with Dignity' (1990) 14 Crim LJ 401, considers the subject in detail.

Suicide Act 1961, s 2(1).[14] In passing, it may be mentioned that there is some doubt as to whether an offence of abetting suicide exists in Scotland, where the Suicide Act never applied – it is difficult to imagine a common law offence of aiding an act which is not, itself, a crime.[15] Concerning ourselves only with England, our current interest lies in the relationship of outside agencies to the would-be suicide and, particularly, to the standing of the doctor. As to the general outsider, it is now clear that, while counselling or assisting a suicide remains an offence, this can only be illegal if conducted on a basis of immediacy and intent – the impersonal distribution of advice or information is unlikely to attract legal sanction.[16]

    We are unaware of any prosecutions of doctors in the United Kingdom. Whether such a prosecution would succeed depends, in our view, very much on the type of assistance given. It might, for example, be perfectly clear to a patient that he would die were he to use a conveniently located switch to disconnect an electrically operated life-sustaining apparatus; the fatal dose of a drug would be far less obvious and its 'successful' use might depend upon advice from the medical attendant – and, in law, counselling, procuring, aiding and abetting are taken as a whole. In practical terms – and, particularly, in view of the British jury's well demonstrated benign attitude to the medical practitioner – it would be very difficult to prove 'beyond reasonable doubt' an intent to commit a crime. 'Leaving the pills' could, certainly, be an offence but, equally, it could be one to which the law might turn, at least, an unseeing eye. The situation is, however, likely to be different when the doctor's assistance necessarily involves some activity. Such instances involve, pre-eminently, cases of progressive neurological disease in which the patient may wish to commit suicide but is physically unable to do so without assistance. These cases constitute a very specific group which has its own special ethical problems.

Progressive neurological disease

In so far as the right of the competent adult to refuse life-saving treatment is now universally established,[17] and that the right to control one's body has found expression in the decriminalising of suicide, it is but a short step to holding that to refuse assistance in dying to a person who is incapable of ending his or her own life is an affront to that person's rights of autonomy. The dilemma has been particularly well aired in Canada, where this proposition was upheld in *Nancy B v Hôtel-Dieu de Québec*.[18] Ms B, who suffered from the Guillain-Barré syndrome, was existing by virtue of ventilation; she sought to have her ventilator disconnected and was

---

14 It is also an offence throughout the US, save in Oregon which has legalised abetting suicide by physicians (see p 444 below).

15 By contrast, a good case can be made out for believing that assisting a person to commit suicide would be considered to be culpable homicide: see R A McCall Smith and D Sheldon *Scots Criminal Law* (2nd edn, 1997) p 171. The topic has been re-assessed recently: P R Ferguson 'Killing "Without Getting into Trouble"? Assisted Suicide and Scots Criminal Law' (1998) 2 ELR 288.

16 *A-G v Able* [1984] QB 795, [1984] 1 All ER 277.

17 For the UK, see *Re T (adult: refusal of medical treatment)* [1992] 4 All ER 649, (1992) 9 BMLR 46. For a recent Canadian decision, see *Ciarlariello v Schacter* [1993] 2 SCR 119.   Examples from the US include: *Re Kathleen Farrell* 529 A 2d 404 (NJ, 1987); *Bouvia v Superior Court of Los Angeles County* 179 Cal App 3d 1127 (1986).

18 (1992) 86 DLR (4th) 385, (1992) 15 BMLR 95.

supported in this by her family and the hospital. In making the required order, Dufour J called upon the Civil Code of Lower Canada, which held:

> 19.1. No person may be made to undergo care of any nature whether for examination, specimen taking, removal of tissue treatment or any other act, except with his consent,

and concluded that this encompassed ventilation. He proceeded:

> What Nancy B is seeking . . . is . . . that nature may take its course; that she be freed from the slavery of a machine as her life depends on it. In order to do this, as she is unable to do it herself, she needs the help of a third person. Then, it is the disease which will take its natural course.

As a result, the person responsible for the actual cessation of treatment would not violate the criminal law in so doing. At the same time, however, the judge ruled that, not only would it not be homicide, it would also be neither suicide nor assisted suicide – which suggests that the case of *Nancy B* is misplaced in this section. None the less, we find it difficult to accept this last use of words and return to the point below.[19]

Clearly, much the same misgiving affected the Supreme Court of Canada in *Rodriguez v A-G of British Columbia.*[20] The arguments in Ms Rodriguez' case, which concerned the setting up of a mechanism she could use to end her life should she become paralysed as a result of her motor neurone disease, were, in the main, based on Canadian constitutional law and, in particular, related to possible conflicts between the Canadian Charter of Rights and Freedoms and the Criminal Code; it is not easy, therefore, to transfer them to the United Kingdom stage.[1] It was held by a majority of 5:4 that, while the patient's autonomy was at stake in such cases, the deprivation of rights consequent on the refusal of such a request was not contrary to the principles of fundamental justice, which required a fair balance to be struck between the interests of the state and those of the individual; neither were the liberty and security of the person compromised – one reason being that the provisions in the Criminal Code, s 241 prohibiting assisted suicide were there as a *protection* for the terminally ill who were particularly vulnerable as to their life and will to live:

> [T]his protection is grounded on a substantial consensus among Western countries . . . that, in order to effectively protect life and those who are vulnerable in society, a prohibition without exception on the giving of assistance to commit suicide is the best approach . . . The formulation of safeguards to prevent excesses has been unsatisfactory and has failed to allay fears that a relaxation of the clear standard set by the law will undermine the protection of life and will lead to abuses of the exception.[2]

Despite the rather narrow basis for the judgment, some of the dissenting opinions express important general principles. In particular, the 'floodgates' argument was

19 See p 424.
20 *Rodriguez v A-G of British Columbia* (1993) 107 DLR (4th) 342.
1   It must be restated that *Nancy B* was heard under the Civil Code of Quebec.
2   (1993) 107 DLR (4th) 342 at 410, per Sopinka J. Note that the Supreme Court rejected Ms Rodriguez' appeal by a majority of 5:4 only.

dismissed, not because it might not occur, but because a person should not be denied a choice which others have open to them simply on the grounds that, as a consequence, others may then abuse such powers as they have over the weak and ill[3] – effectively, each individual person must be treated fairly by the law and not made a scapegoat for the fallibility of others (per McLachlin J). Finally, the opinion of Cory J merits repetition:

> [D]ying is an integral part of living . . . It follows that the right to die with dignity should be as well protected as is any other aspect of the right to life. State prohibitions that would force a dreadful, painful death on a rational but incapacitated terminally ill patient are an affront to human dignity.[4]

Thus, the arguments for and against assisted suicide of this type are finely balanced but all the dissenting opinions in *Rodriguez* stressed that it was for Parliament, not the courts, to make such fundamental decisions.

A third comparable case was heard in New Zealand.[5] The circumstances were very similar to those in *Nancy B,* save that the patient, L – also suffering from the Guillain-Barré syndrome – was incapable of expressing his wishes. His existence depended on artificial ventilation and the question put to the High Court was in the rather stark terms: would the doctors' action in withdrawing ventilator support make them guilty of homicide?[6]

Thomas J approached this issue by asking whether a doctor is obliged to continue treatment which has no therapeutic or medical benefit notwithstanding that the withdrawal of the treatment may result in the clinical death of the patient. He commented that all natural life has ceased in such a case; it was the *manifestations* of life which were maintained artificially and which were brought to an end by the doctor's intervention. He proceeded on the twin principles of humanity and common sense. On this basis, he concluded that life support provided *only* for the purpose of deferring certain death could not be regarded as a necessary of life; moreover, doctors have a lawful excuse to discontinue treatment when there is no medical justification for continuing that medical assistance. Withdrawal of treatment would not be unlawful if it was carried out within the accepted confines of 'good medical practice' – or adhering to a procedure which provided safeguards against the possibility of individual error. Within this scenario, withdrawal of life support would not be the cause of death *as a matter of law* – and this would coincide with the common-sense perception.

Thomas J's admirable analysis attracted particularly favourable comment in the House of Lords in *Bland.* Jurisprudentially, it owes much to the reasoning in PVS cases and this is inevitable in that L's disease state was more advanced than was that

---

3   We do not intend, here, to discuss the bizarre case of Dr Kevorkian in America who is said to have invented and promoted a 'suicide machine' – he faced a Grand Jury (D S Greenberg 'Dying, Doctors, and Politics' (1991) 338 Lancet 1446) and was acquitted of all charges. He has now filmed his operation and is again challenging the authorities to legitimate his actions. See D Whitworth 'Murder Charge for Death Doctor' (1998) The Times, 26 November, p 16.
4   (1993) 107 DLR (4th) 342 at 413.
5   *Auckland Area Health Board v A-G* [1993] 1 NZLR 235, [1993] 4 Med LR 239.
6   Crimes Act 1961, ss 151(1) and 164, NZ.

of Ms Rodriguez or Ms B. The judge was able, however, to medicalise the dilemma fully and thus avoid what is, in our view, the sophistry of the 'best interests' test.

The situation in the United States is interesting in that, as we have already seen, physician assisted suicide remains unlawful in the majority of States. Despite this, there is abundant evidence that removal of life support mechanisms at the request of the patient is not only acceptable but may be obligatory. Thus, in *Farrell*,[7] a motor neurone disease case, not only was a request for disconnection from the ventilator agreed, but the right to professional assistance during the agonal phase was upheld. An equally emphatic case arose in California, where the health care team was instructed to provide full facilities in order to ease the patient's dying.[8] It is thus clear that the United States' jurisdictions recognise a distinction between refusal of treatment and assisted suicide.[9]

It is to be noted that all these cases have it in common that the courts were anxious to ensure that the cause of death was due to natural disease. We suggest, and have argued already in respect of PVS,[10] that the cause of death following withdrawal of any form of life support should depend on whether the support was removed before or after brain stem death has occurred. If the body is dead at that time, the cause of death is clearly the original anoxic or other insult sustained by the brain. When, however, a treatment is discontinued solely by reason of its futility, there is nothing to be lost – and much to be gained by way of intellectual honesty – in attributing death, correctly, to 'Lawful withdrawal of life support systems which were necessitated by [the disease]'. Prevarication is, perhaps, inevitable in the absence of specific legislation – and a major advantage of a statute would be to open the door to greater honesty. This could be particularly easy in England where, it would seem, all that is needed is a subsection in the Suicide Act 1961, which excludes a registered medical practitioner from the provisions of s 2 along the lines suggested below.[11] Similar excluding legislation should be possible in most jurisdictions.

There have been no strictly comparable reported cases in the United Kingdom. The nearest approach was the case of Ms Linsell, which will probably remain unreported.[12] Ms Linsell was in the terminal stages of motor neurone disease when she sought a declaration that her practitioner would not attract prosecution if he gave her potentially lethal analgesics when her condition deteriorated. In the end, she withdrew her application on learning that a responsible body of medical opinion supported her doctor's planned palliative management regime – and her action was 'thoroughly approved and endorsed' by the court. Effectively, therefore, Ms Linsell's case does no more than endorse the well-tried legal concept of necessity.[13] Despite her counsel's statement that her only alternative option was to commit suicide, we are given no indication of the current judicial attitude to PAS. Her practitioner's reported summing up was probably an accurate reflection on the result: 'It's a shame for [her] sake that she didn't end up with a concrete ruling, which is what she would have liked.'

---

7 *Re Kathleen Farrell* 529 A 2d 404 (NJ, 1987).
8 *Bouvia v Superior Court of Los Angeles County* 179 Cal App 3d 1127 (1986).
9 See *Vacco v Quill* (1997) 117 S Ct 2293.
10 See p 406 above.
11 See p 444.
12 E Wilkins 'Dying Woman Granted Wish for Dignified End' (1997) The Times, 29 October, p 3.
13 See also pp 254-255 above.

Active euthanasia

By contrast with the above, there can be no doubt that active euthanasia is unlawful and this has been unequivocally restated in *Bland*, where we have Lord Mustill:

> [T]hat 'mercy killing' by active means is murder . . . has never so far as I know been doubted. The fact that the doctor's motives are kindly will for some, although not for all, transform the moral quality of his act, but this makes no difference in law. It is intent to kill or cause grievous bodily harm which constitutes the mens rea of murder, and the reason why the intent was formed makes no difference at all.[14]

This, then, was the position when Dr Cox was charged with the attempted murder of his patient of 13 years' standing, Ms Boyes.[15] Ms Boyes was suffering from rheumatoid arthritis – not, of itself, a killing condition but one causing intense pain; she had expressed a wish to die and was, indeed, already categorised as 'not for resuscitation'.[16] It was admitted that Dr Cox injected her with two ampoules of potassium chloride, which is known to be potently cardiotoxic but, at the same time, is a substance which the majority of practitioners would regard as having no analgesic value – and, as we have already indicated, it is this which distinguishes Dr Cox's case from any other prosecutions of doctors of which we are aware.[17] The only issue at trial was, therefore, that of intent – as Ognall J put it at the outset of his summing up:

> If he injected her with potassium chloride with the primary purpose of killing her, of hastening her death, he is guilty of the offence charged.[18]

and later:

> If a doctor genuinely believes that a certain course is beneficial to his patient, either therapeutically or analgesically, then even though he recognises that that course carries with it a risk to life, he is fully entitled, nonetheless, to pursue it. If in those circumstances the patient dies, nobody could possibly suggest that in that situation the doctor was guilty of murder or attempted murder.[19]

Essentially, therefore, the problem for the jury was whether the intention was that the patient should be free from pain because she was dead or whether she was to be granted a short pain-free period during the process of dying. In the event, Dr Cox was found guilty of attempted murder.

---

14 *Airedale NHS Trust v Bland* [1993] 1 All ER 821 at 890, (1993) 12 BMLR 64 at 137.
15 *R v Cox* (1992) 12 BMLR 38. Dr Cox was charged with attempted murder presumably because Ms Boyes had been cremated before her death was regarded as suspicious. Any arguments as to the cause of death would, therefore, have been speculative.
16 For which see p 445 below.
17 Another trial concerned with voluntary euthanasia by way of injection of potassium chloride and lignocaine was aborted when the prosecution offered no evidence: *R v Lodwig* (1990) Times, 16 March.
18 *R v Cox* (1992) 12 BMLR 38 at 39.
19 (1992) 12 BMLR 38 at 41.

So, what distinguished Dr Cox from Dr Adams and Dr Arthur? Some aspects of the judge's charge may have had an effect on the jury. He did, for example, exhort the jury not to be mesmerised by experts and, above all, to hold fast to common sense when assessing intention – no one, however, could question his impeccable neutrality. Obviously, we can never know the precise reason for a jury verdict; it is, however, reasonably safe to assume that, while public opinion in the United Kingdom will give great latitude to the medical profession in its fight against suffering, it is not yet prepared to accept the use of a substance which has no analgesic effect, and no known therapeutic purpose but which is known to be lethal when injected in concentrated form.

Even so, sympathy for Dr Cox was widespread.[20] No immediate custodial sentence was imposed; the vice-president of the Voluntary Euthanasia Society castigated what he saw as a supine jury;[1] the General Medical Council was content to admonish him on the grounds that, although his actions had fallen short of the high standards which the medical profession must uphold, he clearly acted in good faith; and the responsible regional health authority offered continued employment subject to certain restrictions.[2] We believe that the jury decision was certainly right in law but that public dissatisfaction ultimately stems from the law's determination to dissociate motive from intent when faced with unlawful killing[3] – as in the case of Dr Arthur, Dr Cox was certainly not a murderer as the word is commonly interpreted. None the less, for reasons which appear elsewhere in this chapter, we cannot accept that individual doctors should be given free rein in this field absent specific legislation.[4] Moreover, any such legislation must, itself, be suspect – one's distrust lying in what Levin has called the fallacy of the altered standpoint.[5] It has been said that current attitudes to euthanasia are comparable to the attitudes to abortion in the early 1960s;[6] it is precisely the fear that current attitudes to abortion may reflect those to euthanasia in the twenty-first century that temper our intuitive sympathy for both Dr Cox and his patient.

Passive euthanasia

By contrast with the positive action thus far discussed, passive euthanasia involves the shortening of life through an omission to act. Few people will find difficulty as

20 It is reported that 11% of doctors in the USA who are closely associated with relevant cases had received requests for a lethal injection and 4.7% had complied with the request at least once: D E Meier, C-A Emmons, S Wallenstein et al 'A National Survey of Physician-Assisted Suicide and Euthanasia in the United States' (1998) 338 New Engl J Med 1193.
1 C Dyer 'Rheumatologist Convicted of Attempted Murder' (1992) 305 BMJ 731.
2 C Dyer 'GMC Tempers Justice with Mercy in Cox Case' (1992) 305 BMJ 1311.
3 This view is central to the persuasive argument in K Boyd 'Euthanasia: Back to the Future' in J Keown (ed) *Euthanasia Examined* (1995) ch 7.
4 For an interpretation of the relationship between the law and the medical profession see Hoffmann LJ in *Airedale NHS Trust v Bland* [1993] 1 All ER 821 at 858, (1992) 12 BMLR 64 at 103: 'The court [has been invited] to decide whether, on medical facts which are not in dispute, [the action] would be justified as being in the best interests of the patient. This is a purely legal (or moral) decision which does not require any medical expertise and is therefore appropriately made by the court.'
5 B Levin 'No Justice in a Merciful Release' (1992) The Times, 24 September, p 12.
6 R Smith 'Euthanasia: Time for a Royal Commission' (1992) 305 BMJ 728.

to what is meant by active euthanasia. A glance at Figure 17.1 will show, however, that the definition of passive euthanasia presents a number of problems in so far as death resulting from inaction of one sort or another is spread across the whole spectrum and includes, inter alia, non-treatment of a treatable condition, withdrawal of treatment and refusal of treatment. Sub-categories exist even within this framework. Thus, treatment can be withdrawn either because it is non-productive or because, based on an anticipated quality of life, it is in the patient's best interests to do so; alternatively, treatment can be refused because the competent patient wishes to die or, simply, because he or she has an aversion to a particular form of treatment.

What one regards as passive euthanasia, then, depends not only on whether one is speaking in legal, moral or medical terms but also on personal preference or prejudice. As to the latter, we have tended to use the death certificate as our benchmark – would the patient have died if the physician had not retreated into his passive mode? On this definition, passive euthanasia is confined to withdrawal of life-sustaining treatment in the incompetent and refusal of further treatment by the competent patient where death is the intended outcome – with the 'do not resuscitate order' providing a virtually distinct category. The concept of 'double effect'[7] is also so bound to the subject of euthanasia that it cannot be ignored in this context. Such a classification will seem unsatisfactory to some; nevertheless, it forms the basis for the discussion that follows.

Whether there is any useful distinction to be made between activity and passivity when the common intention is either an accelerated or a 'better' death depends, as indicated above, largely on the idiom in use. We have already mentioned the moral argument[8] and, while we see the force of the contrary opinion, we believe that there is a morally significant difference between inactivity and action and that this rests on a firmer base than mere intuition. The essence of discrimination lies in the means to obtain the same end, in that the taking of active steps implies an autocratic control over the way in which the event occurs. The doctor who administers a drug intended to end the life of a suffering patient determines the moment and the manner of the patient's death. The process is quite different from allowing another agency – eg illness – to cause death. Activity, moreover, directly confronts those views which concede that death is the one hazard of life which is beyond the ambit of legitimate human intervention.

Speaking in medical terms, while only a very small number of physicians would work actively to end the life of a patient, selective non-treatment is practised fairly widely.[9] The medical profession as a whole sees a difference although the reasons for so doing may be tenuous in the extreme – as one reviewer put it: 'Our gut intuition tells us that there is a difference between active and passive euthanasia and we are not going to be browbeaten into changing our minds by mere logic.'[10] Put in rather less

---

7   See p 437 below.
8   See p 386 above.
9   In one of many such studies, this one undertaken by the BMA, 22 out of 750 doctors admitted to having actively ended the life of a patient on request although a surprising 46% believed that they should be legally permitted to do so. 90% supported passive euthanasia and 75% recognised a moral distinction between active and passive euthanasia: J Coulson 'Till Death Us Do Part?' (1996) BMA News Rev, Sept, p 23.
10 T B Brewin 'Voluntary Euthanasia' (1986) 1 Lancet 1085.   A logical, albeit tenuous, argument can be maintained for a distinction between the two: D P Sulmany 'Killing and Allowing to Die: Another Look' (1998) 26 J Law Med & Ethics 55.

Figure 17.1 ENDING LIFE – A SUGGESTED OUTLINE

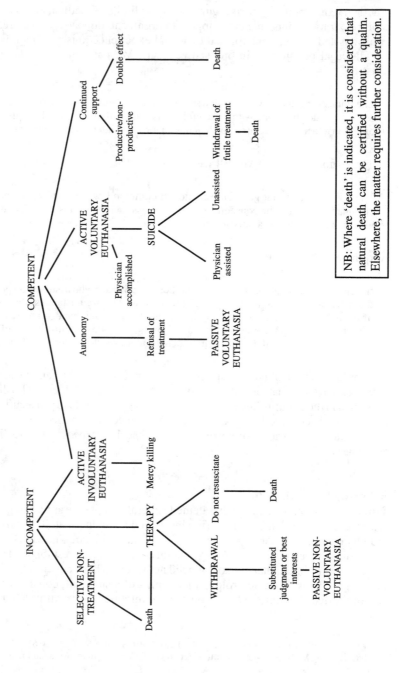

NB: Where 'death' is indicated, it is considered that natural death can be certified without a qualm. Elsewhere, the matter requires further consideration.

practical terms, philosophical argument has its limits in medical ethics: 'We cannot capture our moral judgments by appeal to argument alone . . . in the area of dying, intuitions and conceptions formed by actual experience must be given weight.'[11]

The legal position is, in one sense, clear. We can return to *Bland,* per Lord Mustill:[12]

> The English criminal law . . . draws a sharp distinction between acts and omissions. If an act resulting in death is done without lawful excuse and with intent to kill it is murder. But an omission to act with the same result and with the same intent is in general no offence at all.

So far, so good but Lord Mustill went on to say:[13]

> There is one important general exception at common law, namely that a person may be criminally liable for the consequences of an omission if he stands in such a relation to the victim that he is under a duty to act.

And there is Lord Keith:[14]

> In general it would not be lawful for a medical practitioner who assumed responsibility for the care of an unconscious simply to give up treatment in circumstances where continuance of it would confer some benefit on the patient. On the other hand, a medical practitioner is under no duty to treat such a patient where a large body of informed and responsible medical opinion is to the effect that no benefit at all would be conferred by continuance.

Lord Keith was, of course, speaking of the permanent vegetative state. There is, however, no doubt that, despite his obvious duty of care, the doctor who discontinues treatment in the circumstances envisaged he will not be liable to prosecution provided his inaction is covered by the doctrine of good medical practice.

We can now turn to some of the more specific aspects of so-called passive euthanasia.

Allowing the patient to die

While selective non-treatment has gained general acceptance as part of good medical practice, it is clear that it will not find moral endorsement in all its forms. The issue thus focuses on the distinction between what have become known as ordinary and extraordinary treatments. There is a general consensus, now established in both legal and medical opinion, that the doctor need not resort to heroic methods to prolong the life – or, perhaps better, to prolong the dying – of his patient; considerations of cost and of the distribution of other resources are important here, although they must be

11 G Gillett 'Euthanasia, Letting Die and the Pause' (1988) 14 J Med Ethics 61. This attitude was challenged by M Parker 'Moral Intuition, Good Deaths and Ordinary Medical Practitioners' (1990) 16 J Med Ethics 28.
12 [1993] 1 All ER 821 at 890, (1992) 12 BMLR 64 at 137.
13 Ibid.
14 [1993] 1 All ER 821 at 861, (1992) 12 BMLR 64 at 106-107.

secondary to the well-being and the dignity of the patient.[15] These principles are embodied in the classic expression of the ordinary/extraordinary treatment test which is to be found in the directive issued by Pope Pius XII in 1957:[16]

> Man has a right and a duty in case of severe illness to take the necessary steps to preserve life and health. That duty . . . devolves from charity as ordained by the Creator, from social justice and even from strict law. But he is obliged at all times to employ only ordinary means . . . that is to say those means which do not impose an extraordinary burden on himself or others.

This statement represents the core of Roman Catholic teaching on the matter and it has been widely accepted through the nearly half century of medical progress which has passed since its promulgation. Clearly, however, the difficulty about such a test is to distinguish ordinary from extraordinary treatments and the Pope, himself, qualified 'ordinary' as 'according to personal circumstances, the law, the times and the culture'. Thus, the ordinary/extraordinary test should not and cannot be applied as a general, all embracing rule. Some have, accordingly, suggested that the comparison should be between proportionate and disproportionate therapy; we would take this concept one stage further in preferring the contrast of productive and non-productive means – the test being whether or not a particular treatment is doing the condition any good. This firmly concentrates decision-making within the context of the individual patient and his unique condition; such an interpretation is endorsed both by the Anglican Church[17] and by the Roman Catholic Sacred Congregation.[18] Factors such as the physical and psychological pain involved in the treatment, its claim on scarce resources and the general prospects for the patient and his family may all be taken into account in deciding whether or not a treatment is productive. Clearly, non-productivity and medical futility have much in common as a treatment standard and, as we have already discussed, the arguments for and against their adoption are very similar. The scope for ethical and legal disagreement is wide and, in the long term, social consensus must be sought on ways to resolve the conflicts engendered by the notion of futility[19] – which we are convinced must come to be accepted in some way. Meantime, imperfect as the concepts of futility and non-productivity may be, their practical value should not be discarded for fear of offending what Miles has described as an elitist view of 'autonomy'.[20]

---

15 It is clear from at least two speeches in *Bland* ([1993] 1 All ER 821 at 879, 893, (1992) 12 BMLR 64 at 125, 140, per Lord Browne-Wilkinson and Lord Mustill), that resources might be a legitimate concern of the clinician.

16 (1957) 49 Acta Apostolicae Sedis 1027.

17 Most Rev D Coggan 'On Dying and Dying Well' (1977) 70 Proc Roy Soc Med 75.

18 *Declaration on Euthanasia* (1980). For further criticism of the ordinary/extraordinary treatment test see N L Cantor *Legal Frontiers of Death and Dying* (1987) p 35.

19 For a UK approach, see K R Mitchell, I H Kerridge and T J Lovat 'Medical Futility, Treatment Withdrawal and the Persistent Vegetative State' (1993) 19 J Med Ethics 71. Guidelines have been drawn up in New South Wales to cover cases in which life support treatment is deemed futile. Life supporting therapy is widely defined and includes chemotherapy, radiotherapy and renal dialysis: NSW Department of Health *Dying with Dignity* (1993) discussed by D John (1993) 306 BMJ 1363.

20 S H Miles 'Medical Futility' (1992) 20 Law Med Hlth Care 310.

Whose body is it?
The individual's right of self-determination is now virtually established as the determining factor in any situation of conflict – whether it is a problem of abortion, consent to treatment or euthanasia. Yet the question can still be properly asked – are there circumstances in which the wishes of the individual should be looked upon as being qualified by other considerations?

The theologian might well answer Yes; the Roman Catholic church, for example, allows no right to suicide and declining treatment might be regarded as suicide in certain circumstances. Others might hold that to diminish the seriousness and awe with which we view life is but a step towards the rejection of values which are of crucial importance. We would do well to reflect on the moral steps which are being taken when we pay homage to the cult of self-determination. None the less, the principle of self-ownership is now firmly established and is reflected legally in the offence of battery; any residual limitations of the right to accept or decline treatment have been virtually eliminated[1] – the concept of informed refusal has achieved the same legal standing as that of informed consent in the United States and Canada;[2] the principle is equally well established in the United Kingdom.[3] The common law basis for these decisions lies in the assumption that the rights of the competent individual to self-determination will normally outweigh the interests of the state in the preservation of life.

Pioneering statutory action in this field is to be found in the Medical Treatment Act 1988 of Victoria. The Act has two main thrusts. First, it enables a patient to refuse treatment, on either a general or a specific basis, by way of certification; the certificate may be completed only by persons over the age of 18 who were under no inducement or compulsion at the time and who were fully informed as to the consequences of refusal (s 5). Secondly, it introduces the offence of medical trespass which is committed by a medical practitioner who knowingly treats contrary to the prohibitions of a certificate (s 6); thus, the practitioner cannot plead his own ethos and there is no 'conscience clause'. Simultaneously, however, the Act exonerates the doctor who fails to treat in accordance with a certificate of refusal from professional, criminal and civil liability (s 9).[4]

The Victorian legislation is far-reaching. In particular, no distinction is made between terminal and other illness. Moreover, the right to refuse treatment is unqualified; it is subject neither to the interests of the state nor to those of third

1   See, in general, the very strong Supreme Court decision in *Washington v Glucksberg* 117 S Ct 2258 (1997). For an anecdotal reference, see the case of *Winter* – F Charatan ' "Wrongful life" Man Dies' (1990) 300 BMJ 1095 and D Brahams 'Unwanted Life-sustaining Treatment' (1990) 335 Lancet 1209. For the legal position in England, see *Re T (adult: refusal of medical treatment)* [1992] 4 All ER 649, (1992) 9 BMLR 46 and *Airedale NHS Trust v Bland* [1993] 1 All ER 821, (1992) 12 BMLR 64.
2   *Re Kathleen Farrell* 529 A 2d 404 (NJ, 1987) *State v McAfee* 385 SE 2d 651 (Ga, 1989), where the right to be helped through the resulting pain was also upheld; *McKay v Bergstedt* 801 P 2d 617 (Nev, 1990). For Canada, see *Malette v Shulman* (1990) 67 DLR (4th) 321, at 328 per Robins JA; *Nancy B v Hôtel-Dieu de Québec* (1992) 86 DLR (4th) 385.
3   *St George's Healthcare NHS Trust v S, R v Collins, ex S* [1998] 3 All ER 673 is probably the strongest authority.
4   The power to appoint an agent in the event of supervening incompetence is granted in the Medical Treatment (Enduring Power of Attorney) Act 1990. For description of the 1988 Act, see D Lanham 'The Right to Choose to Die with Dignity' (1990) 14 Crim LJ 401.

parties – non-consensual caesarian section on behalf of the fetus, for example, now has no place in Victorian medical practice.[5] The Act specifically excludes palliative treatment – or the provision of reasonable medical procedures for the relief of pain, suffering and discomfort (s 3) – from that which can be refused but, at the same time, preserves the patient's rights at common law in this respect. On the face of things, therefore, the Medical Treatment Act 1988 is a particularly firm expression of the doctrine of patient autonomy; it is also a remarkable example of the denial of a physician's autonomy – and it is difficult to see it as other than legislative approval of passive euthanasia of either voluntary or non-voluntary type.

It is to be noted that informed lay and medical opinion[6] has rejected the need for a similar statute in the United Kingdom where the common law and the advance directive, an importation from the United States, offer alternative solutions. As we have seen, there is ample evidence that the right of the competent individual to refuse treatment is ingrained in the common law – and this right persists even though it may result in the patient's death;[7] moreover, a refusal can take the form of a declaration of intention never to consent in the future.[8] By contrast, the position of the advance directive or 'living will', which is designed to express the autonomy of the incompetent patient, is uncertain in the United Kingdom.

In theory, the principle of the advance directive is simple – the individual executes a document expressing his or her wishes as to treatment in the event of being disabled from doing so verbally and the physician acts upon it. It is important to remember that, while the advance directive commonly expresses a refusal of treatment, it may, equally, authorise that life-prolonging measures be maintained – though it cannot, of course, *require* that such treatment be given; looked at in this way, the advance directive becomes an aspect of the right to choose rather than the right to die.[9] There seems little doubt that an unambiguous directive being applied in unambiguous circumstances would have the support of common law.

The difficulty is, however, that, while the theory may be simple, practice has its complications. Perhaps the main concern lies in the fact that it is almost impossible to devise an intelligible document which will be unambiguous in all circumstances – in particular, who is to define words such as 'severe', 'advanced' or 'comparable gravity' (for which, see Appendix G). Secondly, there is the persistent concern that the patient has, during the critical phase, changed his or her mind; Dworkin, in his classic *Life's Dominion*,[10] points out that the person who drafts a 'living will' and the incompetent who benefits from it are, effectively, different persons and the one need not necessarily be empowered to speak for the other. Given these imponderables, the doctor's dilemma is summed up in the words of Lord Donaldson:

---

5 Neither has it in England: *St George's Healthcare NHS Trust v S (No 2), R v Collins, ex p S (No 2)* [1998] 3 WLR 936.
6 House of Lords *Report of the Select Committee on Medical Ethics* HL Paper 21-1 (1994).
7 *Re T (adult: refusal of medical treatment)* [1993] Fam 95 at 115, (1992) 9 BMLR 46 at 61.
8 *Re C (adult: refusal of medical treatment)* [1994] 1 All ER 819, sub nom *Re C (mental patient: medical treatment)* (1993) 15 BMLR 77 at 82. The question of the capacity to refuse has been dealt with in chapter 10.
9 An elegantly neutral consideration of advance directives is to be found in A Sommerville 'Are Advance Directives Really the Answer? And What was the Question?' in S A M McLean (ed) *Death, Dying and the Law* (1996).
10 R Dworkin *Life's Dominion* (1993).

... what the doctors *cannot* do is to conclude that, if the patient still had the necessary capacity in the changed situation [he being mow unable to communicate], he would have reversed his decision ... what they *can* do is to consider whether at the time the decision was made it was intended by the patient to apply in the changed situation.[11]

from which it is clear that the doctor should, and probably must, apply his own interpretation to an advance directive.

Thirdly, the legal standing of the advance directive is, at least, in doubt in the United Kingdom. The only official dictum that we can find lies in a practice note:

The views of the patient may have been previously expressed, either in writing or otherwise. The High Court exercising its inherent jurisdiction may determine the effect of a purported advance directive as to future medical treatment ... In summary, the patient's expressed views, if any, will always be a very important component in the decisions of the doctors and the court,[12]

which is scarcely a dogmatic instruction. It is true that two of the Law Lords in *Bland* indicated that the advance directive had legal status[13] but their comments were certainly obiter; in our view, the current status of the 'living will' is indicative rather than binding.[14]

All in all, we believe that the case against legislating for an imperative living will is stronger than that in its favour. As things stand, less than 20% of adults have executed such directives. It would be asking too much of doctors presented with a comatose patient to be required to search for one before beginning treatment; on the other side of the coin, we would hope that the possession of a 'Request for Treatment' card never becomes a prerequisite for admission to the intensive care unit.[15] There does, however, seem little reason why the range of the Enduring Powers of Attorney Act 1985 and the comparable Law Reform (Miscellaneous Provisions) (Scotland) Act 1990, s 71 should not be extended so as to include health care provisions within the remit of proxies appointed to oversee the interests of persons who become incompetent (see chapter 12 for further discussion).

A limited concept?

We have already remarked on how blurred are the boundaries of 'passive euthanasia' and on the subjective nature of its definition. Thus, treatment of the patient in the permanent vegetative state is, in our opinion, best regarded as an example of medical

---

11 In *Re T (adult: refusal of medical treatment)* [1993] Fam 95 at 115, (1992) 9 BMLR 46 at 60.
12 *Practice Note* [1994] 2 All ER 413. Note that considerable 'persuasive' importance has been put on the advance directive by the Court of Appeal in *St George's Healthcare NHS Trust v S (No 2)* [1998] 3 WLR 936.
13 Per Lord Keith and Lord Goff in *Bland* [1993] 1 All ER 821 at 860, 866, (1992) 12 BMLR 64 at 105, 112.
14 The views of the English and Scottish Law Commissions are also to be noted – for which, see chapter 12.
15 Having said all of which, it has to be acknowledged that many of the American states have legislation giving legal status to the advance directive and there is no public outcry.

futility and has been discussed under that heading.[16] At the other end of the scale, we find the removal of life support from the competent patient indistinguishable from physician assisted suicide and continued treatment in the face of refusal comes very close to, or may actually constitute, an assault. Effectively, therefore, 'pure' passive euthanasia is limited to those relatively rare management decisions involving patients who have retained some cortical activity but are unable to make competent decisions and who, at the same time, are not known to have previously expressed an unequivocal preference as to treatment in the prevailing conditions.

So far as we know, there are no apposite legal precedents outside the neonatal field to look to in the United Kingdom, where the lawfulness of non-treatment in such circumstances would be very much determined by good medical judgment. The more frequent recourse to the law courts in the United States has, however, served to demonstrate certain principles and, at the same time, the difficulties which may be encountered.

Certain aspects of the individual circumstances have been given particular attention. In the first place, great emphasis is placed on intentions which have been expressed in life, not only specifically but also by words or attitudes. This is exemplified in the *Eichner/Storar* decisions.[17] In the first of these, the guardian's right to refuse treatment on behalf of an incompetent was upheld on the grounds that the latter had expressed his preferences, albeit only in conversation, when he was healthy. Mr Storar, on the other hand, had never been competent and the appellate court refused his mother's request to abandon blood transfusion therapy for his cancerous condition; it was thought that no one, not even a parent or a sibling, should decide that an incompetent should bleed to death. The authority of an advanced oral directive is, however, not absolute and may be subject to evidence of its being 'clear and convincing' – a condition which was first introduced in the important case of *Cruzan*,[18] which has been discussed in chapter 16. Secondly, some importance is attached to the imminence of death; in general, persons who are likely to survive for more than a year with treatment are maintained on therapy.[19] Thirdly, special provision is made for the permanent or persistent vegetative, regarding which it has been held:

> Life expectancy analyses assume that there are still some benefits to be derived from the continued existence of an incompetent patient. That assumption . . . is not appropriate in the case of persistent vegetative patients.[20]

It is, therefore, probably wrong to regard *Quinlan*[1] as the seminal case in the context of passive euthanasia and we have discussed it more appropriately under futile

---

16 See pp 394 et seq above.
17 *Re Storar* 420 NE 2d 64 (NY, 1981) (Consolidating *Eichner v Dillon*).
18 *Cruzan v Director, Missouri Department of Health* 110 S Ct 2841 (1990). An analysis of the legal effects of *Cruzan* is given in A Meisel 'A Retrospect on *Cruzan*' (1992) 20 Law Med Hlth Care 340. The author cited some 75 'right to die' cases heard in the US courts since 1976.
19 *Re Claire C Conroy* 464 A 2d 303 (NJ, 1983); on appeal 486 A 2d 1209 (NJ, 1985).
20 *Re Hilda M Peter* 529 A 2d 419 (NJ, 1987). Withdrawal of treatment from PVS children is also legally acceptable: N K Rhoden 'Treatment Dilemmas for Imperilled Newborns' (1985) 58 S Cal L Rev 1283.
1 *Re Quinlan* 355 A 2d 664 (NJ, 1976).

treatment. Although there are many other apposite examples,[2] perhaps the most instructive case is that of Ms Conroy;[3] *Conroy* is, admittedly concerned primarily with assisted feeding but we have established that feeding is, for current purposes, an aspect of treatment – and is certainly so regarded in the United States.[4]

Ms Conroy was an elderly incompetent diabetic, severely malformed and with an intellectual capacity above that of a person in the persistent vegetative state – even if only marginally so. Permission to remove her nasogastric tube was sought and granted by the trial court on the grounds that no valid purpose was served by needlessly prolonging a useless life. Although the subject had, meantime, died, the finding was appealed and was reversed – the Court of Appeal considering that death following removal of the feeding tube would have been due to dehydration and starvation; this implied active killing and they were not prepared to condone active euthanasia. Great concern was also expressed as to the knock-on effect which might seriously compromise the standards of treatment of the mentally retarded and of the senile demented. Even so, the Supreme Court of New Jersey reversed the appellate decision, holding that:

> artificial feeding by means of a nasogastric tube . . . can be seen as equivalent to artificial breathing by means of a respirator. Both prolong life through mechanical means when the body is no longer able to perform a vital bodily function on its own.[5]

the extrapolation being that the patient has the right to refuse both. While the Supreme Court commended the appointment of a guardian to act as proxy for the incompetent, it still laid down very strict criteria – including investigation by an ombudsman – before such decisions could be taken by the medical staff and the guardian or relatives. In the absence of *any* indications of the patient's wishes – under what the court referred to as the 'pure objective test':[6]

> the net burdens of the patient's life with treatment should clearly and markedly outweigh the benefits that the patient derives from life. Further, the recurring, unavoidable and severe pain of the patient's life with the treatment should be such that the effects of administering life-sustaining treatment would be inhumane.

The court expressly declined to authorise decision-making based on the personal worth or social utility of another's life, or the value of that life to others:

---

2 Eg *John F Kennedy Memorial Hospital Inc v Bludworth* 452 So 2d 921 (Fla, 1984); *Re Bertha Colyer* 660 P 2d 738 (Wash, 1983); *Re Nancy Ellen Jones* 529 A 2d 434 (NJ, 1987); *Guardianship of Grant* 747 P 2d 445 (Wash, 1987) – particularly describing procedures to follow to avoid judicial involvement in such cases.

3 *Re Claire C Conroy* 464 A 2d 303 (NJ. 1983); on appeal 486 A 2d 1209 (NJ, 1985).

4 Eg *Re Severns* 425 A 2d 156 (Del, 1980); *Re Mary Hier* 464 NE 2d 959 (Mass, 1984); *Brophy v New England Sinai Hospital* 497 NE 2d 626 (Mass, 1986); *Corbett v D'Alessandro* 487 So 2d 368 (Fla, 1986). In *Re Requena* 517 A 2d 893 (NJ, 1986), a hospital was ordered to retain a patient who refused to consent to artificial feeding and to honour her decision.

5 486 A 2d 1209 at 1236.

6 It should be noted that, contrary to our views expressed at p 405 above, the Supreme Court regarded this as a 'best interests' test rather than one of substituted judgment.

We do not believe that it would be appropriate for a court to designate a person with the authority to determine that someone else's life is not worth living simply because, to that person, the patient's 'quality of life' or value to society seems negligible.

Conroy is not an ideal authority, as the case was decided negatively because of the quality of the evidence. It does, however, provide a template by which decisions in similar cases can be measured. As we have seen, the American cases give great importance to the potential life-span of the patient. It is, therefore, appropriate to consider the effect this has on attitudes to euthanasia as a whole.

The terminally ill patient

We have seen that the law condemns active euthanasia on the grounds of intent. The terminally ill are beyond curative therapy by definition, and their management becomes a matter of the relief of suffering. Achieving this may, inevitably, involve some risk to life – but it is the patient's comfort, not his or her premature death, which is the intended outcome. The terminally ill patient thus most clearly sets the scene for the application of the philosophical concept of 'double effect'.[7]

The principle of double effect, in simple form, is that an action which has a good objective may be performed despite the fact that the objective can only be achieved at the expense of a coincident harmful effect. This analysis has, however, to be qualified – the action itself must be either good or morally indifferent, the good effect must not be produced by means of the ill-effect and there must be a proportionate reason for allowing the expected ill to occur. It is implicit in this doctrine that the good effect must outweigh the bad and this may involve a value judgment. Thus, it might well be ethically right to administer pain-killing drugs in such dosage as simultaneously shortens the life of a terminally ill patient; it would not be justifiable to give the same dose to a young man with identical pain who stood a reasonable chance of recovery. Many years ago, Lord Edmund Davies[8] put the counter-argument that death is the worst of all evils and, by implication, that it cannot therefore be a good objective. Such a view would, however, have little support among moral and religious spokesmen – the Archbishop of Canterbury firmly approved the principle at the same time,[9] as did Pope Pius XII, with certain limitations, as far back as 1957;[10] the Sacred Congregation for the Doctrine of the Faith has since confirmed his view.[11] The legal position is now clear.

The seminal case in the United Kingdom is that of *R v Adams*.[12] Dr Adams was thought to have treated a patient, who was incurably but not terminally ill, with increasing doses of opiates. Following her death, he was tried for murder and was

---

7 For a wide-ranging analysis of double effect, see D Price 'Euthanasia, Pain Relief and Double Effect' (1997) 17 LS 323. This paper highlights the difficulties in distinguishing double effect from active euthanasia.
8 'On Dying and Dying Well – Legal Aspects' (1977) 70 Proc Roy Soc Med 73.
9 'On Dying and Dying Well – Moral and Spiritual Aspects' (1977) 70 Proc Roy Soc Med 75.
10 (1957) 49 Acta Apostolicae Sedis 1027.
11 *Declaration on Euthanasia* (1980).
12 H Palmer 'Dr Adams' Trial for Murder' [1957] Crim LR 365.

acquitted. In the course of his summing up, Devlin J said: 'The doctor is entitled to relieve pain and suffering even if the measures he takes may incidentally shorten life', which is a clear direction. Twenty years after the *Adams* verdict, Lord Edmund Davies commented: 'Killing both pain and patient may be good morals but it is far from certain that it is good law.'[13] Williams,[14] by contrast, found the proposition easily justified by necessity. Any conflict has now been resolved. Devlin J's classic direction was followed in *R v Cox*[15] and the charge to the jury in the latter case was cited with approval by the House of Lords in *Bland,* where we have Lord Goff:

> [It is] the established rule that a doctor may, when caring for a patient who is, for example, dying of cancer, lawfully administer painkilling drugs despite the fact that he knows that an incidental effect of that application will be to abbreviate the patient's life . . . Such a decision may properly be made as part of the care of the living patient, in his best interests; and, on this basis, the treatment will be lawful[16]

And this is so whether the management regime is justified under the essentially moral doctrine of double effect or under the very similar legal principle of necessity.

We can also look to the important cases in infancy discussed in chapter 15. The majority of these came to judicial notice only because the patient was a ward of court; indeed, the principle is now so well established that there would be very few occasions outside wardship in which the courts would expect to be involved. The interesting inclusion of the whole caring team in the decision-making process[17] might be thought to be confined to paediatric practice but there is no reason why such a routine should not be extended to hospitals for adults; to do so would not only ensure 'open' decision-making but would also serve to emphasise that the effects of any treatment decisions fall not upon the doctor but on the nursing staff who will care for the dying person.

The incurable patient

The relative simplicity of the euthanasia debate has, thus far, depended upon the use of the adjective 'terminal', which defines a patient status which can only deteriorate – indeed, it is fair to say that attempts to legalise euthanasia in the English-speaking world have seldom, if ever, extended beyond the concept of the management of the dying patient. The problems for the doctor, and for the ethicist, become more complex when discussion is extended to the incurably ill whose condition may certainly get worse but which is also likely to remain static for often long times. Many variations on such a state can be envisaged and different therapeutic solutions adduced. There are, however, two overriding considerations likely to influence one's thinking – first, whether the patient is sentient or non-sentient and, secondly, whether

---

13 See p 437, n 8 above.
14 *Textbook of Criminal Law* p 416, n 12 above, p 581.
15 (1992) 12 BMLR 38.
16 [1993] 1 All ER 821 at 868, (1993) 12 BMLR 64 at 114.
17 *Re C (a minor) (wardship: medical treatment)* [1990] Fam 26 at 34, 37, [1989] 2 All ER 782 at 786, 788, per Lord Donaldson MR.

or not the distinction between incurable illness and death depends upon the use of artificial means.

The incapacitated patient

Thus, at one extreme, we have the fully conscious, incapacitated patient able to breathe naturally, as exemplified by the paraplegic or tetraplegic whose condition results from an accident. The clinical and moral solutions here are based on the same principles as relate to the terminally ill but conscious patient – any differences are those of emphasis. Once again, we are at the grey interface of passive euthanasia, assisted suicide and refusal of treatment and, as a result, major weight must be given to patient autonomy. Much of the discussion in this area is led by lay people and concentrates on the right to die. Most doctors who have been concerned with disabled persons receiving care and love have, by contrast, been impressed by their tenacity to life and their ability to adapt. This was demonstrated vividly in an old, but emotionally influential, study of tetraplegia – a condition which must be as near to wholly intolerable as can be imagined; 18 out of 21 sufferers said that they wished to be resuscitated in the event of their degenerating into coma.[18]

Both the double effect doctrine and the productive/non-productive treatment test are available in the management of the incapacitated patient; their rationale needs to be just that much more firmly based than is so in the case of the terminally ill

The conscious patient maintained artificially

It is fortunate that the interim state – that of mental competence while life is dependent upon a machine – is now rare due to the virtual disappearance of the more serious forms of acute anterior poliomyelitis (infantile paralysis); the least uncommon examples nowadays are those cases of high spinal tetraplegia which cannot be weaned from mechanical ventilation or, as we have seen, advanced cases of motor neurone disease (amyotrophic lateral sclerosis) and the Guillain-Barré syndrome. The medico-legal response to a positive request for the doctor to disconnect the mechanical respirator has already been discussed in some detail. There is now abundant international case law indicating that not to do so would constitute non-consensual treatment and, accordingly, battery – but the underlying implications of compliance are disturbing. It is almost trite to say that the ethical difficulties concerning the removal of mechanical respiratory support from those who can no longer benefit originate from the *provision* of that support – the primary decision is more important than those which follow as a consequence of that action.[19] But the doctor presented with an accident or an acute neurological emergency has virtually no choice of initiative action. He is dealing with a conscious but suddenly paralysed patient and he must provide support because he cannot know whether an individual patient is going to respond either physically or emotionally to heroic treatment – and,

18 B P Gardner et al 'Ventilation or Dignified Death for Patients with High Tetraplegia' (1985) 291 BMJ 1620. See also M Siegler and A J Weisbard 'Against the Emerging Stream' (1985) 145 Arch Int Med 129.
19 I M Kennedy 'Switching Off Life Support Machines: The Legal Implications' [1977] Crim LR 443. See also p 441 below.

if the doctor does not know, the patient cannot give or withhold his informed consent to setting the therapeutic train in motion. Can the doctor, then, accede to a later request to remove support?

It has been suggested that switching off a mechanical support is an act of omission and, therefore, both morally and legally acceptable. This is, in our opinion, untenable in practical terms. It would be an omission not to switch *on* the emergency supply in the event of a central power failure; that is easily distinguished from a deliberate, premeditated decision to remove the power – one has to *act* to turn off the television and the same will apply to the respirator.[20] Kennedy[1] has pointed out that a well-wisher disconnecting a conscious patient from his respirator would be guilty of homicide or perhaps of abetting suicide – and, in the United States, Mr Linares was, at least, brought before a grand jury.[2] The difference adduced by Lord Goff in *Bland*[3] was that, whereas the doctor was allowing the patient to die from his pre-existing condition, the interloper was actively intervening to stop the doctor from prolonging the patient's life. *Bland*, in fact, very nearly solves the problem – albeit indirectly. Thus, if, as was decided, the withdrawal of nasogastric feeding is an omission, it is but a short step to conclude that withdrawal of respiratory support is, likewise, an omission – and Lord Browne-Wilkinson, for one, was happy to see them as similar. The analogy admittedly involves some elasticity of conscience. Lord Browne-Wilkinson further concluded that a nasogastric did nothing, of itself, to sustain life and its removal could not be said to cause death; it is difficult to say the same of the ventilator of which the air-bag is an integral part. The main practical difference between the two must lie in the immediacy and the certainty of death when the respirator is turned off; the care team is, effectively, being asked to suffocate their patient. Lanham[4] has gone so far as to suggest that refusal to turn off a respirator when so requested might be a unique concession to the doctor's ethos allowed within the Victorian legislation which emphatically supports the autonomy of the patient. It is one thing, he says, to prevent doctors from forcing their treatment on an unwilling patient; it is another matter to require them to take what they may regard as unethical positive action to bring a conscious life to an end. As something of an envoi to the discussion, Kennedy and Grubb[5] point out that the omission/commission distinction loses significance once there is a duty to act – as there is in the doctor/patient relationship; in both cases, the doctor is either acting lawfully or he is guilty of manslaughter or murder depending upon intent.

The unconscious patient and the patient in intensive care
The management of the unconscious, breathing patient has been fully discussed in Chapter 16. There remain for consideration those comatose patients who are unable to sustain their cardiorespiratory functions without the aid of mechanical ventilation.

20 For an authoritative alternative view see Williams p 416, n 12 above, p 282.
 1 [1977] Crim LR 443, n 19 above.
 2 Lantos et al, p 416, n 17 above.
 3 [1993] 1 All ER 821 at 867-868, (1992) 12 BMLR 64 at 113-114.
 4 (1990) 14 Crim LJ 401, p 432, n 4 above.
 5 I Kennedy and A Grubb *Medical Law: Text with Materials* (2nd edn, 1994) p 1210.

The vast majority, perhaps all, of living patients with severe brain damage must be offered such care when they present at hospital – recourse is automatic for the purposes of facilitating diagnosis and assessment. If a diagnosis of irretrievable functional brain loss is made, there is no legal or ethical objection to regarding the ventilator as no more than part of the diagnostic machinery and dispensing with it once it has served its purpose. But a decision to treat, which, in this case, is within the doctor's clinical choice, is a different matter carrying with it the inescapable consequence that, at some time and for some reason, the treatment must be withdrawn. The critical point for applying the productive/ non-productive ethical test is, thus, at the beginning. With one exception, any later decisions are based on clinical or technical considerations alone.

This exceptional ethical decision relates to the allocation of scarce resources which include machines, beds, doctors and nursing staff, together with the necessary technical back-up. It may be necessary for a resource-based value judgment to be made at some point. Making a choice between patients may be among the doctor's most agonising moments and the weight to be given to economic and policy considerations can only be judged by the individual physician or surgeon on such factors as are outlined in chapter 11. There are now sufficient obiter statements from a variety of English cases to allow one to say with confidence that the courts will be sympathetic to resource-based management arguments. We do, however, suggest that this relates only to a competition for an *available* facility. There is nothing to support the suggestion that it would be acceptable to *remove* a patient from essential intensive care for no other reason than that a medically more rewarding case required the bed.[6]

Resources aside, the removal of a patient from intensive care depends, primarily, on a simple alternative – either he is dead or he is not dead. It can be taken that the whole brain is dead once the criteria for brain stem death have been met and we have the authority of the Conference of the Royal Medical Colleges and their Faculties[7] that the individual is dead when the whole brain is dead. In such circumstances, continued treatment is no more than treatment of a corpse – far from being unethical to withhold support, it would be positively immoral to continue other than to serve the purpose of beating heart organ donation or, conceivably, of post-mortem parturition. Withdrawal of treatment would also be legally indicated.[8]

However, it may still be proper to discontinue artificial ventilation even if death is not diagnosed. The closely allied considerations of productive/non-productive treatment and of 'death with dignity', untrammelled by tubes and wires, may be regarded by some as being related to the moral sphere and by others as being clinical in nature. Even so, the purely clinical consideration – that the treatment is doing, and will do, no good – will justify removal of support. One of two things may then happen – the patient will either continue to breathe of his own accord or he will die. In the former case, the patient has reverted to the persistent vegetative state, the management of which has already been discussed. No moral or legal problem arises in the latter

6 See Balcombe LJ in *Re J (a minor) (wardship: medical treatment)* [1993] Fam 15 at 30, (1992) 9 BMLR 10 at 20, discussed previously at p 379 above.
7 'Diagnosis of Death' [1979] 1 BMJ 332. Legislation to this effect is generalised in the English-speaking world.
8 *Re A* [1992] 3 Med LR 303.

situation; the outcome will have resulted from a clinical decision taken in good faith and after due deliberation based on a productive/non-productive treatment test. As we have already discussed, consent of the next of kin would be desirable but not essential to the question of lawfulness.

Criminal liability for withholding treatment

The case of *Quinlan*[9] settled the problem of criminal liability for ventilation withdrawal in the United States and there have been many later confirmations of this.[10] The position in the United Kingdom was resolved, first through the Scottish case of *Finlayson*[11] and later in the English case of *Malcherek*,[12] both of which have been discussed in relation to causation in chapter 13. Although *Finlayson* was not cited in *Malcherek*, the two decisions have remarkable similarities in that, in excluding criminality, the judges, first, relied on the concept of good medical practice and, secondly, declined to define death in both cases. This latter omission might, at first glance, be interpreted as vacillation on the part of the law; in fact, it reinforces the former principle in leaving the clinical decision firmly in the hands of the clinician.[13]

There is no reason to suppose that these decisions would not be applied in the civil courts and it would now be necessary to prove negligence – with all that entails – before a doctor could be considered culpable of a ventilator death. There are no United Kingdom authorities but a similar policy line has been adopted in the United States.[14]

A need for legislation?

It will be seen that, throughout this discussion, we have tended to the view that there is little need for legislation in respect of the incurably or terminally ill adult patient; the great majority of life or death decisions can be based on good medical practice which is contained by relatively clear legal and moral guidelines. The movement in favour of voluntary euthanasia is, however, maintaining its momentum. Some unease is apparent as to the capacity of the common law to contain what could become moral turmoil and there are a number of advocates of what can be loosely termed 'allowing to die' legislation; we have, ourselves, advocated defining legislation in the case of

9 *Re Quinlan* 355 A 2d 664 (NJ, 1976). See chapter 16 for discussion.
10 Eg *Re Bertha Colyer* 660 P 2d 738 (Wash, 1983); *Re Nancy Ellen Jones* 529 A 2d 434 (NJ, 1987); *Barber v Superior Court* (1983) 147 Cal App 3d 1006.
11 *Finlayson v HM Advocate* 1978 SLT (Notes) 60.
12 *R v Malcherek* [1981] 2 All ER 422, [1981] 1 WLR 690, CA (*R v Steel* being heard simultaneously on appeal).
13 Some concern was shown in Scotland when the Solicitor General stated that the prosecuting authorities were not in a position to give an assurance that withdrawing life support would not lead to prosecution: G Duncan 'Doctors Warned about Decision to Withdraw Life Support' (1993) Scotsman, 1 April, p 3. We believe, however, that this was no more than a reminder as to procedure, not as to principle.
14 Eg *Lovato v District Court* 601 P 2d 1072 (Colo, 1979).

the neonate in chapter 15. Powerful voices calling for parliamentary action, such as those of Lord Browne-Wilkinson and Lord Mustill, cannot be ignored.[15]

There are, of course, many hazards in legislating for what are broad moral issues. We have seen from the Netherlands' experience that attempts to satisfy all political views result only in confusion for the medical profession. The great majority of 'allowing to die' statutes passed in the United States allow for some professional privilege in interpreting instructions and some feel that this represents an actual reduction in patient autonomy. Many years ago, Lappé, discussing the first of these Acts, suggested that, in addition to eroding the patient's rights, legislation may lead to deterioration in standards of care – by covering poor treatment with the cloak of obedience to a directive – and may lead to the creation of conflict between doctor and patient in so far as both autonomy and paternalism are being simultaneously attacked.[16]

The original California Natural Death Act of 1976 is among those that are, in fact, restrictive. It deals only with 'medical procedures or intervention which utilises mechanical or other artificial means to sustain, restore or supplant a vital function' and can be applied only when 'death is imminent whether or not such procedures are utilised'. United States legislation, either enacted or proposed, covers a wide range – from the limited Californian conditions, through the wide acceptance of patient autonomy, subject only to public policy, as in Alabama, to the potential euthanistic permissiveness of Idaho – and none seems entirely satisfactory. Following the attempt at uniformity introduced by the model Uniform Rights of the Terminally Ill Act 1985,[17] the Patient Self Determination Act was brought into force in the United States at the end of 1991. The Act is relatively unadventurous and, essentially, lays a duty on hospitals to advise patients of their rights to accept or refuse medical treatment and to execute an advanced directive. The difficulties in drafting in such a complex area are clear from both examples.

However, as we have already commented,[18] this is not to say that it should not be attempted, and we now believe that some form of statutory law regulating 'controlled death' is inevitable, and needed, in the United Kingdom. We have sufficient faith in our legislators to believe that they will stop short of a fundamental alteration of the healing face of medicine. It may be better to start with relatively minor modifications of the law.

In this respect, the very great importance of the advanced directive in the United States is to be contrasted with its lack of standing in British law. While we maintain our distrust of the 'living will' as a legally binding document, we acknowledge that an advance directive may be useful to the clinician in charge of the case. We believe it should be incumbent upon a lawyer who is aware of its existence to notify the medical attendant of the fact in appropriate circumstances and that it would not be difficult to make this a legal duty by way of statute. This is by no means a giant step, but it could be a useful way of edging towards more extensive legislation.

We admit, however, to having changed our views in this respect since the last edition of this book and we suggest that there may be a case for legislation which not

15 See chapter 16, p 397 above.
16 M Lappé 'Dying while Living: A Critique of Allowing-to-die Legislation' (1978) 4 J Med Ethics 195.
17 For a full appraisal of this model Act, see I Kennedy and A Grubb *Medical Law: Text and Materials* (1st edn, 1989) p 1137.
18 See p 407.

only assists the practising physician but which, at the same time, serves to erode the holistic attitude to euthanasia which the public commonly adopts. The easiest – and most logical – segment of the 'end of life' issues to isolate is the permanent vegetative state, and we believe that distinctive legislation covering the management of this distinct condition would be valuable from both these points of view. We have intimated in chapter 16 that this should be of enabling type, possibly backed by a Code of Conduct approved by the Ministry of Health. A suitable Bill might be modelled on that which we have suggested could cover selective non-treatment in infancy.[19]

We also consider it important to distinguish suicide with the assistance of the physician, which must be seen as an extended form of personal autonomy, from other forms of arranged premature death – the Netherlands experience indicates the need to separate PAS from euthanasia as it is commonly understood. We have noted that the majority of the United States still prohibit PAS; none the less, Oregon has enacted specific legislation and others may well follow suit – particularly now that the Supreme Court has decided that control of PAS is a matter for the individual State legislatures.[20] Legislation in this field may be difficult to draft – the history of the Oregon Death with Dignity Act 1994 testifies to this[1] – but it is clearly possible to do so.

Once again, we consider it could best be done by permissive action. The opportunity exists in England to insert a sub section in the Suicide Act 1961 amending s 2(1) – which criminalises aiding or abetting suicide. Suitable wording might be:

> The provisions of s 2(1) shall not apply to a registered medical practitioner who, given the existence of a competent directive, is providing assistance to a patient who is suffering from a progressive and irremediable condition and who is prevented, or will be prevented, by physical disability from ending his own life without assistance.[2]

Having said which, we concede that many would regard this as allowing too much discretion to the medical profession and that they would prefer a positive, and possibly restrictive, approach.[3] Either route achieves the desired result of legislating for a specific, relatively uncontroversial aspect of euthanasia and, for our part, we would go no further. Legalising active euthanasia compromises the duty of the state to protect its subjects and the integrity of the medical profession[4] too deeply for general acceptance at the present time. It is often said that the euthanasia debate is at the same state as was abortion before the passing of the Abortion Act 1967 – and that it will progress inexorably in the same way; it is precisely this anticipation that lies at the heart of the euthanasia resistance movement. By addressing the subject in stages

---

19 Set out in J K Mason and D Mulligan 'Euthanasia by Stages' (1996) 347 Lancet 810. See p 407 above.
20 *Washington v Glucksberg* 117 S Ct 2258 (1997); *Vacco v Quill* 117 S Ct 2293 (1997).
1 For which, see C K Smith 'Safeguards for Physician-assisted Suicide: The Oregon Death with Dignity Act' in S A M McLean (ed) *Death, Dying and the Law* (1996) ch 5.
2 See Mason and Mulligan (1996) 347 Lancet 810, n 19 above.
3 For an example, see Professor McLean's draft Bill, p 420, n 4 above. Positive legislation would certainly be needed in the United States and, with this in mind, we have produced our own suggested Bill: see Meyers and Mason, p 419, n 14 above.
4 Most commentators anticipate the active involvement of doctors in carrying out any programme: M Otlowski 'Active Voluntary Euthanasia: Options for Reform' (1994) 2 Med L Rev 161; M Battin 'Voluntary Euthanasia and the Risks of Abuse: Can We Learn Anything from the Netherlands?' (1992) 20 Law Med Hlth Care 133.

as suggested above, we are confining ourselves to the 'core' situations for which it is not difficult to make out a logical case for legalisation; at the same time, we leave open the door for cautious extension of the law in the light of the experience so gained.

The 'do not resuscitate' order

There can be no doubt that it is often undesirable, effectively, to prolong the process of dying[5] – the problem, however, is to establish an acceptable general policy in an area that is so susceptible to subjective judgments. In what is probably the most influential current document on the subject, the British Medical Association and the Royal College of Nursing have issued a statement which is aimed to promote more discussion – and, hopefully, uniformity – on the subject in the United Kingdom.[6] In essence, this recommends that a do not resuscitate (DNR) decision can be considered when cardiopulmonary resuscitation (CPR) is unlikely to be successful, is contrary to the patient's sustained wishes or is likely to be followed by a quality of life which would be unacceptable to the patient; in the absence of a decision or of the patient's wishes, resuscitation should be initiated in the event of arrest; while the overall responsibility for the decision rests with the consultant, the views of the health care staff and the patient's relatives should be canvassed; discussion of CPR facilities with all patients is not obligatory but sensitive exploration of the wishes of those at risk should be undertaken – and recorded in the hospital notes; all members of the health care team should be made aware of a DNR order which should, itself, be reviewed regularly; if the DNR order results from the unlikelihood of any benefit, the clinical decision should be discussed with the patient and others close to him or her; if it derives from quality of life considerations, the views of the patient should be ascertained and, if this is impossible, those of close relatives should be used to assess the patient's best interests.

Well meaning though such guidelines may be, it is clear that they conceal a hornet's nest of moral dilemmas. Exclusion from resuscitation in British hospitals is said to be more likely in patients with a current diagnosis of malignancy, dementia or pneumonia or with a past or present history of stroke.[7] But at what stage of the disease is the patient with cancer to be regarded as not to be salvaged? How are we to assess what is the patient's idea of an acceptable quality of life? To what extent is dementia a contraindication imposed for the benefit of the carers?[8] Perhaps most

5 For a classic example, see the papers associated with R F Weir 'Betty's Case: An Introduction' (1989) 17 Law Med Hlth Care 211. For a recent American review assessing the moral grounds for providing or withholding treatment, see M Hilberman, J Kutner, D Parsons and D J Murphy ' Marginally Effective Medical Care: Ethical Analysis of Issues in Cardiopulmonary Resuscitation (CPR)' (1997) 23 J Med Ethics 361.

6 BMA *Cardiopulmonary Resuscitation – A Statement from the BMA and RCN*' (1993). See also the earlier publication from the Royal College of Physicians: Working Party of the Royal College of Physicians of London 'Resuscitation from Cardiopulmonary Arrest. Training and Organisation' (1987) 21 J R Coll Physic Lond 175.

7 R M Keating 'Exclusion from Resuscitation' (1989) 82 J Roy Soc Med 402.

8 See *Re D (medical treatment)* (1997) 41 BMLR 81, [1998] 2 FCR 178, in which treatment was lawfully suspended in a man whose long-standing mental disability made it impossible for him to commit himself to co-operate in his haemodialysis.

importantly – who is to make the decisions and how deeply involved should the patient be in the process? Despite the BMA's guidance that the patient's consent is highly desirable, one would have thought that obtaining such consent would raise intractable practical difficulties – and only a minority of doctors make the attempt. Surprisingly, however, it appears that the majority of patients actually welcome appropriate consultation.[9]

Finally, we might revert to the question of age. There is little doubt that DNR orders are issued more often and more freely in older patients; irrespective of the diagnosis and prognosis, DNR orders were written in five major American medical centres for 22% of patients under 54 years old, rising to 56% for those aged more than 85.[10] In our opinion, it is particularly important to ensure that junior doctors in the prime of life are trained to understand the needs of the elderly disabled. The somewhat chilling observation of Rhoads, albeit from across the Atlantic and made some time ago, bears repetition: 'How large a factor is age in deciding to relax therapeutic efforts seems to depend somewhat on the age of the physicians making the decisions.'[11]

Cases involving DNR orders come to the attention of the courts only rarely. An exception lies in the significant case of *Re R*,[12] which concerned a 23-year-old man who could not sit up, chew food or communicate in any formal way. He was probably blind and deaf and other physiological disabilities indicated that his condition was appalling. Nevertheless, he could not be regarded as being in the permanent vegetative state. A DNR order in the event of cardiac arrest was signed by the consultant psychiatrist and agreed by the patient's mother. However, a member of the staff at the day centre at which he was treated arranged for an application for judicial review of the order. The health authority then sought a declaration that it would be lawful to withhold life-sustaining treatment – which included resuscitation and ventilation, nutrition and hydration by artificial means and the administration of antibiotics – and to treat the patient so that he suffered minimum distress until his death. The application was later amended so as to exclude withholding of nutrition and hydration – and, in fact, it was proposed to perform a non-consensual gastrostomy.

At the hearing, all the medical witnesses expressed the view that cardiopulmonary resuscitation (CPR) would not be appropriate in R's case, this being largely on the grounds that it was unlikely to be successful. Withholding antibiotics was, however, considered as a separate issue and was recommended subject to the approval of the patient's general practitioner and to the consent of one or both parents – and this distinction was recognised by the court in its determination.

In granting the declaration as sought, the President, Sir Stephen Browne repeated that there was no question of the court being asked to approve a course aimed at terminating life or accelerating death. In tying *Re R* to *Re J*,[13] however, the President

9 M E Hill, G MacQuillan, M Forsyth and D A Heath 'Cardiopulmonary Resuscitation: Who Makes the Decision?' (1994) 308 BMJ 1677.

10 R B Hakim, J M Teno, F E Harrell et al 'Factors Associated with Do-Not-Resescitate Orders: Patients' Preferences, Prognoses, and Physicians' Judgments' (1996) 125 Ann Int Med 284.

11 J E Rhoads 'The Right to Die and the Chance to Live' (1980) 6 J Med Ethics 53. A brief but informative review of patient and physician attitudes is to be found in R Morgan, D King, C Prajapati and J Rowe 'Views of Elderly Patients and their Relatives on Cardiopulmonary Resuscitation' (1994) 308 BMJ 1677.

12 *Re R (adult: medical treatment)* (1996) 31 BMLR 127, [1996] 2 FLR 99.

13 *Re J (a minor) (wardship: medical treatment)* [1991] Fam 33, (1990) 6 BMLR 25.

clearly admitted a 'quality of life' standard for decisions involving adults – approving Taylor LJ in *Re J*:

> [T]he correct approach is for the court to judge the quality of life [the patient] would have to endure if given the treatment and decide whether in all the circumstances such a life would be so afflicted as to be intolerable . . . [14]

Approved management regimes thus seem to be following the course we anticipated in chapter 16. The case also strongly indicates that non-treatment decisions in the case of the incapacitated should normally be taken by health professionals in concert with people close to the patient; it is only in the event of serious challenge to the clinical opinion that court intervention will be required. At the same time, *Re R* raises the question as to whether feeding and hydration are to be seen as different in quality from other medical treatments.[15] Our own tentative view is that any apparent divergence from the House of Lords decision in *Bland* derives from the rather specialised wording of the application in *Re R* and has no significant general application.

Feeding as a part of treatment

We have already referred to feeding as a part of treatment in relation to *Bland* in chapter 16. The definition of artificial feeding was not, however, addressed in either *Bland* or *Re R* – or in any of the other relevant British cases. As Strong[16] has pointed out, when we speak of providing nourishment, we are referring to a continuum which runs from natural breast feeding through feeding by mouth to seriously invasive procedures which may even entail surgical operation. Once discomfort and danger are introduced, so too is balancing the advantages and disadvantages – or, in practice, applying a productive/non-productive treatment test.[17] The fundamental question is, therefore, at what *stage* does the act of feeding become medical treatment?

Increasing invasiveness carries increasing risk – it, therefore, seems logical to classify anything which involves invasion as medical treatment. At the other end of the scale, it is difficult to conceive of purely natural feeding as treatment and, so far as we are aware, no court in either the Commonwealth or America has ever suggested that normal feeding could properly be withheld on clinical grounds from someone able to accept it. None the less, even this distinction is over-simplistic. At one extreme, spoon feeding of a reluctant ament can be regarded as invasive and, accordingly, as medical treatment; at the other, the instillation of fluid through a tube can be seen as simple care involving no risk – but it can be done only as a *result* of invasion. The difficulties are exemplified in the drafting of the Victorian legislation which includes 'the reasonable provision of food and water' under the heading of

14 (1990) 6 BMLR 25 at 42.
15 As suggested by the BMA in their Discussion Paper, p 445, n 6 above.
16 C Strong 'Can Fluids and Electrolytes be "Extraordinary Treatment"? (1981) 7 J Med Ethics 83.
17 K C Micetich et al 'Are Intravenous Fluids Morally Required for a Dying Patient ?' (1983) 143 Arch Int Med 975. The complication rate of intravenous hyperalimentation may approach 50%.

palliative treatment – and, therefore, outwith the statutory control of the patient[18] – and, then, fails to define 'reasonable provision'. An all-embracing definitional solution seems impossible. We can only look to a minimum standard and suggest that any form of feeding which requires some *medical* training and expertise can be considered medical treatment and, accordingly, may properly be subject to selective provision. The insertion of a nasogastric tube involves a surprising degree of skill and, on this basis, nasogastric feeding would qualify as medical treatment; thus, the decision in *Bland* is, to us, unexceptional. By contrast, the provision of food and water by normal means – that is, by mouth and dependent on the patient's swallowing reflexes – is a matter of skilled nursing care. It may also be seen as the quintessential example of kindness and humanity.[19]

---

18 Medical Treatment Act 1988 (Vict), s 3.
19 *Airedale NHS Trust v Bland* [1993] 1 All ER 821 at 856, (1992) 12 BMLR 64 at 101, per Hoffmann LJ.

Research and experimentation

18 Biomedical human research and experimentation

At one time, biomedical experimentation using human subjects proceeded almost without comment. The researchers justified their activities as benefiting mankind; the subjects were generally happy to 'oblige' or to be reasonably recompensed; and research was of manageable quantity. Attitudes and conditions have, however, changed. The reaction against paternalistic medicine has gained momentum pari passu with an increasing concern for the rights of the individual; the potential investigations and the instrumental and other means for conducting them have greatly increased; and there has been something of an explosion not only in the production of new therapeutic agents but also in governmental control of their distribution – witness the copious legislation regulating the marketing of medicines. But the greatest single impulse to regulate experiments on human beings sprang from a realisation of the appalling depths which were plumbed in the genocidal era of the Second World War when, undoubtedly, much valuable information was gathered but only at the cost of immense suffering. The awareness of what had happened in the medical laboratories of Nazi Germany and Japan led to a determination that medical research should never again be tainted by such callous disregard for the rights of the individual, and it is this determination which led to the promulgation of international codes on the ethics of research. Such endeavours were not everywhere supported, however, and the end of the Soviet era in Eastern Europe resulted in a frank acknowledgment in a number of countries that medical science in the Soviet Union and its satellite countries had been far from meeting the ethical standards expected it the West.[1] This has been translated into action in Poland, for example, by the introduction of a code of medical ethics which, in a remarkable judgment of the Polish Constitutional Court in 1992, was held to outrank contradictory provisions of the law.[2]

Ethical codes in human biomedical experimentation

The first internationally accepted set of ethical guidelines in this context was known as the Nuremberg Code and was a direct result of the war-crimes trials.[3] It is, perhaps, unfortunate that this should be so, as it inevitably puts the researcher on the defensive. To minimise this, the tribunal itself adopted the preamble:

1 Z Szawarski 'Research Ethics in Eastern Europe' (1992) 82 Bull Med Ethics 13.
2 The English text of this code is published in (1992) 82 Bull Med Ethics 13; the decision of the Constitutional Court is discussed by E Zielinska at p 25.
3 There is a wide discussion of the problem of the significance of Nuremberg in G J Annas and M A Grodin (eds) *The Nazi Doctors and the Nuremberg Code: Human Rights in Human Experimentation* (1992).

451

The great weight of the evidence before us is to the effect that certain types of medical experiments on human beings, when kept within reasonably well defined bounds, conform to the ethics of the medical profession generally ... All agree, however, that certain basic principles must be observed in order to satisfy moral, ethical and legal concepts.

It was, however, apparent that the medical profession itself should publicly endorse the principles expressed in the ten clauses of the Nuremberg Code; this movement culminated in the Declaration of Helsinki – drawn up by the World Medical Association in 1964 and revised several times between 1975 and 1996 – which is reproduced as Appendix F.[4] Many national authorities have attempted to explain or expand upon the basic principles established at Nuremberg and, for the British reader, the most important of these are the comprehensive set of guidelines issued by the Royal College of Physicians of London[5] and the Medical Research Council of 1992.[6] In the European context, the Council of Europe's Convention on Human Rights and Biomedicine, opened for ratification in 1997, sets out broad principles under which research may be undertaken on human subjects, including those who are unable to give a proper consent, and on embryos.[7]

In addition to these specialised codes, protection for the subject of experimentation is provided by international human rights law. The International Covenant on Civil and Political Rights, which forms part of the International Bill of Rights, includes the provision that 'no one shall be subjected to torture or to cruel, inhuman, or degrading treatment or punishment. In particular, no one shall be subjected without his free consent to medical or scientific experiment'. This prohibition is couched in the most general terms, but the linking of medical research issues to human rights law adds important weight to the protection of the research subject.

All such codes have it in common that they appreciate the need for human experimentation while accepting that this can only be accomplished at the expense of some of the subjects' right to self-determination. Moreover, the doctor's ethical position must show some flexibility. The Hippocratic Oath states: 'I will follow that regimen which ... I consider for the benefit of my patients and abstain from whatever is deleterious and mischievous'; the absolutist could say that this precludes all experimentation on patients, yet it is clear that progress in medicine depends upon some form of trial. A balance is needed and must be sought.

---

4   Other international codes include the International Ethical Guidelines for Biomedical Research involving Human Subjects published in Z Bankowski and R J Levine *Ethics and Research on Human Subjects: International Guidelines* (1992). For discussion of the various guidelines, see K M King 'A Proposal for the Effective International Regulation of Biomedical Research Involving Human Subjects' (1998) 34 Stanford J Int Law 163.

5   Royal College of Physicians of London *Research Involving Patients* (1990). Other useful earlier documents include *Responsibility in Investigations on Human Subjects*, report of the Medical Research Council of 1962-63 (Cmnd 2383).

6   Medical Research Council *Responsibility in Investigations on Human Participants and Material and on Personal Information* (1992).   This replaced the statement of the Council of 1962-63.

7   Council of Europe *Convention for the Protection of Human Rights and Dignity of the Human Being with Regard to the Application of Biology and Medicine* (1997).

What is research?

Research and experimentation are commonly used as interchangeable terms – we, however, believe that there is a distinction to be made. Research implies a predetermined protocol with a clearly defined end-point. Experimentation, by contrast, involves a more speculative, ad hoc, approach to an individual subject. The distinction is significant in that an experiment may be modified to take into account the individual's response; a research programme is more likely to tie the researcher to a particular course of action until such time as its general ineffectiveness is satisfactorily demonstrated.[8]

Research activities can be broadly categorised as clinical research, which is aimed at the improved treatment of a patient or a group of patients and as non-therapeutic – in which the essential object is the furtherance of purely scientific knowledge which may, eventually, have a wider application than patient care. This distinction makes little conceptual difference to the general requirements for ethical research. The mere fact that the research subject, being a patient at the time, may receive benefit does not mean that the programme can be undertaken unregulated by research codes – indeed, the fact that a relatively vulnerable group is involved emphasises the vigour with which controls should be applied. Only the degree of risk to be permitted in proportion to the expected outcome is affected by the nature of the research.

It follows from this classification that research subjects may be of four types: individual patients; a group of patients who are suffering from one particular condition, patients who have no association with the disease or process under review but who are readily available; and, finally, healthy volunteers – a heterogeneous group which is of importance because it may involve other 'captive' populations, including the researchers themselves.

The logical implication of this division of subjects is that researchers should also be categorised. Thus, the individual patient is under the care of a doctor. Any experimentation is, therefore, performed on a care-associated basis and, while there may be difficulties in a hospital setting where 'care' is very much a team concept, the essential doctor-patient relationship is, and should be, maintained. But it cannot be said with reference to any of the other groups that 'the health of my patient is my first consideration' and, consequently, the researchers cannot include the patients' physicians. Even so, when human subjects are involved in medical experimentation, so must doctors be; the danger of non-medical researchers being, not so much callous, as uncomprehending of their subjects' reactions is such that a situation excluding doctors would only be acceptable in the event that the researchers were their own experimental subjects.

The risks involved
All research involves some risk and it is the art of the good investigator to minimise that risk. But there are certain guidelines to be followed which are spelled out in the

8   For discussion, see B M Dickens 'What is a Medical Experiment?' (1975) 113 Can Med Assoc J 635; B Gaze and K Dawson 'Distinguishing Medical Practice and Research: the Special Case of IVF' (1989) 3 Bioethics 301.

Declaration of Helsinki[9] and also in the report of the Royal College of Physicians.[10] A risk/benefit analysis must be undertaken in each case and patients may be involved only when the benefit to them clearly outweighs the inconvenience, discomfort or possible harm which the protocol may impose. The Royal College of Physicians distinguishes between research involving 'less than minimal risk' and that involving 'minimal risk'. The former is the risk of the sort involved in giving a sample of urine or a single venous sample in an adult; the latter arises where there is a reasonable chance of a mild reaction – such as a headache or a feeling of lethargy – or where there is a remote chance of serious injury or death. If the level rises above that of minimal risk, then the College takes the view that patients should be involved only if:

(a) the risk is still small in comparison with that already incurred by the patient as a consequence of the disease itself;
(b) the disease is a serious one;
(c) the knowledge gained from the research is likely to be of great practical benefit;
(d) there is no other means of obtaining that knowledge; and
(e) the patient gives a fully informed consent.

The question of whether healthy volunteers may ever be exposed to serious risks in the course of medical research is problematic. The Declaration of Helsinki seems to rule it out in stating that, in non-therapeutic research, 'the investigator or the investigating team should discontinue the research if in his/her or their judgment it may, if continued, be harmful to the individual'.[11] This would exclude participation by anyone other than the researchers themselves in hazardous research and would render the use of volunteers unethical in, say, potentially harmful research into the development of vaccines against diseases that may affect the community. The European Convention on Human Rights and Biomedicine is more general, and therefore, on one reading at least, more permissive. It states that research involving human subjects may only be undertaken if 'the risks which may incurred by [the participant] are not disproportionate to the potential benefits of the research'.[12] There will clearly be differing views as to what risks are justifiable; it is clear, though, that there will be those who would accept risks of a very high order for admirable altruistic reasons and it is questionable whether they should be prevented from so doing. There are legal limits to the extent to which consent decriminalises the infliction of harm[13] and it is interesting to speculate whether the consent of a volunteer to a dangerous medical experiment would serve as a defence to a charge of assault or homicide.

The AIDS pandemic, and the widespread public concern which it has sparked, has brought the issue of participation in risky research into focus. In one view, the threat which HIV poses justifies the suspension of normal controls on research. This would mean that the normal procedures for investigating the safety of promising drugs might

9 Paras 4 and 5.
10 Paras 5.8-5.26.
11 Para III.3.
12 See p 452, n 7, above, art 16.
13 *A-G's Reference (No 6 of 1980)* [1981] QB 715, [1981] 2 All ER 1057, CA; *Smart v HM Advocate* 1975 SLT 65; *R v Brown* [1994] 1 AC 212, [1993] 2 All ER 75. See also The Law Commission *Consent in the Criminal Law* (Law Com No 131, 1995).

be circumvented and volunteers would be allowed to run risks which would, in normal circumstances, be considered excessive. While it would be unwise, and scientifically inappropriate, to suspend all regulation of AIDS-related research, the necessity of the situation undoubtedly justifies such measures as 'fast-track approval' of therapeutic drugs.[14] It would also be difficult to condemn the participation by fully informed volunteers in vaccine or other trials which involved a high level of personal risk. Such volunteers, if they are also researchers, are likely to be regarded as scientific heroes. In the case of patients, willingness to explore any avenue of treatment – even those that are highly risky – might be regarded as lying within the range of acceptable personal risk-taking. It seems churlish to refuse the slim prospects held out by an experimental treatment if a condition is, otherwise, clearly terminal.[15]

The design of experiments

All experiments cost money and cause some inconveniences both to colleagues and subjects. Badly planned research loses all ethical justification if, as a result, the findings are scientifically useless. So much depends upon planning that it is now a requirement for district health authorities to establish and support local research ethics committees whose function it is to approve any experimental project using NHS patients or resources. Such committees wield considerable power in the United States, where their function is generally expanded to include therapeutic and prognostic decision-making.[16] The situation in the United Kingdom is, however, different. Here, with the occasional exception,[17] committees are established purely to vet research projects and this mainly from the point of view of their moral implications as to the use of subjects and of resources. The majority of the work is undertaken at local level through local research ethics committee (LREC), but the need to extend research so as to include a number of departments has necessitated the establishment of multi-centre research ethics committees. The composition of these committees, along with matters of procedure, are regulated by guidelines issued by the NHS.[18]

14 L C Fentiman 'Aids as a Chronic Illness: a Cautionary Tale for the End of the Twentieth Century' (1998) 61 Albany LR 989.

15 The issue is discussed by C Levine 'Has AIDS Changed the Ethics of Human Subjects Research?' (1988) 16 Law Med Hlth Care 167.

16 For a discussion of procedural aspects of American hospital ethics committees, see 'Ethics Committees' (1992) 20 Law Med Hlth Care 278 (S M Wolf 'Toward a Theory of Process', 278; J C Fletcher 'Ethics Committees and Due Process' 291; C B Cohen 'Avoiding "Cloudcuckooland" in Ethics Committee Case Review: Matching Models to Issues and Concerns' 294; B M Dickens 'Ethics Committees, Organ Transplantation and Public Policy' 300). On the implications of the introduction of such committees in the UK, see A McCall Smith 'Committee Ethics? Clinical Ethics Committees and their Introduction in the United Kingdom' (1990) 17 J Law & Soc 124.

17 'UK's First Hospital Ethics Committee' (1993) 90 Bull Med Ethics 5, reporting the setting up, within an NHS trust hospital, of an ethics committee with the broad remit of considering any ethical dilemmas arising in the course of hospital activity.

18 Department of Health *Local Research Ethics Committees* (1991). See also Royal College of Physicians *Guidelines on the Practice of Ethics Committees in Medical Research Involving Human Subjects* (3rd edn, 1996). For Scotland, Home and Health Department *Local Research Ethics Committees* 1992 (GEN) 3. Guidelines for regional multi-centre REC's in England and Wales are set out in HSG (1997) 23 and for a national MREC in Scotland in NHS MEL (1997) 8. For notes on the relationship between LREC's and MREC's, see 'Research Ethics Committee Update' (1998) 138 Bull Med Ethics 13.

Each local committee should include both sexes and cover a range of ages; the hospital staff and general practitioners should be represented and the committee, of which the ideal size should be between eight and twelve members, must include at least two lay persons – and either the chairman or vice-chairman must be drawn from the lay membership.

The inclusion of 'average citizens' can be seen as no more than a necessary political gesture; on the other hand, lay members may be better placed than professionals to appreciate the effects of different treatments on the day-to-day lives of the patients and their inclusion may, therefore, have definite practical advantages. The overall derivation of committee members is of greater significance but, in view of the language in which proposals are couched, it is inevitable that the medical members, having a greater understanding of what is entailed, will play a leading role in decision-making. Thus, the efficiency of an LREC depends very largely on the capacity and willingness of the latter to explain the proposals to their non-medical colleagues. Neither the composition nor the remit of LRECs in the United Kingdom is uniform, but the setting up by the Nuffield Foundation of a national body – the duties of which include the monitoring of the activities of ethics committees – goes at least some way towards ensuring consistency of approach in such matters as multi-centre trials.

The production of guidelines is not governed by statute and, accordingly, it is not a *legal* requirement that prospective researchers submit their proposals to a local research committee for approval, but there are several reasons why the carrying out of medical research will be effectively impossible without such approval. To begin with, it will not be possible to use NHS patients or resources for an unapproved project.[19] Funding is also likely to be denied unless an ethics committee's imprimatur is obtained, and, perhaps of even greater practical importance, the results of unethical research will not be accepted for publication by reputable scientific journals.

The decisions of ethics committees could be subject to judicial review, in the same way as any other administrative decision; a frustrated researcher could therefore pursue a remedy by that route.[20] The aggrieved research subject may also seek redress, in his case most obviously through an action against the researcher.[1] It could be argued that a relationship exists between the committee member and the research subject which is of sufficient proximity to give rise to a duty of care and that this may, in theory, lead to civil liability in a case where a committee member has failed to exercise due care in the scrutiny of a research proposal. In fact, the courts have tended to avoid imposing liability on those charged with a regulatory role, as has been demonstrated in cases such as *Yuen Kun-Yeu v A-G for Hong Kong*.[2] The anxieties of committee members should be allayed, however, by the Department of Health's suggestion that district health authorities give to those members of the local research ethics committees who are not NHS employees an undertaking to the effect that the authority will take

---

19 The body conducting the research is encouraged to submit its proposals to a LREC even when there is no NHS involvement.
20 *R v Ethical Committee of St Mary's Hospital (Manchester), ex p H* [1988] 1 FLR 512.
 1 Those injured in the course of pharmaceutical trials may be compensated by the company sponsoring the trial, as recommended by the Association of the British Pharmaceutical Industry in its *Clinical Trial Compensation Guidelines* (1991).
 2 [1988] AC 175, [1987] 2 All ER 705.

full responsibility for those acts which are performed in the context of committee membership.[3] The wording of the indemnity is somewhat limiting, excluding acts performed in bad faith or wilful default and acts of 'gross negligence'. The latter term, in so far as it means anything at all, arguably has no place in such an indemnity.

Controlled trials

Biomedical research almost inevitably involves a controlled trial at some time. The principle is simple – in order to decide whether a new drug or other treatment is better than an existing one, or is preferable to none at all, the new treatment is given to a group of patients or healthy volunteers and not given to as similar a group as can be obtained. The subtleties of experimental design are critical to the success of the project and, as stated above, a badly conceived trial is fundamentally unethical. But even the best designed trial has its built-in moral problem – depending on how one looks at it, on the one hand, a relatively untried treatment which may do harm is being given to one group while, on the other, a treatment which may be of considerable benefit is being withheld from a similar group. In one view, this is ethically unacceptable, as there can be no grounds – other than, possibly, those of limited resources – for withholding a treatment which is believed to be beneficial. The doctor must do his best for patients but the problem is to know what is best and, in particular, to know whether the patient's recovery is being hindered by the restraints of the experimental protocol.[4] The first essential for any controlled trial is, therefore, that it must provide its answer as rapidly as possible and it must be terminable as soon as an adverse effect becomes apparent. Conflict may arise between statisticians and doctors, with the former possibly insisting on evidence from many more cases – and possibly observed for longer – than the doctor may feel necessary.

When, then, should randomised trials stop? At what point does the clinician say that enough is enough and that the evidence of benefit is sufficient to justify the conclusion that a treatment does, indeed, do good? Conversely, at what point does the apparent emergence of an adverse effect dictate that the project be abandoned? The patient involved in such a trial will have been informed that he is possibly being denied a potential benefit or possibly given a placebo – yet his consequent consent will have been based on his trust that there is genuine scientific uncertainty. Once this uncertainty is resolved to the extent of a belief – on, say, a balance of probabilities – that the treatment offers clinical benefit, then it becomes questionable whether it can still be denied to some in a continuing quest for statistical significance.[5] In deciding this question, it is important that the researcher bears in mind the fundamental precept which governs ethical medical research – that one does not use patients as a means

---

3   Accountability is considered in a major review: J V McHale 'Guidelines for Medical Research – Some Ethical and Legal Problems' (1993) 1 Med L Rev 160.   One major study has found that anonymity is often sought by committee members: C G Foster, T Marshall and P Moodie 'The Annual Reports of Local Research Ethics Committees' (1995) 21 J Med Ethics 214.

4   H Helmchem and B Muller-Oerlinghausen 'The Inherent Paradox of Clinical Trials in Psychiatry' (1975) 1 J Med Ethics 168.

5   For an analysis, see N Johnson, R J Lilford and W Brazier 'At what Level of Collective Equipoise Does a Clinical Trial Become Ethical?' (1991) 17 J Med Ethics 30.   The standards of proof have been compared to the different standards applied in the civil and criminal courts: The Lancet 'On Stopping a Trial before Its Time' (1993) 342 Lancet 1311.

to a scientific end but treats them as an end in themselves. Even so, the practical dilemma remains – the clinically orientated researcher stands to see his subsequent report criticised for want of scientific support while the more scientifically minded one sleeps uneasily because he worries that his research has reached an inadequate conclusion. Most good trials include plans for periodic analysis; there is a good case to be made for an independent observer, or the ethical committee itself, being responsible for monitoring the trial from this angle.

Two further features are of major importance in ensuring the objective of a trial: the 'double-blind' technique and randomisation. The former is virtually confined to drug trials. It is almost impossible for a doctor not to have some preference in a choice of treatments; the double-blind trial attempts to eliminate this subjectivity by keeping the assigned therapeutic groups secret from the physicians as well as from the patients. Not only does this dictate that the patient's doctor cannot be the researcher, but it also makes it implicit that the ethical justification of the trial is agreed by the 'caring' physicians involved; this leads to considerable difficulty in implementing the second principle – of randomisation – because it involves some form of conscious pre-selection. It has been suggested that no clinical trial can be truly random.[6] Certainly, the subjects, by volunteering, distinguish themselves from those who do not; or it may be necessary to exclude patients on the grounds of the severity of their disease, in which case the trial is limited to establishing the effectiveness of a treatment for the milder forms of the disease.

Randomisation in clinical trials is, in fact, becoming one of the major issues in research; this is particularly so in respect of treatments for cancer. For reasons discussed above, doctors having care – and especially primary care – of patients distrust the process. Most do so for fear that the doctor-patient relationship will be jeopardised; a sizeable minority are, however, concerned with the problems of informed consent.[7] This is discussed in greater detail later[8] but here it can be said that it also has a profound effect on the patient's acceptance of a trialist status. Refusal may be on simple utilitarian grounds but is equally liable to stem from confusion. No randomised therapeutic trial can be ethical unless the professionals genuinely do not know which treatment yields the best results. Given that the doctors are unsure, it may be difficult for the patient to solve what appears to him to be an insoluble problem. The result of the cumulative adverse factors is that accrual rates to important trials are often very low[9] – it is reported that a fundamental research project intended to identify the best treatment for early breast cancer had to be closed after a very low recruitment because the insistence on full informed consent (see below) frightened off both surgeons and patients.[10] Researchers therefore seek devices which will circumvent

6 W Rudowski 'World Health Organisation Biomedical Research Guidelines and the Conduct of Clinical Trials' (1980) 6 J Med Ethics 58.
7 K M Taylor et al 'Physicians' Reasons for not Entering Eligible Patients in a Randomised Clinical Trial of Surgery for Breast Cancer' (1984) 310 New Engl J Med 1363. The problem of consent may be particularly acute where the participants in a randomised trial are illiterate or where they do not share the scientific view of the researcher: see M Barry and M Molyneux 'Ethical Dilemmas in Malaria Drug and Vaccine Trials: a Bioethical Perspective' (1992) 18 J Med Ethics 189.
8 See p 462 below.
9 M Angell 'Patients' Preferences in Randomized Clinical Trials' (1984) 310 New Engl J Med 1385.
10 M Baum, K Zilkha and J Houghton 'Ethics of Clinical Research: lessons for the Future' (1989) 299 BMJ 251.

the confrontation between clinicians and patient and most of these involve some form of pre-selection – or 'pre-randomisation' – prior to discussion of treatment.[11] There are specific ethical and practical objections to such manoeuvres but, in general, it seems doubtfully moral to use what is essentially a ruse in order to obviate an agreed ethical practice which is, in addition, an integral part of the basic principles of the Declaration of Helsinki. The issue is, however, more finely balanced than might be supposed. One perfectly arguable school of thought will hold that this is the penalty we have to accept: 'unless we wish to return to the dark ages when treatment was determined by conceptual rationalism rather than scientific method.'[12] Others would emphasise that care must be taken lest, by attenuating our commitments to present patients in favour of benefits to those of the future, we do not lose overall more than we gain.[13] There is little wonder that the debate persists.

Groups of subjects

There is clearly an advantage whenever possible in using healthy volunteers as experimental subjects but, by definition, their use is limited to non-therapeutic research. Somewhat strangely, the Declaration of Helsinki allows for actual patients being used for such purposes. In this context, we believe that the temptation to use a group of persons who are already under stress and who probably have a sense of obligation to the doctors, simply because of their accessibility, must often bring such research close to unethical practice; non-therapeutic research in patients should be confined to a type which adds no extra burden – for example, through the use of existing blood samples as is discussed below.[14] It has been argued that the use of volunteers is, itself, unjustifiable but we prefer the view that people have a right to exercise altruistic impulses, particularly in a society in which the benefits of free health care are extended to all. None the less, considerable caution is needed, particularly as to the repetitive volunteer who is particularly prone to exploitation even if the researchers are unconscious of this – they may, for example, be quite unaware of marital disharmony caused by frequent absences from home. Motivation of the ever-ready volunteer takes several forms, some good and others bad, and, among these, the problem of recompense looms large. The Declaration of Helsinki is silent on this aspect but it is reasonably certain that, in conditions of present-day society, very few volunteers would come forward in the absence of some inducement; large payments would, however, be clearly unethical and a reasonable balance must be set – if for no other reason than to satisfy the needs of randomisation. It might be noted that the Royal College of Physicians Report *Research Involving Patients* describes payments to patients as 'generally undesirable' but occasionally acceptable in the case of long and tedious studies.[15] Even in such cases, 'payments should not be

11 S S Ellenberg 'Randomization Design in Comparative Clinical Trials' (1984) 310 New Engl J Med 1404. See, in particular, M A Zelen 'A new Design for Randomized Clinical Trials' (1979) 300 New Engl J Med 1242. For a simple explanation of pre-randomisation, see D J Torgerson and M Roland 'What Is Zelen's Design?' (1998) 316 BMJ 606.
12 Baum et al (1989) 299 BMJ 251.
13 Angell (1984) 310 New Engl J Med 1385.
14 See p 469.
15 Royal College of Physicians *Research Involving Patients* (1990).

for undergoing risk, and payments should not be such as to persuade patients to volunteer against their better judgement'.

The topic of inducement does, however, introduce the problems of the use of special populations because of their easy access, malleability and the like. Students, and particularly medical students, provide an example about whom there is little difficulty; they are intelligent and comprehending, they may well have an active interest in the trial and all educational establishments have very stringently controlling 'ethical committees' to protect against, say, repetitive use. Much the same could be said for the armed forces, who may be particularly vulnerable to improper research in war or when war threatens – even in 1990, non-consensual trials were allowed on American troops engaged in the Gulf War.[16] The use of prisoners, however, exposes many ethical issues that are based, essentially, on the argument that some advantage, even if only imagined, must accrue to the prisoner participating in a trial; that advantage may be so great as to induce the prisoner to volunteer for research which involves greater discomfort or risk than would be accepted by a free man and, in particular, it may compromise his inalienable right to withdraw from the trial. The arguments are not, however, entirely one way – it is possible to be paternalistic in an attempt to preserve people's autonomy. Thus, prisoners could well resent protective attitudes on the grounds that it is their right to dispose of their bodies and to take such risks as they please that is being compromised. This could be the subject of lengthy debate but we would suggest that the conditions in today's prisons are such that any process which provides some relief deserves, at least, a sympathetic evaluation and, secondly, that many prisoners might be benefited therapeutically through helping society. But it is also felt that experiments on prisoners should be particularly rigidly controlled by ethical committees which should always contain lay members with experience in criminology. Nowhere is it more important to observe the maxim 'the aims do not justify the method – the method must be judged in its own right'.

When comparing treatments, however, the use of patients is axiomatic. This is what the Declaration of Helsinki calls medical research combined with professional care and for which it lays down clear principles. The therapeutic controlled trial must invoke the Geneva principle: 'the health of the patient will be my first consideration.' Rudowski[17] has quoted:

A patient is assigned to undergo clinical study when, on the basis of our best judgment, an equal possibility exists that each of the compared methods of treatment will be of advantage to the patient.

This is a minimum standard – a clinical trial is rarely undertaken unless there is good reason to suppose that one therapy will show an advantage over others and particularly over those currently accepted as the best available. The advantage need not be direct; it could, for example, be collateral in that the results of the method were not better but were achieved with less disfigurement or with fewer side effects. Anticipation of advantage can, in general, only be based on laboratory or animal experimentation and, while the view is occasionally expressed that the latter is less

16 G J Annas and M A Grodin 'Treating the Troops: Commentary' (1991) 21 Hastings Center Rep (2) 24.
17 (1980) 6 J Med Ethics 58.

moral than is human biomedical research, it represents the first basic principle of the Declaration of Helsinki. The corollary, as we have already emphasised, is that an experimental method must be immediately withdrawn if it is found to be positively deleterious and the patients involved must be transferred, whenever possible, to an alternative regime. The difficulties of such clinical research include, first, the fact that each patient is a unique set of many variables. While a statistical result may be achieved, it would be a remarkably well-designed trial which simultaneously solved the problems of the individual exceptions – for example, the patients' preferences may distort a trial unless they are allowed for.[18] Secondly, the results of the experimental therapies may take a considerable time to filter through and, by then, there may be no turning back. A typical example is provided by the study of the use of folic acid supplements in order to reduce the incidence of neural tube defects in infants. Two pilot studies were undertaken; both showed an apparent marked reduction in recurrence rates in affected families but neither stood up to statistical analysis. The problem then arose as to whether the study should be continued and, if so, whether the clinical impression was sufficient to render the use of placebos unethical. It was decided that the matter was so important that a major randomised trial was indicated, the intent being to study at least 2,000 pregnancies. In the event, after more than seven years, sufficient information had been gained from 1,195 informative pregnancies. Thus, the trial could now be ended, it being clear that folic acid supplements had no adverse effects but had a significant protective effect as regards fetal neural tube defect.[19]

The use of placebos
A placebo is an inert substance without pharmacological action. The use of placebos is occasionally remarkably successful in straightforward therapeutics but, there, the practice is even more difficult to justify morally than it is in the experimental situation where the use of placebos is sometimes essential. The mere taking of medicine may lead to subjective improvement; this is the 'placebo effect', which must be considered whenever a new drug or procedure is on trial. On the other hand, the trial drug may do more harm than inactivity; but, for psychological reasons, inactivity must involve apparently comparable activity if two regimens are to be properly compared. In either case, the controlled giving of a placebo necessarily involves the deception of patients and this raises some complex issues.

The extreme position is that placebos offend against the fundamental rightness of fidelity.[20] If, as is often the case, there is patient resistance to the use of such controls, this should not be regarded as an excuse for further deception but rather as an indication that such experiments are unacceptable to society. To which one could reply that a poor experiment is a worse affront to society and that the simple expedient is to leave out those who object – little is lost, other than, perhaps, absolute numbers,

18 C R Brewin and C Bradley 'Patient Preferences and Randomised Clinical Trials' (1989) 299 BMJ 313.
19 MRC Vitamin Study Research Group 'Prevention of Neural Tube Defects: Results of the Medical Research Council Vitamin Study' (1991) 338 Lancet 131.
20 B Simmons 'Problems in Deceptive Medical Procedures: An Ethical and Legal Analysis of the Administration of Placebos' (1978) 4 J Med Ethics 172.

and, as previously discussed, experimental volunteers are, by nature, already a selected group.

More practical objections are based on the effect of the experiment on patient care; the circumstances in which it is ethical to deprive a patient of treatment must be strictly regulated. It would, for example, be improper to use placebo controls when pain was a feature of the condition under treatment, despite the fact that some patients might derive benefit; many pain killers are available and can be used as reference substances. The basic circumstances in which placebo trials are ethical and, perhaps, necessary are, first, when there is no alternative to the experimental treatment available – it might, for example, be right to include placebo controls in the evaluation of a drug intended for the treatment of AIDS, for which there is no known cure; secondly, the use of a placebo could be justified when the effect of adding a new treatment to an established one is under study. In the majority of instances, however, the purpose of using placebos is to analyse the effect of a treatment on subjective symptoms rather than on organic disease.[1]

Informed consent

It is apparent that the theoretical baseline for an ethical research programme or therapeutic experiment is drawn on free, autonomous participation by the subject and this, in turn, depends upon 'informed consent', the nature of which has been discussed in chapter 10.

The principles in relation to experimentation are similar to those governing therapy; most philosophers would say that the patient's rights are, if anything, greater in the former situation than they are in the sphere of pure patient management. The standard of information provided must certainly be that of the 'reasonable subject' – if not that of the actual subject – rather than that of the 'reasonable doctor'.[2] Even so, there are many and variable difficulties which make it almost impossible to lay down hard and fast rules – these include the essential need for some measure of ignorance in the trial, the seriousness of the condition being treated, the psychology of individual patients and the like. The complexity is such that in Sweden, for example, while the law lays down that the doctrine of informed consent has to be satisfied, no attempt is made to define the extent of the information given.[3] It has been reported that the requirements for informed consent have rendered controlled trials next to impossible in Germany. Confrontation between the back-room and the coal-face is almost inevitable:

> The central dogma [of professional medical ethicists] seems to be that whatever is done for the sake of medical science is alien to the treatment of the individual, and should therefore

1   For further criticism, see K J Rothman and K B Michels 'The Continuing Unethical Use of Placebo Controls' (1994) 331 New Engl J Med 384. A cautious but relatively benign attitude, which, to an extent, parallels our views, is adopted by P P De Deyn and R D'Hooge 'Placebos in Clinical Practice and Research' (1996) 22 J Med Ethics 140.
2   Detailed requirements are set out didactically by A Herxheimer 'The Rights of the Patient in Clinical Research' (1988) 2 Lancet 1128.
3   G Giertz 'Ethics and Randomised Clinical Trials' (1980) 6 J Med Ethics 55.

be labelled an 'experiment', necessitating informed consent by the patient and adjudication by an ethics committee.[4]

Such general problems are amplified in the practical ambience. It is widely agreed that the patient's consent must be based on four main lines of explanation: the purpose of the experiment; the benefits to the patient and society; the risks involved; and the alternatives open to the subject. Who is to impart the information – the patient's physician or the researcher? Should the patient have the benefit of a 'friend' to interpret for him? Should there be confirmation of the consent procedure? It has been fairly widely mooted that, in fact, informed consent is a double-edged weapon – token consent may take the place of the genuine and relieve the researcher of responsibility. Might it not be better to burden the investigator with full responsibility rather than provide such a shield?[5] Many of the states of the United States have enacted 'informed consent statutes', some of which lay down specific disclosure requirements for particular procedures. In the same spirit, United States courts, dealing with claims that inadequate information has been given to experimental subjects, have tended to stress the requirement that there be a considerably higher burden of disclosure in cases involving non-therapeutic research than in therapeutic cases,[6] a view shared by a Canadian court in the well-known case of *Halushka v University of Saskatchewan*.[7] Here the court said: 'There can be no exceptions to the ordinary requirements of disclosure in the case of research as there may well be in ordinary medical practice.'

These difficulties are highlighted in 'care associated' research when, effectively, the doctrine of informed consent implies that the patient has to choose for him- or herself whether to accept an experimental treatment or to be randomised in a comparative therapeutic trial. The philosophical basis of patient autonomy is perfectly clear, but is the ideal end attainable in practice? Ought a patient to be told of a 'last chance' effort? Is the medically naive patient capable of giving consent as required? Can he be expected to understand the risks when the medical profession itself is so divided? Such issues are crystallised in the treatment of cancer, in which respect American legislation as to disclosure is particularly severe[8] – in California, for example, physicians are provided with a summary of medically viable alternative treatments for cancer of the breast which can be used to comply with the relevant statute. Whether such devices are valuable to the patient is doubtful and, while they undoubtedly give protection to the doctors, we can still ask how and why we have reached a situation where that should have to be a major concern.

And this is, perhaps, the nub of the problem. We have already noted that a major cancer trial has been abandoned on mainly consent-based grounds – and this conclusion was, to an extent, foreseen. In this respect, the working party[9] regarded it as intolerable that the burden of accountability should be placed entirely on the

4 Lancet 'Medical Ethics: Should Medicine Turn the Other Cheek?' (1990) 336 Lancet 846.
5 See Helmchem (1975) 1 J Med Ethics 168.
6 Eg *Whitlock v Duke University* 637 F Supp 1463 (NC, 1986); affd 829 F 2d 1340 (1987).
7 (1965) 53 DLR (2d) 436: K Morin 'The Standard of Disclosure in Human Subject Experimentation' (1998) 19 J Leg Med 157.
8 S Taub 'Cancer and the Law of Informed Consent' (1982) 10 Law Med Hlth Care 61.
9 Cancer Research Campaign Working Party in Breast Conservation 'Informed Consent; Ethical, Legal and Medical Implications for Doctors and Patients who Participate in Randomised Clinical Trials' (1983) 286 BMJ 1117.

doctors concerned. As things stand, the physician wishing to do his best for the individual patient and, at the same time, for the community at large, is often left in limbo.[10]

A remarkable example of how this uncertainty may operate in practice came before a coroner's court inquiring into the death of a female patient – a death due, interestingly enough, to a failure to inform a temporary house officer of the research in progress.[11] It came to light that 15 units were involved in a trial treatment of colonic cancer which involved infusing selected but randomised patients with a potent cytotoxic drug post-operatively; all units had submitted the trial protocol to their ethical committees and 11 had decided that 'informed consent' need not be obtained. The Lancet, while, admittedly, concluding that special consent should have been obtained on the grounds of both variance from standard procedures and the degree of risk involved, summed up the dilemma in a series of questions: when, if ever, can informed consent be dispensed with? If a trial is concerned with the treatment of cancer, how can consent be obtained without adding to the patient's distress? At what stage in the trial should consent be obtained? and, finally, Have local ethical committees the authority to override national and international guidelines on the ethics of research? To which we would add – how can you possibly expect a patient to understand such a complex subject? – and the Lancet answers that the patient should not be included in the trial if he or she is not capable of understanding the basic plan of management.[12]

A real problem here is that doubts as to patients' ability to understand complex medical information can very easily result in the striking of an unacceptably paternalistic attitude – sometimes with shocking consequences. Such a situation arose in New Zealand in the course of the Auckland cervical cancer campaign.[13] Here, a senior doctor, believing that cancer in situ would not spread, was strongly of the view that some women with abnormal cervical smear tests were best left untreated. These patients were denied treatment over a period of 15-20 years without being told that they were, in effect, involved in a therapeutic experiment. The doctor in charge of the experimental research believed honestly and firmly in his hypothesis, but his failure to obtain consent was severely criticised both by medical colleagues and by the judicial inquiry which was established to investigate the matter; the impact on medicine in New Zealand and, hopefully, elsewhere, has been profound.[14]

The issue of consent still gives rise to disputes. The involvement of a patient in a British randomised breast cancer study without her informed consent led to allegations by the patient in 1988 that she had been 'abused' by the doctors concerned.

10 Well described by H A F Dudley 'Informed Consent to Surgical Trials' (1984) 289 BMJ 937.
11 Coroner's Court, Birmingham, 19 September 1981. Discussed in Leading Article 'Secret Randomised Clinical Trials' (1982) 2 Lancet 78. See also D Brahams 'Death of Patient who was Unwitting Subject of Randomised Controlled Trial of Cancer Treatment' (1982) 1 Lancet 1028 and 'Clinical Trials and the Consent of the Patient' (1982) 226 Practitioner 1829.
12 (1982) 1 Lancet 1028.
13 Judge S Cartwright *The Report of the Cervical Cancer Enquiry* (1988); discussed by A V Campbell 'An "Unfortunate Experiment"' (1989) 3 Bioethics 59.
14 C Paul 'The New Zealand Cancer Study: Could it Happen Again' (1988) 297 BMJ 533; P McNeill 'The Implications for Australia of the New Zealand Report of the Cervical Cancer Inquiry: No Cause for Complacency' (1989) 150 Med J Austral 264; G Gillett 'NZ Medicine after Cartwright' (1990) 300 BMJ 893.

The Bulletin of the Institute of Medical Ethics took a similar view;[15] by contrast, a leading surgeon, a chairman of an ethical committee and the Assistant Director of the Cancer Research Campaign argued strongly that it is legitimate to dispense with the informed consent requirements when placing the patient within a trial constitutes good medical treatment.[16] It was suggested that to give a patient full information on such a study might add to her distress and that there are circumstances where the principle of non-maleficence should override that of autonomy. Such views, although motivated by concern for patient welfare, are, however, open to the charge that they underestimate the extent to which patients actually want to be informed of what is happening to them; full communication between the patient and researcher is still probably the safer policy.[17]

Research and the incompetent
Particularly difficult ethical and legal problems arise in relation to those patients who cannot give a valid consent to participation in clinical research by virtue of their mental condition. Such patients must be excluded automatically if informed consent is an absolute prerequisite for involvement in research, and yet this would have the effect of halting valuable lines of inquiry into serious and debilitating diseases. One way round this difficulty is to accept that there are special groups of patients who cannot consent but whose involvement is vital if research into a condition from which they suffer is to make progress. Such patients may be used in research provided that certain safeguards are erected; these would be designed so as to ensure that they are not subjected to appreciable risk or inconvenience and would include the agreement of relatives and/or that of some independent supervisory party. Although the 'consent' of relatives is of no legal effect in these circumstances, it is an important check, in that they may be assumed to have the interests of members of their family at heart. The required approval of an independent authority would cover those instances in which it was suspected that uncaring relatives had been thoughtless.

The Working Party on Research on the Mentally Incapacitated, set up by the Medical Research Council, has accepted that non-therapeutic research on the mentally incapacitated is ethically acceptable, subject to the qualification on risk mentioned above and subject to there being no sign that the subject objects to involvement.[18] Yet, even if we accept the morality of this view, the legal position in such cases is considerably more dubious. As the law stands in both England and Scotland, there can be no legal justification – other than, possibly, that of necessity – for any non-therapeutic invasion of the bodily integrity of an incapacitated person. Research of this type is, therefore, probably unlawful at present. This will change in English law if the Law Commission recommendations are accepted; non-therapeutic research

15 Editorial Comment 'Research Without Consent Continues in the UK' (1988) 40 Bull Inst Med Ethics 13.
16 Baum et al (1989) 299 BMJ 251.
17 T M Marteau 'Ethics of Clinical Research' (1989) 299 BMJ 513. An interesting debate, which also considers the ethics of publication in the absence of consent, is summarised in 'Informed Consent: Edging Forwards (and Backwards)' (1998) 316 BMJ 949.
18 Medical Research Council *The Ethical Conduct of Research on the Mentally Incapacitated* (1991). For the US debate, see: E G DeRenzo 'Decisionally Impaired Persons in Research: Refining the Proposed Refinements' (1997) 25 J Law Med & Ethics 139; R Dresser 'Mentally Disabled Research Subjects: the Enduring Policy Issues' (1996) 276 J Amer Med Ass 67.

will then be allowed subject to approval by a mental incapacity research committee. The criteria for such approval will include the existence of negligible risk and the limitation of research to a condition with which the participant is, or may be afflicted. Recommendations are also made for an additional requirement of independent, proxy consent.[19]

The unethical researcher

All that has gone before has assumed that the researcher is acting in good faith with the interests of the profession and of the public at heart. There has, however, been an upsurge of concern not so much as to research of poor quality – which is distinguished relatively easily – but as to frankly fraudulent studies.[20]

Modern doctors are under some pressure in this area. In high-profile areas of research, the competitive spirit may have a lamentable effect. The temptation to falsify results or to suppress the truth may be too much for some scientists, particularly when there is a prospect of high earnings from patents. Even in the more mundane reaches of medicine, the senior academic who publishes frequently is likely to attract more funding than his colleague who does not and the advantage of 'being first' encourages premature reporting. More importantly, advancement in hierarchical medicine now depends heavily on the number of publications to the junior's credit. The fact that this results in ever-escalating multi-authorship is of intra-professional concern only; of far greater public interest is the imposed temptation to look upon an individual patient as a potential notch in one's curriculum vitae. Such influences lead to 'sloppy science' which is, perhaps, understandable. There is, however, no excuse available for the deliberate falsification of results – which are less easy to identify and of which there have been a number of examples.[1] The danger in these cases is that the public, often prompted by the news media, may be led to believe in therapeutic claims which are unsupported by the available data or that, as a result, they may be subjected to valueless or dangerous treatment schedules. The issue is also, understandably, of great interest to pharmaceutical companies, who may be wrongly deprived of profits if a drug is withdrawn from the market on the basis of fraudulent results.[2] This happened in the case of Debendox, which was withdrawn after claims by the Australian gynaecologist, William McBride, that the drug could cause deformities in

19 Law Commission *Mental Incapacity* (Law Com No 231, 1995); Scottish Law Commission *Report on Incapable Adults* (No 151, 1995).
20 J Smith 'Preventing Fraud' (1991) 302 BMJ 362 discussing, inter alia, S Lock 'Misconduct in Medical Research: Does it Exist in Britain?' (1988) 297 BMJ 1531. Between 1987 and 1993, ten cases of scientific fraud were processed through the disciplinary committee of the GMC: S Kingman 'GMC may not pay legal Costs for investigating Fraud' (1993) 307 BMJ 403. The penalties for scientific fraud are severe, and include that of being struck off the register for misconduct: 'Sex, Scandal and Fraud' (1992) 305 BMJ 272.
1 See Smith, n 20 above.
2 The effect of publication of results – genuine as well as fraudulent – on the stock-market has also to be considered. Researchers who also trade in the relevant pharmaceutical shares may find themselves in breach of the Company Securities (Insider Dealing) Act 1985: see D S Freestone and H Mitchell 'Inappropriate Publication of Trial Results and Potential for Allegations of Illegal Share Dealing' (1993) 306 BMJ 1112.

a small proportion of the children of those women to whom it was administered. An inquiry by the New South Wales Medical Tribunal subsequently concluded that McBride claimed statistically significant results where none, in fact, existed.[3] McBride is reported as saying that he had changed his data in 'the long-term interests of humanity',[4] an attempted justification which could appeal to a wide range of miscreants. The fraudulent researcher, of course, faces a variety of sanctions. He may be criminally liable for fraudulently obtaining research funds, and he could, also, face civil action for any loss incurred by drug manufacturers. In addition, there are powerful professional disciplinary procedures that can effectively end a scientific career.

A closely allied problem is that of experimental treatment. This is an even more contentious subject. Medicine is not always scientific; many advances are made fortuitously or as a result of no more than intuition. The difficulty then becomes that of distinguishing courageous innovation from unethical experimentation – and, human nature being what it is, the answer often depends on the outcome. A vivid example of how differing attitudes and understanding can cloud the issues arose in 1987, when Parliamentary questions were asked concerning anaesthesia for children undergoing open heart surgery – emotive words such as 'barbaric' were used. The medical profession was, however, able to point out that the research was humane and that the results had shown the way to improvement in the post-operative status of such infants;[5] the criticisms were withdrawn unreservedly.[6]

We have already noted[7] a less satisfactory defence of an experimental treatment in which a baboon's heart was transplanted into a neonate with congenital heart disease. The parents were unmarried minors and doubts have been expressed as to whether they could give 'informed consent' in the true sense. A consultant summed up the procedure:

> I think this xenograft is premature because I am not aware of any finding in the clinical literature that suggests anything but the prevailing rule – the human body will reject a transplanted animal organ. Baby Fae will reject her baboon heart within the next week or two, and cyclosporine will not prevent it.[8]

Most would agree with this assessment – Baby Fae actually survived for two and a half weeks – but the procedure had been approved by the university's institutional research board and there was some further professional support for the operation. Nevertheless, it does appear to be an example of premature experimental treatment.

At what would seem to be the extreme of dubious practice lies the instance of treating AIDS by an unproven biological method and exaggerating its success in what was described by one consultant as 'the most scientifically unfounded presentation [he had] ever heard'.[9] It is only fair to note, however, that equal criticism was later

3   M Ragg 'Australia: McBride Guilty of Scientific Fraud' (1993) 341 Lancet 550.
4   N Swan 'Australian Doctor Admits Fraud' (1991) 302 BMJ 1421.
5   J O Forfar and A G M Campbell 'Medicine and the Media' (1987) 295 BMJ 659.
6   B Braine 'MP Apologises' (1988) 297 BMJ 865.
7   See p 339 above.
8   Details taken from H S Schwartz 'Bioethical and legal Considerations in Increasing the Supply of Transplantable Organs: From UAGA to "Baby Fae"' (1985) 10 Am J Law Med 397.
9   R Smith 'Doctors, Unethical Treatments, and Turning a Blind Eye' (1989) 298 BMJ 1125.

levelled at the medical profession for failing to bring the matter to the attention of the General Medical Council – doctors have an undoubted distaste for 'shopping' their colleagues but such cases do underline the often expressed concern at the inadequacy of the GMC's powers of investigation.[10]

We are left with the complex problem of whether or not information gained from frankly immoral research should be used for the general good – the classic, and ultimate, examples being data obtained in the concentration camps of the Second World War.[11] The arguments are finely balanced. In the end, we subscribe to the view that the fact that children do not, say, now die from certain forms of hypothermia is best regarded as a monument to those who suffered and died to make it possible; if the material is used, they will, at least, not have done so in vain.

Compensation for personal injury in research

The research volunteer who is injured in the course of a medical experiment may resort to a claim for compensation under the law of tort. Such a route, of course, may prove to be difficult: researchers may have taken every precaution to avoid injury and there may therefore be no evidence of negligence. In the current physician-orientated state of negligence law, an action based on lack of consent would be unlikely to succeed unless the failure of disclosure was of an obviously material nature; *Bolam*[12] as modified in *Sidaway*[13] would be as likely to be followed in experimentation as in treatment, particularly if the research was itself therapeutic in nature. Although the odds against a plaintiff in such actions are not as long as they were before *Sidaway*, the research subject is in a somewhat unfair situation. Quite apart from the problems of expense or uncertainty, he is entitled to believe that he will be looked after in the event of something going wrong – and charity is unpredictable and often ungenerous as a remedy. There is clearly a need for some defined method of compensation as of right, the Pearson Commission[14] favouring strict liability.[15] This is also unsatisfactory from the point of view of the aggrieved subject as it also involves recourse to the courts where the burden of proving causation would fall upon the plaintiff or pursuer. The alternative of a no-fault principle of compensation similar to those schemes discussed in chapter 9 is attractive and, moreover, there would be little or no difficulty in defining an accident within the narrow confines of medical research; but such schemes require funding and administration.

In the United Kingdom, those involved in the funding and regulation of medical research have acknowledged the necessity of compensation outside the framework of

10 The GMC is, itself, concerned at the 'blind eye' mentality. See *Professional Conduct and Discipline: Fitness to Practise* (1993), para 63.
11 A particularly poignant series of interviews with survivors was published in M Gwyther and S McConville 'Can Good Come from Evil' (1989) The Observer Magazine, 19 November, p 18.
12 *Bolam v Friern Hospital Management Committee* [1957] 2 All ER 118, [1957] 1 WLR 582, in which failure to disclose a minimal risk was not considered negligent.
13 *Sidaway v Board of Governors of Bethlem Royal Hospital and the Maudsley Hospital* [1984] QB 493, [1984] 1 All ER 1018, CA; affd [1985] AC 871, [1985] 1 All ER 643, HL.
14 Report of Royal Commission on Civil Liability and Compensation for Personal Injury (Cmnd 7054) at para 1341.
15 See p 218.

tort law and, in theory at least, the injured research subject should be dealt with sympathetically. Some health authorities recommend that ex gratia payments be made under the NHS indemnity scheme and that, where an NHS trust or a health authority has not accepted responsibility for the research investigation, an approach should be made to the sponsoring pharmaceutical company. The Association of the British Pharmaceutical Industry recommends to its members that compensation be paid 'when, on the balance of probabilities, the injury was attributable to the administration of a medicinal product under trial or any clinical intervention or procedure provided for by the protocol that would not have occurred but for the inclusion of the patient in the trial'.[16] Compensation is not payable under these guidelines where there has been a significant departure from the agreed protocol, or where there has been a wrongful act on the part of a third party, including a doctor's failure to deal adequately with an adverse reaction. These limitations, together with the non-legally binding nature of the guidelines, mean that the research subject is by no means guaranteed compensation should anything go wrong.

Random sample testing

One aspect of research which has received little consideration concerns the use of samples which have been removed for defined, usually therapeutic, reasons. The use of such samples for other investigations subjects the patient to no further discomfort and, while a patient could undoubtedly make directions as to the disposal of any biological specimen he has provided, this would be by virtue of no more than an inchoate right.[17] It would be reasonable to assume from silence that the patient was indifferent in the matter, yet there is an element of invasion of the patient's privacy in 'finding out things' about him without his consent – no matter how much it might be felt that the geographic distribution of genes or any cultural alterations in body chemistry, for example, might provide useful research projects. But a balance has, again, to be struck since most patients, even if asked, would be uninterested in consent.

The justification of such projects rests on the consequences of a positive finding. At one extreme is the problem of AIDS which we discuss as a separate issue.[18] At the other, a search for a particular blood group gene in a specific population could make no possible difference to the subjects and would accordingly be permissible. But one would have to think carefully before embarking on, say, a survey of abnormal genetic markers with its consequent possible influences on marriage and having a family.

Other surveys could be of no immediate consequence to the patient but could be of significance were the results to be published. An example would be the routine estimation of blood alcohol as a community study. In the event of the samples deriving from accidents, the results could be of particular interest to the police or insurance companies and would be normally available only by consent of the subjects. Serious consequences might arise if the result of a research project were

16 Association of the British Pharmaceutical Industry *Clinical Trial Compensation Guidelines* (1991).
17 B M Dickens 'The Control of Living Body Materials' (1977) 27 Univ Toronto LJ 142.
18 See p 271 above.

entered in the notes and these were later subject to disclosure;[19] no research of potentially damaging type would be ethical if there was a chance that the subject and the result could later be associated. Practical problems in this field have, in fact, arisen in the United States in relation to drug screening surveys; preservation of the patient's anonymity must be a determining condition under which specimens are used without express consent for purposes other than those originally stated.

19 The evidence might be used in the United Kingdom (*R v Sang* [1980] AC 402, [1979] 2 All ER 1222, HL) but it is doubtful if it could be used specifically under the Road Traffic Act 1988, which requires that a blood specimen be taken by a medical practitioner with the consent of the subject. The doubt arises from the Road Traffic Offenders Act 1988, s 15(2), which refers to account being taken of the analysis of specimens 'not provided in connection with the alleged offence'. The proposition has not, to our knowledge, been tested in the courts.

19　Research on children and fetal experimentation

A child is by no means a miniature version of an adult. Children respond differently to drugs, as they do to a number of other treatments, and it is impossible to say that the effect of a particular therapy on an adult will be mirrored when applied to a child. Medical research on children is, therefore, necessary before a treatment can be approved for paediatric use. As in adults, such research may entail not only therapeutic research on sick children but also essential non-therapeutic research on normal control groups; it is this non-therapeutic research which poses the ethical and legal problems.[1]

Such research involves a variety of procedures, ranging from the completely benign – such as weight and height studies – to those which are frankly invasive. As an example of the latter, the Institute of Medical Ethics cited a French project which involved lumbar punctures on newborn infants for non-therapeutic reasons.[2] Such investigations would not be approved by research ethics committees today, but procedures that are far less hazardous and uncomfortable still raise questions as to the general acceptability of research in this particular group of subjects.

Non-therapeutic research on children

The essential difficulty with non-therapeutic research on children lies, again, in the question of consent. An adult may be able to give an informed, and therefore valid, consent to participation in research – but can the same be said of a child? The Declaration of Helsinki specifically mentions the 'legally incompetent' participant in research, stating that the consent of the guardian should be procured; this approach was also adopted in the guidelines on experimentation issued by the British Paediatric Association,[3] the Medical Research Council,[4] the Royal College of Physicians[5] and, in the United States, by the National Institutes of Health.[6] All these influential bodies accept that non-therapeutic research on children is justified in that it is intended to benefit other children – although it should not be carried out if it could be done equally well using adults. Such research should not be instigated before parental consent has

---

1 For general discussion of the issue, see J K Mason *Medico-Legal Aspects of Reproduction and Parenthood* (2nd edn, 1998) p 319 et seq.
2 See R H Nicholson (ed) *Medical Research with Children: Ethics, Law and Practice* (1990) p 19.
3 British Paediatric Association *Guidelines for the Ethical Conduct of Medical Research Involving Children* (1992).
4 Medical Research Council *The Ethical Conduct of Research on Children* (1991).
5 Report of the Royal College of Physicians of London *Research Involving Patients* (1990) p 19.
6 National Institutes of Health *Policy and Guidelines on the Inclusion of Children as Participants in Research Involving Human Subjects* (1998).

been obtained; in the view of the Royal College of Physicians, parental consent is required in respect of children under 16 years old and also in the case of 'some older children'.

The Institute of Medical Ethics studied the question in depth[7] and recommended that parental consent should be ethically acceptable only when the risks involved in the research are minimal – this being defined by the Institute as a risk of death lower than 1:1,000,000, a risk of major complications less than 1:100,000 and a risk of minor complications of less than 1:1,000. In addition, the Institute thought that the consent of the child should be obtained after the age of seven years. This concern was shared by the Royal College of Physicians, which felt that a child who is capable of giving a consent should also be allowed to refuse to participate in a research procedure – even if parental consent has been obtained. The College does not rule out proceeding with research involving a child who objects but is too young to give consent but it suggests that, in such circumstances, investigators should reconsider whether it is appropriate to go ahead.

Obtaining parental consent is clearly important, but the fact that it has been given does not, of itself, justify carrying out research on children. Our first concern here must be with the welfare of the child, and it need hardly be said that parental consent to something which is obviously to the detriment of the child is unacceptable. Parents do not have an absolute, unfettered right to regulate their children's lives; it is implicit in the modern concept of parenthood that the aim of such parental powers as there are is to protect and enhance the status of the child.[8] It follows that the researcher cannot simply say: 'The parents have consented and this means that I can go ahead'; parental consent may justify the involvement of children in non-therapeutic research but it will do so only because it points to the acceptability of the research in terms of some interest of the child.

One way of assessing parental consent is to see it as a substitute for the child's own judgment which cannot, as yet, be expressed. Under this theory, parental consent does no more than voice what the child would be expected to state, had he the ability to do so. Acceptance of this approach salves any qualms the researcher might have – in effect, the child consents to what is done, the only complication being that this cannot be expressed personally. Critics of theories of proxy consent point out that this involves a blatant fiction. It would be more honest, they argue, to accept that this constitutes non-consensual research and to admit the need to justify it on other grounds. The difficulty cannot be avoided by attempting to justify the child's involvement in terms of his 'future identification' with the decision made on his behalf.[9] It is difficult to see any distinction between 'identification' and 'consent' and, whatever terms one uses to imply future assent, there is no certainty that the child will, in fact, subsequently endorse what his parents have decided.

7   Institute of Medical Ethics 'Medical Research with Children: Ethics, Law and Practice' (1986) Bull no 14, p 8. For discussion of the recommendations, see R J Robinson 'Ethics Committees and Research on Children' (1987) 294 BMJ 1243. See also M A Grodin, L H Glantz and A M Dellinger 'Children as Research Subjects: Science, Ethics and Law' (1996) 21 J Hlth Politics Policy Law 159.
8   See B M Dickens 'The Modern Function and Limits of Parental Rights' (1981) 97 LQR 462; also A McCall Smith 'Is There Anything left of Parental Rights' in E Sutherland and A McCall Smith (eds) *Family Rights* (1991) ch 1.
9   R B Redmon 'How Children Can Be Respected as Ends Yet Still Be Used as Subjects in Non-therapeutic Research' (1986) 12 J Med Ethics 77.

The matter may, however, be approached from an entirely different perspective – one which focuses not on any imagined consent of the child but on what is in that child's best interests. This test would allow the parents to involve the child in that which is in – or, alternatively, that which is not manifestly against – the child's best interests. The first of these would require that the non-therapeutic research secures some benefit for the child – a difficult, though not impossible, case to make. A child is a member of a class within the community – the class of children – and the individual can be said to be a potential beneficiary if research will benefit the class as a whole. It is also possible to extrapolate the reasoning used to justify organ donation (see chapter 14) and to argue that participation in research related to a disease from which, for example, a sibling is suffering will benefit the normal child – it being in his interests that his sibling should recover.

An allied benefit-based theory focuses on the altruistic nature of participation in non-therapeutic research.[10] Here, the issue is, at base, whether or not parents have the right to involve their children in projects by way of imposed unselfishness. Such co-operation is undoubtedly good for the subject, but this would apply only if the child were sufficiently mature to understand the philanthropic nature of what he was doing. An older child may later derive satisfaction from the fact that he helped others when younger, but the same objection applies here as to proxy consent – how can we be sure that this is what he would feel?

The alternative interpretation of the best interests test, which allows for measures which are not to the actual detriment of the child, clearly licenses the child's involvement in non-therapeutic research so long as the risks involved are negligible. This assessment gives a wider discretion to the parent, who may choose to interpret his duty to society as including a duty to engage his children in pro-social activities. Such parents act within their rights, and cannot be regarded as abusing their position until such time as the child suffers actual harm or runs an appreciable risk of harm.[11]

Even if this were not accepted, and the child's interest in non-participation were to be seen as being more significant than any parental social duty, the non-interventionists could still hold that this is an area of the family's activities in which the law has no right to interfere. State intervention may be justified if a child's life is threatened through neglect or through a parental decision which is going to lead to great danger – but these are not the stakes involved in comparatively harmless research. The protagonist of individual self-determination is unlikely to approve of a justification based on relative values but the inevitable consequence of the extreme individualistic position would be the suspension of all non-therapeutic medical research on children – which would benefit nobody, least of all the children themselves.

Discussion thus far has proceeded on the assumption that the child in question is not of an age to give any meaningful consent. Even so, many children of relatively tender age will be able to understand the issues involved and the question then arises as to the weight to be given to any agreement they might give. The age at which a child can appreciate the implications of what he is doing will obviously vary, but some

10 See A McCall Smith 'Research and Experimentation Involving Children' in J K Mason (ed) *Paediatric Forensic Medicine and Pathology* (1989) p 469.
11 The test of acceptability then becomes one of the 'reasonable parent': see J K Mason *Medico-legal Aspects of Reproduction and Parenthood* (2nd edn, 1998) p 324 et seq.

generalisations may be made.[12]   Children under the age of seven are usually considered to be incapable of that degree of morally sophisticated thought required to make consistent altruistic decisions but, above that age, a child may be perfectly able to understand that he is helping doctors to cure others by taking part in the research programme. A child who was not able to grasp the general idea of medical research by the age of 15 would probably be an exception today. This view is supported by a study which was designed to assess the ability of groups of nine- and 14-year-olds to make decisions relating to medical treatment. The 14-year-olds were shown to have the same general level of capacity to make this sort of decision as did adults and a surprising degree of competence was shown in the nine-year-old group.[13]

The ethical issues might be clarified to an extent if the law could give a clear answer to this question. Unfortunately, the law itself is uncertain in this area and this has not eased the difficulties of those involved in paediatric research. In 1962 the Medical Research Council stated that:

> in the strict view of the law, parents and guardians of minors cannot give consent on their behalf to any procedures which are of no particular benefit to them and which may carry some risk of harm.[14]

This was followed by a Department of Health circular which confirmed that interpretation in a negative way:

> Health authorities are advised that they ought not to infer [from a Royal College of Physicians' recommendation that children can be used in certain forms of research provided the consent of the guardian has been obtained] that the fact that consent has been given by the parent or guardian and that the risk involved is considered negligible will be sufficient to bring such clinical research investigation within the law as it stands.[15]

The advice of the Department of Health was roundly attacked by doctors. Lawyers were also critical of this strict view of the law, pointing out the paucity of authority on the point.[16] In these conditions – almost amounting to a legal vacuum – the proper way of approaching the issue is to look at general legal principles governing the parent/child relationship and to infer from these what a court might decide if the matter were to come before it.

We have already seen that the consent of a minor to medical treatment may be adequate even without parental ratification provided that the child has sufficient

---

12 See J Berryman 'Discussing the Ethics of Research on Children' in J van Eys (ed) *Research on Children* (1978) p 85. See discussion by P Alderson and J Montgomery *Health Care Choices: Making Decisions with Children* (1996); M Paul 'Informed Consent in Medical Research. Children form the Age of 5 should be Presumed Competent' (1997) 314 BMJ 1480.

13 L A Weithorn and S B Campbell 'The Competency of Children and Adolescents to make Informed Treatment Decisions' (1982) 53 Child Develop 285. For discussion, see R H Nicholson (ed) *Medical Research with Children* p 146.

14 Report of the Medical Research Council for 1962-3 (Cmnd 2382) pp 21-25.

15 Supervision of the Ethics of Clinical Research Investigations and Fetal Research HSC (5) 153.

16 See eg discussion by G Dworkin 'Law and Medical Experimentation: Of Embryos, Children and Others with Limited legal Capacity' (1987) 13 Monash Univ LR 189.

understanding and intelligence to appreciate what is involved. The judgment of the House of Lords in *Gillick v West Norfolk and Wisbech Area Health Authority*[17] has confirmed this view. 'Parental rights', said Lord Scarman, 'exist only so long as they are needed for the protection of the person and property of the child'. It is not certain whether the *Gillick* principle, which is concerned with consent to treatment, would be applied to cases of non-therapeutic experimentation. Much would, of course, depend on the severity of the procedure – this being one of the factors to be balanced in the assessment of '*Gillick*-competence'. As to statute, it is clear that the Family Law Reform Act 1969, s 8 refers only to diagnosis and treatment[18] – the statutory age of 16 years has, therefore, no relevance as to consent to experimentation. To infer from this that consent to non-therapeutic investigations is impossible below the age of majority would be, again, to accept a total embargo on paediatric research. It is not unreasonable to extrapolate Lord Donaldson's interpretation of the law in *Re R*[19] and to infer that anyone who is capable of doing so may give consent but that demurral by the minor would be a very important consideration in judging whether to carry out the research. Moreover, this would be even more significant than it would be in relation to treatment – to such an extent that it would be improbable in the extreme that a responsible doctor would ignore the minor's negative attitude. The problem then becomes that of deciding whether there is any age below which a person is deemed incapable of consent and, while there is no law on the point, it would be unwise, in our opinion, for a researcher to accept the unendorsed consent of a child under the age of 16; indeed, the circumstances in which such a consent would be acceptable would be exceptional. Hazardous experimentation authorised by the consent of a minor alone might, in fact, be unlawful and actually *restrained* by statute.[20]

To say that a procedure is legal is not to say that it is necessarily morally acceptable; furthermore, there is no reason to assume that the court, if asked, would approve an action which was unethical. The position is, therefore, still delicately balanced. Anticipating a judicial reaction is a matter for ethical committees who may assume that the court would act as a wise parent would act – giving first consideration to the child but being, at the same time, hospitable to good research.[1] Thus, the essential measure is the 'risk-benefit ratio' of the investigation – but, within this, the 'risk' factor must, without doubt, retain primary control. We also suggest that, notwithstanding what the true legal position may be, it would be, in practice, improper to proceed with an experiment involving a child against the wishes of its parents. The only exception might be when that refusal was clearly unreasonable and was jeopardising an otherwise essential trial to which a child who was capable of

---

17 [1986] AC 112, [1985] 3 All ER 402, HL.
18 It is problematic as to whether this limitation applies in Scotland in so far as the Age of Legal Capacity (Scotland) Act 1991, s 2(4) refers to consent by the understanding minor to 'any surgical, medical or dental *procedure* or treatment' (our emphasis).
19 *Re R (a minor) (wardship: medical treatment)* [1991] 4 All ER 177, (1992) 7 BMLR 147.
20 Lord Donaldson distinguished between medical treatment and a severely damaging operation which gave no benefit to the subject: *Re W (a minor) (medical treatment)* [1992] 4 All ER 627 at 635, 639, (1992) 9 BMLR 22 at 31, 35.
1 G Dworkin 'Legality of Consent to Nontherapeutic Medical Research on Infants and Young Children' (1978) 53 Arch Dis Child 443. The author notes the transition in legal thinking from paramount interests to first consideration of the child – the latter indicating that other interests are admissible.

understanding – the 'mature minor' of *Gillick* – had already consented. Such conditions must be extremely rare; in the event of their materialising, a decision to go ahead should be taken only after very careful consideration – and, probably, not even then.

It must not be thought that an ethical assessment of a project is always clear cut. A most apposite example was an experiment in preventive medicine which entailed the deliberate infection with the virus of hepatitis of children in a home for the subnormal. Although the chances of the children being infected naturally within six months of admission were as high as 60%, the project was castigated by some writers.[2] Others disagreed with such an analysis – one of Britain's most respected paediatricians at the time described the experiment as: 'a small, carefully controlled trial for which the director also deserves a great deal of credit for his scrupulous care in securing the truly informed consent of the children's parents.'[3] It is clear that there can be no generalised approach to a subject such as childhood experimentation, the practice of which is governed, in the end, by humane pragmatism.

Fetal experimentation

Several of the legal and moral attitudes to fetal life have already been discussed. The possibilities of fetal research and experiment, which are repugnant to many, extend the area of debate and merit further discussion. Research on the fetus is of considerable importance: just as children are, medically, more than little adults so, or rather more so, are fetuses not just immature children; the environment in which they exist is wholly different and, as has already been discussed, it is within that environment that something in the region of half the morbidity and mortality of infancy is fashioned.[4] Major areas of disease will never be properly understood in the absence of fetal research. Nor will the outstanding dilemma of drug therapy during pregnancy be fully resolved.

Sources of fetal material and the problems of consent

Other than those which are born alive prematurely and with which we are not currently concerned, fetuses become available either through spontaneous miscarriage or as a result of therapeutic abortion. It is axiomatic that any necessary consent to research can only be given by the mother and both her attitude and that of her physicians may be different in the two cases.

The position seems clear in the case of miscarriage. The mother is distressed and, normally, wants everything possible done for her offspring. It seems unlikely in the circumstances that a research project will be contemplated but, were it so, the informed consent of the mother would be required. The therapeutic abortion situation

2   See, for a good review, L Golman 'The Willowbrook Debate' (1973) 9 World Med (1)(79).

3   A W Franklin 'Research Investigation on Children' (1973) 1 BMJ 402 at 405.

4   The Peel Committee, reporting in 1972, listed 53 ways in which fetal research could be valuable, a catalogue which will have increased in the interim: *Report of the Committee on the Use of Fetuses and Fetal Material for Research* (1972).

is rather different. In the majority of cases, the mother will have requested termination and it could be held that, in so doing, she has effectively abandoned her fetus. The Peel Committee made the following recommendation:

> There is no legal requirement to obtain the patient's consent for research but, equally, there is no statutory right to ignore the parent's wishes – the parent must be offered the opportunity to declare any special directions about the fetus.[5]

This recommendation would now be considered inadequate. The very strict rules as to consent to research on the abandoned embryo should, in theory, be extrapolated to the abandoned fetus.[6] Moreover, the Peel Report has now been overtaken by that of the Polkinghorne Committee[7] which detected no material distinction between the results of therapeutic or spontaneous miscarriage.[8] It was firmly recommended that positive consent be obtained from the mother before fetal tissue is used for research or treatment in either circumstance[9] – for it was thought to be too harsh a judgment to infer that she has no special relationship with her fetus that has been aborted under the terms of the Abortion Act 1967;[10] the mother was entitled, at least, to counselling on the point. The Committee also recommended that her consent should include the relinquishing of any property rights – a recommendation which is discussed in greater detail below.[11] Interestingly, the Committee rejected the notion of any control by the father over the disposal of his child – this being on the grounds that paternal consent was not required for an abortion and that his relationship to the fetus is less intimate than is that of the mother.[12] We have already referred to the general denial of paternal interests in the fetus which we see as unreasonable;[13] this seems to be a further questionable extension of the principle of the woman's right to self-determination.

The Polkinghorne Committee was established mainly in response to concerns over fetal brain implants (which we discuss as a separate issue above[14]), and, as a consequence, one of its main concerns was that the research worker seeking consent should be wholly independent of the caring gynaecologist – every moral and public policy principle dictates that it be made absolutely clear that abortions are not being performed in order to provide research or therapeutic material; the timing of a therapeutic abortion should be subject only to considerations of care for the pregnant woman.

---

5 At para 42.
6 Human Fertilisation and Embryology Act 1990, Sch 3.
7 *Review of the Guidance on the Research Use of Fetuses and Fetal Material* (Cmnd 762).
8 At para 2.9.
9 At para 3.10.
10 At para 2.8.
11 See p 488.
12 At para 6.7. For this and several other criticisms of the recommendations, see J Keown 'The Polkinghorne Report on Fetal Research: Nice Recommendations, Shame about the Reasoning' (1993) 19 J Med Ethics 114.
13 See p 76 above.
14 See p 361.

The status of the fetus

The Polkinghorne Committee was fully alert to the fact that conditions for fetal research are not uniform and, in particular, that the fetal subject may be alive or dead – or it may be killed during the process of abortion. The living human fetus should be accorded a profound respect – a conclusion which is based upon its potential for development into a fully formed human being.[15] In so saying, the Committee clearly differentiated the dead fetus but still thought that this commanded respect. Research on the living fetus should be considered in a way broadly similar to that pertaining to children and adults and it was, therefore, recommended that it should not be undertaken if the risk to the fetus was more than minimal; research or experimentation carrying a greater risk should be limited to that which was of direct benefit to the subject. Respect for the dead fetus was recognised by the belief that research in that area should also be considered by ethics committees.[16]

Somewhat surprisingly, the Committee did not seek that the law be used to impose their restrictions. Rather, fetal research was to be overseen by local ethical research committees[17] and here, as we discuss above,[18] conditions are not uniform. Definitions of minimal or of direct benefit are likely to differ – as, indeed, are doctors' interpretations of research and experimentation and of the need for reference to an ethics committee. The general ethical and legal principles involved still merit discussion.

Some useful research is non-invasive and may be coupled with patient care but even then there is no simple answer. Thus, the experimental use of X-rays, at least in the first trimester, would be unethical; ultrasonic investigations seem, by contrast, to be wholly safe – but we cannot yet know, for example, whether fetal ultrasonic investigations will affect the subject at retiring age. Our more immediate concern is with invasive investigations and these, once again, focus attention on the uncertainties surrounding the legal status of the unborn child (see chapter 5).

It is now clear that 'wrongful death' in utero of the fetus that is incapable of being born alive gives rise to no action in the United Kingdom; neither the dead non-viable fetus nor the stillbirth has any right of action of itself and the only redress available is to the parents on the grounds of distress, inconvenience and the like[19] – but this is not to deny the trend towards a moral and legal acceptance of fetal rights which are comparable to those of a self-existent child.[20] If the fetus were born deformed, it would clearly have right of action against a research worker whose defence, assuming causation to have been proved, would rest on the standard of reasonable care having been observed. The matter of consent then becomes paramount and must be judged in the same light as has been discussed in relation to children.

---

15 At para 2.4.
16 At para 7.3.
17 At para 2.3.
18 See p 456.
19 See eg *Bagley v North Herts Health Authority* (1986) NLJ Rep 1014; *Grieve v Salford HA* (1991) 2 Med LR 295. In the United States, however, actions for wrongful death of the fetus have succeeded and a new form of tort – with a largely punitive motivation – may be being developed: *Amadio v Levin* 501 A 2d 1085 (Pa, 1985).
20 The constitutional protection of the fetus may be less extensive than that provided by private law – particularly when the issue is that of abortion: M L McConnell 'Sui Generis: The Legal Nature of the Foetus in Canada' (1991) 70 Can BR 548.

Assuming that the mother has a right of proxy consent to research procedures, the risk/benefit test would have to be very stringently applied, because, whereas the child has at least minimal understanding, the fetus can certainly have none. A negligence action based on a lack of informed consent would be more likely to succeed in these conditions than in many others; if, by contrast, parental consent is impossible, the damaged infant has a cause of action for trespass which will be virtually indefensible other than on issues of causation. In practice, the nature of any invasive experiment of this type is strictly limited on clinical grounds.

But what if the fetus should die? The fetus not being a legal person, there is no offence of feticide as such; but, should the fetus die prior to or during a resultant miscarriage, an offence may lie under the Offences Against the Person Act 1861, s 58 or under the Infant Life (Preservation) Act 1929, s 1 if the subject were capable of being born alive. Both these sections, however, include a requirement of intent, in the former to procure a miscarriage and in the second to destroy life. To prove an offence, it would then be necessary to show that the action amounted to constructive intent – that is, something was done when it was known that fetal death was a very high probability – and this seems a very doubtful proposition. It is, however, quite clear that intentional or reckless intra-uterine injury which results in neonatal death can attract a charge of manslaughter or of culpable homicide;[1] it is at least likely that disregard of the recommendations of the Polkinghorne Committee would give rise to an inference of recklessness. We do, however, see such eventualities as being extremely rare.

The pre-viable fetus
Perhaps it is the pre-viable fetus which attracts most emotion in the general issue of fetal research. Pre-viability implies that the fetus as a whole is incapable of a separate existence but that, nevertheless, there are signs of life in some organs. There can be no doubt that this is the fetal state which offers the greatest research potential; it is also true that the time available for such research is limited and so, therefore, is the opportunity for abuse. But, again, one must ask – is this an ensouled human being with the privacy rights of a human being? And, moreover, do we know that it has no feeling and is incapable of pain and suffering?[2] The Polkinghorne Committee was unable to discern any relevant ethical distinction between the pre-viable and the viable fetus – thereby diverging from the Peel Report. None the less, the status of the pre-viable fetus in relation to the criminal law needs consideration and the door is not quite closed on the moral concerns of the researcher.

We suggest that the criminal law is inadequate in this area. To destroy a fetus outside the terms of the Abortion Act is to destroy life. But, in doing so, what offence is being committed? It is now quite clear that no charge of murder or manslaughter can be raised in respect of a fetus absent its survival after birth;[3] the discussion may,

---

1 *Kwok Chak Ming v R* [1963] HKLR 349; *McCluskey v HM Advocate* 1989 SLT 175. For further discussion, see J Temkin 'Prenatal Injury, Homicide and the Draft Criminal Code' (1986) 45 CLJ 414.
2 The problem of fetal experience of pain seems unresolved and one wonders if it is capable of resolution: Z Kmietowicz 'Antiabortionists Hijack Fetal Pain Argument' (1996) 313 BMJ 188; I Murray 'Guidelines Will Ensure Foetuses Feel no Pain' The Times, 25 October 1997, p 2. The majority opinion seems to be that fetuses of less than 24 weeks' gestation feel no pain.
3 *A-G's Reference (No 3 of 1994)* [1996] QB 581, [1996] 2 All ER 10.

therefore, seem sterile in present conditions. It is doubtful whether the Abortion Act 1967 would be an adequate safeguard in the event of an extension of techniques being coupled with a deterioration in professional standards; it might then be necessary to invent an offence of feticide. The moral dilemma is clear from the questions posed above and, equally, turns on the definition of 'life'. We suggest that the moral problem may be resolved by considering, first, whether or not a placenta is present and whether there is or is not a competent fetal-maternal connection. If there is, the fetus is, subject to normality, clearly alive and destructive research or experimentation would be morally unacceptable; it should be disallowed on these grounds alone. If, however, the pre-viable fetus is separated from its mother, it is no longer capable of an existence; it is, therefore, possible to argue that its state is one of somatic death. Experiments or research conducted on the body are, by this reasoning, conducted during the interval between somatic and ultimate cellular death which has been described in chapter 13. Accordingly, we suggest that the processes involve neither moral nor legal culpability.

The dead fetus and fetal materials

Much useful research can be done on fetuses which are clearly dead or are incomplete; the major debate as to the morality of such research depends on how the fetus came to be dead – any objection on principle to the use of tissue from dead fetuses is almost certainly grounded on an overall objection to abortion.[4] Disposal of the dead fetus and fetal materials[5] must, ultimately, be subject to the mother's discretion but the extent of her authority is currently a matter of legal debate. Despite the strong reservations expressed by the Polkinghorne Committee, it is possible that property rights in respect of such tissues can arise, but recent case law indicates that such rights would vest in the researchers rather than the mother. We discuss this further in chapter 20. The Polkinghorne Committee condemned out of hand the sale of fetal tissues and materials for commercial purposes but, as we discuss later,[6] times have changed and the issue is not as simple as it once appeared to be. There are no rules governing the disposal of fetuses other than those related to offences against public decency. What offends against public decency is dictated by the public mores at the time – the disposal of fetal materials provides a classic example of such changing values.

Embryonic research

Research into human infertility and an understanding of embryonic development and implantation are inseparable. Embryonic research is also essential to the study and conquest of genetic disease. Systematic study in both these fields depends upon a supply of human embryos, for there always comes a time when animal models are

---

4 For discussion of attitudes and practices in relation to fetal tissue research in various countries, see 'Fetal Tissue Research around the World' (1992) 304 BMJ 591.
5 Ie those parts of the products of conception which are discarded by both the mother and the fetus – the placenta and its membranes and the umbilical cord. The Polkinghorne Committee preferred the term 'other contents of the uterus'.
6 See p 488.

inadequate for human research purposes. Essentially, there are two adoptable attitudes: either one can be totally opposed to research and experimentation on what are considered to be living human beings who cannot refuse consent to manipulation, or one can hold that the benefits to mankind are likely to be so great that the opportunity for study must be grasped if it is presented. Given that the case for human research is agreed – and we believe that it must be – the problem then arises as to how the necessary material is to be obtained within an acceptable moral framework. There are, again, two possibilities which are by no means mutually exclusive – either one can use the inevitable surplus of embryos that are produced for infertility treatments, or one can go one stage further and create embryos in vitro for the explicit purpose of using them for research. It is first necessary to look at the general proposition.

Arguments against a policy which prohibits embryo research rely, ultimately, on the view that, although the embryo may have human properties, it is not a human being invested with the same moral rights to respect as are due to other living members of the human community.[7] This approach has a familiar ring to it; indeed, it introduces the same concepts of personhood that have been so much a part of the abortion debate. There is, however, a crucial distinction to be made between lethal embryo research and abortion. The life of the aborted fetus is extinguished because its interests are outweighed by a more powerful and tangible set of interests – namely, those of the pregnant woman. The embryo subjected to experimentation, by contrast, dies because of the far less obvious interests of society in the pursuit of medical knowledge. The justification of feticide in abortion does not necessarily license the taking of in vitro embryonic life – and the legislative concern for the latter in the face of a liberal abortion policy may not be as unreasonable as is sometimes argued.[8]

Yet, if we consider, first, the surplus embryo, we have to ask: 'what is the alternative to embryocide?' The techniques in IVF and the welfare of the patient demand that more embryos are created than are strictly necessary; to say that all must be implanted[9] is to fly in the face of the reality that there are insufficient wombs available for the purpose. The alternatives then lie between embryocide and reduction of multiple pregnancy – of which the former is clearly the less objectionable. We have discussed elsewhere[10] the ethics of obtaining good from a morally poor or doubtful *fait accompli*. It is only the innate public fear of the 'scientist'[11] which stands against the acceptance of such a principle – one which we believe to be valid, perhaps particularly so in respect of the undifferentiated embryo.

But this can only hold so long as the basic tenet of the doctrine of double effect – that the good result must not be achieved by means of the ill-effect – is observed and it is this that distinguishes research on the surplus embryo from that undertaken on the embryo that has been created for the purpose; it follows that the latter needs

---

7 For a statement of this position, see J Harris 'Embryos and Hedgehogs: On the Moral Status of the Embryo' in A Dyson and J Harris (eds) *Experiments on Embryos* (1990) p 65.
8 See eg Mason p 471, n 1, at p 234.
9 As seems to be the case in the Infertility (Medical Procedures) Act 1984 (Victoria), s 6(5). But the section can be read as being directed only at the creation of embryos for non-therapeutic research purposes, which is certainly unlawful in Victoria.
10 See p 468.
11 M Warnock *A Question of Life* (1985) p xiii.

further justification. The proponents of unrestricted research would reply that it is acceptable not only because the embryo fails to satisfy the requirements of personhood which the fetus, similarly, fails to satisfy but also because, at least in its earlier stages,[12] its cells are pluripotential. In other words, until the development of the primitive streak, the conceptus is not a single, identifiable individual; any of its cells can develop along a number of lines, into a placenta, a hydatidiform mole, a human being or, indeed, several human beings. The early embryo thus lacks the essential qualities which go to make the human individual unique and worthy of moral respect.

The counter-assertion is, of course, that the embryo is the first stage of the human being that is born at the end of pregnancy – and that this holds from the moment of syngamy. It has been pointed out that the embryo stage is an essential part of life and that it makes no sense to argue that a person's life begins only with the appearance of the primitive streak on about the fourteenth day after conception.[13] It follows that the use of an embryo for any purpose that does not bear upon its future good constitutes a wrong; the embryo is, otherwise, being treated as a means to an end rather than as an end in itself – a process which offends a fundamental principle governing the way in which we treat other persons. To create human life in the full knowledge that it can have only the most limited future is seen by many opponents of embryo experimentation as an example of amoral exploitation and a first step on yet another slippery slope.

Between the two 'extreme' positions – that of a total rejection of embryo research on the grounds of its inescapable immorality and that of its acceptance in the case of any embryo, however derived – lies the middle view that, whereas research on surplus embryos is acceptable, the creation of embryos for that purpose is not. This is a view which is held by many and one with which we have very great empathy. Even so, it is not easy to establish a valid moral basis for the claim – because in so far as the ultimate outcome is their destruction, the harm done to the embryos is the same in each case. A possible philosophical solution depends on distinguishing harm from wrong. No *wrong* is done to the embryo at the time it is formed with a view to implantation; a later failure to achieve that goal is due to circumstances which are, to a large extent, beyond the control of the person who has brought it into being. By contrast, the embryo which is developed with the express intention of harming it is clearly *wronged* at the moment of its formation. Thus, while the harm done to each is the same, the wrong done is of a different quality. But do those who take the middle road adopt such reasoning in reality? It seems more probable that they accept instinctively that a utilitarian argument which holds that the benefit to mankind exceeds the harm done to what are the unfortunate rejects of a legitimate therapeutic activity cannot be substantiated in the case of specially created research subjects. This problem has raised what has been, perhaps, the most difficult hurdle for the world's legislatures.[14] We see below that the United Kingdom Parliament, in contrast to that of Victoria, has opted in favour of the similarity of in vitro embryos; could it

---

12 The use of the term 'pre-embryo' is suggested for this stage of development. We feel, however, that this smacks of changing words to establish a moral bolt-hole.
13 A Holland 'A Fortnight of My Life is Missing: A Discussion of the Status of the Pre-embryo' (1990) 7 J Appl Philos 25.

be that this disparity mirrors the public intuition unearthed by the intense involvement of community, or peoples', organisations in the deliberations of the preparatory Australian committee?

The legal response

The legal regulation of embryo research in the United Kingdom is embodied in the Human Fertilisation and Embryology Act 1990. The debate on the Bill was a free one in both the House of Lords and the House of Commons and there is no doubt that moral, rather than political, loyalties determined the position of the individual legislators.

We have already discussed this Act at length in chapters 3 and 5. For present purposes it is to be noted that, so great was the dilemma posed by the issue of embryo experimentation, the unusual step was adopted of introducing three mutually exclusive clauses relating to the point in the Bill. As we have seen, the most important overall effect of the Act is to establish an Authority which is responsible for overseeing fertilisation treatment and research services in the United Kingdom. The fundamental principles to be adopted are now clear. It is illegal to conduct any research on human embryos except under licence from the Authority. The Authority can only issue such a licence if the project is thought to be desirable for the purposes of advancing the treatment of infertility, for increasing knowledge of the causes of congenital disease, for studying the causes of miscarriage, for developing methods of contraception, or for developing methods of detecting the presence of genetic or chromosomal abnormalities in embryos before implantation; other reasons may be added by regulation.[15] In the absence of further regulation, no licence may authorise altering the genetic structure of a cell while it is part of an embryo and, while the hamster test for the normality of human sperm is allowed, all products of such research must be destroyed not later than the two-cell stage. There are strict regulations as to the maintenance of experimental records.[16] Overall, licences cannot authorise keeping or using an embryo after the appearance of the primitive streak – taken as being not later than 14 days after the gametes were mixed – nor may any embryo be placed in any animal.[17] Most importantly, in decreeing that research may be carried out, Parliament placed no restrictions on the source of the embryos used; the Authority has no mandate to impose an overall embargo on the creation of embryos for that specific purpose.

A tight regime of licensing and regulation will satisfy those who feel that research of this nature, while being permissible, needs close monitoring. Even so, the 1990 Act demonstrates a legislative approach which is probably more liberal than that existing elsewhere. Much depends upon the ability and motivation of the Human Fertilisation and Embryology Authority; it is doubtful whether the current legislation will go far in quietening the concern of those who feel that we are now allowing the use of human life in a way that is contrary to the spirit of, for example, the Declaration of Helsinki

14 The UK debate is well summarised in D Morgan and R G Lee *Backstone's Guide to the Human Fertilisation and Embryology Act 1990* (1991) ch 3.
15 Schedule 2, para 3(2).
16 Section 15.
17 Section 3.

– though it has to be said that any such expression has been, at best, muted. One thing is certain: the mere existence of an Authority will not end the debate and may, in fact, generate controversy of its own.[18]

18 See eg the controversy raised by the enforced intervention of the Authority in the case of Mrs Blood, discussed on p 60 above.

20 The body as property

We have encountered examples of moral, ethical and legal recognition of the relationship between the concept of 'self' and the physical entity known as 'the human body' at many junctures in our discussion thus far. In particular, the central position in medical law of the principle of respect for the patient's autonomy determines that the individual patient has the ultimate right to control his or her body and what is done with or to it. Primarily, that control is exercised through the twin concepts of consent to and refusal of treatment. Thus, we have seen in chapter 10 that disrespect of a refusal to an invasive procedure can result in actions in negligence or assault at common law and the use and storage of gametes is strictly controlled according to the written consent of the donor under the Human Fertilisation and Embryology Act 1990 (see chapter 3). That said, it is by no means the case that we have an absolute right, either ethically or legally, to do whatever we want with our bodies – we have noted how the Human Organ Transplants Act 1989 prohibits 'trade' in organs and the House of Lords was categoric in *R v Brown*[1] that ritual physical abuse of the body for sexual pleasure remains criminal even when undertaken within the envelope of full and informed consent by the parties involved. The question therefore arises of the limits which exist to the right to control our bodies. In recent years this debate has centred around the very important issue of the status of the body as property. This chapter will consider three aspects of that debate: property in material taken from living persons; property in material taken from cadavers; and the granting of intellectual property rights in human material.

Property in living human material

Intuitively, it is perfectly natural for us to talk of 'my body' and to infer that, because it is 'my' body, I can determine precisely what is done to it or its parts. Moreover, for most people, this feeling is inherently bound up with the proprietary notion that, because my body is my own, I 'own' my body.[2] However, it is far from clear that there is support for this in either legal or ethical terms. No ethical principle or imperative exists in which one can ground a property right in oneself. And, as Harris has pointed out, it is a 'spectacular non sequitur' to deduce that, because no one can make a slave of me and own my body, I necessarily own my body myself.[3] Indeed, the idea of

1 *R v Brown* [1996] 1 All ER 545.
2 Consider, for example the claim of one Peter Wallis, who at the time of writing has alleged that his former lover 'stole' his sperm by intentionally acquiring and misusing it during sexual intercourse with a view to becoming pregnant. The counter-claim to the suit is that Wallis surrendered any right of possession to his sperm when he transferred it during voluntary sexual relations: see B Vobejda 'Court to Decide if a Man has a Right to Choose Fatherhood' Washington Post, 23 November 1998, p A01.
3 J W Harris 'Who Owns My Body' (1996) 16 OJLS 55 at 71.

property is primarily a legal one. It is a construct which allows us to order our society according to a chosen value system, which in turn greatly facilitates the achievement of certain of our social goals – in our case, those of most Western states which encourage commerce and sanction commodification. The role of ethics lies not in grounding a property right but in determining whether it is appropriate to commodify something such as the human body which, for reasons we have already articulated in chapter 1, has a particular moral status deserving of respect. Thus, for many, the idea that one can buy or sell body parts is repugnant in that it shows disrespect for the status of 'the human body'.[4] Trade in body parts also gives rise to the spectre of exploitation, which is ethically unacceptable because it has the potential to harm those who are exploited. The counter to this, of course, is that whereas no one would sanction forced participation in the trade of body parts, it is unduly paternalistic to eschew the consent of individuals who would willingly sell their tissues. It is on just such a basis, amongst others, that the Human Organ Transplants Act 1989 has been criticised as being an unsophisticated knee-jerk reaction to a serious problem with a workable solution.[5]

Matters are further complicated by the opaqueness of the law as to the actual status of body parts in property terms. Thus, while there is evidence in the case law which suggests that regenerative body material such as hair,[6] blood[7] and urine[8] can be the subject of property,[9] the United Kingdom courts and legislature have been, on the whole, reluctant to address this issue directly. The Human Organ Transplants Act 1989 says nothing about property in organs as such and merely criminalises those who would attempt to trade in the material. Similarly, in controlling the use and storage of gametes, the Human Fertilisation and Embryology Act 1990 relies on the expressed written wishes of the donor of gametes but falls far short of acknowledging a property right in any sample. This should be compared with the Court of Appeal of California's decision in *Hecht v Kane*,[10] in which the court held that a deceased man who had previously deposited sperm for the use of his partner had an interest 'in the nature of ownership' of the samples such as to render them 'property' within the meaning of the Probate Code and, accordingly, disposable property on his death.[11] This decision should be contrasted with the French case of *Parpalaix v CECOS*,[12] in

4   S R Munzer 'An Uneasy Case Against Property Rights in Body Parts' (1994) 11 Soc Philosoph Pol 259; cf A Ryan 'Self-Ownership, Autonomy and Property Rights' (1994) 11 Soc Philosoph Pol 241.
5   J Radcliffe-Richards et al 'The Case of Allowing Kidney Sales' (1998) 351 Lancet 1950.
6   *R v Herbert* (1961) 25 JCL 163.
7   *R v Rothery* [1976] RTR 550, (1976) 63 Crim App Rep 231.
8   *R v Welsh* [1974] RTR 478.
9   In each of these criminal cases, the accused was convicted of theft for removing the 'property' of another without permission. Eg in *Rothery* the accused gave a sample of blood to be tested for alcohol levels and then 'stole' it by removing it from the police station.
10   16 Cal App 4th 836 (1993).
11   Similarly, the Tennessee Supreme Court held in *Davis v Davis* 842 SW 2d 588 (1992) that the embryo occupied an 'interim category' as neither 'person' nor 'property', yet which entitled it to a special respect. While the parties were denied 'a true property interest' they retained an interest, 'in the nature of ownership' in relation to the use and disposal of their pre-embryos.
12   JCP 1984.II.20321. In subsequent cases the French court struggled to find a valid basis in law for dealing with embryos and sperm, vacillating between the law of obligations on the one hand and the principle of 'the established family' on the other: see (1996) *La Semaine Juridique* Ed G, No 27, 22666. The current position in France is embodied in Law No 94-654 of 29 July 1994, which was incorporated into the public health code. These provisions make no mention of property rights but require that both the male and female partners be alive and consent to insemination with sperm or use of an embryo created in vitro. In this way, post mortem uses are prohibited.

which the court ordered the return of frozen sperm to the wife of the depositor on the basis of an agreement which had been made between him and the sperm bank. It refused, however, to go so far as to recognise any property interest in the sperm.

The embryo in vitro

The Human Fertilisation and Embryology Authority is equally indecisive as to the disposal of embryos which are created for artificial insemination but which are not used for the purpose. Once again, the 1990 Act avoids any recognition of property rights and control over the use and disposal of the frozen embryos falls to be determined by the will of the parties contributing to their formation. However, unlike gametes, two parties provide the genetic material contained in embryos. Who, then, has the power to dispose of them?

In this respect, Sch 3 to the 1990 Act provides that effective written consent must be given by each person whose gametes have contributed to the embryo.[13] In effect, this gives either contributor an effective veto over its use but provides neither with rights of disposal – the embryos must be allowed to perish if the gamete providers cannot agree and the storage time for the embryo has exceeded the statutory limit.[14]

The regulations which govern storage of gametes and embryos provide that the initial storage period of five years may be extended up to ten years, and in some cases longer, so long as the gamete providers do not lodge an objection when asked to reaffirm their consent to storage. It is important to note here that actual written reconfirmation of such consent is required. This can be problematic at a number of levels, particularly if a couple who have provided gametes has separated or if gametes have been supplied by a donor who is no longer traceable. In each case, the embryos will be allowed to die if no reconfirmation is obtained.[15]

We view this system of consents with a degree of concern. In the absence of any property right in embryos, the aim for which they have been created can be thwarted easily by the withholding of consent by a potentially disinterested, bitter or uncontactable contributor. Thus, the person for whom they were intended, that is the woman who was to carry one or more of them, will be denied the opportunity to benefit from the original treatment proposed. While we do not suggest that a property system would be problem-free, we believe that to recognise a property right in embryos which vests, in the first instance, in the woman who is to receive treatment would go a long way to resolving the current controversies surrounding these issues. It should not be forgotten that a considerable number of embryos had to be destroyed at the end of the first five-year period of storage precisely because of the difficulties outlined above.[16] The mere creation of a facility to extend the storage period will not make the problems go away.

---

13 Schedule 3, para 6(3).
14 Human Fertilisation and Embryology (Statutory Storage Period for Embryos) Regulations 1996, SI 1996/375, r 14(1)(c).
15 Schedule 3, para 6(3).
16 K D Hopkins 'First Batch of Human Embryos Destroyed in UK' (1996) 348 Lancet 399.

The fetus in vivo

Whatever may be said about the embryo in vitro, there should be no support for extending a woman's property right to an implanted fetus. A clear moral distinction is to be made between the in vitro and the in vivo human organism, not least because of the immediate potentiality of the latter to become a complete human being.[17] It is to be noted that the Polkinghorne Committee[18] suggested that provision be made in any consent to fetal research procedures for the relinquishment of property rights 'if, indeed, there be any' (para 8.4). This clearly refers to maternal rights in respect of the fetus. Times have, however, changed since 1989 and, while the Polkinghorne Committee regarded the dissociation of the use of fetal tissues and abortion as the overriding consideration, others might now see it as anomalous if, as we argue tentatively below, a 'profit sharing' agreement were enforceable between a biotechnological institute and the donor when the tissues of a living person were used but the institute could escape any financial duty of recompense by using tissues from a fetus.

But what of a non-viable or stillborn fetus and/or fetal material that is discharged from the mother as result of either a medical termination or a spontaneous miscarriage? The potentiality for viable human life has clearly ended in such a case[19] and we must consider the possibility of property rights afresh. The Polkinghorne Committee refused to address this issue and preferred, instead, to recommend that the full and informed consent of the woman be obtained concerning the use and/or disposal of the material. We confess to something of a *volte face* on this issue since the publication of the last edition of this book. While we acknowledge that, in moral terms, a dead fetus might command greater respect than fetal material *in se*, we do not consider that the recognition of a property interest in either necessarily involves such a degree of disrespect as would lead us to refuse to recognise any such interest. The potential value of any tissue is,[20] nowadays, uncertain but is surely increasing and we suggest that the mother of the fetus should retain any available property claim not only in respect of the fetus itself but also of its associated materials. Of course, the matters of ownership and disposal should be approached cautiously and with sensitivity at such an emotional time.

The Nuffield Report

The themes of abandonment and consent figure large in the April 1995 report of the Nuffield Council on Bioethics, which addressed the question of property in body parts generally, including gametes, embryos and fetal material.[21] After reviewing the legal and ethical position on human tissue, the Council made its recommendations in light of the provisions of the Human Tissue Act 1961, the Human Organ Transplants Act 1989 and the Anatomy Act 1984, which make it clear, first, that any tissue given or taken from individuals is received free of all claims and, second, that the common law position is, as yet, unsettled. It recommended that any disputed claim over material should be settled with regard to the nature of the consent given to the initial procedure for removal. Moreover, it was the Council's view that it should be implied in any

---

17 Although the fetus is not a legal person, the concept of it being 'property' is too close to that of slavery for comfort.
18 *Review of the Guidance on the Research use of Fetuses and Fetal Material* (Cm 762, 1989).
19 The possible exception to this is the living abortus which we discuss in chapter 5, p 132 above.
20 See p 489 below.
21 Nuffield Council on Bioethics *Human Tissue: Ethical and Legal Issues* (1995).

consent to medical treatment which involves the removal of tissue that the tissue has been abandoned by the person from whom it was removed.[1] It was recommended that tissue removed from an individual who is unable to give valid consent should not be the subject of any claim, either by the incapax or his or her representatives.[2]

The Council's recommendations are certainly in keeping with the trend which has emerged in the United Kingdom to date.[3] Yet, we cannot help but feel that the Council, like the courts and legislature before it, was reluctant to face head-on the real issues concerning body ownership.[4] The attitude of a small sample of in-patients says little about the current ethical debate over body parts and nothing about the actual or potential legal position. It is telling, for example, that few of those surveyed had been told about the possible uses of the material. The Nuffield Council's report was based, in the main, on the premise that people see no value in their excised body parts; this premise has long dominated this area of debate, yet it is one which has always been questionable and is easily challenged today. 'Value' exists in a variety of forms. Consider the value which we attach to fetal tissue and the controversy which has surrounded proposed research and therapies using such tissue (see chapter 19). Consider, too, the fact that we find it meaningful to continue to talk about 'my appendix' and 'my gall stones' even when these materials have been removed from our bodies. Perhaps most significantly of all, the advent of the biotechnological age has meant that there can be considerable economic value which accrues to biotechnological products produced using human material. Thus, to assert, as the Council does, that patients should be deemed to abandon their tissues, is to ignore the potential values which those very persons may well hold in retaining control over such material. A system of consents does not permit that control to be exercised as fully as might be desirable.

Commercialism and human material
Gold has noted, for example, that, because the courts tend to ignore sociological, psychological and anthropological attitudes towards the body in their decisions and, instead, reduce everything to economics, they ignore signs of people's ambiguity about technological advancement.[5] It is widely assumed that the interposition of commercial interests between the source of valuable material and its user is unacceptable because it leads necessarily to exploitation. At the same time, it is accepted that the encouragement of commercial profit-making by users, primarily by the biotechnology industry, can only bring benefits to the community in the guise of more therapies and cures. But, as Gold correctly observes, giving property right to biotechnologic researchers focuses the medical industry primarily on cure and shifts attention away from the equally, or more, important pursuit of determining – and eradicating – the underlying causes of illness and disease.[6] Similarly, as we discuss

1 Ibid, ch 9, in particular para 9.14.
2 Ibid, paras. 9.15.–9.17.
3 A recent survey showed that only 10% of hospital patients believed that they retained ownership of tissue removed after surgery, while 47% thought that the material belonged either to the hospital (27%) or to the laboratory (20%). Only 27% of those surveyed were of the opinion that no one owned the material: R D Start et al. 'Ownership and Uses of Human Tissue: Does the Nuffield Bioethics Report Accord with Opinion of Surgical Inpatients?' (1996) 313 BMJ 1366.
4 For a full discussion, see P Matthews 'The Man of Property' (1995) 3 Med L Rev 251.
5 E R Gold *Body Parts: Ownership of Human Biological Material* (1996).
6 Ibid, p 37.

in the context of surrogacy (see chapter 3), it is not necessarily exploitative *in se* to offer financial incentives or rewards to individuals to use their bodies in certain ways. That something is potentially exploitative does not mean that it must always be so, and it certainly does not justify the courts' refusing to deal directly with the real interests and issues.

The case which most clearly betrays the skewed attitude of the judiciary towards these matters is *Moore v Regents of the University of California.*[7]   John Moore suffered from hairy cell leukaemia and his spleen was removed at the Medical School of the University of California at Los Angeles. His doctor, Dr Golde, discovered that cells from the spleen had unusual and potentially beneficial properties and developed an immortal cell-line from them without his patient's knowledge or consent. Moreover, Dr Golde sought, and obtained, a patent over the cell-line which he subsequently sold to a drug company for $15m – and it has been reported that the drugs and therapies which were developed from the patented product are now worth in excess of $3b. Moore brought an action against the researchers, the university and the drug company when he discovered the truth about his cells. He filed 11 causes of action in total but those concerning the questions of property and consent are of most direct interest. In particular, he alleged *conversion* – that, as the 'owner' of the cells, his property right had been compromised by the work carried out on the cells by the defendants. He also alleged breach of fiduciary duty and lack of informed consent because he had never been told of the potential use of his cells and, correspondingly, he had never given his full and informed agreement to the initial operation. The Californian Supreme Court upheld these two last claims but rejected the argument in conversion. The court opined that it was inappropriate to recognise property in the body, first, because no precedent could be found on which to ground such a claim and, secondly, because to recognise individual property rights in body parts would be to hinder medical research 'by restricting access to the necessary raw materials' – a pure utilitarian consideration. Moreover, the court was concerned that a contrary decision would '[threaten] to destroy the economic incentive to conduct important medical research' because '[i]f the use of cells in research is a conversion, then with every cell sample a researcher purchases a ticket in a litigation lottery'.[8] The irony of this decision is pointed out in the dissent of Broussard J:

> ... the majority's analysis cannot rest on the broad proposition that a removed part is not property, but ... on the proposition that a *patient* retains no ownership interest in a body part once the body part has been removed. (emphasis added.)

Thus, while each of us is denied recognition of a property interest in excised parts of our bodies, third parties may not only gain such an interest but can go on to protect such an interest using forms of property law such as the law of patents.

But does not such an example demonstrate precisely the kind of value which individuals could retain in their excised parts? The properties of the patient's cells are a *sine qua non* of the ultimate invention. And, while no one would deny that much time and money would need to be expended in turning the natural material into a

7   793 P 2d 479 (Cal, 1990).   See also, *Brotherton v Cleveland* 923 F 2d 661 (6th Cir, 1991).
8   For comment on *Moore,* see B Hoffmaster 'Between the Sacred and the Profane: Bodies, Property, and Patents in the *Moore* Case' (1992) 7 Intellect Prop J 115.

patentable product, is the view of the Supreme Court in *Moore* not something of an over-reaction to the *possible* consequences of applying property law to the human body? It is entirely reasonable to hold that some financial reward should also be given to the source of the valuable sample while, at the same time, accepting that the majority of the spoils should return to those who have done the work in creating a patentable product. It is *not* reasonable to exclude completely from the equation the one person who can make everything possible.

It is uncertain how far these views would be accepted in the courts of the United Kingdom. As Scowen pointed out,[9] there is no fiduciary duty to disclose information under English law; it is, however, hard to believe that the court would not see the prospect of a monetary fortune as being something so obviously necessary to an informed decision by the patient that no reasonably prudent professional man would fail to mention it[10] – and, to that extent, the courts in California and the United Kingdom would be in accord. But we also agree with Scowen's implication that a British court would conclude that, in equity, the patient should be entitled to a share of the profits arising from an enterprise to which his contribution was an essential prerequisite – although, as we discuss above, that share might well be proportionate to the expertise and resources contributed by the technologists.

This does not, perhaps, take us very far with the question of disposal of the commercially valueless specimen. We suggest, however, that a consent-based action in negligence would be available if, for example, a patient's susceptibilities were outraged by his tissues being used for demonstration purposes. Fortunately, the question is of no more than academic interest in the overwhelming majority of cases.

Tissues at molecular level

As a final point, we bring the reader's attention to the United States federal Genetic Privacy Act 1995, which we discuss in the context of control over genetic information in chapter 7. In an unprecedented move, this piece of legislation vests a right of property in a DNA sample in the source of that sample. Thus, in addition to requiring clear written consent from the sample source in respect of the gathering and use of any DNA material, the Act puts him in a stronger bargaining position in respect of any potentially profitable research work which might be carried out on his sample. Lin argues that this approach promotes, rather than hinders, research because those previously hesitant to provide samples now have an incentive to do so.[11] We would agree, and add that this also clarifies the legal position substantially and makes for a more principled approach to the question of ownership of body parts. While it remains to be seen how many states will implement this legislation, we believe that this Act is but the first step on the road to full recognition of ownership of one's own body and its parts.

9 E Scowen 'The Human Body – Whose Property and Whose Profit ?' (1990) 1 Dispatches 1.
10 See Lord Bridge in *Sidaway v Board of Governors of the Bethlem Royal Hospital and the Maudsley Hospital* [1985] AC 871 at 900, [1985] 1 All ER 643 at 663, HL.
11 M M J Lin 'Conferring a Federal Property Right in Genetic Material: Stepping into the Future with the Genetic Privacy Act' (1996) 22 Am J Law Med 109.

Property in cadavers and cadaver tissues

The concept that third parties can own body parts while the person from who those parts are taken cannot do so, is also to be found in the law relating to cadavers. For a long time the 'no property in a corpse' rule was thought to exclude all possibility of property in a dead body or its parts in England and Wales[12] – although there is authority in Scotland that property can exist in a corpse, at least until it is buried or otherwise disposed of.[13] The case of *R v Kelly*[14] has, however, now established that there are serious limitations to any such rule which may have important consequences for the users of human tissue removed from cadavers. In *Kelly* the Court of Appeal was faced with the question of whether it was theft for a junior technician of the Royal College of Surgeons to remove body parts for use, and ultimate disposal, by an artist who was interested in using them as moulds for his sculptures. The defendants relied on the 'no property' rule as their defence. The Court of Appeal held that the rule refers only to the a corpse or its parts which remain in their natural state, but that:

> . . . parts of a corpse are capable of being property. . . if they have acquired different attributes by virtue of the application of skill, such as dissection or preservation techniques, for exhibition or teaching purposes.[15]

So it was in the *Kelly* case. Work had been done on the body parts in question, such that they became specimens owned by the Royal College. To remove them without authority was, therefore, theft. The court opined, however, that the 'no property' rule is so deeply entrenched in English jurisprudence that legislative action would now be required for it to be changed *in se*. That having been said, the court went so far as to speculate that the common law might recognise property in human body parts even when those parts had not acquired different attributes, but if they had attracted a 'use or significance beyond their mere existence'.[16] What we are not told is who would be the holder of any such right. An answer may be found, however, in an earlier ruling by the Court of Appeal, which was approved of in *Kelly*.

In *Dobson v North Tyneside Health Authority*[17] the relatives of a woman who had died from brain tumours brought an action in negligence against the health authority for failure to diagnose the nature of the deceased's condition properly and in time. In order to succeed, however, it was important to establish whether the tumours were malignant or benign and this could only be done by examining samples from the deceased's brain. The brain had been removed by the hospital at autopsy and preserved in paraffin[18] but it had been disposed of later. The relatives therefore brought a further action against the hospital alleging that it had converted 'property'

12 Nuffield Report, para 10.2. The Australian case *Doodeward v Spence* (1908) 6 CLR 406 is frequently cited in this regard.
13 *Dewar v HM Advocate* 1945 JC 5 at 14.
14 [1998] 3 All ER 741.
15 Ibid at 749-750.
16 Ibid at 750.
17 [1996] 4 All ER 474, (1996) 33 BMLR 146.
18 One of us finds this hard to understand. Normal procedure would be to preserve the brain in formaldehyde and to remove small pieces which would be processed into small 'paraffin blocks' for examination. The latter would present a negligible storage problem.

to which the relatives were entitled and that, at best, it acted as a bailee having no right of unauthorised disposal. In rejecting these claims, the Court of Appeal held that no right of possession or ownership of the brain, or indeed of the corpse, vested in the relatives. At best, a limited possessory right to a corpse is enjoyed by the executor or administrator of a deceased person but this right is only to possess the corpse with a view to its burial or disposal.[19] More importantly, the court held that the next of kin have no such legal right unless they assume the role of executor or administrator. Secondly, the court held that property rights could arise in respect of body parts where some work or skill differentiates the body or its parts from a corpse in its natural state. It quoted with halting approval the following passage from the Australian decision *Doodeward v Spence,* which involved a dispute over the 'ownership' of a two-headed fetus:

> . . . when a person has by lawful exercise of work or skill so dealt with a human body or part of a human body in his lawful possession that it has acquired some attributes differentiating it from a mere corpse awaiting burial, he acquires a right to retain possession of it, at least as against any person not entitled to have it delivered to him for the purposes of burial.[20]

Two elements from this passage are worth noting. First, any such property right which accrues, accrues to the person who does the work. Second, the property right which springs into existence is subject to the right of those with the right to possession for burial. We have already seen that no possessory right for burial purposes existed in *Dobson.* But had the brain become property? Gibson LJ did not seem to think so. The brain had not been preserved for the purposes of teaching or exhibition, nor was the case analogous to a stuffing or an embalming, which displays an intention to retain the part as a specimen. The brain had been removed and preserved only under the obligation to remove material bearing on the cause of death imposed by the Coroners Rules 1984.[1] The hospital intended to abide by these rules and was at liberty to destroy the brain once the material was no longer required by the coroner.

Dobson is as interesting for the questions that it does not answer as it is for those that it does. For example, as to the possessory right of executors, must the body and *all* of its parts be returned? Similarly, what is the role of intention in creating property rights? Reading *Dobson* and *Kelly* in conjunction, it seems that property rights can arise if work is done on a tissue *with the intention* of retaining the sample as a specimen or for some other purpose. But just how much, or little, work needs to be done? In *Kelly* the court indicates that dissection or preservation techniques are enough to make a sample 'property'.[2] If so, then merely to carry out an autopsy or to place a sample in formaldehyde is enough to create 'property'.[3] And, as we have

---

19 No executor or administrator had been appointed in the present case until after the body had been disposed of.
20 *Doodeward v Spence* (1908) 6 CLR 406 at 414, per Griffith CJ.
 1 Coroners Rules 1984, SI 1984/552, r 9.
 2 [1998] 3 All ER 741 at 749-750.
 3 The Nuffield Council is of the view that 'a hospital which has tissue in its possession, for example for transplant, has such property rights over the tissue as to exclude any claim of another to it, as does a coroner or pathologist who has carried out a post-mortem and retains body parts for examination': Report at para 10.6. Without wishing to labour the point, there is a world of difference between placing a brain in preservative and preparing blocks for microscopic examination; the precise conditions of the case are, therefore, of some significance.

seen from *Dobson*, that property belongs to he who would 'use' the goods and certainly not to the source or his/her significant others. Thus, if the Court of Appeal in *Kelly* is correct and the common law does one day move to the position that property rights may arise because of the 'inherent' valuable attributes in tissue samples, it is undoubtedly the case that such rights will vest in the 'discoverer' of those properties.

Intellectual property law and the human body

We end this section with a consideration of intellectual property rights in the human body. We have already seen how in *Moore* a patent was granted over the 'Mo' cell-line produced using Mr Moore's cells. Certainly, patent law has had to adapt rapidly in the last two decades to meet the demands of the biotechnology industry. Astronomical sums are invested in research and development by drug companies and the industry has fought long and hard to ensure that its products receive patent protection. This, it is thought, assures a degree of return on the investment. The earning potential of the industry is tremendous. The revenues of European biotechnology companies exceeded 1,700m ECU in 1996. At the same time, the United States industry was worth over 11,600m ECU.[4]

A patent offers an absolute monopoly for up to 20 years over an invention to the extent that all others can be excluded from competing in the marketplace with the same, or a similar, product. Strict criteria must be met to obtain protection but, once secured, a patent can protect a commercial enterprise against all comers. Yet patenting is not a morally neutral exercise and the biotechnology industry has faced considerable problems in obtaining protection for itself. These problems have been particularly acute in Europe and arise because the work of the industry involves the manipulation of living organisms. Thus, for many, to patent a biotechnological invention is to patent 'life' itself.[5]

The patent law of the United States exemplifies the standard criteria for patentability that are accepted in most of the world.[6] To be patentable, an invention must be new, it must involve an 'inventive step' – in the sense that the development should not be obvious to a person skilled in the particular field – and it must have utility. There is no provision in the law to refuse to register a patent on the grounds of morality. Thus, while it was argued in *Diamond v Chakrabarty*[7] that a patent for a genetically hybridised oil-eating bacterium should be revoked on the grounds that no patent should be given over 'life', the Supreme Court rejected this objection, holding that 'Congress intended statutory subject matter to include anything under the sun that is made by man'. Similarly, when, in 1988, Harvard University sought a patent for its *ONCOmouse* – a mouse genetically engineered with a human cancer gene in such a way that it develops cancer as a matter of course – the US Patent and Trademark Office granted the patent without question.

4   Ernst & Young *Biobusiness* (1997).
5   Compare A J Wells 'Patenting New Life Forms: An Ecological Perspective' (1994) 3 Euro Intellect Prop Rev 111 and S Crespi 'Biotechnology Patents: The Wicked Animal Must Defend Itself' (1995) 9 Euro Intellect Prop Rev 431.
6   35 USC paras 101, 102 and 103. The UK equivalent is found in the Patents Act 1977, s 1(1).
7   447 US 303, 66 L Ed 2d 144 (1980).

Harvard have faired significantly less well in Europe – indeed, at the time of writing, disputes over the ONCOmouse patent remain unresolved some ten years after a patent application was first filed. In essence, the problem of patent protection faced by the biotechnology industry in Europe stems from the 'morality provisions' of the European Patent Convention 1973 (EPC), which embodies the patent law of 18 European countries. Article 53 of the EPC states:

European patents shall not be granted in respect of —
(a) inventions the publication or exploitation of which would be contrary to 'ordre public' or morality, provided that the exploitation shall not be deemed to be so contrary merely because it is prohibited by law or regulation in some or all of the Contracting States;
(b) plant or animal varieties or essentially biological processes for the production of plants or animals; this provision does not apply to microbiological processes or the products thereof.

The Harvard patent has been challenged both on the grounds that it is inherently immoral to patent 'life' under art 53(a) and because it is an attempt to patent an 'animal variety' under art 53(b).[8] Yet, in *HARVARD/ONCOmouse*,[9] the Examining Division of the European Patent Office allowed the patent in respect of (a) because it held that the morality question is to be tested by balancing, on the one hand suffering of the animal, with, on the other, the potential benefits to humanity. The 'carrot' of a potential cure for cancer tipped the scales in favour of patentability. In respect of (b) it was held that the 'invention' being claimed was a 'non-human mammal' and this was much broader than a mere 'animal variety'; therefore, no problem arose under art 53(b).[10] Such linguistic gymnastics are clearly driven by policy concerns as to the attractiveness of Europe to the investor in biotechnology. Laws which are too strict act as a disincentive and encourage more investment in the United States where morality in this field is, seemingly, not a problem.

Patents over human material have been granted for a number of years. For example, over 1,175 human DNA patents were granted in the period 1981-95, mainly in the United States. Yet, as with ONCOmouse, the European Patent Office (EPO) has had to deal with moral objections to such patents. The patent in dispute in *HOWARD FLOREY/Relaxin*[11] concerned H2 Relaxin, a protein produced naturally by women at the time of childbirth which softens the pelvis and so eases the passage of the child. Howard Florey genetically engineered this protein and sought a patent for the artificial chemical. It was argued before the Opposition Division of the EPO, first, that it would be tantamount to slavery to grant a patent for such a product, in that it involved the sale of human tissue; secondly, that this too was exploitative and an offence to human dignity; and, finally, that any patent over DNA is inherently immoral because DNA is 'life'. Each of these arguments was rejected out of hand by the Division. It held that there can be no question of slavery because no woman is forced to surrender material – all the subjects consented. Similarly, it was not

8 *HARVARD/ONCOmouse* [1990] EPOR 4.
9 [1991] EPOR 525.
10 Opposition proceedings were immediately started by 16 groups after this decision, but no resolution has as yet been possible.
11 [1995] EPOR 541.

necessarily exploitative to use human material because free and informed consent was given; the Division pointed out that human material is used in a variety of contexts without the question of exploitation arising. Finally, it was held that DNA is not 'life' but a chemical substance which carries genetic information: 'no woman is affected in any way by the present patent.'[12]

We consider that, well-intended as it is, the morality provision in European patent law is ill-placed. Primarily, this is because it can never attain to that which it designed to achieve. The crucial point is that the refusal of a grant of a patent does nothing directly to prevent the creative process from continuing. Thus, Harvard can continue to produce the mouse for sale on the open market even if ONCOmouse is not given a patent – all that is lost is a chance to monopolise that market. If one is concerned by the act of creation itself, and this must be the main concern in these cases, then attention should be turned not to the point at which protection is offered, but to the point at which the creation takes place.[13] This cannot be done through the law of patents but, rather, through other mechanisms such as the introduction of regulatory schemes or the creation of authorities which can monitor the industry. Making morality part of patent law does nothing to regulate the biotechnology industry.

A European Directive was adopted in July 1998 which seeks to clarify the legal position in respect of biotechnological patents[14] but, whereas guidance is given on the kinds of invention which will never receive patent protection,[15] the morality provision as defined in ONCOMouse remains broadly untouched and relatively imprecise.[16] The Nuffield Council has recommended that the United Kingdom Government join with the other signatory countries to the EPC to adopt a protocol which sets out in some detail the criteria to be used by national courts when applying the morality exclusion test[17] – this is an initiative which merits widespread support.

Conclusion

It seems that whether we are dealing with living or dead human tissue, whether we are looking at humanity at the structured or the molecular level, or whether we are

---

12　Ibid at 550-551.
13　This is argued more fully in G T Laurie 'Biotechnology: Facing the Problems of Patent Law' in H L MacQueen and B G M Bain (eds) *Innovation, Incentive and Reward: Intellectual Property Law and Policy* (1997) Hume Papers on Public Policy 46.
14　Directive of the European Parliament and of the Council on the Legal Protection of Biotechnological Inventions, No 98/44/EC of 6 July 1998.
15　Under art 6 the following are unpatentable: (a) processes for cloning human beings; (b) processes for modifying the germ line genetic identity of human beings; (c) uses of human embryos for industrial or commercial purposes; (d) processes for modifying the genetic identity of animals which are likely to cause them suffering without any substantial medical benefit to man or animal, and also animals resulting from such processes.
16　Article 6 now requires that a *substantial* medical benefit accrue to humanity or animals before the morality test will be satisfied. It is interesting to note that the Dutch government has challenged the validity of the directive on four grounds: (a) legal basis; (b) subsidiarity; (c) breach of international obligations; and (d) conflict with basic/human rights: *Netherlands v EC Council and EU Parliament* C-377/98 (unreported).
17　Nuffield Report, p 488, n 20, para 11.43.

considering domestic or international regulation, we are faced with a schizoid approach to property rights in human material. On the one hand, there is an innate antipathy to the concept; on the other, we accept the inexorable march of 'science' knowing that, if something is there to be discovered, someone will discover it – and with little concern for the consequences. Governments may set up regulatory authorities as the significance of each scientific advance becomes apparent but they are relatively powerless in the face of global international pressures. What does seem clear is that, so far as the domestic scene is concerned, our courts must appreciate that this is a field in which technology and societal attitudes are advancing and being fashioned rapidly – and the common law must keep pace and accelerate as is necessary. Put in a nutshell, the legal issues involving the DNA double helix can no longer be resolved by way of authority derived from the circumstances surrounding a nineteenth-century fairground exhibit.

Psychiatry and the law

21 Human rights, psychiatry and the law

The practice of psychiatry is more vulnerable to criticism than any other area of medicine. The reasons for this are complex; one factor, however, stands out: while treatment for physical conditions almost always depends upon the consent of the patient, the psychiatrist may be called upon to treat the unwilling. The associated powers may involve the involuntary detention of a fellow being for a considerable time, something which is usually reserved to the judiciary in a state governed by law. In addition, psychiatric treatment is likely to be aimed at ameliorating a disturbance of mood or behaviour. In so doing, it sets out to alter the functioning of the human mind and this can be seen as an interference in human autonomy which will be justified only in the most exceptional circumstances. Thus, in the view of some critics,[1] the powers accorded to psychiatric medicine give rise to unnecessary and unwanted intervention in the lives of persons whose situation, although unusual, may be tolerable from their point of view. This criticism of psychiatry, once fashionable, is now more muted. The civil liberties concerns of the critics have, to an extent, been addressed by reforming legislation aimed at restraining professional power, and it is now difficult to find psychiatrists who are not acutely aware of the dangers of excessive intervention in the lives of mentally ill people. Some critics, however, remain unconvinced, and take the view that the 'legalism' of the current approach merely masks an interventionist philosophy and the exercise of power over the vulnerable.

Society favoured the institutional or asylum approach to the management of mental illness until the final decades of the twentieth century. Those diagnosed as suffering from a psychiatric illness were usually sent to 'mental hospitals' where in-patient treatment would be provided. The growth of a large group of patients whose only home was hospital was an inevitable result of such a policy and there grew up increasing calls for the release into the community of as many long- and short-term psychiatric patients as possible.[2] This movement was motivated principally by the desire to save those with mental disability from the indignities of forced 'removal' from the community but the cause was, in due course, taken up by governments which were anxious to keep health costs as low as possible; as a result, many psychiatric hospitals were closed.[3] Thus, the debate related to psychiatry and human rights is

---

1 For classic examples of radical views of mental illness and society's response to it, see T S Szasz *The Myth of Mental Illness* (1972) and R D Laing *The Divided Self* (1965). A more recent critique is contained in C Unsworth *The Politics of Mental Health* (1987); see also T Mason and L Jennings 'The Mental Health Act and Professional Hostage Taking' (1997) 37 Med Sci & Law 58.
2 For the greater part of the UK regulation, see Mental Health (Patients in the Community) Act 1995.
3 While there is evidence that money can be saved by the provision of community-based services, hospital closures have not proved to be a panacea: see M Knapp, D Chisholm, J Astin et al 'The Cost Consequences of Changing the Hospital-Community Balance: the Mental Health Residential Study' (1997) 27 Psychol Med 681.

entering a new phase. Whereas, in the past, the emphasis has been on protecting the patient from what might be considered over-zealous enthusiasm for therapy, the focus has now turned to how the right to proper treatment can be secured. This is not to say that the civil libertarian aspects of the rights of the unwilling individual are no longer a matter for concern; these issues are still important and occupy much of the time of lawyers involved with mental health. Equally important, however, is the plight of those who, while being mentally ill, find help hard to obtain because of the inadequacy of community care arrangements.[4] Prisons have always contained more than a chance proportion of the mentally ill – at least, by way of mental handicap[5] – and this is now exaggerated simply because, with the closure of psychiatric wards, other places become more limited. It is not at all uncommon for those who are discharged from hospital to find themselves quite incapable of living in the community and ending up in prison as a result.[6] Once in prison, access to psychiatric treatment may be inadequate and transfer to a psychiatric hospital practically impossible. This may have tragic consequences, as demonstrated by a New Zealand study which showed than when arrangements for such transfer became inadequate, the prison suicide rate went up by some 500%.[7] This has clear implications as to civil liability in respect of failure on the part of prison authorities to discharge their duty of care towards mentally disordered inmates. Courts are reluctant to extend this duty in such a way that the task of an over-burdened prison service become even more onerous, but it is clear that there is a certain minimal level of care which prisons must meet. In *Kirkham v Chief Constable of the Greater Manchester Police*,[8] liability was imposed on the police for failing to inform a remand centre that a prisoner they were transferring to its care was a suicide risk. By contrast, in *Knight v Home Office*,[9] the Court of Appeal took the view that a prison hospital could not be expected to meet the standard of care expected of a psychiatric hospital in respect of its treatment of a potentially suicidal prisoner. The limitations placed on prison authorities are an inevitable consequence of the overcrowded conditions. It is undesirable enough to house ordinary offenders in such conditions; it becomes frankly unconscionable to treat in this way those who may only be there in the first place because of a mental illness. Such injustices should be every bit as much a matter for concern for civil libertarians as are the rights of those who do not seek treatment.

De-institutionalisation and proper community care is undoubtedly an attractive option for many mentally ill people – and, indeed, the concept has wide support amongst psychiatrists and patients. Yet the danger with such a change is that adequate resources will not be available and that some patients – particularly the more difficult ones – will have inadequate arrangements made for them. A solitary bed-sit with none

---

4   E Murphy 'Community Mental Health Services: A Vision for the Future' (1991) 302 BMJ 1064.
5   R Bluglass 'Mentally Disordered Prisoners: Reports but No Improvements' (1988) 296 BMJ 1757.
6   For discussion, see B G A Weller and M P I Weller 'Prison, the Psychiatric Dumping Ground?' (1989) 139 NLJ 1335, who cite a study of prisoners on remand for violent offences which revealed an incidence of schizophrenia 22.5 times higher than the epidemiological expectation. See also, by the same authors, 'Mental Illness and Social Policy' (1989) 139 NLJ 1382.
7   K Skegg and B Cox 'Impact of Psychiatric Services on Prison Suicide' (1997) 338 Lancet 1436.
8   [1990] 2 QB 283, [1990] 3 All ER 246.   Liability cannot be avoided by a claim that the suicidal act of the deceased amounted to a novus actus interveniens: *Reeves v Metropolitan Police Comr* [1998] 2 All ER 381.
9   [1990] 3 All ER 237, (1989) 4 BMLR 85.

of the facilities or diversions of hospital life, no programme of rehabilitation and nothing but four walls to stare at is not real community care; it is more a washing of the hands on the part of the state. There is also the question of protecting the rights of those in long-term, non-institutional care; their removal from a hospital setting does not necessarily mean that their rights will be adequately protected.[10]

This issue is essentially a political one, but human rights considerations resulted in legal attention being given to community care in *R v Ealing District Health Authority, ex p Fox*.[11] The patient in this case had been detained in a secure psychiatric hospital after he had been convicted of causing grievous bodily harm. Some three years later a mental health review tribunal had ordered his discharge, subject to the relevant health authority making arrangements for him to be supervised in the community. The health authority declined to make these arrangements, offering instead to manage him for 18 months in a regional secure unit. The court held that once the patient had been conditionally discharged, then it was the duty of the health authority to make every effort to ensure that he was able to meet the condition of his discharge. The court accepted, however, that this obligation had to be considered within the limits of the authority's resources. Further support for the community care principle came in the unlikely guise of a lands tribunal decision holding that a covenant restricting the use of a domestic dwelling could be discharged in favour of allowing the house to be used for psychiatric patients in community care.[12] This decision affirms the public interest in community care.

The grounds for intervention

The mere presence of a psychiatric condition will not, of itself, be sufficient to justify compulsory treatment: a person may suffer from psychiatric illness and yet still be able to reach a reasoned decision as to whether or not to undergo therapy. Compulsory treatment is justified only if a person's remaining untreated poses a threat to his own health or safety or to the safety of others.

Danger to others

One problem confronting psychiatrists in this field is the definition of mental illness and, particularly, what practical distinction – in terms of treatment and disposal – is to be made between psychosis and psychopathy (sociopathy). The clinical differentiation may be very difficult and the two conditions are by no means mutually exclusive. In one study, which is admittedly rather old, 24 out of 100 psychopathic prisoners had been diagnosed alternatively at some stage in their criminal careers and the author commented on the ease with which the diagnosis could be changed;[13] the diagnostic conflict with schizophrenia lay at the heart of the important decision in

---

10 See D Dickenson 'Ethical Issues in Long Term Psychiatric Management' (1997) 23 J Med Ethics 300.
11 [1993] 3 All ER 170, (1992) 11 BMLR 59.
12 The decision, sub nom Lloyd, is discussed by G Thornicroft and A Halpern 'Legal Landmark for Community Care of Former Psychiatric Patients' (1993) 307 BMJ 248.
13 D Power 'Psychopathic Disorder' (1988) 12 Criminologist 202.

W v Egdell,[14] which is discussed in detail above.[15] Legislation has, however, gone some way to easing the problem. Psychopathy – defined as abnormally aggressive or seriously irresponsible conduct resulting from a persistent disorder or disability of mind – is now included in a definition of mental disorder which may be treatable;[16] moreover, even if there is no specific therapy available, treatment that is limited to nursing care and rehabilitation can be regarded as 'treatment' for the purposes of the Mental Health Act 1983, s 72.[17] There is thus comparatively little to prevent the compulsory admission of psychopaths for assessment and treatment and, whatever one's views as to the use or abuse of such powers in social terms, this facility is clearly desirable – some psychopaths, at least, are, by definition, likely to expose the public to physical danger.

There is wide social acceptance of the proposition that those who are dangerous should be contained in a way which will prevent their causing harm to others. This principle is observed regularly by the courts when heavy custodial sentences are imposed on violent offenders in the interests of public safety. It is, nevertheless, axiomatic that a person who is dangerous but has not yet committed a crime is entitled to his liberty whatever his potential for future harm may be. We are then left with a paradox: why would so few people argue against the prophylactic detention of a dangerous person who is suffering from a mental illness? The answer must be that, in contrast to the case of the mentally 'healthy' violent person, the illness itself may provide a basis for asserting that certain forms of violent or irrational conduct may be reasonably foreseeable.

Even so, the prediction of dangerousness is an imprecise – and, perhaps, fruitless – exercise. Many attempts have been made to determine an objective concept of dangerousness but none has succeeded in allaying all doubts as to the strong element of subjectivity that is inherent in such judgments.[18] Disparities are frequently detected; in one such study, 60% agreement between a group of assessors was achieved in only four out of 16 case appraisals.[19] Psychiatric assessment of dangerousness must not, therefore, be considered an exact science – although the fact remains that reliable prediction is exactly what courts, parole boards and tribunals may be expecting. It is, indeed, possible that dangerousness is best established retrospectively by way of a history of recidivism; the problem then becomes one for the criminologist rather than the psychiatrist.[20]

The position of the psychiatrist is therefore difficult and, in all but a few exceptional cases, it will be impossible for him to say with any degree of certainty

14 [1990] Ch 359, [1990] 1 All ER 835, CA.
15 See p 195.
16 Mental Health Act 1983, s 3(2).
17 *R v Mersey Mental Health Review Tribunal, ex p D* (1987) Times, 13 April.
18 P E Mullen 'Mental Disorder and Dangerousness' (1984) 18 Austral NZ J Psychiat 8. Opinions differ amongst psychiatrists as to the ethical implications of making predictions of dangerousness. Not all psychiatrists are reluctant to do so; see eg T Grisso and P S Applebaum 'Is it Unethical to Offer Predictions of Future Violence?' (1992) 16 Law and Hum Behav 621. Legislators might prove ready to act on such predictions, providing for the detention of those who *might* offend: M A Bochnewich 'Prediction of Dangerousness and Washington's Sexually Violent Predator Statute' (1992) 29 Cal West Law R 277.
19 G Montadon and T Harding 'The Reliability of Dangerousness Assessments: A Decision-making Exercise' (1984) 144 Brit J Psychiat 149.
20 D J Gee and J K Mason *The Courts and the Doctor* (1990) p 138.

whether violent conduct is to be expected. Harm to others may result from premature release; yet excessive caution may cause injustice to the patient himself. This issue has provoked litigation in the United States where the courts have imposed civil liability upon psychiatrists when patients have been released and have subsequently harmed others.[1]

The American courts have, in fact, been unrelenting in their demands. *Tarasoff v Regents of the University of California*[2] is, perhaps, the best known of the relevant cases and is one which has given rise to widespread debate in North America and elsewhere. In this case, a patient had confessed to a therapist that he intended to harm a woman who had rejected his advances. The therapist failed to warn her of the danger and she was later killed by the patient; her family then sued the therapist's employers successfully. The court in *Lipari*[3] was not persuaded that the inherent difficulties in predicting dangerousness justify denying the injured party relief regardless of the circumstances. Subsequent courts have taken a similar line. The premature release of a psychiatric patient resulted in liability being imposed on a psychiatrist in *Perreira v State*[4] and, in an important decision of the Ohio Supreme Court,[5] a psychotherapist was held liable for damages when an *out-patient* murdered his own parents. A remarkable feature of this decision was the court's willingness to regard the psychotherapist as the best line of defence available against violence by the mentally ill – a role attributed to them because, according to the court, they are best-placed to perform it. Not surprisingly, the psychiatric reaction to such developments results in a tendency to err on the side of caution[6] although, significantly, the court in *Estates of Morgan* was dismissive of this effect, claiming that psychiatrists had shown no increased tendency since the *Tarasoff* ruling to resort to prolonged commitment in order to avoid liability.

Considerable strains could be forced on the health system if it had to bear the costs of harm caused by mentally disordered persons and there are, as yet, few signs of an inclination to impose this role on hospitals and psychiatrists in common law jurisdictions outside the United States. The issue arose in *Clunis v Camden and Islington Health Authority*.[7] The plaintiff, a psychiatric patient, had been discharged into community care, but had missed four appointments made for him by the doctor who was responsible for his care. He was convicted of manslaughter on the grounds of diminished responsibility after he had attacked and killed an innocent stranger. He then sued the health authority responsible for his care, arguing that the authority's negligent failure to assess his mental state had resulted in his suffering losses resulting from conviction and imprisonment. The Court of Appeal upheld the authority's argument that to impose liability in this case would be to allow the plaintiff to profit from his own illegal act, which is contrary to the ex turpi causa rule preventing a wrongdoer from claiming damages in respect of his own illegal act. This is a

---

1 T J Rudegeair and P S Applebaum 'On the Duty to protect: An Evolutionary Perspective' (1992) 20 Bull Amer Acad Psychiat Law 419.
2 529 P 2d 55 (Cal, 1974); on appeal 551 P 2d 334 (Cal, 1976).
3 *Lipari v Sears, Roebuck & Co* 497 F Supp 185 (Neb, 1980).
4 768 P 2d 1198 (Colo, 1989).
5 *Estates of Morgan v Fairfield Family Counselling Center* 673 NE 2d 1311 (Ohio, 1997).
6 For a discussion of criteria for release, see D J Power 'When not to Release Potentially Dangerous Patients' (1992) 16 Criminologist 2.
7 [1998] 3 All ER 180, (1997) 40 BMLR 181.

somewhat unusual application of the exclusionary ex turpi causa rule and it is possible that the court may have had one eye to the policy consequences of allowing the recovery of damages in such circumstances. Policy considerations played an acknowledged role in *Palmer v Tees Health Authority*,[8] in which damages were sought by the mother of a child who had been abducted and murdered by a psychiatric out-patient under the defendant's care. The court was reluctant to impose a duty of care on the basis that the relationship of proximity between plaintiff and defendant had not been established. Not only was the identity of the potential victim unknown to the defendant, thus ruling out proximity, but the judge also suggested that to impose liability could lead to the practice of defensive medicine and could divert the attention of health authorities away from their primary function.

The issue of dangerousness also raises questions of psychiatric confidentiality, an aspect which is discussed more fully in chapter 8. *Tarasoff* concerned a threat to a specific individual, but later cases have extended the principle so as to impose liability on psychiatrists who fail to detect and warn of danger on a general scale.[9] A similar dilemma of confidentiality arose in England in *W v Egdell*.[10] Here, a psychiatrist, who was invited by a patient's solicitors to examine him with a view to an application for transfer from a secure hospital, sent his report to the Home Office in order to prevent what he saw as a danger of the patient's premature release. This action was held to be justified in the public interest – a decision which was upheld in the Court of Appeal. The trial judge, however, made some disturbing observations – in particular:

> I accept that [the conclusion that the weight of public interest prevails over the private right to confidence] places W and persons like him in a position in which the duty of confidence owed by their psychiatrists is less extensive than the duty that would be owed by psychiatrists to other members of the public.[11]

Why, it may be asked, was W not an ordinary patient? Was it because he was in a secure hospital or because he had killed several persons? If it was the latter, the opinion raises doubts as to the rights of any prisoner convicted of violent crime. Or was it because he was now labelled as a psychopathic personality? While the outcome of *Egdell* would probably be approved by the majority, the implications the case raises for the psychiatrist-patient relationship are clearly considerable.

Paternalistic intervention

The compulsory treatment of mental illness in those who pose no threat to others is based on the notion of justified paternalism.[12] A paternalistic act is one which is not sought by the patient but which is provided with the intention of protecting him from harm. Ordinarily, paternalistic action will be considered wrong because it offends the principle of autonomy. It may be justified, however, when the person for whose

8   (1998) 45 BMLR 88.
9   Eg *Durflinger v Artiles* 673 P 2d 86 (Kan, 1983).
10 [1990] Ch 359, [1990] 1 All ER 835, CA.
11 [1990] Ch 359 at 393, [1989] 1 All ER 1089 at 1135, per Scott J.
12 There is a major survey of paternalism in general in D Van De Veer *Paternalistic Intervention* (1976). Other contributions include: B Gert and C M Culver 'Paternalistic Behavior' in M Cohen, T Nagel and T Scanlon (eds) *Medicine and Moral Philosophy* (1981) p 201.

benefit the act is performed is unable to make an informed choice for himself. Thus, paternalism towards a child is accepted on the grounds that a child may not be sufficiently mature to make important decisions about his or her life. The mentally retarded and the mentally ill may be similarly incompetent in that their ability to understand the reality of their situation is compromised by their mental state. The absence of rationality in such cases then warrants action directed towards preventing their being harmed. One approach to the problem is by way of the question: 'Would the patient, were he or she rational, consent to the treatment proposed?' There may be grounds for involuntary treatment if the answer is Yes. This is the American 'substituted judgment' test which is, effectively, autonomy-based in so far as intervention is directed to the higher goal of restoring the patient's already compromised autonomy. The relief of suffering would never be a sufficient justification for paternalistic intervention *by itself* – otherwise, the imposition of medical treatment would be permissible whenever a person refused palliation.

An alternative way of justifying intervention in the face of mental illness is to invoke the doctrine of implied consent. Someone who cannot consent to a procedure while incompetent may later be able to endorse what was done, thereby providing a form of retrospective consent. There are serious objections to this approach. To begin with, there is the difficulty of predicting whether subsequent consent will be given. Many patients who resent involuntary intervention continue to do so after their treatment – and, indeed, may never change their attitude to psychiatric interference. It is also possible that any post hoc consent will be a product of the intervention itself – as, for example, where treatment results in increased docility, compliance or even dependence on the person providing it. For these reasons, it is safer to rely on the autonomy-based arguments identified above.

All such means depend, however, upon the patient having ever had a meaningful degree of autonomy through which to exercise the decision-making function – it is philosophically impossible, or at least extremely difficult, to appeal to substituted judgment in the absence of such a resource. Moreover, it is an ethically dubious ruse to invoke the doctrine of implied consent in the near certainty that there will be no recovery phase in which implication may become reality. In such circumstances, it is more honest to take the opposite, frankly paternalistic, route and apply a 'best interests' test. This is the way followed in statute whereby, subject to the safeguards discussed in detail below, treatment for the mental disorder that has occasioned compulsory admission to hospital may be given without specific consent. In recent years, the courts have increasingly – and, now, almost regularly – been using a best interests rule to justify non-consensual treatment of a non-psychiatric nature and there is no doubt that doctors will continue to rely upon it. The patient, however, is unconcerned in such esoteric argument; the fact is that legitimating paternalism in this way carries the danger of licensing excessive interference in the lives of those afflicted by mental illness. There must, therefore, be limits both as to the determination of incompetence and the extent of treatment. Competence is not necessarily entirely compromised by mental illness and the fact that a psychiatric diagnosis has been made does not mean that the patient, thereafter, loses all capacity to decide upon treatment for himself.[13] On the other hand, there will be conditions which deprive the patient

---

13 See eg *Re C (adult: refusal of medical treatment)* [1994] 1 All ER 819, (1993) 15 BMLR 77, discussed at p 263 above.

of all insight into his plight and where the effect of the illness is so profound as to deny him all chance of an autonomous life. Intervention on a major scale may be justified in the latter case; it may be difficult to accept any paternalistic intervention at all in the former instance.

The happiness of the patient is another limiting factor. One who is psychotically ill, but relatively contented, may dread incarceration in a hospital or may dislike the effects of a drug he has been prescribed. There will be a case for abandoning therapeutic goals if these can only be attained at the expense of extreme and long-lasting unhappiness – therapy should not be allowed to eclipse all other considerations. This is just another way of saying that the mentally ill have their rights, which are significantly affected by their status. Rights may have to be considered, and adapted, in the light of limitations imposed by the illness but the wishes of the patient must always be taken into account when determining a therapeutic regime. Sometimes these wishes will put a stop to a promising line of treatment; at others, they may properly be overruled in the interests of the patient's future happiness.

Pure theory will not necessarily provide the right answer in such a dilemma. An unequivocal commitment to the consensual rights of the mentally ill may result in their being denied treatment on civil libertarian grounds. It may also lead to unnecessary suffering by the families of those afflicted; calls for the recognition of the psychiatric patients' right to reject treatment may well sound hollow to those struggling to cope with their demands in a domiciliary situation. Enthusiasm for a rigid and one-sided doctrine of rights may amount to misplaced kindness, as became apparent in the United States. There, a movement to de-institutionalise the mentally ill resulted in limitation of involuntary admission for those who were a danger to themselves or others; as a consequence, there was strong backlash pressure to reintroduce compulsory paternalistic treatment – including treatment of those who were not dangerous. The American Psychiatric Association bowed to these demands in their 1982 Guidelines for Legislation on the Psychiatric Hospitalization of Adults.[14]

In Canada, considerations of civil liberty have significantly eroded the paternalistic claim of society to treat those who are suffering from mental disorder. In *Fleming v Reid*,[15] the appellants, who had committed crimes of violence, had been diagnosed as suffering from schizophrenia. Their doctor had decided that the appellants were incompetent and proposed to treat them with neuroleptic drugs, a proposal which was vetoed by the patients' substitute decision-maker. The latter pointed out that the patients had had previous experience of this form of treatment and had objected to it at a time when they were competent. Under the relevant mental health legislation, the Ontario Mental Health Act, the substitute decision-maker's refusal to consent could be overridden by a review board and it was the decision by a review board to do just this that led to the legal challenge. In due course, the Ontario Court of Appeal held that this decision contravened art 7 of the Charter of Rights and Freedoms, which protects the right to bodily integrity and personal autonomy. It was only in the absence of any indication of the patient's previously expressed, competent rejection

---

14 For discussion of the reaction against involuntary commitment in the US, see A E Buchanan and
  D W Brock *Deciding for Others* (1989) p 312.
15 (1991) 82 DLR 4th 298.

of treatment, that a best interest argument might be used to justify imposing involuntary treatment on an incompetent person. This means, in effect, that if one expresses an antipathy to any form of drug treatment, and if one subsequently becomes incompetent, psychiatric medicine may be powerless to attempt a cure. Psychiatric treatment is, thus, put on the same footing as the treatment of physical illness, an approach which fails to distinguish those features which make psychiatric disease a special case – namely, that it distorts or destroys the ability to make a *rational* decision.

Controlling treatment

The framework for the treatment of mental illness in the United Kingdom is to be found in the Mental Health Act 1983, the Mental Health (Scotland) Act 1984,[16] and the Mental Health (Patients in the Community) Act 1995. The first two of these statutes introduced major reforms which related principally to the regulation and review of involuntary treatment and to consent to certain forms of treatment. The English Act also established a Mental Health Commission,[17] which was structured along the lines of the long-standing Scottish Mental Welfare Commission[18] – both have the general power to monitor procedures for admission to hospital and to scrutinise the conditions in which patients are detained. The 1995 Act is concerned in the main with the aftercare of patients who have been hospitalised.

Informal treatment
Treatment for mental illness is provided on either a voluntary or an involuntary basis. Informal – that is, voluntary – treatment may be provided by any registered medical practitioner or, indeed, by any layman provided that the provisions of the Medical Act 1983 as to impersonation are observed. Informal hospital treatment is regulated by s 131 of the 1983 Act, which states that a patient may enter hospital for psychiatric treatment without any order being made for that purpose and with freedom to leave at will. Informal patients can object to any particular treatment; they have unhindered access to the courts and enjoy certain other privileges which are denied to those who are detained compulsorily. The proportion of informal patients has increased markedly over the last three decades, this being an objective which was first expressed legislatively in the Mental Health Act 1959.

Many seriously incapacitated psychiatric patients are looked after in nursing homes and other institutions without having any formal order made in respect of their care. In *R v Bournewood Community and Mental Health NHS Trust, ex p L*[19] the House of Lords considered the position of informal patients who lack the

16 Discussion here is principally in terms of the Mental Health Act 1983. The 1984 Act is similar in many respects but has some important differences – eg in the role of the sheriff in compulsory admission (s 21). There is a full treatment of the Scottish provisions in J Blackie and H Patrick *Mental Health: A Guide to the Law in Scotland* (1990).
17 Mental Health Act Commission Regulations 1983, SI 1983/894.
18 Established by the Mental Health (Scotland) Act 1960, s 2.
19 [1998] 3 All ER 289, [1998] 3 WLR 107.

capacity to give a proper consent to treatment but who are, none the less, compliant. In this case, a profoundly retarded autistic adult was admitted for in-patient treatment following upon an outburst of disturbed, self-harming behaviour. He was not detained compulsorily under the provisions of the Mental Health Act as he did not resist admission. Relations between the hospital and the plaintiff's carers deteriorated, with the result that an action was brought against the health trust for damages for unlawful detention. The Court of Appeal allowed damages, but the House of Lords overturned this decision after hearing argument that requiring such patients to be detained under the Act – rather than admitted informally – would pose an immense burden on existing arrangements. In effect, compulsorily detaining such patients would be a luxury which the system simply could not pay for at current levels of funding. In the result, the House of Lords ruled that informal treatment of compliant patients who were, nevertheless, incapable of consenting was justified on the principle of necessity and was in accordance with the Mental Health Act's objective of facilitating informal treatment; the Act does not exclude common law powers relating to the provision of treatment to psychiatric patients. What was seen by some to be a gaping hole in the law had, in effect, been neatly plugged by the flexible doctrine of necessity.

As emphasised by Lord Steyn, patients in this category who are detained – and both Lords Nolan and Steyn, in particular, emphasised that they *are* detained – are denied the statutory protections afforded those who are compulsorily detained; in addition, they do not qualify for many of the benefits derived from supervision by the Mental Health Act Commission. These seem to be unfortunate legacies of the House of Lords decision. None the less, it is clearly the intention of Parliament that hospital treatment should be available to all psychiatric patients and that this should not involve undue formality. What, is needed, then, is a system which allows for flexibility rather than a rigid separation of two classes of patient. The House of Lords in *Re L* noted, with satisfaction, that reform of the law was under active consideration.

The informal status of a patient in a psychiatric hospital may be changed to that of compulsory detention (s 5(1)). This can be effected by the 'doctor in charge' of the patient on the grounds that it appears to him that 'an application ought to be made' for compulsory admission (s 5(2)). Detention under this provision expires after 72 hours. Nurses may also restrain a patient from leaving hospital if this is deemed to be immediately necessary and if it is not practicable to secure the immediate attendance of the doctor in charge or his delegate (s 5(4)). This form of detention may last for only six hours or until a doctor entitled to act under s 5(2) is able to attend.

Compulsory admission

There are three routes to involuntary admission to hospital under the Mental Health Act 1983. These are:

(1) *Admission for assessment under section 2*. Application for such admission must be made either by the patient's nearest relative – or by a person authorised by him or by a court to act on his behalf – or by an approved social worker. It is essential that the applicant has seen the patient within the past 14 days; the application must also be supported by two registered medical practitioners, one of whom must be qualified in psychiatry. Responsibility for getting the patient to hospital rests upon the

applicant, although this may be delegated to others such as ambulance staff; force may be used to this end provided it is not excessive.

The grounds for admission under s 2 are that a patient is suffering from a mental disorder of a nature or degree which warrants detention in hospital for assessment for at least a limited period and that he should be detained in hospital 'in the interests of his own health or safety or with a view to the protection of other persons'. Patients admitted for assessment may be kept in hospital for up to 28 days and such admissions cannot be renewed.[20]

Patients must be informed of their legal position and rights and may apply to have the case reviewed by a mental health review tribunal during the first 14 days of detention. The procedures for admission under s 3 (see below) must be invoked if it is proposed to detain the patient for a further period.

(2) *Emergency admission.* A patient may be admitted in an emergency under s 4 (1984, s 24). This form of admission can be effected on the recommendation of one doctor and is valid for only 72 hours. The doctor need not be a specialist in mental illness but he must, if practicable, have known the patient beforehand (s 4(3)); the applicant must have seen the patient within the previous 24 hours. Emergency admission may be converted to admission for treatment (28 days) by obtaining an additional opinion from a specialist in mental illness; the formalities required for s 2 admission must be complied with at this stage.

(3) *Admission for treatment.* Longer-term compulsory detention for treatment is governed by s 3. Application procedures are similar to those used for admission for assessment although, under s 3, the nearest relative must be consulted when admission is being sought by a social worker. Court authority for admission will be needed if the relative objects. The grounds for admission for treatment are that, in the opinion of the doctors recommending admission, the patient is: (a) suffering from mental illness, severe mental impairment, psychopathic disorder or mental impairment and his mental disorder is of a nature which makes it appropriate for him to receive medical treatment in a hospital; and (b) in the case of psychopathic disorder or mental impairment, such treatment is likely to alleviate or prevent deterioration in his condition; and (c) it is necessary for the health or safety of the patient or for the protection of other persons that he should receive such treatment and it cannot be provided unless he is detained under this section. Treatment for sexual disorders is excluded.

Admission for treatment allows for detention for up to six months. This period is renewable for a second period of six months and, thereafter, for periods of a year at a time. Detention under s 3 can, therefore, last indefinitely; however, on renewal, the responsible medical officer must believe that further treatment is likely to alleviate or prevent deterioration in the patient's condition or that the patient would be unable to care for himself or would be liable to serious exploitation were detention to be ended (s 20(4)(a) and (b)).

The move to a community care philosophy in psychiatric treatment has meant that there is an increasing number of relatively seriously ill patients living outside

---

20 For Scots law and the common law power of detention, see *Black v Forsey* 1988 SC 28, HL.

psychiatric hospitals. These patients need to be supervised and various techniques of supervision have been tried within the framework of the Mental Health Act. Guardianship orders were used as was the practice of granting leave (permissible under the Act) and revoking the leave if the patient became non-compliant. Both of these methods proved unsatisfactory, Guardianship orders lacked teeth and the use of periods of leave in this way was eventually expressly declared to be unlawful – after the decision in *R v Hallstrom*[1] it was not longer possible for doctors to recall patients to hospital shortly before the elapse of a six-month period of detention merely to renew the detention order prior to re-releasing them on leave (the so-called 'long-leash' approach). Dissatisfaction with the inadequacy of supervision powers was fuelled by a series of public inquiries into crimes of violence committed by patients and new provisions aimed at increasing the efficacy of community care were introduced by the Mental Health (Patients in the Community) Act 1995.

The main thrust of this Act is to prevent patients from 'drifting off' into the community without the safeguards and benefits of their progress being monitored. There had been suggestions that new legislation should introduce a community treatment order system which would allow for the enforcement of medication outside hospital, but this has not been accepted. Instead, a system of supervision discharge has been introduced. Under this system, any person who is liable to be detained for treatment under the Mental Health Act may be discharged under a supervision order, which regulates the aftercare arrangements made available under s 117 of the Mental Health Act. A supervision order may only be made if aftercare is necessary to avoid a substantial risk of serious harm to the health or safety of the patient or other persons, or to avoid a risk of serious exploitation. It may specify where the patient is to live and it may also require the patient to attend for treatment, occupation, education or training. It is important to note that the order cannot impose treatment, even though it can require a patient to attend at a place where treatment will be offered. It also appears that there are no in-built means of dealing with non-compliance with the terms of the order. Ultimately, of course, resort may be made to compulsory admission to hospital in cases where supervised discharge is not working. Some critics see the supervision order approach as a worrying extension of psychiatric power outside its traditional (and regulated) domain – the psychiatric hospital.[2] The supervision order system certainly makes it possible for considerable pressure to be brought on the patient to comply; whether or not this leads to the future exercise of unwarranted coercion will depend on the spirit in which it is applied. One thing is clear: the closure of hospitals and the resultant reliance on community care are trends which potentially conflict with the public's concern at the presence within the community of potentially dangerous patients. This points to a stark alternative: either we accept at least some degree of compulsion outside hospital or we ignore the public outrage over well-publicised incidents of homicide or sexual assault by inadequately supervised patients.

Persons without physical illness who are compulsorily detained in hospital – and particularly those who are mentally disturbed – are likely to see themselves as victims of paternalistic injustice. The strong possibility exists that they may institute

1   *R v Hallstrom, ex p W; R v Gardner, ex p L* [1986] QB 1090, [1986] 2 All ER 306.
2   A matter which is discussed by P Fennel *Treatment without Consent* (1996) p 289.

proceedings against those responsible for their committal to and/or detention in hospital. This was foreseen in s 139 of the 1983 Act, which states:

> No person shall be liable . . . to any civil or criminal proceedings . . . in respect of any act purporting to be done in pursuance of this Act . . . unless the act was done in bad faith or without reasonable care.

Bad faith or negligence would, however, be something that the proceedings were designed to establish and sub-s (2) gives further protection in stating that no civil proceedings may be brought against any person without the leave of the High Court. Section 139 thus leaves two questions open: has the patient any legal redress in the absence of bad faith or negligence and by what criteria should the High Court grant leave to proceed? As to the first, it has now been held that Parliament must have intended to retain the court's inherent power to protect the rights of the individual; application for judicial review does not constitute 'civil proceedings' for the purposes of the Act and remains open to an aggrieved patient.[3] The answer to the second 'chicken and egg' problem is of even greater significance to the patient. The Court of Appeal in *Winch*[4] overturned the trial judge's ruling that leave to proceed depended upon there being a prima facie case to bring. The change of wording between the 1959 and 1983 Acts was considered deliberate and the court was no longer required to establish that there were substantial grounds for the patient's contention; the issue was simply whether or not the complaint appeared to be such that it deserved the fuller investigation which would be possible if the applicant was allowed to proceed – in Miss Winch's case, the court went so far as to deny any suggestion that the proceedings were likely to succeed. Section 139 relates only to actions against individuals. No such protection is afforded, for instance, to the Department of Health; this, however, is generally a matter of the criminal law, to which we refer later.

It is, none the less, clear that detention in hospital for long periods is open to abuse without some form of independent review. This is provided for in the establishment of mental health review tribunals, to which patients who wish to have their cases considered can apply.[5] The tribunals have been subject to considerable criticism in the past – a low incidence of appeals has been alleged and patients are said to have experienced difficulty in obtaining adequate representation; current procedures for automatic review and the availability of legal aid now answer many of these shortcomings. It has also been held that tribunals must state their reasons for their decisions,[6] a proposition that provides considerable protection against decisions based on surmise or suspicion. Hospital authorities are now duty bound to explain to patients their right of appeal to a tribunal; a case is now referred automatically if this right is not exercised within the first six months' detention. Hospital managers

---

3   *Ex p Waldron* [1986] QB 824, sub nom *R v Hallstrom, ex p W* [1985] 3 All ER 775, CA. Discussed by Legal Correspondent 'Actions by Psychotic Patients' (1986) 292 BMJ 128.

4   *Winch v Jones, Winch v Hayward* [1986] QB 296, [1985] 3 All ER 97, CA. Discussed by Legal Correspondent 'Legal Proceedings by Mental Patients' (1986) 292 BMJ 820.

5   P F Mawson 'The Function of Mental Health Review Tribunals under the Mental Health Act' (1986) 26 Med Sci & Law 291. For an account of the way in which the tribunals interpret their role and of the supervision by the courts of the process of review, see G Richardson *Law, Process and Custody: Prisoners and Patients* (1993) p 278 et seq.

6   *Bone v Mental Health Review Tribunal* [1985] 3 All ER 330.

are also obliged to refer patients to the tribunal when detention has been renewed and the case has not been considered for three years. In all of this, however, the onus lies on the patient to prove that his continued detention is unjustified, whereas it might be argued that the reverse should be the case.

Conditions justifying compulsory admission

A major civil rights concern in this area is that the boundaries of mental illness should not be drawn so widely as to embrace forms of behaviour that are no more than non-conformist. Compulsory admission should be limited to conditions which amount to an illness that can be said to compromise the mental health of the sufferer. In this respect, the Act distinguishes between admission for assessment and admission for treatment.

In the former case, the patient may be admitted under compulsion if he is thought to be suffering from a 'mental disorder'. This term is widely defined. Not only does it include mental illness, arrested or incomplete development of mind and psychopathic disorder – it embraces, too, 'any other disorder or disability of mind' (s 1(2)). The term 'disorder' could potentially include a number of deviations from the psychiatric norm and its application to conditions such as alcoholism, drug addiction or sexual deviation of themselves is expressly excluded by s 1(3). Admission for treatment is more closely controlled and the Act requires that the patient be suffering from one of four specifically identified disorders: mental illness, severe mental impairment, psychopathic disorder or mental impairment. Those suffering from the first two conditions may be admitted irrespective of the likely effect of treatment; those suffering from psychopathic disorder or mental impairment can be detained only if they are likely to benefit from treatment. The threat of continued detention may not be used to ensure compliance with proposed treatment for a psychopathic condition. In *R v Canons Park Mental Health Review Tribunal, ex p A*[7] it was held that a mental health review tribunal could refuse an application for discharge by a detained psychopathic patient if it considered that the patient's condition was treatable. The Court of Appeal held that the treatability test should not be construed too narrowly; the patient in question was refusing the only available therapy (group therapy) but could be given care in a hospital setting that might lead to compliance in the future. This satisfied the treatability test. This line was followed in *R v Mental Health Review Tribunal, ex p Macdonald*.[8] Here a patient who had previously been the subject of a restriction order was detained in hospital under s 37 of the Mental Health Act 1983. He sought discharge from a tribunal on the grounds that the condition from which he was suffering was psychopathy and that this was not treatable. It was held, however, that the treatability of a *condition* was only one factor to be taken into account in assessing a patient's liability to detention in hospital; a person suffering from an untreatable condition could still be given medical treatment, which included nursing and care within a structured medical environment. His continued detention could be justified on these grounds.

---

7   [1995] QB 60, [1994] 2 All ER 659.
8   (1998) Crown Office Digest 205 (Queen's Bench). For discussion of the issue in Scotland under the Mental Health (Scotland) Act 1984, see *R v Secretary of State for Scotland* 1997 SLT 555.

Such cases illustrate the difficulties attendant upon psychopathic patients who may be considered dangerous to others. Are they to be detained in hospital even if their condition will not respond to treatment? Or are they to be released, on the grounds that the psychiatric hospital can do nothing for them and, then, dealt with by the criminal justice system if they cause harm? There is a clear tension here between the role of the psychiatric hospitals as therapeutic communities and the role of such hospitals as 'containers' for those who, through personality disorder, are dangerous. If mental health legislation is drafted so as to regard the psychopath as untreatable, such a patient will be excluded from hospital and can only be contained within the prison service – provided, of course, that he has committed an offence. The real issue, then, is whether psychiatrists are prepared to offer the psychopath 'treatment' in the broad sense expressed in *ex p A* and *Macdonald*. The problem of what to do with the dangerous psychopath would be greatly simplified were this to be so.

The Act does not define mental illness.[9] There is a wide consensus that it includes psychoses such as schizophrenia – and also anorexia nervosa – but neurotic conditions may well be considered as being unlikely to warrant hospital detention and, therefore, to be beyond its scope. The problem was neatly put by Roth and Kroll,[10] who cited the case of a young man who courted disaster through compulsive risk-taking; this involved having dangerous masochistic sexual encounters with violent men and, ultimately, led to his death. Such conduct is an 'illness' in so far as it affects the subject's health and is beyond his control much as an organic illness would be; it would be classified as illness were it due, say, to hormonal imbalance but not if it were psychological in origin – which, say the authors, is illogical.[11] Personality disorders may be distinguished from mental illness on a variety of grounds. The role of organic factors in the former is controversial;[12] moreover, if one of the criteria of illness is that it 'overlays' the normal self, this cannot be said of a personality disorder which lies at the core of 'self'. There is, in fact, considerable debate as to the categorisation of psychopathy (or sociopathy). The condition, which was identified by psychiatrists of the nineteenth century,[13] is listed as a mental disorder in the American Psychiatric Association's DSM-IV. Yet the precise criteria defining psychopathy are unclear[14]

9 A judicial attempt to do so is to be found in *W v L* [1974] QB 711 at 719, [1973] 3 All ER 884 at 890, CA, where it was said that the words 'mental illness' were ordinary words of the English language with no particular medical significance which should, therefore, be construed in the way in which 'ordinary sensible people would construe them' per Lawton LJ. A definition within the UK jurisdiction is, however, to be found in Mental Health (Northern Ireland) Order 1986, SI 1986/595 (NI 4), art 3(1).
10 M Roth and J Kroll *The Reality of Mental Illness* (1986) p 79.
11 In one view, conditions such as self-destructive behaviour are merely matters of choice. One opponent of the disease model is H Finagarette who, in his *Heavy Drinking: The Myth of Alcoholism as a Disease* (1988), argues strongly against the genetic theory of alcoholism. For a view of drug abuse as chosen, rather than compelled, behaviour, see J Davis *The Myth of Addiction* (1992).
12 See M Dolan 'Psychopathy: a Neuro-biologial Perspective' (1994) 165 Brit J Psychiat 151. A genetic factor may, however, be operating: M Roth 'Psychopathic (Sociopathic) Personality' in R Bluglass and P Bowden (eds) *Principles and Practice of Forensic Psychiatry* (1990). Roth also cites research revealing EEG abnormalities in psychopaths.
13 The historical background is discussed in N Walker and S McCabe *Crime and Insanity in England and Wales* (1973) at II, p 205. See also P Pichot 'Psychopathic Behaviour: A Historical Overview' in R D Hare and D Schalling (eds) *Psychopathic Behaviour: Approaches to Research* (1978).
14 The category of personality disorder is now more differentiated – and refined. For a survey of advances in the diagnosis of conditions of this nature, see P Tyrer, P Carey and B Ferguson 'Personality Disorder in Perspective' (1991) 159 Brit J Psychiat 463.

and there is some concern that the tendency to label a wide range of anti-social conduct as psychopathic may lead to an undue medicalisation of deviant behaviour. One Scottish judge, having listened to a description of the symptomatology of psychopathy, remarked:

> It is, to my mind, descriptive rather of a typical criminal than of a person . . . regarded as being possessed of diminished responsibility.[15]

This is an unscientific view but, in a sense, it points to the difficulty which many people have with the concept of psychopathy – namely, how it is to be distinguished, if at all, from uncomplicated anti-social conduct.

The personality traits which feature most commonly in attempts to characterise psychopathy are a tendency to disruptive or selfish behaviour, inability to form relationships or to learn from experience and an inadequate moral sense. It is doubtful if there is any point in trying to treat the psychopath on an involuntary basis; certainly the Butler Committee[16] took the view that prison is the proper place for the psychopath who has offended and many psychiatrists are unwilling to admit them to their wards.

Mental impairment and severe mental impairment are both defined in the Act (s 1(2)). Mental impairment is not, of itself, a sufficient ground for admission for treatment. To satisfy the requirements, the patient's condition must be associated with 'abnormally aggressive or seriously irresponsible conduct' – the object and effect being to limit compulsory treatment to those who pose a threat to others.

Sexual deviancy is specifically excluded as a sole ground for intervention under the Act (s 1(3)). This means that a person may engage in outrageous sexual practices but will not be liable to compulsory treatment unless he also manifests one of the qualifying mental disorders discussed above. In *Clatworthy*,[17] the appellant had been detained by reason of psychopathic disorder. He argued, successfully, that the only ground for the diagnosis was his sexual behaviour and that this could not, by itself, constitute the basis for his detention by virtue of the explicit exclusion of sexual deviance as a statutory form of mental disorder. Contemporary psychiatry is cautious on this subject following the acrimonious debate on the classification of homosexuality as a psychiatric illness.[18]

Consent to treatment

Previous legislation made no direct reference to the conditions under which a person compulsorily admitted could be given hospital treatment. It is important to note that the Mental Health Acts refer only to treatment given for the mental condition itself and it will have been noted throughout this book that this can cause considerable

15 *Carraher v H M Advocate* 1946 JC 108 at 117, per Lord Normand.
16 Report of the Committee on Mentally Abnormal Offenders (Cmnd 6244) 1975.
17 *R v Mental Health Tribunal, ex p Clatworthy* [1985] 3 All ER 699.
18 M Ruse *Homosexuality* (1988) p 202. The equivalent philosophcal debate has focused on whether homosexuality can be considered a perversion: S Ruddick 'Better Sex' in R Baker and F Eliston (eds) *Philosophy and Sex* (1975); R Scruton *Sexual Desire* (1986).

difficulty – in particular as related to reproductive activity in the female. The rules evolved to regulate the treatment of physical illness in psychiatric patients have been discussed in chapter 10; occasionally, however, psychiatric and physical disease are so intimately associated that the courts may be called upon to decide what is and what is not 'treatment of the psychiatric condition'. Such a situation is exemplified in the condition of anorexia nervosa – a life-threatening eating disorder which affects teenage girls in particular. Several judicial decisions have been called for and the subject merits a small diversion.

Anorexia nervosa

Much depends on the age of the patient. Many sufferers are minors coming within the ambit of the Family Law Reform Act 1969, s 8 – and some are, arguably, *Gillick* competent minors; the courts are then confronted with a conflict between their inherent jurisdiction and the autonomy-orientated terms of the Children Act 1989. On the other hand, the court, in coming to a decision, is concerned only with the welfare of the child; the precise nature of the underlying condition is immaterial. *Re W*[19] is the most important of the 'minor' cases and has already been discussed under the heading of consent.[20] The case concerned a 16-year-old girl who was violent towards the staff of her special residential unit; she was prone to self-injury and, on account of this, had to be immobilised. She refused transfer to a special hospital and the local authority applied under the Children Act, s 100(3) for a direction that it could transfer W if necessary without her consent. The Court of Appeal was in no doubt that, in the exercise of its inherent jurisdiction, it had the power to overrule a minor's refusal of treatment. It went on to say, per Lord Donaldson MR, that it is a feature of anorexia nervosa that it is capable of destroying the ability to make an informed choice:

> It creates a compulsion to refuse treatment or only to accept treatment which is likely to be ineffective. This attitude is part and parcel of the disease and the more advanced the disease, the more compelling it may become.[1]

These are strong words which, we suggest, open the door to non-consensual treatment of *all* cases of anorexia nervosa, irrespective of age.

In respect of adults, however, the court now has no parens patriae jurisdiction. Given, then, that the patient has the capacity to refuse treatment, the courts must decide whether or not force-feeding constitutes a treatment for mental disorder which can be given without consent under the terms of the Mental Health Act 1983, s 63 or, alternatively, is justified within the broad envelope of s 145, which defines treatment as including nursing, care, habilitation and rehabilitation under medical supervision. The problem was addressed in the Family Division in *Re KB*,[2] which involved an 18-year-old suffering from anorexia nervosa who was detained under the Mental Health Act 1983, s 3. Interestingly, she was originally force-fed under s 58 of the Act[3]

19 *Re W (a minor) (medical treatment: court's jurisdiction)* [1993] Fam 64, [1992] 4 All ER 627.
20 See p 259 above.
 1 [1993] Fam 64 at 81, [1992] 4 All ER 627 at 637.
 2 *Re KB (adult) (mental patient: medical treatment)* (1994) 19 BMLR 144.
 3 See p 519 below.

but this was found to be improper;[4] the health authority, therefore, sought a declaration that it was lawful to do so under the terms of s 63. It was agreed by all that nasogastric feeding was medical treatment.[5] The problem was whether the feeding was given as treatment for her mental disorder of for her physical symptoms – that is, to increase her weight. Ewbank J was happy to accept the argument that she was suffering from anorexia nervosa, which is an eating disorder, and that relieving symptoms was just as much a part of treatment as relieving the underlying cause; it was clear that feeding by nasogastric tube in the circumstances of the type of case was treatment envisaged under s 63. By way of an obiter dictum, the judge also followed *Re W* in that the treatment she was refusing was related to her mental illness and that, accordingly, she did not have the capacity to refuse her consent to that treatment. A similar approach was adopted in *Riverside Mental Health NHS Trust v Fox,*[6] concerning a 37-year-old woman who was being treated for anorexia under the 1983 Act. The judge at first instance said:

> I have no difficulty at all in concluding . . . that feeding is treatment within s 145 of the 1983 Act. It is an essential part of nursing and care. It is more difficult to decide whether it constitutes medical treatment for the mental disorder. That disorder is anorexia nervosa . . . [The medical evidence] is clearly not the effect that feeding a person suffering from anorexia nervosa is an essential part of that treatment.[7]

and an order was made accordingly.

Some of the reasoning in these cases may seem to lean towards sophistry. The cases as a whole do, however, demonstrate a judicial anxiety to save lives when that is possible and some distrust of an autonomy which allows patients to take fatal treatment decisions in circumstances in which their competence to do so is, at least, doubtful.

General criteria as to consent to treatment by mental patients

We are, however, concerned mainly with the treatment of mental disorder in involuntary patients. The 1983 and 1984 statutes go some way to clarifying the scope of acceptable intervention by, in particular, delimiting the degree of invasion which is permitted and by, at the same time, defining the nature of consent to the procedures.

As has already been intimated, non-consensual treatment of the underlying mental disorder is permitted by statute (s 63) but the extent of this is limited by the conditions imposed by ss 57 and 58. Section 57 refers to what are loosely known as

---

4   Confirmed in *B v Croydon Health Authority* [1995] Fam 133, [1995] 1 All ER 683, CA – a similar, but in many ways distinct, case involving an eating disorder as a manifestation of borderline personality disorder. It was held that nursing and care concurrent with the core treatment were ancillary to treatment calculated to alleviate or prevent a deterioration of the disorder and, as such, were included under s 63.
5   Relying, perhaps a trifle dubiously, on *Airedale NHS Trust v Bland* [1993] 1 All ER 821, (1993) 12 BMLR 64.
6   [1994] 1 FLR 614, sub nom *F v Riverside Health Trust* (1993) 20 BMLR 1.
7   Quoted on appeal by Sir Stephen Brown P (1993) 20 BMLR 1 at BMLR 5. The judge's order authorising force feeding was, in fact, set aside but this was on technical grounds – the possibility of a further application in the event of need was fully accepted.

irreversible procedures, which include destruction of brain tissue or of its function and the surgical implantation of hormones for the control of the male sex drive;[8] it applies to the treatment of both voluntary and involuntary patients.[9] Consent is needed before such treatment can be given and this must be verified and certified as real by an appointed doctor and two non-medical witnesses who have also been appointed for the purpose.[10] Furthermore, the appointed doctor must certify that the treatment is likely to benefit the patient; he can do this only after consultation with two persons concerned professionally with the patient, one of whom is a nurse and the other neither a doctor nor a nurse. It is apparent that this section presents some difficulties. First, consent is essential. It follows that a patient who cannot consent cannot have treatment even though it may appear appropriate; the regulations can be waived only when the treatment is regarded as life saving (s 62(1)(a)). Secondly, the two confirmatory opinion providers must be *professionally* involved; a certificate cannot be issued if only doctors and nurses are available. The fact and results of irreversible treatments must be notified to the Mental Health Act Commission, who may withdraw the certificate issued by the appointed doctor (s 61(3)). The whole scenario must, however, now be extremely rare.

Section 58 controls 'hazardous' treatments which, currently, include electro-convulsive therapy and long-term drug treatment – which is defined as continuing for three months or more. These may only be given if the patient has consented and either his responsible medical officer or an appointed doctor has verified that consent or if an appointed medical practitioner has certified that the patient cannot give valid consent but that the treatment would be of benefit to him; again, the doctor must consult two other persons as above who have been professionally concerned with the patient. Hazardous treatment can be given in the absence of certification only if it is needed to save the patient's life or, provided it is not irreversible, to prevent a serious deterioration in his condition (s 62(1)(b)). Treatment covered by s 57 or s 58 may be given in circumstances of urgency if it is neither hazardous nor irreversible and is either necessary to alleviate serious suffering on the patient's part or represents the minimum interference necessary to prevent the patient from behaving violently or being a danger to himself or others.[11] The patient may withdraw his consent to s 57 or s 58 treatments at any time – once he does so, the process of certification must start again (s 60).

Behaviour modification

Several methods may be employed by psychologists and psychiatrists in an effort to alter undesirable behaviour. These may be non-intrusive, in the sense that they involve no physical intervention, or they may be very invasive – brain surgery for mental disorder, commonly referred to as psychosurgery, being the most extreme

8 The specific limitations of ss 57 and 58 are laid out in the Mental Health (Hospital, Guardianship and Consent to Treatment) Regulations 1983, SI 1983/893.
9 But the equivalent legislation in the Mental Health (Scotland) Act 1984, s 97 applies only to detained patients.
10 The procedures to be followed in such cases are laid out in the *Code of Practice* approved by Parliament in 1990, para 16.
11 Section 62(1)(c) and (d).

example. Several ethical problems arise in either case: are coercive techniques ever acceptable? to what extent has the therapist the right to impose his model of desirable behaviour on the patient?[12] can consent ever be given to such treatments if they are offered in the form of an inducement – for example, as an alternative to punishment? These questions are posed most dramatically in relation to psychosurgery, which merits separate discussion.

The essential claim of psychosurgery is that it can change behaviour patterns in reasonably predictable ways. Modern techniques avoid the crudities of leucotomy and may involve localised interference with parts of the brain which influence feelings and sexuality. Psychosurgery may be offered for a variety of conditions, most frequently for affective illnesses such as depression; other indications have included aggressive behaviour, intractable pain and unacceptable sexual urges.[13] Any discussion of the effectiveness of the procedure raises, of course, the question of the standpoint from which success is measured. It is important to distinguish the concept of therapeutic success – removal of symptoms without incurring unacceptable side-effects – from that of manageability. It is hardly proper to regard a treatment as successful if its main effect is merely to render the patient passive and compliant. In one sense, this constitutes little more than the 'neutralising' of the patient. Psychosurgery as a method of making uncontrollable patients more quiescent is open to the challenge that it is primarily a means of social control. As one writer has put it, 'Life in "Brave New World"' may be more pleasant for all, but only John the Savage is fully human'.[14]

The utility of psychosurgery is debated. A number of surgeons have reported good results. Depression seems to be the condition in which there is the best chance of success; positive improvement, however, has also been claimed in the case of patients whose unacceptable anti-social behaviour prior to the operation made it difficult for them to live successfully in society. It is, however, rarely used. There were 46 referrals for psychotherapy in England and Wales in the years 1991-93 and 42 certificates of treatment were issued by the Mental Health Act Commission. In the United States, the National Commission for the Protection of Human Subjects of Biomedical Behavioral Research, which considered the subject of psychosurgery in detail, concluded that such surgery should no longer be considered experimental and, although it suggested safeguards in the form of review boards, the Commission recommended that psychosurgery should be available to those institutionalised.[15] The Commission explicitly rejected the *Kaimowitz* decision,[16] in which it was held that an institutionalised person could not give a free consent to psychosurgery by virtue of the fact of being detained there involuntarily.

Even if one accepts that the patient is capable of giving a consent which is valid, in that it is informed and uncoerced, that fact alone may not be sufficient to justify the

12 S Fairbairn and G Fairbairn (eds) *Psychology, Ethics and Change* (1987); A McCall Smith 'Changing the Offender: Ethical Issues in Behaviour Modification' (1988) Acta Juridica 169; J Holmes and R Linley *The Values of Psychotherapy* (1989).
13 E S Valenstein 'Who Receives Psychosurgery?' in E S Valenstein (ed) *The Psychosurgery Debate* (1980) p 89.
14 J Kleinig *Ethical Issues in Psychosurgery* (1985).
15 US National Commission for the Protection of Human Subjects of Biomedical and Behavioral Research Report 1976.
16 *Kaimovitz v Michigan Department of Mental Health* 42 USLW 2063 (1973).

treatment. Consent to a grossly maiming operation which achieves no therapeutic purpose may not justify the operation in the eyes of the law; similarly, psychosurgery could well be seen as a procedure which is unacceptable on grounds of public policy. The patient who is incapable of consenting may not now be given irreversible and hazardous treatments. He may therefore suffer, yet Parliament feels that this is an acceptable price to pay for the protection of the majority from what could turn into abuse were it uncontrolled.

Objections to psychosurgery focus on its drastic and irreversible nature. The consequences of drug therapy, while possibly unpleasant, are usually reversible and a mistake, or a change of mind, can be rectified. Any alteration in behaviour following psychosurgery is likely to be permanent and it is this which gives rise to misgivings. The central issue of the aim of treatment must be confronted before one can make out a case for its use. If it is seen principally as a means of controlling behaviour, then there are sound reasons for objecting to it as representing a draconian and ethically unacceptable method of control. A different conclusion may result if, on the other hand, the therapeutic intention is predominant. There is no reason why patients should be denied a potentially effective treatment purely because it is open to abuse or is hazardous. Such treatments should, of course, be subjected to control – preferably control which embodies an element of outside, lay opinion – but they should not be excluded from the range of those available by virtue only of their nature.

Controversy of almost equal intensity surrounds the use of chemical methods to control the behaviour of actual or potential sex offenders.[17] Opponents of these procedures have described them in such terms as 'chemical castration' and have been especially concerned as to their inherent coercive nature. Certainly, Parliament has expressed this view in specifically including surgical implantation of hormones to control the male sex drive in those 'irreversible' treatments controlled by s 57 of the 1983 Act. On the other hand, it is perfectly possible to see behaviour modification of this type in a properly therapeutic light. The person troubled by sexual inclinations which he cannot control may look upon drug treatment as his only hope of a normal life in the community.[18] On this analysis, the refusal of treatment to someone who genuinely seeks it can amount to unacceptable paternalism.

Just such an instance arose in *R v Mental Health Commission, ex p* X[19] – a case which demonstrates a number of interesting points. X was a compulsive paedophile who sought medical help. Standard antiandrogen treatment was unsuccessful and he was transferred to a new and relatively untried synthetic compound with the proprietary name of Goserelin; this was administered monthly by the subcutaneous insertion of a thin cylindrical implant. A satisfactory response was obtained with three insertions; however, the Mental Health Commission was now concerned as to the validity of his consent and withdrew its approval of the relevant certificates. X applied for judicial review – as a result of which, the Commission's decision was quashed. The court's opinion raised several interesting points; some were, to an extent, peripheral to the main question but they merit note. First, it was held that, despite its action, a synthetic chemical compound could not be described as a 'hormone'; secondly, the subcutaneous injection of a substance through a needle,

17 Mental Health (Hospital, Guardianship and Consent to Treatment) Regulations 1983, SI 1983/893.
18 S L Halleck 'The Ethics of Antiandrogen Therapy' (1981) 138 Am J Psychiat 642.
19 (1988) 9 BMLR 77.

albeit of wide bore, was not a 'surgical implant'. Most importantly, however, the court noted that sexual deviance is expressly excluded from the definition of mental disorder for the purposes of the 1983 Act (s 1(3)); Goserelin was used for the treatment of such deviance and, although success in this respect would inevitably lead to improvement in any associated mental condition, it was not a treatment for mental disorder and was not subject to the controls of s 57. The Commission's decision was irrational.[20] Once again, some of the observations made may be seen as bordering on the casuistic; nevertheless, we feel that the case demonstrates that, if it is possible to do so, the courts will disapprove a bureaucratic attempt to separate a patient from the treatment he genuinely seeks and that they will support the doctors who are supplying it in good faith.

20 For discussion of the case see P Fennell 'Sexual Suppressants and the Mental Health Act' [1988] Crim LR 660; C Dyer 'Mental Health Commission Defeated over Paedophile' (1988) 296 BMJ 1660.

22 Psychiatry and the criminal law

The psychiatrist – and also the clinical psychologist – may become involved with criminal law at a number of points in the process of trial. Most dramatically, he may be called upon to provide evidence to the court of the accused person's mental state; this intimately involves the psychiatrist in the essential function of any criminal trial – the determination of guilt or innocence. In addition to fulfilling this need, psychiatric evidence may be invoked to assist the court in the exercise of its sentencing power. Psychiatric reports on an offender may persuade the court to impose a more lenient custodial sentence or may point to what would be a more appropriate means of dealing with the offender; moreover, the court may ensure, as a result, that an offender gets further psychiatric or other medical treatment. The psychiatrist may be called upon to assist the court in other ways. Even when the sanity of the accused is not in question, evidence may be called as to the mental state of a witness, if that is relevant to the issue of the reliability of his or her evidence.[1] Attempts have been made to introduce psychiatric evidence which is aimed at demonstrating that an accused person's disposition was such that he could not have formed the necessary intention to commit the offence with which he is charged, but the courts have generally been reluctant to allow what they see as the usurpation of their exclusive power to decide such issues of mens rea.

The grounds for strictly limiting the scope of psychiatric evidence were spelled out in *R v Turner,* in which the Court of Appeal warned that:

> The fact that an expert witness has impressive scientific qualifications does not, by that fact alone, make his opinion on matters of human nature and behaviour within the limits of normality any more helpful than that of the jurors themselves; but there is a danger that they think it does.[2]

This sceptical view of psychological or psychiatric evidence has resulted in the rejection by courts of attempts to use expert evidence to interpret the conduct of the accused. In *R v Weightman*[3] the appellant had confessed to the police that she had murdered her young child. The defence sought to adduce psychiatric evidence to the

---

1 This was accepted in *Toohey v Metropolitan Police Comr* [1965] AC 595, [1965] 1 All ER 506, HL. See also *R v MacKenney* (1980) 72 Cr App Rep 78.
2 [1975] QB 834 at 841, [1975] 1 All ER 70 at 74, per Lawton LJ. For discussion, see D H Sheldon and M D MacLeod 'From Normative to Positive Data: Expert Psychological Evidence Re-assessed' [1991] Crim LR 811; D Sheldon 'The Admissibility of Psychiatric and Psychological Evidence' 1992 SLT 301. For an interesting analysis of the defects in the 'common sense' view of human conduct, see R D Mackay and A M Colman 'Excluding Expert Evidence: A Tale of Ordinary Folk and Common Experience' [1991] Crim LR 800.
3 [1991] Crim LR 204.

effect that the appellant suffered from a histrionic personality disorder which inclined her to make theatrical statements intended to draw attention to her herself – a condition which would obviously call her confession into question. This exclusion of this evidence was upheld by the Court of Appeal on the grounds that evidence which disclosed anything less than mental disorder or mental abnormality was not relevant; the reliability of a confession would be determined by the jury on the basis of its own experience of human nature rather than on the basis of any psychiatric insight. A similar view has been taken in provocation cases, where the effect of the decision in *R v Turner* has been to exclude psychiatric evidence of the likely effect of stressful circumstances on a particular individual. In *R v Roberts*,[4] for example, the defence was precluded from relying on psychiatric evidence to establish that an immature person, affected by a particular form of deafness, will react in an abnormal way when subjected to certain forms of stress. There was similar legal resistance to the evidence of psychologists in *R v Hurst*,[5] in which an attempt had been made to introduce evidence of the accused's idiosyncratic reactions. In this case a drug courier, who claimed that she had been coerced into committing the offence, sought to adduce expert evidence that, since she had been trained in her youth to fear men she was, as a consequence, likely to do as she was ordered.

It will be different if it can be shown that the accused suffers from a mental disorder or mental handicap which places him in the category of the 'abnormal'. In *R v Masih*,[6] it was held that psychiatric evidence could be admitted in order to throw light on the state of mind of a mentally defective defendant – with an IQ of less than 70 – because mental abnormality would not be within the jurors' experience. The clarity of the rule has, however, been clouded by later judicial willingness to consider evidence as to mental capacity in the case of defendants who were not classified as being mentally handicapped.[7] The dividing line, then, between the normal and the abnormal is by no means clear and, certainly, a reference to an arbitrary IQ criterion will not resolve the issue. This was made evident in *R v Raghip*[8] where the court observed that it would be impossible to regard as normal an accused aged 19 years who functioned at the level of a child of nine, even if such a person had an IQ which was just within the borderline range.

Other jurisdictions – to their credit – have shown themselves readier to invoke the insights of psychiatry and psychology. In *Murphy v R*,[9] the High Court of Australia distanced itself from the restrictive view expressed in *Turner* and allowed psychological evidence which called into question the admissions made by a defendant who was intellectually limited but not mentally retarded. A similarly receptive view was taken by the Supreme Court of Western Australia, which allowed psychiatric evidence to establish that the defendant was not an 'ordinary man' and could not be expected to form the same intentions as the ordinary man.[10] Psychiatric evidence as to the

4 [1990] Crim LR 122.
5 [1995] 1 Cr App Rep 82. For comment, see (1995) 59 J Crim L 252.
6 [1986] Crim LR 395.
7 See M Beaumont 'Psychiatric Evidence: Over-rationalizing the Abnormal' [1988] Crim LR 290.
8 *R v Raghip, R v Silcott, R v Braithwaite* (1991) Times, 9 December, CA.
9 (1989) 86 ALR 35. This case is discussed in J Hunter and J Bargen 'Diminished Responsibility: "Abnormal" Minds, Abnormal Murderers and What the Doctor Said' in S Yeo *Partial Excuses to Murder* (1991) p 125.
10 *Schultz v R* [1982] WAR 171.

accused's strong antipathy to homosexuality was held to be admissible in a charge involving a homosexual offence in the Canadian case of *R v Lupien*.[11] Such evidence could, of course, be categorised as character evidence – which is admissible in the United Kingdom. Character evidence does not, however, question the ability of the judge or jury to determine the issue according to their own understanding of human nature; by contrast, psychiatric evidence, being expert evidence, clothes its conclusions in scientific language and thereby inevitably acquires a superior status in the eyes of the layman.[12] Even if the courts were to become more receptive to the possibility that psychologists can throw light on obscure or abnormal aspects of human behaviour, this development must not be allowed to introduce prejudice into a trial. The courts should be cautious, for example, in admitting psychological profiling, a technique which has been widely used in the investigation of crime, particularly in the United States – not always with unequivocal results.[13] Psychological predictions as to what sort of person is likely to have committed an offence may help investigators, but is not admissible as prosecution evidence and should also be excluded from the defence.[14] Unfortunately, the decision of the Privy Council in *Lowery v R*,[15] in which one of two accused persons was allowed to bring psychological evidence that he was less likely than his fellow accused to have committed the sort of crime with which they were charged, appears to give it a foothold, but this case was described in *Turner* as turning upon its special facts, which is a courteous rebuff.

The current role of the psychiatrist in the criminal process has its ethical snares. In theory, the psychiatric witness should be required to do no more than pronounce on the presence or absence of a mental abnormality but, in practice, the danger exists that he will be encouraged to address himself to the question of responsibility. There is also the risk that psychiatric questions will be unduly simplified in order to provide the 'key' to the unlocking of certain pleas. This has happened in relation to that of diminished responsibility,[16] in respect of which medical evidence frequently goes unchallenged; the court may be looking for a pretext for the exercise of leniency. It is doubtful if psychiatrists should lend themselves to procedures which might involve moral and professional compromise.[17] The psychiatrist gives evidence to the court as an expert. He does not provide an irrebuttable conclusion as to the state of mind of the accused but, rather, tenders an expression of opinion which will ultimately be

---

11 (1970) 9 DLR (3d) 1. Of course, overt antipathy to something does not mean that one will not do precisely that thing. Psychological insights here might promote suspicion for the person who makes much of his distaste.
12 See R Bluglass 'The Psychiatrist as Expert Witness' in R Bluglass and P Bowden (eds) *Principles and Practice of Forensic Psychiatry* (1990) p 161.
13 Now extending to the psycological autopsy of which possibly the most publicised example was the investigation into the explosion on the USS Iowa, in which 47 people died: see D Canter and M Cremer 'The Psychological Autopsy' in J K Mason and B Purdue (eds) The Pathology of Trauma (3rd edn, 1999) ch 30.
14 For full discussion, see D C Ormerod 'The Evidential Implications of Psychological Profiling' [1996] Crim LR 863.
15 [1974] AC 85.
16 See p 534 below.
17 D Chiswick 'Use and Abuse of Psychiatric Testimony' (1985) 290 BMJ 975. See also J R Rappeport 'Ethics and Foresnic Psychiatry' in S Bloch and P Chodoff (eds) *Psychiatric Ethics* (2nd edn, 1991) p 391.

decided upon by the judge or jury as the case may be. As a Scottish judge said of expert witnesses:

> Their duty is to furnish the judge or the jury with the necessary scientific criteria for testing the accuracy of their conclusions, so as to enable the judge or jury to form their own independent judgment by the application of these criteria to the facts proved in evidence.[18]

While a jury does not have to accept psychiatric evidence, it is not justified in discounting such evidence when it is not contradicted in any way. This has been clearly laid down in a number of cases[19] but forensic psychiatric evidence is sometimes ignored in spite of this legal acknowledgment.[20] Certainly, psychiatric evidence which is favourable to the accused is more likely to be accepted in a case where the accused attracts sympathy – where, for example, a woman is charged with the killing of a tormenting and violent husband – rather than in those where such sympathy is unlikely – as in a brutal murder committed for purposes of sexual gratification.[1]

Mental illness and crime

At the heart of this issue is the question of the extent to which mental illness affects responsibility for criminal conduct. At one extreme is the view that a great deal of such conduct is explained by the psychopathological factors present in the offender's background – the 'crime as disease' position. At the other is the notion that the vast majority of mentally ill offenders are, in fact, responsible for their crimes, on the grounds that their mental abnormality does not necessarily impair their ability to understand the difference between right and wrong and to choose accordingly. Most supporters of the latter position would agree, however, that there can be no question of responsibility where illness is so severe as to distort fundamentally the offender's perception of reality. The controversial cases, then, are those which involve the less serious conditions, such as neuroses or personality disorders.

The problem here is essentially that of identifying a causal relationship between mental illness and crime. Such a relationship cannot be conclusively established, although the association of certain psychiatric conditions with criminal conduct appears to be strong. This is particularly the case with psychopathy, a disorder of the personality which manifests itself in persistent antisocial conduct. As Hare and his collaborators observed on studying the careers of a group of men diagnosed with antisocial personality disorder: 'Psychopaths generally had significantly more convictions for assault, theft, robbery, fraud, possession of a weapon, and escaping

18 *Davie v Edinburgh Magistrates* 1953 SC 34 at 40, per Lord Cooper.
19 *R v Matheson* [1958] 2 All ER 87, [1958] 1 WLR 474, CCA; *Taylor v R* (1978) 22 ALR 599.
20 Psychiatric evidence was discounted by the jury in the trial of Peter Sutcliffe, the so-called 'Yorkshire Ripper'. For discussion, see G Silverman 'Psychiatry after *Sutcliffe*' (1981) 125 Sol Jo 518. Also, H A Prins 'Diminished Responsibility and the Sutcliffe Case: Legal, Psychiatric and Social Aspects (A "Layman's" View)' (1983) 23 Med Sci & Law 17.
1 See p 538 below.

custody than did non-psychopaths.'[2] Other conditions may underlie other instances of criminal conduct. A proportion of those suffering from depressive illness, for example, may engage in violent conduct directed against persons or property; the most likely explanation of this conduct lies not in any defect of character so much as in the irritability which stems directly from the illness. Similarly, a number of shop-lifting incidents, particularly those which are markedly out of character, are thought to be associated with depression.[3] Certain crimes attract a psychiatric explanation by virtue of their unusual nature. Arson may be motivated by a financial motive or by a desire for revenge but it is apparently motiveless in some cases. This suggests that there is a psychopathological explanation, a hypothesis which is borne out by the frequently abnormal psychiatric profile of arsonists – particularly younger ones.[4] In the case of sex offences, the nature of the crime may be so bizarre as to make sense only in terms of a psychiatric explanation. Once again, the backgrounds of many sex offenders reveal a range of defects and abnormalities, many of which are rooted in highly stressful experiences in early life. It is significant that many child abusers were themselves sexually abused as children and, in the midst of a widespread moral panic over the sexual abuse of children, it is salutary to reflect on the fact that paedophilia, the condition which may lead to such conduct, is a psychiatric disorder listed as such in the diagnostic manuals.[5] This fact may not exculpate the offender – it may not be unreasonable to expect people to control unacceptable drives and impulses – but it may be that a therapeutic response, rather than an unambiguously punitive one, is more appropriate in some cases of this nature.

The presence of psychiatric abnormality does not of itself provide grounds for exculpation unless it can be established that the abnormality caused the commission of the offence. Even then, there remains the question of whether the defendant could have chosen not to do as he did. A person may have a strong urge to commit an antisocial act, but society may expect such urges to be controlled. Is it unreasonable to expect similar self-control on the part of the mentally abnormal person? It is certainly not such a person's fault if a desire to commit an offence is prompted by illness – but neither is it the fault of the mentally normal person if he experiences a similar strong antisocial desire, which may spring from his unconscious. In fact, society may expect both to conform to the provisions of the criminal law, provided that both are aware that these provisions exist. What lies at the heart of responsibility is the *ability* of a person to conform, because we do not (or, at least, should not) hold people responsible for that which they cannot do. If the condition from which the mentally abnormal person suffers is such as to prevent him from conforming to the provisions of the law, then it is wrong to hold him to account. The test, then, should not be whether a particular label can be put on the condition from which a defendant

2 R Hare, L McPherson and A Forth 'Male Psychopaths and their Criminal Careers' (1988) 56 J Consult Clin Psych 710.
3 R Bluglass 'Shoplifting' in R Bluglass and P Bowden (eds) *Principles and Practice of Forensic Medicine* (1990) p 787; G H Gudjonsson 'Psychological and Psychiatric Aspects of Shoplifting' (1990) 30 Med Sci & Law 45.
4 H Prins, G Tennant and K Tirck 'Motives for Arson (Fire Raising)' (1985) 25 Med Sci & Law 275. Arson has also been associated with epileptic automatism: R Brook, M Dolan and P Coorey 'Arson and Epilepsy' (1996) 36 Med Sci & Law 268.
5 World Health Organisation *The ICD-10 Classification of Mental and Behvioural Disorders*, F 65.4 (1992); American Psychiatric Association *Diagnostic and Statistical Manual of Mental Disorders* (4th edn, 1994).

suffers, but whether the effect of his illness was to put him in a position where he either did not know what he was doing or could not help doing it. Such a test satisfies the criteria of a humane theory of criminal responsibility but, as will be seen below, the law has not found it easy to apply.

The insanity plea

The plea of not guilty on the grounds of insanity is the most 'extreme' plea available to the mentally disordered offender. Such pleas were quite common in the days of capital punishment for murder, as a verdict of 'not guilty by reason of insanity' provided an escape route from possible execution. The abolition of capital punishment has changed this and the insanity plea has become quite rare. Its rarity is not surprising, perhaps, given the 'all or nothing' nature of this particular defence and the (until recently) inflexible nature of the options available to the courts in disposing of offenders found to be legally insane. The making available of a wider range of possible psychiatric dispositions may lead to a greater use of the defence, although one suspects that the outdated label and the test employed will continue to restrict the defence to relatively extreme cases.

The belief that the insane should not be punished because they are not responsible for punishable acts lies at the root of the insanity defence in criminal law.[6] In simple language, the insane are not 'to blame' for what they do, and for many laymen that intuitive moral assessment will be sufficient. At a more theoretical level, a variety of grounds can be postulated as the justification for acquittal in such cases. By measuring the behaviour of the insane offender against the behaviour of the sane person who commits the same offence, it will become apparent that the state of mind of the insane person is likely to be different in many significant respects and, therefore, mens rea may be absent. The insane offender may be ignorant of the fact that what he is doing is wrong, in either moral or legal terms, or he may be unaware of the consequences of his actions. His intentions or his motives in acting might likewise differ from those of the sane offender if they are clouded by delusions. The acts of the insane may also be analysed in terms of involuntariness. That an act should be voluntary is a pre-requisite for the attribution of responsibility: if it is not willed by the actor, the law takes the view that there is no actus reus and that there can, then, be no criminal liability.[7] The insane offender can therefore be exculpated either on the grounds of lack of mens rea – in that he did not act with the requisite criminal intent – or because there was no actus reus.

Involuntariness is, however, a difficult concept in the criminal law and is generally used to describe only those acts over which the actor has no muscular control. A nervous spasm is classically an involuntary act in the criminal law, as is

6   For a useful discussion of the theoretical basis of the insanity defence, see J Radden *Madness and Reason* (1985). There is an excellent survey in L Reznek *Evil or Ill* (1997), which succeeds in combining philosophical and psychiatric insights. Legal treatments of the issue include R D Mackay *Mental Condition Defences in the Criminal Law* (1995) and F McAuley *Insanity, Psychiatry and Criminal Responsibility* (1993).

7   On voluntary acts, see A R White *Grounds of Liability* (1985) p 48.

an act performed while asleep. The status of acts falling into the category of irresistible impulses is, however, different. A mental disorder may well have prompted an accused to steal or set fire to property but, although this may be something over which he (or his reflective ego) really has no control, it would not be accepted as an involuntary act in terms of the criminal law if it were shown that the act was performed consciously. It is only in those states where somebody is so disturbed as to be 'out of control' that his actions might fit into the usual criminal law category of involuntary acts.

In many cases, a mentally abnormal offender may act in a way which would not exculpate him prima facie in terms of the mens rea and actus reus requirements. The accused may know exactly what he is doing and intend to achieve a very specific and intelligible objective in acting as he does. And yet, in the background, there may be a grossly disturbed personality or a long-standing mental illness. As the Royal Commission on Capital Punishment pointed out, there are many offenders who know what they are doing and who know that it is wrong but who are none the less clearly insane and should not therefore be held responsible for their actions.[8] In considering such cases, there may be an inclination to treat the accused in a way which is different from the way in which we treat sane offenders. The reason for this difference in treatment might lie not so much in the absence of the constituent elements of mens rea but, rather, in the assumption that there is a causal link between the mental disorder and the criminal act. The crime may be seen as the product of a mental disorder and it is arguable that the accused would not have acted as he did if he had not been suffering from the mental condition.[9] In many cases the link between the crime and the psychiatric condition may not be at all specific; in others, however, there will be a clear connection between the accused's disordered thoughts and a criminal act. An example of such a case is *R v Oommen*,[10] a decision of the Supreme Court of Canada. Here a man suffering from psychotic paranoid beliefs that he was being persecuted by a particular group integrated a woman with whom he was living into this delusional belief structure. He now saw her as being under instructions by his persecutors to kill him, and he killed her first, acting in what he saw as self-defence. It was held that, although he knew exactly what he was doing, he did not think that his act was wrong because, as a result of his delusional beliefs, he saw her as an immediate threat to his life.

The place of deterrence is also an important consideration. If it be accepted that one of the principal purposes of the criminal law is to impose sanctions aimed at deterring offenders, then there is no point in convicting the insane because the deterrent effect is unlikely to have significant personal impact. As Barry J put it:

> It is useless for the law to seek to deter persons from committing crimes if they cannot be influenced by the possibility or probability of subsequent punishment because of their psychotic condition. The kind of mental awareness which justly exposes the person to punishment for a criminal act is thus sane awareness not the distorted or confused or unreal awareness of a diseased mind.[11]

8 (Cmnd 8932) para 295.
9 For further discussion of the theoretical basis of the defence of insanity, see H Finagarette and A Hasse *Mental Disabilities and Criminal Responsibility* (1979).
10 [1994] 2 SCR 507.
11 *R v Weise* [1969] VR 953 at 964.

The McNaghten Rules

Merely being insane does not, in itself, qualify as a defence to a criminal charge in English law. In order to benefit from the special verdict, an accused person must satisfy the test laid down in the McNaghten Rules, the controversial text which has dominated English law on the subject since the mid-nineteenth century. The rules originate in the pronouncement of the House of Lords in 1843 in the case of Daniel McNaghten,[12] who had been charged with the shooting of the Prime Minister's secretary in the belief that the secretary was the Prime Minister himself. The House of Lords laid down the basic test that acquittal on the grounds of insanity was appropriate if the accused 'was labouring under such a defect of reason, from disease of the mind, as not to know (1) the nature and quality of the act he was doing, or, if he did know it, (2) that he did not know he was doing what was wrong'. This test, variously formulated and interpreted, has since been applied throughout the Commonwealth as well as in the United States.

Criticism of the McNaghten Rules has been forceful and continuous. At the root of the problem is the very antiquity of the rules; nineteenth-century psychiatric notions differed from those of today in terminology and in substance, and it seems remarkable that Victorian concepts should still dominate the modern test of insanity. At the outset, the rules place too great an emphasis on reason as the controlling element in human behaviour. Secondly, the concept of disease of the mind, which forms a vital part of the rules, is one which is no longer in favour amongst psychiatrists. Nor is there an accepted legal definition of what constitutes such a disease – and this raises the question as to the status of a host of conditions, including psychopathy and other personality disorders. The judges, however, have not necessarily been deterred by this uncertainty. In *R v Kemp*,[13] for instance, the court held that arteriosclerosis was a disease of the mind and could, therefore, provide a defence to a criminal charge. *Bratty v A-G for Northern Ireland*[14] provided another example of a judge determining what is a disease of the mind; Lord Denning considered that this question was one for judicial resolution – but the propriety of bending medical diagnosis to suit judicial policy is doubtful. We discuss this further under the heading of automatism.[15]

More important than the objections on the point of reason are those which refer to the emphasis in the rules on the knowledge of the accused. The controversy here has focused on the interpretation of the word 'know'. Narrowly interpreted – and the majority of the critics of McNaghten have assumed that it is the narrow interpretation which will be favoured by the courts – the word 'know' implies cognitive awareness rather than broader emotional understanding. As a result of this, many insane offenders might be held to fail the McNaghten test on the grounds that, in this sense, they would probably know what they were doing. In fact, courts have tended to take a broader view of the knowledge requirement and have often required something more than an intellectual knowledge of the nature and quality of the act in question. In Canada, s 16 of the Criminal Code essentially embodies the McNaghten test of

12 (1843) 10 Cl & Fin 200, HL. McNaghten experienced delusions of persecution and would probably be diagnosed today as suffering from paranoid schizophrenia.
13 [1957] 1 QB 399, [1956] 3 All ER 249.
14 [1963] AC 386, [1961] 3 All ER 523.
15 See p 541 below.

insanity but states that a defence may be established if it is shown that the accused failed either to know or to appreciate the nature and quality of his act.[16] In interpreting this provision, the Canadian courts have ruled that, in order to be said to appreciate the nature and quality of his act, an accused person must not only know what he is doing but also must be able to understand the consequences of his act. This was taken even further by the Supreme Court of Canada in *Cooper v R*,[17] in which it was said that appreciation involves emotional as well as intellectual awareness and, thus, is not the same as knowledge as conceived in the McNaghten test. This would clearly cause difficulties in the case of psychopaths, who typically lack this ability to appreciate matters emotionally. It is not surprising, then, that in *Kjeldsen v R*[18] the court should have opted for intellectual, as opposed to emotional, appreciation as the criterion for the application of the insanity test in the Criminal Code. Kjledsen was a sexually-motivated psychopath who cold-bloodedly killed his female victim. It was apparent that the killing left him unmoved and that he probably did not appreciate (in an emotional sense) the nature of what he was doing. But if he were to be adjudged insane, then every person who committed a crime and simply felt no remorse or emotional distress over what he had done, or who was simply incapable of empathising with his victim, would be entitled to an acquittal on the grounds of insanity. The court therefore endorsed the view that the requirement that the accused appreciate the wrongfulness of his act did not refer to emotional appreciation.

There has also been some judicial debate over the significance of the term 'wrong' as it is used in the context of the McNaghten Rules. Does the accused have to know that his act is morally wrong or does he have to know that it is legally wrong? English courts have come down in favour of the latter; a successful defence must show that the accused did not know that the act was legally wrong.[19] In theory, at least, this might lead to the absurd result of the denial of the insanity defence to an accused who heard voices commanding him to commit murder and, although he knew murder to be illegal, thought that the voices came from the Prime Minister and acted accordingly.

One avenue of escape from the limitations of McNaghten is to adopt a test which emphasises the actor's control over action. This test concentrates not on the cognitive aspects of the matter but on volitional features – an accused is not to be held responsible if he is shown to be incapable by reason of mental disorder of conforming his conduct to the requirements of law. These theories have long enjoyed support, and indeed a control test is written into a number of statutory statements of the defence, sometimes alongside other criteria. The Criminal Code of Western Australia, for example, allows the defence where the accused can establish either lack of capacity to understand what he is doing, lack of capacity to know that what he is doing is wrong, or lack of capacity to control his actions.[20] One form of the control test is the irresistible impulse doctrine, which was rejected in English law in *Sodeman v R*[1] and,

16 The application of s 16 of the Canadian Criminal Code is discussed by S V Verdun-Jones 'Tightening the Reins: Recent Trends in the Application of the Insanity Defence in Canada' (1991) Med Law 285.
17 (1980) 110 DLR (3d) 46.
18 [1981] 2 SCR 617.
19 *R v Windle* [1952] 2 QB 826, [1952] 2 All ER 1, CCA.
20 Section 27. For discussion of the Western Australian provisions, see Law Reform Commission of Western Australia *Report on the Criminal Process and Persons Suffering from Mental Disorder* (1991).
 1 [1936] 2 All ER 1138, PC.

again, in *R v Rivett*[2] and which has attracted sparse support elsewhere.[3] Control theories need not, however, always be tied to the irresistible impulse concept; this is demonstrated by some American decisions in which the suddenness of the prompting to act has not been regarded as significant.

A final, and wider ranging, difficulty associated with these tests of responsibility which focus on ability to control behaviour lies in the fact that such theories view the cognitive and volitional functions of the mind as being quite separate and isolated. Modern psychiatry rejects this and regards the human personality as an integrated whole – one cannot distinguish these functions and view them in isolation from other mental processes.

Alternative attitudes

The American experience of the insanity defence has been particularly interesting. Criticism of the McNaghten Rules in the United States has been especially intense and the courts have responded by experimenting with a variety of alternative approaches. One test which, although not widely applied, occasioned much discussion was in *Durham v United States*,[4] in which the Court of Appeals of the District of Columbia abandoned the McNaghten approach in favour of what appeared to be the more scientific test of linking the crime with a diagnosed 'mental disease or mental defect'. The problem with this test is twofold: how has a mental disease to be defined – the test takes us no further in this direction – and how can one ascertain a firm causal link between the criminal act and the disease? The mere fact of mental illness need not exculpate; the criminal act must be attributable in some way to the illness and this may be a difficult, if not impossible, task.[5] A more helpful solution was suggested by the American Law Institute in its Model Penal Code.[6] The test outlined in the code is a conventional one, involving a combination of the cognitive and control criteria: an insanity defence will be available if, in the presence of mental disorder, there is a failure to appreciate the criminality of the act or, even in the event of an appreciation of this sort, there is an inability to conform one's conduct to the requirements of the law. There has been a successful move to limit and, in some cases, even to abolish the insanity defence in many parts of the United States. There has always been a degree of grass-roots scepticism about the exculpatory role of forensic psychiatry and this was given a considerable boost after the acquittal of John Hinckley, who has now achieved in an American context much the same sort of immortality as has Daniel McNaghten in this country. Hinckley attempted to assassinate President Reagan, and was acquitted on the grounds of insanity after a long trial, in which psychiatric evidence figured prominently. Public outrage at this outcome resulted in the abolition of the distinct defence of insanity in a number of states where the issue of insanity was subsequently restricted to the role of deciding whether or not there was mens rea.

2 (1950) 34 Cr App Rep 87, CCA.
3 For the fate of the irresistible concept in Canada, see *R v Wolfson* [1965] 3 CCC 304; *R v Borg* [1969] SCR 551.
4 214 F 2d 862 (1954)
5 In those jurisdictions where the *Durham* rule was applied, the courts became disenchanted with its effect and the rule was abandoned; see G Fletcher *Rethinking Criminal Law* (1978) p 840.
6 Model Penal Code, 4.01. See also *US v Brawner* 471 F 2d 969 (1972).

Other states left the insanity defence in place but either reverted to strictly McNaghten-style tests[7] or introduced additional verdicts of 'guilty, but mentally ill'. Such verdicts allowed for the psychiatric treatment of disturbed offenders without denying their responsibility.

An apposite example of legislation in this area is the Insanity Defense Reform Act 1984 (a Federal Act), which states:

> It is an affirmative defense to a prosecution under any Federal statute that, at the time of the commission of the acts constituting the offence, the defendant, as a result of severe mental disease or defect, was unable to appreciate the nature and quality or the wrongfulness of his acts. Mental defect does not otherwise constitute a defence.

It is significant that this provision abandons the volitional part of the American Law Institute's Model Penal Code and it is, therefore, no longer a defence that the defendant was 'unable to conform his conduct to the requirements of the law'. It also refers to 'severe' mental illness or defect, thereby apparently excluding neuroses, behavioural disorders and other conditions falling short of psychotic illness.[8]

The courts in Scotland now seem to have developed a fairly simple test of insanity. The McNaghten Rules have never been part of Scots criminal law and the courts have, therefore, been tied to no specific formula. In *HM Advocate v Kidd*[9] the judge's instruction to the jury, although couched in terms of reason and of alienation – which are not terms which would necessarily be accepted by psychiatrists today – stated quite simply that the defence would be available if the accused was considered to be of unsound mind at the time of the offence. That is language which anybody can understand and, although a psychiatrist might argue that it begs a lot of questions, at least the psychiatrist himself should find it quite possible to give an opinion to a court in terms of mental soundness or unsoundness.

Reform of English law was considered at length by the Butler Committee, which reported in 1975.[10] The committee accepted the fact that there were major flaws in the McNaghten Rules and proposed that a verdict of 'not guilty on evidence of mental disorder' should be introduced; this would be appropriate if there was adequate psychiatric evidence of the existence in the accused of a sufficiently severe degree of mental disorder at the time of the commission of the offence charged. This recommendation is embodied in the Draft Criminal Code, prepared by the Law Commission, which provides for a defence where the accused suffers from severe subnormality or, at the time of the offence, a severe mental illness.[11] It would also be a defence under this draft code if mental disorder is proved to negate the fault element in the offence, the grounds upon which this is to be done being left open. Severe

---

7 American developments are summarised by R D Mackay 'Post-Hinckley Insanity in the USA' [1988] Crim LR 88.

8 For criticism of the removal of the volitional aspect of the test, see R J Simon and D E Aronson *The Insanity Defense* (1988) p 49. There is a survey of the American reforms in R D Mackay *Mental Condition Defences in the Criminal Law* (1995), p 127 et seq.

9 1960 JC 61. For an analysis of the development of the Scottish cases, see G H Gordon *The Criminal Law of Scotland* (2nd edn, 1978) pp 364ff. Also, R A A McCall Smith and D Sheldon *Scots Criminal Law* (2nd edn, 1997) p 135.

10 Report of the Committee on Mentally Abnormal Offenders (Cmnd 6244).

11 *Codification of the Criminal Law* (Law Com no 143).

mental illness is defined in cl 38(e) of the draft and embraces those conditions which lead to significant thought disorder – particularly delusions.

The main attraction of this proposal is that, at least where severe conditions are involved, there is no need to tie the condition to any putative mental state of the accused in relation to the act in question; it will be enough that he has been diagnosed as suffering from a sufficiently serious mental disorder. Another attractive feature of the proposed defence is that diagnostic labels are avoided and the criteria laid out are intelligible to the layman. Any attempt at a statement of an insanity defence will have its critics – but the provisions in the draft code seem to be very much better than many.

Unfortunately, the code remains a draft; the McNaghten Rules remain the governing test of insanity in English criminal law, although the Criminal Procedure (Insanity and Unfitness to Plead) Act 1991 allows a broader range of options to a court once the special verdict has been reached. Under this Act, except where the special verdict follows upon a charge of murder, a court is no longer obliged to order detention in a secure hospital under a restriction order (which had no limit of time); it may choose from a number of options, including a supervision or treatment order, guardianship or the absolute discharge of the defendant.[12] This removes the inflexibility of the previous system and will also help to avoid the absurdity of, say, detaining a diabetic or somnambulist in a psychiatric hospital under the draconian shadow of a restriction order – which is what would have happened following upon a successful defence of insane automatism under the previous system.[13]

Unfitness to plead

In addition to the criticism directed against the actual criteria of the insanity defence, there has been frequent criticism of the rules governing fitness to plead. Until the implementation of the Criminal Procedure (Insanity and Unfitness to Plead) Act 1991, a person who was deemed incapable of standing trial by reason of mental disorder would be sent to hospital under a restriction order without any trial as to whether or not he committed the offence with which he was charged. Now there must be a trial of the facts in order that the jury may decide whether the accused actually committed the offence in question. The 1991 Act makes no changes in the grounds upon which there may be a finding of unfitness to plead. The basis of the plea is an inability to understand proceedings and to defend oneself, but the way in which the criteria for the plea are applied varies greatly.[14]

Diminished responsibility

The plea of diminished responsibility was devised as a means of allowing the court to avoid a conviction for murder where the mental condition of the accused made the attribution of full responsibility inappropriate. The doctrine was first used in

---

12 Similar powers are available under the Criminal Justice (Scotland) Act 1995.
13 See I Mackay 'The Sleepwalker is not Insane' (1992) 55 MLR 714.
14 D Grubin 'Unfit to Plead in England and Wales 1976-1988: A Survey' (1991) 158 Brit J Psychiat 540; 'What Constitutes Fitness to Plead ?' [1993] Crim LR 748.

Scotland in the case of *HM Advocate v Dingwall*[15] in 1867 and was eventually introduced into English law in the Homicide Act 1957, s 2(1). This provides that, in cases of homicide, there should be no conviction for murder if the accused is found to be suffering from:

> such abnormality of mind (whether arising from a condition of arrested or retarded development of mind or any inherent causes or induced by disease or injury) as substantially impaired his mental responsibility for his acts and omissions in doing or being a party to the killing.

The doctrine is justified because of the fixed penalty of life imprisonment for murder; it is not required elsewhere because the degree of culpability can be considered in sentencing. The reduction of the offence to one of manslaughter allows this discretion to be exercised in a homicide charge and the court can then choose a sentence ranging from the leniency of a probation order on the one hand to life imprisonment on the other.[16] Sentencing discretion already exists in respect of most other offences and, as a result, the case for extending the application of the plea is hardly strong. Some have criticised the whole concept of a diminished responsibility plea, arguing that we are either responsible or not responsible for our actions and that there should be no half-way house. It has been pointed out that the killing is both premeditated and intended in many cases where homicide occurs in conditions accepted as qualifying for diminished responsibility. Self-control in such circumstances is still a possibility; it is quite unlike the situation, say, where there is a disorder of thinking as a result of psychotic illness. Such iconoclasm discounts the fact that we do regularly make allowances which influence the extent to which we hold people to account for their acts. More usually, such allowances are described as mitigating circumstances rather than as factors influencing responsibility, but the ultimate effect will be the same. The usefulness of the concept of diminished responsibility lies in its flexibility; through its operation, those who are accused and for whom sympathy is felt can be treated in a lenient fashion on conviction without there being any condoning of their offence. A plea of diminished responsibility will, for example, enable the courts to look with equal mercy on cases of 'mercy-killing'. Inferring diminished responsibility in such circumstances does not involve any diminution of the seriousness with which the taking of life is viewed; what it does say is that something other than a long prison sentence may be appropriate by virtue of the accused's mental condition.

The conditions which may give rise to a successful plea of diminished responsibility vary considerably.[17] Disabilities such as reactive depression or hysterical disassociation, which are unlikely to qualify as mental disorders requiring prolonged psychiatric treatment, have been so accepted on occasion and, at the other end of the scale, psychopathy has also succeeded as the basis of a plea.[18] General guidance as to what

---

15 (1867) 5 Irv 466.
16 S Dell *Murder into Manslaughter* (1984); S Dell 'The Mandatory Sentence and Section 2' (1986) 12 J Med Ethics 28.
17 For an Australian survey which reveals the wide range of conditions on which pleas of diminished responsibility have been based, see K L Milte, A A Bartholomew and F Galbally 'Abolition of the Crime of Murder and of Mental Condition Defences' (1975) 49 A LJ 160 – in the cases studied, the conditions included epilepsy, paranoia, reactive depression and alcoholism.
18 Gordon *Criminal Laws of Scotland* p 395.

constitutes abnormality of mind for the purposes of the Homicide Act 1957, s 2(1) was given by Lord Parker CJ in *R v Byrne*,[19] where he stated that such abnormality existed when there was a state of mind 'so different from that of ordinary human beings that the reasonable man would term it abnormal'. This concept, it was stressed, was wide enough to cover 'the mind's activities in all its aspects', including both the ability to form a rational judgment as to right and wrong and the ability to control behaviour in accordance with that judgment.

The wording of s 2(1) excludes abnormality of mind that derives from the working of the emotions. A person who kills another in a state of rage, or who commits homicide out of passionate hatred or jealousy, will not succeed with a plea of diminished responsibility. Alcoholic intoxication may justify the plea but only if the intoxication (a) has caused an abnormality of the mind by way of organic damage or (b) it results from an uncontrollable compulsion to drink caused by the fact that the person is dependent on alcohol.[20] The evidence of mental abnormality may need only to be slight in 'meritorious' cases in which the courts may be prepared to clutch at whatever psychiatric straws are available to avoid the consequences of a conviction for murder. Yet such a process has its dangers and there have been occasional judicial reactions to what is seen as the over-extension of the concept. In Scotland, where the plea of diminished responsibility lies at common law, the High Court has emphasised that, to be successful, there must be clear psychiatric evidence of mental illness; psychiatric expressions of opinion on the issue are worthless in the absence of such evidence. This severe approach is based on a relatively old case, the meat of which is:

> ... it has been put in this way: there must be aberration or weakness of mind; that there must be some form of mental unsoundness; that there must be a state of mind which is bordering on, though not amounting to, insanity; that there must be a mind so affected that responsibility is diminished from full responsibility to partial responsibility – in other words, the prisoner in question must be only partially accountable for his actions. And I think one can see running through the cases that there is implied ... that there must be some form of mental disease.[1]

All of which may sound a touch archaic; yet, not only has it been restated recently as the law of Scotland, but it has been emphasised that the passage must be read as a whole and that the four criteria cannot be regarded as alternatives.[2]

Many suggestions have been made for reform of the doctrine of diminished responsibility; these range from arguments in favour of its extension to cover offences other than murder to calls for its abandonment – along with the abolition of the fixed penalty for murder. The Criminal Law Revision Committee favoured a less radical change and its suggestions have now been embodied in the Law Commission's Draft

19 [1960] 2 QB 396, [1960] 3 All ER 1, CCA. See also *Rose v R* [1961] AC 496, [1961] 1 All ER 859 and *R v Seers* (1984) 79 Cr App Rep 261, CA, where it was stressed that there need not be a condition 'on the borderline of insanity' in every case. The Court of Appeal in England has addressed the issue of what amounts to an abnormality of mind for purposes of s 2 of the Homicide Act 1957 in *R v Sanderson* (1993) 98 Cr App Rep 325.
20 *R v Tandy* [1989] 1 All ER 267, [1989] 1 WLR 350, CA.
1 *HM Advocate v Savage* 1923 JC 49 at 51, per Lord Alness LJ-C.
2 *Connelly v HM Advocate* 1990 SCCR 504.

Criminal Code.[3] Clause 58 of this draft avoids the term 'diminished responsibility' and provides instead for the reduction of a charge of murder to one of manslaughter when the accused is suffering from a form of mental abnormality substantial enough to warrant such reduction. Mental abnormality is defined as: 'mental illness, arrested or incomplete development of mind, psychopathic disorder and any other disorder or disability of mind, except intoxication.'

Difficult cases: infanticide and the abused woman

'Infanticide' has both a general and a technical legal meaning. In its general sense – as used, for example, in the United States – it means no more than the killing of an infant; in its English legal sense it is restricted to the killing of a child by its mother within the terms of the Infanticide Act 1938. This Act, which was based on earlier statutory provisions and which does not run to Scotland, takes such killing out of the ambit of murder into which it would otherwise fall in the absence of any special factors – such as diminished responsibility. This special treatment is based on the sympathy traditionally shown by the courts to women in this position and on the resulting disinclination to apply the full rigour of the law in such cases.[4] This attitude is dressed up in medical language of very doubtful scientific validity. According to the Act, the crime will be charged as infanticide when the death occurs within 12 months of the birth of the child and the mother is suffering from an imbalance of the mind caused by her not having recovered from the effects of childbirth or by reason of the effects of lactation. Such maternal homicidal behaviour can result from various reasons and psychiatric abnormality cannot be presumed in them all. d'Orban, in his major study of British maternal filicide, categorises six causes of infanticide, including battering in angry response to behaviour on the child's part; mental illness, in the form of depressive psychosis or personality disorder, was a factor in only 24 of the 89 cases studied.[5]

Infanticide is an uncommon crime and there is real doubt as to the need to preserve it as a separate offence. The doctrine of diminished responsibility appears to cope adequately with the problem in Scotland, where the matter will be dealt with in the same way as other cases of culpable homicide when there is evidence of a psychiatric abnormality. The specific question is whether it should be dealt with even more leniently than is the 'average' case of culpable homicide. There is a case for retaining the separate crime if this is the true objective of legal policy – and infanticide, as it stands, attracts very lenient sentences. An objection to this approach, however, is that there will be cases in which the mother deserves to be convicted of murder and it is difficult to justify special treatment for women on grounds of gender. Maternal filicide results probably often from the special stresses experienced by women and this conclusion must attract a deal of sympathy. Yet to allow such factors to mitigate homicide in some cases but not in others would be to establish a fundamental inconsistency in the law.

---

3   See p 533, n 11 above.
4   For general discussion of the background to the offence, see J K Mason *Medico-legal Aspects of Reproduction and Parenthood* (2nd edn, 1998) p 382 et seq.
5   P T d'Orban 'Women who Kill Their Children' (1979) 134 Brit J Psychiat 560. See also P J Resnick 'Murder of the Newborn: A Psychiatric Review of Neonaticide' (1970) 126 Amer J Psychiat 1414; D Maier-Katkin and R Ogle 'A Rationale for Infanticide Laws' [1993] Crim LR 903.

Claims that women should be treated differently from men in matters of criminal responsibility tend to be based on the notion that the existing criminal law is significantly biased in favour of a male view of the world. This issue has been most actively debated in the context of provocation, where it has been suggested that the plea of provocation, with its insistence on an immediate response to provocative conduct, fails to take account of the way in which women respond to ill-treatment. The matter has been medicalised by the concept of the 'battered woman syndrome', a feature of which is the development of helplessness on the part of the victim of prolonged physical and psychological torment. The concept of the syndrome is controversial,[6] but it has now been recognised in Canada and Australia.[7] The Court of Appeal in England has now accepted that the features of the syndrome may be taken into account as characteristics of the victim when assessing the response to provocation.[8]

The emergence of a realistic defence for abused women will satisfy the undoubted need for a more sympathetic legal response to the plight of those who are subjected to intolerable conduct on the part of their partners or spouses. If psychiatry can achieve this by the creation of a new syndrome, then the courts can at least avoid having to impose mandatory life sentences on those who kill in these extraordinary circumstances. It might, however, be preferable to approach the matter from the point of view of self-defence; this would avoid the creation of a further psychiatry-based ground of non-responsibility which could, logically, be applied to many others who take life when exposed to intolerable conditions. To do so could lead to the abandonment of basic notions of responsibility which form the essential foundation of criminal justice and without which systems of criminal law simply could not operate.

The problem of psychopathy

Psychopathy, which is variously known as sociopathy or antisocial personality disorder, is a condition over which there has been considerable disagreement among psychiatrists. Some deny the value of the concept altogether, arguing that it does no more than describe those who behave consistently in an antisocial fashion. The term appears, however, in diagnostic manuals and in mental health legislation and it has been accepted by the courts as grounds for a plea of diminished responsibility;[9] it is also widely accepted and used in criminology. What, then, is psychopathy and is the psychopath to be held legally responsible for his acts? According to the International Classification of Diseases, Injuries and Causes of Death of the World Health Organisation, psychopathy involves:

6   There are those who feel that it perpetuates stereotypes of women: D Nicolson and R Sanghvi 'Battered Women and Provocation: the Implications of *R v Ahluwalia*' [1993] Crim LR 728. See also K O'Donovan 'Defences for Battered Women Who Kill' (1991) 18 J Law and Soc 219.
7   S Yeo 'Battered Women Syndrome in Australia' (1993) 140 NLJ 1380.
8   *R v Ahluwalia* [1992] 4 All ER 889. See also *R v Thornton* [1992] 1 All ER 306.
9   See G Williams *Textbook of Criminal Law* (2nd edn, 1983) p 691. Professor Williams sums up the doubts at p 654: 'The term [psychopathy] can be regarded as a declaration of interest in the subject of habitual criminality by the medical profession.'

deeply ingrained maladaptive patterns of behaviour, generally recognisable by the time of adolescence or earlier, and continuing throughout most of adult life, although becoming less obvious in middle or old age.[10]

The Mental Health Act 1983 defines psychopathic disorder as a:

persistent disorder or disability of mind (whether or not including impairment of intelligence) which results in abnormally aggressive or seriously irresponsible conduct on the part of the person concerned.[11]

Views on the aetiology of the condition differ. There is a growing body of research which points to a biological explanation, and the implications of this for responsibility are considerable.[12] If psychopaths behave as they do because their biology is different, then the issue arises as to whether they should be held responsible for their actions in the same way as normal people are. However, psychopathy compromises moral abilities and the ability to empathise with others; even if a psychopath does not see the need to conform to rules, he is still able to do so – if he chooses. Biology does not effect his understanding of the existence of a rule, nor his ability to conform to it. It might alter the level of inclination to conform but the degree of a person's responsibility is not to be assessed on the basis of weak or strong inclinations.

Psychopathy has caused some difficulty for the criminal courts.[13] One response has been to deny its relevance to the question of criminal guilt, a sceptical approach based on the notion that all that a diagnosis of psychopathy does is to confirm that the patient behaves in a deviant fashion. Legal scepticism can be understood in the absence of more specific clinical features; while a judge or jury may be prepared to accept the presence of insanity when the condition of the accused is described in terms of delusions, hallucinations or blunting of affect, they may be less swayed by a general term such as personality disorder.

The fate of the psychopath in the British criminal process has varied. Psychopathy would have to be accepted as a mental disease in order to justify an insanity plea in McNaghten terms in England or to satisfy the test of insanity in Scots law; the issue has not, however, been decided in a United Kingdom case.[14] In *R v Cooper*[15] the Supreme Court of Canada decided that a personality disorder could fit within the concept of a 'disease of the mind' for legal purposes but, even were this to be generally accepted, it is most unlikely that psychopathy would have such an effect on cognitive capacity as to relieve the accused of responsibility. Indeed, personality disorders are specifically excluded from the scope of the insanity defence in a number of

10 World Health Organisation ICD 9 (1978).
11 Section 1(2). Psychopathy as such is not defined in the Mental Health (Scotland) Act 1984.
12 Eg P A Arnett 'Autonomic Responsivity in Psychopaths: a Critical review and Theoretical Proposal' (1997) 17 Clin Psychol Rev 903; R J R Blair, L Jones, F Clark and M Smith 'The Psychopathic Individual: a Lack of Responsiveness to Distress Cues' (1997) 34 Psychophysiology 192.
13 For discussion, see M Roth 'Psychopathic (Sociopathic) Personality' in Bluglass and Bowden (eds) *Principles and Practice of Forensic Medicine* (1990) p 437.
14 The diagnosis was not clearly established in *A-G for Northern Ireland v Gallagher* [1963] AC 349, [1961] 3 All ER 299, HL.
15 (1979) 13 CR (3d) 97.

jurisdictions.[16] This being so, the only practical implications of psychopathy for the criminal courts relate to the plea of diminished responsibility and, here, there has been occasional willingness to allow evidence of the condition to reduce murder to manslaughter. More usually, however, the courts have declined to accept it as grounds for the plea and the psychopath will most probably be sentenced in the same way as any other offender.[17] This is not to say that such persons will always elude psychiatric attention during their incarceration; in 1990 it was estimated that 143 out of the 577 mentally disordered persons in prison establishments in England and Wales were classified as psychopaths.[18] The Butler Committee concluded that 'the psychopath is, in general, untreatable, at least in medical terms'. That being so, he could expect to find little haven in the psychiatric hospital but whether this view is generally held is unclear since the Mental Health Act 1983, s 3(2)(b) now includes the psychopath amongst those who may be compulsorily admitted – subject to a treatability test.

Although the Butler Committee condoned the sending of psychopaths to prison, another view holds this to be unacceptable. Such persons, it is argued, are suffering from a personality disorder and are therefore not fully responsible for their actions. Conviction and imprisonment are quite different qualitatively from acquittal and admission to a psychiatric institution and it is inadmissible to impose the former on those who offend for that reason. The refutation of this argument takes one to the heart of the issue of responsibility. There is no obvious reason why a personality disorder of this nature should be treated as being any different from what one might loosely term a 'criminal or antisocial disposition' (which is a matter of character). The aetiology of psychopathy is certainly controversial, but the psychopath will probably always have been what he is at the time of the offence – that is his 'nature'. By contrast, the person who is mentally ill is not antisocial 'by nature' – his antisocial behaviour is likely to be connected with his illness. And this leads one to the question as to whether it is wrong to punish somebody for what their character dictates. If one argues that it is wrong, then the entire basis of the system of criminal justice must be seen as being immoral. People are regularly punished because their conduct is bad. The reasons why they are bad may be of some criminological interest but do not affect the basic issue of accountability in the courts; only the determinist will be inclined to argue otherwise. This view may seem unsympathetic but its critics will have to contend with the realities of the penal and hospital systems. If psychiatrists can do little or nothing to the psychopath and, at the same time, the psychopath will be a highly disruptive element within the hospital, then the viable alternatives are those of prison or freedom – and, in excluding the latter on grounds of public safety, one is left

16 As in the American Law Institute's Model Penal Code, which provides that the term 'mental disease or defect' excludes an abnormality 'manifested only by repeated criminal or anti-social conduct' (s 4.01). For further discussion, see P A Fairall and P W Johnston 'Anti-social Personality Disorder (APD) and the Insanity Defence' (1987) Crim LJ 78.

17 See eg *R v Jennion* [1962] 1 All ER 689, [1962] 1 WLR 317, CCA. In *R v Aarons* [1964] Crim LR 484 a reduction to manslaughter was allowed by way of a diagnosis of psychopathy; none the less the accused was sentenced to life imprisonment. For the Scottish position, see D Chiswick 'Criminal Responsibility in Scotland' in Bluglass and Bowden, p 539, n 13 above, p 313. Chiswick suggests that the rejection of the term psychopathic disorder in favour of a synonymous description may increase the chances of this form of personality disorder being accepted as grounds for a plea of diminished responsibility.

18 A Ashworth and J Shapland 'Psychopaths in the Criminal Process' [1980] Crim LR 628.

only with prison and with such attempts at psychotherapy as might be possible within that framework.

Automatism

The difficulty of reconciling legal requirements with medical insights into the nature of human action is also illustrated by the development of the automatism defence in criminal law. Like the insanity plea, this is a controversial defence which raises some awkward problems of balancing justice for the individual against the protection of society.

The basic principle of the criminal law that only voluntary acts will result in criminal liability clearly indicates acquittal if the accused has acted automatically. Automatic behaviour consists of acts of which an actor is not conscious or over which he has no control. Actions of somnambulistic type provide a classic illustration of this sort of behaviour.[19] Sleep-related violence may take place within the context of night terrors, which occur during slow-wave sleep, or it may occur in the course of somnambulistic activity itself. In a night terror, the subject may awake to find his hands round the throat of his sleeping partner and he may have no recollection of events preceding this. The same type of amnesia will occur when he has been sleep-walking. He may have performed complicated actions – operated machinery, opened doors or even fired a gun – and yet none of these will have been executed consciously. It is obvious that there should be no responsibility for such behaviour although it has been observed that somnambulistic behaviour does, in fact, involve a higher level of consciousness than has been supposed previously. Automatic behaviour can result from a number of other causes. These may arise from well-established patho-physiological conditions such as hypoglycaemia, the encephalopathies and post-traumatic states. Cerebral function may also be affected by the state of the blood vessels (arteriosclerosis)[20] and by the ingestion of alcohol and drugs, but offences committed while intoxicated are usually considered in a different context. More legally – and, indeed, morally – controversial are states of dissociation resulting from acute emotional stress; these are sometimes categorised as non-organic automatism.

The main problem with the defence of automatism lies in the difficulty of establishing with certainty that a given physical condition actually produced automatic behaviour. Idiopathic epilepsy may be taken as an example. It is beyond question that complicated actions, of which the subject may later have no recollection, may be performed either during a seizure or in the post-ictal period. These actions are clearly unconscious and are therefore involuntary from the point of view of the law. That, unfortunately, is as far as certainty can go. There is very little concrete evidence of the occurrence of violence in such states[1] but automatism at least provides an explanation of otherwise inexplicable behaviour; its rejection in such circumstances would be substantially unfair to the accused. Whether an acquittal is appropriate in

19 The possibility of violence during sleep is discussed by I Oswald and J Evans 'Serious Violence during Sleep Walking' (1985) 147 Brit J Psychiat 688. See also P Fenwick 'Murdering while Asleep' (1986) 293 BMJ 574. For a full treatment of the issue, see C Shapiro and A McCall Smith *Forensic Aspects of Sleep* (1997).

20 *R v Charlson* [1955] 1 All ER 859, [1955] 1 WLR 317; *R v Kemp* [1957] 1 QB 399, [1956] 3 All ER 249.

1 The form of association between epilepsy and violent or aggressive behaviour is controversial. See P Fenwick 'Automatism' in Bluglass and Bowden, p 539, n 13 above, p 271; also P Fenwick 'Aggression and Epilepsy' in M Trimble and T Bolwiq (eds) *Aspects of Epilepsy and Psychiatry* (1986) p 31.

such cases or whether some other form of disposal is to be preferred involves complicated policy issues.

In principle, a finding that the criminal offence was committed automatically should result in an acquittal. This will, in fact, be the result in some cases but, in others, the reluctance of the courts to release potentially dangerous offenders has led to the development of two conceptual categories of automatism – insane and non-insane. If the automatic behaviour is classified as insane, the court will then be able to deal with the offender in the same way as it deals with other insane offenders and so ensure that society is protected from potential danger. In theory, at least, the non-insane automaton is entitled to acquittal. The question which the courts have, thus, set for themselves is: in what circumstances will automatism count as insanity?

A useful starting point for discussion is Lord Denning's judgment in *Bratty v A-G for Northern Ireland*.[2] The accused in this case was charged with the murder of a girl whom he strangled when what he described as 'a feeling of blackness' came over him. The basis for deciding whether automatic behaviour should be classified as insane, according to Lord Denning, depended upon the question of whether or not it resulted from a disease of the mind. Clearly, if a criminal action derives from a disease of the mind it is appropriate to raise the question of insanity, with all that this entails. In *Bratty*, Lord Denning chose to define disease of the mind in terms of a mental disorder which had manifested itself in violence and which was prone to recur. These criteria indicate the main policy objective behind the distinction – the protection of the public. But the decision is open to criticism in that its logical corollary is that a non-recurrent disorder would not be a disease of the mind; the reasoning is also somewhat circular in that the definition of mental disease depends upon the inference of mental disorder which is, itself, not defined. The case of *R v Quick*[3] highlights the difficulties faced by the courts when trying to evaluate complex medical problems within the framework of a public protection policy. The appellant in *Quick* was a diabetic who, having injected himself with insulin and then failed to eat, went into a hypoglaecemic state during which he committed an assault. The court declined to hold that hypoglycaemia resulting from incorrect therapy was a disease of the mind and ruled that the defence of non-insane automatism was available. The injection of insulin, it was held, was an external factor in the same sense as a blow to the head is an external factor in those cases in which concussion leads to automatic behaviour. Recklessness in failing to eat could, of course, mean that the defence of non-insane automatism would not be available, a point which was stressed in the later case of *R v Bailey*.[4] In this case, the court, by implication, took the view that the defence of insane automatism would be appropriate in those cases where a state of hyperglycaemia resulted from failure of the medical regime; in such cases the abnormal state is produced by disease and not by an external cause such as the injection of insulin. Once again, the court stressed the role of recklessness and emphasised that knowledge of the risks of non-compliance with medical advice in such a case would exclude the defence of non-insane automatism. An attempt to circumvent the strictures of this rule was made in *R v Hennessy*,[5] a decision which, once again, denied the defence of non-insane

2   [1963] AC 386, [1961] 3 All ER 523, HL.
3   [1973] QB 910, [1973] 3 All ER 347, CA.
4   [1983] 2 All ER 503, [1983] 1 WLR 760, CA.
5   [1989] 2 All ER 9, [1989] 1 WLR 287, CA.

automatism to a diabetic who failed to inject himself with insulin. The appellant in this case argued that his condition of automatism was caused not only by this failure but also by stress, anxiety and depression. It was held that these were not external causes for the purposes of the automatism defence but were states of mind that were prone to recur; they were, therefore, relevant to insane rather than to non-insane automatism.

The position of the epileptic is somewhat clearer.[6] In *R v Sullivan*,[7] the House of Lords dealt with the case of an epileptic who had been convicted of assault during an alleged seizure. The judgment of Lord Diplock in this case is unambiguous: any disease-induced state of mind which satisfies the requirements of the McNaghten Rules – in that it impairs the faculties of reason, memory and understanding – amounts to insanity for legal purposes. The permanence or transience of the impairment is irrelevant, as is the question of its having been caused functionally or organically. Acts performed as a result of an epileptic seizure amount, therefore, to insane automatism. This will be the case even if the offence in question is not one involving violence; in this respect the decision in *Sullivan* broadens the concept of insane automatism beyond Lord Denning's definition in *Bratty*, where the condition was required to manifest itself in violence.

The problem of somnambulistic automatism came before the Court of Appeal in *R v Burgess*.[8] The appellant had alleged that an attack he made on a friend was committed while he was asleep. The jury accepted that he was not conscious at the time of the attack but returned a verdict of insane automatism rather than non-insane, as was claimed. The Court of Appeal upheld this verdict on the grounds that the somnambulistic behaviour was a product of a disease of the mind rather than of any external cause. This decision maintains the principle that automatism will be treated as insanity if it results from a mental disorder that is prone to recur – with or without manifestations of violence. The concern of the courts over the acquittal of persons who might pose a future danger are understandable, but the difficulty will always be that of predicting dangerousness in such cases. One episode of somnambulistic violence may provide weak grounds for prolonged detention, particularly when the causative factors in relation to such behaviour are so difficult to identify – and the evidence given in *R v Parks*[9] was that there is no recorded instance of repeated violence during sleepwalking. In *Parks*, a case involving homicide, the Supreme Court of Canada reached the opposite conclusion to that in *Burgess* and held that the loss of mental faculties in somnambulistic automatism is caused by the normal condition of sleep rather than by disease of the mind – it was pointed out that, otherwise, all children and some 2.5% of adults could be said to be affected.[10] The words of Watt J, the trial judge in this case, have a persuasive ring:

> There may be any number of appropriate responses ... in the control and treatment of those who have caused serious social harm while in a somnambulistic state, but a mischaracterization of the disorder as a disease of the mind and the use of the blunt

6 K J M Smith 'Epileptic Action and Criminal Responsibility' (1983) 99 LQR 506.
7 [1984] AC 156, [1983] 2 All ER 673, HL.
8 [1991] 2 QB 92, [1991] 2 All ER 769.
9 (1990) 78 CR (3d) 1, [1992] SCR 871.
10 (1990) 78 CR (3d) 1 at 5, per Brooke JA.

instrument of indefinite confinement by warrant under a special verdict of not guilty by reason of insanity is not one of them.[11]

Following the ruling of the High Court in *HM Advocate v Cunningham*[12] in 1963, Scots law took a particularly harsh view of automatism, denying any defence in such cases other than that of insanity. This changed with the decision in *Ross v HM Advocate*[13] in which the court accepted that acquittal is the appropriate result where non-insane automatism is established. The automatic behaviour in *Ross* resulted from involuntary drugging. In later cases, however, the Scottish courts have sought to limit the scope of this defence by insisting that there should be clear evidence of a complete lack of consciousness on the part of the accused; they have also stressed that the accused should in no way be the author of his own state of impairment.[14]

Non-organic automatism, or psychogenic automatism, has been viewed very much more sceptically by some courts. Such automatism may occur when there is subjection either to prolonged stress or to a sudden shock. In each case, a state of dissociation may result in which actions are performed without the exercise by the subject of conscious control. In a series of decisions, the Canadian courts recognised what became known as 'psychological blow automatism' as being grounds for acquittal as non-insane automatism; more prolonged states of dissociation were treated as insanity.[15] In *R v K*,[16] for example, the accused, who had been undergoing treatment for a severe neurotic condition, killed his wife after the shock of hearing that she planned to leave him. Psychiatric evidence to the effect that the killing took place while he was in a state of automatism was accepted by the jury and the accused was acquitted. Similarly, in *R v Gottschalk*[17] the accused was acquitted of assault after psychiatric evidence was led of his state of depersonalisation which was productive of automatism. A reverse in the trend of the Canadian decisions occurred, however, with the decision of the Supreme Court of Canada in *Rabey v R*,[18] in which it was held that dissociation resulting from a psychological shock should be treated as insanity rather than as non-insane automatism. It is significant in this case that the accused, who assaulted a woman after she had rejected him, did not have the sort of psychiatric record which was produced by the defendants in *K* and *Gottschalk*. It may be suspected, too, that the court wished to restrict defences of psychogenic automatism for policy reasons, as the whole concept is an obvious candidate for abuse and non-meritorious defences.[19]

The High Court of Australia considered the issue of psychogenic automatism in *R v Falconer*,[20] a case involving the killing by a woman of her violent and abusive husband. The High Court ruled that psychiatric evidence of the dissociative state in which the accused had acted should have been admitted – and it was also observed that

11 Quoted by Brooke JA (1990) 78 CR (3d) 1 at 5.
12 1963 JC 80, 1963 SLT 345.
13 1991 SCCR 823, 1991 SLT 564.
14 *Ebsworth v HM Advocate* 1992 SLT 1161, 1992 SCCR 671; *Macleod v Napier* 1993 SCCR 303. See discussion in R A A McCall Smith and D Sheldon *Scots Criminal Law* (2nd edn, 1997) p 28.
15 See M E Schiffer *Mental Disorder and the Criminal Process* (1978) p 101.
16 (1971) 3 CCC (2d) 84.
17 (1974) 22 CCC (2d) 415.
18 (1981) 114 DLR (3d) 193.
19 For a criticism of *Rabey*, see R D Mackay 'Non-organic Automatism – Some Recent Developments' [1980] Crim LR 350.
20 [1990] 65 ALJ R 20.

there was no reason in principle why the law should allow automatism following upon physical trauma and yet disallow it if it proceeds from a psychological cause. In England, the possibility of a non-insane automatism defence based on dissociation was rejected in the Court of Appeal decision in *R v Isitt*.[1] The accused in this case failed to stop after an accident and had attempted to evade the police. In considering his claim to have been in a state of shock, the court took the view that, although the accused's mind might have been 'shut to the moral inhibitions which control the lives of most of us', there was no suggestion that his mind was not working at all and the defence of automatism was, therefore, not available. This concept of 'diminished awareness' has, only recently, been again rejected by the Court of Appeal in a driving case.[2] A vehicle user caused the death of two pedestrians while driving in a state in which his awareness of his surroundings was impaired due to fatigue. The court held that this failed to qualify as automatism, as some conscious control of his actions was still retained.

Psychiatry and the sex offender

Sex offenders present particularly difficult problems in the field of behaviour modification. They are most commonly dealt with by way of imprisonment on the grounds that the prime consideration in sentencing policy must be the protection of potential victims.[3] Such disposal works as a temporary measure but release may well bring a fairly rapid return to antisocial behaviour. Imprisonment of sex offenders also involves more than the usual measure of cruelty because isolation from other prisoners is often needed in order to protect the offender from violence. Successful treatment of the abnormal sexual urge may well be regarded as preferable to simple segregation of the subject.

Psychiatric assistance aimed at overcoming antisocial sexual behaviour may be offered either before the patient has come into conflict with the criminal law or, following conviction of an offence, within the context of punishment and rehabilitation. It may also be available, of course, in the case of a person whose sexual impulses are not necessarily antisocial but which, nevertheless, cause him or her – almost always him – distress or embarrassment. Most homosexuals are satisfactorily integrated into society and are content with their sexual orientation; others, however, regret their preference, and a few even seek to develop heterosexual impulses. Sex therapy may provide the only route to personal adjustment in the latter cases. The fundamental ethical implication underlying any attempt to alter the sexual behaviour of another person is whether intervention of any form is justified.[4] Conventional punishment of offenders presupposes the ability to make free choices and leaves the personality untouched other than by the environment. Inducements to moral change may be

---

1 (1977) 67 Cr App Rep 44, CA.
2 *A-G's Reference (No 2 of 1992)* [1993] 4 All ER 683.
3 Howard League Working Party *Unlawful Sex* (1985) p 87.
4 For discussion, see J Bancroft 'Ethical Aspects of Sexuality and Sex Therapy' in S Bloch and P Chadoff *Psychiatric Ethics* (2nd edn, 1991) p 215. Intervention, in any event, may be pointless, given the difficulties inherent in changing sexual proclivities: A Kaul 'Sex Offenders – Cure or Management' (1993) 33 Med Sci & Law 207.

offered but the subject's capacity to reject the opportunity is not compromised. Behaviour therapy goes considerably further than this. The essence of such treatment is an attempt to change responses to and relationships with the world at large – that is, to effect something which is different in kind from a reformed moral outlook. The aim is to create a different personality and the point from which the patient deals with others shifts significantly if the therapy succeeds.

It would need a rather rigid adherence to the principle of the sanctity of personality to deny the legitimacy of any attempt of this sort. The more acceptable viewpoint would, perhaps, involve accepting the ideal while rejecting any behaviour modification programmes which are not undertaken in the knowledge of – and quite voluntarily – by the patients. As discussed in chapter 10, this requirement might rule out all such programmes being applied to prisoners or to others threatened with penal sanctions on the grounds that consent must contain an element of coercion. But a denial of opportunity might, at the same time, deny the possibility of a genuine change of heart following conviction and of a real desire to undertake treatment which would obviate future offending. There may be doubts as to voluntariness even in the case of the person who is not an offender but who seeks release from sexual inclinations which do no more than trouble him. The search for such treatment by a homosexual may be inspired by pressures from his family or others who have an interest in his conforming to social norms. The same may be true of one whose unfulfilled sexual fantasies are those which might be expected to attract strong societal disapproval – a pederast, for example – but who does not translate his sexuality into practice. He is then likely to seek treatment through externally induced shame or self-disgust and it might be argued that, in such circumstances, it is more appropriate that treatment should be aimed at self-acceptance and understanding than be of a type which is intended to suppress the emotions. But, given the supposition that we accept the propriety of therapeutic intervention in sexuality, the question then arises as to what can be achieved in practice. The most radical form of attempted therapy is that which involves surgery by way of castration or psychosurgery – and both are of dubious value. There are some reported successes in reducing the rate of recidivism in sex offenders subjected to castration[5] but it is naive to assume, as the lay public often does, that a person whose sexual impulses have led him into trouble can be 'neutralised' merely by removing his gonads. There may be a reduction in libido after such an operation but it is seldom completely destroyed and some sexual urge commonly remains. The fallacy is to regard sexuality as being purely a product of the body rather than being, in part at least, a product of the mind. As Meyers put it so graphically: 'The cause of, and answer to, the sexual psychopath's abnormal urges lie in his cranium, not in his scrotum.'[6]

Even so, by extrapolation from the discussion in chapter 21, we see no place, in our current state of knowledge, for psychosurgery in the prophylaxis of abnormal sexuality. Chemical methods which are so targeted are, however, more acceptable and are fairly widely used today. These methods involve the use of anti-androgen drugs which are given either by mouth or through subcutaneous implants; their action is to counter the effects of the male hormones and, as a result, it is hoped they will

---

5 For a European review, see N Heim and C Hirsch 'Castration for Sex Offenders: Treatment or Punishment' (1979) 8 Arch Sex Behav 281.
6 D W Meyers *The Human Body and the Law* (1970) p 46.

diminish the male sex drive. The drugs have several, sometimes distressing, side-effects – notably impotence, enlargement of the breasts and loss of body hair – and it is these which constitute the major drawback to what would, otherwise, be an attractive option in the management of potential recidivists who have not responded to less severe forms of therapy.[7]

Aversion therapy involves less serious physical intervention but may, none the less, make a major inroad into the integrity of the personality. The standard techniques consist, essentially, of an attempt to induce the patient to associate the desired sexual object or situation with pain or discomfort and, thus, to make them less attractive. Some successes have been reported but aversion is nowadays less widely used than is the opposite approach – that is, of positively rewarding appropriate reactions. Psychotherapy involving individual or group counselling is widely used in an attempt to modify antisocial sexual behaviour and treatment in special units designed for this purpose has, in fact, been offered in the United Kingdom. The success of the methods depends upon the patients' self-awareness and willingness to participate. Some sexual offenders are simply too recalcitrant to respond to psychotherapy but others may be successfully dealt with or, at least, 'defused' by such treatment.

A delicate balance?

All forms of 'mental defence' give rise to the same general dilemma. While the non-punishment of the mentally disordered is seen as an attractive goal, the need both for a certain degree of scepticism and a measure of social defence have constantly to be borne in mind. A broad, sympathetic view of excusing conditions of this sort may prevent the unjust punishment of those who are truly not responsible for their actions, but it may also have the effect of blunting our conceptions of responsibility and of imposing upon psychiatric institutions a group of people who should not be there. At the same time, too fine a net will deny a defence to meritorious cases and that, too, is socially damaging. The inescapable task of the criminal law then becomes one of charting an acceptable middle course. To achieve this, the criminal law should adhere to a broad definition of insanity (such as in the Scottish formula) which allows maximum leeway for a court to take into account expert evidence while at the same time avoiding necessarily being bound to an acceptance of psychiatric notions of responsibility. The matter is thus ultimately left in lay hands which, although fettered to an extent by theoretical guidelines, may none the less exercise such discretion as the situation demands. In the final analysis, the question: 'Is the accused responsible for his acts?' is answered not in terms of a McNaghten-style dissection of mental states but in terms of our reaction to the question: 'Should the accused be punished?' Finding the answer to that question, of course, will, in many cases, be as perversely difficult and unsettling as ever.

7   D Torpy and A Tomison 'Sex Offenders and Cyprotene Acetate – A Review of Clinical Care' (1986) 26 Med Sci & Law 279; S S Yang 'Treatability of the Sex Offender: Considerations of Etiology, Pathology, and Treatment in Repealing Sexually Dangerous Offender Status' (1989) 8 Med Law 319. The legality of the use of clinical methods of libido suppression arose in the case of *R v Mental Health Act Commission, ex p X* (1988) 9 BMLR 77, discussed at p 521 above. The issue is dealt with by P Fennell 'Sexual Suppressants and the Mental Health Act' [1988] Crim LR 6.

Appendices

Appendix A
The Hippocratic Oath

'I swear by Apollo the physician, by Aesculapius, Hygiea and Panacea, and I take to witness all the gods, all the goddesses, to keep according to my ability and my judgement the following Oath:

'To consider dear to me as my parents him who taught me this art; to live in common with him and if necessary to share my goods with him; to look upon his children as my own brothers, to teach them this art if they so desire without fee or written promise; to impart to my sons and the sons of the master who taught me and the disciples who have enrolled themselves and have agreed to the rules of the profession, but to these alone, the precepts and the instruction. I will prescribe regimen for the good of my patients according to my ability and my judgement and never do harm to anyone. To please no one will I prescribe a deadly drug, nor give advice which may cause his death. Nor will I give a woman a pessary to procure abortion. But I will preserve the purity of my life and my art. I will not cut for stone, even for patients in whom the disease is manifest; I will leave this operation to be performed by practitioners (specialist in this art). In every house where I come I will enter only for the good of my patients, keeping myself far from all intentional ill-doing and all seduction, and especially from the pleasures of love with women or with men, be they free or slaves. All that may come to my knowledge in the exercise of my profession or outside of my profession or in daily commerce with men, which ought not to be spread abroad, I will keep secret and will never reveal. If I keep this oath faithfully, may I enjoy my life and practice my art, respected by all men and in all times; but if I swerve from it or violate it, may the reverse be my lot.'

Appendix B
Declaration of Geneva
(As amended at Stockholm, 1994)*

At the time of being admitted as a member of the medical profession:
I solemnly pledge myself to consecrate my life to the service of humanity;
I will give to my teachers the respect and gratitude which is their due;
I will practise my profession with conscience and dignity;
The health of my patient will be my first consideration;
I will respect the secrets which are confided in me, even after the patient has died;
I will maintain by all the means in my power, the honour and the noble traditions of the medical profession;
My colleagues will be my sisters and brothers;
I will not permit considerations of age, disease or disability, creed, ethnic origin, gender, nationality, political affiliation, race, sexual orientation, or social standing to intervene between my duty and my patient;
I will maintain the utmost respect for human life from its beginning even under threat, and I will not use my medical knowledge contrary to the laws of humanity.
I make these promises solemnly, freely and upon my honour.

* The authors are grateful to the Medical Ethics Department of the British Medical Association for providing the current updated texts of Appendices B - F.

Appendix C

International Code of Medical Ethics

(As amended at Venice, 1983)

English text

Duties of Physicians in General

A PHYSICIAN SHALL always maintain the highest standards of professional conduct.

A PHYSICIAN SHALL not permit motives of profit to influence the free and independent exercise of professional judgement.

A PHYSICIAN SHALL, in all types of medical practice, be dedicated to providing competent medical service in full technical and moral independence, with compassion and respect for human dignity.

A PHYSICIAN SHALL deal honestly with patients and colleagues, and strive to expose those physicians deficient in character or competence, or who engage in fraud or deception.

THE FOLLOWING PRACTICES are deemed to be unethical conduct:

(a) Self advertising by physicians, unless permitted by the laws of the country and the Code of Ethics of the National Medical Association.

(b) Paying or receiving any fee or any other consideration solely to procure the referral of a patient or for prescribing or referring a patient to any source.

A PHYSICIAN SHALL respect the rights of patients, of colleagues, and of other health professionals and shall safeguard patient confidences.

A PHYSICIAN SHALL act only in the patient's interest when providing medical care which might have the effect of weakening the physical and mental condition of the patient.

A PHYSICIAN SHALL use great caution in divulging discoveries or new techniques or treatment through non-professional channels.

A PHYSICIAN SHALL certify only that which he has personally verified.

Duties of Physicians to the Sick

A PHYSICIAN SHALL always bear in mind the obligation of preserving human life.

A PHYSICIAN SHALL owe his patients complete loyalty and all the resources of his science. Whenever an examination or treatment is beyond the physician's capacity he should summon another physician who has the necessary ability.

A PHYSICIAN SHALL preserve absolute confidentiality on all he knows about his patient even after the patient has died.

A PHYSICIAN SHALL give emergency care as a humanitarian duty unless he is assured that others are willing and able to give such care.

Duties of Physicians to Each Other

A PHYSICIAN SHALL behave to his colleagues as he would have them behave towards him.

A PHYSICIAN SHALL NOT entice patients from his colleagues.

A PHYSICIAN SHALL observe the principles of 'The Declaration of Geneva' approved by the World Medical Association.

Appendix D
Declaration of Tokyo, 1975

Statement on torture and other cruel, inhuman or degrading treatment or punishment

Preamble

It is the privilege of the medical doctor to practise medicine in the service of humanity, to preserve and restore bodily and mental health without distinction as to persons, to comfort and to ease the suffering of his or her patients. The utmost respect for human life is to be maintained even under threat, and no use made of any medical knowledge contrary to the laws of humanity.

For the purpose of this Declaration, torture is defined as the deliberate, systematic or wanton infliction of physical or mental suffering by one or more persons acting alone or on the orders of any authority, to force another person to yield information, to make a confession, or for any other reason.

Declaration

1. The doctor shall not countenance, condone or participate in the practice of torture or other forms of cruel, inhuman or degrading procedures, whatever the offence of which the victim of such procedures is suspected, accused or guilty, and whatever the victim's beliefs or motives, and in all situations, including armed conflict and civil strife.

2. The doctor shall not provide any premises, instruments, substances or knowledge to facilitate the practice of torture or other forms of cruel, inhuman or degrading treatment or to diminish the ability of the victim to resist such treatment.

3. The doctor shall not be present during any procedure during which torture or other forms of cruel, inhuman or degrading treatment is used or threatened.

4. A doctor must have complete clinical independence in deciding upon the care of a person for whom he or she is medically responsible. The doctor's fundamental role is to alleviate the distress of his or her fellow men, and no motive whether personal, collective or political shall prevail against this higher purpose.

5. Where a prisoner refuses nourishment and is considered by the doctor as capable of forming an unimpaired and rational judgement concerning the consequences of such a voluntary refusal of nourishment, he or she shall not be fed artificially. The decision as to the capacity of the prisoner to form such a judgement should be confirmed by at least one other independent doctor. The consequences of the refusal of nourishment shall be explained by the doctor to the prisoner.

6. The World Medical Association will support, and should encourage the international community, the national medical associations and fellow doctors to support, the doctor and his or her family in the face of threats or reprisals resulting from a refusal to condone the use of torture or other forms of cruel, inhuman or degrading treatment.

Appendix E

Declaration of Oslo, 1970

(As amended at Venice, 1983)

Statement on therapeutic abortion

1. The first moral principle imposed upon the doctor is respect for human life from its beginning.

2. Circumstances which bring the vital interests of a mother into conflict with the vital interests of her unborn child create a dilemma and raise the question whether or not the pregnancy should be deliberately terminated.

3. Diversity of response to this situation results from the diversity of attitudes towards the life of the unborn child. This is a matter of individual conviction and conscience which must be respected.

4. It is not the role of the medical profession to determine the attitudes and rules of any particular state or community in this matter, but it is our duty to attempt both to ensure the protection of our patients and to safeguard the rights of the physician within society.

5. Therefore, where the law allows therapeutic abortion to be performed, the procedure should be performed by a physician competent to do so in premises approved by the appropriate authority.

6. If the physician considers that his convictions do not allow him to advise or perform an abortion, he may withdraw while ensuring the continuity of medical care by a qualified colleague.

7. This statement, while it is endorsed by the General Assembly of the World Medical Association, is not to be regarded as binding on any individual member association unless it is adopted by that member association.

Appendix F
Declaration of Helsinki
(Revised 1996)

Recommendations guiding physicians in biomedical research involving human subjects

Introduction

It is the mission of the physician to safeguard the health of the people. His or her knowledge and conscience are dedicated to the fulfilment of this mission.

The Declaration of Geneva of the World Medical Association binds the physician with the words: 'The health of my patient will be my first consideration,' and the International Code of Medical Ethics declares that, 'A physician shall act only in the patient's interest when providing medical care which might have the effect of weakening the physical and mental condition of the patient.'

The purpose of biomedical research involving human subjects must be to improve diagnostic, therapeutic and prophylactic procedures and the understanding of the aetiology and pathogenesis of disease.

In current medical practice most diagnostic, therapeutic or prophylactic procedures involve hazards. This applies especially to biomedical research.

Medical progress is based on research which ultimately must rest in part on experimentation involving human subjects.

In the field of biomedical research a fundamental distinction must be recognised between medical research in which the aim is essentially diagnostic or therapeutic for a patient, and medical research the essential object of which is purely scientific and without implying direct diagnostic or therapeutic value to the person subjected to the research.

Special caution must be exercised in the conduct of research which may affect the environment, and the welfare of animals used for research must be respected.

Because it is essential that the results of laboratory experiments be applied to human beings to further scientific knowledge and to help suffering humanity, the World Medical Association has prepared the following recommendations as a guide to every physician in biomedical research involving human subjects. They should be kept under review in the future. It must be stressed that the standards as drafted are only a guide to physicians all over the world. Physicians are not relieved from criminal, civil and ethical responsibilities under the laws of their own countries.

I. Basic Principles

1. Biomedical research involving human subjects must conform to generally accepted scientific principles and should be based on adequately performed

laboratory and animal experimentation and on a thorough knowledge of the scientific tradition.

2. The design and performance of each experimental procedure involving human subjects should be clearly formulated in an experimental protocol which should be transmitted for consideration, comment and guidance to a specially appointed committee independent of the investigator and the sponsor provided that this independent committee is in conformity with the laws and regulations of the country in which the research experiment is performed.

3. Biomedical research involving human subjects should be conducted only by scientifically qualified persons and under the supervision of a clinically competent medical person. The responsibility for the human subject must always rest with a medically qualified person and never rest on the subject of the research, even though the subject has given his or her consent.

4. Biomedical research involving human subjects cannot legitimately be carried out unless the importance of the objective is in proportion to the inherent risk to the subject.

5. Every biomedical research project involving human subjects should be preceded by careful assessment of predictable risks in comparison with foreseeable benefits to the subject or to others. Concern for the interests of the subject must always prevail over the interests of science and society.

6. The right of the research subject to safeguard his or her integrity must always be respected. Every precaution should be taken to respect the privacy of the subject and to minimise the impact of the study on the subject's physical and mental integrity and on the personality of the subject.

7. Physicians should abstain from engaging in research projects involving human subjects unless they are satisfied that the hazards involved are believed to be predictable. Physicians should cease any investigation if the hazards are found to outweigh the potential benefits.

8. In publication of the results of his or her research, the physician is obliged to preserve the accuracy of the results. Reports of experimentation not in accordance with the principles laid down in this Declaration should not be accepted for publication.

9. In any research on human beings, each potential subject must be adequately informed of the aims, methods, anticipated benefits and potential hazards of the study and the discomfort it may entail. He or she should be informed that he or she is at liberty to abstain from participation in the study and that he or she is free to withdraw his or her consent to participation at any time. The physician should then obtain the subject's freely-given informed consent, preferably in writing.

10. When obtaining informed consent for the research project the physician should be particularly cautious if the subject is in a dependent relationship to him or her or may consent under duress. In that case the informed consent should be obtained by a physician who is not engaged in the investigation and who is completely independent of this official relationship.

11. In case of legal incompetence, informed consent should be obtained from the legal guardian in accordance with national legislation. Where physical or mental incapacity makes it impossible to obtain informed consent, or when the subject is a minor, permission from the responsible relative replaces that of the

subject in accordance with national legislation. Whenever the minor child is in fact able to give a consent, the minor's consent must be obtained in addition to the consent of the minor's legal guardian.

12. The research protocol should always contain a statement of the ethical considerations involved and should indicate that the principles enunciated in the present Declaration are complied with.

II. Medical Research Combined with Professional Care (Clinical research)

1. In the treatment of the sick person, the physician must be free to use a new diagnostic and therapeutic measure, if in his or her judgement it offers hope of saving life, re-establishing health or alleviating suffering.

2. The potential benefits, hazards and discomfort of a new method should be weighed against the advantages of the best current diagnostic and therapeutic methods.

3. In any medical study, every patient – including those of a control group, if any – should be assured of the best proven diagnostic and therapeutic methods. This does not exclude the use of inert placebo in studies where no proven diagnostic or therapeutic method exists.

4. The refusal of the patient to participate in a study must never interfere with the physician-patient relationship.

5. If the physician considers it essential not to obtain informed consent, the specific reasons for this proposal should be stated in the experimental protocol for transmission to the independent committee (I, 2).

6. The physician can combine medical research with professional care, the objective being the acquisition of new medical knowledge, only to the extent that medical research is justified by its potential diagnostic or therapeutic value for the patient.

III. Non-therapeutic Biomedical Research Involving Human Subjects (Non-clinical biomedical research)

1. In the purely scientific application of medical research carried out on a human being, it is the duty of the physician to remain the protector of the life and health of that person on whom biomedical research is being carried out.

2. The subjects should be volunteers – either healthy persons or patients for whom the experimental design is not related to the patient's illness.

3. The investigator or the investigating team should discontinue the research if in his/her or their judgement it may, if continued, be harmful to the individual.

4. In research on man, the interest of science and society should never take precedence over considerations related to the well-being of the subject.

Index

References are to page numbers.

AIDS. *See* HIV
Abortion, 113 *et seq*
  abnormality of fetus, for, 115,
    131-3, 164-5
    failure to sustain living
      neonate, 133
    organ donation issues, 358
    'right' of fetus to, 165
  adult incompetent, 103
  Australia, in, 122, 126
  Canada, in, 121-2, 125
  contraception distinguished, 130
  doctor,
    conscientious objection, 139-40
    duty of care, 143
  failed, damages for, 94
  fetal research, after, 476-80. *See*
    also RESEARCH
  fetal rights, 124-34. *See also*
    FETUS, RIGHTS OF
  genetic abnormality, for, 152, 153,
    154, 155-6, 163-4
  Germany, in, 122-3
  Hippocratic oath proscribes, 9,
    113, 133
  lawful, 115-18, 145
    conditions for, 115-16
    extended availability, 117
    late, for abnormality, 115, 131-3
    time limit, 115, 131-2
  legal background, 114-18
  minor, for, 144-5
    interests of mother prevail, 144
    mentally handicapped mother-
      to-be, 145
    parental consent, 144
    statistics, 144
  multiple fetuses, reduction of, 145-6
  Northern Ireland, in, 118-19
  Peel Committee, 477, 479
  post-coital contraception, 111-12,
    129-30

Abortion—*contd*
  religious objection to, 5
  restrictions on maternal choice, need
    for, 4
  sex selection, for ('gender abortion'),
    116-17
  statistics, 117-18
  third party rights, 139-43
    conscientious objection, 139-41
    doctor, 139-40
    father, 141-3
    nurse, 140-1
  US, in, 113, 119-21, 125
    constitution and right of woman to,
      119-20
    restrictions under State law, 120-1
  viability of fetus, and, 131-4
  wrongful birth action, 143. *See also*
    WRONGFUL BIRTH ACTION
Abuse
  child, 202-3
  elderly person, 311
  woman, 202, 538
Accident
  blood alcohol sampling as research,
    469-70
  industrial, 206
  medical. *See* PROFESSIONAL NEGLIGENCE
  road traffic. *See* ROAD TRAFFIC ACCIDENT
Accident victim, 439-40
Accused person
  confidentialty to, 205
Adultery
  doctor, by, 12
  third party semen use as, 61-2
Advertising, 13-14
**Advisory Committee on Genetic
  Testing**, 169, 174, 183
Age. *See also* CHILD; ELDERLY PATIENT;
  INFANT
  consent to medical treatment, for. *See*
    CONSENT TO TREATMENT

Age—*contd*
  'do not resuscitate' order, and, 446
  homosexuality, consent to, 33, 35-6
  in vitro fertilisation, 71
  resource allocation, as basis for, 302
  resuscitation, and, 446
  transplantation, limits, 341
Alcoholic intoxication
  homicide etc, and, 536, 541
Alcoholism, 514, 536
Amniocentesis, 153, 154
  failure of, 159-60
  failure to recommend, 158
  mortality rate, 155
  time for, 154
Anencephaly, 149, 152-3, 330
  organ removal, 358-60
  US, *Baby K* case, 383-4
Animal
  experimentation, 460-1
  organ/tissue use. *See* TRANSPLANTATION
    OF ORGANS: xenotransplantation
Anorexia nervosa, 517-18
  adult with, 517-18
  feeding as 'treatment', 518
  mental illness, for MHA, as, 515
  minor with, 270, 517
  refusal of treatment, 259-60, 517
    force-feeding, 270, 517-18
Anti-social personality disorder. *See*
  PSYCHOPATH
Armed forces, member of
  confidentialty issues for medical
    officer, 205
  research, use for, 460
Artificial insemination, 57-67
  artificial introduction into the uterus
    (AIH), 57
    licence, 57
    new techniques, 57
    prisoners, and, 58-9
    sex selection, 59
    sperm banking for use after death,
      57-8
  artificial introduction into the uterus
    by donor (AIHD), 57
    Blood, case, 60-1
    Code of Practice factors, 64, 66
    consent of husband, 65
    consent to use by donor, 60
    father, 64-5
    legal position of child, 64-7

Artificial insemination—*contd*
  artificial introduction into the uterus
    by donor (AIHD)—*contd*
    licence, 60, 62, 64
    register of donors, 66
    single/lesbian woman, 63-4
    third party semen use as 'adultery',
      61-2
    'treatment of man and woman
      together', 62-3, 65
  controls and HFEA, 74-6, 487
  in vitro fertilisation. *See* IN VITRO
    FERTILISATION
  ovum donation. *See* IN VITRO
    FERTILISATION
  statistics for conception (AID), 57
  surrogacy, use for, 87-8. *See also*
    SURROGATE MOTHERHOOD
  uterine lavage, 76
Attorney
  incompetent, for, health care
    provisions, 434
Australia
  abortion in, 122
  Debendox trials (McBride), 466-7
  donation of organ by minor, 344-5
  duty of care, 225
  informed consent case, 284-5
  non-treatment of child, law on, 384
  psychiatric evidence, 524
  psychogenic automatism defence,
    544-5
  refusal of treatment (Victoria), 432
  sterilisation cases, 105-7
Automatism, 541-5
  diabetic, 542-3
  'diminished awareness', 545
  epilepsy, 541-2, 543
  insane and non-insane, cases, 542-5
    English cases, 545
    Scots law, 544
  non-organic or psychogenic, 541, 544
    Australian case, 544-5
  public protection, 542
  sleep, crime in, 541, 543-4
  stress or shock, state of, 541, 543,
    544, 545
Autonomy
  euthanasia, and, 432-4
  futility of treatment, and, 364
  importance of concept, 6-7, 485
  mental patient, 501-3, 508-9

Autonomy—*contd*
paternalism distinguished, 244, 255,
311 *et seq*
qualification to, 7, 19

Baby. *See* INFANT; NEONATE; PREMATURE
BABY
Battered woman, 202
syndrome, 538
Battery, 245, 247, 274-5. *See also*
CONSENT TO TREATMENT
Beating heart donor. *See*
TRANSPLANTATION OF ORGANS
Behaviour modification/therapy. *See*
PSYCHIATRIC PATIENT
Bentham, Jeremy, 6
Best interests
compulsory treatment of mental health
patient, 507-8
fetus, of, 157
medical treatment,
Down's syndrome baby, 371-2
futility concept. *See* MEDICAL
FUTILITY CONCEPT
incapax, 254-6, 264
minor, 250-2, 371-4
'no interests' compared, 374-5
pregnant woman, 266-7
See also CONSENT TO TREATMENT
permanent vegetative state patient.
See PERSISTENT/PERMANENT
VEGETATIVE STATE
research on child, and, 473
Biliary atresia
child with, non-treatment, 377-9
Biomedical human research. *See*
RESEARCH
Blood donation
reckless (Canada), 52
Blood products
contaminated, 239, 240
disclosure of donor, 207
US, as supply of service, 240
Blood transfusion
refusal of,
adult, by, 261-2
parent, for child, 249-50
Blood Transfusion Service, 240
Bodily integrity principle, 7, 245, 264.
See also AUTONOMY; CONSENT TO
TREATMENT
Body, property in. *See also* AUTONOMY

Body, property in—*contd*
cadaver, 492-4
autopsy etc, and, 493
conversion case (*Dobson*), 492-4
tissue use from (*Kelly*), 492, 493,
494
cell, 490-1
commercial aspects, 489-91, 494-6
cell-line from removed spleen
(*Moore*), 490-1, 494
See also PAYMENT
DNA sample, 491, 495
embryo, 487
fetus, 478-80, 488
molecules, 491
Nuffield Council on Bioethics
recommendations, 488
organ or tissue removal, 488-90
ownership concept, 485-6, 490
patent, 494-6
DNA, 495-6
European Directive, 496
FLOREY/Relaxin, 495-6
ONCOmouse, 494-5
sperm after death, 486
***Bolam* test**, 280-1, 283-5, 398-9, 400
research, relevance to, 468
Brain damage, 328-9. *See also* NEURAL
TUBE DAMAGE; PERSISTENT/PERMANENT
VEGETATIVE STATE
death, definition of. *See* DEATH
degree of, factors for, 394
non-treatment, adult, 393 *et seq*. *See
also* PERSISTENT/PERMANENT
VEGETATIVE STATE
non-treatment, child, 372-7, 386. *See
also* INFANT; NEONATE
vaccine, from, 236-7
Brain death. *See* DEATH
Brain tissue, fetal
transplant, 361-2
Bristol thoracic paediatric operations,
217
British Medical Association
formation, 10
resuscitation statement, 445
status, 10
Butler Committee, 533, 540

Cadaver
organ donation from, 350-7
property rights in, 492-4

Cadaver—*contd*
use of body parts, case, 492
Caesarian section
court ordered,
impacted fetus, 138
moribund mother, for, 137-8
refusal of mother to undergo, 265
Canada
abortion, 121-2, 125
donation of organ by minor, 344
euthanasia, cases, 422-4
HIV from reckless blood donation, 52
mentally ill, treatment etc in, 508-9,
529, 530-1
non-treatment of child
(hydrocephalus), 384
personality disorder, as 'disease of
mind', 539
psychiatric evidence, 525
Cancer
discrimination against sufferer, 181
gene therapy, 185
ONCOmouse, 494-5
research into,
breast, 458, 463-5
cervical, NZ campaign, 464
colonic, 464
consent of subject, 463-4
Capacity. *See also* COMPETENCY; ELDERLY
PATIENT; MENTAL INCOMPETENT;
MINOR
best interests, 254-6, 264
consent to medical treatment. *See*
CONSENT TO TREATMENT
Cardiopulmonary resuscitation, 445.
See also RESUSCITATION
Cell, 490-1
Child. *See also* MINOR
abuse, 202-3
access to records, 210
consent of/for,
medical treatment. *See* CONSENT TO
TREATMENT
research, 471-2
handicapped. *See* HANDICAPPED CHILD
newborn. *See* NEONATE
research on. *See* RESEARCH
teenager, confidentiality issues, 203-4
very young. *See* INFANT
Chorionic villus sampling, 154, 155
Chromosomal abnormality, 147, 150
detecting, 154

Civil rights. *See also* HUMAN RIGHTS
HIV, and, 22
psychiatric patient, 501-3, 508-9, 514
Cloning, 186-8
legality, UK, 187-8
prohibitions on human, 187
Codes, human research, 451-2, 453. *See
also* RESEARCH
Coma, 329
elective ventilation organ donation,
precondition for, 355
PVS distinguished, 394
pregnant woman in, 335
withdrawal of treatment, 440-2. *See
also* EUTHANASIA
Communicable disease, 193, 206
HIV not notifiable, 198-9
Community care, 298-9, 312, 313
psychiatric patient, for, 501-2, 511-12
Company doctor, 205
Compensation
medical injury/accident, for, problems
with system, 216
no-fault scheme, 216-17
Pearson Commission, 218
research injury, for, 468-9
Competence
gross incompetence, 230, 242
Competency. *See also* CONSENT TO
TREATMENT; GILLICK COMPETENCE
elderly incompetent, 318-19
psychiatric patient, 503, 507
research, for consent to. *See* RESEARCH
Compulsory treatment. *See* CONSENT TO
TREATMENT; PSYCHIATRIC PATIENT
Computer, information on, 209-10
Confession
reliability of, and expert evidence, 524
Confidentiality, 191 *et seq*
abortion (minor), 144-5
child (teenager), 203-4. *See also*
'abortion (minor)' *above*;
CONTRACEPTION
communicable disease, 193, 206
consent to release of information,
193-4
contraception (minor). *See*
CONTRACEPTION
death, after, 213-14
domestic violence, 202-3
child abuse, 202-3
wife battering, 202

Confidentiality—*contd*
  genetic disease, and. *See* GENETIC
    INFORMATION
  HIV, and, 198-202. *See also* HIV
  hospital, in, 192, 194, 199
  legal process, and,
    document disclosure, court order
      for, 207-9
    expert report, 207-8
    legal professional privilege, 208-9
    statutory disclosure, 205-7
  medical research, 205
  obligation of confidence,
    breach, remedies for. *See* 'remedies
      for breach' *below*
    common law, 191
    criminal code protection abroad, 193
    elements of breach of, 191
    exceptions, 193-205
    doctor with patient, 191-3
    intra-professional sanctions, 192
    psychiatrist with patient, 191, 506
    special cases, 205
  origins, 9
  patient's interests to breach, 194
  police, dealings with, 20, 195
  privilege, and,
    legal professional, 208-9
    qualified, 212-13
  remedies for breach,
    damages, 211-12
  society, doctor's duty to, 195-8, 214
    AIDS, and. *See* HIV
    driver being unfit, 197-8
    family violence, 202
    'need to know' principle, 198, 200,
      213
    private vs public interest, 196. *See*
      also PUBLIC INTEREST
    urgent grounds, need for breach, 197
  spouse, 90-1, 204
Consent
  embryo storage, 487
  genetic screening, to, 152, 156, 157-8
  homosexual act. *See* HOMOSEXUALITY
  organ, etc, donation, 343, 348
  research, to. *See* RESEARCH
  sado-masochistic act, to, 29-30
  treatment, to. *See* CONSENT TO
    TREATMENT
Consent to treatment, 244 *et seq*
  anorexia nervosa, 259-60, 270, 517

Consent to treatment—*contd*
  child, for. *See* 'minor, parent as proxy
    for' *below*
  child, of. *See* 'Gillick competent child'
    and 'minor, mature' *below*
  competency, test for, 270. *See also*
    'Gillick competent child' *below*
  court authority, 248, 250-1
    cases, 257-61
    wardship, 258, 260
  elderly patient, 317-18
    dementia, effect, 318
  force-feeding, 270. *See also* FEEDING
  form, 247-8
  '*Gillick* competent' child, 109-11,
    252-3, 258-9
  HIV test, 271-4
    diagnostic tests, as part of, 271-2
    GMC view, 271
    health carers, 23-4, 273
    insurance implications, 272
    legal opinions to BMA, 271
    random/anonymous testing, 273-4
    retrospective consent/secrecy
      options, 272-3
  'informed consent' concept, 277-88
    Bolam principle, 280-1, 283-5,
      398-9
    cases on, 280-6
    details, extent of, 278-9, 280-6
    future of, 286-8
    general standard for information,
      278-9
    psychologically damaging
      information, 282-3
    size of risk, relevance, 282
    warning, element of, 281-2, 284,
      285-6
  legal position, 245
  mental incompetent, 244, 246, 248,
    253-5
    best interests, 254-6, 264, 266
    elderly, 318
    Law Commission reports, 255-6
    psychiatric patient. *See* PSYCHIATRIC
      PATIENT
    Scotland, in, 255-7
  minor, mature, 109-11, 252-3, 258-9
    16-18 year old, legislative
      provision, 259
  minor, parent as proxy for, 248-52, 257
    abortion, 144

Consent to treatment—*contd*
  minor, parent as proxy for—*contd*
    best interests, 250-2, 344
    brain damaged infant, 257
    care proceedings/specific issue
      order to override, 249
    contraception. *See* CONTRACEPTION
    court overriding wish for continued
      treatment, 250-1
    donation of organ, 344
    reasonable use of power, 248
    refusal for child's interests, right,
      251-2
    refusal for parents' religious
      reasons, 249-50
  need for, 245, 246-53
  non-consensual treatment, 244-61,
    266, 274-7
    battery, as, 245, 247, 274-5
    circumstances for, 246-53
    negligence action, 274, 275-7, 280-6
    parens patriae. See 'parens patriae
      jurisdiction' *below*
    paternalistic approach, 244, 255
    social cost, and, 244
  non-treatment, 385. *See also* MEDICAL
    FUTILITY CONCEPT
  'non-voluntary therapy', 246
  parens patriae jurisdiction, 248, 250,
    253-61
    background, 253-4
    removal of, 254-5
  prisoner, 269-70
  refusal of, 261-70
    adult, by, 261-70
    child, for, religious grounds, 249-50
    competence, challenge to, 264
    elderly person, by, 317-18, 322-3
    Jehovah's Witness (adult), 261-2
    minor (mature), by, 259-61
    pregnancy, in, 137-9, 265-9. *See*
      also PREGNANCY
    right, 263-4, 265, 421
  sterilisation, non-consensual, 96-107.
    See also STERILISATION
  tissue etc removal, and property
    rights, 488-9
  unconscious patient, 246-8
    family member, consent by, 248
    necessity principle, 246-8
Consumer protection, 239-40
Contingency fee system, 218-19

Contraception, 107-12
  emergency, 111-12
  female minor, for, 108-11
    confidentiality issues, 108, 110,
      203
    Gillick, 109-11
    parental consent, conditions for
      lack of, 109-10
    post-coital, 111-12, 129
    risks, 107-8
Contract claim, 219
Corpse. *See* CADAVER
Cortex destruction, 394-5
Cost of health care. *See* RESOURCE
  ALLOCATION
Counselling. *See also* GENETIC
  COUNSELLOR
  informed consent, as part of, 278-9
Crime
  automatism defence, 541-5
  confession, reliability of, 524
  euthanasia. *See* EUTHANASIA
  expert medical evidence. *See* EXPERT
    EVIDENCE/REPORT
  fetus, against,
    capable of being born alive. *See*
      FETUS, RIGHTS OF
    pre-viable, 479-80
  fraudulent research trial, 467
  involuntariness concept, 528-9
  McNaghten Rules, 530-2
  manslaughter,
    doctor, by, 241-3
    parent, by, after withholding
      consent, 250
  mentally ill person,
    danger from, 503-6, 515
    diminished responsibility. *See*
      DIMINISHED RESPONSIBILITY
    insanity plea, 528-30, 539-40
    responsibility for, 526 *et seq*
    unfitness to plead, 534
    See also PSYCHIATRIC PATIENT;
      PSYCHOPATH
  murder. *See* MURDER
  negligence, criminal liability for, 240-3
    recklessness, 241-2
  patient committing/about to commit,
    195
  psychiatric evidence. *See* EXPERT
    EVIDENCE/REPORT
  sex offender, 545-7

Crime—*contd*
  sex offender—*contd*
    chemical treatment of, 521
    deviance. *See* SEXUAL DEVIANT
    psychosurgery, 519-21, 546-7
  withholding treatment, 369-71, 416,
    437-8, 442. *See also* EUTHANASIA
Cystic fibrosis, 157

DNA
  information about, 173
  sample, property right in, 491, 495-6
  test for abnormality. *See* GENETIC
    DISEASE
DNR order. *See* RESUSCITATION
Damages
  battery, for, 274-5
  breach of confidence, 211-12
  failed abortion, 94
  failed sterilisation, 91, 93-4
  wrongful birth action, 159-60
  wrongful/diminished life action, 161
Death, 327 *et seq*
  brain damage, and, 328-9
    hypoxia and injury contrasted, 329
  'brain death', 327, 330-3
    Denmark, view in, 332
    Japan, in, 332, 352
    'whole brain death', 330, 331
    withdrawal of treatment, 388
  brain stem death, 328 *et seq*
    'beating heart' donor. *See*
      TRANSPLANTATION OF ORGANS
  cardiac function, maintenance
    after, 335-6
  diagnosis, 331-3
  effect in law, 334
  removal of patient from ventilator.
    See VENTILATOR
  succession law issues, 334-5
  time of death, 334-5
  transplantation of organs, and, 342,
    351-2
  unlawful killing, application in, 333-4
  certificate, 213
  confidentiality issues, 213-14
    legal duty to patient, and, 213
    post-mortem report, 213
    public figure, medical history of,
      213-14
  cortex destruction, 394-5
  definition, 327

Death—*contd*
  definition—*contd*
    Australia, in, 336
    statutory, call for, 336-7
    US, in, 336
  doctor etc causing. *See* PROFESSIONAL
    NEGLIGENCE; UNLAWFUL KILLING
  heart or respiratory failure, from, 327-8
    medical intervention to correct,
      327-8. *See also* VENTILATOR
  posthumous impregnation from sperm
    bank, 57-8
  right to die, 410, 424. *See also*
    EUTHANASIA; PERSISTENT/
    PERMANENT VEGETATIVE STATE
  somatic, 333, 480
  tests for (EC), 331-2
  time of, 334
    survivorship issues, 334-5
  ventilator, 442
Death certificate, 213
Death penalty, 19-20
Declaration of court
  withdrawal of treatment, as to
    lawfulness, 396-7
Defamation, 212
Defence organisation, 221
Dementia. *See* ELDERLY PATIENT
Denmark
  Danish Council of Ethics, and brain
    death, 332
Dentist
  records, 210
Deontological theories, 5-6, 8
Depressive illness, 520
  criminal conduct in, 527
  force feeding, 270
Diabetic, 542-3
Dialysis
  incompetent adult, treatment
    impracticable, 376
  resource allocation, 300-3, 307
'Diminished awareness' defence, 545
Diminished life action. *See* WRONGFUL
  LIFE ACTION
Diminished responsibility, 534-7
  conditions for, 535-6
    'abnormal' state of mind, 536
  expert evidence on, 525-6
  first use, 534-5
  infanticide, 537-8
    battered woman syndrome, 538

Diminished responsibility—*contd*
mercy-killing, 535
murder, reduction to manslaughter, 535
psychopath, 538-41
purpose of, 534
reform proposals, 536-7
Scotland, in, 536, 537
Disability discrimination, 24-5, 180
Disabled child/person. *See* ABORTION;
HANDICAPPED CHILD; GENETIC DISEASE
definition (DDA 95), 180
Disclosure of information. *See*
CONFIDENTIALITY; CONSENT TO
TREATMENT: 'informed consent'
concept; DOCUMENT; RESEARCH:
consent
Discrimination
cancer, etc, sufferer, against, 181
disability, 24-5, 180
genetic disease, on account of, 174,
180-2. *See also* GENETIC
INFORMATION
homosexual, against, 33, 34, 35-6
sex, 180
transsexual, against, 44-7
District health authority
local research ethics committees,
duty, 455-7
resource allocation, 291, 293, 294
Doctor. *See also* PROFESSIONAL
NEGLIGENCE
AIDS, with, 199
abortion, conscientious objection to,
139-40
adultery, 12
confidentiality duty. *See*
CONFIDENTIALITY
counselling. *See* GENETIC COUNSELLOR
duty of care, 158, 164-5
abnormal fetus, as to, 158
abortion, 143
sterilisation, 90-1
hospital, in. *See* PROFESSIONAL
NEGLIGENCE: hospital staff
obligations of, 7
paediatrician. *See* INFANT; NEONATE
patient, and. *See* DOCTOR-PATIENT
RELATIONSHIP
police, for, 195, 205
rights of, 7
vicarious liability for staff, 220
witness, as, 209

Doctor-patient relationship. *See also*
CONFIDENTIALITY
Hippocratic oath, and, 9, 191-2, 193
ideal, 18-19
law defining, dangers of, 18
nature of, 8, 18-19
Document. *See also* CONFIDENTIALITY;
RECORDS (MEDICAL)
disclosure, court ordered, 207-9
legal professional privilege, 208-9
'Double effect' principle, 437, 481
Down's syndrome, 147, 150, 153
damages for shock and distress of
father, 160
test for, limitations, 155
treatment or non-treatment of neonate,
attempted murder charge (*Arthur*),
369-71
best interests of child (*Re B(a
minor)*), 371-2
US, in, 382
Driver. *See also* ROAD TRAFFIC ACCIDENT
disease, doctor reporting, 197-8
Drug
addiction, 514
injury caused by taking, 239-40
intellectual property rights, 494
overdose, 331
screening surveys, US, 470
testing. *See* RESEARCH
Duchenne muscular dystrophy, 157, 160
discrimination against sufferer, 181
Dutch Paediatric Association
non-treatment guidelines, 389

Elderly patient, 310-23
capacity, contractual etc, 319
community care, 312, 313
consent to treatment, 317-18
consolidating legislation proposed,
319-20
dementia, 318-19, 320, 322-23
disability living allowance, 312
euthanasia. *See* EUTHANASIA
family responsibility and abuse, 311
guardian for, 317
institution, in, 312-17
financing, 313-14
local authority duty, 313
Part III accommodation, 313, 315
private homes, 313-14
mentally disordered, options, 317-18

Elderly patient—*contd*
mentally disordered, options—*contd*
hospital, compulsory admission,
318
nursing home, 313
own home,
compulsory removal from, 315-17
keeping in, 312, 315
paternalism versus autonomy, 311-15,
316
receiver for, 318-19
refusal of treatment, 317-18, 322-3
residential care home, 313
resource allocation, 291-2, 302, 321-2
Scotland, 316, 317, 318
sheltered housing, 313
statistics, 310
withholding treatment, 320, 322-3
Embryo. *See also* FETUS, RIGHTS OF
biopsy, 156
implantation of, importance of, 129
in vitro fertilisation, and. *See* IN VITRO
FERTILISATION
research on, 480-4. *See also* RESEARCH
storage, 74-6, 487
Emergency treatment
compulsory admission to hospital, 511
contraception, 111-12
negligence, and, 223-4
Employee
confidentiality issues for company
doctor, 205
genetic disease,
discrimination, 180-1
screening, 178
NHS. *See* NHS STAFF
Epilepsy, 541-2, 543
Ethical basis for medicine, 4-10
ancient Greece, origins in, 8-9
identifying, difficulty of, 4
religion as, 4-5
strands, 5-8
Europe, Council of
protection of medical data, 193, 209
**European Convention on Human
Rights**
homosexuality, 35, 36-7
transsexualism, 40, 42, 43-4, 47-8
European Patent, 495-6
Eurotransplant catchment area, 347
Euthanasia, 413 *et seq*
active, 415, 426-7, 428

Euthanasia—*contd*
active—*contd*
potassium chloride injection (*Cox*),
426-7
advance directive for, 433-4, 435
assisting suicide (PAS), 418-25, 444
distinguished, 420
neurological disease cases. *See*
'progressive neurological
disease' *below*
offence, 421-2
Scotland, 422
surveys of public/medical opinions,
420-1
US position, 425
withdrawal of treatment
distinguished, 419, 424
autonomy, and, 7
Hippocratic oath proscribes, 9, 367
Holland, in, 416-18
MEDL, 418
incurable illness, 437, 438-42
conscious, maintained artificially,
439-40
duty to act, 440
incapacitated, fully conscious, 439
overriding considerations, 438-9
resource-based arguments, 441
unconscious/intensive care patient,
440-2
'involuntary', 414-15
living will, 433-4
meaning, 414
murder and manslaughter charges,
416, 437-8
nasogastric tube, etc removal. *See* FEEDING
PVS patient, and, 406-9
omission to act, 'passive' euthanasia,
415, 427-37, 440
blurred boundaries, 434-5, 439
duty to preserve life, and, 430-1
practise of, 428
self-determination, weight of, 432-4.
See also 'refusal of life-
sustaining treatment' *below*
US, principles in, 435-7
progressive neurological disease, 422-5
Canadian cases, 422-4
New Zealand, in 424
US, in, 425
refusal of life-sustaining treatment,
263, 265, 421, 432

Euthanasia—*contd*
  refusal of life-sustaining treatment—*contd*
    Australian legislation, 432-3
    UK, 433-4, 439-40
  religious objection to, 5, 413, 432
  terminal illness, 437-8, 442
    double effect principle, 437
  ventilator, turning off, 422-3, 439-42
  'voluntary', 414
  withdrawal of treatment contrasted, 378, 386, 406-9
Evidence
  disclosure, 207-9
    expert report, 207-8. *See also* EXPERT EVIDENCE/REPORT
    legal professional privilege, 208-9
Execution, 20, 413
Experience
  theoretical approach contrasted, 8
Experimentation. *See* RESEARCH
Expert evidence/report
  diminished responsibility, on, 525-6
  disclosure before trial, 207-8
  psychiatric, 523-6
    abnormal accused, for, 524-5
    acceptance of, 525-6
    Australia, 524
    Canada, 525
    likelihood of committing crime, on, 525
    limits, 523-4

Father. *See also* PARENT
  abnormal neonate of, position in relation to, 391
  abortion, position in relation to, 141-3
    husband, 141
    jurisdictional differences, 142-3
    unmarried father, 141-2
  artificial insemination, use of. *See* ARTIFICIAL INSEMINATION
  damages for Down's syndrome child, 160
  vasectomy, failure of, 160
Feeding
  force-, 270, 517-18
  medical treatment, as, 370, 385-6, 399, 447-8
    anorexic, for, 270, 518
    stage at which becomes, 447-8
  nasogastric tube,
    anorexic, use on, 517-18

Feeding—*contd*
  nasogastric tube—*contd*
    dislodgement, event forcing withdrawal, 399, 400
    insertion, 448
    withdrawal of, 370, 385-6, 387, 391, 399, 400
      artificially maintained conscious patient, 440
      PVS patient, 398-9
Fertility, control of. *See also* CONTRACEPTION; STERILISATION
  religious objection, 5
  statute law, 17
Feticide, 479-80. *See also* ABORTION
Fetus
  abnormality, with. *See* ABORTION; GENETIC DISEASE; GERMAN MEASLES
  abortion. *See* ABORTION; SEX SELECTION
  best interests, 157. *See also* FETUS, RIGHTS OF
  brain implant, 361-2, 477
  capable of being born alive, 124-5. *See also* FETUS, RIGHTS OF
  embryo stage. *See* EMBRYO
  experimentation on, 476-80
  fetoscopy, 156
  gender abortion. *See* SEX SELECTION
  organ donor, as, 357-60
    neural tissue, 361-2
  property right of mother, 487-8
  research on. *See* RESEARCH
  rights. *See* FETUS, RIGHTS OF
  stillborn/fetal material, rights over, 478-80, 488
  surplus. *See* INFERTILITY; RESEARCH
Fetus, rights of, 124-34, 160-1
  common law, at, 160-1
  implantation of embryo, importance of, 129
  jurisdictional differences, 125
  mother's action causing prenatal injury, 134-7, 161
    fetal neglect cases, 135-7
    road traffic accident, 134, 161
  mother's refusal of treatment, 137-9, 265-9
    competency, and, 139
    fear of needles, 139, 266
    fetus, for, 137, 139
    maternal treatment, 137-9, 265-9. *See also* PREGNANCY

Fetus, rights of—*contd*
  Polkinghorne Committee, 477-8, 479,
      480, 488
  realisation of, by birth, 124-5, 126,
      136-7
    'live birth', 130-1
  religious stances, 124
  right to be born, 164-5
  stabbing of mother, case on, 126-7
  status, UK cases, 126-9
  UK, in, 125-34
  US, in, 135
  viability, 130-4
Finance. *See* RESOURCE ALLOCATION
Forensic medicine, 19, 21
France
  organ donation by minors, 345, 347
Funding. *See* RESOURCE ALLOCATION
Futility. *See* MEDICAL FUTILITY CONCEPT

Gamete
  provider, consent to disposal of
      embryo, 487
  storage and use, 71–2, 485, 486, 487
Gender abortion, 59, 116-17, 157
Gender dysphoria syndrome, 37, 39.
    See also TRANSSEXUALISM
Gender, identifying. *See* SEX
Gender reassignment, 35, 37-8. *See
    also* TRANSSEXUALISM
Gene therapy, 184-6
  ethical implications, 184
  germ-line, 184
    controversial nature, 185, 186
    permitted, scope of, 185-6
  somatic, 184
    goals, 184-5
Gene Therapy Advisory Committee, 174
General Medical Council
  advertising, views on, 13-14
  assessment of standards, 12
  committees, new, 12
  confidentiality advice, 192, 193, 194,
      213-14
    public interest disclosure, 196, 200
  criticism of, 12
    'peer control', 12
    proceedings, limited powers as to,
        12-13
  disciplinary role, 192. *See also*
      PROFESSIONAL CONDUCT COMMITTEE
  establishment, 10

General Medical Council—*contd*
  functions, 11-12
  standards of practice, powers, 217, 242-3
General practitioner. *See* DOCTOR
Genetic counsellor, 150-2
  advisory options, 151-2
    prenatal diagnosis or abortion, 157
  availability, 183
  concept of, 151
  duties, 158
  negligence, 158-66
    damages for, 159-60
    See also WRONGFUL BIRTH ACTION;
        WRONGFUL LIFE ACTION
  role, 150-1, 155-6, 169
  spouse, consent of, 204
  techniques,
    limitations of, 155
    maternally invasive, 152-5
    non-invasive, 152
Genetic disease, 147-52
  'abnormality', 157
  abortion of fetus, 152, 153, 154, 155-6
    judicial antipathy to, 163-4
    negligent failure to advise, 164
  control/prevention(general), 149
    developments in techniques, 157
  counselling, 150-2, 158-66, 169. *See
      also* GENETIC COUNSELLOR
  fetal rights, 161-6. *See also* WRONGFUL
      LIFE ACTION
  genetic engineering. *See* GENE THERAPY
  inbreeding, 149
  prevention. *See* GENE THERAPY
  screening, 150, 151, 157, 169
    consent, 152, 156, 157-8, 204
    employer, by, 178
    national programme, 183
    testing distinguished, 169
  tests during pregnancy, 152-5
    amniocentesis, 153, 154, 155
    chorionic villus sample, 154, 155
    code for, 169
    DNA techniques, 155, 156
    embryo biopsy, 156
    fetoscopy, 156
    maternal serum, 152-3
    quality of, 174
    reason for, 153
    resource allocation, and, 153
    ultrasound scan, 152, 154
    See also GENETIC INFORMATION

Genetic disease—*contd*
  types, 147-9, 154, 156
Genetic information, 167-88
  Advisory Committee on Genetic
      Testing, 169, 174, 183
  conflict, potential for, 167-8
  counselling. *See* GENETIC COUNSELLOR
  DNA sample, 173
  disclosure, 169-72
    avoidance of harm, and, 170-1
    cure availability, effect of, 172,
      183-4
    interest in not knowing, protection
      of, 172
    privacy aspects, 171-2, 175, 183
  discrimination, 174, 180-2
    employer, by, scope, 180-1
    future conditions, 181-2
    legislation, 180
    progressive conditions, 181
  employer, for, 167, 174, 178-9, 180
    pre-employment screening, 178-9
    reasons for wanting, 178
    restrictions, recommendations, 179
  features unique to, 167
  Gene Therapy Advisory Committee, 174
  Human Genetics Advisory
      Commission, 174, 177, 188
  individual/family, for, 167, 168-74
    effect of knowledge, 169
    GP, confidence issues, 169-70
    right to know/not to know, 170-4
    See also 'disclosure' *above*
  insurer, for, 167, 174, 175-8, 180
    Association of British Insurers
      view, 177
    disclosure request, 175, 177-8
    moratorium on testing for, 175-7
    recommendations for, 176-7
    test request, 175
  minor, on, 174, 183
  records, 174
  state interest in, 167, 174, 182-4
    public health aspects, 182
  UK, proposals in, 173-4
  US, Genetic Privacy Act, 172-3
  use of, and motivation for, 168-9
Geneva, Declaration of, 193, 367
Geriatric. *See* ELDERLY PATIENT
German measles
  fetus damaged from mother
    contracting, 163, 164

Germany
  abortion in, 122-3
  germ-line therapy in, 186
  research, informed consent to, 462
***Gillick* competence**, 109-11, 252-3
  research, for consent to, 475
Guillain-Barré syndrome, 422, 424,
  439-40
Gulf War syndrome, 238

HIV, 21-6
  blood donation, reckless (Canada),
    52
  blood products, contaminated, 240
  blood transfusion, doctor's duty to
    warn infected patient, 54-5
  civil rights, and, 22
  confidentiality issues, 198-202
    duty of doctor to warn, 200-1
    hospital records, 199
    'need to know' exception, 200
    prisons, 201-2
    sexual partners, 200-1
    social interests, balancing, 198-
      200
    US/Canada, in, 201
  death certificate, 213
  deliberate transmission, non-sexual/
    criminal act, 50
  deliberate transmission, sexual
    intercourse, 51-5
    Canada, 52-3
    criminal laws, 51
    tort action, 54
    UK, 53-4, 55
  development of AIDS from, 22
  disability discrimination, 24-5, 181
  doctor/surgeon having, 25, 53
  employment law issues, 24
  life insurance, 25-6
  notification, 198-9
  patient's relation with doctor, 23-4
  research into, 454-5, 467-8
  social responsibility/public health
    issues, 22-3
  testing,
    consent to, 271-4. *See also*
      CONSENT TO TREATMENT
    health care workers, 23-4, 273
    immigration, 26
  transmission of virus, methods, 21-2
Haemophilia, 149, 156

Handicapped child
claim by. *See* ABORTION; FETUS, RIGHTS
OF; WRONGFUL LIFE ACTION
medical expenses for rearing, 163
right to be born, 164-5
withdrawal of treatment, 250, 366 *et
seq. See also* MEDICAL FUTILITY
CONCEPT; PARENT
Health Authority
action against, 220, 296-7
psychiatric patient, by, for failure
to assess, 505-6
budget balancing, 296
resource allocation,
ex p B (lymphoma treatment), 379-81
'*Wednesbury* unreasonableness', 297
Heart. *See* DEATH; TRANSPLANTATION OF
ORGANS
Helsinki, Declaration of, 452, 454, 459,
461, 484
Hepatitis, 23
Hippocratic oath, 8-10, 113, 191-2, 193
abortion, 9. 113, 133
euthanasia, 9, 367
experimentation, 452
guidelines in, 9
influence of, 9
versions of, 9
Home
elderly patient,
keeping in, 312, 315
removal from, 315-17
nursing home/sheltered housing, 313
Homosexuality, 33-7
adoption of child, 33-4
age of consent, 33, 35-6
discrimination law issues, 33, 34, 35-6
cases, 34
European equality principle, and, 34-5
employment law issues, 33
European Convention on Human
Rights, 35, 36-7
privacy, 35
psychiatric illness, debate as to, 516
psychiatric treatment, 545
Hospital
access to notes, 211
compulsory admission under Mental
Health Acts, 318, 510 *et seq.*
See also PSYCHIATRIC PATIENT
confidentiality issues, 192, 194
AIDS patient records, 199

Hospital—*contd*
confidentiality issues—*contd*
police access, 206-7
doctor. *See* PROFESSIONAL NEGLIGENCE:
hospital staff
indemnity, 219
waiting lists, and resource allocation,
295-6, 298
Human
body. *See* BODY, PROPERTY IN
cloning, 187
organ, use of. *See* TRANSPLANTATION
OF ORGANS
research using. *See* RESEARCH
**Human Genetic Advisory
Commission,** 174, 177, 188
Human rights, 452
Biomedicine, and, Convention on,
452, 454
European Convention on. *See* EUROPEAN
CONVENTION ON HUMAN RIGHTS
Huntington's disease, 147, 151, 156
test for, reason and use of, 168
Hydrocephalus, child with, 384

In vitro fertilisation, 56, 68-74
age of woman, 71
disability of child, 72-3
embryo,
disposal, 73-4, 75-6
status of, 73-4
storage, 70, 76, 487
transfer (ET), 68, 70-1
use and production of, 75-6, 487
financial implications, 70
mother, legal position, 69
ovum donation, 67, 69-70
donor, legal position, 72-3
difficulties with, 69
single/lesbian woman, 71-2
statistics for conception, 68
Incapax. *See also* ELDERLY PERSON;
MENTAL INCOMPETENT; MINOR
best interests, 254-6, 264
consent to medical treatment. *See*
CONSENT TO TREATMENT
Scotland, in, 255-7
Incest, 30-2
definition, 30-1
Scotland, 31, 32
taboo, reasons for, 31
trust and authority, importance of, 32

Incompetent adult. *See* MENTAL
INCOMPETENT
Incurable illness. *See* EUTHANASIA
Indemnity
hospital, 219
research, scheme for injury payments,
469
Individualism, liberal, 5-6, 7
Industrial poisoning, 206
Infant. *See also* NEONATE
selective non-treatment, 372-7
adults compared, 385-8
Australia, in, 384
best interests, 371-4, 376
biliary atresia, child with, 377-9
brain-damaged child, 372-7, 386
brain dead, 388
Canada, in, 384
circumstances for, list, 388-9
clinical judgment, and, 373-4, 376,
377, 390
dying child, 372
euthanasia distinguished, 386
feeding, 370, 385-6, 387, 391
guidelines, 388-91
leave of court to discontinue
treatment, 375, 376
not prolonging/terminating life,
difference, 373, 386-7
parents' wishes, 375-6, 378, 382
persistent vegetative state, 374-5,
385-6
US, in, 382-4
Infanticide, 369
diminished responsibility plea, 537-8
meaning, 537
Infectious disease. *See* COMMUNICABLE
DISEASE
Infertility, 56 *et seq*
artificial insemination. *See* ARTIFICIAL
INSEMINATION
childlessness distinguished, 56
controls of assisted reproduction, 74-6
female. *See* IN VITRO FERTILISATION
GIFT, 72, 77
hormone treatment, 56, 77
Human Fertilisation and Embryology
Authority (HFEA), 61, 72, 74, 483
male. *See* ARTIFICIAL INSEMINATION
selective reduction of pregnancy, 77,
145-6
surplus fetuses, 77, 145-6, 481

Infertility—*contd*
surplus fetuses—*contd*
embryocide, and alternatives, 481
research on, 481-4
surrogacy. *See* SURROGATE MOTHERHOOD
Information. *See also* CONFIDENTIALITY;
RECORDS (MEDICAL)
computer data, 209
genetic. *See* GENETIC INFORMATION
informed consent. *See* CONSENT TO
TREATMENT
statutory duty to provide, 205-6
Informed consent
research, to. *See* RESEARCH: consent
treatment, to. *See* CONSENT TO TREATMENT
Injury, personal
research, from, compensation, 468-9
Insanity. *See also* PSYCHIATRIC PATIENT
automatism as, 542-5
plea of, 528-9, 539-40
test for, 530-4
English law, reforms, 533-4
Scotland, in, 533
US, in, 532-3
Insurance, 221
Insurer
genetic information, interest in. *See*
GENETIC INFORMATION
medical examination, confidentiality
issues, 205
Intensive care patient
removal from bed, on 'death', 441.
See also DEATH
withdrawal of treatment. *See* MEDICAL
FUTILITY CONCEPT

Japan
brain death, attitude to, 332, 352
Jehovah's Witness, 261-2

Kant, 5-6
Kidney
human,
cadaver, from, 353-4
living donation, regulation, 343-4
sale of, 'Turkish affair', 348-9
US distribution method, 301
US, permission of relatives, 354
machine, resource allocation dilemma,
300-3, 307
Legal adviser
professional privilege, 208-9

Legal aid, 218
Legal involvement/restrictions, 15-18
  judicial approach to clinical freedom,
    16, 17
  morality, law imposing, 15-16
  need for, 3-4, 15-16
  slow development of law/uncertainty,
    15, 16-17
  statutory approach, Britain, 17
Legal professional privilege, 208-9
Life, 'right to', 380
Liver transplant. *See also*
  TRANSPLANTATION OF ORGANS
  Re T case, 377-9, 381
Living will, 433-4
Local research ethics committee, 455-
  7, 478
Locum tenens, 220
Lymphoma
  resource allocation for treatment, 379-81

McNaghten Rules, 530-2
Manslaughter
  diminished responsibility, murder
    reduced for, 535, 540
  doctor, by, 241-3
  euthanasia, 416, 437-8
  parent, by, after withholding consent,
    250
Marfan's syndrome, 157
Marriage
  transsexual, of. *See* TRANSSEXUAL
Medical data. *See also* CONFIDENTIALITY;
  GENETIC INFORMATION; RECORDS
  (MEDICAL)
  computerised, 209-10
  protection of, and Council of Europe,
    193, 209
Medical futility concept, 363 *et seq*
  best interests, and. *See* BEST INTERESTS
  brain-damaged adult, 393 *et seq*. *See*
    also PERSISTENT/PERMANENT
    VEGETATIVE STATE
  brain-damaged child, 372-7, 386. *See*
    also NEONATE; INFANT
  euthanasia, incursion into, 378, 386,
    406-9
  'futility', 364-6, 384
    alternative definitions, 365, 366
    use of term, connotations, 366
  introduction to, 363-4
  life, 'right to', 380

Medical futility concept—*contd*
  medical opinion, court following, 373-
    4, 376, 377
  'non-productive treatment', 366
  quality of life concept, 377. *See also*
    QUALITY ADJUSTED LIFE YEARS
  resource allocation aspects, 379-81
  sanctity of life concept, 367-9
  selective non-treatment,
    circumstances for, list, 388-9
    Common law jurisdictions, in, 382-4
    infant. *See* INFANT
    neonate. *See* NEONATE
    parents' views, 368, 375-6, 378,
      380
    presumption in favour of
      prolonging life, 376
  trends, overview, 377
  withdrawal of treatment (adult). *See*
    EUTHANASIA; PERSISTENT/
    PERMANENT VEGETATIVE STATE
Medical product
  injury caused by, 239-40
Medical research. *See* RESEARCH
Medical Research Council, 452, 465,
  474
Medical treatment. See TREATMENT
Mental disorder
  admission to hospital. *See* PSYCHIATRIC
    PATIENT
  compulsory treatment. *See* PSYCHIATRIC
    PATIENT
  crime by, responsibility, 526 *et seq*.
    See also PSYCHIATRIC PATIENT
  elderly person, 317-18
  feeding, force, 270. *See also* FEEDING
  prisoner, 270, 502
  psychopath. *See* PSYCHOPATH
  resource allocation, and, 291
  schizophrenia, 503-4, 515
Mental handicap. *See* HANDICAPPED
  CHILD; MENTAL INCOMPETENT
**Mental Health Acts, compulsory
  treatment under.** *See* PSYCHIATRIC
  PATIENT
Mental Health Tribunal
  reasons for decisions, 513
  review by, 511, 513-14
Mental illness, 515. *See also* PSYCHIATRIC
  PATIENT
Mental incompetent, 253, 254
  abortion, 103

Mental incompetent—*contd*
consent,
    research, to, 465-6
    treatment, to. *See* CONSENT TO
      TREATMENT: mental
      incompetent
psychiatric illness, person with. *See*
    PSYCHIATRIC PATIENT
research, consent to, 465-6
Scotland, in, 102. *See also* SCOTLAND
sterilisation, 102-7
Minor. *See also* ABORTION; CHILD;
    CONTRACEPTION; NEONATE;
    STERILISATION
best interests, 250-2, 371-4
confidentiality duty of doctor, 194,
    203-4
consent of. *See* CONSENT TO TREATMENT
donation of organ by, 344-7
    Australia, 344-5
    Canada, 344
    France, 345, 347
    UK, 346-7
    US, 344
    WHO ban proposal, 345
Mongol. *See* DOWN'S SYNDROME
Mother. *See also* ABORTION; PARENT;
    PREGNANCY; SPOUSE; STERILISATION
fertility treatment. *See* IN VITRO
    FERTILISATION
fetal rights against. *See* FETUS, RIGHTS OF
infanticide. *See* INFANTICIDE
mentally-handicapped, 145
surrogate. *See* SURROGATE MOTHERHOOD
Motor neurone disease
assisted suicide cases, 423, 425, 439
Multifactorial disease, 149, 150-1
Murder
euthanasia, 416, 437-8
non-treatment of neonate, 369-72
reduction for diminished
    responsibility, 535, 540
Muscular dystrophy. *See* DUCHENNE
    MUSCULAR DYSTROPHY

NHS staff. *See also* DOCTOR; NURSE
dentist, records, 210
health records of, patient access, 210.
    See also RECORDS (MEDICAL)
hospital. *See* PROFESSIONAL NEGLIGENCE
informing on doctor, 12-13
Nasogastric tube. *See* FEEDING

Negligence
disclosure of document for evidence,
    207-9
doctor, of. *See* PROFESSIONAL
    NEGLIGENCE
fetus, claim for. *See* FETUS, RIGHTS OF;
    WRONGFUL LIFE ACTION
Neonate
death after research in utero, 479
organ donor, as, 357-60
selective non-treatment, 366-72
    abortion, relation with, 366-7
    adults compared, 385-8
    Arthur, R v, 369-71
    assumptions involved, 368-9
    brain dead, 388
    circumstances for, list, 388-9
    guidelines and options, 388-91
    killing by omission, 369, 372,
      386-7
    murder/attempted murder cases,
      369-72
    nursing staff, respect for, 391
    parent as decision-maker, 368
    premature baby, 387-8
    sanctity of life doctrine, 367-9, 382
    statistics, 369
    US, in, 382-4
    See also DOWN'S SYNDROME; INFANT
Nervous shock, 238
organ donation from cadaver, relative
    affected, 351
Netherlands
euthanasia in, 416-18
    'medical decisions concerning the
      end of life (MDEL)', 418
    Royal Dutch Medical Association
      on, 416-17
    statistics, 417-18
Dutch Paediatric Association
    guidelines, 389
Neural tube defect, 154, 155, 386
research into folic acid supplements,
    461
Neurological disease, progressive
assisting suicide of sufferer. *See*
    EUTHANASIA
New Zealand, 216, 243
assisted suicide case, 424
cervical cancer study, 464
Newborn. *See* NEONATE
No-fault compensation, 216-17

Non-consensual treatment. *See* CONSENT
TO TREATMENT; PSYCHIATRIC PATIENT
Non-productive treatment. *See* MEDICAL
FUTILITY CONCEPT
Non-treatment. *See* INFANT; MEDICAL
FUTILITY CONCEPT; NEONATE;
RESOURCE ALLOCATION;
RESUSCITATION
Northern Ireland
abortion in, 118-19
Notes, patient. *See* RECORDS (MEDICAL)
Notification
duty on doctor, 193, 206
Nourishment. *See* FEEDING
Nuffield Council on Bioethics, 150,
157, 176, 178-9
property in body parts,
recommendations, 488
Nurse
abortion, role in, 140-1
non-treatment/euthanasia, position of,
391, 438
Nursing home, 313

Offence. *See* CRIME
Omission to act. *See* MEDICAL FUTILITY
CONCEPT; EUTHANASIA; RESUSCITATION
ONCOmouse, 494-5
Organ donation. *See* TRANSPLANTATION
OF ORGANS

Paediatrician
non-treatment decisions. *See* INFANT;
NEONATE
Paedophile
treatment for, 521-2
Paraplegic
euthanasia, 439
Parens patriae
background to, 253-4
consent to treatment, 248, 250, 253-61
sterilisation, to, 98, 103, 104, 145
Scotland, in (tutor dative procedure),
402-3
Parent
consent/refusal of treatment of child.
See CONSENT TO TREATMENT
non-treatment of defective child,
views, 368, 375-6, 378, 380-1
Partner
joint liability, 219
Patent, 494-6

Patent—*contd*
morality, exclusion for, 495-6
ONCOmouse, 494-5
Paternalism, 244, 255, 311-15
best interests test as, 404-5
psychiatric patient, compulsory
admission of, 506-9
Payment
body part/tissue, 348-50, 356-7, 489-90
research, for taking part in, 459-60
surrogacy, for, 80
Pearson Commission, 218, 468
Persistent/permanent vegetative state,
329, 363
adult, withdrawal of treatment, 394-412
borderline PVS case, 400-1, 407-8
cases, 396-7, 399-401
declaration of court, 396-7, 399, 407
euthanasia, as, 406-9. *See also*
EUTHANASIA
events forcing, 399, 400
feeding, 398-9
good medical practice benchmark,
398-9, 400
'omission', as, 398
best interests test, 374-5, 398-9, 403-6
problems with dependence on, 403-4
'substituted judgment' test
alternative, 404-6
Bland, 396-7, 440
coma distinguished, 394
cortex destruction with functioning
brain stem, 394-5
definition/diagnosis, 395-6, 401
'do not resuscitate' order, 411-12. *See
also* RESUSCITATION
infant, withdrawal of treatment, 374-
5, 385-6
legislation to clarify, 444
organ donation, and, 347-8
BMA guidelines, 347
permanency, 394-5
Scotland, position in, 401-3
US, in, 409-11
Cruzan, 410
family views, 411
patient's earlier wishes, 409-11
Quinlan, 409-10
Personal injury
research, in, compensation, 468-9
Personality disorder, 539-40. *See also*
PSYCHIATRIC PATIENT

Physician assisted suicide (PAS), 418-22, 444. *See also* EUTHANASIA

Placebo, 457, 461-2

Police
access to medical records. *See* RECORDS (MEDICAL)
body search, 20-1
relationship of doctor with, 20

Police surgeon, 195, 205

Polkinghorne Committee, 477-8, 479, 480, 488

Post-coital contraception, 111-12, 129-30

Post-traumatic stress disorder, 238

Pregnancy. *See also* FETUS; IN VITRO FERTILISATION
amniocentisis. *See* AMNIOCENTISIS
Caesarian. *See* CAESARIAN SECTION
controlled, 149, 157
ending. *See* ABORTION
genetic abnormalities. *See* ABORTION; GENETIC DISEASE
injury to fetus during. *See* FETUS, RIGHTS OF
multiple, 77, 145-6
pre-natal screening, 150. *See also* AMNIOCENTISIS; CHORIONIC VILLUS SAMPLING; GENETIC DISEASE
preventing. *See* CONTRACEPTION; STERILISATION
refusal of treatment for self, 265-9
'best interests', when arise, 266-7
CA guidelines set out, 267-9
competence, and, 265-9
right to refuse, 266
ventilator support, to achieve fetus viability, 335
'wrongful', action for, 94, 96

Premature baby
selective non-treatment, 387-8
non-resuscitation decisions, 388

Prison medical service. *See* PRISONER

Prisoner, 21
artificial insemination, 58-9
confidentiality issues, 205
AIDS/HIV, 201-2
consent to treatment, 269-70
hunger strike, 269-70
mentally disordered/ill, 270, 502
psychopath, 540
research, use in, 460
sexual offender, 545

Prisoner—*contd*
suicide risk, 502

Privilege. *See* CONFIDENTIALITY

Product liability, 239-40
'state of the art' defence, 239

Professional Conduct Committee, 11, 194

Professional misconduct, serious
definition, 11

Professional negligence, 215 *et seq*
basis of liability, 219-21
criminal prosecution, 240-3
tort claim, 219-40
who to sue, 219-21
battery action contrasted, 274-5
Bolam principle. *See* BOLAM TEST
civil liability, 219-40
compensation, 216-19
no-fault alternative, 216-17
problems with system, 216-19
costs, 221
criminal liability, 240-3. *See also* CRIME
current developments, and, 227
damages, quantification, 237
deterrence element, 217-18
drug or product causing injury, 239-40
elements, 221-33
breach of duty of care/fault, 221-35
causation, 222, 225-6, 235-8, 275-7
custom test, 224-8
objective standard, 232
standard of care, 222-35
emergency treatment, 223-4
error of judgment, 230
experience, degree of, 231-3
failure to read an article, 227
failure to take a precaution, 236
GMC concern with, 11
GP, by, 220
gross mistake, 230, 241, 243
Health Authority, action against, 220
hospital, nature of duty, 220
liability, 220-1
hospital staff, 220
doctor, 219, 221
indemnity, 219
nursing staff, 220-1
innovative technique, use of, 227-8
judicial hostility to, 17-18
misdiagnosis, 228-9
reference to specialist, 229

Professional negligence—*contd*
  NHS staff, by, 219-21
  newly qualified doctor, 231-3, 242
    delegation to, 232-3
  non-consensual treatment, 274, 275-7
    causation, and subjective/objective
      approach, 275-7
    'informed consent' cases, 280-6
    See also CONSENT TO TREATMENT
  non-resuscitation of premature baby,
    388. *See also* MEDICAL FUTILITY
    CONCEPT
  political aspects of, 215
  psychosomatic disease, 238
  'recognised risk avoidance' concept,
    236
  res ipsa loquitur, 233-5
    effect of, 233-4
  research, injury in, 468-9
  statistics of claims, 215
  suicidal patient, duty to, 233
  super-specialist, 226
  'swab cases', 230-1, 235
  treatment, in, 229-31, 237
  ventilator death, 442
  vicarious liability, 220, 221, 232
Professional standards. *See*
    PROFESSIONAL CONDUCT COMMITTEE
Progessive disease. *See* EUTHANASIA
Proxy consent
  research, to, 465, 472
  treatment, to. *See* CONSENT TO
    TREATMENT: minor, parent as
    proxy for
Psychiatric patient
  anorexia nervosa sufferer. *See*
    ANOREXIA NERVOSA
  behaviour modification, 519-22, 545,
    546-7
  behaviour therapy, 546-7
  Canada, in, 508-9
  civil rights, 501-3, 508-9, 514
  community care, 501-3, 511-12
    supervision order, and lack of
      resources, 503
  competence, and, 503, 507
  compulsory admission and detention,
    318, 510 *et seq*
    assessment, for, 510-11, 514
    emergency, 511
    legal proceedings by patient, 512-13
    relative, involvement of, 510-11

Psychiatric patient—*contd*
  compulsory admission and detention—
    contd
    renewal of treatment period, 511
    review rights, 511, 513-14
    treatment, for, 511, 514
  compulsory treatment, 510, 516 *et seq*
    conditions for, 503-9, 514
    limits, 518-19
    mental condition, limited to, 516-
      17, 518, 522
    treatability, relevance, 514
  criminal conduct, responsibility for,
    526 *et seq*
    automatism defence, 541-5. *See*
      also AUTOMATISM
    awareness or knowledge, 530-1
    Butler Committee, 533, 540
    Canada, 529, 530-1
    causal link between crime and
      illness, 529
    control tests, 531-2
    deterrent effect, 529
    dilemma, 547-8
    diminished responsibility. *See*
      DIMINISHED RESPONSIBILITY
    fitness to plead, 534
    insanity, plea of, 528-9, 539-40
    insanity, tests for, 530-4, 547
    involuntariness concept, 528-9, 541
    McNaghten Rules, 530-2
    reforms to English law, 533-4
    Scotland, in, 533
    test for ability to conform, 527-8
    types of crime, 527
    US, in, 532-3
    'wrong', legal or moral, 531
    See also PSYCHOPATH
  'danger to others', 503-6, 515
    accuracy of prediction, 504-5
    confidentiality and public interest
      conflict, 506
    health authority liability for failure
      (UK), 505-6
    psychiatrist's liability (US), 505
    sex offender, 545. *See also* SEX
      OFFENCE; SEXUAL DEVIANT
  'danger to self', 506-9
    best interests, 507-8, 509
    implied consent, 507
    paternalist basis, rationale for, 506-7
    substituted judgment test, 507

Psychiatric patient—*contd*
  discharge application, 514
  guardianship order, 512
  'mental disorder', 514-15
    mental illness, scope, 515-16
    'mental impairment', 516
    sexual deviancy, 514, 516, 521
  psychopath. *See* PSYCHOPATH
  supervision order, 503, 512
    new system, 512
  treatment,
    admission for. *See* 'compulsory
        admission and detention' *above*
    certification of benefit of, 519, 520
    consent to, 516-22
    distorting decision-making ability,
        509
    hazardous, 519
    irreversible, 519
    meaning, 516, 517
    psychosurgery, 519-21, 546-7
    US, in, 505, 508
    voluntary or 'informal' treatment,
        509-10
      changing to compulsory detention,
          510
      consent issues, 510
Psychiatrist, 191, 506. *See also*
    PSYCHIATRIC PATIENT
  expert evidence, 523-6. *See also*
    EXPERT EVIDENCE/REPORT
  US, liability for harm by released
      patient, 505
Psychologist, 210
Psychopath. *See also* PSYCHIATRIC
    PATIENT
  admission for assessment, 514
  Canadian case, 539
  crime by, responsibility for, 526-7,
      531, 538-9
  definition, 538-9
  diagnosis, 503-4, 515-16
  diminished responsibility plea, 538-41
    effect of, 540
  prison as punishment, 540-1
  treatment, 514, 515, 516
Psychosomatic disease, 238
Psychosurgery, 519-21, 546-7
Public health medicine, 5, 9, 22
Public interest
  disclosure for, 196, 200, 207
  doctor's duty, 195-8, 198-9, 506

Public relations, importance of, 13-14
Punishment and torture (political), 19-
    21
  death penalty, 19-20

Quality adjusted life years, 303-5
  aid to decision-making, 305
  criticisms of, 303-4
Quality of life concept, 377

Ramsey, Paul, 5
Receiver
  elderly person, for, 318-19
Records (medical)
  code of practice, Openness in NHS,
      210
  computerised, 209-10
    subject access rights, 209-10
  disclosure of, court order, 207-9
    public interest exception, 207
  hospital, 192, 199, 206, 211
  manual, 210
  ownership, 211
  patient access, 207, 209-11
    child, 210
    inaccuracy, correcting, 210
    medical reports, 210
    'serious harm' exception, 210
  police access, 206-7
    search immunity, 21
    warrant, 206
Refusal of treatment
  elderly patient, 317-18, 322-3
  'passive' euthanasia, 263, 265, 421,
      423
  right. *See* CONSENT TO TREATMENT:
      refusal of
Relative. *See also* PARENT; SPOUSE
  consent of,
    research on incompetent patient,
        465
    treatment of child. *See* CONSENT TO
        TREATMENT
  corpse, property rights in, 493
  mental patient, of, 510-11
  organ donation,
    by, 343
    objection to, from cadaver, 350,
        355-6
  resuscitation, views on, 445
Religion
  Christian, 9-10, 124

Religion—*contd*
consent to child's treatment, and, 249-50
euthanasia, objection to, 5, 413
Jehovah's Witness, 261-2
Judaeo-Christian, 5, 9-10
human life as gift, 413
Judaism, 5, 124, 250
medicine, involvement with, 4-5
monasteries, 10
public health basis, 5, 9
ritualistic practices, 4-5
Roman Catholicism, 5, 89, 124
duty to preserve life, 431
suicide, attitude to, 432
Renal failure. *See* DIALYSIS; KIDNEY
Repetitive strain injury, 238
Report. *See* EXPERT REPORT; RECORDS
(MEDICAL)
Reproduction
cloning, 186-8
control of. *See* CONTRACEPTION;
STERILISATION
genetic counselling, 150-2
genetic engineering. *See* GENE THERAPY
human right. *See* STERILISATION
Res ipsa loquitur, 233-5
Research, 451 *et seq*
AIDS, into, 454-5, 467-8
aggrieved subject, redress for, 456,
468-9
animal experimentation, 460-1
beginnings of age of, 10
cancer. *See* CANCER
central control
need for, 10
professional bodies/rules, origins, 10
child, on, 471-6
best interests, 473
competency to consent, 473-5
consent issues, 471-2, 473-6
legality, 474-5
moral acceptability, 475-6
clinical, 453, 457 *et seq*
codes, 451-2, 453
Convention on Human Rights and
Biomedicine, 452
Declaration of Helsinki, 452, 454,
459, 461, 484
Medical Research Council, 452
Nuremberg, 451
Royal College of Physicians, 452,
454, 472

Research—*contd*
compensation for personal injury
from, 468-9
confidential information, disclosure,
205
consent, 454, 458, 462-5
child, for, 471-2
child, of, 472
dispensing with, 464-5
Germany, 462
incompetent patients, 465-6
'informed', 462-3
Sweden, in, 462
US, in, 463
controlled trials, 457-9
'double-blind', 458
'pre-randomisation', 459
randomisation, 458
rapid answer, need for, 457-8
See also 'subjects' *below*
Eastern Europe, 451
embryonic, 480-4
Australia, 483
created embryos, 482, 483
licence for, 483-4
source of embryos, 481, 483
surplus embryos from IVF, 481-4
UK law, 483-4
use of, 480-1
experimentation, 467
distinguished from, 453
fetus, on, 476-80
abortion, use after, 476-7
brain implant, 361-2, 477
consent of mother, 476-7, 479
dead, 478, 480
death resulting, 479
defect resulting, 478-9
living, 478
miscarriage, use after, 476
Polkinghorne Committee, 477, 478,
479, 480, 488
pre-viable, 479-80
property rights in tissues/disposal,
480
status of fetus, 478-9
fraudulent/unethical, 466-8
Debendox trials, 466-7
liability for, 467
human rights, international law, 452
importance to modern practice, 14-15
indemnity scheme, 469

Research—*contd*
  local research ethics committees
      (LREC), 455-7, 478
    judicial review of decision, 456
    non-NHS members, indemnity for,
        456-7
  meaning, 453-5
  mentally incapacitated, 465-6
  NHS patients, use of, 456
  negligence liability, 468
    Bolam test, application to, 468
  non-therapeutic, 453, 459, 465-6, 471-6
  placebo, 457, 461-2
    deception inherent in, 461-2
    justification, 462
  planning and approval, 455-7
  risks, balancing, 453-5
  samples, use for, 469-70
  subjects, 459-61
    armed forces, 460
    classification of, 453
    payment, 459-60
    prisoners, 460
    students, 460
    volunteers, 459-60
  withdrawal, 461
Resource allocation, 289-309
  allowing patient to die, relevance to,
      430-1, 441
  global issues, 289-90
  individual patients, 299-309
    age basis, 302
    cost-benefit argument, 301
    dialysis, 300-3, 307
    'first come, first served' option,
        305-6
    medical benefit criterion, 302-3
    merits basis, 301-2
    private medicine, use within public
        sector, 307-8
    quality adjusted life years (QALY),
        303-5
    responsibility of individual,
        relevance, 308-9
    saved young life equivalent
        (SAVE), 304
    smokers, 308-9
    triage concept, 300
    withdrawal of treatment, 306-7
  lymphoma, girl with (*ex p B*), 379-81
  nationally, 290-99
    budget balancing, 296

Resource allocation—*contd*
  nationally—*contd*
    community care, effect of, 298-9
    cost evaluation, 294
    court role, 295-8
    elderly patients, 291-2, 321-2
    Health Authority '*Wednesbury*
        unreasonableness*', 297
    hospital waiting lists, 295-6, 298
    mental health patients, 291-2
    mortality as yardstick, 290, 291
    needs, correlation with, 290-1
    political nature of, 290-1
    rationing strategies, 292-4
    Secretary of State's duty, 295, 299
    societal benefit principle, 292, 321
Resuscitation
  BMA/RCN joint statement, 445
  cardiopulmonary (CPR), 445, 446
  'do not resuscitate' order, 411-12,
      428, 445-7
    age, 446
    circumstances for, 445-7
  failure, premature baby, 388
Rhesus disease/immunisation, 154, 162
Rights theory, 7
Risk
  disclosure of. *See* CONSENT TO
      TREATMENT: 'informed consent'
      concept; WARNING
  negligence action, and accepted
      practice. *See* NEGLIGENCE
  research, of, 453-5
Road traffic accident, 206
  alcohol levels research, ethics, 469-70
  'diminished awareness' defence, 545
  fetus injured in, 134, 161
Royal College of Physicians
  research guidelines, 452, 454, 472

Sado-masochistic act, 29-30
Sample
  property rights. *See* BODY, PROPERTY IN
  research use, 469-70, 491
Sanctity of life doctrine, 367-9, 382,
    397
Saved young life equivalent (SAVE),
    304
Schizophrenia. *See also* PSYCHIATRIC
    PATIENT
  diagnosis, 503-4
  mental illness for MHA, as, 515

Scotland
abetting suicide, 422
abortion, 112
automatism defence, 544
breach of confidentiality, 212
child, consent of, 252-3, 259
diminished responsibility plea, 534-5, 536
  infanticide, 537
elderly in, 316, 317, 318-20
  curator bonis, 318-19
father of Down's baby, damages for, 160
fetal rights, 125, 126, 161
incapax, consent of, 255-7
insanity test, 533
PVS, withdrawal of treatment case, 401-3
parens patriae jurisdiction, 402
premature baby, non-resuscitation cases, 388
sterilisation, 102
  failure case, 95-6
Search (body), 20-1
Serious professional misconduct, 11
Sex
criteria for identification, 38-9
Sex discrimination, 180
Sex offence, 521, 545-7. *See also* SEXUAL DEVIANT
prison as punishment, 545
treatment of offender, 545-7
  aversion therapy, 547
  drugs, by, 547
  psychosurgery, 519-21, 546-7
  psychotherapy, 547
Sex selection (fetal), 59, 116-17, 157
Sexual deviant, 29-30, 514, 516
chemical treatment, 521
Sexual intercourse
girl under 16, protection of, 35-6
homosexual. *See* HOMOSEXUALITY
Sexual law, 29 *et seq. See also* HOMOSEXUALITY; INCEST; TRANSSEXUALISM
sexual behaviour, consent principle, 29-30
Sexual orientation. *See also* HOMOSEXUALITY
meaning, 39
sex reassignment distinguished, 37, 49

Sexually transmitted disease
deliberate transmission, 50-5. *See also* HIV
disclosure, and, 208
notification. *See* COMMUNICABLE DISEASE
Sheltered housing, 313
Shock. *See* NERVOUS SHOCK; STRESS
Singer, Peter, 6
Sleep, crime committed in, 541, 543-4
Smoker
health care resource allocation, 308-9
Social services
authority, duty to elderly, 312
removal, from disabled man (case), 298
Society. *See also* PUBLIC INTEREST
constraints of, 7
doctor's duty to, 195-8
Sociopath. *See* PSYCHOPATH
Specialist Register, 14
Sperm
bank, 57-8. *See also* ARTIFICIAL INSEMINATION; GAMETE
deceased man, of,
  Blood, case, 60-1
  France, in, 486
  US, 486
Spina bifida, 149, 151, 152-3
Spouse
confidentiality issues,
  disclosure of treatment, etc, to, 90-1, 204
wife battering, 202, 538
Sterilisation, 89 *et seq*
consent, performed with lack of, 96-107
  Australian cases, 105-7
  'best interests' test 96-8, 99, 101-2, 104-5
  Canadian case, 98
  compulsory measures in US etc, 96
  court intervention, rationale for, 105-6
  declaration by court prior to, 103, 104
  gender-based, 101
  handicapped minor, 96-8, 99, 101-2, 107
  High Court judge, sanction of, 102, 103, 105
  incompetent adult, 102-7, 253
  parens patriae jurisdiction, 98, 103, 104, 145

Sterilisation—*contd*
  consent, performed with lack of—*contd*
    Practice Note, 102
    reproductive 'right', 97, 98, 100-1,
      104
    therapeutic/non-therapeutic
      distinction, 98-9, 102, 106
    United States, in, 96, 97
  ethical objections, 89-90
  failed, liability for, 90-6
    breach of contract basis, 91, 92
    causation, 91
    damages, 91, 93-4
    duty of care, 90-1
    negligence basis, 91-2
    warning of risk of failure, 92-3, 94,
      96, 286
    wrongful pregnancy action, 94, 96
  'human right to reproduce', 97, 98,
    100-1, 104
  reversal, 89
  spouse, position of, 90-1, 204
  vasectomy, failed, 160
Storage. *See* EMBRYO; SPERM
Stress
  offence committed under acute, 541,
    543, 544, 545
Suicidal person
  duty to protect from self, 233
  prisoner, 502
Suicide, 421
  physician assisting, 418-25. *See also*
    EUTHANASIA
  Roman Catholic view, 432
Surrogate motherhood, 77-88
  adoption of child, 79-80
  alternative methods, 78, 86-7
  BMA view, 81-2
  cases (British), 80, 82-3, 85
  commercial elements, 78-80, 81, 82, 86
    'reasonable payments', 80
  contractual position, 80-1
  control of artificial insemination
    aspects, 87-8
    licence, relevance of, 87
  court order procedure, 79
  legal position of parties, 79
  morality of, 85-7
  non-commercial arrangement, 81, 87
  treatment for childlessness, as, 88
  US, in, 83-5
    acceptance of, 78

Surrogate motherhood—*contd*
  US, in—*contd*
    cases, 83-4, 85
    womb leasing, 78, 86-7
Sweden
  informed consent to research, 462

Tay Sachs disease, 157, 159
Terminal illness. *See* EUTHANASIA
Test
  abnormality. *See* AMNIOCENTISIS;
    CHORIONIC VILLUS SAMPLING;
    GENETIC DISEASE
  death, for. *See* DEATH
  HIV, for. *See* HIV
Tetraplegic
  euthanasia, 439
Tissue
  donation. *See* TRANSPLANTATION OF
    ORGANS
  ownership. *See* BODY, PROPERTY IN
Tokyo, Declaration of, 19
Tort action. *See* NEGLIGENCE;
    PROFESSIONAL NEGLIGENCE
Torture
  international law, 452
Transplantation of organs
  'beating heart' donor, 342, 350-1, 354
    brain stem death concept, and, 351-2
    death certificate/evidence of death,
      352
    elective ventilation, use of, 355
  biliary atresia, child with, case, 377-9
  claims of donor, 488
  dead donor, 342, 350-7
    age etc restrictions, 341
    'contracting out' or 'in', 353
    kidney from, 353-4
    objection by relative, 350, 355-6
    payment to next of kin, 356-7
    person 'lawfully in possession of
      the body', 350
    'reasonable enquiry' that no
      objection, 350-1
    statutory regulation, 350
    unauthorised removal, 351
    ventilator, person maintained on.
      See 'beating heart' donor
      above
  fetal brain implant, 361-2, 477
  fetus/neonate donor, 357-60
    anencephalic neonate, 358-60

Transplantation of organs—*contd*
  fetus/neonate donor—*contd*
    living abortus, 358
    stillbirth, 357-8
  homotransplantation, 340 *et seq*
    immunosuppression side effects,
      340-1
    viability of organ, time limits, 341
  kidney. *See* KIDNEY
  living donor, 342-50
    common law, 342-3
    consent of, 343, 348
    heart of, 342, 343
    kidney of, 343-4, 348
    liver of, 342
    minor, 344-7. *See also* MINOR
    payment to, 348-50
    permanent vegetative state, person
      in, 347-8
    relative, 343
    statutory regulation, 343
    unrelated, 343
  tissue immunity reaction, 338-42
  trade in body parts, 486
  Unrelated Live Transplant Regulatory
    Authority, 343, 349
  xenotransplantation, 338-40
    Government policy, 340
    pig, from, 340
    problems, ethical and practical.
      339-40
    regulatory authority (UKXIRA), 339
    transgenic animals, use of, 339, 340
Transsexualism, 37-50
  birth certificate alteration, 39, 44
  criminal law issues, 41, 49
  diagnosis of sex, criteria for, 38-9, 40
  discrimination in employment, 44-7
  Europe, legal differences in, 42-4
  European Convention on Human
    Rights, 40, 42, 43-4, 47-8
  marriage, 40-1, 42-4, 49
  parental rights, 47-8
  public morality, involvement of, 37
  surgery to reassign, 37-8, 39 *et seq*
    France, in, 43-4
    results, efficacy, 48
    statistics, 38
  testicular feminisation syndrome, 40,
    41, 44
Treatment
  compulsory. *See* PSYCHIATRIC PATIENT

Treatment—*contd*
  consent to, and risks. *See* CONSENT TO
    TREATMENT
  feeding, 370, 385-6, 387, 399, 447-8
  infertility. *See* ARTIFICIAL INSEMINATION;
    IN VITRO FERTILISATION
  non-productive. *See* MEDICAL FUTILITY
    CONCEPT
  refusal. *See* CONSENT TO TREATMENT:
    refusal of; EUTHANASIA
  selective non-treatment. *See* INFANT;
    MEDICAL FUTILITY CONCEPT;
    NEONATE
  supply and demand dilemmas. *See*
    RESOURCE ALLOCATION

Ultrasound scan, 152, 154
Unborn child. *See* FETUS
Unconscious patient
  withdrawal of treatment. *See*
    EUTHANASIA; MEDICAL FUTILITY
    CONCEPT; PERSISTENT/PERMANENT
    VEGETATIVE STATE; VENTILATOR
Unifactorial disease, 147-9
United States, 17, 18
  AIDS confidentiality issues, 201
  abortion in, 119-21
    conflict on, 113
  cloning prohibition Bills, 187
  damages for lost chance, 238
  death, definition in, 336
  dialysis, finance for, 307
  donation of organ, 354
    anencephalic neonate, by, 359-60
    living minor, by, 344
    payment to relatives, 357
  donor insemination control, 62
  elderly,
    institutional care, 314-15
    refusal of treatment, 322-3
  euthanasia, 425, 435-7, 443
  execution in, 20
  genetic privacy, 172-3
  HIV testing, 23
  human kidney distribution, 301
  informed consent concept, 280, 286-7
    research, for, 462
  insanity defence, 532-3
  medical futility concept, 364, 365
  mentally ill, 505, 508
  non-treatment of infant, cases, 382-4
    Baby K case (anencephaly), 383-4

United States—*contd*
  non-treatment of infant, cases—*contd*
    circumstances for withholding
      treatment, 383
  PVS in, 409-11
  patent, 494
  physician assisted suicide, 425
  psychosurgery, 520
  refusal of treatment/passive
    euthanasia cases, 435-6
  resource allocation, Oregon plan, 295
  sterilisation,
    cases, 97
    compulsory, 96
  surrogacy, 78
  wrongful birth action, 158-9
  wrongful life action, 162-3
Unlawful killing. *See also* CRIME;
    DIMINISHED RESPONSIBILITY;
    INFANTICIDE
  causation, and brain stem death
    criteria, 333-4
  euthanasia as, 416 *et seq. See also*
    EUTHANASIA
  PVS patient, position regarding, 395
  ventilator death. *See* VENTILATOR
  'year and a day' rule, 334
**Unrelated Live Transplant Regulatory
  Authority**, 343, 349
Uterus
  AIH and AIHD. *See* ARTIFICIAL
    INSEMINATION
  death of fetus in,
    abortion. *See* ABORTION
    wrongful death action, 478
    See also FETUS, RIGHTS OF
  lavage, 76
Utilitarianism, 6

Vaccine
  brain damage from, 236-7
Vasectomy
  failed, 160
Vegetative state. *See* PERSISTENT/
    PERMANENT VEGETATIVE STATE
Ventilator
  'beating heart' donor on. *See*
    TRANSPLANTATION OF ORGANS
  removal of patient from, 332-6
    civil liability, 442
    criminal liability, 442
    ethical issues, 335-6

Ventilator—*contd*
  removal of patient from—*contd*
    patient requesting, 422-3, 439-40.
      See also EUTHANASIA
    pregnant woman and fetus
      viability, 335
    survivorship issues, 334-5
    time of death, 334
    US, in, 409-10, 442
    unconscious patient, 440-2. *See
      also* PERSISTENT/PERMANENT
      VEGETATIVE STATE
    'year and a day' rule, and, 334
  use of, after respiratory failure, 328
Viagra
  NHS, and, 294-5
Vicarious liability
  GP, of, 220
  Health Authority, of, 220-1, 232
Violence, domestic
  doctor's position, 202-3
Violent crime. *See also* AUTOMATISM;
    CRIME; PSYCHIATRIC PATIENT
  doctor's position, patient committing,
    195
Volenti non fit injuria, 284-5

Wardship
  consent to treatment, 258, 260
  new born infant, for, 136
  sterilisation of ward, 98-9, 101
Warning
  HIV, doctor's duty, 54-5, 200-1
  informed consent, element in, 281-2,
    284, 285-6
  sterilisation failure, of, 92-3, 94, 96,
    286
Whistle-blowing, 12-13
Withdrawal of treatment. *See* MEDICAL
    FUTILITY CONCEPT; PERSISTENT/
    PERMANENT VEGETATIVE STATE
  euthanasia distinguished, 419
Witness
  doctor as, privilege, 209
  mental health of, evidence of, 523
  psychiatrist as, 523-6
Womb leasing, 78, 86-7
Woolf Report, 218
World Health Organisation
  organ donation by minors, 345
Wrongful birth action, 94, 96, 143, 158-9
  causation problems, 159

Wrongful birth action—*contd*
  damages, 159-60
  UK, in, 159-60
    quantum, case on, 159
  US, in, 158-9
'Wrongful death'
  fetus in utero, of, 478
Wrongful life action, 159, 160-6
  basis of claim, 162
  Israel, in, 166
  UK, in, 164-6
    damages, 165

Wrongful life action—*contd*
  UK, in—*contd*
    'diminished life' claim preferable,
      165-6
  US, in,
    allowing claim, 163
    rejecting claim, 162-3

Xenotransplantation, 338-40
  consent to, 467
  transgenic animals, use of, 339
  US, in, 383, 467